Anecdotes of British Topography

*Or, an Historical Account of What Has Been Done
for Illustrating the Topographical Antiquities
of Great Britain and Ireland*

RICHARD GOUGH

CAMBRIDGE
UNIVERSITY PRESS

CAMBRIDGE
UNIVERSITY PRESS

University Printing House, Cambridge, CB2 8BS, United Kingdom

Published in the United States of America by Cambridge University Press, New York

Cambridge University Press is part of the University of Cambridge.
It furthers the University's mission by disseminating knowledge in the pursuit of
education, learning and research at the highest international levels of excellence.

www.cambridge.org
Information on this title: www.cambridge.org/9781108064460

© in this compilation Cambridge University Press 2014

This edition first published 1768
This digitally printed version 2014

ISBN 978-1-108-06446-0 Paperback

CAMBRIDGE LIBRARY COLLECTION

Books of enduring scholarly value

Earth Sciences

In the nineteenth century, geology emerged as a distinct academic discipline. It pointed the way towards the theory of evolution, as scientists including Gideon Mantell, Adam Sedgwick, Charles Lyell and Roderick Murchison began to use the evidence of minerals, rock formations and fossils to demonstrate that the earth was older by millions of years than the conventional, Bible-based wisdom had supposed. They argued convincingly that the climate, flora and fauna of the distant past could be deduced from geological evidence. Volcanic activity, the formation of mountains, and the action of glaciers and rivers, tides and ocean currents also became better understood. This series includes landmark publications by pioneers of the modern earth sciences, who advanced the scientific understanding of our planet and the processes by which it is constantly re-shaped.

Anecdotes of British Topography

The leading antiquary of his day, Richard Gough (1735–1809) promoted the history of the British Isles, particularly the Anglo-Saxon period, rather than pursuing the classical interests of contemporaries who had made the Grand Tour. Gough travelled extensively over the years, sketching and taking detailed notes on what he observed. He believed that the Society of Antiquaries, of which he was director from 1771 to 1797, should preserve the nation's heritage without catering to fashion or the interests of dilettantes. He published this major work anonymously in 1768, and it found a receptive readership. The book is in effect a gazetteer of published and unpublished materials for the local history and topography of the whole of Great Britain and Ireland, discussing public records, printed books, manuscripts, maps, and other sources relating to the antiquities of each county.

Cambridge University Press has long been a pioneer in the reissuing of out-of-print titles from its own backlist, producing digital reprints of books that are still sought after by scholars and students but could not be reprinted economically using traditional technology. The Cambridge Library Collection extends this activity to a wider range of books which are still of importance to researchers and professionals, either for the source material they contain, or as landmarks in the history of their academic discipline.

Drawing from the world-renowned collections in the Cambridge University Library and other partner libraries, and guided by the advice of experts in each subject area, Cambridge University Press is using state-of-the-art scanning machines in its own Printing House to capture the content of each book selected for inclusion. The files are processed to give a consistently clear, crisp image, and the books finished to the high quality standard for which the Press is recognised around the world. The latest print-on-demand technology ensures that the books will remain available indefinitely, and that orders for single or multiple copies can quickly be supplied.

The Cambridge Library Collection brings back to life books of enduring scholarly value (including out-of-copyright works originally issued by other publishers) across a wide range of disciplines in the humanities and social sciences and in science and technology.

ANECDOTES

OF

BRITISH TOPOGRAPHY.

OR, AN

HISTORICAL ACCOUNT

Of what has been done for illustrating the

TOPOGRAPHICAL ANTIQUITIES

OF

GREAT BRITAIN AND IRELAND.

LONDON:

Printed by W. RICHARDSON and S. CLARK:

And sold by T. PAYNE, at the Mews Gate, and W. BROWN, in Fleet Street.

————————

MDCCLXVIII.

PREFACE.

AMONG the infinite variety of writers thefe kingdoms have produced in every period for fo many centuries, we might expect that fome in the earlier ones fhould have turned their thoughts to a geographical defcription of them. From the firft eftablifhment of monafteries there wanted not monks to record the tranfactions of their own focieties, and the kingdom in general. The minuteft detail of religious or civil controverfy found a place in their records. Every religious that could write or read, at a time when nobody elfe could, entered in his regifter, like a good houfewife in her almanac, the atchievements or diftreffes of his brethren and countrymen ; and fuch as had not wit enough to be original authors, had at leaft induftry enough to be tranfcribers, or to fuperadd the credulity of others to their own. But logic and divinity being fo effential to their profeffion, we are not to wonder that men fecluded from the world ftudied the arts of life fo little. In an unenlightned age they knew enough to make themfelves of importance to the grofs of mankind, and to maintain their dependance on them. If they were ignorant of the prefent name of a Roman ftation, they well knew the

utmoft

utmoſt extent of their own terrier. Strangers to the value of denarii, not of ſticas, of legionary, not of legendary, inſcriptions, if they could not make better maps of the kingdom than thoſe of the iſle of Thanet, or the four Roman ways in the MS. of Matthew Paris, they could determine the quantity of bovates, hides, and roods given and bequeathed by each benefactor. Bede was better qualified to write an ecclefiaſtical hiſtory, than a geographical deſcription of England. The piece " De ſitu & mirabilibus Britanniæ," in Benet college library, D. I. 173. 205. beginning, " the firſt wonder is Chederhole, the ſecond-Rollendrick," if rightly aſcribed to him, is the oldeſt of the kind. Gildas and Nennius before him had left catalogues of the Britiſh cities, which vary in name and number in every copy. The Saxon chronicle, like later writers, follows Bede, from whom to Gyraldus Cambrenſis, nothing of the kind was even attempted. Gyraldus's topographies of Wales and Ireland are ſo ſtuffed with fiction and marvellous, that one is almoſt deterred from receiving the little real information they give. He made a map of Wales, containing 43 towns, and the parts of England bordering on it, which is ſtill extant, and is probably the oldeſt map made in England. His own account of it may give us ſome idea of the ſtate of map-making at that time. " Expreſſam Cambriæ totius mappam, cum montanis arduis & ſylvis " horridis, aquis & fluviis, & caſtellis electis, cathedralibus etiam eccle- " fiis & monaſteriis multis, maximeque Ciſtercienſis ordinis, copioſa " pariter & artificioſa ſumptuoſitate conſtructis, arto folio ſtrictoque " valde locello & ſpatio breviſſimo, diſtincte tamen & aperte decla- " ravi." Epiſt. ad capitulum Hereford. de libris ſuis, Ang. Sac. II. 441. Wood ſays, he left a map of Ireland too ; but this does not appear in the Bodleian copies. In his piece " De illaudabilibus Walliæ," he promiſes *totius Britanniæ* topographiam, which Leland doubts if he ever finiſhed, though Pits ſays it was in the public library at Cambridge, and thoſe of Peterhouſe and Benet : he even makes it conſiſt of four books : but what he took for it in the laſt of theſe libraries are his other topographies, and two other pieces, marked I. 9. James gives that at Peterhouſe, Nº 1894, the title of *Hiberniæ :* the other copy is not in his catalogue. Leland ſpeaks of a deſcription of England wrote in *Saxon* by

Colman,

Colman, firnamed *The Wife*, whofe age he has fixed to the reign of John, fo that he was cotemporary with Gyraldus. It is pity that diligent man did not make fome extracts from this book, which he read in St. Paul's library, and which fo few of his cotemporaries were acquainted with. It might in its way have been as valuable as the Saxon chronicle. Stephanides or Fitz-Stephen wrote his fhort defcription of London a little before Gyraldus. William of Worcefter took his tour three centuries after both; and Hearne, who laments the indolence and ignorance of our monks in this article, grudged the world a printed copy of it. Simon or Symeon, an Irifh minorite, wrote a journal of his travels with friar Hugh, firnamed *Illuminator*, from Ireland to the Holy Land 1322. MS. c. c. c. C. vii. 6. in which bp. Tanner fays, he gives fome account of the cities and places in England.

The rays that difpelled the gloom of religion illuminated every branch of fcience. It was not till the monks were turned adrift, and the invention of printing had given circulation to every improvement the mind enlarged could make, that we began to be acquainted with the face of our own country. The firft that undertook to open the way was Leland, at the moft critical period, when our antiquities were on the point of being involved in the ruins of our religious foundations. Not content with tranfcribing and extracting hiftorical matter from innumerable regifters foon after deftroyed or difperfed, he made a particular and regular defcription of the places he vifited, marked the courfe of rivers, minuted the ftate of cities, towns, and villages, defcribed the caftles, palaces, churches, with their monuments, and every other building that came in his way. His Itinerary, though in many inftances it only fupplies the ufe of maps, may be faid to have formed our Britifh Paufanias in the fucceeding century. It will be no reproach to Camden if he borrowed from him more than it can be proved he did. Leland's principal works are but the outlines and materials of a greater plan, which he enjoyed neither life nor reafon to finifh. Perhaps he undertook too much for the imperfect ftate of antiquarian knowledge in that age, or the fatigue he had fuffered and apprehended in the courfe of this defign was too much for his conftitution. One fuppofition yet remains;——perhaps the zeal

of

of this great preferver of our antiquities could not ftand the fhock of their devaftation. Though he had encouragement and countenance from Henry VIII. to ranfack the libraries, and even to fave as much of their contents as he could, the diffolving hand of that furious monarch, and the avarice of his minifters, proceeded like a devouring fire, to which his antiquary could oppofe no refiftance. Defolation marked his way; and we muft venerate Leland's indigefted refearches as the firft-fruits of antiquarian fcience among us. "What he did "was faithful; what he defigned was great and noble * !"

Camden, whofe genius for antiquities was innate, and who travelled over great part of the kingdom before he left the univerfity, was firft put upon "reftoring antiquity to Britain, and Britain to antiquity +," by Ortelius, whom he calls the great reftorer of geography. As he could derive but little affiftance from Greek or Roman writers, he found himfelf obliged to apply, where every man muft, who would not be deemed a witling in our antiquities, —— to the Saxon language. Though, where it fubmitted with its people to the Norman invaders, it ceafed to be a living language, the traces of it occur to this day in almoft every fentence we utter. All the efforts of the Conqueror, however fuccefsful among the upper ranks, who were to adopt the ftile of the court they had connections with, could not eradicate from the common people, the fureft maintainers of language and manners, a language they had fpoken 600 years. The few written remains that furvived the difufe of above 400 more, were confined to the libraries of abp. Parker and Sir Robert Cotton, and from thefe Camden acquired his knowledge of it. He fpent 10 years in making his collections, which he firft communicated to the world when he was a little turned of thirty. His edition of fome of our earlieft hiftorians from MSS. in his own poffeffion, his hiftory of his own times, his remains, (the fruit of his refearches for his Britannia) and fome leffer pieces, are fo many fervices rendered by him to his country after his great work had

* Gibfon's life of Camden.
+ His own words in his preface. Daniel Rogers, another correfpondent of Ortelius, drew up " Obfervationes antiquæ Britanniæ," including remarks on the geography and Roman infcriptions. Tanner.

gone

gone through five editions in 15 years, during which he held both the mafterfhips of Weftminfter fchool fucceffively. His foundation at Oxford carried his views for the promotion of hiftorical antiquities to the lateft pofterity.

Thefe two had many imitators.——In 1590 an ANTIQUARIAN SOCIETY was formed of fome of the greateft names in our republic of letters; and though the filly apprehenfions of the timid pedant then on the throne, who muft have all wifdom centre in himfelf, checked their meetings, it laid no reftraint on their fpirit. After above 20 years difcontinuance, it was revived 1614; and during all interruptions, its members produced in their ftudies works that will do honour to themfelves and their country. The fucceeding calamities of civil broils quickened Dugdale and Dodfworth to preferve our monaftic, in which fo many other treafures are included. Their collections on that article rank as much above thofe of Mabillon, as they had greater difficulties to furmount. The voluminous Annales & Acta ordinis S. Benedicti came into the world under the patronage of the fociety whofe hiftory they contain : the Monafticon Anglicanum, refcued from the jaws of war and fanaticifm, lay at the mercy of bookfellers.—— Every one knows what elfe we owe to Sir William Dugdale.

Dr. Plott formed a moft ufeful and extenfive defign of travelling through England and Wales to improve the labours of Leland and Camden. The general plan was for promoting of learning and trade, by a ftrict enquiry after all natural and artificial curiofities. He propofed to fearch all public and private libraries, to make a catalogue of MSS. and obtain as many as he could, or at leaft tranfcripts or abridgments of them, for the Bodleian library; to collect coins and other antiquities, and to examine all the works, as well as the curiofities, of art, to the meaneft inventions. It is eafier to conceive than enumerate the advantages of fo noble and extenfive a defign, and fo worthy of its author, if one man's capacity or life can be fuppofed equal to it;—— an objection in part removed by the encouragement held out by the many focieties of this age to the fearchers after truth in every part of the plan, without the credulity of the preceding one.

If

If we compare the endeavours of our countrymen for the illuftration of our antiquities with thofe of other nations, we fhall find the preference both in number and matter due to us. Continental writers have indeed given furveys of kingdoms, principalities, and provinces; and defcriptions of a few particular cities, towns, churches, religious houfes, and other monuments. But their attention has been chiefly employed in hiftorical or biographical difquifitions, difcuffions of claims, legendary memoirs, and fuch like relations, interefting in a different department. The Italians and French are our only competitors. The latter have acquired, the former are born with, a paffion for antiquities. Both will teach us a ftyle, when we have afcertained our knowlege; and we may borrow from the one a portion of fcepticifm, to contraft with the affiduity of the other. The French, carrying thofe engaging talents they poffefs in the generality of literary purfuits, into their antiquarian refearches, have handled thofe obfcure fubjects with the fame eafe as romances: without going fo deep as graver nations, even their fuperficial knowlege appears to greater advantage by an animated ftyle and pertinent reflections, while our language, as capable of concife judicious remarks, is drawn out into tedious unanimated narrative in fuch compofitions. Bp. Gibfon, in his life of Camden, obferves, that topographical furveys were firft attempted in Italy for elucidating the Roman hiftory. The neighbouring countries on the fame continent had the like advantages in a fmaller degree. But with us, induftry and application were to ftrike out light without other affiftance. France comes the neareft to us in hiftories and defcriptions of particular provinces and cities ‡; fome of them as early as the 16th century. Our Dutch and German neighbours have laboured through topographies, furveys, and defcriptions of their infinitely divided territories. The Spaniards have romanced about the antiquities of their cities. Our topographical knowlege of Portugal is confined to the civil and ecclefiaftical antiquities of its capital, written about the middle of the laft

‡ " La bibliotheque des autheurs, qui ont ecrit l'hiftoire & la topographie de la France, Par. 1618." 8vo. fomewhat anfwers to Nicholfon's hiftorical library, but gives nothing more than the titles of the books. The firft topographical defcription of France fince the Romans was " Gilb. Cognati Nozerchi brevis Galliæ defcriptio. Bafil. 1552." 8vo.

century.

century. Late as the fea-born republic of Venice emerged, fhe wants not hiftorians: but defcriptions of her continental territories are rather to be fought in thofe of Italy. That country can never want defcriptions, while there are travellers: her capital has been planned and rebuilt oftener than any in the world, and her ruins have been fo often ranfacked and laid open, that we begin now to turn our attention from mutilated ftatues to living manners. Almoft every eruption of Vefuvius has produced an effay: there are reckoned up 16, of which 10 relate to the eruption of 1631. Sicily has fomewhat to boaft on the fubject of topography in the late critical and accurate furvey of the whole ifland by Mr. D'Orville.——What fhall we expect of this fort in the north, where the fetters of barbarifm are fcarce loofened? yet the names of Wormius and Bartholinus muft not be forgotten, or ranked with the more modern bifhop of Berghen.——Travellers of every nation in Europe will affift our refearches in other parts of the globe. Our own nation, and our neighbours on the continent, furvey the territories they acquire. In a few ages more we may expect a complete fyftem of geography and natural hiftory for the whole world. Thefe muft fupply the place of civil and ecclefiaftical hiftory among the natives of Africa and America, where pofterity will decide on fuch relations as their conquerors can furnifh them.

While Camden was engaged in a general defcription of the kingdom, Lambarde caught the happy contagion, and fet about the perambulation of *Kent* 1570. Erdefwicke, another intimate of Camden's, collected for *Staffordfhire* early in the laft century; and the fmall part of his labours that he digefted was printed long after in a manner that difcredits his induftry. Carew's hiftory of *Cornwall* appeared about the fame time, and a hiftory of *Pembrokefhire* ftill in MS. is fuppofed to have been drawn up for Camden's ufe. Norden furveyed feven counties in the clofe of the 16th century. Burton undertook *Leicefterfhire* 1622; but as he profeffedly confined himfelf at firft to the hiftory of property, we are left to wifh that the prefent poffeffor ‖ of the author's large improvements and additions, would give them

‖ Sir Tho. Cave.

to the public.   Somner, who in the middle of the laſt century was im-
mortalizing Canterbury, when the confuſions of the times damped his
ardour, and almoſt deprived us of his labours, propoſed a ſurvey of
Kent, the loſs of which we cannot ſufficiently regret.   Notwithſtanding four eminent antiquaries have laboured on this county, we hope
e'er long to ſee an ample harveſt riſe out of their gleanings.   The next
ſurvey after Burton's was that of *Cheſhire* 1656, indigeſted, indeed, and
incomplete; but ſuch as, like thoſe of many other counties, we muſt be
content with, till ſome native antiquary riſes up to enlarge and new
model it.   The ſame year gave us Sir Wm. Dugdale's *Warwickſhire*,——
a perfeʑt pattern for all ſuch works, and imitated 20 years after by Dr.
Thoroton, in his hiſtory of *Nottinghamſhire*, with all the marks of inferior abilities.   At the ſame time a deſign was ſet on foot for *Wiltſhire*, which biſhop Tanner, who was better qualified for ſuch a work
than any of thoſe appointed to undertake it, did not live to finiſh.
Indeed the works he left nearly in order for the preſs were ſufficient
to fill up a life, which ended at the age of 62.   Sir Henry Spelman
ſoon after drew the outlines of a deſcription of *Norfolk*; and Wright
before did little more for *Rutlandſhire*.   Randall Catherall colleʑted for
Oxfordſhire 1625: Silas Taylor for *Herefordſhire* 1645: but we are at
a loſs where to find their papers.   Aſhmole began colleʑting for *Berkſhire* 1667.   Windſor and its order had a claim to his attention.   His
other engagements and extravagancies diverted him from antiquarian
purſuits, and his county notes have been publiſhed juſt as he left them.
Aubrey perambulated *Surrey* 1673.   The preſent century begun with
the hiſtory of *Hertfordſhire*, by Sir Henry Chauncey, who, if we over-
look the pedantry of his digreſſions, has colleʑted a valuable hiſtory of
property there, abridged and improved by Dr. Salmon.   Batteley did the
ſame good office to Somner's labours, by greatly enlarging his hiſtory of
Canterbury.   Sir Robert Atkyns having left a ſurvey of *Glouceſterſhire*
on Chauncey's plan, but conduʑted with leſs ſkill, we are promiſed a
new " Topographical, eccleſiaſtical, biographical, and natural hiſtory"
of it, by Mr. Rudder, bookſeller, of Cirenceſter, not a meer republication of the other, but great part new wrote, continued to the preſent
time.

time. Rifdon's meagre furvey of *Devon* was compiled about the
fame time. Mr. Bridges had been long employed about *Northamptonfhire*, but died before he could arrange his materials. Sir Thomas
Cave has taken up the fatherlefs work, and we are impatient to receive
the 2d vol. with the valuable draughts. Several defcriptions of other
counties, left unfinifhed by their authors, found a patron and publifher
in Dr. Rawlinfon. Among thefe I reckon Afhmole's Berkfhire and
Aubrey's Surrey, and the flimfy incorrect compilations for the cathedrals of Rochefter, Chichefter, Worcefter, Lichfield, and Salifbury.
At this time too it was the fafhion to enter into other men's labours:
Dr. Harris compiled his hiftory of Kent 1719 from all the former
accounts of it, and his own perambulation; but without much judgment or fkill in the ufe or arrangement of his imperfect defigns. Mr.
Peck having put together in a moft uncouth ftile and method, " Antiquarian annals " of Stamford, propofed 1729 fetting about a hiftory
of Leicefter and Rutland fhires, which failed of encouragement, and
upon his death fell to the ground. In 1732 came out a flight furvey
of *Dorfetfhire* by Mr. Coker, which Mr. Hutchins with proper encouragement will certainly improve. At the fame time N. Salmon,
as his laft fhift to live, fet about a furvey of *Effex*, and to the collections made by others, added his own induftry and conjectures. However extravagant thefe laft may appear, I am forry to be obliged to fay
his unfinifhed account of this county, of which fo much might be faid,
is the beft yet extant. The neighbouring county of Norfolk was next
attended to, and had Mr. Blomefield lived we might have feen a valuable work. But as if by the fatality attending antiquarian collectors
" particular efforts on the hiftory of fingle counties have dropt into the
graves of their intended authors "*. Dr. Borlafe in his Natural hiftory
and Antiquities of Cornwall has fhewn, by an example yet unimitated,
how both thefe fubjects may be treated with accuracy and elegance
and,—perhaps a fingle inftance,—is preparing a 2d edition of the latter work with confiderable improvements.

Of the forty counties of England, eighteen have found no antiquary hardy enough to attempt their general illuftration. *Bedfordfhire,*

---

* Kennet's life of Somner.

Shrop-

Shropſhire, and *Suſſex*, ſtill want the very rudiments of geographical and hiſtorical deſcriptions. Only one hundred in *Bucks* has been deſcribed. Blomefield's Collectanea Cantabrigienſia, any more than Layer's MS. are only church notes in a few pariſhes in *Cambridgeſhire*. George Smith, eſq; of *Cumberland* took ſome pains about the antiquities of that northern county ; but if I am not miſinformed, he has been dead eight years. A preliminary diſcourſe to a natural hiſtory of *Derbyſhire* remains in Aſhmole's muſeum ; and Dr. Leigh's is not much better. Dr. Smith's and Dr. Hunter's valuable collections for the hiſtory of *Durham* are yet with-held from the public ; and Mr. Spearman's intention proved abortive. Want of materials muſt not be complained of there. Much might be ſaid of *Hampſhire* : and of Wincheſter, more than the two good, but ſhort, printed accounts afford. As to *Huntingdonſhire*, no ſteps have been taken towards illuſtrating it ſince Sir Robert Cotton, its brighteſt ornament, declined the purſuit. We are quite unacquainted with *Lancaſhire*. Dr. Stukeley gave us all the information about the county of *Lincoln* that was conſiſtent with his other engagements, and this for the extent of it was more than we could get from Peck or Delapryme, whoſe inquiries were confined to a particular town or two, and failed of their due perfection. London has engroſſed all concern about the county of *Middleſex*. The deſign of Dr. Rawlinſon for illuſtrating *Oxford* city and county, which he recommended by his laſt will to the univerſity, remains unexecuted. Sir Simon D'Ewes is ſaid to have collected for *Suffolk* ; but all that remains to this purpoſe in the Harleian library is principally in the law way. Something in Dodſworth's MSS. vol. xxxviii. E. 39, quoted by bp. Kennet in his life of Somner, p. 41, probably led bp. Nicholſon to ſeek for more information in the Bodleian library ; but he was diſappointed : and if what he ſays of three volumes of collections for Eſſex by the ſame antiquary, in the Herald's office, be not as great a miſtake, Mr. Morant has made no uſe of them. Many attempts have been made towards a deſcription of *Somerſetſhire*, that fund of Roman and Britiſh antiquities, but without ſucceſs. All that has been done for *Worceſterſhire* is confined to the capital. *Monmouthſhire* continues in the ſame obſcurity as Wales, of which it once made a part. There
remain

remain in MS. Mr. Machel's collections for *Weſtmoreland*, bp. Nicholſon's for *Northumberland*, archdeacon Todd's for Cumberland, Mr. Dodſworth's and Dr. Johnſton's for *Yorkſhire*, Taylor's, Brome's, and Hill's for Herefordſhire.

Next to deſcriptions of counties ſucceeded thoſe of cities and towns. Stowe, cotemporary with Camden, begun with the metropolis : and his work has been frequently augmented. Somner followed his example for Canterbury. Between theſe a rector of Tottenham drew a ſketch of its hiſtory. After them Butcher made another of Stamford. Izacke, chamberlain of Exeter, put together a trivial account of that city, more like an hiſtorical regiſter than an antiquarian eſſay, often reprinted, but never in the leaſt improved. From theſe, till Thoreſby ſet about the civil and eccleſiaſtical hiſtory of Leedes, we have the long interval of fifty years. This century produced hiſtories of Thanet and Feverſham, Lynne and Thetford, York and Halifax, Stamford, Nottingham, Maidſtone, Colcheſter, Waltham, Dunwich, Buckingham, Worceſter, Arundel, and Leiceſter ; which laſt we wiſh to receive as an omen of future attempts to illuſtrate the county.

Of our two univerſities, Oxford, as if by birthright, has been moſt diſtinguiſhed, if the party prejudices of its hiſtoriographer are to be admitted for an authentic hiſtory of its members, or the collections of Allen, Twyne, and Fulman had arrived at maturity. Mr. Baker, with better temper, was longer collecting for Cambridge, and has left materials not unworthy to ſee the light. Only one college in each univerſity has found an hiſtoriographer ; one more in each has materials prepared for its hiſtory.

Eſſays on particular monuments did not come in faſhion till this century, if we except the injudicious attempt of the great reſtorer of architecture to reduce Stonehenge to Roman mcaſures, and Dr. Charlton's as eager one to make it Daniſh. Archdeacon Batteley begun with a Latin diſſertation on the antiquities of Richborough, compoſed with more elegance of ſtyle than accuracy of ſentiment. The late Mr Wiſe wrote with preciſion about the White horſe, and cther antiquities in Berkſhire 1738. Mr. Rauthmell, with a moſt verboſe quaintneſs, deſcribed the Roman ſtation at Overboro' in Lancaſhire

b 2　　　　　　　　　　　　　　　　　1746.

1746. The druidical æra of antiquity has certainly received as great light as so dark a period is capable of from Dr. Stukeley. Without entering into his hypothesis we may trust his descriptions of the monuments. Yet many of them escaped his examination. He does not seem to have ever visited Cornwall. It was reserved for Dr. Borlase to lay open the whole system of druidism, as well as to trace the progress of the Roman arms, in that county. Stonehenge was the only monument of its kind known to Leland: Camden mentions only Rollrich besides it. Mr. Aubrey seems to have first attended to these things in England and Mr. E. Lluyd in Wales; and to have taught others to take notice of them. The first account we have of Abury is from the former: Mr. Twining in writing about it only exposed his own ignorance.

The Roman geography of this island was not attended to till Dr. Talbot, a great collector of antient writings, cotemporary with Camden, wrote a few notes on the Itinerary of Antoninus, brought to light about thirty years before. Camden made very good use of this table, whose date and design have been so much controverted. Wm Burton of Shropshire, whom bp. Kennet calls " the best topographer since Camden §", published the fullest and most connected comment on it 1658. The great earl of Arundel formed a design of tracing and delineating the Roman roads and stations, and had made a considerable progress; but in the confusion of the times his drawings were lost. The anonymous monk of Ravenna's work, written about the seventh century, which Baxter thought a translation from the Greek, was found by father Porcheron as he was taking a catalogue of the king of France's MSS. and published 1688. Richard of Cirencester's later Itinerary and map have been given to the world by Mr. Bertram and Dr. Stukeley. But even after both these additional helps much remains for the diligence and sagacity of those who would settle the antient places in this island. We have from Leland a curious anecdote of a Roman inscription, perhaps the first discovered or regarded here. " Tun-
" stallus episcopus Dunelmensis vidit saxum repertum apud Barptolo-
" mæanos Londini dum quærerent nova fundamenta ; inscriptum vero

§ Life of Somner, p. 19.

" fuit

" fuit literis Romanis, fed præ vetuſtate pene corruptis & obliteratis *."
Tunſtal was a good ſcholar, and a patron of letters, and had filled the
ſee of London eight years before he went to Durham 1530. Sir Robert
Cotton and Camden took a journey together to the Picts wall 1599, and
not content with tranſcribing the inſcriptions inferted in the Britannia,
conveyed as many as they could purchaſe to Sir Robert's ſeat at Connington. All of theſe that ſurvived to this age, being only 15, are
now in Trinity college library, Cambridge. Thoſe which their friend
and aſſociate in theſe purſuits, William lord Howard, transferred to Naworth caſtle, ſtill remain there. They communicated copies of a few
to Gruter, who publiſhed them very incorrectly. Mr. Gordon copied
all that he met with in Scotland and about both the walls ; and Mr.
Horſley united all in Great Britain in one view, with great exactneſs and in true proportion. Enough have been ſince diſcovered to
make an appendix to this valuable Theſaurus.

Our firſt hints in the map way ſeem likewiſe to be taken from
Camden. Saxton, who ſhared with him the patronage of the munificent Cecil, begun 1574 with his map of Oxford, Bucks, and Berks
united, and in five years ended with Wales. Norden followed him
in a few counties, and was followed in all by Speed, who had not the
merit of adding the hundreds to all the former maps. Succeeding artiſts
rather reduced the ſcale, than improved in point of correctneſs. Ogilby,
from firſt introducing roads into maps, made maps of little elſe but
roads † : and whatever attempts have ſince been pretended to accommo-
date theſe to their preſent courſe, the editors are the only perſons benefited.
Surveys on large ſcales were reſerved for the labours of a Jefferies, a
Rocque, and a Taylor.—I invert the chronological order for the climax of
merit, at the ſame time not ignorant of inſtances, in which even the laſt
artiſt might be corrected, particularly in the orthography of his names.
As to the ſeveral ſets of county maps profeſſing to be drawn from the

* Collect. iv. 46.—Bagford conjectured that a marble headleſs figure, which he
called *Fortitude*, but which may have been any other deity or hero, ſet in a nitch in the
front of a houſe in Alderſgate ſtreet, facing St. Paul's alley, was found thereabouts.
Letter to Hearne, p. lxiii. Theſe two ſpots are not a great way aſunder.

† About the ſame time that Ogilby executed this work, there appeared a ſimilar one
in France, intitled " La guide des chemins, pour aller & venir par tout le royaume de
" France. Lyon. 1696" 12mo.

lateſt

lateſt obſervations, they are almoſt invariable copies of thoſe that preceded them; not excepting Emanuel Bowen's, on whoſe labours one
may now paſs a cenſure without violating the laws of humanity.

In eccleſiaſtical topography, by which I underſtand ſurveys of
churches and religious houſes, deſcribing their ſtructures and monuments, with liſts of their dignitaries, we are under too great obligations
to Sir Wm. Dugdale not   begin with him.   Camden opened the laſt
century with an account of the monuments of Weſtminſter abbey,
where Keepe gleaned after him and the havoc of fanaticiſm.   A better
fate attended St. Paul's cathedral, doomed not to periſh till Dugdale
and Hollar had preſerved every part of that noble pile.   Sir William
was happy enough to take ſurveys of the other cathedrals before the
ravages of a levelling civil war deſpoiled them of their wealth and
honours.   After him Mr. Gunton took an account of Peterborough, publiſhed 1686.   Sir Thomas Brown's Repertorium of Norwich cathedral
was wrote merely for private uſe.   The church hiſtories publiſhed about
1717 are ſcanty compilations haſtily gathered up by Dr. Rawlinſon.
Mr. Thomas's ſurvey of Worceſter is better, and we have higher and
juſter expectations from Dr. Thorpe and Mr. Bentham for Rocheſter
and Ely.   Mr. Southouſe's Monaſticon Feverſhamenſe, 1671, begins
the accounts of religious houſes.   A ſhort, but well written, anonymous
hiſtory of Glaſſenbury 1717, rather ſetting forth what that abbey might
have been, than what it was or is, follows next.   Then came Mr. Thomas's uſeful Latin hiſtory of Malvern priories 1725; and in 1751, Mr.
Widmore's ſenſible ſurvey of Weſtminſter abbey; the only merit of
Dart's book being the draughts.   Our religious foundations are obliged
to Mr. Willis, notwithſtanding the many inaccuracies of dates and epitaphs
ſcattered throughout his mitred abbies and ſurveys of the cathedrals:
but conſidered only in the capacity of a compiler from other men's papers
and notices, he certainly is of great uſe.   One cannot help wiſhing
every dioceſe had ſuch a repertory as Mr. Newcourt has given us for that
of London; and every county ſuch a monaſticon as Dr. Burton has begun for that of York.——While eccleſiaſtical hiſtory, as far as concerns
the ſettlement of our faith and the rights of the church, has been ex-
hauſted, we remain unacquainted with the more amuſing original of
our

our religious rites and usages; and Staveley's first attempt towards a history of churches remains unimproved.

Heraldical visitations began about the middle of the 16th century. The earliest I have met with are those of Devonshire, Hampshire, and Suffex, dated 1530, and the last, that of Northumberland, dated 1666 *: so that the paffion for preserving and authenticating pedigrees and armorial ensigns continued somewhat more than a century. And I cannot help thinking it an useful one, notwithstanding we now affect to put a contempt on the college of arms. The spirit of chivalry, so fertile of generous and honourable atchievements, maintained itself not a little by the diftinctions of rolls and family bearings: these were made at once the guerdons of valour and the guardians of property.—There was a time when our heralds were our censors:—now, they must serve to affift our antiquarian researches.

Natural knowlege dawned upon these kingdoms in the 16th century. Among the Harleian MSS. Nº 585, is an herbal written in Saxon in the 10th. There is another in the Bodleian library, Nº 4125, called by Wanley, " Liber medicinalis de virtutibus & vitiis herbarum:" and a third in the Cottonian, Vitel. C. 3. named " Herbarium Apuleii." These are no more than tranflations of a Latin herbal falfly afcribed to Apuleius, but whofe author is unknown. MSS. of it are in the Harleian library, Nº 4986, 5294. Before the reformation the knowlege of fimples, like phyfic, was in the hands of the religious, who feldom departed out of any beaten track; and, whether in confequence of their ignorance or good living, loft their own blood at the difcretion of their fuperiors. To the 2d edition of Turner's Herbal 1525 is annexed " A moft excellent and perfecte homifh apothecarye or homely phyfick booke for all the grefes and difeafes of the bodye : tranflated out of the Almaine fpeche into Englifh by John Hollybufh §. Collen. 1561." and this may be

---

* Mr. Bigland (Obfervations on regifters, p. 75) fays, the laft vifitations were made between 1660 and 1688. That of Lincolnfhire 1562 confifts moftly of bare pedigrees; the cuftom of regiftering the feals, church-notes, and other proofs of the antiquity and gentry of families not obtaining in thofe earlier vifitations. Wanley's note on Harleian MS. 1190.

§ He publifhed the New Teftament after the vulgar text, with an Englifh tranflation, 1538. 4to. Thorefby's mufeum, p. 504. Tanner. And " An expofition upon the Songe of the bleffed virgin Mary called Magnificat. 1538." 12mo.

deemed

deemed the firſt medical publication in our language. Horticulture and huſbandry were ſcientifically treated about the ſame time. Gerard, who collected a garden of plants, compoſed a general herbal 1597. Lord Bacon ſeems to have inſpired the thought of a natural hiſtory of England; but has hitherto found none to purſue his plan, if we except the partial hiſtory of a county or two, and the materials for ſuch a ſyſtem to be collected from the earlier Tranſactions of the Royal Society, with Mr. Boyle's indefatigable experiments. Dr. Caius begun an inquiry after animals with our dogs; but this branch of natural hiſtory kept no pace with the other. There had been a kind of ſucceſſion of botaniſts in Gerard, Norton, Lyte, Johnſon, Howe, Plat, Lovel, Merret, and others: but the animal part of natural hiſtory lay uncultivated till Willughby reſumed it, and Ray united it with the vegetable. Martin Liſter had indeed made ſome valuable diſcoveries in the tribe of ſhellfiſh ten years before Ray's firſt publication; but his thoughts were not turned to that of inſects till near twenty years after. We are not without hopes that the univerſity of Oxford, who are poſſeſſed of the plates of his ſhells, will give us a new and correct edition. In 1699 Lluyd's Lithophylacium appeared, but to little purpoſe: his collection of foſſils, the nobleſt in its kind, conſiſting intirely of Engliſh ones, lay neglected in the Aſhmolean muſeum, the various ſpecies tumbled out of their papers, and on the point of being loſt or ſtolen, till a new arrangement was made of them, and the book republiſhed ſeven years ago. Dr. Woodward's bequeſt to Cambridge fell into better hands. The firſt inquiry into our mineral waters ſeems to have been Dr. Jones's examination of thoſe of Bath and Buxton 1572. Whatever we can trace of the former to earlier times had more of panegyric than phyſic. Guidot took the moſt pains with them in the laſt century, and in this, their examiners have multiplied. Thoſe at Tunbridge were not diſcovered till 1632, and then Dr. Rowzee celebrated their virtues, as did Dr. Borlaſe thoſe at Latham in Lancaſhire 1670. Tobias Venner's cenſure of Briſtol water, 1662, is the firſt we hear of in print. The Yorkſhire ſpaws were analyſed much about the ſame time, and others of leſs note as they were diſcovered or came

5   in

in vogue. Dr. Short of Sheffield included in one quarto volnme all the mineial waters of England.

Dr. Plot firft attempted the natural hiftory of particular counties; but after executing.that of Oxford and Stafford fhires grew weary of a work in which the frequent appearances of want of judgment muft be afcribed in great meafure to the credulous temper of the age he lived in. The plan he formed for illuftrating the natural hiftory of the whole kingdom deferves the attention of thofe who have fince, with better fuccefs, applied themfelves to thefe purfuits. His excellent fyllabus of queries, an inlargement of his fcheme already printed at the end of Leland's Itinerary, we hope to fee in the improved edition of that book: In the Bodleian library is a tranfcript by Hearne of his Analecta, a kind of common place for illuftrating both our antiquities and natural hiftory. Dr. Moreton in his natural hiftory of Northamptonfhire occafionally touched on the antiquities with a better grace than Plot or Leigh. Dr. Borlafe has done juftice to that of Cornwall. That of Somerfet has been twice attempted without fuccefs, by Beaumont in the laft age, and Sunderland in this. Bp. Tanner included that of Wiltfhire in his plan.

Wales has had fcarce any thing done towards bringing either natives or foreigners acquainted with its remote antiquities. Mr. Rowlands fcruples not to charge his countrymen with fuch an indifference to their antiquities, that unlefs the Englifh, when they invaded their country, had carried off their monuments, they would have been loft or neglected *. Edward Lluyd took a deal of pains about them; but his valuable collections, which were in the hands of the late Sir Thomas Seabright, are difperfed, it is to be feared, beyond recovery. Befides thefe, a general, and not very correct, account of the four cathedrals, communicated to Brown Willis, and Rowlands' view of the earlier hiftory of Anglefea, are all we know of this romantic part of our ifland.

Scotland has but a fmall fhare in topographical illuftration. Sir Robert Gordon of Straloch had, at Bleau's requeft, circulated inquiries all over the kingdom, from the anfwers to which he began to draw up fundry defcriptions, which the troubles prevented both him and

* Mona ant. p. 119, 2d. edit.

c

David

David Buchanan, on whom he devolved it, from compleating. Some of his leſſer compoſitions in Latin were depoſited by his ſon James, miniſter of Rothway, in the hands of Sir Robert Sibbald, who, by command of Charles II. to whom he was phyſician and geographer in ordinary, ſeems to have firſt ſet on foot a regular inquiry into the antiquities and natural hiſtory of his country. Commiſſary Maul, in the beginning of the laſt century, wrote a hiſtory of Scotland, ſtill in MS. in which he ſeems to have ſkilfully touched on its earlier anti- quities. Alexander Gordon, fired by the reflection Dr. Stukeley * had caſt on his countrymen for their remiſſneſs in publiſhing their treaſures of Roman antiquities, collected into one view all ſuch monuments, with thoſe of the Picts and Danes, that came in his way, and deſigned a noble map of the walls. Sibbald publiſhed ſhort views of four ſhires, and left ſeveral more in MS. as they ſeem likely to continue. Captain Slezer's valuable deſign of engraving the principal towns, caſtles, and ruins was cut ſhort by diſappointment or death : thoſe given us by Mr Paul Sandby ſerve but to make us wiſh for a further acquaint- ance with the many wild proſpects of this country from his pencil. Its eccleſiaſtical topography is likely to remain in darkneſs ; and few lights have been thrown on its natural hiſtory.

A more laudable ſpirit has appeared in *Ireland*, inſpired by their great antiquary Sir James Ware, cultivated by Petty and Molyneux, and improved, though not to the utmoſt, by the ſociety at Dublin, inſtituted to promote the intereſt of their country with the knowlege of its anti- quities. What Mr. Smith has produced under its auſpices diſcovers. much ſkill in the plan, and application in the execution †.

Thoſe who have hitherto treated our topographical antiquities ſeem to have trodden only in mazes overgrown with thorns, neglecting the flowery paths with which the wilderneſs of obſcurity is diverſified. Incorrect pedigrees, futile etymologies, verboſe diſquiſitions, crowds of epitaphs, liſts of landholders, and ſuch farrago, thrown together without method, unanimated by reflections, and delivered in the moſt uncouth and horrid ſtyle, make the bulk of our county hiſtories. Such

* In his Graham's dyke, See Gordon's preface.
† See his very ſenſible obſervations in the introduction to his Hiſtory of Cork, p. x.

works

works bring the ſtudy of antiquities into diſgrace with the generality, and diſguſt the moſt candid curioſity. They repreſent their authors as men of uncultivated minds, fit only to pore over muſty records, and grovel among ruined walls ; ſhut up in cloſets from the commerce of life, and ſecluded from information even in their own way. Who-ever ſits down to compile the hiſtory and antiquities of a county or a town, ſhould confirm the evidence he collects from books and MSS. by inſpection of places deſcribed. The face of the country, and the monuments remaining on it, are as intereſting as the progreſs of deſcents or revolutions of property. Injudicious and ſedentary compilers find it much eaſier to arrange materials put into their hands, than to ramble about, and examine every remnant of antiquity. Fatigue and expence are made excuſes for indolence or want of judgment, when a proper correſpondence with intelligent perſons would help to much new in-formation, and correct or confirm that already received. It is acknow-leged ſuch works require time ; and, though there are ſome caſes in which it were to be wiſhed diligent collectors were more forward to oblige the public with their labours, this ſtudy ſuffers by nothing ſo much as by productions hurried into light without proper correctneſs and maturity. Next to the uncertainty ûnavoidable in ſuch purſuits, and an injudicious uſe of materials already collected, nothing is more perplexing than to find no uſe at all made of many monuments and evi-dences, obvious to a careful inquirer, but more expoſed to the ravages of time and accident. We ſhall often find ſuch traditions annexed to theſe as lead to the hiſtory of the monuments themſelves——and tra-ditions are by no means to be deſpiſed !

Antient earthworks, camps, and roads abound in every county. It is well known how much geography owes to a due obſervation of theſe. Many of our Roman ſtations are ſtill unſettled ; and while we labour to adjuſt the opinions of former writers, the actual remains which might fix the preciſe ſpot, and have eſcaped them all, are periſhing apace.——Compared with ſuch negligence the wildeſt conjec-ture is a venial ſin !—The views of ſuch works in Gordon's Itinerary and Wright's Louthiana make us regret the want of them for our own country, where we have a ſufficient number to verify the various periods

of

of antient fortification. Among the defiderata therefore of our antiquarian knowlege, muft be reckoned a notitia of our forts and caftles, with faithful reprefentations, from the earlieft date to the laft century, which levelled fo many. In Henry the Second's time there were in England 1115 caftles. By thefe are meant fortifications of ftone, which were increafed or rafed as the neceffities of the times required. Britifh, Roman, Danifh, and Saxon camps, fortified only by a foffe and vallum of earth, either in their original ftate, or altered by fucceeding works and buildings, are not lefs numerous, though lefs fought after.

One cannot enough regret the little regard hitherto paid to Gothic architecture, of which fo many beautiful models are daily crumbling to pieces before our eyes. England can boaft fpecimens of all its ftages from the fimpleft to the moft improved. We can go back even to the druids, who poifed immenfe weights almoft on nothing, yet wanted courage or contrivance to raife arches. At Stonehenge they fupplied their place with flat impofts of the fame fize with the uprights; all their other temples are but fo many circles of pillars. It was referved for the Norman architects to rear arches without centres, and without thofe fupports which a femicircle finds in itfelf, and which their bold magnificence betrays the want of, when, to furnifh an equal preffure, their walls are obfcured by maffive buttreffes. Had the remains of antient buildings been more attended to, we fhould before now have feen a fyftem of Gothic architecture in its various æras: we fhould have had all its parts reduced to rules; their variations and their dates fixed together. That fine work which, by bringing us acquainted with the fkill and magnificence of former ages, would have given immortality to our own, is laid afide ‡. We penetrate the wilds of Europe,

‡ Mr. Muntz propofed to publifh a courfe of Gothic architecture, demonftrating its fundamental principles and rules, exemplified in defigns and meafures taken from the fineft fabrics and monuments here and abroad, in upwards of fixty plates. It was to have confifted of four parts. The 1ft containing the theory of this ftyle. The 2d, exemplifications of it in various kinds of arches, &c. The 3d, in defigns from actual remains drawn by fcale. The 4th, the ornamental parts in larger proportion. The 3d part was to have exhibited defigns of fome beautiful and curious remains of Morefque buildings in Spain, firft drawn by the author 1748. This defign was offered to the public 1760, at a fubfcription of 300 perfons, three guineas and half each, for one folio volume; and fome beautiful drawings of fundry parts of St. Alban's abbey church, &c. were

Europe, and the defarts of Afia and Africa, for the remains of Grecian, Roman, and earlier architecture, while no artift offers himfelf a candidate for fame in preferving thofe of our forefathers in their own country. Temples and palaces of the polite nations of antiquity engrofs our attention, while the works and memorials of our own priefts and heroes have no effect on our curiofity. If any architectonical draughts of our buildings are preferved, they are in private cabinets. Few of thofe engraved have been executed with fufficient care and fkill. In moft, the effect of the whole is more confulted than the proportions of the parts. While our conventual churches perifh unheeded, our cathedrals fubfift unnoticed.——And yet the tracery of windows, the mouldings and turn of arches, the rich and light dreffings of pinnacles and buttreffes, the foliage of capitals, the cluftering of pillars, the difpofition of pilafters, the variations in the oppofite fide of the fame tranfept, and a thoufand nicer articles both of ornament and ufe, to which we have fcarce affigned diftinguifhing names, are all to be attended to. Mr. Perry's attempt to exprefs the feveral forts of windows fhews what that article is capable of in the hands of a more elegant artift, and with proper illuftrations. The fuperbly ftoried front of Rheims cathedral in Bergier's unfinifhed effay towards its hiftory, is a model to thofe who would exibit draughts of fuch buildings here.

No attempt has yet been made to fettle the age of *brick* buildings in England. Alfred has been thought to have introduced thefe, as well as ftone buildings: but his own hiftorian Afferius calls his ftructures, both for elegance and ftrength, *lapidei & lignei* †. Whether the Romans employed their fubjects in the brick-kilns as a mark of fubjection or not, they certainly introduced the ufe of brick buildings into their provinces. The pyramid of Ceftius muft be one of the few monuments built intirely of brick at Rome, where their greateft edifices were only cafed with marble. The ufe of brick for houfes was pro-

---

were to be feen for fome time at Mr. Webley's, bookfeller, in Holborn; but not meeting with encouragement the author entered into the fervice of the king of Spain, where he ftill continues.

† The Irifh, who would vie with the Chinefe for antiquity and accomplifhments, were three centuries behind us in any kind of building; if they did not even take the firft idea from us. Sir John Davis afcribes their backwardnefs in this article to the uncertainty of Tenure among them.

hibited

hibited there, becaufe the party walls being limited to a certain thick-
nefs * could not be made of it thick enough to fupport an upper
ftory. Out of the city, where they had more room, fuch materials
were allowed; and Vitruvius † defcribes a method of making brick
walls extremely lafting, by fecuring them from the droppings of water
with a coping of burnt brick, or a cornice. He mentions the old wall
of Aretium as a piece of excellent brick work; and thofe on two
fides of Athens: to which inftances Pliny ‡ adds thofe of Mevania,
another town in Italy; and both thefe authors defcribe feveral public
buildings of brick in Greece and Afia. The latter obferves, that the
Greeks, except where they could get flint, preferred brick for walls on
account of its durability. Accordingly Paufanias ‖ mentions a very antient brick temple of Apollo at Megara, rebuilt of marble by the emperor Adrian; and Vitruvius fpeaks of two temples at Athens built of
brick, with ftone pillars and cornices. Though Auguftus fet the fafhion
of building with ftone at Rome, the fucceffors of the twelve Cæfars
feem to have introduced brick again, and we find Caracalla's circus
only cafed with ftone. Thofe antiquaries who call our antient bricks
Britifh, as if peculiar to the Britons, or of their workmanfhip, are
grofly miftaken. Whether every ruin that has fuch laid in regular
ftrata, or carelefly intermixed, be of the Roman times, may admit
of a doubt; but where they are worked into the foundations, as at
Verulam and Chefterford, they may claim as early a date. The
Mint-yard tower at York, and the round towers and outer walls of
Pevenfea caftle, have the fame ftrata, but we have not equal evidence
that both are of Roman erection. The walls of Richborough and
Burgh caftles, with the fame circumftance, may have been erected by
the Saxons on a Roman fcite. Thus far however we may fairly pre-
fume, that whoever difpofed thefe bricks in their prefent fituation,
their meafures correfponding with thofe affigned by Roman authors, is
an argument that they are of Roman manufacture, and that a Roman
ftation was not far from the fpot they are now found in. Whatever
motive the Romans had for making fo much ufe of brick in this country after it was almoft banifhed from their own, the Saxon magni-

* Sefquipedali craffitudine. Vit   † Lib. ii. 8.   ‡ Lib. xxxvi. 6.
‖ Attic. c. 42.

ficence

ficence feems to have rofe above burning a few maffes of clay for the purpofes of building, referving the ufe of fuch as they found in the ftrong holds they had ruined, for occafional ornament, or haftier erection, or to fupply the want of other materials. Thus St. Albans abbey and St. Martin's church at Canterbury were raifed out of the ruins of Verulam and Durolevum. The ftately Normans, who, as fome think, affected greater plainnefs than even the Saxons, appear to have ufed nothing but ftone, and that fetched acrofs the feas from their own country, as if in difdain of the productions of this conquered foil. As Gothic architecture became more improved and ornamented, ftone once wrought into tender purflings and tracery was more likely to retain the form than brick; and after the latter came in vogue, we fee all the mungrel decorations of the Elizabethan age wrought in ftone. Bagford fays, " There were no brick buildings in England, except chimnies §, before the time of Henry VII. and even fuch as were built afterwards, were chiefly in monafteries, or fome few palaces for kings and noblemen, fuch as Henry VIIIth s houfe at Oldford, lord Shower's, or Brook houfe *, and another at Hackney, befides the church houfe in the church yard, all of the fame form, a houfe near Stepney called King John's Court, though certainly not built before the reign of Henry VII. probably the manor houfe, or that of Sir John Collet, father of the dean †." He might have added as of the fame age, Rochford hall in Effex, built by fome of the Boleyn family, the tower of Ingatftone church in the fame county, built a little before the Reformation, part of Downham church there much fooner; and the manfion houfe of the Delapoles, and Henry VIIIth's palace at Hull. Whether the venerable bridge at Plefhey in Effex, the feat of the high conftables of England, be the work of its laft lord of that rank, or raifed for later convenience, older it could hardly be;

§ Harrifon fays, old people in the country took notice of a very great increafe of them in common houfes in Elizabeth's time " In their yong dayes there were not above 2 or 3 if fo many in moft uplandifh towns (the religious houfes and manour places of their lordes alwaies excepted, and peradventure fome great perfonages) but ech one made his fire againft a *reredoffe* in the hall, where he dined and dreffed his meat." Defcription of England, prefixed to Hollinfhed's Chronicle, vol. ii. c. 12.

* Now intirely modernized, except one brick tower.
† Letter to Hearne, p. lxxviii.

con-

confequently it may be prior to the time when this manor was united to the duchy of Lancaster. The gate tower at Layer Marney was built by Henry lord Marney, who died 1523. That to the parfonage at Hadleigh in Suffolk is known to have been built in the reign of Henry VII. by William Pikynham, dean of Stoke college and rector of Hadleigh, 1490 ‡. Ewelme palace, in Oxfordfhire, was built of brick by William Delapole, in the reign of Henry VI. The noble caftle at Hurftmonceaux, Suffex, intirely of brick, is afcribed to Roger Fienes, who lived in the fame reign. Leland fomewhere mentions the walls of Wallingford, built of brick temp. Richard II. an inftance perhaps as fingular as thofe in Italy ‖. Dr. Woodward § refers to this reign, or thofe of Henry III. or John, the prefent wall of London, in which were inferted bricks of a different proportion from the Roman. Stow fays, Ralph Stratford, bifhop of London, inc ofed the burying ground in the Charter-houfe for thofe that died of the plague 1348 with a wall of brick. But the church of St. Botolph at Colchefter, belonging to a priory of Auftin canons founded before 1107, and built in the Saxon ftyle, is of a ftill older æra. A clofe infpection will fhew it to be compofed intirely of Roman bricks, cut or broken into fmall pieces, fo that it would be difficult to find one of its original dimenfions in the whole pile, whereas there are feveral remaining intire in the caftle and in the walls of other churches in the fame town. The fquare tower of Tatterfal caftle, Lincolnfhire, is built of bricks, in colour and hardnefs refembling our grey ftocks: it is 200 feet high, divided into three ftories of a fingle room each, the two lowermoft of which have beautiful chimney pieces charged with coats of arms and other ornaments, and the walls are 15 feet thick. The date of this building is fixed to the time of Hen. III. which is a century after the other. Salmon * finds evident traces of a Roman fortification inclofing the whole fcite of this caftle, with the church and other buildings; and here, he fixes Durobrivæ. Eudo the Norman had poffeffions both at Tatterfal and Colchefter. Drayton, in a note on his epiftle of Rofamond, fays, her labyrinth was built " of vaults under ground arched

‡ Hiftory of C. C. C. Append. Nº xxii. p. 39.
‖ The date on the brick at Walling (Berks) as corrected by profeffor Ward, is of this reign, if the figure taken for ·3 be not 5.
§ Letter to Wren, p. 22.   * Survey of England, p. 256.

and

and walled with brick and ftone." What authority he has for it does not appear : it feems not very likely that a work erected at the king's own expence fhould be compofed of two fuch materials, either of which would have anfwered the purpofe as well by itfelf. Harrifon obferves, that in Elizabeth's reign " the greateft part of our buildings in the cities and great towns confifted onlyof timber, for as yet few of the houfes of the commonalty (except here and there in the weft country towns) are made of ftone *." By *commonalty* he muft mean perfons of the rank of artifts and mechanics ; for at no time were the habi-tations of the rank below thefe built of ftone, though now of brick, which was at firft appropriated to palaces.——We meet with *Tiles* as early as Richard I. when the houfes in London were ordered in Fitz Alwin's mayoralty to be covered with flate or *brent tile,* inftead of ftraw. Their fize was fettled by an act of Edw. IV. 1477. In Thorefby's old MS. of Corpus Chrifti plays, among the trades are *Tylle-thakkers.* As tiles were a common covering among the Romans, they probably introduced them in England. The Saxon ᴛɪᴈɪl is doubtlefs derived from *tegula;* and though þæc ᴛɪᴈɪl is properly a *ridge* tile, tylle-thakkers feem to mean the workmen who laid on tiles in general : þæc, fignifying ftrictly a *ftraw* roof, fuch as roofs originally were, came afterwards to ftand for any roof, as thatching implies covering. When *Pantiles* were firft ufed among us I have not found ; but M. Outhier, a French religious of Befançon, who attended Maupertuis into the north 1734, fpeaks with aftonifhment of fome houfes at Stockholm covered with tiles, *creufes par un bord, &* *convexes par l'autre bord,* and took the trouble to draw and engrave them : the tegulæ hamatæ of Vitruvius † feem to be fuch.

Sepulchral monuments have their feveral æras, from the coffin-fafhioned tomb with no figure at all, or only a crofier, and feldom in-fcribed, to the moft ornamented canopy or chapel, which ended at the Reformation, and funk in the next reign into the univerfal difguife of architecture. Mr. Tate wrote or intended to write of the antiquity of tombs and monuments in England. His lift of heads and collec-

---

* Defcript. of Engl. ii. c. 12. † Lib. vii. 4.

tions

tions were in Mr. Anftis's hands *. In a Harleian MS. N° 2151, is a diftribution of tombs into ranks and claffes by Randal Holme, from the cuts in Dugdale and Thoroton, rather by the figures on them, than their own proper form. One of the moft beautiful monuments I recollect, is that of Margaret Holland and her two hufbands, in St. Michael's chapel at Canterbury, the work of the 15th century, not one reprefentation of which has done it juftice. Still more unfaithful are thofe in Sandford, where we muft transfer the blame from the engraver to the draughtfman. The hand of Hollar has made Dugdale and Thoroton's works moft valuable repofitories of our antient fepulchral monuments. Sir William took furveys of many of our cathedrals in the moft critical time: that of York, in the Herald's office, has been properly made ufe of by Mr. Drake. In the fame office are many valuable notes, and draughts of monuments long fince defaced and loft. Such a fpirit of avarice and outrage accompanied the moft laudable fpirit of reformation, that no pains were taken to preferve family monuments in the churches and chapels of the religious houfes, moft of which being in the higheft prefervation, and of moft excellent workmanfhip, their ruinous ftate could not be pleaded in excufe. How many that furvived the violence of the two laft ages are fuffered to decay in this, removed, broke in pieces, reftored in an aukward manner, or even plain painted and white wafhed. That want of tafte that fuffers beautiful pilafters of Englifh fpeckled marble to be daubed with plaifter, or rich capitals and ornaments to be knocked off in every repair of our cathedrals, will juftify throwing by a mutilated trunk, or felling imperfect braffes—Thus prebends fanctify the facrilege of parifh clerks.

The feveral heraldic remains in windows and other parts of churches, in caftles and manor-houfes, fhould be carefully attended to. As to vifitations, the originals, or authentic copies, are preferved in the Herald's office: and fince they have been difcontinued, and individuals omit to fupply this defect by lodging their pedigrees in the college, very little regard is due to printed genealogies. But arms in ftone or glafs

* Hearne's pref. to Curious Difcourfes, p. 114.

are

are fo many evidences of defcents, benefactions, and property, admitted even in courts of law.

Dates or infcriptions in fingular characters have been hitherto little attended to, or, if given at all, not in the original form.—An antiquarian fhould be afhamed to give them otherwife. But by the lot of human fallibility, every age leaves fomething for the next to find out—if fuch memorials efcape the wreck and changes of fo long a period! A fyllogè of thefe with an alphabet of variations would be a valuable acquifition.

Our enlightened age laughs at the rudenefs of our anceftors, and overlooks the manners of that rank of men whofe fimplicity is the beft guardian of antiquity. Innumerable lights may be drawn from local cuftoms and ufages, which are generally founded on fome antient fact, and ferve to guide us back to truth.—Aids to tradition they are its moft faithful interpreters!—When we condefcend to ftudy the antiquities of the common people, Bourne, the Newcaftle antiquary's, work, though poorly enough executed, may fuggeft the idea of a better, whofe rudiments muft be fought for in the northern or weftern counties.

Among other defiderata in our antiquities muft be reckoned a connected hiftory of the Saxons, both in and out of England. If the traces of this people, before they quitted the continent, are dark and confufed, we have good materials for their hiftory after this ifland fubmitted to them. Every one knows the value of the Saxon Chronicle, publifhed by bp. Gibfon from three MSS. each fuller than the other. Bp. Nicholfon fays there are in the Cotton library three more, if not of the fame work, of others relative to the fame times. Thwaites had tranflated this Chronicle into Englifh; but whether his ftyle was too quaint, or fuch a tranflation not capable of being univerfally circulated, the bifhop, unfortunately for his countrymen, has fhut up in an elegant Latin tranflation, what a literal Englifh one would have made infinitely more intelligible. The fame unhappinefs has attended all the Saxon lexicons fince Somner's. We muft learn Latin to underftand Englifh. A Saxon dictionary with a literal Englifh verfion would contribute more than any thing to bring us acquainted with that lan-

guage,

guage, which, however we have fuffered it to be corrupted by the heterogeneous mixture of Latinifms, Gallicifms, and Scotticifms, is our mother tongue. A proper cultivation of it would raife a noble fuper-ftructure of hiftory on the foundations of the Saxon Chronicle, Bede, and fome others of our earlier writers. There is fcarce a department in our antiquities for which we muft not recur to our Saxon anceftors, who during their refidence here had almoft fupplanted the original Britons. While the manners and language of the latter are confined to the weftern parts of the ifland, nothing is more amufing than to trace thofe of the former among the uncorrupted peafants of the northern counties. The laudable attempt of Sir Henry Spelman, to revive the ftudy of the Saxon language in one of our univerfities in the laft century, failed by the confufion of the times: the like intention of Dr. Rawlinfon in the other in this century defeats itfelf.

The arts of defign, ever cultivated by civilized nations, are the hap-pieft vehicles of antiquarian knowlege. Many MSS. of the Eliza-bethan age contain draughts of public buildings long fince deftroyed. While we regret the want of fuch in Leland and Camden, it was the fingular good fortune of the laft age to have given birth to Hollar, who firft applied the art of engraving in England to views and other fubjects befides portraits. Some artifts whom Mr. Walpole has re-fcued from oblivion, are known by painting Englifh views. Charles II. employed Dankers in drawing the royal palaces and fea ports. Griffiere lived in a yatcht on the Thames, drawing views of London, Greenwich, Gravefend, and Windfor. Vandieft drew for Granville earl of Bath feveral views and ruins in the Weft. Martin Johnfon, a celebrated engraver of feals, cotemporary with Simon, painted many of our moft beautiful landfcapes with much judgment, freedom, and warmth of colouring. Our modern artifts, who have chofen this walk, throw themfelves on the patronage of a curious public. The many views in the three kingdoms annually expofed to criticifm are evidences how favourably fuch performances are received. Gravelot, Smith, Vivares, Bellers, have painted or engraved many profpects in different parts of England. Mr. Samuel Buck and his brother have

com-

completed a noble defign of giving the public near 400 views of religious and other ruins, and 80 profpects of cities and towns; and are poffeffed of a number of other drawings taken at the fame time. The Antiquarian Society during a courfe of fifty years have caufed many antient monuments to be executed on copper by that faithful artift, George Vertue. This is ftill a part of their plan, though the public does not receive fuch frequent prefents from them. Vertue himfelf, who thirfted after our antiquities, did many at his own expence; and publifhed in 1740 propofals for a very valuable work, his hiftoric prints, drawn with extreme labour and fidelity, and executed in a moft fatisfactory manner, of which he finifhed but two numbers. Dr. Rawlinfon was at the expence of engraving many antient monuments and feals, the plates of which, and feveral views in the counties of Oxford, Surrey, Middlefex, and Berks, and of Norwich and Winchefter cathedrals, as well as views by other hands, he left to the univerfity of Oxford; intending all his own plates fhould be worked off into one volume for their benefit—But none have laboured more for the prefervation of our antiquities in this way than the late Dr. Stukeley, whofe pencil was as ready as his fancy was lively——a circumftance which while it puts us on our guard as to his fidelity, pleafes us in the reflection on his defign, and fhould animate others to follow his example.—The pencil is as effential as the pen to illuftrate antiquities. Thofe who contribute plates of antient monuments to county hiftories promote knowlege better than by filling them with views of private houfes, interefting to none but the owner's vanity. Badeflade, Kip, and Harris neglected many curious things, while they laboured on manfion houfes, with full dreffed gentlemen and ladies parading in meanders of diftorted box and yew.

Secretary Pepys firft began to collect all the prints and drawings that any way illuftrate the city of London. This valuable affemblage is now at Magdalen college, Cambridge. The late Smart Lethieullier, efq; of Alderfbrook, Effex, befides three folio volumes of original drawings of churches, monuments, painted widows, Roman pavements, &c. in England, by Gravelot, Green, and other eminent artifts,

ftill

ftill in the hands of his heirs, collected in three more volumes all
engraved maps, plans, views, and monuments, that fell under his
notice, which at the fale of his curious library 1761, paffed into the
royal cabinet. A like collection is the property of the Antiquarian
Society, formed from the donations of its members, and by the induftry of the late lord Colerane, of whofe reprefentative they were
obtained.

The learned and induftrious F. Montfaucon, after having ferved
the interefts of religion and claffical antiquity, applied himfelf to collect
the monuments of the French monarchy. The general plan of this
work was to give, with an abridgment of the French hiftory, the portraits of the kings, princes, and nobility, of whom any monuments remain ; the largeft churches and other principal buildings; the habits,
feftivals, public fports, and military antiquities; illuftrated with reprefentations from original monuments; to conclude with the moft remarkable tombs from the earlieft times to the reign of Henry IV. Of the
five parts of his defign he completed only the firft, in five volumes folio,
publifhed 1733. Two days before his death, he communicated to the
Aacademy of Infcriptions and Belles Lettres the plan and drawings of the
the fecond part, in three volumes, which remain unpublifhed. Our
country is as capable as France of furnifhing fuch a fyftem of its antiquities. Dr. Stukeley lamented * that " only in retrieving the noble
monuments of our anceftors are we behind the other learned nations
of Europe, not that we have a lefs fund of curiofities than they, were
the defcription of them attempted by able hands, and at an adequate
expence." Illuminated MSS. of which our public libraries contain a
valuable treafure, while they exhibit rude and ill-proportioned figures,
are faithful reprefentations of many particularities not otherwife to be
expreffed. Sepulcral · monuments anfwer the fame purpofe ; and
however ungraceful moft of the earlier ones may feem, they are fo
many records of their refpective ages. I am aware, with Mr. Anftis†,
that we fhould be on our guard with refpect to our antient effigies,
and examine into their true age, whether they be really cotemporary

Preface to his Itinerary.　　　　† Black Book, p. 57,

with

with the perfons or facts they reprefent, or erected afterwards, fince
many inftances might be produced of great errors committed by too
hafty credulity in this article. Likenefs of features was not the talent of
thofe days; but, having no Greek or Roman models to miflead them,
they gave faithful reprefentations of the habits of their cotemporaries; while we, as if afhamed to tranfmit to pofterity habits more
unnatural than thofe of the 16th century, impofe upon them by the
borrowed refemblances of thofe we never knew how to wear. If Dr.
Stukeley could find the bufts of founders fupporting the arches of church
doors and windows, what treafures are fcattered on the outfides of Lincoln, York, Exeter, Wells and Lichfield cathedrals, and the W. front
of Croyland church; or in the windows of innumerable churches,
which in their mangled ftate preferve hiftorical knowlege! And in York
and Lincoln minfters are chronicles of their founders and benefactors
to thofe who take the pains to read them. Mr. Torr both read and
committed to writing thofe of the former. The Scripture hiftories in
the N. and S. windows of Canterbury choir are particularly defcribed
in a MS. printed by Batteley, Append. N° xxx. but fome of them at
prefent feem to contain Saxon hiftory. In this and Lincoln cathedral
the hiftories are in rondeaux, like thofe in St. Denis engraved by Montfaucon. Prior Wafhington's defcription of the windows at Durham
long fince deftroyed, is printed in the antiquities of that cathedral.——
Whether we begin the æra of portrait likeneffes with Holbein, or admit it in the works of our earlier painters, Vertue and Houbraken have
fhewn us we cannot want a feries of illuftrious images in the galleries
of antient families. That valuable collection of engraved heads made
by the late Mr. Nichols, in ten volumes, of which Mr. Ames publifhed a minute catalogue, is capable of being continued to the prefent year.

Mr. Anftis made a collection of our antient feals for publication *.
Other nations are before hand with us in fuch an ufeful defign. The
Antiquarian Society and Dr. Rawlinfon have engraved feveral; others
are in Sandford, and difperfed in different works. Mr. Lewis, in his

* Leland's Collect. vi. p. 291. Drake's York, p. 532.

Dif-

Differtation on the antiquity and ufe of feals in England, 1740, 4to has but flightly treated the fubject. Mr. Tate had confidered it before in two MS. differtations prefented to the Antiquarian Society of his time.

Lord Bacon fomewhere obferves that learned men want fuch inventories of every thing in art and nature as rich men have of their eftates. As difcoveries and defcriptions multiply, fome fall back into obfcurity and others prefs forward into light. After a while we wifh to retrieve them; and as our knowlege advances, we would know how far that of our forefathers went, and would derive affiftance from it. Antiquarian literature was in a promifing train among us in the laft century, till our unhappy contefts involved all good learning in one common confufion with religion and good manners. This age is happy in poffeffing fo much of the fpirit of the laft, that the tafte for Britifh antiquities is daily increafing. The eagernefs with which every work on the fubject is fought after is the evidence of this affertion, and my encouragement to offer to the public thefe outlines of a hiftory of the progrefs of topographical inquiries in Great Britain and Ireland.

The firft compiler of a work like this was induftrious John Bagford, who, in the courfe of his collections for a hiftory of printing, furnifhed bp. Gibfon with the very fuperficial lift prefixed to his edition of the Britannia. Such another lift of pieces relative to London and Weftminfter is among his papers in the Harleian library. The chapters in bp. Nicholfon's hiftorical libraries are little better. It is furprizing his lordfhip fhould have made fo little ufe of fo much better opportunities than could be expected to have fallen to the lot of one who was bred a fhoemaker, and afterwards turned bookfeller. Either his inquiries did not extend far, or antiquarian knowlege was then but reviving. So little pains has he taken to inform himfelf about his materials, that the preface to his Englifh part, which pretends to give an account of our moft confiderable libraries, is a mere abftract of thofe imperfect catalogues which were fent to Dr. Bernard, and form his Catalogus MSS. Angliæ & Hiberniæ. In his topographical chapter he

inferts

inserts Diceto's tract " De mirabilibus Angliæ," a kind of introductory chapter to every monkish chronicle; and Thorn's " Chronicle of " all the counties, &c." which is neither more nor lefs than his hiftory. He took no trouble to diftinguifh Gyraldus' topographies of Britain and Wales, nor ever inquired after Botoner's Itinerary. His whole work is indeed capable of very confiderable improvement.——If our topographical writers furnifh fo copious a catalogue, what are we to expect from the other divifions of our hiftory?——Dr. Rawlinfon took up the tafk where the bifhop left off. But when I fay he only profeffed to continue the feries, and has hardly done that, I have made his elogium. Many of the books he mentions in his " Englifh Topogra- " pher *," were only to be found in his own rich library †, and many others are intirely omitted. Not to infift on the ftiffnefs of his ftyle, and the incorrectnefs with which he has given many titles, Scotland and Ireland were not included in his plan, and he does not appear to have attempted to correct his many miftakes by a fecond edition.

Since his lift was compiled, the growing fpirit of antiquarian curiofity has furnifhed ample matter for a new one. Many difcoveries have been thrown out in a fcattered manner. For want of an uniform method of communicating them to the world, like that fuccefsfully purfued by the Academy of Infcriptions and Belles Lettres, the Philofophical Tranfactions and the Gentleman's Magazine have ferved as channels; out of which an ufeful mifcellany of antiquarian fugitive pieces might be formed, with an occafional comment. Many little effays have been publifhed in the form of pamphlets. A confiderable number of prints have been engraved. Several whole counties have been furveyed and defcribed; and copious materials are come to light for doing the fame fervice to others. Future writers on thefe fubjects will not be difpleafed to be told where they may derive affiftance. A comprehenfive view of all thefe pieces, many of which are become extreme-

---

* London, printed in 8vo. 1720.——John Worral, who publifhed feveral editions of a ufeful catalogue of law books, publifhed " Bibliotheca topographica Anglicana, " 1736." 12mo. ranging the books alphabetically, and adding fome relating to the hiftory, &c. of England.

† The fale of it after his death by Samuel Baker, bookfeller, in Covent-garden, 1756, took up *fifty* nights, exclufive of *ten* more the following year.

ly

ly fcarce, cannot be abfolutely ufelefs. An analyfis of them is not to
be expected, much lefs a lift of all the MS. materials concealed in our
libraries both public and private. The catalogues of thofe already publifhed, with all their defects, have their ufe; and it is the duty of
librarians to amend them. We may hope this from the abilities and
application of the prefent keeper of the Bodleian. Few perfons are
acquainted with the treafures of this kind contained there, or the value
of Dr. Rawlinfon's bequeft, which is now laid open to the curious,
and includes all his improvements and continuation of Wood's Athenæ,
and other materials for a complete hiftory both of the city and univerfity of Oxford, many county collections, particularly all thofe made by
Mr. Holman for Effex, digefted for the moft part into a regular form,
and on the proper plan for fuch works. The Harleian library claims
the fecond place after this repofitory; and fuch MSS. as have occurred
there relative to this fubject have been taken notice of.

The prefent attempt pretends to fupply the omiffions of preceeding
ones, to inform the curious what lights have from time to time been
thrown on the topographical antiquities of the three kingdoms, and to
refcue them and their authors from oblivion. Perfect it cannot be
while the number of fuch pieces is daily increafing. It will have obtained one of its ends, if, while it brings to light intentions of illuftrating this department, it does not barely tell pofterity they mifcarried
for want of patronage. The plan is partly the fame with that of the
Englifh Topographer. No pieces are regiftered that do not relate in a
manner ftrictly local to the topography of each county. Domefday is
the hiftory of one æra of geography and property among us. Vifitations
illuftrate in a minuter detail the fucceffion and rights of the feveral
families. Effays in natural hiftory are another branch of topography.
The general furvey and hiftory of counties, and particular accounts of
towns, monuments, or occurrences follow thefe. Views and maps are
fuch interefting reprefentations, and we are fo fenfible what we have
loft by the want of them in earlier ages, that while the curious are induced to preferve them, future artifts will be encouraged to execute
them. What other articles have found a place here, have the fame
claim—that they may poffibly be referred to a general defcription of

each

each county.——Accounts of Witchcraft are inferted after the example of Dr. Rawlinfon, and becaufe it is a part of the curiofity of this age to hunt after fuch monuments of the credulity of the laft.

Curiofity to vifit as much of my native country as I had opportunity excited a defire to know all that related to its topographical antiquities. The fcarcity of defcriptions by the pen or pencil foon appeared not fo great as former lifts reprefented it. A diligent inquiry after every article of this kind, which fome notwithftanding have efcaped, produced the catalogue I now prefent to thofe whofe purfuits are congenial to my own.——If a catalogue of the authors or artifts of Great Britain be interefting to their countrymen, fome account of thofe who have traced its topographical antiquities to their fource may not be unworthy their notice. We are naturally inclined to think what is of importance to ourfelves deferves to be accounted fo to others. Thefe Anecdotes have informed and amufed the colleftor :—if they only amufe the readers I fhall not be abfolutely condemned;—if they inform them, my paffion for Britifh antiquities becomes a zeal to ferve the public.

If under heaven any endurance were,
    Thefe moniments, which not in paper writ,
But in porphyre and marble do appear,
    Might well have hop'd to have obtained it.
      Na'thlefs, my lute, whom Phœbus deign'd to give,
        Ceafe not to found thefe old antiquities :
      For if that time do let thy glory live,
        Well mayft thou boaft, however bafe thou be,
      That thou art *one*, which of thy nation fong
      The old honour of the people gowned long.
SPENCER's Ruins of Rome.

ANECDOTES

ANECDOTES

OF

BRITISH Topography, &c.

Roman Geography of Britain.

WHATEVER antiquity Britain may pretend to in common with the reſt of the world, the Greeks are the firſt in whoſe writings we find any mention of it. The commercial part of that people, whom an intercourſe with the Phœnicians and the advantage of the tin trade brought hither, frequented it as later ages viſited China or America, without giving themſelves much concern about the country or the people. They did not ſo much as know whether it was continent or iſland. What Pliny [a] therefore ſays of their acquaintance with it muſt be underſtood with limitation. Polybius [b], who died above twenty years before Cæſar was born, is the firſt that promiſes a diſtinct deſcription of the Britannic iſles, and the tin-works there, as far as he knew. But Cæſar, who diſcovered our iſland to the Romans, was the firſt that compiled any deſcription of it. He took both its form and dimenſions upon truſt, and ſucceeding geographers and hiſtorians did the ſame, contenting themſelves with a general account of the face of the country, the manners of the people, or the tranſactions of the Romans in it. Diodorus Siculus [c], Strabo [d], Mela [e], and Dio Caſſius [f], treat of it in Cæſar's manner. The firſt of

---

[a] *Britannia clara Græcis Monumentis.* N. H. i. 2. If we believe Camden, we ſhall find Britain and Ireland in Orpheus's Argonautics, and Ariſtotle's piece De Mundo, which may rank together. Hearne (Pref. ad Gul. Neub. p. 22.) would perſuade us that Herodotus (iv. 49.) calls the Cantiani, and from them the inhabitants of the whole iſland, Cynctii.   [b] Hiſt. iii. p. 290.

[c] v. § 21, 22.   [d] iv. p. 303.   [e] iii. c. 6.   [f] lxxxvi. § 11, 12.

B

theſe

thefe refers for a more particular detail to his relation of that conqueror's expedition g, which is loft. The fame may be fuppofed of Livy and Fabius Rufticus. Pliny h contents himfelf with giving the dimenfions of the ifland from a map of the world made by Agrippa, and painted in his portico. Tacitus, in his life of Agricola, interweaving the hiftory with the geography, enters into the fulleft detail of both; agreeable to his profeffion i, to give a faithful relation of what former writers had only reprefented in a florid manner without any certainty. Ammianus Marcellinus k had drawn up a defcription of Britain. As he wrote after it had been long in the hands of his countrymen, we might have expected fome information from him; but the book that contained it is loft. All that the Roman hiftorians have left us has been connected and difcuffed in the firft book of Horfley's Britannia Romana.

Baron Clerk confidered Ptolemy among the moft incorrect of all antient authors. Several things might be pleaded to excufe his inaccuracies; great allowance muft be made for the time in which he wrote, and the errors of tranfcribers muft always be taken into the account . Dr. Gale was the firft that publifhed his Britifh geography by itfelf with notes at the end of his Hiftoriæ Anglicanæ Scriptores. The map of Britain in all the general editions of him is the moft aukward that can be conceived. Mercator, who corrected many errors in it, left the greateft of all, which inclines Scotland to the Eaft m. Horfley has prefixed it to his comment on Ptolemy, with another rectified according to his own idea. This able illuftrator of our Roman antiquities juftly obferves of Antoninus's Itinerary, that we owe more difcoveries of the names of Roman places here to that work, than to all the other authors put together. If any of the princes whofe name it

g Dr. Halley fixed the time and place of his landing to Aug. 26, in the afternoon, An. ante C. 55. in the Downs, and the place he fet out from at Calais. Phil. Tranfact. N° 113. Chifflet had fettled *Portus Iccius* at Mardyk, Somner at Bologne, Du Frefne, Camden, and Ortelius at Witfan. Horfley follows Halley.

h iv. 30. i § 10. k xxvii. 8.

l Agathemeris and Marcianus Heracleota both lived after Ptolemy, and are as fuperficial as Solinus, Orofius, or Jornandes, who do but copy earlier and better writers.

m Richard of Cirencefter obferves, that in Ptolemy's time Britain was fuppofed to refemble an inverted z.

bears

bears compofed the Britifh part, he thinks it muft be Caracalla. Weffelingius, who publifhed an elegant edition of the whole [m], con-jeƈtures with Surita another editor, that from certain internal charaƈters it cannot be placed higher than Severus, or much lower than Con-ftantine. It was firft printed at Paris by H. Stephens 1512, from a very old manufcript in the poffeffion of Longolius [n]. Dr. Robert Talbot, treafurer of the church of Norwich 1547, an eminent antiquary, co-temporary with Leland, was the firft of our own countrymen that illuftrated it with various readings and notes, which were of great ufe to Camden, and printed by Hearne with Stephens's text, and the Englifh names of the ftations as fixed by Dr. Gale, at the end of the third volume of Leland's Itinerary, from a manufcript in the Bodleian library which belonged to J. Stowe, and is in his hand-writing. Two other co-pies are in Benet Col. library; that marked 12—4 in the author's own writing: a fourth is in Caius Col. library, with additions by Dr. Caius [o]. Talbot died 1558, and left his manufcripts to New College Oxford. Camden followed his fettlement of the ftations in moft inftances. But William Burton [p] more frequently differs from him in his " Commen-" tary on Antoninus's Itinerary, or Journies of the Roman Empire, fo " far as it concerneth Britain," illuftrated with " A chorographical map " of the feveral ftations. Lond. 1658." Fol. His text was copied from the edition of the Itinerary at the end of Hollinfhed's Defcription of Bri-tain 1587, and reprinted in the Englifh editions of Camden. The next commentator was Dr. Thomas Gale, Dean of York, who in the feveral manufcripts he collated found but four variations in the diftances, which are the main article. He printed it at the end of his Hift. Angl. Scrip-tores, with Surita's notes. His own notes on it were publifhed after his death, revifed and enlarged by his fon Roger Gale, Efq; 1709. 4to.

[m] Amft. 1735, 4to. in which the modern names of our ftations are taken from Horfley.
[n] The next edit. was at Venice, ap. Ald. 1514. 12mo. the third at Florence 1519, 4to. the 4th at Lyons 1539, 12mo. from Aldus's copy; a fifth at Bafil, by Simler 1575; the fixth by Surita Col. 1600, 8vo. Bertius printed it with Ptolemy at Leyden 1618. fol.
[o] Cat. MS. Angl. tom. i. p. iii. p. 123, N°. 33. Quære if it includes Caius's piece *de antiquis Britanniæ urbibus*, or a lift of their antient and modern names, which Bag-ford fays he enlarged to two volumes kept in this library.
[p] Not the Leicefterfhire antiquary, but a Shropfhire man, L. L. B. and Schoolmafter at Kingfton upon Thames.

who

who added the Chorography of Britain by the anonymous **Ravennas.**
This, which was firſt publiſhed by P. Porcheron, Paris 1688, 8vo. has
been aſcribed to Gallio of Ravenna, the laſt Roman commander here.
But Salmon who propoſes this conjecture, did not conſider that this is
only a ſmall part of a larger geographical work in five books, where
Britain comes in among other iſlands at the end of the laſt. Horſley
has beſtowed a few notes on this part. Dr. Gale likewiſe printed it with
Ptolemy, &c. It is as miſerably corrupted as all the reſt, which Ward
thinks the confuſed compilation of ſome ignorant monk. Richard of
Cirenceſter has a better claim to authenticity. The Tabula Peutingeri-
ana, ſo called from having been found in Conrad Peutinger's library, is
a parchment roll above twenty-two feet long, and one broad, on which
were traced the ſtages or manſions for the Roman army throughout the
empire. It bears great reſemblance to our maps where the miles are
marked. Ward dates it in the reign of Theodoſius the Great, and ſuppoſes Antonine's Itinerary was copied from ſome ſuch table [q]. The
Notitia is a liſt of the ſeveral military and civil officers and magiſtrates in
the eaſtern and weſtern empires lower than the reigns of Arcadius and
Honorius, wrote probably towards the end of Theodoſius the younger's
reign, or about A. D. 445, when the bulk of the Roman forces was
ſtationed on the Kentiſh coaſt againſt the Saxon invaders, and on the
northern barrier, or *per lineam valli.* It ſeems to have been tranſcribed
from the *Latercula,* or regiſters of ſtate.

The names of Roman places in Britain are illuſtrated in Baxter's
" Gloſſarium antiquitatum Britannicarum, five ſyllabus etymologicus
" antiquitatum veteris Britanniæ atque Iberniæ temporibus Romano-
" rum, 1719" and 1723. 8vo. Baxter was a Shropſhire man, and
from his ſkill in the old Britiſh language attempted to determine the
geography by etymology, a method the moſt uncertain, and which too
often miſled Camden before, and others ſince. To his book was annexed
Ed. Lhuyd, another etymologiſt's, " Adverſaria poſtuma de fluvio-
" rum, montium, urbium, &c. in Britannia nominibus."

In p. 5. of " Miſcellanies on ſeveral curious ſubjects, 1714" and
1723, 8vo, is a letter from Aſhmole to Dugdale about the courſe of

---

[q] A correct edition of the whole table was publiſhed by D. Scheyb. Vien. 1753. Fol.

the

the Watling-ftreet.   Hearne printed in the 6th vol. of Leland's Itinerary, p. 93, " An effay towards the recovery of the courfes of the
" four great Roman ways," by Roger Gale; and fome additions to it,
in a letter to him from the author, in the 6th vol. of Leland's Collectanea, p. 473.   Some corrections of it are inferted in the Philofophical Tranf. N° 357.   In the Effay is engraved an old fketch of thefe
ways from the Additamenta to Mathew Paris. Cott. Lib. Nero D. 1. the
maker of which, though aukward enough, was not fo ignorant as
Gale makes him :   for it is eafy to fee he draws a line from Chefter to
Salifbury, and cuts off all to the weftward of it, except the weftern
extremity of Devon ;   what he takes for Dorobernia fhould certainly be Durnovaria, and his *Meridies* is in the original *Oriens.*
Whether Watling-ftreet takes its name from its winding direction
or not, it certainly has fuch a direction.   This way, and Antoninus's
Iter upon it, go from Richborough through London to Chefter
and Anglefea, thence back again to York, and thence to Carlifle.   The
military way in Herefordfhire and thofe in Scotland have the fame
name.   Ermin-ftreet runs ftrait from London to Lincoln, and fo to
Wintringham.   Stukeley begins it at Newhaven in Suffex;   others
carry it on to Carlifle ;   its name however is loft in Scotland.   The Foffe
is carried from Bath or Seaton to Lincoln.   Higden o begun it at Tot-
nefs ;   it fince appears that the Roman roads in Cornwall are part of it;
but how much farther eaft it runs is not certain.   Icknild-ftreet, the
moft uncertain of all, paffes from Caifter near Norwich through Effex
to London, whence it is continued through Hampfhire and Dorfetfhire p.   As it is certain thefe were the four principal roads that in the laws
of Edward the Confeffor divided the kingdom length and breadth wife,
there feems no other way of accounting for the many others out of a
direct line, yet retaining their names, but by fuppofing them fo many
branches of thefe, denominated from that out of which they were firft
turned.   Hence perhaps we come by two Icknield-ftreets, one in Norfolk, the other in Effex, which fome imagine joined at Chefterford.

° Higden has fixed the firft and third of thefe roads pretty accurately ; but he carries
both Ermin-ftreet and Rykeneld from St. David's; the former to Southampton, the
latter through Worcefterfhire, Warwickfhire, &c. to Tinmouth.

P Wife, who derives its name from Agricola, traces it from Oxfordfhire, where Plot
left it, through Berks towards Abury or the Devifes.   Lett. to Mead, p. 44.

" The

" The general hiſtory of the highways in all parts of the world,
' more particularly in Great Britain," &c. 1712, 8vo. would have
been a uſeful compendium ; but only the firſt book was finiſhed,
containing the manner of making them by the Carthaginians, Lace-
dæmonians, Romans, Peruvians, and all other nations, from the remoteſt antiquity to this time ; and only the laſt chapter of this contains
the Britiſh Roman ways. The contents rather ſhew what was deſigned than what was executed.

N. Salmon, eldeſt ſon of Tho. Salmon, rector of Mepſal, Bedfordſhire, and brother to the geographer and hiſtoriographer, who received
his education at Benet Col. Cambridge, and was curate of Weſtmill,
Hertfordſhire, but, ſcrupling to take the oaths to Q. Anne, practiſed
phyſic at Stortford, and died 1742, publiſhed, without his name,
" Roman ſtations in Britain, according to the Imperial Itinerary upon
" the Watling-ſtreet, Ermine-ſtreet, Ikening or Via ad Icianos, ſo far
" as any of theſe roads lead through the following counties, Norfolk,
" Suffolk, Cambridgeſhire, Eſſex, Hertfordſhire, Bedfordſhire, Middle-
" ſex. 1726." 8vo. and " A ſurvey of the Roman antiquities in ſome of
" the midland counties of England. 1726." Theſe he afterwards incorporated into his " New ſurvey of England, in which the defects of Cam-
" den are ſupplied, and the errors of his followers remarked : the opi-
" nions of our antiquaries compared : the Roman military ways traced ;
" and the ſtations ſettled according to the Itinerary, without altering
" the figures : with ſome natural hiſtory of each county." 2 vols. 8vo.
1731. To the firſt of which is annexed, " An examination of the
" Britiſh coins produced in Camden's Britannia, with the foundation
" of a conjecture, that they are not Britiſh, but brought in by the
" Romans and the Saxons." q

But the moſt complete work on this ſubject is John Horſley's
" Britannia Romana, or the Roman antiquities of Britain, in three
" books. The Iſt. containing the hiſtory of all the Roman tranſac-
" tions in Britain. The IId. a compleat collection of the Roman in-

q Very vague and inconcluſive. Dr. Borlaſe, in his Antiquities of Cornwall, has
ſufficiently aſſerted our anceſtors right to coins in all metals. Mr. Pegge allows them
coins, but not ſkill to ſtrike them. He fetches the artificers from Rome ; and a motley
piece of work they made of it.

" ſcriptions

" ſcriptions and ſculptures diſcovered here[r]. The IIId. the Roman
" geography of Britain. The whole illuſtrated with above 100 copper
" plates. 1732." Fol. The author of this well written work was
educated in the public grammar ſchool at Newcaſtle, ſtudied afterwards
in one of the Scotch colleges, where he took his degree, and died paſtor
of a diſſenting congregation at Morpeth, in Northumberland, 1732, a
little before the publication of his book; which might be greatly enlarged from later diſcoveries to be hereafter taken notice of.

John Pointer's pamphlet, intitled, " Britannia Romana, or Roman anti-
" quities in Britain. 1724." 8vo. pretends to give an account of the Roman coins, roads, and ſtations in Britain, and the Roman hiſtory of Oxford city and univerſity; but his pompous title page produces nothing.

Dr. Stukeley's " Itinerarium Curioſum, or account of the antiquitys
" and remarkable curioſitys in nature and art, obſerved in travels
" through Great Britan: illuſtrated with copper prints. Centuria I.
" 1724." Fol. contains many good notices of our Roman antiquities,
tho' the revival of our Celtic and Druidical was his principal objeɛt. Beſides the plates in this he had another ſet, and a number of drawings for a
ſecond part. To him we owe " An account of Richard of Cirenceſter,
" monk of Weſtminſter, and of his works; with his antient map of
" Roman Brittain; and the Itinerary thereof. Read at the Antiquarian
" Society Mar. 18, 1756," and publiſhed 1757. 4to. Richard lived about
the end of the fourteenth century, and appears to have been the Leland
of his age. He ſearched all our monaſtic libraries, and compiled a
hiſtory of the Anglo-ſaxons, in five books, from the arrival of Hengiſt
to Hen. III[s]. The preſent MS. drawn up from memoirs left by a Roman general, who, the Doɛtor perſuades himſelf, was Agricola[t], wants

---

[r] They amount to about 340, above 140 of which were never before publiſhed.
The originals have been all compared more than once; and none but thoſe ſtill remaining have a place in the plates, the reſt being thrown into the obſervations.

[s] The firſt part intitled *Speculum Hiſtoriale*, in four books, the ſecond *Anglo-Saxo-
num Chronicon*, lib. v. Both are in the public library, and that of Benet C. Cambridge,
and in that of the Royal Society. If this be as accurate as his geography, it deſerves to
ſee the light.

[t] Horſley ſeems to authorize this ſuppoſition, when he obſerves, p. 387. that moſt of
our military ways were probably laid by J. Agricola. None certainly were made till after
Claudius's conqueſt. But whether the ways and the ſtations were made together is not
eaſily determined. The latter might be made when the country was a little ſettled to
keep up a communication between the former, and to employ both ſoldiers and ſubjeɛts.

twenty-

twenty-two pages at the beginning, which feem to have contained the
geography of the Roman empire.   It gives the length and breadth of
this ifland in miles, and 18 iters in various directions acrofs it in the
manner of Antoninus's Itinerary, but more exact and particular, and
reaching to Alata Caftra, Invernefs.   Of 500 places which he mentions in Britain and Ireland, 150 are new or more correctly fixed.   Dr.
Stukeley has affigned them modern names, and modernized the map.
What he publifhed was only an extract, not exactly tranfcribed from
the original, which is intitled, " Commentariolum geographicum de fitu
" Britanniæ, & ftationum quas Romani ipfi in ea infula ædificaverunt."
The 2d book is a chronological abftract of Roman tranfactions in Britain,
imperfect.   He prevailed on Mr. Bertram, Englifh profeffor in the Marine
Academy at Copenhagen, who had purchafed it, to give the world a
correct edition of the whole, with two more of our old hiftorians, under
the title of " Britannicarum gentium hiftoriæ antiquæ fcriptores tres :
" Ricardus Corinenfis, Gildas Badonicus, Nennius Banchorenfis : re-
" cenfuit, notifque & indice auxit Carolus Bertramus, S. A. Lond. Soc.
" &c. Havniæ. 1757." 8vo.   The notes on Richard are only on the firft
and fecond chapters of the firft book.   But Mr. Bertram promifes a
compleat commentary, if thefe were well received [u].

The regard for Roman monuments began fo late amongft us that
in the fouthern and more cultivated parts of the kingdom many infcriptions muft have perifhed through inattention.   The many curious ones collected by Camden and Sir Robert Cotton [x], in their travels
about the northern counties, were fixed in an octagon fummer-houfe,
at the end of Sir Robert's garden at Connington ; but the roof falling
to decay expofed the infcriptions to continual damage, and many were

---

[u] Gildas was firft publifhed by Polydore Vergil very unfaithfully 1525. 12mo.   Archbifhop Parker's fecretary Joffeline reprinted him more correctly from two new MSS.
1560. 12mo.   He was a third time printed from a much correcter MS. by Dr. Gale in
his Hift. Angl. Scriptores, where Nennius appeared for the firft time.   Mr. B. followed
the Doctor's edition of both thefe antient writers, but in the latter he has diftinguifhed
the interpolations of Samuel from the genuine text.   Nicholfon mentions a MS. of
Nennius in the Bodleian lib. free from thele interpolations.

[x] A boat or two loaded with thefe precious reliques is faid to have been loft at fea ;
but Camden had tranfcribed them with thofe miffing at Connington.   This magnificent
manfion prefents nothing now but a few wrecks of a portico, and a neat garden-gate in the
ftyle of that age.   Sir Robert and his family lie in the adjoining elegant church.

stolen

ftolen or deftroyed. The few that remained were prefented (1750) by his lineal defcendant, Sir John Cotton of Stratton, Bart. to Trinity College, Cambridge, where they are placed at the foot of the ftairs, and were lately accurately engraved in their prefent ftate and order, by Mr. Lamborn of Cambridge, with numerical references to the tranfcripts in Horfley *x*. This is the oldeft collection. There are others in the univerfity of Glafgow and at Baron Clerk's feat, at Pennicuick, near Roflin. Horfley had about twenty, which I know not where to follow. Thofe affembled at Hexham by Mr. Warburton, who damaged many to render them portable, were lodged in the library at Durham by the care of Dr. Hunter, who added others to them. The two largeft collections in Cumberland are at Naworth caftle and Elenborough hall. Others are at Scaleby caftle, and the late Mr. Appleby's feat at the Cleugh : and fome in the neighbourhood of the ftations. Only two of the many curious ones relating to this county removed to Connington have furvived. Many Yorkfhire ones were collected by Thorefby, and feveral remain at York. Sir Thomas Robinfon, at his feat at Gretabridge *y*, has preferved feveral found in his own park in the burial place of the adjoining ftation ; and fome have been transferred hither from Naworth. The laft place that can fhew any number together is Bath.

Samuel Woodford, of Wadham Col. compiled a collection of Roman infcriptions found in Britain, with this title, " Infcriptionum " Romano-Britanicarum conlectio. auctore S. Woodfordo, Londino- " Wadham. adjecta commentatione; felicibus denuo aufpiciis incepta " kal. Jan. A. S. MDCLIIX. Admonitio ad lectorem. Hic fiftas jubeo, " B. L. nam in ipfo limine paucis te volo : eoq; libentius ut certam " methodum qua in infcriptionibus defcribendis utar, brevi propone- " rem adlocutione. Totum igitur epigrapharum penu in deorum

---

x They are only fifteen, and anfwer to Horfley's Northumberland plate N° 18. 53, 54. 80, 81, 82. 87, 88. 90. 95. Cumb. 55. 59. Yorkfh. 1. 18. Hampfh. 1. The accuracy with which thefe are copied is a reflection on that editor, who feems to have followed Camden implicitly in Northumb. 88. and to have taken the reft too haftily, particularly the images. The other faces and ornaments of 81 are omitted by Lamborn.

y In the fame repofitory is a beautiful altar tomb from the choir of Egglestone abbey in this neighbourhood, which abounds with a moft romantic variety of the works of nature and art.

C " trans-

" transferam & hominum. Sub illis ponam fi quæ aræ votivæ, ftatuæ
" columnæ, fimulacra, templa, eorumq: propriis numinibus dedica-
" tiones. Hos in vivos diftinguam & mortuos: vivorum funt grates,
" laudes, tabulæ honorariæ, & tituli: e mortuis defunctorum me-
" moriæ, manium jura eruantur; integra habebis & fragmenta, ex
" fidiffimis omnia tranfcriptionibus, & fub uniufcujufq; fide unde &
" a quo accepi, utrumne ipfe vidi fuftinebo. Vale." He names the
perfons from whom he had them only once or twice: moft, if not all
the reft appear to have been taken from Camden. The comment
does not contain an explication of them, but is chiefly a defcription of
the antient grandeur of Rome. Then follows an imperfect difcourfe
intitled, " S. W. Wadhamenfis Cippi fepulchrales," in which he
treats of the feveral funeral rites of different nations, illuftrated with
variety of infcriptions. Hearne appears to have feen this MS. by his
account of it, preface to *Fordun's* Scotichr. p. cxxxvii. *Quin & hoc
didicit Fordunus pro falute imperatorum quofdam in Britannia noftra
pofitos fuiffe lapides cum ejufmodi infcriptionibus, quos pene fe habet* Joan.
Murraius *in fchedis viri doctiffimi* S. Woodfordi, *ejufdem fcil.* Woodfordi *qui A. D.* 1658. *fyntagma edere in animo ftatuerat in quo academiæ Oxonienfis epitaphia daturus erat, & urnas fepulchrales per urbis
ecclefias repertas, & privata collegiorum facella.*——*Veteres non raro
cineres fuos ab una plaga in aliam transferre jubebant. Hinc doctifs. W.
in fchedis quas diximus pene Cl.* Murraium *notat quædam temporaria
fuiffe* [monumenta] *idcirco nempe ita dicta, quod ob breve tempus ibi ca-
davera condebantur, dato fixoq; intervallo & certo die quo ad avitas
transferrentur cineres.* Woodford mentions what is here referred to
about the Univerfity of Oxford, in the beginning of his difcourfe on
the Cippi, and therefore certainly intended it: but as it does not appear in the treatife, 'tis probable it was never executed. From
Murray's hands it came to Dr. R. Rawlinfon, who left it with his
other MSS. to the Univerfity of Oxford [z].

The Roman topography of Britain is a field of enquiry ftill open to
diligent inveftigators, who have opportunities to make obfervations on
the fpot, and examine the innumerable camps and roads concealed in

---

[z] MS. note of Prof. Ward in his copy of Horfley now in the Britifh Mufæum.

many

many parts of the ifland, from which, if traced with attention before
time and cultivation have compleated their deftruction, an almoft new
Notitia might be deduced. Talbot firft attempted to affign modern
names to a few ftations of the Itinerary. Camden followed him almoft implicitly, except where he quitted regular diftances to purfue
affinity of found. Burton departed fomewhat from their track: Gale
rather more. Salmon ufed greater freedom of enquiry; but his work
however ingenious is too fyftematical. Stukeley's excurfions give a
good deal of information, as he not only examined what were already
known, but difcovered many new ones; not to mention our obligations
to him for Richard of Cirencefter. Horfley, who fpared neither expence
or labour, by vifiting moft parts of the kingdom and comparing all
former accounts together, as well as by the ufe he has made of infcriptions, has fixed many ftations very juftly. Yet it was referved for
Dr. Borlafe to trace the progrefs of the Roman arms beyond the Tamar,
and for Mr. Pegge to fix the refidence of the Coritani[a], and to trace
the roads through it [b]. Nothing but an actual infpection of the country can fettle what remains. Effex alone affords fufficient conviction
how much light might be thrown on the Roman geography of England were the other counties as attentively examined.

Since nobody has yet undertaken the Saxon topography of Britain
on Dr. Hickes's plan [c], in which the Roman was to be included, we
muft content ourfelves with what information Dr. Gibfon's map in his
editions of Camden, and the Saxon Chronicle, and Dr. Smith's in his
edition of Bede, will afford us for this period.

The next begins with that moft authentic and moft antient record
in this or any other kingdom, Doomfday-Book. Notwithftanding
the laudable defign [d] of ranking that grand repofitory of our topo-

[a] Which he does to Derby, Leicefter, and Lincolnfhire, and the north part of Northamptonfhire, in his differtation annexed to his Effay on Cunobeline's Coins juft publifhed.

[b] Which he promifes fhortly to do.

[c] At the end of his epiftolary differtation.

[d] See Mr. Webb's " Short account of fome particulars concerning Doomfday-Book,
" with a view to promote its being publifhed. 1756." 4to. The expence of publication has been calculated at about 1400 *l.*

graphy

graphy among printed books has not yet met with the encouragement it merits, as the moſt effectual means of preſerving this invaluable MS. kept with leſs ſtrictneſs and ſafety than ever in the old Chapter-houſe at Weſtminſter. It was begun 1080, and finiſhed in ſix years, for the univerſal eſtabliſhment of tenures; in which and the article of tallage its authority ſtands unqueſtioned. It contains a general ſurvey of the greateſt part of the kingdom, divided into counties, rapes, lathes, and hundreds, and ſubdivided into cities, towns, vills, &c. each man's proportion of arable, paſture, meadow, and wood land, with their extent and value d, the number and condition of men in each town, &c. in the time of the Confeſſor and at the making of the ſurvey. The firſt volume, a large folio, finely wrote on 382 double pages of vellum, in a ſmall but plain character and double columns, contains thirty-one counties. The other is in 4to, written on 450 ſuch pages in ſingle columns, and a fair but large hand, containing Eſſex, Norfolk, and Suffolk. Part of Rutland is included in Northamptonſhire, and part of Lancaſhire in Yorkſhire and Cheſhire. Northumberland, Cumberland, Weſtmoreland, and Durham had ſuffered ſo much from the ravages of war that no ſurvey could be taken of them. In the orthography of the places names the Norman ſcribes made many miſtakes, ſeldom copying them from other writings, but ſetting them down from Saxon pronunciation, which they depraved and contracted e. Whether there are any intire and accurate tranſcripts of this record now extant, except one in the hands of Mr. Arthur Trevor, uſed by Dr. Gale f, does not appear. Abridgements and ſome returns from whence it was compiled have been miſtaken for it. Such parts of it as have been printed or remain diſtinct in MS. will be ſpecified under their reſpective counties. Moſt of them ought to be re-examined and compared with the originals previous to the printing of the whole. When that deſirable deſign can be accompliſhed we may hope for the illuſtrations of our antiquaries on the deſcriptions of each county.

---

d Ingulphus takes care to inform us his abbey of Croyland was favoured by the inquiſitors, who gave in an under rate and under meaſurement of their eſtates. We may ſuppoſe many other religious bodies met with the like favour.
  e Kennet's Par. Antiq. p. 64.   f App. ad Hiſt. Angl. Script.

William'

William Botoner, firnamed of Worcefter, a native of Briftol, fecretary, purfuivant, executor, and biographer to Sir John Faftolf, a perfon of learning and curiofity, and the firft that tranflated any of Cicero's works into Englifh, wrote " Itinerarium five liber memorabilium in " viaggio de Briftol ufque ad montem S. Michaelis in anno 1478." His travels include more than his title. He begins with the remarkables of his native city, and gives the meafurements of almoft all the churches in England; but in fuch terms as have puzzled pofterity to reduce them to the prefent proportions. All his meafurements are by *greffus* or *fteppys,* which do not anfwer to our modern paces. B. Willis publifhed them in his hiftory of mitred abbies. There is a copy of his book in the library at Lambeth, among Wharton's MSS. L. p. 107. another long one in an aukward fcrawl, which I fhould take for William's field book, C. C. C. C. Lib. alii xiii. A tranfcript of this, in the fame hand and book with Talbot's notes on Antoninus, ib. Mifc. M. Hearne fays, he was informed by a learned friend this book was not worth publifhing. It is at leaft as fit to fee the light as many he has expofed to view.

At the head of our own countrymen's printed attempts to illuftrate our topography muft be placed a little folio tract called, " The De-" fcription of England, Wales, and Scotland," finifhed by Caxton, 18 Aug. 1480. 20 Edw. IV. confifting of 29 chapters, printed from Trevifa's tranflation of Higden the compiler of the Polychronicon, and reprinted with the Fructus temporum, &c. In Julian Notary's edition of it, 1515, the following rubrics are prefixed. " ¶ Here followeth " a lytell treatife, the whych treateth of the defcription of this londe, " whyche of olde thyme was named Albyon, and after Britayne, and " now is called Englonde, and fpeketh of the noblefe and worthinefe " of the fame. ¶ It is foo, that in many and diverfe places the comyn " cronycles of Englond ben had, and alfo now late prynted. And for-" afmoche as the dyfcrypcyon of this londe, which of olde tyme was " named Albyon and after Brytayne, is not defcryved ne comynly " hadde, ne the noblenefe and worthynefe of the fame is not knowne, " therefore I entende to fette in this boke the defcrypcyon of the fayde

---

⁵ Pref. ad Lib. nig. Scac. p. xix.

" yfe

" yle of Brytaine, with the commodytes of the fame ᵍ." Nothing
but the order of time can give this book precedence of

" The Itinerary of John Leland, the antiquary, publifhed from the
" original MS. in the Bodleian Library, and other authentic copies, by
" T. Hearne, Oxf. 1710, 1711, 1712." 8vo. 9 vols. This work is
the refult of fix years travels of its indefatigable author who led the
way to the illuftration of his country, and let nothing efcape his refearches; penetrating into the recefses of learning in the monafteries
on the eve of diffolution, and preferving in his Collectanea many valuable extracts from books that foon after perifhed, except fuch as he
had intereft enough to refcue and lodge in the royal library. In his
" New Yeere's Gifte," addreffed to Hen. VIII. who had appointed him
his librarian, he promifed a draught or map of England, on a filver
plate; a defcription of the kingdom to reftore the antient names of
places; its antiquities or civil hiftory, in 50 books, anfwering to the
number of counties in England and Wales; a furvey of the Britifh Ifles,
in fix books; and an account of our nobility before the conqueft, in
three. His Itinerary and Collectanea may be confidered as the com-
mon-place books, whence this great plan was to be executed. But his
intenfe application, joined perhaps to an apprehenfion of wanting abilities or encouragement to complete it, turned his head. He lingered
out a few years in this unhappy condition, and, dying 1552, was
buried ʰ in the church of St. Michael le Querne, in which parifh he
had lived. This church was burnt in the great fire, and afterwards
united to that of St. Vedaft; and Leland's afhes blended with the
ftreet. Sir John Cheke, by command of his royal pupil, fecured his
MSS. and gave the four volumes of the Collectanea to Humphrey Pure-
foy, efq; afterwards one of Q. Elizabeth's privy-councellors, whofe fon
gave them to W. Burton of Leicefterfhire. The eight volumes of the
Itinerary, after paffing thro' Lord Paget's and Sir William Cecil's hands,
came alfo to Burton, who, 1632, depofited them all in the Bodleian
Library, except one volume which he had lent out, but which was afterwards united to the reft by Charles King, of Chrift Church, a learned
antiquary. The Itinerary had received fo much damage before it came

---

ᵍ Lewis's Life of Caxton, p. 39, 40. Bp. Nicholfon miftakes Bale's account of Caxton,
which is a high compliment on his induftry.   ʰ His epitaph is in Weever, p. 688.

to Burton's hands, that he caufed fome parts of the firft five volumes to be tranfcribed, as Stowe did the reft [i]; but the wet it had contracted expofing it to continual decay, Hearne undertook a complete tranfcript of it, which he afterwards compared with the others, and printed with all its defects and redundancies. Only 120 copies being printed, it was at one time fold for a guinea a volume. T. Pote, bookfeller at London, publifhed a new edition in 10 vols. 8vo [k], with improvements and additions; the original MS. having been re-examined with the ftricteft care, many places fupplied, and many paffages reftored, by the rev. Mr. Jofeph Sandford, fellow of Baliol, who added two extracts from Stowe's copy, vol. iii. p. 119. vol. iv. p. 126. an account of the infcriptions at Melbury, &c. vol. viii. p. 48. a fragment of the Itinerary in Leland's own hand, Cott. Lib. Vefp. ix. 36. f. 223. at the end of vol. ix. and a general index.

From Leland was borrowed the " Hiftorical defcription of the " ifland of Britaine; with a brief rehearfal of the nature and qualities " of the people of England, and fuch commodities as are to be found " in the fame, comprehended in three books, by William Harrifon," chaplain to Sir William Brook, Lord warden of the Cinque ports, prefixed to both editions of Hollinfhead's Chronicle, 1577 and 1587. Fol. In the firft edition the Ift book contains 17 chapters, the IId 18, the IIId 26; in the fecond edition the Ift has 24, the IId 25, the IIId 16; many of the chapters being tranfpofed [l].

Camden was the firft who took a uniform furvey of his own country, and gave a plan for this method in which he exceeded former, and has been imitated by fucceeding ages. He has fixed the date of the firft edition of his Britannia himfelf to 1586 [m]. He affirms the fame in the preface to his laft edition: yet Wood [n] puts the

[i] Burton's tranfcript in his own writing, fomewhat damaged at the beginning, was given to Dr. Stukeley 1758. A complete tranfcript made t. Eliz. belonging to Mr. Wright, author of the Hiftory of Rutlandfhire, was burnt with other valuable curiofities, in the Temple 1688.

[k] The 10th containing " Joannis Roffi Warwicenfis Hiftoria Regum Angliæ," firft publifhed by Hearne 1716. 8vo.

[l] Tanner Bib. Brit. He quotes (p. 32.) fome particulars about Jerfey and Guernfey from a defcription of Britain by one J. Sulmo or Solimount, a native of the latter ifland, who died 1545.

[m] *Mem. de feipfo* at the end of his life by Smith. [n] Ath. Ox. I. 481, 482.

firft

first edition 1582, and the second 1585, and elsewhere ᵐ he had fixed the first to 1585. Camden himself says he spent ten years in compiling it, and was put upon it by Ortelius; whence it appears he began to digest his materials the year after he came to Westminster ⁿ. A letter from W. Lambarde ᵒ to him, dated July 9, 1585, proves there could be no edition till after that time. He speaks there of Kent as done; and *if you have in purpose to perform the rest,* &c. The dedication to William Cecil Lord Burleigh is dated May 2, 1586. so that he finished this work precisely at the age of thirty-five, employing in it only his leisure hours and holidays. The title of this edition was " Britannia, five florentissimorum regnorum Angliæ, Scotiæ, & Hi- " berniæ, & insularum adjacentium ex intima antiquitate descriptio : " authore Gul. Camdeno. Lond. 1586." 8vo. Succeeding editions bore the same. The 2d 1587, 12mo. " Nunc denuo recognita & " plurimis locis adaucta." The 3d 1590, " Nunc tertio recognita, " & magna accessione adaucta," in a larger size than the two former. It was printed the same year at Francfort by J. Wechel ᵖ. The 4th was at Lond. 1594, 4to. " Nunc quarto recognita, & magna accef- " fione post Germanicam editionem adaucta." Camden made the tour of many of the western counties, and travelled as far as Carlisle to prepare for a 5th edition, but some passages in this were attacked in the mean time by Ralph Brook, York Herald, in his " Discoverie of " certain errors published in print, in the much commended Britannia, " 1594. very prejudiciall to the discentes and successions of the aun- " cient nobilitie of this realme." More influenced by spleen than truth he soon sunk into contempt, tho' Camden took the pains to vindicate himself in a polite Latin reply annexed to the discovery, and to the 5th edition of the Britannia. Lond. 1600. 4to. Brook was a fellow of a violent and implacable temper, who stuck at nothing to gratify his revenge ᑫ. He did not so much resent Camden's getting the place of Clarencieux from him, as his pretending to heraldical

m Hist. & Ant. Ox. II. 270.   n Pref. to the Folio Ed.
o Camd. Ep. p. 28, 29.   p The title page sets forth, " Primumque in
" Germania in lucem edita.   MDLXXXX."
q See more of his character in Anstis's Black Book.   Vol. I. p. 389.

knowledge.

knowledge.   In the three firft editions he had but flightly touched on genealogies, but in the fourth he gave a lift of near two hundred and fifty families.   Tho' he corrected the errors in his fifth from Brook's fuggeftions, he treated his knowledge in heraldry too contemptuoufly. Brook charged him with errors in feveral noble pedigrees, and with not acknowledging the affiftance he received from Glover's and Leland's papers.   Camden replied, that in the firft cafe he had been miſled by Rob. Cook, Clarencieux; and as to the other, he always made honourable mention of thofe he borrowed from, and particularly Leland's Itinerary and other pieces, except where they faid the fame thing from their own knowledge.   He offered to fubmit the difputed points to the Earl Marſhal, the College of Heralds, the Society of Antiquaries, or to any four perfons learned in thofe ftudies.   Brook had prepared a fecond " Difcovery of Errors," in the appendix to which he fets down the paffages objected to in the Britannia 1594. and as corrected in the edition of 1600.   This was firft publiſhed 1723, 4to. from a MS. in Mr. Anftis's poffeffion.   T. Mills, kinfman and executor to R. Glover, Somerfet Herald [r], who died 1588, having printed his collections in an injudicious and incorrect manner 1610, Brook publiſhed " A Catalogue and Succeffion of the Kings, Princes, &c. &c. " Lond. 1619." Fol. and again corrected and enlarged 1622, Fol. with fevere remarks on Mills's errors.   This was anfwered by Vincent, Rouge Croix, in " A Difcovery of Errors in the firft edition of the " Catalogue publiſhed by R. Brook, &c. 1622." Fol.   It is plain from his addrefs to Brook, that the whole of this affair is only a continuation of the old quarrel between him and Camden.   Vincent treats him as he had treated Camden, and this book has the recommendation of all the moft learned heralds and antiquaries of the time. Thus Brook's fplenetic attack on the Britannia produced great advantages to the public, by fifting and bringing to light a good, perhaps, a better and more authentic account of our nobility than had been then given of any in Europe [s].   The Dutchefs of Newcaſtle above fifty years after took up the quarrel.   In her *Unnatural Tragedy* (which

[r] Sir W. Dugdale told Dr. Smith he thought Camden and Glover the only *truly great* among the Heralds.
[s] See Biog. Brit. Camden. n. F. H. U.

D

ſtrictly

strictly answers its title) is a whole scene against the Britannia.   Three or four sociable virgins and matrons criticizing on the speeches in the antient historians, the third proceeds charging " our later chronologers, " such writers as Camden, and the like, with writing not only partially, " but falsly : as for some particular families, some Camden hath mis- " taken, and some he hath falsly mentioned to their prejudice, and some " so slightly, as with an undervaluing, as if they were not worth the " mention, *which is far worse than if he should rail or* disclame *against* " *them.*——To follow the practice of his profession he hath sweetened " his pen as towards his scholars and their families, and it is likely most " towards those scholars that were more beneficial to him ; but to such " whose parents had tutors for them at home, not suffering them to " go to common schools, he hath passed over or lightly mentioned " their families, or hath dipped his pen in vinegar and gall."   The first suggests, " it is likelyer that he might take some pett at those that " did not entertain him at their houses when he went his progress, to " inform him of the several parts of the country, before he writ of " them."   The second observes, " when he mentions such places and " houses, he says, the antient situation of such a worthy family, when " to her knowledge many of those families he mentions bought those " houses and lands, some one descent, some two descents, some three " before, which families came out of other parts of the kingdom or " the city, and not to the antient and *inheritary* families ; but he leaves " those antient families unmentioned."   The fourth surmises, " he " thought it fit, that the memories of those families, that were so ill " husbands, or had so ill fortunes, as they were forced to sell their " antient inheritance, should be buried in their ruins."   Sir Simon D'ewes, in his letter to Archbishop Usher, pretends there is not a page in the Britannia without faults, which he threatened to animadvert upon.   He had better have arranged his own collections relating to the three eastern counties, Suffolk, Norfolk, and Essex, and by pub- lishing them, saved us the trouble of hunting for them with little prospect of success.

The last and best edition of the Britannia was in 1607, Fol. correctly printed, much amended and augmented, adorned with maps of the

counties,

counties. An Englifh tranflation of this edition was publifhed 1610, Fol. by Ph. Holland, who was thought to have confulted Camden himfelf, and therefore great regard was paid to his editions and explanations. But in a later edition of his tranflation, 1637, Fol. he has taken un-warrantable liberties [t]. The original was printed at Amfterdam 1617, 8vo. with maps; again by Bleau at Leyden 1639, 8vo. again much altered and interpolated, inferted with Speed's maps in the 5th volume of Bleau's Theatrum Orbis, Amft. 1662, Fol. without Scotland or Ireland. It was alfo tranflated into French by Salabert and Sorbiere, and printed in the Grand Atlas. But the moft compleat and faithful tranflation is that by Bifhop Gibfon, Lond. 1694, Fol. with large additions and improvements. Holland's moft material notes are placed at the bottom of each page, and the additions at the end of each county: others are inferted in the body of the book, properly diftinguifhed from Camden's own work. As this was grown fcarce, and many improvements [u] communicated to the editor, he publifhed a new edition in two volumes folio, 1722, in which the tranflation was revifed, and the additions, greatly enlarged, incorporated with Camden's text, diftinguifhed by hooks. From this another was printed in two volumes, Fol. 1753. The maps in Gibfon's firft edition engraved by Morden were very faulty: and no notice was taken of the hints for their amendment communicated by Mr. Brokefby, rector of Rowley in Yorkfhire, in a letter to Hearne, printed at the end of the 6th vol. of Leland's Itinerary. I have feen a firft volume of another tranfla-tion in 4to by W. O. efq; printed by R. Penny, in Wine-office court Fleet-ftreet; but I believe never finifhed. Regnerus Vitellius Zirizæus publifhed a trifling abridgement of the Britannia at Amfterdam 1639, 12mo, which was tranflated into Englifh, and publifhed, with maps, 1626, 8vo; and fince, with various alterations and additions from Gibfon's edition with improvements and continuation to the time of publication, lifts of the nobility, a valuation of benefices, and above

[t] Daniel King engraved in a large fheet an orthographical defign of feveral views of buildings, &c. upon the roads in England and Wales, to illuftrate Camden's Britannia. But I believe his fpecimen met with no encouragement.

[u] Particularly in Wales, by E. Lluyd, to whom we owe all our knowledge of that part of the ifland.

60 maps, in 2 vols. Lond. 1701, 8vo. It does not appear the Bishop made any use of a copy of the edition of 1607 enriched with several additions and corrections in Camden's own hand writing, which came into the possession of Dr. Thomas Smith [x], fellow of Magdalen Col. Oxford, and keeper of the Cotton Library, and was by him bequeathed with his other collections to Hearne, who had thoughts of publishing it with many additional remarks of his own. Stowe had a design of writing a description of England, and discoursing at large upon all the religious houses, as appears from many of his notes now remaining [y]. Whatever materials Camden left or others have collected for a new edition, his book certainly deserves one, were it only to unite in one view the many discoveries since his time and those which daily occur. A compleat edition of the Britannia will probably remain among the desiderata of our antiquities, till the person shall be found who furnished with all the requisites to be gained by later discoveries and improvements, shall with due attention and support, undertake what Leland and Camden performed in part, and Plot proposed to pursue, a progress over the whole island, and by actual observations and proper correspondencies do for his native country what states and societies have commissioned their members to do for the desarts of Arabia and Siberia.

In the mean time I venture to rank next after Camden, as a kind of supplement to his imperfections, though itself not compleated, " Magna Britannia & Hibernia antiqua & nova, or a new survey " of Great Britain, wherein to the topographical account given by " Mr. Camden and the late editors of his Britannia, is added a " more large history not only of the cities, boroughs, towns, and " parishes, mentioned by them, but also of many other places of note " and antiquities since discovered : together with the chronology of " the most remarkable actions of the Britains, Romans, Saxons, Danes, " and Normans : the lives and constitutions of the bishops of all our " sees; founders and benefactors to our universities and monasteries;

---

[x] Who published a Latin life of Camden, with the correspondence between him and his learned cotemporaries.

[y] Hearne's pref. to Lel. It. vol. vi.

" the

" the fufferings of martyrs ; and many other ecclefiaftical matters : the
" acts and laws of our parliaments, with the places of their meeting :
" a character of fuch eminent ftatefmen and churchmen as have figna-
" lized themfelves by their wife conduct and writings, and the pedi-
" grees of all our noble families and gentry, both antient and mo-
" dern, according to the beft relations extant. Collected and com-
" pofed by an impartial hand."——This work, which we owe to the
diligence of Thomas Cox, vicar of Bromfield, Effex, 1685—1733, was
firft publifhed in monthly numbers, as a fupplement to Europe in the
Atlas Geographus, afterwards collected into 6 vols. 4to ; of which the
Ift and IId came out in 1720 ; the IIId, 1724 ; the IVth, 1727 ; the
Vth, 1730 ; and the VIth, 1731. It contains only the Englifh counties, and confidered as a compilation from the beft original hiftories
and furveys of England with whatever additions its editor was able to
procure, has a great deal of merit. To each county is prefixed a
map ; befides which there are fome indifferent cuts of antient Britifh
habits, &c.

Hearne printed at the end of Benedictus Abbas, 1735, from a copy
in the hand writing of Lawrence Noel, in the poffeffion of T. Lambarde of Sevenoak, Kent, " The Perigrination of Dr. Andrew Boarde,
[Hen. VIIIth's rambling phyfician] " or a book of every region, coun-
" ty, and province, which fhews the miles, leages, diftance from city
" to city, and from town to town." Wood [z] fays the Doctor intended
to publifh it himfelf if Thomas Cromwell, to whom he lent the original MS. had not loft it. Norden [a] quotes it to prove that Harrow
on the hill was a market town in Boarde's time.

George Coryat, rector of Odcombe in Somerfetfhire, and father of
Tom the mad traveller, wrote in Latin verfe, " Defcriptio Angliæ,
" Scotiæ, & Hiberniæ," dedicated to Queen Elizabeth. But Wood,
who mentions it, does not fay whether it was ever printed. Part of
this may be " Defcriptio Angliæ & Defcriptio Londini : two poems in
" verfe, fuppofed to be written in the xvth century. Publifhed at the
" requeft of feveral learned gentlemen, lovers of antiquity. Lond.

[z] Ath. Ox. II. 57.
[a] Speculum Brit. p. 13.

" 1763."

" 1763." 4to. the editor's account of which is that they were found among the papers of a confiderable family in a weftern county, and fuppofed to be the work of fome perfon in it. The mention of only 15 colleges at Oxford fixes them before 1571.

Paul Hentzner's " Journey into England in 1589," printed at Straw-berry-hill, 1757, 12mo. is that part of his " Itinerarium Galliæ, « Germaniæ, Angliæ, & Scotiæ," (printed at Breflaw 1617, 4to, and at Nuremberg 1629, 8vo) which relates to this ifland. Dr. Birch in his Negotiations of Sir Thomas Edmondes, 1743, p. 213, n. gave a fhort extract from this obfolete author, which for the elegance of the Latin and the remarkable defcription of Queen Elizabeth, has been defervedly admired; her beft portraits fcarce exhibiting a more lively image. Hearne reprinted his account of Oxford in his notes at the end of Fierbert's defcription of that Univerfity, annexed to the ixth vol. of Leland's Itinerary.

Richard Symonds, of Black Notley, Effex, gent. born at Okehamp-ton, was in the King's army during the civil war, writing memoirs of battles, actions, motions, and promotions of officers from time to time, in fmall pocket books; and, through the feveral counties he paffed, memorandums of churches, monuments, painted windows, arms, in-fcriptions, &c. till Jan. 1, 1648, when he went to Paris, Rome, and Venice (always continuing his memoirs) where he ftaid till his return to England 1652. Eight or ten of thefe books are in the Harleian Li-brary, two were in Dr. Mead's, and two or three are in the Herald's Office, where is the pedigree of his family, with his picture (probably) in red wax, from a feal engraved by T. Simons, his namefake but no relation [b]. Of the books in the Harleian Lib. Nº 965. and 966. contain Oxford, Worcefter, Berks, and Shrop fhires 1644. Nº 939, Devon, Dorfet, Somerfet, Wilts, and Berks 1644. Nº 944. York, Notting-ham, Lincoln, Huntingdon, Hereford, Stafford, Salop, Leicefter, Cam-bridge fhires, and great part of Wales 1645. The arms and moft of the monuments are rudely drawn with a pen; but thofe that furvived the havock of the times evidence the care with which they were taken.

[b] Walp. Anecd. of Paint. II. p. 95. n.

Three

Three " Itineraries or accounts of journies over feveral parts of England and Wales, by Mr. Ray," in 1661 and 1662, are printed among his " Select Remains," by Geo. Scott, efq; 1760, 8vo.

In the Harleian Library is faid to be " A Journal of travels over " great part of England in 1677, 1678, by Thomas Bafkervile, efq; " of Sunningwell in Berkfhire," a gentleman of learning and curiofity, efpecially in his younger years; known at Oxford by the nick name of The King of Jerufalem. He died about 1705, aged upwards of ninety, as appears from a print c of him. His father was Hannibal Bafkervile of Brazen Nofe Col. a melancholy retired charitable man, fo great a cherifher of wandering beggars that he was feveral times indicted at Abindon for harbouring them d.

" Poly-Olbion, or a chorograpical defcripton of tracts, rivers, " mountaines, forefts, and other parts of this renowned ifle of Great " Britaine, with intermixture of the moft remarkable ftories, antiqui- " ties, wonders, rarityes, pleafures, and commodities of the fame. " Digefted in a poem, by Michael Drayton, efquire. With a table. " Lond. 1612." Fol. To the 2d edition 1622, were added 12 more books never before printed. The firft 18 are illuftrated with notes by Selden. The whole was reprinted together with thefe notes in a folio edition of Drayton's works publifhed by fubfcription 1748: and in an 8vo edition in 4 volumes 1753. This poetical defcription has many particulars which efcaped Camden's notice.

Fuller's " Hiftory of the worthies of England, 1662." Fol. being digefted alphabetically under the feveral counties, of which it con- tains many geographical and hiftorical particulars, may come in here. A trifling abridgement and continuation of it intitled, " Anglorum " fpeculum, or the worthies of England in church and ftate," by G. S was publifhed 1684. 8vo.

Here our original defcriptions and furveys fail: what follow are meagre compilations, many of them by foreigners or natives; book-

---

c Not in Ames' Catalogue of heads.

d See Wood's life, at the end of Hearne's edition of Caii Vindiciæ Ac. Ox. vol. ii. p. 516. Wife's letter concerning fome antiquities in Berkfhire, p. 58, and n. where is a curious extract from this journal, which I cannot find in the Britifh Mufeum.

fellers

fellers catchpennies, or to fpeak moft favourably of them, perfectly
uninterefting.

" Defcriptio Britanniae, Scotiae, Hyberniae, & Orchadum, ex libro
" Pauli Jovii, epifcopi Nucer. de imperiis & gentibus cogniti orbis,
" cum ejus operis proemio, ad Alexandrum Farnefium card. ampliff.
" Venet. 1548." 4to.

" Magnæ Britanniæ deliciæ feu infularum & regnorum quæ M.
" Britanniæ nomine & fereniff. regis Jacobi, &c. imperio hodie
" comprehenduntur defcriptio : ex variis auctoribus collectæ, & reli-
" quarum Europæ nationum jam ante editis deliciis additæ. Colon.
" 1613." 12mo.

" A fhort relation of a long journey made round or ovall by encom-
" paffing the principality of Wales, &c. began 13 July 1652 and ended
" Sept. following, performed by the riding, going, crawling, running,
" and writing of John Taylor, dwelling at the fign of the Poet's head
" in Phenix-alley, near the middle of Long-aker, or Covent-garden."
12mo.

" England defcribed, or the feveral counties and fhires thereof
" briefly handled, 1659." 8vo. moftly copied from Camden by Edw.
Leigh, author of the Critica Sacra.

" Britannia Magna ; five Angliæ, Scotiæ, Hiberniæ, & adjacentium
" infularum geographico-hiftorica defcriptio. Amft. 1661." 2 vols. by
Rutgerus Hermannidas, hiftory profeffor in the Univerfity of Hardero-
wick in Guelderland.

Richard Blome's " Britannia, or a geographical defcription of the
" kingdoms of England, Scotland, and Ireland, with the ifles and
" territories thereunto belonging, &c. The like never before publifhed,
" 1672." Fol. A moft notorious piece of plagiarifm on which Thomas
Blount, author of the antient tenures, wrote animadverfions ; but whether they were printed Wood e could not tell.

" England's Remarques ; giving an exact account of the feveral
" fhires, &c. 1682."

Dunftar's " Anglia rediviva, or full defcription of all the fhires, &c.
" 1699." 8vo.

e Ath. Ox. II. 73.

Seller's

Seller's " Particular defcription of the counties," annexed to his " Hiftory of England."

Rogers's " Three years travels over England and Wales." 8vo.

James Brome's " Travels over England, Scotland, and Wales." 1707 and 1726. 8vo.

" A relation of a journey into England and Holland in 1706 and " 1707, by a Saxon phyfician, in a letter to his friend at Drefden, by " C. H. E. D. phyfician in ordinary to the King of Poland, tranflated " from the Latin, 1711." 8vo. giving a trifling account of London, Oxford, &c.

" Britifh curiofities in art and nature, 1713, 1721, and 1728." 12mo, with a fcheme of 22 columns of things to be obferved by ftrangers in a folding fheet.

Bickham's " Britifh monarchy, or a new chorographical defcription " of all the dominions fubject to the King of G. Britain, 1743." Fol. a fpecimen of engraved penmanfhip, going no further than Devonfhire.

" The beauties of England, divided into their refpective counties. 1757." 12mo.

Hanway's " Journal of eight days journey from Portfmouth to King-fton upon Thames, 1756." 4to. and 2 vols. 8vo. 1757

William Toldervey's " England and Wales defcribed in a feries of letters," propofed to be publifhed in 3 vols. 8vo. by weekly numbers, of which only nine came out, which had nothing to recommend them but tolerable cuts.

In 1714 was publifhed " A Journey through England, in familliar " letters, from a gentleman here to his friend abroad," 8vo. reprinted 1724, 1732. A 2d volume was afterwards added, reprinted 1724, 1732. A 3d, containing a Journey through Scotland," on the fame plan and by the fame author, reprinted 1723, 1729. The plan was followed in " A Tour through the whole Ifland of Great " Britain; divided into circuits or journies, giving a particular ac-" count of whatever is curious and worth obfervation, by a gentle-" man." 2 vols. 8vo. A 2d edition 1738, 4 vols. 12mo. another 1748; a 5th 1753, with the Iflands. After it had gone through five editions a fet of maps of England, Scotland, the iflands, and the counties were

E   engraved

engraved for it. To the 6th edition were added an account of the medicinal fprings and Scilly. The additions bring it down to the end of 1761. A work on this plan, compiled by one who had actually vifited the feveral parts of the kingdom, or received authentic information from fuch as had, or from the beft furveys, might be made a very ufeful pocket companion to all kind of travellers. The other editions of this book, with all their defects, far exceed two wretched compilations, called " The Englifh traveller," with maps, and Simpfon's " Agree-" able hiftorian, or compleat Englifh traveller ," both in 3 volumes, 12mo. 1746.

Dodfley printed " The geography of England, done in the manner " of Gordon's geographical grammar," with a compleat map, from the lateft and beft obfervations, by J. Cowley, prefixed to each county : a feparate map of England, the roads, and the Channel, and a plan of London : and, by way of introduction, a view of our conftitution, and every branch of the legiflature. 1744. 8vo. He re-publifhed it 1765, 8vo. with the title altered to make it pafs for a new work. The fecond part contains a concife hiftory of England, or the revolutions of the Britifh conftitution, befides the introduction. The fame year he put out a work in 2 vols. 4to. pretended to be upon a new plan, intitled, " England illuftrated, or a compendium of the natural hiftory, geography, topography, and antiquities, ecclefiaftical and civil, of England and Wales ; with maps of the feveral counties, and engravings of many remains of antiquities, remarkable buildings, and principal towns." This is nothing more than an abridgement of Camden, in a different method, all his errors adopted, and many new ones committed [f]. The views are copies of thofe by Meffrs. Buck, and the maps of little value.

Herman Moll's " New defcription of England and Wales, with the " adjacent iflands, &c. with many hiftorical and critical remarks, and " a new and correct fet of maps [g] of each county, their roads, and " diftances ; their margins adorned with a great variety of very re-

[f] See the Monthly Review, Apr. 1764.
[g] The map intitled Antonini Itinerarium per Britanniam is by Dr. Stukeley : the reft, except thofe of Flint and Denbigh fhires, are the fame which make his quarto fet of Englifh counties.

" markable

" markable antiquities, 1724." Fol. allowing for the types and engravings, is at leaſt of as much, if not more value.

In the firſt vol. of " A complete ſyſtem of geography," with maps
by E. Bowen, 2 vols. Fol. 1747. is a better deſcription of Great Britain and Ireland, with many particulars not uſually inſerted in ſuch
general ſurveys.

In 1757 were publiſhed at Newcaſtle " Four topographical letters,
" written in July 1755, upon a journey through Bedfordſhire, North-
" amptonſhire, Leiceſterſhire, Nottinghamſhire, Derbyſhire, War-
" wickſhire, &c. from a gentleman of London to his brother and
" ſiſter in town, giving a deſcription of the country thro which he
" paſſed, with obſervations on every thing that occurred to him ei-
" ther curious or remarkable," 8vo. containing ſome unborrowed particulars.

Foremoſt among what our neighbours have wrote about us ſtands
" Relation d'un voyage en Angleterre, ou ſont touchées pluſieurs
" choſes, qui regardent l'eſtat de ſciences, & de la religion, & autres
" matieres curieuſes. Paris 1664.." 12°. by Samuel Sorbiere, a vain
Popiſh prieſt, remarkable for nothing but ridiculous obſervations and
ſuch abuſive reflections on the Engliſh, that Lewis XIV. whoſe hiſtoriographer he was, baniſhed him out of his dominions.   Biſhop Spratt,
who was then writing the hiſtory of the Royal Society, of which Sorbiere boaſted himſelf a member, made ſome good ſtrictures on this
book in a letter addreſſed to Dr. Wren, profeſſor of aſtronomy at Oxford, 1665, annexed to the firſt tranſlation of it, intitled, " A voyage
" to England, containing many things relating to the ſtate of learning,
" religion, and other curioſities of that kingdom, by Monſ. Sorbiere.
" With a letter of M. Sorbiere, concerning the war between England
" and Holland in 1652 : To all which is prefixed his life, writ by M.
" Graverol.   Done into Engliſh from the French original. Lond.
" 1709." 8vo.   Several ſpurious tranſlations were publiſhed before.

The firſt edition of Dr. Liſter's journey to Paris, 1697, was full of
ſimilar impertinencies, ſmartly ridiculed by Dr. King, in his Journey to
London, fictitiouſly aſcribed to Sorbiere, which did not prevent the
2d edition having many more.

E 2   " Memoires

" Memoires et obfervations faites par un voyageur en Angleterre,
" fur ce qu'il a trouvé de plus remarquable, tant a l'egard de la reli-
" gion, que de la politique, des moeurs, des curiofitez naturelles, et
" quantité de faits hiftoriques. Avec une defcription particuliere de ce
" qu'il y a de plus curieux dans Londres. Le tout enrichi de figures.
" A la Haye 1698." 8vo. Tranflated by Ozell, and publifhed 1719,
under the title of " M. Miffon's Memoirs and obfervations in his travels
" over England; with fome account of Scotland and Ireland; difpofed
" in alphabetical order." 8vo.

" Les Delices de la Grande Britaine & de l'Ireland ou font exacte-
" ment décrites les antiquitez, les provinces, les villes, les bourgs, les
" montagnes, les rivieres, les portes de mer, les bains, les forterefles,
" abbayes, eglifes, academies, colleges, bibliotheques, palais, les prin-
" cipales maifons de campagne, et autres beaux edifices des familles
" illuftres avec leurs armoiries, &c. la religion, les moeurs des habi-
" tans, leurs jeux, leurs divertiffemens, et genéralement tout ce qu'il
" y a de plus confiderable a remarquer. Par Jaques Beeverell, M. A.
" le tout enrichi de tres belles figures, et cartes geographiques, deffi-
" nées fur les originaux. Leide 1707." 8vo. 9 vols. and 1727, in 8
vols. The cuts are the beft part of this work.

" Le Guide d'Angleterre, ou relation curieufe du voyage de M. de
" B * * *, contenant un detail exact de tout ce que la campagne & les
" principales villes de ce royaume ont de plus remarquable, avec une
" expofition fidele des genies & des coutumes de la nation, & une de-
" fcription circonftanciee de la ville de Londres, & des amufemens
" des eaux de Tunbridge & d'Epfom. Enrichi d'une carte geogra-
" phique pour l'intelligence du pais. Amft. 1744." 12mo.

" Effai geographique fur les ifles Britanniques, contenant une defcrip-
" tion de l'Angleterre, l'Ecoffe, & l'Irlande, tant pour le navigation
" des coftes, que pour joindre aux cartes reduites de ces ifles, qui ont
" ete dreffées au depoft des cartes, plans, & journaux de la marine
" pour le fervice des vaiffeax du roy, par ordre de Monf. de Machault,
" garde des fceaux de France, miniftre & fecretaire d'etat, ayant le
" departement de la marine, par M. Bellin, ingenieur de la marine &
" du depoft des plans, cenfeur royal de l'academie de marine, & de
" la

" la fociete royale de Londres. 1757." 4to. Befides a general and three diftinct maps of the Britifh ifles this work is adorned with neat views of Cambridge, London, Chatham, Weftminfter, Dover, Oxford, Windfor, Canterbury, Edinburgh, and its caftle, Carrickfergus, King-fale harbour, Portfmouth, Plimouth, and the light-houfe, Briftol, Harwich, Deptford, Invernefs, York, the Sorlingues bearing N. W. 3 leagues, Pomona, Mountains of Dundrum at the entrance of Carling-ford bay bearing N. N. E. 2 leagues, *Laftiffe* [Loweftoff] the church bearing N. W. Loknour bay, Faro bearing N. E. 3 leagues, Port S. Pierre [Jerfey] Gulph of Edinburgh, and plans of London, Berwick, Newcaftle, Dublin, Kingfale, Galway, Yarmouth, Caernarvon, and Leith, engraved by W. Chaffaud and J. de la Crux. The large maps referred to are five large fheets comprehending the three king-doms; England and Scotland in two each, and Ireland in the 5th, and made to ufe feparately or together. Bellin obferves that the French maps of England are worth very little: he ufed Moll's maps 1710, Speed's theatre, Morden, Kitchen, and Jefferey's fmall Englifh atlas 1751, Bowen's maps in the Syftem of geography, and Jefferey's fix fheet map, the lateft and beft; which, he fays, proves the want of exactnefs in the others. His work is divided into three parts. 1. A geographical defcription of the three kingdoms. 2. A defcription of the coafts, harbours, foundings, &c. 3. An analyfis of the larger maps; but for want of fufficient materials he confiders it as only an effay, though the firft of the kind. By the affectation peculiar to his coun-trymen, or the negligence of his printer, he has given directions fcarce intelligible to us, though copied from Englifh guides. Thus he lays down the road from London to *la Rye* [Rye], by *Lefham* [Lewifham], Riverhoad [Riverhead], &c. to Shoram by Croydon, Eaft Grimfted, and *Newchapgo* [h] : from E. Grimftead to Lewis by *Foreftrow* [For-reft row], *Shelfortgo* [h] [Sheffield green], Offa ftreet [Offam ftreet] : from Bagfhot to *Hailleron* [Hartley row] to Bafingftoke. P. 104. from Cranborn to Beaufort, through *Alhallon Wabon* [Allhallows Wimborn], *Middleaffet* [Middle-guffet]. And perhaps the moft curious of all is

---

[h] Thefe two ftand in Ogilby's map N. *gr.* and S. *gr.* which Bellin miftakes for *go.*

his route from London to Waltham crofs, p. 106, &c. " de Londres a
" Edmonton, m. 6. paffant par Kingfland, Newington, & Tottenham
" crofs. De Edmon ton a Waltham crofs, m. 6, paffant par *Lacmorand*
" [Lackmore-end] & *Infiel-Dwafh* [Enfield-wafh;]" and fo on, " a
" Hodfdon, m. 6, paffant par Turner's-hill, *Chefton*-ftreet, Wormley,
" end, & *Brokton* [Broxbourne]." He calls Stilton, *Stilfon*; Hollo-
way, *Holwais*; Whetfton, *Vefton*; Uppingham, *Upagham*; Higham
Ferrers, *Higfham*; Melton-mowbray, *Mittomowbray*; Tring, *Ering*;
Bramber, *Bomber*; Bottefdale, *Buddefvale*: and fays, Dunftable is only
a village, with a caftle, which is built on the fcite of the antient Magio-
vinium. It is to hoped he is more exact in the names in his Maritime Atlas for the whole world, publifhed laft year, by order of the
Duke de Choifeul, in 4 vols. 4to. of which a fifth is to comprehend
France alone.

Since this there has been publifhed " Defcription hiftorique & geo-
" graphique des ifles Britanniques, ou des royaumes d'Angleterre,
" d'Ecoffe, & d'Irelande, par M. l'abbe Expilly, de la fociete royale
" des fciences & belles lettres de Nancy, avec des cartes geogra-
" phiques. Paris 1759." 12mo.

Among the Harleian MSS. No 6281. is " A booke of the citties,
" burroughs, villages, and hundreds, their names, and who were lords
" of every manor throughout all the counties of England, from 1316
" [10 Ed. II.] to 1559 [3 Eliz.]" A tranfcript of the book called
" Nomina Villarum," kept in the remembrancer's office in the Exchequer.

" Villare Anglicum, or a view of the townes of England. Col-
" lected by the appointment of Sir Henry Spelman, Kt. Lond. 1656."
4to. Reprinted 1678, with fome alterations in the title, and the addition of the bifhopricks, number of parifhes in each diocefe and county, boroughs and members, and other corrections and amendments.
It is alfo inferted in Gibfon's edition of Spelman's Englifh works 1698
and 1727. Fol. under its original title. Nicholfon fays it was afcribed
to Spelman and Dodfworth jointly; but he thinks it was chiefly drawn
out of Speed's tables on the back of his maps.

Tho.

Tho. Gore [i], a Wiltſhire gentleman, who ſtudied at Magdalen Col. Oxf. and publiſhed a Catalogue of antient Engliſh families, Ox. 1667. 8vo. and another of all the writers on heraldry in all languages 1668, 1674, printed likewiſe " Nomenclator geographicus Latino-anglicus " & Anglico-latinus, alphabeticè digeſtus, complectens plerorumq; " omnium M. Britanniæ & Hiberniæ regionum, comitatuum, epiſ- " copatuum, oppidorum, fluviorum, nomina & appellationes (quæ ſci- " licet apud ſcriptores occurrunt Latinos) ex libris qua MSS. quam " typis excuſis, chartis geographicis, aliiſque rei antiquariæ monumentis " ſumma diligentia collectas. Ox. 1667." 12mo. of which he intend- ed a 2d edition.

" A book of names of all the pariſhes, market towns, villages, ham- " lets, and ſmall places in England and Wales, alphabetically ſet down, " &c." was publiſhed 1668. 4to.

But the beſt book of this kind, tho' not without faults, is " Index " Villaris, or an alphabetical table of all the cities, market towns, pa- " riſhes, villages, and private ſeats in England and Wales. By Mr. " Adams of the Inner Temple. Lond. 1680." Fol. In the dedica- tion to James II. he tells him, he intends not only to make this cor- rect, but to preſent to his view a compleat map of England and Wales, upon an actual ſurvey. Accordingly he offered to the Royal Society, Apr. 27, 1681, propoſals for making a ſurvey of England, by mea- ſuring the bounding line, the diſtances between places both in the round and the ſtrait lines, and taking the latitudes and angles of po- ſition; and deſired their directions and encouragement. Biſhop Ni- cholſon ſays " his map [k], with the contraction of it afterwards, muſt be " acknowledged to be done with great pains, judgment, and exactneſs." It were to be wiſhed his Index Villaris had no more errors nor omiſ- ſions in it: but great improvements upon it by the induſtrious and learned Mr. Aubrey (now in his Muſeum) were expected to be pub- liſhed. Somewhat of the ſame kind is the " Dictionarium Angliæ " topographicum & hiſtoricum : An alphabetical deſcription of the

[i] Of whom ſee Ath. Ox. II. 758.
[k] It was ſix feet ſquare: the computed and meaſured miles entered in figures. Phil. Tranſ. N° 135. p. 886.

" chief

" chief places in England and Wales; with an account of the moft
" memorable events which have diftinguifhed them. By the celebrated
" antiquary William Lambarde, formerly of Lincoln's Inn, efq; and
" author of the Perambulation of Kent. Now firft publifhed from a
" MS. under the author's own hand. Lond. 1730" 4to. This, as
the author tells us, is but a breviate for ftore, and was meant to be enlarged, as the Perambulation of Kent is, which was for the moft part
drawn out of this, after which fort alfo the reft of the fhires might
be defcribed. It is a kind of common place of extracts from our hiftorians, &c. under each article, and many curious particulars not felected
by other antiquaries occur in it.

The laft work of this kind was " England's Gazetteer, or an accu-
" rate defcription of the cities, towns, and villages of the kingdom,
" in 3 volumes. Vol. I. and II. contain a dictionary of the cities, cor-
" porations, market towns, and moft noted villages, &c. Vol. III. a
" new Index Villaris, or alphabetical regifter of the lefs noted villages.
" Including all the chief harbours, bays, forefts, hills, mines, medi-
" cinal fprings, moors, and other curiofities both of nature and art,
" and not only taking notice of moft of the manors and feats in the
" kingdom both antient and prefent, but alfo pointing out the old mi-
" litary ways, camps, caftles, and other remarkable ruins of Roman,
" Danifh, and Saxon antiquity; and particularly fhewing the eftates that
" were formerly abbey land, 1750." 12mo. A hafty compilation in
which many confiderable places are omitted.

In the Phil. Tranf. N° 330, p. 266, is Dr. Grew's demonftration of
the number of acres in England or South Britain, viz. 46 millions
80,000. Its length from Newhaven (Suffex) to Berwick 395 miles;
breadth from the South Foreland to the Land's end, 367 miles. Of all
the antient dimenfions of the ifland thofe in Cæfar approach neareft the
truth. Agrippa from the Greeks made the breadth 300 miles, which
Mr. Bertram [a] underftands of a line drawn from Wales to Norfolk, its
greateft breadth. Dio puts its leaft at 300 ftades, and its greateft at

---

[a] Note on Rich. of Cir. p. 163.

2310 ftades, which anſwer to 289 Roman miles [b]. Cæſar makes the S. coaſt about 500 miles long. Grew's 367 miles anſwer to about 400 Roman ones, and with him agrees Richard of Cirenceſter. We may ſuppoſe Cæſar allowed for the irregularities of the ſhore [c]. The weſt ſide is 700 miles long [d], including Scotland : Agrippa makes the length of the whole iſland 800 Roman miles, which anſwer to about 730 ſtatute miles. Our maps of the laſt age carried it to 700 ; but its true length from the Lizard to Dungſby or Dannet-head, the extremity of Orkney, has been ſince fixed to 590 ſtatute miles [e], which make but 650 Roman ones. Cæſar, perhaps from the Druids, makes the circumference 2000 miles, Pliny from Iſidorus Characenus 3825 [f].

A letter from Dr. Wm. Brackenridge to G. L. Scott, eſq; concerning the number of people in England, was publiſhed in vol. xlix. of the Phil. Tranſ. art. 45. Calculating them by the number of houſes and the quantity of bread conſumed, he makes them amount to about ſix millions. In another letter to the ſame gentleman (art. 113.) he ſhews there is no increaſe of our people at preſent, and that in England in particular they would decreaſe if not ſupplied from Ireland and Scotland. The 43d, 57th, and 58th articles of vol. l. contain a controverſy between the Doctor and Mr. Forſter, rector of Great Shefford, Berks, on the number of cottages, which the latter ſuppoſes 400,000 more than the former.

John Norden, who intended the deſcription of famous England, but lived or had leiſure only to publiſh deſcriptions of a few counties to be

[b] Marc. Heracleota meaſures its *breadth* from the Lizard point to the Mull of Galloway 3083 ſtades or 386 miles. Richard makes it 1000.

[c] Strabo and Diodorus exceed all probability when they make it from 5000 to 7500 ſtades, *i. e.* from 600 to 800 miles.

[d] Dio Caſſius had made it 7132 ſtades or 891 Roman miles, anſwering to about 820 Engliſh. Diodorus makes it 20000 ſtades or 2500 miles : Strabo 4300 ſtades. Diodorus makes the Eaſt ſide 15000 ſtades or 1875 miles, and Richard moſt erroneouſly 2200 miles.

[e] According to the geometrical meaſure of Engliſh ſtatute miles, which is 69 miles and 864 feét to a degree, the true length of the iſland is 622½ miles : the true breadth 284 miles. Bowen's Compl. Syſt. of Geogr.

[f] Solinus and Bede ſay 3275. Pytheas of Marſeilles, that credulous liar whom Strabo thought worth quoting, makes it 40000 ſtades or 5000 miles. Pliny muſt be corrected when he ſays Pytheas and Iſidorus agreed. Diodorus gives 42500 ſtades or 5312 miles. Marcianus Heracleota puts it between 28604 and 20526 ſtades, *i. e.* 3575 and 2576 miles. Richard follows his greater number, ſetting it down roundly 3600.

F

here-

hereafter mentioned, compiled the firft pocket companion for travellers, over this ifland, intitled, " England: an intended guide for Englifh tra-
" vailers; fhewing in generall, how far one citie, and many fhire-townes,
" in England, are diftant from other ; together with the fhires in parti-
" cular, and the chief townes in every of them ; with a generall table of
" the moft of the principall townes in Wales. Invented and collected
" by John Norden. *Voluntas pro facultate.* Lond. 1621." 4to. This was
copied exactly on copper plates, and, with the names of all the cities,
towns, villages, and hamlets, publifhed under the title of " A direc-
" tion for the Englifh traviller, by which he fhall be inabled to coaft
" about all England and Wales; and alfo to know how farre any
" market, or noteable towne in any fhire lyith one from another, and
" whether the fame be eaft, weft, north, or fouth, from the fhire-
" towne : as alfo the diftance betweene London and any other fhire or
" great towne; with the fcituation thereof, E. W. N. or S. from
" London. By the help alfo of this worke one may know (in what
" parifh, village, or manfion houfe foever he be in) what fhire he is
" to pafs through, and which way he is travell, till he come to his
" journies end. Lond. 1643." 12mo. The fcheme of the market
towns, &c. their diftance from London and one another, at the end of
each county in the Magna Britannia, is copied from this work.

" A new booke of mapps; being a ready guide or direction for any
" ftranger, or other, who is to travel in any part of the common-
" wealth of England, Scotland, and Ireland. Wherein are, I. Alpha-
" betical tables, fhewing the longitude and latitude of all the towns
" named in the faid maps; with eafie and ready directions how to find
" any of them. II. Tables of the highwayes alphabetically metho-
" dized. III. Tables as eafie as an almanack, which may fupply the
" ufe thereof for 100 years, that is to fay, from anno 1600 to 1700,
" and other ufeful tables. By Thomas Porter. Lond. 1655." 12mo.

" The Englifh traveller's companion, or a ready and fure guide
" from London to any of the principal cities and towns in England and
" Wales; containing all the grand roads, with their feveral branches,
" and the towns and villages they pafs through : to which is affixed
" the

" the computed diftances from one to another, exhibited in five tables,
" of a new and accurate method. By a lover of his countrymen.
" Lond. 1676." 12mo.

John Ogilby, born near Edinburgh 1600, and through his father's
extravagance bred a dancing-mafter, teaching in Lord Strafford's family was by him made mafter of the revels in Ireland, where he built a
play-houfe : but lofing all his fortune in the Irifh rebellion 1641, he
came to Cambridge, tranflated Virgil and Homer, and by pompous
editions of them and the Bible recovered his fortune and place in Ireland, and rebuilt his theatre. The fire of London reduced him to 5 *l.*
but getting appointed King's cofmographer, and geographic printer,
he publifhed an Atlas, in feveral parts, and defigned a noble defcription of England, in 3 vols. of which the firft only was publifhed, intitled, Britannia, &c. Lond. 1674. Fol. containing an ichnographical
and hiftorical account of all our great roads on 100 large copper cuts :
the 2d was to have given us the like view of our cities : and the 3d a
topographical defcription of the whole kingdom [1]. His Britannia was
reprinted in the " Traveller's guide, or a moft exact defcription of the
" roads of England, being Mr. Ogilby's actual furvey, and menfura-
" tion by the wheel, of the great roads from London, to all the con-
" fiderable cities and towns in England and Wales ; together with the
" crofs-roads from one city or eminent town to another. Wherein is
" fhewn the diftance from place to place, and plain directions given,
" to find the way, by fetting down every town, village, river, brook,
" bridge, common, foreft, wood, copfe, heath, moor, &c. that oc-
" cur in paffing the roads. And for the better illuftration thereof, are
" added tables, wherein the names of the places, with their diftances,
" are fet down in a column, in fo plain a manner, that meer ftrangers
" may travel all over England, without any other guide. Lond.
" 1674." Fol. Since reprinted in 8vo. without the plates, and intitled " Mr. Ogilby's and Mr. William Morgan's pocket-book of the
" roads, with their computed and meafured diftances, and the diftinc-
" tion of market and poft towns. To which is added, feveral roads,
" and above five hundred market towns; with a table for the ready

[1] Nicholfon, Hift. Lib. p. 6.

F 2

" finding

" finding any road, city, or market town, and their diſtance from
" London, and a ſheet map of England, fitted to bind with a book.
" By William Morgan, coſmographer to their Majeſties. Lond. 1689.'
8vo. The eleventh edition of this uſeful book was printed 1752, 12mo.
with a liſt of the poſt towns, &c.

" Britannia depicta, or Ogilby improved ; being a correct copy of
Mr: Ogilby's actual ſurvey of all the direct and principal croſs roads in
England and Wales : wherein are exactly delineated and engraven all
the cities, towns, &c. ſituate on or near the roads ; with their reſpective diſtances in meaſured and computed miles, a full and particular
deſcription and account of all the cities, &c. With ſuitable remarks
on all places of note, drawn from the beſt hiſtorians and antiquaries.
By John Owen of the Middle Temple, gent. The arms of the peers
of this realm, who derive their titles from places lying on, or near the
roads : the arms of all the biſhopricks and deanaries, their foundation,
extent, yearly value, number of pariſhes, &c. the arms, and a ſuccinct
account of both univerſities. Laſtly, particular and correct maps of all the
counties of South Britain, with a ſummary deſcription of each county,
&c. By Em. Bowen, engraver. Lond. 1720." 8vo. This has gone thro'
ſeveral editions ; the 4th 1736, the laſt 1764. It was preceeded a year
by " Gardner's Pocket guide to the Engliſh traveller, being a compleat
" ſurvey and admeaſurement of all the principal roads and moſt con-
" ſiderable croſs roads in England and Wales, in 100 copper plates,
" 1719." 4to. and followed by " The traveller's guide, or Ogilby's
roads epitomiſed : a ſet of tables, in which are deſcribed all the grand
roads and ſeveral of the croſs roads of England and Wales ; the diſtance
between every town in meaſured and computed miles, &c. with a
correct map of England. By I. V. Kircher." 12mo.

" Chorographia Britanniæ, or a ſet of maps of all the counties in
England and Wales ; to which are prefixed an accurate chart of the
ſea coaſt, &c. a map of England and Wales as divided into counties,
with the names of the cities and county towns, and the length, breadth
and ſuperficial contents of the whole, and each county ſeparately ;
a map of the roads from London to all parts of South Britain, with
tables ſhewing the diſtance of each city and town on the road from the

metro-

metropolis, both in computed and meafured miles; a map of all the crofs roads from one great town to another, with their diftances both by computation and meafurement. With the particular maps of each county is an account of all the cities, &c. therein, the number of members, the market and fair days, and an account of the univerfities: to the whole is added an alphabetical index of all the cities, &c. This collection was firft drawn and compiled into a pocket-book by order and for the ufe of his late majefty King George I. by Thomas Badeflade, furveyor and engineer and now neatly engraved by W. H. Toms. Lond. 1742." 12mo.

Dodfley publifhed in 1756 and 1759, 12mo. what he called " A " new and accurate defcrption of the prefent great roads and crofs " roads of England and Wales, with the feveral branches leading out " of them, and a defcription of the feveral towns thereon, divided in- " to four parts, weftern, northern, eaftern, and fouthern: to which " are added the antient Roman roads and ftations in Britain; fome " general rules to know the original of the names of places in Eng- " land, a lift of mitred abbots, and an alphabetical lift of fairs regu- " lated by the new ftyle." This leads through many ways long fince difufed, and differs in meafurement from the mile-ftones.

Another " Traveller's pocket-book, or Ogilby and Morgan's book of roads improved and amended; containing, I. the diftances in mea- fured miles from London according to the new erected mile-ftones, and an account of the feats near the road fide. II. The crofs roads in England and Wales. III. An alphabetical lift of all the cities, &c. with a whole fheet map of the roads, &c." came out 1759.

The laft on the fubject is " The traveller's affiftant, being the moft " general and compleat director extant, to all the poft, principal, and " crofs roads in England, Wales, Scotland, and Ireland; giving the " true names, and exact diftances from the ftandard in Cornhill for " Great Britain, and from Dublin for Ireland, to all the feveral cities, " towns, villages, &c. in the three kingdoms. The whole collected " and computed in a new manner, more clear and intelligent than any " yet publifhed. By J. Rocque, topographer to his Majefty. Lond. " 1764." 12mo.

Bagford

Bagford [m] fays, the firft ftep that was made towards a knowledge of our coafts was by an Almanac with a chart of the coafting part of England, in a fmall portable volume bound and printed on vellum or parchment by Wynkin de Worde, 1520. This was the firft he had feen of the kind [n]; and Hearne thinks it defigned principally for the Council [o].

" A defcription and plat of the fea-coaft of England, from London,
" up all the river of Thames, all along the coaft to Newcaftle; and fo to
" Edinburgh all along Scotland, the Orcades, and Hitland; where the
" Dutch begin their fifhing," was publifhed Lond. 1653. 4to.

Capt. Greenville Collins, hydrographer in ordinary to K. William and Q. Mary, publifhed in 1693, " Great Britain's coafting pilot, the
" firft part; being a new and exact furvey of the coaft of England,
" from the river of Thames to the weftward, with the iflands of Scilly,
" and from thence to Carlifle, defcribing all the harbours, rivers, bays,
" roads, rocks, fands, buoys, beacons, fea marks, depths of water,
" latitudes, bearings, and diftances from place to place, the fetting and
" flowing of the tides, with directions for the knowing of any place,
" and how to harbour a fhip in the fame with fafety, with directions
" for coming into the Channel between England and France." The fecond part is a furvey of the fea-coaft of England and Scotland from the Thames to the northward, with the iflands of Orkney and Shetland, &c. &c. Both were republifhed 1760.

A chart of the Channel, faid to be corrected by Dr. Halley, was publifhed in 1721.

In confequence of an act of parliament, 14 Geo. II. for furveying the chief ports, headlands, &c. of Great Britain, to determine the latitude and longitude thereof, and impowering the commiffioners of longitude to apply 2000 l. for this purpofe, Whifton employed John Renfhaw, who went round the coaft, and furveyed it trigonometrically

---

[m] Letter to Hearne, Pref. to Leland's Itin. vol. I. p. lxxx.

[n] Spicileg. ad G. Neubrig. p. 749.

[o] A piece *De fluxu et refluxu maris*, Pits adds *Anglicani*, is afcribed by Leland to Walter Burley, preceptor to Edw. III. and a great commentator on Ariftotle. There are two MSS. of it at Oxford, but Bp. Tanner doubts whether it was not wrote by Rog. Bacon. That afcribed to the latter in the Bodleian Lib. begins differently. Tan. B. B. p. 142. n. *k*. comp. with p. 63. n. *i*.

from

from the N. Foreland to the Land's end, and Scilly: but could not be conveyed to Cape Clear on the S. W. of Ireland, which Whiston said was only to be determined by the eclipses of Jupiter's satellites, and was done at his expence by Renshaw 1744 p. The chart, which is large, was published 1745, and includes the French coast before published by Dr. Halley from an incorrect chart of our coast by the French astronomers' observations of such eclipses.

" Plans of the harbours, bays, and roads in St. George's Channel,
" lately surveyed under the direction of the Lords of the Admiralty,
" and now published with their permission: with an appendix concern·
" ing the improvements that might be made in the several harbours,
" &c. for the better securing the navigation on those parts: together
" with a short account of the trade and manufactures on the coast.
" By Lewis Morris. Lond. 1748." 4to.

Very little regard is to be paid to maps made before the reformation. The religious had too little occasion for the art of making them to cultivate it much. We don't find they drew plans of their estates or convents, and when they attempted to delineate particular countries, or routs through them, it was in the rudest manner. In the most complete MS. of Giraldus Cambrensis's description of Ireland, in Benet Col. library, I. IX. is a rude map of Britain and Ireland. He wrote this piece about 1176. In an abridgement of Matthew Paris's history, supposed to be wrote with his own hand, Cott. Lib. Claud. D. VI. is a curious map of England and Scotland, the latter contracted for want of length in the page. Dover, Canterbury, and Rochester are placed in a line due S. of London, as St. Albans, Dunstable, and Northampton are due N. of it. The Medway runs from the W. into the Thames, and in the whole tract westward of the latter are only three places, Exon, Tintacol [Tintagel] and Bristol. All the places are expressed by names only, except London and Dover, which are rudely drawn. At the end of the fine MS. of the same author's Lives of the

p I have seen a survey of the British Channel from the N. Foreland to Cape Clear in six sheets, without date or maker's name. Quære, if this?

2 the

two Offas and the abbots of St. Albans, in the fame library, Nero, D. I is a kind of itinerary from London through France to Rome, thence to Otranto, and back to Naples, by above 60 ftages of a day's journey, which, by its following on the fame page pleas of the crown, temp. Ed. II. cannot have been made later than the fourteenth century. The date of the old map of Thanet printed by Lewis from a MS. formerly in St. Auftins abbey, Canterbury, is uncertain. That of Richard of Cirencefter's has been fixed before. One of the oldeft Hearne had feen was in MS. in Jefus Col. Oxford: rude, and not much to be gathered from it, yet a curiofity. He looked on the antient map of Merton Col. mentioned by Harrifon [q], where the river Sore is called Brember water, to be equally curious; but could not determine whether it were a map of all or only part of England [r].

Dr. William Cunningham, phyfician at Norwich, in his " Cofmo" graphical glaffe, conteinyng the pleafant principles of cofmographie, " geographie, hydrographie, or navigation," printed by Day 1559. Fol. fays he was the " firft that ever in our tongue have written of this " argument." His article of chorography is illuftrated by " an accu" rate map of the excellent city of Norwich, as the form of it is 1558," with many alphabetical references to an explanation of the places at the bottom. He gives the neceffary directions for map-making, the whole procefs of a map of England, Helvetian compared with Englifh miles, and a tide table for the coafts of Britain, Ireland, Dutchland, and France.

Geo. Lilly (fon of William, the famous grammarian) who lived fome time at Rome with Cardinal Pole, publifhed the firft exact map of this ifland [s]. The map of England in Ortelius' Theatrum orbis. Antv. 1570, was the work of Humphrey Lhuyd of Denbighfhire [t].

The firft fet of maps of England was that collected by Chriftopher Saxton of Yorkfhire, who [u] fpent nine years in travelling over the whole kingdom, of which he made a general furvey, and feparate ones of the

[q] Defcrip. of Brit. p. 54. col. 1. 1586.
[r] Not. & Spicil. ad G. Neubrig. p. 749, 750.
[s] Nicholfon's hift. lib. p. 3.
[t] Walpole's cat. of engr. p. 8.
[u] Wood.

counties

counties. Thomas Seckford, mafter of the requefts to Q. Elizabeth, was the promoter of this undertaking, procuring him a licence x to imprint maps for England or any county therein for ten years. Harrifon y fays he begun with Kent, which he furveyed and publifhed 1575; but this is a miftake: for Norfolk, Oxford, Buckingham, and Berk fhires are dated 1574. Saxton himfelf engraved only the Welfh counties; and Herefordfhire in conjunction with one Nich. Reynold. The reft are engraved by Corn. Hogius, Remigius Hogenbergius, Leonard Tervoort of Antwerp, Francis Scaterius, Auguftine Ryther, and Wm. Bourough, whofe labours will be fpecified under the refpective counties, with their dates. Each map has his patron's arms. To the whole fet are prefixed 84 coats of arms of the nobility, a Latin catalogue of cities, bifhoprics, market towns, caftles, parifh churches, rivers, bridges, groves, forefts, inclofures in each county in England and Wales; and an alphabetical and other index of the maps, and the judges circuits. There is a copy moft curioufly painted among the Bodleian MSS z. Another, formerly Lord Burleigh's, is in the King's Library a in the Britifh Mufeum b, having on the back of each map a lift of the juftices in each county; and feveral plans of harbours and maps of particular counties drawn and painted on paper and vellum, viz. a plan of Falmouth haven and county painted on vellum: one of Lyme, the Ifle of Wight, and Southampton, on paper: one of Sandwich, Tanet, and Newhaven: one of Windfor Foreft, and the arms of the caftle in trick: Humber mouth and the coaft up to Flamboro' and beyond it, painted on paper: Scarborough and its port: plan of Salopia:

---

x Printed in Ames's Hift. of print. p. 541. and dated July 28, anno reg. 15. Among Afhmole's MSS. N° 858. is a patent of arms granted to Chr. Saxton, efq; by the name of C. S. of Dunningley, in the county of York, gent. who by the Queen's command had made a geographical defcription of the feveral fhires of England. Tanner, Bibl. Brit. He is faid by fome to be a native of Leeds. Thorefby Vic. Leod. p. 89.

y Defcrip. of Britain, p. 55.

z Hyde's catalogue, p. 151.

a D. III.

b The late Dr. Birch, whofe communicative difpofition and intimate refearches into our hiftory and antiquities, will make his untimely end regretted by all who had the pleafure of his acquaintance, told me Martin Folkes wrote a differtation on Saxton's maps, publifhed in the Phil. Tranf. about fifteen years back; but I have fought it in vain.

G

foreſt of Clun with Clun caſtle and river : the country about Oſ-
weſtry : the Gill of St. Gillyers·: Scotia, Rom. 1578, by Natalis
Bonifacius Sibenicenſis from Leſley's hiſtory of Scotland.

There is another ſet of neat maps of the three kingdoms in the Cotton Library, Dom. XVIII. England in thirteen, Scotland and Ireland
in three each : the former diſtributed according to the nobility who
take their titles from or had property in the counties. They have
the degrees of longitude and latitude marked on the ſides, and in the
northern counties of England the Saxon names and writing are retained.

Saxton's maps were copied by Geo. Biſhop and John Norton for the
5th edit. of Camden's Britannia in 1600, and in " The theatre of the em-
" pire of Great Britain: preſenting an exact geography of the kingdomes
" of England, Scotland, Ireland, and the iles adjoyning ; with the ſhires,
" hundreds, cities, and ſhire-townes within the kingdome of England,
" divided and deſcribed by John Speed." Lond. 1611 and 1650. Fol.
Theſe are the firſt maps wherein all the counties are divided into hundreds. Saxton's miſtakes are reformed in many ; particularly in Eſſex,
Middleſex, Kent, and Surrey. Jodocus Hondius, a Flemiſh graver, executed many of them ; others were done by Abraham Goos ᶜ, though
his name is not to them. This collection makes a noble apparatus to
his hiſtory. The deſcriptions of the ſeveral counties are moſtly abridgements of Camden ; but that of Norfolk he had from Sir H. Spelman.
The maps of the four counties of Cornwall, Eſſex, Middleſex, and
Suſſex, made by J. Norden, who was cotemporary with Camden, are
copied in Speed's Theatre : the reſt of Norden's will be mentioned
hereafter. The map of the Iſle of Wight was made by Wm. White,
gent. that of Man by Tho. Durham ; that of Cheſhire by J. Speed
aſſiſted by Wm. Smith ; and as only thoſe of Norfolk, Worceſter,
Radnor, and Montgomery ſhires have Saxton's name retained, one
would ſuſpect that Speed ſo intirely new modelled the reſt as not to
leave their original maker any title to them. There is a map of Britain under the Heptarchy : and at the ſides of thoſe of the three kingdoms are the dreſſes of their inhabitants.

ᶜ Walp. cat. of engravers, p. 33.

Hearne

Hearne d mentions among maps Henry Lyte's " Light of Britain," engraved in about twenty fheets, and wonderful fcarce. James I. gave the author, when he prefented it to him, his own picture fet with dia- monds, valued at 300 l.

Mercator publifhed a curious map of the Britifh ifles after his Atlas Major, 1636.

Speed's book was abridged, or the maps of the counties alphabetical- ly ranged, 1627. 8vo. by Blome 1676. 8vo. 1681, 1685. 4to. John Philips, nephew to Milton, made a fupplement to it 1676 e.

There is a map of England printed by Overton 1660, Chr. Saxton defcripfit, Petrus Kærius cælavit.

Hollar's maps of England and Wales, commonly called the Quar- ter-mafter's map, compiled by order of O. Cromwell, were publifhed 1676. Vertue f calls this " The kingdom of England and principality " of Wales defcribed, with every fhire, and the fmall towns in every " one, ufeful for all commanders and quartering of foldiers, in fix " maps and the title. Printed and fold by J. Garrett. W. Hollar fecit, " only in the title." He engraved on a fingle fheet a map of Great Bri- tain, " containing the three kingdoms of England, Scotland, and Ire- " land, with the principality of Wales, &c. as alfo an addition of feveral " of the chief cities belonging to the faid kingdomes. Lond. printed " and publifhed by J. Overton." 1667. This has a view of Edin- burgh, plans of York, Dublin, Oxford, Cambridge and London, and a profpect of the latter " as appearing in the time of its flames."

Another map of England, in half a fheet, 1667.

Another fmall map of England, with thirty fmall views of the principal cities round it; fans date. This I take to be " A new " map of the kingdome of England and principality of Wales, " taken out of J. S. [John Speed,] printed and fold by J. Overton, " 1673." with views of London, Canterbury, Chichefter, Salifburie, Exceftre, Bath, Briftol, Glocefter, Hereford, Worcefter, Shrowefburie, Coventre, Oxford, York, Durham, Newcaftle, Carlifle, Chefter, Lych-

d Not. & Spicil. ad G. Neub. p. 750.
e Ath. Ox. II. 1118.
f Lift of Hollar's works.

G 2

feld,

feld, Lincolne, Nottingham, Peterborow, Northampton, Colcheſter, Ipſwich, Norwich, and Cambridge.

Another ſingle ſheet map of England, with the kings heads round it in ſmall ſquares; ſans date.

" Great ſums were expended this way by Seller and Morden 8." The latter drew thoſe in the Engliſh editions of the Britannia, and a ſet of the Engliſh and Welſh counties in ſmall 4to.

A correct map of South Britain by Charles Price, 1712.

A large map of England in eight ſheets by H. Moll, 1714.

One of Great Britain and Ireland by Geo. Willdey, 1715.

Another of G. Britain and Ireland by John Elphinſton; ſans date.

An accurate map of England and Wales drawn from all the particular ſurveys hitherto publiſhed, illuſtrated with many additional improvements, and regulated by numerous aſtronomical obſervations made by the members of the Royal Society. By Thomas Kitchin, geographer.

Whiſton intended a new ſurvey of England and Wales by the application of his method for finding the longitude at land, which could be eaſier done than at ſea, and by improving Derham's tables of the velocities of ſounds to 30 or 50 miles diſtance. The rectilinear canal called New Bedford River in the Iſle of Ely, and the Watling-ſtreet paſſing nearly in a ſtrait line through the plain county of Stafford, were pitched upon for theſe experiments. Propoſals were publiſhed for a ſet of correct maps according to this method at two guineas: but the deſign met with no encouragement.

Maps of England, Scotland, and Ireland, in ſeven ſheets, containing all the cities, market towns, &c. with the roads and diſtances in computed miles from town to town; ſhewing all the ſea coaſt of Great Britain and Ireland, with the coaſts of France in the Engliſh Channel, compiled, drawn, and improved from actual ſurvey, in ſeven ſheets and a half, reduced to ſix ſheets and a half. By R. W. Seale.

Another of the ſame kind by Wm. Knight.

" A map of the counties of Surry, Kent, Suſſex, Hampſhire, and
" Berkſhire, with part of Dorſet, Wiltſhire, &c. with the roads, rivers,

8 Nich. H. L. p. 6.

" ſea

" fea coafts, &c. taken from the lateft and beft maps extant," was publifhed from the drawings of the late John Senex, F. R. S. 1746.

In 1748 came out " The fmall Englifh Atlas, being a new and accurate fet of maps of all the counties in England and Wales, defigned and engraved in a portable fize for the ufe of travellers," 12mo. To the fecond edition were added two new maps of the rivers, and feaport towns and harbours; and of all the crofs roads through the kingdom.

S. Wale engraved " Geographia Britanniæ, or correct maps of all " the counties in England, Scotland, and Wales, with general ones " of both kingdoms, and of the feveral adjacent iflands, 1748." 2 volumes 12mo

H. Moll's fet of fifty maps of the Englifh and Welfh counties in 4to.

Kitchen and Jefferies put out an Englifh Atlas, being a new and accurate fet of maps of all the counties of England and Wales, 1751. 12mo.

Another fet called the Britifh Atlas was executed by Rocque 1753.

" The large Englifh Atlas; containing a general map of England, " and particular maps of all the counties of England and Wales. " Taken from all the furveys hitherto made, on a large fcale, fhew- " ing all the cities, towns, villages, and churches, whether rectories " or vicarages, chapels, noblemen and gentlemen's feats, &c. &c. " On each map is engraved hiftorical extracts relative to the trade, " manufactories, government of the cities, principal towns, &c. En- " graved by Emanuel Bowen, geographer to his Majefty, Thomas " Kitchen, and others. Lond. 1763." Fol. Thefe maps are alfo reduced to a fmaller fcale, and may be had feparately.

" The fmall Britifh Atlas, being a new fet of maps of all the coun- " ties of England and Wales, with a general map with tables of " length, breadth, area, cities, boroughs, and parifhes in each county; " likewife a particular map of England, with tables of the produce of " the land-tax, &c. by J. Rocque. 1764." 8vo.

" The Englifh Atlas, or a compleat fet of maps of all the counties " in England and Wales, containing all the cities, towns, parifhes, " rivers, roads, feats, and in general every other particular that is " ufually

" ufually fought for or to be found in maps. The whole engraved in
" the neateft and moft accurate manner, from drawings after actual
" furveys, and other the beft authorities, by Thomas Kitchen. Lond.
" 1765." 4to.

" Ellis's Englifh Atlas, or a compleat chorography of England and
" Wales, in 50 maps, containing more particulars than any other col-
" lection of the fame kind; the whole calculated for the ufe of travel-
" lers, academies, and of all thofe who defire to improve in the know-
" ledge of their country: from the lateft furveys by and under the di-
" rection of J. Ellis. Lond. 1766." long 4to. There is a map of
England and Wales, another with poft roads, and Britain under the
heptarchy: Bucks, Hertfordfhire, Huntingdonfhire, Kent, Warwickfhire, and N. Wales are engraved by W. Palmer; Cornwall by de la
Rochette; others by J. Ellis; others have no name.

Notwithftanding the affertions of Bowen and Kitchen that their
maps are framed from actual new furveys, there is fcarce a fingle one
which does not abound with faults: and a fet of correct maps remains
to be hoped for from the encouragement given to the abilities and induftry of Mr. Taylor, of which feveral fpecimens will occur in the
courfe of this work; with the like labours of others in this age of improvement.

" Britannia illuftrata: or Views of feveral of the Queen's palaces,
" and principal feats of the nobility and gentry of Great Britain, on
" eighty copper plates, Lond. 1714." Fol. drawn by [h] L. Knyff, and
very indifferently engraved by J. Kip. A fecond volume with the
fame number of plates and above 300 coats of arms, was publifhed the
year after, the views in which were both drawn and engraved by J. Kip.
Both volumes were republifhed 1724 with a French title by Jofeph
Smith, bookfeller, at In. Jones's head, near Exeter Change. The Ift
contains 80, the IId 68 plates. Two more volumes of plates were
afterwards added by Badeflade, &c. 1736.

[h] Leonard Knyff was a native of Amfterdam and a dealer in pictures, and died 1724
at Weftminfter. John Kipp (whofe chriftian name Mr. Walpole did not know) was his
countryman, died in the fame place the year after: both lived to near 70. Walp. cat.
of engravers, p. 113.

I have

I have feen five fmall quarto volumes of maps, views, and plans of cities, &c. about England, &c. ranged alphabetically according to the order of the counties, with explanations in Dutch, and this title: " Gefichten der fteeden London, Canterbury & Colchefter, en an- " dere omleggende plaatzen, met haare voornaamfte kirken, pala- " cien, gebouwen, luft huizen en andere aanmerkelyke zaaken. In " 82 zeer naauwkeurige prenten afgebeeld, verdeeld in twe deelen. Te " Amfterdam." q. d. " Views of the cities of London, &c. and other places adjacent, with their principal churches, palaces, buildings, pleafure-houfes, and other remarkable places, delineated in 82 very accurate prints, divided into two volumes." The 3d and 4th contain views of colleges, &c. in Oxford and Cambridge after D. Loggan, the 5th views in Scotland and Ireland.

" Vitruvius Britannicus, or the Britifh Architect," contains the plans, elevations, and fections of the regular buildings both public and pri- vate in Great Britain, with variety of new defigns in 200 large folio copper plates, engraven by the beft hands, and drawn either from the buildings themfelves, or the original defigns of the architects. In two volumes. A 3d volume contains the geometrical plans of the moft confiderable gardens and plantations, alfo the plans, elevations, and fections of the moft regular buildings not publifhed in the 2d vol. with large views in perfpective of the moft remarkable edifices in Great Britain, engraven by the beft hands, in 100 large folio copper plates, by Colen Campbell, efq; architect to his royal highnefs the Prince of Wales. Lond. 1725. Fol. A 4th volume is now publifhing by Gandon and Wolfe.

J. Paine, architect, is now engraving by fubfcription the plans, elevations, and fections of noblemen and gentlemen's houfes, ftabling, bridges public and private, temples, and other garden buildings, by him executed in the counties of Derby, York, Lincoln, Nottingham, Northumberland, &c. &c. The whole to confift of 74 large folio plates. To which will be added the name of the proprietor of each building, a defcription of the feveral fituations, and an account of the time when they were begun and finifhed.

Ecclefiaftical

Ecclesiastical Topography.

" THE history of churches in England; wherein is shewed the
" time, means, and manner of founding, building, and endow-
" ing of churches, both cathedral and rural, with their furniture and
" appendages. By Thomas Stavely, late of the Inner Temple, esq;
" Lond. 1712." 8vo. This useful essay on ecclesiastical antiquities, tho
capable of great improvement, has an undoubted right to begin this
article. The author was a barrister, who spent the latter part of his life
in the study of English history, and acquired the reputation of a diligent, judicious, and faithful antiquary.

The episcopal sees are enumerated in " Tabula chronologica archi-
" episcopatuum & episcopatuum in Anglia & Wallia ortus, divisiones,
" translationes, &c. breviter exhibens; una cum indice alphabetico
" nominum, quibus apud authores insigniuntur, concinnata per Sam.
" Carte, vic. S. Martini Leicestr. & explicata per eundem." Fol. sans
date.

Andrew Allam, vice president of S. Edmund's hall, Oxford, laid the
foundation of a " Notitia ecclesiæ Anglicanæ," giving an account of all
cathedrals, with their statutes and customs, and a list of the bishops,
deans, archdeacons, and canons, &c. to his own time; but death
prevented him from compleating this useful work, of which Le
Neve's Fasti is so small a part. As a supplement to the latter
Brown Willis, who in his pilgrimages, as he used to call them, had
visited all our cathedrals, published " A survey of the cathedrals of
" York, Durham, Carlisle, Chester, Man, Lichfield, Hereford, Wor-
" cester, Gloucester, and Bristol; giving an account of their founda-
" tions, builders, antient monuments and inscriptions, endowments,
" alienations, sales of lands, patronages; dates of confecration, admif-
" sion, preferment, deaths, burials and epitaphs of the archbishops,
" bishops, deans, precentors, chancellors, treasurers, archdeacons, and
" prebendaries: an exact account of all the churches and chapels in
" every diocese; distinguished under their proper archdeaconries and
" dean-

" deanaries : the patrons of them, to what religious houfes impropri-
" ated, and to what faints many of them are dedicated.   The whole
" extracted from numerous collections out of the regifters of every par-
" ticular fee, old wills, records in the Tower and Rolls Chapel : and
" illuftrated with twenty curious draughts of the ichnographies and
" uprights of every cathedral, newly taken, to rectify the erroneous
" reprefentations of them in the Monafticon and other authors. Lond.
" 1727." 4to. and three years after a like furvey of thofe of Lincoln
Ely, Oxford and Peterborough, with twelve draughts of the ichnographies, &c. Lond. 1730. 4to.   Thefe two works were united 1742
under fuch a title as would lead one to think the thirteen remaining
cathedrals therein mentioned had been furveyed like the others,
whereas there is only the lift of the churches and chapels in their
refpective diocefes, making his Parochiale Anglicanum, to be hereafter mentioned : nor were any of thefe, except the four Welfh cathedrals, furveyed as the reft.   The ufefulnefs of thefe furveys is greatly
leffened by the many errors occafioned either by his hafte and inaccuracy, or the careleffnefs of the printers ; but the remiffnefs of correcter
antiquaries obliges us to take up with them, fuch as they are, in moft of
the diocefes.

   In the public library at Oxford is a fair antient MS. valuation of all
the benefices in England, 19 Edw. I. 1291.   It once belonged to Sir
H. Spelman, and is intitled " Taxatio omnium beneficiorum in Anglia
" tempore Regis Edv. I."   Propofals (dated June 25, 1717) were
publifhed with a fpecimen by Edw. Burton, late commoner of Oriel
Col. and barrifter of the Middle Temple, who was very accurate in
collating this with other MSS. in the Bodleian library.   This excellent
MS. is imperfect, and confifts of 197 folio leaves, containing the ftates
of the diocefes of York, Durham, Carlifle, Canterbury, Rochefter i,
Chichefter, London, Norwich, Ely, Lincoln, Winchefter k, Salifbury l,
Worcefter m, part of Exeter, part of Exeter and Wells, part of Exeter

---

i Printed in p. 78, 79, &c. of the antiquities of the church of Rochefter.
k Printed p. 324. of the 5th vol. of Aubrey's antiq. of Surrey.
l Printed p. 383. of the 3d vol. of Afhmole's Berkfhire.
m Printed p. 4. of the antiquities of the church of Worcefter.

and

and Bath, Coventry and Litchfield ⁿ, Chefter, Llandaff, St. David's, part of St. David's and Bangor, part of Bangor, St. Afaph, Hereford º.

In King's defcription of Chefhire, p 91. is a valuation of benefices from a MS. in St. John's Col. Cambridge. A lift of all the churches in England, their valuation in the King's books, and tenths, by Le Neve, who defigned to add the patrons and epitaphs, is in the Harleian Library, in eight books, Nº 3617—24.

" A book of the valuations of all the ecclefiaftical preferments in
" England and Wales, intitled Nomina & valores omnium & fingu-
" lorum archiepifcopatuum, epifcopatuum, archidiaconat. decanat. præ-
" bendarum, ecclefiarumque parochialium infra regnum ac dominia
" Angliæ, ac omnium aliarum promotionum quarumcunque fpiritua-
" lium infra eadem, quæ ad folutionem decimæ partis earundem do-
" mino Regi & Reginæ nuper tenebantur. Lond. 1680." 8vo. This having been furreptitioufly and incorrectly printed, a new edition was publifhed intitled " Valor beneficiorum : or a valuation of all eccle-
" fiaftical preferments in England and Wales. To which is added
" a collection of choice precedents relating to ecclefiaftical affairs.
" Lond. 1695." 12mo ᴾ. Mr. T. Rawlinfon had a MS. valuation different from both thefe, and never printed.

John Ecton, receiver-general of the clergy's tenths, publifhed " Liber
" valorum & decimarum : being an account of the valuations and
" yearly tenths of all fuch ecclefiaftical benefices in England and
" Wales, as now ftand chargeable with the payment of firft fruits
" and tenths ; alfo the true yearly valuations of all fmall ecclefiaftical
" benefices, as they have been lately certified into her Majefty's Court
" of Exchequer, in order to their difcharge from the payment of firft-
" fruits and tenths. To which are added, the tenths formerly charged
" upon fuch laft mentioned fmall benefices. Carefully collected and
" examined. Lond. 1718." 8vo. republifhed 1723 and 1728. 8vo. and again under the title of " Thefaurus rerum ecclefiafticarum :
" being an account of the valuations of all the ecclefiaftical benefices
" in England and Wales, as they now ftand charged with or lately

---

ⁿ Printed p. 2. of the antiq. of the church of Lichfield.
º Printed p. 145. of the antiq. of the church of Hereford.
ᴾ The benefices in Calais and the earldom of Guifnes are included in thefe two.

" were

" were difcharged from the payment of firft-fruits and tenths. To
" which are added the names of the patrons and the dedications of
" the churches: with an account of procurations and fynodals, ex-
" tracted from the records in the reign of Henry VIII. To the whole
" are fubjoined proper directions and precedents relating to prefentation,
" inftitution, induction, difpenfations, &c. Lond. 1742 and 1754."
4to. A 4th edition, wherein the appropriations, dedications, and patronages of churches have been revifed, corrected, and placed in regular order under their refpective archdeaconries, with numerous additions, by Brown Willis, L. L. D. to which is added a compleat alphabetical index, came out 1763. 4to.

Ecton publifhed alfo " The ftate of the proceedings of the Corpo-
" ration of gove nors of the bounty of Queen Anne for the augmenta-
" tion of the maintenance of the poor clergy, giving a particular ac-
" count of their conftitution, benefactions, and augmentations, with
" directions to fuch as defire to become benefactors to fo pious and
" charitable a work. The 2d edition, with a continuation to Chrift-
" mas 1720. Lond. 1721." 8vo. Mr. Walpole p fays the late Lord
Harvey publifhed an account of this bounty.

Bafket publifhed in 1736 " The return made by the Governors,
purfuant to an order of the Houfe of Lords, with an account of what
fums have been received by them for the firft fruits and tenths, and of
what they have received, and from whom, for the increafe of the faid
bounty, in each year, fince their incorporation; what have been laid
out in each year, and to what ufes, and what is now in hand, and
where depofited; alfo an account of what livings are capable of being
augmented according to the act, and their refpective value; the charter
and rules of the faid corporation; an account of what licences have been
granted by the crown, and for what values refpectively to any perfon
or perfons, bodies politic or corporate, their heirs and fucceffors, to
aliene, purchafe, take and hold in mortmain in perpetuity any lands,
&c. fince the act of the 7th of K. William, intitled an act for the encou-

p Catal. of royal, &c. authors, vol. II. p. 145. Dr. Cobden celebrated it in a poem 1756.

ragement

ragement of charitable gifts and difpofitions." Fol. Since which no account has been communicated to the world.

During the civil war was publifhed " Impropriations purchafed, with
" a lift of fuch perfons from whom the commiffioners for compofition
" with delinquents at Goldfmiths-hall have purchafed any revenue
" for increafe of maintenance to the miniftry : allowing for the fame
" proportionably, by deduction out of the fines impofed on them.
" Publifhed for the ufe of thofe whom it may concern. 1684." 4to.
Reprinted in Morgan's Phœnix Britannicus 1732. p. 81.

Some years ago large collections were made by Dr. Peter Needham,
of St. John's Col. Cambridge, for an account of the patrons, &c. of
benefices in England and Wales. Of this nature are thofe lifts publifhed at the end of each county in the firft volume of Magna Britannia, of which that relating to Buckinghamfhire was communicated to
the editor by B. Willis q, who alfo drew up and publifhed " Paro-
" chiale Anglicanum, or the names of all the churches and chapels
" within the diocefes of Canterbury, Rochefter, London, Winchefter,
" Chichefter, Norwich, Salifbury, Wells, Exeter, St. David's, Landaff,
" Bangor, and St. Afaph; diftinguifhed under their proper archdea-
" conries and deanries : with an account of moft of their dedications,
" patrons, and to what religious houfes the appropriations belonged.
" 1732." 4to. The fame kind of lifts are annexed to his furveys of
the other cathedrals.

An accurate account of the fale of lands belonging to the fees and
cathedrals during the civil wars, was in the library of Mr. Rawlinfon,
who permitted feveral parts of it to be printed in the hiftories of the
cathedrals of Winchefter, p. 16. Hereford, p. 1. Rochefter, p. 119.
Worcefter, p. xxvi. Litchfield, p. xxxii. St. Davids, p. 187. Llandaff, p. 212. St. Afaph, p. 265.

So many monuments fell a facrifice to avarice under the colour of
reforming zeal in the reigns of Hen. VIII. and Edw. VI. that Elizabeth
was obliged to iffue out a proclamation to check fuch demolition, not

---

q B. Willis fays in his introduction to the diocefe of Exeter, that thefe lifts gave the
patrons and incumbents of livings only in Cornwall and Devonfhire ; whereas they are in
the whole firft volume, which reaches to Effex inclufive.

only

only of funeral monuments but even any images painted on glafs [r], and to oblige the demolifhers to repair them, or do penance in the church two or three times: and that the ftock of collegiate or cathedral churches not particularly appropriated, might be applied to this pur-pofe. But either the wealth or the zeal fell fhort, and we hear of no inftance in which her Majefty's injunction though repeated twelve years after was attended to. Not to mention the ravages of the civil wars, the mutilated church at Plefhey in Effex is an inftance of fuch rapine in our own time. The many monumental braffes there which fur-vived both thofe fatal æras were ftolen and fold when Bifhop Comp-ton's liberality repaired the fhattered edifice. Thofe which perpetuate the obfcurer branches of the Delapole family at Wingfield have been carefully depofited in the church cheft as they happened to get loofe [s]. I have feen fome impreffions of braffes rolled off as copper plates, which is both an effectual and correct method of preferving them.

John Weever, a native of Lancafhire, educated at Queen's Col. Cam-bridge, emulous of the honour foreign nations had received from the publication of their monumental antiquities, travelled over moft parts of England and fome parts of Scotland [t], to collect the funeral infcrip-tions of all the cathedral and parochial churches, but being much dif-couraged by the many malignant and avaricious defacements of thofe venerable remains, and the many obftructions and troubles he met with from impertinent churchwardens for want of a commiffion, he was on the point of fuppreffing all his collections, had he not been en-couraged by the moft eminent antiquaries his cotemporaries, who af-fifted him in finifhing the firft part of his " Ancient funeral monu-" ments within the united monarchie of G. Britaine, Ireland, and the " iflands adjacent. 1631." Fol. It contains only the diocefes of Can-terbury, Rochefter, London, and Norwich, and part of Lincoln to com-pleat the county of Hertford. Wharton [u] charges him with grofs mif-takes in the numerical letters and figures. He or thofe who examined

---

[r] Some figures were preferved from the parliamentarians by taking out their faces.
[s] The fame care is taken of braffes at moft of the churches in Norfolk. Blomef. III. p. 267.
[t] He had before vifited fome parts of the continent with the fame defign.
[u] Angl. Sac. I. p. 668.

the monuments for him appear not to have been able to read many
which are printed imperfectly [x]. To complete his work he sollicited
the communication of the public, but died the next year [y]. Such as
it is, he has preserved so many epitaphs since lost, that we cannot help
regretting he did not give us the like surveys of other dioceses. Dr. Plot
proposed to carry on his design and save the remaining inscriptions.
One Tooke, a printer, is now re-publishing Weever in weekly quarto
numbers, and sollicits assistance. But unless the author's errors are reformed, and something said about the present state of his inscriptions, all
we can expect from this new edition must be that it will raise the
price instead of the real value of Weever's book. Such surveys of
churches as have been printed since his time have corrected his mistakes, and given us further information [z]; and where none have appeared this edition will hardly supply their place.

John Le Neve in some sort carried on Weever's design, but in a
more dry immethodical manner in his five volumes of " Monumenta
" Anglicana; being the inscriptions on the monuments of several emi-
" nent persons deceased, in or since the year 1600 to the end of the
" year 1718, deduced into a series of time by way of annals." In the
last volume but one he added at the end of each year an obituary of
memorable persons who died therein, and whose epitaphs, if erected,
were not come to hand: but this on account of its uncertainty was
omitted in the rest. One from 1678 to 1706 remain MS. in the Harl.
Lib. N° 3625.

The first catalogue of our religious houses was drawn up by [a] Burton
and Leland, published in Speed's History, and translated into Latin, at
the end of Harpsfield's Church History, and though faulty in many
places commended in general. Richard Broughton was a Hunting-

---

[x] Flagrant instances of this are in Lord Audley's epitaph at Walden, Lady Joyce Tip-
toft's at Enfield; some of the Harricks at Southacre, and the Spelmans at Narburgh, in
Norfolk, are omitted.

[y] His little body, says Wood, being in a manner worn out with continual motion.
He was buried towards the west end of St. James's, Clerkenwell.

[z] Ames had a copy of Weever with drawings and additions in Kent by Lewis; but
into whose hands it passed from his sale I cannot say.

[a] The foundation of several religious houses in England, collected by Burton, remain in MS. in the Cotton Lib. Jul. C, VI. 19.

donshire

donfhire man, born and buried b at Great Stukeley, where his epitaph celebrates him as *Antiquariorum fui fæculi exquifitiffimus*. He wrote a rhapfodical indigefted ecclefiaftical hiftory of England, fome things in favour of popery; and " Monaftichon Britannicum, or a hiftoricall nar-
" ration of the firft founding and flourifhing eftate of the ancient mo-
" nafteries, religious rules, and orders of Great Britaine, in the times
" of the Brittaines and primitive church of the Saxons. Collected out
" of the moft authentick authors, lieger books, and MSS. By that
" learned antiquary R. B. Lond. 1655." 8vo. But that year produced a much more valuable work in the Monafticon Anglicanum : the Ift vol. of which contains the foundations of the Benedictines, Cluniacs, Cifter-cians, and Carthufians, to the diffolution, from their original MSS. in the Tower of London, St. Mary's Tower at York, the Exchequer, and Augmentation-office, the Bodleian, King's, and Bennet Col. the Arun-dellian, Seldenian, and Hattonian libraries, Lond. 1655." Fol. The IId, the Canons Regular of St. Auftin, the Hofpitalers, Templars, Gil-bertines, Præmonftratenfes, Maturines or Trinitarians; with an appendix to the firft volume containing certain religious houfes in France, Ireland, and Scotland, and fome omitted in England. Lond. 1661. The IIId volume is made up of additions to the two former, with the foundations and endowments of divers cathedral and collegiate churches. 1673. Though the title pages of the two firft volumes afcribe this noble work to Dodfworth and Dugdale, they are chiefly the work of the former; the latter only methodizing the deeds, correcting the prefs, and com-piling the indexes. Dodfworth died in Auguft 1654, before a tenth part of the firft volume was printed; and thereby probably loft the credit of the whole, which Dugdale gained by publifhing it. The third volume appeared in his name only; but it is not to be doubted he was greatly indebted to Dodfworth's collections. Great part of the impreffion of this volume, which contains chiefly foundation charters, (thofe relating to particular donations being omitted as too numerous) was accidentally burnt. The firft volume was reprinted with large ad-ditions 1682. The whole was abridged in 1695, Fol. by James Wright,

---

b He died 1634. Wood's Fafti, I. 235.

author

author of the History of Rutlandshire.   Another epitome by an anonymous writer came out, under the title of " Monasticon Anglicanum,
" or the history of the antient abbies, monasteries, hospitals, cathe-
" dral and collegiate churches, with their dependencies, in England
" and Wales.   Also of all such Scotch, Irish, and French monaste-
" ries, as did in any manner relate to those in England.   Containing
" a full collection of all that is necessary to be known concerning the
" abby-lands, and their revenues, with a particular account of their
" foundations, grants, and donations ; collected from the original
" MSS. &c. &c.   Illustrated with the original cuts of the cathedral
" and collegiate churches, and the habits of the religious and military
" orders.   First published in Latin, by Sir William Dugdale, Kt. late
" Garter principal king at arms.   To which are now added, exact
" catalogues of the bishops of the several dioceses, to the year 1717.
" The whole corrected, and supplied with many useful additions, by
" an eminent hand. Lond. 1718." Fol.

Great additions were made to the Monasticon itself in " The history
" of the antient abbeys, monasteries, hospitals, cathedral and collegi-
" ate churches, being two additional volumes to Sir Wm. Dugdale's
" Monasticon Anglicanum, containing the original and first establish-
" ment of all the religious orders that ever were in Great Britain, be-
" ing those treated of in the Monasticon Anglicanum, as also of the
" Franciscans, Dominicans, Carmelites, Augustinian Friars, Regular
" Canons of Arroasia, Brigittins, Monks of Fontevraud, Savigni,
" Crouched Friars, Friars of Penance or of the Sack, and Bethleem-
" ites ; not spoken of by Sir W. Dugdale and Mr. Dodsworth : the
" foundations of their several monasteries, a very large collection
" of many hundred grants and charters belonging to them, besides
" several thousands abridged : the final suppressions of all those places ;
" with some account of the manner how their vast lands and possef-
" sions were disposed of.   There are added perfect catalogues of the
" abbots and other superiors of those religious houses, and of all per-
" sons eminent and distinguished for piety, learning, and other ac-
" complishments, in the several orders ; with short lives of as many
" of them as have been transmitted down to us.   Collected from above

" 200

" 200 of the beft hiftorians extant, and from MSS. in the Bodleian
" and Cotton Libraries, and many more in the hands of learned anti-
" quaries, and other curious gentlemen, whofe names may be feen in
" the preface : adorned with a confiderable number of copper plates
" of the feveral habits of the religious orders, the ichnographies of
" cathedral and collegiate churches, and the ruins of facred places
" deftroyed or gone to decay, and the profpects of others ftill ftanding.
" By John Stevens, gent. 1722." The collections of this gentleman,
who was of the Romifh communion, and had a captain's commiffion
under James II. in Ireland, fell into the hands of the late Mr. Warburton, and were fold with his books, &c. by S. Paterfon 1759. Mr.
Peck promifed a fourth volume of the Monafticon, which he told the
world 1735 was in great forwardnefs.

Bifhop Tanner before he was twenty-two drew up and publifhed an
excellent compendium of our religious houfes, fetting forth when and
by whom they were founded, their dedications, orders, and value :
intitled " Notitia Monaftica ; or a fhort account of the religious houfes
" in England and Wales. Oxford 1695." 8vo. This was fo favourably received that within twenty years it became extremely fcarce ; fo
that at the requeft of his friends he fet about revifing and enlarging it
in 1715. His attention to the duties of his ftation as chancellor of
Norwich prevented a clofe application to it, and his infirmities afterwards occafioned it to be left at his death very far from finifhed. It
came out, however, thirty years after under the fame title, giving an
account of all the abbies, priories, and houfes of friars ; alfo of all the
colleges and hofpitals founded before 1540, being publifhed by John
Tanner, A. M. vicar of Loweftoff in Suffolk, and precentor of St. Afaph.
Lond. 1754. Fol. The editor, his lordfhip's brother, completed and
enlarged it from the many collections and notes he left, with confiderable additions of his own. The regifters of the feveral houfes and
other papers relative to them, pointed out fo exactly under each article,
are alone fufficient to recommend this valuable and comprehenfive repofitory. The Bifhop was an indefatigable fearcher into our antiquities, for which he had great opportunities, and left as many printed
volumes and bundles of MS. collections as filled feven carts on their

removal

removal from Norwich to Chrift Church library, Oxford. Among them were 300 volumes of MSS. purchafed by him of Bateman, the bookfeller, who bought them of Archbifhop Sancroft's nephew for 80 guineas, being moftly written by the Archbifhop's own hand. The Bibliotheca Britannico-Hibernia, publifhed after Bifhop Tanner's death by Dr. D. Wilkins, canon of Canterbury, from materials collected by him, is a ufeful repofitory of our writers, as far as it goes, which is only to the beginning of the laft century.

A lift of the mitred abbots by Wharton, intended to have been inferted in the 3d vol. of his Anglia Sacra, is among his MSS. at Lambeth.

In Leland's Collectanea, vol. vi. p. 51. is " A view of the mitred " abbeys, with a catalogue of their refpective abbats, by Brown Willis, " with fome preliminary obfervations by the publifher Tho. Hearne." This was foon after revifed by the author, and from ten fheets improved into two octavo volumes, of " An hiftory of the mitred parliamentary abbies, and conventual cathedral churches, fhewing the times of their refpective foundations, and what alterations they have undergone. With fome defcriptions of their monuments, and dimenfions of their buildings, &c. a catalogue of their abbats, priors, &c. lifts of the principals of divers monafteries; number of monks at the furrender; names of the laft abbats, priors, &c. who figned the fame; as far as they have come to hand : with an exact account of thofe religious men and women, and chantry priefts, receiving penfions throughout England and Wales, 1553. 1718." the fecond 1719. 8vo. To thefe accounts are added, brief furveys of the dimenfions and monuments, in all the remaining cathedrals not treated of in vol. I. that were not conventual, or re-founded at the diffolution, viz. St. Afaph, Bangor, St. David's, Hereford, Landaff, Litchfield, Lincoln, London, Salifbury, Wells, and York.

The laft thing on the fubject is intitled " A fummary of all the re- " ligious houfes in England and Wales, with their titles and valua- " tions at the time of their diffolution, and a calculation of what they " might be worth at this day; together with an appendix concerning " the feveral religious orders that prevailed in this kingdom. Lond. " 1717."

" 1717." 8vo. afcribed to Bifhop Burnet, who was dead two years before it came out.

An account of fome particular orders here may be feen in " Frag-
" menta, five hiftoria minor provinciæ Angliæ fratrum minorum."
1658. 8vo. and Douay 1661. 8vo. in the firft volume of the fcholaf-
tical and hiftorical works of Francis a Sancta-Clara ; and

" Supplementum hiftoriæ provinciæ Angliæ in quo eft chronofticon
" continens catalogum & præcipua gefta provincialium fratrum mino-
" rum provinciæ Angliæ. Duaci 1671." Fol. Both wrote by Chriftopher
Davenport, an Englifh Francifcan, chaplain to Charles the Ift's Queen [c].
Wood lent him for the latter work a MS. then in his hands, " De
" primo adventu fratrum minorum in Anglia, & eorum geftis," by
Thomas Eccleftone, a Minorite. He always calls him in his own life,
p. 593. 595. Fr. a S[ta] Clara.

" Collectanea Anglo-minoritica ; or a collection of the antiquities of
" the Englifh Francifcans, or Friars Minors, commonly called Grey
" Friars : in two parts, with an appendix concerning the Englifh nuns
" of the order of St. Clare. Compiled and collected by A. Parkinfon.
" Lond. 1726." 4to.

The 3d volume of Britannia Illuftrata is made up of views of all the
cathedrals, and fome of the chapels of Great Britain, on copper plates.
Lond. 1712. Fol. J. Harris did views of all our cathedrals in a
fmaller fize with an Englifh and French title. Thefe as well as the remains of the principal religious houfes and the churches formerly belonging to them, now made parochial, were wretchedly executed by
Daniel King, for the Monafticon. The latter have been fince accurately
engraved, and publifhed by fubfcription in fets by Samuel and Nathaniel Buck, who fpent upwards of thirty years in drawing thefe and
other remains about England, which will be particularized in their refpective counties. This however fhould be obferved that their firft fet
of views publifhed 1721 are by no means equal to the reft, and ought
in juftice to the originals to be executed again.

[c] Ath. Ox. II. 652.

I 2

Natural Hiſtory.

LORD Bacon was the firſt that ſuggeſted the ſtudy of the natural hiſtory of England. Though the liſt of general notices of our proficiency therein does not profeſs to be perfect, and particular ones will be found in the ſeveral counties, I believe we have done at leaſt as much if not more on this article than our neighbours on the continent. The firſt herbal in Engliſh was only a tranſlation, full of faults and miſtakes, intitled " The Great Herbal, &c. 1525." Fol. Dr. William Turner, ſtudent at Pembroke-hall, dean of Wells, and phyſician to Edw. VI. was the firſt of our countrymen that compiled one, which was intitled, " A new Herbal; wherein are contained " the names of herbes in Greek, Latin, Engliſh, Dutch, and French, " and in the apothecaries and herbaries, with the properties, degrees, " and natural places of the ſame," in two parts; Part I. Lond. 1551 Part II. Colon 1562. 1568. He tells us Botany was ſo much neglected that he could not find a phyſician in Cambridge capable of telling him the Greek, Latin, or Engliſh names of any plants he produced as he gathered them for his Latin ſkeleton of this work, 1548, a ſmall account of the names of herbs in the five languages. His " book of " herbs will always grow green and never wither, as long as Dioſco- " rides is held in mind among us mortal wights," ſays his cotemporary Dr. Bulleyn [d]. This eminent phyſician, whom the authors of the Biographia Britannica have reſcued almoſt from oblivion, was born in the Iſle of Ely, ſtudied at Cambridge, travelled over England, Scotland, and Germany, at length ſettled and practiſed with great ſucceſs at Durham, till he came to London, where after ſeveral traverſes of fortune he died 1576, and was buried in St. Giles's church Cripplegate, in the ſame grave where Fox the martyrologiſt was laid eleven years after. Among his numerous publications his " Bulwark of de- " fence againſt all ſickneſs, &c." 1562, a collection of many of his

[d] Book of Compounds, f. 46, 47. Dr. Stukeley had a ſmall plate of him engraved 1722, in a fur gown, and the Bulleyn arms behind him.

other

other pieces, feems to hold the firft rank. In that part which is intitled the Book of fimples, a herbal in form of a dialogue with
wooden cuts of plants, &c. he makes many curious obfervations on our
natural productions, remarkable for their plenty, excellence, or other
qualities, not fufficiently attended to before e.

John Gerard, citizen and furgeon of London, and author of the
Hiftory of plants publifhed 1597. Fol. under the patronage of Lord
Burleigh, feems to have been the firft that cultivated a phyfic garden.
He had a large one near his houfe in Holborn, where he raifed near
1100 different plants and trees. John Norton printed a Latin catalogue of the trees, fhrubs, and plants, both native and foreign, growing in it, 1599. Fol. Gerard's Herbal was republifhed by Johnfon
1636, before which Hen. Lyte had put out, " A new herbal, 1619,"
a tranflation from the German of Dodoens. Parkinfon's Herbal
followed, 1640. Thefe treat of the properties of plants in general,
and are mentioned here merely as inftances of our progrefs in the
fcience of botany. " The garden of health, containing the rare and
" hidden vertues of all forts of plants, 1684." 4to. is of the fame kind.

" The perfect platteform of a hoppe garden, and neceffarye inftruc-
" tions for the making and mayntenaunce thereof, &c. by Reginalde
" Scott. Lond. 1578." 4to. One hundred and fifty years before, under Hen. VI. the Parliament petitioned againft hops as a wicked weed f,
and fo late as Q. Elizabeth's reign they were fetched from the Low
Countries.

Cherries are fuppofed to have been brought over from Flanders by Richard Hains,
fruiterer to Hen. VIII. and planted at Tenham in Kent, whence they had the name of
Kentifh cherries. Our Kentifh pippins and other fruits are of the fame extraction. But
Dr. Bulleyn fhews there were plenty of good native cherries at Ketreinham near Norwich,
pears called the Blackfriars in and about that city †, and excellent grapes at Blaxhall in
Suffolk, where he was rector from 1550 to 1554. Lord Cromwell introduced the Per-
drigon plum in the reign of Hen. VII. and Wolfe, the King's gardener, firft brought
in Apricots. Artichokes came in at the fame time: in the Harl. Lib. N° 676. is a treatife on " The beft fettynge and kepinge of Artychokes," wrote in Q. Mary's reign. Our
Levant traders brought over Currants from Zante, temp. Hen. VIII. Archbifhop Grin-
dal brought the Tamarifk plant from Germany 1560; and the Tulip root came firft
from Vienna 1578.

f Fuller's Worthies, Effex.

† The arms of Wardon abbey, Bedfordfhire, as given by Tanner, are Arg. 3 Pears, Or. Quære,
If thefe are the fpecies called Wardons, or if they are peculiar to that part of England?

We

We may date the æra of gardening in the reign of Q. Elizabeth, though many table greens were even then fetched from Holland, whither they are now as frequently exported. Lord Burleigh was the Mæcenas of this as well as other arts. In 1579 one Hill publiſhed " The art of gardening." 4to. I find no other piece on the ſubject till almoſt a century after appeared " The garden of Eden, or an ac-
" curate deſcription of all flowers and fruits now growing in England;
" with particular rules how to advance their nature and growth, as
" well in ſeeds and hearbs, as the ſecret ordering of trees and plants.
" In two parts. By that learned and great obſerver Sir Hugh Plat,
" knight. Lond. 1652." 12mo. 1655 the 5th 1659, the 6th 1675.
12mo. A work like Miller's or Whitmill's Gardener's Calendar. Sir John Evelyn publiſhed another 1676, 1683.

" Phytologia Britannica, natales exhibens indigenarum ſtirpium
" ſponte emergentium. Lond. 1650." 8vo. By Wm. Howe, M. D. a noted herbaliſt of his time g.

Robert Lovel, ſtudent of Chriſt Church, Oxon, and phyſician at Coventry, publiſhed " A univerſal index of plants, ſhewing what grow
" wild in England: annexed to his Enchiridion botanicum, or a com-
" pleat herbal. Ox. 1659 h " 8vo.

" Britannia Baconica, or the natural rarities of England, Scotland,
" and Wales, according as they are to be found in every ſhire, hiſto-
" rically related, according to the precepts of the Lord Bacon, metho-
" dically digeſted; and the cauſes of many of them philoſophically at-
" tempted; with obſervations upon them, and deductions from them,
" &c. By. J. Childrey i. Lond. 1661." 8vo. There is a French tranſlation of this work intitled, " Hiſtoire des ſingularites naturelles d'An-
" gleterre, d'Eſcoſſe, & du province de Galles: raiſonement qu' ex-
" plique les cauſes naturelles des choſes qui paroiſſent les plus ſingu-
" lieres. Ce qui fait avec l'hiſtoire naturelle d'Ireland k, que l'on a
" donne au public depuis peu, une hiſtoire naturelle entiere de tous

g Athen. Ox. II. 204.
h Athen. Ox. II. 857.
i Of him ſee Athen. Ox. II. 468. Shaw's abridgment of Bacon's phil. works, iii. p. 31. n.
k A tranſlation of Boate's Natural hiſt. of Ireland.

2   " les

" les provinces & de tous les etats que poſſede le roy de la G. Bre-
" tagne. Traduite de l'Anglois de Mr. Childrey par M. P. B. Par.
1667.

The ſcience of botany was greatly improved among us by the phyſic
garden at Chelſea about 1670 [1]; and that at Oxford, founded under
Charles II. where Robert Moriſon was appointed botanical profeſſor and
read lectures, intending to publiſh a ſyſtem of botany, " ſeu herba-
" rum diſtributio nova per tabulas cognitionis & affinitatis ex libro na-
" turæ obſervata & detecta ;" but did not live to compleat it.

" Pinax rerum naturalium Britannicarum, continens vegetabilia,
" animalia, & foſſilia, in hac inſula reperta, inchoatus. Authore
" Chriſtophoro Merret, M. D. Utriuſque Societatis Regiæ Socio, pri-
" moque muſæi Harveani cuſtode. Lond. 1667." 8vo. This is the
ſecond edition ; the firſt I have not met with. The Doctor ſeems to
have been a diligent ſearcher into natural knowlege in its infant ſtate [m];
though Ray has left a ſevere cenſure on this book [n]. The firſt book
of that great maſter of the botanical ſcience in the laſt century was his
" Catalogue of plants about Cambridge 1660," which by exciting an
attention in many to thoſe neglected ſubjects revived the ſcience, and
laid the foundation for the ſtudy of botany among us. The next was
the reſult of three journies with his learned friends over moſt part of
England ; " Catalogus plantarum Angliæ, et inſularum adjacentium :
" tum indigenas, tum in agris paſſim cultas complectens. In quo præ-
" ter ſynonyma neceſſaria facultates quoque ſummatim traduntur, una
" cum obſervationibus & experimentis novis medicis & phyſicis. Lond.
" 1670." 8vo. The counties are ranged alphabetically with their
plants. It was republiſhed 1677. The great demand for it ſoon made
it ſo ſcarce that he prepared a third edition ; but meeting with ſome
oppoſition from the bookſeller who had the right of the copy, to
ſatisfy the importunity of his friends, he inſtead of it publiſhed his
" Methodus plantarum nova, brevitatis & perſpicuitatis cauſa ſynoptice

[1] Biog. Brit. VI. I. 3697.
[m] Many of his papers of a more general kind are in the Philoſophical Tranſactions.
[n] In a letter to Dr. Liſter he ſays, " At preſent the world is glutted with Dr. Merret's
bungling Pinax." Ray's life by Derham, p. 20.

" in

" in tabulis exhibita, cum notis generum tum fummorum tum fubal-
" ternorum chara&erifticis; obfervationibufque nonnullis de feminibus
" plantarum, & indice copiofo. Lond. 1682." 12mo. and his " Faf-
" ciculus ftirpium Britannicarum poft editum catalogum plantarum
" Angliæ. Lond. 1688." 8vo. In this he promifed a work which
he had prepared the fame year; but the delays and artifices of the
bookfellers and printers prevented it appearing till two years after. It
was his catalogue thrown into a new form, agreeable to the method
of nature, intitled, " Synopfis methodica ftirpium Britannicarum, in
" qua tum notæ generum chara&erifticæ traduntur, tum fpecies fin-
" gulæ breviter defcribuntur. Lond. 1690." A fecond edition was
afterwards publifhed with large improvements and additions, intitled
" Raii fynopfis methodica ftirpium Britannicarum, tum indigenis, tum
" in agris cultis, locis fuis difpofitis; additis generum chara&erifticis,
" fpecierum difcriminibus & virium epitome: editio fecunda: in qua,
" præter multas ftirpes & obfervationes curiofas paffim infertas, mufco-
" rum hiftoria, negligenter ha&enus & perfun&oriè tradita, plurimum
" illuftratur & augetur; additis defcriptis centum circiter fpeciebus
" (totidemque fucorum etiam atque fungorum) novis & indi&is; ac-
" ceffit cl. viri D. Aug. Rivini ° epiftola ad J. Raium de methodo,
" cum ejufdem refponforia in qua D. Tournefort elementa botanica
" tanguntur. Lond. 1696." 8vo. and a third edition corre&ed and
enlarged, with near 450 new fpecies, and cuts. Lond. 1724. 8vo.
Between the two laft editions he publifhed his " Methodus plantarum
" emendata & au&a, in qua notæ maxime chara&erifticæ exhibentur
" quibus ftirpium genera tum fumma tum infima cognofcuntur, & a
" fe mutuo dignofcuntur, non neceffariis omiffis: accedit methodus
" graminum, juncorum, & cyperorum fpecialis, eodem au&ore. Lond·
" 1703." 8vo.

His works have lately been enlarged and methodized according to
the Linnæan fyftem by Dr. Hill, in his " Flora Britannica: five fynopfis
" methodica ftirpium Britannicarum: fiftens arbores & herbas, indi-

---

° Rivinus had publifhed his own method of claffing plants by the number of petals
in the flowers in his introdu&ion 1692, in which he obliquely run down Ray's. Tournefort had done the fame in his Elements of botany: his method was alfo taken from
the form of the flowers.

" genas

" genas & in agris cultas in claſſes & ordines, genera & ſpecies re-
" dactas ſecundum ſyſtema ſexuale : additis nonnullis noviter detectis ;
" cum claſſium, ordinum, & generum characteriſticis, ſpecierum de-
" ſcriptionibus, & virium epitome : tabulis æneis illuſtrata : poſt ter-
" tiam editionem ſynopſeos Raianæ, opere Dillenii concinnatam, nunc
" primum ad celeberrimi Caroli Linnæi methodum diſpoſita. Lond.
" 1760." 8vo. and by Mr. Wm. Hudſon, in his " Flora Anglica ex-
" hibens plantas per regnum Angliæ ſpontè creſcentes diſtributas ſe-
" cundum ſyſtema ſexuale cum differentiis ſpecierum, ſynonimis auto-
" rum, nominibus incolarum, ſolo locorum, tempore florendi, offici-
" nalibus pharmacopæorum. Lond. 1762." 8vo.

" A ſynopſis of Britiſh plants, in Mr. Ray's method, with their
" characters, deſcriptions, places of growth, times of flowering, and
" phyſical virtues, according to the moſt accurate obſervations of the
" beſt modern authors, together with a botanical dictionary; illuſtrated
" with ſeveral figures : By John Wilſon," was printed at Newcaſtle
1744. 8vo.

" Specimen botanicum quo plantarum plurium rariorum Angliæ in-
" digenarum loci natales illuſtrantur authore J. Blackſtone, pharm.
" Lond. 1746." 12mo.

" Medicina Britannica : or a treatiſe on ſuch phyſical plants as are
" generally to be found in the fields or gardens in Great Britain ; con-
" taining a particular account of their nature, virtues, and uſes : to-
" gether with the obſervations of the moſt learned phyſicians as well
" ancient as modern; communicated to the late ingenious Mr. Ray,
" and the learned Dr. Sim. Pauli : adapted more eſpecially to the
" occaſions of thoſe whoſe condition or ſituation of life deprives them
" in a great meaſure of the helps of the learned. To which are added
" three indexes : the firſt containing the Engliſh and Latin names of
" the plants treated of; the ſecond of the diſeaſes and remedies; the
" third to the notes. By Tho. Short of Sheffield, M. D. Lond. 1746."
8vo.

" The Britiſh herbal : an hiſtory of plants and trees, natives of Bri-
" tain, cultivated for uſe or raiſed for beauty. By John Hill, M. D.
Lond. 1756." Fol.

K   The

The internal application of the folanum lethale in a cancerous cafe 1745, by profeffor Lambergen at Groningen, who publifhed a journal of the cure at the end of his Inaugural Oration, Groning. 1745, gave rife to " Obfervations on the internal ufe of the folanum or night-fhade, by Thomas Gataker, furgeon to Weftminfter hofpital. Lond. " 1757." 8vo. and " An account of the Englifh nightfhades, and their " effects, with the original cafe of Dr. Lambergen, as delivered in his " inaugural thefis : alfo practical obfervations on the ufe of corrofive " fublimate and farfaparilla, &c. &c. By William Bromfield, furgeon " to her R. H. the Princefs of Wales, and to St. George's and the " Lock hofpitals. 1757." 12mo.

Dr. Turner, the herbalift, drew up in Latin a fhort and fuccinct hiftory of the principal birds mentioned by Pliny and Ariftotle, with the Greek, German, and Englifh names, addreffed to Prince Edward. Col. 1544. 12mo. Mr. Francis Willoughby, who had dedicated his talents to the improvement of the animal part of natural hiftory, but was cut off in the prime of life, has treated of our birds in his three books of Ornithologia, illuftrated with 78 copper plates from the life, revifed and enlarged by Ray. Lond. 1676. Fol. who alfo tranflated it into Englifh, and publifhed it 1678. Fol. with the plates, and large additions, particularly three confiderable difcourfes of the art of fowl-ing, with a defcription of feveral nets in two large copper plates ; the ordering of finging birds; and of falconry. Dr. Birch fays P, the cuts in this book and his hiftory of fifhes were not drawn from the life, but picked up here and there out of books : but in Willoughby's article in Biogr. Brit. they are exprefly affirmed to be drawn by himfelf. Walter Moyle ¶ was preparing a hiftory of birds either Englifh or paffengers, to be communicated to the Royal Society, to rectify the miftakes in this work, which is only the general hiftory of birds, in which the Englifh are included, as they are in three 4to volumes of prints by Eleazar Albin, with notes and obfervations by Dr. Derham. Lond. 1738 and 1740 ; and in the later beautiful collection by Mr. Edwards. " A na-

---

P Hift. of the Royal Society, vol. iv. p. 382.
¶ Biog. Brit. Moyle.

" tural

" tural hiftory of Englifh fong-birds, and fuch of the foreign as are
" ufually brought over and efteemed for their finging; to which are
" added figures of the cock, hen, and egg of each fpecies, exactly
" copied from nature by Eleazar Albin, and curioufly engraven on
" copper," was publifhed 1737. 8vo. and preceded by other like accounts without figures.

John Moore publifhed 1725, 8vo. " Columbarium, or the pigeon-
" houfe: being an introduction to a natural hiftory of tame pigeons,
" giving an account of the feveral fpecies known in England, with the
" method of breeding them, their difeafes and cures." Confiderable
improvements and additions were made to this now fcarce tract in
" A treatife on domeftic pigeons, comprehending all the different fpe-
" cies known in England, defcribing the perfections and imperfections
" of each, agreeable to the great perfection they are at this time ar-
" rived at, &c. Illuftrated with a frontifpiece and cuts elegantly and
" accurately engraved from life, by the moft able and eminent artifts,
" under the immediate infpection of an experienced fancier. 1765."
8vo.

Our fifh are treated of in Willoughby's three books De hiftoria
pifcium, illuftrated with copper plates, revifed and enlarged by Ray,
who added the two firft books, and printed at the expence of the Royal
Society. Oxon 1686. Fol. Cromwell Mortimer, their fecretary, had
the title page reprinted 1743, and added an index of the fifh, with
their names r in Englifh and moft other modern languages from Tancred Robinfon's MS. notes in a copy in their library, and from Ray's
Synopfis, and the works of our later naturalifts, with a view of the
feveral claffes.

Ray himfelf compiled and left ready for the prefs " Synopfis metho-
" dica avium & pifcium; opus pofthumum, quod vivus recenfuit ipfe
" infigniffimus author; in quo multas fpecies in ipfius ornithologia &
" ichthyologia defideratas adjecit; methodumq; fuam pifcium naturæ
" magis convenientem reddidit: cum appendice & iconibus. Lond.
" 1713." 8vo. This lay in the hands of the bookfeller who bought

---

r Pafted alfo at the bottom or fides of the plates.

the

the copy, till after the author's death, when Innys found it among their ſtocks which he had purchaſed, and engaged Mr. Derham to prepare it for the preſs. Two of the plates contain fiſh lately diſcovered on the coaſts of Cornwall by the Rev. Mr. Iago; but the book treats principally of American and foreign animals.

Martin Liſter engraved our ſhells in his " Hiſtoria conchyliorum. " Lond. 1655." conſiſting only of copper plates; which we are not without hopes of ſeeing republiſhed. Liſter printed alſo a piece " De " cochleis tam terreſtribus quam fluviatilibus exoticis ſeu quæ non " omnino in Anglia inveniuntur. Lond. æri inciſ. ſumpt. authoris " 1685." and " Exercitatio anatomica in qua de cochleis maxime ter- " reſtribus, & limacibus agitur; omnium diſſectiones tabulis æneis ad " ipſas res affabre inciſis illuſtrantur. Lond. 1695."

Some of our inſects are treated of in his " Hiſtoriæ animalium An- " gliæ tres tractatus, unus de araneis; alter de cochleis tum terreſtriis, " tum fluviatilibus; tertius de cochleis marinis; quibus adjectus eſt " quartus de lapidibus ejuſdem inſulæ ad cochlearum quandam imagi- " nem figuratis. Lond. 1678." 4to. Mr. Wm. Lodge of Leeds drew 34 different ſorts of ſpiders for the Doctor, beſides ſnails, ſhells, and figured ſtones, communicated to the Royal Society, and inſerted in No 88. 100. and 112 of their Tranſactions, of which the drawings were in Thoreſby's Muſeum [s].

" Johannes Goedartius of inſects, done into Engliſh, and metho- " dized, with the addition of notes: the figures etched upon copper " by Mr. F. Place. York printed by John White 1682, for M. L." The preface ſigned M. L. The original MS. was in Thoreſby's Muſeum, and is now in the hands of G. Scott, eſq; of Wolſton-hall, near Chigwell, Eſſex. Only 150 copies were printed. The Doctor pubpubliſhed 1685. 8vo. Goedart's book of inſects in the original Latin, with ſhort notes, and a new edition of the appendix to his own Hiſtoria animalium Angliæ, two new plates, and a new deſcription of the genus of the muſculi fluviatiles and the pholas kind: and four tables of the beetle kind in England, without any deſcription. Ray pubpubliſhed " Methodus inſectorum, ſeu inſecta in methodum aliquam di-

---

[s] Walp. cat. of engr. p. 53.

" geſta.

" geſta. Lond. 1705." 8vo. and after his death the Royal Society printed his " Hiſtoria inſectorum ; cui ſubjungitur appendix de ſcarabæis Britannicis : autore M. Liſtero, S. R. S. ex MSS. Muſæi Aſhmolæani. Lond. 1710." 4to. republiſhed in the ſame ſize 1726.

" A natural hiſtory of Engliſh inſects. Illuſtrated with 100 copper " plates curiouſly engraven from the life, and (for thoſe that deſire it) " exactly coloured by the author, Eleazar Albin, painter : to which " are added large notes, and many curious obſervations, by W. Der- " ham, F. R. S Lond. 1724." 4to.

" An account of Engliſh ants, which contains, 1. Their different " ſpecies and mechaniſms. 2. Their manner of government, and a " deſcription of their ſeveral queens. 3 The production of their eggs " and proceſs of the young. 4. The inceſſant labour of the workers " or common ants. With many other curioſities obſervable in theſe " ſurpriſing inſects. By the Rev. William Gould, A. M. of Exeter " Col. Oxford. Lond. 1747." 12mo.

" The Engliſh moths and butterflies, together with the plants, " flowers, and fruits whereon they feed and are uſually found, all " drawn and coloured in ſuch a manner as to repreſent their ſeveral " beautiful appearances, being copied exactly from the ſubjects them- " ſelves, and painted on the beſt atlas paper ; together with an at- " tempt towards a natural hiſtory of the ſaid moths and butterflies. " This work conſiſts of 120 copper plates, with a particular account " of the flies repreſented in the ſaid plates, ſetting forth the true times " of their appearing in the caterpillar, chryſalis, and fly ſtate, the moſt " ready means of finding them, the method of managing and pre- " ſerving them, their way of feeding, the ſeveral plants they feed " on ; in a word, every thing known relating to their natural hiſtory, " together with the names of the plants, flowers, and fruits. By Ben- " jamin Wilkes. Lond. 1742." 4to. James Duffield publiſhed 1748 ſix 4to numbers of " A new and complete natural hiſtory of Engliſh " moths and butterflies through all their progreſſive ſtates and changes ; " with plates neatly coloured from life, with the plants, &c. on which " they are found."

Ou

Our quadrupeds have been treated of in a general way in Ray's
" Synopſis methodica animalium quadrupedum & ſerpentini generis;
" vulgarium notas characteriſticas, rariorum deſcriptiones integras ex-
" hibens: cum hiſtoriis & obſervationibus anatomicis perquam curio-
" ſis: præmittuntur nonnulla de animalium in genere ſenſu, genera-
" tione, diviſione, &c. Lond. 1693." 8vo.

John Kay wrote a little treatiſe " De canibus Britannicis," which together with his " De rariorum animalium & ſtirpium hiſtoria," he
drew up in a haſty manner for his friend Conrade Geſner, who dying
of the plague 1565, he reviſed, enlarged, and publiſhed them Lond.
1570. 12mo ᵗ. together with the following tracts, " De libris propriis,
" liber unus. De pronunciatione Græcæ & Latinæ linguæ cum ſcrip-
" tione nova, libellus." All reviſed from the beſt copies and republiſhed by Dr. S. Jebb. Lond. 1729. 8vo.

" Of Engliſhe dogges, the diverſities, the names, the natures, and
" the properties: a ſhort treatiſe written in Latine by Johannes Caius
" of late memorie, doctor of phiſicke in the univerſitie of Cambridge,
" and newly drawne into Engliſhe by Abraham Fleming, ſtudent.
" Imprinted at London 1576 by Richard Johnes, and are to be ſold
" overagainſt Sepulchre's Church without Newgate." 4to. Fleming
was a Londoner, who reviſed and made indexes to the ſecond edition
of Hollingſhed's Chronicle 1585, wrote ſeveral moral eſſays, and tranſlated ſeveral pieces of the antients and moderns in natural hiſtory ᵘ.

The Society of Cymmrodorion in London inſtituted 1751 for promoting natural knowledge and uſeful charities among the deſcendants
of the Antient Britons, agreed to publiſh (under the direction of
Thomas Pennant, eſq; of Flintſhire, who employs a painter on purpoſe, and draws up the explanations himſelf) for the uſe of their charity-
ſchool on Clerkenwell-green, " Britiſh zoology, or a natural hiſtory of
" the quadrupeds and birds of G. Britain and Ireland, illuſtrated with
" 100 copper plate cuts of the moſt rare animals on half a ſheet of
" imperial paper, drawn, engraven, and coloured from nature by the
" beſt hands." The firſt part, containing 24 plates of birds and one

---

ᵗ There has been another edition Hanov. 1610. Fol.
ᵘ See them enumerated in Tanner, p. 287.

of the pole-cat, was delivered to the fubfcribers 1763, with a fmall 4to pamphlet, giving a bare explanation, with references to the natu-ralifts that have treated of each more fully, and a pretty copious and entertaining account of the Soland goofe. Part II. came out 1764, containing defcriptions of a number of quadrupeds and thirty birds; the figures of which are to appear in the following parts. The IIId was publifhed 1765; the IVth 1766.

Webfter, in his " Metallographia, or [general] hiftory of metals, " Lond. 1671." 4to. has touched upon our foffils, earths, ores, metals, and minerals. The firft are in part arranged in " Edwardi " Luidii apud Oxonienfes cymeliarchæ lithophylacii Britannici ich-" nographia, five lapidum aliorumq; foffilium Britannicorum fingulari " figurâ infignium quotquot hactenus vel ipfe invenit, vel ab amicis " accepit, diftributio claffica : fcrinii fui lapidarii repertorium cum locis " fingulorum natalibus exhibens, additis aliquot rariorum figuris ære " incifis : cum epiftolis ad clariffimos viros de quibufdam circa marina " foffilia & ftirpes minerales præfertim notandis. Lond. 1699." 8vo. There being but 120 copies of this book printed at the expence of the author's patrons, it foon became very fcarce. A fecond edition was publifhed at Oxford 1760. 8vo. with new plates of fpecimens, and the author's " Prælectio de ftellis marinis," &c.

Dr. Lifter communicated to the Royal Society his plan of a foil or mineral map of the kingdom, with counties, rivers, cities, &c. the foils coloured, his fcheme of fands and clays, and an account of certain pebbles like ombriæ or brontiæ, or rough pearls as they are called in leafes of Royal mines, printed in N° 164 and 20 of their Tranfactions, and other remarks by him in N° 110 and 120. Ob-fervations made by John Hutchinfon, founder of the fect that bears his name, moftly in 1706, while he traverfed feveral parts of England as fteward to the Duke of Somerfet, were publifhed, with many ufeful mar-ginal notes by Dr. Woodward. He had made a good collection of foffils, which he put into the Doctor's hands to arrange : Woodward, under pretence of proving from them the truth of the Mofaic account of the creation of the earth, the deluge, and the re-formation of the earth after it, kept poffeffion of the collection, and with held from Hutchin-fon

fon even the credit of having made it. The Doctor had ranfacked the greateft part of the ifland for foffils, and made a particular and correct difpofition of them, in his " Attempt towards a natural hiftory of the " foffils of England, in a catalogue of thofe in his own collection : " containing a defcription and hiftorical account of each ; with obfer- " vations and experiments, made in order to difcover as well the ori- " ginal and nature of them, as their medicinal, mechanical, and other " ufes." Vol. I. Lond. 1729. 8vo. Part I. containing, the foffils that are real and natural, earths, ftone, marble, talcs, coralloids, fpars, cryftals, gems, bitumens, falts, marcafites, minerals, and metals. Part II. exhibiting the foffils that are extraneous, the parts of vegetables and animals digged out of the earth ; in particular the fhells of fea-fifhes ; as alfo the ftoney, mineral, and metallic bodies formed in them : ranged and difpofed in a claffical method, according to their feveral kinds and alliances ; with an hiftorical account of each : as likewife various obfervations and reflections. Vol. II. Lond. 1728. contains three additional catalogues of native and three of extraneous Englifh foffils, and a catalogue of the foreign foffils in the Doctor's collection, brought as well from feveral parts of Afia, Africa, and America, as from Sweden, Germany, Hungary, and other parts of Europe ; in two parts, in the fame order as the Englifh. The catalogues of Englifh foffils in the firft volume contain thofe given in two cabinets to the univerfity of Cambridge : the Englifh and foreign ones in the fecond volume being put up to fale, agreeable to his will, in two other cabinets, with his library and antiquities, were bought by the fame univerfity for 500 l. The oration by the firft Woodwardian profeffor, Dr. Middleton, was publifhed in 1732. 4to. and in his works. His fucceffor Dr. Charles Mafon publifhed his Cantabr. 1734. 4to.

The general accounts of our mineral waters are " M. Lifteri de " fontibus medicatis Angliæ exercitationes duæ. Lond. 1684." 8vo. The firft part was originally printed at York 1682.

Dr. Plott's " De origine fontium tentamen philofophicum in præ- " lectione habitâ coram focietate philofophicâ nuper Oxonii inftitutâ " ad fcientiam naturalem promovendam. Oxon. 1685." 12mo. This learned author's fcheme for a natural hiftory of England, in a letter to

Dr.

Dr. Fell, then dean of Chriſt Church, giving an account of his intended journey through England and Wales, for the diſcovery of antiquities and other curioſities, was publiſhed by Hearne from a MS. in the Bodleian Library, at the end of Leland's Itinerary, vol. II.

" The natural hiſtory of the chalybeat and purging-waters of Eng-
" land, with their particular eſſays and uſes; among which are treated
" at large, the apoplexy and hypochondriaciſm: to which are added,
" ſome obſervations on the Bath waters in Somerſetſhire. Dedicated
" to the right honourable the Earl of Mancheſter. By Benjamin Allen,
" M. B. Lond. 1699." 8vo.

Dr. Short of Sheffield publiſhed " The natural, experimental, and
" medicinal hiſtory of the mineral waters of Derbyſhire, Lincolnſhire,
" and Yorkſhire, particularly thoſe of Scarborough. Wherein they
" are carefully examined and compared; their contents diſcovered, their
" uſes ſhewn and explained; and an account given of their diſcovery
" and alteration together with the natural hiſtory of the earths, mine-
" rals, and foſſils through which the chief of them paſs: the ground-
" leſs theories and falſe opinions of former writers are expoſed, and
" their reaſonings demonſtrated to be injudicious and inconcluſive.
" To which are added, large marginal notes, containing a methodi-
" cal abſtract of all the treatiſes hitherto publiſhed on theſe waters,
" with many obſervations and experiments, as alſo four copper plates
" repreſenting the cryſtals of the ſalts of 34 of theſe waters. 1734."
4to. And " A treatiſe on various cold mineral waters in England, but
" more particularly on thoſe at Harrogate, Thorp-arch ˣ, Dorſt-hill ʸ,
" Wiggleſworth ᶻ, Nevill-holt, and others of the like nature; with
" their principles, virtues, and uſes. Alſo a ſhort diſcourſe on ſolvents
" of the ſtones in the kidneys and bladder. 1765." 8vo.

The fenny parts of England are treated of in Dugdale's " Hiſtory
" of imbanking and drayning of divers fenns and marſhes, both in
" foreign parts and in this kingdom; and of the improvements there-

---

ˣ A village on the weſt ſide of the Wherfe, a mile E. of Clifford moor, ſulphureous and chalybeat, p. 52.
ʸ Two miles from Tamworth, p. 114.
ᶻ The only bituminous water in England, p. 94.

" by.

" by. Extracted from records, manuſcripts, and other authentick
" teſtimonies. Lond. 1662." Fol. drawn up at the inſtance of Lord
Gorges and other principal adventurers in that coſtly and laudable undertaking of draining the Great Level, extending into a conſiderable
part of the counties of Cambridge, Huntingdon, Northampton, Norfolk, and Suffolk: of which places ſo drained there are ſeveral exact
maps in it.   Romney and other marſhes in Kent are treated of p. 16
——83 ; the marſhes on the Thames in Surrey p. 66; thoſe in Middleſex and Eſſex p. 69 —- 74; in Suſſex p. 83——87 ; in Somerſetſhire
p. 104; in Glouceſterſhire p. 113; Yorkſhire, Weſt-riding, p. 115;
Nottinghamſhire p. 138 ; Lincolnſhire p. 141 ; Norfolk p. 244; Suffolk p. 298 ; Cambridgeſhire p. 299; Huntingdonſhire p. 365.

In 1757 came out a trifling book fit only for children called " Rural
" beauties, or the natural hiſtory of the four following counties, viz.
" Cornwall, Devonſhire, Dorſetſhire, and Somerſetſhire, with addi-
" tional remarks by Theophilus Botaniſta, M. D." 12mo.

BRITAIN

BRITAIN [a] was originally parcelled out into regions and nations, certain tracts, of territory occupied by collective bodies under one chief. Severus divided it in upper and lower; Theodosius into five provinces; Canute into four kingdoms; and Alfred into shires, at least all that lay north of the Thames; for the kingdom of the West Saxons was parcelled out into such divisions before [b]. He took a general survey of the kingdom united under him; the record of it, called *Dome boc*, was long preserved in Winchester cathedral, and imitated by the Conqueror. At first there were but thirty-two [c] shires, the northern parts being independant of Alfred; and in the hands of the Scots at the conquest: though at William's survey two more were added. They took their names from the people in whose kingdoms they were included, as Surry, Suffex, Effex, and Middlefex; or from the situation of those people with respect to each other, as Suffolk and Norfolk; or from the capital towns, or some remarkable particularity in the county. The nine southern ones were governed by the laws of the West Saxons, whose kingdom seven of them had composed: the fifteen midland and easternmost by the laws of the Danes, to whom most of them had been subject under the name of the kingdom of Mercia, by the laws of which the eight westernmost were governed. Northumberland, Cumberland, Westmoreland, and Durham were added afterwards, and Lancashire taken out of Yorkshire and Cheshire. Hen. II. when he appointed justices itinerant made a new division, or rather allotted the shires to six circuits, not very different from the present distribution of them.

---

[a] Ptolemy, in his mathematical constructions, is the first writer that speaks of *Great Britain*; but it is in opposition to Ireland, which he calls *Little* Britain. The writer, who by epitomizing has preserved Strabo, and lived near the end of the Xth century, is the next that may be called antient who mentions this name, which afterwards became familiar. If we follow Hearne's reading of the Chichester inscription, *Magna Britannia* was in use under Claudius.

[b] Spelman s life of Alfred by Hearne, p. 110.

[c] It is very remarkable that the island was parcelled out into just so many partitions under the Heptarchy. Camd. Britan. p. ccxxv.

BEDFORD-

BEDFORDSHIRE.

THE county of Bedford was firſt viſited 1556 by William Harvey, Clarencieux : again 1585 and 1623 by different officers at arms. It does not appear that any thing has been done towards a general ſurvey of it. All that we have relative to the chief town, is two accounts of calamities with which it has been viſited. " A true relalation of what hapned at *Bedford*, on Munday laſt, Aug. 19 inſtant, while thundering, lightning, and tempeſtuous winds tore up the trees by the roots, &c. Lond. 1672." 4to. and " Strange and terrible news from Bedford, or a true and particular narrative and accompt of a wonderfull and prodigious tempeſt and hurricane there. Lond. 1672."

A view of the bridge was engraved by Francis Perry.

" A ſhort yet true and faithful narrative of the fearefull fire that fell in the towne of *Wooburne*, in the county of Bedford, on Saturday the 13th of September laſt, anno 1595. Lond. 1595. 12mo. By Thomas Wilcock."

An antique coffin and Runic inſcription found at Woburne Abbey are deſcribed in the Gentleman's Magazine, April 1749, p. 157.

William Foulkes, L.L.D. intended to write the hiſtory of *Dunſtable* town and priory; but died before he had accompliſhed his deſign: nor could his papers after diligent enquiry be found by Hearne, who publiſhed in 2 vols. 8vo. Lond. 1731, " Chronicon ſive annales pri- " oratus de Dunſtaple, una cum excerptis ex chartulario ejuſdem ;" from MSS. in the Harleian Library ; with an appendix, according to his uſual method of emptying his immenſe common place books. This antient chronicle ſeems to be different from the private hiſtory of this monaſtery quoted by Camden, and was written in great part by Richard de Morins [d], prior here, who died 1252. H. Wanley tranſcribed it from this MS. N° 1885, collated it with another in the Cotton Library, ſince greatly damaged by the fire 1731, and illuſtrated it with ſhort notes, intending, if he had lived, to publiſh it, together with Bene-

---

[d] Leland does not appear to have ſeen this work ; neither he nor Tanner mention the writer, of whom Wanley gives a full account in the Harleian Catalogue.

dictus.

dictus Petroburgenſis and Annales de Lanercoſt, from the Cottonian MSS. Lord Weymouth put him upon the deſign, and gave him 100l. promiſing him as much more for a dedication, and to take fifty copies. He propoſed to have illuſtrated the whole with large notes, charters, ſeals, monuments, epitaphs, and as much unprinted matter as he could meet with; alſo an index and gloſſary: but it being thought theſe would take too much time, he was ordered to publiſh the text alone: after he had agreed with the bookſeller and printer, his Lordſhip died, and left no money for the copies: ſo they all flew off [e].

In p. 419 of N° 379 of the Philoſ. Tranſ. we have an account of the fullers-earth pits in this county: and in p. 224 of N° 486 Mr. Ward's remarks on a Teſſera found at *Market Street.*——In vol. LIV. p. 118. is an obſervation of an extraordinary degree of cold at *Cardington* Nov. 22, 1763, by John Howard, eſq; Farenheit's ſcale by Bird's thermometer being at 10 and $\frac{1}{4}$ juſt before ſun riſe.

Among Dr. Stukeley's unpubliſhed plates was one of Ravenſbury, a Roman camp, near Hexton in this county [f]. 1724.

Meſſrs. Buck have given the following views. 1730.

$$\left.\begin{array}{l} \text{N. W. Dunſtable} \\ \text{S. E. Chickſand} \\ \text{E. Bedford} \end{array}\right\} \text{Priories.}$$

N. E. Harwood   Nunnery.
N. E. Wardon   Monaſtery.

Saxton included this in his map of Northampton and the adjacent ſhires 1576, none of which have the hundreds: they were firſt ex-preſſed in Speed's map, which has a plan of Bedford. Another map has been publiſhed by Em. Bowen, in concentric circles.

[e] His own account among his letters MS. Harl. 3778. 65. in the Muſeum.
[f] Deſcribed in his Itinerary, p. 74.

BERKSHIRE.

THIS county was visited by Harvey 1566: by Chitting and Philipot, Chester and Somerset heralds, deputies to Camden 1623: and by Elias Ashmole, as Windsor herald 1665. The latter's account of it was transcribed from three folio volumes, in his library, N° 850. intitled, " Verum exemplar insignium epitaphiorum, venerandæque " antiquitatis inscriptionum aliquot in omnibus ecclesiis & aliis locis " Bercheriensis comitatus; A. D. 1666, ibidem existentium, per E. A. " arm. Windesorii heraldum ad arma, deputatum marescallumque ab " Edoardo Byshe, milite, armorum rege Clarencieux pro comitatu " prædicto." The monuments, &c. are all drawn by his own hand. A duplicate of it is in the Heralds College, and from both these collated, with the addition of many whole parishes, was published in three volumes 8vo. " The antiquities of Berkshire, with a large appendix of " many valuable original papers, pedigrees of the most considerable " families of this county, and a particular account of the castle, col- " lege, and town of Windsor. Lond. 1719." reprinted at Reading 1736 in folio, under the title of " The history and antiquities of Berk- " shire, &c. By E. Ashmole, esq; with his life :" which is also in the former edition. A transcript of Domesday is in Ashmole s library, N° 822.

Many particulars relative to this county were inserted in the new edition of the Britannia from Aubrey's MS. intitled Monumenta Britannica. This work, which he intended to publish, was to have given a particular account of our earlier antiquities, the temples, religion, and manners of the Druids ; the camps, castles, &c. of both Britains and Romans [f]. What he proposed has been since more fully executed by Dr. Stukeley, in whom amazing industry, lively invention, and a happy talent of designing concurred to produce a complete system of Druidism.

[f] Nicholson's Eng. hist. lib. p. 39 Great use was made of it by Bishop Gibson in his Camden.

Among

Among Bishop More's MSS. Cat. MSS. Angliæ, tom. II. 365. is a survey of the manor of *Blewberrie*, being parcel of the Prince of Wales s estate, taken July 1617 by John Norden, sen. and jun. deputed by Sir James Fullerton, surveyor-general of the said estate.

Hearne published in the review of Leland's Itinerary annexed to the 9th vol. of the first edit. p. 197—202, some account of G. Barbour's contributions to the bridges at *Abingdon*, and verses thereon in the hall of St. Helen's hospital there; and in p. 594. Ap. xii. of his Liber niger Scaccarii, Ox. 1728. 8vo. are some notes relating to this town, its bridges, and cross, from a register taken 1638, lent him by Ja. West, esq; He had a scarce poem, in one sheet, " In honour of Abing- " don, or the seaventh day of September's solemnization 1641. by " John Richardson, serjeant of Abingdon, in the county of Berks. " Printed in the yeare 1641." The Parliament had ordered that every parish should keep that day in memory of the accommodation with the Scots: the 106th Psalm was sung at the cross by 2000 choristers ᵍ. The new cross at Coventry was built, temp. Hen. VIII. after the model of this beautiful one, of which there is a particular description in Symmond's pocket-book, Harl. MS. 965. The late Mr. Francis Perry, engraver, who was a native of this very antient town, had some drawings of St. Helen's church, the town-hall, and remains of the abby, which his executor proposes to publish. He engraved the seal and counter seal of the abbey, in the hands of Dr. Rawlinson, which were re-engraved by Vertue for the Antiquarian Society.

Of *Reading* abbey and its gatehouse we have a view in plate xxiii. and xxvi. of Stukeley's Itin. Curiosum, and a south view of the town among Buck's large views.

At the end of the first volume of Leland's Itinerary is a letter containing an account of some antiquities between Windsor and Oxford, first published in " The monthly miscellany, or memoirs for the curious, 1708." 4to. vol. ii. p. 335.

Hearne published two inquisitions of the manor of *Feenes* in White Waltham parish from a MS. in the hands of John Loveday; and from a MS. of Mr. West's, the rents assigned to O Philippa out of the manors

ᵍ Note on Wood s life, p. 550.

of

of *Braye* and *Cookham*, 32 and 33 Ed. III. in the appendix to his edition of T. Otterburne, &c. Oxf. 1732. p. 133. At the end of his edition of Roper's life of More, Ox. 1716, is an account of monuments in the churches of *Aldworth, E. Hakborn,,* and *Bright-well,* and *Hogshaw,* in Buckinghamſhire Thoſe in the firſt church are treated of in the Gent. Mag. Oct. 1760, p. 458 and 525 [h]. At the end of his J. Glaſtonienſis Chronica, Oxf. 1726, p. 567. is a copy of a paper relating to the manor of *Aſh-downe* or *bury,* the ſcene of that battle commemorated by the White Horſe. In the pre-face to the Hiſtory of Glaſtenbury, p. xxiii—xxv. is ſome account of *Camp's chapel,* and another ſuppoſed to have belonged to Noion ab-bey. A print of the ruins of *Littlemore* minchery or nunnery, with the nuns table; and the regiſter of *Thatcham* pariſh, in the appendix. A grant from *Poghly* convent of a tenement in S. Denchworth, ib. N° xvi. H. Tubbeney's grant of lands there to the ſaid priory, pref. p. lxxxi. an indenture conſtituting a ſteward of the priory, and an in-ventory of the goods. App. N° VI. [i]

Mr. Francis Wiſe, fellow of Trin. Col. Oxf. in his " Letter to Dr. " Mead concerning ſome antiquities in Berkſhire, Oxf. 1738." 4to. ſhews, that the White Horſe, which gives name to the vale, is a monu-ment of the Weſt Saxons, made in memory of a victory obtained by Alfred over the Danes, A. D. 871. He touches on the name of Berkſhire, the Ickneild-ſtreet traced by him hereabouts, the Roman antiquities of Wantage, where Salmon had fixed Glevum ; and other Roman and Saxon fortifications. In his " Further obſervations upon the White Horſe, and other antiquities in Berkſhire; with an account of White-leaf croſs in Buckinghamſhire : as alſo the Red Horſe in Warwickſhire, and other monuments of the ſame kind, Oxf. 1742." 4to. he con-firms his former account of this monument, and ſuppoſes the Buck-inghamſhire croſs a ſimilar memorial of ſome victory not ſpecified in hiſtory, gained probably by Alfred's ſon and ſucceſſor, Edward the elder, his father having changed the former national ſtandard for this.

[h] The Beche family are further mentioned in the appendix to Hemingii Chart. p. 665.
[i] The ſeal of this convent, not in Tanner, was a religious treading on a dragon. Kennet's Paroch. Ant. p. 234.

There

There is another White Horfe under Bratton caftle, Wiltfhire, of very
modern make; and the Red Horfe in Warwickfhire Mr. Wife thinks
a monument of Sir Richard Nevil, the king-making Earl of Warwick.
The firft of thefe pieces was as rudely as fillily animadverted upon in a
pamphlet called, " The impertinence and impofture of modern anti-
" quaries difplayed, or a refutation of the rev. Mr. Wife's letter to
" Dr. Mead, concerning the White Horfe, and other antiquities in
" Berkfhire, in a familiar letter to a friend.   By Philalethes Rufticus.
" With a preface by the gentleman to whom this letter was addreffed.
" Lond." 4to. faid to be wrote by Mr. Afplin, vicar of Banbury, and
replied to by Mr. Geo. North, curate of Coddicote, Hertfordfhire, in
his " Anfwer to a fcandalous libel, intitled, The impertinence and impofture of modern antiquaries difplayed, &c. Lond. 1741." 4to.

The Order of the Garter makes the greateft figure in this county. The
firft printed account of it is Dr. Heylin's " Hiftory of that moft famous
" faint and foldier of Chrift Jefus St. George of Cappadocia, afferted from
" the fictions of the middle ages of the church, and oppofition of the
" prefent.   To which is fubjoined the inftitution of the moft noble
" order of St. George, named the Garter; and a catalogue of all the
" knights from its firft inftitution until this prefent; as alfo of the prin-
" cipal officers thereto belonging. 1631." 4to.   Anftis fays the pains
he took to clear up and compleat a catalogue of the knights are fo
commendable, that it is to be lamented he did not proceed in farther
enquiries of the fame nature.   Dr. Hakewill having attacked this book,
Charles I. took the author's part, who, after examining the records at
Windfor, reprinted it with additions and corrections 1663: his antagonift thought proper to retract his printed objections, and confined his
abufe to private letters publifhed afterwards [k].   Dr. Fairclough, for
treating the ftory of St. George as a figment in one of his books of devotion 1626, was forced to cry peccavi, and fall upon his knees before
Laud [l].   From Heylin's book was ftolen a " Hiftory of St. George,
&c. 1661." 4to. and a " Hiftory of the life and martyrdom of St.

[k] See Ath. Ox. II. 280. Prince doubts if his book on the fubject was printed.
Worth. of Devon. p. 407.
[l] Ath. Ox. II. 2. 78. After all Heylin gives up the faint's exiftence, and confiders
the enfign only as a fymbol.

M   George,

George, the titular patron of England, &c. Lond. 1664." 4to. a poem by Tho. Lowick, gènt. [m].

" St. George for England; or a relation of the manner of the elec-
" tion and inftallation of the knights of the moft noble order of St.
" George, called the Garter, which is to be folemnized on the 18 and
" 19 of Apr. next at Windfor. 1661." 8vo.

" A perfect catalogue of all the knights from the firft inftitution of
" the order until the prefent April 1661; whereunto is prefixed a
" fhort difcourfe touching the inftitution, the patron, habit, and fo-
" lemnities, with many other particularities which concern the fame.
" Collected and continued by J. N. 1661. [n]"

" The order of the ceremonies ufed at the celebration of St. George's
" feaft at Windfor, when the Sovereign of the moft noble Order of the
" Garter is prefent." [By Sir Edw. Walker, Garter King at arms.] Lond.
1671 and 1674. 4to. He wrote alfo the acts of the knights in the civil
wars, MS. in Afhmole's mufæum: as is a journal of feveral proceedings of the knights of the Garter, by Sir Tho. Rœ, cited frequently
in " The inftitution, laws, and ceremonies of the moft noble order of
the Garter: collected and digefted into one body by Elias Afhmcle, of
the Middle Temple, efq; Windfor herald at arms. A work furnifhed
with variety of matter, relating to honor and nobleffe. Lond. 1672."
Fol. with many beautiful engravings by Hollar. Afhmole in the
prime of his life was a very Monf. Oufle in chemiftry, then turned
antiquary and herald, and wrote this hiftory, which was placed by the
Pope in the Vatican, and tranflated into High Dutch by order of Fre-
deric-William Elector of Brandenburgh. Thirty-nine folio volumes of
MSS. collections ufed in compiling it are preferved in his mufeum:
many others which he had been thirty years gathering for this and other
works, were burnt with his library, &c. at his chambers in the Middle
Temple 1678 [o]. This moft authentic and compleat account was contracted

[m] Ath. Ox. II. 280.
[n] Catalogue of pamphlets in the Harleian Mifcellany. Perhaps thefe two books are the fame. Sir Chriftopher Wren being regiftrary of the order drew up a catalogue of the knights. MS. in Caius Col.
[o] Burman, Dr. Plot's fon in-law, publifhed his Diary or memoirs of his own life; containing fome interefting particulars among many filly minutiæ never intended to be made

tracted and republished in 8vo by Walker, compared with the author's corrections in his library at Oxford, faithfully digested and continued down to this present time : the whole illustrated with proper sculptures· 1715. Hollar's prospects of the castle, inside views of the chapel, habits, &c. were omitted in this edition.

Tho. Salmon p in his " New historical account of St. George for " England, and the original of this order Lond. 1704." 8vo. labours hard to prove that the story of George, the Arian bishop of Alexandria, whom the pagan mob tore to pieces, has been confounded during the ignorance of the twelfth century with that of George bishop of Ostia, whom Pope Adrian sent hither to revive Christianity among the Anglo-Saxons, and whose acts with those of the council of Ceoltide, which dismembered the see of Canterbury, were purposely suppressed by succeeding writers.

Dr. T. Dawson's " Memoirs of St. George, the English patron ; and of the most noble order of the Garter : being an introduction to an intended history of the antiquities of the castle, town, and borough of Windsor, with the parts adjacent. 1714." 8vo. is only an abridgement of Ashmole ; the account of the patron taken from Selden's Titles of honour.

Ashmole confined himself chiefly to the ceremonial and legal parts of the Order : and as after his harvest in them, there remain gleanings enough in the antiquarian part to fill up some volumes, as well as to correct his mistakes, John Anstis, esq; Garter herald, proposed, or rather drew out a plan for, compiling the lives of the several knights, which Vincent q had before promised, but did not live to finish. Ashmole made a laborious and expensive collection of materials for the same purpose, but failing in his application to be made historiographer and remembrancer of the order, waved the prosecution thereof. Anstis begun with publishing in two folio volumes, 1724, " The register of the most noble order of the Garter, from its cover in black velvet

made public. Such memorandums of Camden's have been mistaken for the outlines of his annals of James I. Ashmole's third wife was Sir William Dugdale's daughter.

P Rector of Mepsal, in the county of Bedford, &c.
q Dedicat. to his Discovery of Brooke's errors.

　　　　　　　　　usually

uſually called the Black book; with notes placed at the bottom of the pages, and an introduction prefixed by the editor." The annals of the Order prior to 4 Hen. V. were loſt, probably in the plundering of the chapel by the Parliament's ſoldiers, when this, with the Blue and Red books and other papers were reſcued from the commiſſioners for ſelling the King's goods by Dean Wren. This regiſter is wrote in Latin (of which a tranſlation is added here) in a large pompous folio and a ſtrong character on vellom, beautifully illuminated and adorned with whole-length figures of all the Sovereigns, except Edw. VI. A copy of it is in Aſhmole's muſæum, with his notes and additions. In p. 268 are engraved two draughts of the ſovereign in chapter, and the proceſſion to the altar 26 Hen. VIII. explained No XII. The firſt part of it is a looſe, incorrect, and confuſed abridgment and tranſlation of the French paper regiſter by Dr. Robert Aldrydge, provoſt of Eton, canon of Windſor, and continued by him from 26 Hen. VIII. as long as he was regiſter. All the other materials for a hiſtory of the knights are the plates in the ſtalls (which deſerve to be engraved) copies of the Windſor tables in Heylin and Aſhmole (the originals being worn out and loſt) wardrobe entries, and ſome ſcattered notices in records. Mr. Anſtis has given ſpecimens of his lives of the knights in thoſe of fifteen in the twelfth ſtall, and of Sir John Faſtolf in the third, with the arms from the plates; and a ſupplement to Aſhmole's diſcourſe of Garter herald. Many particulars relative to our antient habits may be learned from this book.

One Dr. Mondonus Belvaleti, a Cluniac monk, orator or chargè d'affaires from ſome foreign court to ours, allegoriſed all the habits and ornaments of the order in his " Catechiſmus ordinis equitum periſcelidis Anglicanæ ſeu ſpeculum Anglorum;" which he ſent to Whethamſtead, abbot of St. Albans, for his corrections, not having one book of his own by him. It was publiſhed by Boſquieri, Colon. 1631, from a beautifully illuminated MS. which would probably have exhibited drawings of the ſubjects, the deſcription of which is the only merit of this myſtical rhapſody [r].

Draughts of arms aſcribed to our knights have been publiſhed abroad in large books, according to the conjectures and fancies of the

[r] Heylin, p. 349. Anſtis, p. 119. and his letter to Hearne, app. to Otterburn, No 16.

authors; in " Les noms, furnoms, qualites, armes, & blafons de tous
" les princes, feigneurs, commandeurs, chevaliers, & officiers de
" l'ordre & milice de la Jartierre depuis l'inftitution, &c. Paris 1647."
a large folio, containing on each fide the titles, in the middle the arms
in a garter, and below the blafons.——" Armoiries & blafons de tous
" les chevaliers, de l'ordre du Roy de St. Efprit, de la Jartiere, & de
" la Toifon d'Or, depuis le commencement d'iceux jufqu'a prefent,
" par Charles Soyer, enlumineur du Roi. Par. 1643." Fol. in John
Boiffeau's " Promptuaire armoriel" for thefe three orders and that of
the Annunciada 1658, and P. Danet's " Noms & armes" of the Garter
and Holy Ghoft. Par. 1652. 4to.

Dr. Pettingal's " Differtation on the original of the equeftrian figure
of the George and of the Garter. Lond. 1753." deriving it from Egyptian and Grecian mythology corrupted by the Bafilidians, is more ingenious than probable : he has not proved that the antients reprefented
the fun by an equeftrian figure, though the horfe was the fymbol of
his fwiftnefs : he thinks his influence over the noxious vapours is alluded
to in this fymbol of victory, and will not allow us a patron faint,
becaufe George, if he exifted at all, was an Arian ᶳ : when he makes
the garter an amulet he does not diftinguifh between a charm and a
fymbol.

The Order has been celebrated in verfe in " The honour of the
" Garter difplaied in a poem gratulatorie; entituled, to the worthy and
" renowned Earle of Northumberlande created knight of the order,
" and inftalled at Windfor 26 June, 35 Eliz. by Geo. Peele, maifter of
" artes, in Oxenford. Lond. 1593." 4to. and in Gilbert Weft's fine
dramatic poem on its inftitution. 1742. 4to. reprinted in Dodfley's
Collection of poems, vol. iii. p. 107.

Pote, bookfeller at Eton, publifhed " The hiftory and antiquities
" of *Windfor* caftle, and the royal college and chapel of St. George;
" with the inftitution, laws, and ceremonies of the moft noble order
" of the Garter; including the feveral foundations in the caftle : with
" an account of the town and corporation of Windfor, the royal

---

ᶳ Dawfon fhews our martyr lived feventy years before the Arian bifhop.   Heylin gives
him quite up.

" apart-

" apartments and paintings in the caſtle; the ceremony of the inſtalla-
" tion of a knight of the Garter; alſo an account of the firſt founders
" and their ſucceſſors the knights companions to the preſent time,
" with their ſeveral ſtalls or lay-titles at length from the plates in the
" choir of St. George's chapel, and the ſucceſſion of the deans and
" prebends of Windſor, the alms knights, the monumental and antient
" inſcriptions; with other particulars not mentioned by any author.
" The whole intirely new wrote, and illuſtrated with cuts. Eton
" 1749." 4to. abridged in " Les delices de Windſore, or a deſcription of Windſor caſtle, and the country adjacent, &c. Eton 1755."
12mo. In the third volume of Aſhmole's Antiquities is a good hiſtory
of the dean and canons of Windſor from their own original regiſter
drawn up by Tho. Fryth, canon here 1610, rector of Elmeley in Kent,
his native county, who died 1631. Wood calls him a moſt judicious
and induſtrious man; and ſays that Geo. Evans, another canon, and
others, continued the catalogue from 1628 to his time[t]. It comes
down to 1718.

Among Le Neve's MSS. and in Harl. MS. 3749, is " A deſcription
" of the honour of Windſor, viz. the caſtle, foreſt, parks, rayls, lodges,
" towns, pariſhes, hamlets, houſes of note, woods, rivers, and hills,
" extending into Berks, Surrey, and Bucks, done by John Norden,
" A.D. 1607. being an actual ſurvey of the caſtle, foreſt, and each
" park, in 17 maps, exactly delineated."

The painting in St. George's hall is deſcribed in a Latin copy of
verſes by Mr. Sparke, ſtudent of Chriſt Church, intitled " Aula Winde-
foriæ D. Georgio inſtaurata," printed in the Muſæ Anglicanæ. Oxon
1699. 8vo. vol. ii. p. 64.

" Windſor-Caſtle, a poem, inſcribed to the immortal memory of
" Q Anne. 1708." Fol.

There is a Latin tranſlation of Pope's " Windſor Foreſt," intitled
" Vinſorium nemus, carmen autore Alex. Pope, Latine reddidit Guil.
" Patterſon in academia A. Pollok, M. D. linguarum profeſſor.
" Lond. 1758." 4to.

[t] Faſti. I. 169.

Hollar

Hollar engraved a small view of the castle 1644, in a set with three other views of London, Lambeth, and Tothill-fields; and a south prospect of it having at the bottom a new map of the county, on a large sheet, 1666: another, together with a view of St. George's chapel, and two of the choir, 1660, 1663, distinct from those in Ashmole's book: he also engraved a great hollow tree, 26 feet round at bottom, with a door in the trunk and stairs within up to the top, 33 feet high, with a square turret 34 feet about, and people in it, in Langley Park near Windsor. 1653.

Four views of the castle from the N. S. E. and W. with a plan and elevation, drawn by B. Langley, engraved by T. Langley, 1743.

Another of the town and castle, and little park, with the town and college of Eton; and the east prospect of the castle, and plan of the gardens, as proposed to be executed in the reign of Q. Anne, drawn and published by Wm. Collier, of Eton. 1742.

Another plan of the castle and park by Rocque.

A view of the palace and castle by Buck. 1732.

Eight views of the great park by T. Sandby, viz. the lodge and stables, engraved by Mason; view from the north side of the Virginia river near the manor lodge, by P. Sandby; great lake, by W. Austin; new building on shrub's hill near the lodge, by Canot; the moat island; and the lodge and garden from the great lake, by Vivares; the great bridge over the Virginia river, by P. Sandby; cascade and grotto, by ditto and E. Rooker.

In p. 484 of N° 261 of the Phil. Transf. is part of two letters from Dr. Brewer concerning the beds of oyster-shells near Reading.——In p. 603 of N° 490 is Mr. Ward's account of a date in Arabic numerals at *Walling* near Aldermaston.——In vol. L. Dr. Collet's description of a peat-pit near *Newbury*.——In Birch's history of the Royal Society, vol. I. p. 438, is a description of an elm partly petrefied at *Wadley* near Farringdon.

Sir John Denham's " *Cooper's-hill* " was printed at Oxf. 1643, in one sheet and half, 4to; again with additions, Lond. 1650 and 1655. 4to; 1667 and 1668, 8vo. and frequently since: and translated into Latin verse by Moses Pengry, of Brazen Nose Col. printed at Oxford 1676.

1676. 4to. under the title of " Cooper's-hill, Latine redditum ad no-
biliffimum Dominum Gulielmum Dominum Cavendiſh, honoratiſſimi,
Domini Gulielmi, Comitis Devoniæ ᵘ, filium unicum."

" St. Anne's-hill, a poem."

" St. Leonard's-hill, or the hermitage, a poem, humbly inſcribed to
———— ———— by Robert Morris. Lond. 1743." 4to.

" Heliocrene, a poem, in Latin and Engliſh, on the chalybeat well
at Sunning-hill in Windſor foreſt. Lond. 1744."

A braſs lamp, found at St. Leonard's-hill near Windſor, and preſented to the Antiquarian Society by Sir Hans Sloane, has been engraved
at their expence by Vertue.

A N.E. view of Dunnington caſtle, the ſeat of Chaucer and the
Delapoles, by Buck 1732.

Two views of Datchet bridge, upon the Thames, and the five bells of
Oſeley [a public houſe] on the ſame river, by W. Oram. 1745.

Two views of the gardens of Tho. Hart, eſq; at Warfield, by J.
Wood 1751, from paintings by J. Harris.

Saxton's map of this county is included in thoſe of Oxfordſhire and
Bucks, 1574, and wants the hundreds, which are inſerted in Speed's,
with a view of Windſor caſtle : a plan of Reading is at the corner of
his map of Bucks. Hollar engraved a ſmall map 1670. Another was
publiſhed by E. Bowen 1756.

John Rocque, topographer to the King, engraved " A topographical
ſurvey of the county of Berks, in 18 ſheets : in which are expreſſed
his Majeſty's royal palace of Windſor, its parks and foreſt, the ſeats of
the nobility and gentry, towns, villages, hamlets, farms, cottages, with
the main and croſs roads, bridle-ways, pales, hedges, hills, valleys,
rivers, brooks, canals, ponds, bridges, ferries, wind and water mills,
woods, commons, and greens appertaining to each pariſh, &c. to which
is added a topographical and hiſtorical index of all the remarkable places
in the ſaid county, with their bearings and diſtances to the next market
town or well-known place ; the length, breadth, circumference, and
contents in acres and ſquare miles, of the county, Windſor foreſt, and
each pariſh. 171."

Another was done by I. Taylor. 1763.

ᵘ Whoſe chaplain he was.

BUCK-

BUCKINGHAMSHIRE.

THIS county was visited by Harvey 1566; by R. Lee, Portcullis, 1574; by Philipott and Ryley, Somerset and Blewmantle, 1634. Browne Willis, after labouring indefatigably many years to procure materials, and circulating queries, dated April 8, 1712, published " The history and antiquities of the town, hundred, and deanry of " *Buckingham :* containing a description of the towns, villages, ham- " lets, monasteries, churches, chapels, chantries, seats, manors; their " antient and present owners; together with the epitaphs, inscrip- " tions, and arms in all the parish churches; and state of the rec- " tories, vicarages, donatives; their patrons, and incumbents, terriers, " and valuations in the king's books. Also some account of the earls " and dukes of Buckingham, and high-sheriffs of the county. With " a transcript of Domesday-book, and the translation thereof into Eng- " lish, &c. Lond. 1755." 4to.

In 1717 were published proposals for " Historia, antiquitates, & " Athenæ *Etonenses;* or the history, antiquities, &c. of the famous " college of St. Mary, near Eton, from its first foundation, 1440, to " the present time; wherein are preserved all the inscriptions on the " monuments and grave-stones formerly in this college chapel; with " an exact account of all the persons who have been educated at Eton, " and thence elected to King's College in Cambridge; as also of the " provosts, fellows, and schoolmasters, representing the births, for- " tunes, preferments, and obits of all those authors, bishops, and states- " men, and others, the great accidents of their lives, and an impartial " account of their writings : the whole compiled from the best autho- " rities, as well MSS. as printed; with an appendix, consisting of ori- " ginal charters, and papers from the Tower, the Rolls Chapel, the " Augmentation-office, the Bodleian and Cottonian libraries, and other " MSS. communicated from private gentlemen, as well as from pub- " lick offices."

N   J. Pote,

J. Pote, bookſeller at Eton, publiſhed 1730 " Catalogus alumnorum
" e coll. regali B. Mariæ de Etona in coll. regale B. Mariæ & S. Nico-
" lai apud Cantabrigienſes cooptatorum, ab A. D. 1444 ejuſdem col-
" legii Etonenſis fundationis primo uſque ad an. 1730." 4to.

A catalogue of the MSS. in this college is in Cat. MSS. Angliæ, tom. II. p. 46. Richard Topſham of Windſor, eſq; bequeathed
a valuable collection of books, drawings, &c. 1736, on condition that
ſuch as are ſtudious in antiquities ſhall have free acceſs to them ˣ.

" Muſæ Etonénſes, ſive poemata," were printed in two vols. 1755.

Hollar engraved a north view of the college and church 1672, in
one ſheet : another on half a ſheet, undated.

Copy of an illumination on a charter granted to the provoſt and fellows of Eton by Hen. VI. and confirmed by act of parliament, engraved by Pine 1740.

Dr. Rawlinſon had a charter of confirmation and protection from Abp.
Becket to the nuns of Ivingehou (*Ivingho*), which he cauſed to be engr.

In the library of the Heralds College among Vincent's MSS. Nº 85.
has this note by the donor, A. Wood, 1674. " This book is tranſcribed
" from an antient leiger-book, belonging to the lords of Borſtall in
" Bucks, which leiger I peruſed in 1668, in order to obtain matter
" for Mr. Dugdale's Monaſtic. Anglican. the Lady Penelope Dynham
" being then lady of Borſtall.". The original chartulary, a large
folio on vellom, was made temp. Hen. VI. and has at the beginning a
drawing of the manſion-houſe moated, and the lord of the manor
John Fitz Nigel iſſuing out, and on his knees preſenting a boar's head
on a ſpear to the king, who returns him a coat of arms, in alluſion to
the cuſtom of the manor, which is ſuppoſed to have been antiently a
thick wood and retreat for wild boars : the garriſon ſurrendered this
houſe to the Parliament 1646 ʸ.

ˣ Biog. Brit. Mead, n. Q.

ʸ See Wood's life, publiſhed by Hearne, p. 464 and 578. The boar s head was
carved on an old bedſtead in this houſe; of which laſt there is a view in Kennet's Parochial Antiquities. p. 679. An antient horn, tipped with ſilver, gilt, and fitted with
leather wreaths to hang about it, with the arms of the Liſures, who had the manor after
the conqueſt, was preſerved as Nigel's horn by the lords of this eſtate to the end of the
laſt century, when Sir John Aubrey, then lord, ſhewed it to Dr. Kennet. One that
pretends to older date is preſerved in a Berkſhire family. Camd. Berks.

Some

Some places in this county are taken notice of in Bifhop Kennet's " Parochial antiquities attempted in the hiftory of *Ambrofden, Bur-* " *cefter*, and other adjacent parts in the counties of Oxford and Bucks. " Oxon. 1695." 4to.

Some antiquities at or near *Hitchendon* are defcribed in the Gent. Mag. Oct. 1758. p. 466.

The crowded gardens at *Stow* are celebrated in a poem called by their name, addreffed to Pope. 1732. 8vo. and in " The triumphs of " nature," another poem, in the Gent. Mag. June, July, and Auguft, 1742. Defcriptions of them were printed at Lond. 1745. 8vo. Northampton, 1747. 8vo. Another, containing forty views of the buildings and houfe : and a dialogue upon the gardens. 1749. 8vo. Another, with views, &c. 1756. Geo. Bickham publifhed " The " beauties of Stow." 1750. 12mo. with cuts. Rigaud and Baron engraved eight large views of thefe gardens, with a plan, from draw-ings made immediately under the earl's direction, by Chatelain; pub-lifhed by S. Bridgman. 1749.

Four views of Lord Defpenfer's houfe and gardens at *W. Wick-ham*, and two of Mr. Waller's at *Hall-Barn* near Beconsfield, by Woollett.

A view of Lord Inchiquin's feat at *Cliefden* by L. Sullivan. 1761.

The N. E. profpect of St. Martin's Chapel, at *Fenny Stratford* de-figned by Ed. Wing of Aynhoe, drawn by J. Gofley, engraved by G. Hulett. This chapel was raifed and endowed by Browne Willis, and dedicated May 27, 1730, to St. Martin, becaufe his grandfather Dr. Tho. Willis was born in the parifh of St. Martin's in the Fields, Lon-don, and buried here, with this uncouth epitaph :

> In honour to thy memory, bleffed fhade,
> Was the foundation of this chapel laid.
> Purchafed by thee, thy fon and prefent heir
> Owe thefe three manors to thy facred care.
> For this may all thy race thanks ever pay,
> And yearly celebrate St. Martin's day.

S. W. view of *Hambleden* parfonage, by S. Wale and Vivares, 1752.

Buck engraved an E. view of Nutley abbey, and a W. one of Burnham priory, 1730.

" The multiplying wheel-bucket engine, for raifing water to fupply gentlemen's feats and gardens, which moves continually by a fmall fall of water without the help of any man or beaft, &c. &c. &c. erected at Chichley, Bucks, the feat of Sir John Chefter, made by Geo. Greves, 1725. H. Beighton del. E. Kirkall fc."

Saxton's map of this county is included in that of Oxfordfhire and Berks 1574, and wants the hundreds, which are added in Speed's 1610, with a plan of Buckingham. Another was publifhed by E. Bowen 1756.

CAMBRIDGE.

CAMBRIDGESHIRE.

A short defcription of part of this county by Mr. Layer, rector of
Shepreth near Royfton, containing the hundreds of Armingford,
Long Stowe, Papworth, N. Stowe, Chefterton, Wetherley, and Triplow,
is among the Harl. MSS. N° 6768. other collections, N° 6772-4-5.

Francis Blomfield, the Norfolk antiquary, printed in his own houfe
at Norwich his " Collectanea Cantabrigienfia, or collections relating
" to Cambridge univerfity, town, and county, containing the monu-
" mental infcriptions in all the chapels of the feveral colleges, and
" parifh churches in the town; with a lift of the mayors; the moft
" antient charters of the town; and other hiftorical memoirs of feveral
" colleges, &c. 1751." 4to.

Edmund Carter, a fchoolmafter in Cambridge, by the affiftance of
fome academical friends, compiled a " Hiftory of the county from
the earlieft account to the prefent time, &c. alfo a particular account
of the antient and modern Cambridge, with the city of Ely, and the
parifhes therein: and an account of the feveral towns and villages, in
an alphabetical order. Cambr. 1753." 8vo. Under each parifh are the
particulars of the ravages committed in the churches by W Dowfing,
employed by the government 1643 to deftroy all the antient monuments, &c. as miniftring to fuperftition; of which ravages he kept a
particular account, publifhed by Dr. Grey 1739 [z].

There are vifitations of this county by Cooke 1575; and by Hen. St.
George 1619.

Befides what is faid of the fenny part in Dugdale's hiftory of imbanking and draining, &c. there have been publifhed " The hiftory
" or narrative of the great level of the fens, called Bedford-Level,
" with a large map of the faid level, as drained, furveyed, and de-

---

[z] In the appendix to " Schifmatics delineated from authentic vouchers, &c." 8vo.
and fince in " The ornaments of churches confidered, 1761, appendix, N° VI. Bifhop
Hall faved the windows of his chapel at Norwich from deftruction by taking out the
heads of the figures: and this is the reafon we fee fo many faces in church windows
fupplied with white glafs.

" fcribed

" scribed by Sir Jonas Moore[a], knight, his late Majesty's surveyor-
" general of his ordnance. Lond. 1685." 12mo. to which is annexed, a poetical " true and natural description of the great level of the
" fens."   The map of this level of the fens extending itself into the
counties of Northampton, Norfolk, Suffolk, Lyncolne, Cambridge, and
Huntingdon, and the Isle of Ely, as drained by Sir Jonas, was published
in several sheets, and is to be found reduced in Magna Britannia and
other books.

" Proposals and inducements for a considerable number of people to
" joyn in the purchas of several thousand acres, of drein'd and derelict
" lands in several counties of England, which will redound to the
" vast advantage of the purchasors.   For that end application will be
" made to the King and Parliament that the purchasors may be made
" a body corporate, in nature of that of Bedford Level.   And most of
" these lands proposed having been under the same circumstances with
" those of Bedford Level, the history of that Level is annexed, which
" will give a just and proper idea of what may be expected from this
" undertaking.   The whole will be entertaining, and let people see
" they are invited to honour, pleasure, and profit. Lond. 1726." 8vo.

" An essay on draining; more particularly with regard to the north
" division of the great level of the fens called Bedford Level.   Lond.
" 1729." 8vo.

" The result of a view of the great level of the fens, taken at the
" desire of the Duke of Bedford, &c. governor and the gentlemen of
" the corporation of the fens in July 1745.   By Charles Labelye, en-
" gineer. Lond. 1745." 4to. with Moore's map.

" The result of a particular view of the level of the fens taken in
" August 1745. [By the same.] Lond. 1748." 8vo.

---

[a] Sir J. Moore was an eminent mathematician, appointed by Charles I. 1647, to teach
the Duke of York arithmetic, geography, &c. till his escape from St. James's 1648 : by
the recommendation of Col. Giles Strangeways, prisoner in the Tower, to other eminent
fellow prisoners, he was appointed chief surveyor of the draining the great level of the
fens : sent to Tangier 1663; at his return appointed surveyor of the ordnance, and
knighted by Charles II. he was chosen fellow of the Royal Society 1674, and was a
great patron of Flamstead, for whom he obtained the place of royal astronomer, with
a salary of 100 l. per ann.   He died 1681. Birch's Hist. of the Roy. Soc. IV. p. 106.
where this work is dated 1683.

Charles Nelson Cole, efq; of the Inner Temple, barrifter, and regifter to the corporation, publifhed in 1761 " A collection of laws
" which form the conftitution of the Bedford-Level corporation, to-
" gether with an introductory hiftory thereof." 8vo.

" A new method of making the banks in the fens almoft im-
" pregnable, fo as in time to refift the force of rivers in the moft
" impetuous floods, and prevent all future inundations: with a new
" but certain method of preparing the lands therein for the growth
" of our moft valuable timber, viz. oak, elm, afh, &c. particularly
" thofe extenfive tracts of land in the counties of Cambridge and
" Lincoln. Alfo fome obfervations on the river Cam; how to con-
" fine its bounds and improve its navigation: which may ferve as a
" plan for any other inland river, &c. By John Harrifon, botanift and.
" nurferyman in Cambridge. 1766."

The firft effay towards a botanical hiftory of the county was Ray's
" Catalogus plantarum circa Cantabrigiam nafcentium; in quo exhi-
" bentur quotquot hactenus inventæ funt, quæ vel fponte proveniunt
" vel in agris feruntur; una cum fynonymis felectioribus, locis natali-
" bus, & obfervationibus quibufdam oppido raris: adjiciuntur in gra-
" tiam tyronum, index Anglico-Latinus, index locorum, etymologia
" nominum, & explicatio quorundam terminorum. Cantab. 1660."
12mo. Three years after he publifhed an appendix of 42 more plants
obferved here: another edition 1685 had 60 more added to it by
Peter Dent, apothecary at Cambridge. Dr. Stukeley, who fimpled
here with Dr. Hales while ftudents, made great additions to this catalogue, which he was folicited to print, with a map of the county, but
was prevented by family engagements. John Martyn, profeffor of botany in this univerfity, difpofed the plants in alphabetical order, agree
able to Ray's method, intitling his book " Methodus plantarum circa
" Cantabrigiam nafcentium. Lond. 1727." 8vo. b including Ray's
appendix; but no new plants, only moffes, fungi, and graffes, inferted
in an intended new edition, of which only one fheet and half was
printed. Several plants have fince been found by Ifrael Lyons, jun
who publifhed " Fafciculus plantarum circa Cantabrigiam nafcen-

b In the Gent. Mag. Mar. 1766, is a table ranging the plants in this book according
to Ray's method in preference to that of Linnæus.

" tium

" tium quæ poſt Raium obſervatæ fuere. Lond. 1763." 8vo. All
theſe ſeveral works are comprehended in " Plantæ Cantabrigienſes, or
" a catalogue of the plants which grow wild in the county of Cam-
" bridge, diſpoſed according to the ſyſtem of Linnæus. Herbationes
" Cantabrigienſes, or directions to the places where they may be found:
" comprehended in thirteen botanical excurſions: to which are added,
" liſts of the more rare plants growing in many parts of England and
" Wales. By Thomas Martyn c, M. A. fellow of Sidney Col. and
" profeſſor of botany in Cambridge. Lond. 1763." The firſt of theſe
conſiſts of three columns, containing the generical and marginal names
from Linnæus, J. Martyn, and Ray. Dr. James Douglas gave an account of the cultivation of ſaffron in Cambridgeſhire in Phil. Tranſ.
Nº 405. p. 566. as others had done before him in Nº 138 and 380.

T. Dawkes, ſurgeon, publiſhed " Prodigium Willinghamenſe; or
" authentic memoirs of the more remarkable paſſages in the life of a
" boy born at *Willingham* near Cambridge, Oct. 31. 1741. who be-
" fore he was three years old was three feet eight inches high, and
" had the marks of puberty. With ſome reflections on his underſtand-
" ing, ſtrength, temper, memory, genius, and knowlege. Lond."
8vo. In the Phil. Tranſ. Nº 475. p. 251. is a letter about this boy
from Mr. Almond, vicar of Willingham to Ph. Miller, and another
from Dawkes to Dr. Mead.

" A ſad relation of a dreadful fire at *Cottenham*, four miles diſtant
" from Cambridge, Saturday the 10th of April 1676. which in five
" hours conſumed above 100 dwelling houſes, beſides barns, &c.
" written by an eye-witneſs, &c. 1676." 4to. one ſheet.

" Nundinæ *Sturbrigienſes*, anno 1702. Authore T. Hill, Col. S.
" Trin. Soc." in the Muſæ Britannicæ, p. 1. is a good deſcription of
this famous fair, the inſtitution of which Dr. Stukeley d aſcribes to the
Romans.

In p. 79 of Nº 474 of the Phil. Tranſ. are Mr. Ward's remarks on a
date at the Half-moon inn near Magdalen Col.

In the Gent. Mag. Sept. 1754. p. 424. was inſerted for explanation
an inſcription on the front of Serj. Leeds's houſe at *Croxton*.

c Son of the former.   d Hiſt. of Carauſius. I. p. 207.

The

The rev. Mr. James Bentham, minor canon of Ely, has been long engaged in writing the hiſtory and antiquities of that cathedral, to be illuſtrated with near fifty views and ſections of the buildings, monuments, &c. to explain the antient and preſent ſtate of this fabric, and the various ſtiles of Gothic architecture uſed in England from the foundation of the church to the reformation, with occaſional remarks on the ſtile of building in general. His propoſals were publiſhed 1761, and we eagerly expect an account of a building which is the chief inſtance of the elegance and variety of our antient architecture. The ſtate of the dioceſe, in Latin, by Biſhop Wren, is among the Harl. MSS. 6885. King engraved the N. and S. Harris the S. N. E. and W. ſides of the church, and Buck a large S. E. view of the city 1743.

In the Gent. Mag. Mar. 1766, is a letter from Dr. Stukeley to Mr. Collinſon about certain Britiſh antiquities found at *Chateris* 1757, and then in his poſſeſſion [e], with a cut : the Doctor ſuppoſes the Britiſh king to whom they belonged reſided and was buried on the ſcite of Chateris nunnery.

In the appendix to Hearne's Annales de Dunſtaple, N° 5. is a copy of K. John's charter to the town of *Cambridge* for a præpoſitus or mayor with Hen. IIId's charter confirming the ſame : both copied from the originals among the town archives, by Mr. Baker : among whoſe collections in the Britiſh Muſeum, N° 7037. 15. 7053, 12. is a petition of this town to be made a city.

" Cambridge, a poem. Lond. 1757." Fol. By a lady.

The beſt plan of the town ſeems to have been in Markant's MS. de privilegiis & ſtatutis univ. Cantabrig. but now cut out. Dr. Caius [f] made another, whereon are in hiſtorical inſcriptions the names of the hoſtles, ſtreets, and lanes, with their reſpective ſituations, the arms of the univerſity and town, the Queen, and Archbiſhop Parker, which was engraved by Jo. Lyne [g] 1574, the expence of the Archbiſhop, in whoſe

---

[e] Since purchaſed at the ſale of his curioſities by Guſtavus Brander, eſq;

[f] See Hiſt. of C. C. C. p. 42. Markant was proctor about 1472.

[g] This workman, who has eſcaped Mr. Walpole, is doubtleſs the ſame with Richard Lyne, employed by Archbiſhop Parker, who engraved a genealogical hiſtorical map intitled " Regnum Britanniæ tandem plene in heptarchiam reductum a Saxonibus, &c." with a map called Angliæ Heptarchia. Strype, who ſaw it at Ruckholt, ſays it was done in wood very plain and well, and under it was Richardus Lyne, ſervus D. Matth.

Archiep.

whofe hands the Doctor left it, and prefixed to the 4to edition of his piece on the antiquity of the univerfity. Ralph Aggas, furveyor, publifhed a plan of Cambridge, three feet by four, about 1578 according to Mr. Walpole, or 1589 as Mr. Ames.

Hollar engraved a profpect of Cambridge from the London road, with the ground plan, arms of the colleges, and earls of Cambridge, on a half fheet.

David Loggan, a Dantzicker, drew and engraved views of the colleges and other public buildings in this univerfity, and a plan of the town: his work intitled " Cantabrigia illuftrata" was publifhed at Cambridge 1690. Fol. in the title of which he ftiles himfelf utriufque academiæ chalcographus.

Buck engraved a N. W. view of the town and univerfity 1743, and a N. E. view of the caftle h 1730.

P. S. Lamborne of Cambridge engraved the following fix views in and about the town. 1. Part of Barnwell. 2. Part of Chefterton. 3. Clarehall from Queen's grove. 4. King's new building from the grove. 5. Trinity library and St. Mary's from St. John's back-gate. 6. King's college chapel and Clare-hall from Erafmus's walk. He is at prefent engaged about four large views of public buildings belonging to the univerfity, to be publifhed by fubfcription, viz. Clare-hall new building to the river—Trinity library and the new cycloidical bridge—the fenate-houfe and fchools—the S. fide of King's chapel i.

Of Pythagoras School, or, as it fhould more properly be called, Merton-hall, in Cambridge, the remains of a college founded before the conqueft for the revival of learning here, we have a fection and ichnography drawn and publifhed by the rev. Mr. Mafters, with the feals of this houfe, and Merton college, Oxford, to which it belongs. Buck engraved a S. W. view of the fame building 1730, a S. W. view of Thorney abbey, N. E. of Denny priory, and N. E. of Camps caftle.

Archiep. Cant. fc. 1574. In the map were defcribed the feven kingdoms in feven columns, with the diocefes and counties in each: and the genealogy was threefold, the Britifh kings, the Norman dukes, and the Norman kings to Q. Eliz. with the dates of their reigns; making a fuccinct hiftory of England. Life of Parker, 541.

h Edw. I. was the firft of our kings that ever lodged in this caftle. Lib. de Bernewell in Lel. Coll. II. 444. Sir J. Huddleftone built his houfe at Sawfton with its ruins given him by Q. Mary.

i Loggan is faid to have hurt his eye fight in delineating this chapel.

The

The pedeftal of a crofs at *Hadenham* is engraved in pl. XI. of Stukeley's It. Cur.

Saxton's map of this county is included in that of Northamptonfhire, &c. 1576, and wants the hundreds, which are fupplied in Speed's, 1610, with a plan of the town, arms of the colleges, and four figures of the academical habits. Another very faulty one has been publifhed by E. Bowen, with a S. E. profpect of Ely. 1753. Jefferies engraved a map of the country twenty miles round Cambridge.

Univerfity of Cambridge.

The firft accounts of the univerfity are pieces of controverfy about its antiquity. The difpute was begun by Nicholas Cantelupe, who is fuppofed to have drawn up the hiftoriola k in the black book, and was anfwered by John Rofs in a piece now loft. Leland's work De academiis Britannicis and his Life of Sigebert have fhared the fame fate. In this laft he probably exhaufted the fubject. In that prince's article l in his account of our writers, he fpeaks modeftly in favour of this univerfity, whereof himfelf was a member; and without carrying its foundation to old Granta, where the Britons and Romans are fuppofed to have ftudied together m, inclines to make him founder. When Q. Elizabeth was at Cambridge n 1564 the public orator in his fpeech before her happening to extol the antiquity of this univerfity above that

k A note of Bale's in Leland's MS. at Trinity Col. afcribes it to Cantelupe or Thomas Aulaby, of whom nothing is faid in Tann. Bib. Brit. Oxford has a like hiftoriola, which Wood prudently declined bringing in evidence.

l He there quotes an Englifh poem on the antiquity of this univerfity by a German, lately printed at Cambridge.——John Herrifon or Harrifon, a phyfician, about the middle of the fixth century, wrote a piece on the foundation of this univerfity. MS. Caius Col. 1094. Another piece on the univerfity in general is Phineas Fletcher's " De literis anti- " quæ Britanniæ legibus, præfertim qui doctrina claruerunt, quique collegia Cantabri- " giæ fundarunt, Cantab. 1633." 12mo. dedicated to King's and Eton colleges.

m Almoft 400 years before Sigebert was born: it cannot be fooner, for Dr. Stukeley does not allow Granta to have exifted before Caraufius. According to the hiftoriola Maximian deftroyed Cambridge with all its churches, and it remained deftitute of ftudents near 150 years. In the fame book we have Anaximander and Anaxagoras for profeffors, ftudents carried to Rome by J. Cæfar, and Amphibalus for the firft chancellor.

n " The triumphs of the Mufes, or Q. Elizabeth's entertainment at Cambridge 1564." was printed in Peck's Defid. Cur. II. B. 7. N° 15. p. 40. from Baker's Harleian Collections, 7037.

of

of Oxford, Thomas Key, mafter of Univerfity Col. at the requeft of
a friend, compofed in a week's time a little piece on the antiquity of
his own univerfity, whofe foundation he carried back to the Greek
profeffors that accompanied Brute to England, and its reftoration to
Alfred about 870. Having given the MS. to his friend, who did
not return it, he wrote out another copy, which notwithftanding all his
precaution came into the hands of the Earl of Leicefter, from which
Dr. John Caius, mafter of Caius Col. having obtained it, fet himfelf
to prove that the univerfity of Cambridge, being founded by Cantaber
394 years before Chrift, was 1267 years older than that of Oxford. His
work was publifhed under a feigned name together with the piece it
was intended to confute, and intitled " De antiquitate Cantabrigienfis
" academiæ libri 2. in quorum 2do de Oxonienfis quoque gymnafii
" antiquitate differitur, & Cantabrigienfe longe eo antiquius effe de-
" finitur, Londinenfi authore: adjunximus affertionem antiquitatis
" Oxonienfis academiæ ab Oxonienfi quodam annis jam elapfis duobus
" ad reginam confcriptam, in qua docere conatur, Oxonienfe gym-
" nafium Cantabrigienfi antiquius effe: ut ex collatione facilè intel-
" ligas, utra fit antiquior. Excufum Londini, A. D. 1568, menfe
" Augufto, per Henricum Bynneman." 12mo.   As foon as this came
to Thomas Caius' hands he drew up a defence[o] of his Affertio, intending to have printed it in the form of notes with an appendix of animadverfions on his antagonift's work : but dying 1572, his obfervations
remained in MS. till induftrious Hearne gave them to the world.
John Caius died a year after him ; and the year following appeared
under Archbifhop Parker's patronage a new edition of his work, with
large additions which he left behind him ; intitled " De antiquitate
" Cantebrigienfis academiæ libri duo, aucti ab ipfo autore plurimum,
" in quorum fecundo de Oxonienfis quoque gymnafii antiquitate dif-
" feritur, & Cantebrigienfe longe eo antiquius effe definitur : Johanne

---

[o] Tanner and Wood calls this reply " Examen judicii Cantabrigienfis cujufdam qui
" fe Londinenfem dicit, nuper de origine utriufque academiæ lati ;" what he calls an
apology for his writing both the Affertio and this piece is only the introduction to the
Animadverfiones, intitled " hujus concertationis ratio." The MS. paffed thro' feveral
hands into Archbifhop Ufher's : his grandfon Tyrrel gave it fome time before he died
to a friend, who left it to Hearne to publifh it.

" Caio

" Caio Anglo authore. Adjunximus affertionem antiquitatis Oxoni-
" enfis academiæ, ab Oxonienfi quodam, &c. &c. 1574." 4to. At
the end is, " Hiftoriæ Cantebrigienfis academiæ ab urbe condita
" lib. 2. p. authore Johanne Caio Anglo. Lond. 1574." 4to. with a
plan of the town and fchools, and arms of the colleges. Hearne's edition comprehends all that both difputants wrote on the fubject: the
principal title is only " Thomæ Caii vindiciæ antiquitatis academiæ
" Oxonienfis contra Joannem Caium, Cantabrigienfem." 2 vols. Ox.
1730. 8vo. The firft vol. contains the pieces in Bynneman's and the
4to edition, with Thomas Cay's ftrictures as notes at the bottom of the
Vindiciæ: his animadverfions are in the 2d: fome additions are alfo
inferted in the Affertio. Hearne, who boafts of the Oxford advocate's
clear and nervous manner of writing, imagines our Cambridge parti-
fan broke his heart when he found how able an adverfary he had
engaged with; though he does not believe he faw his ftrictures [q].
It muft be confeffed that John Caius is bewildered in the pomp and
pedantry of a phyfician of the laft century; but whether either of
them has cleared up this obfcure fubject may be queftioned. The
difpute was revived by a paffage inferted in the fecond edition of Affer's
life of Alfred by Camden 1602, from a MS. the date of which he
fixed to Rich. IId's time [r]. Archbifhop Parker had before publifhed
Affer from a MS. which he afterwards depofited in Benet Col. library,
and which Mr. Wife [s] allows to be a copy of that in the Cotton library,
the oldeft MS. of Affer extant. Sir John Spelman [t] and Dr. Smith [u]

[p] The firft book contains the antient ftate of the place, a defcription of the town,
hiftory of the univerfity, and foundation of the colleges: the fecond defcribes the town
as in the author's time, the officers of the univerfity, exercifes, &c. fchools, library, &c.

[q] He thinks T. Caius eftablifhed the antiquity of Oxford by proving Cambridge and
Grantchefter different places, as if it was at all to the purpofe whether the univerfity
was founded exactly to a mile on the prefent fpot. T. Caius allows a grammar fchool
at Cambridge before Alfred.

[r] It is moft probable it was inferted into that MS. from Higden, who firft broached
the ftory of Alfred's founding Oxford, and lived near the date affigned by Camden.
That editor's fidelity therefore is nothing to the purpofe: the late date of his MS. is a
fufficient objection, though Hearne thought it fo valuable as to have been deftroyed by
the enemies of that univerfity.

[s] Apolog. Afferii Camdeniani at the end of his edition of Affer.

[t] Life of Alf. Engl. ed. p. 176—190.

[u] Append. to Bede. Nº XIV.

have

have expofed the inconfiftencies in this passage, and their objections have received no fatisfactory anfwer. The latter has with equal fairnefs and perfpicuity fhewn the right this univerfity has if not to fuperior, at leaft to equal, antiquity with the other ; and if not to Sigebert for its founder, at leaft to Edward fon of Alfred, for its reftorer [x], which is more than his father was to Oxford. Sir Simon D'Ewes in a fpeech in parliament [y] inferred the antiquity of the univerfity from the confiderable figure Caer Grant makes in the lift of Britifh cities, and in Domefday ; and offered to prove it a renowned city at leaft 500 yeras before there was a houfe in Oxford. If the queftion is to be decided by the number of books publifhed about this univerfity, we muft yield the palm of feniority to her fifter : the librarian of the Vatican within thefe fifty years could not perfuade himfelf that Cambridge was any thing more than a grammar fchool till Dr. Middleton appeared at Rome.

Dr. Hatcher of King's Col. a phyfician, and able antiquary of the 16th century, had compiled fome Latin memoirs of the eminent perfons educated here, in two books, in the manner of Bale [z]. Mr. T. Baker of St. John's [a] intended a work of the fame fort, upon the plan of the

[x] The earlieft authors who make Alfred founder of Oxford univerfity lived at the end of the 14th century. Rofs, who lived at the end of the 15th, and is brought to prove the antiquity of Oxford, exprefly fays the Chriftian mafters taught in the religious houfes fecundum formam ftudiorum antiquorum, Grekladiæ, Lechladiæ, Staunfordiæ, Caerleon, *Cantebrigiæ* & Bellofiti, & aliorum quot prius in infula fuerunt hujufmodi ftudia. Ed. Hearn. p. 77. compared with p. 96. What is this but putting all thefe learned focieties on a level in point of time, and Alfred's foundation later than any ?

[y] Printed erroneoufly by John Thomas ; reprinted 1642, 4to. more correctly, with another concerning privilege of parliament in caufes civil and criminal.

[z] Tanner, 384.——In the Harl. Library, Nº 7176—7, are two volumes of lives of illuftrious perfons educated at Cambridge from its foundation to 1715, collected from printed books by Morris Drake Morris, of Mount Morris, in Kent, efq; late fellow commoner of Trinity college.

[a] He was a native of Lanchefter, in the bifhoprick of Durham, born Sept. 14, 1656 ; chofen into a fellowfhip founded in this college by Dr. Afhton, dean of York 1522, for a native of that county, but loft it on the acceffion of Geo. I. for refufing to take the oaths to the government. As he could not perfuade himfelf but that the mafter might have fhewn the fame indulgence to his fcruples on that occafion, as he had done before, he retained a lively refentment of this deprivation, and wrote himfelf in the books he gave to the library *Socius ejectus*. He continued to refide in the college as commonermafter till his death, July 2, 1740, and was buried in the outer chapel, where he ftill wants an epitaph. Dr. Grey is collecting materials for his life.

Athenæ

Athenæ Oxonienfes. Had he lived to compleat his defign it would have far exceeded that work, notwithftanding the reflection [a], as unjuft as fevere, with which the writer of Wood's article in the Biographia Britannica infults us. To the application and induftry of Wood Mr. Baker united a penetrating judgment and great correctnefs of ftyle; and thefe improvements of the mind were crowned with thofe amiable qualities of the heart candour and integrity. Though he lived to above fourfcore [b], he had not time enough to digeft his voluminous collections, which are divided between the Britifh Mufeum and the public library at Cambridge, the former poffeffing twenty-four folio volumes [c], which he prefented to his friend and patron Lord Oxford, and the latter 16 in folio and 3 in 4to. which he bequeathed to the univerfity.

Among Mr. Baker's MSS. in the Harleian library, N° 7048, is a tranfcript of a very fcarce tract printed in 1571, intitled " A defcrip-" tion of the foundation and privileges of the univerfity," fuppofed to be written by Dr. Perne and Dr. Caius.

Hearne printed at the end of Sprott's Chron. Oxf. 1719. 8vo. p. 122, Nich. Cantalupe's before-mentioned " Hiftoriola de antiquitate & origine " univerfitatis Cantabrigienfis. Præmittuntur bullæ quædam papales, " aliaque ad univerfitatis ejufdem hiftoriam fpectantia." This was fince publifhed in Englifh, in 8vo. under the title of " The hiftory and an-" tiquities of the univerfity of Cambridge, containing its original and pro-" grefs, defcription of the prefent colleges, &c. &c. by the rev. Mr. " Richard Parker, B. D. and fellow of Caius Col. in 1622. to which " are added feveral charters granted to the colleges; with an account of " the authors above-mentioned: as alfo a catalogue of the chancellors, " and a fummary of all the privileges granted to this feminary of learn-" ing by the Englifh monarchs; from a MS. in the Cotton library." This piece of Parker's is a tranflation of his " Σκελετος Cantabri-" gienfis, five collegiorum umbratilis delineatio, cum fuis fundato-

---

[a] Mr. Baker's " feeble attempt of the like kind undoubtedly reflects the higheft ho-" nour upon Mr. Wood's performance."

[b] Wood died at fixty-three, and had publifhed the hiftory and antiquities of Oxford and the Athenæ in his life-time.

[c] See a particular detail of their contents in the Harleian Cat. from N° 7028 to N° 7054. He wrote a fingular hand, but remarkably fair and diftinct.

2 " ribus

" ribus & benefactoribus plurimis; in qua etiam habes hofpitia acade-
" miæ antiqua; a tergo vero epifcopos, qui ex hac academia prodie-
" runt fupra annum abhinc centenarium," publifhed by Hearne 1715
in Leland's Collectanea, vol. v. p. 185. from a MS. in the library of Sir
Phil. Sydenham, of Brumpton d'Eurcy, Somerfetfhire. This author,
fon of John Parker, archdeacon of Ely 1568—1592, was an excellent herald, hiftorian, and antiquary, but of a melancholy difpofition, neglecting all preferment to enjoy himfelf: Fuller fays the bare
bones of his fceletos are flefhed with much matter, and were of fo
much ufe to him in his hiftory of this univerfity fince the conqueft to
1655 ᶜ, that he wifhed fome perfon would print it for the benefit of
pofterity.

Mr. Tho. Rawlinfon had a paper MS. intitled " The foundation
" of the univerfity of Cambridge, with a catalogue of the principal
" founders and efpecial benefactors of the colleges, publick fchools,
" and library now in the fame; and the names of all the prefent
" mafters and fellows of every particular college; together with the
" number of magiftrates, governours, and officers thereunto belong-
" ing, and the total number of ftudents now therein refiding: collected A.D. 1621. by John Scot." Fol.   Wood ᵈ fays this was printed
1622: there are three copies of it among the Harleian MSS. with the
arms of the colleges and founders, marked 4283. 6080. 7053: this
laft, dated Apr. 10, 1619, is among Baker's collections, who fays it
was compiled by or with the affiftance of R. Parker.   From thefe
tables principally was taken by Dr. Langbain " The foundation of
" the univerfity of Cambridge, with a catalogue of the principal foun-
" ders, and fpecial benefactors of all the colleges, and total number of
" ftudents, magiftrates, and officers therein being; and how the re-
" venews thereof are and have been increafed from time to time, and
" by whom, with buildings, books, and revenues, as no univerfitie
" in the world can in all points parallel: thefe are the nurferies of
" religion, and feminaries of good literature. Lond. 1651." 4to.   The
Doctor, though an Oxford man, gave Cambridge the precedence.

ᶜ At the end of his Church hiftory of Britain.
  Ath. Ox. II. 221.

Mr.

Mr. Rawlinson had a folio MS. which (as appears by his arms and a dedication) belonged to George Villars duke of Buckingham, chancellor of this univerſity, finely illuminated with the arms of the colleges, and intitled " The foundation of the univerſity of Cambridge, with a " catalogue of the principal founders, and ſpecial benefactors of all " the colleges, and total number of ſtudents, magiſtrates, and officers " therein ; being collected by John Ivory 1671." ſince printed on a ſingle folio ſheet.

At the end of Abp. Parker's book, " De antiquitate Britannicæ eccle- " ſiæ, 1672." Fol. republiſhed by Drake 1729; is a Latin catalogue of chancellors, vice-chancellors, proctors, and doctors, and a liſt of all the graduates, &c. from 1550, 15 Hen. VII. to 1571, 14 Eliz. The preſent maſter of Emanuel Col. to whom we owe the elegant edition of Godwin de præſulibus continued to 1743, has compiled a catalogue of graduates, which it is hoped will one day or other ſee the light. A regiſter of the doctors of phyſick in both univerſities from 1659 to 1694, was printed Lond. 1694. 12mo.

The laſt hiſtory of this univerſity is a flimſey account, from its original to the year 1753, by Edmund Carter, then removed to Chelſea, 1753. 8vo. of a piece with " Salmon's foreigner's companion through the two univvrſities. 1748." 12mo. both which are better than " Can- " tabrigia depicta : a conciſe and accurate deſcription of the univerſity " and town of Cambridge, and its environs, &c. Cambr. 1763." 12mo; a very incorrect compilation by the Cambridge bookſellers. Among the plates in this laſt, which are engraved by Lambourn, is a plan of old Granta, whoſe ſcite is very traceable about the caſtle.

Dr. Rawlinson [f] mentions a poem, " attempting ſomething upon the rarities of the moſt renowned univerſity of Cambridge. Lond. 1673." 4to.

An extract from the large book of ſtatutes for the uſe of graduates was printed 1684. 12mo. again 1714, with the ſtatutes reſpecting undergraduates : and 1732 and 1748 were printed " Excerpta e ſtatutis " academiæ Cantabrigienſis, præfectorum interpretationibus, ſenatus de-

[f] Eng. Topogr. p. 23.

P

" cretis

" cretis, & literis regiis, ad fcholarium officia pertinentia. Cant. 1748."
8vo.

" An argument to prove that the 39th fection of the 50th chapter
" of the ftatutes given by Q Elizabeth to the univerfity of Cambridge
" includes the old ftatutes of the univerfity, and that all the old ftatutes
" are not repealed by the ftatutes of Q Elizabeth : together with an
" anfwer to the arguments, and the author's reply to that anfwer.
" Lond. 1727." 4to. by Mr. John Burford, of King's college.

" A briefe treatife concerning the burnynge of Bucer and Phagius,
" at Cambrydge, in the time of Q Mary, with theyr reftitution in the'
" time of our moft gracious foverayne lady that now is : wherein is
" expreffed the fantafticall and tirannous dealynges of the Romifhe
" churche, together with the godly and modeft regiment of the true
" Chriftian church, moft flaunderouflye diffamed in thofe dayes of
" herefye. Tranflated into Englyfhe, by Arthur Goldyng. Lond.
" 1562." 8vo. g. An ample narrative of that ridiculous proceeding,
with many hiftorical anecdotes of the principal perfons of the univerfity
concerned in it.

In Somers's tracts, 3d coll. vol. 1. p. 443, is the humble petition of
the univerfity of Cambridge to the Parliament, to be exempted from
contributions to the war, and to be kept free. Hearne h printed Dr.
Spencer s fpeech to the D. of Monmouth, inftalled chancellor at Wor-
cefter-houfe 1674.

" Proceedings againft the vice-chancellor, &c. of Cambridge for
" refufing a degree to a monk, with taking the oaths. 1689" Fol.

" The life of William Moore i, late fellow of Caius Col. and keeper
" of the univerfity library, as it was delivered in a fermon preached at
" his funeral folemnity, Apr. 24, 1659, at St. Maries church, Cam-
" bridge. By T. Smith, his fucceffor. Cambr. 1660." 12mo. Upon

g Catal. of Harleian pamphlets, No 2.
h Append. to Caius, No X.
i He collected into one body the univerfity ftatutes, and made a catalogue of all the
MSS. in the public library, except the oriental, writing the whole with his own hand,
notwithftanding a fevere illnefs: he defired to be buried in his own college chapel, but
being refufed by Mr. Dell, the mafter, the ufe of the liturgy, which was his laft requeft,
was laid in St. Mary's church, under the ftone he ufed to kneel on. Carter's hift. of
the univ. p. 232.

the

the donation of Bp. More's library by George I. who purchased it for 6000 l. ᵏ Dr. Middleton, being appointed principal librarian, drew up a plan for difpoſing all the books together in the new projected build-ing, intitled, " Bibliothecæ ordinandæ methodus," printed among his works. A catalogue of the MSS. in the publick library, many of them Abp. Parker's gift, is in Cat. MSS. Angliæ, p. 164—174. an appendix to it, MS. Harl. 694. Wanley apologiſes for the incorrectneſs of theſe catalogues of MSS. in all the Cambridge libraries, becauſe the members of this univerſity had an intention of publiſhing an account of their own MSS. with thoſe at Lambeth themſelves ˡ.

Views and ſections of the library and ſenate-houſe, and a perſpective view of the new building as intended, by H. Hulſberg.

" Oratio habita coram academia Cantabrigenſe in templo B. Mariæ, " die ſolenni martyrii Caroli I. regis, A. D. 1730. a Joanne Taylor, " A. M. Coll. D. Joannis Evangeliſtæ ſocio. Lond. 1730." 8vo.

" The muſic ſpeech, ſpoken at the public commencement in Cam-bridge Jul. 6, 1714, by Jer. Long. Lond." 8vo.

" The muſic ſpeech at the public commencement at Cambridge, " July 6, 1730: to which is added " an ode deſigned to have been ſet " to muſic on that occaſion. By John Taylor, M. A. fellow of St. " John's Coll. Lond, 1730." 8vo.

The ode wrote by the rev. Mr Maſon of Pembroke-hall, and per-formed in the ſenate-houſe at the inſtallation of the D. of Newcaſtle, on the commencement-day 1749, was firſt printed ſeparately in 4to. and afterwards in Dodſley's collection of poems, vol. iv.

Certain orders and regulations paſſed in the ſenate on this occaſion gave riſe to the following ſevere pamphlets;

" The Capitade, a poem."

" A fragment."

" A key to a fragment by Amias Riddinge, B. D. with a preface by " Peregrine Smyth, eſq; Lond. 1751." 8vo.

" Another fragment." 8vo.

ᵏ It was offered to Lord Oxford for 8000 l. Letter from Dr. S. Clark to Wanley, in the Britiſh Muſeum.

Pref. ad Cat. MSS. Ang.

Frag-

" Fragmentum eft pars rei fractæ. Lond. 1751." 8vo.

" David's prophecy relating to C——b——e; with an account of its
" accomplifhment in that u————y. By Ifaac van Sampfon, a learned
" Dutch commentator. Dedicated to the vice chancellor, heads, and
" Mr. B—— the proctor. Camb. 1751." 8vo. A profane application
of fome texts of Scripture.

" The academic, or a difputation on the ftate of the univerfity of
" Cambridge and the propriety of the regulations made in it on the
" 11th day of May and the 26th day of June 1750. Lond. 1750."
8vo. replied to in " Remarks on the Academic. Lond. 1750" 8vo.

" An occafional letter to the rev. Dr. Keene, mafter of Peter-houfe
" and vice-chancellor of the univerfity of Cambridge. Lond." 8vo.
anfwered in " Confiderations on the expediency of making, and the
" manner of conducting the late regulations at Cambridge. Lond.
" 1751.' 8vo.

A number of gentlemen educated at Weftminfter fchool having met
at the tavern Nov. 17, 1750, according to cuftom, to celebrate queen
Elizabeth's anniverfary, the fenior proctor came after eleven o'clock
at night, and ordered them to depart, it being an irregular hour.
Thinking himfelf affronted by them, he fummoned feveral before the
vice-chancellor, whofe primanded four and fined others : the late Mr.
Anfell, fellow of Trinity-hall, for adding a fhew of contempt in making
his defence, was fufpended from every degree. Upon this was publifhed " An authentic narrative of the late extraordinary proceedings at
" Cambridge againft the W————r club. Lond. 1751." 8vo. denying the charge of irregularity and infult, and cenfuring the proctor's
behaviour as rigorous and unprecedented. Mr. Anfell's right of appeal
being denied in a pamphlet, intitled " An inquiry into the right of
" appeal from the chancellor or vice-chancellor of the univerfity of
" Cambridge in matters of difcipline : addreffed to a fellow of a col-
" lege; to which is added an appendix, containing fome obfervations
" on the Authentic Narrative, &c. Lond. 1751." 8vo. was defended
in another, intitled " 'The opinion of an eminent lawyer concerning
" the right of appeal from the vice-chancellor of Cambridge to the
" fenate ; fupported by a fhort hiftorical account of the jurifdiction of

2   " the

" the univerfity. By a fellow of a college. Lond. 1751." 8vo. This was replied to in " A further inquiry into the right of appeal, &c. " Lond. 1752." 8vo. anfwered in " A letter to the author of a further " inquiry, &c. Lond. 1752." 8vo. " Some confiderations on the " neceffity of an appeal in the univerfity of Cambridge. Lond. 1752." 8vo. There came out on the fame fubject " An epiftle to a fellow- " commoner at Cambridge, occafioned by the difpute there. Lond. " 1751." 8vo. and " The friendly and honeft advice of an old tory " to the vice-chancellor of Cambridge. Lond. 1751." 8vo.

The chancellor's difmiffion from public affairs produced " A letter " to the univerfity of Cambridge, on a late refignation. By a gentle- " man of Oxford. Lond. 1756." 8vo.

The late contefted election of a high fteward occafioned the follow- ing pieces. " Cam an elegy. Lond. 1764." 4to.

" The conteft : a poem. Lond. 1764." 4to.

" An addrefs to the members of the fenate of the univerfity of " Cambridge, on an attention due to worth of character from a religious " fociety, with a view to the enfuing election of a high fteward : to " which is added a letter of Mr. Jofeph Mede, formerly of Chrift's " Coll. (copied from a MS. in the Harleian collection) giving a very " particular account of the circumftances attending the D of Buck- " ingham's election in K. Charles the Ift's time. By a mafter of arts. " 1764." 8vo.

Five weekly numbers of " Terræ filius," feveral of the " Scrutator," and one extraordinary " Occafional Refpondent."

A propofal for giving fellows of colleges leave to marry being agitated in this univerfity produced a pamphlet called " The council " in the moon. Camb. 1765." 4to.

A MS. hiftory of the mafters and fellows of PETER-HOUSE, by Dr. Matthew Wren, mafter there 1625, fucceffively Bifhop of Hereford, Norwich, and Ely, and their greateft benefactor, is in the college li- brary: a tranfcript of it among Baker's Harleian collections, 7029 ; with a continuation by Mr. Attwood, fellow there, ib. 7033 ; and other particulars, ib. 7034. Some extracts from the college regifters and fta- tutes were printed in " Corporations vindicated in their fundamental li-

" berties

" berties, from a negative voice, and other unjuft prerogatives of their
" chief officers, deftructive to true freedom : or a difcourfe proving that
" the chief officer affuming to himfelf the power of, 1. calling or dif-
" folving of meetings : 2. propofing or refufing of queftions offered to
" the debate : 3. granting or denying of affent to the conclufions of
" the major part of the affembly, at the fole pleafure of his own private
" difcretion, is of right to be abolifhed in all other corporations, as it
" hath been by this prefent parliament in the fupreme council of the
" nation, and common council of the city of London ; argued firft
" and more properly in the cafe of Peter-houfe in Cambridge, but is of
" general import to all the bodies incorporated throughout the whole
" nation ; and of great conducement to the fure and more firm efta-
" blifhment of this nation in form of a commonwealth. By Charles
" Hotham, late fellow of that college. To which is annexed a
" true narrative of the proceedings of the committee for the univerfi-
" ties againft him for his publication of the faid book, with the grounds
" and reafons of his appeal to the Parliament againft their cenfure ;
" and his preface and petition to the honourable Parliament : in the
" former of which are largely fet forth fome of the chief grounds of
" his conftant adherence to the Parliament's caufe. Lond. 1651." 12mo.
A catalogue of the MSS. in this library from Dr. James is in Cat. MSS.
Angliæ, p. 147—156. The E. front of the college built by Sir James
Burroughs, drawn by R. Weft, is engraved by P. Fourdrinier.

Dr. Nath. Vincent, fellow of CLARE HALL, publifhed " The right
" notion of honour, as it was delivered in a fermon before the king
" at New-Market, on the 4th of October 1674. A general addrefs
" to all bountiful encouragers of religion and learning, in the behalf
" of Clare-hall in Cambridge : which remains half built, after all the
" endeavours of the fociety for more than forty years to finifh it. Lond.
" 1675." 4to. The feal of this college has been engraved for the
Society of Antiquaries, together with thofe of Cottingham abbey, Yorkfhire, and of the chapter of Ely : their noble foundrefs lies at Ware,
almoft as undiftinguifhed as Hugh de Balfam at Ely.

" An abftract of the cafe of Mr. Freeman's foundation of fellow-
" fhips and fcholarfhips in Clare-hall ; appropriated by his will, next
" after

" after his kinfmen, to natives of Northamptonfhire and Lincolnfhire,
" and the definitive fentence or final decree of the right worfhipful
" and rev. Tho. Chapman, L. L. D. vice-chancellor of the univerfity
" of Cambridge and vifitor of Clare-hall, upon the cafe; and feveral
" letters; never before printed, from the late worfhipful Dr. Andrew,
" with a preface upon them and the cafe. To which are added, the
" extract out of the founder's will, a larger extract out of the inden-
" ture betwixt his executors and the college; and extracts out of three
" of the mafter's letters. Publifhed for the benefit of the two univer-
" fities. Lond. 1749." 4to.

Of PEMBROKE-HALL we have only a catalogue of 271 MSS. in its
library, moft of them given by William Smart, alderman of Ipfwich,
1599. in Cat. MSS. Angliae, p. 156—161.

A fhort account of CORPVS CHRISTI or BENET college was drawn
up by Archbifhop Parker's order by his fecretary Joffelyn, intitled,
" Hiftoriola C. C. C. C." containing the tranfactions from its foundation to 1569, but full of inaccuracies [m]; there is a tranfcript of it among
Baker's Harl. MSS. 7046. Better fortune has attended this antient
houfe than the reft of its neighbours. The rev: Mr. Mafters, late fellow, has given us a hiftory of it " from its foundation to the prefent
time; in two parts. 1. Of its founders and benefactors. 2. Of its other
" principal members. Cambr. 1753." 4to. He has annexed a plan of
a new building defigned by himfelf, and promifed [n] an account of that
valuable collection of MSS. given to this fociety by Abp. Parker [o],
which Fuller juftly ftiled " the fun of Englifh antiquity before it was
" eclipfed by that of Sir Rob. Cotton." A catalogue of them was publifhed by Dr. James, and inferted in Cat. MSS. Angl. p. 131—146.
an appendix to it in MS. Harl. 694. Dean Stanley when mafter
drew up another, and printed it at his own expence 1722. Fol. but
even this is capable of great enlargement.

The MSS. at TRINITY-HALL are in the Cat. MSS. Angl. p. 162.
The W. view of this hall, as propofed to be rebuilt on a plan of Sir James
Burroughs, drawn by James Effex, jun. was engraved by Toms 1743.

[m] See Mafters's hift. p. 99.   [n] Ib. p. 173.
[o] Strype compiled the life of that great prelate, who received his education in this
houfe, which juftly gives him the preference as founder.

The

The founder of CAIUS college tells us he wrote its annals, intending to publish them; but what is become of them does not appear. A catalogue of the MSS. in this library is in Cat. MSS. Ang. 107—130: among them are five classes given by Wm. Moore, the public librarian, already mentioned; and several good visitations and heraldical books, given by Dr. Knight, serjeant surgeon to Charles II.

Thomas Hatcher, before-mentioned, drew up a list of the provosts, fellows and scholars of KING's college, from the foundation to 1572 [p]: continued by J. Scot to 1620; and by Geo. Goad to 1646: of which Fuller and Wood made great use. The few MSS. here are in Cat. MSS. Angl. p. 162 [q]. The anthems used in the chapel were printed Camb. 1746. The general plan of the college as intended with the upright of the W. side of the quadrangle next the river, from a design of Gibbs, drawn by John Essex, jun. was engraved by H. Hulsberg. The E. prospect of it as intended to be finished from the same design, by Fourdrinier 1741. A very good large S. view of the chapel, dedicated to lord Francis Godolphin, with an account of it in Latin below: sold by Richard Caldwall, print and map seller, opposite Warwick-lane, near Newgate street.

"Oratio habita in funere rev. & doctiss. viri Gul. George, S. T. P. "Coll. regalis præpositi 7 kal. Oct. 1756. a Gul. Barford, M. A. Coll. "regal socio. Cant. 1756." 4to.

"The form of consecration of the chapel at ST. KATHERINE's-HALL "performed Sept. 1, 1704, by Symon [Patrick] Bishop of Ely, pub- "lished from the register of the college by his lordship's permission;" annexed to a sermon preached the 1st of Sept. 1704, on that occasion by John Leng, B. D.

Dr. Sherman, who died president of JESUS college 1671, left a Latin history of it in MS. A list of seven MSS. here is in Cat. MSS. Angl. p. 162. a fuller list MS. Harl. 694.

[p] There is such a list among Baker's Harl. MSS. 7038. and a supplement ib. 7045. In a letter to Stowe, Harl. MS. 374, he mentions his own history of this college. Other lists are among the Harl. MSS. 6114. and 6865; a copy of their statutes, and account of the foundation, ib. 7323.

[q] I have a Delphin edition of Eutropius collated by Beaupre Bell with a MS. here, not mentioned in the catalogue, which contains but seven.

Mr.

Mr. Baker's Harl. MS. 7048, begins with particulars relating to the foundation, &c. of QUEEN's college. There is an unpublished catalogue of their MSS. in MS. Harl. 694.

The liberality of the foundress of ST. JOHN and CHRIST's colleges has been celebrated in her funeral sermon, preached by Bishop Fisher, and printed by Mr. Baker, with a preface, containing some further account of her charities and foundations, and a catalogue of her professors both at Oxford and Cambridge, and of her preachers at Cambridge. Lond. 1708. 8vo.o. This piece is a sufficient specimen of the editor's skill in antiquities to make us regret that he did not live to publish his "History of the college, from the foundation of old St. John's house to the present time; with some occasional and accidental account of the affairs of the university, and of such private colleges as held communication or intercourse with the old house or college: collected principally from MSS. and carried on through a succession of masters to the end of Bishop Gunning's mastership, 1678." The original, fit for the press, is among the Harleian MSS. N° 7028: N° 7302 and 7051 contain their statutes and those of the university, with interpretations, decrees, &c. Mr. Thomas Rawlinson had a copy of their statutes, with Q. Elizabeth's confirmation, extracts from wills, or regulations and instructions of the founder and benefactors p.

A catalogue of the MSS. at TRINITY college, including those given by Sir Henry Puckering, bart. drawn up by Henry Laughton, public librarian, is in Cat. MSS. Angl. p. 93—103: a different one MS. Harl. 694 q. Besides the Roman inscriptions from Connington already mentioned, this library possesses a curious marble brought by Lord Sandwich from Athens 1739, containing an account of the money received, disbursed, and due for the celebration of Apollo's festival at Delos in

---

o The Bishop's life was wrote by R. Hall, of Christ's Coll. almost transcribed by Fuller in his Church history, vol. v. p. 202, and printed under the name of T. Bailey at London 1655. Tanner. Four others, MSS. Harl. 6382. 7047. and 7049. Another by Geo. Lilly, before-mentioned, p. 40, unpublished.

p Some verses prefixed to it are printed in the English Topographer, p. 16. No catalogue of their MSS. has been printed, but a MS. one, taken 1675, is in Harl. lib. 694.

q In N. Hooke's collection of poems, Lond. 1653. 8vo. is "Elogium seu sciographica " descriptio Coll. S. S. & undiv. Tria. Cantab." Another by J Cropley, follow, Harl. MS. 6839. f. 241.

Q

the

the 101ſt Olympiad, above 370 years before Chriſt, illuſtrated by the late Dr. Taylor of St. John's in a learned Latin commentary, 1743. 4to.

Certain regulations attempted by Dr. Bentley, when maſter of this college, giving offence to ſome of the ſociety, occaſioned a long conteſt, and no leſs than eight pamphlets on both ſides. The Doctor having notice that the fellows intended to complain of him to the Biſhop of Ely, their viſitor, and get him removed by their 40th ſtatute, *De magiſtri, ſi res exigat, amotione*, went beforehand to Biſhop Patrick with his own ſtory; and withal to let him know he had no buſineſs with the college, which the want of a precedent and a copy of the ſtatutes in his archives ſeeming to confirm, the affair was dropt during his lordſhip's life. The college exhibited to his ſucceſſor Dr. More, 1709, a number of articles about dilapidations againſt the maſter, afterwards printed, and intitled " A true copy of the articles againſt Dr. Bentley, exhibited to John " lord biſhop of Ely, by many of the fellows of Trinity college in " Cambridge. Together with the college ſtatute, *De amotione magiſtri*, " and ſeveral other clauſes of the college ſtatutes, with references to " the articles. Lond. 1710." 8vo. The Doctor declined giving his anſwer, alledging the want of form in the charge, as brought only by the ſenior fellows; but having in the mean time diſtributed written copies of an anſwer with the petition among ſome of his friends, both were afterwards printed together under the title of " The preſent ſtate " of Trinity college, in a letter from Dr. Bentley, maſter of the ſaid " college, to the right rev. John lord biſhop of Ely. Publiſhed for " general information by a gentleman of the Temple. Lond. 1710." 8vo. This was animadverted upon in " Some remarks upon a letter, in- " titled, The preſent ſtate of Trinity college, written by Richard Bent- " ley, D.D. now maſter of the ſaid college, to the right rev. John lord " biſhop of Ely. With ſome remarks alſo upon the preface, pretended " to be written and publiſhed together with the letter, by a gentleman " of the Temple. By Mr. Miller ʳ, fellow of the college. Lond. 1710."

" the

ʳ Miller was a great oppoſer of Bentley's deſigns, and chief manager of the proſecution againſt him, by which he was conſiderably out of pocket, though the college paid him 100 l. Bentley ſuſpended him from his fellowſhip: but the offer of 400 l. three years after, on pretence of charges, being moſt of the income of his fellowſhip during ſuſpenſion,

8vo.—" Some confiderations humbly offered in a letter to John lord
" bifhop of Ely, on a book, intitled, The prefent ftate of Trinity col-
" lege: in a letter to a refiding fellow of that fociety: wherein the
" trifling impertinencies, malicious afperfions, and bold falfhoods of
" Dr. Bentley are anfwered, in fuch a manner as they deferve: pub-
" lifhed for the information of the ftudents, fcholars, and fellows of
" both univerfities. Lond. 1710." 8vo.—" A full view of Dr. Bent-
" ley's letter to the bifhop of Ely. In a difcourfe to a friend; wherein
" the whole ftrain of that celebrated piece throughout is fairly, fami-
" liarly, and largely confidered. By Thomas Blomer, M.A. fellow of
" Trinity college, Cambridge. Lond. 1710." 8vo.—" An humble and
" ferious reprefentation of the prefent ftate of Trinity college, in a letter
" to a noble Lord. Lond." 8vo.——" A true and impartial account of
" the prefent differences between the mafter and fellows of Trinity col-
" lege in Cambridge confidered, in a letter to a gentleman fometime
" member of the fociety. Lond. 1711." 8vo.——" The rights of the
" fcholars of Trinity college afferted, and feveral abufes detected, in a
" 2d letter to the rev. John lord bifhop of Ely, by a mafter of arts and
" fellow of the faid college." 8vo. The Bifhop not thinking this a
fufficient plea, and infifting on his anfwer, the Doctor began to queftion his lordfhip's authority over him or the college, and petitioned the
Queen to take both under her protection, and maintain her fole right
of jurifdiction over her royal foundation and the mafters thereof. In
the mean time came out " A vindication of the Lord bifhop of Ely's
" vifitatorial jurifdiction over Trinity college in general and the mafter
" in particular." As the Queen's counfel could not determine the
point fo foon, the Doctor, to prevent a total neglect of order and bufinefs in the college, fubmitted to be tried under any vifitor appointed
by her Majefty, and even under the Bifhop *falvo jure regio*. But his

fion, brought him over to his intereft. He wrote " An account of the univerfity of Cam-
" bridge, and the colleges there, being a plain relation of many of their oaths, ftatutes,
" and charters, by which will appear the neceffity the prefent members lie under, of en-
" deavouring to obtain fuch alterations as may render them practicable, and more fuit-
" able to the prefent times: together wirh a few natural and eafie methods, how the
" legiflature may for the future fix that and the other great nurfery of learning in the
" true intereft of the nation and proteftant fucceffion. Moft humbly propofed to both
" houfes of parliament. By Edmond Miller, ferjeant at law., Lond. 1717." 8vo.

lordfhip

lordſhip would not proceed on theſe terms, till obliged by the court of King's-bench. Aftei a long and expenſive trial, death prevented his giving ſentence; and ſo the affair reſted. Dr. Middleton, whoſe pen had firſt reduced Bentley to the condition of the meaneſt member in the univerſity, could not let ſlip this further opportunity to inſult him, and publiſhed anonymouſly, " A true account of the preſent ſtate of " Trinity college under the oppreſſive government of their maſter " Richard Bentley, late D. D. Lond. 1720." 8vo. of which he was ſoon compelled to own himſelf the author, and juſtify his aſſertions. Fourteen years ' after the death of biſhop More the college preſented the ſame charge to his ſucceſſor Green, and the former proceedings were revived, the college now engaging againſt the Biſhop, who petitioned to be heard touching his right. He was accordingly referred to a committee; but juſt before the day of hearing a 4to pamphlet, intitled, " The caſe of Trinity college, whether the Crown or the Biſhop of " Ely be the general viſitor; to be heard before the right hon. the " committee of his Majeſty's privy-council, on Thurſday March 13, " 1728-9. Lond. 1729." was put into the hands of the commiſſioners, who referred it to the court of King's-bench. The judges unanimouſly determined it in favour of the Biſhop as to his viſitatorial power over the Doctor, and the fellows accordingly exhibited their complaints before his lordſhip. But it being urged that he was going to exerciſe a general viſitatorial power, the maſter and fellows petitioned the king and council, and obtained a further hearing in the King's-bench that year, which was determined againſt the Biſhop, who appealed to the Houſe of Lords 1731. And " A defence of the Biſhop of Ely's viſitatorial " juriſdiction over Trinity college in general and over the maſter there- " of in particular," came out 1732. 4to. The crown at length put an end to the whole by taking both maſters and fellows into its own juriſdiction. During theſe conteſts with his own ſociety Dr. Bentley found himſelf involved in 1717 in a diſpute with the univerſity about the fees uſually paid by doctors of divinity on their creation, and his ſuppoſed contempt of the vice-chancellor's authority when cited before him, for not returning the extraordinary fees, as he had engaged, when-

' 1728.

5   ever

ever they were determined not to be his due. The irregularity of the
proceedings againſt him was crowned by ſuſpenſion from all his degrees
in a manner equally irregular. Dr. Middleton, who was the moſt dangerous antagoniſt he had to deal with, drew up and publiſhed " A full
" and impartial account of all the late proceedings in the univerſity of
" Cambridge againſt Dr. Bentley, by a member of the univerſity.
" Lond. 1719." 4to. and 8vo. " A ſecond part of the full and im-
" partial account, &c. &c. Lond. 1719." 4to. and 8vo. both occaſioned partly by ſome ſevere letters in the St. James's Evening Poſt, and
partly by Dr. Bentley's petition to the king and council, at the end of
the ſecond pamphlet. Somebody elſe publiſhed " The proceedings of
" the vice-chancellor and the univerſity of Cambridge againſt Dr. Bent-
" ley ſtated and vindicated, in a letter to a noble peer. Lond. 1719."
Fol. Two of theſe were anſwered in " The caſe of Dr. Bentley, regius
" profeſſor of divinity, truly ſtated: wherein two late pamphlets, inti-
" tled, The proceedings of the vice-chancellor and the univerſity, &c.
" and A full and impartial account of the late proceeding, &c. are ex-
" amined. Lond. 7719." 8vo. " A review of the proceedings againſt
" Dr. Bentley, in anſwer to a late pretended full and impartial account,"
and " The caſe of Dr. Bentley further ſtated and vindicated." On the
laſt Dr. Middleton printed " Some remarks; wherein the merits of
" the author and his performance, and the complaint of proctor Laugh-
" ton, are briefly conſidered. Lond. 1719." 4to. This complaint of
the celebrated tutor of Clare-hall, when ſenior proctor, was an old ad-
venture of the year 1710, when Dr. (then only Mr.) Middleton and
ſome others of reſpectable characters one ſummer's evening having met
Mr. Anneſly (afterwards Earl of Angleſey) then candidate to repreſent
the univerſity in parliament, at the Roſe tavern, were viſited more than
once by Laughton, who charged them with contempt of his office, and
printed the ſtate of the caſe nine years after, purely to prejudice Dr.
Middleton; whoſe anſwer to it turned greatly to his advantage. Dr.
Bentley's petition before-mentioned was referred to a committee, and
thence to the court of King's-bench, who after ten years agitation reſtored him 1728 to his degrees, and whatever he was deprived of;
which he enjoyed till his death 1742. To the laſt edition of Dr.
                                                                Bentley's

Bentley's propofals for a new edition of the Greek Teftament was fub-joined " A full anfwer to all the remarks of a late pamphleteer,' figned J. E. charging Dr. Colbatch, fenior fellow of Trinity Coll. and cafuiftical profeffor, with writing the remarks, of which it was known Dr. Middleton was the author. As this charge was fupported with virulence, and condemned in a congregation, the act of indemnity intervening before any legal difcovery could be made of the author, when the Doctor moved for fatisfaction, an inhibition from the King's-bench was put on the proceedings : on which the Doctor publifhed " Jus aca-
" demicum : or a defence of the peculiar jurifdiction that belongs of
" of right to univerfities in general, and hath been granted by royal
" charters, confirmed in parliament to thofe in England in parti-
" cular : fhewing that no prohibition can lie againft their acts of judi-
" cature, nor appeal from them in any caufe like that which is now
" depending before the vice-chancellor, with a full account and vin-
" dication of the proceedings in that caufe. By a perfon concerned.
" Lond. 1722." 4to.

A profpective view of the great court, with the E. front of Nevile's and King's gates, and of Nevile's court with the Bifhop's hotel from the north, and the tribunal againft the weft fide of the hall : in two plates, by Weft. 1739. The W. front of the college drawn by Wm. Burroughs, engraved by Toms. 1743.

A catalogue of the MSS. at EMANVEL are in Cat. MSS. Angliæ, p. 89—92. a different one, MS. Harl. 694. The life of Dr. Cha-derton, the firft mafter, was wrote by Dr. Dillingham, and printed Cant. 1700, with the life of Ufher, the original MS. is in the Har-leian library, N° 7052.

Among Baker's Harleian MSS. N° 7037, p. 413—420, is " Tabula
" Sidneiana, five hiftoria col. Sidneiani ex adverfariis, T. Sherman,
" S. T. P. Col. Jefu præfids & archidiac. Sarum concinnata, tranfcripta
" ex MS. T. Harrifon, S. T. B. col. Sidn. foc. digniff." A catalogue of the MSS. by Jofeph Craven, fenior fellow, is in p. 133—1c6 of Cat. MSS. Angliæ ; a different one, MS. Harl. 694.

CHESHIRE.

CHESHIRE.

THE antiquities of this county were firſt collected 1585 by William Smith, Rouge Dragon purſuivant, by the encouragement of Mr. Ranulph Crew, ſon to Sir Ranulph Crew, chief juſtice of the King's-bench, in whoſe hands the copy was left, and from whom it came to the Heralds college ˢ. William Webb, clerk in the mayor's court at Cheſter, encouraged by that eminent patron of antiquaries, Sir Simon Archer, of Tamworth in Warwickſhire, was the next collector. The labours of theſe two were united under the title of " The Vale-
" royal of England, or the county palatine of Cheſter illuſtrated ;
" wherein is contained a geographical and hiſtorical deſcription of that
" famous county, with all its hundreds, and ſeats of the nobility, gen-
" try and freeholders ; its rivers, towns, caſtles, buildings antient and mo-
" dern. Adorned with maps and proſpects, and the coats of arms be-
" longing to every individual family of the whole county. Performed by
" Wm. Smith and Wm. Webb, gentlemen : publiſhed by Mr. Daniel
" King ᵗ. To which is annexed an exact chronology ᵘ of all its rulers
" and governors both in church and ſtate, from the time of the
" foundation of the ſtately city of Cheſter, to this very day : fixed by
" eclipſes and other chronological characters. Alſo an excellent diſ-
" courſe of the iſland of Man, &c. Lond. 1656." Fol.

" Hiſtorical antiquities, in two books : the firſt treating in general
" of Great-Brittain and Ireland ; the ſecond containing particular re-
" marks concerning Cheſhire, faithfully collected out of authentick
" hiſtories, old deeds, records, and evidences, by Sir Peter Leyceſter

---

ˢ There is another copy of it in the Harleian library, Nº 1046, with proſpects of Cheſter, and a map of the county 1585. A tranſcript of Domeſday, Nº 6128.

ᵗ Dugdale, in a letter to Wood, ſpeaks of King, who engraved the plates in this work and the Monaſticon, as *a moſt ignorant ſilly knave.* Ath. Ox. II. 251 : his engravings are certainly neither elegant or exact ; yet we owe the publication of this work intirely to him. Wood ſays the original MS. was in Sir R. Cotton's library, till Sir Thomas Cotton gave it to a certain perſon ; after which it came into Aſhmole's hands and is now in his muſeum, Nº 765. Ath. Ox. I. 434.

ᵘ By Sam. Lee, fellow of Wadham Col. Ath. Ox. II. 882.

" bart.

" bart. Whereunto is annexed a tranfcript of Doomfday-book ˣ, fo
" far as it concerneth Chefhire, taken out of the original record.
" Lond. 1673." Fol. The fecond part is divided into four: of
which the three firft relate to the county in general; but the fourth
treats only of the antiquities of Bucklow hundred. Sir Peter having
impeached the legitimacy of Amicia, daughter of Hugh Cyveliock
Earl of Chefter, an hiftorical conteft was commenced between him
and his coufin Sir Thomas Mainwaring, which ended not till the former's death ʸ. The following pieces were wrote on both fides:

1. " A defence of Amicia, daughter of Hugh Cyveliock Earl of
" Chefter; wherein it is proved, that Sir Peter Leycefter, bart. in his
" book, intituled, Hiftorical antiquities, in two books: the firft treat-
" ing in general of Great Britain and Ireland; the fecond containing
" particular remarks concerning Chefhire, hath without any juft
" grounds declared the faid Amicia to be a baftard. By Sir Thomas
" Mainwaring, of Peover in Chefhire, bart. Lond. 1673." 12mo.

2. " An anfwer to the book of Sir Tho. Mainwaring, of Peover in
" Chefhire, bart. intitled, A defence of Amicia, daughter of Hugh
" Cyveliock Earl of Chefter, wherein is vind cated and proved, that
" the grounds declared in my former book, concerning the illegiti-
" macy of Amicia, are not evinced by any folid anfwer or reafon to the
" contrary. By Sir P. Leycefter, bart. Lond. 1673." 12mo.

3. " A reply to an anfwer of the defence of Amicia, daughter of
" Hugh Cyveliock Earl of Chefter. Wherein it is proved, that the
" reafons alledged by Sir P. Leycefter in his former books, and alfo in
" his faid anfwer, concerning the illegitimacy of the faid Amicia, are
" invalid and of no weight at all. By Sir T. Mainwaring of Peover
" in Chefhire, bart. Lond. 1673." 12mo.

4. " Addenda: or fome things to be added to the former anfwer to
" Sir T. Mainwaring's book; to be placed immediately after p. 90.
" Lond. 1673." 8vo.

ˣ As it was tranfcribed 1649 by Mr. Squire from the record itfelf, then in the Tally-
office, Weftminfter, in the cuftody of the treafurer and two chamberlains of the Exchequer.

ʸ At Nether Tabley, in this county, Oct. 11, 1678; in which church he was interred.

5. " A

5. " A reply to Sir Tho Mainwaring's book, intitled, An anfwer
" to Sir P. Leycefter's Addenda."

6. " Sir T. Mainwaring's law cafes miftaken by the faid Sir P. Ley-
" cefter, and the antient law mifunderftood, and the new mifapplied.
" 1674." 12mo.

7. " An anfwer to two books, the firft being ftiled A reply to Sir
" T. Mainwaring's book, intitled, An anfwer to Sir P. Leycefter's Ad-
" denda. The other ftiled, Sir Tho. Mainwaring's law cafes miftaken,
" written by the faid Sir T. M. Lond. 1675." 12mo.

8. " An admonition to the reader of Sir P. Leycefter's books. Writ-
" ten by Sir T. M. Lond. 1676."

9. " A reply to Sir T. Mainwaring's anfwer to my two books. Writ-
" ten by Sir P. Leycefter, bart. A. D. 1675."

10. " The fecond reply : together with the cafe of Amicia, truly
" ftated. Lond. 1676." 12mo.

11. " An anfwer to Sir T. Mainwaring's book, intitled, An admo-
" nition to the reader of Sir P. Leycefter's books. Written by the fame
" Sir P. Leycefter. Lond. 1677." 12mo. This momentous controverfy was ridiculed in a humorous ballad : the laft piece was fent,
by Mainwaring, to Leycefter's executors a few days after the latter's
death, to know whether they would continue this controverfy ; but
they had the fenfe to drop it [z].

This county was vifited 1566 and 1580 by Wm. Flower and Rob.
Glover : 1613 by H. St. George. Some arms, monuments, &c. collected in it by E. Afhmole 166$\frac{2}{3}$, are in his mufeum, N° 854.

Henry Bradfhaw, monk of St. Werberg's, wrote feveral books " De
antiquitate & magnificentia urbis Ceftriæ, & chronicon," &c. and compiled in Englifh verfe " The life of the glorious virgin St. Werberg ;
" alfo many miracles that God hath fhewed for her. Lond. 1521." 4to.
Webb has quoted him largely, and calls him their beft antiquary.
His book contains a good deal of true hiftory.

---

[z] Wood fays, it did not end without a fuit at law, in which, at the Chefter affizes
1675, the right of the matter was adjudged to Mainwaring. Athen. Ox. II. 622.
638.

Ames

Ames [a] mentions " The death of the rood of Weſt-cheſter," printed by Wm. Griffith, 1565. 8vo.

" A ſummary of the life of St. Werburgh, with an hiſtorical ac-
" count of the images [b] upon her ſhrine (now the epiſcopal throne) in
" the choir of Cheſter. Collected from antient chronicles and old
" writers. By a citizen of Cheſter [c]. Publiſhed for the benefit of the
" charity ſchool, Cheſter. 1749." 4to.

James Chaloner, author of the deſcription of the Iſle of Man, made collections of arms, &c. in this city, which came into Vincent's hands [d].

A Roman monument in a rock near the bridge, and the outſide front of the Roman gate of the Watling-ſtreet called Eaſt-gate, Cheſter, as ſtanding Aug. 2, 1725, are among Dr. Stukeley's unpubliſhed plates.

Buck engraved a N. W. view of the caſtle 1727: and a larger S. W. one of the city, 1729 ; of which there is another by J. Boydell, 1750. Another S. E. by J. Bowen, engraved by C. Duboſc, and publiſhed by Wm. Williams, who dedicates it to the Earl of Plymouth.

A plan of it by Alex. de Lavaux, engraved by Parr : with the addi-tional new work, by order of the Earl of Cholmondeley, and a pro-jection of four baſtions, to defend the antient walls againſt a regular ſiege. A plan and view of the caſtle, by the ſame.

In the third volume of Aſhmole's Berkſhire, appendix, p. 393, is a Latin explanation of an inſcription on a Roman altar, found at Cheſter 1653, by Mr. John Grenehalgh, printed from a MS. in the Bod-leian library, B. 67. The Miſcellanies on ſeveral curious ſubjects, 1714 and 1723, begin with a letter of Dr. Langbain to Dugdale, and another from Selden to Langbain about it, printed In the ap-pendix to Hearne's Ann. de Dunſtable, Nº III. Marmora Arunde-liana, p. 282, and Horſley, p. 315 : the altar, with the inſcrip-tion quite ſcaled off, is now at Oxford. In p. 316 of Nº 222 of Phil. Tranſ. is a letter from Dr. Halley, dated Cheſter, Oct. 26, 1696,

---

[a] Hiſt. of printing, p. 316.
[b] Repreſenting her family, &c. in number thirty, juſt then repaired.
[c] Dr. William Cowper.
[d] Ath. Ox. II. 252.

giving

giving an account of another Roman altar, found there, and preserved by Mr. Prescot and since by his son, and printed in Horsley, p. 314. In N⁰ 76. p. 2274. are Ray's observations on the anatomy of a porpoise at West-chester.—In p. 216 of vol. XLVII. we have an account of the Roman stations in Cheshire and Lancashire, by Tho. Percival, esq;—In N⁰ 2293. p. 370. two letters from Dr. Halley about a hail storm at Chester 1697 —In N⁰ 156. p. 485. is Dr. Lister's remarks on the midland salt springs of Worcestershire, Staffordshire, and Cheshire.—In N⁰ 66. p. 2015. Martindale's account of a rock of natural salt at *Rotherton.*—In N⁰ 53 and 54 are Dr. Jackson's answers to queries about the salt springs and works at *Namptwich.* Ray annexed to his collection of English local words, an account of the salt works at Namptwich. Of the increase of the river *Weever*, and discovery of a Roman pavement and coins, and a skeleton of a stag, near Nantwich, see Birch's history of the Roy. Soc. vol. II. p. 185. In the Gent. Mag. 1762. p. 563 and 616, is a description of *Eastham* and *Bromborough* parishes.

Some records of this county palatine are in Booth's " Nature and practice of real actions, &c. 1701 and 1704." Fol. and a discourse concerning its earldom in Sir John Dodderidge's " History of the an-" tient and modern estate of the principality of Wales," p. 123.

" A brief narrative of a strange and wonderful old woman, who hath
' a pair of horns growing upon her head, giving a true account how
" they have several times after their being shed grown again : declar-
" ing the place of her birth [*Shotwick*], her education, and conversa-
" tion ; with the first occasion of their growth, the time of their con-
" tinuance ; and where she is now to be seen, viz. at the sign of the
" Swan near Charing-cross. Lond. 1679." 4to. reprinted in Morgan's Phænix Britannicus. 1732. p. 248.

A grant of lands in *Congilton* by Hen. de Lacy Earl of Lincoln to Benedict Fitz-walter of Stanley 1300, 28 Ed. I. pen. Dr. Rawlinson was engraved at his cost.

A description of *Beeston* castle, of which Buck published a S. view, is annexed to Erdeswicke's survey of Staffordshire. Other collections by this antiquary relative to Chester remain in the Harl. library, N⁰ 473. 506. 1990; where are more voluminous materials for this than any

R other

other county, and fome for Lancafhire, made by Randall Holmes, and his father and grandfather, who were all three citizens and arms-painters of Chefter, in the laft century, and purchafed by Lord Oxford of the fon's executors. Wanley has given a particular detail of them in the Harleian catalogue. In N° 2073 are drawings of buildings in Chefter by the third R. Holmes.

Buck's views in this county, 1727, are

> Combermere abbey. W.
> Ince ruin. S.
> Norton priory. W.
> Birkenhead priory. S. W.
> Halton caftle e. S.
> Frodfham caftle. N.

A view of *Eaton-hall*, the feat of Lord Grofvenor, by Badeflade and Toms. 1740. and a plan of the gardens, containing above forty acres, in two fheets.

Another of *Dunham Maffey*, the feat of the Earl of Warrington, by John Harris, engraved by Boydell 1751.

Another of *Crewe-hall* by W. Yox, engraved by Toms 1742.

A view in *Lyme* park belonging to Peter Legh, efq; with the extraordinary manner of driving the ftags, by Vivares from a painting by Smith. 1745.

" Ceftriæ comitatus (Romanis legionibus & coloniis olim infignis) " vera & abfoluta defcriptio. C. Saxton del. F. Scatterus fc. 1577." wants the hundreds, which are added with a plan of the city in Speed's map. A later map has been publifhed by Em. Bowen.

---

e A furvey of the honor, caftle, and manor of Halton, Chefhire : being part of the Dutchy of Lancafter, and the revenue thereof, 16 H. VIII. Harl. MS. 7391.

CORNWALL.

THE hiſtory and monuments of this county were faintly touched by Richard Carew, of Antonie, eſq; a perſon extremely capable of deſcribing them, if the infancy of thoſe ſtudies at that time had afforded him light and materials [d]. His " Survey of Cornwall" was publiſhed Lond. 1602. 4to. reprinted, in the ſame ſize, 1723, with " an epiſtle concerning the excellencies of the Engliſh tongue, then " firſt publiſhed from the MS. and the life of the author, by H. C. " eſq;" Mr. Thomas Rawlinſon had a copy of the firſt edition, with arms tricked by Burton, the Leiceſterſhire antiquary : but this work was expected with large continuations to the beginning of this century by Mr. Killigrew of Somerſet-houſe, who long laboured to illuſtrate the antiquity of this his native county. Large aſſiſtance might have been afforded from many curious MS. collections, particularly of in-ſcriptions from the late Mr. Anſtis's library.

John Norden ſurveyed this county about 1584: his work was printed 1728, intitled, " Speculi Britanniæ pars : a topographical and " hiſtorical deſcription of Cornwall, with a map of the county, and " each hundred ; in which are contained the names and ſeats of the " ſeveral gentlemen then inhabitants ; as alſo thirteen views of the " moſt remarkable curioſities in that county. By the perambulation, " view, and delineation of John Norden [e]. To which are added the " W. proſpect of the ſometime conventual church of St. German's, and " a table of the diſtances of the towns from each other : with ſome " account of the author." 4to. I apprehend from Bateman's dedica-

---

[d] Borl. pref. to antiquities of Cornwall.

[e] This induſtrious topographer, of whom we might have expected ſome account in the Biographia Britannica, ſeems to have been a native of Wilts about 1548, and ad-mitted of Hart hall, Oxf 1564, where he proceeded A. M. 1573. He had patronage, but little elſe, from the great Burleigh, and in his old age obtained jointly with his ſon the place of ſurveyor to the prince of Wales. Beſides the ſurveys of the kingdom, ſeven counties, and two manors, he wrote and publiſhed the ſurveyors dialogue, 1607 1610. and 1618. 4to. and fifteen devotional pieces, mentioned by Wood, Ath. Ox. I. 450. He lived in narrow circumſtances at Fulham and Hendon, and died about 1626.

tion

tion to Lord Oxford that he publifhed it from a very old MS. in the Britifh Mufeum [f] (MSS. Harl. 6252) with coloured drawings of all the plates, except the front of St. German's church, and the general and particular map by Norden: that by Norden and Speed [g] with the arms, &c. and thofe of the hundreds are in it engraved: the frontifpiece is alfo a coloured drawing, and the capital letters throughout gilded imitations of print: in the printed copy is added another title and the author's life; the conclufion, " touching your Majefty's mineralls in " Cornwall," fronts the title page in the MS. The better part of this moft finifhed of his works is a mere tranfcript of Carew; from the other parts very little of moment is to be learned, and no ftrefs is to be laid on his drawings [h]. He wrote an account of the eftates of the dutchy of Cornwall, the right by which the duke holds his eftates, and many of the cuftoms of the manors; which was once repofited in the dutchy-office.

In the fecond part, p. 77. of Sir J. Doderidge's book, before-mentioned in Chefhire, is included the hiftory of this dutchy. Lond. 1630. reprinted 1714. 8vo.

Cornwall was vifited about 1570 by Cook: 1620 by S. George and Lennard.

A tranfcript of its domefday is in Exeter cathedral library. Cat. MSS. Angliæ, p. 11. N° 2093. Dr. Borlafe fays this was in all probability a copy of the original furvey of the weftern counties, whence the greater in the Exchequer was compiled.

MS. defcriptions of this county by Mr. Hals [i], and Mr. Scawen of Molinek (the latter, intitled Cornu-britannick antiquities, in the hands of Francis Gregor, of Trewarthenik, efq;) are frequently quoted by Dr. Wm. Borlafe, rector of Ludgvan, who has given the compleateft and beft written accounts in his " Obfervations on the antiquities, hif-

[f] Dr. Rawlinfon fays the beft copy of this furvey was prefented by the author to James I. and after the difperfion of the royal library fell into private hands. Quere, If this be the fame or one of thofe he mentions in Gale's poffeffion and in the hands of Mr. Cowfe, bookfeller in London?

[g] Inferted in Speed's Theatre, with a view of Launcefton, the other half ftone, hurlers, and cheefe-wring.

[h] Borl. antiquities of Cornwall, p. 326.

[i] Borl. Nat. Hift. p. 295, n. q.

" torical

" torical and monumental, of the county of Cornwall, confifting of
" feveral effays on the firft inhabitants, Druid-fuperftitions, cuftoms,
" and remains of the moft remote antiquity in Britain and the Britifh
" ifles, exemplified and proved by monuments now extant in Corn-
" wall and the Scilly iflands, faithfully drawn on the fpot, and en-
" graved according to their fcales annexed, with a fummary of the re-
" ligious, civil, and military ftate of Cornwall before the Norman
" conqueft: illuftrated by the plans and elevations of feveral antient
" caftles, an eaftern view of the monaftery and fcite of St. Michael's
" Mount, and a vocabulary of the Cornu-britifh language. Oxf. 1754."
Fol. and his " Natural hiftory of Cornwall, the air, climate, waters,
" rivers, lakes, fea, and tides: of the ftones, femi-metals, metals,
" tin, and the manner of mining: the conftitution of the ftannaries:
" iron, copper, filver, lead, and gold found in Cornwall; vegetables,
" rare birds, fifhes, fhells, reptiles, and quadrupeds; of the inhabi-
" tants, their manners, cuftoms, plays or interludes, exercifes and fefti-
" vals: the Cornifh language, trade, tenures, and arts: illuftrated with
" a fheet map of the county, and 28 folio copper plates from original
" drawings taken on the fpot. Oxf. 1758." Fol. Ray, who made
confiderable additions to the hiftory of this county in Gibfon's edition
of the Britannia [k], diligently took a lift of the fifh and plants. E.
Lhwyd made fome difcoveries in each department. The late rev.
Mr. Jago of Loo intended an hiftory of the Cornifh fifh [l]. It is to be
feared his notes and obfervations are loft: the few drawings that were
found were communicated to Dr. Borlafe by Mr. Dyer, vicar of St.
Clare and chaplain of E. Loo, and fuch as are rare and not in Ray's
Synopfis are inferted in this natural hiftory, with proper acknowledge-
ments. The Doctor at the end of his firft work promifes fome account of the religious houfes in this county fince the conqueft as well
as thofe before it. His Antiquities of Cornwall contain the moft con
fiftent and fatisfactory account of Druidifm, fupported by the beft
vouchers, the remains of it fcattered up and down this county, where it
feems to have fubfifted in its greateft purity and fplendor, as well as to

[k] See his philofophical letters, p. 277.
[l] See Ray's Synop. meth. pifcium, p. 162.

have

have maintained its empire longeſt. We have here no ſtreſs laid on the errors and ſuppoſitions of continental writers, nor the fancies and reveries of our arch-druid Dr. Stukeley.

Beſides what is ſaid of the tin mines in theſe books[m], at the end of Ray's northern words, and in N° 69 and 138 of the Phil. Tranſ.[n] there was printed in half a ſheet " The caſe of the ſtannaries ſtated ; " with the grounds and reaſons of their petition to the honourable " houſe of Parliament; together with the anſwers to ſeveral objections " that are uſually made againſt them, humbly propoſed."

" Laws of the ſtannaries of Cornwall made at the convocation or " parliament of tinners at Truro, Sept. 13, A° 27° Georgii II. in " which the laws made 22° Jacobi I. 12° Caroli I. 4° Jacobi II. are " recited and confirmed : to which are added the laws made at Truro " 2° Annæ. Printed by order of the convocation." 8vo.

" A ſtate of the proceedings of the convocation or parliament for " the ſtannaries of the county of Cornwall, held at Leſtwithiel on " Tueſday the 28th of Aug. 1750, and at Helſtone by prorogation on " Saturday the 20th of October following, and alſo the point in diſ- " pute between the lord warden and the houſe of ſtanators, impar- " tially ſtated and fairly diſcuſſed : together with ſome obſervations. " By a Corniſh man." Lond. 1751."

" The laws and cuſtoms of the ſtannaries in the counties of Corn- " wall and Devon, in two parts : containing the charter of Ed. I. for " erecting the tinners of Cornwall and Devon into a corporation : the " rights of the prince as duke of Cornwall, &c. By Thomas Pearce, gent. 1725 and 1750." Fol.

A ſtrange celeſtial phænomenon is mentioned in a ſmall piece, a ſheet and a half, intitled, " Somewhat written by occaſion of three " ſuns ſeen at *Tregnie* in Cornwall, the twenty ſecond of December " laſt ; with other memorable occurrents in other places. Imprinted " MDCXXII." 4to.

---

m Dr. B. ſuppoſes the *Ictis* of Diodorus Siculus to be ſomewhere near this coaſt, *Ik* being Corniſh for *Cove, Creek*, or *Port :* or it may have been ſome place loſt now. It certainly could not have been *Vectis* or the iſle of *Wight*. MS. Harl. 6380 is an hiſtory of the tin works in Cornwall, beginning with their manner of working by the Saxons.
a The latter by Dr. Chriſtopher Merret.

" An

" An account of Anne Jefferies, now living in the county of Corn-
" wall, who was fed for fix months by a fmall fort of airy people called
" Fairies ; and of the ftrange and wonderful cures performed with
" falves and medicines fhe received from them, for which fhe never
" took one penny of her patients. In a letter from Mofes Pitt, to Dr.
" Edward Fowler, Bifhop of Gloucefter. Lond. 1696." 4to. reprinted
in Morgan's Phænix Britannicus, p. 545.

In N° 113 of the Phil. Tranf. is a method of improving Cornwall by
fea fand. In N° 242, Mr. Newton's account of the effects of Papaver
corniculatum luteum growing here. In N° 336. p. 527, a letter from
Edw. Lhwyd to Dr. Tancred Robinfon, giving an account of fome uncommon plants growing about *Penzance* and *St. Ives.* In N° 458,
p. 459, Dr. Williams's attempt to examine the barrows in Cornwall
1740. In N° 493, p. 49 , we have Dr. Borlafe's o remarks on the
Cornifh diamonds ; and in p. 86 of vol. XLVIII. his account of a ftorm
of thunder and lightening near *Ludgvan,* Dec. 20, 1752. In p. 51.
of vol. L. he gives an account of fubterraneous trees at *Mount's-bay*
and p. 499, of an earthquake felt in the weftern parts of Cornwall,
July 15, 1757. There are alfo in p. 104 and 198, relations of ftorms
of thunder and lightening in *Bucklawren, Lanreath,* and *Leftwithiel,*
parifhes. In the firft part of vol. LI. we have his account of fome Roman antiquities found at *Boffen,* in the parifh of St. Erth, near St. Michael's Mount p. In the fecond part of vol. LII. his relations of extraordinary agitations of the waters in Mount's-bay and other places in this
county March 31 and July 28, 1761 ; and of two thunder ftorms in
Cornwall. Art. 7. in vol. LIII. his account of the late mild weather in
Cornwall, and the quantity of rain fallen there 1762 ; and vol. LIV.
p. 59, the quantity of rain at Mount's-bay and the weather there 1763.

The rev. Mr. Moore printed in 1760 " A fea piece, written on the
" coaft near Mount's-bay." 4to. and verfes on Mr. Percival's foffilry at
Tendarves, Gent. Mag. Dec. 1755. p. 567. In the fame Mag. May 1761,
p. 205. were directions for entering the port of *Padftow,* by John
Griffin.

o Such of his communications as appeared before the publication of his larger works
are fince incorporated into them with additions.

p The Patera among them is now at Oxford, and engraved in the Marmora Oxonienfia.

Views

Views in this county publiſhed by Buck 1734 are St. Michael's Mount, N. and E. (and two larger, S. E. and S. W. 1739); St. German's Priory, S. W.; W. Launceſton; N. W. Trematon; E. Pengerſick; N. E. Pendennis; E. St. Maws; W. Leſtormel; S. E. Fowey; and W. Tintagel Caſtles; and S. E. Leſtwithiel Palace. Of theſe caſtles Tintagel, Trematon, Leſtormel, and Launceſton are exhibited in pl xxv. xxvi. xxvii. xxviii. and a plan of the laſt in pl. xxvi. and St. Michael's Mount pl. xxix. of Borlaſe's antiquities, and the firſt and laſt in Norden, p. 80 and 93.

Four views of *Mount Edgecumbe* by Chatelain after Lambert. Another by Badeſlade and Toms, ſans date.

A view of *Penzance* by R. Scaddon, engraved by W. H. Toms 1748.

A N. E. view of *St. Michael's Mount* by the ſame, engraved by T. Morris.

A chart of *Mount's bay* by Dion. Williams, ſurveyor, and others.

A plan of *Helſton's Loch* was engraved by the late Mr. Warburton, and two inſtruments for drawing up tin out of the lake, invented by him, but never publiſhed.

Saxton's map of Cornwall, is dated 1576, and engraved by Leonard Tervoort of Antwerp.

Speed's, engraved by Jod. Hondius 1610, has a view of Launceſton, or antient Dunhevet, the other half ſtone, the hurlers, and the cheſe-wring.

A map of this county, newly ſurveyed by Joel Gaſcoyne, engraved by J. Harris, and dedicated to Charles Bodville Earl of Radnor.

A new and accurate map from an actual ſurvey made by Thomas Martyn in 174$\frac{4}{9}$. with the arms of the ſubſcribers, dedicated to the late prince of Wales, in two ſheets: the ſame reduced, dedicated to Robert Hoblyn, of Nantſwyhdon, eſq; member of parl. for Briſtol; and on a ſmaller ſcale, dedicated to Jon. Raſhleigh, eſq; of Menabilly.

Dr. Borlaſe has given another in his Natural hiſtory; " not, he ſays, " to correct thoſe already done, of which Martyn's has been of great uſe to him."

The laſt is that by Kitchen for the Britiſh Atlas.

C U M B E R-

CUMBERLAND.

A MS. defcription of this county, with the pedigrees of the principal families, conveyances of eftates, manors, and other more general and earlier antiquities, was wrote in the laft century by Mr. Denton of Cardew, with care and judgment according to Bifhop Nicholfon. A copy of it is in the cathedral library at Carlifle. We were encouraged to expect a full and accurate account of this county from Geo. Smith, efq; who occafionally communicated feveral of its antiquities to the public in the Gentleman's Magazine. It was vifited with Weftmoreland 1615 by S. George. Bifhop Nicholfon wrote the natural hiftory in Dr. Plott's method, ftill in MS. in private hands. Something on that fubject is included in the natural hiftory of Weftmoreland by the rev. Mr. Robinfon, of which by and by.

A fhort hiftory of the cathedral of *Carlifle* may be feen at the end of Dugdale's Hiftory of St. Paul's, 1716. Collections concerning it by Dr. Hugh Todd[q], prebendary of the church, are carefully preferved by the corporation, and mentioned as in the church library, in the catalogue communicated to Dr. Bernard, inferted in the fecond volume of his Cat. MSS. Angliæ. Wood gives thefe titles of them[r]: " Notitia ec-
" clefiæ cathedralis Carleolenfis una cum catalogo priorum dum con-
" ventualis erat & decanorum & canonicorum, quum collegiata."——
" Notitia prioratus de *Wedderhall*[s], cum catalogo omnium benefac-
" torum qui ad ambas has facras ædes ftruendas, dotandas & ornandas
" pecuniam, terras & ornamenta vel aliqua alia beneficia pie & muni-

---

[q] Whofe MS. notes on the Saxon verfion of Bede's Ecclefiaftical hiftory are frequently referred to in Bede's life in the Biographia Britannica. Several of his letters to Wanley are preferved in the Britifh Mufeum [MS Harl. 3779.] In one, dated May 25, 1702, he tells him he could not difpofe of the MS. account of Cumberland, an imperfect collection, the property of the dean and chapter of Carlifle : but he hoped in time to have a more perfect account of thefe parts. In another, 1712, he mentions fending Lord Oxford two folio volumes of charters of confiderable abbies in this county, to be followed by two more, in which would be the account of the county taken temp. Eliz. In another, 1713, he fays he was upon a work relating to the province of York.

[r] Athen. Ox. II.

[s] The regifter of this priory is in the fame library. A tranfcript of it by Mr. Todd MS. Harl. 1881.

" fice

" fice contulerunt." Thefe two in 4to. written 1688, and dedicated
to the dean and chapter.——" Hiftory of the diocefe of Carlifle, con-
" taining an account of the parifhes, abbies, nunneries, churches, mo-
" numents, epitaphs, coats of arms, founders, benefactors, &c. with
" a perfect catalogue of the bifhops, priors, deans, chancellors, arch-
" deacons, prebendaries, and of all the rectors and vicars of the feveral
" parifhes in the faid diocefe. Written 1689." If thefe MSS. are
correctly written and properly methodized, we may hope that under
the patronage of the prefent diocefan a part of the ifland fo well
furnifhed with curious fubjects, will e'er long be brought more into
public view. King engraved the S. profpect of the cathedral before
the civil wars, and Harris, from Kyp, the N. Buck did a S. W. profpect of the city 1745, and a N. E. view of the caftle 1729.

The foundation charter and ftatutes of *St. Beghe*'s fchool, 25 Eliz.
are among Bifhop Barlow's MSS. at Queen's Col. Oxford.

" A poetical profpect of the coaft, town, and harbour of *Working-*
" *ton :* to which is annexed a correct edition of the poetical profpect
" of Whitehaven. By James Eyre Weekes, formerly of Trinity Col.
" Dublin. Whitehaven 1752." 8vo.

" A defcriptive poem, addreffed to two ladies t at their return from
" viewing the mines near *Whitehaven*. To which are added fome
" thoughts on building and planting, to Sir James Lowther, of Low-
" ther-hall, bart. By John Dalton, D. D. Lond. 1755." 4to. In
N° 429, p. 109, of Phil. Tranf. is an account of a damp in thefe
mines.

A catalogue of the MSS. belonging to the Earl of Carlifle, at his feat
at *Naworth* caftle may be feen in the Cat. MSS. Angliæ, tom. II. p. 14.
An E. view of the caftle by Buck. 1739.

In p. 1287 of N° 178 of Phil. Tranf. and p. 1029 of Gibfon's Camden
1722 is a letter, dated Nov. 2, 1685, from Mr. Wm. Nicholfon to Mr.
Walker, mafter of Univerfity Col. concerning a Runic crofs with an infcription in *Beaucaftle* church-yard, drawn and publifhed in the Gent.
Mag. March, June, and Oct. 1742. p. 132, 318 and 529, by Geo. Smith,
efq; The firft of thefe has the Runic infcription on the W. fide, of which

---

t The late Lord Lonfdale's daughters.

Dr.

Dr. Nicholſon could find but five letters legible [u]. On this and the other two ſides Mr. Smith promiſes a diſſertation, which has not yet appeared. In p. 1201 of the aforeſaid N° of the Phil. Tranſ. and p. 1007 of Camden, is another letter from Nicholſon to Dugdale, dated 23 Nov. 1685, concerning a Runic inſcription on the font in the church at *Bridekirk*, ſince publiſhed in the Gent. Mag. Apr. 1749, p. 152.—In p. 813 of N° 356 are ſome obſervations on a Roman inſcription, found near Lannercoſt-abbey, by Dr. Jurin,. Horſley, Cumb. xxvii. p. 258. In N° 200, p. 737, are Dr. Liſter's obſervations on the copper mines, and in N° 240, p. 103, Dr. Plot's on the black-lead mines at *Keſwic*. In p. 362 of N° 494 a relation of a ſurpriſing inundation in St. John's valley, near Keſwic, Aug. 22, 1749. Another account of this in the Gent. Mag. Oct. 1754, with a view.—In p. 194 of vol. L. an account of a ſtorm at *Wigton*, Dec. 6, 1756.—Art. 4 of vol. LIII. mentions a remarkable decreaſe of the river *Eden*, Dec. 28, 1762, communicated by Wm. Milbourne, eſq; Art. 28 of the ſame volume conſiſts of obſervations by the rev. Dr. Taylor on two Roman inſcriptions at *Netherby*.

In the Gent. Mag. for Dec. 1741, p. 650, is a Roman altar, found by the river *Cambeck*, communicated by Mr. Smith; explained by him and Mr. Ward in that for Jan. 1742, p. 10. A further account of it by Mr. Smith, Feb. 1742, p. 76. and explanation by Mr. Gale, Mar. p. 135.——In that for June 1744, p. 340, is a Roman inſcription in a houſe at *Naworth*; and in that for July, p. 369, another at *Lannercoſt* abbey, with a Latin one relating to Edw. II. all communicated by the ſame curious gentleman, who was engaged in a deſcription of the county.——In that for Oct. 1746, p. 537, a Roman inſcription at *Naworth* and two at *Burdoſwald*, communicated by the ſame gentleman.— In thoſe for May, June, and July the ſame year was publiſhed, " A

[u] The Doctor ſays there are only ſix or ſeven lines. Mr. Smith gives nine, and in them many well known Runic letters, and many characters not ſo intelligible, but equally perfect. Part of it was publiſhed by Wormius, Mon. Dan. p. 161. The Doctor refers the monument to the expulſion of the magical Runæ; and their converſion to Chriſtianity. Mr. Smith ſuppoſes it belongs to a Daniſh king ſlain in battle about 865, whoſe death might be followed by his people's converſion. In the Cott. Lib. Dom. xviii. 7. is the inſcription on the head of a croſs found at Beaucaſtle 1615: from the head 16 inches, upper end 12 inches broad, and four thick 
May not this croſs have ſtood on the top of the obeliſk?

letter to a friend, containing an account of the march of the rebels into England, a defcription of the caftle of Carlifle x, and a differtation on the old Roman wall; with refpect to the map of it, and the adjacent country, the plan of Carlifle, and the view of its caftle juft publifhed, in two fheets; the draughts of which were favourably received by the Duke of Cumberland on his forming the attack on the caftle. and now are dedicated to his Royal Highnefs, by Geo. Smith;" with the larger map reduced to a fmaller fcale.——In that for Aug. 1747, p. 384, is a defcription of *Crofs-fell* mountain; in that for Nov. p. 522, a journey to *Caudebec-fells,* with a map; and in that for Dec. p. 583, an account of the wadd or black-lead mines; on which fubject two MS. letters of Bifhop Nicholfon's are there referred to.——In that for Jan. 1748, p. 4, a defcription of *Skiddaw.* In that for Apr. p. 178, are certain Roman antiquities found at *Coningarth,* with an infcription, explained in the following month, p. 266. In the fame Magazine for Aug. 1749, p. 367, is a Roman infcription at *Burgh on Sands:* two other infcriptions found in the cathedral at Carlifle in that for Sept. p. 403; explained by Geo. Smith, efq; Dec. p. 155.——In that for Jan. 1750, p. 27, an account and draught of a hypocauft found at *Netherby* 1732.—In that for Feb. 1751, p. 51, is a journey to the black-lead mines, with a map, by Geo. Smith, efq; who in the following Magazine, p. 112, communicated an infcription in the church-window at *Deerham,* which Mr. Pegge explained in that for June, p. 254. Mr. Smith publifhed an account of *Long Meg and her Daughters* y, near Little Salkeld, in the Magazine for July 1752, p. 311.——In that for Dec. 1754, p. 505, is a defcription and draught of *Chriftenbury Crags.*—— In that for Sept. 1755, p. 392, a Roman infcription at *Nunnery;* ex-

---

x A narration of the memorable fiege of it 1645, when, after forty-one weeks, Sir T. Glemham delivered it to the Scots, MS. Harl. 6798: 62.

y Dr. Stukeley took a drawing of this Celtic temple 1725, in which a fmaller circle appears W. of it. At Shap, further to the S. of it, he found an alate temple; near Kefwic a circle of ftones, which he took for an archdruid's burial place; and on the banks of the Lowther near Perith a Britifh circus, confifting of an amphitheatre and a circular entrenchment, of which he had an unpublifhed plate. This laft is probably called in the maps Arthur's round table. He had three unpublifhed plates of his own drawings of the monuments at Elenborough, &c. marked in Horfley, Cumb. lxv. lxviii. lxix. lxx. lxxii. lxxiii. The draughts are very different, particularly of the firft and fecond. He gives the infcription on lxix.

DEAE SETICENIAE L. ABAFIVS. G. V. S. L. M.
and feveral flight variations in the others.

plained

plained by Mr. Pegge in the following Magazine, p. 438. in which, at p. 440, is another infcription near the fame place; explained by the fame, p. 452.—In that for May 1757, p. 220, we have a more correct account and drawing of two Roman altars, found near Carlifle 1755, in which year Mr. Smith communicated them to the public in this Magazine for Aug. p. 360.—In p. 520 of that for Nov. 1760 is an authentic account of a water-fpout which moftly fell upon *Brackenthwaite*, in this county, on Sept. 19, 1760, by an eye-witnefs.——Some of the curiofities in the neighbourhood of *Kefwic* are pointed out in that for Nov. 1761, p. 500.

From paintings of Wm. Bellers Chatelain and Ravenet engraved 1752 a view of Derwentwater towards Borrowdale near Kefwic. Another of ditto from Vicar's Ifle by Skiddaw 1753, by Chatelain and Grignion.

Views of Derwentwater from Crow-park; Thirlmeer, Ennerdale, Broadwater, and Winder or Winander meer, lakes in this county, painted by T. Smith of Derby, were engraved 1761.

Buck's views 1739 are,

S. E. Home z ⎫
W. Calder ⎬ abbey.

N. W. and S. E. Lanercoft ⎫
S. E. St. Bees ⎬ priory.

W. Wetherall priory, and Corby caftle.

S. W. Egremont ⎫
N. W. Cockermouth ⎪
N. Penrith ⎪
N. W. Rofe ⎪
N. W. Kirkofwald ⎬ caftles.
N. E. Dacre ⎪
N. E. Scaleby ⎪
N. E. Millum ⎪
N. E. High-head ⎭

This county is included in Saxton's map of Weftmoreland, engraved by Auguftine Ryther 1576, without the hundreds, which are added in Speed's map of Cumberland 1610, with a plan of Carlifle, and five Roman infcriptions found in this county. The two counties were engraved together 1760 by an anonymous hand for the Britifh Atlas.

z Or Holm Cultrum. Three other views of it are in the 2d vol. of Stevens's Monaft.

D E R B Y.

DERBYSHIRE.

IN the Aſhmolean library, Nº 788, is " A natural hiſtory of " Derbyſhire, by Philip Kynder ᵃ "; or rather a preliminary diſcourſe to an intended natural hiſtory. In the ſame library, Nº 854, are collections of arms, &c. by E. Aſhmole, 166²⁄₁, and 816 notes relating to this county. The viſitations were performed by Flower and Glover 1569; by St. George 1611; and by Sir Wm. Dugdale 1662.

Among Dr. Rawlinſon's printed books I find, Nº 3608, " The " noneſuch wonder of the *Peake* in Derbyſhire;" without author or date. Hobbes of Malmeſbury's Latin verſes, " De mirabilibus Pecci," addreſſed to William Earl of Devonſhire, were printed 1636 and 1666. 4to. afterwards tranſlated into Engliſh verſe, and printed together in 8vo. 1678, in 12mo. 1683, the 5th edit. Charles Cotton alſo wrote the wonders of the Peak. Lond. 1681. 4to. reprinted in all the editions of his works from 1709 to 1765, with miſerable views of Chatſworth and the Devil's Arſe. Bagford ᵇ was told he firſt wrote it in the dialect of the county, and made a gloſſary to it; but what became of it he had not heard. In Leigh's natural hiſtory. Oxf. 1700. Fol. p. 187 and 192, are views and deſcriptions of this laſt and *Poole's hole*. In Nº 2 of the Phil. Tranſ. p. 7, is Dr. Plot's account of *Elden hole*. The moſt accurate and particular deſcription of theſe three caverns is in Dr. Short's hiſtory of the mineral waters of England, 1736, p. 29—34.

In p. 22 of Nº 406 of Phil. Tranſ. we have J. Martyn's obſervations in natural hiſtory, in a journey to the Peak, 1728.

" The benefit of the auntient bathes of *Buckſtones*, which cureth " moſt greevous ſickneſſes, never before publiſhed, compiled by John " Jones, phiſition at the King's Mede, nigh Derby, Aº Salutis 1572. " 4to. Lond. imprinted by Tho. Eaſt and Hen. Middleton, for Wm. " Jones."

ᵃ Many phyſical and religious pieces by him are in the ſame library.
ᵇ Liſt prefixed to the Britannia.

" A trea-

" A treatise on the nature and virtues of Buxton waters, with a pre-
" liminary account of the external and internal use of natural and arti-
" ficial warm waters among the antients: by a physician, 1761." 8vo.
At the corner of Speed's map of Derbyshire is a view of Buxton-hall or
inn and St. Anne's well.

" Tentamen hydrologicum, or an essay upon *Matlock*-bath in Derby-
" shire. Whereto are prefixed, three short preliminary dissertations,
" upon, 1. Water in general. 2. The tactile qualities (so called.) 3.
" Minerals. Further demonstrating, from the fundamental principles
" of philosophy and physick, the excellent qualities of these waters, in
" the cure of several diseases incident to the human body. By John
" Medley, M.D. Nottingham, 1730." 8vo. [c]

In N° 456 of the Phil. Transf. p. 352, is an account of petrefactions
near Matlock, with conjectures concerning baths in general, by Moreton Gilkes. Views of this bath were engraved and published by J. Boydell 1749, and by Vivares after Smith 1743.

Concerning the lead-mines have been printed " The liberties and
" customs of the myners: with extracts from the bundles of the Ex-
" chequer and Inquisitions taken in the reign of king Edward the
" First, and continued ever since, under the most favourable kings and
" queens of this kingdom of England. Lond. 1649." 4to.

" The liberties and customs of the lead-mines, within the wapen-
" take of Wirksworth, in the county of Derby, part thereof appear-
" ing by extracts from the bundles of the Exchequer and Inquisitions
" taken in the 16th year of the reign of king Edward the First, and in
" other kings reigns, and continued ever since. Composed in meeter
" by Edward Manlove, esq; heretofore steward of the Barghmoot-
" court for the lead-mines, within the said wapentake. Lond. 1653."
4to.

The laws of the miners in Derbyshire were printed long before
(1680) by Thomas Johnson, clerk of the New River Company, in a
book intitled " The Barmoot-court [d]".

[c] Of this author and his book see Short's history of mineral waters, p. 81. *n*
[d] Birch's Hist. of the Roy. Soc. IV. 75.

Thomas

Thomas Houghton's "Rara avis in terris, or the compleat miner, in
" two books : the firſt containing the liberties, laws, and cuſtoms of
" the lead-mines within the wapentake of Wirkſworth, in Derbyſhire,
" in 59 articles, being all that ever was made : the ſecond teacheth
" the art of dialling and levelling grooves ; a thing greatly deſired by
" all miners; being a ſubject never written on before by any. With
" an explanation of the miners terms of art uſed in this book. The
" 2d edit. corrected. Lond. 1736." 12mo. was inſerted in " A col-
" lection of ſcarce and valuable treatiſes on metals, mines, and mine-
" rals, with Albaro Alonſo Barba's art of metals, tranſlated from the
" Spaniſh by the E. of Sandwich, 1669 : and Gabr. Platte's diſcovery
" of ſubterranean treaſure."

Geo. Steer publiſhed " The compleat mineral laws of Derbyſhire,
" taken from the originals. 1. The High Peak laws, with their
" cuſtoms. 2. Stony Middleton and Eame, with a new article made
" 1733. 3. The laws of the manour of Aſhforth i'th' Water. 4. The
" Low Peak articles, with their laws and cuſtoms. 5. The cuſtoms
" and laws of the liberty of Litton. 6. The laws of the lord-
" ſhip of Tidſwell. And all their bills of plaint, cuſtoms, croſs-bills,
" arreſts, plaintiffs caſe or brief ; with all other forms neceſſary for
" all miners and maintainers of mines, within each manour, lordſhip,
" or wapentake. Lond. 1734." 12mo.

Hearne printed in the appendix to Annales Glaſtonienſes. Ox. 1726.
p. 557, a calendar of *Beauchief* monaſtery, founded by the barons of
Alfreton, from a MS. of Dugdale's in the Aſhmolean muſeum : and
Buck engraved a S. W. view of its ruins 1727.

Peck reprinted in the ſecond vol. of his Deſiderata curioſa, b. xv.
Nº 1. p. 1. the chronicle of *Dale* abbey, by Thomas de Muſca, ſometime canon there, with corrections and additions not in Dugdale's edition of it in the Monaſticon, tom. ii. p. 616. An E. proſpect of this
abbey is among Buck's views : and its hermitage in pl. xiv. of Stukeley's Itinerarium Curioſum.

A deſcription of a monſtrous giant, diſcovered by a certain labourer
in this county was publiſhed in 1661.

A diſ-

A difcourfe upon the twelve months fafting of Martha Taylor, a famous Derbyfhire girl, at *Overhaddon*, not far from Bakewell, by John Reynolds, 1669, 12mo. See a letter from Hobbes about her in Birch's Hift. of the Roy. Society, vol. ii. p. 334. and another in Latin from Dr. Johnfon, ib. p. 389. In the Phil. Tranf. Nº 400, p. 363, is an account of a human fkeleton nine feet long, found in a repofitory at *Repton*, with 100 common-fized ones pointing to its feet. In Nº 434, p. 413, an account, by Dr. C. Balguy of Peterborough, of the dead bodies of a man and woman preferved four years in the moors in *Hope* parifh. In Nº 475, p. 266, Mr. Gale's account of a foffil fkeleton difcovered at *Lathdill Dale*. In the 2d part of vol. LII. a defcription of a remarkable monument found near *Afhford* by Mr. Evatt of that place. In Nº 331, p. 320, Thorefby's account of a lunar rainbow in this county. In Nº 100, p. 6179, are Dr. Lifter's remarks on uncommon mineral fubftances found in coal and iron mines in this county and Yorkfhire.

" An account of a large filver plate, of antique baffo relievo Roman workmanfhip, found in *Rifley* park, Derbyfhire, in a letter to Roger Gale, efq; 1729, read before the Antiquarian Society 8 April, 1736, by Wm. Stukeley. 1736." 4to. with two cuts by Vandergucht. On this difh or falver, which probably belonged to fome heathen temple, and is adorned with rural fcenes, is an infcription fetting forth that Exuperius bifhop of Bayeux and Touloufe, A. D. 405, gave it to the church of Bouges, where the battle was fought 1421, between the Scots under the Duke d'Alenfon, quartered in the church, and the Englifh under Thomas Plantagenet Duke of Clarence, brother to Hen. V. who was flain there : fo that it was probably given as a trophy to Dale abbey, which is five miles from the place where it was found.

A print of *Melbourn* caftle was publifhed by the Society of Antiquaries from a draught in the Dutchy of Lancafter's office ; and N. E. and W. views of *Bolfover* ; N. W. *Caftleton*, and the Devil's-arfe ; and W. *Codenor* caftles, and a large E. view of Derby, 1728, by Buck.

The S. front of *Chatfworth* houfe by Campbell.

Vivares engraved after Smith, 1744, a S. W. view of Chatfworth, and N. W. view of the duke of Rutland's at *Haddon*.

T   An

An ichnography of Derventio *(Littler-chefter)* by Derby, is in Stuke-ley's Itin. Cur. pl. lxxxvi.

Smith of Derby painted, 1743, the following extraordinary prof-pects in the mountainous parts of Derbyfhire and Staffordfhire, commonly called the Peak and Moorlands :

One in Dovedale, 3 miles N. of Afhton, engraved by Benoift.

One in the upper part of Dovedale, 5 miles N. of Afhdown, by Roberts.

One on the river Manyfold at Wetton-mill, etched by Smith, finifhed by Scotin.

Matlock bath from the lovers walk, by Vivares.

A view of the beautiful cafcade below Matlock [fince broke down] by ditto.

A profpect on the river Wie in Monfal dale, 2 miles N. W. of Bakewell, ditto.

A profpect of Chee-torr, &c. on the Wie, 2 miles below Buxton, etched by Smith, finifhed by Scotin.

A profpect of the rocks and that vaft cavern at Caftleton, called Peak's or the Devil's arfe, by Granville.

Vivares engraved after Smith, 1745, Dunning cliff on Trent, 5 miles S. E. of Derby.—Anchor church, a large cave in a beautiful rock on Trent, 4 miles S. of Derby, near Foremark, a feat of Sir Robert Burdett.—Hopping-mill ware on the Derwent, 4 miles N. W. of Derby.

Thorpe cloud and Matlock torr were engraved after Smith by Mafon, 1751.

Univerfi Derbienfis comitatus graphica defcriptio 1577 by Saxton, without the hundreds, which are inferted in Speed's map, with a plan of Derby.

A later incorrect map by Bowen, 1748.

D E V O N-

DEVONSHIRE.

" A chorographical defcription, or furvey of the county of Devon,
" with the city and county of Exeter, collected by the travel
" of Triftram Rifdon, of Winfcot, gent. for the love of his country-
" men in that province," difperfed into various hands, each copy differing from the other, was collated with the beft belonging to John
Prince, vicar of Berry Pomeroy, and fome others, and printed, Lond.
1714. 8vo. 2 vols. republifhed in the fame fize 1723, the 2d vol.
from a compleater MS. in Prince's poffeffion. Rifdon was twenty-five
years engaged in it, and we muft take up with it for want of a better.

Of Hooker's " Synopfis chorographica, or an hiftorical record of the
" province of Devon: giving an account of the foil, air, commodities,
" natives, government ecclefiaftical, civil, and military, &c. &c." many
MS. copies remained in Prince's time: he faw one corrected for the prefs
by judge Dodderige, whofe recommendatory letter to one Z. Pasfield,
probably a printer, was prefixed to it. He mentions [a] A view of Devonfhire by T. W. Thomas Weftcott, of Raddon, who was put upon
it by Edw. Earl of Bath: after an elaborate introduction he derives
the name of Devonfhire from its many rivers, by which he defcribes
the towns, &c. on them, and then the foil, inhabitants, government,
&c. with much induftry and fancy, a folio MS. and another of pedigrees [b]
The MS. of Sir —— Northcott, bart. fo often quoted by Fuller in his
Worthies, is yet in being; though bifhop Nicholfon contradicts the
doctor with one of the loweft puns. There was a copy in the hands
of Mr. Hefkett, late of the Herald's-office; and Sir Henry Northcott
of Taviftock near Barnftaple, fome years ago, revifed his anceftor's
papers, and was inquifitive after materials to compleat them; fo that
there was reafon to hope he would publifh them.

[a] Worthies of Devon. p. 388.
[b] Ib. p. 586.

A tranf-

A tranfcript from Domefday-book is in the library of Exeter cathedral [c]. Another in the hands of Mr. Tutet, F. A. S.

The county was vifited 1530 with Cornwall by Wm. Tonge, Norroy: 1565 by Rob. Cooke, Clarencieux, and Edm. Knight, Chefter: 1620 by S. George and Lennard.

An anceftor and namefake of Sir William Pole, high-fheriff ult. Eliz. wrote with great judgment and faithfulnefs, a defcription of Devonfhire in 2 vol. folio, of great ufe to Rifdon. He left alfo a very large folio of deeds and charters, pedigrees and arms; and the knights fees taken 31 Edw. I. copied out of an old roll 1616: a thinner folio collection of arms of the Devonfhire gentry: a thicker of Torr abbey, charters, domefday, and an extract of Cheiverton's book of Cornifh obits. His collection of genealogies and pedigrees of the moft noted families in this county was lately in the hands of Mr. Anftis. Other MSS. by him and his fon Sir John, who made additions to the defcription of Devon, were loft during the civil wars; nor does it appear what is now become of the reft [d]. In the Harl. Lib. N° 3967 is pedigrees of Devonfhire gentry by Hugh Cotgrave, Richmond herald, with additions by R. Brooke. N° 4278 is a parochiale 1602, and inquifitions 9 Edw. II.

The ftate of this county under the Romans may be found in Dr. W. Mufgrave's " Belgium Britannicum, in quo illius limites, fluvii, " urbes, viæ militares, populus, lingua, dii, monumenta, aliaque per- " multa clarius & uberius exponuntur Ifcæ Dunm. 1719." 8vo.

The lives of the moft celebrated natives of this county were written by Mr. Prince, in his " Danmonii orientales illuftres, or the worthies of " Devon. Exeter 1701." Fol. The undeferved ill fuccefs this laborious and induftrious author met with difcouraged him from venturing his fecond volume, which was fome years prepared for the prefs.

Dr. John Huxham publifhed, 1752, " Obfervationes de aere & " morbis epidemicis, ab anno 1728 ad finem anni 1737 Plymuthi " factæ. His accedit opufculum de morbo-colico Damnonienfi [e]."

[c] Cat. MSS. Angliæ, p. ii. p. 56; N° 2093.
[d] Prince, p. 506.
[e] In a letter to Dr. Jurin 1738. This difeafe was very epidemic 1724.

8vo.

8vo. and a fecond volume from 1738 to 1748. The firft volume was tranflated into Englifh, and publifhed with the Doctor's approbation Lond. 1759. His obfervations on the anomalous epidemic fmall pox, which prevailed at Plymouth from Aug. 1724 to Sept. 1725, were inferted in the Phil. Tranf. N° 390, and his account of an aurora borealis at Plymouth N° 395, p. 157.

John Hooker, chamberlain of Exeter, wrote in 1584 the antiquities and defcription of this city, afterwards reprinted in Holingfhed's Chronicle. It remains alfo in MS. in the Afhmolean library, N° 762. His catalogue or hiftory of the bifhops of Exeter from Wereftan or Adulph to Walton, is in Hollinfhead. His pamphlet of the offices and duties of every particular fworn officer of the city of Exeter, was printed in 4to. 1584. The three pieces have been reprinted together at Exeter, under the title of " The antique defcription and account of the city of Exeter:
" in three parts. Part I. containing the antient hiftory, &c. of the city,
" together with relations of the fundry great affaults and fieges it time
" after time fuftained; and moft efpecially by the conjoined rebels of
" Devonfhire and Cornwall in 1549, the various circumftances of
" which long and dreadful fiege are amply and minutely detailed.
" Part II. containing a large and curious account of the antiquity,
" foundation and building of the cathedral church of St. Peter: to
" which is added a regular and orderly catalogue with authentic me-
" moirs of the bifhops, down to bifhop John Wolton in 1583, then
" living. Part III. contains the offices and duties (as of old) of thofe
" particular fworn officers, &c. of the city; viz. a freeman, the mayor,
" ftewards, receiver, recorder, the common-council, and every of
" them, an alderman, chamberlain, town-clerk, the ferjeants, &c.
" All written purely by John Vowell, alias Hooker, chamberlain and
" reprefentative in parliament of the fame. Exon. Now firft printed
" together by Andrew Brice, in Northgate, 1765." 4to.

Richard Izacke, another chamberlain, collected " Remarkable anti-
" quities of the city of Exeter: giving an account of the laws and
" cuftoms of the place; the offices, courts of judicature, gates, walls,
" rivers, churches, and immunities: together with a catalogue of all
" the

" the bifhops, mayors, and fheriffs, from 1049 to 1677." Lond. 1677.
and 1681. 8vo. ᶠ. The 2d and 3d editions of this book have the title
enlarged, as was the work itfelf, and continued to 1723, by Samuel
Izacke, efq; then chamberlain: with a new and correct map of the
city and a profpect of the cathedral on copper plates, and the freeman's
oath, both honorary and common. Lond. 1731, 1734, 1741. 8vo.

Sam. Izacke publifhed his grandfather's " Alphabetical regifter of
" divers perfons who by their laft wills, grants, feoffments, and other
" deeds have given tenements, rents, annuities, and monies towards
" the relief of the poor of the county of Devon, and city and county
" of Exon; and likewife to many other cities and towns in England,
" &c. Lond. 1736." 8vo

A ground plot of Ifca Dumnoniorum and a view of Exeter make the
73d and 74th plates of Stukeley's Itinerarium Curiofum. The Doctor
mentions an old plan of this city, taken in Q. Elizabeth's time. Another
by Fairlove was engraved by Cotes. Another by J. Rocque, engraved
by R. White 1741, in two fheets, with N. and W. views of the cathedral, Ex bridge, workhoufe, guildhall, caftle, city hofpital, city and
county hofpital ᵍ, and the cuftom-houfe from Trew's ware.

Meffrs. Buck engraved a W. and S. W. view of this city 1736.

Mr. Pafmore's collections out of the records, charters, regifters, and
papers of the cathedral are mentioned in Bagford's lift. A catalogue of
MSS. belonging to it is in the Cat. MSS. Angl. T. II. p. 55. Hollar
and Vertue engraved fmall views of it, and King the W. N. and S.
fides.

To a fermon of J. Prince's againft felf-murder, Lond. 1709. 8vo. is
added " A prodigy of providence, containing the wonderful preferv012-
" tion of a woman of *Totnes*, who endeavoured, Jan. 25, 1707, to
" drown herfelf, by leaping over the bridge near twenty feet high into
" the river running by that town."

ᶠ Mr. Rawlinfon had the author's own copy, with additions by his fon, and the figure
of a conduit, mentioned p. 85, which being in very few if any other copies was re-
engraved, and inferted in Rifdon's furvey, vol. i. p. 10.

ᵍ See an account of this hofpital in the Gent. Magazines for Sept. and Dec. 1741,
p. 474. 652.

The

The antient borough of *Lidford* has been celebrated in some humorous verses by Wm. Browne [h], of Taviftock, printed in his article in Prince's Worthies, p 96.

The three fucceffive devaftations of *Tiverton* by fire are recorded in " The true lamentable difcourfe of the burning of Teverton in Devon-" fhire, the 3d day of April laft paft, about the hower of one of the " clocke in the afternoone, being market-day, 1598 : at which " time there was confumed to afhes about the number of 400 houfes, " with all the money and goods that was therein, and fyftie perfons " burnt alive, through the vehemencie of the fame fyre. Lond. 1598." 4to.——" Wofull newes from the weft partes of England, being the " lamentable burning of the town of Teverton in Devonfhire, upon " the 5th of Aug. laft ; whereunto is annexed the former burning of " the faid town the 3d of April 1598. Lond. 1612." 4to.——" An ac-" count of the late dreadful fire there, the loffes, the contributions for " the fufferers, and the manner how they have been applied ; with an " addrefs of thanks to the contributors, &c. By Samuel Smith, mafter " of the free-fchool at Tiverton. 1730." 8vo.

Hen. Kiddel wrote a poem on the town 1754.

Buck engraved a S. E. view of the caftle 1734.

A feal, in the poffeffion of Dr. Rawlinfon, publifhed in the Englifh Topographer, p. 41, infcribed *Si: comunitatis: burgi: de Trile* round a fhield with three chevronels, feems to imply that the little village of *Trill* in this county [i] was once more confiderable.

" A true and certaine relation of a ftrange birth which was borne at " *Stonehoufe*, in the parifh of Plimouth, 20 Oct. 1635, together with " notes of a fermon preached Oct. 23, in the church of Plimouth, at " the intering of the faid birth. By Th. B. B. D. Pr. Pl. 1635." 4to. with a cut of the two boys united from the breaft to the belly, ftillborn of one J. Perfons, a fifherman's wife.

" Hell opened, or the infernal fin of murder punifhed : being a " true relation of the poyfoning a whole family at Plymouth ; for " which the malefactors were condemned before lord chief juftice

h Author of Britannia's Paftorals, 1616. The Shepherd's Pipe, 1614, &c.
i Rifdon, II. 309.

2

" North

" North at Exeter, one to be burnt, the other to be hanged. By John
" Quick, minifter of the gofpel. 1676." 12mo.

Hollar engraved " A true map of the town and port of *Plimouth*,
" with the fortifications in the time of the late fiege, 1623," inferted
in John White's narration thereof, 1644. 4to. alfo part of Plimouth
found; another view by Plimouth and a third by it at Catwater, with
Plimftoke in profpect, 1676.

Eight views and plans of Plymouth were publifhed 167¾, with a
letter from the officer of the yard to the hon. Edw. Dummer, efq;
furveyor of his majefty's navy, about the true circumftances of the
Barton of Montwife, with a plan of it, a chart of the harbour, and
view of the yard near Plymouth from the river or weftward, engraved
by J. Kip

Two views of Plymouth fort, and St. Nicholas's ifland, from Mount
Edgecumbe, and of Hamoaze and Plymouth, painted by Lambert and
Scot, and drawn by C. W. Bampfylde, efq; engraved by Mafon.

A large N. view of the town, and W. one of the dock,   Buck,
1736.

The citadel of Plymouth, drawn by Sandford Mace, engraved by
Charles Mofley 1737, with the found and haven at the corners.

" A true relation of thofe fad and lamentable accidents which hap-
" pened in and about the parifh church of *Withycombe in the Dartmoors*
" in Devonfhire, on Sunday the 21ft of Oct. laft, 1638. Lond. 1638."
4to. This pamphlet, which has been reprinted in the Harleian Mifcellany,
vol. iii. p. 211, includes a former account of the fame accidents which
were occafioned by lightening, adding and explaining fome paffages
omitted or left obfcure, by way of appendix. Hearne printed at the
end of Adam de Domerham 1727, p. 676, a poetical defcription of this
town and ftorm, by Rich. Hill, fchoolmafter, part of it fet up in two
tables in the church. Mr. Lyde, the vicar, who was in the pulpit
when the ftorm happened, wrote a long poetical defcription of the
parifh and accident. MS. Fol. k.

" A true relation of two moft ftrange and fearfull accidents lately
" happening; the one at *Chagford* in Devonfhire, by the falling of

k Prince's Worth. of Devon. p. 449.

" the

" the ftannary court-houfe, the 6th day of March laft: the other at
" Branfon, within a mile of Burton upon Trent in Staffordfhire, this
" prefent year 1618." 4to.   The latter was the fudden firing of a hay-
rick, &c. belonging to a farmer who had wronged a dumb brother.

In p. 253 of vol. xlvii of the Phil. Tranf. is an account of a body
found in *Staverton* church.   J. Kirkpatrick, M. D. honorary member
of the fociety of navy furgeons publifhed " Some reflections on the
" caufes that may retard or prevent the putrefaction of dead bodies:
" occafioned by an account of a body found entire and imputrid at
" Staverton, in Devonfhire, eighty years after its interment, in a let-
" ter to the fociety of navy furgeons.   With an atteftation of the fact,
" and of the fimilar ftate of three bodies difcovered fourteen years fince
" in St. Martin's, Weftminfter, and interred the laft century. Lond.
" 1751." 8vo.

" Here folowyth the confirmation of the charter perteyninge to all
" the tynners wythyn the county of Devonfhyre, with there ftatutes
" alfo made at Crockeryntorre, by the hole affent and confent of al the
" fayd tynners.   Yn the yere of the reygne of our fovereygne lord
" kynge Henry VIII. the fecund yere.   Here endeth the ftatutes of
" the ftannary imprented yn Tavyftoke [1], the xx day of Aug. the
" yere of the reygne off our fovereygne lord kygne Henry VIII. the
" xxvi yere.   God ffave the kyn."   This fingular book, confifting of
fixteen leaves 4to. was communicated by the rev. Mr. Jofeph Sandford of Baliol Col. Oxf. to Mr. Ames, who mentions it in his Hiftory
of printing, p. 468; as alfo p. 430, " The laws and ftatutes of the
" ftannaries of Devon." beginning with the charter granted to the
tinners there by Edw. III. and fince confirmed by divers kings, and
ending with acts made 42 Eliz. 1600. Fol. probably the fame with
" The laws touching the ftate of the mines and ftannaries, during the
" wardenfhip of the Earl of Bedford, in the reign of Q. Elizabeth,"
mentioned by Dr. Rawlinfon as a very fcarce tract.

[1] The additions to Camden fay in the beginning of the late civil wars a Saxon grammar was printed in this town, where the famous Saxon fchool and lecture was eftablifhed,
and continued till the fifteenth century. I fhould be glad to have this anecdote better afcertained.

U   A true

" A true and impartial relation of the information againſt three
" witches, viz. Temperance Lloyd, Mary Trembles, and Suſanna
" Edwardes, who were arraigned and convicted at the aſſizes at Exe-
" ter, Aug. 12, 1682, with their ſeveral confeſſions taken before
" Thomas Giſe mayer and John Davie alderman of Biddeford, as alſo
" their ſpeeches and confeſſions and behaviour at the time and place
" of execution, on the 25th of the ſaide month. Lond. 1682." 4to.

" The caſe of the county of Devon with reſpect to the conſequences
" of the new exciſe duty on cyder and perry," by Mr. Benj. Heath,
was publiſhed by the direction of the committee appointed at a general
meeting of the county to ſuperintend the application to parliament for
the repeal of that duty. Lond. 1763. 4to.

In the Phil. Tranſ. N° 23, 1666, is archdeacon Cotton's account
of a load-ſtone of ſixty pounds weight, moving a needle nine feet
diſtant, dug out of the earth in this county.—In N° 69 are mineral
obſervations on the mines here and in Cornwall.——In p. 908 of
N° 204 is a letter from Dr. William Oliver, concerning the ſtrange
ebbing and flowing of a well near *Torbay*.—In p. 28 of N° 215 is
Zachary Mayne's account of a water-ſpout that he ſaw at *Topſham*, on
the river, between the ſea and Exeter, Aug. 7, 1694.—In N° 316,
p. 142, is a method of manuring land by ſea-ſand, communicated by
Dr. Bury.—In p. 528 of N? 336 are related the effects of a thunder-
ſtorm at *Sampford-Courtney*, Oct. 7, 1711, communicated by John
Chamberlayne, eſq; F. R. S.—In p. 1101 of N° 363 and p. 186 of
N° 368 are deſcriptions of an aurora borealis ſeen Feb. 6, 1720, at
Cruwys Morchard, by S. Cruwys, eſq;—In p. 171 of N° 439 is a regiſter of the births, burials, and inhabitants of *Stoke Damarel*, communicated by Mr. Barrow.—The 52d article in the xlviith vol. is an account of the effects of lightning at *Southmolton*, by Joſeph Palmer, eſq;
—The 64th art. of vol. xlix is the caſe of a man who died by the
melted lead running into his ſtomach when *Eddyſtone* light-houſe was
burnt 1755.—In p. 642 of vol. xlix. is an account of the extraordinary
agitation of the ſea at *Ilfracombe* Feb. 27, 1756, and at *Dartmouth* Nov.
1, 1755.—In vol. li. part 2d. is a deſcription of a foſſil found in Devonſhire called Bovey coal.——Art. 3 of vol. xlix. is a letter from Dr. Hux-

ham

ham to Mr. Watſon on the effects of lightning at Plymouth, Dec. 15, 1754.—Art. 29 is Dr. Parſons's account of a monſtrous ſheep bred in this county, ſhewn alive to the ſociety, and its ſkin preſerved in their muſæum.—Art. 61 in vol. l. are Mr. Smeaton's remarks on the different temperament of the air at the Eddyſtone and Plymouth July 1757.

In the Gentleman's Magazine for June 1745 is an inſcription found at *Slaughter*'s or *Sloven*'s bridge, near Worthvale and Camelford, the ſpot where K. Arthur received his mortal wound, communicated by Joſeph Pomeroy. Dr. Borlaſe republiſhed this in his Antiquities of Cornwall, p. 360, much more correct, reading it in Roman letters, *Catin hic jacit—filius magari*, and taking it intirely away from Arthur. In thoſe for June, July, and Aug. 1746, p. 297. 352, and 405, a dialogue in the Devonſhire dialect uſed near *Exmore* foreſt in Somerſetſhire. In that for May 1748, p. 214, an account of human bones filled with lead found at *Axminſter*. In that for Mar. 1750, an account of an aurora borealis, ſeen at *Biddeford*, by B. Donn. In that for Oct. 1755, p. 445, and Dec. p. 564, is an account of Biddeford, in anſwer to the queries relative to a more compleat account of the natural hiſtory and antiquities of England, propoſed in the Magazine for April that year: in July 1751, p. 296, is a view of its bridge.

" A proſpect of *Eddy-ſtone* light-houſe near Plymouth, being 80 " foot high, erected and contrived by Henry Winſtanley of Littlebury, " in the county of Eſſex, gent. [1696] drawn at the rock by Jaaziell " Johnſton, painter," engraved by Sturt. This being blown down by the great ſtorm 1703, another was erected by John Rudyard, gent. purſuant to an act of parliament, 4 and 5 An. the lights put up therein July 28, 1708. Sturt engraved a proſpect and ſection of it from a drawing of B. Lens. This being burnt Dec. 2, 1755, Mr. Smeaton raiſed a third, of which I have ſeen no draught.

A S. E. view of *Taviſtoke* by Ch. Delafontaine, engraved by R. Parr, 1741. A W. view of the abbey 1734 by Buck, who at the ſame time publiſhed

S. Ford
E. Buckfaſtre ⎱ abbies,

U 2

S. W.

S. W. Ottery }
E. Buckland } priories,
S. E. Frithelſtoke }
E. Dartington temple.
S. Okehampton }
E. Powderham }
S. Berry Pomery } caſtles,
S. E. Dartmouth }

and a large S. E. view of Sir Wm. Courtenay's ſeat at *Powderham* caſtle, 1745.

There is a good proſpect of *Torr* abbey in the Monaſticon, II. 652.

Proſpects of *Seaton* and *Lyme* make the 75th and 76th plates of Stukeley s Itin. Cur.

Saxton's " Devoniæ comitatus rerumque omnium in eodem memo-" rabilium recens, vera, particulariſq; deſcriptio. 1575." engraved by R. Hogenbergius, is not divided into hundreds; but they are added in Speed's map, with a plan of Exceſter, and the arms of ſuch nobles as have borne the titles of them.

Another by E. Bowen, with a plan of Plymouth.

A new and accurate map, from an actual ſurvey by Benjamin Donn, was engraved by Jeffereys 1765, on twelve ſheets.   At the corners are plans of the town and citadel of Plymouth, Stoke town, and Plymouth dock, and the city and ſuburbs of Exeter

DORSET.

DORSETSHIRE.

MR. Anthony Etricke communicated some particulars about this county to Bishop Gibson, who inserted them in the Britannia The rev. Mr. Coker of Mapowder left in MS. " A survey of Dorset-" shire, containing the antiquities and natural history of the county; " with a particular description of all the places of note and antient " seats, and a copious genealogical account of 300 of the principal fa-" milies, with their arms, on six copper plates, with a map : " pub-lished 1732. Fol.   Mr. Hutchins, rector of Wareham, has for some years been preparing a fuller history of the county, which lies ready for the press, whenever the author can prevail with himself to encoun-ter the difficulties of such a publication.   MS. Harl. 5227 is a valua-tion of benefices in Dorsetshire by Francis Neve.   There are visitations 1562 by ———— : 1623, by St. George and Lennard.

Dr. Rawlinson engraved in his English Topographer, p. 43, an old seal in his possession, inscribed *S: Convent de Pool*.   It is also inserted. in the additions to the folio edition of Tanner's Notitia Monastica; where is mentioned a priory of St. George at *Pool*.   Sir Peter Thomp-son has collections for a history of this town.

Malachi Blake, dissenting minister at *Blandford*, published " A brief " account of the dreadful fire at Blandford-Forum June 4, 1731; with " a sermon preached there June 4, 1735, being the day set apart by " the protestant dissenters there for prayer and humiliation under the " remembrance of that sad providence.   To which is added a serious " address to the inhabitants of that town.   The 2d edit. Lond. 1735." 12mo with a plan of the town.

Mr. Richard Russel, attorney, of *Wimburn-minster*, has collected the antiquities of that antient town, which it were to be wished he would oblige the world with.

The Roman amphitheatre at *Dorchester* is largely treated of by Dr. Stukeley, in his Itinerarium Curiosum, p. 155—168. and plates l. li. lii. liii. lxxvii. and lxxviii.   This account was at first drawn up and

read

read to a fociety of free mafons 1723, and printed in 4to. with a geo-metrical ground plot, but much enlarged in the Itinerarium.

A profpect from Dike-hills, Dorchefter, the Britifh Curfus, drawn by Dr. Stukeley 21 May 1755 was engraved by Hulett.

S. Gould, bookfeller at Dorchefter, publifhed a view of the town by Boydell.

Another of Dr. Stukeley's unpublifhed plates is the Roman camp on *Woodbury-hill* near Bere regis, the Ibernium of Ravennas. Itin Cur. p. 182.

In Peck's Defid. Cur. vol. ii. b. xiv. Nº 6. p. 5, is the ftrange curfe belonging to *Shirburne* caftle, which Ofmund, who from a Norman knight became a bifhop, and gave that caftle with other land to the church of Salifbury, laid on all who fhould alienate or diminifh his donation: with inftances wherein it has been verified. K. Stephen took it from Niger, bifhop of Salifbury, and his reign was a feries of ufur-pation and confufion. After his death the Montacutes, earls of Salif-bury, held it, and moft of them died violent deaths. The duke of Somerfet, beheaded under Ed. VI. was another unfortunate proprietor. Bifhop Capon recovered it from Sir John Horfley, to whom that king gave it. Sir Walter Raleigh and Carr earl of Somerfet poffeffed it with equal ill luck. If the firft of thefe obtained it of bifhop Coldwell by artifice, the fecond got it from him by greater injuftice: Prince Henry, who never ceafed importuning his father till he obtained it, on purpofe to reftore it to Sir W. which nothing but his untimely death prevented, fhould furely be exempted from the curfe. Charles I. confirmed his father's grant of it to John Digby, whom he created earl of Briftol, and whofe titles and honours became extinct in half a century. The prefent proprietor advances inftead of declining in his. Buck engraved a S. view of this caftle 1733. Mr. Tomkins exhibited a painting of it at Spring-gardens 1765.

Hearne in the review of Leland's Itinerary, at the end of the 9th volume, p. 156, has printed three charters relative to the abbey, and an extract, as fuppofed, from Domefday, from a MS. containing many other charters to the fame foundation; and the offices ufed in the church, and thought to be wrote about the time of Bifhop Poore.

The

The feals of Shireburne, *Shaftsbury*, and *Abbotsbury* abbies were engraved by Vertue among others for the Antiquarian Society, 1741.

Two bad views of the S. and W. fides of the church by D. King.

An account of the Roman coins found at *Corton* in §. xi. of Hearne's preface to Heming's Chartularium.

In the Phil. Tranf. N° 56, p. 1128, is Dr. Highmore's account of a medicinal fpring at *Farringdon*. In N° 231, p. 659, Sir Robert Southwell's account of damage done to *Portland* pier by rain. In N 454, p. 229, a relation of a terrible whirlwind at *Cerne Abbas* Oct. 30, 1731. In vol. lii. p. 1, an account of an uncommon phænomenon, a fmoke and fometimes a vifible flame iffuing from the cliffs near *Charmouth*: by John Stephens. M. A.

In the Gentleman's Magazine for June 1744, p. 329, are verfes on *Br—ne* cliff on Stoure river, by whofe fide is a walk under the cliff. In that for Feb. 1750, p. 78, is an account of an aurora borealis feen at *Stalbridge* Jan. 15, by Samuel Bolton, rector. In that for July 1764, p. 336, we have the figure and dimenfions of the giant cut out on Nant hill, near *Cerne*, 180 feet high, which Dr. Stukeley calls Melcartus or Hercules.

Berwick, the feat of James Gollop, efq, between Abbotfbury and Burton, was celebrated in a Latin poem intitled " Barvicea villa feu " Golloppianum, 1753." 4to. by Paul Jallange.

Concerning a harbour at *Chrift Church* fee Yarrington's " England's " improvement, 1675." 4to. and the Gent. Mag. Feb. 1745. p. 95.

Meffrs. Buck engraved 1733,

N. W. Milton ⎫
N. Abbotfbury ⎬ abbey,
S. Bindon ⎭

N.E. Lulworth [a] ⎫
N. E. Chidioc ⎬ caftle,
S. Corfe ⎪
N. Sanford ⎭

---

[a] Built by Tho. Howard earl of Suffolk after a defign of Inigo Jones.

Another

Another view of Lulworth caftle, the feat of Henry Weld, efq; delineated by the lady of the feat, 1721. fold by Smith at Exeter-change.

J. Banks, efq; of Kingfton, in this county, has a drawing of *Corfe* caftle before the civil war. None of the engraved views have done this noble ruin juftice; three good paintings of it by Mr. Richards were exhibited at Spring-gardens 1764 and 1766.

F. Perry engraved in one plate Portland old and new caftle, and the vicar's houfe there, and Weymouth caftle.

" Dorceftriæ comitatus vicinarumq; regionum nova veraq; defcrip-
" tio," by Saxton, 1575, without the hundreds; added with a plan of Dorchefter in Speed's map 1610.

Another, very incorrect, by Em. Bowen.

A capital furvey of this county was publifhed by I. Taylor 1765, in fix fheets, having at the fides views of Corfe caftle, the amphitheatre at Dorchefter, Maiden caftle, Lulworth caftle, the obfervatory at Horton, and Shirborn caftle.

DURHAM.

DURHAM.

THE late John Mickleton [a], of Grey's-inn, efq; had many valuable papers, moftly collected by his grandfather, who held a public poft in the city of Durham. They confifted of regifters, charters, church-antiquities, and other original papers, in about twenty folios. Mr. Rudd communicated fome extracts out of them to bifhop Gibfon, who inferted them in his Britannia. In the dean and chapter's library are as many volumes of Collectanea made by the late Dr. Hunter, an eminent phyfician of this city, wrote in a very fair and curious hand. Dr. Smith, editor of Bede, made fome progrefs in writing the antiquities of Durham; for which undertaking bifhop Nicholfon obferves he was the moft proper perfon. In one of his letters to Wanley [b], dated Durham, June 6, 1702, he fays they have fair regifters from the foundation of the prefent church by bifhop William, under the conqueror [c], and the originals of moft charters that are in them; but no Saxon wills or inftruments, except that he fent to Dr. Hickes.

Mr. John Spearman, who was under-fheriff of the county twenty-nine years and deputy-regifter of the court of chancery here forty-two years, at the requeft of bifhop Nicholfon, drew up in 1697 an abftract of the antient ftate of the county from records, and printed it under the title of " An inquiry into the antient and prefent ftate of the county " palatine of Durham, wherein are fhewn the oppreffions which at- " tend the fubjects of this county by the male-adminiftration of the

---

By a letter from R. Sare to H. Wanley, dated Dec. 3, 1719, Harl. MSS. 3782. 217, this gentleman feems to have come to an " unfortunate death; being in bad cir- " cumftances he took to drinking: his eftate in the bifhopric was mortgaged, and upon " his death there were many claims on his effects, till the arrival of his brother, a mer- " chant at Newcaftle. Mr. Spearman, an intimate friend of his, delighting in fuch " curiofities as he had, would probably endeavour to purchafe them." What became of them afterwards does not appear.

[b] MS. Harl. 3782. 254.
[c] A. D. 1093.

X " prefent

" prefent minifters and officers of the faid county palatine; with fome.
" reafons humbly offered to the freeholders, leafeholders, and copy-
" holders of the faid county to confider of ways and means to remedy
" the faid abufes, or take away intirely the faid county palatine, and
" the bifhop's temporal power and jurifdiction herein, whereby their
" fortunes and tenures may be rendered more eafy and fecure. 1729."
4to. The fecond and third parts were compiled in hafte, the collector
defigning to publifh a larger and more correct account of the faid
county palatine and its antiquities in due time.

The life d of the patron faint was wrote by Bede both in verfe and
profe, printed in the third volume of his works, Colon. 1612, and at the
end of Smith's edition of his hiftory, 1722. B. R. efq; publifhed
1663, 12mo. " The legend of St. Cuthbert; with the antiquities of
" the church of Durham," by Robert Hegge, native of this city, and
fellow of C. C. C. Oxford, who died in 1629. A copy of it which
belonged to Dr. Edward Pocock, canon of Chrift-church, has a preface dated July 1, 1626, and many confiderable corrections and additions, miftakes in proper names amended, and feveral paffages tranfpofed by the author's own hand. The book was printed from
another MS. in the author's own hand in Lord Fairfax's library, the
editor B. R. being one of his retinue. Another fair copy was lately in
the library of Sir John Evelyn of Wotton in Surry. Bifhop Tanner had
prepared a genuine and correct edition of it, with large additions from
the MS. and notes and obfervations of his own, and a learned preface.
Another copy, with large additions, &c. by Dr. Hunter, is in the hands
of Mr. Ifaac Thompfon, printer at Newcaftle, who had thoughts of
publifhing it.

In the cathedral library is a MS. collection of the antiquities of this
church tranfcribed by order of bifhop Cofin, intitled " A defcription
" of all the antient monuments, rites and cuftoms belonging to the
" monaftical church of Durham before the fuppreffion," and dated
1597. It differs confiderably from " The antient rights and monu-
" ments of the monaftical and cathedral church of Durham, collected

---

d In the Harleian library, N° 4843, is a life of St. Cuthbert, compiled from various
authors : others of St. Ofwald and St. Aidan, bifhop Wm. Carileph, &c. and the writing under the images in the church of Durham : other lives of Cuthbert and Ofwald by
Reginald monk here about 1160 are in the Bodleian.

" out

" out of ancient manuscripts, about the time of the suppression, pub-
" lished by John Davis of Kidwelly. Lond. 1672." 12mo. which
seems to have been compiled about the end of the 16th century [e], by
an eye-witness of all that passed at that time. As to the anachro-
nism charged on it by Wood, in the account of the defacing Nevil's
cross 1639, this might be inserted by the editor. It was reprinted
at the expence of the late Mr. Richardson, bookseller and alderman
of this city, with additions by Dr. Hunter, and intitled " The history
" of the cathedral church of Durham, as it was before the disso-
" lution of the monastery; containing an account of the rites, cus-
" toms, and ceremonies used therein : together with a particular de-
" scription of the fine paintings in the windows [by Prior [f] Wasington],
" likewise the translation of St. Cuthbert's body from Holy-island, with
" the various accidents that attended its interment here ; with an ap-
" pendix of divers antiquities, collected from the best MSS. The 2d
" edition with additions. Durham." 12mo. The additional description
of the windows is dated Durham 1733. The appendix contains
the inscriptions under the pictures of the kings and bishops in the
choir; a list of churches dedicated to St. Cuthbert; the epitaphs of
dean Sudbury, Sir Geo. Wheeler, archd. Basire, and Mr. Spearman,
bishop Hugh's charter, &c. and in the body of the book are interspersed many additional particulars. Another short account of this church
is at the end of Dugdale's history of St. Paul's, 1716.

Mr. Rawlinson had a 4to paper MS. intitled, " Origo episcopatus
" Dunelmensis, A.D. 1616." and at the end of it K. James's confirmation of bp. Tobias Matthews's charter granted to the city of Durham,
44 Eliz. 1602. The MS. in Bagford's list intitled, " The original
and succession of the bishops of Durham, together with their lives and
actions, collected out of the antient and late records of the cathedral
church of Durham, and for the most part translated out of the Latin
into English, at the charges of Mr. J. Hall, of Conset, in the county of
Durham, A. D. 1603 [g]." is Harl. MS. 1694.

[e] See p. 49.
[f] He was prior here from 1416 to 1446, and wrote a book of the rights and privileges of this church, now in the Cotton library, marked Vitellius, A. ix.
[g] Quære, If this be a translation of Mr. Rawlinson's MS.?

Mr.

Mr. T. Bedford published 1732, 8vo. from a very valuable MS; in the cathedral library, which he supposes to be either the original or copied in the author's life time [h], " Symeonis monachi Dunhel-" mensis libellus de exordio atque procursu Dunhelmensis ecclesiæ :" with a continuation to 1154, and an account of the hard usage bishop William received from Rufus from the same MS. to which he prefixed a learned dissertation by Thomas Rud, rector of Washington, proving the author to have been Symeon, monk and præcentor here. about the end of the 12th century, against Selden,. who in a dissertation prefixed to Twisden's edition of it among the Decem scriptores 1652, laboured to make Turgot, who was prior here 1087—1109, its author. It begins with the conversion of Oswald king of Northumbria, A. D. 634, and gives the history of the see of Durham to A. D. 1096. The latter part of the continuation in Twisden's edition differing considerably from this MS. is printed in the appendix [i]; where is likewise a letter from Bernard and William abbots of Clareval and Rievaulx 1137 —1149, to prior Roger, recommending Laurence for bishop, but without success.

The Cotton library is hardly better stocked with the records of any cathedral in England than that of Durham; whereof the chief is a large catalogue [k] of their benefactors from K. Edwin to the reign of Hen. VIII; the beginning is in an old Saxon character as antient as K. Æthelstan, in whose possession it is very probable it some time was, from his name in the title page supposed to be wrote by himself. There is also a curious miscellany relating to St. Cuthbert and his successors in the see, the visitatorial contests between the priors and bishops, &c. [l].

A catalogue of the MSS. of the cathedral is in the 2d volume of the Cat. MSS. Angliæ. p. 5—12.

[h] There are copies of it in the publick library at Cambridge, and the Cotton library, Calig. A. VIII. which Twisden used.

[i] Other continuations by two monks here, Jeoffrey Coldington from 1144 to 1214, and Rob. Greystanes from 1213 to 1336, were published by Wharton; Ang. Sac. I. 714, & 732. Laurentius, prior about 1150, wrote a poem De civitate & episcopatu Dunelm. which seems to be lost.

[k] Dom. XII.

[l] Nich. Hist. Lib. p. 129.

In a curious MS. among thofe given by Dugdale to the Herald's office are beautifully drawn all the arms in this church, comprifing 117 coats; and bifhop Hatfield's monument in the choir. In Smith's edition of Bede are two views of St. Cuthbert's altar, and the fcreen behind the high altar, feen from the former, alfo of Bede's tomb in St. Mary's chapel. I am informed the fine fcreen, or lardofe, at the back of the high altar, has been drawn by fome London architect, who it were to be wifhed would engrave it. King drew and engraved the N. fide of the church, with the W. fpires; Harris the N. fide B. Willis in his furvey of this cathedral refers to a draught of it publifhed by Buck, infcribed to the late dean Mountague; but no fuch draught was ever made publick, though Mr. Buck painted feveral views of the cathedral for bifhop Crew. The whole church deferves to be correctly engraved, as a fine remain of Saxon architecture.

A large plan of the city was drawn and publifhed by T. Forfter, furveyor there, 1754, engraved by J. Mynde, with a view of the cathedral from the caftle walks, N.W. view of the city from the gardens above Framwell gate, N. W. view of the caftle from a field called Hollow croft above Framwell gate, and an E. view of the city from Pelloewood hill; alfo on one fheet without the views.

A S.W. view of this Englifh Zion 1745, and S. of its caftle 1729, by Buck.

The prefent dean has publifhed " A perpetual table of the fun's " rifing and fetting in every degree of declination for this city," with this view of the city at the head of it.

Mr. Jonathan Story having, 1705, rebuilt a chapel for the iron manufacturers at *Winlaton*, which had lain in ruins ever fince the earl of Weftmoreland's rebellion in Q. Elizabeth's time, printed the account of its erection and endowment, addreffed to bifhop Crew 1710, under the title of " The intereft of the church defended againft the " attempts of papifts and others : being the remarkable account of " the late rebuilding of Winlaton chapel in the bifhoprick of Durham. " Lond. 1721." The income of this chapelry is 50 l. per annum, of which 20 l. goes towards a free fchool.

Dr. Rawlinſon engraved 1752 a grant of lands in *Wotton, Eſcumbe*, and *Stanhope*, from biſhop Bek to Walt. de Berinſtone, and his heirs, between 1283 and 1310.

The county was viſited by Flower and Glover 1575: and by St. George 1615.

All that we have of natural hiſtory is in Dr. Edward Wilſon's "Spa " dacrene Dunelmenſis; or a ſhort treatiſe of an ancient medicinal " fountain, or vitrioline ſpaw, near the city of Durham. Together " with the conſtituent principles, virtues, and uſe thereof. Lond. " 1675." 12mo. and in p. 726 of N° 163 of the Phil. Tranſ. an account of a ſalt ſpring, and a medicinal one on the banks of the river Ware, from Dr. Tod of Univerſity college.

In p. 70 of N° 145 is an account of a Roman monument found near *Shields* [m], and of ſome Roman antiquities at York, by Dr. Liſter. In p. 666 of N 266 a letter from Mr. (afterwards Dr.) Chriſtopher Hunter, dated from Newcaſtle, Nov. 6, 1700, to Dr. Liſter, concerning ſome Roman inſcriptions found near Durham [n]. In N° 278 part of another letter from the ſame gentleman concerning Roman antiquities found at *Ebcheſter*. In p. 701 of N° 354 an extract of a letter, dated July 5, 1717, from Mr. Hunter to Dr. Woodward, concerning a Roman inſcription found near *Lancheſter* 1715. In p. 823 of N° 357 are Roger Gale's remarks on it. In p. 173 of N° 486 we have another Roman inſcription on an altar near *Stanhope*.

In the Gentleman's Magazine, Oct. 1763, p. 492, is an account of a human ſkeleton nine feet ſix inches long, found with ſundry coins at *Fulwell* hills, near *Muncremouth*, communicated by Mr. Collinſon.

Views in this county by Buck 1728 are, S. Holy iſland monaſtery and caſtle; S. W. Yarrow monaſtery; W. Finchale [o] priory; S. Bi-

[m] Horſley, Durh. II p. 287.

[n] Of which ſee Horſley, Durh xi. xii, p. 289. where the antiquities in theſe three numbers are treated of. Dr. Stukeley had a plate engraved by Sturt of three inſcriptions in Durham library, Horſley's Durh. 13. 15. and North. 55. on which laſt he reads R A E T I C V S.

[o] King's view of this priory in the Monaſticon has nothing to recommend it, but that it exhibits the tower intire. The ſcene of the holy Godric's miracles, who from an itinerant merchant turned hermit and wore out three ſuits of iron clothes, is now the retreat of the ingenious Mr. Spence, being part of his prebendal eſtate. His life by Reginald is in the Bodleian library.

ſhop-

ſhop-Aukland palace ; S. W. Lumley ; S. E. Raby ; W. Barnard ;
E. Ravenſworth; W. Hilton ; S. W. Brancepeth ; and S. E. Norham
caſtles.

In 1753 was publiſhed a perſpective view of the ruins of *Skinkliff*
bridge, near Durham, built by biſhop Skirlaw about 1400, two arches
of which were forced down by a violent flood Feb. 17, 1755, occaſioned by a ſudden thaw and heavy rain the day before.

The *High Force*, a cataract on the Teeſe, falling down a granite
rock twenty-three feet high into a circular baſon, was engraved by J.
Maſſon, 1751, from a painting by T. Smith of Derby.

Saxton's map of this county was engraved by Aug. Ryther 1576,
without the hundreds.

There is an old map of Durham, with the ſeals of the biſhop, count-
palatine, church, and city round it, engraved by Matthew Patteſon in
1595, and dedicated to biſhop Matthews P.

Speed's 1610 has a plan of the city.

T. Kitchen engraved another map for the Britiſh Atlas

P Engliſh Topog. p. 44.

ESSEX.

E S S E X.

A MS. ſurvey of this county by John Norden, in a thin folio, in Sir John Turner's library, is frequently referred to by ſucceeding writers, none of whom tell us where it now is. Mr. James Strangeman of Hadley caſtle [a] had written on the ſame ſubject: Salmon, who made great uſe of his collections though he cites him but twice by name, calls him a good antiquary. The moſt conſiderable progreſs was made by John Ouſely, rector of Pantfield, Springfield-Boſwell, and Little Waltham, in the laſt century and beginning of the preſent, whoſe eminent ſkill in our antiquities is acknowledged by his cotemporaries [b]. He ſpent a conſiderable time in making collections, and received aſſiſtance from ſome of the gentry, but principally from Nicholas Jekyll of Caſtle Hedingham, who juſt before the civil wars amaſſed a great deal of matter for this purpoſe. Ouſely's papers were in the year 1710 in the hands of William Holford, his ſon-in-law and ſucceſſor at Little Waltham, who offered them to Lord Oxford [c], and afterwards communicated them to William Holman, a diſſenting miniſter at Halſted, who ſpent 20 years in a diligent ſearch after every thing curious throughout the county, having made ſeveral journies about it, but publiſhed only the hiſtory of Hinckford hundred [d].

Thomas

---

[a] In Eſſex, not Suffolk, as in Bagford's liſt.

[b] Particularly Gibſon and Newcourt, who were greatly beholden to him.

[c] In a letter to Wanley, now in the Britiſh Muſeum, he ſays, " Jekyll's grandſon claimed " a great many of them :" but adds, " I am certain he is willing to part with them for " a valuable conſideration : he has a very great quantity of them." In another, dated Feb. 7, 170⅚, he acquaints him, that Ouſely being ſecurity to the Stamp-office for a perſon who went off, they had prevented the ſale of them. A catalogue of them is in Cat. MSS. Angliæ, T. II. p. 103.

[d] I have not met with this work, but am well aſſured of its being in print. By a letter of his to the hon. John Morley, eſq; dated Oct. 13, 1713, deſiring to be acquainted with Wanley, and aſſiſted with communications from Lord Oxford's library, it appears he was about this hundred, of which there is a ſcheme MS. Harl. 6677. In one to Wanley June 5, 1722, we find him almoſt deſpairing of carrying on the antiquities of ſo large a county. " If I had foreſeen the difficulty I ſhould not have " undertaken it ; and if it not were for your noble lord and Mr. Morley's kindneſs " I ſhould ſoon be blown up." The ſame year he ſent Lord Oxford two boxes of original

Thomas Jekyll, efq; of Bocking, fecondary in the King's-bench, who fpent great part of his life in the ftudy of antiquities, wrote with his own hand above forty volumes in folio, relating chiefly to Effex, Norfolk, and Suffolk e. From thefe valuable materials Mr. Nicholas Tindal f, vicar of Great Waltham, propofed to compile in 3 volumes 4to. price one guinea each, " The hiftory and antiquities of Effex, " containing, I. Domefday of Effex. II. Hiftory of the manors, and " the families through which they have fucceffively paffed from the " Conqueft to this day. III. Antiquities, ecclefiaftical hiftory, charitable " donations, free-fchools, funeral infcriptions, &c. with an introduction " or general hiftory of the county from J. Cæfar's invafion to the prefent " time," &c. Only two numbers came out as fpecimens, the firft containing the hiftory of Felfted and Pantfield, with a large and exact map of Hinckford hundred ; the fecond the hiftory of Raine, Braintree, Stebbing, and part of Bocking. Mr. Strype, who was vicar of Layton, has accounted for fome of the parifhes within his circuit walk round London. About 1739 were publifhed nineteen numbers of a hiftory of this county, containing the hundreds of Becontree, Waltham, Ongar, Harlow, Uttlesford, Clavering, Frefhwell, Dunmow, Chafford, Barftaple, Rochford, Dengy and Winftree, Havering liberty, and part of Thurftable hundred, by N. Salmon, who left it unfinifhed at his death 1742. This being thought by many too contracted and fuperficial g, the collections above-mentioned, with many others equally valuable by Sam. Dale, Rich. Symons, H. Wanley, Smart Lethieullier, efq; were put into the hands of Philip Morant, rector of St. Mary's, Colchefter, who began to publifh, in folio numbers, " The hiftory and antiquities of the county " of Effex : compiled from the beft and moft ancient hiftorians ; from " Domefday-book, inquifitions poft mortem, and other the moft va-

ginal charters. The laft of his five letters now among Wanley's correfpondencies in the Britifh Mufeum, dated Apr. 10, 1723, gives a fketch of his hiftory of Effex, which he propofed to comprehend in one volume lefs than the Britannia.

e Mr. Tindal promifed an account of them in this parifh, which was not finifhed in his hiftory of Effex. Morant fays not a word about the author or his works.

f Who tranflated and continued Rapin.

g Such as it is I wifh he had lived to finifh it, or that his republifher had made as good ufe of fuch valuable materials as he would have done, and followed his method of inferting the epitaphs in the refpective parifhes, as well as in other particulars.

Y " luable

" luable records and MSS. &c. particularly from the collections, and:
" the great improvements of the late moſt accurate Mr. John Booth ᵇ.
" The whole digeſted, improved, perfected, and brought down to the
" preſent time." The three numbers that compoſe the firſt volume,
dated 1766, contain the hundreds of Chelmsford, Witham, Lexden,
Hinckford, Dunmow, Harlow, Froſhwell, Uttlesford, and Clavering; with maps of each, and views of ſeveral ſeats, &c. ⁱ.

This county was viſited by Harvey 1558; by Cook 1583; by John
Raven, Richmond herald, deputy to Camden, about 1615; by Geo.
Owen, York, and Hen. Lilly, Rouge-roſe, 1634; and by Sir Edward
Byſhe 1664. The funeral monuments were imperfectly collected by
Weever, p. 597—660. The 2d volume of Newcourt's Repertorium,
1710. comprehends its eccleſiaſtical hiſtory.

Mr. Morant publiſhed " The hiſtory and antiquities of *Colcheſter*, in
" three books, collected chiefly from MSS.. with an appendix of records
" and original papers ᵏ. 1748." Fol.

Of the memorable ſiege of this town in 1648 we have accounts in
" A relation of that as honourable and unfortunate expedition of Kent,
" Eſſex, and Colcheſter. 1650." 12mo. and " A true relation of that
" honourable though unfortunate expedition of Kent, Eſſex, and Col-
" cheſter, in 1648. By Matthew Carter, quarter-maſter general in the
" king's forces, and other perſons of repute. Colcheſter printed, and
" ſold by J. Pilborough in High-ſtreet." 12mo. A plan of the town
during the ſiege with a journal thereof, &c. round the ſides was engraved 1648.

A copy of a teſſelated pavement found about three feet under the
ſurface in the garden of Mr. John Barnard, ſurgeon, at Colcheſter.

ᵇ He was many years under ſheriff of the county, and had a tranſcript of its Domeſday: another is among Dodſworth's MSS. a third MS. Harl. 5167.
ⁱ Theſe plates being preſents to the author, it is to be hoped the many curious monuments in the county will not want patrons to tranſmit them to poſterity. Among theſe
may be reckoned the tombs of the Veres, Ratcliffes, and Fitzwalters, at Earl's Colne,
Hedingham, Boreham, and Dunmow, the venerable keep and bridge at Pleſhy, the
priories at Latton, Bileigh, &c. the ſeveral Roman and other entrenchments, of which
only that at Danbury has yet been engraved.
ᵏ Thomas Rawlinſon, eſq; had the original books of the affairs of the corporation of
Colcheſter, from 1638 to 1642, in two volumes, which do not appear to have been
made uſe of in this work.

1763,

1763, drawn by Dunthorn, engraved by Larken, fince inferted in Morant's hiftory of Effex[1].

In p. 287 of N° 255 and p. 677 of N° 266 of the Philofophical Tranfactions is a letter from Thomas Luffkin of Colchefter, concerning an ancient date (1090) in an old window of the market-houfe, confirming Dr. Wallis's opinion, that numeral figures were ufed in Europe long before 1250 or 1300, as Mabillon and Voffius fixed them. This was fupported by a paper inferted in Bibliotheca Literaria 1724, N° viii. p. 7; but retracted in N° x. p. 35. Mr. Ward, in N° 439, p. 120, of the Philofophical Tranfactions, contending for the introduction of Arabic numerals into England after 1333, introduced this date in fupport of his opinion: but afterwards difcovered earlier in Hertfordfhire and Cambridgefhire. Morant, who has given an exact copy of the Colchefter date, and mentions others in the fame place, imagines it was fet down from tradition, or copied from an older date when the houfe was rebuilt.

Colonel Tuke's hiftory of the ordering and generation of green, commonly called Colchefter, oyfters, is inferted in Sprat's Hiftory of the Royal Society, p. 307, and from thence abridged in the Hiftory of Colchefter, B. I. p. 87.

The new charter granted to this town 1763 was printed 1764. 12mo.

There is a good plan of Colchefter at the corner of Speed's map, 1610.

A new and exact plan of this antient borough by Wm. Fidgett, 1724.

Dr. Stukeley engraved a plan of Roman Colchefter, or the track of the Roman walls. One of the prefent town, a S. E. view of the caftle, a N. W. of St. Botolph's priory, and one of St. John's abbey gate, are in Morant's hiftory. The Antiquarian Society publifhed three views and a ground plot of the caftle, in two plates. A N. W. view of the caftle, one of St. John's abbey gate, and a larger S. E. of the town have been engraved by Buck 1738 and 1741.

[1] That beautiful one difcovered 1730 in W. Merfey church yard, in Merfey ifland, was drawn by Dr. Cromwell Mortimer, and Salmon defcribes it, p. 434. It was near 20 feet fquare, but only part of a larger one.

The

The stupendous earth works on *Lexden* heath were surveyed, tho' not so far as they reach, in 1759 by Dr. Stukeley, who takes them for Cunobeline's circus, &c. and had six plates of them engraved by P. Benazech for his intended history of the British kings, viz. a map of the works; three prospective views of K. Cunobeline's circus on the heath; a section of the works of the circus; and the British amphitheatre called K. Coil's kitchen [m]. He had engraved by the same a place of an alate temple on *Navestock* common. described in his Abury, p. 96, and history of Carausius, I. 218.

At the end of Fuller's Church history, Lond. 1665. Fol. we have an history of *Waltham* abbey, wrote by him when curate there, republished in " The history of the antient town and once famous abbey of
" Waltham, from the foundation to the present time : containing
" many curious extracts from records, leger-books, grants, charters, acts
" of parliament, approved authors, and from inscriptions on the monu-
" ments in the church; together with the inquisition taken [17 Char. I.
" 1642] of the perambulation of the forest of Waltham, setting forth
" all and singular the meers, metes, bounds, &c. of the said forest:
" to which is added the history of abbies [n], abridged, from the year
" 977 to their dissolution, and down to the reign of Q. Eliz. illustrated
" with many curious copper-plates [o]. By J. Farmer, of Waltham
" abbey, gent. 1735." 8vo.

The Chartulary or leger-book of this abbey by Rob. Fuller last abbot (so often quoted by his namesake) was in B. Willis's hands 1718. The English Topographer mentions it in the Harleian library. Nº 3739 there is a very fair folio MS. on parchment, intitled Registrum chartarum Waltham; probably one of those mentioned in this

---

[m] He seems to have made the circular entrenchment at Bergholt the capital of Cynobeline, whose tumulus he places E. of the circus, but within the principal banks, and more eastward without them the tomb of Prasutagus. A survey of these works 1722 by Mr. Luffkin and Pailor Smith, esq; who took them for a Roman camp, was printed in Morant's history of Colchester. Morant likewise ascribes them to the Romans, and thinks Birch castle belongs to them. Hist. of Essex, p. 182, and map of Lexden hundred.

[n] From Fuller's Church history.

[o] Among others a piece of Harold's tomb, found in the gardens of the abbey then in the author's possession, and since fixed in a vault supposed to have communicated with Cheshunt nunnery. Another fragment is fixed in the wall of a house in the town.

library

library by Tanner, Not. Mon. p. 119 : the other may be N° 4089. N° 3776 is the life and miracles of its founder. Holman tells Wanley his hiftory of this abbey was pretty large, and that he had taken a great deal of pains with the monumental infcriptions. We certainly have very little fatisfaction from what has yet been printed about it.

A S. E. profpect of the church was publifhed by J. Peak 1758.

The abbey feal is among others engraved by the Antiquarian Society p.

A view of the crofs, drawn by Dr. Stukeley, was engraved at their coft 1721, and in pl. xii. of the Itin. Cur. Another is prefixed to Farmer's Hiftory; and a third, drawn by Peter Tillemans, engraved by J. Harris 1720.

Concerning the foreft there is a 4to fheet, dated May 9, 1665, intitled, " Some reafons and arguments, why the records of the claims " and prefentments made before the late juftice in eyre in the foreft " of Waltham, in the county of Effex, and fome other forefts, now " remaining as publique records in the Tower of London, and pre- " ferved from the fpoyle and ravage of the late times of ufurpa- " tion, ought not to be delivered out of the faid Tower, to the now " lord chief juftice in eyre of all his majefty's forefts, chaces, and " parks, on this fide Trent." A large collection of extracts from records in the Tower and other publick offices, relating to it, was in the poffeffion of Dr. Rawlinfon. In the Harleian library are a MS. treatife concerning Waltham foreft, with copies of leafes made between Fr. Stonard q, of Stapleford-abbot, efq; &c. N° 6705. Articles given in charge to the grand jury at Waltham foreft, concerning foreft laws, A. D. 1634, N° 1634 and 6839. An account of deer in Waltham foreft, given in by the keeper at feveral courts held at Chigwell, 31 Eliz. N° 6853 : 103.

" The hiftory and antiquities of *Harwich* and *Dovercourt*, topogra- " phical, dynaftical, and political; firft collected by S. Taylor, alias " Domville, gent. keeper of the king's ftores there, and now much " enlarged in all its parts with notes and obfervations relating to na-

---

p They have another coat in the 2d edit. of Tanner's Notitia Mon. from Fuller.
q More particulars refpecting his eftates here, Ib. 6850 f. 129. 6853. f. 587.

" tural

" tural hiftory: illuftrated with many copper plates. By Samuel Dale.
" 1730." 4to. reprinted 1732. 4to. with an appendix. In p. 1568
of N° 291 of the Philofophical Tranfactions is Dale's letter to Ed.
Lhuyd about the foffils in Harwich cliff.

Three places in the county claim a fhare in the following piece:
" The honourable 'prentice; or this taylor is a man: fhewed in the life
" and death of Sir John Hawkwood, fometime 'prentice of London;
" interlaced with the famous hiftory of the noble Fitzwalter, lord of
" Woodham in Effex, and of the poifoning of his faire daugh-
" ter: alfo of the merry cuftomes of *Dunmow*, where any one
" may freely have a gammon of bacon that repents not marriage in
" a yeere and a day. Whereunto is annexed the moft lamentable
" murther of Robert Hall at the high altar in Weftminfter abbey."
Hearne[r] had feen two impreffions of this book, one in 1615 and the
other 1616, both printed at London for Henry Goffon, in five fheets
4to[s]. He fays it was written by a curious antiquary; W. V. being at
the end of the dedication to Mr. Robert Valens, perhaps the author
was William Valens; but whoever he was he had certainly fearched
antient records with more than ordinary diligence, and feems to have
been acquainted with the regifters of the Herald's office. Morant in
his account of Sir J. Hawkwood, at Sible Hedingham, takes no notice
of this piece.

A caricatura of the ceremony and proceffion at Dunmow, when
T. Shakefhaft of Weathersfield and his wife had the flitch, June 20,
1751, drawn by David Ogborne of Chelmsford, and engraved by
C. Morley 1752.

A Grub-ftreet account of a fpectre in *Canvey* ifland was publifhed
in 1717. 8vo.

Cafley engraved at the end of his catalogue of the king's library
the charter of Hodelredus, father of Sebba king of the Eaft Angles, to
Barking abbey, from a MS Cott. library, Aug .II. 26. It was before
printed in Edw. IVth's confirmation charter, Mon. Ang. I. 79.

<hr>

[r] Pref. to Leland's Itin. vol. III. p. v.
[s] Among Ames's books, N° 258, is an edition 1743, 4to. dated probably by miftake.

Two

Two stones found in the ruins of this abbey 1720 and 1745 were engraved, I believe at Mr. Lethieullier's charge. On the first, which is circular, is inscribed round a cross, *dñs thomas bewford dux de exceft. an. dñi* M° CCCC° XXX°. On the other, long and smaller,

m̃ harri bewford
mi·¹ ..... wych.

The first is a memorial of Thomas Beaufort duke of Exeter, earl of Dorset, &c. third son of John of Gaunt, and half uncle to Henry IV. who died at Greenwich 5 Hen. VI. [t] and was buried at St. Edmond's-bury: and the other, of his only son Henry, who died young.

" A true report and exact description of a mighty sea monster or
" whale cast upon *Langor* shore, over-against Harwich in Essex, this
" present month of February 1617, with a brief touch of some other
" strange preceding and present occurrents." 4to.

" Strange news from the deep, being a full account of a large prodigious
" whale lately taken in the river *Wivner*, within six miles of Colchester;
" declaring the strange manner of its coming up, and by what means it
" was seized upon by the neighbouring inhabitants, &c. 1677." 4to.

Some poor wretches having been sacrificed to the credulity of the last age in this as in other counties, there was published by authority, 1645,
" A true and exact relation of the several informations, examinations,
" and confessions of the late witches arraigned and executed in the
" county of Essex, who were arraigned and condemned at the late
" sessions holden at Chelmesford, before Robert earl of Warwicke,
" &c. July 29, 1645. Lond. 1745." 4to.

The pamphlet intitled, " Some memorandums of matters of fact
" relating to the original and preliminaries of a suit in Doctors Com-
" mons, between Sir Hugh Everard, baronet, promoter, and John
" Oswald, vicar of *Much Waltham* in Essex. Lond. 1702." 4to. is rather of a private than a local nature. Oswald lost his vicarage by the suit, and was succeeded by the plaintiff's son-in-law.

Concerning the breach at *Dagenham* in the winter 1707, and the manner of stopping it, see " An impartial account of the frauds and

[t] Sandford, p. 263, makes him die 1424, 5 Hen. VI. but the 5th of that king was 1426; p. 296 he puts his death 1428. perhaps this stone fixes it 1430.

5

" abuses

" abufes at Dagenham breach, and the hardfhips fuftained by Mr. Wm.
" Bofwell, late undertaker of the works there : in a letter to a member
" of parliament. Lond. 1717." 8vo   After Bofwell had fpent above
1600 l. on it Capt. J. Perry effected it with a great deal of trouble and
expence, and publifhed " An account of the ftopping of Daggenham
" breach : with the accidents that have attended the fame from the firft
" undertaking : containing alfo proper rules for performing any the
" like work : and propofals for rendering the ports of Dover and Dub-
" lin (which the author has been employed to furvey) commodious
" for entering large fhips.   To which is prefixed a plan of the levels
" which were overflowed by the breach. 1721." 8vo.

" An effay upon *Witham* fpa ; or a brief enquiry into the nature,
" virtues, and ufes of a mineral chalybeate water at Witham in Effex ;
" 1737." 8vo. by James Taverner, M. B. late of Clare-hall, Camb.

" An account of the *Tilbury* water ; containing a narrative of the dif-
" covery of the medicinal qualities of this fpring, experiments on the
" water, obfervations on the experiments ; the vertues of the water,
" interfperfed with various cafes ; the manner of drinking it ; and,
" laftly, feveral remarkable cures. 1742." 8vo. by Dr. John Andree.
The third edition with additions came out 1764.

Robert Winftanley of Walden wrote a fhort poetical defcription of
part of this county, with hiftorical explanatory notes, intitled " Poor
Robin's perambulation from Saffron-walden to London, performed this
month of July 1678. Lond. 1678." 4to.

" A poem on *Knoll's hill,* in Effex, the feat of the hon. Sir John
" Fortefcue Aland, knight, L. L. D. F. R. S. and one of the juftices
" of his majefty's court of common pleas, by R. Barford, A. B. Lond.
" 1745." Fol.   This was formerly the feat of Henry Spencer, the
military bifhop of Norwich ; but the humble poet, difclaiming all
pompous themes, has made no ufe of this circumftance.

In N° 205, p. 970 of the Phil. Tranf. is a letter from Mr. S. Dale
to Mr. John Houghton, about bread made of turnips in a fcarce feafon
1693.   In p. 91 of N° 238 his account of two large eels at Crickfea
and Maldon, the firft 5 feet 8 inches long, and 22 inches round ; the
other 7 feet long, 27 inches round, and 36 pounds weight.   In p. 45

of

of N° 249 a letter from Dr. Derham to Sir Hans Sloane with a regifter of the weather, winds, height of the barometer, and quantity of rain falling at Upminfter 1698. In N°s 262, 288, and 297 are fimilar regifters for 1699, 1700, 1701, 1702, 1703, compared with one kept at Townley in Lancafhire by R. Townley, efq; In N° 298, p. 1917, is Mr. Locke's regifter of weather for 1692 at Oates. In p. 924 of N° 274 is a letter from Mr. Luffkin concerning fome very large bones found in a gravel pit at Wrabnefs, near Colchefter, 1701. Some fuch were difcovered 1763, in a bed of fea fhells at Stanway, and Camden p. 351 mentions others found hereabouts, t. Rich. II. and Eliz. In p. 2411 of N° 310 is an account of a pyramidal appearance in the heavens feen in Effex, Apr. 3, 1707, by Dr. Derham. In p. 140 of N° 316 is Mr. Jof. Nelfon's account of the effects of a ftorm of thunder and lightning at Colchefter, July 16, 1708. In p. 478 of N° 335 are Derham's obfervations concerning fubterraneous trees found near Dagenham, and in other marfhes in this county, and mentioned in Perry's book. In p. 130 of N° 341 his calculation of the quantity of rain fallen there for eighteen years, compared with De la Hire's obfervations at Paris. In N° 399 his account of an aurora borealis feen at Upminfter. In p. 288 of N° 455 an account of an explofion at Halftead, Mar. 12, 1731, by A. Vievar, minifter there: and in p. 289 a relation of the fame explofion at Springfield, by S. Shepheard, efq; In p. 136 of N° 464 Lord Petre's account of lightning at Thorndon. In p. 611 of N° 497 an account of the burning of Danbury fteeple by lightning Feb. 5, 1750, by Smart Lethieullier, efq; who with great probability conjectures that the horrible raging of the devil in the fame fteeple A. D. 1402, mentioned by Walfingham and Weever, was juft fuch an accident. Art. 27 of vol. XLVII. is a letter concerning Mr. Bright, the fat man of Maldon, In p. 198 of vol. LIV. is Dr. Heberden's account of the effects of lightning at S. Weald June 18, 1764.

In the Gentleman's Magazine for Sept. and Oct. 1733, p. 490, is a poem on *Plaiftow*, by J. D. efq; In that for Jan. 1747, p. 46, an account of a phænomenon which happened in digging a well at *High Eftre*. A fingular coin found at *Earle's Colne* is engraved in that for April 1763, p. 156.

Plans,

Plans, elevations, and particular profpects of *Audley-ende* [u], when a royal palace, were engraved by H. Winftanley 1676, in 23 plates, dedicated to James II. The plates are preferved by the defcendants of the earls of Suffolk, but the prints become fo extremely fcarce that Dr. Mead's copy was fold for 50 l.

A view of the hunting tower in the Roman camp near *Littlebury*, and the ichnography of Camboritum *(Chefterford)* make pl. xlv and lix of Stukeley's Itinerarium Curiofum.

The Antiquarian Society have given us three views of the wooden church at *Greenfted*, near Ongar, fuppofed to have been at firft only a temporary refting place for the body of St. Edmund in its way to Bury : and a bell belonging to a nunnery in this county, 1366.

Meffrs. Bucks views 1738 are, W. of St. Ofyth's and Leigh's priories ; S. W. Hedingham and N. of Hadleigh caftles. Another view of Hedingham caftle by R. Fox, with a hiftory of it underneath.

A miferable perfpective view of the town of *Chelmsford*, with the proceffion of the judge, &c. was drawn by David Ogborne, and engraved by Ryland.

A plan for making the river Chelmer navigable, by —— Yoman, 1765.

A N. view of the beautiful church at *Thaxted*, by A. Baldry, was engraved by T. White, at the expence of Lord Maynard and others, 1764, and inferted in Morant's Hiftory, with a particular account of it from the larger collections of Reyner Heckford, efq; of that town.

A map of the coach roads within fix miles of *Harlow*, by Mr. Fifher, apothecary there, was engraved by T. Kitchen 1741.

Saxton's map of this county 1576 has the hundreds. That in Speed's Theatre was made by Norden and augmented by Speed.

Ogilby and Morgan publifhed, a furvey of Effex, with the roads therein exactly meafured, and the arms of the gentry on the borders.

---

[u] Built by Thomas Howard, firft earl of Suffolk of the name, grandfon of chancellor Audley, in the beginning of the laft century, at the charge of 190,000 l. The model in wood made in Italy coft' 500 l: The greateft part of it and the gallery, which was 226 feet long, was taken down by Henry earl of Suffolk and Bindon about fixty years ago.

A new

A new map of Essex by actual survey and dimensuration, with the coats of arms and seats of the nobility and gentry, together with the courses of the several Roman ways, and the stations thereon, the present roads, rivers, rivulets, &c. was published about 1749, by John Warburton, esq; Somerset herald, on two sheets of imperial atlas.

A new and correct map of Essex, Middlesex, and Hertfordshire, with the roads, rivers, sea coasts, &c. actually surveyed by John Warburton, esq; and Jos. Bland and Payler Smith, gent. with the arms of the nobility and gentry on the borders.

A later one by E. Bowen.

GLOUCESTERSHIRE.

JOHN Smith efq; of Nibley left in three folio volumes a full account of the ftrength and ftate of this county, the names of the lords of manors, and the number of all the men in each parifh fit to bear arms: in two other folios the ftate of the militia, and the fums paid to fubfidies temp. Eliz. and James; and in a fourth an account of controverted elections. He alfo drew up a moft elaborate account of Berkeley hundred, where his feat was, in a thick folio, relating the cuftoms of the feveral parifhes and manors, and the pedigree of almoft every tenant, which he was almoft forty years compiling. Atkyns fays the MSS. were in the cuftody of his great grandfon Sir George Smith, who generoufly communicated them to all that defired a perufal of them. He alfo collected the pedigree of the Berkeley family in three large folios, abridged by Dugdale in his baronage, as the beft warranted pedigrees[a]. Judge Hales' collections relative to the antiquities of this county, left by him with his other MSS. to the library of Lincoln's inn, confift only of fome quo warrantos and liberties, with the pleas of the chace of Kingfwood, and a tranfcript of Domefday for this county and Herefordfhire; all contained in two folio volumes. Abel Wantner, freeman of Gloucefter, and inhabitant of Minchin-Hampton, after he had been twelve years collecting materials, chiefly in the heraldical way (though bifhop Nicholfon thought him unequal to the tafk) publifhed propofals for a defcription of the county in 1683, which met with no encouragement. The MS. remained fome time in the hands of Jonathan Colley, M. A. chantor and chaplain of Chriftchurch, Oxford, and was fince fold in Le Neve's library. Some of it was probably incorporated into Atkyns's book. Dr. Richard Parfons, whofe office as chancellor of this diocefe gave him great opportunities for fuch a work, undertook a hiftory of this cathedral and diocefe at the requeft of Mr. Wharton, who was to have publifhed it in another

[a] Atk. Gloc. 579.

volume

volume of his Anglia Sacra. Biſhop Nicholſon [b] ſays he collected two volumes, which were digeſted into ſo good a method that they well deſerved the title of a compleat hiſtory. The firſt was intitled " Me-" moirs of the antient abbey and preſent cathedral of Glouceſter : " the other " A parochial viſitation of the dioceſe." Whatever his plan was, his death, June 12, 1711, put a ſtop to it, as his ill ſtate of health had prevented him from digeſting his collections. The moſt compleat account is Sir Robert Atkyns's " Ancient and preſent " ſtate of Gloſterſhire. Lond. 1712." Fol. publiſhed by his executors. Sir Robert having once conceived the uſe of ſuch a hiſtory thought him-ſelf obliged to carry it on, and purſued it with unremitted attention. Some have imagined there is a larger proportion of merit due elſewhere, than is thought fit to be acknowleged. This large work was very ex-penſive to the undertaker, who printed it in a pompous manner, adorn-ing it with variety of views and proſpects of the ſeats of the gentry and nobility, with their arms ; and he has inſerted ſome which very little deſerve it. It were to be wiſhed that more authorities had been given, and the charters and grants publiſhed in the original language. The tranſcripts of all theſe were collected by Parſons. The value of this work has been greatly raiſed by an accidental fire which deſtroyed moſt of the copies.

The ſame year was printed at Oxford, though but few copies got abroad, a very trifling " Topographical deſcription of Glouceſterſhire, " containing a compendious account of its dimenſions, bounds, air, " ſoil, and commodities, &c." 8vo.

Glouceſter was viſited 1569 by ————— ; 1633 by Chitting and Philpot for Camden.

For ſome famous cuſtoms of this county ſee " Annalia Dubrenſia, " upon the yeerely celebration of Mr. Robert Dover's Olympick " games upon Cotſwold-hills : written by Michael Drayton, eſq; John " Truſſell, gent. William Durham, Oxon. William Denny, eſq; " Thomas Randall, gent. Ben. Johnſon, John Dover, gent. Owen " Feltham, gent. Francis Izod, gent. Nicholas Wallington, Oxon. " John Ballard, Oxon. Timothy Ogle, gent. William Ambroſe, Oxon.

[b] Hiſt. Lib. p. 130.

" William

" William Bellas, gent. Thomas Cole, Oxon. William Baffe, gent.
" Capt. Menefe, John Truffel, gent. William Cole, gent. Ferriman
" Rutter, Oxon. John Stratford, gent. Thomas Sandford, gent. Robert
" Griffin, gent. John Cole, gent. Robert Durham, Oxon. A. Sirinx,
" Oxon. John Monfon, efq; Walton Poole, gent. Richard Wells,
" Oxon. William Forth, efq; Shackerley Marmion, gent. R. N.
" Tho Heywood, gent. Lond. 1636." 4to. Dover was an attorney at
Barton on the heath in Warwickſhire, and being of an active and
public ſpirit obtained leave of James I. to inftitute thefe games, which
he conducted in perfon habited in a fuit of his majefty's old cloaths :
they were reforted to by the nobility and gentry for 60 miles round, and
continued for forty years, even, fays Wood[c], " till the rafcally rebellion
was begun by the prefbyterians." To this book is prefixed a cut reprefenting the various games and fports, dancing and hunting, with a
wooden caftle on a hill, and guns firing ; and the great director Dover
on horfeback.

Andrew Horne, a perfon well fkilled in the hiftory and law of England, who wrote notes on the Mirror of Juftices, on which account
fome have made him author of that book, compiled a Chronicle of the
city of Gloucefter, long fince loft. Dr. Rawlinfon mentions a good
furvey of the cathedral, taken in 1717, by a private hand, which
would make a proper fupplement to Atkyns's account of the church.
There is a defcription of the whifpering place by Mr. Powle, with a
fcheme of it in Birch's Hift. of the Royal Society, i. p. 120. Hearne
publifhed at the end of Robert of Gloucefter's Chronicle, 1724, the
hiftory of the foundation of this abbey, and the changes of the fame
before the fuppreffion thereof in the reign of Hen. VIII. by William
Malverne, abbot there : Harl. MS. 539. f. 111. King and Harris
have engraved S. views of the church.

The behaviour of this city to Charles I. is recorded in " An
" hiftorical relation of the military government of Gloucefter, from
" the beginning of the civil warre betweene King and Parliament, to

[c] Athen. Ox. II. 812. There is a book wrote by Clement Barkfdale, vicar of Haw-
ling in this neighbourhood, called " Nympha Libethris, or the Cotfwold mufe, prefent-
" ing fome extempore verfes to the imitation of young fcholars : in four parts. Lond.
" 1651." 8vo. but it has no relation to Cotfwold or the games, Wood, ibid.

" the

" the removal of Colonel Maffie from that government to the com-
" mand of the Weftern forces: by John Corbet d, preacher of God's
" word. Lond. 1645." 4to. with the Colonel's head prefixed.

Some remarkable paffages may be feen in a collection of " Certain
" fpeeches, made upon the day of the yearly election of officers in the
" city of Gloucefter, being in the charter-language of the faid city,
" die lunæ prox. poft feftum S. Michaelis archangeli. By John Dor-
" ney, efq; town-clerk of the city. Lond. 1653." 12mo.

A plan of Glevum by Dr. Stukeley, an unpublifhed plate.

White Friars and Black Friars at Gloucefter are inferted in his Itin.
Cur. pl. xxii and xxxii. and of the latter, with Lantoni abbey without
the walls, we have a N. view by Buck 1732, and a large N. W. view
of the city 1734.

" Rules for the government of the Infirmary, Glouc. 1755." 12mo.
At the head of the ftate of this infirmary for 1764 is a view and plan
of it engraved by John Cook. Another plate of it will fhortly be publifhed alone by S. Gamidge, bookfeller at Worcefter.

" The cuftomes of the manor of *Painfwick*, in the countie of
" Gloucefter. Lond. 1660." I fuppofe as fettled by act of parliament.
1624 e.

The regifter of *Winchcombe* abbey, wrote by Richard Kedermyn-
fter the laft abbot, contained the hiftory of its foundation, printed in
part in the Monafticon, vol. i. p. 188, with a catalogue of the abbots.
It fell into the hands of judge Moreton, and was confumed in the fire
of London, at his chambers at Serjeant's inn. His lordfhip fhewed
Wood feveral extracts from it by his clerks, but not to be depended
on: and bifhop Fell had a copy of it on vellum or parchment about
1630.

---

d He wrote likewife " A vindication of the magiftrates of the city of Gloucefter from
the calumnies of Robert Bacon, printed in his relation of his ufage there, intitled, The
fpirit of prelacy yet working, or truth from under a cloud. Lond. 1646." 4to. Ath.
Ox. II. 674. Chillingworth at the fiege of Gloucefter advifed making *Teftudines cum
pluteis*, to affault the town in the Roman manner. Rufhworth. Corbet calls him the
jefuitical doctor. He was a zealous royalift, and fell into the hands of as zealous parliamentarians.

e Atkyns's Gloc. 598.

A view

" A view of the antient and prefent ftate of the churches of *Door*,
" *Home-lacy*, and *Hempfted*, endowed by the right hon. John lord
" vifcount Scudamore, with fome memoirs of that antient family; and
" an appendix of records and letters. By Matthew Gibfon, M.A. rector
" of Door. 1727." 4to.

Concerning *Fairford* church fee p. 3 of bifhop Corbet's poems 1672:
and in p. 247 of Roper's life of More is a defcription of the painted windows from a MS. in the hands of Mr. John Murray of Sacombe, a great
collector of fcraps of antiquity; to which are prefixed fome occafional
remarks by the publifher T. Hearne, who thinks it a tranfcript of an old
roll laid there ever fince the foundation of the church, but carried off by
fome light-fingered antiquarian about 1716. His remarks defcribe monuments in Berks, Bucks, and Oxfordfhire. A defcription of thefe
windows in verfe is mentioned to be in Univerfity Poems [f]. A more
particular and correct account of thefe beautiful paintings was faid to
be preparing five years ago, and there certainly wants one. A fmall
view of the S. E. fide of the church, drawn by H. Beighton 1715, was
engraved by T. Harris.

Some defign feems to have been on foot for the honour of *Tewkfbury*
abbey, fome old charters with their feals having been engraved
at the expence of that generous and experienced antiquary Richard
Greaves [g], of Mickleton in Gloucefterfhire, efq; whofe letter to Hearne
concerning *Campden* in this county is publifhed at the end of Langtoft's chronicle. Oxf. 1725. p. ccxiij. N° xx.

An ichnography of the church is in Stevens's Monafticon, I.
513.

The tomb and figures of George duke of Clarence (brother to
Edw. IV.) and his wife Ifabella (daughter of the king-making earl of
Warwick) not exhibited in Sandford, were engraved by S. Wale 1745.
The repofitory of fo many of our antient nobility deferves a further
illuftration.

[f] Life of Wood, p. 532.
[g] Vertue engraved prints of this gentleman, who died 1731; his father Richard,
who died 1669; and his grandfather John, who died 1616, aged 102: alfo the monument of Mrs. Eleanor Greaves, &c.

Buck

Buck has engraved a N. W. view of the abbey 1733, of which King did a wretched N. view.

Lord Gage's " Letter to the gentlemen, clergy, and others, voters " for this borough. Lond. 1753." Fol. is a remonſtrance on an illegal aſſociation to ſell their votes to mend their roads.

At the end of Hearne's edition of Benedictus Abbas, Ox. 1735, p. 751, is " An authentick evidence concerning the relick of the blood " of *Hales*, with proper remarks; ſhewing that by the help of their " evidence the miſtakes of ſeveral hiſtorians might be rectified, and " ſome of the many calumnies that have been thrown upon the reli- " gious houſes detected." Hugh biſhop of Worceſter certifies to Crom- well, on the evidence of the prior of Hales and three more, that they found it to be an " unctuowſe gum colouryd, which beinge in the glaſſe " appeared red like blood, but out of it gliſtering yellow like amber."

A S. view of this abbey by Buck 1733.

" A true and perfect account of the examination, confeſſion, trial, " condemnation, and execution of Joan Perry, and her two ſons, John " and Richard Perry, for the ſuppoſed murder of William Harriſon, " gent. being one of the moſt remarkable occurrences which hath hap- " pened in the memory of man, ſent in a letter by Sir T. O. [Thomas " Overbury] of Burton, in the county of Glouceſter, knight, to T. S. " [Thomas Shirley] doctor of phyſick, in London. Likewiſe Mr. Har- " riſon's own account how he was conveyed into Turkey, and there " made a ſlave for above two years, and then his maſter which brought " him there dying, how he made his eſcape, and what hardſhips he en- " dured: who, at laſt, through the providence of God, returned to " England, while he was ſuppoſed to be murdered: here having been " his man ſervant arraigned, who falſly impeached his own mother and " brother as guilty of the murder of his maſter: they were all three " arraigned, convicted, and executed on Broadway hills in Glouceſter- " ſhire. Lond. 1676." 4to. reprinted in the Harl. Miſc. vol. iii. p. 519. and ſince in 8vo. ſans date. John Perry the ſervant was thought to have been out of his ſenſes; his mother and brother denied the fact to the laſt, the wiſe judge cauſing the old woman to ſuffer firſt, in compli- ance with the vulgar prejudice that by her ſkill in witchcraft ſhe pre- vented her ſons from confeſſing. Harriſon's tranſportation is ſuppoſed

A a

to have been brought about by his eldeſt ſon, who might ſuſpect the ruffians had killed him, and ſo proſecute the innocent to prevent diſcovery. He ſucceeded his father both in his eſtate and place as ſteward to lord Campden at Campden, and by his miſbehaviour in it increaſed the ſuſpicion againſt him.

" A candid enquiry concerning the benefactions of the late Mrs. " Rebecca Powell, in favour of the town of Cirenceſter. By a native of " the place. Lond 1765." 8vo.

" The *Cirenceſter* Conteſt. Lond. 1753." 8vo. is a collection of letters, papers, verſes, ſongs, &c. relative to a conteſted election there.

" An experimental diſſertation on the nature, contents, and virtues " of the *Hyde* ſpaw, near Cheltenham in Glouceſterſhire. By Diede- " rick Weſſel Linden. Lond. 1751," 8vo. In Nº 461 of the Philoſo- phical Tranſactions is an examination of the Cheltenham waters, by C. H. Senckenberg.

A deſcription of the *Severn* and its navigation by Mr. G. Perry is in the Gentleman's Magazine, June 1758, p. 277; and in Birch's Hiſtory of the Royal Society, vol. iii. p. 122, is part of a letter from Mr. Caſwell to Mr. Flamſtead, mentioning his having taken the fall of the Severn three yards and three inches in five miles.

" A ſtrange and wonderful diſcovery of houſes under ground at " *Cotton's Field* in Glouceſterſhire." ſans date.

" The laws and cuſtoms of the miners in the foreſt of *Dean*," were printed 1687. 12mo. Dr. Rawlinſon had in MS. the " Proceedings at large of a juſtice ſeat for the foreſt of Deane, holden at Michel- Deane within the foreſt, 10 Julii, 10 Car. 1634, and adjourned from thence to Glouceſter caſtle, and there continued until xviij° Julii, and then adjourned de die in diem." 4to. There is another copy among the Harl. MSS. 738, p. 23. MS. Harl. 4849 is a book of preſent- ments and laws relating to this foreſt: and 6939 : 65. copy of a return of a commiſſion concerning it Apr. 12, 1662.

In p. 931 of Nº 137 of the Phil. Tranſ. is an account of the iron- works in this foreſt, by Henry Powle, eſq; In p. 1 of Nº 143 is a defcription and draught of *Pen-park-hole*, by Sir Robert Southwell. In p. 279 of Nº 243 Ed. Lluyd's account of ftones in this county.

In the Gentleman's Magazine, Feb. 1762, p. 54, is an account of a large old chefnut tree at *Tortfworth*, engraved in that for July 1766, with a defcription of it by Mr. P. Collifon.

Jofeph Trapp, fellow of Wadham and poetry profeffor at Oxford, wrote " Ædes *Badmintonianæ*: a poem, moft humbly prefented to " his grace Henry duke of Beaufort, &c. and to her grace Mary " dutchefs-dowager of Beaufort, &c. upon their magnificent and de- " lightful feat in Gloucefterfhire. Lond. 1701." Folio.

To the 3d edition of Mr. Chandler's poem on Bath, 1736, 8vo. are annexed fome verfes addreffed to Mrs. Jacob on her feat called *the Rocks*, in Gloucefterfhire.

Buck engraved 1733,
  S. W. view of Malmefbury abbey,
  S. E. Lacocke nunnery [h],
  N. Bradenftoke priory,
  S. E. Berkeley ⎫
  E. St. Briavel's ⎪
  S. Thornbury ⎪
  S. W. Sudley ⎬ caftles.
  N. Beverfton ⎪
  S. E. Wardour ⎭

Mr. Walpole [i] fays that Henry Gravelot, a faithful copier of antient buildings, tombs, and profpects, was for fome time employed in draw-ing churches and antiquities in this county. If he engraved any it has not been my good fortune to meet with them.

Gloceftriæ five Claudioceftriæ comitatus (Claudii Cæfaris nomine ad-huc celebrati) verus typus, by Saxton, 1577, engraved by A. Ryther, without the hundreds, which are in Speed's map, with plans of Glou-cefter and Briftol at the corners. That in Atkyns' book feems to be the work of H. Moll. Another including Monmouthfhire for the Britifh Atlas is anonymous.

[h] The moft intire in England.
[i] Catal. of engravers, p. 124.

    HAMP-

HAMPSHIRE.

I know of no general defcriptions of this county except Vifitations by T. Benolt, Clarencieux, 1530 or 1561; by Cook 1576; by Philpot 1622. A copy of Domefday MS. Harl. 1904.

Tho Rudburn, monk at *Winchefter* in the middle of the fifteenth century, wrote a hiftory of the affairs of that city from Lucius to Hen. 6. and an abftract or outline of it. Wharton publifhed the firft from two imperfect copies in his Anglia Sacra, I. 181, and part of the latter. Ib. 179. 285. Wood fays [a] that Truffel the hiftorian, who was alderman of Winchefter, continued to bifhop Curll's time, 1632, an old MS. hiftory of the fees and bifhops in the cathedral library. He alfo wrote, " A defcription of the city of Winchefter; with an hiftorical relation " of divers memorable occurrences touching the fame;" and prefixed to it, " a preamble of the original of cities in general." Bifhop Nichol-fon guefles it was too voluminous, and bifhop Kennet too imperfect to be publifhed. The former mentions fomething on the fame fubject by Dr. Bettes, whofe book is ftill in MS. Mr. Butler of St. Edmonds-bury made obfervations on the ancient monuments of this city under the Romans. T. Rawlinfon, efq; had a MS. terrier on vellum made 1408 intitled, " Terra regis in civitate Winton."

" The hiftory and antiquities of the cathedral church of Winchefter,
" containing all the infcriptions upon the tombs and monuments:
" with an account of the bifhops, priors, deans, and prebendaries;
" alfo the hiftory of Hyde abbey, begun by the right hon. Henry late
" earl of Clarendon, and continued to this time by Samuel Gale, gent.
" Lond. 1715." 8vo. Gale, who was only the editor, was largely affifted by Cranley, regifter of this church, who fupplied the Claren-donian MS. with a continuation of the monumental infcriptions, and feries of the dignitaries; and B. Willis furnifhed the account of the priory and Hyde abbey. The learned editor added an hiftorical introduction

[a] Ath. Ox. I. 448.

concerning

concerning the antient and prefent ftate of this church, the lands given to it, and the fale of them in the civil wars, and adorned the whole with feveral views of the church and monuments drawn by C. Woodfield, engraved by Vandergucht. Gale's original MS. was fold among Dr. Stukeley's books.

The MS. leger-book of *St. Crofs*'s hofpital, which was in the hands of Henry Worfely, efq; of Lincoln's Inn, 1694, is now among the Harleian MSS.

About fix years ago Mr. Wharton publifhed a very ufeful fhort " Defcription of the city, college, and cathedral of Winchefter, ex- " hibiting a complete and comprehenfive detail of the antiquities and " prefent ftate: the whole illuftrated with feveral curious and authen- " tic particulars collected from a MS. of Anthony Wood [b], preferved " in the Afhmolean mufeum [c] at Oxford, the college and cathedral " regifters, and other original authorities never before publifhed."

A catalogue of MSS. belonging to the cathedral is in the Cat. MSS. Ang. tom. II. p. 30.

Of the crofs we have a print by the Antiquarian Society.

An E. view of the palace by Buck 1733.

An E. view of the city, 1736, is among Buck's large views; and another in Stukeley's Itin. Cur. pl. 88. A S. W. view by E. Kirkall, in Stevens's Monafticon, I. 217. A view of the cathedral by King from Newcomb.

There is a map of the city by Wm. Godfon, 1750, with views of the king's houfe, the county hall, guild hall, market crofs, St. Mary's college, the college for minifters widows, the bifhop's palace, N. fide of the cathedral, St. John's houfe, and thofe of Edw. Sheldon, efq; Mr. Townfend, Wm. Prefcot the recorder, and Mr. Penton.

In 1715 propofals were publifhed for a hiftory and antiquities of St. Mary's college, and large collections were made for that purpofe. At the end of fome Latin poems by Richard Willey, addreffed to Sir Wm. Burghley. Lond. 1573. 8vo. is the life of the founder by Dr. Chr. Johnfon, phyfician at Winchefter, and head-mafter of the fchool,

[b] Who vifited this college 1684.
[c] N° 8518.

and

and a series of the wardens and schoolmasters in Latin verse [d]. Other lives of this eminent prelate have been written in Regiſtrum Wykeham, MS. in two large folio volumes at Wincheſter in the chancellor's regiſter's office. " Libellus ſeu tractatus de proſapia, vita & " geſtis venerabilis dom. W. Wykeham nuper epiſcopi Winton. editus " A. D. MCCCCXXIV. qui fuit annus XX poſt obitum ejuſdem patris, " & regni regis Hen. VI. ſecundus." Dr. Lowth aſcribes this MS. which is alſo at Wincheſter, to Rob. Heete, fellow of Wincheſter college 1420, who died 1432. A manuſcript in New college library contains " Brevis cronica de ortu, vita & geſtis nobilibus rev. domini " W. de Wykeham, olim epi. Winton;" and " Collocutiones de lauda- " bili vita & moribus, & chriſtiana perfectione W. de Wykeham; [e] auc- " tore Thoma Chaundeler, utriuſq; collegii cuſtode, dein Oxon. poſtea " Wellenſi cancellario." The firſt has been publiſhed by Wharton in the 2d vol. of his Anglia Sacra, p. 351. who by miſtake aſcribes it to Chaundeler, as does alſo Tanner, B.B. p. 171. Dr. T. Martin, [f] chancellor of this dioceſe under biſhop Gardiner, wrote another life in Latin, printed in 1597. 4to. ſeveral years after the author's death; reprinted at Oxford 1690. 4to. without any correction or improvements, by Dr. Nicholas, warden of New college, intitled " Hiſtorica deſcriptio, complectens vitam " ac res geſtas beatiſſimi viri Gul. Wicami, quondam Vintonienſis epiſ-

---

[d] Printed firſt on a broad ſheet with Wykeham's arms in the garter 1564, and again at the end of Sir John Harrington's Brief view of the ſtate of the church of England, &c. Lond. 1653. 8vo. Ath. Ox. I. 289.

[e] In the Cotton MS. Tit. A. xiv. whence Wharton publiſhed them, they have not the form of dialogues, tho' the title is, " Collocutiones 7 de laudibus W. de Wyckham fun- " datoris ducentorum clericorum," addreſſed to Beckington bp of Wells, whoſe praiſes make up the firſt book. Leland ſaw in the library at Wells, " Joannis" (it ſhould be Thomæ) " Chaundelarii cancellarii Wellenſis opuſcula continentia laudes & celebria facta " epiſcopi Wycham." Collect. iv. 156.

[f] There is a copy of this book in New college library, and in a leaf before the title are curiouſly delineated with a pen the effigies of Wykeham ſitting in a chair, with Chicheley, founder of All Souls, on his right, and Waynfleet, founder of Magdalen, on his left hand, holding the pictures of their reſpective colleges, and preſenting them to him, in whoſe college they were educated. Ath. Ox. I. 219. Among Dr. Plott's MSS. 2896, is a letter to Dr. Wm. Muſgrave, fellow of New Col. giving an account of divers alterations and additions that might be made in this life of the founder.

" copi

" copi & Angliæ cancellarii, & fundatoris duorum collegiorum Ox-
" oniæ & Wintoniæ." The poetical life above-mentioned was prefixed
to this, of which Thorefby had a MS. wrote, as he thought, about
1597, which might be the original. He bought it with an old MS.
of the ftatutes of New college out of the library of one of the fellows.
Peck publifhed his will from a MS. of Sir P. Thompfon's in the appendix to his life of O. Cromwell, N° II. All thefe feveral accounts
were inferted in that judicious, compleat and learned " Life of
" Wykeham, bifhop of Winchefter. Collected from records, regifters,
" manufcripts, and other authentic evidences. By Robert Lowth, D.D.
" prebendary of Durham, and chaplain in ordinary to his majefty.
" Lond. 1758." 8vo. A poem on the genealogy of Chrift, as it is
reprefented on the eaft window of Winchefter college chapel, written
at Winton fchool, by the fame elegant writer, is inferted in The
Union or felect Scots and Englifh poems. Edinb. 1753. 12mo. p.
13—23.

The prayers ufed by the poor children of this foundation are prefixed to a piece printed for the ufe of this fchool, intitled, " I. Preces.
" II. Grammaticalia quædam. III. Rhetorica brevis. IV. Antiquæ
" hiftoriæ fynopfis. Oxon. 1616." 4to. all drawn up by Dr. Hugh
Robinfon, mafter of the fchool in the beginning of the laft century,
and author of the Winchefter phrafe book.

" A manual of prayers for the ufe of the fcholars of Winchefter
" college, and all other devout chriftians. Lond. 1681." 12mo. By
bifhop Ken, when fellow there.

A catalogue of MSS. in the library compiled by Mr. Eyres, is in
the Cat. MSS. Angliæ, tom. II. p. 31.

For fome difputes relative to elections fee " An account of Mr. Har-
" ris's election at Winchefter college, laft May, in a letter to a perfon of
" quality in London, dated New college, Oxon. Jan. 12, 170$\frac{4}{5}$." 4to.

" The plea of the fellows of Winchefter college againft the bifhop
" of Winchefter's local and final vifitatorial power over the faid
" college. Lond. 1711." 4to. In the appendix are accounts of Bp.
Wainfleete's vifitation 19 Sept. 1449. Abp. Cranmer's 16 June, 1535.
Bancroft's 11 Jan. 160$\frac{2}{1}$, Laud's 16 July, 1635.

A fhort

" A short address to the society of New college in Oxford, occafioned by a paragraph in a late dedication. Lond. 1758." 8vo.   This with the following relates to another contested election, and ridicules the dedication of Dr. Lowth's life of Wykeham.

" A letter to the rev. Dr. Lowth, prebendary of Durham, in vindi-
" cation of the conduct of the fellows of New college in Oxford, in
" their late election of a warden of Winchester. Lond. 1758." 8vo.

" A defence of the warden of Winchester college, in accepting of
" that wardenship, occasioned by a letter to Dr. Lowth, and written
" by himself. Lond. 1758." 8vo.

" An answer to the anonymous letter to Dr. Lowth, concerning the
" late election of a warden of Winchester college. Lond. 1759." 8vo.

" The law and equity of a late appointment of a warden of Win-
" chester confidered. Lond. 1759." 8vo.

" A defence of the conduct of the warden of Winchester college in
" accepting that wardenship: the 2d edition corrected. Lond. 1759."
8vo.

" A reply to Dr. Golding and Dr. Lowth's answers to the anonymous
" letter. By a Wykehamist. Lond. 1759." 8vo.

" An impartial review of the controversy concerning the warden-
" ship of Winchester college.   Lond. 1759." 8vo.

There is a print of the grotesque emblematical figure in the kitchen. Toms engraved a view and ichnography of the college.

John Speed, M D. of St. John's college, Oxford, and son of the historian, wrote " Batt upon Batt: a poem upon the parts, patience, and
" pains of Barth. Kempster, clerk, poet, and cutler of Holy-rood
" parish, in *Southampton* : by a person of quality.   To which is an-
" nexed the Vision, wherein is described Batt's person and ingenuity ;
" with an account of the ancient and present state and glory of South-
" ampton ; by the same author.   Dedicated to the gentry of Hamp-
" shire, for their diversion, but more especially to the inhabitants of
" Southampton."   The first editions were in 4to. but the fifth and last Lond. 1706. 8vo.   Wood says, both these were esteemed very ingenious things [h].

[h] Ath. Ox. II. 1083.

A prospect

A profpect of Traufantum or Southampton, from the eaft, makes the lxxixth plate of Stukeley's Itin. Cur.

" The cafe, or an abftract of the cuftoms of the mannor of *Merdon*,
" in the parifh of Hurfely in the county of Southampton, which are
" to be obferved and performed by the lord and the cuftomary tenants
" of the faid mannor, their heirs and fucceffors for ever, as they were
" taken out of a decree made and enrolled in the hon. court of chancery,
" for ratifying and confirming the fame cuftoms. Together with fome
" remarkable paffages, fuits at law, and in equity, and the great dif-
" ferences and expences therein. By Matthew Imber, gent. Lond.
" 1707." 8vo. Printed for private ufe.

We might probably have feen in print a good account of the ancient Vindomis, or *Silchefter*, had not an unfortunate death [i] overtaken the learned Mr. Robert Betham, formerly of St. John's college, Cambridge, and by that fociety prefented to this rectory, where he had frequent opportunities of confidering the various Roman remains, and of collecting a large number of medals on the fpot. It is faid he had made fome progrefs in digefting his collections. Hearne, who frequently vifited thefe parts, could alfo have given the world fome conjectures. Dr. Stukeley gave a defcription and plan of it in his Itinerarium Curiofum, p. 169. pl. lxi. a fide view of the amphitheatre was among his unpublifhed plates: but the learned profeffor Ward gave the moft particular account of this place in N° 490 of the Philofophical Tranfactions, illuftrated with a plan: and in p. 200 of N° 474 an explanation of a Roman infcription here.

Sir Francis Knollys, who died in 1596, drew up a defcription of the ifle of *Wight*, and a fair copy of it was fold amongft the late earl of Anglefea's books. An account of its antiquities was attempted by Dr. Richard James [k], who was excellently qualified for fuch a work. His MS. is preferved in the Bodleian library, N° IX. confifting of feventeen 4to pages, which Wood fays is but a fpecimen or foundation for a larger work. In the preface to this imperfect piece he fays, " Primo,

[i] He was drowned in Fleet ditch.

[k] A diligent and fkilful antiquary, nephew to Tho. James, firft keeper of the Bodleian library. He died at Sir Thomas Cotton's at Weftminfter, 1638.

[j] Ath. Ox. I. 617.

" ex quibufdam libris & hiftoriis antiquis ea excerpo, quæ ullo modo
" ad infulam, aut infulanos fpectent: Secundo, ftatuo omnes archivas
" infulæ explorare diligenter, & fi quid ex privatis chartis aut inftru-
" mentis generoforum ibi habitantium poterit illuc conducere: Tertio,
" dabo topographiam exactam totius infulæ, cum rivulis, vicis, & civi-
" tatibus: Quarto, quicquid peregrinum in natura illic vifitur latere
" ulterius non finam ; Quinto, dabo anthropologiam Vectenfium, qui
" aut literis, aut armis, aut alia gratia ibi aliquandiu floruerint. Deus
" faveat cæptis."

" Vectis, or the ifle of Wight, a poem in three cantos, by Henry
" Jones. Lond. 1766." 4to.

In N° 450 of the Philofophical Tranfactions, p. 379, is an account
of a damp in a well here.

In the Gentleman's Magazine, April 1757, p. 176, we have an account and print of *St. Catharine*'s tower, part of an hermitage founded
before 1312, now a lighthoufe [m]: and in that for Dec. 1760, p. 522,
an account and view of *Carifbrook* caftle, of which Buck engraved a
N. view 1733. The entrance and an infide view, painted by A. Me-
nagett, were engraved by J. Hulett, 1755. Three profpects of Hurft
and Portchefter, and the W. fide of Cowes caftle, by Hollar, after
F. Place. An E. view of Hurft, S. of Calfhot, W. of Cowes caftles, by
Buck 1733. I have a print of *Appledorecome*, the feat of Sir Robert
Worfley, as it was rebuilt 1710. There is a map of the ifland by William White, gent in Speed's theatre. Mr. Taylor has publifhed a neat
little one, diftinct from that in his furvey of the county.

Prefixed to Hearne's edition of Langtoft's Chronicle, Ox. 1725, p. cci.
is an extract of a letter from the rev. Mr. Richard Furney of Winchefter
to the editor, about the election of an abbefs of *Rumfey*, A. D. 1333,
confirming an affertion in this Chronicle that K. Edgar founded it for
100 nuns; and p. cciii. N° 18, another letter from the fame, concerning the number of nuns there in 1523, being only thirteen. Buck
engraved a N. E. view of this nunnery 1733.

---

[m] It feems to have been the tower of a church or chapel, and is Tanner's hermitage,
on Chale hill. Not. Mon. p. 170.

" News from *Basingstoke* of one Mrs. Blunden, a malster's wife,
" who was twice buried alive: for which neglect several persons were
" indicted at the last assizes held at Winchester, and the town of
" Basingstoke compelled to pay a great fine :" an undated pamphlet.

" The history of the brotherhood or guild of the Holy Ghost, in
" the chapel of the Holy Ghost near Basingstoke in Hampshire, dis-
" solved by K. Edward VI. and re-established by K. Philip and Q
" Mary; wherein is contained the history and antiquities of Holy
" Ghost chapel near Basingstoke, and an enquiry into the patronage of
" that chapel: with an account of another religious house founded at
" the same place by King Henry III. [By Samuel Loggon.] Reading
" 1742." 8vo.

" *Portsmouth:* a descriptive poem: by R. Maxwell. 1755." 4to.

Hollar engraved Portsmouth in prospect, and over to the isle of
Wight. We have a W. view of Portsmouth by Buck 1749; others
in Stukeley's Itinerary, pl. lxxx. and lxxxii. A geometrical plan and
W. elevation of his majesty's dock yard at Portsmouth, with part of
the common, by T. Milton. 1754.

A view of the fleet at Spithead July 25, 1744, from Stone common,
near Exbury, distant upwards of three leagues, by T. W. engraved
by Fourdrinier.

To this place belongs " The borough; being a faithful though hu-
" morous description of one of the strongest garrison and sea port towns
" in Great Britain; with an account of the temper and commerce of
" the inhabitants: left by a native of the place, who was lost in the
" Victory man of war, and now published for the benefit of the gen-
" tlemen of the navy, and the entertainment of the rest of mankind,
" by Robert Wilkins."

A description and print of the royal hospital for sick and wounded
seamen at *Gosport* is in the Gentleman's Magazine for Sept. 1751, p. 400.

In p. 1212 of N° 177 of the Philosophical Transactions is an account
of some remarkable effects of a great storm of thunder and lightning
at Portsmouth, Oct. 23, 1685. In p. 652 of N° 459 an antient date
in Arabic figures on the N. front of *Rumsey* church, communicated
by the rev. Mr. William Barlow. This date Mr. Wray in the same

number

number fays he could not find, but only fome characters in a wooden model of a window in a ftable; which characters Mr. Ward, N° 474, p. 79, took for the names of Jefus and John. In p. 273 of N° 475 are obfervations on two antient camps in this county near *Buckland* caftle, or the rings, by Mr. Wright.

Mr. Richards of Jefus College Oxford, wrote a burlefque poem, in anfwer to the Mufcipula, intitled " Hoglandia, or a defcription of Hamp-" fhire; a mock heroic poem, &c." with an Englifh tranflation, 1728. 8vo.

" *Stokes bay*, a poem." By Mr. Gafelee, late of Gofport, is in the Gentleman's Magazine for May 1739.

" Scapin triumphant, or a journey to Petersfield and Portfmouth. " By Wm. Rover. Lond. 1757." 4to.

" The ruins of *Nettley* abbey. By Geo. Keate, efq; Lond. 1764." 4to. who exhibited feveral neat views of it at Spring-gardens 1766. A N. view by Buck 1733. Another painted by Wm. Bellers, and engraved by Toms and Mafon 1755.

" *Mons Catharinæ* prope Wintonam carmen. Lond. 1760." 4to. at-tempted in Englifh in the Gentleman's Magazine, Nov. 1762, p. 544 ⁿ.

" Verfes on a view of the environs of the E. of Portfmouth's fine feat " at *Downe Hufbourne*, in Hants, infcribed to lord Lymington, by " Hannah Purver," were inferted in that for Sept. 1759, p. 431.

" *Hackwood park*, a poem, Lond. 1766." 4to. A S. E. view of the houfe, painted by P. Sandby, was exhibited at Spring-gardens 1764.

A profpect and plan of *Farnham* [Caleva Atrebatum] 1723, by Dr. Stukeley, an unpublifhed plate.

Other views in this county by Buck, 1733, are, S. E. Tychfield abbey; N. W. Portchefter caftle. Another view of the laft was en-graved in 1763 by James Peake, from a drawing taken on the fpot by an officer.

A view of *Pilewell*, the feat of Sir Thomas Worfley, by Rocque.

A view of *Langfton* harbour, near Havant in Hampfhire, at funfet, engraved by J. Mafon, after a drawing by William Bellers 1763.

ⁿ To this hill, which formerly had a chapel of St. Catherine and a Danifh circumval-lation, the fcholars refort on holidays.

Southamptoniæ comitatus (præter infulas Vectis, Jerfey, & Garn-fey, quæ funt partes ejufdem comitatus) cum fuis undique confinibus, oppidis, pagis, villis, & fluminibus vera defcriptio, by Saxton, engraved by Leonard Tervoort of Antwerp, has neither date nor hundreds. The latter are fupplied in Speed's map, with a plan of Winchefter.

Another was publifhed by T. Kitchen, 1753, for the Britifh Atlas.

Ifaac Taylor engraved an accurate furvey of this county 1759, in fix fheets, with views of the Needles, Calfhot caftle, Netley abbey, Carefbrook and Portchefter caftels; a S. and another view of Silchefter walls, a plan of Silchefter as it now appears, with the outworks, and a view of the amphitheatre.

HEREFORD-

HEREFORDSHIRE.

NO perſon has yet given a general hiſtory of this county. Silas Taylor left large materials, which his rank in the parliament's army in the civil war enabled him to collect and preſerve from the plundered libraries of this and Worceſter cathedral, 1645. As his mild exertion of his ſequeſtring power in this part of the country procured him the eſteem of the Royaliſts at that time, and the king's favour at the reſtoration. Dr. Rawlinſon underſtood they were depoſited in lord Oxford's library, and part of his hiſtory of Herefordſhire is mentioned at the end of MS. Harl. 6766, and extracts from Domeſday N° 6856. But Dale when he publiſhed the hiſtory of Harwich from Taylor's papers, 1730, ſpeaks of theſe collections as being *lately*, if not *now*, in the hands of Sir Edw. Harley of Brompton Brian ͣ, grandfather of the firſt earl of Oxford. He was upwards of four years collecting various antiquities, arms, inſcriptions, &c. throughout the county. Perhaps they were peruſed by the learned William Brome, eſq; of Ewithington in this county, who is ſaid to have made a large and judicious collection to do honour to his native country ᵇ. N° 6868 of the Harleian MSS. is a thin quarto, containing the names of the pariſhes in all the hundreds of Herefordſhire, with collections and materials for compiling a hiſtory of it. 'Tis very ſhort, ſomewhat in Norden's method, but not alphabetical, and gives the arms and epitaphs in ſome churches. N° 6726 contains an account of ſeveral

---

ͣ When the parliament's forces 1643 ſacked and burnt this caſtle (the ſeat of the Harleys ever ſince Edw. I.) a very valuable library of books and MSS. collected through many deſcents of a family who united the ſtudy of letters with the exerciſe of arms, periſhed in the flames. Lady Brilliana, ſecond daughter of lord viſcount Conway, third wife of Sir Robert, and mother of Sir Edward Harley above-mentioned, obliged a powerful army to raiſe a ſeven weeks ſiege, which nothing but her death ſoon after encouraged them to renew. The counteſs of Derby rivalled her valour in an eighteen weeks defence of Latham houſe the year after.

ᵇ Hearne, p. 11. of his dedication to Leland's Collectanea, ſpeaks of him as " Vir " utique harum rerum, ut & politioris literaturæ, peritiſſimus, & à quo agri Herefordenſis " deſcriptionem accuratiſſimam expectare debemus, ſi modo ne in lucem proferatur, non " obſtet modeſtia."

hundreds,

hundreds, tenures of lands, foundations of churches, and statutes of the cathedral in the same hand. But all the labours of Brome and others were swallowed up in large proposals published in 1717, by Mr. James Hill of the Middle Temple, for a history of the city of Hereford, to contain an exact and regular account of it from its most early age to his time, divided into two parts; the first treating of its ecclesiastical, the second of its civil state; the plan of which is inserted in the English Topographer, p. 71.

The county was visited 1569 by Cooke; by other heralds 1619 and 1634.

N° 4046 of the Harleian MSS. treats of the city of Hereford, and has some loose leaves relating to the county. N° 4056 has arms of Herefordshire families, and a history of the bishops to 1602.

A N. E. view of this city has been published by Buck, 1732. A plan of it by Isaac Taylor, engraved by R. Benning 1757, with views of an antient chapel adjoining to the bishop's palace (published also by the Antiquarian Society 1738, but since pulled down); a view of the cathedral, White-friars cross, and that in Lady Arbor, St. Peter's, St. Nicholas, and All Saints churches, the town-hall, a view of the cathedral, palace, and part of the town, and a general view from Broomy hill.

" The history and antiquities of the city and cathedral church of
" Hereford: containing an account of all the inscriptions, epitaphs,
" &c. upon the tombs, monuments, and grave-stones: with lists of
" the principal dignitaries; and an appendix consisting of several
" valuable original papers" was published. Lond. 1717. 8vo. Among other papers are the obits of several benefactors to this cathedral transcribed from a folio Missal secundum usum Hereford in Hearne's possession [c], wrote about the reign of Edw. III. printed on vellum 1502. The work is concluded with 71 charters, or grants of land to this church, from Bodleian MSS. Some years after it came out it was attacked in a most ungenerous manner by a member of this church in a very warm and angry preface to a sermon preached in Landaff cathedral, fathering it on B. Willis, with some uncharitable reflections,

[c] He published from it in the appendix to the history of Glastonbury, N° XV. p. 309—325. the form of matrimony, which was then celebrated at the church-door.

which

which were anſwered in Willis's account of this church in his ſurvey
of the cathedrals, &c. 1727. p. 500. where he diſclaims all concern in
the book.   He refers to a weſt proſpect of the church taken by a
gentleman, who had engraved ſeveral of the monuments, and promiſed draughts of all the tombs, arms, and every thing curious in it.
Dr. Rawlinſon mentions a collection of the monuments by Mr. Dingley
1680, which has preſerved ſome inſcriptions now loſt, but is moſt
remarkable for its fine drawings.   King engraved the N. ſide, Harris
the N. and W. and Vertue the ſeals of the dean and chapter, and of
the biſhops Benet and Coke.   In the Bodleian library, among Jones's
MSS. Nº XXI. is a folio on vellum, intitled " Inquiſitiones & literæ
" patentes ad eccleſiam Herefordenſem pertinentes:" depoſited there
ſince the publication of Bernard's catalogue, in which the MSS. here
are inſerted tom. II. p. 43. MS. Harl. 4343. contains Statuta eccleſiæ
Heref. & hoſp. S. Ethelberti, and Nº 6233 charters from the old regiſter, Nº 7519 collections from Domeſday and other records, relative
to this county and parts adjacent, by Dr. Matthew Hutton.

 " The life of James Parry, late organiſt at *Roſs* in Herefordſhire.—
" 12mo."

 " A moſt ſtraunge and true diſcourſe of the wonderfull judgment
" of God, of a monſtrous deformed infant begotten by inceſtuous
" copulation between the brother's ſonne and the ſiſter's daughter,
" both being unmarried perſons, which childe was borne at *Colwall,*
" in the countie and dioceſſe of Hereford, upon the 6th daye of Janu-
" arie laſt, being the feaſte of Epiphanie, commonly called Twelfth-
" day, 1599.   A notable and moſt terrible example againſt inceſt
" and whoredome, 1600." 4to.

 " The late commotions of certain papiſts in Herefordſhire, occa-
" ſioned by the death of one Alice Wellington, a recuſant, who was
" buried after the Popiſh manner in the town of *Allens Moore* near
" Hereford, upon Tueſday in Whitſun week laſt paſt. London 1605."
4to.

 " A ſhort narrative of the diſcovery of a college of Jeſuits at a
" place called *the Come,* in the county of Hereford, which was ſent

" up

" up unto the lords affembled in parliament at the end of the laft
" feffion, by Herbert lord bifhop of Hereford, according to an order
" fent unto him by the faid lords to make diligent fearch, and return
" an account thereof. To which is added a true relation of father
" Lewis the pretended bifhop of Landaff, now a prifoner in Mon-
" mouth caftle. Lond. 1679." 4to.

" Strange news from Lemfter in Herefordfhire. Being a true nar-
" rative, given under feveral perfons hands there, of a moft ftrange
" and prodigious opening of the earth in divers places thereabouts.
" Alfo a true relation of feveral wonderful fights, viz. a hand, and
" arm and fhoulder of the bignefs of a man's, and fadles of blood-
" colour, which were feen to iffue out of the earth, and afcend up to the
" fkies. Likewife a ftrange and wonderful noife of fighting, which
" was heard during this furprizing accident. All attefted by feveral
" perfons of worth and reputation, and exhibited for public informa-
" tion." fans date.

In the article of its cyder Herefordfhire has great obligations to Dr.
John Beale, in whofe family, natives of the county, a zeal for the
plantation of orchards was hereditary. Two letters of his to Samuel
Hartlib were printed 1656 and 1724. 8vo. intitled " Herefordfhire
" orchards, a pattern for all England," by which he fo raifed and
extended their reputation, that within a few years the county gained
fome hundred thoufand pounds by it. Many of his letters to Mr.
Boyle are publifhed in the 5th vol. of Boyle's works ; and others in
the Philofophical Tranfactions, and in Birch's hift. of the Royal Society, I. 145. 172. Col. Long was defired by the Society 1663, tc
reduce all the papers on cyder into one hiftory, and application was at
the fame time made to capt. Silas Taylor for the continuance of his
obfervations on that fubject. Thofe fince made by R. Bradley may be
found in a diftinct treatife. Hugh Stafford, efq; of Pynes in Devonfhire, publifhed " A treatife on cyder-making, founded on long prac-
" tice and experience, with a catalogue of cyder-apples of character in
" Herefordfhire and Devonfhire, &c. To which is prefixed a differ-
" tation on cyder and cyder fruit. Lond. 1753." 4to.

C c " The

" The complete planter and cyderift, or a new method of plant-
" ing cyder-apple and perry-pear trees; and the moft approved way
" of making cyder, in two parts. The firft treating of the cultiva-
" tion of orchards. The 2d, of the various ways of making cyder
" and perry as practifed in Devonfhire and Herefordfhire, &c. how
" to diftil cyder fpirits: with a propofal for making a ftrong-bodied
" cyder as a noble antifcorbutic for the navy. By Wm. Ellis, of Little
" Gaddefden in Hertfordfhire. Lond. 1757." 8vo.

John Philips has immortalized this liquor in an elegant poem that
bears its name, in which he has interwoven many epifodes and digreffions in honour of the county and its principal inhabitants, and which
fince its firft publication 1706 has paffed through many editions, and
was tranflated into Italian by a nobleman of Florence.

In N° 229, p. 579 of the Ph. Tranf. is an account of a hail ftorm
in this county 1697.

A feal found at *Ecclefwall* caftle, and fent by a perfon inveftigating
the antiquities of this county, is in the Gentleman's Magazine for
Dec. 1749, p. 536. An infcription in the old preceptory of *Dynemore*
explained in the fame Magazine, for Aug. 1755. p. 347. A view and
plan of *Wilton* bridge over the Wye near Rofs may be feen in that
for Aug. 1753.

In an heraldic MS. of R. Holmes MS. Harl. 2152. is a note of a
tree in *Afhperton* park, Herefordfhire that was 60 feet high before it had
any bough; then one grew out fo long, that a man on the ground
might touch the end with his hand; then it was 15 ½ feet before it
had any more; the body was three fathom round, and very upright.

Views by Buck 1731 are S. E. Goodrich, S. E. Brompton-Brian,
and S. W. Brønftill caftles, and S. Wigmore caftle and priory.

A plan of Ariconium [*Kentchefter*] is in plate lxxxv. of Stukeley's
Itin. Cur. Concerning this place fee Sir Theod. de Vaux's account of
a cinereous fubftance found at Kentchefter walls: and the Roman
baths there in Birch's hift. of the Royal Society, vol. II. p. 274 and 347.
A draught of the ruins at that time difcovered there is mentioned
p. 301.

" Frugiferi

" Frugiferi ac ameni Herefordiæ comitatus delineatio," by Saxton, engraved by Remig. Hogenbergius 1577, without the hundreds, added with a plan of the city in Speed's map, 1610.

Another was publifhed by E. Bowen.

A much correcter furvey than any of thefe by Ifaac Taylor 1754, in four fheets, with arms at the fides, and a plan of the city.

HERTFORD-

HERTFORDSHIRE.

THE firft effay towards a delineation of this county was attempted by the travail and view of John Norden, who in 1593 pub-lifhed " Speculum Britanniæ: the firfte parte: an hiftoricall and cho-
" rographicall defcription of Middlefex and Hartfordfhire; wherin are
" alfo alphabeticallie fett down the names of the cyties, tounes, pa-
" rifhes, hamletes, houfes of name, &c. with directions fpedilie to
" finde anie place defired in the mappes, and the diftance betwene
" place and place without compaffes." 4to. illuftrated with maps and the arms of the principal perfons interred in the county engraved by Peter Vanden Keere. It was reprinted 1637, and again 1723, with the addition of " A preparative to this work, intended [as] a reconciliation
" of fundrie propofitions by divers perfons tendred, concerning the
" fame, by the faid author [a]."

But the compleateft defcription is " The hiftorical antiquities
" of Hertfordfhire; with the original of counties, hundreds, or
" wapentakes, boroughs, corporations, towns, parifhes, villages, and
" hamlets: the foundation and origin of monafteries, churches, ad-
" vowfons, tythes, rectories, impropriations, and vicarages in generall;
" defcribing thofe of this county in particular: as alfo the feverall ho-
" nors, mannors, caftles, feats, and parks of the nobility and gentry;
" and the fucceffion of the lords of each mannor therein: alfo the
" characters of the abbots of St. Albans. Faithfully collected from
" public records, leiger-books, antient manufcripts, charters, eviden-
" ces, and other felect authorities. Together with an exact tranfcript
" of Domefday book, fo far as concerns this fhire, and the tranflation
" thereof in Englifh. To which are added, the epitaphs and me-
" morable infcriptions in all the parifhes, and likewife the blazon of
" the coats of arms of the feveral noblemen and gentlemen proprietors
" in the fame. Illuftrated with a large map of the county; a profpect
" of Hertford; the ichnography of St. Albans and Hitchin; and many

---

[a] The Englifh Topographer by miftake mentions a MS. copy of this furvey with fome additions by Wm. Burton in Mr. Rawlinfon's library.

" fculp-

" fculptures of the principal edifices and monuments. By Sir Henry
" Chauncy, kt. ferjeant at law. Lond. 1700." Fol. It were to be
wifhed more care had been taken in the engravings. The author had
by him confiderable additions and continuations, which came afterwards into the hands of N. Salmon, and were the chief foundation of
his " Hiftory of Hertfordfhire; defcribing the county, and its antient
" monuments, particularly the Roman: with the chara&er of thofe
" that have been the chief poffeffors of the lands; and an account of
" the moft memorable occurrences. Lond. 1728." Fol.

The county was vifited 1572 by Cooke; 1634 by St. George.

The funeral monuments in it are imperfe&ly treated of by Weever,
p. 542—597. The benefices under the bifhop of London's jurifdi&ion
may be feen in Newcourt's Repertorium, vol. I.

" A tale of two fwannes. Wherein is comprehended, the original
" and increafe of the river *Lee*, commonly called Ware river: toge-
" ther with the antiquitie of fundrie places and townes feated upon
" the fame. Pleafant to be read, and not altogether unprofitable to
" be underftood, by W. Vallans. Lond. 1590." 4to. This imitation
of Leland's Cygnea cantio was publifhed by Hearne from a copy
amongft Mr. Rawlinfon's books, and prefixed to the fifth volume of
Leland's Itinerary.

" Extra&s from the books of the mayor and aldermen of Hertford,
" together with copies of papers relating to the navigation of the river
" Lea between Hertford and Ware. 1734." 4to. with a map of the
river between the toll-bridges of each town by William Whittenberg,
1733.

John Jones, ufher of the free-fchool at *St. Albans*, wrote " Fanum
" St. Albani, poema carmine heroico. Lond. 1683." 4to.

Dr. Rawlinfon had a vellom MS. relating to feveral manors of this
abbey, from which Hearne printed in p. 278 of his notes on Leland's
Colle&anea, " Proceffus declarans formam & modum quibus manerium
" de Makereyende ortum habebat, & inicium, fuamque primariam
" originacionem." He prefixed to Otterburn and Whethamfted's
hiftories of England a long extra& from a MS. Cott. Lib. Nero D. VII.
of the a&s of the latter, who was twice abbot here, and fpent above
4000 l.

4000l. on the houfe.   He alfo publifhed [a] from a report book of He-neage Finch a procefs of T. Newland prior here againft Eliz. Bywell, for defamation in charging him with an attempt upon her chaftity: a charge Hearne will by no means believe.

The abbey church is engraved on half a fheet by King, with fome account of it below in three columns, 1680.   An elevation of the N. front and a plan by Hawkfmoor, 1721.   N. and S. fides by King for the Monafticon; and two fmaller views by J. Harris [b], and S. W. by Buck 1737.   I am told Mr. Lightoler has taken accurate draughts of all the principal parts of this beautiful but neglected remain of the Saxon architecture in its various periods [c].   Dr. Stukeley engraved two views of the high altar in pl. xxx and xxxi of his Itinerarium Curiofum.

At the corner of Speed's map 1610 is a good plan of old *Verulam*. The Antiquarian Society publifhed another taken 1721 by Dr. Stukeley, who inferted it in pl. xcv. of his book above-mentioned.   In p. 436 of N° 333 of the Philofophical Tranfactions are the dimenfions of fome very large human bones, fuppofed to belong to a perfon eight feet high, found near an urn infcribed Antoninus, in the Roman camp near St. Albans, communicated by Mr. W. Chefelden, furgeon.   Among the curiofities collected by Ebenezer Muffel, efq; fold at Langford's in the fpring 1765, was a beautiful little vafe in form of a cup of whitifh earth, full of coins of the lower emperors.

R. Benning engraved an elevation of the E. and W. fronts and plan of a building defigned for a feffion-houfe for the county at *Hertford*, infcribed to lord Wm. Cowper by John Kirby and Abraham Andrews.

Dr. Stukeley had an unpublifhed plate of *Berghamftead*, where he places Durocobrivis.

---

[a] Ap. to Caius, N° IV.

[b] Harris's view and an ichnography are inferted in Stevens's Monafticon, I. 233.

[c] At the Crown inn is preferved a groupe reprefenting the martyrdom of St. Amphibalus, who is attended by two executioners: each figure ftands on a pilafter, in an arched niche (at the corners of which are the bufts of Offa and his queen) which formed the roof of a fpacious fubterraneous room in the abbey orchard, difcovered 1729; the tiles of which are now laid in the abbey church.   There is a drawing of it by James Blackamore, 1760.

" Three

" Three ftrange wonders, or newes upon newes, being a brief and true
" relation of three memorable accidents which have lately happened,
" viz. Two mandrakes found at a town called *Abery*, near unto
" Bifhop Starford in Hertfordfhire. 2. Many dung carts full of fnakes,
" adders, and other venomous creatures, bred in a dung heap near
" unto Linton, a market town in Cambridgefhire. 3. A ftrange ac-
" cident by thunder and lightning at mafter Coulman's, at Denton-
" hall, near Tiltey in Effex. Lond. 1669." 4to.

The accidental difcovery of a kind of well at *Royfton* 1742 gave
birth to a controverfy about its antiquity and ufe. Dr. Stukeley in his
" Palæographia Britannica: or difcourfes on antiquities in Britain.
" Number I. Origines Royftonianæ, &c. Lond. 1743." 4to. labours
hard to prove it an oratory of lady Roifia, who is fuppofed to have retired to it about 1167, to have carved figures about it relative to the
hiftory of that time, and her own family in particular, and to have
been buried there. Mr. Charles Parkin d, rector of Oxburgh, Norfolk, in " An anfwer to, or remarks upon Dr. Stukeley's Origines Roy-
" ftonianæ; wherein the antiquity and imagery of the oratory lately
" difcovered at Royfton in Hertfordfhire are truly ftated and accounted
" for. Lond. 1744." 4to. affirms it was the oratory of an hermitage
long before Roifia's time, the figures reprefenting the faints who had
five altars in it; and that her ladyfhip was not buried here, but at her
priory at Chickfand. The Doctor replied to it in " Palæographia Bri-
" tannica: &c. number II. Origines Royftonianæ, part II. or a defence
" of Lady Roifia de Vere foundrefs of Roifton, againft the calumny
" of Mr. Parkin, rector of Oxburgh : wherein his pretended anfwer
" is fully refuted; the former opinion further confirmed and illuftrated.
" To which occafionally are added, many curious matters in antiquity:
" and fix copper plates. Stamford 1746." 4to. His antagonift clofed
the controverfy with " A reply to the peevifh, weak, and malevolent
" objections brought by Dr. Stukeley, in his Origines Royftonianæ,
" N° 2. againft an anfwer to, or remarks upon, his Origines Royfto-
" nianæ, N° 1. wherein the faid anfwer is maintained; Royfton proved
" to be an old Saxon town, its derivation and original: and the hiftory

---

ᵈ He died 1765.

" of

" of Lady Roifia fhewn to be a meer fable and figment." Norwich " 1748." 4to.

Dr. Stukeley had two plates engraved by Hulett from his drawings of a Britifh gymnafium at Royfton, 1741 ; another of the fix barrows near *Stevenage*, 1724, by Vandergucht.

Francis Taverner in the laft century wrote a good account of the antiquities of *Hexton* in this county, which hangs up in a wooden tablet in the family chapel in the church there, and was inferted in Sir H. Chauncey's work.

Mr. T. Rawlinfon had the accounts of the churchwardens of *Tring* from 1495 to 1548.

In Murden's " Collection of the Burghley papers from 1571 to " 1596, tranfcribed from originals at Hatfield houfe. Lond. 1756." Fol. p. 375—378, is an account of " Roomes and lodgings in the two " courts at Teobalds, 27 May, 1583." in lord Burghley's own hand.

" The entertainment of K. James and the K. of Denmark here 1666, " and of K. James and Q Anne, when the houfe was delivered up to " her majefty, 22 May, 1607." both by Ben. Johnfon. are printed in his works.   What remained of this fumptuous palace was pulled down 1765 by the prefent proprietor Geo. Prefcot, efq;   Among the reft was the room in which James I. died and a portico with a genealogical tree of the houfe of Cecil painted on the walls.

The S. profpect of *Hatfield* houfe by T. Sadler, jun. was engraved by Collins.

Elizabeth in her 10th year, and James in his 3d and 4th, had paffed feveral acts enabling the city to bring a river from any part of Middle-fex or Hertfordfhire, which they defpairing to effect, transferred their licence to Sir Hugh Middleton, who had acquired a confiderable for-tune by fome Welfh mines.   He begun Feb. 20, 1608, and carried on his work from the united ftreams of Amwell and Chadwell, for a winding courfe of near 39 [e] miles, and under 800 [f] bridges.   The pro-

---

[e] It was originally reckoned 60 miles, but Mr. Mills, furveyor, found this to be the exact courfe 1723, of which 660 feet are taken up in a wooden aqueduct at Winchmore hill, and 462 in another at Highbury.

[f] Now reduced to 215, and 43 fluices.

jector's

jector's fortune having fuffered greatly by it notwithftanding the affift-ance of the crown, James incorporated him, his brother, and fon, five more of his name, and 19 others; and the profits of the work were at firft divided into 36 fhares, which now fell for 30 years purchafe.

"The manner of the lord mayor's entertainment on Michaelmas day "laft, being the day of his honourable election, together with the worthy "Sir John Swinarton, knight, then lord maior, the learned and judi-"tious Sir Henry Montague, maifter recorder, and many of the right "worfhipfull the aldermen of the citty of London. At that moft fa-"mous and admired worke of the running ftreame from Amwell head "into the cefterne neere Iflington, being the fole invention, coft, and "induftry of that worthy maifter Hugh Middleton, of London, gold-"fmith, for the general good of the citty. By T. M. Lond. 1613." 4to. One Wm. Garbot wrote a poem called "The New River." 8vo fans date.

"The tryal of Spencer Cowper, efq; John Marfon, Ellis Stevens, "and Wm. Rogers, gent. upon an indictment for the murther of "Mrs. Sarah Stout, a quaker, before Mr. baron Hatfell, at Hert-"ford affizes, July 18, 1699; of which they were acquitted: with "the opinion of the eminent phyficians and chirurgeons on both fides, "concerning drowned bodies, delivered in the tryal; and the feveral "letters produced in court." was printed Lond. 1699. Fol. followed by "Some obfervations on it, together with fome other things relating "thereunto" Lond. 4to. reprinted in the Harleian Mifcellany, vol. viii. p. 414. "A letter from Hertford," on the fame fubject; and "A "reply to the Hertford letter: wherein the cafe of Mrs. Stout's death "is more particularly confidered; and Mr. Cowper vindicated from "the flanderous accufations of being acceffary to the fame. Lond. "1699." 4to.

A filly ftory of witchcraft in this county, too much countenanced by fome well-meaning credulous people, was canvaffed in feveral pam-phlets, and gained fo much influence on the minds of the populace, that the trial went through five editions, under the title of "The witch "of *Walkerne*. Being, I. A full and impartial account of the difco-"very of forcery and witchcraft, practifed by Jane Wenham of Wal-

D d   "kerne

" kerne in Hertfordſhire, upon the bodies of Anne Thorn and Anne
" Street, &c. alſo the procedings againſt her from her being firſt appre-
" hended till ſhe was committed to goal by Sir Henry Chauncy; with
" her tryal at the aſſizes at Hertford, before Mr. juſtice Powell, where·
" ſhe was found guilty of felony and witchcraft, and received ſentence
" of death for the ſame, March 4, 1711-12. II. Witchcraft farther
" diſplay'd: containing, 1. An account of the witchcraft practiſed by
" Jane Wenham ſince her condemnation upon the ſame women; and
" the deplorable ſtate in which they ſtill remain. 2. An anſwer to the
" moſt general objections againſt the being and power of witches:
" with ſome remarks on the caſe of Jane Wenham in particular, and
" on Mr. juſtice Powell's procedure therein. To which are added,
" the tryals of Florence Newton, a famous Iriſh witch, at the aſſizes
" held at Cork, 1661; as alſo of two witches at the aſſizes held at
" Bury St. Edmonds in Suffolk, 1664, before lord chief baron Hale,
" who were found guilty and executed."

" The caſe of the Hertfordſhire witches conſidered; being an exa-
" mination of a book, entitled, A full and impartial account of the diſ-
" covery of ſorcery and witchcraft practiſed by Jane Wenham, &c."

" A defence of the proceedings againſt Jane Wenham: wherein the
" poſſibility and reality of witchcraft are demonſtrated from ſcripture,
" reaſon, and the concurrent teſtimonies of all ages, in anſwer to two·
" pamphlets, intitled, The impoſſibility of witchcraft; plainly proving
" from ſcripture and reaſon that there never was a witch, and that it is
" both irrational and impious to believe there ever was: in which the
" depoſitions againſt Jane Wenham are confuted and expoſed g. and
" A full confutation of witchcraft, more particularly of the depoſitions
" againſt Jane Wenham; in which the modern notions of witchcraft
" are overthrown, and the ill conſequences of ſuch doctrines are ex-
" poſed, by arguments proving that witchcraft is prieſtcraft. In a letter
" from a phyſician in Hertfordſhire to his friend in London. 1712. A
" general preface to the whole, by Francis Bragge, B. A. late of
" Peter-houſe in Cambridge, and once of Hart-hall in Oxford [and
" vicar of Hitchin]. Lond. 1712." 8vo. Dr. Hutchinſon, in his Hiſ-

g Aſcribed to Mr. Pittis, formerly fellow of New Col. Oxford.

torical essay concerning witchcraft. 1718. 8vo. chap. x. p. 129, has again discussed this affair. Our more enlightened legislators avenged the murder of a poor wretch sacrificed fifteen years ago at Tring in this county to the same ridiculous prejudice of a frantic mob: the law in the same century authorizing a judge to condemn criminals for real and for impossible outrages. On this occasion was printed " The " tryal of Thomas Colley before Sir Wm. Lee at Hertford 1751, for " the murder of Ruth Osborne, under supposition of her being a " witch. 1751." 4to.

In Nº 229, p. 577, of the Philosophical Transactions is Mr. Tailor's account of a hail storm at *Hitchin* 1697. In p. 119 of Nº 439 are observations by Mr. Cope on an antient date over a door-way at *Widgell* hall, pulled down in 1733 when the house was on fire, and given to the Royal Society by Mr. Gulston; and in p. 120 are Mr. Ward's remarks on it. In p. 349 of Nº 476 is an attempt to explain some antiquities found 1743 in a chalk-pit near *Rooky* wood in Barkway parish, by Mr. Ward, with a print of them. Art. 26 of vol. xlix. contains Dr. Parsons's remarks on a singular petrified echinus found in *Bovingdon* parish [h], transcribed, with a cut of it, in the Gentleman s Magazine for Sept. 1756. In p. 684 of vol. xlix. is an account of a remarkable agitation of waters at several places in this county, Nov. 1, 1755. In p. —— of vol. li. is an account of the effects of thunder and lightning at *Rickmansworth* June 16, 1759.

Hartfordiæ comitatus nova, vera ac particularis descriptio, by Saxton, 1577, engraved by Nich. Reynolds of London, has the hundreds.

Speed's map has plans of Hertford and Verulam.

Hollar engraved a smaller map 1670.

Mr. Warburton published one engraved by Nath. Hill on one sheet of imperial atlas, and afterwards joined it with Essex and Middlesex. He also had engraved a view of *New Place* at East Barnet, the seat of John Sharp, esq; which was never published.

Another map of the county was engraved by Kitchen, among the set of county maps published by Bowen.

Purchased at the sale of bp. Pococke's curiosities May 1766 by Gust. Brander, esq;

HUNTING-

HUNTINGDONSHIRE.

WHETHER Sir Robert Cotton wrote the defcription of this county inferted in Speed is not certain; he feems to have collected for fuch a work ª. Nobody has taken up what this great antiquary's engagements prevented him from purfuing, and very little has been publifhed relative to the county. It was vifited by Hugh Cotgrave, Richmond herald, for Hervey 1566: by N. Charles, Lancafter herald, 1613.

The Englifh Topographer mentions a piece, intitled " The Hunt-" ingdon divertifement, or an interlude for the general entertainment of " the county-feaft, held at Merchant-Taylors hall, June 30, 1678."

Some account of a family that made much noife at the beginning of the civil wars, and was objected to Laud as an inftance of his affection to popery, may be feen in " The Arminian nunnery, or a " briefe defcription and relation of the late erected monafticall place, " called, The Arminian nunnery, at *Little Gidding* in Huntingdon-" fhire, hun.bly recommended to the wife confideration of this prefent " parliament. The foundation is by a company of Farrars at Gidding. " Lond. 1641." 4to. reprinted by Hearne at the end of Langtoft's chronicle. Oxf. 1725. p. cxxiv. Nº X. It was taken, with unwarrantable alterations, from a letter figned H. S. wrote by Edw. Lenton to Sir Tho. Hedley, knt. ferjeant at law, " on his requeft to certifie " as he [the letter-writer] found concerning the reputed nunnerie at " Gidding, Huntingdonfhire ᵇ;" printed alfo by Hearne in the fame book, p. cix. Nº IX. and p. 702 of Caii Vindiciæ. The editors of the catalogue of lord Oxford's pamphlets feem to infinuate that Hearne did not reprint the former pamphlet with exactnefs ᶜ. In p. 679 of the 2d vol. of Caii Vindiciæ are papers relating to this Proteftant nunnery, tranfcribed and given to the publifher by Mr. John Worthington;

ª " Cottonus de notitia comitatus Huntingdonienfis, in quo natus erat, edenda olim " cogitâffe, facile inducor ut credam ex materia congefta è libro cenfuali aliifque, fed " aliis ftudiis impeditus, non ultra proceffiffe videtur." Smith vita Cott. p. 3.

ᵇ See Lenton's letter to John F. the eldeft fon about it. Caii Vindiciæ, p. 695.

ᶜ P. 22. Nª 87.

to which are prefixed an epitaph to the memory of Dr. John Worthington ᵈ (who preserved those papers) and some historical notes about the Farrars, particularly that mirrour of piety Mr. Nicholas Farrar. Some more particulars of this useless enthusiast may be seen in B. Oley's prefatory view of Herbert's life prefixed to Herbert's " Country par-" fon :" in bp. Hacket's life of archbp. Williams, part II. p. 50. and in Stephens's abridgment of the same *1715,* p. 153. Dr. Turner bp. of Ely had an intention of writing his life ; but what advances he made towards it does not appear. Mr. Peck informs us that he himself composed a work, intitled " The complete church of England man " exemplified in the holy life of Mr. Nicholas Ferrar, of Little Gidding " in the county of Huntingdon, gent. commonly called The Proteftant " St. Nicholas, and the pious Mr. Geo. Herbert's brother ;" but in whose hands his papers at present are I have not been able to learn. We might have expected some account of this remarkable person in the Biographia Britannica, where is only a flight note about him in the Supplement, p. 126. This religious family confifted of an old matron, widow of Nichoals Farrar, of London, merchant, two fons, of whom the fecond Nicholas during his travels had been ftrongly follicited to go over to the church of Rome, an only daughter and her hufband Mr. Colet, with their 15 children (of whom fix daughters and two fons were married) and three or four fervants. They had a handfome houfe and chapel, with fine walks and gardens, and an eftate of about 500 l. a year purchafed by the mother. Thus declining all calling or employment that might render them ufeful in the world, which Nicholas accounted *a nothing between two diſhes,* they devoted their whole time to fafting, watching, prayer, and reading, accounting this method of worfhip, with fome external ceremonies, as lighting of tapers, and performing certain proftrations and genuflections the moft perfect and acceptable fervice of God, and their beft calling. Nicholas employed himfelf in compiling fcripture harmonies and hiftories in his own and 21 other languages, with literal tranflations in Latin, of which fee an account Caii Vindiciæ, p. 812.

ᵈ Prefident of Emanuel, and mafter of Jefus col. Camb. Died 1671.

and

and his brother John's ᵉ letter to Dr. Bafire for all the tranflations of the bible he could collect, p. 697. One of thefe patch-work harmonies prefented to abp. Laud, was by him depofited in St. John's coll. library, Oxford, adorned with variety of cuts, and intitled " The " whole law of God, as it is delivered in the five books of Moyfes, " methodically diftributed into three great claffes, morall, ceremoniall, " and politicall ; and againe each of thefe fubdivided into feveral heads, " as the variety of the matter requires ; wherein each particular fub- " ject difperfedly related in the 'forefaid books is reduced to its proper " head and place : alfo every head of the politicall law referred to " which precept of the morall law it properly belongs : to which are " added fundry pictures, expreffing either the facts themfelves, or " their types and figures, or other matters appertaining thereto. Done " at Little Gidding, An. 1640." Some remains of the maiden-fifters exercifes, a parcel of rhapfodical enthufiaftic converfations, were printed by Hearne, Ib. p. 713.

In Peck's Defiderata Curiofa I. B. VI. N° XIX. is bp. Kennet's account of the very antient monument at *Overton Longueville*, reprefenting a lord Longueville lying in armour, with his entrails twifted round his left arm, alluding to a wound he received fighting with the Danes there, notwithftanding which he continued the engagement till he had flain their king, and foon after expired.

The hiftory of *Ramfey* abbey by an anonymous author was publifhed in Dr. Gale's Hiftoriæ Britannicæ, Scriptores XV. Ox. 1691. p. 385. It confifted of four *telæ*, or parts, of which the laft is not now to be found, tho' quoted by Spelman in his gloffary. A fmall regifter of its charters MS. Harl. 5071. was printed by Hearne at the end of Sprot's chronicle. Dr. Stukeley has given us a print of the ftatue of Aylwin its founder. Itin. Cur. pl. xvii. and a view of the abbey among his unpublifhed plates; and Buck a N. W. view of its ruins 1730.

Of a very ridiculous piece of witchcraft, which is pretended to have happened in this county, we have an account in " The moft " ftrange and admirable difcoverie of the three witches of *Warbeys*,

---

John's fon Nicholas died 1640 at the age of 21, when he was upon the point of emulating his uncle's piety. His elogium by Crafhaw was printed by Hearne. Ib. p. 810.

" arraigned,

" arraigned, convicted, and executed at the laſt aſſizes at Huntingdon,
" for the bewitching of the five daughters of Robert Throckmorton,
" eſq; and divers other perſons, with ſundry divelliſh and grievous
" torments ; and alſo for the bewitching to death of the lady Crum-
" well, the like hath not been heard of in this age.   Printed Lond.
" 1693." 4to. f.

Cowper Thornhill has been conſigned to immortality in a poem
called " The *Stilton* hero. Lond. 1745."

In p. 851. of N° 461. of the Philoſophical Tranſactions we have an
account of a violent hurricane in this county, Sept. 8. 1741.

Huntingdon bridge is engraved in the Gent. Mag. for Dec. 1753.
N. E. view of Hitchinbrook priory, and a W. one of Buckden palace,.
by Buck 1730.

An eaſt view of *Bluntſham* church, drawn by Joſ. Eayre, engraved
1738 by Vertue.

A geometrical elevation of the W front of *St. Neot*'s church, by
P. S. Lamborn 1764.

This county is included in Saxton's map of Northampton, and other
ſhires 1576, and wants the hundreds : ſupplied in Speed's 1610, with
plans of Huntingdon and Ely.

Another by Gordon.

Another in concentric circles by Bowen.

T. Jeffereys propoſed 1766 to publiſh a new map conſtructed from
a ſcale of two inches to a mile, drawn from his own ſurvey, to be
delivered in May.

---

f See chap. 3. of vol. i. of a complete hiſtory of magick, &c. Lond. 1715. 12mo.
and Hutchinſon on witchcraft, p. 130.

KENT.

K E N T.

NORDEN made a furvey of this county, ftill in MS. The firft printed defcription was Wm. Lambarde's ᵃ " Perambulation of " Kent, containing the defcription, hiftorie, and cuftomes of that " fhyre, written in the yeere 1570 : firft publifhed in the yeere 1576," by Henry Middleton. 4to. containing an account of the nobility of the county omitted in fucceeding editions, of which one was " increafed and altered after the author's owne laft copy. Lond. 1596." 4to. The laft edition 1640 has the charters, &c. of the Cinque Ports.

Richard Kilburne, of Hawkhurft, efq; publifhed " A topographie, " or furvey of the county of Kent, with fome chronological, hiftorical, " and other matters touching the fame, and the feveral parifhes and " places therein. Lond. 1659." 4to. He had before publifhed in an oblong form in various columns 1657, " A brief furvey of the county, " viz. the names of the parifhes in the fame ; in what bailywick, hun- " dred, lath, divifion of the county, and divifion of juftices, every of " the faid parifhes is ; what liberties do claim in the fame ; the day on " which any market or fair is kept therein ; the antient names of the " parifh churches ; in what hundred or what townfhip every of the " faid churches doth ftand ; and in what dioceffe every of the faid " parifhes was."

Thomas Philipot, efq; of Clare hall, Cambridge, publifhed " Villare " Cantianum, or Kent furveyed and illuftrated : being an exact de- " fcription of all the parifhes, burroughs, villages, and other refpective

ᵃ He was fon of an alderman and fheriff of London, eminently verfed in the Arme- nian language, and admitted of Lincoln's inn, where he made a confiderable progrefs in the law. Tanner has enumerated feveral treatifes which he wrote about this and other fubjects. His principal work is a collection of Saxon laws, firft made by Laurence Noell dean of Litchfield, who going abroad in 1567 left them to him to tranflate and publifh, which he did under the title of Αρχαιονομια, &c. Lond. 1568, 4to. revifed by Wheloc. Cantab. 1644. Fol. Somner's tranflations of them into Englifh and fimpler Latin ftill extant in MS. deferve to fee the light with the confiderable additions that might be made to the laws themfelves. His pofthumous alphabetical defcription of England has a good head of him by Vertue.

" mannors

" mannors included in the county of Kent, and the original and inter-
" mediate poffeffors of them, even until thefe times; drawn out of
" charters, efcheat-rolls, fines, and other publick evidences; but
" efpecially out of gentlemens private deeds and muniments: to
" which is added an hiftorical catalogue of the high fheriffs of Kent,
" collected by John Philipot, efq; father to the author. Lond. 1659"
and 1664. Fol. Bp. Kennet b fpeaks very flightingly of Philipot, and
calls both him and Kilburne modern and fuperficial; he fays the whole
was the work of this John, who was Somerfet herald, and died in
1645, having married a niece of Robert Glover, Somerfet herald, that
" moft fkillfull genealogift c."

Wm. Somner has done the moft for his native county, of which
he intended a hiftory; but " being foon after overtaken by that impetuous ftorm of civil war, he was neceffitated to betake himfelf to
other thoughts d." It is fuppofed we have all he did of it in his
" Treatife of the Roman ports and forts in Kent, publifhed by James
" Brome, M. A. rector of Cheriton, and chaplain to the Cinque Ports.
" Oxon. 1693," 12mo. Bp. Gibfon added fome good notes to it.
An accurate account of the author by Bp. Kennet is prefixed by way
of letter to the editor, interfperfed with inftructive digreffions on our
antiquities. This eminent antiquary was born on the eve of a period
for which he feems to have been referved to refcue our antiquities
from that fecond and more defolating ftorm of civil war and fanaticifm
which threatned them with a more fweeping ruin than the diffolution.
Camden gives the honourable title of reviver of the Saxon language to
Alexander Nowel, dean of Litchfield, who only compiled an imperfect vocabulary: but Somner's indefatigable application and great pro-
ficience in it, intitle him to the more extenfive praife of having revived Saxon antiquities. To write his life is to write a panegyric on
that ftudy, without which the antiquities of England could be hardly
difcovered, or at leaft but imperfectly known. He imbibed his firft
inclination to antiquity with his grammar rudiments under John Twine,

b Life of Somner, p. 37.
c Wood's Fafti, I. 285.
d Pref. to his Gavelkind.

E e

mafter

mafter of the free-fchool at Canterbury, who wrote De rebus Albioni-
cis, and made collections for a hiftory of this city. His appointment
by Laud to a confiderable office in the archbifhop's court ᵉ gave him
great opportunities in purfuits where the way was to be opened altogether by his own induftry. So early as the feventh century the manners and language of France were imported among us. Ingulphus
400 years after complains that the great refort of foreigners to the
Confeffor's court made it unfafhionable to act or fpeak as an Englifhman. The Conqueror gave out his laws in French, and forbad the
teaching children to read or write Saxon : fo that in the next reign the
very letters were almoft worn out. Henry the firft's charter of confirmation to William archbifhop of Canterbury is the laft in that language and character. When Edw. III. appointed the law pleadings
to be in Englifh he could not reftore our original language, which was
preferved no-where but in monafteries founded before the Conqueft,
whofe intereft it was to keep it up, that they might defend their titles
againft arbitrary claimants ᶠ Somner therefore, as Bp. Kennet obferves, had the Saxon language almoft to invent ; and the fcarcity of
books in it, and the confufion and corrupt tafte of the times to ftruggle
with. His intimate acquaintance with the Saxon manners and polity
appears in his treatife of Gavel-kind, and his great improvements of
Lambarde's code of their laws. His mafterpiece and the refult of all
his refearches is his Saxon lexicon, printed at Oxford 1659. Fol. the
want of a new edition of which moft ufeful work is only fuperfeded by
that valuable one of Junius's Etymologicum Anglicanum by Edw. Lye,
rector of Little Houghton, Northamptonfhire. Oxf. 1743. Fol. Upon
his death 1669, at the age of feventy, the dean and chapter of Canterbury
purchafed his books and MSS. now repofited in the church library ᵍ.

Norden

ᵉ Where his father was regiftrary.

ᶠ Thus they had a Saxon tutor at Croyland, and a Saxon lecture at Taviftock. Sir
H. Spelman in 1639 founded one at Cambridge, with a falary of 10 l. a year and the
living of Middleton in Norfolk annexed : the profeffor to read or publifh Saxon books.
Upon the death of Wheloc the firft profeffor, Sir Henry's grandfon divided it between
a lecturer and a publifher, giving the former the living, and the latter, who was Somner,
the falary. The confufion of the times when the Spelman eftate was fequeftred feems
to have diffolved the inftitution.

ᵍ A lift of them is at the end of his life. Many loofe notes and letters lodged in the
chapter-houfe were accidentally burnt there foon after. His " Difcourfe of Portus
" Iccius,

Norden made a furvey of this county, ftill in MS. and large collections towards a natural hiftory by Dr. Plot are mentioned among his MSS. h

The laft work of this kind was " The hiftory of Kent, in five parts " containing, I. An exact topography, or defcription of the county " II. The civil hiftory of Kent. III. The ecclefiaftical hiftory of Kent. " IV. The hiftory of the royal navy of England. Vol. I. Lond. 1719." Fol. by Dr. John Harris, who died before he had compleated more than half his defign, fo that not quite three parts out of the five were publifhed. The 2d vol. was to have contained the hiftory of Rochefter cathedral, an account of the eminent perfons of the county, the religious foundations in alphabetical order, and the hiftory of the royal navy. The materials for all thefe heads were got ready, and good part of them tranfcribed before the author's death, which happened Sept. 7, 1719, before the publication of the firft volume. He was only eight years compiling this work from the former defcriptions of Kent, with little alteration, and few continuations of families. The alphabetical difpofition of the places is liable to many objections. The defign met with no fmall oppofition at firft, and the Doctor complains of the want of proper affiftance from thofe who had materials in their hands. What is publifhed has barely merit enough to make the 2d volume regretted. Moft of the plates are engraved by Kip, except a few by Harris, and all drawn by T. Badeflade. A copy of Domefday book for this county is faid to be in the hands of the Doctor's heirs. There is another MS. Harl. 1905. In the Cotton library, Vitel. C. VIII. 13

" Iccius, wherein the late conceits of Chiffletius in his topographical difcourfe are exa- " mined and refuted; the judgment of Cluverius concerning the fame port afferted and " embraced, and the true fite thereof more clearly demonftrated," was tranflated into Latin by Bp. Gibfon, with another differtation by Du Frefne fixing it at Witfan, and publifhed Oxf. 1694. 12mo. Chifflet contended for Mardyk, Somner for Bologne.

h Cat. MSS. Angliæ, &c. part II. p. 73. N° 2895. This defign is alfo hinted at in his epitaph, " Cantii natalis foli, antiquitatibus, fi fata fiviffent, illuftrior iftiturus;" and in p. 45 of " Mifcellanies on feveral curious fubjects. 1714." is a copy of his letter to the Royal Society, giving an account of Roman antiquities about Richborrow, &c. All that Dr. Harris could get from his collections was only a catalogue of MSS. relating to Kent, and a difcourfe on the Roman ways in the county, which he vifited 1690. The former, enlarged from Harris's own inquiries, was to have been printed at the end of his 2d volume.

is

is " Pars libri cenfualis continens defcriptionem Cantii." Cafley engraved a fhort fpecimen of the character of this MS. which he thought one of the rolls out of which Domefday was made, but Mr. Webb finds it to be no more than a verbatim copy of great part of Domefday for this county, tranfcribed fo literally as to infert marginal references in the text, and probably for fome great lord's private ufe. The county was vifited by Glover 1574; by Philipot 1619; by Byfhe 1663.

We have fome account of the ftate of botany here in " Defcriptio " itineris plantarum inveftigationis ergo fufcepti in agrum Cantianum. " Lond. 1632." 8vo.

A curious collection of plants is defcribed in " Hortus Elthamenfis " five plantarum rariorum quas in horto fuo Elthami in Cantio collegit " vir ornatiffimus & præftantiffimus Jac. Sherard, M. D. Soc. Reg. & " Coll. Med. Lond. Soc. Gulielmi P. M. frater, delineationes & de- " fcriptiones quarum hiftoria vel planè non, vel imperfecte a rei herba- " riæ fcriptoribus tradita fuit, auctore Jacobo Dillenio i, M. D. Lond. " 1732." 2 vol. Fol.

Concerning the marfhy part of this fhire fee " A fummary relation " of the paft and prefent condition of the upper levels, lying in the " counties of Kent and Suffex: by Sir Nathaniel Powel, bart." &c. Anfwered in " Animadverfions on feverall material paffages, in a book " written by Sir N. P. bart. Together with a more exact narration of " the ftate of thofe levels; by Thomas Herlackenden, efq; Lond. " 1663." 4to.

" The charters of Romney marfh, Lat. and Eng printed by J. " Wolfe. 1597."

" The charter of Romney marfh: or the laws and cuftoms of Rom- " ney marfh: framed and contrived by the venerable juftice Henry de " Bathe: very ufeful for all profeffors of the law, and alfo for all lords " of towns, and other land-holders within Romney marfh, Bedford " level, and all other marfhes, fenns, and fea-borders. Lond. 1686." 8vo. annexec to the " Laws of fewers." 1726 and 1732. 8vo.

The famo is cuftom of Gavel kind, which obtains no where elfe in England, is fully difcuffed by Somner, in his " Treatife of Gavel kind,

---

i Botany Profeffor at Oxford.

" both

" both name and thing: shewing the true etymology and derivation
" of the one, the nature, antiquity, and original of the other: with
" sundry emergent observations both pleasant and profitable to be
" known of Kentishmen and others, especially such as are studious of
" the antient customs or the common law of this kingdom. By a well-
" wisher to both, William Sumner. Lond. 1660." 4to. To the 2d edition 1726. 4to. newly revised and much enlarged, is added his life
by Bp. Kennet [k]. Silas Taylor in his " History of Gavel kind, with
" the etymology thereof; containing also an assertion, that our Eng-
" lish laws are, for the most part, those that were used by the antient
" Brytains, notwithstanding the several conquests of the Romans, Sax-
" ons, Danes, and Normans. With some observations and remarks
" upon many especial occurrences of British and English history. To
" which is added, a short history of William the Conqueror, written in
" Latin by an anonymous author in the time of Henry the First. Lond.
" 1663." 4to. carries both the name and custom further back: in all
material points he confirms the opinion of Somner, who answered his
objections in marginal notes on a copy of his book, which with a correct copy of his own is now in Canterbury library.

Thomas Robinson, esq; of Lincoln's inn published " The common
" law of Kent, or the customs of Gavel kind; with an appendix, con-
" cerning Borough English. Lond. 1741." 8vo.

As *Canterbury* was the most antient royal city and the first episcopal
church of the Saxon Christians, so both were the first whose antiquities
were published to the world [l].

Gervase, a monk there in the 13th century, wrote an account
of the burning and rebuilding the cathedral A. D. 1070, the difputes between the monks and archbishop Baldwin, and the lives of
the archbishops from Austin to Hubert [m]; all published among the
Decem Scriptores 1652. Thomas Sprott or Spott, another monk about

---

[k] The Bishop had told us in his life of Somner prefixed to his Roman ports, &c.
that the first edition came abroad so complete that it did not admit of one correction
(except errors of the press) alteration, or addition from his own pen.

[l] Kennet's life of Somner, p. 20.

[m] Ralph Diceto's lives of the archbishops takes in the same period, but is a very super-
ficial work.

1270, wrote the hiſtory of his monaſtery loſt before Leland's time, but abridged by Thorn, a third monk, a century later. A ſmall fragment of Sprott's work, containing about fifty years, is ſaid by biſhop Tanner to remain in the Cotton library, Vitel E. IV.ⁿ but both this hiſtory and the collections for a hiſtory of Canterbury°, made by John Twine, maſter of the freeſchool there, were loſt before Somner "for the honour of that ancient metropolis, and his good affection to antiquities, ſought out and publiſhed" "Antiquities of Canter-"bury; or a ſurvey of that antient citie, with the ſuburbs and cathe-"dral; containing principally matters of antiquity in them all; col-"lected chiefly from old manuſcripts, leiger-bookes, and other like re-"cords, for the moſt part never as yet printed: with an appendix here "annexed, wherein (for better ſatisfaction to the learned) the manu-"ſcripts and records of chiefeſt conſequence are faithfully exhibited. "Lond. 1640." 4to. A new title page was printed 1662, but not a new edition. Many years after, it was republiſhed with very conſiderable additions both from Somner's own papers, and the labours of the editor, (who according to bp. Nicholſon, intirely compiled the ſecond part himſelf) and intitled "The antiquities of Canterbury, in two "parts: the firſt part, The antiquities of Canterbury, or a ſurvey of "that antient city, with the ſuburbs and cathedral, &c. ſought out by "the induſtry and good-will of William Somner: the ſecond edition, "reviſed and enlarged by Nicholas Battely, M. A. Alſo Mr. Somner's "diſcourſe, called Chartham news, or a relation of ſome ſtrange bones "found at Chartham in Kentᵖ. To which are added ſome obſerva-"tions concerning the Roman antiquities of Canterbury; and a pre-"face giving an account of the works and remains of the learned an-

---

ⁿ Bale and Pits make Wm. Gillingham, monk here about the end of the 14th century, to have written De rebus Cantuarienſibus. Leland aſcribes to him only an account of the writers of his order: all his writings however are loſt. Archbp. Parker's learned book "De antiquitate eccleſiæ Britannicæ & privilegiis eccleſiæ Cantuarienſis cum archiepiſcopis 70 ejuſdem" muſt not be forgot. It was three times printed in London and once at Hanau before Mr. Drake's elegant edition 1724. Tann. B. B. 575.

° Mr. T. Rawlinſon had an antient MS. of the cuſtoms, &c. of Canterbury, ſuppoſed to be wrote about the time of Hen. VII. as appears from a petition to the king mentioning Sir John Dinham lord Dinham, who was his treaſurer from 1486 to 1500.

ᵖ See hereafter p. 222.

"tiquary.

" tiquary Mr. William Somner, by N. B.   The fecond part, Cantu-
" aria Sacra, or the antiquities, I. Of the cathedrall and metropo-
" litical church. II. Of the archbifhoprick. III. Of the late priory of
" Chrift church ; and of the prefent collegiate church founded by K.
" Henry VIII. with a catalogue of all the deans and canons thereof.
" IV. Of the archdeaconry of Canterbury.   V. Of the monaftery of
" St. Auguftine : of the parifh churches, hofpitals, and other religious
" places, that are, or have been, in or near that city, enquired into by
" Nicholas Battely, vicar of Beakfborn.   Illuftrated and adorned with
" feverall ufeful and fair fculptures. Lond. 1703." Fol. [q]   Many of
Somner's collections relating to this city, and other towns and churches
in Kent, were publifhed in Thorn's Chronicle of the abbey from the
coming of Auftin down to 1375 among Twifden's Decem Scriptores:
his extracts out of this chronicle, the obituary, and other regifters of
this and Rochefter church, and the Saxon annals, in Wharton's Anglia Sacra.

The rev. Mr. John Dart publifhed " The hiftory and antiquities of
" the cathedral church of Canterbury, and the once adjoining monaf-
" tery, containing an account of its firft eftablifhment, buildings, re-
" edifications, repairs, endowments, benefactions, chapels, altars,
" fhrines, reliques, chauntries, obits, ornaments, books, jewels, plate,
" veftments, before the diffolution of the monaftery, and the manner
" of its diffolution : a furvey of the prefent church and cloyfters, mo-
" numents, and infcriptions, and other things remarkable, which,
" with the feveral profpects of the church, are engraven by the beft
" hands ; the lives of the archbifhops, priors, &c. of Chrift church ;
" with an account of learned men there flourifhing in their feveral
" times ; and an appendix of antient charters and writings relating to
" the church and monaftery ; a catalogue of the church's wealth in
" prior Eftrey's time ; an antient Saxon obituary, and a large one
" continued thence downward. 1726." Fol.   Weever gives the funeral monuments in this and Rochefter diocefe, p. 197 and 301.

[q] In this edition is omitted the fine draught of a font given by Dr. Warner, the liberal
bp. of Rochefter 1636, inferted in the former, p. 181.   The parliament foldiers having
pulled it down, Somner bought the pieces, and at the reftoration prefented them to the
archbifhop, who replaced it, and firft baptifed a daughter of its preferver in it.

Dr.

Dr. Rawlinſon engraved a charter of king Egelred granting lands in Sandwich and Eſtree to Chriſt church, Canterbury, from the beginning of a very old Latin MS. of the Goſpels in St. John's library, Oxford. 1754.

" A repertory of the endowments of vicarages in the dioceſe of Can-
" terbury. By Andrew Coltee Ducarell, L.L.D. F.R.S. and F.S.A.
" commiſſary of the city and dioceſe of Canterbury. Lond. 1763," 4to.
is a ſpecimen of the method propoſed by the author for a general repertory or liſt of the endowments of vicarages throughout the kingdom.

The Antiquarian Society have engraved in two plates a view of the cathedral and monaſtery, as they were between 1136 and 1174, with the effigies of Eadwin, probably a monk there about that time, both drawn by himſelf in an antient curious MS. given by dean Neville to Trinity Coll. Cambridge, with a printed account by Dr. Jer. Milles. Rude as this draught is it correſponds with Gervaſe's deſcription of the buildings, and gives a good idea of the diſpoſition of religious houſes [r].

Becket's ſhrine from a MS. in the Cotton library engraved by Vaughan, and the high altar from one in Trinity Coll. library, are in the Monaſticon.

E. and N. views of the abbey, Winchup and Riding gates, the caſtle, St. Gregory's priory, St. Thomas's chapel by F. Perry, Two more views of the abbey in Stukeley's Itinerary, pl. xxiv. xxv. and St. Martin's church, pl. xlviii. The ſingular font in the latter by Perry 1760.

A N.E. view of the abby by Buck 1735.

A catalogue of the MSS. belonging to this cathedral, among which are all Somner's collections, may be ſeen in Cat. MSS. Angliæ, tom. ii. p. 223 and 389.

John Green engraved for the Antiquarian Society the third ſeal of this cathedral from a curious impreſſion of it, formerly Sir A. Fountain's, exhibiting a beautiful view of the church and the murder of Becket: alſo a plate of coins ſtruck by archbiſhops of Canterbury in the ninth century.

[r] Mabillon mentions ſuch an one of the monaſtery of St. Gaul, in the library there, 1683, of which he had a copy. Iter Germ. p. 37. edit. 1717. 8vo. Two views of the monaſtery on Mount Athos, taken 1716, and brought over by Doſithers the archimandrite are in the Bodleian library.

5

A plan

Hollar engraved a N. profpect of Canterbury, with a ground plot of the city; a view of the S. fide of the cathedral and the ichnography of it after Tho. Johnfon [s], dedicated to archbp. Sheldon, by John Ogilby, on a large fheet. There is a S. profpect of the cathedral [t] after Johnfon by Hollar on a half fheet. The N. and W. fides of the cathedral, and a profpect of the abbey from the tower of Chrift church by King after Johnfon. A S. W. profpect of the metropolitical church by James Collins 1715. A plan of Durovernum (Canterbury) with a view of the Roman gate called Riding gate is in Dr. Stukeley's xcvith plate, and another Roman gate called Worth gate in the livth. A S. W. view of Canterbury is among Bucks larger views 1738. and a N. E. of its caftle among the fmaller, 1735.

All that has yet appeared in print relating to *Rochefter* is " The " hiftory and antiquities of the cathedral, containing the local ftatutes " of that church; the infcriptions upon the monuments, tombs, and " grave-ftones; an account of the bifhops, priors, deans, and arch- " deacons; an appendix of monumental infcriptions in the cathedral " church of Canterbury, fupplementary to Mr. Somner's and Mr. Bat- " tely's accounts of that church: fome original papers, relating to " the church and diocefe. Lond. 1717." 8vo. republifhed 1723. The moft venerable monument of antiquity that belongs to this church is the Textus Roffenfis, written by Bp. Ernulf, who died A. D. 1124, publifhed by Hearne at Oxford 1720. 8vo. to which were added " Profeffionum antiquorum Angliæ epifcoporum formulæ de canonica " obedientia archiepifcopis Cantuarienfibus præftanda," and " Leo- " nard Hutten's differtation of the antiquities of Oxford." Befides the affairs of this cathedral it furnifhes us with the laws of four Kentifh kings omitted by Lambard, together with the Saxon forms of oaths, &c. An extract of it was publifhed by Wharton, Angl. Sac. part I. p. 329, intitled " Ernulphi epifcopi Roffenfis collectanea de rebus ec- " clefiæ Roffenfis, a prima fedis fundatione ad fua tempora, ex textu

---

[s] Mr. Johnfon of Canterbury fhewed the Royal Society 1685 a curious profpect of the cathedral, and feveral views of the adjacent country drawn by himfelf in oil colours. Birch's Hift. of the Roy. Soc. iv. p. 399.

[t] In which the feveral pillars of the choir, &c. with their different capitals are diftinct-ly expreffed.

" Roffenfi

" Roffenfi quem compofut Ernulphus;" confifting of the following particulars, 1. Nomina epifcoporum Roff. from Juftus's death 624 to Ernulphus. 2. Donationes ecclefiæ Roff. 3. De placitis apud Pinendenam inter Lanfrancum archiepifcopum Cant. & Odonem Baiocenfem. epifc. [in Hearne's edit. p. 140, c. 83.] 4. Quomodo Lanfrancus terras ecclefiæ S. Andreæ extraCtas, &c. contradidit, & de Gundolfo epifcopo [H.'s edit. p. 141. c. 86.] 5. Quomodo Willielmus rex Willielmi filius conceffit ecclefiæ Roff. manerium de Hedenham, & quare Gundulfus epif. caftrum Roff. lapideum totum de fuo proprio regi conftruxit. [H.'s edit. p. 144. c. 87.] 6. Conceffio Willielmi magni regis [H. p. 148. c. 89.] 7. Contentio inter Gundulfum & Pichot. [H. p. 149. c. 91.] 8. Donationes. Bp. Nicholfon fays this is the " Chronicon clauftri Roffenfis" of the Monafticon, and fuppofes that during the civil wars this book was lodged in the hands of Sir Roger Twifden, where Dugdale in his Origines Juridiciales frequently refers to it. Hearne printed it from a tranfcript in the hands of Sir Edw. Dering, by his great grandfather's father, from the original at that time [1632] in the hands of one Dr. Leonard, a phyfician, and now among the Harleian MSS. 6523. Nicholfon fpeaks of a MS. chronicle of Rochefter, chiefly colleCted from this by Wm. Bedenham, efq. Wharton publifhed almoft the whole of Dean's hiftory of this church and its bifhops from 1314 to 1351 [u], and extraCts on the fame fubjeCt from Hadenham the monk's general chronicle [x].

Propofals are now circulated for printing by fubfcription " Regiftrum " Roffenfe:" containing a curious and valuable colleCtion of all fuch records, charters, grants, feoffments, endowments, appropriations, and other deeds and inftruments hitherto unpublifhed, as are neceffary for illuftrating the ecclefiaftical hiftory and antiquities of the diocefe and cathedral church of Rochefter; faithfully tranfcribed from the originals in the Tower of London, the chapel of the Rolls, the Augmentation office, the king's and treafurer's remembrancers offices in the Exchequer, the Bodleian, Cottonian, and Harleian libraries, the refpeCtive regifter books of the archbifhop and dean and chapter of Can-

[u] Ang. Sac. I. 356.
[x] Ib. I. 341.

terbury, thofe of the fee and cathedral church of Rochefter, and other public and private repofitories : by John Thorpe, M.D. F.R.S. late of Rochefter, and prepared for the prefs by his fon John Thorpe, efq; A.M. F.S.A. To which will be added, the monumental infcriptions in the feveral churches within the diocefe : the effigies of the author elegantly engraved, together with fome account of his life, will be pre-fixed to the work.

The W. and N. views of this cathedral were drawn and engraved by D. King.

A large N.W. profpect of the city and N. and S. views of its caftle by Buck 1735.

Another view of the caftle by Dr. Stukeley, Itin. Cur. p. vi.

Two others by Perry. I have another very neat one, which feems to have been done by F. Place, but has under it only Philip Lea in Cheapfide, ex. Dr. Stukeley had an unpublifhed plate of a piece of Roman wall here 1724.

" Monafticon Faverfhamienfe in agro Cantiano, or a furveigh of the " monaftery of *Faverfham* in the county of Kent; wherein its barony " and right to fit in parliament is difcovered. Together with its an-" tient and modern ftate defcribed ; as alfo its founder and benefac-" tors remembred: by Thomas Southoufe of Greys-inne, efq; To " which is added, an appendix of the defcent of king Stephen : by " Thomas Philipot, efq; Lond. 1671." 12mo.

The rev. Mr. John Lewis, vicar of Mynftre, publifhed " The hiftory " and antiquities of the abbey and church of Faverfham, the adjoin-" ing priory of Davington, and Maifon Dieu of Ofpringe, and parifh of " Bocton fubtus le Bleyne : to which is added a collection of papers " relating to the abbey, &c. and of the funeral monuments, and other " antient infcriptions in the feveral churches of Favrefham, Shelwich, " Boeton under le Bleyne, Ofpringe, Graveney, and Throwley; with " the charitable benefactions thereto given. 1727." 4to. Somner furnifhed the Monafticon with Stephen's original foundation charter.

The oldeft and the prefent feals of this corporation, the mayor's feal, the arms of the Cinque ports, the oldeft and the laft feal of Faverfham abbey, and the feal of St. Katherine's hofpital by the Tower of London

were

were all engraved in one plate by J. Mynde, and dedicated to the corporation of Faverſham by Edward Jacob. We have a view of the
abbey in Dr. Stukeley's Itin. Cur. p. xxvii. a N. view by Buck 1735.
and two of the abbey and gate by Perry.

Mr. Lewis wrote likewiſe " The hiſtory and antiquities, as well ec
" cleſiaſtical as civil, of the iſle of *Tenet* in Kent, with many cuts.
" Lond. 1723." 4to. of which a 2d edition with additions came out
in 1736 y. 4to. From this has been compiled " A deſcription of the
" iſle of Thanet, and particularly of the town of Margate; with an
" account of the accommodations, manner of bathing in the ſea, &c.
" the antiquities and remarkable places to be ſeen on the iſland. With
" a deſcription of Sandwich, Deal, Dover, Canterbury, Rocheſter,
" Chatham, and other places. Illuſtrated with a correct map of the
" iſland, a plan of Ramſgate peer, and a repreſentation of the machines
" for bathing. Lond. 1763." 12mo. In Harris's hiſtory of Kent is
a map of this iſland, with the N. W. proſpect of St. Mary's minſter
at the corner, drawn and given by J. L. 1717, and engraved by S.
Parker. Alſo the old monkiſh map, inſerted in the Monaſticon and in
Lewis's book.

Perry engraved a view of *Reculver* church.

" The hiſtory and antiquities of *Maidſtone*, the county-town of
" Kent, from the MS. collections of William Newton, miniſter of
" Wingham in the ſame county, vicar of Gillingham in Dorſet, and
" chaplain to the right hon. Margaret viſcounteſs Torrington. Lond.
" 1741." 8vo. A large appendix is promiſed at the end of the preface, which has not appeared. Buck engraved a N. W. view of the
town 1738.

Archdeacon Batteley's well written poſthumous work, intitled " Anti-
" quitates Rutupinæ," publiſhed by Dr. Terry, canon of Chriſt church
and Greek profeſſor at Oxford, in 1711. 8vo. diſcovers the author to be
well verſed in the Roman antiquities and hiſtory, and gives an entertaining account of the antient Rutupiæ and Regulbium, with other
cities and ports on the coaſt of Kent well known to the Romans,

y Mr. Ames had the original MSS. of both theſe books, interleaved with many additions and drawings by the author. See his catal. Nº 1295, 1296.

whoſe

whofe coins, &c. are here daily difcovered, and were plentifully col-
lefted by the curious author. It was reprinted Oxf. 1745. 4to. with
the antiquities of St. Edmund's Bury in Suffolk by the fame author.
Mr. Lewis before-mentioned had written fomething on the antiquities
of *Richborough, Sandwich,* and *Stoner,* MS. in the hands of his friend
Mr. Ames[a]. Mr. Stephen Gray defcribes the foffils at *Reculver* caftle
Philofophical Tranfactions, N° 268, p. 762. A view of the old caftle
here is given by Dr. Stukeley in pl. xcvii. of his Itin. Cur. A S. W.
view of Rutupiæ, another of it from Sandwich 1722, and the Caftren-
fian amphitheatre here, Cæfar's paffage over the Stour by Chilham, &c.
and a profpect of Julaber's grave, are among his unpublifhed plates.
A N. W. view by Buck 1735.

As to *Deptford,* we have printed the act concerning fea-marks and
mariners, enabling the mafter, wardens, and affiftants of the Trinity-
houfe in Deptford-ftrond to fet up beacons, marks, and figns for the
fea, 8 Eliz. 1566. cap. 13, intitled, " The charter of the Trinity-houfe
" of Deptford-ftrond. With the bye-laws. Lond. 1685." 12mo.

In p. 75 of N° 371 of the Philofophical Tranfactions is an account
of the manner of bending planks by a fand heat in the dockyards here,
invented by capt. Cumberland.

A large N. W. view of the town by Buck 1739.

A N. W. view of St. Paul's church, Deptford, with the rector's
houfe, by T. Allen; engraved by W. H. Toms.

A geometrical plan and elevation of the dockyard, with part of the
town, by T. Milton, 1753.

" Rules and orders for the royal academy at *Woolwich.* Lond. 1741."
4to.

A geometrical plan and elevation of the dockyard by T. Milton,
1753.

A N. view of Woolwich by Buck 1739.

" A true defcription of his majefty's royal fhip built this year 1637
" at Woolwich in Kent, to the great glory of the Englifh nation, and
" not parallelled in the whole Chriftian world. Publifhed by autho-
" rity. Lond. 1637." 4to. T. Haywood, a celebrated actor, author

[a] Ames's Cat. N° 685.

of

of 220 plays, was employed in contriving the emblematical devices about this veffel, which was 1637 tons burden befides tonnage; 128 feet long, 48 broad: from the fore end of the beakhead to the after end of the ftern 232 feet: from the bottom of the keel to the top of the lantern 76 feet: it had five lanterns, of which the biggeft would hold ten perfons upright: three flufh decks, a forecaftle, half deck, quarter deck, and roundhoufe: the lower tier had 60 ports, the middle one 30, the third 26, the forecaftle 12, half deck 14, and as many more within, befides 10 pieces of chace ordnance forward, and 10 right off, and many loop holes in the cabin for muſkets: eleven anchors, one weighing 4400 lb.

" An abſtract of the rules and ordinances of the new colledge of " Cobham in the county of Kent, of the foundation of the late Wil- " liam baron Cobham: reprinted 1687, by the order and at the ex- " pences of Sir Joſeph Williamſon of Cobham-hall in the ſaid county, " knight, one of the preſidents of the ſaid colledge.—Morning and " evening prayers, uſed in the colledge. Lond. 1617." 4to. reprinted 1733. 4to.

A copy of the inſtitution, ſtatutes, and endowments of *Dulwich* college in folio is among the Pepyſian MSS. at Magdalen Col. Camb. Another copy, late Thoreſby's, was bought at his ſale by Dr. Ducarell, See an account of this college in the Gentleman's Magazine, Aug. 1745. p. 426, and in the Biog. Brit. Allen. The founder played the capital parts in the moſt excellent dramatic pieces, and was one of the original actors of Shakeſpear's plays.

" Chatham news: or a brief relation of ſome ſtrange bones there " lately digged up in ſome grounds of Mr. John Somner's of Canter- " bury; written by his brother Mr. Wm. Somner, late auditor of Chriſt " church, Canterbury, and regiſter of the archbiſhop's court there be- " fore his death. Lond. 1669." 4to. with a print of two large teeth. Publiſhed alſo with his diſſertation on the iſthmus between England and France in the Philoſophical Tranſactions, N° 271, p. 882. and il- luſtrated by Dr. Wallis, N° 276.

Mr. Warburton had a MS. diſcourſe concerning the Weald of Kent by Sir Roger Twyſden, bart. on 50 pages: and a treatiſe of the Wealde,

and

and the marle therein, drawn out of the experience of Edw. Batcoat of Hawkhyrſt, yeoman, 1592.

" Magna & antiqua charta quinque portuum domini regis & mem-
" brorum eorundem. Cantab. 1675." 8vo.

" Charters of the Cinque ports, two antient towns, and their mem-
" bers, tranſlated into Engliſh, with annotations hiſtorical and critical
" thereupon ; wherein divers old words are explained, and ſome of
" their antient cuſtoms and privileges obſerved. By Samuel Jeake,
" ſen. of Rye, one of the ſaid antient towns. Lond. 1728." Fol.

A plan of the intended harbour between Sandwich town and San-down caſtle by C. Labelye, engraved by J. Harris. In the Gentle-man's Magazine, 1745, p. 95. are extracts from " A treatiſe containing reaſons for making a harbour from Sandwich into the Downs, near Sandown caſtle, for which commiſſioners were appointed in purſuance of an addreſs from the houſe of commons to the king, Apr. 24, 1744."

The hiſtory of *Dover* caſtle and the Cinque ports by Fran. Thynne, Lancaſter herald, in his own hand, is in the Pepyſian library.

In Harris's hiſtory is a draught of Dover caſtle, t. Eliz. from a MS. in the Herald's office, " De caſtellis Cantiæ," by Wm. Darel, chaplain to Q Eliz. dedicated to Cobham, lord warden.

" A diſcourſe of ſea ports; principally of the port and haven of Dover,
" by Sir W. Raleigh ; written and addreſſed to Q. Elizabeth : with
" uſeful remarks on that ſubject, by the command of his late majeſty
" K. Charles the ſecond. Lond. 1700. 4to.

Hollar drew views of the cliff, and a proſpect from ſea ; the caſtle, and another proſpect from the W. ſide ; Deal caſtle, and a view on the river Chatham by Shireneſs, ſome of which were engraved by himſelf 1651 and ſome by Tempeſta.

The tower in Dover caſtle is in Stukeley's Itin. Cur. pl. xlvi. xlvii. xlviii. he ſent his draught of it to Montfaucon, who inſerted it in his Antiquite expliquè. The appearance of Roman Dubris is among the Doctor's unpubliſhed plates.

Buck engraved 1735 the W. and N. views of the caſtle, N. W. of the tower, S. E. of Maiſon Dieu at Dover : alſo a large S. proſpect of the town and port.

Another

Another view of the town and caftle, engraved by J. Mafon, from a painting by G. Lambert. 1762.

Two of the caftle and its antient chapel by F. Perry.

As to the medicinal waters of this county we have " A treatife of " *Lewifham*, but vulgarly called *Dulwich* wells, in Kent, fhewing " the time and manner of their difcovery, the mineralls with which " they are impregnated, the feverall difeafes experience hath found " them good for, with directions for the ufe of them, &c. by John " Peter, phyfician. Lond. 1681." 12mo. In p. 835 of N° 461 of the Philofophical Tranfactions is an account of a new purging fpring at the Green man at Dulwich 1739, by Mr. Martyn.

" Some experiments on the chalybeat water lately difcovered near " the palace of the lord bifhop of Rochefter at *Bromley* in Kent. " With obfervations on chalybeat waters in general, and the moft fuc- " cefsful method of drinking them: in which an expedient is offered " to reconcile the different opinions of Dr. Hoffman and Dr. Short, " concerning the exiftence of alkaline falts in thofe chalybeat waters, " which are commonly, but improperly, called acidulæ. With fome " plain and eafy directions to make artificial chalybeat waters, and to " diftinguifh with abfolute certainty the factitious from the native. To " which are added fome directions for difcovering the unwholfome " contents of common water, and fome method of correcting them, " fo as to render them more fafe for alimentary purpofes. By Thomas " Reynolds, furgeon. Lond. 1756." 8vo.

Tunbridge waters, firft difcovered by lord North, were recom- mended by Lodowick Rowzee, phyfician at Afhford, in " The " queenes welles b; that is, a treatife of the nature and vertues of " Tunbridge water: together with an enumeration of the cheifeft di- " feafes which it is good for, and againft which it may be ufed, " and the manner and order of taking it." Lond. 1632. 1658. 1670. 12mo. and in the Harleian Mifcellany, viii. 316. This was fol-

b He gave them this name from Charles the firft's queen Henrietta Maria, who fpentfix weeks here after the birth of Charles II. Kilburne calls them Frant-wells, probably from their rifing on the borders of an eftate in Frant parifh, belonging to lord Aberga- venny, who firft interefted himfelf about making them ufeful to the public.

lowed

lowed by Dr. Patrick Madan's " Philofophical and medicinal effay
" of the waters of Tunbridge, written to a perfon of honour. Lond.
" 1687." 4to.

" Metellus his dialogues: the firft part containing a relation of a
" journey to Tunbridge wells, alfo a defcription of the wells and place,
" with the 4th book of Virgil's Æneids in Englifh verfe; written un-
" der that name by a gentleman of this nation, fometime gentleman
" commoner of Chrift church in Oxford. Lond. 1693." 12m.

In the Mufæ Britannicæ, Lond. 1711. 8vo. p. 17. are " Tunbrigialia,
" authore P. Caufton," printed in Englifh in 1688. 4to.

Tunbrigialia, or Tunbridge mifcellanies were publifht 1737, 1738,
1739.

" Defcription of Tunbridge, a poem, 1727.

There has juft appeared a " Hiftory of Tunbridge wells. Lond.
" 1766." 8vo. by Thomas Benge Burr, a native of the place, and
journeyman to Mr. Hawkins the bookfeller.

A view of thefe wells with the company en grotefque by Badeflade
is in Harris's hiftory.

Meffrs. Buck have given fouth views of the priory and caftle, 1735.

" The ftrange witch of Greenwich (ghoft, fpirit, or hobgoblin)
" haunting a wench, late fervant to a mifer, fufpected of a murtherer
" of his late wife: with curious difcuffions of walking fpirits, and
" fpectars of dead men departed : for rare and myfticall knowledge
" and difcourfe. By Hieronymus Magomaftix. 1650." 4to.

Mr. Manning wrote a poetical defcription of Greenwich hill 1697.
Folio. Another folio poem on Greenwich park was infcribed to the
duke of Montague, 1728.

There are four plates of the Royal Obfervatory ; one of the houfe,
with a view towards London ; the others infide views, with draughts
of the telefcopes and other aftronomical inftruments.

Hollar engraved a profpect of Greenwich for many miles to London,
&c. with four Latin verfes, in two fheets, near a yard long. 1637.

A head of profeffor Flamftead from a painting of Gibfon by Vertue, 1721.

G g

A view

A view of the front of the royal hofpital, engraved by R. Parr 1739.
Another view and plan by Rocque.

A profpect of the hofpital, dedicated to Q Caroline, by Thomas Lauranfon, 1734. A perfpective view of the colonades by ditto, engraved by Toms 1740.

" Remarks on the founding and carrying on the buildings of the " royal hofpital at Greenwich, by N. Hawkfmoor, deputy furveyor, for " the perufal of parliament. 1728." 4to.

" An explanation of Sir James Thornhill's paintings there : publifhed " for the benefit of the charity boys." 8vo.

A N. W. view of Greenwich by Buck.

Another from the Obfervatory by Rigaud, engraved by S. Torres.

Another from one-tree-hill in the park, engraved by J. Wood from a painting by Pond.

The monument of Sir John Lethieullier, kt. fheriff of London 1674, his wife and children, &c. erected in Greenwich church yard, was engraved at the expence of Smart Lethieullier, efq; his defcendant.

" Orders to be obferved by the penfioners and fervants in the hofpi- " tal," printed on a broad fheet.

Thomas Churchyard wrote " A fpark of friendfhip and warm good- " will ; with a poem concerning the commodity of fundry fciences ; " efpecially concerning paper and a paper mill lately fet up near Dart- " ford by a High German called Mr. Spilman, jeweller to the Queen's " majeftie :" addreffed to Sir Walter Raleigh. Lond. 1558 and 1588. 4to. His " Wonders of Wiltfhire and the earthquake of Kent" were printed 1580. 8vo.

Fanfcomb barn, (near Pickanden a valley below Wye downs) formerly by cuftom a privileged retreat for beggars, and famous for breeding white fparrows and white mice, but now pulled down, has been celebrated, together with the neighbouring fine fpring, much frequented by the youth of Wye freefchool, by the late countefs of Winchelfea, in p. 58 of her " Mifcellany poems on feveral occafions. Lond. 1713." 8vo. and inferted in Harris's hiftory, p. 344.

" Sevenoke a poem, humbly infcribed to his grace the duke of Dorfet, by W. Harrold. Lond. 1753." 4to.

Penfhurft,

Penſhurſt, or rather the hoſpitality of its lord, has been celebrated in epigrams by Ben. Johnſon [c], and ſince in a poem inſcribed to William Perry, eſq; and the hon. [d] Mrs. Elizabeth Perry. Lond. 1750. 4to. by the late Mr. F. Coventry, reprinted in Dodſley's Miſcel. iv. p. 50. There is a view of this retreat of the Sidney family by J. Kip in Harris's hiſtory; and another has been ſince engraved by Vertue. The oak planted on Sir Philip's birth-day is now no more to be found than that which ſhould have immortalized Chaucer at Dennington. Collins [e] ſays it was known ſo lately as his time by the name of Bear's oak.

An old braſs ſeal found on Blackheath, ſuppoſed to belong to the ſpiritual court held annually at *Clyff* for proving wills in that pariſh, and then in the hands of Mr. John Murray of Sacombe, is engraved in the Engliſh Topographer, p. 94. Dr. Rawlinſon ought to have availed himſelf of it in behalf of thoſe who place Cloveſho here inſtead of Abingdon.

There is a print by Hollar, 1652, of a monumental column in memory of Elizabeth wife of Robert Cole of *Wye,* with arms.

In p. 32. of Caſaubon's notes on Antoninus's Meditations, book ii. Lond. 1625. 4to. is an account of ſome Roman urns found about *Newington* near Sittingbourn, with the figures of them; and in p. 42 and 43 of the 4th edition, Lond. 1673. 8vo. the ſame account is reprinted without the figures: alſo in Harris's hiſtory, p. 218, with a fourth urn; and in Burton's Antoninus, with a draught of two, of which the largeſt was given to Burton by H. Dearing, vicar of the pariſh.

In MS. Harl. 1106 are draughts of a very antient graveſtone of one Northwood in the choir of *Minſter,* Shepey, and of Elizabeth counteſs of Athol 1377 at *Aſhford.*

" Newes from Graveſend and Greenwich, being an exact and more
" faithfull relation of two miraculous and monſtrous fiſhes, firſt diſco-
" vered in Rainham creek, and afterwards purſued by fiſhermen in
" the Thames, and the biggeſt killed and boiled for oil at Graveſend:
" the other at Greenwich, which was one and twenty feet in length

---

[c] Works, III. 177. VI. 306.
[d] Niece to the laſt Sidney earl of Leiceſter.
[e] Memoirs of the Sidney family. p. 98.

" and

" and fix feet over, and likewife a lefs than either which made its
" efcape to the fea again." 4to.

" A mirrour of mercy and judgement, or an exact true narrative of
the life and death of Freeman Sonds, efq; a youth of nineteen, fonne to
Sir George Sondes, of *Lees Court* in Shelwich, executed at Maidftone
Aug. 21, 1655, for murthering his elder brother," 4to. wrote by R.
Bowman, B. D. fellow of Trin. C. Cambridge, with a mifcellany of
divers remarkable paffages and practices of mafter Freeman by Theo.
Higgons, rector of Hunton.

" Strange and wonderfull news ; being a true account of the great
" harms done by the violence of the thunder at *Afhurft* in Kent,
" Bleachinley in Surrey, and at Kennington in the fame county; or a
" full and true relation how a man and his wife walking together in
" the fields at Kennington were both flain with a thunderbolt on Sun-
" day the 5th of this month July 1674." 4to.

The " Defcription of the ftorm in Weft Kent Aug. 13, 1763, by John
" Hedges, A. M. vicar of Tudeley cum Capella, Kent. Lond. 1763."
4to. is miferable nonfenfe, the writer of which muft be out of his head.

Charles Clarke, late of Baliol Col. publifhed his " Conjectures rela-
" tive to a very antient piece of money lately found at *Eltham* ; endea-
" vouring to reftore it to the place it merits in the cimeliarch of Eng-
" lifh coins, and to prove it a coin of Richard the firft king of Eng-
" land of that name. To which are added, fome remarks on a differta-
" tion (lately publifhed) on Oriuna, the fuppofed wife of Caraufius,
" and on the Roman coins here mentioned. Lond. 1751." 4to. anfwered by the rev. Mr. Geo. North in " Remarks on fome conjectures,
" &c. fhewing the improbability of the notion therein advanced ; that
" the arguments produced in fupport of it are inconclufive or irrelative
" to the point in queftion, &c. &c. Lond. 1752." 4to.

In Nº 243 of the Philofophical Tranfactions, p. 289, is a letter from
Dr. R. Conny to Dr. Plot about a fhower of fifh at *Cranftead* near
Wrotham 1666. In p. 964 of Nº 275 is a letter from Dr. Wallis to Dr.
Sloan, concerning the ifthmus or neck of land, which is fuppofed to
have formerly joined Dover and Calais. In p. 2462 of Nº 312 is a
letter from Dr. Scipio des Moulins to Dr. Sloan, concerning a mineral
water

water found at Canterbury 1696. In p. 469 of N° 349 is a letter from the rev. Mr. John Sackette, M. A. to Dr. Brooke Taylor, secretary, giving an account of a very unusual sinking of the earth near *Folkstone*, the cliffs, &c. sliding insensibly into the sea. In p. 462 of N° 155 we have a letter from Dr. Griffith Hartley to Dr. Grew, concerning a bed of shells six feet under ground at *Hunton*, five miles from Maidstone and one from the Medway, which he supposes lapides sui generis, and not shells petrefied. In N° 270, p. 805, is Patrick Gordon's relation of a waterspout in the *Downs*. In N° 399, p. 305, an account of a shock of an earthquake felt near *Dartford* 1727, and in p. 307 an account of a subterraneous fire in *Flinx-hill* parish, near Canterbury. In p. 79 of N° 474 Mr. Ward's remarks on an antient date in *Ashford* church. In p. 551 of N° 405 a relation of an uncommon sinking of the earth at *Lymne*. In p. 191 of N° 411 a letter from the king's officer at Sheerness and Chatham, giving an account of discoveries made in opening an antient well near *Queenborough* castle 1729 [f]. In N° 446 is Mr. Brown's account of a Scolopendra aquatica scutata found in a pond on *Bexley* common. In p. 828 of N° 461 is A. Godfrey's examination of *West Ashton* well water, four miles from Holt. In p. 489 of N° 403 an account of the various strata of earth and fossils found in sinking Holt mineral wells : and in p. 43 of N° 408 we have observations on these waters by Mr. Lewis. In p. 626 of vol. xlviii. a description of elephants bones found at *Leysdown* in the isle of *Shepey*. Art. 86 of vol. xlix. is an account of an earthquake felt Feb. 18, 1756, along the coast between Margate and Dover. In p. 396 of vol. l. a description of fossil fruits, &c. found in the same island. In p. 523 of vol. xlix. an account of the irregularities of the tides at Chatham, Sheerness, Woolwich, and Deptford, communicated by lord Anson. In p. 614 of vol. l. an account of an earthquake felt at *Edenbridge* Jan. 24, 1758.

In the Gentleman's Magazine for Jan. 1747, p. 33, is an inscription in the churchyard wall at *Alkham* near Dover. In that for May 1763, p. 248, we have a view and account of *Kits Coity House*, or the grave of Catigern, of which there are two unpublished views by Dr. Stukeley.

---

[f] There is a view of this castle by Hollar in a set.

In

In that for July, p. 340, an infcription in *Hythe* church.   In that for Aug. 1760, p. 371, an account of fkeletons found near *Milky Down* near Hythe.   In that for Apr. 1762, p. 155, an account of a piece of human flefh petrefied, found in a grave at *Folkftone*.

Other views by Buck 1735, are,

S. Allington
N. Leeds
W. Hever ᵍ
S. Cowling
S. E. Saltwood   } caftles.
S. Sandown
N. W. Deal
N. W. Walmer
N. W. Sandgate
N. E. Eltham palace.
N. E. Malling   } abbies.
S. Reculver

An unpublifhed view of the court at Malling abbey by Dr. Stukeley.

F. Perry engraved Milkhoufe chapel, near Cranbrook; Well chapel, near Wingham, and Upnor caftle, among his Kentifh views before-mentioned.

A large S. profpect of the town and port of Sheernefs, N. W. of Gravefend, and W. of Chatham dock, by Buck, 1738, 1739. Geometrical plans and elevations of the dock yards at Sheernefs and Chatham with the village of Brompton, by T. Milton, 1753.

Dr. Stukeley gives *Lapis Tituli* (Folkftone) pl. xcviii. *Lemanis portus* (Limne) p. xcix. of his Itinerary.

Another view of Saltwood caftle was engraved by J. Mafon from paintings of G. Lambert, 1762, by whom a view of the ruins of Radegund's abbey, near Dover, was exhibited at Spring-gardens 1761.

An outfide view of *Siffinghurft* caftle engraved by James Peake from a drawing on the fpot by an officer was publifhed 1763.

Coombank, near Sevenoaks, the feat of the duke of Argyle, and

---

ᵍ In Hever church is buried Sir Thomas Bulleyn father to Henry VIIIth's queen, who lived here at the beginning of her courtfhip, and was fucceeded here by the divorced Anne of Cleeves.

Foot's

Foot's Cray place, late the feat of Bouchier Cleeve, efq; have been drawn and engraved by Woolet, in a fet with four others.

An exact furvey of the river *Medway* from Maidftone up to Penfhurft, in the county of Kent, and alfo of the ftream falling thereinto from For-reftrow, Suffex; by John Brown at Tunbridge, 1739: engraved by Toms.

Saxton has included this county in his map of Suffex, Surry, and Middlefex, 1575, omitting the hundreds; fupplied with plans of Canterbury and Rochefter by Speed.

A new defcription of the county of Kent, divided into its laths, bailywicks and hundreds, comprehending all the cities, market towns, parifhes and poft towns, the feats of the nobility and gentry, and the nature of the foil whether plain, hilly, or woody, is more particularly obferved; with a view of Dover and Rye; by Philip Symondfon of Rochefter, gent.

Another with views of Dover town and caftle, and a profpect of Rye, drawn by Vandyke and etched by Hollar [h], in two fheets.

A fourth by Sellers.

A fifth by E. Bowen for the Britifh Atlas, with a correct draught of the Downs and of the adjacent coaft from the N. to the S. Foreland, with the foundings and variations of the compafs as obferved in 1736.

Dr. Packe, a phyfician, publifhed 1737 " A differtation upon the " furface of the earth, as delineated in a fpecimen of a philofophico- " chorographical chart of Eaft Kent;" which was prefented to the Royal Society, and received with approbation, 1738; containing a graphical delineation of the county fifteen or fixteen miles round Canterbury: wherein are defcribed the progrefs of the vallies, the directions and elevations of the hills, and whatever is curious both in art and nature, that diverfifies and adorns the face of the earth. This curious perform-ance was to be printed on four fheets of atlas paper, and publifhed in November following, for one guinea: but nothing more came out than the fpecimen in one fheet accompanied with an effay called " Ανκογραφια five convallium defcriptio; in which is briefly and " fully explained the origine, courfe and infertion, extent, ele- " vation and congruity of all the vallies and hills, brooks and rivers,

" as

---

[h] See Philpot's Villare Cantianum.

" as an explanation of a new philofophico-chorographical chart of Eaſt
" Kent. Occaſionally are interſperſed ſome tranſient remarks that re-
" late to the natural hiſtory of the county, and to the military marks
" and ſigns of Cæſar's rout through it in his deciſive battle in Kent.
" Canterb. 1743." 4to.

LANCASHIRE.

LANCASHIRE.

DR. R. Kuerſden, a phyſician, publiſhed propoſals in the beginning of this century for " Brigantia Lancaſtrenſis illuſtrata, or
" a hiſtory of the honourable dukedom or county palatine of Lan-
" caſter," which he ſaid was ready for the preſs, in five volumes: but
he ſeems not to have met with encouragement. Some of the papers
came into the hands of John Hare, Somerſet herald, who left them to
the Herald's office. Some particulars concerning the northern parts of
the county were communicated to the new edition of Camden by Sir
Dan. Fleming, knt. who was a perſon of great curioſity and judgment
in ſuch matters, and made large collections.

It was viſited 1533 by Wm. Fellowe for T. Benolt ᵇ: 1567 by
Flower : 1613 by Richard and Hen. St. George.

Dr. Rawlinſon mentions a MS. wrote by Mr. Urmſton, and preſerved by Thomas Brotherton, eſq; of Heye, relating to the ſtate of
religious affairs in it about the beginning of James I.

Somewhat of the natural hiſtory may be learnt from Dr. Charles
Leigh's " Phthiſiologia Lancaſtrienſis, cui acceſſit tentamen philoſo-
" phicum de mineralibus aquis in eodem comitatu obſervatis. Lond.
" 1694." 12mo. the beſt part of which was incorporated into his
" Naturall hiſtory of Lancaſhire, Cheſhire, and the Peak in Derbyſhire:
" with an account of the Britiſh Phænician, Armenian, Greek, and
" Roman antiquities in thoſe parts. Oxford 1700" Fol. in which
his account of this ſhire is the fulleſt: what he ſays of Derbyſhire
being only a trite and trifling account of its wonders. Bp. Nicholſon
ſpeaks of both with deſerved contempt.

Edm. Borlaſe, who practiſed phyſic at Cheſter ᵃ, publiſhed a piece
on " Latham ſpaw in Lancaſhire, with ſome remarkable caſes and
" cures effected by it. Lond. 1670" 12mo.

ᵃ He wrote " The reduction of Ireland," " Hiſtory of the Iriſh rebellion, and " Brief
" reflections on lord Caſtlehaven's memoirs. Wood's Faſti II. 129."
ᵇ MS. Harl. 2076. f. 19.

H h   In

In p. 209 of Ray's " Northern Words," we have the manner of making falt of fea-fand in this county.

The hiftory of *Manchefter*, by Rich. Hollingworth, is preferved in MS. in the college library b. A more perfect account of this college may be collected from their charters and other authorities, publifhed on the late bifhop of Chefter Dr. Gaftrell refufing to inftitute' to the wardenfhip Dr. Peploe, afterwards bp. of Chefter, prefented by the chancellor of the duchy under Geo. I. whofe cafe was printed at Oxford 1721, and privately difperfed by the bifhop, dated 26 Jan. 17$\frac{1}{2}\frac{0}{0}$, wrote with great ftrength of argument, and entirely fubverting that ancient illegal legatine power of conferring degrees claimed by the archbifhops of Canterbury. The foundation-charter requires hat the warden be. batchelor of divinity : Dr. Peploe, inftead of taking his degree at Oxford, tho' he had prepared beft part of his exercife, took it at Lambeth ; notwithftanding this the King's bench determined in his favour.

The college MSS. are in Cat. MSS. Angliæ, tom. II. p. 222.

A S. W. view of the town by Buck 1728.

We have fome fhort account of *Hawkefhead* in the preface to " The " fatal nuptiall; or mournefull marriage. Relating the heavy and " lamentable accident lately occurring by the drowning of 47 perfons, " and fome of thofe of efpeciall quality, in the water of Windermere, " in the north, Oct. 19, 1635. Lond. 1636." 12mo. The foundation-charter, ftatutes, &c. of its free-fchool are among the original papers added to the antiquities of Worcefter cathedral 1717 and 1723. 8vo. p. 163, from a MS. in the hands of Dr. Rawlinfon. Hearne printed in his appendix to the hiftory of Glaftonbury, p. 289, extracts from the regifter of this parifh.

" Strange newes of a prodigious monfter born in the townfhip of " *Adlington* in the parifh of Standifh, in the county of Lancafter, Aprill " 17, 1713, teftified by the rev. divine W. Leigh, D. D. and preacher " of God's word at Standifh aforefaid, 1613." 4to. with a wooden cut of a double child.

b Another copy probably quoted by Wood Ath. Ox. I. 653. in his account of bp. Stanley, one of the wardens, is in the Heralds college.

" The

" The happineſs of retirement, in an epiſtle from Lancaſhire to a
" friend at court, to which is ad led an encomium on the town of *Preſton*,
" Lond. 1733." An account and views of the guild merchant of
Preſton, &c. with a liſt of the company at the balls, &c. Sept. 1762,
were publiſht that year. 8vo. Buck engraved 1728 a S. view of this
town, and S. W. of *Liverpool*. There is a deſcription of the latter in
the Gentleman's Magazine for June 1764, p. 278. and the charter has
been printed at large. A S. profpect of its charity-ſchool drawn by
Joſ. Mollins was engraved by Hulſberg. A ſmall plan of the town
1766.

John Lucas, ſchoolmaſter, left behind him many good MS. collections, eſpecially a large folio hiſtory of *Warton*, his native town, and
the parts adjacent in this county, which by the great variety of obſervations ecclefiaſtical, civil, and natural interſperſed throughout it, he
rendered a very uſeful work [c].

" A true purtraiture of ſundrie coynes found the 8. of Aprill and
" other daies following in the yeare 1611, in a certaine place called
" the *Harkirke*, within the lordſhip of Litle Croſbie in the pariſh of
" Sephton in the county of Lancaſter : which place Wm. Blundell,
" eſq; of the ſaid Litle Croſbie, incloſed from the reſidue of the ſaid
" Harkirke for the buriall of ſuch catholick recuſants deceaſing, either
" of the ſaid village, or of the adjoyning neighbourhood, as ſhoulde
" be denied buriall at their pariſh church of Sephton." This print, of
which there is a copy MS. Harl. 1437. contains 35 coins, 32 of which
are Anglo-Saxon ; Wanley knew many to be incorrectly engraven,
the publiſher, who endeavoured to diſpoſe them in form of a croſs,
having more ſuperſtition than learning.

In Mr. Walpole's liſt of Vertue's works is mentioned " A plan of
" a Roman military way in Lancaſhire."

" Antiquitates Bremetonacenſes ; or, The Roman antiquities of
" *Overborough* ; wherein Overborough is proved to be the Bremeto-
" nacæ of Antoninus ; the year when, and the Romans who erected
" this ſtation proved out of Tacitus : an account of the garriſon there ;
" alſo of the idol who was tutelar deity of Overborough ; to which is

[c] Biograph. Brit. THORESBY. Note E.

" added

" added a defcription of as many monuments of antiquity as have
" been dug up or difcovered there lately, tending to illuftrate the
" hiftory of that once famous ftation. By Richard Rauthmell 1746."
4to. Some pertinent remarks are here delivered in moft uncouth
language. The author's explanation of an infcription on an altar
found here was controverted by Mr. Pegge, who in the Gentleman's
Mag. for Sept. 1759, p. 407, changes the name of the deity and the
dedicator, in which laft particular he was fupported by another critic
in the Magazine for the following month, p. 451.

" A view of the advantages of inland navigations: with a plan of a
" navigable canal, intended for a communication between the ports
" of Liverpool and Hull. Lond. 1765." 8vo. with a plan from a
furvey by Mr. Brindley, engineer to the D. of Bridgewater; drawn
by Hugh Henfhall, engraved by Kitchen. This pamphlet and plan
have been pirated in " The hiftory of inland navigations, particularly
" thofe of the D. of Bridgewater; and the intended one promoted
" by earl Gower, &c. in Staffordfhire, Chefhire, and Derbyfhire.
" Printed for Lowndes 1766." 8vo.

" The advantages of inland navigation; or, fome obfervations
" offered to the public, to fhew that an inland navigation may be
" eafily effected between the ports of Briftol, Liverpool, and Hull;
" together with a plan for executing the fame. By R Whitworth,
" efq. Lond. 1766." 8vo.

In p. 483 of N° 26, and p.   of N° 245 of the Phil. Tranf. is
Mr. Thomas Shirley's defcription of a well and earth about a mile
from Wigan, in the road between Warrington and Chefter. Both
this burning well and that at Brofeley are now loft [d]. In p. 695
of N° 199, is an extract of a letter from Mr. John Sturdie, dated
14 March 1674, concerning the iron ore and hæmatites wrought into
iron at Milthrop forge. Some obfervations on the Roman ftations in
Chefhire and this county, byThomas Percival, efq; were inferted in p. 216
of vol. xlvii. In N° 155, p. 457, we have a Roman infcription near

---

[d] See an account of fome water and earth in Mr. Molyneux's eftate at Hawkfley near
Wiggan, that would light a candle at half a yard's diftance, in a letter from Mr. Brad
fhaigh at Haigh, in Birch's Hift. of the Royal Society. Vol. i. p. 301.

Man-

Manchefter communicated by Dr. Lifter, of which fee Horfley, p. 301. In Nº 244, is a letter from Mr. Thorefby concerning fome Roman coins found in this county. In Nº 245, is a letter from Dr. Cay concerning fome waters. In Nºs 208, 249, and 297, is the quantity of rain falling monthly here for feveral years. In p. 1097 of Nº 363, is Dr. R. Richardfon's relation of a wonderful fall of water from a water-fpout on the moors. In p. 257 of Nº 422, an account of a ftag's horn taken out of the fea on this coaft. In Nº 452, p. 59, Dr. Clayton's experiments on the Wigan coal, in a letter to Mr. Boyle. In p. 282 of Nº 475 an account of a moving mofs near Church-town.

" The mayor of Wigan, a tale, &c. By Hilary Butler, efq. Lond. " 1760." 8vo. A dirty ftory, poorly told.

" Knowfley, a poem on the E. of Derby's feat," in the Gent. Mag. for May 1760, p. 241.

" A burlefque view of the Lancafhire dialect by way of dialogue, " with a gloffary of all the words and phrafes, by Tim. Bobbin, fel- " low of the Sifyphian fociety of Dutch loom-weavers," was printed Lond. 1746. 8vo. 4th edit. 1750.

Among Dr. Richard James's MSS. in the Bodleian library Wood mentions " Iter Lancaftrenfe," in Englifh verfe 1636. in two fheets and a half.

In Rawlet's poetic mifcellanies. Lond. 1687. 8vo. p. 86. are " Verfes " on the fight of Furnefs Fells, June 19, 1671."

John Darrell, who turned Popifh prieft becaufe by his own con- feffion he was fit for nothing elfe, and fet up the trade of an exorcift in this county about a century and an half ago, having driven the devil out of a whole family at once, recorded it in " A brief and " true difcourfe, contayning the certayne poffeffion and difpoffeffion " of feven perfons in one familie in Lancafhire, as namely of John " Starkie, Ann Starkie, Margaret Hurdman, Ellynor Hurdman, Ellen " Holland, Margret Byrom, and Jane Afhton, which may ferve (as " an interim) for a peece of an anfwer to that fraudulent difcoverie " lately come out, which depraveth thefe, as well as the reft of thofe " great and mighty works of God, which be of the fame kinde. Lond. " 1595."

" 1595." 12mo. This ſtory was re-publiſhed under a different form
and title of " A true narration of the ſtrange and grevous vexation by
" the devil of ſeven perſons in Lancaſhire, and William Somers of
" Nottingham : wherein the doctrine of poſſeſſion and diſpoſſeſſion
" of demoniakes out of the word of God is particularly applied unto
" Somers, and the reſt of the perſons controverted : together with
" the uſe we are to make of theſe workes of God. By John Darrell,
" miniſter of the word of God. 1600." 4to. " The diſcovery of
" the fraudulent practices of John Darrell, batcheler of artes, in his
" proceedings concerning the pretended poſſeſſion and diſpoſſeſſion
" of Wm. Somers at Nottingham ; of Thomas Darling, the boy of
" Burton, at Caldwall ; and of Cathrine Wright at Mansfield, and
" Whittington ; and of his dealings with one Mary Cooper at Not-
" tingham, detecting in ſome ſort the deceitfull trade of theſe latter
" days of caſting out devils. Lond. 1599." 4to. wrote by Samuel
Harſnet, who was raiſed for it to the ſees of Chicheſter, Norwich and
York, was anſwered in " The triall of maiſter Dorrell, or a col-
" lection of defences againſt allegations not yet ſuffered to receive
" convenient anſwers : tending to cleare him from the imputation of
" teaching Somers and others to counterfeit poſſeſſion of devils, that the
" miſt of pretended counterfeiting being diſpelled, the glory of Chriſt
" his royal power in caſting out devils (at the prayer and faſting of
" his people) may evidently appeare. 1599." 12mo. againſt which
came out " A detection of that ſinfull, ſhamefull, lying, and ridi-
" culous diſcourſe, intitled A diſcovery of the fraudulent practices of
" John Darrell, &c. 1600 " 4to.

This county ſo fertile in ſorcery and witchcraft produced " A
" wonderful diſcovery, with the arraignment and trial of 19 notorious
" witches at the aſſizes and general gaol delivery held at Lancaſter
" caſtle, Munday Aug. 6, 1612, before Sir James Altham, and Sir

ᵉ Ath. Ox. I. 732. Wood mentions John Dorel or Darrel dean of Agen. Ib. 383.
In his Faſti I. 108. he aſcribes the true diſcourſe, &c. printed 1600, to one Geo. More,
a miniſter, who at that time had been priſoner in the Clink about two years for bearing
witneſs to and juſtifying the ſaid matters. Harſnet when bp. of Norwich had a like controverſy about Popiſh poſſeſſions with Edmondes alias Weſton, a jeſuit. Ath. Ox. I.
591.

" Edw.

" Edw. Bromley, with the arraignment and trial of Jennet Preſton at
" the aſſizes held at Yorke, with her execution for the murther of maſter
" Aſton by witchcraft, publiſhed by command of his majeſty's juſtices
" of aſſize in the northern parte. By Thomas Potts, eſq; 1612." 4to. and
" A particular declaration of the moſt barbarous and damnable prac-
" tices, murtherous, wicked, and diveliſh conſpiracies practiſed and
" exerciſed by the moſt dangerous and malitious witch Elizabeth
" Sowthernes alias Demdike, of the foreſt of Pendle in the county of
" Lancaſter, widow, who died in Lancaſter caſtle before her trial.
" 1612." 4to.

About the end of the laſt century appeared " The Surey demoniack ;
" or an account of Satan's ſtrange and dreadfull actings in and by the body
" of Richard Dugdale of Surey near Whalley in Lancaſhire, and how
" he was diſpoſſeſſed by God's bleſſing on the faſtings and prayers of
" divers miniſters and people ; the matter of fact atteſted by the oaths
" of ſeveral credible perſons before ſome of his majeſty's juſtices of
" the peace in the ſaid countie. 1697. 4to" The Puritan party being
the dupes, and charged with being the managers of this poſſeſſion,
were attacked in " The Surey impoſtor, being an anſwer to a late
" fanatical pamphlet, intitled The Surey demoniack. By Zach. Tay-
" lor, A. M. and one of the king's preachers for the county palatine
" of Lancaſter. 1697." 4to. " Popery, ſuperſtition, ignorance, and
" knavery confeſſed and fully proved on the Surey diſſenters from the
" ſecond letter of an apoſtate friend to Zachary Taylor. To which
" is added A refutation of Mr. Thomas Jollie's vindication of the
" devil in Dugdale, or the Surey demoniack. Lond. 1699." 4to. This
refutation was firſt printed by itſelf the ſame year. " A vindication
" of the diſſenters from Mr. Taylor's charge in the Surey impoſtor
" 1698." 4to. and ſome tracts prior to theſe two I have not ſeen.

The Society of Antiquaries have publiſhed among other antient
ſeals that of Burſcough priory : views of Lancaſter and Clithero caſtles
from drawings in the dutchy office, and of the ruins of Furneſe abbey
from a drawing taken 1727 by order of the duke of Montague. Buck
has given a S. E. view of the former, and S. views of the two latter,

1727.

1727. with a S. view of Whalley abbey, S.E. Cockerſand abbey, Cartmele and Holland priories, N. W. of Peele, W. of Gleaſton, and E. of Hornby caſtles: and a larger N. E. view of Lancaſter town. 1728.

Saxton's map of this county was engraved 1577 by R. Hogenbergius without the hundreds, which Speed has added in his 1610, with a 'an of Lancaſter, and eight ill-favoured heads of its dukes, &c.

Bowen publiſhed another ſurvey 1753.

LEICESTER-

LEICESTERSHIRE.

William Burton [a], efq; of Lindley in this county, publifhed in folio, 1622, " The defcription of Leicefterfhire; containing " matters of antiquity, hiftory, armory, and genealogy, &c." A fair copy of it was in the poffeffion of Walter Chetwynd of Ingeftry in Staffordfhire, much augmented with Roman, Saxon, and other antiquities by the author before his death, and came afterwards to Mr. Charles King. Dr. Rawlinfon had the original MS. with numerous notes, and feveral pedigrees in MS. Another is in Jefus Col. library, Cambridge, with large emendations and additions to the pedigrees by Richard Gafcoigne of Branham Biggen, Yorkfhire, tranfcribed fair in a fourth copy 1656: and many of them in Dodfworth's MS. collections at Oxford. In ecclefiaftical matters Burton followed an old valor compiled 1220, a tranfcript of which is in the Cotton library. This county was vifited by Leonard and Vincent 1619. A tranfcript of Domefday is in the hands of Mr. Mores, F. A. S. Mr. Peck, rector of Godeby, had prepared the natural hiftory and antiquities of this and Rutlandfhire, for which he printed a folio fheet of queries 1729, reprinted in the appendix to his life of Cromwell 1740, N° 39, where he fays he had made a confiderable progrefs in his new furvey, and collected many records, papers, infcriptions, &c. and intended to vifit each parifh, and take draughts of all the churches, arms, monuments, feats, natural rarities, &c. many of which he had already done, and to prefix a new and accurate map of each county, with arms. His papers are probably in the hands of Sir Thomas Cave, bart. who reprefents this county in parliament, and is I am well affured engaged in the fame defign.

The rev. Mr. Farmer, fellow of Emanuel Col. Cambridge, has juft publifhed propofals for printing by fubfcription in 4to. " The hiftory " and antiquities of the town of *Leicefter*; originally collected by

---

[a] Mr. Peck had collected materials for the life of this gentleman and his brother Robert.

" William

" William Staveley, efq; barrifter at law, formerly of Peter-houfe in
" that univerfity : and now firft offered to the public from the author's
" MS. with large additions and improvements, and an appendix of
" papers relative to the fubject," to be illuftrated with copper plates
of the ancient and prefent town, Roman remains, teffelated pavements,
coins, feals, &c.

Dr. Stukeley has given a very incorrect view of what is called the Jewry-
wall, which he thinks part of a temple of Janus, in Leicefter, It. Cur.
pl. lv. and the ichnography of Ratæ Coritanorum (the antient Leicefter)
pl. xcii. A view of the other fide of the Roman building is among his
unpublifhed plates, as alfo two views of the Britifh curfus at Leicefter,
called Rawdikes, from the hills above and from the other fide the
river by the fofs road, and a plan of it, 1722.

A view of *Bow* bridge at Leicefter in Peck's Defid. Cur. vol. i. book
vii. p. 15. A S. view of Leicefter abbey 1730, and a large S. view of
the town by Buck 1743.

'' In 1679 was publifhed in one fheet " A brief relation of a wonder-
" full accident, a diffolution of the earth in the foreft of *Charnwood*,
" about two miles from Loughborough in Leicefterfhire, lately done
" and difcovered, and reforted to by many people both old and young.
" Publifhed by two lovers of art, J. C. and J. W. 1679." 4to. reprinted in the Harl. Mifc. II. 178.

There is fome account of *Difeworth* at the beginning of Lilly's
" Hiftory of his life and times. 1715."

A defcription and S. view of the church of *Market Harborough*; fuppofed to have been built by John of Gaunt 1370, as a penance for
keeping Kath. Swinford, is inferted in the Gentleman's Magazine,
June 1765, p. 283, and p. 253 an account of Thomas Sampfon,
rector of *Keym*, near Loughborough, who from the account of the
births of his eight children is fuppofed to have been 114 years old :
but this fuppofition was confuted in the General Evening Poft, Dec.
10—12, 1765, by another, that he probably tranfcribed the regifter
from 1563 and fet his name to each page, which might make him
pafs for rector there ever fince 1563.

" Plans

" Plans for a public library and garden at *Church Langton*," were publifhed by the rev. Mr. Hanbury. Lond. 1760. 8vo.

" The contents, virtues, and ufes of *Nevil Holt* fpaw water further
" proved, illuftrated, and explained from experiments and reafon.
" With fome hiftories of its fignal effects in various difeafes. Collected
" by feveral hands. Alfo rules and directions for its more eafy ufe
" and greater fuccefs. The 2d edition, with feveral emendations and
" great additions. Lond. 1749 " 8vo. with a poftfcript printed 1750.

In p. 324 of Nº 331 of the Philofophical Tranfactions is a letter from Samuel Carte, rector of St. Margaret's church, Leicefter, to Humphrey Wanley, concerning a teffellated pavement found there. In p. 803 of vol. xlix. we have an account of rare plants found in this county by Richard Pulteney, apothecary at Leicefter.

Loughborough, an ode, infcribed by John Duick to Ambrofe Philips, efq; of Garrenton near it, knight of the fhire for this county, is in the Gentleman's Magazine, Aug. 1735, p. 494.

" *Belvoir:* a Pindaric ode upon Belvoir caftle, the feat of the earls
" of Rutland, made in the year 1679." was printed from the MS. in the Harleian Mifcellany, iv. 527. E. and S. views of the caftle were engraved by Buck 1730. A N.W. profpect by Badeflade and Toms 1731.

Two views of *Dunnington* cliff, on the Trent, five miles S. E. of Derby, belonging to the earl of Huntingdon, were publifhed 1745 by Vivares, from paintings by Smith.

A view of the parifh church of *Hufbands Bofworth*, Leicefterfhire, as damaged by a dreadful ftorm July 6, 1755, drawn by Samuel Turner and engraved by T. Jefferies.

A view of Benonis *(High Crofs)* Stukeley's It. Cur. pl. xciii.

Buck engraved, 1730,
> S. W. view of Olvefton priory.
> N. Ulvefcroft priory.
> N. W. Grace Dieu nunnery.
> S. and N. Afhby de la Zouch caftle.

Saxton's

Saxton's map of this county is included in that of Warwickſhire, engraved 1576 by Leon. Tervoort, without the hundreds : Mr. Burton ſupplied theſe, and added eighty towns in another map, engraved by Jod.Hondius at Amſterdam 1602, inſerted in his book on a ſmaller ſcale by Kip, and copied by Speed 1610, with a plan of Leiceſter.

Another including Rutlandſhire has been publiſhed by E. Bowen 1756.

LINCOLN-

LINCOLNSHIRE.

IN the British Museum, MS. Harl. 6829, is a large folio, containing the antiquities of the county of Lincoln, particularly the inscriptions on the tombs in the several parishes throughout the county, with the arms of the gentry painted. The names and arms of the Lincolnshire gentry are alphabetically disposed at the end of Yorke's Union of honour : the author of which was a blacksmith at Lincoln. A transcript of Domesday for this county is among Dodsworth's MSS. in the Bodleian library, Cat. MSS. Angl. I. p. 212. N.º 5017. 11. Mr. Becket the surgeon observed more wills in the prerogative office relating to this county than any other [a]. It was visited 1562 by Cook : 1592 by Lee : 1615 by————

In 1614 was published " Lamentable newes out of Lincolnshire, " of the over-flowing of waters breaking from the seas, which " drownded five villages, &c. November 1613." 4to. and in 1671 " A true and impartial relation of the great damages done by the late " great tempest and overflowing of the tide upon the coast of Lincoln- " shire and Norfolk, &c."

Dr. Stukeley in his Itinerary [b] expressed his hopes that Wm. Pownal, esq; of Lincoln, would one day favour the learned with an accurate account of that city, as it highly deserves.

" The history and antiquities of Lincoln cathedral, containing an " exact copy of all the antient monumental inscriptions there (in num- " ber 163) as they stood in 1641, most of which were soon after torn " up or otherwise defaced : collected by Robert Sanderson, S. T. P. " (afterwards bishop of that church) and compared with and corrected

---

[a] Stukeley's Itin. Cur. p. 25.
[b] Page 86. where he has given the Roman inscription on St. Mary's steeple : the modern one over it was engraved for him by Harris in an unpublished plate; not having seen it elsewhere I add it for explanation.

MARIE
OFEISCE
NERIS IEIO
+ VIPIOSCSI / R
+ ERII GMEIEIRIPE   " by

" by Sir W. Dugdale's MS. furvey. Communicated by Nich. Lambert " L. L. D. fellow of St. Peter's Cambridge." is inferted in Peck's Defid. Cur. vol. ii. b. viii. N° 1. with notes and additions by the editor. Dugdale's furvey was taken 1641, when he and Wm. Sedgwic the arms-painter fervant to Sir Chriftopher Hatton, drew in a moft exact and curious manner all the monuments and infcriptions here and in the other churches mentioned in his life. The book was in lord Hatton's library; extracts from it are in Willis's furvey of this cathedral, and two draughts of bp. Smith s graveftone and bp Hugh's fhrine in Stukeley's Itin. Cur. pl. xvi and xxix. Hearne publifhed in Ap. to Caius, N° 171, the fize of the great bell and dimenfions of the church. The E. S. and W. fides were engraved by King, the S. and W. by Harris. Vivares executed a beautiful view of the W. front drawn 1750 by Jofeph Baker, mafter of the comedians at York.

A Roman fudatory difcovered thirteen feet under ground near the W. end of this cathedral 1740, was publifhed by the Society of Ant - quaries: Mr. T. Sympfon gave an account of it in p. 855 of N° 461 of the Philofophical Tranfactions.

Meffrs Buck gave 1726 a N. view of the bifhop's palace; a S. W. one of the caftle, an E. one of John of Gaunt's palace, now almoft pulled down: and a larger S. W. view of the city 1743. They have a drawing of the *Mint wall*, part of a Roman building near the caftle, 63 feet long, about 30 high, and 3½ thick, with 5 layers of brick between the ftones. An ichnography of Lindum Colonia makes pl. lxxxviii and Newport gate, a Roman work, pl. liv. of Stukeley's Itin. Cur.

" The furvey and antiquitie of the towne of *Stamford*, in the " county of Lincolne, written by Richard Butcher, gent. fometimes " towne-clarke of the fame towne. Lond. 1646." 4to. A republication of this piece with numerous additions was expected from Mr. Fofter, rector of St. Clements Danes, native of this town and fometime warden of Brown's Hofpital, who had long promifed it, though it does not appear he left ought behind him towards fuch a work. He begun to revife it in 1706; and afterwards formed a defign of a new work: but an inveterate palfy in his head prevented him from digefting his extenfive reading. All that Peck could find compleated

among

among his papers was only a letter to Dr. Tanner, proving that there was neither Roman or Britifh town here, and the contents of another to Stevens, author of the fupplement to the Monafticon; both which he printed at the end of his Antiquarian Annals. At laft, without fo much as a continuation of the lift of aldermen, the work came forth under the altered title of " The furvey and antiquity of the " town of Stamfurd, in the county of Lincoln, with its ancient found- " ation, grants, priviledges, and feveral donations thereunto belong- " ing: alfo a lift of the aldermens names, and the times when they " were chofen, with the names of the ten lord mayors of the honour- " able city of London, born in the aforefaid county of Lincoln: writ- " ten by Richard Butcher, gent. &c. Lond. 1717." 8vo. Butcher himfelf revifed the piece, and made feveral additions about 1660. After his death his fon promifed to publifh it: which promife Peck performed by inferting it with his own notes, at the end of his " Aca- " demia tertia Anglicana, or the antiquarian annals of Stamford in " Lincoln, Rutland and Northampton fhires; containing the hiftory of " the univerfity, monafteries, gilds, churches, chapels. hofpitals, and " fchools there, with memoirs of the lords, magiftrates, founders, " benefactors, clergy, and other antient inhabitants; interfperfed with " many new and curious particulars touching the Britons, Romans, " Saxons, Danes, French, Jews, church-hiftory, parliaments, coun- " cils, pleadings, occurrences in the barons wars, and the wars be- " tween the two houfes of York and Lancafter; as alfo the acts and " anceftry of divers lord chancellors, knights of the garter and bath, " abbats of Peterborough, priors of Durham, bifhops of Lincoln, and " fundry other famous perfons and antient families; being not only a " particular hiftory of Stamford, and feveral other old towns, but an " uncommon feries of civil and ecclefiaftical affairs under each reign, " gathered from the beft accounts print and MS. with a large chrono- " logical table of contents, and variety of fculptures, in fourteen books. " 1727." Some of his friends of the Antiquarian Society advifed him to throw this work into the aukward form of annals. He had pre- pared a fecond vol. but died before he could publifh it. The publi- cation of the firft having been delayed five years after the fubfcription

was

was opened, Francis Howgrave, a bookfeller of the town, publifhed
" An effay of the antient and prefent ftate of Stamford; its fituation,
" erection, diffolution, and re-edification; antient and prefent fports,
" endowments, benefactions, churches, monuments, and other curi-
" ofities; monafteries, colleges, fchools, and hofpitals: fome account
" of a monaftic life, when the monks firft appeared in the world,
" what orders of them fettled here, and the time of their coming into
" England.   The whole gathered from the printed accounts as well as
" original MSS. particularly the regifters of Durham and Peterborough,
" the rolls in the Tower and Cotton library, old writings belonging to
" Brown's hofpital, the corporation books, Mr. Fofter's papers, Ste-
" vens's fupplement to Dugdale's Monafticon, and many other private
" repofitories.   Stamford 1726." 4to.   In the preface to this fuperficial compendium is a long detail of what paft on this occafion between
the author and Peck, who thought it intended to prejudice his performance, and is moft unmercifully handled by Howgrave.

A S. view of Stamford by Buck 1743.

An indifferent print of St. Leonard's hofpital without the walls of
Stamford, with its fine Saxon W. front, is in Stevens's Monaft. vol. i.
p. 226.

A flight defcription of *Burghley* houfe is in Peck's Defid. Cur. I. b. vi.
Nº xxii.   The S. front towards the gardens is engraved from a draw-
ing by John Lungton, the buildings too much fhortened.   Mr. Bridges,
the Northamptonfhire antiquary, had another by Tillemans from the
S. W. gate of the park, taking in the gardens.   The tapeftry after
the defigns of Albano has likewife been engraved.   In this book of
Peck's is a view of this houfe from the gardens, a N. profpect and
ichnography of Burghly hofpital, Stamford, 1594, the monuments of
Richard Cecil and his wife, of William lord Burghley, and of Henry
Wykes, vicar of All Saints 1508.

Mr. Peck promifed the " Hiftory and antiquities of the town and
" foke of *Grantham*," which were in great forwardnefs in 1735.

We have an account of the famous abbey of *Croyland* in Ingulphus's
hiftory, and the continuation of it.   But what cannot be enough regretted

gretted is the want of a good view of its magnificent front. Peck [c] tells us that Mr. Bridges had caused one to be taken by the curious hand of P. Tillemans, which is probably with all his other collections and draughts in the hands of Sir Thomas Cave. The execrable S. and W. views in the Monasticon might pass for any other building: nor are the small W. and S. W. ones by Buck 1726 very correct. Harris engraved a much better for Dr. Stukeley, who inserted the head of abbot Turketyl in his Palæographia Brit. N° II. The triangular bridge is engraved in the Itin. Cur. pl. vii. and in the Gentleman's Magazine, July 1751, p. 296, and further remarks on it, with a ground-plot, in that for Apr. 1763, p. 179. also in that for Dec. 1759, p. 570, a draught of St. Guthlac's cross the boundary of the abbey lands, which with Edenham and Ivy cross is in Dr. Stukeley's plate of crosses. In the Philosophical Transactions, N° 490, the doctor gave an account and plate of an antient shrine belonging to this abbey, afterwards in his possession, and since bought at his sale by Gust. Brander, esq;

Ames [d] has printed from the original in the hands of Dr. Rawlinson (who takes no notice of it in the English Topographer) " A deed by " which the prior and convent of *Kyrkeby*, Lincolnshire, admitted " William Husse and Anne his wife to the benefit of an indulgence " granted by Boniface IX. to which is annexed this absolution. " *D. Ihesus Christus te absolvat, & auctoritate Dei patris omnipot. &* " *beat. Petri & Pauli apostolor. ejus, ac virtute papalis indulgentiæ ego* " *absolvo te ab omnibus peccatis tuis, & penis purgatorii, & quæ tibi in* " *purgatorio debentur propter culpas & offensas quas contra deum com-* " *missisti, & restituo te illi puritati & innocentiæ in quibus eras quando* " *baptizatus fuisti. In nomine Patris, & Filii, & Spirit. S. Amen.*" The seal, two keys in saltire. He mentions also " An [e] indenture or deed printed on a broad sheet of vellom for the use of the gild or brotherhood of St. Mary's at Boston, in Latin, dated Mar. 8, 1505." and " The admission of Richard Woolman into the gild of St. Mary's

---

[c] Antiq. of Stamford, b. viii. § 38.
[d] History of Printing, p. 134.
[e] Ibid. A register of C. C. C. gild there begun 1335, MS. Harl. 4795.

in

in the church of St. Botolph at Boſton, with all the privileges thereof:
printed on vellom with blanks for the perſon's name and the date, as
follows. *Univerſis Xpi pntes literas inſpecturis, nos aldermannus &*
camerarii gilde ſive confraternitas in honore B. M. V. in ecc. ſci Botoul-
phi de Boſton, Lincoln. dioces. inſtitute, ſalut. in communi ſalvatore.
Dudum ſiquid poſtquam felicis recordationis, Nic. V. Pius II. & Sextus
IV. Rom. pontifices univerſis confratribus conceſſerant utriuſq. ſexus con-
fraternitatis, gratioſe conceſſerant. Ac deinde Innocent. eo Rich. Wool-
man intra noſtr. confratrum numerum eligimus, & admittimus & in-
dulti ſuperad. ac noſtrorum indulgentiarum omniumq. aliorum ſuffra-
giorum & bonorum operum ſpiritualium noſtrorum ſemper fore participes
volumus, & innoteſſimus per præſentes in quorum teſtimonium cmnium &
ſingulorum premiſſorum ſigillum comm. dicte gilde preſentibus eſt appenſus.
Dat. apud Boſton x die menſis Dec. ann. dni MVCIII.

A good S. view of the church was drawn and publiſhed by Dr.
Stukeley, who dedicated the plate to Peregrine marquis of Lindſey,
and lord Willoughby of Ereſby, eldeſt ſon of Robert duke of Ancaſter,
with a brief hiſtory of it annexed. A ſmaller view is inſerted in his
Itin. Cur. pl. xix.

There are two others of different ſizes, the largeſt drawn by W.
Stennit, jun. 1715, the ſmaller probably copied from the Doctor's.
Mr. Walpole mentions another engraved by Vertue.

A plan of the town ſurveyed 1741 by Robert Hall, engraved by
Toms, with views of the market croſs and church. Harris engraved
the croſs for Dr. Stukeley. The ſeal of the ſtaple here, in the hands
of Samuel Gale, was engraved 1736. Dr. Stukeley had unpubliſhed
plates of the Roman roads through Lincolnſhire, Holbeach croſs, and
a monument of a Littlebury in the church, which makes pl. xxi. of his
Itinerary. The churchwardens account from 1453 to 1597 [f], and the
town book wrote by Mr. John Stukeley 1676, one of his anceſtors, are
in the hands of the Doctor's ſon-in-law Mr. Fleming.

There is an ichnography of the remains of *Spalding* abbey in the
Monaſticon. Dr. Stukely inſinuates [g] that a particular account of this

[f] There is an extract from it Itin. Cur. p. 18.
[g] Ib. p. 22.

town

town was expected from Maur. Johnson, esq; an eminent antiquary, native of it. In the Philosophical Transactions, Nº 279, is an account of Roman cisterns found there [h].

The MS. history and antiquities of *Winterton*, collected by Abraham Delapryme, corrected and enlarged by Warburton, was purchased at the sale of the latter's books 1759 by Mr. Goodman. The Antiquarian Society have engraved three tessellated pavements found at this place.

" The report of Messrs. John Grundy, Langley Edwards, and John " Smeaton, engineers, concerning the present ruinous state and con- " dition of the river Witham, and the navigation thereof, from Lin- " coln through Boston, to its outfall into the sea; and of the fen lands " on both sides the said river. Together with proposals and schemes " for restoring, improving, and preserving the said river and naviga- " tion, and also for effecting the drainings of the said fen lands. To " which is annexed a plan and proper estimates of the expences in " performing the several works recommended for those purposes." was printed at Lincoln 1761. 4to.

" An Act for draining and preserving certain low lands called the " Fens lying on both sides of the river Witham, in the county of " Lincoln, and for restoring and maintaining the navigation of the " said river, from the High Bridge in the city of Lincoln, through the " borough of Boston to the sea. 1762." Fol.

Hatfield chace, the largest in England, containing within its limits above 180,000 acres, one half of which was yearly drowned and surrounded with water, Char. I. sold to Vermuiden, without the consent of the commissioners and tenants, to dischace, drain, and cultivate; which to the general surprize and advantage he at length effected at the expence of about 400,000 l. He published 1642 " A discourse " concerning draining the great fens." 4to. There afterwards came out against him " The long and tedious decree in the Exchequer of " the participants within the level of Hatfield chace, made in the " 12th year of the late king upon the award of Sir John Banks, kt.

[h] Itin. Cur. p. 12.

K k 2 " then

" then attorney general, againſt ſome of the tenants of Epworth in
" the iſle of Axholme, with the recitals therein contained, in Mr.
" Gibbon's fourteen ſkins of parchment, and the means uſed by Sir
" Cornelius Vermeuden, the Dutchman, with the help of Mr. Gib-
" bon, then ſecretary to the lord treaſurer Weſton, to obtaine the
" ſame; and the proceedings thereunto truly and briefly ſtated, where-
" upon ſeveral quæries are raiſed, and humbly ſubmitted to the grave
" wiſdom and judgment of this honourable parliament, whether the
" 370 perſons therein named to have ſubmitted, are, or ought by law
" or equity to be bound, and exempted from their antient right of
" common in the 7400 acres of ground now in queſtion by that de-
" cree, and why it ought to be wholly reverſed and of no force, hav-
" ing already little or no ſtrength, as appears from the parliament's
" own laſt decree or decretal order of the 10th of Feb. 1750.   Pub-
" liſhed to inform the truth, and to prevent the miſinformation of
" Mr. John Gibbons, and to rectifie his breviate formerly given in to
" the hon. committee, tending to the ſubverſion of truth. Lond.
" 1657."

" Thunder, haile, and lightning from heaven againſt certaine co-
" vetous perſons inhabitants of *Humerſton*, Lincolnſhire, five miles
" from Grimſby, thought to be a juſt puniſhment from God in
" the behalf of the poore, the 3d of July laſt 1610; how the corne
" was deſtroyed, the like never heard of in any age, only one man's
" eſtate preſerved, who gave them reliefe, as it was juſtified before
" the knights and juſtices of the countie at the ſeſſions held at Lowth
" the 10th daye of July; with the lamentable end of John Corniſh,
" his wife, and two children, who were moſt ſtranglie conſumed in a
" daye at Strow in Staffordſhire 9 May 1616. 1616." 4to.

" God's wonderfull judgment in Lincolnſhire; or a dreadful warn-
" ing to children that are undutifull to their parents : being a true ac-
" count of the ſad end of a young man about ſeven miles from Lin-
" coln [near Grantham] who having been very diſobedient, and ſo
" very unnatural as to ſtrike his own father, and otherwiſe a notorious
" ill-liver, the devil on Saturday 22 March laſt viſibly appeared to
" him, and thenceforward he fell into deſpair of God's mercy, ac-

5   " knewledging

" knowledging he had given himfelf to the devil ever fince he was
" ten years old, and fo after a fortnight'scontinuance in that miferable
" condition dyed. Lond. 1679." 4to.

One of the moſt capital pieces of witchcraft in the laſt century, which
made James I. a convert to its reality, was practifed in the earl of Rutland's family at Belvoir caſtle by Joan Flower and her daughters Phil-
lipa and Margaret, in revenge for the difmiſſion of the latter from his
fervice, for which thegirls were hanged. Their caſe was printed 1618,
4to. and 1621 a 4to pamphlet, intitled " Strange and wonderful
" witchcrafts: difcovering the damnable practices of feven witches
" againſt the lives of certain noble perfonages, and others of this king-
" dom; with an approved trial how to find out either witch or any
" aprentice to witchcraft."

In N° 67, p. 2050, of the Philofophical Tranfactions is a relation of
wood found under ground in the Iſle of *Axholme*. In N° 484, p. 571,
an account of the body of a woman and an antient ſhoe found in the
fame iſle; inferted in the Gentleman's Magazine for May 1749, with
a cut. In N° 223 is a letter from Mr. Chriſtopher Merret [i], mentioning
feveral obfervables in natural hiſtory in Lincolnſhire, not taken notice of
by Camden or any other author. In N° 263, p. 561, is a letter from Mr.
De la Pryme, dated Hull Aug. 2, 1700, to Mr. G. D. of York concerning the Roman road from Lincoln to the Humber, and a Roman pavement found at *Roxby*, afterwards drawn by C Mitley under the direction of Mr. Drake, and engraved by the Antiquarian Society 1747.
In N° 266, p. 677, is a letter from the fame gentleman concerning
the village of *Broughton*, with obfervations on ſhells found in the quarries there. In N° 278, p. 1129, another letter from the fame concerning fome trees found under ground in *Hatfield* chace. In N° 224
we have a table of the Lincolnſhire waſhes, by C. Merret. Dr. Stukeley improved this table, and had it engraved for the benefit of travellers on a handſome copper plate by John Redman in 1721. The
Doctor publiſhed 1723 a map of the levels here, commonly called
Holland, defcribed by himfelf. In N° 279, p. 1156, is part of a

[i] Surveyor of Boſton port and fon of Dr. Merret.

letter

letter from Mr. Raftrick concerning fome Roman coins, &c. found near *Fleet* and *Spalding*; and R. Thorefby's remarks on them. His amendments and additions to the above account were inferted in N° 377, p. 344. In N° 402, p. 428, is an account of a Roman pavement difcovered at *Denton* near Grantham 1727, and the œconomy of the Roman times in this part of England, by Dr. Stukeley. In vol. xlvii. p. 447, is an account of a water fpout raifed off the land in *Deeping* fen, communicated by the rev. Mr. Ray.

An E. view of *Tatterfal* caftle was publifhed by Buck 1726, and another in the Gentleman's Magazine, Dec. 1759, p. 560. The antiquities of this place, with the monuments in the defolated choir, and the hiftories in the rich, but ruined, windows of its church deferve the attention of the curious.

Other views by Buck are N. Somerton caftle; S. Torkfey hall; W. Thornton college; N. Barling's abbey; N. W. Tupholme priory; S. Moore Tower k; Temple Bruer church ; N. Scrivelfby hall m; W. Louthpark and Kirkfted abbies, N. E. and E. A weft profpect of Lowth church 1725.

A view and plan of Kirkfted abbey and of Tupholme abbey gatehoufe may be feen in Stukeley's Itin. Cur. pl. xxviii. Colfterworth church, where Sir Ifaac Newton was baptized, pl. xx. The form of the decoys in Lincolnfhire, pl. ii. Ichnographies of Banovallum (Horncaftle) pl. lxxxix. and at p. 76 of his Abury, &c. are two fanciful views of an alate druid temple at Barrow on the Humber, with an account of it. Unpublifhed plates of the fcite of the Roman town at Wintringham (Abontrus), and Brough (Crocolana) from Potter hill; a profpect of Cafter or Thongcafter, a metzotinto of Syfer fpring there, and an infide view of Thornton college 1724; which is particularly defcribed Itin. Cur. 94, and of which Buck's is a very indifferent view.

A view of lord Tyrconnel's new waterworks, &c. at Belton, engraved by Vivares from a painting of Smith's was publifhed 1749.

k Dr. Stukeley had an engraving of this brick building, which feems a fragment of a manor houfe.
l Now reduced to a fteeple and the whole town to one farm houfe.
m Burnt down 1766.

Vertue

Vertue engraved a N. W. view of Gainſborough.

A S. proſpect of Hatherthorp, the ſeat of Sir Michael Newton, by Badeſlade and Toms.

A plan of the road from the city of Lincoln over the heath through Duntſby lane, through Sleaford, Folkingham, Bourn, and Market Deeping to Peterborough; and alſo from Bourn through Edenham, Grimſthorp park by Swinſted and Corby to Colſterworth by S. Bee, dedicated to Peregrine Bertie duke of Ancaſter, by Robert Auſtin.

Saxton's map of Lincolnſhire is included in that of Nottinghamſhire, engraved 1576 by Rem. Hogenbergius, without the hundreds, ſupplied in Speed's 1610, with a plan of the city. Hollar engraved a ſmall map of this county with part of York and Nottinghamſhires, and a view of Hull and the Humber at the corner. E. Bowen another 1753, with Dr. Stukeley's perpetual tide table for the waſhes.

MIDDLESEX.

MIDDLESEX.

JOHN Norden began his labours with " Speculum Britanniæ:
" the 1ſt parte, an hiſtorical and chorographical deſcription of
" Middleſex. Wherein are alſo alphabeticallie ſet down the names
" of the cyties, townes, pariſhes, hamletes, howſes of name, &c.
" With direction ſpedeilie to find any place deſired in the mappe, and
" the diſtance betwene place and place, without compaſſes ; by the
" travail and vew of John Norden, anno 1593." 4to. with maps by
Senex, and the arms of the principal perſons intetred here 1723. 4to.
His deſcription of Hertfordſhire was annexed to it. A copy of this
book among the Harleian MSS. N° 570, ſuppoſed to be Norden's
own writing, differs from the printed books both in the arrangement,
and the additions made to it.

John Bowack, writing-maſter to Weſtminſter ſchool, attempted in
monthly numbers " The antiquities of Middleſex ; being a collection
" of the ſeveral church monuments in that county : alſo an hiſtorical
" account of each church and pariſh ; with the ſeats, villages, and
" names of the moſt eminent inhabitants, &c. Part I. Beginning
" with Chelſea and Kenſington. Lond. 1705." Fol. The ſecond part
contained the monuments and deſcriptions in Fulham, Hammerſmith,
Chiſwick, and Acton churches. 1705. Fol. A third was promiſed,
containing the pariſhes of Ealing, New Brentford, Thiſtleworth, and
Hanwell but the author proceeded no further, not finding or de-
ſerving encouragement. His principal talent ſeems to have been
writing a good hand, a ſpecimen of which may be ſeen in Harleian
MS. 1809. a thin vellum book containing ten neat drawings in Indian
ink, and divers ſpecimens of Engliſh text and print hands, ſent to
lord Oxford 1712, with a letter (now at the beginning) from the
author.

Propoſals for publiſhing the antiquities of this county with Norden's
book, and on the ſame plan, dated Feb. 29, 17$\frac{1}{2}$, with a ſpecimen
of the pariſh of Finchley.

Weever

Weever has given the funeral monuments, p. 522—542. One in Iflington church was republifhed more correctly in the Gent. Mag. Aug. 1751. p. 368.

Middlefex was vifited 1634 by H. St. George, 1664 by Wm. Ryley and H. Dethick.

Dr. Plott defigned to write its natural hiftory, and his collections were faid to be left in the hands of his fon-in-law Burman.

Dr. Johnfon at the end of his " Defcriptio itineris plantarum," mentioned in Kent, gives " Enumeratio plantarum in ericeto " Hamftediano locifque vicinis crefcentium. Lond. 1632." 12mo.

J. Blackftone publifhed " Fafciculus plantarum circa Harefield " fponte nafcentium, cum appendice ad loci hiftoriam fpectante. Lond. " 1737." 8vo.

" A fhort and plain account of the late found balfamick wells at " Hoxdon, and of their excellent virtues above other mineral waters; " which make them effectually cure moft difeafes, both inward and " outward. With directions how to ufe them. By T. Byfeild, M.D. " Lond. 1687." 12mo.

" A true and exact account of Sadler's-wells : or, the new mineral " water lately found out at Iflington; treating of its nature and vir- " tues. Together with an enumeration of the chiefeft difeafes which " it is good for, and againft which it may be ufed, and the manner " and order of taking it. Publifhed for publick good, by T. G. doctor " of phyfick. Lond. 1684." 4to.

" Experimental obfervations on the water of the mineral fpring " near Iflington, commonly called New Tunbridge Wells. Lond. " 1751." 8vo.

" Hampftead Wells : or directions for the drinking of thofe waters, " &c. With an appendix relating to the original of fprings in general; " with fome experiments on the Hampftead waters, and hiftories of " cures. By John Soame, M. D. Lond. 1734." 8vo.

" An experimental enquiry concerning the contents, qualities, and " medicinal virtues of the two mineral waters lately difcovered at " Bagnigge Wells near London ; with directions for drinking them,

L l   " and

" and fome account of their fuccefs in obftinate cafes.   By John Bevis,
" fellow of the Royal Academy of Sciences at Berlin. Lond. 1760." 8vo.

    " A brief de cription of the towne of *Tottenham High Croffe*, in
" Middlefex.   Together with an hiftorical narration of fuch me-
" morable things as are there to be feen and obferved.   Collected,
" digefted, and written by Wilhelm Bedwell, at this prefent paftour
" of the parifh.   To which is added, The turnament of Tottenham ;
" or, The wooing, winning, and wedding of Tibbe, the reeve's daugh-
" ter there.   Written long fince in verfe, by Mr. Gilbert Pilkington,
" at that time, as fome have thought, parfon of the parifh.   Taken
" out of an ancient manufcript, and publifhed for the delight of others,
" by Wilhelm Bedwell, now paftour there. Lond. 1631." 4to.   fince
reprinted in 8vo. Lond. 1718.   This turnament is inferted in " Reliques of antient Englifh poetry," Vol. 2. p. 13. 1765. the editor of
which thinks it a fatire on turnaments : I rather take it for a humorous
relation of a country wedding, and the ruftick fports at it, without any
further view ; Hearne, who printed part of it in his preface to G. Neu-
brigienfis, thinks it might have happened under H. 5. or 6. or Ed. 4.
The ftile and verfification rather incline me to fix it to the age of maifter
Skelton, whofe Tunning of Eleanor Rumminge it much refembles.
Pilkington is not in Newcourt's lift of vicars of this parifh.

    In T. Ofborne's catalogue of the late lord Coleraine's library, Nᵒ
1418, was a " MS. hiftory of the parifh and town of Tottenham
High Crofs, by lord Coleraine, curioufly wrote, neatly bound, with his
lordfhip's arms on the cover."   What this was or in whofe hands it is
at prefent I have not learnt.

    Edmonton has furnifhed matter for a play called " The merry divel
" of Edmonton, as it hath beene fundry times acted, by his maiefties
" fervants, at the globe on the banke-fide. Lond. 1617 and 1626."
reprinted among Dodfley's old plays. V. xi. 1744. from a 3d edition
1655.   One Kirkman, a bookfeller, who about 80 years ago collected
and publifhed many old plays, affirms it to have been wrote by Shakefpear : but his claim to it is now generally given up.   " The life and
" death of the merry devil of Edmonton was printed 1631." 4to.
                                                                " The

" The witch of Edmonton, a known true ftory, compofed into a
" tragi-comedy, by divers well-efteemed poets, Wm. Rowley, Tho.
" Dekker, John Ford, and acted by the prince's fervants, often at the
" cock-pit in Drury-lane, and once at Court, with fingular applaufe.
" Never publifhed till now. Lond. 1658." 4to.

Concerning *Enfield* we have " The cafe of the earl of Stamford
" relating to the wood lately cut in Enfield-Chace; to which is an-
" annexed a plan of the chace, and the intended ridings therein. Lond.
" 1701." Fol. A plan of it as intended to be parcelled out into
farms under the common-wealths among the records in the Tower.
Another among the Harl. MSS. but by a falfe reference in the index
not to be found.

" The auncient feverall cuftomes of the feverall mannors of *Steb-*
" *bunhuth* and *Hackney*, within the countie of Middlefex; which were
" perufed, viewed, and approved by the lord of the faid mannors, and
" by all the copyhold-tenants of the faid feveral mannors, manie years
" paft; and which cuftomes be now againe newlie and fullie con-
" fidered of, ratifyed, allowed and approved by the right honourable
" Henrie lord Wentworth, lord of the faide feverall mannors, and all the
" copiehold-tenants of the faid mannors, as in the feveral articles and
" agreements hereafter following are exprefled, the 10th day of No-
" vember 1587; and in the 29th yeare of the raigne of our foveraigne
" ladie Elizabeth, by the grace of God, queene of England, Fraunce,
" and Ireland, defender of the faith, were printed 1587 and 1617."
4to. and reprinted with great alterations and additions and an introduction of 12 pages, under the title of " The free cuftoms, benefits,
" and privileges of the copyhold-tenants of the mannors of Stepney
" and Hackney, in the county of Middlefex, within this compofition.
" To which. is prefixed, An abftract, or brief relation of the affurance
" given by the right honourable Thomas lord Wentworth, lord of
" both the faid mannors, unto his lordfhip's faid tenants (within this
" compofition) for the ratifying and perpetual eftablifhing of the
" fame. Whereunto two alphabetical tables are fitted; the one con-
" taining the names of the copyhold-tenants, now having com-
" pounded: the which (with the marginal notes in the book) ferveth

" for

" for the ready finding of any note-worthy matter herein contained.
" Lond. 1675." 4to.

" Cuſtoms and priviledges of the manors of Stepney and Hackney,
" &c.   To which is prefixed an act for perpetual eſtabliſhment of the
" ſaid copyhold eſtates and cuſtoms of divers copyholders of the ſaid
" manors according to certain indentures of agreement, and a decree
" in the hon. court of chancery made between the lord of the ſaid
" manor and the copyholders.   With two alphabetical tables. Lond.
" 1736." 12mo.

Three plates of monuments of the Rowe family in Hackney church,
and one in the church of St. Lawrence Jewry, were engraved at the
expence of Edw. Rowe Mores, eſq; F. A. S. by James Mynde, 1752.

The ſtatutes and by-laws of the French Proteſtant Hoſpital at
Hoxton were printed in French and Engliſh. 1741. 8vo.

" A copy of the remarkable laſt will and teſtament of Francis
" Bancroft." purſuant to which his alms-houſes at *Mile-end* were
erected by the Drapers company in 1735, was printed 1754. 8vo.

" Ayme for *Finſburie* archers, or an alphabetical table of the names
" of every marke within the ſame fields, with their true diſtances,
" both by the map, and dimenſuration by the line, publiſhed for the
" eaſe of the ſkilfull and behoofe of the younger beginners in the
" famed exerciſe of archerie, by J. J. and B. E. Lond. 1594." 16mo.

Bagford mentions " The neceſſity and excellence of archery, by
" J. S. dedicated to the nobility and gentry of England by the com-
" pany of Bowyers and Fletchers of London."

" The artillery garden, a poem, dedicated to the honour of thoſe
" gentlemen who practiſe military diſcipline, written by Tho. Dicker.
" 1616." 4to. and

" Aim for the archers that uſe to ſhoot in S. George's fields."

We have a full account of the firſt deſign of *Chelſea* College, with
the frontiſpiece of the model by which it was to have been built, in
" The glory of Chelſey-College revived : where is declared its original,
" progreſs, and deſign, for preſerving and eſtabliſhing the church of
" Chriſt in purity, for maintaining and defending the Proteſtant reli-
" gion

" gion againſt Jeſuits, Papiſts, and all Popiſh principles and argu-
" ments, &c.   By what means this excellent work, of ſuch incom-
" parable uſe and publick concernment, hath been impeded and ob-
" ſtructed.   By John Darley, B. D. and of Northill, in the county of
" Cornwall, rector. Lond. 1662." 4to.

" The rat-catcher of Chelſea-College, a tale : alluding to the man-
" ner in which the out-penſioners of Chelſea have been a long time
" oppreſſed by uſurers and extortioners : with letters from John Sam-
" ford, eſq; ſhewing by what eſtabliſhed rules thoſe uſurers and ex-
" tortioners, with the help of the buyers of the penſions, may beggar
" the penſioners, and enrich themſelves.   As, alſo, a ſcheme to pay
" the out-penſioners after a method whereby, among 4000 of them,
" they may be paid 4560 l. 15 s. a year more than they can get after
" the manner in which they have been hitherto paid, and that too,
" ſo that neither they, nor thoſe appointed to pay them, can either
" defraud the government, or be defrauded the one by the other, and
" likewiſe, ſo that, upon any emergency, all thoſe who are able,
" may be ready to do garriſon-duty, or re-enter into the ſervice, with-
" out doing ſuch injury to them or others, as at preſent is, and has
" heretofore been done upon ſuch occaſions.   With remarks there-
" upon, and letters to the lords commiſſioners of Chelſea-Hoſpital,
" &c.   By John Woodman, who in the year 1723 contrived the
" regulation of the books in the ſecretary's office at Chelſea-College.
" Lond. 1740." 8vo.

" A narrative of ſome proceedings in the management of Chelſea-
" Hoſpital, as far as relates to the appointment and diſmiſſion of
" Samuel Lee, ſurgeon. Lond. 1754." 8vo.   " The true account of
" all the tranſactions before the commiſſioners of Chelſea-Hoſpital, as
" far as relates to the admiſſion and diſmiſſion of Samuel Lee, ſur-
" geon : to which is prefixed a ſhort account of the nature of a rup-
" ture.   By John Ranby and Cæſar Hawkins, ſerjeant-ſurgeons to
" his majeſty. Lond. 1754." 8vo.   " A proper reply to the ſerjeant-
" ſurgeons defence of their conduct at Chelſea-Hoſpital.   By Samuel
" Lee, ſurveyor to his majeſty's Royal Hoſpital at Greenwich, and

" Iſaac

" Ifaac Rand, fuperintendant of the gardens, and botanic reader.
" Lond. 1754." 8vo.

" The trial of Wm. Mitchell, furgeon, for perjury, tried at the
" fitting after Trinity term 1754, in the King's-bench. Lond. 1754."
4to. Lee having brought an action againft Ranby for calling him
impoftor, it was decided by mutual agreement 1753; but by a fecond
action Lee got 100 l. The defamatory words were fworn to by
Mitchell, but an alibi was proved both of place and time, and that
the firft action was partly founded on thefe words: however, in confideration of his univerfal good character, and Ranby s acknowledging
he believed he meant no harm, he was acquitted.

A profpect of this hofpital by R. Ingiifh, comptroller thereof, engraved by J. Sturt. A ground-plot by the fame.

Sir H. Sloane gave the Apothecary's company the phyfic garden,
which they rented of him, on condition it fhould always be kept up,
in evidence of which they were to prefent yearly to the Royal Society
50 plants grown there the preceding year, fpecifically diftinct from
each other, till they amount to 2000, to be carefully preferved by the
Society. Philip Miller publifhed " Catalogus plantarum officinalium
" quæ in horto botanico Chelfeyano aluntur. Lond. 1730.' 8vo.

" Horti medici Chelfeiani index compendiarius exhibens nomina
" plantarum quas ad rei herbariæ præcipue materiæ medicæ fcientiæ
" promovendam ali curavit Societas Pharmacopæorum Londinenfium.
" Confcripfit Ifaacus Rand, horti præfectus, & prælector botanicus.
" Lond. 1739." 8vo.

" An accurate furvey of the botanic garden at Chelfea, with the
" elevation and ichnography of the green-houfe and ftoves, and an
" explanation of the feveral parts of the gardens, fhewing where the
" moft confpicuous trees and plants are difpofed. Surveyed and de-
" lineated by John Haynes." 1751.

" A letter from a councellor at law to his client, about purchafing
" fome lands in *Shadwell*. Lond. 1685." 4to. relates to the fuit between lady Ivy and Dr. Whitchcot, and Sir Anth. Bateman, on the
lady's fide. In Ames's catal. N° 666, is " The famous trial in the

King's-

" King's-bench between Thomas Neale, efq; and the late lady Theo-
" dofia Ivy, June 4, 1684. for part of Shadwell in the county of
" Middlefex, together with a pamphlet heretofore writ by Sir Tho.
" Ivy her hufband, and here now reprinted again with the plans.
" 1696." Fol.

" *Iftleworth*'s Syon's peace, containing articles of agreement between
" Algernoon earl of Northumberland, lord of the manor of Iftleworth
" Syon, and Sir Tho. Ingram, and other copyhold tenants of the faid
" manors."

" A catalogue and plans of all the demefne lands (with the feveral
" erections thereon) of the late William duke of Powis, in the parifh
" and manor of *Hendon*, &c. &c. fold by Langford. Oct. 1756." 8vo.

" A relation of the impofture of Sufanna Fowles of *Hammerfmith*,
" who pretended a poffeffion. Lond. 1698." 4to.

" Innocentia patefacta, & malitia detecta : being the cafe of Mr.
" Charles Dean, practifer at law, who was lately (but innocently)
" executed at Tyburn, for breaking open the houfe of Mr. John Stone,
" at *Shepperton*, 15 miles from London, with an account of feveral
" remarkable paffages relating thereunto. Written by an impartial
" hand, and lover of juftice, now made publick in vindication of Mr.
" Deans innocence, as to the fact for which he died. Lond. 1711."
8vo.

Henry Ford, who under Cromwell's patronage laid the Thames
water into the ftreets of London by pipes, and erected the great waterworks by Somerfet-houfe for fupplying the neighbourhood, projected
and publifhed " A defign for bringing a navigable river from Rick-
" manfworth in Hartfordfhire to S. Giles's in the Fields near London :
" the benefits of it declared, and the objections anfwered. Lond. 1641."
with an anfwer to the whole. 4to. both reprinted 1720. 8vo. A revival of this ufeful defign has been attempted in our age.

In N° 332, p. 375. N° 333, p. 416. N° 337, p. 33. 177. N° 343,
p. 229. of the Philofophical Tranfactions, are accounts of divers rare
plants obferved in feveral curious gardens about London, and particularly in the phyfic-garden at Chelfea, by Mr. James Pettiver, F. R. S
and

and in p. 241. of vol. xlvii. is an account of bp. Compton's botanical garden at *Fulham*.

The eaſt proſpeſt of Fulham bridge is in the Gent. Mag. July *1751*, p. 296.

" An account of the new manufaſture of tapeſtry, after the man-
" ner of that at the Gobelins ; and of carpets, after the manner of
" that at Chaillon, &c. now undertaken at Fulham, by Mr. Peter
" Pariſot. Lond. 1753." 8vo.

" A plan of Mr. Pope's garden as it was left at his death, with a
" plan and perſpeſtive view of the grotto, all taken by J. Serle, his
" gardener ; with an account of all the gems, minerals, ſpars, and
" ores of which it is compoſed, and from whom and whence they
" were ſent : to which is added a charaſter of his writings," from
Thompſon's poem on ſickneſs : alſo R. Dodſley's cave of Pope. Lond,
1745. 4to.

Three views of Mr. Pope's, the counteſs of Suffolk's, and gov. Pitt's houſes at Twickenham, by A. Heckell, engraved by J. Maſon. 1749.

Of a bituminous earth and water on the ſcite of a painter's ſhop, burnt down near the new ſquare at *Hockſdon* by Moorfields ſee Sir H. Sloane's letter to Ray, and his anſwer, in Ray's Philoſophical letters, p. 193. 196. 1713. and Birch's Hiſt. of the Roy. Soc. IV. 398. 405.

" *Pimlyco*, or runne red cap : 'tis a mad world at Hogſdon. 1609."
4to. A poem like Elynor Rummin, which is inſerted in it.

" *Iſlington* : a poem addreſſed to Mr. Benjamin Stappe. To which
" are ſubjoined ſeveral other poetical eſſays by the ſame author. Lond.
" 1763." 4to.

A view of Iſlington by the water-ſide ; two of the water-houſe there, a proſpeſt on the N. ſide of London, and two views of London by Iſlington : by Hollar. 1665. in a ſet.

A view of the new church there in the Gent. Mag. Feb. 1754.

In p. 80. of Mannings " Poems upon ſeveral occaſions. 1701."
8vo. are " Verſes on *Tuddington-houſe*, inſcribed to Sir Charles Dun-
comb."

" *Hounſlow* Heath, a poem, the 2d edition carefully correſted and
" enlarged, by the rev. Mr. Wetenhall Wilkes, M. A. miniſter of the
" chapel

" chapel at Hounflow, in the patronage of Richard Bulſtrode, eſq.
" Lond. 1748." 4to.

" An ode to a grove at Finchley," Gent. Mag. July 1764, p. 343.

The magnificent ſeat of James Brydges, duke of Chandos, levelled
with the ground by publick auction 1747, was celebrated by Gildon in
" *Canons:* or, the viſion, a poem, addreſſed to the right honourable
" James earl of Caernarvan, &c. Lond. 1717." 8vo. and by S. Humphreys in a folio poem under its name, inſcribed to the duke of
Chandos. 1728. Here was preſerved Sir James Ware's valuable collection of MSS purchaſed by the earl of Clarendon when lord lieut.
of Ireland, and ſince by the late John Bridges, eſq; of Lincoln's-inn.
They chiefly concern the affairs of Ireland. A catalogue of them was
printed at Dublin. 1648. 4to. with the books given by Dugdale to the
muſæum at Oxford; another intitled " Librorum MStorum in duabus
" inſignibus bibliothecis, altera Tenniſoniana Londini, altera Dugda-
" liana Oxonii catalogus. Oxon. 1692." 4to. Mr. (afterwards bp.)
Gibſon took this while they were for ſafety depoſited in St. Martin's
library, then lately built by abp. Tenniſon; but his ſtiling them Tenniſoniana offended the honourable owner, and the MSS. were immediately removed. The catalogue was republiſhed in the 2d or Iriſh part
of the 2d vol. of the Cat. MStor. Angliæ, p. 3—15. and the catalogue
of Dugdale's in the firſt volume, p. 292—298.

Tickell's poem on *Kenſington* gardens is in Dodſley's miſcellanies.
I. 43. 1751. and the works of the minor poets II. 247. 1749.

" A walk in Kenſington gardens: a poem. Lond. 1738."

A plan of the palace and gardens by Rocque. 1736.

" Deliciæ Britannicæ; or the curioſities of Hampton-Court and
" Windſor-Caſtle delineated, with occaſional reflections, and embel-
" liſhed with copper-plates of the palaces, &c. By George Bickham,
" Lond. 1742." 12mo.

" Apelles Britannicus" was to have been " A new and ample deſcription of all the moſt valuable paintings, ſtatues, buſtos, and other
curioſities of the royal palaces of Hampton-Court, Windſor, Richmond, Kenſington, St. James's, Whitehall, and Somerſet-Houſe, with
the ſeats of the nobility and gentry, and all the other moſt remarkable
publick edifices throughout Great Britain. With the hiſtory of the

ſubjects,

subjects, &c. and the lives of the most eminent painters, sculptors, architects, and other artists, with the dates of their performances. The whole to have been illustrated with a great variety of large folio copper-plates, exactly drawn from the capital and most valuable originals in each building by Henry Gravelot, and other celebrated hands. In two folio volumes." But only a few numbers came out. " The " English connoisseur: containing an account of whatever is curious " in painting, sculpture, &c. in the palaces and seats of the nobility " and principal gentry of England both in town and country. 1766." 2 vols. 8vo. is on the same plan, but very unequally executed.

In the Pepysian library are two fine drawings by Hollar of the river and garden fronts of the old palace at *Hampton-Court*. Sutton Nicholls engraved the new garden front. Eight views of Hampton-Court and Kensington, drawn by Highmore, were engraved by John Tinney. Rocque engraved a plan of the first of these palaces and gardens 1736.

A perspective view of the magnificent Gothic hall at Hampton-Court, built by Henry VIII. for the reception of ambassadors, was engraved from a design of Mr. Kent, by J. Vardy 1749.

" The circus : or British Olympicks. A satire on the ring in *Hyde-* " *Park*. 1709." 8vo. " An accurate plan of Hyde-Park, the royal palace and gardens at Kensington; together with the town and parish, from a scale so large, that it shews every minute object, hill, dale, grove, &c. and (contrary to the usual method of plans) every object which conveniently can, is thrown into perspective, and will be both useful and picturesque. By Joshua Rhodes, land-surveyor at Kensington." In eight large plates, engraved by Bickham 1763.

Two views of the D. of Argyle's gardens, &c. at *Whitton*, drawn and engraved by Woollet. Four more of the cascade, great canal, bridge, and orangery, painted by Rasbrake, engraved by Du Bois, published by J. Tinney.

A S. prospect of *Holland*-House, by P. Foudrinier 1757.

Burlington-House at Chiswick, dr. by P. Brookes, engr. by J. Fougeron 1750. A plan of the house and gardens by Rocque.

A perspective view of the inside of the amphitheatre in *Ranelagh*-gardens, drawn by W. Newbond, was engraved by Walker 1761. Eight large views of these and *Vauxhall*-gardens by Canaletti and Rooker 1751.

A S.

A S. W. view of Sion abbey by Buck 1737. An etched view of the W. front in the Pepyſian library.

In the ſame library is a drawing, aſcribed to Hollar, of St. Pancras church, commonly called the mother of St. Paul's : and an etching of Highgate church.

A plan of the great road from Tyburn to Uxbridge, and from Brent-bridge to Brentford, in the county of Middleſex. Surveyed by T. Lediard jun.

Plans of Cæſar's camps at Shepparton, on Hounſlow-heath, on Green-field com. between Aſhford and Lalam near Stanes 1723, and that called the Brill at Pancras 1758, are among Dr. Stukeley's unpubliſhed plates.

Saxton has included this county in his map of Kent, Suſſex, and Surrey 1575, without the hundreds, which are inſerted in Speed's, at the corners of which are plans of the moſt famous cities of London and Weſtminſter, and elevations of their cathedrals.

Hollar engraved a large map of Middleſex 1667, and a ſmaller 1670. That in the Britiſh atlas is by R.W. Seale, with the arms of the companies.

A map of thirty miles round London, by C. Price. Another in two ſheets, with an alphabetical table

The counties 25 miles round London by Bowen and Kitchen. Another map of the ſame extent by Ellis. Another of the country from 31 to 42 miles by Kitchen.

Mr. Warburton publiſhed 1749 a map of Middleſex on two ſheets of imperial atlas, with the arms of the nobility and gentry on the borders. Some objeĉtions to the authenticity of theſe arms being raiſed by the then garter king of arms, the author, by order of the deputy earl marſhal, drew up to juſtify them " London and Middleſex " illuſtrated by a true and explicit account of the names, reſidence, " genealogy, and coat armour of the nobility, principal merchants, " and other eminent families, travelling within the precinĉts of this " moſt opulent city and county (the eye of the univerſe) all blazoned " in their proper colours, with references thereunto ; ſhewing in what " MS books, or other original records of the heralds office, the right " of each perſon reſpeĉtively may be found. Lond. 1749." 8vo.

Another ſurvey of this county has been publiſhed by Rocque, in four ſheets, and reduced to one.

WESTMINSTER.

WESTMINSTER.

THE city of Weſtminſter has been generally included in hiſtories of London, but there are ſome diſtinct accounts of it. Great materials are ſaid to have been collected for a full deſcription by a pariſh-clerk of St. Margaret's. I preſume this is Henry Turner mentioned in Widmore's account of the writers of the hiſtory of Weſtminſter abbey, who ſays he was a man of good natural parts, very diligent in making enquiries relating to his ſubject, and had collected a great deal; but had no learning, and underſtood only Engliſh; and was not in many caſes able to diſtinguiſh between truth and falſhood. His book was only a ſurvey of the city of Weſtminſter, purpoſely omitting the hiſtory of the church, which he wiſhed might be written by the late receiver Charles Batteley. He had, however, an account of the abbots, and ſeveral things relating to the officers, and other buildings of the abbey. Rich. Ware, abbot here from 1258 to 1283, cauſed a book of the cuſtoms of his monaſtery to be made, eſteemed a very uſeful work, which were it now in being would have given light to the hiſtory of the place: it conſiſted of four parts, the laſt and principal of which was kept very carefully in the monaſtery; but deſtroyed by the fire in the Cotton library 1731. The firſt printed account of this church is by Camden, in " Reges, reginæ, nobiles, & alii in eccleſia " collegiata B. Petri Weſtmonaſterii ſepulti, uſque ad annum reparatæ " ſalutis 1600. Lond. 1600." 4to. This is ſaid to be enlarged from a collection begun by J. Skelton the poet, probably when this abbey ſheltered him from Wolſey's vengeance; tho perhaps he only amuſed himſelf in ſcribbling epitaphs for the great people there. Camden for fear of offending Elizabeth omitted the coronation chair brought from Scotland. This book was republiſhed with additions 1603 and 1606; of which laſt edition Dr. Rawlinſon had a fair copy on large paper, its margin adorned with the arms of the perſons mentioned in it finely illuminated, and painted in their proper colours.

The next accounts are, " Mauſolea regum, reginarum, dynaſtarum, ' nobilium, ſumptuoſiſſima, artificioſiſſima, magnificentiſſima, Lon-

" dini

" dini Anglorum, in occidentali urbis angulo ſtructa, h. e. eorundem
" inſcriptiones omnes in lucem reductæ cura Valentis Arithmæi pro-
" feſſoris academici. Literis & ſumptibus Joannis Eichorn. Francof.
" Marchion. 1618." 12mo.

" Monumenta Weſtmonaſterienſia : or, An hiſtorical account of
" the original, increaſe, and preſent ſtate of St. Peter's, or the abbey
" church of Weſtminſter. With all the epitaphs, inſcriptions, coats
" of arms, and atchievements of honour belonging to the tombs and
" grave-ſtones : together with the monuments themſelves, faithfully
" deſcribed and ſet forth by Henry Keepe, gent. of the Inner-Temple,
" 1681. Lond. 1682." 8vo. All his merit lies in his faithful copies
of the inſcriptions : he intended a new edition of it in folio like Dugdale's S. Paul's, and had drawn up a ſcheme of the deſign and charge,
which if he had lived to finiſh it would have been a noble work.
Francis Barlow and others drew the monuments, &c. for it. Keepe
wrote alſo under a feigned name " A true and perfect narrative of
" the ſtrange and unexpected finding the crucifix and gold chain of
" that pious prince S. Edward the king and confeſſor, which was
" found after 620 years interment, and preſented to his moſt ſacred
" majeſty K. James the ſecond. By Charles Taylour, gent. Lond.
" 1688." 4to. reprinted at the end of " The antiquities of Weſt-
" minſter abbey." 1722. p. 16. Bagford mentions a 2d part by Gy-
bon. 4to. 1688.

" The antiquities of St. Peter's, or the abbey church of Weſt-
" minſter : containing all the inſcriptions, epitaphs, &c. upon the
" tombs and grave-ſtones ; with the lives, marriages, and iſſue of the
" moſt eminent perſonages therein repoſited ; and their coats of arms
" truly emblazoned, adorned with draughts of the tombs curiouſly
" engraven. By J. Crull, M.D. F.R.S. Lond. 1711." 8vo. A ſupplement to this was printed 1713. 8vo. A 2d edition 1722, in two
volumes, by H.S. and J.R. A 4th in 1741 ; a 5th 1742, with twelve
new monuments. Weever has printed many of the epitaphs ; and
the monuments of the kings, &c. are engraved in Sandford's Genealogical hiſtory. The fulleſt deſcription was given by John Dart, in
his " Weſtmonaſterium, or the hiſtory and antiquities of the abbey
" church of St. Peter, Weſtminſter. Containing an account of its
" antient

" ancient and modern buildings, endowments, chapels, altars, reliques,
" cuftoms, privileges, forms of government, &c. with copies of the
" ancient Saxon charters, &c. and other writings relating to it.   To-
" gether with a particular hiftory of the lives of the abbots, collected
" from ancient MSS. of the convent, and hiftorians; and the lives of
" the deans to this time, and alfo a furvey of the church and cloifters
" taken in the year 1723, with the monuments there, which with
" feveral profpects of the church, and other remarkable things, are
" curioufly engraven by the beft hands. In two volumes." [a] To which
is added, " Weftminfter abbey, a poem, by the fame author. Lond.
" 1740." Fol.   For this pompous but very inaccurate work Dart had
affiftance from the Cotton library, the church records, and the papers
of Mr. Charles Batteley, who had begun fomething relative to its
antiquities, for which he wanted neither abilities nor opportunities, but
died before he could finifh it.

Richard Widmore, M. A. librarian to the dean and chapter, publifhed " An enquiry into the time of the firft foundation of Weft-
" minfter abbey, as difcoverable from the beft authorities now remain-
" ing, both printed and MS.   To which is added an account of the
" writers of the hiftory of the church. Lond. 1743." 4to. and " An
" hiftory of the church, chiefly from MS. authorities. Lond. 1751."
4to.   In this laft is inferted " An hiftorical and architectonical account
" of it, and of the repairs, in a letter from Sir C. Wren to bp. Atter-
" bury, principal commiffioner for them about 1714," [b] with additional
notes by Widmore.

" The hiftorical defcription of Weftminfter abbey, publifhed by
" Newbery. Lond. 1753." 12mo. is a ufeful pocket companion, and
good abftract of larger works.

John Maurer drew and engraved a large print of Shakefpeare's
monument, erected two years after Dart's book came out.   There is
another very ordinary one with verfes from Pope on the fcroll, and
Dryden's character of Shakefpeare at bottom.   Sir Ifaac Newton's was
drawn by the defigner Wm. Kent, and engraved by Fourdrinier.

[a] Firft publifhed by itfelf 1721. 8vo.
[b] Firft publifhed in the Parentalia, or memoirs of the family of the Wrens. Lond.
1750. Fol. p. 294—303.

William

William Illidge drew, and Sturt engraved the five coffins of the Stuart family, in " A plan of the royal vault in Henry VIIth's chapel; wherein are interred the bodies of Charles II. Mary II. William III. Prince George and Q. Anne:" dedicated to bishop Atterbury, dean of Westminster.

A plan and perspective of the royal vault under Henry VIIth's chapel, built 1737, drawn by If. Ware, and engraved by P. Fourdrinier. An exact plan of it, with a view of the late queen and prince of Wales's coffins, printed for Dickinson.

A print of the chapel itself, by J. Schynvoet.

A catalogue of the MSS. belonging to this cathedral, by Maittaire, is in Cat. MSS. Ang. T. ii. p. 27. A different one Harl. MS. 694.

Dr. Rawlinson caused to be engraved 1752 a copy of a lease dated Christmas 1399, of a tenement in a garden adjoining to St. Mary's chapel here, from Robert Hermodesworth chaplain, to Geoffrey Chaucers for 53 years, at the yearly rent of fifty-three shillings and four-pence, if the said Chaucers lived so long, with liberty to distrain for a fortnight's arrears, and for want of due satisfaction then, to enter upon the premises again, as also on the death of Chaucers, which happened the year after: the said tenant not to let the said tenement, or any part thereof during that term, nor to lodge in it any invader of the churches privileges without leave of the said chaplain and sacrist of the church. The same curious collector published from the Exchequer and abbey records two tallies dated 1229 and 1232, and the following order from Edw. III. to the abbot and convent, to give up the famous coronation-stone to the queen-mother, when that infamous peace was made with Scotland under her influence 1328, by which all records, &c. were to be restored. " Edward, par la grace de Dieu, roi
" d'Engleterre, seignr d'Irlaunde, et duc d'Aquit. a nos chers en Dieu
" abbe & covent de Westmostr' saluz. Por ce qe nadgaires acordez
" feut par nos & notre conseil a notre   parlement tenuz a
" Northt. [Northampton] que la piere sur quele les rois descose seulei-
" ent seer au temps de lour curonement, et la quele est en vostre garde
" soit envoiee en Escoce & avons mandez as viscountes de notre cite
" de Loundres qils rescevrent de vous la dite piere par endente, & qils
" la facent carer a la roine d'engletere nostre tres chere dame & mere
" vous mandoms qe quele heure qe les dits viscountes veignent par-
" devans

" devans vous pour cete caufe lour facez livrer la dite piere en la
" forme avantdite. Donc en nulle maniere ne leffez. Donne fous
" notre prive feal a Bordefleic le premier jour de Juyl' lan de notre
" regne fecound.

  " As abbè & covent de Weftm.   Par le roy."

     Indorfed.   " O d. Re. Ed. pro regal. fcocie.

The three fides of this church in the Monafticon were done by Hollar
the ichnography by Newcomb and King : the N. door appears to have
been then incumbered with a projecting porch. A N.W. profpect, with
the fpire defigned by Wren, drawn by T. James, and engraved by
Fourdrinier, is inferted in Maitland's Hiftory of London. A view and
account of the two towers added at the W. end 1745, are in the fupplement to the Gentleman's Magazine 1751.

In Sandford's Hiftory of the coronation of K. James II. and Q.
Mary, is a ground-plot of part of the city of Weftminfter, containing the abbey, hall, court of wards, court of requefts, painted
chamber, houfes of lords and commons ; but particularly the way
from the hall to the church ; and a ground-plot of the church as prepared for the coronation.

A view of the court of wards and liveries, with the other perfons
there affembled, from a painting on parchment near a yard fquare, in the
poffeffion of the late duke of Richmond, was engraved for the Antiquarian Society 1747, by Vertue, with an account of it at the bottom
by profeffor Ward.

Wm. Lodge executed a fmall view of the hall and abbey. There are
in the Pepyfian library two old views of it, with ftatues in front on each
fide of the door, and on two wings that formerly occupied the fcite of
the two coffee-houfes. Alfo a view of it and the abbey from the park.

Hollar engraved " Civitatis Weftmonafterii pars" (the parliament-
houfe, hall, and abbey) and a diftinct view of the hall 1647, in a fet
with two others : a view of Tothill fields 1644, in a fet with three
others. Alfo views of the trials of Strafford, Laud, and Charles I. in
it, and their executions ; the manner of conducting lord Delamere to
his trial [1615], and Jefferies to prefide thereat, with the order of
the whole court, among the Pepyfian collections. A view of the court
erected here for the trial of lord Lovat, March 9—19, 174$\frac{6}{7}$, drawn
by S. Wale, engraved by J. Bafire, publifhed by Pine.

The

The N. front and plan of an old gate in King's-street, taken down 1723, has been engraved by the same society 1725, who have also given us plates of the portrait of Richard II. c, from an ancient painting in the abbey choir 1718, drawn by Gioseppi Grisoni, ex coll. Talm. and the shrine of Edward the Confessor, drawn by Talman 1724, engr. by Vertue.

A view of the gate at the end of the banquetting-house, by Silvester.

" The tapestry hanging of the house of lords, representing the several " engagements between the English and Spanish fleets MDLXXXVIII, " with the portraits of the lord high admiral, and the other noble " commanders, taken from the life." To which are added, from a book intitled, " Expeditionis Hispanorum in Angliam vera descriptio, " A. D. 1588 d, done, as is supposed, for the said tapestry to be worked " after, ten charts of the sea-coasts of England, and a general one of " England, Scotland, Ireland, France, Holland, &c. shewing the places " of action between the two fleets; ornamented with medals struck " upon that occasion, and other suitable devices. Also an historical " account of each day's action, collected from the most authentic " MSS. and writers e. By John Pine f, engraver. Lond. 1739." Fol. who also engraved 1749, a view of the house of peers, K. Henry VIII. on the throne, the commons attending, from a drawing ordered by the then garter, in the hands of John Anstis, esq; king at arms: another view with Q. Elizabeth on the throne, from a painted print in the Cotton library: a plan of the houses of lords and commons: a view of the house of commons in the session 174½: another of

---

c The royal hart, the badge or device of this prince, who shewed several instances of kindness to this church, is painted in an arch on the N. side: the mere gilding of his own and his queen's figures on their tomb here, amounted to above 400 marks. Widmore, hist. p. 102. ex regist.

d I suppose these are the charts or representations of the several actions while the armada was on our coasts, drawn and engr. by Rob. Adams, and published by Aug. Ryther 1588, ment. by Walp. Cat. of Eng. 15.

e By Philip Morant.

f Gravelot gave the designs where invention was necessary. Walp. Cat. of Engr. p. 124. Vertue first suggested this work.

the

the houfe of peers, the king on the throne, the commons attending him, at the end of the fame feffion g.

Bagford's MS. of which hereafter, mentions a poem called " Pro-
" teftant divifion, or party againft party ; with a view of the old build-
" ings at Weftminfter, and a defcription of the hall and pictures of
" capt. Turner's auction-room, by the court of requefts. Fol. 1702."

" Reafons for fuppreffing the yearly fair in Brookfield, Weftminfter,
" commonly called May Fair, recommended to the confideration of
" all perfons of honour and virtue. Lond. 1709." 8vo.

" The ornaments of churches confidered, with a particular view
' to the late decoration of the parifh-church of St. Margaret, Weft-
" minfter ; to which is fubjoined an appendix, containing the hiftory
" of the faid church ; an account of the altar-piece, and ftained glafs
" window h erected over it ; a ftate of the profecution it has occafioned ;
" and other papers. Oxf. 1761." 4to.

" An indulgence and pardon granted to the bleffed faint Cornelius,
" of the parifh-church of S. Margaret's in the town of Weftminfter,
" in the county of Middlefex, in H. 8th's days, with the picture of
" St. Cornelius curing the falling ficknefs." Bagford's MS.

" The repertory of records remaining in the four treafuries on the
" receipt fide at Weftminfter, the two remembrancers of the Ex-
" chequer, with a brief introductive index of the records of Chancery
" and Tower. Alfo a moft exact calender of all the records in the
" Tower. Compiled by Tho. Powell. Lond. 1631." Bagford's MS.

The Antiquarian Society engraved the ftandard of ancient weights and meafures from a table in the Exchequer, but at that time in lord Oxford's poffeffion. In the Philofophical Tranfactions, N° 470 and 541, is an account of a comparifon lately made by fome gentlemen of the Royal Society of the ftandard of a yard, and the feveral weights lately made for their ufe, with the royal ftandard of meafures and

---

g In the Harl. library, N° 37, are two prints of the houfe of commons fitting; another of the houfe of lords, with James on the throne, defigned by J. Speed ; another
with Charles I. and a third of the convocation.

h The Antiquarian Society have a beautiful drawing of this window, which came
from Mr. Conyers's chapel at Copthall. In the Gent. Mag. Dec. 1758, p. 572, is an
account of a dried female body found in the church that fummer.

weights

weights in the Exchequer, and others for publick use at Guildhall, Founders-hall, the Tower, &c.

In the Musæ Anglicanæ, vol. ii. p. 231. is, " Scholæ Westmonaste- " rienfis defcriptio ad Thomam ep. Roff. & eccl. coll. Weftm. de- " canum."

" Scholæ Weftm. alumn. lufus Weftmonafterienfis five epigram- „ matum & poematum minorum delectus, quibus adjicitur nunc " primum edita i Solitudo regia a mufis Weftmonafterienfibus adum- " brata anno regni regis Georgii II. 6to 1732. Lond. 1730" 12mo. 1740. 8vo.

" A review of the project for building a new fquare at Weftminfter ; " faid to be for the ufe of Weftminfter fchool. By a Sufferer. Part I. " 1757." 8vo.

There are two views of Whitehall by Hollar, 1644 and 1647.

A furvey and ground-plot of the royal palace of Whitehall, with the lodges and apartments belonging to their majefties 1680, furveyed by John Fifher, was engraved by Vertue 1747.

Several plates of the palace intended by Jones were publifhed by lord Burlington, but Mr. Walpole thinks from no good defigns ; the fide next Charing-crofs 1743, and the Park fide 1749, engraved by T. M. Muller jun. the Weftminfter fide 1748 by ditto, and A. Benoit ; the water fide 1748 by ditto, Rooker, and Canot. A N. W. view of the fame defign drawn by Elias Ferris, was engraved by Fourdinier. Jones's original defigns for the banquetting-houfe are in the Vitruvius Britannicus. The cieling painted by Rubens was engraved in two plates by S. Gribelin 1726. Mr. Highmore publifhed " A critical ex- " amination of them, in which architecture is introduced fo far as " relates to the perfpective, together with the difcuffion of a queftion, " which has been the fubject of debate among painters. Written " many years fince, but now firft publifhed. Lond. 1754." 8vo.

" The defcription and ufe of his majefty's dial in Whitehall-garden, " by Edmund Gunter. Lond. 1624." 4to. Gunter's dials were on a ftone about four feet and an half fquare at the bafe ; five on the upper part, viz. one at each corner, and the great horizontal concave one in

---

i A poem on the hermitage at Richmond.

the

the middle; and four more on the four fides: there were others in the
fame place before, but his lines, except thofe that fhewed the hour of
the day, were different. He made them by order of Charles I. when
prince of Wales, and wrote this account of them at the king's command. The ftone was but lately removed; but the dials were moftly
defaced by the drunken frolicks of a nobleman in Charles IId's time.
Some others were afterwards made of glafs in fix ranks, pyramidically
difpofed one above another, by Fra. Hall, a Jefuit, 1669; and placed
in the fame garden: but for want of a cover they foon decayed. One
of them Mr. Walpole [m] thinks may be ftill extant. Vertue faw them
at Buckingham-houfe, from whence they were fold. They are defcribed in " An explanation of the dial fet up in the king's garden
" at London, anno 1669; in which very many forts of dials are con-
" tained; by which, befides the hours of all kinds, diverfly expreffed,
" many things alfo belonging to geography, aftrology, and aftronomy,
" are, by the fun's fhadow, made vifible to the eye; amongft which,
" very many dials, efpecially the moft curious, are new inventions,
" hitherto divulged by none. All thefe particulars are fhortly, yet
" clearly, fet forth for the common good, by the reverend father
" Francis Hall, otherwife Line, of the Society of Jefus, profeffor of
" the mathematicks. Printed at Liege, by Guillam Henry Streete,
" in the year of our Lord 1673. Superiorum permiffu." 4to.

The Antiquarian Society have given us the N. front, and a plan of
the gate at Whitehall, lately taken down.

Of the fire at Whitehall 1698, we have " A full and true account,
" licenfed according to order: printed by J. Bradford in Little Britain
" 1698." two folio pages: reprinted in the Harl. Mifcel. vol. vi. p. 367.
It is alfo poetically defcribed by T Brockwell, king's fcholar at Weft-
minfter-fchool, in " Incendium Palatinum pridie Nonas Januarius (fcil.
" die 4) 1697," p. 29 of the Mufæ Britannicæ.

Vertue engraved the font in St. James's church made by Gibbons,
from a drawing by C. Woodfield in Mr. Gale's hands. The N. front
of this church, with upper and lower plans by A. Griffin, was engraved by Hulfberg.

[m] Anecd. of Paint. II. p. 5.

Vertue

Vertue engraved a plan, and W. and S. profpects of the old church of St. Martin's in the Fields.

The W. profpect of Marlborough houfe, drawn by James Light-body, was done by J. Harris.

A view of the new building at the horfe-guards, with elevations of the E. and W. fronts, was publifhed 1753 by J. Vardy, clerk of his majefty's works at Whitehall.

Bagford's MS. mentions " The gateway of St. James's houfes, the " prefence-chamber, the infide of it reprefented at an entertainment " of Mary of Medici at her firft coming into England 16 . . to vifit " her daughter Henrietta, Charles the Ift's queen: in a large thin " folio in French, performed by a Frenchman in feveral views, as her " landing at Harwich, and other places of note where fhe lodged, " with her paffage through London, wherein is a view of Cheapfide " crofs and ftandard, to be found no where elfe. This book is feldom " feen." Alfo the infide of the chapel built for her, etched by Kip; and the garden of pleafure made by And. Mallet, mafter of his ma-jefty's garden in his park of St. James's.

St. James's Park and Hampton-Court, by J. Ricaud.

A plan and elevation of the royal fireworks, performed in St. James's Park, Apr. 27, 1749, on occount of the general peace figned at Aix-la-Chapelle, Oct. 7, 1748. Wm. Halfpenny del. R. Parr fc. Ano-ther by G. Vertue.

Upon application to parliament to erect the beautiful bridge here 1735, was publifhed " A defign of the bridge at New Palace-yard, " Weftminfter, compofed of nine arches independent of each other, " whofe nature is fuch, that the greateft weight poffible cannot break " them down, admitting 880 feet water-way for the flux and reflux " of tides, by which an expence of 24,174 l: is faved, and the build-" ing ftronger. 1736."

A fhort hiftorical account of London-bridge, with a propofal for " a new ftone-bridge at Weftminfter; as alfo an account of fome " remarkable ftone-bridges abroad, and what the beft authors have " faid and directed concerning the methods of building them. Illuf-
" trated

" trated with proper cuts, in a letter to the members for Weftminfter.
" 1736." 4to.

" A fhort narrative of the proceedings of the gentlemen concerned
" in obtaining the act for building a bridge at Weftminfter; and of
" the fteps which the commiffioners appointed by that act have
" taken to carry it into execution. In a letter to a member of par-
" liament in the country : together with his anfwer. 1738." 8vo.

" A fhort hiftorical account of London-bridge, with a propofition
" for a new bridge at Weftminfter, with defigns engraved on copper-
" plates, very ufeful for artificers; in a letter to a member of parlia-
" ment for Weftminfter. By Nicholas Hawkfmoor. 1739" 4to.

" The prefent ftate of Weftminfter-bridge; containing a defcription
" of the faid bridge as it has been ordered into execution by the com-
" miffioners, and is now carrying on, with a true account of the
" time already employed in the building, and the works which are
" now done : in a letter to a friend. 1743." 8vo. By C. Labeleye.

" The downfal of Weftminfter-bridge, a poem. 1747."

" A furvey of Weftminfter-bridge, as it is now finking into ruin;
" wherein the caufe of the foundation's giving way under the finking
" pier, and its diflocated arches, is not only accounted for, but alfo
" that the whole ftructure is likewife fubject to the fame immediate,
" if not unavoidable ruin : with remarks on the piratical methods
" ufed for building the piers, and a juft eftimate of the expence for
" which all the foundation might have been made fecure with piles
" until every ftone, with which the bridge is built, was torn into
" atoms by the hungry teeth of devouring time. By Battey Langley,
" of Meard's Court, Dean-ftreet, Soho, architect. 1748." 8vo.

" A defcription of Weftminfter-bridge; to which are added, an
" account of the methods made ufe of in laying the foundations of
" its piers, and an anfwer to the chief objections that have been made
" thereto; with an appendix, containing feveral particulars relating to
" the faid bridge, or to the hiftory of the building thereof; as alfo
" geometrical plans, and the elevation of one of the fronts as it is
" finifhed, correctly engraved on two large copper-plates : drawn up

" and

" and publifhed by order of the commiffioners. By Charles Labeleye.
" 1751." 8vo.

" Gephyralogia. An hiftorical account of bridges, antient and
" modern, from the moft early mention of them by authors down
" to the prefent time. Including a more particular hiftory and de-
" fcription of the new bridge at Weftminfter, and an abftract of the
" rules of bridge-building, by the moft eminent architects : with
" remarks, comparative and critical deduced both from the hiftory
" and the rules, and applied to the conftruction of Weftminfter-bridge.
" To which is added, by way of appendix, an abridgment of all the
" laws relating thereto. 1751." 8vo.

The defign of a wooden bridge approved by the commiffioners, by
James King, was engraved by Foudrinier. 1739.

A perfpective view of the engine for driving the piles, invented and
delineated by Jofeph Vauloue, watchmaker. 1738. drawn by Gravelot,
and engraved by Toms.

A view of this bridge, with the places adjacent, as in 1747, from
a painting by S. Scott, engraved by Canot 1758.

A S. E. profpect of it, with the lord mayor's fhow on the Thames,
from a painting of Canaletti, drawn by S. Wale, and engraved by R.
Parr 1747.

Another view by Parr 1751.

An intended center arch in the Gent. Mag. Feb. 1754.

" Some obfervations on the fcheme, offered by Meff. Cotton and
" Lediard, for opening the ftreets and paffages to and from the intended
" bridge at Weftminfter, in a letter from one of the commiffioners to
" Mr. Lediard, and his anfwer. With the fcheme and plan pre-
" fixed : to which is added a plan of the lower parts of the parifhes
" of St. Margaret and St. John the Evangelift, from the Horfe Ferry
" to Whitehall ; wherein feveral farther improvements are delineated,
" and a propofal for eftablifhing a perpetual fund, to defray the ex-
" pences of paving, watching, and lighting the faid bridge, and keep-
" ing it in repair. By Tho. Lediard, efq. 1738." 4to.

A plan of the ancient city of Weftminfter from College-ftreet to
Whitehall, and from the Thanes to St. James's Park, in which are
delineated

delineated the new ſtreets laid down and intended to be built by order of the commiſſioners. Surveyed 1740, by T. Lediard, eſq; agent and ſurveyor of the ſtreets and ways for the ſaid commiſſioners. Drawn by T. Lediard jun. and engr. by Foudrinier.

There is a map of Weſtminſter in Norden's Middleſex.

LONDON.

LONDON.

THE earliest account of this city was wrote in Latin by William
Fitz-Stephens, native thereof and monk of Canterbury [a], who
died 1191, intitled " Defcriptio nobiliffimæ civitatis Londoniæ;" a
tranflation of it was inferted in the folio editions of Stowe's furvey, and
the original in the 4to. ones : but fince republifhed, with obfervations
and notes, at the end of Leland's Itinerary, vol. viii. from a more correct MS. on vellum given by Dr. Marfhall to Hearne, and the only
one he ever faw. Robert Bale, recorder of London 1461, compiled
a large account of its hiftory and antiquities; but of his pieces, which
were long preferved in the city library or archives, only the titles have
come down to us. Alderman Fabian's Annals of London have fhared
the fame fate, unlefs we fuppofe with bp. Nicholfon that they are incorporated into his printed Chronicle. Bagford perfuades himfelf Leland wrote a particular account of London, now loft, though it does not
appear in the lift of his works : he thinks Stow was greatly beholden
to it without acknowledgement [b]. That honeft induftrious taylor,
who " feeing the confufed order of our late Englifh chronicles
and the ignorant handling of antient affaires, leaving his owne peculiar ganes, confecrated himfelf to the fearche of our famous antiquities," was the firft that attempted a regular and particular defcription of this city. He begun his ftudies with his Annals about 1560,
for which he travelled over the kingdom on foot, perufing and purchafing innumerable papers juft before difperfed out of the monaftic libraries, and fold for pennyworths. When he had almoft ruined himfelf he
found an efpecial benefactor in abp. Parker. But pecuniary difficulties
were not all he had to ftruggle with : his antiquarian collections and
his younger brother's villainy brought his life into danger on a pretence

---

[a] Whence he is called Gulielmus Cantuarienfis. He is faid to have wrote three treatifes on the life and martyrdom, the apparitions and miracles of Becket; one of which
Sparke publifhed 1733, others are in the Quadrilogium Par. 1495. 4to. Thofe taken for
them in the Cotton library feem rather to belong to Joannes Carnotenfis or Sarifburienfis.
Biog. Brit. Becket. n. A.
[b] Letter to Hearne, p. p. lxviii. lxix. He infers this from his frequent reference to
Leland in his Annals, which proves the contrary.

of

of religion. His fummary of the chronicles of England was firft publifhed 1565, frequently reprinted, abridged, and continued to 1618.
His larger chronicle or annals, of which he printed only an abftract,
leaving the intire work fitted for the prefs, paffed into Sir Simond
D'ewes hands, but feems to have been fince loft. His curious and
valuable account of this city, which coft him many years of clofe application, of which he fpent eight in fearching out antient records relative to the fubject, was firft printed under the title of " A furvay of
" London, contayning the originall, antiquity, increafe, moderne eftate,
" and defcription of that citie ; written in the year 1598, by John
" Stow, citizen of London : alfo an appologie (or defence) againft the
" opinion of fome men, concerning that citie, the greatneffe thereof ;
" with an appendix, containing in Latine, Libellum de fitu & nobili-
" tate Londini, written by William Fitz Stephen in the raigne of
" Henry the Second. Lond. 1598." 4to. A fecond edition came out
in the author's life-time 1603. 4to. in which he intended large improvements, but was prevented by his own ill health and the death of
his able friend John Dalton, efq; from inferting any, except a few additions about the civil government of the city out of his own learned
ftorehoufe c. Stow furvived this edition but two years. The city and
nation he had immortalized neglected him. James I. indeed granted
him a brief or licence, authorizing him or his deputy to receive at the
church doors the benevolence of well difpofed people, in recompence
of his painful labours, and for encouragement to the like : but he died of
poverty, the gout, and ftone, in his 80th year, 1605, and was buried
at his parifh church of St. Andrew Underfhaft, where his widow erected
a monument. Anthony Munday, fometime the Pope's fcholar at Rome,
afterwards converted, which feems to have been Stow's cafe, undertook to enlarge his work, from papers which he pretended were delivered to him by Stow himfelf, and after twelve years put out a new
edition, intitled, " The furvey of London, containing the original,
" antiquitie, encreafe, and more moderne eftate of the fayd famous
" citie. As alfo the rule and government thereof, (both ecclefiaftical
" and temporall) from time to time. With a briefe relation of all the

---

c His collections for this furvey are now in the Harleian library, N° 538.

" memorable

" memorable monuments, and other efpeciall obfervations, both in
" and about the fame citie. Written in the yeere 1598, by John Stow,
" citizen of London; fince then continued, and much enlarged with
" many rare and worthy notes both of venerable antiquity and later
" memorie, fuch as were never publifhed before this yeere 1618.
" Lond. 1618." 4to. But his additions confifted chiefly of fome epitaphs, a continuation of the lifts, and fome tranfcripts out of Stow's
Summary and Annals. A fourth edition, very much augmented, was
afterwards publifhed, intitled " The furvey of London: containing the
" originall, increafe, moderne eftate, and government of that city,
" methodically fet downe. With a memoriall of thofe famoufer acts of
" charity, which for publicke and pious ufes have beene beftowed by
" many worfhipfull citizens and benefactors. As alfo all the antient
" and moderne monuments erected in the churches, not onely of
" thofe two famous cities, London and Weftminfter, but (now newly
" added) foure miles compaffe; begunne firft by the paines and in-
" duftry of John Stow, in the yeere 1598; afterwards inlarged by the
" care and diligence of A. M. [Anthony Munday] in the yeere 1618,
" and now completely finifhed by the ftudy and labour of A. M. H. D.
" [Henry Dyfon] and others, this prefent yeere 1633. Whereunto,
" befides many additions (as appeares by the contents) are annexed
" divers alphabeticall tables; efpecially two: the firft, an index of
" things: the fecond, a concordance of names. Lond. 1633." Fol
John Strype, who in his particular department was as induftrious as
Stow, publifhed another edition of this " Survey of the cities of Lon-
" don and Weftminfter; corrected, improved, and very much in-
" larged, and the furvey and hiftory brought down from 1633 to the
" prefent time; illuftrated with exact maps of the city and fuburbs,
" and of all the wards and outparifhes, with many other fair draughts
" of more eminent and publick edifices and monuments: in fix books:
" to which is prefixed the life of the author, writ by the editor. At
" the end is added an appendix of certain tracts, difcourfes, and
" remarks concerning the ftate of the city of London, with a peram-
" bulation or circuit walk, four or five miles round London, to the
" parifh churches, defcribing the monuments of the dead there, with

" other

" other antiquities obfervable in thofe: with an appendix, as a fupply
" and review; and a large index. In two volumes. Lond. 1720." Fol.
The 6th edition 1754 has very little variation in this laft title.

The next compilation was Edw. Hatton's " New view of London;
" or an ample account of that city, in two volumes or eight fections:
" being a more particular defcription thereof than has hitherto been
" known to be publifht of any city in the world. Lond. 1708" 8vo.
Very erroneous in monumental infcriptions, many of which are
abridged and many omitted. I take this to be the book mentioned
by Bagford [c], as a " modern treatife fet forth by a gentleman of the fire-
office, wherein he gives an account of churches new built, with all
the terms of architecture, in two volumes, 8vo. the map of which is
taken from Braun and Hogenbergius, which is copied from the firft
wooden one done in Holland: there are neither alterations nor additions in it, but if compared together it will be found to be only contracted into a fheet: the plate was bought in Holland by Mr. Lee and
ufed in the above book."

Robert Seymour, efq; publifhed " A furvey of the cities of London
" and Weftminfter, borough of Southwark, and parts adjacent: con-
" taining, 1. The original foundation, and the antient and modern
" ftate thereof. 2. An exact defcription of all wards and parifhes,
" parifh churches, palaces, halls, hofpitals, publick offices, edifices,
" and monuments, of any account. 3. A particular account of the
" government of London, its charters, liberties, privileges, and cuf-
" toms; and of all the companies, with their coats of arms, &c. &c.
" The whole being an improvement of Mr. Stowe's and other furveys,
" by adopting whatever alterations have happened in the faid cities, &c.
" to the prefent year, retrenching many fuperfluities, and correcting
" many errors in the former writers. Illuftrated with feveral copper
" plates. In two volumes. 1735." Fol. republifhed in one volume
4to. 1736.

This was foon followed by " The hiftory of London from its
" foundation by the Romans to the prefent time; containing a faith-
" full relation of the publick tranfactions of the citizens, accounts of

[c] Letter to Hearne, p. lxxxi.

" the

" the feveral parifhes ; parallels between London and other great
" cities ; its government, &c. With the feveral accounts of Weft-
" minfter, Middlefex, Southwark, and other parts within the bills of
" mortality. In nine books. The whole illuftrated with a variety of
" fine cuts. With a compleat index. By William Maitland, F. R. S.
" 1739." Fol. A fecond edition 1756, Fol. enlarged to 2 vols. continued to the time of publication, and illuftrated with plans of the city
and wards, views of the former at different times, and of all the churches
and public buildings, and a map of the country ten miles round.

" A new and compleat furvey of London, in ten parts ; in two vols.
" by a citizen and native of London. 1742." 8vo.

" London in miniature : being a concife and comprehenfive de-
" fcription of the cities of London and Weftminfter, and parts ad-
" jacent for 40 miles round, &c. collected from Stowe, Maitland,
" and other large works, with feveral new and curious particulars ;
" intended as a complete guide to foreigners, &c. 1755." 8vo.

" London and its environs defcribed, containing an account of
" whatever is moft remarkable for grandeur, elegance, curiofity, or
" ufe in the city or country twenty miles round it, comprehending
" alfo whatever is moft material in the hiftory and antiquities of this
" great metropolis ; decorated and illuftrated with a great number of
" views in perfpective, engraved from original drawings taken on
" purpofe for this work ; together with a plan of London, a map of
" the environs, and feveral other cuts. In fix vols. 1761." 8vo.

There is now publifhing in monthly numbers " A new and accurate
" hiftory and furvey of London, Weftminfter, Southwark, and places
" adjacent: containing whatever is moft worthy of notice in their
" ancient and prefent ftate : illuftrated with a variety of heads, views,
" plans, and maps. By the rev. John Entick, M. A."

Bolton, author of Nero Cæfar, wrote " Vindiciæ Britannicæ, or
" London righted by refcues and recoveries of antiquities of Britain in
" general, and of London in particular, againft unwarrantable pre-
" judices and hiftorical antiquations amongft the learned ; for the more
" honour and perpetual juft ufes of the noble ifland and the city, in
" feven chapters," to fhew that London was in Nero's time too confiderable

fiderable to have been what Cæfar defcribes a Britifh oppidum. The MS. was in the hands of Hugh Howard, efq; d and fold among T. Rawlinfon's to Endymion Porter.

Bp. Stillinfleet's " Difcourfe of the true antiquity of London, and its " ftate in the Roman times," was printed in the fecond part of his Ecclefiaftical Cafes.

" Londinopolis; an hiftoricall difcourfe or perluftration of the city " of London, the imperial chamber, and chief emporium of Great " Britain : whereunto is added another of the city of Weftminfter, " with the courts of juftice, antiquities, and new buildings thereunto " belonging. By James Howel, efq; Lond. 1657." Fol.

" Camera regis : or a fhort view of London ; containing the anti- " quity, fame; walls, bridge, river, gates, tower, cathedral, officers, " courts, cuftoms, franchifes, &c. of that renowned city ; collected " out of law and hiftory, and methodized for the benefit of the pre- " fent inhabitants. By John Brydall e. Lond. 1676." 8vo.

" Angliæ metropolis, or the prefent ftate of London : with memo- " rials comprehending a full and fuccinct account of the antient and " modern eftate thereof, &c. by Tho. Delaune, gent. Lond. 1681." 8vo. has views of the gates and principal buildings, which in the 2d edit. 1690. 12mo. were omitted.

" Londinum triumphans ; or an hiftorical account of the grand in- " fluence the actions of the city of London have had upon the affairs " of the nation, for many ages paft : fhewing the antiquity, honour, " glory, and renown of this famous city ; the grounds of her rights, " privileges, and franchifes ; the foundation of her charter, the impro- " bability of its forfeiture or feizure ; the power and ftrength of the " citizens, and the feveral contefts that have been betwixt the magi- " ftracy and the commonalty; collected from the moft authentick " authors, and illuftrated with variety of remarks, worthy the perufal " of every citizen. By William Gough, gent. Lond. 1682." 8vo.

---

d Gen. Dict. Bolton III. 446. and Biog. Brit. Bolton II. 850. note E. Maitland has proved London did not exift in Claudius's time, but is firft mentioned after Suetonius Paulinus had reduced Anglefea.

e His Collection of the laws of lunatics, 1700, calls him ftudent of Lincoln's-inn.

5

" The

" The way to make London the moſt flouriſhing city in the uni-
" verſe. By —————— Moreton. Lond. 1729." 8vo.

Robert Burton, author of the " Civil wars of England," publiſhed
" Hiſtorical remarks and obſervations on the antient and preſent ſtate
" of London and Weſtminſter 1682." 12mo. The 2d edition is intitled " A new view and obſervations on the antient and preſent ſtate,
" &c. of London, continued by an able hand. 1730." 12mo.

" Remarks on London by Wm. Stow, 1722." 12mo. " New
remarks collected by the company of pariſh-clerks. 1732." 12mo.
" A new guide to London, or directions for ſtrangers. 1726. 1730.
" 1740. 1752. 1762." Theſe three laſt are no more than ſhort ab-
ſtracts, liſts of ſtreets, &c. &c. and may rank with N. Bailey's " Anti-
" quities of London and Weſtminſter. 1722." 12mo. and George
Reeves's " New hiſtory of London and Weſtminſter, by queſtion and
" anſwer. 1763." 12mo.

Of the cuſtoms of this city Pynſon about 1521 printed a large
quarto ᶠ, without date, containing other miſcellaneous papers, and beginning thus : " In this boke is conteyned the names of the baylyfs,
cuſtoſe, mayirs, and ſherefs of the cyte of Londonn, from the tyme of
kyng Rychard the firſt. And alſo the artycles of the chartour and
lybirtys of England ; wyth other dyvers maters, good and neceſſary
for every cytyzen to underſtonde and knowe, whiche ben ſhewid in
chaptirs after the fourme of this kalendyr folowynge." Some of theſe
contain the names of bailyfs, &c. as above, being 112. The copy
of the whole chartour of London of the firſt graunt, and of the con-
firmacyon of divers kingis. The acte for correction of the errours and
wrong judgments in London. The acte for trees above twenty yeres
growyng to pay no tythys. The charge of every warde in L. at a fyveten.
The ordynance for aſſyſe of brede in L. Copy of pope Nicholas his
bulle for the offryng to the curatts of the pariſhes in the city of L.
in Lat. and in Eng. 1453. P. Innocent's letter for the ſame. The com-
poſycyon of all offryng in L. and ſuburbys 1457. The ordynaunce for
brokers occupying in L. The number and names of all the parys

ᶠ So the laſt edition of the Bodleian catalogue. Ames ſaw two editions in folio, and
one in 4to. with wooden cuts : but no date or printer's name.

Chirches

chirches and other chirches in L. and fub. Articles defired by the
comouns of L. for reformacion of thynges to the fame. The charge
of the queft of warmote in every warde. Articles of the good go-
vernaunce of the cite. Art. of preeftes and other mounkes in the
cite. Againſt the perel of fyer. The othe of the bedel of the warde
of the conftables, the fherefs fergeaunts, of frank pledg of foryners,
of the fcavengers, of every freeman made in the cite, for brokers in
L. Ordynances for the affyze of tall wood and bellet in L. Mar-
chaundyces whereof fcavage ought to be taken in L. Thefe thynges
that longeth to tonage and poundage of the kyng in the cyte of L.
Divers forms of law, fupplications to the K. &c. Ordynance of the
cyte for tenauntes of houfes what things they fhall remove at their
departyng. Copy of the othe gyven to the mayre and aldyrmen, &c.
the tyme of king Herry 6. Matters of chronology and hiftory, not of
London; receipts for wines, ypocras, clary, *braket*, gunpowder, *or-
chell*, pygell to keep fturgeon, vinegar, ynk, foape, beer, *percelye to
growe in an owre fpace*, meafures of foreign wines, weight of iron, and
difference of weights in England. Rate of the cuftoms. Ballad of the
notbrown mayde. Charter of the forefts and magna charta. The
valewe and ftynt of the benefyce of St. Magnus at London bridge
yerely to the perfon 1494. Articles found by the inquyfytours at the
vifitacyion there, and other articles of vifitation, &c. &c. &c. This
book is commonly called Arnolde's Chronicle, his name and initials
frequently occurring in it [f].

　　" A briefe difcourfe declaring and approving the neceffarie and in-
" violable maintenance of the laudable cuftoms of London; namely
" of the one, whereby a reafonable partition of the goods of hufbands
" among their wives and children is provided : with an anfwer to ob-
" jections, &c. 1584." 8vo.

　　" The liberties, ufages, and cuftomes of the city of London, con-
" firmed by efpeciall acts of parliament, with the time of their con-
" firmation : alfo divers ample and moft beneficiall charters granted
" by K. Henry VI. K. Edw. IV. and K. Henry VII. not confirmed
" by parliament, as the other charters were : and where to find every

---

[f] Ames's hift. of print. p. 122, &c. Britifh Librarian, p. 22.

　　　　　　　　　　　　　　　　　　　　　　　　　" par-

" particular grant and confirmation at large. Collected by Sir Henry
" Colthrop, knt. fometime recorder of London, for his private ufe,
" and now publifhed for the good and benefit of this honourable city.
" Lond. 1642." reprinted in Somer's tracts, 3d coll. vol. i. p. 351.

A later and more exact account of the privileges and by-laws of this
city is in " Lex Londinenfis ; or the city law : fhewing the powers,
" cuftoms, and practice of all the courts belonging to the famous city
" of London. And alfo a method for the minifters within the faid
" city to recover their tythes. With a table to the whole book.
" Lond. 1680." 8vo

" Abridgement of the charter of the city of London ; being every
" freeman's privileges. Lond. 1680." 4to.

" The royal charter of confirmation granted by K. Charles II. to the
" city of London, wherein are recited verbatim all the charters to
" the faid city granted by his royal predeceffors, taken out of the re-
" cords and exactly tranflated into Englifh by S. G. gent. together with
" an index or alphabetical table, and a table explaining all the obfolete
" and difficult words in the faid charters, Lond. 1664." 8vo. Maitland has taken the charters out of this book, the collector of which
had a place in the town-clerk's office : an edition of it 1680 is dedicated
to Sir Robert Clayton, mayor.

" The forfeitures of London's charter ; or an impartial account of
" the feveral feizures of the city charter ; together with the means and
" methods that were ufed for recovery of the fame ; with the caufes
" by which it became forfeited ; as likewife the imprifonment, de-
" pofing, and fining the lord mayor, aldermen, and fheriffs, fince the
" reign of Hen. III. to the prefent year 1682 : being faithfully col-
" lected out of ancient and modern hftiories, and now feafonably pub-
" lifhed for the fatisfaction of the inquifitive upon the late arreft made
" upon the faid charter by writ of quo warranto. Lond. 1682." 4to.

" The city of London's plea to the quo warranto (an information)
" brought againft their charter in Michaelmas term 1681. wherein it
" will appear that the liberties, priviledges, and cuftoms of the city
" cannot be loft by the mifdemeanor of any officer or magiftrate
" thereof : nor their charter be feized in the king's hands for any

" mifufage

" mifufage or abufage of their liberties and priviledges, they being
" confirmed by divers ancient records and acts of parliament made
" before and fince Magna Charta. Alfo how far the commons of the
" faid city have power of chufing and removing their fheriffs. Pub-
" lifht both in Englifh and Latin. Lond. 1682." Fol.

" The priviledges of the citizens of London contained in the charters
" granted to them by the feveral kings of this realm, and confirmed by
" fundry parliaments. Comprehending the whole charter, only words
" of form left out. Now feafonably publifht for general information,
" upon occafion of the quo warranto brought againft the faid city.
" Lond. 1682." 4to.

" A defence of the charter and municipal rights of the city of
" London, and the rights of other municipal cities and towns of
" England. Directed to the citizens of London. By Thomas Hunt.
" Lond." 4to.

" Reflections on Hunt's defence of the city charter, and writ of
" quo warranto; together with a vindication of the late fheriffs and
" juries. Lond. 1682." 4to.

" A fermon at the funeral of the quo warranto. 1683." 4to.

" Rights and privileges of the city of London, charters, &c. with
" a preface, fhewing how fatal the proceedings in Weftminfter-hall
" were to the Englifh conftitution. 1689." Fol.

" The pleadings and arguments, and other proceedings in the
" court of King's bench upon the quo warranto, touching the charter
" of the city of London, with the judgment entered thereupon, and
" the whole pleadings faithfully taken from the record. 1690." Fol.

" The priviledges of the lord mayor and aldermen of the city. The
" advantages of the freemen thereof. A method for freemen to
" make their wills. If die without a will, how their eftates muft be
" divided. The ufage of the mayor's court, and orphan's court, and
" all other courts. The chamberlain's clerk his fees. The coroner's
" duty and fees. How to make diftrefs for rent. With feveral acts
" of parliament, acts of common-council, and other matters never
" before publifhed. Alfo the minifter's tythes in every parifh in
" London, and how to recover the fame. With a table of the whole.
" By

" By J. Green, fometime attorney in rhe mayor's court. Lond-
" 1722." 8vo.

" Privilegia Londini, or the rights, liberties, privileges, laws, and
" cuftoms of the city of London; wherein are contained, 1. The fe-
" veral charters granted to the faid city from K. William the Firft to
" the prefent time. 2. The magiftrates and officers thereof, with
" their refpective creations, elections, rights, duties, and authorities.
" 3. The laws and cuftoms of the city, as the fame relate either to the
" perfons or eftates of the citizens, viz. of freemens wills, feme fole,
" merchants, orphans, apprentices, &c. 4. The nature, jurifdiction,
" practice, and proceedings of the feveral courts thereof, with tables
" of fees relating thereto. 5. The feveral ftatutes concerning the faid
" city and citizens.alphabetically digefted. The 3d edition, with large
" additions: by William Bohun, of the Middle Temple, efq; Lond.
" 1723." 8vo. The firft edition was in 1702.

" City liberties, or the rights and privileges of freemen. 1732." 8vo.

" The charters of the city of London which have been granted by
" the kings and queens of England fince the Conqueft, taken verba-
" tim out of the records, exactly tranflated into Englifh, with notes,
" explaining antient words and terms, and the parliamentary confirm-
" ation by K. William and Q. Mary. To which is annexed an ab-
" ftract of the arguing in the cafe of the quo warranto. Lond. 1738 '
8vo. To the 2d edition 1745, 8vo. is annexed the charter of the
15th of Geo. II. and the author is called J. E.

" The laws and cuftoms, rights, liberties, and privileges of the city
" of London: containing the feveral charters granted to the city from
" William the Conqueror to the prefent time, the magiftrates and
" officers thereof, and their refpective creations, elections, rights, du-
" ties, and authorities; the laws and cuftoms of the city, as the fame
" relate to the perfons or eftates of the citizens; the nature, jurifdic-
" tion, practice, and proceedings of the feveral courts in London, and
" acts of parliament concerning the cities of London and Weftmin-
" fter, alphabetically digefted. Lond. 1765." 12mo.

" The cities advocate, in this cafe or queftion of honour and arms,
" whether apprenticefhip extinguifheth gentry: containing a clear re-

" futation of the pernicious common error affirming it : with the
" copies or tranfcripts of three letters that gave occafion to this
" work. Lond. 1629." 4to. and 12mo. By John Philpot, Somerfet
herald ᵍ.

   " The cafe of the apprentices of London, and others, in relation
"ᐧto the complaints made to the court of aldermen of the exactions in
" the chamberlain's office : humbly offered to the confideration of
" the lord mayor, court of aldermen, and common-council. 1606."
Half a folio fheet.   Bagford.

   " The city remembrancer : containing animadverfions upon the
" oaths of the ward-officers of the city of London, and the duties and
" charges thereby impofed; refpectfully addreft to the right hon. the
" lord mayor, the court of aldermen, and common-council of this
" city. Lond. 1753." 8vo. reprinted from a former edition.

   " The order of my lord mayor, the aldermen, and the fheriffs, for
" their meetings and wearing of their apparel throughout the whole
" year. Lond." 12mo. frequently reprinted for their ufe.

   " London's liberties in elections of mayor, &c. according to the
" opinion of judge Hale, &c. 1683.

   " The city law, or the courfe and practice in all manner of juridi-
" ciall proceedings in the huftings in Guildhall.   Englifhed out of
" an ancient French MS.   Alfo an alphabet of all the offices difpofed
" of and given by the lord mayers. 1647." 4to.   Stow perufed the
original.

   " The practice of the fheriff's court at London, containing the
" manner of entering actions, making attachments and fequeftrations,
" with all the proceedings thereon, and the feveral fees. Alfo the de-
" faults, and garnifh fees, upon an attachment for default.   Lond.
" 1657." 12mo.

   " The method and rule of proceedings on all the elections, polls,
" and fcrutinies at common-halls and wardmotes within the city of
" London. Lond. 1743." 8vo.

   " The hiftory of the fherifdom of London and Middlefex, contain-
" ing the original method of election, &c. Lond. 1723." 8vo.

ᵍ Cat. of Harl. pamphlets, N° 32.

" A true

" A true account of the proceedings relating to the late election
" of sheriffs for the city of London and county of Middlesex. Lond.
" 1723." Fol. relates to a contested election of Sir John Williams
and Mr. Lockwood, Sir Richard Hopkins and Mr. Feast, the former
bring returned, but the latter sworn in.

" A letter to the right hon. the lord mayor, occasioned by his lord-
" ship's nomination of five persons disqualified by act of parliament as
" fit and proper persons to serve the office of sheriffs. In which the
" nature and design of the corporation act is impartially considered and
" stated. Lond. 1738." the 2d edit. 8vo.

Of the populousness of London we have the following estimate.
" Natural and political observations, mentioned in a following index,
" and made upon the bills of mortality, with reference to the go-
" vernment, religion, trade, growth, air, diseases, and the several
" changes of the said city. Lond. 1661:" 4to. This book went thro'
five editions in less than 15 years. In the 2d 1662. 4to. the author
owned himself to be John Graunt, citizen of London. The 3d much
enlarged was in 8vo. in 1665, the plague year, by order of the Council
of the Royal Society; the author is there stiled Capt. John Graunt, Fellow of the Royal Society. In the 4th edition 8vo. he is called Major:
having both these ranks in the trained bands. The 5th was published
1676, 8vo. after his death, by Sir Wm. Petty, whose referring to it
on this account as his own occasioned Burnet [a] to call it his. But
this is neither the only nor the least mistake of that historian, who
charges poor Graunt with being a Papist, and stopping the New
River water at the fire of London, from which he is fully vindicated
in the Biographia Britannica.

" Proposals modestly offered for the full peopling and inhabiting the
" city of London; and to restore the same to her ancient flourishing
" trade; which will suit with her splendid structure. 1672." 4to. [b]

" An essay in political arithmetic concerning the growth of the city
" of London, with the measures, periods, causes, and consequences
" thereof. By Sir W. Petty. Lond. 1682." 4to. 1680. 8vo.

---

[a] Hist. of his own times, I. 231.
[b] Cat. of Harl. pamphlets, 101.

" A fur-

" A further affertion of he propofitions concerning the magnitude,
" &c. of London, contained in two effays in political arithmetic ; to-
" gether with a vindication of the faid effays from the objections of
" fome learned perfons of the French nation." publifhed in the Philofophical Tranfactions, N° 185. p. 237. 1686. by the fame author,
who alfo wrote " Two effays in political arithmetic concerning the
" people, houfing, hofpitals, &c. of London and Paris, the firft tend-
" ing to prove that London hath more people and houfing than the
" cities of Paris and· Rouen put together : the 2d tending to prove
" that in the hofpital called L'Hotel Dieu at Paris there die above 3000
" per annum by reafon of ill accommodation. Lond. 1687." 8vo. An
extract of thefe two effays was publifhed in the Philofophical Tranfactions, N° 183. p. 152.

" Obfervations upon the cities of London and Rome. Lond. 1687."
8vo. three leaves.

" Five effays in political arithmetic, viz. 1. Objections from the
" city of Rey in Perfia" [by the author of the Republique des Lettres]
" and from Monf. Auzout" [in his Letters from Rome] " againft two
" former effays anfwered ; and that London hath as many people as
" Paris, Rome, and Rouen put together.   2. A comparifon between
" London and Paris in fourteen particulars.   3. Proofs that at London
" within its 134 parifhes named in the bills of mortality there live
" about 696000 people. 4. An eftimate of the people in London
" Paris, Amfterdam, Venice, Rome, Dublin, Briftol, and Rouen, with
" feveral obfervations upon the fame. 5. Concerning Holland and
" the reft of the feven United Provinces. In French and Englifh."
Publifhed with the effays before recited, and others in political arithmetic. Lond. 1699. 8vo. Sir William fuppofes that London doubles
in forty, and England in three hundred and fixty years : that in 1682
there were about 670000 fouls in London, and in England and
Wales about 7 millions 400,000 to about 28 millions of acres of profitable land : that the growth of London muft be at its greateft
height in 1800, and ftop before 1842, when it will be 8 times more
than in 1682, with above 4 millions for the fervice of the country and
ports : that the affeffment of London is about $\frac{1}{11}$ of all England and

Wales :

Wales : that in 1840 there will be in London 10 millions 7,180,880, and in the whole kingdom only 10 millions 9,17,389. Then he proposes how to make London invincible, and to establish an uniformity of religion therein. He supposed in 1682 there were upon the face of the earth 320 millions of souls, and in the next 2000 years the world would be so fully peopled, that there should be one head for every two acres in the habitable part, and then the Scripture predictions of great wars and slaughters would be fulfilled.

" Old Rome and London compared; the first in its full glory, and
" the last in its present state; by which it plainly appears, that Lipsius
" and Vossius are egregiously mistaken, in their overstretched, fulsom,
" and hyperbolical account of old Rome; and that London, as it is
" at present, exceeds it much, in its extent, populousness, and many
" other advantages. To which is added, a comparison between the
" beauties, &c. of old Rome and London c. By a person of quality
[De Souligne, grandson to Mr. Du Plessis Mornay.] Lond. 1710." 8vo.

" A computation of the increase of London, and parts adjacent;
" with some causes thereof, and remarks thereon; particularly with
" respect to the influence such increase of the capital may have on the
" body of the nation, its constitution and liberties. Lond. 1719." 8vo.

" Observations on the past growth and present state of the city of
" London. To which are annexed a complete table of the christen-
" ings and burials within this city from 1601 to 1750, both years in-
" clusive; together with a table of the numbers which annually died
" of each disease from 1675 to the present time, and also a further
" table representing the respective numbers which have annually died
" of each age from 1728 to this year: from which is particularly
" attempted to be shewn the increasing destruction of infants and
" adults in this city; and consequent thereto the excessive drain which
" it continually makes upon all the provinces of this kingdom for
" recruits: to which are added, some proposals for a better regulation
" of the police of this metropolis. By the author of a letter from
" a bystander. [Corbyn Morris, esq.] Lond. 1751." Fol.

---

c First published under the title of " A comparison between old Rome in its glory,
" as to the extent and populousness, and London, as it is at present. By a person of
" quality, and native of France. Lond. 1706." 12mo.

" A col-

" A collection of yearly bills of mortality from 1657 to 1758 in-
" clufive, together with feveral other bills of an earlier date : to which
" are fubjoined, 1. Natural and political obfervations on the bills of
" mortality, by John Graunt, F.R.S. reprinted from the 6th edition
" 1676. 2. Sir W. Petty's political arithmetic from the edition of
" 1683. 3. Obfervations on the paft growth and prefent ftate of
" London, by Corbyn Morris 1751. with a continuation of the tables
" to the end of the year 1757. 4. A comparative view of the difeafes
" and ages, and a table of the probabilities of life for the laft 30 years.
" By J.P. [James Poftlewhaite] efq. F.R.S. Lond. 1759." 4to.

" Obfervations natural, moral, civil, political and medical on city,
" town' and country bills of mortality. To which are added large
" and clear abftracts of the beft authors who have wrote on that fub-
" ject, with an appendix on the weather and meteors. By Thomas
" Short, M.D. Lond. 1750." 8vo.

In p. 407 of Nº 450 of the Philofophical Tranfactions, is Wm.
Maitland's anfwer to that part of Kerffeboom's effay on the numbers of
people in Holland and Weft-Friezland which treats of thofe in London, which he made fewer than in Paris 1684. In vol. xlviii. part II.
is a letter from Dr. Brakenridge concerning the number of inhabitants
in London and Weftminfter.

" An anfwer to Dr. Wm. Brakenridge's letter concerning the num-
" ber of inhabitants within the London bills of mortality; wherein
" the doctors letter is inferted at length, his arguments proved incon-
" clufive, and the number increafing. [By George Burrington, efq.
" formerly governor of N. Carolina.] Lond. 1757." 8vo. d.

d In a MS. in the Harleian library, 7017, p. 44. is the following calculation of the number of houfes in London, Weftminfter, Southwark, and Middlefex.

	inhabited	empty	total.
In the city and liberty of London —	19917	1123	21040
In Weftminfter — — — —	14484	1203	15687
Middlefex within the bills of mortality —	24005	2583	26588
Southwark — — — —	17815	1374	19189
Total in the bills of mortality —	76221	6283	82504
Total out of ditto — — —	9043	1557	10600
	85264	7840	93104

Sir

The beneficent Sir John Evelyn wrote " Fumifugium : or, The
" inconveniency of the air and fmoke of London, diffipated : together
" with fome remedies, humbly propofed by J. E. efq; to his facred
" majefty, and to the parliament now affembled. Publifhed by his
" majefty's command. Lond. 1661." 4to. ᵉ.

" A fhort and pithie difcourfe concerning the engendering, tokens,
" and effects of all earthquakes in generall ; particularly applyed and
" conferred with that moft ftrange and terrible worke of the Lord,
" in fhaking the earth, not only within the city of London, but alfo
" in moft partes of all England : which hapned upon Wenfday in
" Eafter-week, laft paft ; which was the fixt day of April, almoft at
" 6 a clock in the evening ; in the year of our Lord 1580. Written
" by T. T. the 13 of April 1580. Lond. 1580." 4to. The fhock
lafted about one minute ; the motion was from E. to W. and it was
felt about Rochefter and Windfor.

" A warning for the wife, a feare to the fond, a bridle to the lewde,
" and a glafs to the good. Written of the late earthquake chanced in
" London and other places the 6th of April 1580 : for the glorie of
" God and benefite of men that warily can walke, and wifely can
" judge. Set forth in verfe and profe, by Thomas Churchyard, gentle-
" man. Lond. 1580." 8vo. Wood knew nothing of this tract, which
is dedicated to Alex. Nowel, dean of St. Paul's, and followed by " A
" fhort difcourfe upon the earthquake," with a pious introduction and
prayer ; and a poetical improvement of other accidents, figned by
Richard Tarlton, the Queen's jefter, and the moft humorous comedian
of his time ᶠ.

The two principal plagues with which London has been vifited are
defcribed in " The wonderfull yeare 1603, wherein is fhewed the picture
" of London lying ficke of the plague. At the end of all, like a merry
" epilogue to a dull play, certaine tales are cut out in fundrie fafhions,
" of purpofe to fhorten the lives of long winter nights that lye watch-

ᵉ Edw. I. upon the complaint of the nobility and gentry that they could not go to
London on account of the noifome fmell and thick air, iffued out a proclamation forbid-
ding the ufe of fea coal in the fuburbs, on pain of fine and lofs of their furnace, &c.
Maitland, p. 69, from Stowe's Annals.
ᶠ Both thefe tracts are from the Harleian Cat. of pamphlets, N° 178 and 222.

Q q   " ing

" ing for us in the darke. Lond. 1603." 4to. reprinted in Morgan's
Phænix Britannicus, p. 27.

" London's dreadful vifitation; or a collection of all the bills of
" mortality from Dec. 20, 1664, to Dec. 19, 1665, as alfo the ge-
" neral or whole year's bill, according to the report made to the king
" by the company of parifh clerks, 1665." 4to.

" London's deliverance predicted by Gadbury: a difcourfe fhew-
" ing the caufes of plagues in general. 1665. 8vo.

" London's Lord have mercy upon us. A true relation of feven
" modern plagues or vifitations in London, with the number of thofe
" that were buried of all difeafes: viz. the 1ft in the year of Q.
" Eliz. A. 1592: the 2d in the year 1603: the 3d in (that never to
" be forgotten year) 1625: the 4th in A. 1630: the 5th in the year
" 1636: the 6th in the years 1637 and 1638: the 7th this prefent
" year 1665." Printed 1665. reprinted in Somer's tracts, 2d collect.
vol. iii. p. 53.

Geo. Withers, the fatyrift, wrote a poem called " Memorandum
" to London, occafioned by the peftilence in the year 1665." 8vo.

" Λοιμολογια, five peftis nuperæ apud populum Londinenfem graf-
" fantis narratio hiftorica. Lond. 1672." 8vo. By Dr. Nath. Hodges,
who practifed with great fuccefs at London during the plague : but
died poor in Ludgate about 1684 s.

" Loimologia, or a hiftorical account of the plague in London
" 1665 : with precautionary directions againft the like contagion : by
" N. Hodges, M. D. and fellow of the college of phyficians, who re-
" fided in the city all that time. To which is added, An effay on the
" different caufes of peftilential difeafes, and how they become con-
" tagious : with remarks on the infection now in France, and the
" moft probable means to prevent its fpreading here. By John Quincy,
" M. D. Lond. 1720." 8vo.

" A collection of very valuable and fcarce pieces relating to the laft
" plague in 1665, viz. 1. Orders drawn up and publifhed by the lord
" mayor and aldermen of the city of London, to prevent the fpread-
" ing of the infection. 2. An account of the firft rife, progrefs, fymp-

s Ath. Ox. II. 768.

" toms,

" toms, and cure of the plague: being the fubftance of a letter from
" Dr. Hodges to a perfon of quality. 3. Neceffary directions for the
" prevention and cure of the plague, with divers remedies of fmall
" charge by the college of phyficians. 4. Reflections on the weekly
" bills of mortality, fo far as they relate to all the plagues which have
" happened in London from 1592 to the great plague 1665, and fome
" other particular difeafes. With a preface fhewing the ufefulnefs of
" this collection, fome errors of Dr. Mead, and his mifreprefentations
" of Dr. Hodges, and fome other authors: to which is added an ac-
" count of the plague at Naples in 1656, of which there died in one
" day 20,000 perfons; with the fymptoms that appeared upon diffec-
" tion, and the approved method of cure. The 2d edit. Lond. 1721."

" A journal of the plague year; being obfervations or memorials of
" the moft remarkable occurrences, as well public as private, which
" happened in London during the laft great vifitation in 1665. Writ-
" ten by a citizen who continued all the while in London. Never
" made publick before. Lond. 1722." 8vo. This is profeffed to
be wrote by a fadler in White-chapel, but the real author was Daniel
Defoe. It was lately reprinted with the following fmall alterations in the title, and other aditions: " The hiftory of the great
" plague in London 1665; containing obfervations and memorials of
" the moft remarkable occurrences that happened during that dread-
" full period. By a citizen, that lived the whole time in London.
" To which is added, A journal of the plague at Marfeilles 1720.
" Lond. 1754." 8vo.

On the late *influenza* was publifhed " De catarrho & de dyfenteria
" Londinenfi epidemicis utrifque anno 1762. libellus, auctore Geor-
" gio Baker, Coll. Reg. Med. Lond. & Coll. Reg. Cant. Soc. &
" R. S. S. Lond. 1764." 4to.

The " Account of the burning of the city of London, as it was
" publifht by the fpecial authority of the king and council in the
" London Gazette, Sept. 3, 1666 [h]." feems to have been reprinted
1733.

" A re-

---

[h] Wm. Goffing, engineer, in his " Seafonable advice for preventing the mifchief of
" fire. 1693." 4to. ordered to be hung up in every houfe, recommends having in

each

" A relation of the late dreadful fire in London, as it was reported
" to the committee in parliament. Lond. 1667." 8vo. By —— Rolles.

" A narrative of the burning of London 1666. By Edward Water-
" houfe. i Lond. 1667." 8vo.

" A fhort narrative of the late dreadful burning of London, toge-
" ther with certain confiderations remarkable therein, and deducible
" therefrom : not unfeafonable for the perufal of this age. Written
" by way of letter to a perfon of honour and virtue. Lond. 1667."
8vo.

" A true and faithful account of the feveral informations exhibited
" to the honourable committee appointed by the parliament to inquire
" into the late dreadfull burning of London, together with other in-
" formations touching the infolency of the popifh priefts and jefuits,
" and the increafe of popery, brought to the hon. committee appointed
" by the parliament for that purpofe. Printed in the year 1667." reprinted in Somer's tracts, vol. xiv.

" Obfervations both hiftorical and moral upon the burning of London
" Sept. 1666, with an account of the loffes : and a moft remarkable
" parallell between London and Mofcow, both as to the plague and
" fire. Alfo an effay touching the eafterly wind. Written by way of
" narrative, for fatisfaction of the prefent and future ages. By Rege
" Sincera. Lond. 1667." 8vo. reprinted in the Harl. Mifc. III. 282 k.

" Difcourfes and meditations on the fire of London by —— Rolles.
" 1667." 8vo. Abp. Sancroft's fermon before the king on the faft in
October following was likewife printed.

" London's

each parifh *a great fquirt on wheels* ; which feems to have fuggefted the invention of
fire engines ten years after. John Lofting, merchant of London, had a patent from
K. William for a new fucking-worm engine and for a common one.

i Of him fee Birch's Hift of the Roy. Soc. II. 460.

k Among other curious Obfervations this author makes the following calculation of the
loffes. " The bookfellers who dwelled for the moft part round about the cathedral had
fheltered their books in a fubterranean church under it, called St. Faith, which was propt
up with fo ftrong an arch and maffy pillars that it feemed impoffible the fire could do
any harm to it ; but having crept into it through the windows it feized on the pews,
and did fo try and examine the arch and pillars, by fucking the moifture of the mortar
that bound the ftones together, that it was calcined into fand; fo that when the top of
the cathedral fell upon it, it beat it flat, and fet all things in an irremediable flame. I
have heard judicious men of that trade affirm, that the only lofs of books in that place,
ftationers-

" London's lamentations, or a ferious difcourfe concerning the late
" fiery difpenfation, that turned our (once renowned) city into a
" ruinous heap, alfo the feveral leffons that are incumbent upon thofe
" whofe houfes have efcaped the confuming flames. By Thomas
" Brooks, late preacher of the word at St. Margaret's, New Fifh-
" ftreet; where that fatal fire firft began that turned London into a
" ruinous heap. Lond. 1670." 4to.

" A fhort defcription of the fatal and dreadfull burning of London,
" divided into every day and night's progreffion. Compofed by Samuel
" Wifeman. Four fheets folio. Sold in White-friars-ftreet, near Crip-
" plegate. With the map of London as in its profperity, by Robert
" Prick."

" The papift plot of firing difcovered, in a perfect account of the
" late fire in Fetter-lane, London, the 10th day of   laft, where-
" by it plainly appears who were the inftruments of this work, as alfo
" the rewards they are to have, and what would be the difmal effects
" if this firing trade had gone on. Publifht by way of caution to all
" mafters of families to beware what fervants they entertain into their
" houfes. Lond. 1679." 4to.

" London's flames revived, or an account of the feveral informa-
" tions exhibited to a committee appointed by parliament, Sept. the
" 25th, 1666, to enquire into the burning of London, with feveral
" other informations concerning other fires in Southwark, Fetter-lane,
" and elfewhere; by all which it is apparent that the faid fires were

---

ftationers-hall, publick libraries, and private houfes could amount to no lefs then 150,000l.
—I could hear of but half a dozen perfons that perifhed.—The city within the walls being feated on about 4600 acres, wherein were built about 15000 houfes, befides churches,
chapels, fchools, halls, &c. 12,000 houfes were thought to be burnt, which is four
parts in five, each houfe being valued one with another at 25 l. per ann. rent, which at
12 years purchafe makes 300 l. the whole amounting to 3,600,000 l. 87 parochial
churches, befides St. Paul's cathedral, the Exchange, Guildhall, the Cuftom-houfe,
companies halls, and other publick buildings, amounting to half as much, i. e.
1,800,000 l. The goods that every private man loft one with another, valued at half
the value of the houfes, i. e. 1,800,000 l. about twenty wharfs of coals and wood,
valued at 1000 l. apiece, 20,000 l. About 100,000 boats and barges, 1000 cart loads,
with porters to remove the goods to and fro, as well for the houfes that were burning as for thofe that ftood in fear of it, at 20 s. a load, 150,000 l. In all 7,335,000 l
In French money (at one pound fterling for 13 livres) 10,569,675,000 livres:"

" con-

" contrived and carried on by the papifts : now humbly offered to the
" confideration of all true proteftants. Lond. 1689." 4to.

" A proteftant monument erected to the immortal glory of the
" whigs and the Dutch : it being a full and fatisfactory relation of the
" late myfterious plot and firing of London, taken from the feveral
" records, depofitions, narratives, journals, trials, ftate tracts, hiftories,
" predictions, fermons, and confeffions under their hands and from
" their own mouths, proving that a medley of whigs with a glorious
" fet of protefting common-wealth men of Holland did in their turn
" not only attempt to burn London, but many other places in Eng-
" land, and did fire the city, Southwark, and Wapping; but likewife
" his majefty's royal fleet as it lay difarmed in Chatham river, while
" peace was treating at Breda.   Printed in the year 1712." reprinted
in Somers's tracts, vol. xiv. p. 24.

" Londinenfes lacrymæ : London's fecond tears mingled with her
" afhes. A poem. By John Crouch. Lond. 1666." 4to.

" Conflagratio Londinenfis poetice depicta : the conflagration of
" London poetically delineated, and directed to the moft noble and
" deferving citizen Sir J. L. kt. and bart. Lond. 1667." 4to. " Lon-
" dini quod reliquum : or London's remains : in Latin and Englifh.
" Lond. 1667." 4to.   " Londini renafcentis imago poetica ad ferenif.
" Britanniarum monarcham Carolum II. Lond. 1668." 4to.   The
author of thefe three poems was one Dr. Ford, who wrote a Latin
poem on the fire at Northampton five years after.

" Ακαμαιον Πυρ : or the dreadfull burning of London defcribed in
" a poem. Lond. 1667." 4to. by J. G. M. A. [Jofeph Guillion.] k.

" Annus mirabilis : a fhort and ferious narrative of London's fatal
" fire, with its diurnal and nocturnal progreffion from Sunday morn-
" ing, being the 2d day of Sept. untill Wednefday night following :
" a poem   As alfo London's lamentation to her regardlefs paffengers.
" 1667."   Probably the excellent methodical defcription of the fire,
written in verfe by S. Wifeman before-named, mentioned by Bagford l.

---

l Wood's Fafti, II. 175.
k Letter to Hearne, p. lxxxiv.

Jofbua

Joſhua Barnes wrote a Latin poem on the fire of London and the plague [m]. There are two others on both by —— Tabor, 1667. 4to.

Hollar publiſhed a view of the ruins 1666.

Sir John Evelyn preſented to the king a week after the fire two plans, with a diſcourſe now in the paper-office: the plans were engraved by the Antiquarian Society 1748: one of them contains 25 churches only, reſerved on their old foundations, with all the principal ſtreets almoſt in the ſame part they formerly were, and ſpaces for the reſt of the houſes, lanes and alleys of note, according to the dimenſions there expreſſed ; though, by reaſon of the narrowneſs of the plan, the meaſures are not exact.

A plan of the city after the fire, according to the deſign and propoſal of Sir Chr. Wren, for rebuilding it, ſhewing the ſituation of the great ſtreets and publick buildings, makes the ſecond plate of the " Synopſis ædificiorum publicorum C. Wren," and was engraved again by the Antiquarian Society 1748, and ſince by Rocque.

" A new model for rebuilding the city of London with houſes, " ſtreets, and wharfs, to be forthwith ſet forth by his majeſty's and " city ſurveyors, with the advantages that will accrue by building the " ſame accordingly." The project deſigned by one Knight, who was committed to priſon by order of parliament. Printed by S. Leach, for S. Speed, at the Rainbow in Fleet-ſtreet. 1666. Bagford.

Wm. Lodge engraved the beſt view of the monument [n]. A large print of it with the inſcription, and an hiſtorical account of the fire, was printed by Geo. Larkin 1683 : the bas relief makes a diſtinct plate. Two other views of it drawn by N. Hawkſmore 1723, make plates iii. and iv. of the Synopſis above-mentioned. An elaborate inſcription for this pillar in proſe and verſe by Adam Littleton, is printed at the end of his Dictionary.

" A catalogue of moſt of the memorable tombs, grave-ſtones, plates, " eſcocheons or atchievments in the demoliſht or yet extant churches " in London, from St. Katharines beyond the Tower to Temple-bar,

---

[m] Catalogue of his works prefixed to the firſt edition of his Anacreon.
[n] Walp. Cat. of eng. p. 54.

2

" the

" the out-parifhes being included. Lond. 1668." 4to. Wood fays this was compiled moftly from Stowe by Payne Fifher, the Toldervey of the laft century, and is a confufed piece, mentioning neither the dates of the epitaphs, nor the churches where they ftood º.

Richard Newcourt, notary publick, one of the procurators-general of the Arches-court of Canterbury and principal regiftrary of the faid diocefe near twenty-feven years, compiled a ufeful and valuable " Repertorium ecclefiafticum parochiale Londinenfe : an ecclefiaftical " parochial hiftory of the diocefe of London to 1700, in an alphabeti- " cal order. Lond. 1708." Fol. Vol. ii. 1710, contains the county of Effex.

Mr. Rawlinfon had a fair folio MS. on vellom, with miniatures, containing injunctions to the clergy of this diocefe from their bifhop, 1201, intitled " Statuta felicis recordacionis domini Rogeri Nigri epif. " Londonienfis ex confenfu domini Petri archidiaconi London edita et " univerfis rectoribus, vicariis, capellanis parochialibus in archidiaco- " natu London conftitutis directa A. D. MCC primo." At the end " Richardus Francifcus fcripfit, A. D. 1445."

" Pietas Londinenfis : or the prefent ecclefiaftical ftate of London ; " containing an account of all the churches, and chappels of eafe, in " and about the cities of London and Weftminfter ; of the fet times " of their publick prayers, facraments, and fermons, both ordinary and " extraordinary ; with the names of the prefent dignitaries, minifters, and " lecturers ; with hiftorical obfervations of their foundation, fituation, " antient and prefent ftructure, dedication, and feveral other things " worthy of remark. To which is added, a poftfcript, recommending " the duty of publick prayer. By James Paterfon, A. M. 1714." 8vo.

" A brief account of the maintenances arifing by the tithes, glebe, " and other profits, to the feveral minifters of the parifh churches de- " molifhed by the late dreadful fire of London ; together with the " names of the prefent incumbents thereof : drawn from the certifi- " cates of the faid feveral parifhes, and other informations ; occafioned " by a paper lately printed (by way of complaint) touching the faid " minifters maintenance ; wherein they have difingenuoufly fet forth

---

º Ath. II. 901.

" part

" part for the whole.   As alſo the conſent and agreement of ſome
" aldermen of the ſaid city to the augmentations by the ſaid miniſters
" propounded ; which is hereby diſcovered."   In two broad ſheets.

Samuel Brewſter, eſq; publiſhed " Collectanea eccleſiaſtica : being
" a collection of very curious treatiſes in MS. relating to the rights of
" the clergy of the church of England, and eſpecially of thoſe who
" are beneficed in London : to which is ſubjoined a large appendix,
" containing ſeveral original papers, records, &c. illuſtrated with notes,
" and interſperſed with diſſertations concerning the original and extent
" of the office and authority of archdeacons and rural deans in Eng-
" land ; concluding with an eſſay on the office and duty of pariſh-
" clerks : to which is added the charter of Edw. VI. for their incor-
" poration in London. 1752." 4to.   In this is a treatiſe concerning
the payment of tythes in London by Dr. Bryan Walton p :   the fire
and plague prevented its publication, as the regulation it propoſed could
not be attempted, and the new method of tything introduced by act
of parliament 1680 ſuperſeded it q.   Here is alſo the grievances of the
miniſters of London, in two treatiſes ; one delivered to the lord mayor,
the other to chancellor Elleſmere, printed 1745.

A proviſion for the widows and families of the poor clergy by in-
ſurance, was lately propoſed in " A letter to the fellows of Sion Col-
" lege, and to all the clergy within the bills of mortality and in the
" county of Middleſex ; humbly propoſing their forming themſelves
" into a ſociety for the maintenance of the widows and orphans of
" ſuch clergymen.   To which is added a ſketch of ſome rules and
" orders ſuitable to the purpoſe.   By Ferd. Warner, L. L. D. rector of
" Queenhith, and preſident of Sion College. 1764." 8vo.

Of St. Paul's cathedral we have " Monumenta ſepulchraria Sancti
" Pauli : the monuments, inſcriptions, and epitaphs of kings, nobles,
" biſhops, and others, buried in the cathedral church of St. Paul, Lon-
" don, until the preſent yeere of grace 1614. Together with the founda-

---

p See Wood's Faſti. II. p. 47.

q The decree for payment of tithes in London was printed by Wolfe 1596. It was
enacted 1545 that the citizens within the liberties ſhould for every 10 s. annual rent of
houſes, ſhops, cellars, and ſtables pay to their vicar 1 s. 4 d. and for every 20 s. yearly
rent 2 s. 9 d. and ſo in proportion. Raſtal's Stat. 37 H. VIII.

R r   " tion

" tion of the church; and a catalogue of all the bifhops of London,
" from the beginning, until this prefent. Never before, now with autho-
" ritie, publifhed. By H.H.[r] Lond. 1614." 4to. In the 2d edition 1634.
4to. is added a catalogue of all the archbifhops, alfo of all the deans of
the fame church, and the monuments continued until that year, a copy
of the pope's pardon to Sir Gervais Braybrook 1390; together with a
preface touching the decays, and for the repairing of this famous church.

Some of the monuments are collected together in p. 123 of
Arithmæus's book before-metioned. But for the moft finifhed and
compleat account of this cathedral we are obliged to Sir William
Dugdale, who firft publifhed it in 1658. Fol. A fecond edition
was introduced by a fhort preface by Dr. Edward Maynard, rector
of Boddington, Northamptonfhire, and intitled, " The hiftory of
" St. Paul's cathedrall in London, from its foundation; extracted
" out of original charters, records, leiger-books, and other manu-
" fcripts : beautified with fundry profpects [s] of the old fabrick;
" which was deftroyed by the fire of that city in 1666. As alfo with
" the figures of the tombs and monuments therein; which were all
" defaced in the late rebellion. Whereunto is added, a continuation
" thereof, fetting forth what was done in the ftructure of the new
" church to the year 1685. Likewife an hiftorical account of the
" northern cathedralls, and chief collegiate churches in the province
" of York. By Sir William Dugdale, kt. &c. The fecond edition,
" corrected and enlarged by the author's own hand. To which is
" prefixed his life, written by himfelf. Lond. 1716." Fol.

About 1684 was publifhed " The tombs, monuments, and fepul-
" chral infcriptions, lately vifible in St. Paul's cathedral and St. Faith's,
" under it; compleatly rendred in Latin and Englifh; with feveral
" hiftorical difcourfes on fundry perfons intombed therein. A work
" never yet performed by any author, old or new. By P. F. [Payne
" Fifher] ftudent in antiquities, batchelor of arts, and heretofore one
" of his late majefty's majors of foot to the late honourable Sir Patri-

---

[r] Hugh Holland, eldeft fon of Philemon.
[s] Thefe views were copied by Dan. King, on one fheet, round Latin and Englifh
verfes figned Benevolus.

" cius

" cius Curwen, C. Cumb. baronet. London printed for the author,
" and properly prefented to the kind encouragers of fo worthy a
" work." 4to. This is moftly ftolen from Dugdale. I have feen another edition, in which it is faid to be by " Major P. Fifher, ftudent
" in antiquities, grandchild to the late Sir Wm. Fifher, and that moft
" memorable knight Sir Thomas Neale, by his wife Elizabeth, fifter
" to that fo publick fpirited patriot the late Sir Thomas Freke, &c.
" Vide the laft fheet." All thefe connections could not keep Cromwell's poet laureat and hiftoriographer out of the Fleet u, from whence
this is figned. This edition is dedicated to Thomas Newcome, one
of the mafters and proprietors of the royal printing-houfe.

" The hiftorical defcription of this church," printed for Newbery
1753. 12mo. contains befides the hiftory of the old cathedral an account of the manner of proceeding in taking down its vaft ruins, with
the difcoveries and obfervations made upon the fpot by Sir C. Wren;
and a full defcription of the building of the prefent ftructure: with obfervations on its beauties and defects, &c. To which are added, a
defcription of the Monument; fome conjectures concerning London-
ftone, and other Roman relicks; and a review of the antient wall and
gates about the city.

" The burnynge of Paule's church in the yeere 1561, the 4th and
" 5th day of June, by lightenynge, at 3 of the clock afternoon; which
" continued terrible and helplefs until night. Lond. 1563." 12mo.
The fexton before he died confeffed that this accident was not occafioned by lightning. Bagford mentions additions to this book, with an
" Apology for the caufe of burning Paul's church, with a confirmation
" of the fame. 1563." 8vo.

" St. Paul's church her bill for the parliament, as it was prefented
" to the king's majefty on Midlent Sunday laft, and intended for the
" view of the moft high and honourable court: and generally for all
" fuch as bear good-will to the flourifhing eftate of the faid church.
" Partly in verfe, partly in profe, penned and publifhed for her good

---

u His father, who printed many encomiums on the royalifts, died there before him,
if Wanley does not miftake. Harl. MS. 1460. where is a book of Scotch colours taken
at Prefton and Dunbar, in their proper blazon: a prefent book to the protector.

" by

" by Hen. Farley, author of her Complaint. Lond. 1621." 4to.   A ſtrange farrago of prayers, petitions, dialogues with the church, and dreams and viſions about it, for eight years together, viz. from before 1615, when he preſented St. Paul's Complaint to the lord mayor, till he got into Ludgate by his ſchemes about it.   Charles II. coming to it on the day before-mentioned, its repairs were carried into execution. " His majeſties commiſſion for giving power to enquire of the de-" cayes of the cathedral church of St. Paul in London, and for the " repairing the ſame," was printed 1631. 4to.   His " Commiſſion and " further declaration concerning the reparation of St. Paul's church. " 1633." 4to.   K. William's and Q. Mary's, 1692: Q. Anne's, 1703, both in folio.

An account of bp. Braybrook's body, buried 1404, found dry and found in a vault of St. Faith's after the fire, communicated to the Royal Society by Oldenburg, their ſecretary, is printed in Birch's Hiſt. of the Roy, Soc. p. 121. in Gibſon's Camden, and in the 2d edition of Dugdale.

Hearne publiſhed in the appendix to the hiſtory of Glaſtonbury 1722, p. 160—223, from a Latin MS. of Sir Edward Filmer's, the foundation and ſtatutes of the chantry founded by Walter Sherrington, chancellor of Lancaſter t. H. VI. who alſo gave a library to this church. His epitaph from the beginning of this MS. is in the preface, p. xc. ˣ.

" Frauds and abuſes at St. Pauls.   In a letter to a member of par-" liament. Lond. 1712." 8vo.

" Fact againſt ſcandal: or a collection of teſtimonials, affidavits, " and other authentic proofs, in vindication of Mr. Richard Jennings, " carpenter, Langley Bradley, clockmaker, and Richard Phelps, bell-" founder: to be referred to in an anſwer which will ſpeedily be pub-" liſhed to a late falſe and malicious libel, intitled, Frauds and abuſes " at St. Pauls.   To which is added an appendix relating to Mr. Jones " and Mr. Spencer: and the copy of a certain agreement between the " minor canons, &c. of the ſaid cathedral. Lond. 1713." 8vo.

" An anſwer to a pamphlet, intitled, Frauds and abuſes at St. Paul's: " with an appendix relating to the revenues and repairs of that cathe-" dral. Lond. 1713." 8vo.

ˣ See more of him in Stowe's Survey, p. 329—338. edit. 1603.

" An

" An abstract of an answer lately published to a pamphlet, intitled,
" Frauds and abuses at St. Paul's. Lond. 1713." 8vo.

" A continuation of frauds and abuses at St. Paul's; wherein is con-
" sidered at large the attorney-general's report in relation to a prosecu-
" tion of Mr. Jennings, the carpenter: in answer to Fact against
" scandal. With some remarks on the second part of the same work,
" intitled, An answer to Frauds, &c. in a postscript. Lond. 1713." 8vo.

For an account of the bishops and deans see " Historia de episcopis
" & decanis Londinensibus, a prima sedis fundatione ad annum 1540.
" Autore Henrico Wharton, A. M. Lond. 1695." 8vo.

There was printed 1662 " A poem on the fall of the S. side of St.
" Paul's cathedral. To which is added a satyr against the fanatical
" boutefeus of those times, and a memorial offered up to the tomb of
" the incomparable Mr. Cleaveland, never before exactly printed. By
" T. P. 1662." two folio sheets. And soon after the fire, 1666, " A
" poem: being an essay on the present ruins in St. Paul's cathedral, by
" J. Wright *y*. Lond. 1668." 4to. To this is annexed " The misfor-
" tunes of Paul's cathedral," in heroic verse. Both were reprinted
with two others under the title of " Three poems of St. Paul's cathe-
" dral, viz. the ruins, the rebuilding, the choire. Lond. 1697." Fol.
all by the same author. Another poem on it was published 1750.

In the " Synopsis ædificiorum publicorum dom. C. Wren," are
nine plates of his first design for this church, a model of which is
preserved in the present building over the north chapel. Pl. v. vi.
vii. are the plan, orthography to the S. and section of the church.
Pl. viii. a view of it, engraved by J. Schynvoet. Pl. ix. a plan of the
church, with the vaults and peristyle of the dome, engraved by H.
Hulsberg. Pl. x. a section wherein the dome is represented according
to the original design. Pl. xi. a section of the cross isle, engraved by
S. Gribelin. Pl. xii. elevation of the W. front. Pl. xiii. elevation of
the E. end. The original plates, though first published in 1749, are
already become extremely scarce. Many of this architect's drawings
of St. Paul's were sold in his son's auction a few years ago *z*. Unhap-

---

y Author of the history and antiquities of Rutlandshire, &c.
z Walp. Anecd. of paint. vol. iii. p. 93.

pily for Sir Chriſtopher, Hollar has preſerved every part of the antient pile.

A S. view by Wm. Emmett 1702. E. W. and S. views and a plan
of St. Paul's by Schwert Fager, engraved by Parr 1747. A S. E. view
by P. Fourdrinier 1743. A W. view by Toms.

A proſpect of the choir, with the Queen and both houſes of parliament, on the general thankſgiving Dec. 31, 1706.

An inſide view of the choir, drawn by A. Gwynn and S. Wale, engraved by Rooker 1755.

Sir J. Thornhill's paintings in the cupola have been engraved in
eight plates by ᶻ Beauvais, Baron, Simoneau, and ᵃ Vandergucht.

Bagford's MS. in the Harleian library, before referred to, containing
titles of books relative to London and Weſtminſter, among his collections for a hiſtory of printing, mentions the four ſides of this church
done in large by Sir C. Wren, copied in little in Holland. Robert Trevitt,
painter in Coleman-ſtreet, did four views of it, viz. a general one from
W. to E. the morning chapel on the N. ſide, the N. ſide, the choir ;
and a ſection from W. to E. One of the windows by Short. The N. E.
end, before the ſcaffold were ſtruck, by Sutton Nichols, in one ſheet.
The church, as firſt deſigned, in Ogilby's maps of London ; and alſo
by J. Sellers.

In the Pepyſian collection of prints relative to London and Weſtminſter, at Magdalen college, Cambridge, are two wooden prints and
a drawing of Paul's croſs and preaching there : alſo Sir Philip Sidney's
funeral proceſſion to St. Paul's 1587, drawn and invented by Tho. Lant,
gent. ſervant to the ſaid hon. knight, and graven on copper by Theod.
de Brij in the city of London, 1587. Lat and Eng. Dated at the end
1588.

A ſhort account of Trinity-chapel, Alderſgate-ſtreet, was collected
from the evidences and records not ſeen by Stowe, in a half ſheet, by
the rev. Mr. Robert Orme, M. A. miniſter of a nonjuring congrega-

---

ᶻ Mr. Walpole did not know this particular of Beauvais when he ſays he finds no
other mention of him but aſſiſting Duboſc to engrave the D. of Marlborough's battles.
Cat. of engr. p. 111.

This was Gerard, brother to the preſent John. Ib. p. 116.

tion

tion who meet there, intitled, "An account of the foundation of
" Trinity-hall, now the place where the moſt antient Court of Inqueſt
" is kept, for the ward of Alderſgate; humbly preſented to the wor-
" ſhipful Sir Daniel Wray, knight, foreman, and the reſt of the gen-
" tlemen of the aforeſaid court, for the year 1709." The figures
of a man in a fur gown, and his wife, praying, with the inſcription
under them b, remaining in the eaſt window, were engraved on copper at Dr. Rawlinſon's expence.

" Ordinance of parliament for making Covent-garden church paro-
" chial, printed for Wm. Beeſby, in the new Piazza, 1646," confirmed by act of parliament under Charles II. See more about this
chapel, which was built before 1636, MS. Harl. 1831.

" Reaſons againſt the bill for erecting a church for the French in
" the church-yard of St. Martin Orgar. Lond. 1703."

" The hiſtory of the veſtry of St. Dunſtan's in the weſt. Lond.
" 1714." 8vo.——" Veſtry proceedings in the pariſhes of St. Dunſtan's
" in the weſt In 1712 and 1713, and St. Botolph without Biſhopgate.
" Lond. 1723." 8vo.

" The caſe of the erectors of a chapel or oratory, in the pariſh of
" St. Andrew's, Holborn. Lond. 1722." 8vo.

" The caſe of the patron b and rector c of St. Andrew's, Holborn. In
" anſwer to a pamphlet, intitled, The caſe of the erectors, &c. Humbly offered to the conſideration of all the clergy and patrons in England.
" 1722." 8vo.

" The caſe concerning the ſetting up of images or painting of them
" in churches, written by the learned Dr. Thomas Barlow, late biſhop
" of Lincoln, upon his ſuffering ſuch images to be defaced in his dio-
" ceſe, wherein 'tis diſapproved and condemned by the ſtatutes and
" eccleſiaſtical laws of this kingdom, and the book of homilies. Pub-
" liſhed upon occaſion of a painting ſet up in Whitechappel church.
" Lond. 1714." 8vo First printed in Barlow's " Caſes of conſcience.
Lond. 1692." 8vo.

---

b *Orate pro bono : ſtatu Rogeri Hillet : londin civ. et Anne uxoris : ſue.* Above
theſe figures is a good whole length of S. Baſil in epiſcopalibus.
  b The Duke of Montague.
  c Dr. Sacheverell.

" A let-

" A letter from a parifhioner of St. Clement's Danes to Edmund lord
" bifhop of London, occafioned by his lordfhip's caufing the picture
" over the altar to be taken down: with fome obfervations on the ufe
" and abufe of church paintings in general, and of that picture in par-
" ticular. 1725. 8vo."

Fourteen views of London churches which efcaped the fire, drawn
by R. Weft 1736, were engraved by W. H. Toms, and publifhed
1739, with accounts below. Smaller ones by Harris and Boydell.

Cavendifh Weedon, fellow of Lincoln's-inn, projected a mufical
fervice of voices and inftruments to be performed in Lincoln's-inn
chapel every Sunday at 11 o'clock, except during Lent and the vaca-
tion, under the direction of Dr. Edw. Maynard, by fubfcription, the
propofals for which were engraved on a folio fheet; and on two others
the plan of Lincoln's-inn-fields, with the figures of the twelve apoftles,
and waterworks at each corner, to be fupplied from Hampftead water,
and the model of St. Mary's chapel, to be erected in the centre *for
praife*, on a defign of Sir C. Wren, engraved by Sturt 1698.

Profpectus interior templi Dano-Norwegici Londinenfis, by J. Kip,
1697. Cibber built this church.

A plan, elevation, and profile of Bow fteeple; and a plan and view
of Bow church, with the arcade fronting Cheapfide, originally intended by Sir C. Wren, make the xivth and xvth plates of his Synopfis.
To which is prefixed a catalogue of the churches in London, palaces,
hofpitals, and public edifices, built by him during thirty years, from
1688 to 1718, and a lift of the exact fums laid out for rebuilding each
church, referring to their names and numbers in rondeaux on a pyramid.

Views of St. Giles's Cripplegate by Hollar and Seller.

A N. W. view of St. Giles's in the Fields, built by Mr. Flitcroft,
drawn by Donowell, engraved by Walker 1753.

St. Mary, the new church in the Strand, by J. Gibbs arch. J. Harris fc. Another engraved by Toms in Maitland.

A particular account of the damage done to St. Bride's fteeple by
lightning June 18, 1764, may be feen in Dr. Watfon's obfervations on
the effects of lightning, and in Mr. Delaval's letter to Mr. Wilfon,

with

with draughts, inferted in the livth vol. of the Philofophical Tranfactions, p. 201—235. and the effects of the fame lightning in Effex-ftreet, in a letter from Dr. Thomas Laurence. Ib. p. 235.

" A critical review of the public buildings, ftatues, and ornaments " in and about London and Weftminfter: to which is prefixed the " dimenfions of St. Peter's church at Rome and St. Paul's cathedral at " London. 1734." 8vo. The 2d edition 1736 was enlarged with fome reflections on the ufe of fepulchral monuments; a preface, being an effay on tafte; an appendix, containing a difpute between the Weekly Mifcellany and the author; and a compleat alphabetical index.

" Englifh architecture: or the public buildings of London and " Weftminfter, with plans of the ftreets and fquares, reprefented in " 123 folio plates, with a fuccinct review of their hiftory; and a can" did examination of their perfections and defects." Fol. The plates of Maitland's Hiftory thus dreffed up by the bookfellers art.

" London and Weftminfter improved, illuftrated by plans. To " which is prefixed a difcourfe on public magnificence; with obfer" vations on the ftate of arts and artifts in this kingdom, wherein the " ftudy of the polite arts is recommended as neceffary to a liberal educa" tion: concluded by fome propofals relative to places not laid down " in the plans. By John Gwynn. Lond. 1766." 4to.

The Royal Exchange, with Latin and Englifh verfes in the compartment for the title, and appendant thereto Sir Thomas Grefham's head as in a little medal, by Hollar, with a fmaller view of it. Another of the Tower, and another of St. Mary Overies church, Southwark, 1644: the original is in the hands of Mr. Weft. In Overton's lift is a map of the Royal Exchange by T. Cartwright, the builder. A plate from a drawing belonging to the Antiquarian Society, 1566, the year it was firft finifhed by Sir Thomas, engraved by Vertue in Ward's Hiftory of the Grefham profeffors. The Royal Exchange as defigned 1569 was engraved by Hollar; alfo as it was built, infcribed " Byrfa Londinenfis, vulgo Royal Exchange," with verfes Latin and Englifh, by H. Peacham. 1644. There is another view of it drawn and engraved by R. White 1671, dedicated by Cartwright to Sir Tho. Ford, mayor. An elevation of the S. portico by an unknown hand. An ichnographical draught by J. Seller. A folio plate of Charles IId's ftatue by Vandrebanc.

Great

" Great Britain's glory; or a brief defcription of the fplendor and
" magnificence of the Royal Exchange: with fome remarkable paf-
" fages relating to the prefent engagement. Humbly prefented to the
" feveral merchants of the city of London, who daily meet to traffick
" and converfe in the faid place. Lond. 1672." 4to.

Three views of Domus Hofpitaliorum S. Joan. Jerufal. Londini, in
a half fheet, 1660. and one of St. Katherine's Hofpital, 1672, in the
Monafticon.

In the Pepyfian library are Hollar's drawings of Suffolk, York, Durham, Salifbury, Worcefter, and Somerfet houfes.

A print of the Cuftom-houfe by John Dynftall.

The houfe by Blackfriars ftairs, where Salmon, author of the Dif-
penfatory lived, by B. Lens, infcribed Ars chirurgica a Guil. Salmono.
Καινον γυμνασιον ιατρικον.

Mercers chapel, and Sir Robert Clayton's houfe in the Old Jewry.

Cripplegate: ex dono { Jo. Lichfield, } { Tho. Tarrant.
                       { Pet. Leaver,   } { Tho. Carter.
                                    Convivatorum 1688.

Thanet houfe in Alderfgate ftreet.

The equeftrian ftatue of Charles II. in Stocks market.

The front of Northumberland houfe next the Strand, by J. June,
engraved by Jefferies, 1752.

Grofvenor and Bloomfbury fquares, by Sutton Nichols.

Defign for the lord mayor's manfion-houfe, by I. Ware, 1737.

A plan and elevation of the Fleet-market, by Geo. Dance, 1737,
W. H. Toms, fc.

Edw. Rooker propofes to engrave feveral views in London and Weftminfter: the firft four, views of St. James's gate, W. St. Paul's, Covent-
garden, Scotland-yard with part of Whitehall, and Blackfriars bridge
July 1766.

Bagford mentions [d] a defcription of a Roman camp and place of exercife in the old artillery ground, without Bifhopfgate, by a judicious
author, whofe name he forgot, in the latter end of Q. Elizabeth's
reign; a valuable 4to pamphlet.

[d] Letter to Hearne, p. xii.

Hearne

Hearne publifhed at the end of the 8th volume of Leland's Itinerary Dr. Woodward's " Account of fome Roman urns, and other antiqui- " ties, lately digged up near Bifhopfgate ; with brief reflections upon " the antient and prefent ftate of London, in a letter to Sir C. Wren." It was reprinted 1713. 8vo. with a letter from the Doctor to the editor, and in Somers's Tracts, 1723, vol. iv. p. 15. He printed it firft at the defire of Sir Chriftopher, whofe obfervations have fince ap- peared in the Parentalia. Wren could not be perfuaded that the temple of Diana ftood on the fcite of St. Paul's, though Woodward had prepared a differtation on her image dug up near that cathedral, and an account of the Roman antiquities in his collection, found in feveral parts of England, but chiefly about London ; but thefe were never printed. John Conyers, apothecary, one of the firft collectors of antiquities, efpecially thofe relating to London, when the city was re- building, gave the labourers who dug the foundations encouragement to fave whatever they found for him, and from the W. end of St. Paul's and Goodman's-fields he got a great many Roman utenfils, &c. In his walks about London, and vifits to the bookfellers fhops, he picked up many rare books and MSS. He infpected moft of the gravel- pits near town for different forts and fhapes of ftones. In one near the fign of Sir J. Oldcaftle about 1689 he difcovered the fkeleton of an elephant, which he fuppofed had lain there only fince the time of the Romans, who in the reign of Claudius fought the Britons near this place, according to Selden's notes on the Poly- olbion. In the fame pit he found the head of a Britifh fpear of flint, afterwards in the hands of Dr. Charlett, and engraved in Bagford's let- ter. He drew the form of the Roman tile-kiln for making the facri- ficing veffels, and part of a mould for the ornaments, found near the weft end of St. Paul's in the vacant fpace near the petty canons hall. The kiln was in Dr. Woodward's, the draught and remarks in Sir Hans Sloane's poffeffion d. The late Mr. Empfon, who was librarian to Sir Hans, told me Conyer's MS. on the antiquities of London was in the Britifh Mufeum, though he could not readily find it. Maitland has

u Bagford's letter to the publifhers of Memoirs for the curious, vol. ii. and to Hearne, p. lxviii.

made

made extracts from it. Many things were bought out of his collection after his death by Dr. Woodward; particularly the famous iron shield[e], of which the Doctor had a print engraved at Amsterdam 1705, by Van Gunst, from a drawing by Mr. Howard, and communicated to Cuper. A copy of it contracted was inserted in Hearne's Livy, vol. vi. p. 226. Drakenborch's Silius Italicus, L. iv. 153. p. 196. and Spon's Miscellanea eruditæ antiquitatis.

In Hearne's introduction to Leland's Collectanea, p. 58, is " A let-" ter to him, written by the ingenious Mr. John Bagford; in which " are many curious remarks relating to the city of London, and some " things about Leland."

Ames's observations on a Hebrew inscription found in London-wall 1753 may be seen in the Gentleman's Magazine, July 1753, p. 369. In that for March 1748, p. 122, are certain dates on St. John's Gate, Clerkenwell, engraved in one plate with those at Widial, Helmdon, Colchester, and Worcester. The arms on this gate are exhibited in the Magazine for Dec. 1746. The seal of the priory was engraved by Vertue.

---

[e] Hearne published at Oxford 1713, 8vo. Henry Dodwell's " Dissertatio de Parma " equestri Woodwardiana, &c." left unfinished at his death, and prefixed to it an account of Dodwell's works: some passages of which giving offence, the book was suppressed by a meeting of the heads, March 23, 1712-13; but at length leave was obtained to publish it without the catalogue. Theophilus Downes, fellow of Baliol differed from Dodwell as to the antiquity of this shield; and since his death were published in two leaves, 8vo. his " De clipeo Woodwardiano stricturæ breves." In the Appendix to Ward's lives of the Gresham professors (N° XVII.) is a letter from Dr. Woodward to Abbe Bignon, defending its antiquity against the learned at Paris, of whose doubts the Abbe had informed him. Ainsworth abridged Dodwell's Dissertation, and inserted it at the end of the Museum Woodwardianum, or catalogue of the Doctor's library and curiosities, when sold by auction at Covent-garden, 1728. 8vo. He afterwards enlarged the piece, considered the objections, and reprinted it with this title, " De clypeo Camilli antiquo, operis elegantissimi, & cum per tot secula duraverit, in-" tegritatis plane mirandæ, e reliquiis musei Woodwardiani apud Cl. V. Ric. King, " trib. mil. adservato dissertatio. Præmittitur ejusdem monumenti argumentique limbo " insculpti descriptio. Lond. 1734." 4to. Spanheim and Abr. Seller had both begun to write dissertations on it, but were prevented by death. Ward is the last that made any remarks on it; he thinks it a votive shield probably made before the time of Plutarch, who first mentions the circumstance of the Gaulish general's belt being thrown into the scale as a make-weight: Gronovius imagined a *prop* under the scale was mistaken for it on the shield. Moyle's objection to its antiquity from the ruins of an amphitheatre has not been removed by Dr. Ward. No antient artist could be so ignorant as to ascribe such buildings to that period.

A stone

A ftone found in digging the foundation of the Manfion-houfe 1739, on the fcite of St. Mary Woolchurch, deftroyed 1666, was drawn by R. Weft, and engraved by Toms. The infcription feems to commemorate the foundation of this church.

In the Harleian library, N° 1096, are the epitaphs in the churches of St. Mary Magdalen, Old Fifh-ftreet St. Nicholas Cold abbey, St. Michael Royal, and Queenhith, St. Mary Mountfhaw, and Somerfet, St. Nicholas Olave's, St. Leonard's Shoreditch, and St. Catherine Coleman, 1597, more perfect than in Weever, who had omitted fome. The title expreffes all the churches in London, but only thefe appear.

A graveftone found in the cellar at the Queen's-arms tavern, St. Martin's le Grand, the cloyfter to the collegiate church, 1672, is publifhed ex MS. Afhmol. 860. p. 442, by Hearne in his Appendix to the Hiftory of Glaftonbury, N° VII. The infcription wants the firft half: the remainder may be read, *Tous* or *vous qui par ici paffe pur lalme*, &c. the two laft words are unintelligible.

In the Gentleman's Magazine for April 1758, p. 166, is an account communicated to the Antiquarian Society by Benj. Radcliffe, apothecary, of certain bones, fuppofed of elephants, found under-ground in Pall-Mall; other fimilar ones were found in St. James's-fquare many years before.

The crypts of a church at the corner of Leadenhall and Bifhopfgate ftreets, mentioned by none but Maitland, and difcovered by a dreadful fire there Nov. 1765, were qngraved in the Gentleman's Magazine, Feb. 1766.

The particulars of Sir Thomas Grefham's foundation are contained in " An account of the rife, foundation, progrefs, and prefent ftate of " Grefham-college, in London; with the life of the founder Sir Tho- " mas Grefham: as alfo of fome late endeavours for obtaining the re- " vival and reftitution of the lectures there; with fome remarks there- " on. Lond. 1707." 4to.

Andrew Tooke, geometry profeffor, publifhed " An exact copy of the laft will and teftament of Sir T. Grefham, kt. to which is added, an abridgement of an act of parliament, 23 Eliz. A.D. 1581. for the better performing the laft will of Sir T. G. as alfo fome accounts concern-

ing

ing Grefham college, taken from the laft edition of Stow's Survey of London (printed in the year 1720) and elfewhere. Lond. 1724." 4to. The act faid to be abridged is inferted at length : the extracts from Stow were firft fent by Tooke to Strype, who printed them in his 2d appendix, with the author's initials.

John Ward, rhetoric profeffor, wrote " The lives of the founder and the profeffors : with an appendix of orations, lectures, and letters writen by the latter, with other papers ferving to illuftrate the lives. Lond. 1740." Fol.

" The third univerfitie of England, or a treatife of the foundations of " all the colledges, auncient fchooles of priviledge, and of houfes of " learning and liberall arts within and about the moft famous citie of " London. With a briefe report of the fciences, arts, and faculties " therein profeffed, ftudied, and practifed. By Sir Geo. Buc." at the end of Howe's edition of Stowe's Annals. Lond. 1615 and 1631. Fol.

As to fchools, we have " A catalogue of all the books in the library " of St. Paul's fchool, London, with the names of the benefactors, " as given in by Geo. Charles, L. L. D. high mafter in the time of " John Nodes, efq; furveyor, accomptant of the faid fchool. Dated " the 2d day of March, 1743." This collection was begun 1670.

" Preces quotidianæ in ufum fcholæ Paulinæ : " and " Preces " fcholæ Mercatorum fcifforum." William Dugard, late fchool-mafter in the laft, printed " The fchools probation : or, rules and " orders for certain fet exercifes, to be performed by the fcholars on " probation-days ; made, and approved by learned men, for the ufe " of Merchant-Taylors fchool, in Lond. 1661." Lond. 8vo.

John Sturt engraved a S. E. view of the charity-fchool of Portfoken ward, erected by alderman John Cafs.

" Mr. Rawlinfon had a fair MS. intitled, " Liber Hofpitalis Sancti " Egidii Lond. A° 1402." Its age is determined by thefe words at the beginning : " Frater Walterus Lyntonn magifter Hofpitalis de Burtonn Sancti Lazari f Jerlm in Anglia ordinavit iftum librum fieri cartarum et munimentorum Hofpitalis Sancti Egidii leproforum extra barram vete-

---

f Jerufolimæ. Burton-Lazar hofpital in Leicefterfhire was founded for lepers of St. Lazarus without the walls of Jerufalem. The mafterfhip of St. Giles's was granted to it by Edw. I.

ris

ris Templi London. Anno Dom. Millimo CCCCmo fecundo, anno regni regis Henrici Quarti poft Conqueftum quarto, fecundo die Marcii." In this valuable collection were feveral charters and papers giving a good account of the ftate of feveral parifhes in London at that time.

For an account of the firft hofpital in London, founded as early as 1102, by Rahere, founder of the adjoining priory, fee " The ordre of " the hofpital of S. Bartholomewes, in W. Smythefielde, in London, " erected for the benefit of the fore, and the difeafed; and re- " venue of 100 marks; and that the citizens fhould add v hundred " marks by the year; which they received with thanks. Printed by " R. Grafton. 1553." 12mo.

" The order of the hofpitals of K. Henry the viiith, and K. Edward " the vith. viz. St. Bartholomews, Chrifts, Bridewell, St. Thomas's, " by the maior, cominaltie, and citizens of London, governours of " the poffeffions, revenues, and goods of the faid hofpitals. Lond. " 1557." 12mo. Since reprinted in the old characters and fize.

" Orders and ordinances for the better government of the hofpital " of Bartholomew the Lefs; as alfo orders enacted for orphans, and " their portions, 1580: together with a brief difcourfe of the laudable " cuftomes of London. Lond. 1652." 4to.

The picture of Edw. VI. giving his palace of Bridewell to the city for an hofpital and workhoufe, painted by Holbein, and hung up in the hall there, was engraved by Vertue, with a printed account of it. An abftract of his grant of the hofpitals to the city in the Gentleman's Magazine, Feb. 1766.

A general plan of the new building intended for this hofpital by Gibbs and Toms.

" A true copy of the laft will and teftament of Thomas Guy, efq; " late of Lombard-ftreet, bookfeller, containing an account of his " publick and private benefactions. Lond. 1725." 8vo.

" St. Thomas's and St. George's hofpitals compared. Lond. 1760." a fingle folio fheet.

A view of the London hofpital in Whitechapel road, with the ground and country adjacent, defigned by Boulter Mainwaring, efq; painted by Wm. Bellers, and engraved by Chatelain and Toms. 1753.

Of the Savoy hofpital Hollar engraved a view from the Thames: the Antiquarian Society publifhed a fimilar view 1750; two others 1753, with the chapel; alfo a plan of the ground and buildings, all drawn by Vertue 1736.

Of Sutton's-hofpital, or the Charter-houfe, we have " The Charter-
" houfe; with the laft will and teftament of Thomas Sutton, efq;
" taken out of the Prerogative-court, according to the true original.
" Lond. 1614." 4to. re-printed in 4to. 1646, with this title " Sutton's
" hofpital; with the names of fixteen mannors, many thoufand acres
" of land, meadow, paftures, and woods; with the rents and here-
" ditaments thereunto belonging ; the governors thereof, and number
" of fcholars, and others, that are maintained therewith : as alfo the
" laft will and teftament of Thomas Sutton, efq;" &c. Thefe two
pieces are comprized in " Domus Carthufiana : or, an account of the
" moft noble foundation of the Charter-houfe, near Smithfield, in
" London, both before and fince the reformation; with the life and
" death of Thomas Sutton, efq; the founder thereof, and his laft will
" and teftament. To which are added feveral prayers, fitted for the
" private devotions and particular occafions of the antient gentlemen. By
" Sam. Herne, fellow of Clare-hall, in Cambridge. Lond. 1677." 8vo.

The moft correct and compleat piece on this fubject is " An hifto-
" rical account of Thomas Sutton, efq; and of his foundation in
" Charter-houfe. By Philip Bearcroft, D. D. preacher at the Charter-
" houfe. Lond. 1737." 8vo.

" Sutton's fynagogue, or the Englifh centurion : fhewing the un-
" parallelled bounty of Proteftant charity ; a commemoration fermon
" at the Charter-houfe, by Percival Burrel, A. M. preacher there.
" Lond. 1629." 8vo.

" A dramatick piece by the Charter-houfe fcholars, in memory of
" the powder plot, performed at the Charter-houfe Nov. 6, 1732.
" Lond. 1732."

Dr. Rawlinfon engraved a grant of obituary prayers from the prior and convent here to the priors of the hofpital of St. John of Jerufa-lem, for leave granted by the latter for a water-courfe, 1430.

In 1686 was publifhed a project, intitled, " An account of the ge-
" neral nurfery, or college of infants, fet up by the juftices of peace
" for

" for the county of Middlefex ; with the conftitutions and ends thereof.
" Licenfed 3 Octob. 1686."

" The ftate and cafe of a defign for the better education of thoufands
" of parifh children fucceffively in the vaft weftern fuburb of London
" vindicated ; and humbly dedicated to all the honourable and pious
" perfons that have or may be inclined to be favourers and encouragers
" of it." 4to. This hofpital at Highgate, called the Ladies Charity-fchool,
was erected by one Blake, a woollen-draper in Covent-garden, who
purchafed Dorchefter-houfe, and having fooled away his eftate in building was thrown into prifon, whence he wrote this account, to which
profpects of Dorchefter-houfe and the hofpital are prefixed.

In the Harleian Mifc. vol. iv. p. 136, is reprinted " A fcheme for
" the foundation of a royal hofpital, and raifing a revenue of 5 or
" 6000l. a year, by and for the maintenance of a corporation of fkil-
" ful midwives, and fuch foundlings or expofed children as fhall be
" admitted therein, as it was propofed to his majefty K. James II. by
" Mrs. Eliz. Cellier, in June 1687. Now firft publifhed from her
" own MS. found among the faid king's papers." Fol. containing 9
pages. Cellier was a popifh midwife, in whofe houfe the plan of the
meal-tub plot was found : her part in it was to ftab lord Shaftfbury
with a confecrated dagger concealed under her gown, while pretending to pay him a vifit of thanks : though acquitted of the plot fhe
was fined and pilloried for a libel on fome perfons in power in a narrative of her trial. She propofed in this fcheme that parents fhould
redeem their children under 5 years old for 25 l. under 7 for 40 l. and
every year after the age of 10 to advance 10 l. but after 15, 100 l. or
lefs : all parifh-found children under 3 years old were to be taken in
for 2 s. per week or 15 l. paid by the parifh, and, unlefs allowed to
marry or depart, to continue there 21 years as apprentices to the houfe,
to learn the feveral arts and trades. The only article copied in the
prefent foundation is that of regiftering the child.

" An account of the foundation and government of the hofpital for
" foundlings in Paris ; drawn up at the command of her late majefty
" Q Caroline, and now publifhed for the information of thofe who
" may be concerned in carrying on a like defign in this city. 1739."
8vo. Copies of their charter were printed that and the following years.

T t   " Some

" Some confiderations on the neceffity and ufefullnefs of the royal
" charter for the hofpital for foundlings. 1740." 8vo.

" Regulations for the managing of it," were printed by order of the
governors. 1746. 1752. 1757. 8vo.

Plan and elevation of the building approved and ordered to be
erected at a general quarterly committee of the governors, June 30,
1742, was engraved by Fourdrinier.

A profpective view of the hofpital, with embellifhments, drawn by
S. Wale, engraved by Grignion and Rooker 1749.

" Private virtue and publick fpirit difplayed, in a fuccinct effay on
" the character of capt. Thomas Coram, who deceafed the 29th of
" March, and was interred in the chapel of the Foundling hofpital
" (a charity eftablifhed by his follicitation) April 3, 1751. Lond.
" 1751." 8vo.

" The tendencies of the Foundling hofpital in its prefent extent
" confidered in feveral views, juft as they occur, en paffant, in epifto-
" lary addreffes, attempting to preferve the lives of baftard infants,
" to continue the cuftom of matrimony, to ftrengthen the community
" in its population, and to better it in its induftry and trade, in its
" opulence, and moft of all in what fhould be moft regarded, in its
" morals. In feveral letters to a fenator. Part I. [containing 3 letters.]
" P. II. [fix concluding letters] fhewing what is bad in the plan, and
" pointing out a new one to be fubftituted inftead of it, or to be united
" to what is good in it; this new one tending to make the poor be-
" come a full fupport to the poor, not only not burdenfome to the
" publick, but great benefactors to it. Lond. 1760. 4to. Printed for
private ufe." By the late Dr. Tunftall.

" The rife and progrefs of the Foundling hofpital confidered ; and
" the reafons for putting a ftop to the general reception of all children.
" 1761." 8vo.

The benevolent Mr. Hanway publifhed " A candid hiftorical ac-
" count of this hofpital ; reprefenting the prefent plan of it as produc-
" tive of many evils, and not adapted to the genius and happinefs of
" this nation : fhewing, on the other hand, the great importance of
" the eftablifhment, if put under proper regulations, as the moft effec-
" tual means of preferving the lives of a great number of fuch infants
" as

" as have ufually perifhed within the bills of mortality. With a pro-
" pofal for carrying a new defign into execution. To which is added
" a letter from a country gentleman to a governor of the hofpital :
" containing many obfervations relating to foundlings born, educated,
" or employed in the country; collected from real facts. With his
" opinion concerning the amendments neceffary. The fecond edition.
" 1760." 4to. on which fome remarks appeared foon after.

" An earneft appeal for mercy to the children of the poor, particu-
" larly thofe belonging to the parifhes within the bills of mortality,
" appointed by an act of parliament to be regiftered : being a general
" reference to the deferving conduct of fome parifh officers, and the
" pernicious effects of the ignorance and ill-judged parfimony of others.
" With fome comparative views of thofe parifhes and the Foundling
" hofpital, and reafons for the neceffity of fuch an hofpital in thefe
" cities, to be maintained for certain purpofes only, and under certain
" reftrictions. Alfo a propofal for the more effectual preferving the
" parifh-children here and in other great cities and manufacturing towns,
" and rendering the children of the poor in general pious, ufeful, and
" good fubjects. By Jonas Hanway, efq; 1766." 4to.

" An account of the inftitution and proceedings of the guardians of
" the Afylum, or houfe of refuge, fituated on the Surry fide of Weft-
" minfter bridge, for the reception of orphan girls refiding within the
" bills of mortality, whofe fettlements cannot be found. Printed by
" order of the guardians. 1761." 8vo.

" The original defign and progrefs of the Scots corporation near
" Fleetditch, with their benefactors, mafters, treafurers, &c. Lond.
" 1714." 4to.

" The plan of the Magdalen-houfe for the reception of penitent
" proftitutes. By order of the governors. 1758." 4to. Accounts of
the rife, progrefs, and prefent ftate of this charity, with the rules, and
lift of fubfcribers, and a print of one of the women prefixed, are printed
yearly, for the benefit of the houfe.

" Thoughts on the plan for a Magdalen-houfe for repentant profti-
" tutes, with the feveral reafons for fuch an eftablifhment : the cuftom
" of other nations with regard to fuch penitents, and the great ad-
" vantages, which will probably arife from this inftitution upon poli-

" tical

" tical and religious principles. Addreſſed to the promoters of this
" charity. 1758." 4to.

" A letter to J. Hanway, eſq; in which ſome reaſons are aſſigned,
" why houſes for the reception of penitent women, who have been
" diſorderly in their lives, ſhould not be called Magdalen-houſes.
" 1759." 8vo.

" The hiſtories of ſome of the penitents in the Magdalen-houſe, as
" ſuppoſed to be related by themſelves. Lond. 1760." 12mo. 2 vols. A
catchpenny.

" The Magdalens: an elegy. Lond. 1763." 4to.

" Propoſals for eſtabliſhing a Benevolent Corporation in London, &c.
" to aſſiſt the pariſh-officers throughout the kingdom to provide more
" effectually for the relief of the poor, to reſtrain and employ wander-
" ing beggars and gypſies, and to forward the purpoſes of moſt of the
" preſent charitable eſtabliſhments in the metropolis through the ſeveral
" counties." Intended for the preſs.

Dr. Caius, who was preſident of the College of Phyſicians ſeven
years, tells us he had an intention of publiſhing their annals in Latin.
Dr. Merret ᵍ publiſhed " A collection of acts of parliament, charters,
" tryals at law, and judges opinions, concerning thoſe grants to the
" college of phyſicians in London, taken from the originals, law
" books, and annals. Lond. 1660." 4to. Great part of it is included
in " The royal college of phyſicians of London, founded and eſtab-
" liſhed by law ; as appears by letters patents, acts of parliament, ad-
" judged caſes, &c. Lond. 1684." 4to. To which is generally joined
" An hiſtorical account of the college's proceedings againſt empiricks,
" and unlicenſed practiſers, &c. in every prince's reign, from their
" firſt incorporation, to the murther of the royal martyr, king Charles
" the Firſt. By Charles Goodall, M. D. and fellow of the ſaid college
" of phyſicians. Lond. 1684." 4to.

" The ſtatutes of the college of phyſicians, London ; worthy to be
" peruſed by all men, but more eſpecially phyſicians, lawyers, apothe-
" caries, ſurgeons, and all ſuch that either do, or ſhall, ſtudy, pro-
" feſs, or practice phyſick. Lond. 1653. 1663. 1693." 12mo.

ᵍ See his conteſt with Stubbes in defence of the college. Ath. Ox. II. 930.

" Statuta

" Statuta moralia coll. medicorum. Lond. 1722." 8vo.

" The catalogue of the fellows, and other members" was printed
1695. In p. 8 is inferted " A fhort account of the inftitution and
" nature of the college of phyficians, London; publifhed by themfelves,
" 1688." and " An appendix to the ftatutes; wherein are contained
" feveral more new laws promulgated in the college, Sept. 30. 1696."

" A fhort account of their proceedings in relation to the fick poor
" of the faid city and fuburbs thereof; with the reafons which have
" induced the college to make medicines for them at the intrinfick
" value. Lond. 1697." 4to.

" Some remarks on their charter, and the act of parliament which
" confirms it, wherein the cafe is truly ftated betwixt the univerfities
" and the college. Lond. 1714. 8vo."

" An impartial enquiry into the legal conftitution of the college of
" phyficians in London; fhewing, from their charter, acts of parlia-
" liament, and their own ftatutes, how much they have deviated from
" their original inftitution. Lond. 1753." 8vo.

" A letter from a phyfician in town to his friend in the country,
" concerning the difputes at prefent fubfifting between the fellows and
" licentiates of this college. Lond. 1753." 8vo. Remarks on it. Lond.
1753. 8vo.

" A vindication of the college in reply to the fpeech of the follicitor-
" general on opening the petition and appeal of Dr. Ifaac Schomberg,
" alias Schamberg, to the right hon. the lord high chancellor, the lords
" chief juftices, the lord chief baron, as vifitors of the college; in-
" tended to have been addreffed to their lordfhips in Lincoln's-inn-
" hall after the counfel fhould have concluded their arguments againft
" the jurifdiction. By Sir William Browne, fellow, elect, cenfor, trea-
" furer. Lond. 1753." Fol. " Minutes of the proceedings of the col-
" lege relating to Dr. Schomberg. Lond. 1754."

" Bibliothecæ collegii regalis medicorum Londinenfis catalogus.
" Lond. 1757." 8vo.

" A charter granted to the apothecaries of the city of London, the
" 30th of May, 13 Jac. I. tranflated and printed, for the better in-
" formation of the faid apothecaries, in their duty to the city of London,
" the college of phyficians, and their own fociety. Lond. 1695." 4to.

Bifhop

Biſhop Sprat has written a moſt florid and admired " Hiſtory of the
" Royal Society of London, for the improveing of natural know-
" ledge. Lond. 1667." 4to. reprinted 1702. 1722. and 1734. and
tranſlated into French. Gen. 1699. 12mo. ʰ.　This hiſtory and the
Society were violently attacked by H. Stubbe ⁱ, phyſician at Warwick,
the Hill of the laſt century, in " Legends no hiſtories: or a ſpecimen
" of ſome animadverſions upon the hiſtory of the Royal Society. Lond.
1670." 4to.——" Campanella revived, or an enquiry into the hiſtory
" of the Royal Society, whether the virtuoſi there do not purſue the
" projects of Campanella for the reducing England unto popery:
" being an extract of a letter to a perſon of honour from H. S.　With
" another letter to Sir N. N. relating the cauſe of the quarrel be-
" twixt H. S. and the Royal Society; and a poſtſcript concerning the
" quarrel between him and Dr. Chriſtopher Merrett. Lond. 1670." 4to.
——" A cenſure upon certain paſſages contained in the Hiſtory of the
" Royal Society, as being deſtructive to the eſtabliſhed religion and
" church of England.　To the 2d edition of which is added, The let-
" ter of a virtuoſo in oppoſition to the cenſure, a reply unto the letter
" aforeſaid, and reply unto the præfatory anſwer of Ecebolius [Joſeph
" Glanville] chaplain to Mr. Rouſe of Eaton (late member of the
" rump parliament) rector of Bath, and fellow of the Royal Society.
" Alſo an anſwer to the letter of Dr. Henry More, relating to Henry
" Stubbe, phyſician at Warwick. Oxf. 1671." 4to.

" A review of the works of the Royal Society of London; contain-
" ing animadverſions on ſuch of the papers as deſerve particular obſer-
" vation, in eight parts; under the ſeveral heads of arts, antiquities,
" medicine, miracles, zoophytes, animals, vegetables, minerals.　By
" John Hill, M. D. acad. reg. ſcient. Burd. &c. ſoc. Lond. 1751." 4to.

" At the end of " Chariſmatum ſacrorum trias ſive bibliotheca An-
" glorum theologica," by Martin Kemp, hiſtoriographer to the elector
of Brandebourg. Regiomont 1677. 4to. is an appendix containing an
epiſtolary diſcourſe upon the Royal Society.

ʰ I ſuppoſe by Du Moulin, who had a certificate from the Society that he had tranſlated their hiſtory into French at their deſire, March 3, 16⅞. Birch's Hiſtory of the
Roy Soc. II. 426.
　Biog. Brit. Sprat. n D. He was drowned going from Bath to viſit a patient at Briſtol
one ſummer evening.　Wood ſays, his head was intoxicated with bibbing, but more with
talking and ſpuffing of powder.

　　　　　　　　　　　　　　　　　　　　　　　" The

" The hiftory of the Royal Society of London, for the improving of
" natural knowledge, from its firft rife. In which the moft confider-
" able of thofe papers communicated to the Society, which have hi-
" therto not been publifhed, are inferted in their proper order, as a
" fupplement to the Philofophical Tranfactions. By Thomas Birch,
" D. D. fecretary to the Royal Society. London." 4 vols. 4to. 1756
and 1757. The Doctor has inferted the lives of the principal members of the Society at the time he treats of, which is only part of the
laft century, ending 1687: for the reft, this collection contains very
few papers worth publifhing.

" Bibliotheca Norfolciana, five catalogus libb. manufcriptorum &
" impefforum in omni arte & lingua, quos illuftriff. princeps Henricus
" dux Norfolciæ, &c. Regiæ Societati Londienenfi pro fcientia naturali
" promovenda donavit. Lond. 1681." 4to. By William Perry: inferted alfo in Cat. MSS. Angliæ, tom. ii. p. 74—84. Bagford fays k
Marmaduke Fofter, who underftood printed books as well as moft men
in Europe, took a catalogue of them 1687; but before it was printed it
was curtailed by fome who knew nothing of the matter. This valuable
library, great part of which came out of that of Matthew Corvinus's,
K. of Hungary, at Buda, belonged to Bilibaldus Pirkeimerus, counfellor
to Charles V. whofe great learning and extenfive abilities both in the field
and cabinet were equal to his piety and probity. Of his heirs it was purchafed by the celebrated earl of Arundel, whofe grandfon Henry duke
of Norfolk prefented it to this Society. Later benefactions making a
more full and perfect catalogue neceffary, one was prepared for the
prefs, but never printed. Lifts of the fellows are annually given out:
one called " A lift of the Royal Society of London, inftituted by his
" majefty king Charles II. for the advancement of natural knowledge,
" with the places of abode of moft of its members; as alfo an adver-
" tifement, fhewing what fubjects feem moft fuitable to the end of its
" inftitution. Lond. 1718." 8vo. was privately handed about, but foon
fuppreffed as it gave offence, by " diftinguifhing the *moft proper* and *able*
" perfons for the feveral arts and fciences."

" Diplomata & ftatuta Regalis Societatis Londini. Juffu præfidis &
" concilii edita. Lond. 1752." 8vo.

An

An imperfect account of their repository is in " Musæum Regalis
" Societatis; or, a catalogue and description of the natural and artificial
" rarities belonging to the Royal Society, and preserved at Gresham-
" college, made by Nehemiah Grew, M.D. fellow of the Royal Society,
" and of the College of Physicians. 1681." Fol. with cuts. The mummy,
which makes the first article in this catalogue, was taken to pieces and
examined by several eminent physicians and others, Dec. 16, 1763, at
the house of the late Dr. Hadley, whose account of it in a letter to Dr.
Heberden, communicated to the Society, was printed in the livth vol. of
their Transactions, art. 1. with a cut of the foot, and a bulbous root
found under it; the original drawing of which hangs up in the public
library at Cambridge. The Philosophical Transactions were begun
March 166$\frac{1}{4}$, by Oldenburg, about four years after the Journals and Registers commence. He went to N° 136, and they were discontinued
from Jan. 167$\frac{4}{5}$ to Jan. 168$\frac{4}{5}$; but supplied in a great measure by Hooke's
Philosophical Collections, of which N° i. came out 1679, ii. and iii.
1681, iv. v and vi. 168$\frac{1}{4}$, vii. and last. Grew and Plot carried them
on from N° 136 to N° 166. when Dr. Musgrave, and after him Dr.
Halley, continued them. They were discontinued three years more,
from Dec. 1687 to Jan. 169$\frac{0}{1}$, besides other smaller interruptions of near
a year and half more before Oct. 1695, since which they have been regularly carried on in 497 numbers, till 1751, when the method of publication was changed to volumes, beginning with vol. xlvii. The Collections and Transactions, from the beginning to 1701, were abridged
and disposed under general heads by John Lowthorp, A. M. F. R. S. in
3 vol. 4to. 1705. 3d edit. 1722; 4th, 1731: from 1700 to 1720, very
incorrectly, by Benj. Motte, a printer [a], in 3 vols. 4to. 1721; and better
by Henry Jones, late fellow of King's Coll. Camb. 1721. 2d edit. 1731.
2 vols. 4to: from 1719 to 1733, by J. Eames, F. R. S. and J. Martyn,
F. R. S. late professor of botany at Cambrigde, 1734. 2 vols. [vi. vii.]
4to. from 1720 to 1732, by ——Reid and John Gray, 2 vols. 1733. 4to.
from 1732 to 1750 by Martyn alone, 4 vols. 4to. [viii. ix. 1747. x. xi.
1756.] An abridgment for 1732, being a supplement to these, came
out 1747. 4to. A general index to the 7 volumes of Lowthorp, Jones,
Eames, and Martyn's abridgements 1736. 4to.

[a] Motte published " A reply to Jones's preface to his Abridgement. Lond. 1732." 4to.

The

The Antiquarian Society, which began about the clofe of Elizabeth's reign, but was fuppreffed by that timid pedant her fucceffor, was incorporated by his late Majefty 1751. The charter and ftatutes were printed by order of the Society for the ufe of the members 1752. 8vo. The prints of various antiquities engraved at their expence form two folio volumes; the firft, intitled " Vetufta monumenta quæ ad rerum " Britannicarum memoriam confervandam Societas Antiquariorum " Londini fumptu fuo edenda curavit. Volumen primum. His accef- " fit fodalium focietatis ab anno MDCCXVII catalogus. Lond. 1747." The fecond is intitled " Collectanea antiquitatum fumptibus Societatis " Antiquariæ Londinenfis impreffa." It were to be wifhed they would refolve at length to indulge the publick with fome of the many interefting communications laid before them.

" De Societate Antiquaria Londinenfi ad virum celeberrimum Joan- " nem Erhardum Kappium, prof. eloqu. ordin. in acad. Lipfienfis & " collegii majoris principum collegiatum epiftola Chriftiani Kortholti, " A. M. ordinis philofophia Lipfienfis affefforis & collegii minoris " principum collegiati. Lipfiæ 1735." 4to.

" Sion college, what it is and doth; together with a vindication of " that fociety from the flanderous defamation of the two fell and fiery " fatyrs, the one called, Sion college vifited, the other, The pulpit " incendiary. Alfo a little taft by the way, of a little thing of Mr. " Goodwin's running about with the fhell on the head before it is all " hatcht, under the name of the Youngling Elder. By C. B. who " accounts it an honour to be a member of Sion college. Lond. 1648." 4to. This book gives an account of the foundation and ufe of this college, intended for the London divines. Bagford.

" Catalogus univerfalis librorum omnium in bibliotheca collegii " Sionii apud Londinenfes. Una cum elencho interpretum S. S. fcrip- " turæ, cafuiftorum, theologorum, fcholafticorum, &c. omnia per " J. S. [Joan. Spenfer] bibliothecarium (quanta potuit diligentia) or- " dine alphabetico difpofita, in unum collecta, & propriis fumptibus " in ftudioforum ufum excufa. Londini 1656." 4to. Moft of thefe books were loft in the fire 1666: of the few that efcaped a catalogue is inferted in the Cat. MSS. Angliæ, &c. tom. ii. p. 106. We have an

U u   account

account of the collection that succeeded them, in " Bibliothecæ cleri
" Londinensis in collegio Sionensi catalogus duplici forma concin-
" natus.　Pars I. exhibet libros juxta ordinem scriniorum distributos,
" & ad proprias classes redactos.　Pars altera, omnium auctorum &
" rerum præcipuarum capita ordine alphabetica complectitur.　Auctore
" Gulielmo Reading, bibliothecario. Lond. 1729" Fol.

For the library belonging to the dissenting clergy see " Bibliothecæ
" quam vir doctus & admodum reverendus Daniel Williams, S. T. P.
" bono publico legavit catalogus. Lond. 1727." 8vo.　" A true copy
" of the Doctor's will. Lond. 1717." 8vo.　" Memoirs of his life
" and eminent conduct; with some account of his scheme for the
" vigorous propagation of religion as well in England as in Scotland,
" and several other parts of the world. Addressed to Mr. Peirce. Lond.
" 1718."　Other accounts of him in his funeral sermon by Dr. Evans,
$17\frac{1}{16}$, and Calamy's Continuation, vol. ii. and prefixed to his Practical
Discourses, in 2 vols. Lond. 1738. 8vo.

" Catalogus librorum manuscriptorum bibliothecæ Cottonianæ, cui
" præmittuntur illustris viri, D. Roberti Cottoni eq. aur. & baronetti
" vita, et bibliothecæ Cottonianæ historia & synopsis, scriptore Thoma
" Smitho, ecclesiæ Anglicanæ presbytero. Oxon. 1696. Fol."　Hearne
had a copy of it, corrected and enlarged by Smith himself, who was
librarian; as also his catalogue of the charters in this library omitted in
the other catalogue.　Another copy, which was Humphrey Wanley's,
1698, enriched with his additions and notes, and given by him to
Dr. T. Grainger 1715, was sold among Dr. Leatherland's books last
spring.　Dr. Smith drew up a preface, shewing the ill use made by bp.
Burnet of the papers preserved here [m]; which was to have been prefixed to his book, but remains among his other papers, which he bequeathed to T. Hearne.　Vertue engraved for the Antiquarian Society
an original picture of Sir Robert Cotton, and two plates, containing the
fragments of a very antient MS. of Genesis adorned with beautiful
paintings, that were rescued from the fire: these are accompanied
with a Latin dissertation by professor Ward on this MS. which from
a note of James's in the first leaf appears to have been a present to

---

[m] See what Dr. Smith says on this subject in his letter to Hearne, preface to Leland's
Collectanea, p. 25.

Henry

Henry VIII. from two Greek bifhops, who faid it was Origen's: Elizabeth gave it to John Fortefcue, her Greek reader, who gave it to this library.

In 1732 was printed " A report from the committee appointed to " view the Cottonian library, and fuch of the publick records as they " think proper, and to report.to the houfe the condition thereof, with " what they will judge fit to be done for the better reception, pre- " fervation, and more convenient ufe of the fame. Publifhed by order " of the Houfe of Commons." Fol. In the appendix is a narrative of the fire at Afhburnham-houfe Oct. 23, 1731, and an account of fuch MSS. and other curiofities of this library as were deftroyed or injured thereby, by David Cafley, deputy librarian ; and the ftate of the records of the courts of Chancery, common law, the Exchequer, and the Dutchy court of Lancafter, in their refpective offices. Two years after Cafley publifhed " A catalogue of the MSS. in the King s " library : with an appendix to the catalogue of the Cottonian library, " together with an account of the books burnt or damaged by a late " fire; 150 fpecimens of the manner of writing in different ages, from " the third to the fifteenth century, in copper-plates; and fome ob- " fervations upon MSS. in a preface. Lond. 1734." 4to. Hen. VII. and VIII. Edw. VI. and Elizabeth laid the foundation of this library, to which James I. added lord Lumley's books, partly collected by H. Lhuyd, who married his fifter, and partly confifting of thofe of Henry Fitz-Alan, earl of Arundel, his father-in-law, cotemporary with the diffolution, from which he recovered many MSS. Patrick Young, an eminent Grecian, who was appointed librarian by James, made a catalogue of the books, and procured Ifaac Cafaubon's books and MSS. for it. He intended an edition of the Alexandrine MS. in the exact form of the original letters, and printed a fpecimen of the firft chapter. Dr. Grabe completed the edition on another plan, and inferted Young's notes as far as they went. This library being feized among the King's effects 1648, was committed to the care of Whitelock. After the re- ftoration (when only a third part of the medals could be recovered, and many books were miffing) Roffe, tutor to the duke of Monmouth, held this place till 1675 by his deputy, bp. Pearfon's brother, and Fre-

derick

dérick and James Thynne, by Juſtel, till 1692, when it was given to Dr. Bentley, who left a catalogue of the books and MSS. found in Bryan Fairfax's hands 1748, and reſigning it to his ſon, he ſold to it Claude Amyand, who enjoyed the ſalary till 1760, when the King gave the reverſion to the Britiſh Muſeum.

The MSS. in theſe three collections, augmented by thoſe of the late earl of Oxford, are now depoſited in the Britiſh Muſeum. " The ca- " talogue of the Harleian collection of MSS. purchaſed by authority " of parliament for the uſe of the publick, and preſerved there;" was printed in two volumes, Fol. 1753 : the preface and index added 1762, by Mr. Aſtle. This catalogue was begun by the induſtri- ous Humphry Wanley [n], librarian to the earls Robert and Edward, who gives a particular abſtract of the contents of each article, and lite- rary anecdotes, as far as he goes. Caſley reſumed the work after his death, and followed his method in ſome meaſure. Mr. Hocker, the preſent deputy-keeper of the Tower records, carried it on ſomewhat further, and the librarians of this department in the Muſeum have com- pleated it. Lord Oxford's books and pamphlets were purchaſed by T. Oſborne, who publiſhed a catalogue of them by ſubſcription in twelve numbers, at a ſhilling each, or 4 volumes, 8vo. at ten ſhillings, intitled; " Bibliothecæ Harleianæ catalogus in locos communes diſtributus, cum " indice autorum. 1743." The moſt intereſting pamphlets were re- duced to eight 4to. volumes, intitled, " The Harleian Miſcellany," with

<hr>

[n] He was ſon of Nathaniel Wanley, vicar of Trinity church, Coventry, author of " The wonders of the little world," and born 1671. What time he could ſpare from the handicraft trade to which his father put him, he employed in turning over old MSS. and copying the various hands. Dr. Lloyd, his dioceſan, ſent him to St. Edmund's hall, Oxford, of which Dr. Mill was then provoſt, whom he greatly aſſiſted in his collations of the N. T. but afterwards removed by Dr. Charlet's advice to Univerſity Col. When admitted to the Bodleian library he made large extracts from the MSS. and promiſed a ſupplement to Hide's Catalogue of the books, which Hearne completed and publiſhed. He intended a treatiſe on the various characters of MSS. with ſpecimens, Mabillon's work on that ſubject being corrupted by the conceits of the engravers, who inſerted characters that never were or could be uſed. Upon leaving Oxford he travelled over the kingdom in ſearch of Anglo-Saxon MSS. at Dr Hickes's deſire, and drew up the cata- logue of them in his Theſaurus and Grammar. Bagford mentions ſome deſign of his relating to a Saxon bible. He was ſoon after employed in arranging this library for lord Oxford, who allowed him a handſome penſion till his death, 1726. He is buried in Marybone church.

hiſtorical

hiftorical, political, and critical notes, a table of contents, and an alphabetical index, firft publifhed in weekly numbers, and at the end
of each, part of " A copious and exact catalogue of pamphlets in the
" Harleian library," giving a fhort account of their contents, ranged
numerically, that perfons might apply for the publication of any particular one.   They were computed at 400,000.   The coins, medals,
pictures, prints and drawings, collected by Mr. Talman, with Roman,
Greek, and other antiquities out of the Arundelian collection, were fold
by auction by Cock in Covent-garden, March 174½.   Lord Oxford's
library filled thirteen handfome chambers and two large galleries:
Mazarine's books, amounting to 40,000, including the MSS. only fix
rooms and a gallery; Naudè in vain follicited the parliament of Paris to
purchafe them °

" Statutes and rules relating to the infpection and ufe, and for the
" better fecurity and prefervation" of the Britifh Mufeum, were printed
by order of the truftees, 1759. 8vo.   " The general contents of the
" Britifh Mufeum, with remarks, ferving as a directory in viewing
" that noble cabinet. 1761." 8vo. 2d edition, enlarged, 1762. 8vo.
is a fuperficial account.   The mummy given by Smart Lethieullier, efq;
was engraved in five views on two plates by Vertue, 1722 : four views
in two plates by Baron are in Alex. Gordon's Effay on it, 1737. Fol.

The MSS. belonging to the College of Heralds are inferted in the
Cat. MSS. Angliæ, &c. tom. ii. p. 175—178.   Thofe given to the
Society of Lincoln's-inn by Sir Matthew Hale, ib. p. 179.

Dugdale publifhed a compleat hiftory of all the inns of common
law and chancery in his " Origines Juridiciales, or hiftorical memorials
" of the Englifh laws, courts of juftice, forms of tryal, punifhment
" in cafes criminal, law writers, law books, grants and fettlements of
" eftates, degree of ferjeants, innes of court and chancery : alfo a
" chronologie of the lord-chancellors, and keepers of the great feal,
" lord-treafurers, juftices itinerant, juftices of the King's-bench and
" Common-pleas, barons of the Exchequer, mafters of the Rolls,
" king's attorney and follicitors, and ferjeants at law   Lond. 1666."

° See his letter defcribing it, tranflated into Englifh, 1652. 4to. Cat. Harl. pamph.
N° 39.

Fol.

Fol. with copper plates of the feveral halls, the pourtraits of the then judges, chancellor, &c. by Hollar. This was abridged and continued in Chronica Juridicialia, 1685 and 1739. 8vo.

The books of the Middle-Temple library are contained in " Biblio-
" theca illuftris Medii Templi Societatis in ordinem juxta rerum natu-
" ram redacta ac v. iduum Sept. MDCC. aufpicio & fumptu Barth.
" Shower militis, hujus ædis quæftoris. Lond. 1700." 8vo. reprinted
under the title of " Catalogus librorum bibliothecæ hon. Societatis Me-
" dii Templi, Londini, ordine dictionarii difpofitus. 1734." 4to.

" Certaine devices and fhewes prefented to her Majeftie by the gen-
" tlemen of Grayes-Inne, at her Highneffe court at Greenwich, the
" 28th days of Februarie, in the 30th yeere of her Majefties moft
" happy reigne. Lond. 1587. 4to.

The antient manner of keeping Chriftmas in the inns of court may
be feen in the " Gefta Grayorum, or the hiftory of the high and
" mighty prince Henry, prince of Purpoole, archduke of Stapulia and
" Bernardia, duke of High and Nether-Holborn, marquifs of St. Giles
" and Tottenham, count palatine of Bloomfbury and Clerkenwell,
" great lord of the cantons of Iflington, Kentifh Town, Paddington,
" and Knights-Bridge, knight of the moft heroical order of the Hel-
" met, and fovereign of the fame; who reigned and died A. D. 1594.
" Together with a mafque, as it was prefented (by his highnefs's com-
" mand) for the entertainment of Q. Elizabeth; who, with the nobles
" of both courts, was prefent thereat. Lond. 1688." 4to.

The MSS. in Gray's-inn library are in Cat. MSS. Angliæ, &c. tom.
ii. part i. p. 41. A large view of the garden by Sutton Nicholls.

Vertue engraved a view of the chapel at Lincoln's-inn.

For the prifons, fee " Ludgate what it is, not what it was; or a full
" and clear difcovery and defcription of the nature and quality, orders
" and government, duties of officers, benefits and priviledges, fees
" and charges, of that prifon; alfo an exact catalogue of the legacies
" now belonging to the faid prifon, the names of the feveral donors,
" and the perfons appointed to pay them; very ufeful and profitable
" to all forts of perfons, efpecially in London, whether creditors or
" debtors. Humbly prefented to the right hon. Thomas Allen, lord

5

" mayor

" mayor of this honourable city, by M. Johnſon, typograph. a late pri-
" ſoner there. Lond. 1659." 24°. Bagford dates it 1657, and mentions
" A companion for debtors and priſoners, with a deſcription of New-
" gate, the Marſhalſea, the two Counters, Ludgate, the Fleet, and
" King's-bench priſon. 1699." 8vo.

" An account of the fire at the New-priſon by Clerkenwell, where-
" by the greateſtpart of the houſe was burnt down, on Friday night,
" May 9, 1697, preſumed on very violent ſuſpicions to be ſet on fire
" by a papiſt that was there in cuſtody, and by that means eſcaped.
" Taken from the mouth of the keeper of the ſaid priſon. Lond.
" 1679." 4to.

" Reaſons offered for the reformation of the houſe of correction in
" Clerkenwell; ſhewing, I. the preſent ſtate of this gaol, the de-
" bauchery of the priſoners, and the miſerable condition they are in
" from the want of a ſufficiency of food, &c. II. Propoſals in what
" manner theſe evils may be prevented for the future; humbly ſub-
" mitted to the conſideration of the magiſtrates and inhabitants of the
" county of Middleſex. To which is prefixed, a plan of the ſaid
" priſon engraved on copper, with references deſcribing the manner
" in which this gaol ſhould be altered for the purpoſes propoſed, with
" a calculation of the expence thereof. 1757." 8vo.

" An account of ſeveral workhouſes for employing the poor. Lond.
" 1725." 8vo.

" The laws of the markets of the city of London" were printed
1595. 12mo. Bagford found " The aſſize of bread," on vellum
with wooden cuts, ſet forth and printed 12 Hen. VII. 1496, at the
requeſt of Mich. Engliſh and Jo. Rudeſtone, Aldermen. 1ſt impreſſion. In an old book, called " The cuſtoms of London," it is ſaid
that Wm. Hubert, abp. of Canterbury, invented the aſſize for bread.
There is a large table for it in Mr. ſecretary Harley's library, which he
ſuppoſes was the ſtandard for the whole kingdom, with a baker in a
pillory of a different form from thoſe now uſed. He ſays the aſſize of
bread was firſt ſet forth and publiſhed in black letter by Hugh Jackſon °.
4to. The 2d impreſſion 1610 like the 1ſt; the 3d, with additions by
J. Powell, 1614, with wooden cuts. 4to. Ames had one 1621. The

° The firſt dated aſſize is 1528, the next I have ſeen 1591.

4th

4th by ditto, printed by Wm. Stanſbey 1632. 4to. with the ſame cuts. The 5th by J. Penkethman, 1636. The 6th by the ſame, 1638, with " a plane introduction to the art of numeration, and of dearths " and famines in this kingdom." The 7th by his ſon, 1671. The 8th by J. Powell 1684. 4to. " The new book declaring the aſſize of " bread, with the table of the market prices of wheat from 1646 to " 1706." Ames's Cat. 614. I have another 1714. 4to. The title at large is " The aſſize of bread. Together with ſundry good and need- " full ordinances for bakers, brewers, inholders, victuallers, vintners, " and butchers: and alſo other aſſizes in weights and meaſures, which " by the lawes of this realme, are commanded to be obſerved and " kept by all manner of perſons, as well within the liberties as with- " out. Whereunto there are alſo added, ſundry good and needfull " orders, in making and retayling of all kinds of lawfull bread, ven- " dible unto his Majeſties ſubjects in the commonwealth, agreeing " with the ſtatutes, lawes, and antient orders and cuſtomes of this " realme of England. The which ſtatutes, &c. have been heretofore " ſeene, allowed, and are commanded to be kept, by the right hon. " the lords and others of the king's hon. privie counſell. Newly cor- " rected and enlarged, from 12 pence the quarter of wheate, unto " three pounds and ſix pence the quarter, according to the riſing and " falling of the price thereof in the market, by ſixe pence altering in " every quarter of wheate. Joh. Cant. Ch. Hatton, W. Burley, " H. Derby, Cha. Howard, H. Hunſdon, Tho. Buchurſt, Sir Fra. " Knowles, Sir Tho. Heneage, Sir J. Forteſcue, Sir J. Woolley."

Mr. Webb cauſed to be engraved in 1756 letters patents of Edw. IV. 20 Aug. anº r. 20. [1481] confirming others of Rich. II. which confirmed an ordinance of Edw. III. 10 May, anº r. 1º in favour of the *Girdlers* company, that no body ſhould be allowed to work girdles with any worſe metal than *de laton baterie feer & aſſer*, it having been the practice to uſe lead, pewter, and copper *(plum, peautre, & d'eſtain)*; and empowering them to have one or two ſearchers in all the cities, boroughs, and towns in the kingdom, to ſearch, preſent, and burn all ſuch girdles, and puniſh the makers at their diſcretion.

" A ſhort

" A fhort account of the company of *Grocers*, from their original ;
" together with their cafe and condition (in their prefent circum-
" ftances) truly ftated : as alfo how their revenues is fettled, for pay-
" ment of their charities, and provifion made for the well governing
" their members and myftery, to preferve a fucceffion in their fociety;
" defigned for information of all, and benefit of the members; and
" for fatisfaction and encouragement of their friends and benefactors.
" Lond. 1686." Fol. 1689. 4to. By Wm. Ravenhill, clerk of the
company. Dedicated to K. Wm. and Q Mary.

" The orders, rules, and ordinances, ordained, devifed, and made
" by the mafter, and keepers or wardens, and commonalty, of the
" myftery or art of *Stationers* of the city of London, for the well go-
" verning of that fociety. Lond. 1678." 4to.

" The [P] charter and grants of the company of Stationers of the city
" of London, now in force, containing a plain and rational account of
" the freemens rights and privileges faithfully produced, and, where
" neceffary, impartially explained, in order to afcertain the authority
" annexed to the office of mafter and wardens, and to redrefs the hard-
" fhips and miferies of the injured and oppreffed freemen. To which
" is added an appendix, fhewing that the court of affiftants was im-
" pofed upon the freemen by a charter granted by Charles II. which,
" becaufe it was found unreafonable, oppreffive, and illegal, was re-
" voked and made null and void by an act of parliament 2 Wm. and M.
" So that it will be found to be exprefly ordained and granted, that
" the faid company muft be governed by mafter and wardens only :
" that the mafter and wardens muft be elected and removed at pleafure,
" by the freemen for ever : and that the profits of the Englifh ftock
" muft be for the help and relief of the poor freemen, and not for the
" fupport of the mafter, wardens, and affiftants, and their relations and
" dependants. Lond. 1741." 8vo.

[P] The company of Stationers fubfifted long before the invention of printing. Ames
could not find their privileges or charter, though feveral of the old printers are faid to
have been of the Stationers company; nor had they any authority over printed books
granted them as a body corporate till the charter of 1546, 3 Ph. and M. now in the
Rolls Chapel, inferted in Ames's Hift. of Printing, p. 520—525.

" The

" The honour of the *Merchant Taylors*; wherein is set forth the
" noble acts, valliant deeds, and heroick performances of Merchant
" Taylors, in former ages; their honourable loves and knightly adven-
" tures, their combating with foreign enemies, and glorious successes
" in honour of the English nation: together with their pious acts, and
" large benevolences, their building of publick structures, especially
" that of Blackwell-hall, to be a market place for the selling of wool-
" len cloaths. Written by William Winstanley Lond. 1668." 8vo.
With the head of Sir Ralph Blackwell.

" The representation of the promoters, contrivers, and inventers of
" the art or trade of *Frame-work knitting*, or making silk stockings,
" in a petition to the lord protector Cromwell, that they may be united
" and incorporated by charter. Printed for their own use 1657." 4to.
In it is the story of the first inventer of the engine or frame, Wm. Lee,
of Calverton, Nottinghamshire, gent. The workmen were sent to
France just before Henry IVth's death. Lee went thither with nine
workmen, and left some at Roan, to provide for themselves, of whom
seven returned to England with their frames, the other two remained
in France, and one was then living. The Venetian ambassador gave
500l. for the remaining time of one Hen. Mead and Ab. Jones, settled
at Amsterdam. The company was incorporated about 1664.

" Opera mineralia explicata: or the mineral kingdom within the
" dominions of Great Britain displayed; being a compleat history of
" the antient corporations of the city of London of and for the mines,
" mineral and battery works; with all the original grants, leases, &c.
" by M. S. [Moses Stringer] 1718." 8vo.

Richard Wallis, citizen and arms painter of London, in his " London's Armory. 1677." Fol. engraved the arms of every distinct company and incorporated society in London, collected from their several
patents, approved and confirmed by divers kings at arms. Those of
the twelve companies were engraved by Hollar in as many plates, and
for S. Bower, painter, in Budge-row, 1698.

The first pageants we meet with in London were exhibited when
the Black Prince made his entry with his royal prisoners 1357.
Another when his son Richard II. passed along Cheapside 1392. A

3d when Hen. IV. made his entry 1415, after the battle of Agincourt. A 4th when Henry VIII. received the emperor Charles V. 1522 q. A 5th when he and A. Boleyn paſſed through the city to her coronation 1532.

"The paſſage of our moſt ſoveraygne lady queen Elizabeth through "the city of London, to Weſtminſter, the daye before her coronation· "Lond. 1558." 4to. contains an account of all the pageants erected to adorn the proceſſion, with the verſes and orations.

"The whole magnificent entertainment given to K. James, Q. Anne "his wife, and Henry Frederick the prince, upon the day of his Ma-"jeſties triumphant paſſage (from the Tower) through his honor-"able citie (and chamber) of London, the 15 of March 1603, as well "by the Engliſh as by the ſtrangers, with the ſpeeches and ſongs de-"livered in the ſeveral pageants ; and thoſe ſpeeches that before were "publiſhed in Latin, now newly ſet forth in Engliſh, by Tho. Dekker: "Lond. 1604." 4to.

Strype in his edition of Stowe's Survey deſcribes a pageant in the mayoralty of Sir Wolſtan Dixie 1585 : the next he mentions is the firſt in Bagford's MS. liſt of pageants from the firſt printing and pub-liſhing of them by the city poets.

"Chryſo triumphos : the triumph of gold at the inauguration of Sir "James Pemberton to the dignity of lord mayor of London, Fryday "29 Oct. 1611, at the charge of the worſhipfull and antient com-"pany of Goldſmiths, deviſed and written by A. Munday 1611."

"Troja nova triumphans at the receiving Sir John Swinnerton, kt. into the city of London, 1612." 4to.

"The triumphs of truth : Sir Tho. Middleton mayor : wrote by "Tho. Middleton ²: with his lordſhip's entertainment at Iſlington, at "the charge of the Grocers, 1613. 4to.

"Triumphs of old drapery, or the rich clothing of England, at the

---

¹ In C. C. C. C. library, Nº vii. 10. is a MS. deſcription of the pageants made in the city of London at receiving of the moſt excellent prince Charles V. emperor, and Henry VIII. king of England. 1522.

² The firſt lord mayor that went by water to Weſtminſter was John Norman, 1453. There is a drawing of the ſhow on the river in the Pepyſian library.

Brother to Sir Hugh.

X x 2   "charge

" charge of the right worſhipfull the company of Drapers at the iir
" ſtallation of Tho. Hayes, by A Munday, 1614."

" Metropolis coronata in the triumphs of antient drapery or rich
" clothing in England, in two years performance at the inſtallation of
" Sir John Jolley, the firſt that received the dignity, by A. Munday,
" 1615 : with the ſtory of Robin Hood. Printed by Geo. Purſtowe."

" The golden fiſhing, or the honours of the fiſhmongers. Sir John
" Lemon lord mayor, by A Munday, 1616."

" Της ειρηνης τροφαια, or the triumphs of peace. Sir Francis Jones
" lord mayor, Oct. 30, at the charge of the worthy and antient com-
" pany of Haberdaſhers, made by John Squires, 1620."

" The monument of honour at the confirmation of the right worthy
" brother John Goare in his high office of his majeſty's lieutenant over
" his royal chamber, at the charge and expence of the right worthy
" and worſhipfull fraternity of eminent Merchant Taylors. Invented
" and written by John Webſter, taylor, 1624."

" Triumph of health and proſperity at the inauguration of the moſt
" worthy brother, the right hon. Cuthbert Haſket, draper ; compoſed
" by Tho Middleton, draper, 1624. 4to."

" London's jus honorarium expreſſed in ſundry pageants and ſhews
" at the initiation of the r. h. Sir Geo. Whitmore, at the charge of
" the right worſhipfull ſociety of Haberdaſhers, by J. Heywood, 1631."

" Londini artium & ſcientiarum ſcaturigo : or London's fountain of
" arts and ſciences ; expreſſed in ſundrie triumphs, pageants, and
" ſhews, at the initiation of the r. h. Nich Raynton into the maiorty
" of the famous and far-renowned city London. All the charges and
" expence of the laborious projects both by ſea and land being the ſole
" undertaking and charge of the r worſhipfull company of Haber-
" daſhers ; written by T. Haywood, 1632. 4to." ‡.

" London imp : or London mercatur explained in ſundry tri-
" umphs, pageants, and ſhews at the inauguration of the r. h. Ralph
" Freeman, at the charge of the right worſhipfull company of Clothiers;
" by T. Heywood, 1633. 4to."

‡ At the end of this is a panegyric on maiſter Gerard Chriſtmas for bringing the pageants and figures to ſuch great perfection both in ſymmetry and ſubſtance, being before
but unſhapen monſters made only of ſlight wicker and paper.

" Triumphs

" Triumphs of fame and honour at the inauguration of Rob. Park-
" hurſt, clothworker ; compiled by John Taylor. 1634."

" Londini ſpeculum, or London's mirror, expreſſed in ſundrie tri-
" umphs at the initiation of the r. h. Rich. Fenn into the mayoralty of
" the famous and renowned city of London, at the ſole charge of the
" company of Haberdaſhers, bo h by land and water ; written by T.
" Haywood 1637."

" Porta pietatis : Sir Maurice Abbot lord mayor, by the Drapers
" company ; by T. Heywood, 1639."

" Londoni ſtatus pacatus : Hen. Garaway lord mayor ; the ſame
company and compoſer, 1640."

" London's triumph : Rob. Titchburn mayor.   Skinners company.
By J. B. 1657."

The entertainment of Tho. Alleyne by the Grocers ; writ by J.
" Tatham 1690."

" The royal oak : Sir Rich. Brown mayor : J Tatham poet. The
undertakers were capt. And. Duke and Mr. Wm. Lightfoot, painters,
Tho. Whiting, joiners, and Rich. Clarke, carver, 1661."

" The antient honour of the city of London recovered by the noble
" Sir John Robinſon, kt. and baronet, lord mayor for the year 1663,
" in the truly Engliſh and manlike exerciſe of wreſtling, archery,
" ſword and dagger ; with the ſpeeches of Mr. Wm. Smith, maſter
" of the game and clerk of the market.   Intermitted 24 years, ſince
" Garaway was mayor."

" London's reſurrection : Sir Geo. Waterman mayor ; by the Skin-
" ners company, compoſed by Tho. Jorden. 1672."

" London s triumph, or the city in jollity and ſplendor, expreſſed
" in various pageants, ſhapes, ſcenes, ſpeeches, and ſongs, invented
" and performed for the congratulation and delight of Robert Hanſon,
" kt. at the coſt and charge of the worſhipfull company of Grocers ;
" by Jorden, 1673.

" London in its ſplendor : Sir Wm. Hooker mayor : by the Grocers
company, and T. Jorden. 1674."

" The Goldſmith s jubilee : Sir Rob. Vyner mayor : Mr. Stevenſon
painter and undertaker : T J. poet. 1675."

" Another

" Another for Sir Joseph Sheldon, draper." 1676.

" London's triumphs at the instalment of Sir Tho. Davies, draper, lord mayor of Lond. 1677. T. J. poet."

" London's triumphs : Sir Fran. Chaplin, clothworker : T. J. poet. 1678."

" The triumph of London : Sir James Edwards, mayor."

" London in luster : projecting many bright beams of triumph : " disposed into several representations of scenes and pageants : per- " formed with great splendor on Wednesday, October xxix. 1680, at " the initiation and instalment of the right hon. Sir Rob. Clayton, kt. " lord mayor of the city of London. Dignified with divers varieties " of presenters, with speeches, songs, and actions, properly and punc- " tually described ; all set forth at the proper cost and charges of the " worshipfull company of Drapers. Devised and composed by Tho. " Jorden, gent. Lond. 1679. 4to."

" London's glory : Sir Patience Ward : T. J. 1681."

" London's royal triumph : Sir James Smith 1685."

One for Sir Rob. Jeffreys : Mat. Taubman poet. 1686.

" The triumphs of London : performed on Saturday, Oct. 29, " 1693, for the entertainment of the right hon. Sir John Fleet, kt. " lord mayor of the city of London : containing a true description of " the several pageants ; with the speeches spoken on each pageant. " All set forth at the proper costs and charges of the worshipfull com- " pany of Grocers : together with an exact relation of the most splen- " did entertainments prepared for the reception of their sacred ma- " jesties. By E. Settle. Lond. 1692. 4to." There is a drawing of this procession in the Pepysian library, and of Sir Humphry Edwin's 1698.

Richard Johnson's " Nine worthies of London, 1592." 4to. celebrates the honourable actions of nine other citizens : Sir Wm. Wallworth, Sir Hen. Prichard, Sir Wm. Sevenoake, Sir Tho. White, lord mayors, Sir John Bonham, Sir Christopher Croker, Sir John Hawkwood, Sir Hugh Calverley, and Sir Henry Maleverer.

Stephen Harrison, who calls himself joiner and architect, invented the triumphal arches erected in London for the reception of James I.

engraved

engraved by Kip, in a few folio leaves, 1603. which Mr. Walpole ᵘ never faw but in the library at Chatſworth. There is another in the Pepyſian library. The ſpeeches, &c. compiled by B. Johnſon are printed among his works. vol. iii. p. 203.

" The entertainment of his moſt excellent majeſtie Charles II. in
" his paſſage through the city of London to his coronation : contain-
" ing an exact accompt of the whole ſolemnity; the triumphal arches,
" and cavalcade, delineated in ſculpture; the ſpeeches and impreſſes
" illuſtrated from antiquity. To theſe are added a brief narrative of his
" majeſties ſolemn coronation : with his magnificent proceeding and
" royal feaſt in Weſtminſter-hall. By John Ogilby. Lond. 1662."
The plates engraved by Hollar : among the reſt is an inſide view of the choir of Weſtminſter abbey at the coronation. Ogilby being appointed by the commiſſioners for the coronation of Charles II. to prepare the poetical part of this entertainment, drew up firſt a relation of it and deſcription of the arches, deſigned by Sir Balthazar Gerbier, in ten ſheets, enlarged afterwards as above by the king's command.

" London's artillery, briefly containing the noble practice of that
" worthy ſocietie, with the moſt eminent martiall exerciſes, natures of
" arms, vertue of magiſtrates, antiquitie and glorie and chronogra-
" phy of this honorable cittie. By R. N. [Richard Niccolls ˣ.] Oxon.
" 1616." 4to. A poem with illuſtrations.

" A letter of K. Philip and Q. Mary, 1 & 2 reg. to the lord mayor
" [Thomas White], with his precipe to the ſeveral wards, for putting
" in execution the laws againſt the inhabitants for not putting out
" lanterns and candles, (2 ſheets, paſted lengthwiſe) 1554." Bagford.
Sir H. Barton, mayor, firſt ordered lanthorns to be hung out in the ſtreets at night 1416.

" The civil wars of the city, wherein you have an account of the
" diſſenſions between the pope's head, who had ſummoned in a coun-
" ſell of caterpillars, and called all the ſigns in and about London to
" his aſſiſtance." A thin 4to. printed about 1640. Bagford.

ᵘ Anecd. of paint. vol. ii. p. 86. Cat. of eng. p. 113.
ˣ Wood mentions one of both theſe names, L, L. D. 1663. and groom of the bed-chamber to James duke of York, Faſti, II. 156.

" J. Taylor,

" J. Taylor, the water poet's travels through London, to visit all
" the taverns in the city and suburbs, alphabetically disposed, with the
" names of all the vintners at that time. 1636." 8vo. Another perambulation, by the same, 20 miles near London. 16 . . . Richard
Ames turned the same kind of perambulation into a search after claret,
in two parts, printed for H. Newman. 16 . . . 4to. Bagford.

In the Pepysian library are two very antient sets of cries cut in wood,
with inscriptions: among others, My rope of onions, white Sir Thomas' onyons—rosemary and bays—bread and meat for poor prisoners—
ends of gold or silver—markyng stones—a mat for a bed—maids
hang out your lights—glasses, fine glasses—a tanker bearrer—maribones, maids, maribones—ells or yeardes—bandestrings or hankercher
buttons—a bresh or a table booke—small coal a penny a peke—I
have screenes if you desier to keepe your butey from the fire—buy a
cocke or a gelding. Another set of cries was engraved by Tempesta,
after Mauron. The last set by P. Sandby.

" The pleasant walks of Moorfields, the gift of two sisters, now
" beautified, to the continued fame of this worthy city. Compiled by
" Richard Johnson, and dedicated to the right worshipfull the knights
" and aldermen of this honourable city of London. 1617." black letter:
a dialogue between a gentleman and a citizen. Bagford. Stowe mentions [y] a map or plan of Moorfields as intended to be laid out by one
Leate, a citizen, which he was to have inserted in his book.

" The London almanac for the meridian of London, for 1673,
" by Mercurius Civicus: printed by Tho. Ratcliff and Nat. Thomson,
" for the company of stationers, and dedicated to Sir Richard Ford;
" with observations touching the antiquities of London, and the several
" waters, conduits, mills, and rivers." Bagford.

" The inscriptions upon the tombs, grave stones, &c. in the dis-
" senters burial ground, near Bunhill-fields, Lond. 1717." 8vo.

" A description of the Duke of York's] bagnio [in Long-acre], and
" of the mineral bath, and new spaw thereunto belonging; with an
" account of the use of sweating, rubbing, bathing, and the medi-
" cinal vertues of the spaw, by Samuel Haworth, M. D. Lond.
" 1683." 12mo.

[y] Edit. 1633, p. 302.

" A ca-

" A catalogue of many natural rarittes, with great induſtry, coſt, and
" thirty years travel in foreign countries, collected by Robert Hubert,
" alias Forges, gent. and ſworn ſervant to his majeſty, and daily to be
" ſeen at the place called the Muſick-houſe, at the Miter, near the
" weſt-end of St. Paul's church. Lond. 1664." 12mo.

Of John Kemp's muſeum ᶻ, near the Haymarket, when ſold by
auction, Oct. 13, 1717ᵃ, a catalogue was drawn up by Robert Ainſ-
worth, in two parts, intitled " Monumenta vetuſtatis Kempiana, ex
" vetuſtis ſcriptoribus illuſtrata, eoſque viciſſim illuſtrantia in duas
" partes diviſa : quarum altera mumias, ſimulacra, ſtatuas, ſigna, lares,
·" inſcriptiones, vaſa, lucernas, amuleta, lapides, gemmas, annulos,
" fibulas, cum aliis veterum reliquiis ; altera nummos materia modo-
" que diverſos continet. 1720." 8vo. To the 2d part, which contained the medals, and was firſt publiſhed ſeparately 1719, is prefixed
" De aſſe & partibus ejus commentarius," by profeſſor Ward, which
had alſo been printed by itſelf 1719. Six antient inſcriptions bought
here by Dr. Rawlinſon are now at Oxford. Several others purchaſed by
Eben. Muſſel, eſq; were reſold at the auction of his curioſities laſt ſpring.

" The London Spaw, giving an account of the water and its
" properties : compiled by Dr. Jones and Mr John Conyers, 1685."
half a ſheet folio.

" A deſcription of the playhouſe in Dorſet-gardens, a poem," in
one folio ſheet, 1706. A view of it in the Pepyſian library.

" An account of the laſt Bartholomew Fair, and the late city orders
" for regulating the ſame : with four letters to a citizen of London on
" that occaſion. [by G. S.] Lond. 1702." 4to.

" Reaſons formerly publiſhed for the punctual limiting of Bartholo-
" mew fair to thoſe three days to which it is determined by the royal
" grant of it to the city of London, now reprinted with additions, to
" prevent a deſign ſet on foot to procure an eſtabliſhment of the ſaid
" fair for fourteen days. Humbly addreſſed to the preſent right hon.
" the lord mayor, court of aldermen, and common council of the ſaid
" city. Lond. 1711" 12mo.

ᶻ Of which ſee Memoirs for the curious, vol. ii. p. 259.
ᵃ For 1090 l.

Cheap-

Cheapſide croſs and conduit; and the manner of the Queen mother of France paſſing therethrough. Entree royalle de la Reyne mere du Roy tres chreſtien dans la ville de Londres [b].

A drawing of this croſs is in the Pepyſian library; likewiſe a print of the pulling it down [c], and the burning the book of ſports there 1643. This croſs being taken down for repair 1600, the city conſulted both univerſities whether the crucifix ſhould be erected again. Dr. Abbot (afterwards abp.) then vice-chancellor of Oxford, was againſt it: the iſſue was that the croſs was reſtored without the body or dove. This produced a pamphlet called " Cheapſide croſs " cenſured and condemned by a letter ſent from the vice-chancellor, " &c. of Oxford, in anſwer to a queſtion propounded by the citizens " of London, &c. Lond. 1641." 4to.

D. Loggan engraved a deſign of a fountain for the carrefour of Corn-hill and Leadenhall ſtreet.

Newbery printed " An hiſtorical deſcription of the Tower of Lon-" don, and its curioſities, 1759."

A liſt of the records kept in it, drawn up by Wm. Petit, record-keeper, is inſerted in the Cat. MSS. Angliæ, tom. ii. p. 183.

Vertue engraved for the Society of Antiquaries the portrait of Mr. George Holmes, deputy-keeper of theſe records 60 years, who died 1748, aged 87, painted by R. Van Bleak 1743. Alſo a true and ex-act draught of the Tower liberties, from a ſurvey by Wm. Haiward and J. Gaſcoigne in 1597.

Meſſrs Buck publiſhed S. and W. views of it 1737.

Payne Fyſher wrote in heroics " Deſcriptio luculentiſſima Turris " Londinenſis;" but Wood [d] is not explicite whether this is to be ranked among his printed or unprinted works.

" A brief enquiry relating to the right of his majeſty s royal chapel, " and the privilege of his ſervants within the Tower, in a memorial " addreſſed to the right hon. the lord viſcount Lonſdale, conſtable of " his majeſty's Tower of London. 1728." Fol. Signed H. Haynes.

[b] In the ſame library is a print of Charles I. receiving her. He wears his crown, and ſtretches out a ſceptre to her as ſhe ſtands under a canopy, a lady holding her crown, a knight with a collar of SS kneeling holds a ſword.
[c] Copied in the Supplement to the Gentleman's Magazine, 1764.
[d] Ath. Ox. II. 902

" Lon-

" London, K. Charles' Augufta; a poem : by Sylvanus Morgan.
" Lond. 1648."

" Venceflai Clementis a Libeo-montis Trinobantiados Auguftæ, five
" Londini civitatis libri vi. quibus urbis nobiliffimæ antiquitas, ortus,
" progreffus, gloriæ famæque incrementa, tanquam in fciographia
" luculenter exprimuntur, prætori, regi, fenatui populoque. 1636.
" 1673." 4to. The date expreffed in this quaint legend; " Ne
CoLLVCtentVr TrInobantIaDopoLItanI InteftabILIbus foLLIcItV-
DInIbus."

" The glories of London furveyed, in an heroick poem. Lond.
" 1674. 4to."

" A poem upon the new marble ftatue of his prefent majefty (king
" Charles II.) erected in the Royal Exchange, by the fociety of mer-
" chants adventurers of England; together with a copy of the infcrip-
" tion on the pedeftal. Lond. 1684." One fheet folio.

" London : a poem, in imitation of the third fatire of Juvenal. [By
" Samuel Johnfon.] Lond. 1737." This had two editions in a week,
and is inferted in Dodfley's Collection of poems, vol. i. p. 192. 1751.

" London; a fatire. Lond. 1751." Fol.

" Londinum heroico carmine perluftratum. Per Johannem Adam-
" um Tranfylvanum, dedicatumq; literarum, peregrinorum, virtu-
" tumq; patronis. The renowned city of London furveyed and illuf-
" trated in a Latine poem. By J. Adams, a Tranfylvanian, and tranfla-
" ted into Englifh by W. F. of Gray's-inn, J. C. dedicated to the
" patrons of ftrangers, learning, and inginuity. Lond. 167-." 4to.

" The morning walk, or the city encompaffed : a poem, in blank
" verfe; with a prologue and epilogue from the beft poetical fimilar
" fubjects. Dedicated to the earl of Bath. [By William Henry Dra-
" per.] Lond. 1751." 8vo.

" Monuments of honour derived from antiquitie, and celebrated in
" the honourable citie of London. 1624." 4to.e.

" The fpeech of the pales of Somerfet-houfe upon the reparation and
" enlargement of it by her majefty : a poem. 1665." Fol. Bagford.

e Ames' Cat. 954.

　　　　Among

Among J. Barnes' sacred poems. Lond. 166 . is one on the Royal
Exchange.

" A dialogue between the dragon on Bow steeple and the grass-
" hopper on the Royal Exchange: a poem. 1679." Fol.   Bagford.

" A poem on the stately structure of Bow church and steeple, burnt
" 1666, rebuilt 1679, or a second poem upon nothing. 1679."   A
folio sheet.   Bagford.

" A dialogue between the flag at St. Martin's steeple and the stan-
" dard at the Tower: a poem. 1698." 8vo.   Bagford.

" The 2d and 3d part of the building of the Poultry Counter: a
" poem, by Thomas Gifford. 1670."

" Bethlem hospital: a poem in blank verse. 1717." 4to.   By the rev.
Mr. John Rutter of Dublin.   Printed but never published.   Bagford's
MS. mentions " Indulgences of several popes to the benefactors of
" Bethlem *hospital.* 1519 f." a 4to leaf, in lord Clarendon's collections.

" The orations, anthems, and poems, spoken and sung at the per-
" formance of divine musick at stationers hall, for the month of May,
" 1702. undertaken by Cavendish Weedon, esq; Lond. 1702." 4to.
The ticket-money was applied to the relief of decayed gentlemen, and
for a school for teaching youth religion, musick, and accounts.

Concerning the river *Thames* Roger Griffiths, water-bailiff, published
" An essay to prove that the jurisdiction and conservacy of the river of
" Thames, &c. is committed to the lord mayor and city of London,
" both in point of right and usage, by prescription, charters, acts of
" parliament, decrees upon hearing before the king, letters patent,
" &c. &c.   To which is added a brief description of those fish, with
" their spawning-time, that are caught in the Thames, or sold in
" London: with some few observations on the nature, element, cloath-
" ing, numbers, passage, wars, and sensations peculiar to fish in gene-
" ral ; and also of the water-carriage on the river Thames to the se-
" veral parts of the kingdom ; with a history of the keys, wharfs, and
" docks adjoining to the same. 1746." 8vo.

---

f He means *priory*, for such it originally was.

2   Robert

Robert Binnel publiſhed " A deſcription of the river Thames, with
" the city of London's juriſdiction and conſervacy thereof proved, both
" in point of right and uſage, &c. To which are added, rules, orders,
" and ordinances made in purſuance of an act, 30 Geo. II. for the
" more effectual preſervation and improvement of the ſpawn and fry
" of fiſh ; and for the better regulating the fiſhery thereof. 1758." 8vo.

" The preſent ſtate of navigation on the Thames conſidered, and
" certain regulations propoſed. By a commiſſioner [Dr. Burton.] Oxf.
" 1764." 4to.

" The great froſt. Cold doings in London, except it be at the
" lottery : with newes out of the country. A familier talk between a
" countryman and a citizen, touching this terrible froſt, and the great
" lottery, and the effect of them. The deſcription of the Thames
" frozen over. Lond. 1608." 4to. In front is a wooden print of the
citizens at their ſports on the frozen river : the prizes in this lottery
were all of plate ; the higheſt 150 l. and the tickets one ſhilling,
apiece g.

" An hiſtorical account of the late great froſt, in which are diſ-
" covered in ſeveral comical relations, the various humours, loves,
" cheats, and intreagues of the town, as the ſame were managed upon
" the river of Thames during that ſeaſon h Lond. 1684." 12mo.

Leland's Cygnea Cantio, or a voyage of a principal ſwan and ſix
others on the Thames from Oxford to Greenwich, deſcribing poetically
the ſeveral places they paſs by, which are further illuſtrated by the
author's commentary at the end in alphabetical order by their antient
names, was firſt printed in the author's life. Lond. 1545. 4to. again
Lond. 1658, by the care of Selden, or Lamphire, Camden's profeſſor
at Oxford after the reſtoration, and a third time by Hearne in the ninth
volume of Leland's Itinerary.

In p. 222 of Nº 397 of the Philoſophical Tranſactions is an account
of a pair of horns found at Wapping, communicated by Sir H. Sloane.
In p. 68 of Nº 393 are obſervations on the tide in the Thames by

---

g Catal. of Harl. pamph. Nº 186. Matth. Paris mentions a froſt on the Thames
from December to March 1150, when the river bore horſes and carriages.

h There is a wooden print of this fair by Ja. Moxon, in the Pepyſian library, and
another on copper by Ja. Croom.

Mr.

Mr. Saumarez and Capt. Jones : the latter's obfervations on a high tide Feb. 16, 173½, are in Nº 440, p. 136 : and in p. 530 of vol. xlix. are obfervations on the irregularities of the tides at London and Weftmin- fter, Feb. 12 and 13, 1756, by Robert Dingley, efq;

Robert Adams, furveyor of the buildings to Q. Elizabeth, publifhed a plan (yet extant) dated 1588, intitled " Thamefis defcriptio," on a fmall parchment roll, drawn with a pen, fhewing by lines crofs the river how far and from whence cannon balls may obftruct the paffage of any fhip on an invafion from Tilbury to London ; with proper dif- tances marked for placing the guns.

Sir Jonas Moore made an actual furvey of this river from its mouth to its head ; of which Bagford fays Mr. Pepys had a copy. Among his collections are two drawings of it; a third of the manner of upping the fwans of Thames ftream the Monday before Lammas-day, with the owners marks on their bills, ftamped on flips of parchment : another of Milford-ftairs, and a view of the city and bridge from thence.

Mr. Thomas Hall in his " Account of new inventions and improve- " ments now neceffary in England for the improvements of rivers, " 1690." 8vo. gives a large account of this river. Bagford.

In Collins's " Survey of all the coafts" is a map of the Thames, and the rivers and brooks running into it.

It has been celebrated in verfe in " Thamefeis," a poem, in 3 books, by S. W. by fome afcribed to Camden. Bagford. Quære, if thefe are the verfes on the marriage of Thame and Ifis, which bp. Gibfon afcribes to him.

A fea fight on this river at the marriage of James the Firft's daughter was engraved; as alfo the folemnity of lord Sandwich's embaffy to Lifbon to conduct Catharine to England ; with her reception and the king's proceffion on the river from Hampton court to Whitehall. 7 plates. By Theodore and Roderigo Stoop, in Spanifh, Latin, and Englifh.

" The entertainment of the king and queen by the city of London on the Thames, expreft and fet forth in feveral fhews and pageants, the 3d of April. By J. Tatham, gent. 1662." Bagford.

i Painter to the queen of England.

The

The Thames water was firft conveyed into the city by a machine erected in an arch of the bridge by Peter Maurice, a German engineer, 1582. Bevis Bulmar, twelve years after, fet up a large horfe-engine of four pumps at Broken wharf, Thames-ftreet, which foon proved too expenfive to be worked. The works at the bridge are particularly defcribed by Henry Beighton, in N° 417 of the Philofophical Tranfactions.

Peter de Colechurch, chaplain of St. Mary Colechurch, begun London bridge 1176, 22 Hen. II. Ifembert, mafter of the fchools of Xante, who had lately built a bridge there and at Rochelle, was appointed by K. John to finifh it, which he did 1209. Vertue drew and engraved 1747 two profpective views of the infide of St. Thomas's chapel in the ninth pier of the bridge, in its then ftate, and 1748 a a view of the W front and the infide; and of the original ftone bridge 1209. Two other views of this chapel were inferted in the Gentleman's Magazine, Sept. and Oct. 1753. The lovers of antiquity muft regret the demolition of this fingular and perhaps unparalleled monument in the late alterations of the bridge. It was 65 feet by 20, and 14 feet high, divided into two ftories; the upper in modern times ferving for a dwelling houfe, the lower for a warehoufe. Under the ftaircafe was found the tomb of Peter, the architect; without brafs or infcription. The chapel on Wakefield bridge, built about 200 years after this, is rather annexed to than made in a pier.

Bagford mentions a draught of London bridge, expreffing the mill at the end, in the Pepyfian collection: as alfo a very old drawing of this bridge on fire, on vellum. A miferable view of it after the temporary bridge was burnt, with a chronological and hiftorical account of it at the bottom, was engraved 1758.

A view of it before the late alteration in 1757, from a painting of S. Scot, by P. C. Canot, 1758.

Certain antient dates found in pulling down part of it 1758 may be feen in a letter from Mr. Ames, fecretary to the Antiquarian Society, to Dr. Bevis, publifhed in the Gentleman's Magazine, Oct. 1758, p 458; with the Doctor's anfwer, and the figures of the dates.

" The expedience, utility, and neceffity of a new bridge at or near
" Blackfriars: all objections thereto fully anfwered, and the requifite
" difpofition

difpofition exemplified. Lond. 1756." 8vo. See alfo a paper by Sam. Dicker, efq; Gentleman's Magazine, 1751, p. 116.

The infcription on the firft ftone was animadverted on in " City " Latin, or critical and political remarks on the Latin infcription, &c. " By the rev. Bufby Birch, L.L. D. F. R. S. &c. 1761." 8vo.

" The antiquarian fchool: or the city Latin electrified. A ballad. " Dedicated by permiffion to Sir Nicholas Nemo, kt. By Erafmus " Hearne, A. M. F. A. S. 1761." Fol. And

" Plain Englifh; in anfwer to city Latin: fhewing the feveral appli-" cations made or propofed to be made to the univerfities of Oxford, " Cambridge, &c. &c. the London clergy, the lawyers, the college of " phyficians, &c. for a proper Latin infcription. Likewife pointing " out the fuppofed author of .the infcription firft in Englifh, and the " real tranflator of it afterwards into Latin. By a deputy. 1761." 8vo.

The ingenious mechanifm of the central timbers in the two principal arches, drawn by Mylne, the architect, and engraved by Piranefi at Rome, was publifhed 1766: alfo plans and an elevation of this bridge, drawn and engraved by Richard Baldwin.

Southwark being included in the furvey of Surrey we have but few diftinct tracts on it. A Grubftreet legend, called " The true hiftory " of the life and fudden death of old John Overs, the rich ferryman " of London, fhewing how he loft his life by his own covetoufnefs, " and of his daughter Mary, who caufed the church of St. Mary Overs, " in Southwark, to be built: and of the building of London bridge. " 1744." 8vo.

A fuperficial compilation intitled " Hiftory of the antiquities of St. " Saviour's; containing annals from the firft founding, to the prefent " time: lifts of the priors and benefactors: a particular defcription of " the building, ornaments, monuments, remarkable places, &c. with " notes !, &c. By Arthur Tyler. Lond. 1765." 12mo.

" An account of the receipts and difburfements of the free grammar " fchool of St. Olave's, Southwark. Lond. 1733."

" Vindication of the governors of the faid fchool."

" A defence of the account of the receipts," &c. m.

And a view of the W. end.
Ames' Catal. p. 259.

" The

" The manner of holding the court leet and court baron for the
" libertie of Southwark. 1561." 4to. printed by Cawode. Bagford.

" An appeal from a few of the meaneſt and moſt inconſiderable of
" the governors of St. Thomas's hoſpital (for they differ each from other
" in glory as the ſtars are ſaid to do) to the generality of the nobleſt,
" wiſeſt, wealthieſt, and beſt of them, occaſioned by ſome great in-
" juſtice and high affronts which two or three biggots of that hoſpital
" have endeavoured to put upon Dr. Samuel Rolls, the miniſter there-
" of." 4to.

" An argument in defence of the hoſpitaller of St. Thomas's, South-
" wark, and of his fellow-ſervants and friends in the ſame houſe.
" Lond. 1684." 4to.

" A ſecond repreſentation of the hoſpitaller of St. Thomas's, South-
" wark. Lond. 1689." 4to.

Samuel Pepys, eſq; ſecretary to the admiralty under Charles II. and
his brother, was at a conſiderable expence to collect all the prints and
drawings that could illuſtrate his native city; which he left, with all his
other collections and library, to Magdalen Coll. Cambridge, where he
was educated. He arranged them in 1700 in two large folio volumes,
under the following heads: Vol. i. maps, views, and plans—buildings, monuments, and churches—Thames and its views. Vol. ii.
Regalia and habits of the city—lord mayors ſhews—companies arms—
ſeſſions houſe, Newgate, &c.—parliament and convocation—corona-
tions and publick entries—cavalcades and triumphal arches—proceſ-
ſions — habits—cries—vulgaria [n]. Induſtrious Bagford appears to have
ſeen more views of London than fell into the ſecretary's hands, which
he deſcribes at large in his letter to Hearne. He found in a MS. in-
ventory of Henry VIIIth's furniture a view or ground-plot of London,
painted on board. Hearne engraved in Leland's Collectanea, II. p. 451.
a moſt rude ground-plot of ſome ſquare building with round towers
at the corners, which he thought repreſented Durham city or caſtle,
and Bagford the tower which J. Cæſar built at London, or the city
itſelf. pl. lxxx. A fanciful ichnography of London as under the Romans, is in pl. lvii. of Stukeley's Itin. Cur. Bagford begins with an

[n] Or miſcellaneous articles.

old

old view of London in fix fheets cut in wood, which by the fpelling feems to have been done in Holland, and of which he had feen three impreffions, but could not determine whether it was the firft finifhed draught; tho' he was certain the arms of James I. were inferted fince the firft cutting. He mentions another draught in one fheet, cut alfo in wood, different from the former. This may be the wooden profpect before the burning of Paul's fteeple among the Pepyfian views.

The next he knew of is on one fheet on copper, which he efteemed the beft and perhaps the antienteft, taking in only London and the liberties from Temple-bar to St. Catherines's, and the Bankfide, South-wark. More of the old part of London is feen by this than any other, and he thinks it comes neareft to Leland's intended defcription of London.

The next draught for its antiquity taken notice of by Bagford is that publifhed in the cities of the world by George Braun and Francis Hogen-bergius 1573 in one fheet, including Weftminfter with the Tower to the flaughter-houfe, and having the arms of Q Elizabeth and London. By this he obferves one might fee the nakednefs of the buildings on the Bankfide, and in the outparts, from E. to W. St. Giles's in the Fields ftanding by itfelf furrounded with trees: Paris garden (at firft called Palace garden) juft overagainft Bridewell court, a pleafure gar-den of the Greyfriars, exchanged for fome other piece of land by Henry VIII.

Ralph Aggas, the furveyor, who made plans of Oxford and Cam-bridge, drew one of London, which, though referred to the time of Henry VIII. or Edw. VI. appears from feveral circumftances to have been made early in Elizabeth s reign, about 1560. It is both a plan and view of London, with the river and adjacent parts; and intitled " Civitas Londinum." It was republifhed 1618 with alterations, par-ticularly the arms of James I. (England, France, and Scotland) fub-ftituted to thofe of Elizabeth: and the letters of reference fhew that the firft impreffion had explanations of the remarkable places in the city and fuburbs, which feem to have been printed on flips of paper to be added at bottom. This plan, which is 6 feet 3 inches by 2 feet 4 inches, on fix fheets and two half fheets, was re-engraved by Vertue 1748,

1748, (from whose Memoirs ° this account is taken) on six sheets, with this inscription " Londinum antiqua. This plan shews the ancient extent of the famous cities of London and Westminster, as it was near the beginning of the reign of Q Elizabeth. These plates for their great scarcity are re-engraved to oblige the curious, and to hand to posterity the old prospect, whereby at one view may be seen how much was built of this populous city and parts adjacent at that time. Radulphus Aggas in his Oxonia antiqua, published 1578, says, near ten years past the author made a doubt whether to print or lay this work aside until he first had London platted out. These remarkable buildings were not erected when this plan was taken: Whitehall banquetting-house: the first building was of timber, A° ...... Royal Exchange not built before 1570. Moorfields not divided nor planted. Lamb's conduit on Snowhill about 1580. Paget place, so called till the death of lord Paget 1563." ᴾ. The impression of this plan in the Pepysian library has these lines at the right corner:

New Troy my name when first my fame begun
   By Trajon Brute : who then me placed here,
On fruitfull soyle, where pleasant Thames doth run.
   Sith had my lord, my king and lover dear
Encreast my bounds :· and London (far that rings
   Through regions large) he called then my name.
How famous since (I stately seat of kings :)
   Have flourish'd aye: let others that proclaim,
And let me joy, thus happy still to see
   This vertuous peer my soveraign king to be.

The next plan of London seems to have been that inserted in Norden's Survey of Middlesex, with the arms of the twelve companies at the sides. It reaches from St. Catherines, east, to Leicester house, west, which was without Temple-bar, with a description of all the

   Walp. Cat. of eng. p. 9, 10.
ᴾ Bagford confounds R. Aggas with Augustin Ryther, and makes him author of a survey of Oxford 1588, of London 30 Eliz. and of Cambridge In Randal Holmes Cheshire collections, MS. Harl. 2059. f. 249. are " Notes received from ..... Agas, stationer, in Poule's church yard, 1581."

out-lets

out-lets or ways into the fields; and at that time Shrewſbury houſe next on this ſide to the Old Swan was in being. This was firſt engraved 1593, but has ſince fallen into the hands of Peter Stent[r], who added the names of churches, ſtreets, lanes, &c. with letters and figures of reference, which are inſerted in the laſt edition of the book, 1723, and were copied into the map of Middleſex, 1611, by Speed; who in his map of England has inſerted a neat miniature view of London and Southwark. There is another copy of Norden's map of London by Peter Vanden Keere, engraver, 1623, wherein Norden's name is retained, and the title is " A guide to countrymen in the famous city " of London, by the help of which plot they may be able to know " how far it is to any ſtreet, as alſo how to go to the ſame without " farther trouble." Norden publiſhed another view of London in eight ſheets, having at bottom a repreſentation of the lord mayor's ſhew, all on horſeback, and the aldermen in round caps. Bagford ſays this view is ſingular and was taken from the pitch of the hill towards Dulwich college going to Camberwell from London, about 1604 or 1606, and that he had not met with any other of the kind: he adds that he ſaw it on the ſtaircaſe at Dulwich college, and that ſecretary Pepys went afterwards to ſee it, and would have purchaſed it: but that ſince it is quite decayed and deſtroyed by the damp of the wall: it was given to the college with the library by William Cartwright, an eminent comedian and bookſeller, a friend of the founder's[s]. Vertue[t] ſpeaks of ſuch a map in Bagford's collection, where he ſaw another plan by T. Porter, of which he has not given the date; but as he obſerved in it at the upper end of the Haymarket a large building called Peccadilla-hall, at the end of Coventry ſtreet a gaming houſe, afterwards the manſion houſe and garden of lord keeper Coventry, and where Gerard ſtreet is, an artillery ground or military garden made by prince Henry, it probably came out not long after the date of the laſt. In Rymer's Fœdera, vol. xvii. is a patent granted 1618 to

[r] Later printers added the E. and W. views paſted at the ſides, and called it The countryman's travelling guide through the city of London; with figures engraved, 1 : 2 : A : B : but ſeldom affixed dates. Bagford, lxxxii.
[s] Biog. Brit. Alleyn [G]. Aubrey's Surrey, vol. v. p. 356.
[t] Anecd. of Painting, vol. ii. p. 31

Aaron

Aaron Rathburne and Roger Bruges for making a true and perfect defcription of London and Weſtminſter in a map[u].

Maitland has a plan of London as fortified by the parliament 1642
and 1643.

Hollar etched a large view of London, from Weſtminſter to beyond
St. Catharine's, with Latin verſes at bottom by Edward Benlowes, eſq;
dedicated to Q. Henrietta Maria and William prince of Orange, and
ſold at Amſterdam by Corn. Danckers: two yards and a half long in
ſeven ſheets. 1647 [x].

In the Pepyſian library are three views of this city done abroad:
one intitled " Londinum vulgo London," with a Latin account of it:
the other, larger, " Londini Angliæ regni metropolis noviſſima & ac-
" curatiſſima, autore Jac. De la Feuille," at Amſterdam,; with heads
of William and Mary, and a S. view: the third is " Profile de la ville
" de Londre, cappitalle du royaume de Angleterre;" undated: which
Mr. Pepys calls the long Antwerp proſpect.

Corn. Boll, under one of the Charles's, painted views of London
before the fire: Vertue, who ſaw them at Sutton place in Surrey, ſays
they were in a good free taſte, repreſenting Arundel and Somerſet
houſes, and the Tower [y]. At Burlington houſe is a long proſpect of
London before the fire, taken from Southwark, and exhibiting the
great manſions of the nobility then on the Strand. Vertue thought it
the beſt view he had ſeen of London. It was by Thomas Van Wyck.
Mr. Weſt has a print of it, but with ſome alterations [z].

In 1658 came out " An exact delineation of the cities of London and
Weſtminſter and the ſuburbs, together with the borough of Southwark, and all the thorough-fairs, highways, ſtreets, lanes, and common alleys within the ſame: compoſed with a ſcale, and ichnographically deſcribed by Richard Newcourt, of Somerton, in the county
of Somerſet, gent. [a]; with a genealogy from Brute, a chronology,
with the arms of London, the ſeveral churches within the walls, St.

[u] Walpole's Cat. of engr. p. 32. Quære, Whether their ſurvey was engraved by
T. Porter ?
[x] Vertue's Cat. of Hollar's works, Nº 1.
[z] Walp. Anecd. III. 7.
[z] Ib. p. 135.
[a] I ſuppoſe the ſame that drew many views for the Monaſticon.

Paul's

Paul's and Weftminfter abbey; alfo fix windmills (for fo many there were at that time) in eight ᵃ fheets, engraved by Mr. Wm. Faithorne ᵇ.

Another S. profpect of London was drawn by Hollar ᶜ 1664, in fix fheets, and etched by Robert Precke ᵈ. This fhews from E. to W. all the views from Whitehall garden, the outfide walls of Suffolk, York, Savoy, Somerfet, Arundel, and Effex houfes, and the Temple, all next the Thames: likewife a fite of the Bridge as it was before the fire, a view of Nönfuch houfe, with another fine houfe curious in its building next Southwark; and on Southwark fide are the tops of the houfes from St. Olave's church fteeple, Winchefter houfe or the palace of the Clink, with all the other buildings thereto belonging, as alfo the gardens, fountains, and trees. There is nothing extant that fo exactly fhews the buildings of old London before the fire; and many obfervations might be made from this view to good purpofe. Hollar was at no fmall pains in taking the feveral profpects, views, and ground-plots of this city, particularly from the fteeples of St. Tooly's, St. Mary Overey's, and Lambeth churches. He likewife defigned a ground-plot of about four fheets, but never finifhed it. There are two other views by him on flips, as it was before the fire, and under them another view as it appeared in its ruins after it. On a large fheet etched on iron (copper not being then to be had) he defcribed ichnographically the quantity of acres occupied by the ruins within the city, as alfo the churches, halls, and other publick buildings. He has alfo etched another draught of this city on half a fheet, affixed to a poem on the rebuilding of London ᵉ.

Hollar engraved in 1665 a fmall view of London from over the water, chiefly below and as far as St. Paul's, and two views of London by Iflington ᶠ; and the next year " A map or ground-plot of the city

ᵃ Vertue fays fix fheets and two half fheets. Walp. Cat. of engr. p. 32.
ᵇ Bagford, lxxxiii
ᶜ Bagford has all along nick-named him William Hallyer, as his friend Hearne takes notice. Pref. to Rofs of Warwick, p. 18.
ᵈ So Bagford: but it has only R. Pricke, fec. & exc. At the left corner is a figure of Juftice, and Solomon's judgment below: at the right a view of a dock and a very large fhip: at the top Mercury, and the four quarters of the world expreffed by boys.
ᵉ Bagford, p. lxxxiii.
ᶠ Vertue's Cat. N° 11. 16. 17. The two laft and his other four views of Iflington were fince copied by E. Kirkall.

and

and fuburbs within the jurifdiction of the lord mayor; fhewing the
prefent condition fince the laft fad accident of fire; the blank fpace,
fignifying the burnt part, and where the houfes are expreffed yet ftanding: with a general map or ground-plot of the whole city of London
and Weftminfter, and all the fuburbs (in a little compartment below)
by which may be computed the proportion of what is burnt with what
is ftanding," in a fmall fheet; and another like map, but fmaller: alfo
" A true and exact profpect of the famous citty of London from St.
Mary Over's fteeple in Southwarke, in its flourifhing condition before
the fire," in a view about three quarters of a yard long, and underneath
another profpect of the faid citty, taken from the fame place, as it ap-
peareth now after the faid calamity and deftruction by fire in the year
1666 g.

" An exact furveigh of the ftreets, lanes, and churches contained
within the ruines of the city of London, firft defcribed in fix plates
by John Leake, John Jennings, William Marr, William Leyburn, Thomas Streete, Richard Shortgrave, in Decemb. A^{o} 1666, by the order
of the lord mayor, aldermen, and common council of the city, reduced
here into one intire plat by John Leake, the city wall being added, as
alfo the places were the halls ftood are expreffed by the coats of arms,
and all the wards divided by Jonas Moor and Ralph Graterix, furveyors. W. Hollar, fec. 1667. Publifhed, with a defcription of the
wards, by the care, induftry, and charge of N. Brooke, ftationer," in
two fheets: at top is a view of the fire from Southwark. It was
republifhed by Vertue, " Ut memoria faltem priftinæ Londinii
formæ dirum quo fubfidit incendium fupervivat, tabulam ejufdem
umbratilem Societati Antiquariæ Londinenfi dedicat Georgius Vertue. MDCCXXIII." This is embellifhed with views of old buildings
near the Temple-gate, Baynard's caftle, old S. W. view of St. Paul's,
Cheapfide and the crofs before the fire, S. front of Guildhall, and the
Royal Exchange as built by Grefham.

Hollar engraved 1675 " A new map or ground-plot of the cities of
London and Weftminfter and the borough of Southwark, with the

---

t Vertue, N° 28. 29 35. The 2d of thefe is one of thofe mentioned by Bagford
in the preceding page.

2   fuburbs;

suburbs; shewing the streets, lanes, alleys, courts, with the other re-marks, as they are now truly and carefully delineated; and the pro-spect of London, as it was flourishing before the destruction by fire." Sold by Robert Green and Robert Morden. A large sheet [h]. The "New map of London and Westminster, with the borough of South-wark and all the suburbs; shewing the several streets, lanes, alleys, and most thorough-fairs: being a ready guide for all strangers to find any place therein: drawn first by W. Hollar in 1675. Sold by Robert Greene. 2 sheets; Vertue's N° 37, is a copy of this.

The nine following have no dates, but were all the work of Hollar [i].

A small ground-plot, without any other title or references.

A map of both cities, London and Westminster, before the fire, with references; about the same size.

London and the liberties of Westminster, another ground-plot, with references: somewhat larger.

London, inscribed in a compartment, with a distich in it, shewing this to be the landscape and true profile, with references. About half a sheet.

The prospect of London and Westminster, taken from Lambeth, beginning at Peterborough-house, and ending at St. George's, South-wark; in a large draught of four sheets; the whole about a yard and three-quarters long, with figures and letters referring to the chief buildings mentioned at the bottom.

A small prospect, long and round at the ends.

London, in a small ground-plot of one mile to an inch.

London, from the top of Arundel-house.

Part of a view of London below bridge.

In 1677 came out a long quarto, intitled "London surveyed, with "an explanation of the same; giving a particular account of the "streets and lanes in the city and liberty, with the courts, yards, allys, "churches, halls and houses of note in every street and lane, and di-"rections to find them in the map, with the names and marks of the "wards, parishes, and precincts therein described; with a map of "London, Westminster, and Southwark, at one mile in an inch:"

[h] Vertue, N° 30.　　　Vert. N° 31. 32. 33. 34. 36. 39. 26. 27. 22.

etched

etched by Hollar. This map is Vertue's Nº 26. The authors of this
furvey were Ogilby and Morgan[l], who fome time after publifhed another map, with feveral additions eaft and weft, befides other material
ornaments of publick buildings [m].

A plan of London by Ogilby, in 20 fheets : 16 plates nearly done
by Hollar ; the others finifhed by the graver of another hand [n]. The
fhort defcription of London in Ogilby's Britannia is all that he did of
his intended Hiftory and Antiquities of England [o].

Befides thefe they feem to have likewife publifhed a new and accurate map of the city of London, diftinct from Weftminfter and
Southwark, fix feet fquare : and there goes under Ogilby's name " A
new map of the city of London as it is new built."

J. Sellers publifhed " A mapp of the cities of London and Weftminfter and burrough of Southwark as rebuilt."

An actual furvey of London by R. Morden and Ph. Lea.

There have been feveral other views taken, as that by James Howel
in his Londinopolis ; and Mr. Dunfton took a view before the fire,
underneath which is a profpect of the ruins [p].

Other ichnographical draughts and defcriptions of London were
made by John Oliver, —— Lee [q], and Chriftopher Brown, of which
Bagford waves any further defcants, to celebrate a ground-plot or rather the upright of the city of Amfterdam carved in wood, I fuppofe
like that of Paris by Le Quoi.

" Urbis Londini, fluvii Thamefis, templi, palatii, viridarii Greno-
" vicenfis ab auftro confpectus; qualem delineavit, illuftriffimoq. dom.
" Archib. Grant, eq. bar. Alex. Gordon in animi grati teftimonium,
" d. d. d. 1731. Cl. du Bofc. fc."

---

[l] Quere, if Morgan the mapmaker? Mr. Walpole finds only this plan of London
by him. Cat. of engr. p. 70. There is a very long profpect of London and Weftminfter, taken at feveral ftations to the fouthward thereof, by William Morgan, in the
Pepyfian library.

[m] Bagford, ib.

[n] Vertue, Nº 38.

[o] Bagford, p. lxxxv.

[p] Bagford, ib. His MS. mentions " London's remarks by Dutton, alias Cronbie,
8vo." alfo feveral views by Sellers.

[q] I fuppofe Philip Lea.

A a a   A view

A view of London through one of the centers of the arches of Weftminfter bridge, from a painting of Canaletti, by S. Wale and R. Parr, 1747.

Meffrs. Buck engraved five large views of London and Weftminfter, to be united in one, from Millbank to the Tower, 1749.

A new profpective view of London from the fouth, with the navigation on the Thames London and Blackfriars bridges. 3 fheets.

A S. view of London from Chelfea to Limehoufe, taken from Dulwich hills: etched by Wm. Auftin, finifhed by P. C. Canot, publifhed by Al. Cozens by fubfcription, 1763.

An exact furvey of the cities of London and Weftminfter, and borough of Southwark, and the country ten miles round; begun 1741, ended 1743, by John Rocque, land-furveyor: engraved by R. Parr.

" A new and accurate furvey of the cities of London and Weft-
" minfter, the borough of Southwark, with the country 60 miles
" about it, for 19 miles in length and 13 in depth; in which is con-
" tained an exact defcription of St. James's, Kenfington, Richmond,
" and Hampton Court palaces, all the main and crofs roads, lanes
" and paths, bye-ways, walls, pales, hedges, hills, vallies, rivers,
" bridges, ferries, brooks, fprings, ponds, woods, heaths, commons,
" parks, avenues, churches, houfes, gardens, &c. 1748. in 16 fheets,
" by John Rocque, furveyor. Begun 1741, finifhed 1745." Reduced to four fheets and one fheet 1763. Another furvey of London and Weftminfter, and the country 19 miles round it. was done by the fame hand in 1751, in 24 fheets.

Another furvey of London and the country ten miles round, engraved by John Tinney and John Pine, in eight fheets.

A plan of London and Weftminfter, by J. Pine and J. Tinney, 1749, Dedicated to Martin Folkes.

A plan of London and Weftminfter, and borough of Southwark, and the contiguous buildings; with all the new roads that have been made on account of Weftminfter bridge; and the new buildings and alterations to the prefent year 1755: engraved from an actual furvey by J Rocque, in 24 fheets, 13 feet by 6¾, by J. Pine. This plan extends from E. to W. near 6 miles, and from N. to S. a little more than 3, and contains about 11500 acres of ground, and is laid down

by

by a scale of 200 feet to an inch. To it is added a contracted sketch of it in one sheet, and an alphabetical index of the names of the streets, &c. in 16 4to. sheets.

An accurate and comprehensive plan of London, Westminster, and Southwark with the contiguous buildings, engraved from the same actual survey; with all the new roads to Westminster and Blackfriars bridges, and other additions and alterations to 1766; on eight sheets 6 feet by 4 : the same index serves both.

Another copy on one sheet : another on one sheet, and a third on a half sheet, printed by J. Gibson. The city guide is copied from these.

A new and exact plan of London, Westminster, and Southwark; with rates of coachmen and watermen, alphabetical list of streets, and views of buildings ; three sheets: also on two sheets.

Vertue had taken much pains to settle the antient extent of London, and the scite of its several larger edifices at the various periods. Mr. Walpole, who found among his papers many traces relating to this matter, observes that such a subject extended by historic illustrations would be very amusing; and that " Les anecdotes des rues de Paris" is a pattern for such a work. I wish we could construe this into a probability that Vertue's papers would be one day improved into the same form.

MONMOUTH-

MONMOUTHSHIRE.

ALL that has been printed about this county is a very fuperficial piece, called " Memoirs of Monmouthfhire, anciently called " Gwent, and by the Saxons, Gwentland ; fhewing when this county " was fubdued by the Romans, but never by the Saxons or Danes, " nor by the Normans, till king Henry II. That this was the firft " place in Great Britain in which Chriftianity was planted. That a " college of 200 philofophers was firft of all founded at Caer-Leon, " the ftation of the Romans chief legion in this ifland, called Augufta " Secunda : and that the firft academy in Britain was at Caer-Went, " the Venta Silurum of the ancients. With an hiftorical account of " the moft important affairs there tranfacted ; the feveral rarities of " nature in this county, of its feveral kings and princes, and other " eminent men born and bred therein ; and that the kings of England " and Scotland, fince Henry VII. derive themfelves from this county. " With an appendix, of the cafe of Wentwood, with the fevere ufage " and fuffering of the tenants in the late reigns for defending their " rights. Lond. 1708." 12mo. By N. Rogers.

" Lamentable newes out of Monmouthfhire in Wales. Contayn- " ing the wonderfull and moft fearfull accidents of the great over- " flowing of waters in the faide countye, drowning infinite numbers " of cattell of all kinds, as fheepe, oxen, kine, and horfes, with " others ; together with the loffe of many men, women and children, " and fubverfion of xxvi parifhes, in January laft. Lond. 1607." 4to.

In N° 229 of the Philofophical Tranfactions, p. 579, is Ed. Lhuyd's account of a hail ftorm at *Pontypool* 1697. In N° 359, p. 954, a letter from Mr. Rice, rector of *Caerleon*, about a Roman infcription there, with Dr. John Harris's conjectures publifhed in Hearne's preface to Gul. Neubrigenfis, p. liv. and in Horfley, p. 320. In p. 547 of vol. xlix. is an account of the finking of the river *Frooyd*, near Pontypool.

In

In the Gentleman's Magazine for Feb. 1765, p. 72, is an account and draught of the monuments of Urian de St. Pere, lord here temp. Hen. III. by Mr. Row.

In p. 194 of Ray's " Englifh Words" is an account of the wire-works at *Tintern*.   In Stevens's Monafticon, vol. ii. p. 57, is a W. view and ichnography of its beautiful abbey, which owes its prefervation to the good tafte of its proprietor the late duke of Beaufort.   A better N. E. view by Buck, 1732.   A more particular view and account of it are ftill wanting.

Buck engraved likewife a

N. W. view of Lantony priory.

W. Ragland	
N. E. Chepftow [a]	
W. White	
W. Grifmond	caftles.
N. Skinfrith	
S W. Caldecot	
W. Ufk	
E. Newport	

Saxton's map of this county is dated 1577, and wants the hundreds, fupplied in Speed's, 1610, with a plan of the town.   Tis alfo included in the late map of Gloucefterfhire.

[a] A painting of it by Mr. Richards was exhibited at Spring-gardens 1765.

NORFOLK.

NORFOLK.

WHAT Sir Symonds D'ewes intended for this county remains undigefted among his papers in the Harleian library. Sir Henry Spelman's " Icenia five Norfolciæ defcriptio topographica," a flight fketch of a furvey of this county, was printed among that learned antiquary's Reliquiæ. Oxf. 1698 and 1727. Fol. by bp. Gibfon, who made ufe of it and of Dr. Tanner's obfervations in his edition of the Britannia. A volume of hiftorical and heraldical collections for this county by one Robert Kemp 1575, are in the Harleian library, N° 901 ª.

A more ample and exact hiftory was long hoped for from the large materials collected by Peter le Neve, Norroy ᵇ, who fpent above forty years in amaffing at great expence and trouble the greateft fund of antiquities for his native county that ever was collected for any fingle one in the kingdom ᶜ, now in the hands of that induftrious antiquary Mr. Thomas Martin of Palgrave, Suffolk, who married his widow. They were made good ufe of by Francis Blomefield, rector of Fersfield, in his " Effay towards a topographical hiftory of the
" county of Norfolk, containing a defcription of the towns, villages,
" and hamlets, with the foundations of monafteries, churches, chapels,
" chanteries, and other religious buildings : alfo an account of the an-
" tient and prefent ftate of all the rectories, vicarages, donatives, and
" impropriations ; their former and prefent patrons and incumbents,
" &c. and an hiftorical account of the caftles, feats, manors, &c. the
" epitaphs, infcriptions, and arms of all the parifh churches and cha-
" pels, with feveral draughts of churches, monuments, arms, antient

---

ª A monk of Peterborough having attacked Norfolk and its inhabitants in a poem beginning *Exiit edictum ab Augufto Cafare*, John de St. Omer defended his county in another poem, beginning *Edictum fingitur factum a Cafare* : both are in the Cotton library. Tit. A. xx. 43, 44.

ᵇ Dr. Smith in his Synopfis Bib. Cottonianæ, p. 42, mentions it as preparing for the prefs, and calls it *Ampla & accurata comitatus Norfolcienfis hiftoria & defcriptio.*

ᶜ Among thefe were a very old copy of Domefday in the hand of the original, and a lift of ecclefiaftical taxations, with a tranfcript thereof, Cat. MSS. Angl. tom. ii. p. 87, N° 3532-3. A later copy of Domefday is among the earl of Carlifle's MSS. ib. p. 14. N° 917. and MS. Harl. 1406.

5   " ruins,

" ruins, and other relicks of antiquity : collected out of leiger books,
" regifters, records, evidences, deeds, court rolls, and other authentic
" memorials." Printed in his own houfe at Fersfield 1739, in 3 volumes
Fol. Vol. i. contains the hundreds of Difs, Giltcrofs, Shropham, the
burgh of Thetford, Grimefhoe, Wayland, and Forehoe. Vol. ii. thofe
of Humbleyard, Depwade, Earfham, Henfted, S. Greenhoe, and S.
Erpingham : the remaining nineteen hundreds being left unfinifhed.
The 2d vol. contains the hiftory of Norwich, dated 1745. He was
greatly affifted by bp. Tanner, who having been chancellor of this diocefe was acquainted with innumerable records relative to the county ;
but died as well as the author before this work was finifhed. Other
valuable materials were collected by J. Kirkpatrick, merchant at Norwich, a judicious antiquarian, and an intimate friend of Le Neve's. Mr.
Blomefield intended to join his own collections with Le Neve's, for
future infpection ; but dying in bad circumftances they were put into
the hands of the late Mr. Parkyn, rector of Oxburgh, who had drawn
up the account of Cranwich and Furcham deanries d, in that part that
was unfinifhed, and completed the reft, which he intended to publifh
laft year. It is now in the hands of Mr. Whittingham, bookfeller at
Lynn, who propofes to give it to the world very fhortly.

Weever has given an imperfect account of the antient funeral monuments in this county and diocefe.

" A defcription of the diocefe of Norwich, or the prefent ftate of
" Norfolk and Suffolk ; giving an account of the fituation, extent,
" trade, and cuftoms of Norwich in particular, and the feveral market
" towns in thofe two counties, according to alphabetical order. By a
" gentleman of the Inner-Temple and native of the diocefe of Nor-
" wich. Lond. 1735." 8vo. Very flight and trifling.

We are told Dr. John Caius wrote, or intended to write, an account
of the city of *Norwich*. Bartholomew Cotton, monk there about the
end of the 13th century, compiled from Malmfbury a hiftory of England in three books, out of which Wharton collected what he pub-

---

d Dr. Hen. Briggs, rector of Holt, collected Holt hundred. Anth. Norris, efq; carefully examined many churches. Blomefield's work feems to have been publifhed in
monthly numbers, but a complete copy is not eafy to meet with.

lifhed

lifhed in his Anglia Sacra, I. 397. 430. under the title of Annals of Norwich, and a hiftory of its bifhops.   Tanner fays there is.a copy in the
cathedral library, containing one page of chronology, and then a hiftory
of Norwich, word for word anfwering Wharton's Annals, but fuller,
containing many facts worthy to appear from the Norwich prefs.

The firft printed account of this city is " Alexandri Nevylli Norvicus.
" Lond. 1575." 4to. printed at the end of his book called " Kettus
" five de furoribus Norfolcienfium, Ketto duce." Lond. 1575. 4to.
1582. 12mo.   This has towards the end an engraved map of the
defcent of the Britifh and Saxon kings ; and " Al. Neville ad Walliæ
" proceres apologia, 12 Maii, 1576; " and to it is prefixed a poem
on the archbifhop's death : the cuts by R. Lyne, fervant to abp.
Parker 1574. to whom Nevill was fecretary ᵉ.   It was again printed at
the end of Ocland's Anglorum prælia ab A. D. 1327. ad A. D. 1558.
1582.   Thefe two have been tranflated and publifhed under the titles
of " The hiftory of the Norfolk rebels, by Alexander Nevil, a Kentifh
" man ; with the hiftory of Norwich, and a catalogue of the mayors.
" Lond. 1575." 4to.   " Norfolk's furies, or a view of Kett's camp,
" with a table of the mayors and fheriffs of Norwich, &c. done out
" of Latin into Englifh by R. Wᶠ. Lond. 1615." 4to.   " The Nor-
" folk furies and their foyle under Kett their accurfed captain;
" with a defcription of the famous city of Norwich, englifht by Rich.
" Wood, minifter of Fretnam, out of the Latin of Alex. Nevil,
" Lond. 1623 ᵍ."

F. Burgefs's " Obfervations on the origin and firft ufe of printing,
" particularly at Norwich," was the firft piece printed there, 1701, and
was reprinted in the Harleian Mifcellany, vol. iii. p. 148.

" Q. Elizabeth's progrefs to Norwich 1576, collected by B. G.
" [B. Goldingham] and T. C. [Thomas Churchyard.] Imprinted at
London by Bynneman." 4to. with a map of Norwich, by John Day:
inferted alfo in Stowe's fupplement to Hollinfhed, II. 1287, and in
Blomefield's hiftory of Norwich, p. 226.

ᵉ When he was fixteen he tranflated Seneca's Oedipus, printed 1581, and intended a
tranflation of Livy.   Tanner.
    ᶠ Richard Wood, as in the next title.   Nicholfon has knighted this tranflator.
    ᵍ Ames's Hift. of Print. p. 330.

The

The mayor's fhare of a bill of fare 17 years before, for treating the duke of Norfolk and other nobility on the mayor's day, amounting to 1 l. 12 s. 9 d. was printed from the Norwich Regifter, in Leland's Itinerary, vol. vi. and more correctly in Blomefield's Hiftory, II. 199.

Amongft Sir Tho. Browne's pofthumous works, publifhed from his papers in the poffeffion of Owen Brigftock, efq; F. R. S. 8vo. 1712, is " Repertorium; or fome account of the tombs and monuments in " the cathedral church of Norwich, begun by Sir Thomas Browne, and " continued from the year 1680 to this prefent time, illuftrated with " feverall copper plates of the principal monuments, &c. moftly at the " expence of the nobility and gentry of this county. Lond. 1712." 8vo. To this are annexed " Antiquitates capellæ divi Johannis Evangeliftæ, " hodie fcholæ regiæ Norwicenfis. Authore Joanne Burton, A. M. ejuf- " dem ludimagiftro;" communicated by his fon the rev. Mr. Jofhua Burton. At the end is a lift of the dignitaries of this church, with large alterations and corrections, firft publifhed by dean Prideaux in a broad fheet.

The ftate of the city library, founded in the laft century, with the names of the benefactors, may be feen in " A catalogue of the books " in the library of the city of Norwich in the year 1706. Norwich " 1706." 8vo. Mackerell, the Lynn antiquarian, publifhed another catalogue 1732. 4to [h].

" A compleat hiftory of the famous city of Norwich, from the ear-lieft accounts to this prefent year 1728. with a large chronology of occurrences in and near the city, an exact lift of the bifhops, mayors, and fheriffs, &c. and of the pofts and carriers; alfo of the prefent bifhops and deans in England, and of all the judges; to which is an-nexed an exact map; publifhed at the requeft of feveral ingenious gentlemen and other curious perfons. Norwich 1728." 8vo. After p. 38 follows " An appendix to the chronological hiftory, taken from an authentick MS. found in the ftudy of a late noted antiquary in this county:" and " An abridgement of Neville's Norfolk furies."

" The records of Norwich, containing the monuments in the cathe- " dral, the bifhops, the plagues, fires, martyrs, hofpitals, &c." was printed at Norwich 1736. 8vo. in two parts. Price three pence.

[h] Blomefield's Norwich. p. 601.

B b b

" An

" An authentic account of the antient city of Norwich. By Thomas Eldridge. Norwich 1738." 8vo.

" An eſſay on the antiquity of the caſtel of Norwich; its founders, " and governors from the kings of the Eaſt Angles down to modern " times. Norwich 1728." 8vo. Blomefield, vol. ii. p. 6, ſays this is by an ingenious author, but does not tell his name.

In p. 520 of Nº 477 of the Philoſophical Tranſactions we have Mr. Baker's deſcription of the Bridewell, built of flints hewn ſquare. In Nº 486, p. 244, an account of the chalk-hills near this city by Mr. Arderon, and in the 51ſt vol. a relation of the effects of a ſtorm of thunder and lightning on a houſe near *Sandling-ferry* in Norwich.

Kirkpatrick's N. E. view of the cathedral was engraved by J. Harris, 1742.

A print of Blackfriars in Norwich, now St. Andrew's hall, with its ſpire that fell down 1712, by D. King, is in ſome copies of the Monaſticon.

Kirkpatrick publiſhed a large N. E. proſpect of the city, and died 1728. A N. E. S. E. and a third were engraved by Buck 1741.

In Dr. Cunnyngham's Coſmographical Glaſs, 1559. Fol. is a fine map of the excellent city of Norwich.

An ordinary proſpect of the croſs, built by Mr. Rightwiſe 1501, and pulled down 1632, was drawn by J. Stark, and engraved by T. Hill-yard. A very good one drawn 1732 by Timothy Sheldrake, was en-graved by A. Mott.

The ſeal of the biſhops of Norwich, in the hands of the corporation of Lynne, communicated by Le Neve, makes pl. x. of Stukeley's Iti-nerary. It is remarkable for having an inſcription on the edge[i]. On one ſide is inſcribed, *Sigillum : eccleſie : ſancte : trinitatis : Norwici.* On the other, *Eſt michi : numen idem. tribus uni : laus : honor : idem : et : benedico : gregi : famulatur : qui : michi : regi.* On the edge, *Anno domini : milleſimo : ducenteſimo : quinquageſimo : octavo : factum : eſt : hoc : ſigillum :* In the xith plate is the pedeſtal of a ſtone croſs at *Drayton,* near Norwich.

---

[i] Thoſe of St. Auſtin's, Canterbury, and St. Andrew's, Rocheſter, had the ſame.

In

An actual survey of the city of Norwich by James Corbridge, with elevations of the public buildings, on two sheets of imperial paper, 3¼ feet by 2¼.

In 1766 was published a new and accurate plan of the city of Norwich, shewing the exact length and breadth of all the streets and lanes, with their bearings, bendings, and proper names, ornamented with the prospects of several publick buildings in the said city, from an actual survey taken by Samuel King, land-surveyor, and laid down by a scale of three chains (or 66 yards) in an inch. Likewise a copy from the same, on a small scale or six chains in an inch.

" An account of the lamentable burning of *East Derham*, in the " county of Norfolk, July 1, 1581," in verse, printed in black letter 1582.

" A description of the town of *Great Yarmouth*; with a survey of " Little Yarmouth, incorporated with the Great," in one sheet.

" Nashes Lenten stuff, containing the description and first procrea- " tion and increase of the town of Great Yarmouth in Norfolk: with " a new play, never played before, of the praise of the red herring: " fit of all clerks of noblemens kitchens to be read; and not unnecef- " fary by all serving-men, who have short board wages, to be remem- " bered. Lond. 1599." 4to. Reprinted in the Harleian Miscellany, vol. vi. p. 129.

The W. prospect of this town, with elevations of all the public buildings, on three sheets imperial, 5 feet by 2¼. A S. W. view of it by Buck 1741. A short account of the town, transcribed from a table hanging in the town-hall, was communicated by Dr. Rawlinson to Hearne, who published it amongst his notes on Leland's Collectanea, vol. vi. p. 285, &c. The Doctor had a seal of Edmund duke of Somerset, marquis of Dorset, governor of Bayeux in the minority of Hen. VI. found near this place, which he inserted in the English Topographer, p. 161. and in Leland's Collectanea, vi. 291, where Hearne seems to promise some collection of seals to be published by Mr. Anstis, who has engraved in his edition of the Black book of the Garter, vol. ii. p. 175, the monument of Sir Simon Felbrigge and his lady, t. Hen. VI. at *Felbrigge*.

Hearne

Hearne publifhed a grant from Rich. de Pafton to *Brombolm* abbey, of twelve pence a year rent charge on his eftates, to ᵏ *keep their books in repair.* A S. E. view of its ruins by Buck 1738.

The ftory of the pedlar of *Swaffham*, printed by Hearne, App. to Caii Vind. vol. i. p. 84, is properly exploded by Blomefield, who confiders the carving alleged to confirm it as a rebus of the name of Chapman.

Mr. Benjamin Mackerell, a gentleman of Norwich, publifhed " The " hiftory and antiquities of the flourifhing corporation of *King's-Lynn*; " containing whatever is or hath been curious and remarkable in every " refpect in this town: a particular account of whatever is contained " in each parifh church or chapel, &c. the feveral charters from time " to time, with a catalogue of all the mayors, &c. with a particular " defcription and account of K. John's fword and cup. 1738." 8vo. with cuts. It contains great part of Mr. Green's hiftory of that place from his MS. then in the hands of Mr. Squire, rector of Congham, Norfolk. A letter to the mayor about St. James's chapel inferted in this hiftory was reprinted in the Gentleman's Magazine for July 1741, and better explained in that for September.

" Ichnographia burgi perantiqui Lennæ Regis in agro Norfolcienfi " accuratè delineata a Gulielmo Raftrick," adorned with views of the exchange, market-houfe, &c. was publifhed in 1725. A S. view of St. Margaret's church before the fpire was blown down in 1741, was engraved by H. Mackworth from a draught by H. Bell. Bagford's lift prefixed to the Britannia mentions a W. profpect of this town on one fheet. There is an E. profpect by Buck, 1738.

" The defigne for the perfect draining of the great level of the fens " (called Bedford level) lying in Norfolk, Suffolk, Cambridgefhire, " Huntingdonfhire, Northamptonfhire, Lincolnfhire, and the Ifle of " Ely, as it was delivered to the honourable corporation for the drain- " ing of the faid great level the 4th of June 1664: as alfo feveral ob- " jections anfwered fince the delivery of the faid defigne; with objec- " tions to the defigne now in agitation, and as for the new works in-

---

ᵏ Ad emendacionem librorum. Ap. ad Ad. de Domerham. Nᵖ iii.
ˡ Hift. of Norf. vol. iii. p. 508.

" tended

" tended in this defigne appears in the annexed map: and the charge of
" the whole calculated. By collonel Wm. Dodfon. Lond. 1666."

" The antient and prefent ftate of the navigation of the towns of
" Lyn, Wifbeach, Spalding, and Bofton, of the rivers that pafs through
" thofe places and the countries that border thereupon, truly, faithfully
" and impartially reprefented, and humbly propofed to the confidera-
" tion of the inhabitants ; with a way laid down to remedy all the in-
" conveniencies and defects which they now labour under." [By Nathaniel Kinderly.] Lond. 1721. 1751. 8vo.

" A report of the prefent ftate of the great level of the fens, called
" Bedford level, and of the port of Lynn ; and of the rivers Oufe and
" Nean, the two great fewers of that country. With confiderations
" on the fcheme propofed by the corporation of Lynn for draining the
" faid fens, and reinftating that harbour. And alfo a fcheme humbly
" propofed for the effectual draining thofe fens, and reinftating that
" harbour or port: from a furvey thereof made in Auguft 1724, by
" Mr. Charles Bridgeman." On the oppofite pages is printed " An
" anfwer, paragraph by paragraph, to the report and fcheme, drawn
" from authentic teftimonies of the ftate of that level, harbour, and
" river, before and fince Denver dam and fluices were built, &c. and
" from a furvey made in the years 1723, 1724." To the whole is
annexed " Colonel Armftrong's report, with propofals for draining the
" fens, and amending the harbour of Lynn, 1724." Fol. with maps
of the fens, cuts, and new propofed rivers, furveys of the Humber,
Oufe, and Thames from their fources to the fea.

" The hiftory of the antient and prefent ftate of the navigation of
" the port of King's Lyn, and of Cambridge, and the reft of the
" trading towns in thofe parts, and of the navigable rivers that have
" their courfe through the great level of the fens, called Bedford-level:
" alfo the hiftory of the antient and prefent ftate of draining in the
" level, in the province of Marfhland, and the hundred and parts ad-
" jacent, from authentic records and antient MSS. and from obferva-
" tions and furveys carefully made on the fpot thefe three years laft
" paft; with the method propofed for draining the faid fens, and
" amending the harbour of Lyn, by col. John Armftrong, chief en-
" gineer

" gineer of England: illuftrated with maps. [By Thomas Badeflade.]
" 1725." Fol.

" A fcheme for draining the great level of the fenns, called Bedford
" level; and for improving the navigation of Lyn-regis: founded up-
" on felf-evident principles in experimental philofophy and practical
" mathematicks, and upon hiftorical facts; and farther demonftrated
" by comparing the river Oufe with the river Thames, &c. and Lyn-
" harbour with the harbour of Rye. With reflections upon all the
" fchemes hitherto propofed for draining the fens, fhewing wherein
" they are defective. Alfo obfervations upon artificial fcours[m]; fhew-
" ing where and in what cafes they are or can be of ufe; where not.
" Illuftrated with a map. By Tho. Badeflade, author of the hiftory of
" Lynn-regis and of draining in the fens. Lond. 1729." Fol.

" Obfervations on the decay of the outfalls or lofs of the channels
" of divers weak rivers, particularly of the river *Neen*, otherwife Wif-
" bech river, and Shire-drain, humbly offered to the confideration of
" the hon. corporation of adventurers, and of all gentlemen, merchants,
" and others interefted in the preferving the navigation of the faid river,
" and in draining the lands thereto adjacent, in the great level of the
" fens called Bedford great level; with a fcheme to recover the faid
" navigation, and drain the faid lands effectually. To which is added
" the form of a refervoir lately invented for the fcouring the fands out
" of the mouths of any weak rivers. By Richard Edwards. Lond.
" 1749." 8vo.

" An actual furvey of the north level, part of the great level of the
" fenns, commonly called Bedford level, alfo of Crowland, Great Por-
" fand, and part of South Holland, in the county of Lincoln, and of
" Wifbeach, north fide of the Ifle of Ely, and county of Cambridge;
" wherein is defcribed the feveral drains, fewers, fluices, &c. by which
" the lands contained in this furvey drain to their outfalls at fea. Taken
" Aug. 1749, by John Wing, Nath. Hill, &c."

A draught of Lynn-Deeps by Mitchell.

" The hiftory of the antient city and burgh of *Thetford*, in the
" counties of Norfolk and Suffolk: fhewing its rife, increafe, decreafe,

---

[m] Examining captain Perry's fcheme delivered to the corporation of Adventurers,
Feb. 172¾.

" and

" and prefent ftate. By Francis Blomefield, rector of Fersfield in Nor-
" folk. Printed at Fersfield 1739." 4to.   Inferted likewife in the 1ft
vol. of his Hiftory of Norfolk: with Dr. Plott's letter to the earl of
Arlington concerning the old Sitomagus, printed in Hearne's Antiquities of Glaftonbury, p. 227.   Blomefield hints that a more exact account of this town was to be expected from the large collections and
abilities of Mr. T. Martin.   The abbey was engraved by Hollar, in a
fet with five other views: and a S. E. profpect of it by Buck.

" Ædes Walpolianæ: or a defcription of the collection of pictures
" at *Houghton-hall* in Norfolk, &c.   The 2d edition with additions.
" Lond. 1752." 4to.   [By the hon. Horace Walpole.]   The meafures
of the pictures are more correct in this than the former editions.   There
is annexed " A fermon on painting, preached before the earl of Orford
" at Houghton 1742." and " A journey to Houghton, &c. a poem,
" by the rev. Mr. Whaley."

" The plans, elevations, and fections, chimney-pieces, and cielings
" of Houghton-hall, defigned by Thomas Ripley, efq; delineated by
" Ifaac Ware and William Kent, and engraved by Fourdrinier; with
" a defcription of the houfe and pictures. Lond. 1760." Fol.

The plan and elevations of the late earl of Leicefter's houfe at *Holkham* were engraved and publifhed by —— Brettingham, architect. Lond.
1761. Fol.   A fmall view of the front drawn and engraved by R.
Baldwin, clerk to Brettingham.   Mr. Potter addreffed to his lordfhip
a poem on this houfe, Lond. 1758. and celebrated the river *Kymber*,
and the feat of the Wodehoufe family on its banks, in " Kymber: a
" monody: to Sir Armine Woodhoufe, bart. Lond. 1758." 4to.

" The moft lamentable and dreadfull thunder and lightning in the
" county of Norfolk and city of Norwich on July 20, being the Lord's
" day, in the afternoon; the whirlwind and thick darknefs, and moft
" prodigious hailftones, which being above five inches about, did fo
" violently batter down the windows of the city that 3000 l. will hardly
" repair them: diverfe men and women ftruck dead; the firing of
" fome towns and whole fields of corn by lightning; which alfo de-
" ftroyed the birds of the air and the beafts of the field.   Together
" with another moft violent ftorm, which happening on Saturday laft
" in

" in the fame county for almoft thirty miles together performed the " like terrible effect, &c. Lond. 1646." Reprinted in the Harleian Mifcellany, vol. ii. p. 272.

The difcovery of near 50 urns, bones, &c. in a field at *Old Walfing-ham*, five miles from Brancafter, the antient Brannodunum, 1657, occafioned Sir T. Browne's " Hydriotaphia, urne-burial : or, a difcourfe of the fepulchral urnes lately found in Norfolk. Lond. 1658." 8vo. Reprinted in his works 1686. Fol. In his pofthumous works pub-lifhed from his original MS. in the hands of Sir Hans Sloane, 1712, is another difcourfe concerning fome bones found in *Brampton-field* in Norfolk 1667.

Thomas Lawrence, an eminent phyfician in Norfolk, wrote a letter to Sir T. Browne, printed under the title of " Mercurius Cen-" tralis : or, a difcourfe of fubterranean cockle, mufcle, and oyfter-" fhells, found in the digging of a well at Sir Wm. Doilie's [at Shotes-" hall] in Norfolk, many foot under ground, and at confiderable dif-" tance from the fea. Lond. 1664." 24to. In p. 257 of N° 337 of the Philofophical Tranfactions is an account of a large number of trees dug up at *North-Elmham* about February 1711, communicated by P Le Neve, who in p. 766 of N° 355 communicated an account of the finking of three oaks at *Mannington* July 23, 1717. In p. 183 of N° 465 is a defcription of a meteor feen near *Holkham* Aug. 1741, communi-cated by Thomas lord Lovel. In N° 475, p. 331, and N° 482, p. 432, Mr. Baker's defcriptions of a very large foffil tooth of an ele-phant found near *Munfley*, and of a curious echinites found at *Ba-borough*. In p. 275 of N° 481 we have fome obfervations on the cliffs on the N. coaft of Norfolk by Mr. Arderon. In N° 484, p. 576, his account of grubs that deftroyed the grafs in Norfolk 1687. In N° 495, p. 467, his account of John Coan, the Norfolk dwarf. In p. 527 of N° 477, his relation of an extraordinary finking of the earth near *Horsford*. In p. 196 of N° 493 his defcription of the pre-fent ftate of the Roman camp at *Caftor* 1749, with a plan. In vol. liii. art. 5, his eftimate of the quantity of rain fallen in a foot fquare at Norwich from 1749 to 1762. In vol. li. part i. is an account of thun-der and lightning at Norwich July 13, 1758. Art. 65 of vol. xlviii.

part

part ii. is Mr. Arderon's obfervations on the fevere cold weather felt there in the winter 1754.

The Antiquarian Society have drawings of the chancels of *Tunfted* and *Upton*, remarkable for their fimplicity; the monuments of Herbert Scott in the latter church; of Thomas Holditch at *Ranworth*; and of lady Calthorpe, bifhops Lozinga and Overall, prior Bofville, and Richard Brome in Norwich cathedral, all by Mr. Talman, 1705: alfo a drawing of the ruins of St. Edmund's chapel near *Hunftanton*. They have engraved the feals of *Weftacre* priory.

Views of *Caftle-acre* abbey; E. and W. of *Caftle-acre* caftle; *Pentney* priory gatehoufe; the front and back of *Weft Dereham* abbey; *Caftle-Rifing* caftle; and *Middleton* tower, drawn by W. Millecent, were engraved by E. Kirkall.

S. E. views of Wymondham; E. of Caftle-acre, and Walfingham: W. of Creak, and S. W. of Binham priories; S. E. of Caftle-Rifing and S. of Caftle-acre caftles, 1738: and Melton Conftable, Sir Jacob Aftley's feat, 1741, have been publifhed by Meffrs. Buck.

Vaughan engraved for the Monafticon a drawing of *St. Bennet in the Holm* abbey from a MS. in the Cotton library. The Antiquarian Society have given us three views and a ground-plot of the gatehoufe (of which now remains only the lower ftory much fhattered, fupporting a wind-mill) and a view of *Walfingham* abbey, 1720, by Badeflade and Vandergucht. Alfo the tomb of Robart Colles and Cecili his wife at *Foulfham*. An infcription on a tomb in this church-yard was publifhed in the Phil. Tranf. N° 189, p. 361, by Sir P. Skippon.

A S. profpect of *Cromere* church, with an ichnography, T. Blomfield del. W. H. Toms fc. infcribed to Dr. T. Tanner.

A S. view of St. Peter's at *Walpole*. W. Stennitt del. Vertue fc. 1730.

A S. view of *Redenhall* church was drawn by T. Milton and engraved by Toms, but never publifhed. The plate was laft in the hands of Ryall, printfeller, in Fleet-ftreet, who bought it at the fale of Milton's effects 1766. Thomas Brotherton earl of Norfolk and William Neuport built this church early in the fourteenth century; its lofty fquare tower, the moft beautiful of any parochial one in this county, was the work of the next century; and though fplit from top

to

to bottom by a ftorm 1616, was fo well repaired as to receive very little injury from the accident ᵐ.

The famous fign of the White Hart at *Scole* inn, carved by one Fairchild, at the expence of John Peck, efq; 1655, was drawn by Jofhua Kirby, and engraved by John Teffer 1740 on a large fheet, and fince publifhed in the Imperial Magazine, June 1762. The inn itfelf was alfo drawn by Kirby at the fame time and engraved by John Fiffey. The two porches have fince been removed, and fome other improvements made.

I have a plate belonging to Blomefield's hiftory, vol. iii. p. 532, containing the monument of Erafmus Earle, efq; lord of the manor of *Cawfton*, and the two maces carried before the lord or his fteward when they hold the courts, one of them furmounted with the gauntlet, (the rebus of John of Gaunt) holding a plowfhare, becaufe the manor is held in free focage of the dutchy of Lancafter; the other with a bearded arrow, by which tenure part of the town is held of the faid dutchy. The compiler of Magna Britannia, vol. iii. p. 270, mentions the firft of thefe maces, but could give no account of their origin.

Norfolciæ comitatus continentis in fe oppida mercatoria 26, pagos & villas 625, una cum fingulis hundredis & fluminibus in eodem vera defcriptio. C. Saxton del. Corn. Hogius fc. 1574.

Hollar engraved a map of Norfolk 1670. Speed's map 1610 has a plan of Norwich.

Norfolk furveyed by James Corbridge, with a lift of the towns at the fides, and the N. E. profpect of Norwich, W. of Lynn, and W. of Yarmouth, on two fheets of atlas, 4 feet by $2\frac{1}{4}$: alfo on one fheet, with circular meridian lines three miles from Norwich, and the lift: and on two fheets, with the views.

Other maps were publifhed at Norwich 1731. 1740. The laft was made by E. Bowen 1749.

ᵐ Blomefield's Hift. vol. iii. p. 244.

NORTHAMPTON-

NORTHAMPTONSHIRE.

NOrden wrote " A delineation of Northamptonſhire, with certaine " neceſſarie obſervations thearin, copied out of a book your " worſhip a had of Sir Vallentine Knightlye in October, and ended " Wenſdaye the xiiiith of November 1610." Mr. Anſtis had a copy of it; and another has been communicated to the publick by a gentleman of the county, in whoſe library it was, intitled " Speculi Britanniæ pars " altera: or a delineation of Northamptonſhire, being a brief hiſtori- " call and chronographicall diſcription of that county: wherein are alſo " alphabetically ſett downe the names of cyties, townes, pariſhes, ham- " lets, houſes of note, and other remarkables. By the travayle of John " Norden in the year M DC X. Lond. 1720." 8vo. This is the moſt ſuperficial of all maſter Norden's ſurveys, except in a few towns; nor were the map, and plans of Peterborough and Northampton referred to in it ever engraved. Auguſtin Vincent, Windſor herald, had ſome view this way b. Among Wood's MSS. are " Nomina hydarum com. " Northamptona à Franc. Tate" c.

Among the Harleian MSS. N° 6713, contains a collection of in- ſcriptions in 32 churches in the hundreds of Newbottlegrove, Fawſley, Towceſter, Wimerſley, Warden, and Norton, with the length and breadth of the churches and chancels, number of bells, number and form of pillars, deſcription of veſtries, letters and arms in windows, &c. by Wm. Taylor, maſter of the grammar ſchool at Heyford.

But the moſt accurate account of its antiquities was expected from that able antiquary John Bridges, eſq; of Barton Seagrave, near Ketter- ing, who ſpent many years in collecting materials, and ſpared no ex- pence in ſurveying every pariſh, &c. But dying July 30, 1741, only the hundreds of Daventry, Warden, and Norton were publiſhed in

---

a Sir William Hatton, kt. to whom this ſurvey is dedicated.

b Of which ſee Aubrey's Survey, vol. v. p. 231. Burton's Leiceſterſhire, ep. to the reader: and the dedication of Lee's Chronicon Ceſtrenſe in King's Antiquities of Che- ſhire. Aubrey ſays he died while thus employed, and left great materials, which with all his other collections are lodged in the Heralds office.

c Of him ſee Ath. Ox. I. 409.

C c c

160 folio pages, with views of Daventry church and priory (now both pulled down) and Catesby monastery, drawn by Peter Tillemans, and engraved by Paul Fourdrinier. His collections being put 1755 into the hands of a committee of twelve gentlemen of the county with Sir Thomas Cave, bart. at their head, the rev. Mr. Peter Whalley compiled from them an history of the county, continued to the present time. The first volume appeared about 1762, containing the hundreds of Fawsley, Wardon, Sutton, Norton, Towcester, Cleyley, Wimersley, Spelho, Newbottle, and Guilsborough. The promised plates of buildings and ruins are reserved for the second, for which we must wait some time longer.

" The natural history of Northamptonshire, with some account of " the antiquities. To which is annexed a transcript of Doomsday- " book, so far as it relates to that county, by John Moreton, M. A. " rector of Oxendon in the same county, and fellow of the Royal So- " ciety, formerly of Emanuel Coll. in Cambridge. Lond. 1712." Fol. Some remarks on a Roman pavement at Nether Heyford, described p. 517—532, are in the review of Leland's Itinerary, at the end of vol. ix. p. 197—202. The map of the county was drawn and engraved by J. Harris, a native, and bordered with arms. Bp. Nicholson passes great encomiums on this book.

The county was visited 1566 by Hugh Cotgrave, Richmond herald, deputy for Harvey: 1594 by Lee: 1618 by A. Vincent.

Of the principal town we have " The state of *Northampton* from " the beginning of the fire, Sept. 20, 1675 to Nov. 5; represented in " a letter to a friend in London; and now recommended to all well " disposed persons, in order to christian charity, and speedy relief for " the said distressed town and people: by a country minister. Lond. " 1675." 4to.

" Carmen funebre ex occasione Northamptoniæ conflagrantis, com- " positum opera S. Ford, S. T. D. autoris poematis de conflagratione " Londinensis. Lond. 1676." 4to.

" The fall and funeral of Northampton, in an elegy; first published " in Latin, since made English, with some variations and additions. " Lond. 1677." 4to.

" Statutes,

" Statutes, rules, and orders for the government of the county hof-
" pital for fick and lame poor, eftablifhed in the town of Northamp-
" ton. North. 1743." 8vo.

Dr. Rawlinfon had the original feal of a religious houfe in this town,
not mentioned in the Monafticon, or by Tanner, with this infcription
round it: *Sigillum fanĉte crucis in muro Northamptonie.* An exaĉt
draught of it is exhibited in the Englifh Topographer, p. 166.

Buck engraved a large view of the town 1731.

A plan of it by Noble and Butlin was engraved in 1746 by J. Jefferies, with the number of houfes and inhabitants, from an accurate
furvey, exhibiting every ftreet, lane, yard, barn, garden, and the
ground-plot of the outhoufes, barns, &c. alfo the divifion of the parifhes: decorated with the perfpeĉtive views of the churches and other
remarkable ftruĉtures, viz. St. Sepulchre's, St. Peter's, St. Giles's, the
county hall, infirmary and goal, and the cotton mill.

" The hiftory of the church of *Peterborough*: wherein the moft re-
" markable things concerning that place, from the firft foundation
" thereof: with other paffages of hiftory, not unworthy publick view,
" are reprefented. By Simon Gunton, late prebendary of that church.
" Illuftrated with fculptures, and fet forth by Symon Patrick, D. D.
" now dean of the fame (afterwards bifhop of Ely). Lond. 1686." Fol.
Among the papers of Mr. Mickleton of Gray's-inn was a folio MS. concerning the affairs of this church, to which Gunton was much indebted,
feveral of his letters appearing in it. Among 1700 books in the library
were feveral pieces of Cicero, Virgil, Ovid, Seneca's tragedies and
other works, and Q Serenus. All the records of this church were
deftroyed by Cromwell's foldiers 1643, except one MS. called Swap-
ham (preferved under the notion of its being a Latin fcripture-book
or bible) wrote by Hugh White, fub-prior here temp. Hen. II. and
continued to 1249, with the addition of many records: publifhed by
Jofeph Spark, regifter of this church, 1738. Mr. Gunton was a native
of this city, and fpent almoft his whole life in it, and died 1676.
In his book are E. W. and N. views of the church by D. King d, the

---

d Of which the two laft are in the Monafticon.

beau--

beautiful high altar, deſtroyed 1643, and a N. view of the city.   His publiſher added a large ſupplement to it in the ſame order as the parts of the book [d].   Wood ſays he had ſeen divers collections made by Fra. Thynne, Lancaſter herald, of monuments in this cathedral, ſeveral of which were defaced before Dugdale or Gunton made their ſurveys [e]. Biſhop Patrick would have publiſhed the latter's draughts, if the ſubſcription to his book would have defrayed the expence.   Gunton profeſſedly omits ſuch inſcription as are incomplete or contain only dates or names, many of which ſtill remain.   Dugdale's ſurvey and draught of 31 monuments, and the arms in the cloiſter and hall, in lord Hatton's library, were engraved in about 30 or 40 plates with proſpects of the church, at the expence of Mr. Bridges for the hiſtory of the county [f]. B. Willis, in his ſurvey of this church, has publiſhed many of theſe inſcriptions and others remaining 1718.

The Antiquarian Society engraved 1720 a ſeal in the poſſeſſion of Mr. Sparkes, of a monk holding a banner with St. Peter.   Inſcription *Non ſine cauſa gladium portat.*

A view of the W. front of this church was engraved by Collins.

A large S. W. proſpect of the city by Buck 1731.

Wellingborough ſpa or Redwell was recommended by Sir Theodore Mayerne in his writings [g].

" The great flood, or ſad and lamentable news from Northampton,
" Buckingham, Banbury, Daventry, Brackley, and other places; be-
" ing a true and perfect relation of the great inundation of waters
" which broke forth in its violent and mighty ſtreams on Tueſday and
" Wedneſday the 5th and 6th of this inſtant May, and the manner
" how it came pouring down the countries with a mighty force, and
" after a great ſtorm of thunder and lightning, breaking down divers
" ſtone bridges, water mills, and other ſtrong buildings, the people
" being forced to betake themſelves to the upper rooms, crying out at
" the windows, Horſe, horſe, horſe, for the Lord's ſake: together with
" the great miracle that happened at the ſame time near Aino on the

---

[d] Dr. Kennet when dean here made large additions to both.
[e] Ath. Ox. I. 376.
[f] Willis's Survey of Peterborough cathedral, p. 478.
[g] Moreton. Short. 48.

" hill;

" hill ; the great lofs fuftained by thefe inundations of water. Pub-
" lifhed to prevent all falfe copies. 1663." 4to.

" A brief account and feafonable improvement of the late earth-
" quake in Northamptonfhire, Jan. 4, 167⅚, in a letter to a friend in
" London. 1676." 4to.

" The ghoft, or a minute account of the appearance of the ghoft
" of John Croxford, executed at Northampton Aug. 14, 1764, for
" the murder of a ftranger : wherein many particulars relative to that
" affair, and known only to the parties concerned, are now firft made
" public from the confeffion of the ghoft, &c. &c. By a minifter of
" the gofpel near Northampton, perfonally concerned in the conference
" with Croxford's ghoft. Lond. 1764." 8vo. A catchpenny pamphlet, full of trite arguments and fuperfluous evidence, to which the
minifter feems to have been afhamed to fet his name.

In p. 2156 of N° 71 of the Philofophical Tranfactions is an account
of two confiderable hurricanes at *Afhley* and *Braybrook*, by Mr. John
Templer, rector of the latter ; and in Moreton, p. 334. In p. 399 of
N° 154 is a letter from Dr. Wallis to Dr. Plott, concerning the date ʰ
1133 [M° 133] on an old mantle-tree in the rectory-houfe at *Helmdon*, whence he fixes the ufe of Arabic numerals to the middle of the
eleventh century. In p. 800 of N° 166 is another letter from and to
the fame, concerning an antient large ftone chimney at *Edgecot*. In
p. 710 of N° 199, and in Moreton, p. 347, is a relation of a ftorm
of thunder, lightning, and hail at *Oundle*, March 20, 169⅚, by Mr.
W. R. In p. 824 of N° 202 is an account of fome tubera terræ, or
trufles, found at *Rufhton*, by Dr. Tancred Robinfon. In p. 192 of N°
212 is a letter from *Warrington*, concerning the effects of an unufual
whirlwind Aug. 1, 1694. In p. 5 of N° 236, and in Moreton, p. 346,
is a letter from Dr. Wallis, dated Jan. 11, 1697, concerning the effects
of a great ftorm of thunder and lightning at *Everdon*, wherein feveral
perfons were killed, July 27, 1601. In N° 305, p. 210, is a letter
from Dr. Moreton about fhells dug up in a bituminous meary earth at
Mears-Afhby. In 2147 of N° 306 are Dr. Keil's obfervations on the
death and diffection of J. Bailes, button maker, of *Northampton*, aged

---

ʰ Which he had mentioned in his Treatife of Algebra, p. 12.

130. Moreton mentions feveral inftances of longevity in the county, p. 472 ; but makes him only 119. In N⁰ 392, p. 366, is Mr. Waffe's account of the effects of lightning at *Mixbury*. In N° 348 Mr. Lynn's account of an Aurora Borealis feen at *Southwick*. In N⁰ 444, p. 367, an account of the earthquake in this county 1731.

A particular entertainment of the queen and prince at *Apethorp*, at the houfe of the lord Spencer, July 25, 1603, as they came firft into England; by Ben. Johnfon, is among his works, vol. iii. p. 242.

The memory of a charitable benefaction to feveral parifhes in this county is preferved in " A copy of the laft will and teftament of Sir " George Bufwell, bart. of *Clipfton* in the county of Northampton : " to which is prefixed an epiftle dedicatory to the feveral inhabitants " of Clipfton, Kelmarfh, Oxenden magna, Marfton-Truffel, Hafle- " beech, and Eaft-Farndon, in the faid county of Northampton. " Lond. 1714." 8vo. Printed for private ufe.

Mr. Jof. Pullen, late vice-principal of Magdalen hall, Oxford, had the original feal of abp. Chichele's college at *Higham-Ferrers*, with this infcription : *S. fraternitatis be Marie de Hiccham*, engraved in the Englifh Topographer, p. 167, and in the additions at the end of the 4th vol. of Leland's Collectanea, p. 405. Buck engraved an E. view of this college 1729. A S. view of the church by Hollar is in the Monaft.

An account of fkeletons, &c. difcovered in making the road from Thrapfton to Market Harborough is in the Gentleman's Magazine for January, 1757, p. 19.

A Roman teffelated pavement found near *Cotterftock* 1736, drawn by Geo. Lynn fen. and jun. and Wm. Bogdani, efq; was publifhed by the Antiquarian Society. Another found at *Weldon* 1738, with feveral coins of Conftantine and Conftans, was drawn by John Lens and en- graved by J. Cole, at the expence of lord vifcount Hatton.

A defcription of *Eafton Nefton*, the feat of the earl of Pomfret, with the ftatues and pictures may be feen in Bathoe's Catalogue of the duke of Buckingham's pictures, &c. Lond. 1757. 4to. This houfe was built in 1692 by Sir William Fermor lord Lempfter, who bought the ftatues moftly out of the Arundelian collection. They were given to the Univerfity of Oxford by the late countefs dowager of Pomfret in 1755,

and

and the pictures [i] had before been fold by auction. Two pieces of antiquity in this collection have been defcribed in " Marmor Eftonianum, " feu differtatio de fella marmorea votiva Eftoniæ in agro Northampto- " nienfi confervatâ. Autore J. Nixon, A. M. Lond. 1744." 4to. and " An effay on a fleeping Cupid, being one of the Arundelian marbles " in the collection of the (late) right hon. the earl of Pomfret. By John " Nixon, M. A. F. R. S. rector of Cold Higham in Northamptonfhire. " Lond. 1735." 4to. Others of thefe monuments were made a head-piece for the Oxford Almanac 1757, and all have been fince engraved in the Marmora Oxonienfia 1764, of which hereafter. The ftatue of Cicero was fince drawn and engraved by Worlidge.

An E. profpect of lord Cullen's feat at *Rufhton*, by Winftanley, was engraved by Toms 1741.

Buck's views for this county are W. Daventry, N. Billing priories, S. Holdenby palace, S. Barnwell, and E. Rockingham caftles, and S. Drayton houfe 1729. They have correct drawings of *Geddington* and *Queen*'s croffes [k]: the latter defcribed in the Gentleman's Magazine for March 1765, p. 124. We have no view of the fine collegiate church and ruined caftle of *Foderingay:* the firft abridged of half its length; and the monuments of Edward duke of York flain at Agincourt, and his nephew Richard duke of York, who fell at Wakefield, with his wife Cecilie, and their fon Edmund earl of Rutland, in the ftyle of the 17th century, fubftituted to the original ones: the other reduced to a moat and keep, the laft fcene of the unfortunate queen of Scotslife, and facrificed to her manes by her fon. It makes one fmile to read the pageantry with which this royal convict was interred in Peterborough cathedral, fix months after her execution, the countefs of Bedford attending as chief mourner, the bifhop of Lincoln preaching her funeral fermon ; " of whofe life and death he had not, at that time, much to fay, becaufe he was not acquainted with the one, nor prefent at the other," yet charitably hoping the beft for her foul. Her body was removed 25 years after to Weftminfter, and lodged under a more pomp-

[i] From among thefe Mr. Walpole bought the marriage of Hen. VII. engraved in his Anecd. of Paint. vol. i. p. 50.

[k] Mr. Walpole has drawings of all Q. Eleanor's croffes by Vertue, who intended to engrave them.

5

ous,

ous, but far lefs elegant monument, than the cenotaph which remains at Peterborough unviolated by the fucceeding devaftations.

Lilford, near Oundle, the feat of Tho. Powis, efq; taken from Ay-church, engraved by R. Pranker 1758, from a painting by J. Harris.

A plan of *Great Harrowdon*, the feat of the marquis of Rockingham, dedicated to Thomas lord Malton by Jofeph Smith, engraved by J. Harris, fans date.

A profpect of Benavona *(Weedon)* 1725, is among Dr. Stukeley's unpublifhed plates.

A large S. W. view of the parifh church of *Ecton*, five miles from Northampton, in Hamford hundred, built in the 15th century, drawn by J. Shipley, was engraved by Toms 1749, with an account of it below; a coin of Ethelred, found in an adjoining antient burying place, and the head and arms of John Palmer, efq; of the Inner-Temple, patron, from a picture of Hogarth, by Baron.

Saxton's map of Northamptonfhire, including Rutland and the other adjoining counties, was publifhed 1576, without the hundreds, added in Speed's 1610, with plans of Northampton and Peterborough.

A moft inaccurate map was publifhed by E. Bowen 1753.

NORTHUM-

NORTHUMBERLAND.

JOhn Currar, of Bamffhire, an officer under the Conqueror, who promoted him to the government of this county, took a furvey of it, and drew up an account of its 78 fortified caftles and their lords. He likewife wrote a tract on the duty of the governors of the Marches, and fome letters to his fovereign mentioned by Dempfter and Pits, but not as then extant [a]. Bagford in his catalogue prefixed to Gibfon's edition of the Britannia 1695, advertifed as ready for the prefs, but ftill remaining in the dean and chapter's library at Carlifle, a defcription of the antient kingdom of Northumberland, by bp. Nicholfon, when archdeacon of Carlifle, confifting of eight parts: the firft intitled, " Northanhymbria; or an account of the bounds and natural hif- " tory of the county. The 2d, Northanhymbri: the original, lan- " guage, manners, and government of the people. The 3d, Annales: " the fucceffion and hiftory of the feveral dukes, kings, and earls, " from the firft inftitution of the government down to the conqueft. " The 4th, Ecclefiaftica: religious rites obferved by the inhabitants " before the eftablifhment of Chriftianity; together with the ftate of " the church, and the fucceffion of bifhops in it afterwards. The 5th, " Literæ & literati: the ftate of learning; with a catalogue of the " writers. The 6th, Villare: the cities, towns, villages, and other " places of note, in an alphabetical catalogue. The 7th, Monumenta " Danica: Danifh remains; in the language, temples, courts of judi- " cature, Runic infcriptions, &c. To the whole is prefixed a prefa- " tory difcourfe of the condition thefe parts of the ifland were in upon " and fome time before the coming in of the Saxons: wherein no- " tice will be taken of many pieces of Britifh and Roman antiquities " never yet obferved."

Northumberland was vifited 1575 by Flower and Glover: 1615 by Sir R. St. George: 1666 by Dugdale.

The antient ftate of thefe utmoft limits of the Englifh kingdom may be feen in bp. Nicholfon's " Leges Marchiarum, or border laws; con-

[a] Tann. B. B. p. 213.

" taining

" taining feveral original articles and treaties made and agreed upon by
" the commiffioners of the refpective kings of England and Scotland,
" for the prefervation of the common peace and commerce, upon the
" marches of both kingdoms, from the reign of Hen. III. to the union
" of the two crowns in James I. with an appendix of charters and re-
" cords relating to the faid treaties. Lond. 1705." 8vo.

Sir Robert Shaftoe, and Mr. Clavering of Callaly collected materials
for an hiftory of the county. Bourne endeavoured to get a fight of the
former's papers, but they were not to be found. He mentions large collections made by Dr. Ellifon, who was vicar of St. Nicholas, Newcaftle,
and died 1721; of which he could fee but very few. Among the late
Mr. Warburton's collections was an account of the lands and tenements in the county of Northumberland 1584, by —— Lawfon, MS.
folio, and a MS. hiftory of *Newcaftle*, wrote about the time of Charles
II. by Richard Thompfon.

There is in print William Grey's " Chorographia : or a furvey of
" *Newcaftle upon Tine*. The eftate of this county under the Ro-
" mans. The building of the famous wall of the Piⅽ̆ts, by the Ro-
" mans. The antient town of Pandon. A briefe defcription of the
" town, walls, wards, churches, religious houfes, ftreets, markets,
" fairs, river, and commodities; with the fuburbs. The antient and
" prefent government of the town : as alfo a relation of the county of
" Northumberland; which was the bulwark for England againft the
" Scots: their many caftles and towers; their antient families and
" names. Of the tenure in cornage ; of Cheviot hills ; of Tinedale,
" and Reedfdale, with the inhabitants. Newcaftle 1649." 4to. A furvey of the river Tyne, leading from the fea on the eaft to Newcaftle
on the weft by Hollar, is prefixed to fome copies of this piece, which
is reprinted with a few additions in the Harleian Mifcellany, vol. iii.
p. 256. Dr. Rawlinfon fays it was reprinting " with others as valuable
of the fame nature, "when he publifhed his Englifh Topographer; but
I never faw this edition. Ames had two MS. copies of it, folio and
4to. [b]. In 1715 the S. profpect of St. Nicholas's church was engraved
on copper for Overton, and dedicated to Dr. Talbot, bp. of Durham.

[b] See his Catal. Nº 86.

" England's

" England's grievance difcovered in relation to the coal trade; with
" the map of the river Tine, and fituation of the town and corpora-
" tion of Newcaftle. The tyrannical oppreffion of thofe magiftrates,
" their charters and grants, and feveral trials, depofitions, and judge-
" ments obtained againft them; with a breviate of feveral ftatutes
" proving repugnant to their acting; with propofals for reducing the
" exceffive rates of coals for the future; and the rife of their grants
" appearing in this book. By Ralph Gardiner, of Chriton, in the
" county of Northumberland, gent. Lond. 1655." 4to.

We have fome few notes of this town in " The Encænia of St.
" Ann's-chappel in Sandgate; or a fermon preached May 3, 1682,
" before the mayor, &c. of the town and county of Newcaftle upon
" Tyne, upon their erecting a fchool, and a catechetical lecture for
" the inftruction of poor children, and fuch as are ignorant. By John
" March, B. D. and vicar of St. Nicholas there. Lond. 1682." 4to.

" The hiftory of Newcaftle upon Tyne, or the antient and prefent
" ftate of the town. By the late Henry Bourne, curate of Allhallows
" in Newcaftle. Newcaftle 1736." Fol. The feal of this corporation
was engraved by the Society of Antiquaries 1741.

A particular relation of the taking of Newcaftle 1644. 4to.

A large N. E. view of the town by Buck 1745. I am informed a
very correct plan was taken foon after the rebellion, by order and at
the expence of the late Duke of Cumberland, and is now in the hands
of Mr. Thompfon of Newcaftle, who drew it.

The lives of the five firft abbots of *Weremouth* and *Jarrow*, written
by Bede in Latin, were publifhed by Sir James Ware at Dublin, 1664.
8vo. with Bede's letter to Egbert, and a preface containing various particulars of his life and writings, illuftrated with fhort and ufeful notes.
Being grown fcarce, Wharton reprinted them, with fome other pieces
of Bede, under the title of " Bedæ venerabilis opera quædam theolo-,
" gica, nunc primum edita, necnon hiftorica antea femel edita: accef-
" ferunt Egberti archiepifcopi Eborac. dialogus de ecclefiaftica infti-
" tutione, & Adhelmi epifcopi Scireburnenfis liber de virginitate ex
" codice antiquiffimo emendatus. Lond. 1693." 4to. Dr. Smith annexed them to his edition of Bede, corrected from three very old MSS.

" Account

" " Account of certain charities, containing a catalogue of feveral be-
" nefactors who have given or left any thing to the church, the poor,
" or freefchool in Tynedale ward, Northumberland." 8vo.

Hexham has been defcribed in the Gentleman's Magazine, July 1755,
p. 297, and *Alnwick* with its neighbourhood in that for Feb. 1756,
p. 73, in anfwer to queries propofed for obtaining a more perfect natural hiftory of England. Whether Hexham has had juftice done it
in this defcription I am not able to determine; but Alnwick is very
fuperficially treated. No mention is made of the old priory, nor the
monuments in the church. King engraved the N. fide of Hexham
church.

" A true report of a ftrange and monfterous child, born at *Aberwich*
" in the parifh of Eglingham, in the county of Northumberland, this
" 5th of January 1580." in one fheet, black letter c.

" A moft pleafant defcription of *Benwell* village, in the county of
" Northumberland. Intermixed with feveral diverting incidents, both
" ferious and comical. Divided into ten books. By Q. Z. late com-
" moner of Oxon. Newcaftle upon Tyne. 1726." 12mo. A defcription of a Sunday's journey to this village in a low ballad ftyle; the humour altogether local. The author was Dr. Ellifon.

" Vallum Romanum: or the hiftory and antiquities of the Roman
" wall, commonly called the Picts wall, in Cumberland and Northum-
" berland, built by Adrian and Severus, the Roman emperors, feventy
" miles in length, to keep out the northern Picts and Scots. In three
" books: I. contains the antient ftate of the wall; with an account of
" the legionary and auxiliary forces employed here in building of it,
" and the 18 cities or ftationary towns ftanding thereon, called the
" Stations per lineam valli, with 81 caftles and 316 forts, ftill vifible.
" II. contains a large account of the prefent ftate of the walls and mi-
" litary roads; more particularly that now re-edifying at a national ex-
" pence, for the paffage of troops and carriages from Carlifle to New-
" caftle upon Tyne. III. contains a compleat collection of the Roman
" infcriptions and fculptures which have been hitherto difcovered on
" or near the wall, with the letters engraved in their proper fhape and
" proportionate fize, and the reading thereof explained in words at

---

c Catalogue of Harleian Pamph. No 517.

" length ;

" length ; as alſo an hiſtorical account of them, with explanatory and
" critical obſervations. Collected and abſtracted from all writers on
" the ſame ſubject, as an inducement to the young nobility and gentry
" of Great Britain to make the tour of their native country before they
" viſit foreign parts : to which are added two letters from the late
" honourable and learned Roger Gale to the compiler, relating to the
" antiquities in the North of England. The whole illuſtrated with a
" map of the walls, military ways and ſtations laid down by a new
" geometrical ſurvey, and near 200 other ſculptures on copper plates.
" By John Warburton, eſq; Somerſet herald, and F.R.S. Lond. 1753."
4to. This is no more than d Horſley's account of the walls reprinted
and all the inſcriptions of each ſtation thrown together, as a pocket
companion for thoſe who viſit them. The compiler in company with
Horſley ſurveyed this county, of which he publiſhed a map in 1716,
on three ſheets, with the arms of the nobility and gentry, and a great
number of Roman altars and inſcriptions. He cauſed a ſurvey and plan
of this wall and military way to be made 1715, to ſhew the neceſſity of
repairing the latter ; but on the ſuppreſſion of that rebellion his ſcheme
was no more thought of till the late one revived it, and an act paſſed
1751 to make the road.

A collection of inſcriptions, &c. made about this wall by the late
Mr. Wharton, who was beneficed near it, have been purchaſed ſince
his death by the dean and chapter of Durham for their library. His
MS. account of theſe antiquities was miſlaid. The ſurvey of the wall
in Gibſon's Camden was made by one Mr. Smith of Durham. Dr.
Smith in the appendix to his edition of Bede has a long diſcourſe on
both the walls.

In p. 661 of N° 231 of the Philoſophical Tranſactions is a letter
from Mr. Thoreſby to Dr. Liſter, July 10, 1697, concerning two Roman altars found at *Collerton* and *Blenkintop* caſtle, with notes by Dr.
T. Gale e. In p. 291 of N° 330 is a letter from Dr. H. Todd, Feb. 17,

d Horſley in his Britannia Romana frequently charges Warburton with incorrectneſs
in copying his map ; to which he replies in his preface that they were all ſubmitted to
him before they were engraved, which obliged him to copy his remarks and obſervations
here. Gordon who ſpends the whole 8th chapter of his Itinerarium Septentrionale on this
wall complains of the great inaccuracy of Warburton's tranſcripts.
e See Horſley, p. 218. 231.

1710-

1710-11, to Dr. Halley, giving an account of some Roman antiquities lately found at *Colchester*, a mile west of *Corbridge* [f]. In p. 813 of Nº 356 is an inscription.found in the Picts wall, mentioning the Cattivallani. In Nº 278 are letters from Dr. Hunter concerning some inscriptions and antiquities found about the wall [g]. In p. 161 of Nº 474 are his observations on a Roman inscription at *Rochester* and two at *Rifingham* [h]. In p. 344 of Nº 482 is an explanation of another inscription at *Rutchester* by Dr. Taylor. In p. 215 of Nº 318 is a letter concerning a colliery in *Fatfield* parish near Chester le Street, that took fire and killed 69 persons Aug. 18, 1708, communicated by Dr. Charlet, master of University College. In Nº 130, p. 762, are observations on a subterraneous fire in a coal mine near Newcastle by Dr. Hodgson, physician there: and in p. 221 of Nº 480 an account of a like accident in another coal mine near the same place; of the blue well, and a subterraneous cavern near Weredale. In p. 328 of Nº 377 is the depth of rain fallen from April 1, 1722, to April 1, 1723, observed at *Widdrington* by Mr. Horsley.

In the Gentleman's Magazine, March 1752, p.105, are several inscriptions discovered at *Burdoswald* (Amboglana) and *Carrvorran* (Magna) by Dr. Francis Swinhow: and in that for May 1753, p. 224, others at *Rifingham* castle, communicated by Mr. Lionel Charlton. In that for Oct. 1765, p. 450, is a letter from Mr. Chr. Richardson, describing certain large bones and teeth found in this county.

Morpeth has been celebrated by E. W. in p. 6, 7. of " Poems writ-" ten upon several occasions. Lond. 1711." 8vo.

The late election at Berwick in some pitiful verses called " The " constituents : a poem. By P. Stockdale. Lond. 1765." 4to. Buck published a S. view of the town 1745. Bagford and Nicholson say this and some other places of note in this county are described in a MS. in the earl of Carlisle's library at Naworth.

---

[f] Horsley, p. 245. The Greek inscription Ηρακλει, and large teeth and bones.
[g] See Horsley, p. 217. 219. 221. 225. 228. 236. 240.
[h] The large bas relief and inscription found here in Camden's time, and removed to Connington and since to Trinity Coll. Cambridge, has been engraved by Camden, 351. Dr. Stukeley in an unpublished plate, Horsley, North. 88, and Lamborne, each copy differing though not materially from the other.

Hollar

Hollar engraved a view of *Tinmouth* caftle, town, and fhipping, " with the wrecks of captains Vicars and Grey : more particularly in a " compartment above, fhewing the manner how the water curled and " fmoakt while one of thofe fhips burnt after it funk." 1673. Thorefby mentions a view of the caftle and light-houfe from the N. by F. Place. A view of this caftle and haven, drawn by T. Smith, was engraved by Vivares 174⁶⁄₇.

A N. view of Tinmouth monaftery and caftle ; S. W. Brinkburn priory ; S. E. Alnwick ; S. Prudhoe ; N. Bothal ; W. Chillingham ; S. W. Dunftanburgh ; S. Warkworth ; S. Belfo ; S. E. Horton ; E. Widdrington ; and S. W. Bamburgh caftles by Buck.

A print (20 inches by 15) of a filver plate, wt. 148 oz. found 1735 in Tyne fanvls near Corbridge, now in the poffeffion of the duke of Northumberland, lord of that manor, with the figures of Vefta, Apollo, Ceres, Diana, and Minerva on it, drawn by W. Shaftoe, was engraved by Vandergucht, and dedicated to Charles duke of Somerfet.

Wm. Lodge engraved a view of Newcaftle ; with leffer views of Tinmouth caftle, Alnwick, Holy-ifland, Berwick, Carlifle, and Bernard caftle ; all which were finifhed, and a fpecimen printed before the plate was fpoiled by an accident. In the middle was defigned a map of Northumberland, and at bottom a profpect of Durham of the fame dimenfions with that of Newcaftle [i]

Northumbriæ comitatus (Scotiæ contiguæ) nova veraq. defcriptio, by Saxton, undated, and without the hundreds, fupplied in Speed's map 1610 ; with plans of Newcaftle and Berwick by Wm. Matthew, and four Roman infcriptions, N° 53, 54, and 88 in Horfley.

Another map by Warburton 1716, before-mentioned. A later by T. Kitchen for the Britifh Atlas.

Mr. Robert Cay and his friend Horfley began a map of the county ; but the latter dying before it was finifhed his furveyor continued it. Mr. Cay caufed it to be engraved in two fheets at Edinburgh, for cheapnefs, for the benefit of Mr. Horfley's numerous family, which occafioned its being executed fo very incorrectly that an index was printed to rectify the miftakes. Edinb. 1753. 8vo.

* Walp. Cat, of eng. p. 55.

NOTTING-

NOTTINGHAMSHIRE.

Domesday book for this county was transcribed by sergeant Gilbert Boun, feodary of the county, who made a few short notes upon each town, which Mr. Gervas Pigot of Thrumpton, Boun's son-in-law, communicated to Robert Thoroton [a]. M. D. who, having improved and augmented them according to the plan of Burton's Leicestershire, published " The antiquities of Nottinghamshire, extracted out of re-" cords, original evidences, leiger books, other manuscripts, and au-" thentick authorities ; beautified with maps, prospects, and pourtraic-" tures [b]. Lond. 1677." Fol. It is principally a history of property and epitaphs, divided by the hundreds and towns. The author has not intermixed any observations relating to the British, Roman, and Saxon antiquities, writing only after the printed copy of Burton's book.

Some arms, monuments, &c. collected in this county by E. Ashmole, 166½, are in his library, N° 854. It was visited by Flower 1569 : by St. George 1614.

" Nottinghamia vetus & nova ; or an historical account of the an-" tient and present state of the town of *Nottingham*, gathered from " the remains of antiquity, and collected from authentic MSS. and " antient. as well as modern history : adorned with beautiful copper " plates ; with an appendix, containing besides extracts of wills and " deeds relating to charities divers other curious papers. By Charles " Deering, M. D. Nottingham 1751." 4to. The Doctor published a Catalogue of plants about Nottingham. Nottingham 1738. 8vo.

" Queries and reasons offered by Sir Tho. Parkyns, of Bunny, bart. " why the county-hall, goal, &c. should be built in the county of " Nottingham, and on the new purchased ground for that very pur-" pose, and not in the market-place of the town and county of the " town of Nottingham, and out of the county at large ; and why he

---

[a] Ousely the Essex antiquary was his cousin. Nott. 319.
[b] Most of them drawn by Richard Hall and etched by Hollar 1676.

" could

" could not join with his brethren the justices of the peace in signing
" the order of sessions at Rufford, Apr. 24, 1724. With the addition
" of subordination, or an essay on servants, their rates and wages, and
" the great conveniency which would accrue to every county, by re-
" cording with all the chief constables of the same. The 3d edition,
" with amendments and large additions. Lond. 1724." 4to.

" Castri Nottinghamiensis descriptio" is in p. 75 of " Epigramma-
" twn opusculum duobus libellis distinctum, &c. authore Hunting-
" dono Plumptre, A. M. Cantab. Lond. 1629." 8vo. A plan of it
1617 in Deering's history.

A new plan of Nottingham by John Badder and Tho. Peat, 1744,
with a S. view of the town, and an E. one of the castle, St. Mary's
church, Collins's hospital, the new 'Change, Mr. Plummer's and Mr.
Willoughby's houses, St. Peter's and St. Nicholas' churches, and the
charity school. St. Mary's church in Thoroton is thought to be one
of Hollar's last works. Buck engraved a S. prospect of it 1743.

An account of the hospital of St. Mary Magdalen, near *Scroby* d,
by John Slacke, master, by order of Neile abp. of York, and a letter from Dr. Richardson to Mr. Thoresby about it, are in the appendix
to Langtoft's Chronicle 1725, Nᵒ xvii. p. 207.

Among Ben. Johnson's works is a mask performed at *Welbeck*.

Dr. Rawlinson engraved a lease from the prior and convent of *Wyrksopp* to H. Ellys of the grange and manor of *Shyrokes*, a hamlet in
Wyrksopp, 1438.

For *Newark* we have " An account of the donations to the parish
" of Newark upon Trent, by a Parishioner. Lond. 1748." 4to. on
which were published " Remarks by a m—b—r of p—l—t." Printed
[by one of the churchwardens] not for the author, but the real use
and lasting service of the parishioners. 1751. 4to. This was followed
by " An impartial relation of some late transactions at N——k: containing a full and circumstantial answer to a " late libel, entituled,
" Remarks on a book, entituled, An account of the donations to the
" parish of N——k. 1751." 8vo.

A W. view of the castle, 1726, and a large view of the siege by
Buck. A S. view of the church and W. one of the town by Hollar in
Thoroton.

d In Harworth parish near Bawtry, as Tanner Not. Mon. Nottingh. p. 688.

A nar-

A narrative of a furprifing effect of lightning at *Barton in Fabis*, near Gotham, 1734, is in Peck's Defiderata Curiofa, vol. ii. book xiv. N° 16, p. 54.

A feal found in this county is engraved in the Gentleman's Magazine for June 1753, p. 280.

The hiftory of the collegiate church of *Southwell* may be feen at the end of Dugdale's Hiftory of St. Paul's, 1716. Peck ᵉ gives an account of a body found in the S. aile of this minfter 1717, in a ftone coffin, dreffed in cloth of filver tiffue, with leather boots, a wand by his fide, and on his breaft fomething like the cover of a filver cup with an acorn or bunch of leaves on its top. He fuppofes this one of the family of Cauz, referring to that family in Dugdale's Baronage. The N. W. and N. E. views of this church by Hollar and Rich. Hall, 1672, are in Thoroton , N. and W. profpects of it in the Monafticon, vol. iii. Buck engraved a S. view of the palace 1726.

In p. 963 of N° 360 of the Philofophical Tranfactions is an account of the impreffion of the almoft intire fkeleton of a large animal on a very bard ftone, prefented to the Royal Society by Dr. Stukeley from Nottingham.

Buck's other views for this county are W. Newftead, W. Welbeck, S. W. Radford or Workfop abbies ; W. Thurgarton priory; and the cells in Nottingham park, with the caftle. Thefe cells make the 29th plate of Stukeley's Itinerary ; Agelocum (Littlebury) pl. 87. Ad pontem (by Bridgeford) pl. 90. Margidunum (by Willoughby) pl. 91. the crofs at Willoughby pl. 11.

Thoroton has a view of Radford church, and a miferable S. view of Workfop. The N. and S. views of Workfop manor, built by the firft earl of Shrewfbury, the hero of Henry Vth's wars, by Buck, 1745. A view of the menagery as defigned by the dutchefs of Norfolk, painted by P. Sandby, was exhibited at Spring-gardens 1764; as were two views of Welbeck park and the great tree there by Mr. Barret, 1766. A plan and four views of the great oak called the *Greendale* oak, in the lane near Welbeck, Aug. 31, 1727, have been engraved. A view of lord Byron's park at Newfted, painted by Smith, was engraved by Mafon 1749.

      • Defid. Cur. book vi. N° xvii.

OXFORD.

OXFORDSHIRE.

WE have no compleat general defcription of this county. Large collections for an account of its antiquities are faid to have been made by Randall Catherall, (who died 1625) and communicated to bp. Sanderfon; but after the ftricteft fearches they could not be found. Wood [a] was told the bifhop himfelf had collected the monuments in the county and city; and that Henry Symons his fecretary had them. A copy of Domefday is in Afhmole's library [b]. The county was vifited 1566 by Harvey: 1574 by Lee: 1634 by Philipot and Ryley. Bp. Kennet, who communicated fome obfervations on this county to bp. Gibfon, has fully defcribed fome parts in his " Parochial " antiquities. Oxf. 1695." 4to. This firft volume goes only to 1640: the collections for the other were to be left to the author's fucceffor at Ambrofden. In the appendix is a " Hiftory of *Allchefter* and *Bur-* " *cefter*, in Oxfordfhire, with fuch other occurrents as are contigu- " ous and appendant to the fame, ad Francifcum Crane, eq. aur. auli- " cum, wrote 1622." quoted by Dr. Plot, and at the publication in the hands of Mr. Blackwell of Brampton, Northamptonfhire. Dr. Stukely had unpublifhed plates of *Aldchefter* (Alauna), *Banbury* (Branavis), and *Tame* (Tamefe), 1724. He has defcribed the Britifh circular temple at *Rowldrich* in his Abury, chap. ii. with five plates of it, and had an unpublifhed profpect of it from the fouthern hill.

One Bufhell, who had been lord Bacon's fervant, and applied himfelf much to mineralogy, cleanfing a fpring in his eftate at *Enfton*, difcovered a rock capable of much artificial improvement, which he accordingly beftowed on it, and when Charles I. and his queen vifited this neighbourhood, 1636, he prefented it to her majefty, with all the pageantry of thofe times, of which a detail may be feen in Ath. Ox. II. 526. The fpeeches and fongs on the occafion were printed, Oxf. 1636. The latter were made by Bufhell himfelf, and fet to mufick by Samuel

[a] Athen. Ox. II. 322.
[b] Cat. MSS. Angl. part. i. p. 348, Nº 808.

Ive,

Ive, a celebrated mafter. We fhall hear of Bufhell again in Wales, where he held the place of farmer of the king's minerals.

In Leland's Itinerary, vol. ii. p. 64, is an account of feveral antiquities in and about the Univerfity of Oxford; with obfervations on the mona-fteries of *Ofeney* and *Rewley*, the villages of *Wolvercote* c, *Sandford*, and *Einfham* d, St. Bartholomew's hofpital, and *Godftow* nunnery; of which laft Hearne has given a plan and views, with notes, in p. 769 of the 3d volume of his edition of Neubrigenfis, and an infcription found at Rewley at the end of Leland's It. ii. Mr. Aubrey preferved at his own expence a curious draught of the ruins of Ofeney abbey, where Henry VIII. firft fixed the fee of Oxford, etched by Hollar, and in-ferted in the Monafticon, vol. ii. p. 136, with this infcription: *Infignes hujufce fabricæ ruinas quas antiquitatis ergo plurimum fufpexit adolefcen-tulus jam tunc Oxonienfibus afcriptus (& quod commodum accidit) paulo antequam bello civili funditus e medio tollerentur delineandas curavit pofteris quafi redivivas L. D. C. Q. Joannes Albericus de Efton Pierfe in agro Wilts arm.* Many copies want it. There are an E. and W. view of the remains of S. Ofeney, and four of thofe of N. Ofeney, taken 1720, in-ferted in Hutten's Antiquities of Oxford at the end of Hearne's Textus Roffenfis, and copied in Stevens's Monafticon, vol. ii. p. 51. That filly, confufed, imperfect piece publifhed by Hearne at the end of Roper's Life of More, Ox. 1716. under the name of " Chronicon God-ftovianum," he calls fo only becaufe he met with it in a walk to God-ftow. There is one under this name in the Harleian library, and an antient hiftory of this nunnery among Sir J. Ware's books e. Another W. view of Godftow nunnery by Buck 1729. Hearne's plan is copied in Stevens's Mon. I. 523. An infcription found in the ruins, publifhed by Hearne at the end of Leland's It. ii. with another found 1757 is in the Marmora Oxonienfia 1764. " A poetical picture of its ruins, taken as it fhould feem on the fpot, and worthy the hand of Paul

---

c See p. 7 and 8 of Hearne's pref. to Roffi hiftoria regum Angliæ. Ox. 1716. 8vo.

d See p. 111 and 112 of Hearne's pref. to his edition of Camden's Elizabetha. Wood took a profpect of the abbey juft before it was pulled down 1657. which was lately en-graved from the Afhmolean Mufeum, but without any notice of Wood. See his life, p. 568. note (H).

e Nicholfon Eng. hift. lib. pref.

Bril,"

Bril," is quoted by Mr. Wharton [f] from Carmina Quadragefimalia. Oxon. 1748, p. 5.

A view of *Bampton* caftle by Wood 1664 is in Afhmole's mufeum.

In Hearne's Gul. Neubrigenfis we have remarks on *Binfey* chapel, with a view of it, and fomewhat on *Littlemore* s; alfo on *Goring* church, p. 736, *Heddington* p. 726, *Eynfton* p. 781, *Ofeney* p. 793.

Epitaphs and arms in *Dorchefter* church taken by Wood are among his MSS. 8505. 8548. 8565. 8586.   He alfo drew the church and cloifters, &c. 1657.   A N. view and ichnography of the church is in Stevens's Monafticon, vol. ii. p. 95.   Hearne has preferved fome old infcriptions there in his letter concerning fome antiquities between Windfor and Oxford, reprinted at the end of Leland's Itinerary, vol. ii. Some obfervations on Dorchefter, *Benfington*, and *Ewelme* may be feen p. 258, &c. of the occafional remarks prefixed to the account of Fairford windows publifhed with Roper's life of More.   A profpeċt from Dike hills, Dorchefter, the Britifh curfus, drawn by Dr. Stukeley May 1755, and mentioned in his Stonehenge, p. 43, was engraved by Hulett [h].

The foundation and ftatutes of the alms-houfe at *Ewelme* has been publifhed by Hearne from an old MS. in the Harleian library at the end of his edition of Otterburne, &c. Oxf. 1732. 2 vols. 8vo. p. 541. In §. xi. xii. of his preface to Hemingi chartularium, Oxf. 1723, is an account of coins found on *Harcourt* hill in Ewelme warren, over which the Ickneild ftreet paffes, where he fuppofes was fome Roman building. The antiquities of *Chilfwell*, near Oxford, in the appendix to his Liber niger Scaccarii, Oxf. 1728, p. 599.   An account and draught of a ftone coffin found at *Bowney*, near Henley, was inferted in the Gentleman's Magazine 1751, p. 703.

" The cuftome of the mannor of *Woodftocke*" is publifhed out of bp. Barlow's MSS. Bodl. Nº 9, p. 125, in the preface to the 8th vol of Leland's Itinerary, p. 36—39.   A tranfcript of a very antient roll relating to this manor, t. Edw. I. is at the end of Hearne's edition of Robert de Avefbury. Oxf. 1720.

[f] Effay on the Genius of Pope. p. 21.
[g] Alfo in his Hiftory of Glaftonbury, p. 16—23
[h] This was placed by miftake in Dorfetfhire.

" The

" The Woodſtock ſcuffle; or moſt dreadful apparitions, that were
" lately ſeen in the manor houſe at Woodſtock near Oxford, to the
" great terror and wonderfull amazement of all that there did behold
" them. 1649." 4to. a poem, in one ſheet, inſerted in Plot's Hiſtory
of Oxfordſhire and the Gentleman's Magazine for 1762, p. 63, ridi-
culing the parliament commiſſioners, who were bitterly frightned,
till having accidentally burnt their rent-roll they were obliged to return
without doing their buſineſs.　See alſo a letter about it from Liddall to
Aubrey in " Miſcellanies on ſeveral curious ſubjects. 1714." p. 13.
and " The juſt devil of Woodſtock; or a true narrative of the ſeveral
" apparitions, the frights and puniſhments that were inflicted upon
" the rumpiſh commiſſioners ſent thither to ſurvey manors and houſes
" belonging to his majeſty." Lond. 1649. 4to. a diary kept by one
Widdowes, parſon of Woodſtock, and printed 1660, after his death,
though 1649 ſtands in the title page.　Wood ſays " this book is very
impartially written, and therefore worth the reading by all, eſpecially
the many atheiſts of this age."　So groſly was the credulity of that
enthuſiaſtic age impoſed upon by the contrivance of Joe Collins, an
artful fellow, who carried on the whole affair by a few chymical pre-
parations, having hired himſelf to the commiſſioners for ſecretary.
Widdowes wrote likewiſe " A ſhort ſurvey of Woodſtock," taken from
antient authors, and printed with the above-mentioned piece.

A poem on Woodſtock park, by W. [i] Harriſon, 1706, is in Dodſley's
Miſcellanies, vol. v. p. 188.

Hearne wrote " A diſcourſe concerning the *Stunsfeld* teſſellated
" pavement, &c. diſcovered near Woodſtock Jan. 25, 17$\frac{1}{4}$." prefixed
to vol. viii. of Leland's Itinerary, with an exact draught of it, much
correcter than a larger coloured one.　John Pointer, M. A. chaplain
of Merton college in Oxford, and rector of Slapton in Northamptonſhire, attacked this in " An account of a Roman pavement late-
" ly found at Stunsfield, in Oxfordſhire, proved to be 1400 years
" old. Oxf. 1713." 8vo.　The diſpute regarded the figure on the
pavement, which Pointer would have to be Bacchus, and Hearne,

---

[i] It ſhould be Thomas.　He was of Queen's coll. Oxf. ſecretary to the embaſſy at
Utrecht, and died of an inflammatory fever ſoon after.　See Swift's letters by Dr. Hawkſ-
worth, vol. i. lett. 79. 83.

Apollo.

Apollo   The former fupported his opinion with a few witticifms and puns, and was animadverted on and refuted from good authorities by the latter in his preface to Leland's Collectanea.   The pavement was engraved by Vertue 1712.

Dr. Plot's " Natural hiftory of Oxfordfhire; being an effay towards " the natural hiftory of England. Oxf. 1677." Fol. touches very flightly on its antiquities.   A fecond edition with additions and corrections was printed at Oxford 1705. Fol. after the doctor's death by his fon-in-law Mr. Burman [f], fellow of Univerfity Coll. who prefixed a fhort life of the author.   In the epiftle dedicatory he feems to promife a like account of the other counties, but performed only that of Staffordfhire.

Dr. Rawlinfon, who brought many MS. defcriptions of counties to light, intended a defcription of this county fome years ago, and collected great materials, had many plates engraved, an actual furvey taken, and printed queries circulated; which in fome degree anfwered the defign, and encouraged him to purfue it.   In this work were to be included the antiquities of the city of Oxford, which Wood [g] promifed when the Englifh copy of his Hiftoria & Antiquitates Oxon. was to be publifhed, and which have fince been faithfully transcribed from his papers, and much enlarged and corrected from antient original authorities [h].   Camden's collections of the monuments in the churches and chapels were in the hands of Henry St. George.

" An account of the charity fchool in Oxford (maintained by the " voluntary fubfcriptions of the vice-chancellor, heads of houfes, and " other members of the univerfity) for two years, viz. from the feaft " of St. Michael 1707, to the feaft of St. Michael 1709. Oxf. 1710."

The vault under the chancel of St. Peter's church, intended for a burying place by Grymbald, who built the church [i], the old font now turned out and put over a well, and the church itfelf, of which the E. end is fuppofed to be the original building, are engraved in three plates in the preface to Leland's Collectanea, p. 21, 29.

[f] Who died vicar of Newington and Bobington in Kent April 13, 1726. ætat. 45.

[g] In p. 28 of the fecond volume of his Athenæ.

[h] Hearne printed in the appendix to Liber niger Scaccarii, p. 571, fome notes relating to this hiftory by Wood in a MS. of his own writing in Hearne's poffeffion ; a medley of memorandums, quæries, notes croffed out and inferted in other books, &c.

[i] In the reign of Alfred, when building with ftone was fo uncommon that people came from far and near to fee this church, which was efteemed a fine piece of work.

In p. 88 of Hearne's preface to Neubrigenfis are two views[k] of the ruins of Oxford caftle, defcribed p. 38. A N. view by Buck 1729. Dr. Rawlinfon engraved the feals of the Whitefriars or Carmelites in his poffeffion: alfo 1753 a grant of lands by Rob. d'Oyley temp. Wm. Conq. to St. George's college in this caftle: alfo 1754 a N. view of St. Giles's church, built before 1189, where antiently degrees were conferred; and the vault and infcription in the N. aile intended for himfelf. Hearne printed a prefentation of Wm. Marclogh to this vicarage by the nuns of Godftow about 1480, appendix to Caius, N° v.

Stürt engraved a view of All-fouls church, with propofals for a tower by N. Hawkfmoor.

The N. fide of Chrift church by King and Harris.

The oldeft plan of the city of Oxford extant is that included in R. Aggas's plan of the Univerfity 1578[m].

Another cut in wood temp. Hen. VII. mentioned by the Oxford antiquary, who fhewed it Dodwell, is now loft.

Hollar engraved on one fheet a ground plot of it from the E. with the arms of the colleges. A plan of the city with its fortifications while it was a garrifon for the king in the civil wars, was drawn by Henry Sherburne (younger brother to Edward who tranflated Manilius); and this, or another drawn by Rich. Rallingfon, was engraved by the care of bp. Fell, and inferted in the Hiftoria & Antiq Univ. Oxon. p. 364[n]. There is another plan by Wm. Jackfon, Geo. Anderton, and Ifaac Taylor, with views of the city from the Park and Haddington hill; Magdalen college new building from the Grove; the Radcliffe library and Exeter college S. W. A view by Buck 1731.

Hearne printed in the appendix to the Annales de Dunftaple, N° 7 and 8, a copy of John and Henry IIId's charter of liberties and privileges to this city from the regifter of Ofeney abbey, copied by Mr. Hare, among his MSS. in the library at Caius coll. Cambridge.

---

[k] One of the caftle intire from Aggas's plan, the other taken by King during the civil war.

[l] A tranfcript of its ftatutes is among Wood's MSS.

[m] Wood was in vain follicited to illuftrate with his notes a new edition of it. The Univerfity revived the intention fince, but never executed it. Hearne's preface to Rofs, p. 11.

[n] Wood's Faft. II. 19.

To

To Cogan's " Haven of health." Lond. 1587. 1605. 1612. 4to. is annexed " A prefervative from the peftilence, with a fhort cenfure of the late ficknefs at Oxford." [in 1575] p. Dr. Birch publifhed in the Philofophical Tranfactions, vol. li. p. 699, an account of the black affize, from Merton Coll. regifters, with remarks. The morbus campeftris, or epidemical diforder that raged here in 1643, while the king and court were here, is treated of in " Morbus epidemicus an. 1643, " or the new difeafe, with figns, caufes, remedies, &c. Ox. 1643." by Dr. Edw. Greaves, younger brother to John Greaves, and phyfician in ordinary to Charles II. q.

" News from the dead : or a true and exact narration of the mira-
" culous deliverance of Anne Greene, who being executed at Oxford
" Dec. 14, 1650, afterwards revived ; and by the care of certain phy-
" ficians there, is now perfectly recovered. Together with the man-
" ner of her fuffering, and the particular means ufed for her recovery.
" Written by a fcholar in Oxford [Richard Watkins, of Chrift church r]
" for the fatisfaction of a friend, concerning the truth of the bufinefs.
" Whereunto are annexed certain poems caufually written on that
" fubject." Oxf. 1650. 4to. twice printed that year, and reprinted in Morgan's Phœnix Britannicus, p. 233. Wood, or his elder brother, wrote fome lines on her s.

" A ftrange relation of a fudden and violent tempeft which hap-
" pened at Oxford May 31, 1682. Together with an inquiry into the
" probable caufe and ufual confequences of fuch like tempefts and
" ftorms. Ox. 1682." 4to. By Robert Harrifon t.

" An addrefs to the freemen and other inhabitants of the city of
" Oxford. Lucern, printed for Abraham Lightholder." [1764.] 4to.
A humorous reprefentation of the inconveniencies of the dark and dirty ftreets of this city, equally applicable to Cambridge.

p Ath. Ox. I. 342.
q Ath. Ox. II. 669.
r Wood's Fafti. II. 59. Dr. Derham, Phyfico-theol. p. 157, by miftake, afcribes it to Dr. Ralph Bathurft, who only prefixed fome lines.
s See his life, p. 483.
t Wood's Fafti. II. 219.

At

At the end of Boyle's Hiſtory of the air, 1692. 8vo. is a regiſter of the changes of the air obſerved at Oxford from June 24, 1660, to March 28, 1677. In the Philoſophical Tranſactions, Nº 10, p. 166, is Dr. Wallis's and Nº 11, p. 199, Mr. Boyle's account of an earthquake near Oxford. In Nº 13, p. 222, the former's relation of lightning there. In Nº 135, p. 863, are extracts of ſeveral letters from Dr. Wallis concerning the meteor ſeen in and near Oxford and elſewhere in England Sept. 20, 1676. In Nº 151, p. 310, is an account of the earthquake at and near Oxford Sept. 17, 1683, by Thomas Pigott, of Wadham Coll. vicar of Yarnton, near Oxford. In Nº 366, p. 229, Dr. Langwith's account of a rainbow ſeen on the ground in this county. In Nº 200, p. 756, epiſtola E. Lhuydii ad D. Chr. Hemmer de lapidibus aliquot perpetua figura donatis quas nuperis annis in Oxonienſi vicinis agris adinvenit. In Nº 169, p. 930, is a hiſtory of the weather at Oxford 1684, or obſervations of a full year, made by Dr. Plot by order of the philoſophical ſociety there. In vol. lii. part i. art. 16. an account of an anthelion obſerved by John Swinton, D. D. of Chriſt church. Art. 18. is a relation of a remarkable meteor ſeen near Oxford Sept. 21, 1760, by the ſame gentleman; whoſe account of two more ſeen at Oxford March 5. and April 23, 1764, (the firſt an aurora auſtralis) are in vol. liv. p. 326. 333.

Buck engraved an E. view of Eynſham abbey; S. W. Cold Norton, S. W. Clattercote, and N. Minſter Lovel priories; S, E. Ewelme palace, and N. E. Boughton caſtle.

A plan of the vaults in *Bleinheim* houſe was inſerted in the Gentleman's Magazine, 1750, p. 83. The E. front drawn orthographically engraved by J. Harris. Another view by Maurer and Fourdrinier 1745. N. and N. W. views of the houſe and high lodge by Boydell 1752.

" Bleinheim, a poem, inſcribed to the r. hon. Robert Harley, eſq; " Lond. 1705." Fol. Another in Dodſley's Miſcell. vol. ii. p. 21.

A view of lord Litchfield's ſeat at *Ditchley*, drawn and engraved by Sullivan.

Saxton's map of this county, including Bucks and Berkſhire, was made 1574; but wants the hundreds, which are ſupplied, with a plan of the city and arms of the colleges, in Speed's map 1710.

A new

A new map was published 1715, with views of the public fchools, Stunsfield pavement, the city from the E. and Blenheim houfe and bridge.

A new improved map by T. Kitchen for the Britifh Atlas.

An actual furvey, with views of public buildings and of the city.

Univerfity of Oxford.

The firft general account of the Univerfity is a parcel of rhyming verfes by one Trevytlan or Trevytham, a Francifcan friar, publifhed by Hearne at the end of Hiftoria vitæ Ric. II. p. 344.

Thomas Cay's defence of it againft the public orator of Cambridge was firft printed, with John Caius' refutation of it, by Bynneman 1568. 4to. again under the title of " Affertio antiquitatis Oxonienfis academiæ " incerto authore ejufdem gymnafii : ad illuftriff. reginam anno 1566. " Jam nuper ad verbum cum priore [t] edita; cum fragmento Oxonienfis " hiftoriolæ. Additis caftigationibus authoris marginalibus ad afterifcum " pofitis. Inter quas libri titulus eft, qui ante caftigationem (quam edi- " tionem fecundam dicimus) nullus erat. Omnia prout ab ipfis authoris " exemplaribus accepimus, bona fide commiffa formulis. Lond. 1574." 4to. Hearne republifhed it with his " Vindiciæ antiquitatis academiæ Oxonienfis contra Joannem Caium Cantabrigienfem," from the ori- ginal MS. with additions to the Affertio by the author, and other curious papers. Ox. 1730. An account of her majefty's entertainment at this vifit was printed in Peck's Defiderata, II. vii. p. 46. Another more particular, intitled " Commentarii five ephemeræ actiones rerum " illuftrium Oxonii geftarum in adventu fereniffimæ principis Elizabe- " thæ: ad ampliffimos viros dom. Gul. Broke dom. de Cobham & dom. " Gul. Petreum regium a fanctioribus fecretis confiliarium, per J. B. " [Johannem Bereblock [u]] collegii ibidem Exonienfis focium." was printed by Hearne at the end of Hiftoria vitæ Ric. II. Oxf. 1729, from a MS. in the hands of Mr. Ward of Warwick. A third by R.

[t] John Cay's refutation.

[u] A Kentifh man, admitted at St. John's 1560: an excellent draughtfman, who drew the views of the colleges hereafter mentioned, and one of the city of Rochefter extant in Wood's time.

Stephens

Stephens is among Baker's Harleian MSS. 7033. The relation of her grand reception and entertainment 1592, written by Mr. Stringer, one of the gentlemen that attended lord Burleigh, then chancellor of Cambridge, is at the end of Peck's life of Cromwell, N° iv.

"D. Tho. Mori epiſtola ad acad Oxon. de ſcholaſticis quibuſdam "Trojanos ſeſe appellantibus," a ſet of men who oppoſed the ſtudy of Greek 1519, was firſt printed by Richard James among "Poemata quædam in mortem R. Cottoni & T. Alleni. Ox. 1633." 4to. and ſince by Hearne with Roper's life of More. Ox. 1716.

Hearne publiſhed 1713 "Collegium ſcholarumque publicarum aca- "demiæ Oxonienſis topographica delineatio per Thomam Nelum," from a Bodleian MS. intitled, "Dialogus in adventum reginæ ſere- niſſimæ dominæ Elizabethæ gratulatorius, inter eandem reginam & dom. Rob. Dudleium comitem Leceſtriæ & Oxon. acad. cancella- rium;" wrote in Latin verſe, and preſented to the queen on her firſt viſit to the Univerſity. It contains views of all the colleges before 1590 (in which year the author died) drawn by Bereblock; that of the old ſchools is engraved in the notes to Hearne's edition of Fierebert, p. 124. Some part of this delineation was wrote by Miles Wyndſor, M. D. grandſon to lord Wyndſor, who intended to write the antiquities of the Univerſity: but that being undertaken by Brian Twyne he gave him his papers, and was thought to have had a hand in his Apologia[x]. Both their collections[y] are in the library of C. C. C. where they were fellows.

Henry Lyte wrote about 1592 "The myſtical Oxon of Oxford, alias a true and moſt antient record of the original of Oxford, and all Britain; or rather thus: certain brief conjectural notes touching the original of the Univerſity of Oxford, and alſo of all Britain, called Al- bania and Calydonia ſilva." MS. abounding, ſays Wood[z], with "pro- per fancies, which may be of ſome uſe by way of reply for Oxon againſt the farfetcht antiquities of Cambridge."

[x] Ath. Ox. I. 489.
[y] Among Twyne's are the collections of his father John, a good antiquary but a vio- lent papiſt, ſchool-maſter, and mayor of Canterbury 1553. Seven years after he had ſerved this office he was "ordered to abſtain from riot and drunkenneſs, and not to in- termeddle with any public office in the town." Miſc. C. C. C. C. Tanner.
[z] Ath. Ox. I. 343.

2　　　　　　　　　　　　　　　　　　　　A diſ-

A difcourfe of the antiquity of the Univerfity of Oxford, by way of
" letter to a friend, written by Dr. Hutten, canon of Chrift church,
" 1599." printed at the end of Hearne's Textus Roffenfis, p. 275--278.
gives an account of the city and univerfity, but not of the colleges particularly. In the appendix, N° vii. p. 392, is an account of the author
from Wood, who charges him with ftealing from Twyne: againft which
Hearne defends him, pref. p. 38. Wood mentions [a] another MS. on
the fame fubject, divided into three books, taken chiefly from Twyne,
which he'had feen in the hands of a fellow of Brazen-nofe. Hutten
left in MS. " Hiftoria fundationum ecclefiæ Chrifti, Ox. una cum epifcoporum, decanorum & canonicorum catalogo."

" Nicolai Fiereberti [b] Oxonienfis in Anglia academiæ defcriptio ad
" perilluftrem & reverendiff. D. D. Bernardum Paulinum, S. D. N.
" Clementis VII. datarium. Romæ 1602." 12mo. This being very
fcarce, and containing many circumftances not to be met with elfewhere, was reprinted in Leland's Itinerary, vol. ix. p. 100.

Albericus Gentilis, an Italian refugee and profeffor of law at Oxford,
wrote " Laudes academiæ Parifienfis & Oxonienfis. Hanov. 1605." 8vo

An account of James the Firft's entertainment here was printed under the title of " Rex Platonicus, five de potentiffimi principis Jacobi
" Britanniarum regis ad illuftriffimam academiam Oxonienfem adventu
" Aug. 27, 1605, narratio ab Ifaaco Wake [c] publico academiæ ejuf-
" dem oratore tunc temporis confcripta, nunc iterum in lucem edita,
" multis in locis auctior, & multo emendatior. Editio fexta. Oxon.
" 1663." 12mo. The firft edition was at Oxford 1607. 4to. in
which are interfperfed feveral remarkable obfervations on the antient
and prefent ftate of the univerfity. John Sandfbury, fellow of St.
John's, addreffed another compliment to James in Latin verfe, under
the arms of each college, intitled " Ilium in Italian: Oxonia ad pro-
" tectionem regis fui omnium optimi filia pedifequa. Ox. 1608." 12°.

---

[a] Ath. Ox. I. 571

[b] Grandfon of Sir Anth. Fitzherbert the great lawyer: his epitaph at Florence is
printed at the end of Domerham, p. 724.

[c] He was afterwards James's embaffador *extraordinary* in Savoy and Piedmont, *ordinary* for Italy, Helvetia, and Rhetia, *felect* for France, 1719; and left difcourfes on the
ftate of the Swifs Cantons and Italy. Ath. Ox. I. 574.

Brian

Brian Twyne was the firſt that treated the affairs of this Univerſity like a profeſſed antiquary, for which he was rewarded with the place of keeper of its archives. His "Antiquitatis academiæ Oxonienſis apologia, in 3 libros diviſa," was printed Ox. 1608. He intended a 2d edition with large additions, but his interleaved copy is ſuppoſed to be loſt during our civil confuſions. Hearne boaſts that he has defended the antiquity of Oxford with irrefragable and undeniable proofs: yet Twyne allowed the authority of that MS. that makes againſt it [c].

Dr. Langbaine, who ſucceeded him in his office, wrote "The "foundation of the Univerſity of Oxford, with a catalogue of the "principal founders, &c. 1651." 4to. as he did that of Cambridge before-mentioned.

In the appendix to Hearne's Annales de Dunſtaple, Nº ix. is an account of the muſterings of the Univerſity of Oxford, with other things that happened there, from Aug. 9, 1642, to June 15, 1653, incluſively: from an original MS. that belonged to Wood, written as it ſeems by Brian Twyne.

Under the adminiſtration of the parliament appeared "Pegaſus, or "the flying horſe from Oxford; bringing the proceedings of the viſitors "and other Bedlamites there, by the command of the earl of Mont- "gomery. Printed at Montgomery, heretofore called Oxford;" in one ſheet, 4to. 1648, written by way of letter dated Oxford Apr. 18, 1648, by Dr. John Barlow, of Queen's. With it was printed a ſecond part in another letter of one ſheet and half, dated Oxf. Apr. 17, 1648, ſigned Baſilius Philomuſus, as Dr. Pierce ſubſcribed the third and fourth parts of "Pegaſus taught by Bankes his ghoſt to dance in the Doric "mood to the tune of lachrymæ, in two letters from Oxford, July 1, 1648." one ſheet 4to. [d].

"Tragicomœdia Oxonienſis. 1648." 4to. one ſheet: a Latin poem on the proceedings of the parliament's viſitors, by Adam Littleton, author of the Dictionary [e].

"Ruſtica academiæ Oxonenſis nuper reformatæ deſcriptio: una cum "comitiis ibidem 1648, habitis," by Dr. Allibond, maſter of the free-

[c] See his letter to Camden. Camd. ep. cccxxi.
[d] Ath. Ox. II. 859. 877.   [e] Ib. II. 915.

ſchool

fchool near Magdalen Coll. and rector of Bradwell, Gloucefterfhire, twice printed.

" Anfwer of the chancellor, mafters, and fchollars of the Univerfity " of Oxford to the petition, and articles of grievance, and reafons of " the city of Oxford, prefented to the committee for regulating the " Univerfity of Oxford, 25 July, 1649. Oxf. 1649." 4to. reprinted 1678. By Dr. Langbaine [f].

" The cafe of the Univerfity of Oxford; fhewing that the city is " not concerned to oppofe the confirmation of their charters by parlia- " ment. Prefented to the hon. houfe of commons on Friday the 24th " of January 16$\frac{8}{9}$. Oxf. 1690." Fol. and 4to. By James Harrington : as are alfo another " Cafe of the Univerfity of Oxford," on one fheet ; and " A defence of the rights and privileges of the Univerfity of Ox- " ford ; containing an account of the petition of the city. of Oxford, " 1649." Oxf. 1690. 4to. [g].

In 1664 Mr. Fulman [h] publifhed his " Notitia Oxonienfis acade- " miæ," and another edition, very much corrected and augmented. Lond. 1675. both in 4to. In the laft the dedication to the Spanifh embaffador was omitted [i].

But we owe the moft compleat work to that induftrious antiquary Anthony a Wood, whofe " Hiftoria & antiquitates Univerfitatis Ox- " onienfis duobus voluminibus comprehenfæ. Oxon. è Theatro Shel- " doniano. 1674." Fol. was publifhed at the expence of the Univerfity. The firft volume contains the antiquities of the Univerfity in chronolo- gical order to 1648 ; the fecond, thofe of the colleges. It was wrote

---

[f] Ath. Ox. II. 220.
[g] Ath. Ox. II. 909.
[h] He was a native of Penfhurft in Kent, ejected from his fcholarfhip in C. C. C. Ox. by the parliament vifitors 1648 : after the reftoration he was chofen fellow, and pre- fented to the rectory of Meyfey Hampton, Glouc. where he refided till his death, in ftudious retirement, carelefs about preferment fince it did not court him. Burnet's Hif- tory of the Reformation received his corrections, which were publifhed in the appendix to the fecond volume; but not without great alteration. He publifhed under bp. Fell's patronage the firft volume of the Hiftoriæ Anglicanæ Scriptores; was prevented by the fmall pox from writing a life of Charles I. to be prefixed to his works, and by indo- lence from compleating the lives of Hales of Eton and bp. Fox. Ath. Ox. II. 823.
[i] Bp. Nicholfon quotes 21 vols. in the Cotton library, Fauft. C. 7. relating to the an- tiquities of this Univerfity, but they can be only fo many tracts in the fame volume.

in

in Englifh; but bifhop Fell [k] employed Wafe and Peers to tranflate it into Latin, and was alfo at the expence of printing it, when it could not be done by fubfcription. Wood in feveral paffages of his Athenæ complains heavily of the liberties taken in this tranflation, which was modelled intirely by the bifhop, who not only corrected and almoft compofed it, but inferted and left out paffages as he pleafed, fo that he was obliged almoft to difclaim the whole [m], and determined to publifh that other work juft as he wrote it. He had 100 l. for the original from the delegates of the printing-houfe, of whom the bifhop was one, and for that he was to furnifh them witn tranfcripts of the original charters, and the very words of the authors cited by him, alfo with the lives of the writers belonging to their refpective houfes, and the hiftory of all the religious houfes, and fraternities in Oxford, fo that while this tranflation was in hand, his life, he tells us, was day and night in a continual agitation. Mr. Wharton, who had examined the original Englifh MS. now in the tower of the fchools in two volumes folio, as tranfcribed by the author for the prefs, laments that the bifhop ever propofed this tranflation, which is both incorrect and affected; whereas in the plain natural drefs of its artlefs, but accurate, author, it would have been infinitely more pleafing. His lordfhip's defign was to circulate a complete account of the Univerfity in foreign parts. But there are many unavoidable particulars which read ridiculoufly and often unintelligibly, in Latin. The minutenefs of local defcriptions, fo interefting to an Englifh reader, and perfons familiarly acquainted with the fpot, appears fuperfluous and tirefome to others. A more

[k] He introduced Wood to abp. Sheldon at Lambeth as a mafter of arts who had done the Univerfity a great deal of honour by this book.

[l] Particularly in the account of Hobbes, whom Wood informed of it, pointing out the paffages. Hobbes publifhed this to the world in a Latin letter to Wood, dated April 20, 1674, full of warm and bitter complaints againft the bifhop; who immediately publifhed an anfwer, afferting that the article in the Englifh copy was not wrote by Wood, but by Hobbes himfelf, or his great friend and difciple Aubrey. This fpirited but abufive anfwer he annexed to his edition of the Hiftoria & Antiquitates Oxoniæ. Wood pofitively affirms in his Athenæ, II. 645. that he himfelf wrote the article relating to Hobbes.

[m] See his lives of Fell and Peers, Ath. Ox. II, 799. 853. and his life by himfelf, p. 594, and 602, 603. in which laft page he fathers a ftrange abufe of Wickliff on the bifhop.

general

general and compendious detail might have been abftracted and tranflated for foreign ufe ⁿ. Bp. Barlow in two of his letters pointed out
fome grofs miftakes both in the hiftory and tranflation ᵒ. But the beft
examination of it was by the learned William Fulman, who fent the
author his additions, emendations, and expurgations, which with a large
and full index, collected by Wood, remain among the numerous collections in his library. The 2d edition of Fulman's book contains many
additions and corrections from Wood's two works, the feveral fheets
of which were fent him by the author as foon as they were worked
off. Burnet having fallen upon feveral paffages of Wood's writings,
in his anfwer to H. Wharton, who in an attack upon the Hiftory
of the Reformation under the name of Harmer, made Wood a
party, the latter under another feigned name ᵖ publifhed " A vin-
" dication of the hiftoriographer of the Univerfity of Oxford, and
" his works from the reproaches of the lord bp. of Salifbury, in his
" letter to the lord bifhop of Coventry and Litchfield, concerning a
" book lately publifhed, called A fpecimen of fome errors and de-
" fects in the Hiftory of the reformation of the church of England, by
" Anthony Harmer. Written by E. D. (20 Mar. 1622.) To which
" is added the hiftoriographer's anfwer to certain animadverfions made
" in the before-mentioned Hiftory of the reformation, to that part of
" Hiftoria & Antiquitates univerfitatis Oxon.. which treats of the di-
" vorce of Q. Catherine from K. Henry the Eighth. Lond. 1693." 4to.
and prefixed to the laft edition of the Athenæ, though without the initials
or date. A copy corrected by Wood himfelf as defigned for the prefs
before the licenfer handled it, is in his mufeum at Oxford, among
his printed books, Tract. 7. Nᵒ 614.

William of Worcefter, who was educated at Hart-hall 1434, drew
up a hiftory of the learned men educated at Oxford, intitled, " Poly-
andria Oxonienfis," of which Twyne publifhed an extract in his Apologia I. 11. § 144. But the fulleft hiftory of the members of this uni-

---

ⁿ Life of Bathurft, p. 146.
ᵒ P. 181. 183 of his genuine remains publifhed by Sir Peter Pett 1693. 12mo.
ᵖ Ath. Ox. II. 874.

verfity

verfity is tranfmitted to pofterity by an hiftoriographer who fpared neither friend nor foe, but with an unwearied induftry has thrown together, though not in the beft method, or moft agreeable ftyle, a ufeful fyftem of Englifh biography in " Athenæ Oxonienfes: an exact " hiftory of all the writers and bifhops who have had their education " in the moft famous univerfity of Oxford, from the 15th year of " Henry the Seventh, A. D. 1500, to the end of the year 1690; re- " prefenting the birth, fortune, preferment, and death of all thofe au- " thors and prelates; the great accidents of their lives, and the fate " and character of their writings : To which are added, the Fafti or " annals of the faid univerfity for the fame time. In two volumes. " Lond. 1692." Fol. To the firft volume is prefixed the author's account of himfelf with his head in a border at the top, inferted in very few copies, and thofe moftly prefents from himfelf. This head was copied and prefixed to " Mifcellanies on feveral curious fubjects, 1714;" where may be feen the proceedings of the univerfity againft him 1692, for infinuations of bribery and corruption againft their chancellor Edward earl of Clarendon, when chancellor of the kingdom. Wood defended himfelf in a fhuffling manner, alledging that the licenfer was anfwerable for all that was in the book after it had paffed through his hands; that Bennet the London bookfeller, Mr. Harrington, abp. Tillotfon, &c. had altered the MS. as they pleafed ; that the paffage referred to chancellor Lifle, and that he himfelf neither was, nor had been confidered as a member of the univerfity for near 20 years paft. This defence not being proved to the fatisfaction of the univerfity, they condemned it, together with a copy of the 2d volume containing thefe infinuations, to be publicly burnt in the theatre-yard, and banifhed the author as a difturber of the peace, befides fining him 35 l. which was laid out on the two ftatues of Charles I. and lord Danby at the phyfic-garden gate. Mr. Anftis gave Dale the herald, without keeping copies of them, many original letters from Wood to Sir Peter Pett, king's advocate for Ireland, about his method of defending himfelf againft thefe profecutions[q]. Mr. Harrington of Chrift Church, who wrote the preface to the 1ft and introduction to the

[q] Hearne's notes at the end of Caius, p. 806.

2d volume of the Athenæ, having publifhed " A vindication of Wood, Lond. 1693." Dr. Pope, in his life of bp Ward, fell upon this book, which was defended in an appendix to the fame life, in a letter to the author, 1697. 8vo. The Athenæ were reprinted 1721 in two volumes folio, continued down to Wood's death 1695, from the copy now de-pofited in the Mufæum Afhmoleanum, in which the author had with his own hand inferted a great number of additions and amendments; and 500 new lives were communicated to the editors by bifhop Tanner, to whom Wood on his death-bed bequeathed it[r]. He intended to have thrown thefe additional lives and the innumerable corrections of the two firft volumes into a third, to which his own life by him-felf was to have been prefixed, and the whole to have been printed abroad. The corrections relative to the Welch bifhops, communicated by Dr. Humphreys, bifhop of Bangor, were printed at the end of Caii Vindiciæ, p. 605—678, by Hearne, who received them from Mr. Baker, and he from bifhop Kennet. Dr. Rawlinfon bequeathed to the Univerfity, on condition the trunks were not opened till feven years after his deceafe[s], [1755] his own collections for a continuation of the Athenæ and Hiftory of Oxford; a fit fupplement to Wood!

" The life of Mr. Anthony à Wood (from the time of his birth, " Dec. 17th, 1632, to July 6, 1672) written by himfelf, and now firft " printed from a copy, tranfcribed by the publifher from the original " in the hands of the rev. Dr. Thomas Tanner," was publifhed by Hearne in the 2d volume of Caii Vindiciæ This is in good meafure extracted, with enlargements by Wood, from his Diary, the firft part of which to 1659 is preferved in the Harleian library, N° 5409, given to lord Oxford by Mr. Anftis 1712, who had it from Dale: the other part was never found. It abounds with anecdotes and charac-ters[t] of the writer's cotemporaries, and particularly of the moft eminent muficians,

[r] Hearne affects to call this a fpurious edition, though Mr. Baker thought otherwife. Preface to Caii Vindiciæ, § 29. 34. App. to Heming's Chartulary, p. 671, 672.
[s] Wood took the fame precaution about his private papers.
[t] Among thofe who with him attended the noted chymift and roficrufian Peter Staehl's chymical lectures 1663 was John Lock, of Chrift church, " afterwards a noted writer,

a man

muſicians ᵘ, with whom he conſorted, having a " natural and inſatiable genie to muſick ˣ;" which with the " rare books he found in the publick library made his life a perfect elyſium ʸ. Wood's father was a civilian of ſome little property at Oxford, deſcended from a younger branch of a wealthy family, and died there aged 62, 1642, leaving Anthony and Chriſtopher by a ſecond wife, and three other ſons by a former. Our antiquary continued at Tame freeſchool till his admiſſion at Merton 1647. His mother in vain endeavoured to prevail on him to follow ſome trade or profeſſion : his prevailing turn was to antiquity : " heraldry, muſic, and painting did ſo much croud upon him that he could not avoid them ; and he could never give a reaſon why he ſhould delight in thoſe ſtudies, more than others ; ſo

a man of a turbulent ſpirit, clamorous, and never contented. The club wrote notes from their maſter's mouth, but he ſcorned to do it ; ſo that while every man elſe was writing he would be prating and troubleſome," p. 558.—A man of more credulity than Locke would laugh at a Roſicrucian !—When Wood was recommended to Wm. Prynne, 1667, for a peruſal of the Tower records, he " received him with old-faſhioned compliments, ſuch as were uſed in the raigne of James I. and ſeemed to be glad that ſuch a young man, as he called him, ſhould have inclination towards venerable antiquity :" calling again next morning at eight by appointment, he found Prynne " in his black taffaty cloak, edged with black lace at the bottom : they went together from Lincoln's-inn to the tower through the city, then lying in ruins ; but by his meeting with ſeveral citizens and prating with them it was ten before they got there," p. 573. Aubrey meeting at Oxford with the Notitia Acad. Oxon. falſely aſcribed to Wood, and having been cotemporary with his elder brother at Trinity Coll. would needs be acquainted with him. " He was then in a ſparkiſh garb, lived high, and flung out Wood at all reckonings : but his eſtate of 700 l. per ann. being ſold, and reſerving none of it to live on, he was forced to rub out by hanging on his friends." He calls him " a pretender to antiquity, ſhiftleſs, roving, and magoty headed, and ſometimes little better than crazed, and being exceedingly credulous would ſtuff his many letters to Wood with fooleries and miſinformations." P. 577.

ⁿ " When he learnt on the violin 1656, it had not been uſed in concert among gentlemen ; only by common muſicians who played but two parts. The gentlemen at private meetings which A. W. frequented played 3, 4, and 5 parts, with viols, as treble viol, tenor, counter tenor, and baſs, with an organ, virginals, or harpſichord joined with them ; and they eſteemed a violin to be an inſtrument only belonging to a common fiddler, and could not endure that it ſhould come among them, for fear of making their meetings to be vaine and fidling. But before the reſtoration, and eſpecially after, viols began to be out of faſhion, and only violins uſed, as treble violin, tenor and baſs violin : and the king according to the French mode would have 24 violins playing before him, while he was at meals, as being more airy and briſk than viols." P. 501. When W. waited with letters of introduction on Sir John Cotton for the uſe of his father's library, he found him practiſing on his lute with his inſtructor." P. 572.

ˣ P. 486   ʸ P. 500.

pre-

prevalent was nature, mixed with a generofity of mind and a hatred to all that was fervile, fneaking, or advantageous for lucre fake." His firft effay was a furvey of Bledlow church, Bucks, 1649, and in 1657, 1658 he made a perambulation of Oxfordfhire. As he refided altogether at Oxford he perufed all the evidences of the feveral col- leges z and churches, from which he compiled his two great works, and affifted all who were engaged in the like defigns; at the fame time digefting and arranging all the papers he perufed; thus doing the caufe of antiquity a double fervice : his drawings preferved many things foon after deftroyed. As a collector he deferves highly of pofte- rity : but his narrownefs of mind and furious prejudices are unpardon- able: and we want correctnefs both of judgment and ftyle in his works. Many errors in his Athenæ muft be charged to falfe intelligence : in many articles he could receive no information at all. His tittle-tattle is a picture of the manners of his age; his fcandal holds forth no example but his own depraved mind. The impertinencies and invidious re- flections with which he has ftuffed this book make it more than pro- bable that the bifhop was in fome fort to be juftified in the liberties he took with his Hiftoria & Antiquitates. He died 1695 of a retention of urine, under which he lingered above a fortnight. He left his pa- pers and books to the charge of Dr. Charlett a, Mr. Biffe, and Mr. (afterwards bp.) Tanner, to be placed in the Afhmolean library. Two bufhels full of notes and letters were burnt before his face, and he gave great charge to deftroy any loofe reflecting notes :—a poor atone- ment for the injuries he had printed! Hearne, who inherited his fpirit, but exceeded him in the non-importance of his publications b, printed

Dr.

---

z Dr. Millington of All Souls told him that if he had been at home when he perufed their regifters he fhould never have feen them : becaufe his Hiftory and Antiquities of Oxford would breed as much trouble and law fuits as the Monafticon had done. P. 599.

a Hearne infinuates that the Doctor artfully over perfuaded him to nominate him. *forfan ipfius Charletti fuafu: de fraude hac in re (fi tamen fraus ulla fuerit) dicant alii.* Ad. de Dom. p. 730.

b This indefatigable raker-up of the gleanings of our antiquities was fon of the parifh- clerk of White Waltham, Berks, adopted by Mr. Cherry, lord of the adjoining manor of Shotefbrook, who fent him to Oxford, where he held feveral lay places as long as his fcruples would permit. He begun his editorfhip with publifhing feveral of the claffics from Bodleian MSS. but foon devoted himfelf to Englifh antiquities, on the fubject of which he printed in the courfe of 35 years 32 feveral works. To all thefe he has

pre-

Dr. Charlet's letter to abp. Tennifon, giving an account of his death, in App. to J. Glaftonienfis, N° i. p. 455. his will at the end of Domerham, p. 731. and a memorandum of his dying in the communion of the church of England, App. to Caius, N° vii. This laft article was of fome importance to the world, as he appears in his writings to favour

prefixed and annexed variety of fcraps totally unconnected with them. Inflamed with that virulence of party fpirit which infected the antiquarians of the laft century, his mifcellaneous prefaces for the moft part conclude with libels: facrificing fenfe to accuracy he retains the groffeft errors of his authors, for fear of lofing their very words. Dr. Wilkins fpends a whole chapter of his preface to Tanner's Bibliotheca Britannica on the *dignity*, value, and ufe of his many publications. Nobody will condemn him for the pains he took to preferve Leland's pieces, for a complete edition of all which Bp. Tanner, publifhed propofals, 1693, but did not live to purfue the defign. Rofs's compendium contains very little interefting. Alfred of Beverley, if genuine, is legendary. Hearne himfelf was almoft afhamed of Sprott's Chronicle, to which however he has tacked a valuable anonymous fragment relating to the eight firft years of Edw. IV.'s reign. Avefbury and Elmham's relations of Edw. III. and Hen. V. s atchievements are accurately and methodically put together: Livius Forojulienfis's life of the laft prince is an elegant abridgement of Elmham's too pompous work. Fordun's Chronicle, whofe greateft merit is its antiquity, he has given intire, with the continuation. Heming's Chartulary and the Textus Roffenfis are valuable collections of the moft antient monuments of their refpective churches. Robert of Gloucefter's Chronicle takes precedence of all Englifh poets. The two monks of Glaffenbury are hiftorians of their own houfe, of which its Englifh hiftory by an anonymous later hand gives a tolerable account. Wm. of Worcefter's annals at the end of that valuable affemblage of public records the Black book of the Exchequer, are mere notes of the affairs of his own times. The monk of Evefham's account of Richard II. except in the proceedings of one feffion of parliament, is a verbatim extract from Knighton and Walfingham: the other two lives of that prince by Henry Blandford and a monk of Malmfbury have more merit: many particulars of him and Hen. VI. may be learned from Thomas Gafcoigne's Dictionary, from which fome paffages are printed at the end of Hemingford's hiftory of the three Edwards. This laft hiftorian has a great deal of merit: but the anonymous life of the laft prince of that name annexed to it is a tranfcript of Murimuth and Walfingham. Whethamfted, abbot of St. Albans, has interwoven with the hiftory of his own fociety many interefting tranfactions of Hen. VI. and Edw. IV. With him Hearne has coupled Otterburn's trifling compilation and Blackman's detail of Hen. VI.'s *manfuetudines & boni mores*, which could not get him a faintfhip. The Chronicle of Dunftaple has the fame recommendation as Whethamftede's. He only publifhed a fifth and correcter edition of Nubrigienfis's Hiftory of England to 1197, a laboured attack on Geoffrey of Monmouth and Britifh antiquities in general, for the lofs of a Welfh bifhopric where Geoffrey fat before him. Death prevented him from encumbering our libraries with a meagre hiftory of England, or additions to Martin Polanus' Annals, afcribed to one John Murelynch, a monk of Glaftonbury, and another from Brute or Ina, to Edw. I. by John Bever, monk of Weftminfter, borrowed from the Flores Hiftoriarum. His laft publication was the beft prefent to the public, Benedict, abbot of Peterborough s, well written and faithful hiftory of Hen. II. and Rich. II. He died June 10, 1735. aged 55.

2   the

the church of Rome; if that unequal temper which befpatters and perfumes the fame party can be faid to favour any.

John Ayliffe, L. L. D. and fellow of New Coll. c compiled from Wood " The antient and prefent ftate of the univerfity of Oxford, &c. &c. Lond. 1714." 2 vols. 8vo. the many mifreprefentations and fcandalous afperfions in which occafioning him to be degraded and expelled, he wrote a vindication of himfelf, or " The cafe of Dr. Ayliffe at Oxford, giving an account of his profecution in the vice-chancellor's court, and the proceedings againft him in his own college in confequence thereof. Lond. 1716." 8vo. The tranfports of his paffion made this rather a fatire on himfelf than thofe againft whom his refentment was pointed.

Salmon, author of the Modern Hiftory, intended " The prefent " ftate of the univerfities, and of the five adjacent counties of Cam- " bridge, Huntingdon, Bedford, Bucks, and Oxford; " but publifhed only the firft volume, 1744. 8vo. which contains the hiftory of this county and univerfity: and from which fome bookfellers ftole " The " gentleman and lady's pocket-companion for Oxford. 1747." 12mo. He publifhed likewife " The foreigner's companion through the uni- " verfities of Cambridge and Oxford. 1749." 12mo. as did Mr. Pointer " Oxonienfis academia, or the antiquities and curiofities of the " univerfity of Oxford. 1749." 12mo In ridicule of fuch works came out " A companion to the guide, and a guide to the companion: being " a compleat fupplement to all the accounts of Oxford hitherto pub- " lifhed: containing an accurate defcription of the feveral halls, libraries, " fchools, public edifices, bufts, ftatues, antiquities, hieroglyphics, feats, " gardens, and other curiofities omitted or mifreprefented by Wood, " Hearne, Salmon, Prince, Pointer, and other eminent topographers, " chronologers, antiquarians, and hiftorians. The whole interfperfed " with original anecdotes and interefting difcoveries, occafionally re- " fulting from the fubject: and embellifhed with perfpective views " and elevations neatly engraved. Lond. 1760." 12mo.

Richard Aungervylle, bp. of Durham 1333, tutor to Edw. III. lord treafurer and chancellor of England 1344, having in his embaffy to

* Author of " A new pandect of Roman civil law, printed by Ofborne 1736." Fol.

France

France collected a great number of MSS. left to Durham college, just founded here by certain religious of his diocese, a larger library than all the rest of the bishops together were possessed of [d]. This was the first public library at Oxford, if not in England. It was not however set up till the time of Hen. VI. [e] The bp. drew up in very indifferent Latin and a declamatory style a little tract containing rules for the management of the library, the preservation of the books, and the conditions on which they were to be lent to students, intitled "Philo-"biblon Richardi Dunelmensis five de amore librorum & institutione "bibliothecæ tractatus pulcherrimus, finished at Aukland, Jan. 24, 1344, when he was 58 years old [f]. It was printed at Spires 1483, and at Paris 1500. Thomas James, first keeper of the public library 1602, published a correct edition of it Oxf. 1599. 4to. which he calls the 2d, and to which he has added an appendix about the MSS. at Oxford. It was reprinted a 4th time at Leipsic 1674, at the end of "Philologicarum epistolarum centuria ex bibliotheca M. Haimens-feldi."

Thomas Cobham, bp. of Worcester, about 1320, begun a library in a building converted into a domus congregationis when the books were removed to that noble library which good old Glocester gave to the university, and which they possessed till the commissioners of reformation under Edw. VI. plundered it so compleatly that it was determined in full convocation 1555 to sell the seats and cases. These were succeeded towards the end of Elizabeth's reign by Bodley's munificence. "The life of Sir Tho. Bodley, the honourable "founder of the publique library in the university of Oxford" was printed at Oxford 1647. 4to. John Chamberlayn, who has abused Sir Thomas because he did not think fit to leave him just as much as he pretended to claim on the foot of old acquaintance, says this was written on seven sheets of paper, by which it seems

[d] Hist. & Ant. Ox. II. 48.

[e] At the dissolution the books were divided between the public library, Baliol Coll. and Dr. Owen, who bought Durham Coll. and its estates of Edw. VI.

[f] Note in the Cottonian MS. The same note is in the MS at C. C. C. Ox. where it is ascribed to Richard Holcot, his lordship's chaplain, as also by Leland, It. iii. 64. who has made extracts from it in his Collectanea, ii. 315.

to have been curtailed in printing ᵍ. The preface of one leaf and
the poſtſcript by the editor are omitted in Hearne's " Reliquiæ Bod-
" leianæ : or ſome genuine remains of Sir T. Bodley, containing his
" life, the firſt draught of the publick library at Oxford (in Engliſh)
" and a collection of letters to Dr. James, &c. publiſhed from the ori-
" ginals in the ſaid library. Lond. 1703." 8vo. More letters from
Bodley, Q. Elizabeth and others relative to this library are publiſhed
in the liſt of Hearne's works at the end of J. Glaſtonienſis. A life
of Sir Thomas wrote by himſelf to 1609, is printed in Prince s account
of him among the worthies of Devon ʰ, Dr. Hakewill, his kinſman's, Latin tranſlation of another life is among the Bodleian MSS. ⁱ.
That prefixed with the hiſtory of his library to Bernard s Catalogus
MSS. Angliæ, was wrote by bp. Gibſon. His funeral oration by the
famous Hales is in Bates's " Vitæ ſelectiores," p. 420. The verſes
made by the Oxonians on his death were printed under the title of
" Juſta funebria Ptolomæi." 1613. Sir Henry Saville had introduced
Bodley to Sir Rob. Cotton, who ſeems to have offered ſome additions
to his collection. Hearne has printed a letter from Saville to Cotton ap-
pointing an interview for Bodley, and cautioning Sir Robert " if he held
any book ſo deare as that he would bee loath to have him out of his
ſight, to ſet him aſide beforehand." A like anecdote is told of the late
bp. Moore: a gentleman calling on a friend who had a very choice
library, found him unuſually buſy in putting his beſt books out of ſight ;
upon aſking his view in this, he was anſwered, Don't you know the
biſhop of Ely dines with me to-day ?

Tho. James publiſhed " Catalogus librorum bibliothecæ publicæ quam
" vir ornatiſſimus Thomas Bodleius, eq. aur. in acad. Oxonienſi nuper
" inſtituit ; continet autem libros alphabetice diſpoſitos ſecundum qua-
" tuor facultates : cum quadruplice elencho expoſitorum S. Scripturæ,
" Ariſtotelis, juris utriuſq: & principum medicinæ, ad uſum almæ
" academiæ Oxonienſis. Ox. 1605." 4to. reprinted ſome years after
under the title of " Catalogus univerſalis librorum in bibliotheca Bod-

ᵍ Winwood's Mem. iii. 422.   Page 75.
ⁱ Prince, ib. 407. Ath.Ox. II. 125.

H h h   " leiana

" leiana omnium librorum linguarum, & scientiarum genere refertissima,
" sic compositus ut non solum publicis per Europam bibliothecis, sed
" etiam privatis musæis, aliisque ad catalogum librorum conficiendum
" usui esse possit: accessit appendix k librorum qui ex munificentia ali-
" orum vel censibus bibliothecæ recens allati sunt: auctore T. James,
" S. T. D. nuper proto-bibliothecario Oxoniensi. Ox. 1620." 4to.

" Catalogus impressorum librorum bibliothecæ Bodleianæ cura &
" opera Thomæ Hyde e coll. reginæ, Oxon. proto-bibliothecarii. Ox.
" 1674." Fol. Hearne l says this catalogue, though published under
Hyde's name, was really the work of Emanuel Pritchard, and that
Wanley intended an appendix to it, which he himself had drawn up
and designed to incorporate with it. When Wood solicited a free perusal
of the Bodleian MSS. Hyde applied to the vice-chancellor that he should
make him promise to assist him in his catalogue of them, which Wood
partly did : but the other seeing he was engaged in a public work
never urged him again m. A more ample catalogue of the books
since drawn up by Robert Fisher, assisted by Joseph Bowles, fellow
of Oriel and chief librarian, and after his decease by Emanuel Langford, vice-principal of Hart-hall, was printed at Oxford, in two volumes folio, 1738.

James published " Ecloga Oxonio-Cantabrigiensis, tributa in libros
" duos ; quorum prior continet catalogum confusum librorum manu-

---

k Another appendix seems to have been added 1635-6. Ath. Ox. I. 338. James published likewise " Index generalis librorum prohibitorum a pontificiis, una cum editionibus
" purgatis vel expurgandis, juxta seriem literarum & triplicem classem, in usum biblio-
" thecæ Bodleianæ, & curatoribus ejusdem specialiter designatus. Ox. 1627." and " Ca-
" talogus interpretum S. Scripturæ, juxta numerorum ordinem quo extant in bib Bodl.
" Ox. 1635." 12mo. This last was improved and reprinted under the title of a " No-
" menclator of such tracts and sermons as have been printed and translated into English
" upon any place or book of holy Scripture, now to be had in the most famous and
" public library of Sir T. Bodley in Oxford. Opera, studio & impensis Joh. Vernulii.
" editio 2da. correctior & duplo auctior. Oxf. 1642." 12mo. Vernueil was a refugee
from Bourdeaux, admitted of Magdalen 1608, and appointed 2d keeper of this library.
Ath. Ox. II. 108. James was fellow of New Coll. one of the most industrious writers
against popery that had been educated at Oxford since the reformation. When he could
not prevail on the convocation to collate the MSS. of the fathers published by the papists,
in order to detect their forgeries, he set about it himself.
l Pref. to Ann. of Dunst. p. xii. §. ii.
m Life of Wood, p 568.

" scriptorum

" fcriptorum in illuftriffimis bibliothecis, duarum florentiffimarum aca-
" demiarum, Oxoniæ & Cantabrigiæ: pofterior, catalogum eorundem
" diftinctum & difpofitum fecundum quatuor facultates, obfervato tam
" in nominibus quam in operibus ipfis alphabetico literarum ordine.
" Oftenfum eft præterea in hoc fecundo libro, quid a quoque viro
" fcriptum fit, quo tempore, ac poftremo, quot ejufdem libri exem-
" plaria quibufque in locis habeantur. Lond. 1600." 4to. It contains a catalogue of all the MSS. in each college, but not of thofe in
the public library here; and of thofe both in the public and college
libraries at Cambridge. This indefatigable perufer of MSS. had ranfacked all the public libraries in England. As he had liberty of accefs
to all at Oxford, he took many MSS. from thofe colleges which
he thought carelefs of them, particularly from Baliol and Merton ",
and lodged them in the public library. There was a defign in the laft
century of uniting thefe MSS. in one catalogue with thofe in the feveral
libraries at Cambridge and at Lambeth to be drawn up by fome members of that univerfity o. Of the MS. treafures fince lodged in the
Bodleian library catalogues by bp. Tanner and others are inferted in the
Cat. MSS. Ang. tom. i. p. 1—374 P. Dr. Langbaine made an abftract
of all the MSS. Mr. Chilmead drew up, 1636, a very ufeful catalogue of all the Greek ones in this and the Baroccian libraries, ranged
alphabetically by the author's names q. A general catalogue was long
laboured upon, and left unfinifhed by Mr. Crabb of Exeter, under-
librarian. Dr. Hudfon, the late librarian, had caufed one to be tranfcribed fair in fix volumes, now in the library, intending if he had
lived to publifh it. A new one has been fome time printing at Oxford
in four volumes folio r.

Afhmole drew up, 1659, three folio volumes of " Familiarum illuftrium imperatorumq. Romanorum numifmata, Oxoniæ in Bodleianæ
bibliothecæ archivis defcripta & explanata:" which he gave to the
public library 1666, where they ftill remain, and copies of them in his

n Ath. Ox. I. 538.
o Wanley's pref. to Bernard's Cat. MSS. Angl.
P This work, to which H. Wanley wrote a preface and index, contains 30,000 titles.
q Ath. Ox. II. 169. Hearne's pref. to cur. difc. p. xxiv.
r Biog. Brit. art. Bodley, n. H.

mufeum.

mufeum ˢ. Hearne continued Afhmole's catalogue, adding later benefactions ᵗ. He arranged and drew up a catalogue of thofe given by conful
Ray, moftly Greek. Mr. Wife, fub-librarian, publifhed " Nummo-
" rum antiquorum fcriniis Bodleianis reconditorum catalogus cum
" commentario, tabulis æneis & appendice. Oxf. 1750." Fol.

This library received a great addition 1755, on the death of Dr.
Richard Rawlinfon, who bequeathed to it all his MSS. coins, reliefs,
marbles, feals Englifh and foreign with their impreffions, drawings,
printed books with MS. notes, and his copper plates relating to Ox-
f rdfhire, Middlefex, Surrey, and Berks ᵘ. Browne Willis, many years
before his death, gave the compleateft collection of Englifh coins in
the kingdom, which he had been forty years collecting: the univerfity
however thinking fuch a prefent would injure his family paid him for
150 gold coins at the rate of four guineas per oz. He vifited the
cabinet every year on St. Fridefwide's day ˣ, and befides enlarging it,
gave 1200 tradefmen's tokens and fundry MSS. exclufive of his own,
which he left by will to this library ʸ.

In " The monthly mifcellany, or memoirs for the curious. Lond.
1718." vol. ii. p. 359, is a lift of the pictures in the gallery of the
public library at Oxford, with the feveral infcriptions put under them,
publifhed by Hearne; reprinted with corrections in his letter about antiquities between Windfor and Oxford. 1725. 8vo. A fmall catalogue
of the pictures, ftatues, and bufts here and in Afhmole's mufeum is fold
at the gallery.

The antient marbles that form the moft authentic hiftory of Greece,
collected by Thomas Howard earl of Arundel, and given to this univerfity by his grandfon Henry duke of Norfolk, were firft illuftrated
with a learned comment the year after they came over, by Selden,
affifted by R. James and Patrick Young ᶻ, at the defire of Sir Robert

---

ˢ Ath. Ox. II. 890. Thefe were part of abp. Laud's medallic gift to the Bodleian
library in five cabinets. Mr. Freke, fon of Sir Tho Freke, of Hannington, Wilts. gave
500 gold and filver coins 1657.

ᵗ Pref. to Cur. Difc lxv. lxvi.

ᵘ A curious ivory Mufcovite cup now among thefe curiofities was engraved while in
the doctor's poffeffion.

ˣ Oct. 19.

ʸ He died Feb 5, 1760, aged 78.

ᶻ Who was librarian to the earl thirty years.

Cotton

Cotton. They begun with the treaty between the Magnefians and Smyrneans to ftand by Seleucus, whom all his fubjects, except the laft, had deferted, till his ill fortune brought them round again. Copies of this being foon follicited, Selden, to prevent the inaccuracy of tranf-cribers, printed it with 28 other Greek and 10 Roman infcriptions (fome of them his own) under the title of " Marmora Arundeliana, five " faxa Græce incifa ex venerandis prifcæ Orientis gloriæ ruderibus au-" fpiciis & impenfis herois illuftriffimi Thomæ comitis Arundelliæ & " Surriæ comitis marefcalli Angliæ pridem vindicata, & in ædibus ejus " hortifque cognominibus ad Thamefis ripam difpofita. Accedunt in-" fcriptiones aliquot veteris Latii ex locupletiffimo ejufdem vetuftatis " thefauro felectæ; auctariolum item aliunde fumptum, publicavit & " commentariolos adjecit Joannes Seldenus. Lond. 1628." 4to. Philip earl of Arundel, father of the noble collector, was the greateft anti-quarian in Europe, except Ferdinand de Medici. Perfecuted by the in-trigues of a jealous court, to which his own father the great duke of Norfolk had fallen a victim, he was preparing to retire from England, and indulge his only ambition the ftudy of polite literature: Elizabeth remanded him, and not content with a heavy fine and imprifonment, had him tried for treafon ; being unable to convict him of any thing but popery, fhe left him to languifh nine years in prifon, where he funk under her difpleafure and his own aufterity. Among the celebrated libraries of the age in this kingdom his was the completeft in the antiquarian way. His fon Thomas inherited his fpirit and tafte with better for-tune. Too much of a patriot to be efteemed by James, too little of a parafite to cringe to his favourite, too honeft and difinterefted to have many friends in their parliament, he could not attain to the feals after the great Bacon, who drew his laft breath in his houfe at Highgate: In Charles's firft parliament he was inftrumental to the eftablifh-ment of the fundamental privileges of the peerage, and the king feems to have obferved his father's conduct towards him, advancing him to employments unimportant in themfelves or in which he was not left free to act. After prefiding with unimpeached im-partiality at the trial of the favourite minifter, as the ftorm of civil diftractions gathered round, he retreated from a fcene where moderation could not be heard, to purfue thofe ftudies to which he had

always

always given the preference at home: the friend and patron of his learned cotemporaries, he introduced the elegance and arts of Greece and Rome into this angle of the world; superior to ambition, with abilities and revenues equal to its largest views. Clarendon, without intending him so much honour, has drawn in his character the picture of an independant English nobleman. William Petty, afterwards knighted, whom he sent into Asia in quest of antient monuments, bought these of a Turk, who took them from the agent of the famous Peiresk, who had paid fifty pieces of gold for them, and was afterwards thrown into prison and cheated of them. Petty lost one shipload of his collections, and narrowly saved himself[z]. After the earl retired to Italy 1641 many of these curious monuments which lay at Arundel house in the Strand, were stolen, or cut up by masons and worked into houses. Above 130, which was scarce half, surviving this calamity, Hen. Howard, earl marshal, grandson to the noble collector, when he pulled down Arundel house[a], at the instigation of John Evelyn, esq; of Baliol, made a present of them to this university[b]. They were
ranged

[z] Among Sir Thomas Roe's Negotiations are several letters to this earl and the duke of Buckingham, who were competitors in the pursuit of antiquities, strongly expressive of the infant state of that branch of virtu, in which the French preceded us. Sir Thomas mentions a head of Germanicus he had got from Angora, and another from Corinth, supposed L. Mummius, but owns he was frequently imposed on. The rules he prescribed to his agents were " beauty and hard marble." He says. " he could have laden ships with such things as Petty digs, but good things undefaced were rare." He spared no art to get down from the golden gate of Constantinople six bas reliefs which Petty was greatly struck with, but failed of success and only raised a mob about his ears. He procured him admission into the best libraries in Greece, from whence he conveyed 22 MSS. chiefly of the fathers. Sir Thomas, who paid his court to the favourite, complains he had not an equal share of what Petty collected. It would be amusing to trace the statues, &c. he particularizes to their present station.

[a] Hollar engraved a N. and S. prospect of it 1646, and the earl's monument at Arundel in Sussex.

[b] The other parts of this collection were preserved at Tart hall, near St. James's park-gate by Buckingham-house, where some of the statues were buried in the court yard during Oates's plot: the best of them being disposed of as above-mentioned, those that were too much injured by time to deserve a place at Oxford or Easton, when the scite of Arundel-house was converted into a street, were removed to Cuper's gardens, where they were much abused. Here Mr. Aubrey lost sight of them: but when Dr. Rawlinson published his history of Surrey, he inserted, vol. v. p. 283, 8 plates of beautiful fragments of statues and bas reliefs. Some are or were lately at those gardens, and the statue of a Roman senator, which in its present mangled state shews a fine drapery, in the garden at Somerset-house, is believed to have come out of this collection. A colossus
of

ranged in the wall furrounding the court of the theatre, marked with the initial letter of the donor's name, and a pillar erected with an infcription under his arms ᶜ. Upon Selden's death 1654 his executors added his collection of antiquities ᵈ : Sir Geo. Wheeler gave thofe he had collected chiefly at Athens, and the univerfity bought feveral other marbles of merchants who brought them over. A perfon was employed to prepare a new edition of Selden's commentary, which had been found very incorrect, and to infert the additional marbles. This being delayed three years, bp. Fell employed Prideaux, who publifhed them under the title of " Marmora Oxonienfia ex Arundellianis, Sel-
" denianis, aliifque conflata, recenfuit & perpetuo commentario expli-
" cavit Humphredus Prideaux ædis Chrifti alumnus, appofitis ad eorum
" nonnullis Seldeni & Lydiati annotationibus. Acceffit Sertorii Urfati
" Patavini de notis Romanorum commentarius. Oxon. 1676. Fol. ᵉ.
This book growing fcarce, Mr. Pearce of Edmund-hall undertook

of Apollo, whofe head is at Oxford, is faid to lie under the houfes in Arundel ftreet; and I think I have fomewhere read that an intire fmall obelifk is covered by the houfes of one fide of that ftreet. The Antiquarian Society have a drawing of a farcophagus, of white marble, belonging to Mr. Rogers, apothecary, in Howard ftreet, 1742. The earl endeavoured to procure the obelifk fince erected in the Piazza Navona, and would have removed feveral other ftatues had not the pope oppofed it. The remaining curiofities lodged at Tart-hall were fold by auction about thirty years ago, and there Dr. Mead bought his fine head of Homer, purchafed at his fale for 36l. by the prefent earl of Exeter, who has repofited it in the Britifh Mufeum. The cameos and intaglios were by the dutchefs of Norfolk before-mentioned bequeathed to her fecond hufband Sir John Germayne, and are now in the hands of his widow lady Elizabeth Germayne.

ᶜ Lydiat while confined in the king's bench for a debt of furetyfhip for his brother, wrote annotations on the Parian Chronicle, which were firft publifhed by Prideaux. Wood fays he had criticized feverely on Selden's remarks, and inftead of calling him a moft judicious author, only ftyled him an induftrious one, which Selden was weak enough to refent fo highly as to refufe to contribute towards his releafe. Ath. Ox. II. 89. This feems to be a piece of mere tittle-tattle; for in the printed notes, p. 13, he calls him *Induftrius & eruditus amicus nofter* Seldenus. " In an ifland called Augufto near *Paris* [Paros] in the Arches, I have heard of two great marbles, and have taken command to fetch them by the bifhop of Naxia." Roe's letter to the duke of Buckingham, May 1626. Negot. p. 512.

ᵈ Selden's library was lodged in the Bodleian 1659, and Wood affifted Dr. Barlow in forting and ranging it. They found in the books feveral pair of fpectacles which Selden had put in and forgot to take out, and Barlow gave Wood one which he kept in memory of Selden to his laft day. Life of Wood, p. 524.

ᵉ Many infcriptions in Selden's book not having reached Oxford, were thrown with others into an appendix.

3

1721 to reprint it, with leave of the author now advanced in years. Prideaux proposed to him to correct the many errors occasioned by his own youth and the hurry of the press ; but on his declining this, Dr. David Wilkins undertook it 1726, intending to add the Pomfret and Pembroke collections. Mattaire performed the first part of the design 1732, inserting the conjectures and corrections of various learned men, but never consulting the marbles, and totally omitting Wheeler's monuments. His book is intitled " Marmorum Arundelianorum, Seldenia- " norum aliorumque academiæ Oxoniensi donatorum, una cum com- " mentariis & indice　Editio 2d. Lond. 1732." Fol. The statues belonging to the Pomfret collection being part of the inheritance of the eldest branch of the family, since dukes of Norfolk, fell into the hands of the dutchess who was divorced 1699, and being by her sold to the last earl of Pomfret's father were some time preserved at his seat in Northamptonshire ; but since given by the late countess dowager of Pomfret to this university.　These, with the antient inscriptions collected by Sir Geo. Wheeler, and Messrs. Dawkins, Bovery. and Wood during their travels, some which Dr. Rawlinson bought out of lord Oxford's or Kemp's collection, and various fragments of our own antiquities, have been all united together, and engraved by Millar, at the university's expence, in the " Marmora Oxoniensia. Ox. 1763." Fol. a work the design of which will immortalize the university, the nation, and the age.　It were to be wished as much could be said for the execution as far as the engraver is concerned.　The inscriptions are transcribed with great exactness, revised by Mr. Richard Chandler of Queen's, a short account of each with critical notes annexed, an historical preface by Mr. S. Chandler, and a copious index by Mr. Loveday of Magdalen.　Of this collection Bishop had published the statues of Minerva, Clio, and Marius [f].　Price (whom Sir Wm. Petty introduced to Hen. Howard) has engraved a Venus, and a bas relief representing some punishment, in his notes on Apuleius' apology.　The statue of Cicero is etched singly by Worlidge.　Besides the collections above specified, here are sundry Egyptian figures given by Mr. Goodyear, Turkey merchant, three heads by Dr. Shaw, a Citiean inscription

[f] Part i. plate i. iii. vol. iii. pl. xxiii.

brought

brought from Cyprus by Dr. Porter g, the alabaster figure engraved in
Camden's Britannia, p. 725, found at Caerleon; a Greek inscription engraved Muf. Veron. 442, when lord Oxford's, and afterwards, 1742, by
Dr. Rawlinfon, who bought it; the Cornifh patera given by Dr. Borlafe,
and feveral Roman and other infcriptions found in Britain, fpecified in
the refpective counties. Several infcriptions printed by Maittaire having
fince difappeared are inferted from his book. Anthony Thompfon h,
late fellow of Queen's, and author of a collection of poems, 8vo.
celebrated lady Pomfret's donation in a poem intitled " Gratitude."
Another perfon publifhed a namelefs and very indifferent " Poem on
the countefs of Pomfret's benefaction to the univerfity of Oxford.
1756." 4to. intended to have been fpoken in the theatre at the commemoration. Three years after came out " A poem on the Pomfret
ftatues: to which is added another on Laura's grave. Oxf. 1759."
4to. intended alfo for public delivery at the fame time.

" Carmen Pindaricum in theatrum Sheldonianum in folennibus
" magnifici operis encaeniis recitatum Julii, die 9. 1669. à Corbetto
" Owen, A.B. æd. Chr. alumno, authore. Ox. 1669." 4to. reprinted
in the Mufæ Anglicanæ, vol. i. p. 99. and at the end of Wren's Parentalia, p 339.

" Urania: or a defcription of the painting of the top of the theatre at
" Oxford, as the artift laid his defign, by Rob. Whitehall i, fellow of
" Merton college. Lond. 1669." Fol. in verfe. Vertue engraved a fmall
view of the theatre, printing-houfe, and Afhmolean mufeum.

Lhwyd the foffilift took a catalogue of the books, medals, and pictures in the Afhmolean mufeum k. A lift of the books and MSS. is in
Cat. MSS. Angliæ, tom. i. p. 315—370. The latter amount to 620,
of which half relate to Englifh hiftory and antiquities. Here were alfo
lodged Dr. Lifter's and Aubrey's books.

g Illuftrated by Mr. Swinton of Chrift Church, in his " Infcriptiones Citieæ, five in
" binas infcriptiones Phœnicias inter rudera Citii nuper repertas conjecturæ, &c. Oxf.
" 1750." 4to.
h Afterwards dean of Raphoe, where he died 1756.
i Author of " Verfes on Mrs Mary More, on her fending Sir Thomas More's picture,
of her own drawing, to the long gallery at the public fchools here. Oxf. 1674." printed
on one fide of a half fheet. Ath. Ox. II. 786.
k See his letter to Ray, among Ray's letters, p. 265.

" Cata-

" Catalogus librorum MSStorum viri clariſſimi Antonii A Wood;
" being a minute catalogue of each particular contained in the MS.
" collections of Anthony a Wood depoſited in the Aſhmolean muſeum
" at Oxford. By William Huddeſford, M. A. keeper of the ſaid
" muſeum. Oxf. 1761." 8vo.

Another part of the collection is in a ſmall book intitled " Muſæum
" Tradeſcantianum; or a collection of rarities preſerved at South-
" Lambeth, near London, by John Tradeſcant. Lond. 1656" 12mo.
In this is inſerted an ample catalogue of Tradeſcant's plants, ſhrubs,
and trees in Engliſh and Latin, and a liſt of benefactors to this collection, the proprietor of which and his ſon looked after the phyſic garden
at Lambeth, and ſold theſe curioſities to Aſhmole, who lodged with
them, and gave them afterwards to this univerſity. Alexander Mar-
ſhall [1] painted on velom a number of the choiceſt flowers and plants.
Mr. Watſon has publiſhed in the Philoſophical Tranſactions, Nº 492.
p. 160, an account of ſome curious plants yet remaining in this garden.
In the Pepyſian library are drawings of Tradeſcant's monument in
Lambeth church-yard, the ſides decorated with ruins and natural
curioſities, the end with his arms. The heads of both father and ſon
by Hollar are inſerted in the book.

The very large magnet given to this muſeum by the counteſs of
Weſtmoreland was engraved 1756.

The ſeal of Macarius, patriarch of Antioch, inſcribed Μαχαριος ελεω
3εʊ ϖατριαρχης της μεγαλης ϖολεως Αντιοχειας χ̣ ϖασης ανατολης, by
Dr. Rawlinſon 1750.

Two fragments of Egyptian figures on marble in this muſeum are
in tab. vi. of Gordon's deſcription of a mummy, and four views of another in tab. iii.

In the Muſæ Anglicanæ, vol. ii. p. 16, are verſes by Mr. John Dol-
ben, ſtudent of Chriſt Church, ſon to the abp. of York, intitled Muſæum Aſhmoleanum.

" The deed of truſt and will of Richard Rawlinſon, of St. John
" Baptiſt College, Oxford, L.L.D. containing his endowment of an
" Anglo-Saxon lecture, and other benefactions to the college and
" univerſity. Lond. 1755." 8vo.

[1] Walp. Anecd. of Painting, vol. iii. p. 66.

Of

Of the laſt library erected in this univerſity ſee " Bibliotheca Rad-
" cliffeiana, or a ſhort deſcription of the Radcliffe library at Oxford,
" containing its ſeveral plans, parts, ſections, and ornaments, in 23
" copper plates, with an explication to each. By James Gibbs, architect,
" F. R. S. Lond. 1747." Fol. and five large prints of it by Vertue.

" Oratio in theatro Sheldoniano habita idibus Aprilibus 1749, die dedi-
" cationis bibliothecæ Radclivianæ. Lond. Oxon." 4to.

" Remarks on Dr. K——'s ſpeech before the univerſity of O——d at
" the dedication of Dr. R———'s library, on the 13th of April, 1749.
" By Phileleutherus Londinenſis. Lond. 1750." 8vo. aſcribed to Dr.
Burton of Eton.

" A tranſlation of a late celebrated oration, occaſioned by a libel
" intitled, Remarks on Dr. K——'s ſpeech ; with a ſeaſonable intro-
" duction. Lond. 1750." 8vo. A correct tranſlation of this ſpeech
was publiſhed ſoon after.

" Oxford honeſty ; or a caſe of conſcience, humbly put to the wor-
" ſhipfull and rev. the vice-chancellor, the heads of houſes, the fel-
" lows, &c. of the univerſity of Oxford, whether one may take the
" oaths to king George, and yet, conſiſtently, with honour and con-
" ſcience, and the fear of God, may do all one can in favour of the
" pretender ? Occaſioned by the Oxford ſpeech and Oxford beha-
" viour at the opening of Radcliff's library, April 12, 1749." The 2d
edition with additions. Lond. 8vo.

" A ſatire upon phyſicians, or an Engliſh paraphraſe, with notes and
" references, of Dr. King's moſt memorable oration, delivered at the de-
" dication of the Radclivian library in Oxford. To which is added
" a curious petition to an hon. houſe in favour of Dr. King. Lond.
" 1755." 8vo. A burleſque poetical verſion of the oration : the petition
is an indifferent imitation of Swift's humble petition of Frances Harris.

The ſtate of the printing preſs is publiſhed yearly ; and 1695 was
printed at Oxford " A ſpecimen of the ſeveral ſorts of letter given to
" the univerſity by Dr. John Fell ſometime lord bp. of Oxford. To
" which is added, the letter given by Mr. F. Junius." Hearne intended ſome obſervations on the original of printing at Oxford, but
left it to Bagford, who was collecting a general hiſtory of printing.

In

In the botanic way we have " Catalogus plantarum horti medici Ox-
" onienfis, fcil. Latino-Anglicus & Anglico Latinus. Ox. 1648." 8vo.
by Jacob Bobart, keeper of the phyfic gardens.   This was augmented
in " Catalogus horti botanici Oxonienfis, alphabeticè digeftus, duas,
" præterpropter, plantarum chiliadas complectens, priore duplo auctior,
" idemque elimatior; necnon etymologiis, qua Græcis, qua Latinis,
" hinc inde petitis, enucleatior; in quo nomina Latina pariter & Græca
" vernaculis; & in ejus fequiore parte, vernacula Latinis, proponuntur.
" Cui accefsere plantæ minimum fexaginta fuis nominibus infignitæ,
" quæ nullibi, nifi in hoc opufculo, memorantur.   Cura & opera focia
" Philippi Stephani [m], M. D. & Gulielmi Brounei. A. M. adhibitis
" etiam in confilium D. Boberto, patre [n], hortulano academico, ejufque
" filio, utpote rei herbariæ callentiffimis. Oxon. 1658." 12mo.

Edm. Gayton, the poetafter, wrote a poem or fong upon Mr. Jacob
Bobart's " Yew-men of the guards to the phyfic garden, to the tune
" of the Counter fcuffle. Ox. 1662." on one fide of a fheet: and a
ballad " on the gyants in the phyfic garden in Oxon; who have been
breeding feet as long as Garagantua was teeth. Ox. 1662." [o].   Gayton's
friend John Drope of Magdalen wrote " A poem on the moft hope-
" full and ever-flourifhing fprouts of valour, the indefatigble centries
" of the phyfic garden of Oxon. 1664." [p]

[m] Stephens was born at the Devifes, educated at St. Alban's hall, fellow of New Coll.
principal of Hart hall 1653. M. D. 1655. [Wood's Fafti. II. 109.] and died at London after the reftoration.   Brown was a native of Oxford, fenior fellow of Magdalen, and
one of the beft botanifts of his time, and died fuddenly 1678. Ibid. 161.

[n] Jacob Bobart before mentioned wrote a volume of the " Plantarum hiftoria univerfalis Oxonienfis feu herbarum diftributio nova."   The firft volume was compiled by Dr.
Robert Morifon, a native of Aberdeen, who quitting Scotland in the troubles ftudied at
Paris, took a degree in phyfic at Angers, and directed the royal gardens at Blois till the
death of the duke of Orleans.   At the reftoration he was appointed overfeer of the king's
gardens, fellow of the college of phyficians, and 1669 profeffor of botany in this univerfity, where he read lectures till he fet about publifhing the " Univerfal knowledge of
fimples."   Upon his death 1683 Bobart continued his hiftory in 1694, and was to have
added a 3d volume on trees. Wood's Fafti, II. 1-8

[o] Ath. Ox. II. 388.   William the IIId's Dutch tafte has been charged with the extravagant diftortion of trees into all kind of fhapes.   We fee it was brought from another part of Germany about twenty years before.   Perhaps it was thought an improvement on the unnatural practice of clipping trees introduced at Rome in the Auguftan
ge by the elegant Matius, and ftill followed in the beft gardens at Rome. The late Sir
Gerard Napier's houfe at More Critchel, Dorfetfhire, is guarded by two troopers on horfe-
b ck in yew.   At Ludham in Norfolk is a fun-dial in box.   The well known date in
Belfont lane is fomething like the box cut into names at Pliny's Tufcan villa, Epift. v. 6

[p] Wood's Faft. II. 130.

Dr.

Dr. Abel Evans, fellow of St. John's and vicar of St. Giles's, Oxford, wrote a poem on this garden, intitled " Vertumnus: an epiſtle to Mr. " Jacob Bobart, botany profeſſor of the univerſity of Oxford, and " keeper of the phyſick-garden. Oxf. 1713." 8vo. and fronting the title is a view of the ruſtic gate leading into it.

The univerſity ſtatutes printed on velom are placed in each of the college libraries. The body of ſtatutes confirmed by a charter of Charles I. 1636, was collected by Bryan Twyne, and tranſlated into Latin by Dr. Peter Turner, Savilian profeſſor. " Statuta ſelecta è corpore ſtatu- " torum univerſitatis Oxon. ut in promptu, & ad manum ſint, quæ " magis ad uſum (precipue juniorum) facere videntur. Oxon. 1638." 12mo. an abſtract for the uſe of the members, delivered to them on their matriculation. Various editions of it have been ſince printed under the title of " Parecbolæ ſive excerpta e corpore ſtatutorum univ. Oxon." Ox. 1718. 1729. 1749. 8vo. In p. 20 of the firſt edition i a ſcheme engraved on copper by T. Cecill, dedicated to Laud, then chancellor, intitled " Cyclus prælectorum tam indotatorum quam dotatorum ex " corpore ſtatutorum depromptus & delineatus, accurate indicans dies, " horas, libros, auditores, mulctas, &c. quorum cognitio quotidiano " ſtudioſorum uſui & utilitati expedite inſerviat," copied in a later edi- tion by Michael Burghers, engraver to the univerſity. Other parts of the ſtatutes were privately printed by Dr. Charlet, maſter of Univerſity coll. but by the univerſity's command the publication was ſtopped. It contained the laſt charter of Ch. I. the ſtatuta aularia, bib. Bodleianæ, Saviliana, lecturæ anatomicæ & muſicæ, and others concerning the vice-chancellor's court. At the end of Hearne's edition of Robert de Aveſbury, Ox. 1720. p. 299, are a tranſcript of an old beadle's book formerly belonging to Wood, containing many curious things ; a col- lection of MS. notes about the orders of the univerſity, p. 314; a letter from Dr. Chriſtopher Potter relating to the univerſity's privileges, and the form of degrading Wm. Prynne, p. 328. In the appendix to the Textus Roffenſis, p. 394. N° viii. is the manor that the univerſity of Oxford uſed in creating the right hon. Sir Chriſtopher Hatton, kt. of the garter, lord chancellor of England, maiſter of arte and ſo chancellor of the ſaid univerſity, 1588 : in N° ix. the order of chuſing abp. Bancroft

their

their chancellor 1608, both communicated by Mr. Baker. In the appendix to Caius is part of the speech p of a professor of arts and philosophy, temp. Hen. V. to the inceptors in arts, vesperiarum tempore, with the five questions: it consists of ridiculous characters and comparisons of the five inceptors supposed of Magdalen Coll. and puns on their names; and has nothing to recommend it but its antiquity. The respondents used to sit with their hoods over their eyes. The Latin prayers used by the university are printed in " Litania & ordo administrandæ cœnæ " domini. Oxon. è Theat. Sheldon. 1705." 8vo.

" A catalogue of all the graduats in divinity, law, and physick; " and of all masters of arts, and doctors of musick, who have regu- " larly proceeded, or been created in the university of Oxford, be- " tween Oct. 10, 1659, and July 14, 1688. Oxf. 1689." 8vo. by Richard Peers, before-mentioned. It was continued to 1713 by the superior of arts, his successors, beadles (particularly by Gerard Langbaine, to Aug. 6. 1690) and since by others in a later edition to Oct. 10, 1726: to which are added the proceeders between Oct. 10, 1726, and Oct. 10, 1727: likewise the chancellors, high stewards, vice-chancellors, and proctors, from 1659 to 1727; also the members of parliament for the university from 1603 to 1727: a third edition continues the whole to 1735.

The first Oxford almanac was drawn up by Maurice Wheeler, one of the petty canons of Christ Church, 1673. It seems to have contained a short history of the university taken from Wood's history and antiquities, and had so great a sale to the prejudice of the other almanacs that the London booksellers bought up the copy; and ever since there have been only the present sheet almanacs on copper plates, the first of which was engraved 1674 by Robert White q; succeeding ones by G. Vertue r, who introduced views of public buildings and histories of events; and others by John Green, who died immaturely s.

John Faber the elder executed in mezzotinto the portraits of the founders of the colleges here and at Cambridge.

p Cited by Twyne, Apol. iii. 339.   q Walp. cat. of eng. p. 92.   r Life of Vertue, p. 5.   s Cat. of eng. p. 127.

" Cele-

" Celeberrimæ Oxonienfis academiæ, aularum & collegiorum ædifi-
" ciis totius Europæ magnificentiſſimis, cum antiquiſſima civitate con-
" junctæ elegans fimul & accurata defcriptio, Radulpho Agafo autore.
" 1578." three feet by four.

" Oxonia antiqua reſtaurata, five urbis & academiæ Oxonienfis topo-
" graphica delineatio, olim a Rad. Agafo impreſſa A. D. 1578, nunc
" denuo æri incifa A. D. 1728. Huic in margine acceſſit e cod. MS.
" Bodl collegiorum & fcholarum fcenographia amplior & accuratior a
" T. Neale, S. T. B. calamo defcripta 1566." 2 ſheets. At the bottom, A. Ryther, Angl. del. 1588.

David Loggan making a draught of All Souls college for his own ufe,
was defired to undertake plates of the publick buildings here, and firſt
diſtinguiſhed himfelf by his " Oxonia illuſtrata, five omnium celeber-
" rimæ iſtius univerfitatis collegiorum, aularum, bibliothecæ Bodleianæ,
" fcholarum publicarum, theatri Sheldoniani, nec non urbis totius
" fcenographia. Oxon. 1675." Folio. He alfo engraved the habits of
the feveral orders in eleven plates [t].

" Oxonia depicta feu collegiorum & aularum in inclyta academia
" Oxonienfi ichnographica, orthographica, & fcenographica delineatio
" lxv tabulis æneis expreſſa a Gulielmo Williams [u], cui accedit uniuf-
" cujufque collegii aulæque notitia." Fol.

There are fome fmall undated views of the colleges, by Robert Whit-
tlefey. John Donowell, architect, publiſhed a collection of the moſt
confiderable public buildings in Oxford.

General poetical defcriptions are " Oxonium poema, authore F. V.
" [Franc. Vernon] [x] ex æde Chriſti. Oxon. 1667." 4to.

" Oxonii encomium ab Edw. Bendlowes [y] olim coll. D. Jo. Bapt.

[t] In the matriculation book is this entry, " David Loggan, Gedanenfis, univerfitatis
Oxon. chalcographus, Jul 9. 1672." He had a licence for 15 years for vending this
fet of views. Walp. cat. of engr. p 80.

[u] He publiſhed alfo a map of Flint and Denbighfhire, and died of the gout in his
ſtomach at Hatherlin, near Namptwich in Cheſhire, Dec. 27, 1738.

[x] The author's abfence from the prefs occafioned this poem to be very incorrectly
printed. See an account of him in Birch's hiſt. of the Royal Society, vol. iii. p. 357.
and Ath. Ox. II. 599.

[y] Benlowes lived in the beginning of the 17th century, and having fquandered away
an eſtate of near 1000 l. a year on poets, muficians, virtuofi, and parafites, turned poet
and difputant in divinity, and at laſt funk under a load of debt at the age of 73, and
was buried by contribution. Wood's Faſt. II. 204.

" foc.

" foc. commenfal. Oxon. 1672." four fheets folio. " Oxonii elogia.
" Ox. 1673." by the fame author, on one fide of a large fheet, confifting of 12 ftanzas, followed by " Oxonii elegia: academicis fereni-
" tas: academicis temperantia: ftudiofis cautela." &c.

" The humours of Oxford: by Mrs. Danvers. Lond. 1691."

In the collection of univerfity exercifes, or " Theatri Oxonienfis en-
" cænia, five comitia philologica, Julii 6; anno 1667, celebrata," is a
copy of verfes by Charles Finch, fon of Heneage earl of Nottingham,
intitled " Bellofitum, five de regione Oxonium circumjacente·" reprinted in Mufæ Anglicanæ, p. 7.

" Oxford, a poem, infcribed to lord Lonfdale, by Mr. Tickell,
" fellow of Queen's. Lond. 1707." Fol.

" Oxford the feat of the mufes, a poem, by John Heany, book-
" binder. Lond. 1758." 4to.

" Ifis: an elegy, written in the year 1748, by Mr. Mafon. Lond.
" 1749." 4to. republifhed in " The union. Edinb. 1753." p. 42, where
is at p. 47, " The triumph of Ifis: occafioned by the foregoing poem:
" by Thomas Warton of Oxford."

" The praifes of Ifis: by a gentleman of Cambridge. Lond. 1755." 4to.

" The Oxford Act, 1733; being a particular and exact account of
" that folemnity. Lond. 1736." 8vo.

An infide view of the theatre at the public act at the inftallation
of the earl of Weftmoreland chancellor, drawn and etched by T. Worlidge, 1764.

UNIVERSITY COLLEGE.] Afferius, abp. of St. Davids, wrote in Latin
the annals of Alfred, whofe patronage and friendfhip repaid the cultivation his mind received from his learned and agreeable converfation.
This work was firft printed as wrote in Saxon characters by abp. Parker,
at the end of Walfingham's hiftory. Lond. 1574. Fol. which foon
growing fcarce, was reprinted by Camden in his Anglica, Normanica,
&c. Francf. 1603. Fol. " Annales rerum geftarum Alfredi magni,
" auctore Afferio Menevenfi, recenfuit Francifcus Wife, A. M. Coll.
" Trin. foc. Oxon. 1722." 8vo. z.

z The oldeft MS. of this work was burnt at the Cotton library 1731. Hearne thought
Camden's copy the beft by far; but deftroyed by fome enemies to this univerfity—becaufe
in it alone was the evidence of Oxford's fuperior antiquity to Cambridge.

" The

" The life of Alfred, or Alured; the firſt inſtitutor of ſubordi-
" nate government in this kingdom, and refounder of the univer-
" ſity of Oxford : together with a parallell of our ſoveraign lord king
" Charles untill this yeare 1634, by Robert Powel of Wels, one of
" the ſociety of New Inne. Lond. 1634." 12mo. Sir John Spelman
wrote his life in Engliſh and depoſited it in the Bodleian library. A
Latin tranſlation by Chriſtopher Waſe, ſuperior beadle of the civil law,
with an ample comment and ſeven appendixes relating to that king's
life by Obadiah Walker, maſter of this college, was publiſhed under
the title of " Ælfredi magni Anglorum regis invictiſſimi vita, tribus
" libris comprehenſa, a clariſſimo D. Johanne Spelman Henrici F. pri-
" mum Anglice conſcripta, dein Latinè reddita, et annotationibus il-
" luſtrata ab Ælfredi in collegio magnæ aulæ univerſitatis Oxonienſis
" alumnis. Oxon. 1678." Fol. Hearne publiſhed the original Engliſh MS. with conſiderable additions, and ſeveral hiſtorical remarks
by himſelf Oxf. 1709." 8vo. Some objections to the genuineneſs of
a bearded head of Alfred prefixed to this edition delayed the publication ſome time [a]. Sir John and Dr. Walker maintain that Alfred
was the firſt founder of the univerſity itſelf: Camden, Powel, Wood,
and Hearne, zealous for its greater antiquity, allow him only the
honour of reſtoring it. Both parties were attacked in " The annals
" of Univerſity college, proving William of Durham the true founder,
" and anſwering all their arguments who aſcribe it to king Alfred. By
" William Smith, rector of Melſonby, and above 12 years ſenior fel-
" low of that ſociety. Newcaſtle 1728." 8vo. Hearne has poured out
a deal of abuſe on this book in his preface to Hiſtoria Ric. II. Oxf.
1729. 8vo. §. vi. Certain forms of admiſſion, &c. to this college
were printed for their private uſe in 8vo.

BALIOL.] " Balliofergus, or a commentary upon the foundation,
" founders, and affaires of Baliol colledge, gathered out of the records
" thereof, and other antiquities, with a brief deſcription of eminent
" perſons, who have been formerly of the ſame houſe. Whereunto
" is added an exact catalogue of all the heads of the ſame colledge,
" never yet exhibited by any: together with two tables, one of en-

[a] Hearne's liſt of his own works at the end of Caius.

K k k   " dowments,

" dowments, the other of miscellanies. By Henry Savage, master of
" the said colledge. Oxf. 1668." 4to. The author wanting both skill
and materials (for the college registers go no further back than 1520)
has made several great mistakes, particularly in his account of its
members [b]. Wood supplied him with many materials. The petition
of the master and scholars of this college, and the incumbent and
parishioners of St. Lawrence, Jewry, London, and an act for settling
the payment of tythes to the said college about 1692, are printed in
Brewster's collectanea ecclesiastica. The MSS. in this library in Cat.
MSS. Angliæ, tom. i. part ii. p. 6 — 11.

Wood who was of MERTON seems to promise a particular history
of it in his Hist. & Ant. Ox. ii. p. 85. but it does not appear that he
performed his promise. Sir Henry Saville, another member, intended
a life of the founder, either for his own or public use; but what progress he made does not appear [c].

The statutes are prefixed to a speech at the Greek lecture here, intitled " Philologiæ Ἀνακαλυπτήριον oratione celebratum inaugurali,
" quam publice habuit ad Oxonio Mertonenses, Henricus Jacobius [d];
" publicavit a quindecennio H. B. [e] e coll. Omnium animarum: cum
" appendice luculentâ. Oxon. 1652." 4to. A print of the monument
of Dr. William Smith, of Merton, 1580, in Magdalen church, is published in Hearne's append. to the history of Glastonbury, and the epitaph
pref. §. 43. In The natural history and antiquities of Surrey, vol. iv.
p. 167, is " Hortus Mertonensis," a Latin poem, by Dr. Earl, afterwards bp. of Salisbury. And just before were published two English
ones, called " Merton Walks; or the Oxford beauties; a poem. Lond.
" 1717." 8vo. and " Merton gardens. Oxon. 1718." 8vo. The MSS.
in this library are in Cat. MSS. Angliæ, tom. i. p. 12—24.

[b] Ath. Ox. II. 500.   [c] Camd. epist. p. 220.
[d] A great Orientalist, totally helpless in the world, ejected by the parliament visitors,
alike ill treated by his friends and enemies, who published his learning for their own:
he ended his days at Canterbury, where he was relieved by the kindness of a physician
his namesake, whom his apparition almost frighted out of his wits, if we may believe
the Oxford historian. He ought rather to have visited his false friend Birkhead. Ath.
Ox. II. 161. Some of his poetry is in the print of the Royal Sovereign.
[e] Henry Birkhead, the author's intimate friend, who prefixed some account of his
other works in MS. Wood says there are in this book several Greek and Latin poems,
and an English one describing *Oaky hole* near Wells, written 1632.

EXETER.]

EXETER.] For its MSS. fee Cat. MSS. Angliæ, tom. i. p. 25, 26. Wood tranfcribed a MS. catalogue of the fellows, in the library.

John Colmar, M. B. and fellow here, having been expelled the fociety for getting a baftard, a great clamour was raifed againft Dr. Bury the rector, and the reft of the fellows. The doctor publifhed " An " account of the unhappy affair which hath drawn fuch clamours as " difcry him and his affeffors in behalf of one of the fellows, who they " fay is injurioufly or at leaft too feverely expelled. Feb. 1689." in half a fheet in double columns. The year following the doctor himfelf was expelled by Dr. Trelawney, bp. of Exeter, their vifitor, for fome Socinian notions advanced in his book called " The naked gofpel," which feems to have been a hiftory of the corruptions of Chriftianity, and was publicly burnt. " An account of the procedings of Jonathan lord bp. of Exeter, in his vifitation of Exeter college in Oxford," was publifhed by James Harrington, Oxf. 1690. 4to. anfwered in " The " account examined: or a vindication of Dr. Arth. Bury, rector of Exe- " ter college, from the calumnies of a pamphlet, intitled, An account " of the bp. of Exeter's proceedings, &c. Lond. 1690." 4to. Dr. Bury wrote likewife " The cafe of Exeter college related and vindicated. " Lond. 1691." 4to. Wood fays, fome afcribed this to one Jofeph Wafhington of the Temple, a favourite of lord Somers [f]. All thefe three pieces were anfwered by Harrington, in " A vindication of James " Colmar, batchelor of phyfick and fellow of Exeter college in Oxford, " from the calumnies of three late pamphlets, 1. A paper publifhed by " Dr. Bury 1689. 2. The account examined. 3. The cafe of Exeter " college related and vindicated. To which are annexed the authen- " tick copies of the affidavits relating to that affair. Lond. 1691." 4to. Harrington afterwards publifhed " A defence of the proceed- " ings of the right reverend the vifitor and fellows of Exeter college " in Oxford; with an anfwer to, 1. The cafe of Exeter college related " and vindicated. 2. The account examined. Lond. 1691." 4to. At the end is a copy of the proceedings of Dr. Edw. Mafter, chancellor of Exeter, on the commiffion of appeal. Bp. Stillingfleet's fpeech in the houfe of lords, when the affair was brought thither by appeal from the

[f] Ath. Ox. II. 910. 951.

K k k 2

king's-king's-bench, was printed under the title of the " Cafe of vifitation of " colleges," in his ecclefiaftical cafes, part ii. p. 411.

As many pamphlets have been wrote about the fhare this college had in a later affair. " A defence of the rector and fellows of Exeter col-" lege from the accufation brought againft them by the rev. Dr. Hud-" desford, vice-chancellor of Oxford, in his fpeech to the convocation " Oct. 8, 1754, on account of the conduct of the faid college at the " time of the late election for the county. Lond. 1754." 8vo.

" The conduct of —— college confidered; with fome reflections " on a late pamphlet, intitled, A defence of the rector and fellows of " Exetor Coll. In a letter from a Cambridge foph to a gentleman in " Hampfhire. Lond. 1754." 4to.

" A letter to the author of the defence of Exeter college, by way of " notes upon his pamphlet, interfperfed with ferious advice. Lond. " 1755." 8vo.

" A proper reply to a pamphlet, intitled, A defence of the rector and " fellows of Exeter college, &c. By George Huddesford, D. D. vice-" chancellor of the univerfity of Oxford. Oxf. 1755." 4to.

" The laft blow, or an unanfwerable vindication of the fociety of " Exeter college, in reply to the vice-chancellor, Dr. King, and the " writers of the London Evening poft. Lond. 1755." 4to.

" Dr. King's apology or vindication of himfelf from the feveral " matters charged on him by the fociety of reformation g. Lond. " 1755." 4to.

" A letter to Dr. King, occafioned by his late apology, and in parti-" cular by fuch parts of it as are meant to defame Mr. Kennicott, fel-' low of Exeter college. By a friend to Mr. Kennicott, and lately a " member of the univerfity of Oxford. Lond. 1755."

QUEEN's.] Thomas Bifpham, gent. com. here, dedicated to Dr. Bar-low, provoft, whom he accompanied with the reft of the fociety in their progrefs into Hampfhire, &c. h a poetical account of that journey, intitled, " Iter auftrale à Reginenfibus. Oxon. anno 1658, expeditum." 4to.

g The authors of libels publifhed in the Evening Advertifer, and " A defence of the " rector aud fellows of Exeter college."
h Wood's Fafti. II. 21.

Upon

Upon the election of Dr. Wm. Lancaster into the headship of this college was published by Mr. Thompson, who stood for it and lost it, " A true state of the case concerning the election of a provost of Queen's " college in Oxford. Oxon 1704." Dr. Lancaster having quitted his fellowship some time before, Thompson thought him not properly qualified to be chosen provost, and appealed to the abp. of York, then visitor; but his grace upon hearing the opinion of his commissary Dr. Bourchier, professor of civil law at Oxford, confirmed the election i.

Of the new building six small views were engraved by M. Burghers; also at private expence an exact ichnography of the old chapel before it was pulled down. An orthography and plan 1695. Dr. Smith, late provost, drew up a state of the college buildings, with an ichnography of the whole, and had plates of the several parts engraved in 4to. Three views of the entrance into the college and the chamber of the Black Prince over it (since pulled down) were executed by John Green, at the expence of Edw. Rowe Mores, esq; F. A. S. 1751.

Tickell wrote a poem on her majesty's rebuilding the front of the college adjoining to the lodgings of the Black Prince and Henry V. k at Queen's college, published Lond. 1733.

A view of the front of the college to the street makes a head piece to the dedication of Dr. Shaw's Travels.

For the MSS. in the library see MSS. Angliæ, tom. i. part ii. p. 29. and for those given by bp. Barlow, many of which are of his own writing l, p. 79—83. Wood took a compleat catalogue of them 1669.

" An historica character relating to the holy and exemplary life of " the right honourable the lady Elizabeth Hastings m. To which are

i Biog. Brit. Jof. Smith. [G].

k Henry V studied in the same room; and his picture in brass with an inscription remained there till lately.

l He gave these last to his two chaplains, desiring they would not publish any of them after his death. Athen. Ox. II. 879. They gave them to the college. One of them in Latin concerning the Neocori, and another from the public library at Cambridge, being a letter to a friend with directions for the study of history and antiquities, have been published by Dr. Taylor, at the end of his Commentarius ad legem decemviralem, &c. Lond. 1742. 4to.

m Daughter of Theophilus 7th earl of Huntingdon. She died 1739. Her character is drawn in the Tatler, N?. 42, under the name of Aspasia.

5

" added,

" added 1. One of the codicils of her laſt will, ſetting forth her deviſe
" of lands to the provoſt and ſcholars of Queen's college in Oxford, for
" the intereſt of 12 northern ſchools. 2. Some obſervations reſulting
" therefrom. 3. A ſchedule of her other perpetual charities; with the
" principal rules for their adminiſtration. By Thomas Barnard, M. A.
" maſter of the free ſchool in Leedes. Leedes 1742." 12mo.

Hearne publiſhed ſome extracts from the ſtatutes of NEW college
about the library and gates, Append. to pref. to Ad. de Domerham.
N° iv. Their MSS. are in Cat. MSS. Ang. tom. i. part ii. p. 31—38.
What relates to their founder has been mentioned in Hampſhire.

Robert Hoveden, fellow of ALL SOULS, 1565, wrote the life of the
founder, preſerved in MS. in the library, and made uſe of by Dr. Duck,
an eminent civilian of the laſt century, chancellor of Wells and London, and fellow of this college [n], in his " Vita Henrici Chichele archi-
" epiſcopi Cantuarienſis ſub regibus Hen. V. & VI. Oxon. 1617." 4to.
reprinted by Bates at the beginning of his Vitæ ſelectorum virorum.
1681. 4to. tranſlated into Engiſh, with a table of contents. Lond. 1699.
8vo. Dr. Rawlinſon [o] mentions a copy of Latin hexameters on the
founder, in two folio ſheets, intitled, " Chichlæus," ſubſcribed H.
Randolph, A. B. ex æde Chriſti.

In honour of their munificent benefactor col. Codrington [p] are printed
" Orationes duæ Codringtono ſacræ, in collegio omnium animarum
" nuper habitæ. 1. Oratio funebris habita in ſacello collegii omnium
" animarum Junii die 19. annoque 1716. pro celebrandis exequiis cl.
" v. Chriſtophori Codrington, arm. a Digbeo Cotes, A. M. publico
" univerſitatis oratore, collegii ejuſdem ſocio, rogatu conſanguinei &
" hæredis ſui digniſſimi edita. 2. Oratio habita poſtero die, cum jacta
" ſunt bibliothecæ fundamenta. ab Edw. Young, L. L. D. coll. omn.
" anim. ſocio. edita rogatu hæredis digniſſimi. Oxon. 1716." 8vo. To
the latter is prefixed an Engliſh preface addreſſed to the ladies.

---

[n] Prince's Worthies of Devonſh. p. 268.
Eng. Topog. p. 202.
[p] He left 10000 l. for the library, beſides his own books, valued at 6000 l. His
funeral ſermon, preached at St. Michael's church, Barbadoes, by William Gordon, rector of St. James's there, 1710, was printed the ſame year. 4to. See more of him
Biog. Brit. II. 1374.

An

An unsuccessful candidate for a fellowship wrote " The case of
" founders kinsmen, with relation to the statutes of ——— college, in
" the university of ———, humbly proposed and submitted to better
" judgments. Lond." 4to. sans date. It was intended to obstruct the
election of a gentleman whose alliance to the founder was indisputable;
but has neither argument nor law in it. The conduct of this society
in rejecting persons who alledged themselves to be founder's kinsmen
has been defended in " An essay on collateral consanguinity; its limits,
" extent, and duration; more particularly as it is regarded by the
" statutes of All Souls college, Oxford. Lond. 1750." 8vo. By Dr.
Blackston.

" Stemmata Chicheleana; or, general account of some families de-
" rived from Thomas Chichele, of Higham Ferrers, in the county of
" Northampton; all whose descendants are held to be intitled to fel-
" lowships in All Souls college, Oxford; by virtue of their consan-
" guinity to abp. Chichele the founder. Oxf. 1765." To obviate some
difficulties in the qualifications for fellowships here bishop Fleetwood
published his " Chronicon Preciosum: or, an account of English
" money, the price of corn, and other commodities, for the last 600
" years. In a letter to a student in the university of Oxford. Lond
" 1707." and 1745. 8vo. To the latter edition are added the plates
of Martin Leake's " Historical account of English money."

Mr. Pointer having in his account of the antiquities of Oxford, 1749,
degraded the famous mallard into a goose, a year or two after came
out " A complete vindication of the mallard of All-Souls college
" against the injurious suggestions of the rev Mr. Pointer. Lond. 1750."
8vo. and a 2d edition 1751. At the end of this was advertised as to
be speedily published " An apology for the conduct of the rev. J. S.
" [John Swinton] M. A. wherein the reasons and particular circum-
" stances, which provoked him to make use of some unguarded and
" unjustifiable expressions (highly reflecting on the mallard of All-Souls
" and the author of the Vindication) in a sermon preached before the
" university of Oxford at St. Mary's on Sunday Dec. 16, 1750, will
" be fully explained, and submitted to the candour of the publick."

For

For their MSS. fee Cat. MSS. Angliæ, tom. i. part ii. p. 44, 45. The picture of John of Gaunt in the library window was engraved by Vertue.

The great S. front of the college, upright and plan, in two fheets: the N. fide and cloifter joining the chapel and library, the middle portico from the high ftreet to the chapel and hall porch: with the S. fide of the inner court were drawn by N. Hawkfmoor, and engraved by Vandergucht and Hulfberg 1717. 1721. The E. fide of the court, built by Hawkfmore, was engraved by Dubofc. The plan, the two N. fronts to the court and green, and the two W. fronts, by J. Cole.

MAGDALEN.] The MSS. in this library may be found in Cat. MSS. Angliæ, tom. i. part ii. p. 71--78. A fuller catalogue MS. Harl. 695.

John Budden ᴾ wrote " Gulielmi Patteni, (cui Waynfleti agnomen " fuit) Wintonienfis ecclefiæ præfulis quondam pientiffimi, fummi " Angliæ cancellarii, collegiique divæ Mariæ Magdalenæ, apud Oxoni- " enfes fundatoris celeberrimi, vita obitufque. Oxon. 1602." 4to. re- printed in Bates's collection.

" A true accompt of the proceedings (and of the grounds of the " proceedings) of the prefident and officers of St. Mary Magdalen " college in Oxford, againft Dr. Yerburie, late a fellow of the fame: " printed only to fave the labour of tranfcribing many copies, and to " prevent the miftakes, thereby apt to be incurred, and merely for the " fatisfaction of private friends, who either want or defire a moft im- " partial information of that affair. Lond. 1662." Fol. This was wrote by Dr. Pierce, mafter of the college from 1661 to 1671, whofe domineering temper made fo much confufion that he was obliged to refign. Yerburie was a phyfician and fenior fellow, and unjuftly ex- pelled by the mafter; whofe account he anfwered by another, never printed. Pierce then employed one of his own friends to write two lampoons covertly complimenting himfelf, and abufing Yerburie, who anfwered them likewife in MS. ᑫ.

ᴾ Philofophy reader in this college, principal of New inn 1609, king's profeffor of civil law, and principal of Broadgate hall, where he died 1620. Wood fays, he was a perfon of great eloquence, and a moft noted civilian. Ath. Ox. I. 451.
ᑫ Ath. Ox. II. 860.

The

The noble ftand againft arbitrary power in this college occafioned the following tracts. "An impartial relation of the whole proceed-"ings againft St. Mary Magdalen colledge in Oxon, in the year of our "Lord 1687. containing only matters of fact as they occurred. Printed "in the year 1688." 4to. Soon after, in defence of the difpenfing power, came out "The king's vifitatorial power afferted; being an "impartial relation of the late vifitation of St. Mary Magdalen college "in Oxford. As likewife an hiftorical account of feveral vifitations "of the univerfities, and particular colleges. Together with fome "neceffary remarks, according to the laws and ufages of this realm. "Lond. 1688." 4to. by Dr. Johnfton, the antiquarian phyfician at Pontefract, who was employed by the commiffioners to vindicate their proceedings. Next year appeared, "An impartial relation of the ille-"gal proceedings againft St. Mary Magdalen colledge in Oxon, in the "year of our Lord 1687. containing only matters of fact as they oc-"curred. The fecond edition. To which is added, the moft remark-"able paffages, omitted in the former, by reafon of the feverity of the "prefs. Collected by a fellow of the faid colledge. Lond. 1689." 4to. Dr. Smith drew up a fuller detail, the original MS. of which is in the hands of his family, and an abftract publifhed in the Biographia Britannica, vi. p. 3727, &c. n. [I.] art. John Smith, to whom he gave a copy. The doctor and Mr. Charnock (afterwards executed for plotting againft K. William) were the only two fellows that fubmitted to the authority of the commiffioners, and fo remained unmolefted till Gifford was chofen prefident, who turned Smith out for refufing to affociate with the popifh fellows. He was reinftated within two months, but four years after loft both his fellowfhip and living in Wilts, by refufing to take the oaths to K. William. He labours to vindicate himfelf from the charge of popery, but profeffes an unbounded and abufive devotednefs to royalty.

The altar-piece in this chapel painted by Fuller, is defcribed by Mr. Addifon in a poem, intitled "Refurrectio delineata ad altare coll. "Magd. Oxon." Mufæ Angl. p. 157. reprinted with a tranflation by Nicholas Amhurft, efq; ʳ. 8vo. 1718.

ʳ Author of Terræ filius.

L l l

Amongſt the original papers printed with the antiquities of Wor-ceſter cathedral, p. 192, is " The form of prayer uſed in the year 1666, " at the confecration of BRAZEN NOSE Coll. chapel, with the cloiſter " adjoyning, for a burial-place; by the late right rev. father in God " Walter Blandford, bp. of Oxford, afterwards bp. of Worcefter." The MSS. in the library are in Cat. MSS. Angliæ, &c. tom. i. part ii. p. 46.

CORPUS CHRISTI.] William Fulman, once fellow of this col-lege, defigned an account of it in a life of bp. Fox its founder, which remains imperfect in the library. Another on the fame plan Dr. Rawlinfon fays' is in MS. in the hands of a private gentleman. John Shepreve, fellow here and Hebrew profeffor, 1538, wrote in long and fhort Latin verfes the life of John Claymond, the firft prefident. The MS. is in the library'. Robert Hegge, probationer fellow 1714, drew up a MS. catalogue of the fellows and fcholars, now in the library, as is alfo his MS. treatife of dials and dialling, with a picture of the dial in this college garden, made by Nich. Kratzer 1550, and a difcourfe on it; and a picture and account of that other cylindrical one in the court of the college, made by Charles Turnbull 1605ᵘ. Dr. Turner, prefident 1687, and a very great benefactor, is commemorated in " Oratio funebris habita in facello C. C. C. Oxon. fecundo die menfis " Maii, an. 1714. in exequiis rev. atque optimi viri Thomæ Turner, " S. T. P. ejufdem collegii præfidis nuperrime defuncti per Gu. Tilly, " S. T. P. C. C. C. Oxon. focium, rectorem de Albury in com. Oxon. " & prænobili viro Montague com. de Abindon à facris domefticis, " rogatu curatorum teftamenti, aliorumque eruditorum edita. Oxon. " 1714." Fol. A copper plate of his monument in Stow church, Northamptonfhire, was engraved by Sturt.

The " Proceedings of C. C. C. Oxon, in the cafe of Mr. Ayfcough, " vindicated. Lond. 1730." 4to. Mr. Ayfcough was ftatutably refufed a fellowfhip, and unftatutably appealed to the bp. of Winchefter the vifitor, who alike unftatutably reftored him to what he had no right to, and fined the college the cofts in a manner as unjuftifiable. The author, an unknown friend, ably vindicates the college, who had acquiefced after vain remonftrances which only obtained a reduction of the cofts.

ˢ Eng. Top. p. 206.　ᵗ Ath. Ox. I. 61.　ᵘ Ib. p. 533.

For

For the MSS. in this library fee Cat. MSS. Ang. tom. ii. part ii. p. 48—58, including 12 vols. of Twine's and Windfor's MS. collections.

Thomas Storer, M. A. ftudent of CHRIST CHURCH, wrote in ftanzas of feven verfes " The life and death of Thomas Woolfey, cardinal, " divided into three partes; his afpiring, triumph, and death. Lond. " 1599." 4to. principally borrowed from Cavendifh : Wood w fays, he was had in great renown for his moft excellent vein in poefy.

Wm. Cavendifh, anceftor of the dukes of Devonfhire, a moft faithful fervant to this prelate to his laft moments, drew up an account of his life and death x, firft printed at the beginning of the civil war under the title of " The negotiations of Thomas Woolfey, the great car- " dinall of England, containing his life and death, viz. 1. The originall " of his promotion. 2. The continuance in his magnificence. 3. His " fall, death, and burial; compofed by one of his owne fervants, being " his gentleman ufher. Lond. 1641." y 4to. A 2d edition, dedicated by N. D. to Henry, marquis of Dorchefter, great grandfon to the author, had the title thus varied " The life and death of Thomas Woolfey, car- " dinal; once abp of York, and lord chancellour of England; con- " taining, 1. the original of his promotion, and the way he took to ob- " tain it. 2. The continuance in his magnificence. 3. His negotiations " concerning the peace with France and the Netherlands. 4. His fall, " death, and burial. Wherein are things remarkable for thefe times. " Written by one of his own fervants, being his gentleman ufher. Lond. 1667." 8vo. Thefe two editions have the cardinal's head prefixed, and are divided into chapters, both which were left out in fucceeding ones.

---

w Ath. Ox. I. 327. Hearne's account of antiquities in and about Oxford, at the end of Leland's Itin. vol. ii.

x It was reprinted without a date, " with many errours corrected, and fome additions " enlarged. Whereunto is added a parallell between Thomas, lord abp. of York, and " William, lord abp. of Canterbury. Lond. Printed for the good of the common- " wealth." 8vo. The Parallel was printed by itfelf, intitled " A true defcription, or " rather a parallell between cardinal Woolfey, abp. of York, and Wm. Laud, abp. of " Canterbury. Lond. 1641." and in the Harleian Mifcellany, iv. 482, and in Somers's tracts, 3d. coll. i. 263. The life of Woolfey was reprinted in the Harleian Mifcellany, v. 115.

y Stowe and lord Herbert have made large extracts from the MS. The latter calls him George, as does bp. Tanner, who gives a very imperfect account of him : the copy he faw in the Bodleian library begins differently from the printed book. He was advanced and knighted by Hen. VIII. His 3d wife was afterwards the famous countefs of Shrewf- bury, who built Chatfworth and the two other feats of the duke of Devonfhire.

Strype,

Strype, who gave lord Oxford an antient MS. of it, which feemed to be the original, and is now in the Britifh Mufeum, MS. Harl. 428 z, fays, " by the dedication it appears to be then newly reprinted. The preface is the author's own. This book is much mifprinted, as I have given a fpecimen in my marginal notes at the beginning. It was reprinted 1706, with this title, " The memoirs of that great favourite, cardinal Woolfey; " with remarks on his rife and fall; and other fecret tranfactions of his " miniftry in church and ftate. Together with a memorial prefented to " Q Elizabeth by Wm. Cecil, lord Burleigh, then lord high treafurer of " England, to prevent her majefty's being engroffed by any particular " favourite." 8vo. Neither the ftyle nor the freedom of this fpeech agree with thofe times; but it was plainly levelled at Q Anne's minifters. He adds, " this book is divided into chapters a (which the other is not) " and copies the errors, and changes the words in the preface b." An edition of it in the fame fize two years after had this different and fuller title, " Sir Wm. Cavendifh's memoirs of the life of cardinal Woolfey, " legate for the pope, abp. of York, bp. of Winchefter, lord high " chancellor of England, and principal minifter of ftate in the reign of " K. Hen. VIII. containing, 1. His rife and exceffive power. 2. His " embaffies, negociations, and treaties of peace with Germany and " France, &c. 3. His fecret tranfactions in church and ftate. 4. The " plots of the nobility againft him. 5. The king's defcent into France. " 6. An account of the perpetual peace, &c. 7. The cardinal's con- " trivances to humor the king's amours and entertainments. 8. His " fall, laft fpeech, and death. To which is added, a Memorial, &c. The 2d edit. 1708." Dr. Rich. Fiddes, rector of Halfham in Holdernefs, and chaplain to Robert earl of Oxford, wrote " The life of cardinal Woolfey, " Lond 1714." Fol. Dr. Jortin c, comparing this with a life of card. Pole, fays it was wrote at a critical time by a proteftant-papift to pre- pare us for popery and the pretender, a book which had no other

---

z Collins (Peer. i. 300) fays the oldeft MS. is in the Pierpoint family, into which the author's daughter married. In the Harleian library, N° 599, is an original inventory of Woolfey's rich houfhold ftuff by his own officers.

a He means the edition of 1667. The original preface is the fame in the two firft editions and omitted in the two laft, to which the editor has prefixed a new one, and inferted at the end fome lines out of Shakefpear and Corbet, as if quoted by the original author.   b Memorials, i. 128.

c In Appendix to Dr. Neve's Animadverfions on Philips's Life of Pole.

3   effect

effect than to expose the author and his patrons. The doctor was attacked about it on the same account in his life-time, and since by Dr. Knight d, who says, that bp. Atterbury suggested the plan and execution to blacken the reformation. He has found a defender in that vindication of British worthies the Biographia Britannica. In this book are views of the hall and kitchen of this college engraved by Fourdrinier, and of Magdalen Coll. tower by M. Burghers.

" The life and infamous actions of card. Woolsey. Lond. 1731." 8vo.
The last account of this great prelate is a heavy compilation called " The history of the life and times of cardinal Woolsey. In which are " interspersed the lives and memorable actions of the most eminent " persons, and the whole illustrated with political and moral reflec- " tions. Collected from antient records, MSS. and historians; adorned " with cuts, and a complete index. By John Grove. Lond. 1742." 4 volumes, 8vo. Mr. Grove wrote also " Dialogues in the Elysian " fields between card. Woolsey and card. Ximenes, interspersed with " critical remarks and observations: to which are added historical ac- " counts of Woolsey's two colleges, and the town of Ipswich." Printed since his death, with copper plates. Lond. 1761. 8vo. Two views of this college and the account of it are in the appendix A. p. 85.

The Latin prayers used in the morning are printed under the title of " Liber precum ecclesiæ cathedralis Christi, Oxon. Ox. 1688. 1726." 12mo. The great bell Tom, brought from Oseney abbey, is celebrated by Mr. Spark, student of this house, in the 2d volume of the Musæ Anglicanæ, p. 115. " In Thomam Clusium, sive campanam " magnam ædis Christi." The fine painting of the E. window of the chapel is described by Mr. Peter Foulkes, p. 180, in a copy of verses, " In historiam nativitatis delineatam in fenestra orientali ecclef. cathe- " dral. Christi Oxon. Ex munificentia rev. D. Petri Birch, S. T. P. " ecclef. Westmonast. prebendarii."

" A serious inquiry into some late proceedings in vindication of the " honour, credit, and reputation of the university of Ox—d, relative " to an offence of a certain member of the same. Lond. 1751." 8vo. " An answer to the serious inquiry into some late proceedings relating " to the university of Oxford. Lond." 8vo.

d Life of Erasmus.

" A

" A letter to * * * * * * * * * * *, M. D. heretofore of * * * * * *
* * * * * * college in the univerfity of O* * * * *d. Lond. 1752."
8vo. Thefe three pamphlets relate to the charge of an unnatural crime
againft a phyfician of Chrift Church.

James Green engraved a large profpect towards the E. from the
lodgings of Dr. Barlow of Chrift Church, 1754.

For the MSS. at TRINITY college fee Cat. MSS. Angl. tom. i. part
ii. p. 64—66.

" Decretum de collegio gratiis rependendis, figned by Ralph Kettle,
" D. D. &c. 1602." was printed on half a fheet.

" A letter from a ftudent in Oxford to his friend in the country;
" containing a fhort account of the late proceedings of Trinity-college,
" in that univerfity. Lond. 1709." 8vo. Dr. Lancafter, then vice-
chancellor, publifhed a programma, dated March 7, 1708, calling this
an infamous libel, and prohibiting the fale of it in Oxford.

The cafe of WORCESTER College, or Gloucefter-hall changed into
Worcefter college, was printed in a broad fheet. Lond. 1702. A fecond edition in 8vo. was intitled " The cafe of Worcefter-college, as
" it was prefented to the members of the houfe of commons;" Both
were wrote by Benj. Woodroffe, D. D. principal of Gloucefter-hall.
" A letter from a member of the univerfity, enquiring how the bill for
" fettling Sir Thomas Cooke's charity of 10000 l. for the erecting and
" endowing of Worcefter-college in Oxford, came to be rejected."
The doctor replied in " A letter from a member of the houfe of com-
" mons; in anfwer to a letter from a member of the univerfity, &c.
" &c. Lond. 1702." 4to. Soon after came out " The cafe of Glou-
" cefter-hall in Oxford, rectifying the falfe ftating thereof by Dr.
" Woodroffe, Oxon." 4to. without title or date, probably 1703.

Dr. Hen. Wilkinfon, junior, principal of ST. MARY MAGDALEN
Hall, drew up " Catalogus librorum bibliothecæ aulæ Magdalenenfis
" Oxon. Ox. 1661." 12mo. A very fhort one of the MSS. is in Cat.
MSS. Ang. tom. i. part i. p. 84.

" The fubftance of two actions and the proceedings therein, in the
" univerfity court of Oxford; together with certain queries relating to
" the fame; humbly fubmitted to the free judgment of every reader.
" Lond.

" Lond. 1749 " 8vo. relates to a fuit between the burfar and a fcholar of this hall about battels, which fhould have been brought againft the principal and not the burfar.

" A letter to Dr. Wm. King, L. L. D. principal of St. Mary's hall " in Oxford, containing a particular account of the treafonable riot at " Oxford in February 1747. By Richard Blacow, M. A. F. R. S. " canon of Windfor. The 2d edition Lond. 1755." 8vo.

Under the article of this hall may be inferted Dr. King's " Tres " oratiunculæ habitæ in domo convocationis, Oxon. viz. xviii kal. April. " 1743, cum illuftriffimus princeps Jacobus Hamilton dux de Hamil- " ton & Brandon : xviii kal. Maii 1743. cum vir nobiliffimus Geo. " Hen. Lee comes de Lichfield, & viii kal. Auguft. ᶠ 1743 cum vir " nobiliffimus Johannes Boyle comes de Orrery præfentarentur ad gra- " dum doctoris in jure civili honoris.caufa." 4to. Before the doctor publifhed thefe, he amufed himfelf and the univerfity with two pieces in the affumed character of the late abp. Gilbert, then canon of Chrift Church, who had reflected on him. The firft is intitled, " Epiftola canonici reverendi admodum ad archidiaconum reverendum " admodum. Lond. 1744." 4to. in barbarous Latin, which is pretend- ed to have occafioned the printing of the fpeeches, and was followed by " Epiftola objurgatoria ad Guil. King, L. L. D." in the character of a friend employed by the abp. to vindicate him. The doctor carried on the joke in Englifh in " A letter to a friend occafioned by Epiftola " objurgatoria, &c. By S. P. Y. B. Lond. 1744." 8vo. and " A " chiding letter to S. P. Y. B. in defence of Epiftola objurgatoria. Lond. " 1744." 4to.

Dr. Griffin Higgs wrote in Latin verfe, " Nativitas, vita & mors D. " Thomæ White, mil. & alderm. civit. Lond. & fundatoris Coll. " S. Johannis Bapt. Oxon." and in profe " A true and faithfull " relation of the rifing and fall of Thomas Tooker, prince of Alba " Fortunata, lord of St. John's, with the occurents which happened " throughout his whole dominion." Both pieces bound together in

---

ᶠ The dates are wrong printed: the firft fhould be *Maii* : the 2d viii kal. *Septem.* the 3d *Septem.* ᵍ Alluding throughout to the epithet fixed on him in the Dunciad.

MS.

MS. are in the custody of the president. The latter contains verses. speeches, plays, &c. and a description of the Christmas prince of this college, 1607, whom the juniors used annually to elect from its first foundation; which custom prevailed likewise in other colleges[h].

Edmund Gayton, a poetaster, fellow here, wrote a song set to music in two parts, called " Epulæ Oxonienses: or a jocular relation of a banquet presented to the best of kings by the best of prelates in the year 1636, in the mathematical library at S. John Baptist's college. [i].

" Σκελετος utriusque sexus πολυκες-ος." A MS. poem by Dr. John Speed, son of John Speed the chronologer, and fellow of this house, on two skeletons of a man and woman made and given by him to the library [k].

" Verses spoken to the king, queen, and dutchess of York in St. " John's library in Oxon 1663, by Thomas Laurence;" printed at the end of " Verses spoken at the appearance of the king and queen, " duke and dutchess of York in Christ Church hall, Oxford, 29 Sept. " 1663. By Thomas Ireland." Oxf. and Lond. 1663. 4to.

In Pointer's description of the university, p. 92, is a list of curiosities in the Museum Pointerianum given by him to this college. Their MSS. are in Cat. MSS. Ang. tom. i. part ii. p. 59—63. Dr. Rawlinson caused to be engraved 1754 a figure of St. John at the beginning of a very antient Latin MS. of the Gospels, and some singular characters at the end: also some unknown characters at the end of another very antient Latin MS. of the Gospels. To this college the doctor left the bulk of his estate, amounting to near 700 l. a year, a plate of abp. Laud, 31 volumes of parliamentary journals and debates, a set of the Fædera, all his Greek, Roman, and English coins not given to the Bodleian library, all his plates engraved at the Antiquarian Society's expence, his diploma, and his heart[l], which is placed in a beautiful urn against the chapel wall, with this inscription:

[h] Ath. Ox. II. 239.   [i] Ath. Ox. II. 388.   [k] Ib. I. 631.
[l] His body, with Dr. Layer's head in his right hand, was buried in the vault before-mentioned in St. Giles' church. He was third son of Sir Thomas Rawlinson, mayor of London 1706, whose picture painted by Kneller was engraved by Vertue, and his monument in St. Dionis Backchurch, Fenchurch street, by an anonymous hand.

Ubi

Ubi thefaurus, ibi cor.
RIC. RAWLINSON, LLD. & AN. S.S.S.
Olim hujus collegii
Superioris ordinis commenfalis
Obiit vi Apr. MDCCLV.

Dr. Borlafe has made this library a prefent of his curious drawings of Cornifh monuments, and intends depofiting his other collections here..

" Ordinationes & ftatuta coll. ORIELENSIS, in quibus & ftatuta uni-
" verfitatis Oxonienfis ab Edw. VI. latas & fancitas, e cod. MS. pen.
" editorem." are at the end of Hearne's edition of J. de Trokelowe. Ox. 1729. 8vo. p. 295. Their MSS. are in Cat. MSS. Ang. tom. i. part ii. p. 27. A fuller catalogue MS. Harl. 695. Thomas Gafcoyne, fellow commoner of Oriel about 1430, prebend of Wells and thrice chancellor of Oxford, left many valuable MSS. to his own, Lincoln, and Baliol colleges: in the fecond of thefe is his Dictionarium theologicum, which Dr. Langbaine wifhed to have printed, as containing many particulars of our kings and prelates not to be found elfewhere: Hearne publifhed fome extracts at the end of Hemingford.

A Latin hiftory of the foundation, benefactions, rights, and privileges of LINCOLN college is among the Harleian MSS. N° 6664. The MSS. are in Cat. MSS. Ang. tom. i. part ii. p. 39, and a catalogue of thofe given to them by Sir George Wheler, MS. Harl. 694.

" An account of Mr. Parkinfon's expulfion from the univerfity of
" Oxford in the late times. In vindication of him from the falfe
" afperfions caft on him in a late pamphlet, intituled, The hiftory of
" paffive obedience. Lond. 1689." [n]. James Parkinfon, fellow of this college, was expelled Sept. 1683, for feditious words, juftifying the murder of Charles I.

The MSS. in JESUS and WADHAM colleges Cat. MSS. Ang. tom. i. part ii. p. 67 and 85.

Some account of the effects of a ftorm of thunder and lightning in PEMBROKE college, Oxford, June 3, 1765, in a letter from Mr. Griffiths of the faid college to the rev. Mr. Swinton, is in the Philo-

[n] Wood fays this account was afcribed to Dr. Hickes. Athen. Ox. II. 1005.

fophical

fophical Tranfactions, vol. lv. art. 30. Three views of the college by Burghers.

" A fcheme of difcipline with ftatutes intended to be eftablifhed by
" a royal charter for the education of youth in HART-HALL in the
" univerfity of Oxford. 1720." Fol.

" Rules and ftatutes for the government of Hertford college in
" the univerfity of Oxford : with obfervations on particular parts of
" them ; fhewing the reafonablenefs thereof. By R Newton, D. D.
" principal of Hertford college. Lond. 1747." 8vo. Thefe were
drawn up 1725.

" The characters of Theophraftus, with a ftrictly literal tranflation
" of the Greek into Latin, &c. with notes and obfervations on the
" text, in Englifh : for the benefit of Hertford college. By the late
" R. Newton, D. D. and principal. Oxf. 1754." 8vo.

" Univerfity education ; or an explication and amendment of the
" ftatute which under a penalty infufficient and eluded prohibits the
" admiffion of fcholars going from one fociety to another, without the
" leave of their refpective governor, or of their chancellor : humbly
" propofed to the chancellor, mafters, and fcholars of the univerfity
" of Oxford, as a means neceffary to the good education of youth in
" the faid univerfity. On account of the late irregular admiffion of
" W—m S—n—, commoner of Hart hall, into O——l c——e. By
" Richard Newton, D. D. principal of Hart hall. The 2d edition.
" Lond. 1726." 8vo. reprinted 1733.

Nicholas Amherft °, who was expelled from St. John's for his irregularities, vented his refentment on the univerfity in general in a poem
called " Oculus Britanniæ," printed in 1724, and in two profe volumes,
intitled " Terræ filius ; or the fecret hiftory of the univerfity of Ox-
" ford ; in feveral effays. To which are added, remarks upon a late
" book, intitled, Univerfity education, by R. Newton, D. D. princi-
" pal of Hart hall. Lond. 1726." 12mo. Thefe remarks, partly
ferious, partly ludicrous, were made by an unknown hand on the
firft edition of the doctor's book, and anfwered in the fecond.

° Amherft diftinguifhed himfelf greatly in the Craftfman ; but being neglected by the
party whofe drudge he had been near twenty years, died broken-hearted, and was
buried by his bookfeller.

5

Exeter college claiming part of the ground of Hart hall, the attorney-general (the late lord Hardwick) certified, 1724, that they had a right only to an annual rent of 1 l. 13 s. 4 d.; and that no further obftruction fhould lie to the incorporation of this hall. In this Dr. Hole, rector of Exeter, acquiefced; but Mr. (afterwards bp.) Conybeare, and two other fellows, with their vifitor Dr. Wefton, bp. of Exeter, would not.

Upon Conybeare's fucceeding to the rectorfhip an appeal was made to the publick in " A letter to the rev. Dr. Holmes, vice-chancellor of " the univerfity. By R. Newton, D. D. principal of Hart hall. The " 2d edition. Lond. 1734." Fol.

" Calumny refuted, or an anfwer to the perfonal flanders publifhed " by Dr. Richard Newton, in his letters to Dr. Holmes, vice-chancel- " lor of the univerfity of Oxford, &c. in which alfo the conduct of the " lord bp. of Exeter, and of the fociety of Exeter college, in relation " to Hart hall, is vindicated. By John Conybeare, D. D. dean of " Chrift church, Ox. Lond 1735." 8vo.

" A reply to Dr. Conybeare, the dean of Chrift church, his defence " of the conduct of the lord bp. of Exeter, and of Exeter college, " with regard to the obftruction given by them to the incorporation " of Hart hall. Lond. 1735." 8vo.

" The grounds of the complaint of the principal of Hart hall, con- " cerning the obftructions given to the incorporation of his fociety " by Exeter college, and their vifitor, as lately fet forth in a letter to " Dr. Holmes, vice-chancellor of the univerfity of Oxford, and vifitor " of the faid hall, more fully reprefented and juftified, in anfwer to " the mifreprefentations of Dr. C———re, dean of Chrift church, in " his pretended vindication of the conduct of the lord bp. of Exeter " and the fociety of Exeter college, in relation to the faid hall. By " Richard Newton, D. D. principal of Hart hall. The 2d edition. " Lond. 1735." Fol.

A lift of the MSS. in this college may be found in Cat. MSS. An- gliæ, tom. i. part ii. p. 27.

RUTLANDSHIRE.

THIS small tract, which was not taken out of Northamptonshire till Henry the IId's time, is described by James Wright, barrister, in his " History and Antiquities of the county of Rutland ; collected " from records, antient MSS. monuments on the place, and other " authorities : illustrated with sculptures. Lond. 1684." Fol. He is greatly beholden to the collections which Sir Wingfield Bodenham of Ryhall here, an eminent antiquary², made during his confinement in the Tower in the civil war out of Dodsworth's papers. But his book is very far from perfect. He published three sheets of additions 1687, and some " Verses anniversary to the venerable memory of his ever " honoured father Mr. Abraham Wright," with his epitaph at Oke-ham, in half a sheet 8vo. 1690. An interleaved copy of this book, with MS. additions, was bought at Dr. Stukeley's sale by the bp. of Hereford.

What Mr. Peck intended to do for this county has been mentioned in Leicestershire. A. Vincent's notes taken in his visitation as deputy to Camden 1618 are in the Herald's office. Philipot and Ryley visited it together 1634.

Mr. Whiston gives an account in the Philosophical Transactions, N° 369, p. 212, of two mock suns, and an inverted rainbow with a halo and its brightest arc, seen Oct. 22 and 23, 1721, at his son-in-law's at *Lyndon*. In N° 493, p. 248, is an account of a meteor like a waterspout, seen Sept. 15, 1749.

Ben. Johnson's mask of the Gypsies was first acted by the nobility before James I. at *Burley*, the seat of the duke of Buckingham, burnt by the parliament's forces when they evacuated it, 1645.

Jefferey Hudson, Charles the Ist's dwarf, born at Okeham has been celebrated by Davenant in his Jeffreidos, a poem of three cantos.

---

² Dr. Stukeley had three MS. lists of our nobility by him, one of them said to be " in painefull manuscript."

Views

Views of *Ketton* and *Okeham* churches, and Okeham caftle are in Wright. A S.E. view of the latter was engraved by Buck 1730.

A view of *Exton* park, belonging to the earl of Gainſborough, by Maſon, after Smith.

Saxton has included this county in his map of Northamptonſhire, &c. Speed's map of it has the hundreds, and plans of Okeham and Stamford. It is alſo included in Bowen's map of Leiceſterſhire 1756.

SHROP-

SHROPSHIRE

WAS early celebrated by Thomas Churchyard, in his poem on " The worthinefs of Wales." James Chaloner, who wrote the defcription of the Ifle of Man, made collections of arms, monuments, &c. in this county, which fell afterwards into Vincent's hands, and probably paffed among his papers into the Herald's office. Some other fuch collections by E. Afhmole, 166$\frac{1}{7}$, remain in his Mufeum, N° 854. Mr. Mytton has a tranfcript of Domefday for Shropfhire It was vifited 1584 by R. Lee : 1623 by A. Vincent and A. Trefwell, Somerfet ; and 1663 by Dugdale.

Some charters of *Shrewfbury* with a catalogue of its bailiffs from 1372 to 1614, formerly belonging to bp. More, are in the public library at Cambridge. There is a fhort defcription of this town in the Gentleman's Magazine, Oct. 1763, p. 481. A plan of it by Rocque was engraved by R. Parr, with views of the market-houfe, freefchool, and caftle. A large S. W. view of the town, an E. one of the abbey, and a N. W. view of the caftle, by Buck, 1731. Four profpective views of Shrewfbury by John Bowen, viz. from Cotton-hill, from Kingfland-bank, from the abbey fteeple, and from the Coneygreen, engraved by Kip.

MS. Harl. 6693 contains the charter, ftatutes, &c. of the hofpital founded at *Clonn* 5 Jac. I.

" The lamentable ruines of the town of *Shuffnal*, alias *Idfall*, in " Shropfhire, by fire ; with the moft rare and wonderfull burning of " the parifh church ftanding on the other fide of the water, and mi-" raculous prefervation of certaine houfes which ftoode clofe by the " faide church : fet forth by Edw. Mullard, parfon of Idfall, alias " vicar. Lond. 1591." 4to.

Taylor, the water-poet, wrote " The old, old, very old man : or the " age and long life of Thomas Parr, the fon of John Parr of Winning-" ton, in the parifh of *Alberbury*, in the county of Salop, or Shrop-" fhire : who was born in the reigne of K. Edward IV. in the yeare
" 1483.

" 1483. He lived 152 yeares, nine monthes, and odd days; and de-
" parted this life at Weftminfter Nov. 15. 1635. and is now buried
" in the abbey at Weftminfter. His manner of life and converfation
" in fo long a pilgrimage: his marriages, and his bringing up to Lon-
" don about the end of September laft 1635. Whereunto is added a
" poftfcript, fhewing the many remarkable accidents that hapned in
" the life of this old man. Lond. 1634." 4to. reprinted 1703 in the
fame fize, and fince in the Harleian Mifcellany vi. p. 66. The firft
edition has a wooden print ᵃ of him, fitting in a chair in a black cloak.
His father John Parr was a hufbandman, and fent him at feventeen to
a neighbouring farmer, with whom he lived till his father's death,
1518. He held his father's farm 63 years, and at the end of the 3d
leafe took a 4th for life. By his wife Jane Taylor he had a fon and
daughter, who died young. At 122 he married a Welfh widow, and
at 125 did penance in his parifh church for getting a handfome girl
with child. That great lover of antiquities Thomas earl of Arundel
brought him to London in a horfelitter, and introduced him to Charles
the firft. Being then blind and decrepid he ended his life fix weeks
after, probably fhortened by the change of air and living. Peck collected fome further particulars of him, Defid. Cur. book xiv. p. 16.
and a note from a MS. chronicle of Mr. Harrifon, painter in Norfolk;
Appendix to his life of Cromwell, N° xi.

" Alarme for finners; containing the confeffion, prayers, letters,
" and laft words of Robert Foulkes, late minifter of *Stanton-Lacy*, in
" the county of Salop, tried ᵇ, convicted, and fentenced at the Old
" Bailey, London, Jan. 16, 176$\frac{1}{9}$, and executed the 31ft following,
" with an account of his life, publifhed from the original written with
" his own hand during his reprieve, and fent by him at his death to
" Dr. Lloyd, dean of Bangor. Lond. 1674." 4to.

Whitchurch, *Wellington*, and *Tong* are defcribed in the Gentleman's
Magazine for March, 1756, p. 120, Dec. 1758, p. 574, and April,

---

ᵃ Luke Vofterman engraved a print of him. Ames mentions another by G. White,
and a third of the father by a namelefs mafter.
ᵇ For the murder of a baftard child by his own maid. See Ath. Ox. II. 634.

1763, p. 162; and *Newport* in those for Aug. and Sept. 1763, p. 386 and 446.

A description of the *Leasowes*, the seat of the late Mr. Shenstone, by R. Dodsley, is inserted in his works, vol. ii. p. 333, with a plan, and in Woodhall's poems, 1764. 4to.

In the Philosophical Transactions, N° 109, p. 193, is an account of a strange bleeding in a little child at *Lilleshall* by Sam. Dugard[c]. In N° 228, p. 544, is a method of making pitch, tar, and oil out of a blackish earth in this county, communicated by Mr. Martin Ele, the inventor. In N° 310, p. 2418, are some observations in natural history in the parishes of *Kinardsey* and *Donington*, by Mr. Geo. Plaxton, rector of the latter, communicated by Ralph Thoresby. In N° 306, p. 2226, is a description of a Roman hypocaust found at *Wroxeter*, with an account of the ancient Uriconium sent 1701 by T. Lyster to John Harwood, L.L.D. F.R.S. with a letter from Baxter about it; which is no more than is printed in his Glossary in voce Veroconium. In N° 334 is a letter from Mr. Richard Hopton to Mr. John Batchelor, Sept. 28, 1711, giving an account of the eruption of a burning spring at *Broseley*, discovered June preceding, and described by Dr. Mason Woodwardian professor, N° 482, p. 371, and by Mr. Perry, in the Gentleman's Magazine, July 1755, p. 302. In N° 464, p. 127, is an extract of a topographical account of *Bridgnorth*, by Mr. Stackhouse, minister of St. Mary Magdalen there; containing the situation, soil, air, births, and burials, and some tumuli sepulchrales near it, from the papers of the rev. Mr. Richard Cornes, his predecessor. Another account of this town is in the Gentleman's Magazine, July 1764, p. 262; and Buck engraved a large S. view of it. In N° 483, p. 557, is Mr. H. Baker's description of some clay moulds, for forging Roman coins found in this county. In vol. xlix. p. 196, are professor Ward's observations on four Roman inscriptions found at *Wroxeter*. In vol. lii. p. 1. art. 25. is an extract of the register of *Holy Cross* parish from Michaelmas 1750 to Michaelmas 1760, by Robert More, esquire.

Messrs. Buck have engraved S. W. views of Wenlock and Bildewas, and E. Halesowen abbies; W. Lilleshull; N. W. Haghmon priories;

[c] Rector of Forton, Staffordshire. See Ath. Ox. II. 1073.

N. W.

N. W. Ludlow, E. Tong; S. W. Stoke; N. W. Clun; S. Acton-Burnell and E. Hopton castles, 1731: and a large S. W. view of Burton upon Trent 1732.

Joseph Smith engraved a W. prospect of Ludlow castle 1719. Two prospects and the ichnography make pl. iv. and v. of Stukeley's Itinerary, Sutton Nicholls engraved a S. W. prospect of the town and castle.

Hollar did on half a sheet *Boscobel* house and *White Ladies*, the retreat of Charles II. from the battle of Worcester. A simple unaffected detail of this battle and the king's adventures, collected from persons on the spot, was published soon after by Thomas Blount, under the title of " Boscobel d," with plans of Worcester as fortified by the royalists, and a view of the king's two retreats. Another detail of his majesty's adventures related by himself has just been given us from the Pepysian library. The gate at Worcester, which has nothing to recommend it but its contributing to his escape, was lately threatned with demolition.

A S. E. prospect of *Hales Owen* by James Green.

A prospect of *Whitechurch* church, drawn by J. Downs, engraved by And. Johnston.

A N. view of the church of Mary in the *Battlefield*, near Shrewsbury, drawn by James Bowen, Salop, engraved by F. Perry. This church (lately rebuilt) belonged to a little college and hospital founded 11 Hen. IV. on the spot where that prince overcame Henry Percy and other rebels on the eve of St. Mary Magdalen.

A view of the upper works at *Coalbrook* dale, designed and published by G. Perry and T. Smith, and engraved by Vivares: also a S. W. prospect of this dale and the adjacent county, 1758; with a table of subscribers and an explanation.

Basire engraved for the Antiquarian Society, 1763, a round shield a foot diameter, found a foot under ground within the area of the camp at *Hendinas*, near Oswestree, together with trumpets found in Ireland, and other curiosities.

Saxton's map without the hundreds is dated 1577. Speed's 1610 has supplied this defect, and added a plan of Shrewsbury.

A survey of this county in 4 sheets was engraved by Rocque 1752. Another map by Bowen.

---

d It was reprinted 1662, and a 4th time 1725, with Mr. Wyndham's account of the king's concealment at Trent, &c.

SOMERSET-

SOMERSETSHIRE.

" MR. Mufgrave, in a letter to Mr. Afton from Oxford 1684,
" mentioned an account given to the Philofophical Society
" there of a defign carried on by feveral of the moft learned men in
" Somerfetfhire to write the natural, civil, and ecclefiaftical hiftory of
" the county, the whole to be profecuted by feveral hands, but the
" matter to be digefted by one of them : that Mr. Pafchal, who lived
" near Bridgewater, was the principal undertaker; and that they would
" be glad of any affiftance or direction from the Royal Society."[a].
Mufgrave communicated many particulars relative to this as well as the
other weftern counties to bp. Gibfon.

Thomas Palmer, efq; a native of this county, is faid to have undertaken a defcription of it.

A tranfcript of its Domefday is in Exeter cathedral library, Cat. MS.
Ang. part ii. p. 56. N° 2093, and another in the hands of Mr. Hen.
Strachey.

It was vifited 1573 by Cook : 1591 by Brook : 1601 by ————— :
1623 by St. George and Lennard. The original of the laft is in the
Harleian library, N° 1141.

Propofals had been formerly publifhed for a natural hiftory of it by
Mr. John Beaumont, who gave a fpecimen in his letter concerning
Ochey-hole, and other caverns in *Mendip-hills*, printed in N° ii. of the
Philofophical Collections, 1681, and the draught of his defign was
communicated to the Royal Society about three years afterwards. Bp.
Nicholfon fays, " the world had juft caufe to hope for a moft excellent performance;" but feems to fear his other literary engagements
took him off from it. He was a phyfician, and publifhed fomething
about fpectres and Burnet's theory.

In 1761 were publifhed other propofals in this department by J.
Stephens, M. A. being " an introductory effay to a natural hiftory of
England, compofed from an actual furvey, and illuftrated with twenty

[a] Birch's Hift. of the Royal Society, vol. iv. p. 316.

copper

copper plates of views, antiquities, curious foffils, rare plants, and quadrupeds, and alfo a new and correct map of the county." It was to
have confifted of 8 chapters : 1. A general defcription of the county.
2. On its antiquities. 3. On the foil and its cultivation. 4. On the
vegetables. 5. The minerals. 6. The animals. 7. The inhabitants.
8. The trade and manufactures : with a fcheme for the cultivation of
flax and madder in this county. The work was faid to be then in the
prefs, and to be ready by the end of the year.

The virtues of *Bath* waters have been experienced from the days of
Bladud. Leland faw in MS. in the library at Wells, " Johannis b
" Chaundelarii, cancellarii Wellenfis orationes de laudibus Baiarum &
" Fonticulorum civitatum c."

The firft phyfical examination of them was " A booke of the na-
" tures and properties, as well of the bathes in England as of other
" bathes in Germanye and Italye, very neceffarye for all fyck perfones
" that can not be healed without the helpe of natural bathes : gathered
" by Wm. Turner, doctor in phyfick. Imprinted at Collen by Arnold
" Birckman, in the yeare of our lorde 1562." Fol. A 2d edit. " lately
" overfene and enlarged. Collen 1568." Fol. The author was born
at Morpeth, and educated at Pembroke-hall, Cambridge, where he
took orders, and was imprifoned for preaching the reformation doctrines; but obtaining his liberty retired to Italy, and took a degree at
Ferrara. During the reign of Hen. VIII. he continued in Germany,
but on the acceffion of his fon came home, and among other preferments obtained the deanry of Wells 1550. About the fame time he proceeded M. D. at Oxford, and was appointed phyfician to the protector,
Edward duke of Somerfet, to whofe fon Edward earl of Hertford he
dedicates the firft edition of his book. He wrote feveral polemical
tracts againft the papifts, the herbal before-mentioned [p. 60], and
other medicinal pieces, and died 1568. He fpeaks of thefe baths as

b It fhould be Thomæ. He was chancellor of Wells 1454,

c Collect. vol. v. 156. Alex. Necham, in the beginning of the thirteenth century,
comprehends the virtues of Bath waters in this epigram:
> Bathoniæ thermis vix præfero Virgilianas.
> Confecto profunt balnea noftra feni.
> Profunt attritis, collifis, invalidifq;
> Et quorum morbis frigida caufa fubeft

little

little known and much neglected, not having so much as heard of
them till his return from abroad. " After that I had bene in Itali
" and Germany and sene there diverse natural bathes, and was called
" by youre father's grace at that tyme the duke of Summerset and
" protector of his nepvoy king Edward the sixt our most christen lorde
" and governer into Englande to his service after that I hard tel that
" their was a natural bathe within your father's dukedome; I ceased
" not untyl I gat licence to go to se the same bathe, which done, I
" caried certaine diseased persones with me, with whom I taried as long
" as I could, and tryed for the shortnes of the tyme (for I had very
" short tyme granted me) the nature and workinge of it. And after
" being dean of Welles, which place is not far from bathe, and having
" liberty to tary ther so long as I list, I tried the same bathes a litle
" further, and found it by experience, that they were a verye excel-
" lent tresure, but unworthely estemed and judged of al men, and
" namely of suche as have moste plenty of other tresure, but not to
" be compared with this precious gift of God. But after that for the
" safegard of my lyfe, I was compelled now of late in my age to fly
" into hygh Almany, occupying the office of a phisicion, was with
" diverse sick folke in the bathes of Germanye; where as I trust I
" learned sumthynge besyde it that I knew before, which knowledge
" allthowgh the extreme niggishnes and illiberalitie of sum that had
" moste in the time of my bannisshement, and the ungentle hand-
" lying of me of sum, sence my returning into England hath very
" lytle deserved to have either in part or in hole. Yet for theyrs sake
" that are honest and vertuous men, I have writen a small treatishe of
" the bath of Baeth here in England." Dedication dated at London,
1560. " The preface of the auther unto his welbeloved neighbores
" of Bathe, Bristow, Wellis, Winsam ᵈ, and Charde," in both editions,
is dated from Basil 1557. He says " The chefe matter whereof these
" bathes have theyr chefe vertue and streingth, after my judgment is
" brimstone.—If there be anye thynge lightly menged with the brim-
" stone, which thynge I coulde not perceyve, it muste be copper "
Then he recites the opinions of Aetius and Agricola of brimstone
baths. " But nowe in this our lightye and learned tyme, after that

---

ᵈ Not *Windsor*, as in Tanner Bibl. Brit. art. Turner.

" fo many learned phyficiones have fo greatly commended thefe bathes,
" I doute whether the negardifhe illiberalite or the unnaturall unkind-
" nes of the riche menne of Englande is more to be difprayfed, which
" receiving fo many good turnes of almightye God, now after that they
" know that the bathes are fo profitable, will not beftowe one half-
" penny for God's fake upon the bettering and amending of them.——I
" have not hearde tell that anye riche man hath fpente upon thefe noble
" bathes—one grote thefe twintye years." The improvements he fug-
gefts are that holes be made in the bottom of every bath for cleanfing
it, and fhifting the water every 24 hours overnight; that no perfon
be fuffered to ufe the principal bath; that every bath have a roof over
it to keep off rain, &c. yet not let out the ftream; that lofts or upper
apartments be built for women and fuch as chufe to bathe in private,
the water being drawn up from the bath below in buckets, and conveyed away without returning to it again: that vapour baths and diftinct baths for infected patients be contrived: and, laftly, baths for
horfes.

Dr. Caius fays he himfelf wrote De thermis Britannicis, treating
of the effects and difcovery of the baths in Britain; but had not publifhed it [e].

" The bathes of Bathes ayde, wonderfull and moft excellent againft
" very many ficknefles, approved by authoritie, confirmed by reafon,
" and dayly tryed by experience; with the antiquittee, commoditee,
" propertie, knowledge, ufe, aphorifmes, diet, medicine, and other
" thinges thereto belonging, confidered and obferved. Compendiouf-
" ly compiled by John Jones, phifition, anno falutis 1572, at Afple-
" hall befyde Nottingham. Printed at London for Wm. Jones 13
" Maii."

Dr. Edw. Jorden employs the four laft chapters of his " Difcourfe of
" naturall bathes and minerall waters. Lond. 1631." 1633. 4to. on the
nature and ufes of our baths at Bath in Somerfetfhire. Guidot republifhed it 1669. 8vo. adding, by way of appendix, " A treatife con-
" cerning the Bath, wherein the antiquity both of the baths and the

[e] De lib. prop.

city

city is difcurfed, with a brief account of the nature and virtues of the hot waters there."

" The baths of Bathe: or a neceffary compendious treatife con-
" cerning the nature, ufe, and efficacie of thofe famous hot waters.
" Publifhed for the benefit of all fuch as yeerely, for their health, re-
" fort to thofe baths, with an advertifement of the great utility that
" commeth to man's body, by the taking of phyfick in the fpring, in-
" ferred upon a queftion moved, concerning the frequencie of ficknefe
" and death of people more in that feafon, than in any other: Where-
" unto is alfo annexed, a cenfure, concerning the water of St. Vincent's
" rocks, neere Briftoll, which is in great requeft and ufe againft the
" ftone. By To. Venner, Dr. of phyfick in Bathe." Lond. 1628. 4to.
annexed to his Via recta ad vitam longam. 1637. 1650. 4to. and fince
reprinted in the Harl. Mifc. vol. ii. p. 295. Wood fays [f], his great
eminence and practice at Bath was owing to the laft of thefe ufeful and
popular treatifes. His " True ufe of our famous bathes of Bathe," is
only a fhort introduction of 15 pages, about " the nature and choife of
habitable places," in the 2d edition of it 1622. 4to. He adds his epitaph in the abbey, made by Dr. Pierce, was printed by Guidot in his
difcourfe of Bath 1676, p. 170, with moft envious notes.

Dr. Thomas Johnfon's [g] " Thermæ Bathonicæ, five earum defcrip-
" tio, vires, utendi tempus, modus, &c." is printed at the end of his
" Mercurius botanicus: five plantarum gratia fufcepti itineris anno
" MDCXXXIV defcriptio. Cum earum nominibus Latinis et Anglicis.
" Lond. 1634." 8vo.

" Thermæ redivivæ: the city of Bath defcribed: with fome obfer-
" vations on thofe foveraign waters, both as to the bathing in, and
" drinking of them, now fo much in ufe; by Henry Chapman, gent.
" Lond. 1673." 4to.

" Bathonienfium & Aquifgranenfium thermarum comparatio variis

---

[f] Athen. Ox. II. 245.

[g] Before mentioned in the botanical hiftory of Kent and Middlefex. He was a native
of Hull, and kept an apothecary's fhop on Snow-hill. He enlarged and amended
Gerard's Herbal 1636. His fkill in botany procured him a doctor of phyfic's degree
at Oxford 1643: and the fame year commanding a party of the royalifts in garrifon in
Bafing-houfe he loft his life by a wound in his fhoulder. Wood's Fafti. II. 39.

3

" adjunctis

" adjunctis illuſtrata. R. P. i. Epiſtola ad illuſtriſſimum virum Roge-
" rum Caſtlemaini comitem. Lond. 1676." 12mo.

Dr. Guidot, who revived the uſe of theſe waters and practiſed with
ſome eminence at Bath as long as he could refrain from abuſe and impertinence, has left ſeveral treatiſes relating to the place and the waters.
The firſt of them has been already mentioned; others are " A quære
" concerning drinking Bath water at Bath reſolved. Lond. 1673." 8vo.
2 ſheets, publiſhed under the name of Eugenius Philander.

" A letter concerning ſome obſervations lately made at Bathe,
" writen to his much honoured friend Sir E. G. [Edw. Greaves]
" M. D. kt. and bart. by Tho. Guidott, M. B. Lond. 1674." reprinted in the Harl. Miſc. ii. 306. with the appendix to Jorden's
book, and in " A diſcourſe of Bathe, and the hot waters there. Alſo
" ſome enquiries into the nature of the water of St. Vincent's Rock,
" near Briſtol; and that of Caſtle-Cary. To which is added, a cen-
" tury of obſervations, more fully declaring the nature, property, and
" diſtinction of the baths: with an account of the lives and characters
" of the phyſicians of Bathe k. By Tho. Guidott, M. B. phyſician there.
" Lond. 1676." 8vo. Dr. Rawlinſon l ſays he enlarged this with the
addition of ſeveral Roman antiquities in 1691. and that he is ſaid to
have wrote in Latin the antiquities of this city, ſtill in MS. Wood
does not mention this among his MS. works, unleſs it be the " Trac-
" tatus amplus de balneis Bathonienſibus." 4to. m.

" Thomæ Guidotti Anglo Britanni de thermis Britannicis tractatus,
" acceſſerunt obſervationes hydroſtaticæ, chromaticæ, & miſcellaneæ
" uniuſcujuſque balnei apud Bathoniam naturam, proprietatem, & diſ-
" tinctionem curatius exhibentes. Experientiæ diuturnioris opus, &

---

i Robert Pugh, native of Caernarvonſhire, confeſſor to Henrietta Maria, queen mother of England. He died in Newgate, where he was confined upon Oates's plot. Ath.
Ox. II. 425.

k " From the year 1598 to the preſent year 1676, in which, within the compaſs of
" fourſcore years, is comprehended great part of the lives of ſeventeen phyſicians, which
" confirms the words of Hippocrates, in his firſt aphoriſm, Ars longa, vita brevis. By
" T. G. M. B. Lond. 1677." His letter to Greaves makes the 8th chapter.

l Engl. Topog. p. 217. Dr. John Mayow, phyſician at Bath, about 1670, in his
book " De ſale nitro & ſpiritu nitro acerbe. Ox. 1674." 8vo. denied any mixture of
nitre and ſulphur in theſe waters, which Dr. Guidot refuted in his Diſcourſe of Bathe.

m Ath. Ox. II. 1102.

" plurium

" plurium annorum penſum cum indicibus neceſſariis ad Regale Col-
" legium Medicorum Londinenſium. Lond. 1691." 4to.[n]. The doctor deſigned an Engliſh tranſlation of his work, but did not execute it.

A few years after he publiſhed the appendix to his Thermæ
Britannicæ in Engliſh, under the title of " The regiſter of Bath, or
" two hundred obſervations, containing an account of cures performed,
" and benefit received, by the uſe of the famous hot waters of Bath,
" in the county of Somerſet, as they, for the moſt part, came under
" the obſervation and knowledge of Thomas Guidott, phyſician there.
" Being great part of his experience of the effects of the baths of
" Bath, for 27 years laſt paſt. Lond. 1694." 12mo. He publiſhed in
4to. the ſame year, " Epiſtolarum medicarum ſpecimen de therma-
" rum Bathonienſium effectis ad clariſſ. medicos D. Bate, Fraſer,
" Wedderburne, &c." Among theſe letters are ſome by Dr. Maplet,
principal of Gloceſter-hall, whoſe travels into France and the Low
Countries, with Lucius and Henry lords Falkland, Dr. Guidott [o] promiſed to publiſh.

[n] In p. 209 he mentions a pillar erected, in the Croſs Bath, by John earl of Melfort,
on James the IId's queen proving with child ; and gives a copper plate of it, but not
the bombaſt inſcription, which is as follows.

In perpetuam
Reginæ Mariæ memoriam
Quam, cælo in Bathonienses thermas
Irradiante, ſpiritus domini qui fertur
Super aquas
Trium regnorum hæredis
Genetricem effecit.
Utrique parenti natoque principi
Abſit gloriari
Niſi in cruce domini noſtri Jeſu Chriſti ;
Ut plenius hauriant
AqVaS CUM gaVIDo
eX fontIBVs ſaLVatorIs   [1688.]
Deo trino & uni
Tribus digitis orbem appendenti,
Ac per crucem redimenti,
Hoc tricolumnare trophæum
Vovet dicatque
JOHANNES comes de MELFORT.

[o] Diſc. of Bath, p. 181. Ath. Ox. II. 466.

" An

" An apology for the Bath. Being an anſwer to a late enquiry into
" the right uſe and abuſes of the baths in England p, ſo far as may
" concern the hot waters of the Bath in the county of Somerſet. With
" ſome reflections on freſh cold-bathing, bathing in ſea-water, and
" dipping in baptiſm. In a letter to a friend. By the author of the
" Latin tract De thermis Britannicis. Lond. 1708." 8vo. Theſe two
tracts of Dr. Guidott's, with his others before mentioned, and Chapman's deſcription of Bath, were reprinted together in one volume by
Leake at Bath 1725. 8vo. under the title of " A collection of treatiſes
" relating to the city and waters of Bath."

In Nº 49 of the Philoſophical Tranſactions are obſervations on the
Bath ſprings by Dr. Glanville. In Nº 169, p. 944, an account of
their efficacy for curing palſies and lameneſs by Dr. R. Peirce, who
publiſhed " Bath memoirs, or obſervations on three-and-forty years
" practice at the Bath; what cures have been there wrought by bath-
" ing and drinking theſe waters by God's bleſſing on his directions.
" Briſt. 1697." 12mo. Republiſhed with this title, " The hiſtory and
" memoirs of the Bath; containing obſervations on what cures have
" been wrought there, both by bathing and drinking thoſe waters.
" An account of king Bladud, ſaid to be the firſt founder of the
" baths: with a philoſophical preface, of ſeveral experiments and re-
" marks relating to the origin, quality, and nature of baths in general,
" and of theſe in particular. By Robert Peirce, M. D. near ſixty years
" phyſician in Bath. Lond. 1651." 1713. 8vo.

" A practical diſſertation on Bath-waters. Treating of the antiquity
" of Bath: and its waters. Of the original of ſprings. Of the cauſe of
" the heat of Bath-waters; and of their ingredients. Of drinking
" Bath-waters. Of bathing. Of the city of Bath, its ſituation, baths,
" &c. To which is added, a relation of an extraordinary ſleepy per-
" ſon at Tinſbury, near Bath. Deſigned for the uſe of the nobility,
" gentry, &c. who reſort to the Bath. By William Oliver, M. D. and
" F. R. S. Lond. 1719." 12mo. Firſt ſubjoined to the doctor's treatiſe of fevers, &c. 1707.

" Obſervations concerning the nature and due method of treating
" the gout, for the uſe of my worthy friend Richard Tenniſon, eſq;

p The author of which " ſet up colder waters in greater oppoſition to the hot baths
" than the thing will bear."

O o o　　　　　　　　　" together

" together with an account of the nature and quality of Bath-waters.
" By Geo. Cheyne, M. D. and F. R. S. Lond. 1720." The 6th edit.
1724, was revifed, corrected, and enlarged to more than double the
former, and intitled " An effay on the true nature, &c."

" Cyclus metafyncriticus: or an effay on chronical difeafes; the
" methods of cure: and herein, more fully, of the medicinal waters
" of Bath and Briftol, their feveral virtues and differences. By John
" Wynter, M. B. e coll. Chrifti. Cantab. Lond. 1725." 8vo.

" Of bathing in the hot baths, at Bathe: chiefly with regard to the
" palfie, and fome difeafes in women. In a letter, addreffed to a friend.
" By John Wynter, M. B. e coll. Chrifti. Cantab. Lond. 1728." 8vo.
In this are two views of the head of Apollo, and an infcription erected
by the author to the memory of Dr. Guidott.

" A treatife of warm bath water, and of cures made lately at Bath,
" in Somerfetfhire: particularly proving that it is more probable to
" cure difeafes by drinking warm mineral waters and bathing in them
" than in cold mineral waters. By John Quincy, M. D. vol. i. Oxf.
" 1733." 4to. " A treatife of warm bath water, : in which is more
" than 200 cures made at Bath in Somerfetfhire, by bathing, pump-
" ing, and drinking the waters. With a philofophical account of the
" elements, fubterraneous fires, and fermentations of metals, mine-
" rals, &c. Taken from Sir I. Newton, Jones, Baccius, Guidot,
" Boerhave, Miller, Lifter, Cheney, Oliver, Wynter, Willis, Floyer
" and Baynard, Quincy, Sydenham, Lodwick, Rowzee, and many
" others. By J. Quincy, M. D. vol. ii. Oxf. 1734." 4to.

" An effay towards a defcription of the city of Bath. In two parts.
" Wherein its antiquity is afcertained: its fituation, mineral waters,
" and Britifh works defcribed: the antient works in its neighbour-
" hood, the gods, places of worfhip, religion, and learning of the
" Britons occafionally confidered: the rife of the Britifh Druids demon-
" ftrated: the devaftations committed by the Romans at Bath; their
" encamping on the hot-waters, and their turning their camp into a
" city, fully fet forth: and the works of the Saxons and their fuccef-
" fors briefly related. Illuftrated with 13 octavo plates, engraved by
" Mr. Pine. By John Wood, architect. Bath 1742." The 2d part,
printed 1743, treats of the publick buildings, ftreets, &c. which are

par-

particularly defcribed, and illuftrated with a plan of Queen's fquare.
Both parts were republifhed with the enlarged title of " An effay to-
" wards a defcription of Bath, in four parts : wherein the antiquity of
" the city, as well as the reality and eminence of its founder; the
" magnitude of it in its antient, middle, and modern ftate, the names
" it has borne; its fituation, foil, mineral waters, and phyfical plants;
" the general form and fize of its body; the fhape of its detached
" parts ; its Britifh works, and the Grecian ornaments wherewith they
" were adorned ; its devaftations and reftorations in the days of the
" Britons, Romans, Saxons, Danes, and Normans; its additional
" buildings down to the end of the year 1748 ; its baths, conduits,
" hofpitals, places of worfhip, court of juftice, and other publick edi-
" fices ; its gates, throngs, bridges, lanes, alleys, terrafs walks, and
" ftreets; its inferior courts, and its open areas of a fuperior kind are
" refpectively treated of.   The gods, places of worfhip, religion, and
" learning of the antient Britons occafionally confidered : and the
" limits of the city in its prefent ftate ; its divifions, fubdivifions, laws,
" government, cuftoms, trade, and amufements feverally pointed out.
" Illuftrated with the figure of king Bladud, the firft founder of the
" city, as defcribed by the orator Himerius under the name of Abaris;
" together with proper plans and elevations from 22 copper plates.
" By John Wood, architect. The fecond edition corrected and en-
" larged. Lond. 1749." 8vo. in two volumes.   A 3d edition, Lond.
1765. 8vo. in 2 volumes.

  " An enquiry into the medicinal virtues of Bath waters, and the in-
" dications of cures which it anfwers.   By George Randolph, M. D.
" late fellow of All Souls college, Oxford. Lond. 1752."

  " An effay on the external ufe of water. In a letter to Dr. ****,
" with particular remarks upon the prefent method of ufing the mine-
" ral waters at Bath in Somerfetfhire ; and a plan for rendering them
" more fafe, agreeable, and efficacious.   By T. Smollet, M. D. Lond.
" 1752." 1767. 4to.

  " A treatife on the Bath waters, wherein are difcovered the feveral
" principles of which they are compofed, the caufes of their heat, and
" the manner of their production. By Rice Charlton of Bath, M. B.
" F. R. S. Lond. 1754." 8vo.

" Practical

" Practical reflections on the ufes and abufes of Bath waters, made
" from actual experiments and obfervations : to which is added, by
" way of appendix, a narrative of facts relative to the phyfical confe-
" deracy in Bath in the year 1757. By William Baylies, M. D. Lond.
" 1757." 8vo.

" Letters of Dr. Lucas and Dr. Oliver : occafioned by a phyfical
" confederacy difcovered in Bath. Lond. 1757." 8vo.

" A narrative of facts, demonftrating the actual exiftence and true
" caufe of that confederacy made known to the public in the printed
" letters of Dr. Lucas and Dr. Oliver. By Wm. Baylies. M. D. Lond.
" 1757." 4to.   This was an impertinent complaint, that Dr. Oliver
had declared he would not confult with Dr. Lucas, and Dr. Charlton
with Dr. Baylies, and that Dr. Moyfey fided with the recufants.

" A treatife on the mineral qualities of Bath waters: in 3 parts.
" By J. N. Stevens, M. D. of Bath, and fellow of the Royal Academy
" of Sciences. Lond. 1758." 8vo.

" Attempts to revive antient medical doctrines : 1. Of waters in
" general. 2. Of Bath and Briftol waters in particular. 3. Of fea voy-
" ages. 4. Of local remedies. 5. Of the non-naturals ; with an ap-
" pendix on plaiftering in the fmall-pox.   The whole confirmed by
" hiftories of facts. By Alex. Sutherland. M. D. of Bath and Briftol
" hot wells. Lond. 1763." 8vo.   In this is inferted a ground-plot of
ruins difcovered at Bath 1755, exhibiting the whole plan of the Roman baths, which may be had diftinct from the book.   Part of this
work has been reprinted under the title of " An attempt to afcer-
" tain, as well as to extend the virtues of Bath and Briftol waters by
" experiments and cafes.   The fecond edition, new modelled and im-
" proved. Lond. 1764." 8vo.   The author propofes to print the other
three parts in feparate effays.

In the Gentleman's Magazine for May 1762, p. 193, was publifhed
a letter from Dr. W. Linden to Dr. Sunderland, concerning a remarkable phænomenon of the Bath waters.

" Curfory remarks on the method of inveftigating the principles and
" properties of Bath and Briftol waters: fet forth in attempts to revive
" ancient medical doctrines : and in an attempt to afcertain and extend

" the

" the virtues of these waters: both by Alex. Sutherland, M. D. of
" Bath and Bristol hot wells. By C. Lucas, doctor of physic of
" Rheims, Leyden, and Dublin, and member of the Royal college
" of Physicians in London. Lond. 1764." 8vo.

" A seasonable and modest reply to Dr. Lucas's cursory remarks on
" Dr. Sutherland's treatise on Bath and Bristol waters. In which the
" innocence of brimstone is vindicated, and Dr. Sutherland's experi-
" ments on the existency of that mineral in Bath waters, are con-
" firmed. By Diederick Wessel Linden, M. D. Lond. 1765." 8vo.

" Prayers for the use of all persons that come to the baths for cure,
" &c." were published about 1713.

" An inquiry into the contents and mineral virtues of *Lincomb* spa
" waters, near Bath. By Wm. Hillary, M. D. Lond. 1742." 8vo.

" Characters at Bristol in Sept. and at Bath in Oct. 1723. Lond.
" 1724." 4to.

" The life of Richard Nash, esq; late master of the ceremonies at
" Bath. Extracted principally from his original papers. Lond. 1762."
and 1763. 8vo. with a print of him, from an original picture by
Hoare, presented to the corporation.

" The jests of Beau Nash, late master of the ceremonies at Bath.
" Consisting of a variety of humorous sallies of wit, smart repartees,
" and bons mots; which passed between him and personages of the
" first distinction, and the most celebrated for true wit and humour.
" Dedicated to the right hon. the earl of Chesterfield. Lond. 1763."
8vo.

" Epitaphium Rich. Nash, Bath. 1764. Bristol." 4to. A banter
on monumental inscriptions.

" An historical account of the rise, progress, and management of the
" general hospital or infirmary in the city of Bath: with some queries
" to the principal conductors of that charity. By William Baylies,
" M. D. Lond. 1759." 8vo.

" A short answer to a set of queries annexed to a pamphlet lately
" publisht, pretending to be an historical account of the rise, progress,
" and management of the general hospital or infirmary in the city of
" Bath. By a governour of the said charity. Lond. 1759." 8vo.

" A full

3

" A full reply to a pamphlet, entitled, A short answer *to a set of*
" queries directed to the principal conductors of the general hospital,
" or infirmary, in the city of Bath. By Wm. Baylies, M. D. and fellow
" of the Royal College of Physicians in Edinburgh. Lond. 1759." 8vo.
A plan of this hospital was published by Mr. Wood, 1738; which, to
gain a point in the purchase of the land, was made different from that
intended and afterwards carried into execution.

" Scholæ Bathoniensis primitiæ: seu excerpta quædam è Walleri &
" Miltoni poematibus, Latino carmine, à scholaribus quibusdam scholæ
" grammaticalis Bathoniensis, donata." sans date.

The famous inscription at the east-end of the church has employed the learning and pens of some of our best antiquaries. Hearne
first published it with his remarks the year after its discovery, at
the end of Spelman's life of Alfred. Dr. Musgrave of Exeter wrote
a distinct treatise on it, intitled, " Julii Vitalis epitaphium cum notis
" criticis, explicationeque V. C. Hen. Dodwelli & commentario Guil.
" Musgrave. Quibus accedit illius ad cl. Goetzium, de Puteolana &
" Baiana inscriptionibus, epistola. Iscae Dunmoniorum, 1711." 8vo.
The substance of all these and other comments by Wynter, Gale, and
Stukeley is inserted in Horsley, p. 323, &c. with remarks by professor
Ward. Dr. Musgrave fancied another ancient monument [q] near the
former represented Geta, and treated of it in his " Geta Britannicus.
" Accedit domus Severianæ synopsis chronologica, & de icuncula [r]
" quondum m. regis Ælfredi dissertatio. Iscae Dunmoniorum.
" 1716." 8vo. Chapters 18. 19. of his Belgium Britannicum contain other Roman antiquities found in this city, and mentioned by
Camden, Guidot, and Horsley p. 328. Some Roman inscriptions
taken here by Lister are in the Philosophical Transactions, N° 155.
Another communicated by Dr. Stukeley in N° 488, p. 409, and in
the Gentleman's Magazine, Oct. 1736. p. 622. In vol. xlviii. p. 332,
are Mr. Ward's observations on a third found here 1753, inserted in

---

[q] Horsley, N° ix. p. 328.
[r] Of this British antiquity, now at Oxford, the doctor had before communicated an
account to the Royal Society, printed in their Transactions, N° 443, and in Hickes's
Thesaurus, vol. i. præf. p. 144, and the figure of it p. 173. See also the addenda to
Wise's edition of Asserius, p. 171.

Stukeley's

Stukeley's hift. of Carausius, i. 184, and in vol. xlix. p. 285, his remarks on two more on altars in Dr. Oliver's poffeffion.

The Antiquarian Society publifhed 1730 a print of the head of Apollo[s], dug up here 1727, drawn by A. Gordon, and engraved by Vertue, and in Horfley: alfo three plates of teffelated pavements, found at *Wellow*, near Bath, 1737, one of which is in Gale's Antoninus, p. 89. Vertue engraved thirteen famp es of antique filver chafed plate found at Bath.

The antiquities and monumental infcriptions of the abbey church are annexed to "The antiquities of Salifbury," 1719 and 1723. Some charters of Bath priory, tranfcribed by archdeacon Archer, are publifhed in Hearne's edition of Domerham, p. 278. Wharton printed in Ang. Sac. ii. 553. a hiftory of the bifhops of Bath and Wells to 1453, from the Cotton Library. E. and S. views of the church were engraved by King. A view of the infide on a large fheet of imperial paper, drawn and defigned by James Vertue, painter, and engraved by his brother George, was publifhed 1762: alfo a fmall view of the altar piece, the gift of general Wade.

The plan and view of Aquæ Solis make plates 70 and 71 of Stukeley's Itinerary.

A large plan of the city was engraved before 1713 on 4 fheets, with views of the principal buildings at the fides.

Mr. Reynolds took a plan of Bath for the duke of Kingfton 1725, but J. Wood, who mentions it, does not fay whether it was publifhed.

Jofeph Gilmore of Briftol took a plan at the fame time, and publifhed a view of Bath 1726.

Another, copied from the original furvey of John Wood 1735, was engraved by Pine, after the manner of the celebrated plan of Paris.

Mr. Thorpe publifhed an actual furvey of the city and five miles round; wherein are laid down all the villages, gentlemens feats, farm houfes, roads, highways, rivers, watercourfes, and all things worthy of obfervation, in ten fheets, circular.

An elevation to the S of the buildings in Queen's fquare in Bath, as defigned by Wood, has been engraved by Fourdrinier.

[s] Dr. Stukeley takes it for the genius or fortune of the city, buried for luck-fake: and fays there was originally a mural crown on it.

A S.

A S. E. profpect of this city by Buck 1734.

" A journey to Bath and Briftol: an heroicomico-hiftorical, and " geographical poem. To which are added, Love-poems, &c." 8vo. undated.

" A defcription of Bath. A poem, humbly infcribed to her royal " highnefs the princefs Amelia. Lond. 1734." Fol. By Mrs. Mary Chandler ᵗ, who put her name to the 3d edition: to which are added, " Poems by the fame author. Lond. 1736." 8vo. A 4th edit. 1738. 8vo. A 6th, 1744. 8vo. to which is added, A tale, by the fame author.

" Bath: a poem. Lond. 1748." 4to.

" The new Bath guide; or memoirs of the B-r-n-d family, in a " feries of poetical epiftles. 1766." 8vo. By Mr. Ainfty, of Trump-ington. Imitated in " Poetical epiftles to the author of The new " Bath guide, from a genteel family in ——fhire. 1757." 4to.

Propofals for an account of the city of *Briftol* were publifhed fome time before the year 1720: but whether the defign was laid afide or not does not appear. Among Wood's MSS. in the Afhmolean library, Nᵒ 8518, are " Contents of the Antiquities of Briftol, col-" lected by N. Friend."

In 1736 was publifhed " Briftol. The city charters: containing " the original inftitution of mayors, recorders, fheriffs, town-clerks, " and all other officers whatfoever, as alfo of a common-council, " and the ancient laws and cuftoms of the city: diligently compared " with, and corrected according to the Latin originals. To which are " added, the bounds of the city, by land, with the exact diftances " from ftone to ftone, all round the city." 4to. Q. Anne's charter to this city, anno reg. 9. was printed feparately. 4to.

" The exercifes performed at a vifitation of the grammar-fchool of " Briftoll on Thurfday the 7th of April, 1737. To which are added, " Verfes on the grammar-fchool, fpoken at a former vifitation. Pub-" lifhed by A. S. Cattcott, mafter of the faid fchool. Briftol." 4to.

" A defcription of the exchange of Briftol: wherein the ceremony " of laying the firft ftone of that ftructure: together with that of

---

ᵗ Millener at Bath, and fifter to the late Dr. Chandler.

" opening

" opening the building for publick ufe, is particularly recited.   By
" John Wood, architect. Bath 1745." 8vo.

   " Briftollia : or memoirs of the city of Briftol, both civil and eccle-
" fiaftical.   In two parts.   Part i.   An effay towards an account of the
" hiftory and antiquities of that eminent city, from the conqueft to
" the prefent times : containing the moft remarkable occurrences,
" general and fpecial, in every reign : together with complete feries's
" of the kings of England, lords of Briftol, abbats of St. Auguftine,
" mayors,. præpofitors, fenefchals, bayliffs, fheriffs, &c. members of
" parliament, bifhops, deans, chancellors, &c. chronologically di-
" gefted by way of annals.   Part ii.   A topographical view of Briftol,
" defcribing the city in general, with every parifh, and extra-parochial
" precinct in particular; containing their refpective extents, bounda-
" ries, fquares, ftreets, lanes, number of houfes, and inhabitants;
" parochial and other officers; annual taxes; publick edifices; and
" felect private buildings : alphabetically digefted according to the
" parifhes.   Together with a brief account of its fhipping, navigation,
" commerce, riches, and government, civil, ecclefiaftical and mili-
" tary.   The whole collected from records, MSS. hiftorians, &c. and
" illuftrated with notes critical and hiftorical.   To which is prefixed,
" a differtation on the antiquity of Briftol; wherein Mr. Camden's
" opinion of the late rife of that antient city is fhewn to be not only
" contradictory to general tradition, and the opinion of all the anti-
" quaries before him ; but alfo inconfiftent with his own authorities,
" as well as other pofitive and authentic teftimonies.   By Andrew
" Hooke, efq; native thereof.   Lond. 1748 and 1749 " 8vo.   Only
the differtation and another Nº were publifhed.   The author had the
management of the printing office at Briftol, and wrote " A dialogue
" concerning the window tax," and " An effay on the national debt.
" 1750." 8vo. and died 1753.

   A catalogue of the few MSS. belonging to this city is in Cat. MSS.
Angliæ, tom. ii. part ii. p. 40.

   " An account of the election and return of Thomas Cofter, efq;
" member of parliament for Briftol in 1734, with his head."

P p p   The

The fhare this city had in the civil wars may be feen in the following pamphlets. " The fpeech or relation made by col. Nathaniel Fiennes " in the houfe of commons, concerning the furrender of the city and " caftle of Briftol, 5 Aug. 1643; with the tranfcripts and extracts of " certain letters, wherein his care for the prefervation of the city doth " appear. Lond. 1643." 4to. The colonel was fentenced to lofe his head for furrendering Briftol to prince Rupert, but pardoned at the interceffion of his father vifcount Say and Sele. Clement Walker, who with Prynne brought him to his trial, publifhed " An anfwer to " col. Nathaniel Fiennes' relation, concerning his furrender of the city " and caftle of Briftol. Lond. 1643." 4to. The colonel anfwered this in " A reply to a pamphlet, intitled, An anfwer to col. N. Fiennes's " relation concerning his furrender of the city of Briftol. Lond. " 1643." and " A letter to the lord general [Effex] concerning Briftol. " Lond. 1643." one fheet 4to. Walker publifhed " Articles of im- " peachment and accufation, exhibited in parliament againft col. N. " Fiennes touching his difhonourable furrender of the city and caftle " of Briftol. Lond. 1643." 4to. at the end of which is Prynne's letter to the colonel. " A true and full relation of the profecution, ar- " rangement, tryal, and condemnation of N. Fiennes, late colonel, " and governor of the city and caftle of Briftol, before a council of " war held at St. Albans during nine days fpace in Dec. 1643. Lond. " 1644," 4to.

" A defcription of the antient and famous city of Briftol. A poem. " By W. Goldwin, A. M. revifed, with large additions, by I. Smart. " M. A. the 3d edition. Lond. 1751." 8vo.

In the Philofophical Tranfactions for 1754 is inferted a calculation of the number of people in this city from the burials for ten years fuccef- five, and from the number of houfes, by John Browning, efq;

A copy of Edw. Colfton, efquire's, fettlements for the maintenance of 12 men and 12 women in his almfhoufe on St. Michael's hill, and 6 poor men in the merchants-hall alms-houfes in King-ftreet, Briftol, 1708. 1712. 4to. Mr. Colfton was eldeft fon of an eminent Spanifh merchant, whofe family had the two moft valuable branches of the trade in that kingdom, the fruit and the oil, in their hands at the

3   end

end of the laſt century. See his life in Biographia Britannica, vol. ii. p. 1407. Hearne publiſhed in the appendix to his Curious Diſcourſes, N⁹ x. p. 304. a letter from the mayor and aldermen to lord Peircy to ſave the bells in this city.

"An hymn to the nymph of Briſtol ſpring. By Mr. W. White-"head. Lond. 1751." 4to.

Ames mentions ᵘ a map of the city of Briſtowe by Geo. Hoefnagel, one ſheet, 1575.

A brief hiſtory of the city under a plan of all its ſtreets, &c. long ſince publiſhed, was revived about 1720.

Another plan was publiſhed 1742 from a ſurvey, in four ſheets, by John Rocque, engraved by Pine, with four elevations of the Exchange, views of the High croſs, the Cliff and Brand hill, from the S. ſide of Avon, Radcliffe church, great crane and ſlip, St. Vincent's rocks, the cathedral, and college walks.

Of the mutilated cathedral an exact ſurvey was taken 1717. King and Harris did a N. view of it.

Toms engraved, 1745, a large S. view of St. Mary Radcliffe church by J. Halfpenny, and another S. proſpect by James Stewart the ſame year.

A print of the croſs, and S. W. and N. E. views of the city, by Buck, 1734.

A N. W. proſpect of Briſtol high croſs, with a proſpect of the cathedral and pariſh church of St. Auguſtin, drawn by Weſt 1737, engraved by W. H. Toms 1743.

To Venner's "Via recta ad vitam longam" is annexed "A cenſure "of the water of St. Vincent's rock near Briſtol, growing in great re-"queſt againſt the ſtone." firſt publiſhed in 1662. 8vo. and ſince inſerted in the Harleian Miſcellany, vol. ii. p. 295.

"Johannis Subtermontani thermologia Briſtolienſis : or Underhill's "ſhort account of the Briſtol hot well water; its uſes and hiſtorical "cures. Briſtol 1703." 8vo.

ᵘ Hiſt. of Printing, p. 538.

"An

" An enquiry into the nature and virtues of the medicinal waters
" of Briftol, and their ufe in the cure of chronical diftempers. By P.
" Keir. M. D. Lond. 1739." 8vo.

Againft this came out " A new analyfis of the Briftol water, toge-
" ther with the caufe of the diabetes, and hectic; and their cure,
" as it refults from thofe waters, experimentally confidered. By John
" Shebbeare, chemift. Lond. 1740." 8vo.

" An enquiry into the medicinal virtues of Briftol water, and the
" indications of the cures which it anfwers. By George Randolph,
" M. D. late fellow of All Souls college, Oxford. Lond. 1745." and
1750.

" The nature and qualities of Briftol waters, illuftrated by experi-
" ments and obfervations; with practical reflections on Bath waters
" occafionally interfperfed. By A. Sutherland, M. D. of Bath. Briftol
" 1758." 8vo.

" Obfervations on the earth, rocks, ftones, and minerals for fome
" miles about Briftol; and on the nature of the hot well, and the vir-
" tues of its water. By Mr. Owen. Lond. 1753." 12mo.

A N. E. profpect of Briftol hot well, impenf. S Pye, W. Melton
fc. 1747. typis F. Farley.

A view of Briftol hot well houfe, and St. Vincent's rock, taken from
the lead works near Rownham ferry, publifhed by John Palmer, bookfeller at Briftol.

A S. view of St. Vincent's rocks, and the hot wells, &c. engraved by
Benoit 1750, from a painting by Smith. Alfo a S. E. view from Durd-
ham down near Briftol, looking down the Avon to King-road and the
Welfh mountains, by Chatelain and Vivares.

" The hiftory and antiquities of *Glaftonbury*. To which are added;
" (1.) The endowment and orders of Sherington's chantry, founded
" in St. Paul's church, London. (2.) Dr. Plot's letter to the earl of
" Arlington concerning Thetford. To all which pieces (never before
" printed) a preface is prefixed, and an appendix fubjoined, by the
" publifher Thomas Hearne, M. A. Oxf. 1722." 8vo.. The title of
this account, whofe author ftudioufly concealed his name, is " A little
" monument to the once famous abbey and borough of Glaftonbury:

" or,

" or, a fhort fpecimen of the hiftory of that antient monument and
" town, giving an account of the rife and foundation of both.   To
" which is added, the defcription of the remaining ruins, and of fuch
" an abbey as that of Glaftonbury is fuppofed to have been: with an
" account of the miraculous ˣ thorn that blows ftill on Chriftmas-day,
" and the wonderfull wallnut tree, that annually ufed to blow upon
" St. Barnaby's day.   Together with an appendix, confifting of char-
" ters and inftruments, to ftrengthen the authority of what is related.
" Whereto is annexed, the life of K. Arthur, who there lay buried,
" and was a confiderable benefactor to this abbey.   Collected out of
" our beft antiquaries and hiftorians, and finifht April the 28th, 1716."
	Several charters, &c. relating to this abbey are publifhed in the
appendix to Heming's Chartulary, p. 602. 605. 618.   Copy of a furvey of all the eftates of this abbey, taken at the diffolution by order of
Hen. VIII. in Langtoft's chronicle, p. 343.
	" Adami de Domerham hiftoria de rebus geftis Glaftonienfibus. E
" codice MS. perantiquo ʸ in bib. coll. S. Trinitatis Cantabrigiæ de-
" fcripfit primufque in lucem protulit Tho. Hearnius.   Qui & (præter
" alia, in quibus differtatio de infcriptione perveteri Romana Ciceftriæ
" nuper reperta) Gulielmi Malmefburienfis librum de antiquitate ec-
" clefiæ Glaftonienfis, & Edmundi Archeri excerpta aliquam multa
" fatis egregia e regiftris Wellenfibus, præmifit.   Duobus volumini-
" bus. Oxon. 1727." 8vo.   This author lived about the midd.e of the
13th century.   Wharton publifhed ᶻ his " Hiftoria controverfiæ inter
epifcopos Bathonienfes & menachos Glaftonienfes," which was no
more than an abftract of this work by John before-mentioned, or rather the intire compofition of fome other hand.   Domerham's hiftory
is only a continuation of Malmefbury's, which being printed by Gale
among others Ox. 1691. Fol. very incorrectly.   Hearne republifhed it
with large additions from other MSS. a detail of the proceedings on

---

	ˣ Bp. Goodman, in his " Two great myfteries of the Chriftian religion 1652." thinks
this miraculous thorn firft appeared at the diffolution as an emblem that religion fhould
furvive that event, no antient author having mentioned it.   Afhmole fays Gerard, Parkinfon, and Camden are the firft that fpeak of it.   Append. to hift of Glaft. p. 301.
	ʸ Hearne takes this for the original MS. wrote by Adam and abridged by John.
	ᶻ Ang. Sac. i. 578.

abbot More's election 1456, tranfcribed from Wells regifter by archdeacon Archer: fundry charters refpecting this abbey from the fame:
and the inftrument of abbot Whiting's election, communicated by Dr.
Tanner.

An antient fair and very large leiger book of this abbey, called
Secretum abbatis, becaufe always in his cuftody, is in the Bodleian
library [a], among Wood's books bought by the univerfity.

" Johannis, confratris & monachi Glaftoninefis, chronica, five hif-
" toria de rebus Glaftonienfibus. E codice MS. membraneo antiquo
" defcripfit ediditque Tho. Hearnius. Qui & ex eodem codice hifto-
" riolam de antiquitate & augmentatione vetuftæ ecclefiæ S. Mariæ
" Glaftonienfis præmifit, multaque excerpta e Richardi Beere (abba-
" tis Glaftonienfis) terrario hujus cænobii fubjecit. Accedunt quæ-
" dam, eodem fpectantia, ex egregio MS. nobifcum ab amicis eruditis
" Cantabrigienfibus communicato, ut & appendix, in qua, inter alia,
" de S. Ignatii epiftolarum codice Medicæo, & de Johannis Dee, ma-
" thematici celeberimmi, vita atque fcriptis agitur. Duobus volumini-
" bus. Oxon. 1726." 8vo. Hearne publifhed this chronicle from a
MS. belonging to lord Charles Bruce, collated with another in the
Afhmolean library. There is an imperfect copy in the Cotton library
and one at Trinity college, Cambridge, both quoted by Spelman. The
hiftory reaches from the foundation of the abbey to 1400, continuing
Domerham, who leaves off at 1290. The additions from the Cambridge MS. are the order of the lights burnt here: an index of charters in the time of abbot John de Taunton, at the end of the 13th century: a catalogue of books 1247, and reliques. Among the books
appear Livy, Salluft, and fome of Bede's pieces *fo old as to be ufelefs.*
Among the reliques was *Sanctus Beda doctor* intire, except his blade
bones, and his head had received fome damage: Sanctus Gildas no-
bilis hiftoriographus, & *folum deficiunt harchia:* and almoft all St.
Dunftan, of whofe bones there is an exact tale [b].

Mr. Baker

---

[a] Hearne printed from it Hen. IIId's charter. Joh. Glafton. p. 419.
[b] Append. N° viii. Wharton printed in Ang. Sac. ii. p. 222, a curious letter from
Eadmer the hiftorian to the religious of this abbey againft their claims to this faint's
body, which they pretended fome of their fociety ftole from Canterbury after the Danes
had

Mr. Baker found among Dr. Brady's papers a copy of a licence from Edw. III. anno r. 19. to John Blome of London, to dig within the precincts of the abbey for Jofeph's body, agreeable to a divine revelation to him made. Hearne printed it in the lift of his own works prefixed to Caius, art. Johannes Glafton. It is alfo in Rymer, iv. 458.

" A compleat and authentick hiftory of the town and abbey of Glaf-
" tonbury, the magnificence and glory of which was formerly the
" admiration of all Europe : giving an account of its firft founders, the
" means whereby it rofe to fo much glory, the high veneration it
" was held in by both chriftians and infidels ; the immenfe riches
" given to it by kings, queens, and emperors ; the holy men who
" lived in it, and many other curious particulars collected from Sir
" Wm. Dugdale, bp. Ufher, bp. Godwyn, Mr. Hearne, bp. Tanner,
" and other learned men. To which is added an accurate account of
" the properties and ufes of the mineral waters there, confirmed by
" proper experiments ; with fome directions how they fhould be made
" ufe of, fo as to be moft ferviceable, and an authentick account of
" many remarkable cures performed by them, with remarks. By a
" phyfician. The 2d edition corrected " 8vo. A meagre compilation,
written to recommend the aforefaid water difcovered by the dream of
one Matthew Chancellor 1750 ; the fuccefs of which was circulated
in a pamphlet intitled, " Wilt thou be made whole ? Or the virtues
" and efficacy of the water of Glaftonbury in the county of Somerfet,
" illuftrated in above twenty remarkable cafes faithfully defcribed, of
" perfons who by the ufe of that water have been cured of diforders of
" the moft obftinate and deplorable kinds : fuch as the afthma, rheu-
" matifm, dropfy, king's-evil, deafnefs, blindnefs, wens, cancers, ul-
" cers, old fwellings, leprofy, &c. Thefe cafes, being but a few out
" of a vaft number and variety that may be collected, are certain facts,

had defolated it. It is a fine fatire on relique collectors. Abp. Warham had Dunftan's grave at Canterbury opened 1508, and an attefted declaration of all that was found there publifhed to the world. He fent a letter on this occafion to Glaftonbury, advifing the monks to own their miftake and prefumption ; but they knew better than to give up a faint whofe bones they had in much better prefervation, and paid no more regard to the threats of excommunication, which in a fecond letter he darted againft all who fhould affert the genuinefs of their relics, than to the expoftulations in his firft. Wharton has printed his letters and atteftation, and their anfwer.

" and

" and fairly proved, either by the affidavits and hand writing or marks
" of the perſons cured, taken in the preſence of ſenſible honeſt people,
" who knew them and their caſes both before and after their cure; or
" by the atteſtations of the miniſters and church-wardens of their re-
" ſpective pariſhes; or by credible and impartial witneſſes, living in
" parts too remote from Glaſtonbury, to have any connexion with the
" private intereſts of the place, that ſhould in any ſenſe weaken the
" ſufficiency of their teſtimony. To which is prefixed a letter of an
" ingenious and ſenſible clergyman, taken from the Sherbourn and
" Yeovil Mercury of the 29th of April laſt. Collected by an inhabit-
" ant of Bath. Lond. 1751." 8vo. The elevation of a pump-room
erected here on this occaſion by ſubſcription may be ſeen in the Gentleman's Magazine for February 1751, p. 64.

A ſeal found among the ruins of the abbey was publiſhed in this
Magazine for Sept. 1754, p. 410, by Thomas Hare of Crewkherne,
explained by Mr. Pegge in p. 459; which explanation was criticiſed
in that for Oct. 1759. p. 451.

In the Monaſticon, i. 3. are two proſpects of the town, &c. by
Hollar. In Steven's continuation, i. 419. 452. two miſerable views of
the ruins engraved by Vandergucht. Dr. Stukeley has given five views
in his Itinerary; the ichnography, pl. xxxiii. the kitchen, pl. xxxiv. the
inſide ſection of St. Joſeph's chapel, pl. xxxv. and two proſpects of the
ruins, pl. xxxvi. and xxxvii. Another plan by B. Willis is inſerted in
Adam de Domerham, vol. i. The laſt view of theſe venerable remains is a S. one taken by Meſſrs. Buck 1733; ſince which they have
have ſuffered only by the gradual decays of time. Mr. Richards exhibited at Spring-gardens 1763 E. and S. views of them.

Dr. Rawlinſon mentions c a ſurvey of the cathedral of *Wells* taken
ſome time ago, in private hands. A N. W. view, with the ichnography, poorly drawn by T. Fourd, and engraved by Toms, has been ſince
publiſhed: the beſt is that drawn by Newcourt, and engraved with the
S. ſide by King.

A good idea of the revenues of this ſee may be formed from " A caſe
" concerning the buying of biſhops lands, with the lawfullneſs there-

c Eng. Topog. p. 222.

" of;

" of; and the difference between the contractors for fale of thofe
" lands, and the corporation of Wells (ordered anno 1650, to be re-
" ported to the then parliament) with the neceffity thereof, fince
" fallen upon Dr. Corn. Burges. Lond. 1659." 4to.

A S. view of the bifhop's palace, and N. W. one of the city, by Buck,
1733. Dr. Beale wrote to the Royal Society about Ochey hole, and the
hot baths and cool fprings at Wells [d]. This cavern was defcribed 1632
in a poem by Henry Jacob, already mentioned in Oxfordfhire, p. 200,
and has fince given occafion to a copy of verfes called ' The witch of
' Wokey, printed in a fmall collection of poems intitled " Euthemia,
" or the power of harmony, &c. 1756." by an ingenious phyfician
near Bath ; reprinted with fome alterations by Mr. Shenftone in the
Reliques of antient Englifh poetry, 1765, vol. i. p. 310.

The charter for the foundation of Trinity hofpital at *Ivelchefter*, of
which fee Tanner's Not. Mon. p. 474, has been publifhed by Hearne
at the end of J. de Trokelowe, Oxf. 1729. 8vo. p. 265.

At the end of his edition of Langtoft's chronicle, p. 439, is " A dif-
" courfe concerning fome Roman antiquities difcovered near *Conqueft* in
" Somerfetfhire," fuppofed to be the place where the Romans finifhed
the conqueft of Britain. It was fince the property of A. Pafchal, who
mentions it in his letter about the Athelney difcoveries, Curious Mifcellanies, p. 17, and now in the hands of James Weft, efq; Hearne afcribes it to Mr. Gibbons, author of the treatife on Stonehenge, to be
hereafter mentioned.

In the preface to Domerham, p. xxv—xxxvi. is an account of
fome of the abbots of *Muchelney*; and p. lxvii. fome extracts relative
to this houfe from two old breviaries. A perambulation of *Selewood*,
Neracchift, *Exmore*, *Mendip*, and *North Petherton*, 1298, from the
regifters of Wells, ib. p. 184—201. and 685.

" The antient laws, cuftoms, and orders of the miners in the king's
" foreft of *Mendipp*, in the county of Somerfet. Lond. 1687." 12mo.

" A true report of certaine wonderfull overflowing of waters now
" lately in Summerfetfhire, Norfolke, and other places in England,
" deftroying many thoufands of men, women, and children, over-

[d] Birch's Hift. of the Royal Society, vol. i. p. 198.

Q q q
" throwing

" throwing and bearing down whole townes and villages, and drown-
" ing infinite numbers of fheep and other cattle." 4to. fans date.

" More ftrange newes of wonderfull accidents happening by the late
" overflowing of waters in Summerfetfhire, Gloucefterfhire, Norfolke,
" and other parts of England; with a true relation of the townes'
" names that are loft, and the number of perfons drowned; with
" other reports of accidents, that were not before difcovered, happen-
" ing about Briftow and Barftable." 4to. fans date.

" To the king's moft excellent majefty, and the honourable houfes
" of parliament, a mediterranean paffage, by water, from London to
" Briftol, and from Lynne to Yarmouth, and fo confequently to the
" city of York; for the great advancement of trade and traffique: by
" Francis Mathew, efquire. Lond. 1670." 4to.

" A modeft reprefentation of the benefits and advantages of making
" the river *Avon* navigable from Chrift Church to the city of New
" Sarum. Humbly fubmitted to the confideration of the city afore-
" mentioned and the counties bordering upon the faid river, and to all
" other perfons that are or may be concerned therein, for their incou-
" ragement jointly to carry on fo noble a work. By J. H. [James
" Hely] a real well wifher both to the city and county. Lond. 1672."
4to.

" Avona: or, a tranfient view of the benefit of making rivers in this
" kingdom navigable. Occafioned by obferving the fcituation of the
" city of Salifbury upon the Avon, and confequence of opening that
" river to the city; communicated by a letter to a friend at London.
" By R. G. Lond. 1675." 8vo.

In p. 276 of N° 150 of the Philofophical Tranfactions is an account
of fome rock-plants growing in the lead mines of Mendipp hills, by
John Beaumont, jun. of Stoney-Eafton, in this county. In p. 968 of
N° 360 is a letter from John Strachey, efq; to Robert Welfted, with
a curious defcription of the ftrata obferved in the coal mines of Mendipp. Mr. Strachey's obfervations on the ftrata in coal mines in other
parts of the kingdom were inferted in N° 391. In p. 54 of Mifcellanies on feveral curious fubjects is a letter from A. Pafchal to Mr. Aubrey about gold mines, &c. near Glaftonbury. Another letter,

p. 13, mentions a thunder ftorm at *Polden* hill, and a third, p. 15, gives an account of an old tomb, &c. found at *Athelney* 1674. In p. 1 of the 2d N° of the Philofophical Collections is his account of a monftrous human birth at *Hilbrewers*. In N° 18, p. 323, of the Philofophical Tranfactions are promifcuous obfervations on this county by Dr. Beale on fubterraneous oaks between Yeovil and Bridgewater, a vitriolic pool, &c. In N° 39, p. 767, are Glanville's remarks on Mendip mines. In p. 5138 of N° 90 his letter concerning a freezing rain followed by great warmth, Dec. 1672, about Briftol. In N° 56, p. 1128, Mr. Highmore's brief account of a falt fpring near *Eaft Chenock*. In p. 672 of N° 198 an account of the digging and preparing the lapis calaminaris near *Wrington*, by Dr. Giles Pooley. In N° 41, p. 813, are capt. Sturmy's obfervations on tides in *Hong road* near Briftol. In N° 488 is an account of an earthquake at *Taunton* July 1, 1747, in a letter from the rev. Mr. John Fofter to Mr. Henry Baker. Art. 32 of vol. li. is an account of a meteor feen at Bath Oct. 20, 1759. Art. 30. in vol. lii. is an account of a remarkable fifh of the fea-lion kind, taken at *King-road* near Briftol, by Mr. Ferguson. In p. 83 of vol. liv. is an account of a remarkable tide at Briftol Feb. 11, 1767, by the rev. Dr. Tucker.

In the Royal Society's repofitory is a copy of fome Mofaic pavement found in Sir E. Hungerford's lands near Bath 1683 [e]. A large one was found about twelve years ago at *Eaft Coker*, a village a little out of the road from Yeovil to Crewkherne and about five miles from the former, in a field belonging to Mr. Forbes, mafter of the Angel at Yeovil. It was near fifteen feet fquare, formed into figures of perfons lying on a bed furrounded with torches, and a border of dogs, hares, and other animals. It lay on each fide the entrance of a room which they called a chapel, and was difcovered by digging a ditch, together with a fuda-tory with its pipes and flews, and many coffins and bones: the founda-tions of other buildings are faid to remain undifturbed in the fame field. Dr. Denham, phyfician at Yeovil, drew up a defcription of it; but the tenant, a poor man, after numbers of people had feen it, ploughed it up on pretence that it fpoiled his field. I could not learn whether any draught of it was taken.

e Birch's Hift. of the Royal Society, vol. vi. p. 25.

In

In the Gentleman's Magazine for the year 1749, p. 405, is an account of Roman coins found at *North Curry*, near Taunton, July 12, 1748, by J. Pile.

Meffrs. Bucks engraved, 1733, S. Montacute priory; N. E. Dunfter; W. Stokecourci; N. Farley; N. E. Nunny caftles.

In pl. xliv. of Stukeley's Itinerary Cur. is a view of *Montacute* hill: in pl. xliii. *Camalet* caftle (which is alfo in Mufgrave's Belgium Brit. tab. x.): pl. lxxii. *Ifchalis* (Ilchefter).

The monument erected on *Lanfdown* near Bath to the memory of Sir Bevill Grenville flain there, was engraved 1746. the infcription extracted from the Oxford verfes on his death.

Mr. Richards exhibited at Spring-garden, 1764, a view of *Halwell*, the feat of Sir Charles Kemeys Tynte, bart. as did Mr. Lambert, 1763, a view of the entrance into the *Chedder* cliffs.

Saxton's map of this " fruitfull" county was engraved by Leon. Tervoort, 1575, without the hundreds; added in Speed's with a plan of Bath, and the baths; that of Briftol being inferted in his map of Gloucefterfhire.

Another map with the ichnography of Bath by E. Bowen.

STAFFORD-

STAFFORDSHIRE.

SAmpſon Erdeſwick, eſq; of Sandon, whom Camden calls *antiqui-tatis cultor maximus*, collected the antiquities of his native county 1603. His original MS. or a copy, was in Wood's time in the hands of Walter Chetwynd of Ingeſtree, eſq; who was himſelf long engaged in the ſame deſign, but did not live to compleat it. Afterwards George Digby of Sandon, eſq; had it, and lent it to Sir Simon Degge, who re-turned it with the letter annexed to the printed edition. This " Survey " of Staffordſhire, containing the antiquities of the county, with a " deſcription of *Beeſton* caſtle ª," was " publiſhed from Sir Wm. Dug- " dale's tranſcript of the author's original copy. To which are added, " ſome obſervations upon the poſſeſſors of monaſtery lands in Stafford- " ſhire : by Sir Simon Degge, knt. Lond. 1717." 8vo. Only the lat-ter part of this moſt incorrect edition was printed from Dugdale's copy; the other from a MS. in Thoreſby's muſeum, N° 44. bought at his ſale by John Wightwick, eſq; of Tunſtall in this county, which has ſome corrections in a different hand, and goes no further than p. 201 of the printed book, reſuming the hiſtory again in Degge's letter, which ends, but does not begin, in the epiſtolary form. Both parts were reprinted 1723. 8vo. Among the Harleian MSS, N° 1990, is a very correct copy of this ſurvey, with many conſiderable additions, which deſerve a new edition.

James Chaloner, mentioned in Shropſhire, made collections of arms, &c. here; which likewiſe were in Vincent's hands. The arms, epi-taphs, feneſtral inſcriptions, with draughts of tombs, &c. in ſome churches and houſes by E. Aſhmole, when he accompanied Dugdale 166$\frac{2}{7}$, written moſtly in his own hand, are in his muſeum, N° 853. Such collections by Erdeſwick were in Mr. Chetwynd's poſſeſſion. Tho. Aſtle, eſq; F. A. S. another native of this county, has collected many materials for a hiſtory of it, which he is ready to communicate to any who are diſpoſed to undertake the taſk.

ª Boydell engraved a large view of this caſtle, from an old drawing in the poſſeſſion of Wm. Cowper, eſq; F. R. S. This ſhould have been mentioned in Cheſhire.

" The

" The natural hiftory of Staffordfhire, by Robert Plott, L.L.D.
" keeper of the Afhmolean mufæum, and profeffor of chymiftry in the
" univerfity of Oxford. Oxon. 1686." In the epiftle dedicatory to his
hiftory of Oxfordfhire he feems to promife an account of the other
counties; but clofes this work, the refult of nine years ftudy and travel, with a refolution to publifh no more of thefe hiftories (though I
think, fays he, I never was fo fit as now) unlefs commanded by a
power that he muft not refift; meaning James II. whofe approbation
of his natural hiftory of Oxfordfhire encouraged him to compile this,
which was publifhed by fubfcription of a penny a fheet, a penny a
plate, and fix-pence the map, amounting to 10s. or 12s. the copy.

Staffordfhire was vifited 1566 by Glover: 1583 by Flower: 1614
by St. George: 1664 by Dugdale.

The firft draught of a furvey of *Pirehill* hundred by Mr. Chetwynd,
not quite finifhed, with a collection of fair drawings of all the monuments, &c. and two folios of deeds, &c. for the faid hundred (one of
them having a tranfcript of Domefday for the whole county) are mentioned in the catalogue of his library. Cat. MSS. Ang. part ii. p. 105.
Some other tranfcripts from Domefday are in Afhmole's mufeum. Ib.
p. 343. N° 7841. p. 333. N° 7459, p. 348. N° 8087. and the late
Dr. Vernon of Bloomfbury had a correct copy of it.

MSS. Harl. 568. is a book relating for the moft part to the honour
of *Tutbury*, from an older copy. The Antiquarian Society have given
us a view of the caftle, from a draught taken in Elizabeth's time. We
have another of it, with the priory, by Buck, 1731.

We were promifed " The ftate of St. Mary's church in *Stafford*, from
" the time of Q. Elizabeth's grant to this day; faithfully reprefented,
" and humbly fubmitted to the judgment of the right hon. the lord
" high-chancellor of Great Britain, under his majefty, the undoubted
" patron of that church, and to the confideration of all other lovers of
" truth and juftice. Together with a true copy of the faid grant, and
" fome remarks on the management of the fchool revenues, and of
" feveral charities given to the inferior burgeffes, and to the poor of the
" town. By Jofeph Walthorne, M.A. rector of St. Mary's in Staf-
" ford, for his own vindication [b].

[b] Engl. Topog. p. 224.

Afhmole

Afhmole intended to write the hiftory and antiquities of *Litchfield,* his native city : his collections are in his mufeum ; and Hiftoria Ecclefiæ de Lichfeld, bib. Bodl. 3553. Thomas Chefterfield [c], canon of Litchfield about 1340 wrote a hiftory of the kings of Mercia, and the bifhops of Mercia or Litchfield, to A. D. 1347, commonly called Chronicon Lichfeldenfe, and publifhed by Wharton, Angl. Sac. i. 423. as is the continuation by Wm. Whitlock, prebendary here, 1560, in the fame volume, p. 444. In Afhmole's mufeum is a tranfcript of Chefterfield's book by Whitlock, with his additions, both fuller than the printed copies. The black book quoted by Spelman [d], and the defcription of the clofe and two monafteries there cited by Dugdale [e] do not appear to exift : two regifters formerly Le Neve's are in the Harleian library, 3868, 4799. The antiquities of this cathedral are annexed to that of Worcefter, Lond. 1717. 1723. 8vo. A catalogue of MSS. belonging to it is in Cat. MSS. Ang. tom. ii. p. 32. In the Gentleman's Magazine, Sept. 1746, p. 465, is an old gravefone and infcription found in the ruins of the Grey friars, explained by Mr. Pegge in that for Oct. p. 545, and by another perfon in that for Dec. p. 646. Accounts of two coffins in the cathedral by Mr. Richard Greene are in that for Sept. 1751, p. 398, and Jan. 1759, p. 4. and Mr. Pegge's obfervations on the latter in that for Feb. 1759, p. 66. Bp. Hacket's monument was engraved by Hollar for his life prefixed to his " Century of fermons," publifhed by Dr. Plume 1675. Fol. King engraved the W. and Harris the N. fides of the church. A large print of the W. front and a fmaller of the S. fide was executed by the late Francis Perry, who afterwards deftroyed the plates. Buck engraved a S. W. profpect of the city 1732. An E. view of the cathedral ard clofe from Stowpool, near St. Chad's church, 1745, by R. Greene, engraved by J. Wood.

One Wheeler a popifh prieft publifhed " A faithfull relation of the " proceedings of the catholick gentlemen with the boy of *Bilfon*, &c. " 1620." reprinted in " The boy of Bilfon, or a true difcovery of the

---

[c] Not Chefterton, as Nicholfon, H. L. 132. tioned by Tanner, who mentions white and red books.

[d] Gloff. v. Putura, not mentioned by Tanner, who mentions white and red books. [e] Mon. Ang. iii. 216.

" late

" late notorious imposture of certain Romish priests in their pretended
" exorcism or expulsion of the divell out of a young boy named Wil-
" liam Perry, sonne of Thomas Perry of Bilson, in the countie of Staf-
" ford, yeoman : upon which occasion hereunto is premitted a briefe
" theological discourse, by way of caution for the more easy disarming
" of such Romish priests, and judging of their false pretences both in
" this and the like practices. 1622." 4to.

" A just narrative or account of the man whose hands and legs rotted
" off, in the parish of *King's Swinford,* in Staffordshire, where he died
" June 21, 1677, carefully collected by James Illingworth, B. D. an
" eye and ear witness of most of the material particulars in it. Lond.
" 1678." 12mo. Lately republished under the title of " A genuine
" account, &c. To which is added (occasioned by this remarkable
" instance of divine vengeance) a discourse concerning God's judg-
" ments preach'd (in substance) at Old Swinford in Worcestershire, a
" neighbouring parish to King's Swinford. By Simon Ford. D. D. and
" rector of the said parish. To the whole is prefix'd the rev. Mr.
" Wm. Whiston's remarkable mention of this extraordinary affair; with
" his reasons for the republication thereof, taken from his memoirs.
" Lond. [1751.]" 8vo. We have another account of it in " Strange
" and true news from Staffordshire : or a true narrative concerning a
" young man lying under almighty God's just vengeance for impre-
" cating God's judgment upon himself, and pleading his innocency,
" though he knew himself guilty. Written by W. Vincent, minister
" of God's word at Bednall, in the county of Stafford, who saw and
" discoursed the same person upon the 2d day of April 1677, the sad-
" dest spectacle that ever eyes beheld. Lond. 1677." 4to. reprinted in
the Harleian Miscellany, vol. ii. p. 311.

" Fons sanitatis; or the healing spring at *Willow-bridge* in Stafford-
" shire; found out by the right hon. the lady Jane Gerard, baroness of
" Bromley: published for the common good by Samuel Gilbert, chap-
" lain to her honour, and rector of Quat. Lond. 1676." 12mo.

" A true relation of the terrible earthquake at *West Brummidge* in
" Staffordshire, and the parts adjacent, on Tuesday the 4th of this in-
" stant January 167⅚, as it was lately sent by several letters from those

" parts

" parts to divers eminent citizens in London ; and likewife a true ac-
" count of the terror of the earthquake at Kidderminfter in Worcefter-
" fhire, as it was communicated in a letter to an eminent artift in
" London from his correfpondent there." 4to. eight pages.

At the end of Erdefwicke's furvey is " A fcheme or propofal for
" making a navigable communication between the rivers of Trent and
" Severn in the county of Stafford. By Dr. Thomas Congreve of Wol-
" verhampton." reprinted 1753. with obfervations on the rivers-be-
tween Oxford and Bath, and a map, not mentioned in the title. In
the Gentleman's Magazine for Feb. 1760, p. 65, are conjectures concerning the Roman names of the river Trent.

A plan of the navigable canal, intended to be made, for opening a
communication between the interior parts of the kingdom and the ports
of Briftol, Liverpool, and Hull.

In the Philofophical Tranfactions, N° 145, p. 96, are Dr. Plott's
obfervations on the fand found in the brine of falt works of this county.
In N° 150, p. 281, is a letter from Mr. Sampfon Birch, apothecary at
Stafford, concerning a monftrous birth at *Heywood*; with Dr. Tyfon's
remarks. In N° 156, p. 489, are Dr. Lifter's obfervations on the midland falt fprings. In N° 245, p. 384, is a Clog, or Staffordfhire almanac, with a copper plate, by Dr. Plott; inferted in his hiftory. In
N° 336, p. 541, is Mr. F. Bellers's account of the fcattered ftrata of
earth, coal, ftone, &c. at *Dudley*. In N° 496, p. 598, defcriptions of
a foffil found there; and in vol. xlviii. p. 286, Mr. De Cofta's obfervations on it.

In the Gentleman's Magazine for May 1748, p. 218, is an account
of a fhower of very large hail-ftones at *Seighford* July 3, 1719. In
that for July 1751, p. 296, a view and account of *Burton* bridge. In
that for Sept. 1763, p. 445, a defcription of the parifh of *Wefton*.

A plan of *Wolverhampton*, by If. Taylor, 1750, was engraved by
Jefferies, with the number of houfes and inhabitants, and a S. view of
St. Peter's church, and the fchool.

Dr. Rawlinfon engraved the foundation charter of *Croxton* abbey by
Rog. de Verdun 1179, in his poffeffion 1743. A N. E. view of the
ruins by Buck 1731.

A view

A view of the ruins of the church of *Fairfeld*, olim Fagrovella, drawn by R. Green of Lichfield, engraved by F. Perry.

The steam-engine near Dudley castle, invented by Capt. Savery and Mr. Newcomen, erected by the latter, was drawn and engraved by T. Barnes 1719.

Trentham, the seat of earl Gower, J. Harris delin. J. Bonneau scrip. 1751.

A view and plan of *Sandwell*, lord Dartmouth's, by Lightoler and Benazech.

Buck's other views in this county are,

S. W. Dudley priory.

S. Dudley ⎱
           ⎰ castles.
S. W. Alton

And a large S. W. prospect of Burton 1732.

Saxton's map was engraved 1577 by Scatterus, without the hundreds; added with plans of Stafford and Lichfield in Speed's 1610. Hollar engraved a small map 1670. The most accurate is that prefixed to Plott's book by Joseph Brown, with the arms of the gentry and an index. Em. Bowen engraved another.

S U F F O L K.

S U F F O L K.

BISHOP Kennet, in his life of Somner, feems to hint that Sir Simond D'Ewes defigned a furvey of this county. What progrefs
he made is not known, there being but few pieces on this fubject among
his collections in the Harleian library. Bp. Nicholfon was difappointed
in his fearch for them, I know not on what authority, among Dodfworth's at Oxford. One Mr. Tilleyfon or Tillotfon of this county is
faid to have written fomething on its antiquities [a]. Dr. Tanner communicated many particulars to bp. Gibfon. A tranfcript of Domefday
is mentioned in the earl of Carlifle's library, Cat. MSS. Angl. ii. p. 14.
Nº 17. Another among Dodfworth's MSS. in the Bodleian ib. i. p.
120, Nº 5946. 17. It was vifited by Harvey 1561 : by Cooke 1577:
by Raven 1612 : by Byfhe 1664.

It was furveyed in 1732 and the two following years by John Kirby
of Wickham, who publifhed " The Suffolk traveller, or a journey
" through Suffolk ; in which is inferted the true diftance in the roads
" from Ipfwich to every market town in Suffolk, and the fame from
" Bury St. Edmond's. Likewife the diftance in the roads from one
" village to another ; with notes of direction for travellers, as what
" churches and gentlemen's feats are paffed by, and on which fide of
" the road, and the diftance they are at from either of the faid towns :
" with a fhort hiftorical account of the antiquities of every market town,
" monafteries, caftles, &c. that were in former times. Ipfwich 1735."
12mo. But this is no more than a compilation from other books by
the publifher's friends. A new edition was lately printed by fubfcription, with many alterations and large additions by feveral hands. Lond.
1764. 8vo. Though much improved beyond the former, it is by no
means equal to what might be done.

A hiftory of *Ipfwich* from the Saxon times down to the death of
Charles I. in 800 folio pages, by Mr. Bacon, its recorder, town clerk,

---

[a] Wanley in Cat. Harl. MSS. Nº 793. who fays Dr. Keurden mehtions him.

and

and reprefentative under Cromwell, is likely to remain in MS. according to the character given of it for inaccuracy by the editors of Kirby's book [b]. All that has been publifhed about this place is " An account of the gifts and legacies that have been given and be- " queathed to charitable ufes in the town of Ipfwich: with fome ac- " count of the prefent ftate and management, and fome propofals for " the future regulation of them. Ipfwich 1747." 8vo. By Mr. Cannings, minifter of Sir Laurence, and " The principal charters which " have been granted to the corporation of Ipfwich in Suffolk, tran- " flated. Lond. 1754." 8vo. By the fame.

A S. W. view of the town by Buck 1741. A plan in nine fheets, drawn and publifhed by John Kirby. Another, and a fhort hiftorical account of it in Grove's " Dialogue between Woolfey and Ximenes. " 1761." p. 121. and a plan of the ftreets through which the procef- fion paffed from Cardinal college to our Lady of Ipfwich; with up- rights of St. Laurence, Nicholas, Stephens, and Peter's churches and the college gate. Dr. Rawlinfon engraved at bottom of one of his York- fhire deeds his feal of the Dominican convent at Ipfwich, mentioned only by Tanner, N. M. p. 528.

Weever had his information about *Dunwich* from a large treatife about it, then in the hands of Sir S. D'Ewes, written in the time of Q. Mary by an anonymous author.

" An hiftorical account of Dunwich, antiently a city, now a borough; " Blithburgh, formerly a town of note, now a village; Southwold, " once a village, now a town corporate; with remarks on fome places " contiguous thereto; principally extracted from feveral antient re- " cords, MSS. &c. which were never before made public. By Tho. " Gardner [c]. Illuftrated with copper plates. Lond. 1754." 4to.

Vertue had feen on a large fkin of velom a plan of the town and boundaries of Dunwich, with its churches, adjacent villages, &c. and feveral remarks, made by Radulphus Aggas in March 1589 [d]. His report of the ftate of the town and harbour is printed in Gardner's book, p. 20.

---

[b] Second edition, p. 15. n.   [c] An officer of excife there.
[d] Walpole's Anecd. of paint. vol. i. p. 157. n. Ames's Hift. of print. p. 389.

" A pro-

" A proper newe fonet, declaring the lamentation of *Beckles*, a
" market towne in Suffolke, which was in the greate winde upon
" S. Andrewe's eve laft paft, moft pittifullie burned with fire, to the
" loffe by eftimation 20,000 l. and upwarde, and the number of four-
" fcore dwelling houfes. To Wilfon's tune. 1586." A half fheet of
fourteen ftanzas of eight lines each.

" The hiftory and antiquities of the ancient villa of *Wheatfield* in
" the county of Suffolk. Lond. 1758" 4to. A humorous account of
a village near Ipfwich by the rector Mr. Club, in ridicule of the hiftory
and antiquities of Colchefter.

" The woefull and lamentable waft and fpoile done by a fuddaine
" fire at *St. Edmund's Bury* in Suffolke, on Munday the 10th of April,
" 1608." 4to.

In 1719 were printed in one fheet fome notes concerning St. Edmund's Bury, collected from lord Oxford's library by M. Wanley.

Dr. John Batteley, mentioned in Kent, was engaged in writing the
hiftory of its famous abbey. What he left finifhed at the death of
Hen. III. in it, 1272, was publifhed by his nephew Oliver Batteley at
the end of the fecond edition of the Antiquitates Rutupinæ. Ox. 1745.
4to. with an appendix, and the lift of abbots, continued by Sir James
Burroughs, late mafter of Caius coll. whofe ichnography of the abbey
church drawn 1718. and a view of the abbot's palace 1720, now intirely demolifhed, are alfo annexed [e]. The doctor's papers are faid in
the preface to remain in the hands of his heirs, ready to be communicated to any who will undertake the work. We have five views of the
gate: one by W. Millicent, engraved by E. Kirkall, with this infcription: " A view of the gate-houfe belonging to the abbey in St. Ed-
" mund's Bury in Suffolk. It being uncertain when this was built, I
" fhall leave it to the more learned to judge whether before or after
" Edw. I. the wall which inclofed the abbey being built in his time."
A fecond by Meffrs. Buck, 1738, dedicated to Sir Jermyn Davers, bart
then proprietor of the abbey ruins, which his lady is now tearing to

---

[e] I fuppofe thefe were done by Vertue, and are the fame with thofe mentioned in
the catalogue of his works by Mr. Walpole, with a fmall view of St. Edmund's Bury:
Quære, if the headpiece to Dr. Batteley's book.

pieces,

pieces, and deforming the ſcite by a fantaſtic diſpoſition of it. This view was engraved in the Univerſal Magazine, 1759, and though only a perſpective one is much the moſt accurate in the ſtyle and ornaments of the building; though it has not done them the juſtice they deſerve. A third is prefixed to Dr. Batteley's book, but when taken is not ex-preſſed: it exhibits the two unmeaning towers formerly placed on the gateway, but is in other reſpects indifferent enough. A 4th and 5th very imperfect views of it appear among other public buildings in Warren and Downing's plans of the town. It were to be wiſhed ſome able hand would oblige the world with a geometrical draught of this fine building.

An E. proſpect of the town by Buck 1741.

The Antiquarian Society have engraved a fragment of the abbey ſeal in the viith plate of their 2d volume.

" Bury and its environs, a poem. Lond. 1747." By Dr. Winter, late phyſician at Bath.

A new and accurate plan of the ancient borough of Bury St. Ed-mund's, in the county of Suffolk, by Alex. Downing 1740. engraved by Toms, and adorned with views of the croſs and abbey gate.

Another ſurvey 1747 by Thomas Warren, in two ſheets, adorned with views of the S. front of the hoſpital, the S. front of the market croſs, the E. front of the grammar ſchool, the S. E. ſide of St. James's church, part of the abbot's palace 1720: S. W. view of St. Mary's church: N. front of the earl of Briſtol's houſe: W. front of the abbey gate: N. front of the grand-jury houſe. Mr. Warren left drawings of ſeveral other antiquities here, now in the hands of his widow; his ſon, a writing maſter and ingenious draughtſman in this town, being de-prived of them by an unhappy diſpute about his father's will.

The eaſtern counties ſeem to have been more fertile in ſorceries than Lancaſhire itſelf. " A true relation of the arraignment of 18 witches, " that were tryed, convicted, and condemned at the ſeſſions holden at " St. Edmund's Bury in Suffolk, and there by the judges and juſtices " of the ſaid ſeſſions condemned to die; and ſo were executed. As " alſo a liſt of the names of thoſe that were executed; and their ſeveral " confeſſions before their execution: with a true relation of the man-

" ner

" ner how they find them out. 1645." 4to. Among the unhappy
fufferers were Mr. Lowes, an innocent aged clergyman of Brandeſton,
a cooper and his wife, with 15 more women. Hopkins [f], the witchfinder and his aſſociates made people by their tortures confeſs the greateſt
extravagancies, and then they were hanged. The parliament of 1645
adopted James the Iſt's nonſenſical notions, and Baxter ſanctified them.
At the end of judge Hales's ſhort treatiſe touching ſheriffs accompts,
is " A tryal of witches [g], at the aſſiſes held at Bury St. Edmonds, for
" the county of Suffolk, on the 10th day of March, 1664. before Sir
" Matthew Hale, kt, then lord chief baron of his majeſties court of
" Exchequer. Taken by a perſon then attending the court. Lond.
" 1682." 8vo. Sir Tho. Brown, who wrote againſt vulgar errors, is
here ſaid to have declared in court, he " was *clearly* of opinion that
the fits of the plantiffs were *natural*, but heightned by the devil co-
operating with the malice of the witches, at whoſe inſtance he did the
villanies:" he confirmed it by a ſimilar caſe in Denmark, and ſo far
influenced the jury that the two women were hanged. The hardſhips
and inconſiſtencies in both theſe tranſactions are ſufficiently expoſed
in Dr. Hutchinſon's " Hiſtorical eſſay concerning witchcraft, 1720."
chap. iv. and viii. [h].

Some verſes on *Mendleſhan* games were printed in the Gentleman's
Magazine for June 1735.

" A wonderfull and ſtraunge newes which happened in the county
" of Suffolke and Eſſex, Feb. 1. being Fryday, where it rayned wheat,
" the ſpace of vi or vii miles compas : a notable example to put us in
" remembraunce of the judgments of God, and a preparative ſent to
" move us to ſpeedy repentance : written by Wm. Averell, ſtudent in
" divinity. Lond. 1583." 4to.

[f] In the Pepyſian library is a print of this witchfinder general with two witches.
One of them named Holt ſays, " My impes names are, 1. Ilemauzar. 2. Pye-wackett.
3. Pecke in the crown. 4. Griezzell Greedigutt." Four animals attend : Jarmara, a
black dog; Sacke and Sugar, a hare; Newes, a ferret; Vinegar Tom, a bull-headed
greyhound. Hopkins publiſhed, 1647, an account of his commiſſion and exploits. At
laſt ſome gentlemen put the Lex talionis in execution, and cleared the country of
him. The women at Exeter were the laſt who ſuffered death for witchcraft in England.
As the devil loſt his empire among us, he exerciſed it with greater violence among the
Indian Pawwaws, and our New England coloniſts.

[g] Amy Duny and Roſe Cullender.

[h] See alſo Catalogue of Harleian pamphlets, Nº 437.

" move

" A difcourfe of the queene's majefties entertainment in Suffolke
" and Norfolke; with a defcription of many things that were then
" prefently feen.　Devifed by T. Churchyard, gent. 1587." i. 4to.

" Hydro-fidereon: or a treatife of ferrugineous waters, efpecially
" the Ipfwich fpaw; being an excellent fpring of that nature, there
" lately difcovered; with the vaft difference of fuch medicinal waters,
" their proper medical ufes in various difeafes, grounded on feveral cu-
" rious experiments and nice obfervations never before made; with a
" plain demonftration alfo of the great vanity and folly in buying and
" cheat in felling　erman fpaw water in England. Lond. 1717." 8vo.

A letter from N. Fairfax at Woodbridge concerning a young lady
that attempted to ftarve herfelf; but after ten weeks trial (from April
1 to June 16) defifted, and recovered, is in Birch's Hiftory of the Royal
Society, vol. iii. p. 386. n.

In the Philofophical Tranfactions, N° 189, p. 281, is Sir Ph. Skippon's account of fome Saxon coins found in the church-yard of *Honedon*,
near Clare, and Dr. Wotton's remarks on them. p. 361; and in N°
203, p. 874, Mr. Dale's account of three not mentioned by Sir Philip.
In p. 137 of N° 316 is a letter from Orlando Bridgeman, efq; concerning a ftorm of thunder and lightning at *Ipfwich*, July 16, 1708.　In
N.° 17, p. 722, a relation of a land flood, which overwhelmed a great
tract of land in and near *Downham*, by Thomas Wright, efq; abridged
in Kirby's Suffolk Traveller, 2d edit. p. 239.　In p. 191 of N° 474
an account of pits having feveral ftrata of fhells from the bottom to
within nine feet of the furface in a farmer's ground near *Woodbridge*,
by the rev. Mr. Roger Pickering, with a fcheme for manuring land
with fuch foffils, which were firft difcovered with their ufe at *Leving-
ton* in this county 1710.　In N° 424 J. Machin's account of a boy
with a fcaly fkin fhed every autumn. In p. 443 of N° 464 is an account of Margaret Cutting at *Wickham Market* fpeaking intelligibly
without a tongue, in a letter from Mr. B. Boddington to Mr. Baker.
The remarkable cafe of a poor family at *Wattifham* was communicated
to the publick by the rev. Mr. Bones, minifter of the place, and the
late Dr. Wollafton, in vol. lii. art. 83, 84, 85. 98. and the Gentle-

i Ames's Hift. of Printing, p. 332, not mentioned by Wood.

man's

man's Magazine, May, 1762, p. 230. It was suppofed to have arifen from eating bad bread, and paralleled by other cafes in Swifferland in Dr. Tiffot's letter to Dr. Baker, Philofophical Tranfactions, vol. lv. art. 17.

Dr. Rawlinfon engraved 1742 a bell-metal pot with a Hebrew infcription round it, found in a brook in this county feventy years before, and by him bought out of lord Oxford's collection, and left to the Bodleian library.

" An hiftorical account of the 12 prints of monafteries, caftles, an-
" tient churches, and monuments, in the county of Suffolk, which
" were drawn by Jofhua Kirby, painter in Ipfwich, and publifhed by
" him, March 26, 1748. Ipfw. 1748." 8vo. Thefe were engraved by the late Mr. Wood, and exhibit a N. W. view of *Sudbury* priory : W. view of *Chrift* hofpital i, Ipfwich : S. view of *Blithburgh* church and priory : N. W. view of *Bungay* church and priory, and a W. view of the caftle : S. view of St. James's and the priory church at *Bury* : S. W. view of *Lavenham* church : S. E. view of *Clare* priory and caftle : the monuments of Henry Fitzroy duke of Richmond and Somerfet, and bafe fon of Henry VIII ; Thomas Howard, 3d duke of Norfolk of this family, and Henry Howard earl of Surrey, and his wife Frances daughter of John earl of Oxford, in *Framlingham* church k, and that of lord Bardolph in *Dennington* church. Thofe of the Delapoles earls of Suffolk. in *Wingfield* church deferve to be perpetuated in the fame manner.

The brafs plate and figure of Humphrey Sackville, efq; in *Wickham Market* church was engraved by G. Vandergucht.

Lord chief juftice Holt's monument in *Redgrave* church was engraved 1710.

Vertue engraved a perfpective view of the Gothic font in *Worlingworth* church.

Meffrs. Bucks other views in this county, 1738, are,

---

i Great part of the buildings were pulled down laft year.

k There is another for Thomas Howard, the ambitious duke of Somerfet, beheaded by Q. Elizabeth, and two of his wives, but without any effigies. Weever promifed draughts of all thefe monuments, if the haftineffe of the preffe would have permitted. They are all omitted in the account of the town fent to the compiler of Magna Britannia.

E. Leifton

E. Leiſton abbey.
E. Butley priory.
W. Orford caſtle and priory.
W. Framlingham
S. Wingfield
N. Mettingham
S. Burgh
} caſtles.

A ſmall view of *Framlingham* caſtle is in Kirby's Perſpective.

Plate lviii. of Stukeley's Itin. Cur. exhibits a plan of Garionenum, *Borough caſtle*, near Yarmouth.

A draught of the channels of *Cockle* and *St. Nicholas' Galls*, with the buoys, ſands, and ſea-marks between Winterton thwart lights and Pakefield, ſurveyed June 1751 at the expence of the Trinity houſe, by captains Major, Winter, Parker, and Hancock, and drawn by Mr. Daniel Lounder. 2 ſheets.

Suffolciæ comitatus continens in ſe oppida mercatoria 25, pagos & villas 464 una cum ſingulis hundredis & fluminibus in eodem vera deſcriptio, by Saxton, 1572.

A map by Norden, augmented by Speed 1610, with a plan of Ipſwich.

An actual ſurvey of this county was publiſhed 1736 by ſubſcription, by John Kirby, who contracted it to half that ſcale 1737, which was engraved by J. Baſire. He publiſhed another ſmaller, ſince inſerted in the laſt edition of his Suffolk Traveller. Another has been done by Em. Bowen.

Suffolk with part of Norfolk ſurveyed by James Corbridge, with circular meridian lines from Bury to Norwich : one ſheet.

Propoſals were publiſhed 1756 for engraving by ſubſcription a new and correct map of this county, three feet and an half by two feet four inches, one-third leſs than Kirby's.

S U R R E Y.

SURREY.

JOhn Norden made a furvey of this county, which fome curious Hollander purchafed at a high price foon after the Reftoration. The map was engraved by Charles Whitwell at the expence of Mr. Robert Nicolfon, and was much larger and more exact than any of Norden's other maps. It had the arms of Sir William Waade, Mr. Nicolfon, and Ifabella countefs dowager of Rutland who died in 1605[a]. Sir Edward Byfhe, a native, gave out that he defigned another furvey, for which he probably made collections, fome fragments of which are interfperfed in his notes on Upton de ftudio militari. Lond. 1654. 4to. His office of garter into which the parliament thruft him 1645, though five years before he with other members had voted it illegal [b], diverted him from this defign. It was refumed before his death by Mr. Aubrey, who perambulated the whole county: his labours were revifed, corrected, and publifhed by Dr. Rawlinfon, under the title of " The natural hiftory and antiquities of the county of Surrey, begun in " the year 1673 by John Aubrey, efq; F. R. S. and continued to the " prefent time. Illuftrated with proper fculptures. In five volumes. " Lond. 1719." 8vo.

Nicholas Salmon publifhed " Antiquities of Surrey, collected from " the moft antient records; with fome account of the prefent ftate and " natural hiftory of the county. Lond. 1736." 8vo. Its Domefday, in the hand of the original, was among Le Neve's MSS. It was vifited 1572 by Cooke: 1623 by Camden, or his deputies S. Thompfon, Windfor, and A. Vincent: 1630 by Benolt.

" A difcourfe on the feveral kinds and caufes of lightning, written " by occafion of a fearfull lightning, which, on the 17th day of this " inftant Nov. 1606, did in a very fhort time burne up the fpire-fteeple " of *Blechingley* in Surrey, and at the fame time melt into infinite " fragments a goodly ring of bells. By Simon Harwood, A. M. " Lond. 1607." 4to.

[a] Engl. Topog. p. 228.   [b] See more of him, Ath. Ox. II. p. 648. and Anftis Black book of the Garter, I. 405—407. He died 1679.

" A true

" A true and particular account of a ſtorm of thunder and lightning,
" which fell at *Richmond* in Surꝟey, on Whitſunday laſt in the after-
" noon, being May 20th, 1711. With an exact deſcription on a
" copper-plate, of the hurt done by it, both to the perſons of the
" killed and wounded, and the building on which it fell. Where-
" unto are added, ſome ſhort hints concerning the nature, cauſes, and
" effects of thunder and lightning ; and ſome practical reflections upon
" the whole. Lond. 1711." 8vo.

" The king's and queen's entertainment at Richmond, after their
" departure from Oxford : in a maſque, preſented to the moſt illuſtri-
" ous prince, prince Charles, Sept. 12, 1636. Oxford 1636." 4to.
performed by lord Buckhurſt and Edw. Sackville.

" Two hiſtorical accounts of the making New Foreſt in Hampſhire,
" by K. William the Conqueror, and Richmond New Park in Surrey,
" by K. Charles the Iſt. Containing, I. An enquiry into the origin of
" foreſts, chaces, purlieus, warrens, and parks, and the cruel and un-
" juſt laws that were firſt made for the government of thoſe places.
" Some account of the reigns of the kings from William I. to Edw. I.
" ſo far as relates to foreſt laws, and that of obtaining the two great
" charters. II. The hiſtory of the oppoſition that was raiſed againſt
" making the park, and the troubles that immediately enſued. Ex-
" tracted from lord Clarendon and other hiſtorians. An account of
" the privileges the ſubjects enjoyed after the park was made to the
" time of putting in execution certain meaſures for ſhutting it up.
" Addreſſed to the citizens of London ; and adorned with a view of
" Richmond Park. Lond. 1750." 8vo.

Stephen Duck wrote poems on the park, gardens, and grotto 1731,
inſerted in his works.

" The royal hermitage, or temple of honour. A poem addreſſed to
" her majeſty. To which is prefixed, an epiſtle to the right hon. Sir
" Rob. Walpole. By Mr. Mitchell. Lond. 1732." 8vo.

" The rarities of Richmond : being exact deſcriptions of the her-
" mitage and Merlin's cave in the gardens there. Lond. 1735." 8vo.
with his life and propheſies. 1736. 8vo.

" Merlin :

" Merlin: a poem : humbly infcribed to her majefty. To which
" is added, the royal hermitage, a poem. Both by a lady. With
" feveral curious reprefentations both of the cave and hermitage. Lond.
" 1735." 8vo.

A fmall plan and eight views of thefe gardens by Benoit, engraved
by Toms. 1741.

A large plan by Rocque in two fheets, 1748, reduced to one 1754.

Mr. Walpole has drawings of old Richmond and Greenwich ᶜ. Hollar engraved a view of Richmond on a half fheet : Stent another, between 1620 and 1660.   The Antiquarian Society publifhed 1765 two
views of the original palace : one of the front to the green, from an
old painting in poffeffion of lord Fitzwilliams, fuppofed to be done
by a fcholar of Reubens t. Charles I. the other of the water front
from an antient drawing belonging to the prefent duke of Montague,
with a printed account, including the return of the parliament commiffioners, 1649,

" Tractatus de falis cathartici amari in aquis *Ebefhamenfibus* & hu-
" jufmodi aliis contenti natura & ufu, authore Nehemia Grew, M. D.
" utriufque Regiae Societatis focio. Lond. 1695." 12mo.

" A treatife of the nature and ufe of the bitter purging falt, con-
" tained in Epfom, and fuch other vaters. By Nehemiah Grew, M.
" D. Coll. Med. Lond. & R. S. S. Lond. 1697." 8vo.

Obfervations and experiments on this falt by Mr. John Brown, chemift. Philofophical Tranfactions, N° 377 and 378.

" The defcription of Epfom, with the humours and politicks of the
" place. In a letter to Eudoxa. Lond. 1711." 8vo. By Mr. Toland:
inferted in his pofthumous works, vol. ii. p. 91. Lond. 1720. and in
his mifcellaneous works, 1747, vol. ii. p. 60—119. but fo much corrected, enlarged, and explained, that it is almoft a new work: for
which reafon he called it " A new defcription of Epfom."

For *Lambeth* palace fee " The true copies of fome letters occafioned
" by the demand for dilapidations in the archiepifcopal fee of Canter-
" bury. In two parts. Lond. 1716." 4to. and " A letter to Mr. arch-
" deacon Tennifon, detecting feveral mifreprefentations in his pamph-

ᶜ Cat. of engr. p. 35.

" let

" let relating to the demand for dilapidations. Lond. 1717." 4to. This
laft was wrote by Mr. Henry Farrant d.

Mr. Wharton drew up an accurate catalogue of the MSS. here, with
tranfcripts of all the unprinted tracts, and an exact collation of all the
printed ones. His own MSS. were purchafed with this catalogue by
abp. Tennifon, and lodged here.

Hollar engraved a view of the palace 1644, in a fet with four
others. A fmaller one from the Thames by Wm. Lodge, engraved by
Tempefta. A N. W. by Buck 1737. There is an etching of it in
the Pepyfian library, and two drawings of Tradefcant's tomb in the
churchyard, the fides decorated with ruins and natural curiofities, and
the end with his arms. In the Philofophical Tranfactions, N° 492,
p. 160, is Mr. Watfon's account of the remains of Tradefcant's garden
here 1749. It was the next botanical garden in England after Gerard's,
the founder having in feveral years travelling introduced a variety of
foreign feeds and plants, fome of which ftill bear his name.

The Annales *Waverleienfes* were publifhed from a MS. in the Cotton library, Vefp. A. xvi. 14. in the firft volume of Gale's Hiftoriæ
Anglicanæ fcriptores. Ox. 1687. p. 129. They begin at the year 1066,
though the abbey was not founded till 1128, and end 1292. A N. W.
view of the ruins of this abbey is among Buck's views 1737. Mr.
Hunter has as much as lay in his power expiated Mr. Aiflabie's depre-
dations on this venerable fpot. F. Perry engraved another view, together with Martha chapel near Guildford, Newark abbey; and Katha-
rine hill chapel: and this laft by itfelf. Hollar engraved a view of Newark priory in a fet with five others; Buck a S. E. view 1737.

Letherhead had been celebrated by Skelton, on account of its old
ale-wife miftrefs Eleanor Rummin in " The tunning of Elynor Rum-
" min, the famous ale-wife of England." One of the many fingle
impreffions of this droll piece was Lond. 1624. 4to. having in the
title page the picture of an old ill-favourld woman holding a black pot
of ale, and underneath her thefe verfes:

When Skelton wore the laurel crown
My ale put all the ale-wives down.

d Aubrey's Survey, vol. v. p. 273.

5

Another

Another is intitled " The tunning of Elenor Rumming, by Skelton, " laureat. Lond. 1718." 8vo. It was reprinted from this copy in the Harleian Miscellany, vol. i. p. 402. and with all " The pithy, plea- " saunt and profitable workes of maister Skelton. Lond. 1736." 12mo.

" Case of the inhabitants of *Croydon* in Surrey, concerning the great " oppression they lye under, by reason of the unparallelled extortions, " and violent, illegal and unwarrantable prosecutions of Dr. Clewer, " vicar of the said parish." 1673.

The town of *Godalming* will for ever be rendered memorable by the grossest imposture ever practised on human credulity in an enlightened age[e], which produced the following tracts.

" A short narrative of an extraordinary delivery of rabbets performed " by Mr. John Howard, surgeon at Guildford, published by Mr. St. " Andrè, surgeon and anatomist to his majesty. Lond. 1726." 8vo. 1727. 8vo. St. Andrè saved Howard the trouble of publishing the ac- count himself, which he says here he intended.

" Remarks on A short narrative of an extraordinary delivery of " rabbets, performed by Mr. John Howard, surgeon at Guildford, as " published by Mr. St. Andrè, anatomist to his majesty, with a proper " regard to his intended recantation. By Thomas Braithwaite, sur- " geon. Lond. 1726." 8vo.

" Some observations concerning the woman of Godlyman in Surrey, " made at Guildford on Sunday, Nov. 20, 1726. tending to prove her " extraordinary deliveries to be a cheat and imposture. By Cyriacus " Ashley, surgeon to his majesty. Lond. 1726."

" An exact diary of what was observed during a close attendance " upon Mary Toft, the pretended rabbet-breeder, of Godalming in " Surrey, from Monday Nov. 28 to Wednesday Dec. 7. following. " Together with an account of her confession of the fraud. By Sir " Richard Manningham, kt. fellow of the Royal Society and of the " college of physicians. Lond. 1726." 8vo. Dated Dec. 8.

" An advertisement occasioned by some passages in Sir R. Manning- " ham's diary lately publish'd. By J. Douglas, M. D. Lond. 1727."

[e] Whiston reckoned it the accomplishment of a prophecy, Esdras ii. *Menstruous women shall bring forth monstrous births.* He was then near sixty.

8vo.

8vo. This is a vindication of Dr. Douglas, who in the main agreed with Sir Richard, from one or two miſtakes charged on him.

" The ſeveral depoſitions of Edw. Coſten, Rich. Stedman, John
" Sweetapple, Mary Peytoe, Eliz. Maſon, and Mary Coſten, relating
" to the affair of Mary Toft of Godalming in the county of Surrey,
" being delivered of ſeveral rabbits; as they were taken before the
" right hon. the lord Onſlow, at Guildford and Clandon in the ſaid
" county, on the 3d and 4th days of this inſtant December 1726.
" Lond. 1727." 8vo.

" The anatomiſt diſſected: or the man-midwife fairly brought to
" bed: being an examination of the conduct of Mr. St. Andrè, touch-
" ing the late pretended rabbit-bearer: as it appears from his own
" narrative. By Lemuel Gulliver, ſurgeon and anatomiſt to the kings
" of Lilliput and Blefuſcu, and fellow of the academy in Balnibarbi.
" The 2d edition. Lond. 1727." 8vo.

" Much ado about nothing: or a plain refutation of all that has
" been written or ſaid concerning the rabbit-woman of Godalming.
" Being a full and impartial confeſſion from her own mouth, and un-
" der her own hand, of the whole affair from the beginning to the
" end. Now made publick for the general ſatisfaction. Lond. 1727."
8vo.

" St. A--d--è's miſcarriage: or a full and true account of the rabbit-
" woman. Lond. 1727." Fol. A poem.

" The diſcovery, or the ſquire turned ferret: an excellent new bal-
" lad to the tune of Hey boys, up we go, Chevy Chace, or what you
" pleaſe. The 2d edition. Weſtminſt. 1727."

" A ſhorter and truer advertiſement by way of ſupplement to what
" was publiſhed the 7th inſtant: or Dr. D--gl--s in an extaſy at La-
" cey's bagnio, Dec. 4, 1726. Lond. 1727."

" A letter from a male phyſician to the author of the female phyſi-
" cian in London; plainly ſhewing that for ingenuity, probity, and
" extraordinary productions he far ſurpaſſes the author of the narra-
" tive. To which is added a ſhort diſſertation on generation, where-
" by every childbearing woman may be ſatisfied, that it is as impoſ-
                                                                     " ſible

" fible for women to generate and bring forth rabbits, as 'tis for rabbits
" to bring forth women."

There were 13 paltry prints with explanatory verfes under each, engraved on this occafion, and a hieroglyphical epiftle from Mary Toft,
with an anfwer to it.   Dr. Bulleyn [f], who wrote about the middle of
the 16th century, has recorded a Popifh juggle fo much refembling
this that one would think Tofts' tutors had read and improved it,
as much as 17 young rabbits produced by one woman can exceed a full
grown cat with bacon in its belly brought into the world by a butcher's
daughter at Harborough.

The counter feal of *Chertfey* abbey was engraved by the Antiquarian
Society 1741.   An old feal found near Newington buts, infcribed
Prive fun poucenu, round a chalice in a fhield, in the Englifh Topo-
grapher, p. 231, from the original in the hands of Dr. Rawlinfon.

In the Gentleman's Magazine, April 1754, p. 157, is an infcription at *Merton* abbey, with obfervations by Mr. Pegge.   In that for May
1763, p. 220, an account of *Dorking* parifh and its environs, on the
plan propofed for a natural hiftory of England.   In the Philofophical
Tranfactions, vol. xliv. art. 53, is an account of the effects of lightning
in this town July 16, 1750, in a letter from Mr. Wm. Child.   In Dr.
Birch's hiftory of the Royal Society, i. 279, is Sir Robert Moray's account of a fpring covered with an oleaginous matter, two miles from
Chertfey.   In the Philofophical Tranfactions, N° 464, p. 138, Dr.
Tho. Milner's account of a ball of fire feen at *Peckham* Dec. 11, 1741,
defcribed by lord Beauchamp at Kenfington, and Mr. Fuller in Suffex;
by Mr. Goftling in Kent, N° 461. by Mr. Chrift. Mafon in Suffex; and by
a gentleman in the Ifle of Wight, N° 462. and by capt. Gordon at London, N° 463.   In N° 363, p. 1107, an account of an aurora borealis feen
at *Streatham* by Mr. Tho. Hearne.   In N° 495, p. 446, an examination
of the ftrength of the purging waters of *Jeffop's well* on Stoke-common,
near Claremont, by Dr. Hales.   In vol. l. p. 614, an account of an
earthquake at *Lingfield* Jan. 24, 1758.

[f] Dialogues both pleafaunt and pietifull, &c. 1564. 8vo.   Biog. Brit. ii. 1027. n. E

" Forreft

" Forresta de Windsor, in com. Surrey. The meers, meets, limits,
" and bounds of the forrest of Windsor, in the country of Surrey, as
" the same are found, set out, limited, and bounded by inquisition;
" taken by vertue of his majesties commission, in pursuance of one act,
" made in the parliament begun at Westminster, in the 16th year of
" the reign of our sovereign lord, king Charles, intitled, An act for
" the certainty of forrests, and of the meets, limits, and bounds of
" forrests, as the same now remains upon the record, in his majesties
" high court of chancery. Lond. 1646." 4to. g.

In Braunii " Civitates orbis terrarum. Colon. 1572." book v. pl. i
is an old view of *Nonesuch*, with this inscription, " Palatium regium in
" Angliæ regno appellatum Nonciutz, hoc est, nunquam simile; effi-
" giavit Georgius Hogenbachius. 1582." It seems to represent the
back front, a wall running before the entrance. On the fore ground
is the queen in a calash, and a prince or nobleman following her in
another. At the bottom of the plate are figures representing the
women's dress in that age : " modus vendendi lupos pisces apud
Anglos ;" by cutting open their bellies to shew their fat, which by
the touch of tenches and their glutinous slime closed together again,
without killing the fish [h]: and a " Paremptitius," or a person belonging to some of the city companies. There is a confused draught of this
and Richmond palace at the corner of Speed's map of the county.
A large fine print of Nonesuch palace by G. Hoefnagel (probably sold
by Stent) is in the Antiquarian Society's library [i].

Hollar engraved in 1645 the W. prospect of *Albury* house, then the
seat of the great earl of Arundel, now of the earl of Ailesford; and six
views about it, and *Hascomb* hill, which has an antient camp on it.

Sir John Evelyn etched a view of his own seat at *Wooton*, and another
of Putney [k].

---

[g] Harl. Cat. of pamph. N° 546.
[h] Camd. in Mid. p. 394.
[i] Walp. Anecd. Overton's Cat. of Stent's engravings, 1672. He engraved also views
of Whitehall, Wansted, Oatlands, Hampton-court, Theobalds, Westminster, Windsor,
Greenwich, Eltham, Woodstock, and Basinghouse, all extremely scarce, and the more
valuable as many of the edifices themselves no longer subsist. Ib.
[k] General Dict. Evelyn. Walp. Cat. of Engr. p. 80.

Lone-

Lonefome lodge at Wootton, belonging to Theodore Jacobfon, efq; defigned by himfelf, engraved by Fourdrinier.

"A Pindaric ode upon his majeftie's review of his forces at *Putney* "heath. Lond. 1684." a folio half fheet.

A copy of verfes on *Barn-Elmes* is in p. 10, &c. of "Otia Votiva; "or poems upon feveral occafions. Lond. 1705." 8vo.

"Cæfar's camp, or *St. George's hill*: a poem. By the rev. Mr. Duck, "rector of Byfleet. Lond. 1755." 4to.

The duke of Newcaftle's feat has been celebrated in a poem called "Claremont, addreffed to the right hon. the earl of Clare. Lond. 1715." Fol. There is a perfpective view of the houfe and gardens by Auften and Toms 1747, and a furvey of them with two views of the houfe by John Rocque, engraved by J. Bonneau 1750.

Rocque publifhed 1737 one of the late Mr. Pelham's at *Efher*, with two views of the houfe built by card. Wolfey when bp. of Winchefter; of which there is another drawn by Kent and engraved by Fourdrinier; an E. view by Buck 1737, and another by L. Sullivan 1759.

A furvey of the earl of Portmore's houfe at *Weybridge* has been engraved by Rocque.

A view of lord Lincoln's at *Oatlands* by Sullivan 1759. A view of part of the gardens, with a profpect of *Walton*-bridge; and a view from thence, drawn by Pillement, have been engraved by Elliot.

A view of Mr. Southcote's houfe at *Wooburn* by the fame.

A view of Mr. Hamilton's gardens at *Painfhill* near Cobham by Sullivan. There is one of lord Baltimore's houfe at *Woodcote*, without name or date.

"Plans, elevations, fections, and perfpective views of the gardens "and buildings at *Kew*, the feat of her royal highnefs the princefs "dowager of Wales. Defigned by Wm. Chambers, architect to his "majefty, and elegantly engraved on 46 large folio copper-plates, by "Grignion, Major, Rooker, Woollet, &c. Lond. 1763." Fol.

Four views in thefe gardens, drawn by Woollet, engraved by Canot.

"Kew gardens: a poem. By George Ritfo. Lond. 1763." 4to.

T t t 2   " Kew

Kew garden, a poem in two cantos. By Henry Jones, author of the " Earl of Effex, the Ifle of Wight, &c. Lond. 1767." 4to.

A view of *Walton*-bridge over the Thames by L. Sullivan 1753. Another in the Gentleman's Magazine 1750.

Other views by Buck are,

N. Farnham ⎫
N. W. Guildford ⎬ caftles.
E. Betchworth ⎭

And a larger S. W. view of the town of Guildford. A S. W. profpect of Guildford, dedicated to Arth. Onflow, efq; recorder, by John Harris, 1738, with views of the three churches, the hofpital, caftle, grammar fchool, town hall, and friary. An ichnography or ground-plan of Guldeford, the county town of Surrey, 1739, by Matthew Richardfon, engraved by J. Harris. A N. W. profpect of the town, with the fame views as in Harris's profpect, engraved by J. Mafon, from a painting of John Ruffel there, 1759, dedicated to Sir John Elwell, bart. and Geo. Onflow, efq; The bridge is engraved in the Gentleman's Magazine for Jan. 1754.

There is a print of the chapel of St. Mary adjoining to the S. fide of the parochial church of *Kingfton upon Thames*, in which feveral Saxon kings are faid to have been crowned, reduced to ruins 1730 by the fall of one of the pillars and arches next the church; taken 1726.

Saxton included this county in his map of Kent, 1575. Speed has a map of it 1610.

Hollar engraved a map of Surrey with the hundreds 1667, on a quarter of a fheet; and a fmaller 1670.

A large new and actual furvey of this county by Senex. Another by Bowen.

A topographical map of the county of Surry, in eight fheets, to a fcale of two inches to a mile: in which are expreffed, all the main and crofs roads, lanes, paths, walls, pales, hedges, hills, valleys, rivers, brooks, ponds, bridges, mills, woods, heaths, commons, parks, churches, noblemen and gentlemens feats, houfes, gardens, cottages, &c. By John Rocque, 1762.

SUSSEX.

SUSSEX.

IN the Englifh Topographer, we are told that a learned phyfician of Chichefter had made fome progrefs towards a full defcription of this county. Mr. Harris communicated his own obfervations to bp. Gibfon.

A copy of its Domefday is MS. Harl. 1907. It was vifited 1530 by Benolt: 1633 by Philipot and Owen, or R. St. George.

There is an Index Villaris, or lift of the feveral places in it, without date, intitled, " A defcription of Kent and Suffex; or a view of all " the cities, towns and villages in each county, alphabetically com- " pofed; fo that naming any city, town, or village, you may readily " find in what lath or rape they are in: to which is added, the num- " ber of parifhes in each county, and what cities and borroughs return " parliament-men; with an exact account of all the market-towns in " each county, and what days the markets are kept. Written for the " ufe of his countrymen, by Robert Ruffell of Suffex. Lond."

Dr. Rawlinfon had a MS. account of St. Mary's hofpital at *Chichefter*, founded by dean William Flefhmonger 1543, intitled, " Fundatio " hofpitalis beatæ Mariæ infra civitatem Ciceftrenfem fideliter exem- " plata in forma autentica." Bp. Tanner quotes another copy, or the original, of this inftrument (among abp. Sancroft's papers in the Bod- leian library) which calls it " Fundatio five reformatio, &c. per W. F. " &c. 1528."[a].

Fourteen monumental infcriptions in the cathedral are inferted in the antiquities of Worcefter, p. 230. 1717 and 1723: all the older bifhops are omitted, and but imperfectly fupplied in Willis' mitred abbies, II. 348. The N. profpect was engraved by King.

In N° 379 of the Philofophical Tranfactions, p. 391, is Roger Gale's account of a Roman infcription found here; engraved alfo in pl. xlix. of Stukeley's Itinerary: likewife in the preface to Hearne's edition of Domerham, 1728, p. xxxvii. &c. with remarks by Dr. E. Bayly of

[a] Not. Mon. p. 558.

Havant,

Havant, who firſt took a copy of it, and aſſerted his reading againſt Gale.   Hearne waſted a few pages upon it, in which he tells us nothing new or to the purpoſe.   Horſley republiſhed the inſcription, with Gale's and Stukeley's remarks at large, and profeſſor Ward's corrections of the former.

Stukeley exhibits (pl. lxxi.) a plan of this city, under its antient name Mantantonis.   There is a large S. W. view of it by Buck 1738. A plan by William Gardiner and ———— Jeakyl, on two ſheets, with views, will ſhortly appear.

The Antiquarian Society have publiſhed a print of the croſs, built by bp. Story t. Edw. IV. and repaired, with the addition of a new top, after the reſtoration.   At the bottom of the plate is this inſcription: " Prima hujuſce crucis delineatio Aº 1715. 2ᵈᵃ Aº 1724 formam ejus " horologio & campana nundinali ornatæ, prout hodie manet, expri- " mens; poſtrema Aº 1743 quæ ſumptibus Soc. Antiq. Lond. æri in- " ciſa hic exhibetur."

E. W. and S. views of it, drawn by Wm. Ride, were engraved in one plate by Vertue, and dedicated to the duke of Richmond 1749.

" The antiquities of *Arundel:* the peculiar privileges of its caſtle " and lordſhip; with an abſtract of the lives of the earls of Arundel, " from the conqueſt to this time.   By the maſter of the grammar- " ſchool at Arundel ᵇ. Lond. 1766." 8vo.   The account of the town and caſtle are compriſed in 20 pages, charters of religious foundations take up 20 more: the remaining 226 contain the lives of the earls, moſt aukwardly compiled from printed books.   The church antiquities are ſlightly paſſed over, only three of the many epitaphs being mentioned ᶜ.   Buck engraved an E. view of the caſtle 1737.

Hollar engraved a W. proſpect of Arundel town and caſtle, on a half ſheet, dated 1644; and a view of *Bramber* caſtle, with another of its ruins.   Alſo a proſpect of *Old Shoreham.*

ᵇ Charles Carraccioli.   ᶜ The following is the true reading of the only epitaph he has printed :

        Sir adm Ertham p mayeſter de ceſte college giſt ycy
        Dieux de ſalme eyt mcy amen.

Two parliamentary judgments, Gul. Conq. & Rufi, concerning funeral oblations arifing to *Brembre*, Suffex, and the claim thereof by the abbey of Fifcanne in the parifh church of that place, in Brewfter's Collectanea Ecclefiaftica.

" True and wonderfull: A difcourfe relating to a ftrange and mon-
" ftrous ferpent (or dragon) lately difcovered, and yet living, to the
" great annoyance, and divers flaughters both of men and cattell by
" his ftrong and violent poyfon: in Suffex, two miles from Horfam, in
" a woode called *S. Leonard's Forreft*, and thirty miles from London.
" this prefent month of Aug. 1614. With the true generation of fer-
" pents. Lond. 1614." reprinted in the Harl. Mifcel. vol. iii. p. 106.
This monfter was above nine feet long, fhaped like an axle-tree, with bunches at his fides like foot-balls, which they feared might turn to wings: he caft his venom four rods, and his principal food was the rabbits of a neighbouring warren. It had been feen by the Horfam carrier and others, three of whom attefted this account. As good a relation might be made of a fnake faid to have been feen on Lexden heath, Effex.

" The paffage of the hurricane, from the fea fide at Bexhill in Suf-
" fex, to Newingden level, the twentieth day of May 1729, between
" nine and ten in the evening. Containing, 1. A particular account of
" the damage and devaftations of the buildings, timber, &c. that ftood
" in the way of its courfe. 2. An account of the weather, and bear-
" ings of the winds that preceded the hurricane; with the celerity of
" its circular and progreffive motion, the time taken up, and diftance
" it paffed along, over the E. end of Suffex. 3. Some obfervations on
" the way and manner of its courfe. 4. By way of inquiry, fome
" account attempted of the caufes of tempefts, whirlwinds, and hur-
" ricanes. To which is added an account of a new engine to work
" by the wind; which, by the regularity and fteadinefs of its motion,
" will not only be proper to apply to any kind of waterwork, but for
" moft mechanick ufes where any confiderable force is required: alfo
" an account of a chain and buckets only, to raife water to any height
" required, without any kind of attendance or affiftance of force, be-
" fides that of a fmall fall of water. By Richard Budgen. Lond.
" 1730. 8vo. With an exact plan of the hurricane's courfe.

The

The method of preparing iron in this county is annexed to Ray's collection of Englilh local words, 1674. 12mo.

In p. 961 of N° 138 of the Philofophical Tranfactions is a relation of a monftrous birth at *Petworth*, 20 Dec. 1677, by Dr. Sam. Morris of that place. In p. 549 of N° 351 is an account of a teffellated pavement, bath, and other Roman antiquities, difcovered in March, 1717, near *Eaftbourne*, being part of a letter from the learned John Tabor, M. D. of Lewes, to John Thorpe, M. D. 26 Jan. 1717. In p. 783 of N° 356 is the reft of this letter, concerning the fite of the ancient city of Anderida (which he fixes at Eaftbourne) and other remains of antiquity. In N° 395, p. 142, Dr. Langwith's account of an aurora borealis feen at *Petworth*, and other meteors there, N° 399. In N° 419, p. 108, the ftate of *Haftings* after the fmall pox had been there one year and half, by Mr. Frewen. In p. 361 of N° 444, an account of a fhock of an earthquake felt in this county Oct. 25, 1734, by the duke of Richmond, and by Dr. Baylie at Havant. In N° 462, p. 1, a letter from Mr. Chriftopher Mafon, about a ball of fire and explofion in *Warbledon* parilh 1741.

In p. 158 of vol. xlvii. we have an account of *Brighthelmftone* by Dr. Coe. There has been fince publifhed " A fhort hiftory of " Brighthelmfton ; with remarks on its air, and an analyfis of its " waters, particularly of an uncommon mineral one, long difcovered, " though but lately ufed. By Anthony Relhan, M. D. fellow of the " royal college of phyficians in Ireland. Lond. 1761." 8vo.

Canot engraved 1766 a profpective view of Brighthelmftone and the fea coaft as far as the Ifle of Wight, from a drawing taken on the fpot by James Lambert, painter at Lewes.

In the Gentleman's Magazine, Aug. 1763, p. 396, is a letter figned Stephen Vines, about the barrows on *South Downs* and at *Aldfrifton*; and in that for Nov. 1765, p. 524, a further account by the fame of difcoveries on thefe Downs, and fkeletons near *Wolfonbury hall*, a camp ten miles W. of Lewes. In that for Sept. 1767, p. 443, the antiquities and barrows at Aldfrifton, with a cut, figned D. H.

A plan of the park, garden, and plantations of the duke of Richmond's feat at *Goodwood*. Ca. Campbell del. H. Hulfberg fc.

Buck's

Buck's views 1737 are,

S. W. Battle ⎫
N. Begeham ⎬ abbies.

S. Lewes priory d and caftle.

N. W. Boxgrove priory.

S. Winchelfea monaftery.

N. and S. Pevenfey e ⎫
N. E. Bodiham ⎪
W. Winchelfea ⎬ caftles.
S. W. Hurftmonceaux ⎭

An infide view of Winchelfea caftle by F. Perry f. The feal of John abbot of Battle, and the abbey counter feal, and another of an abbot of *Robert's-bridge,* have been engraved by the Antiquarian Society.

A morning view of a lake at *Iping* in Suffex was engraved by J. Mafon, from a drawing by Wm. Bellers 1763.

Saxton's map of this county is included in that of Kent, &c. 1575. Norden's is augmented by Speed 1670. Hollar engraved a fmall one. A larger was publifhed by Richard Budgen in fix fheets.

A draught of the fea-coaft from Arundel in Suffex to St. Aldhams, Dorfetfhire, by Jer. Avery.

A correct map of this county by Charles Pine 1730, with an ichnography and N. profpect of Chichefter, and an ichnography and S. profpect of Lewes.

A later by E. Bowen, with the fame plans and views.

Suffex divided into rapes, hundreds, and deaneries, on which the longitude and latitude of the moft remarkable places are delineated: alfo a complete furvey of the fea-coaft, &c. with profpects of Chichefter, Lewes, &c.

d A very fair regifter of this priory, 1444, is in the Cotton library. The dimenfions of its magnificent church in a letter from John Portmarus, employed by Cromwell, to whom Hen. VIII. gave it, to demolifh it. App. to Willis' mitr ab. ii. 26.

e Among Dugdale's collections in the Afhmolean mufeum, N° 78, is " The ufages " and cuftoms of the town, port, and lege of Pevenfey, 30 Ed. III. Dr. Tabor intended to have added to his account of Anderida a defcription of this caftle, which he fuppofes the greateft and moft intire remain of Roman building in Britain.

f Mr. Perry died Jan. 3, 1765; and befides the views mentioned in the courfe of this work, engraved two or three numbers of a feries of Englifh medals, with defcriptions, 1762, and fix plates of windows, expreffing the fafhion of thofe in England from before the conqueft to Elizabeth's time, with a very indigefted account of them. The drawings of Abingdon and two views near Lichfield are ftill in the hands of his executor.

WARWICK-

WARWICKSHIRE.

SIR William Dugdale's " Antiquities of Warwickſhire illuſtrated
" from records, leiger books, MSS. charters, evidences, tombes
" and armes: beautified with maps, proſpects and portraitures. Lond.
" 1656ᵃ." Fol. muſt ſtand at the head of all our county-hiſtorians.
It was reprinted in two volumes folio Lond. 1730, from a copy corrected by the author himſelf, reviſed, augmented, and continued by
Dr. Wm. Thomas, rector of Exhall in this county, with compleat
liſts of the members of parliament and ſheriffs from the original records, an alphabetical index and blazonry of the arms on the ſeveral
plates, the original plates, the greateſt part of which were done
by Hollar, and ſeveral additional proſpects of ſeats, churches, tombs,
and new and correct maps of the county, and the ſeveral hundreds from
an actual ſurvey by Henry Beighton, F. R. S. The original edition,
with Hollar's plates, was reprinted 1765 by a bookſeller at Coventry by
ſubſcription ; but in ſo negligent a manner that ſome of the laſt ſheets
were worked off on the coarſeſt paper.

Mr. S. Newſham of Warwick aſſiſted bp. Gibſon in his deſcription of this county. It was viſited by Cook 1533 : by Lenard and
Vincent 1619. A valor beneficiorum for it 1292, may be ſeen in p.
xi. of the antiquities of the church of Worceſter 1717, 1723, and p.
xiii. of thoſe of Lichfield.

John Roſs, chantry prieſt at Guycliffe, wrote the antiquities of *Warwick* and *Guycliffe*, and of the earls of Warwick: the two firſt are loſt;
the other, with the pictures and arms curiouſly painted, remains in the
Cotton library, Jul. E. IV. 6. Dugdale ſaw a copy of it in the hands
of Robert Arden of Park hall, eſq; Nicholſon mentions a third in
the Bodleian library.

ᵃ Sir William left 48 volumes of collections for this and other counties to the
Aſhmolean muſeum. See Cat. MSS. Ang. I. 292. The ſtory of St. Auſtin's raiſing
two dead bodies at Compton, Oxfordſhire, inſerted p. 445, to prove the great antiquity of tithes, and of Long Compton church, has been clearly ſhewn by H. Wanley
(ad MS. Harl. 1288.) to be of no older date than John of Tinmouth, 1366. Lydgate
collected and tranſlated a " goodlie narration" of it, printed at St. Auſten's, Canterbury.
4to. Tanner.

A ca-

A catalogue of MSS. belonging to St. Mary's church, Warwick, drawn up by H. Wanley, is in Cat. MSS. Angl. vol. ii. p. 213.

A large S. E. view of this city, and S. E. and N. E. ones of the castle by Buck, 1729.

An undated view of the city from a drawing by J. Fish of Warwick.

About 1710 proposals were published for an account of *Coventry*, in which was to have been included a copy of the deed of gift of Sir Tho. White, mayor of London, and founder of St. John's college, Oxford, to the corporation, who were charged with misapplying his charity; but this imperfect work died with its author: and there has been since published " An account of the many and great loans, benefactions, " and charities belonging to the city of coventry : to which is added " a copy of the decretal order of the court of Chancery relative to the " memorable charity of Sir Tho. White. Lond. 1733." 8vo. A small 4to. formerly belonging to H. Wanley (who was born here) giving an account of the charter of this city, and the common grounds and other privileges belonging thereto, together with a list of the mayors from 1348 to the Revolution is among the Harleian MSS. N° 6388.

" A learned, elegant, and religious speech delivered unto his most " excellent majestie at his late being at Coventry. By Philemon Hol- " land, doctor of physike ; the right hon. the recorder his deputy for " the time. When as his royall majestie was graciously pleased to " grant and command the erecting a military garden therein ; and " sithens, to enlarge the aforesaid citie's charter. Together with a " sermon preached in the audience, and published at the request of the " worthie companie of the practisers in the military garden of the said " well-governed citie of Coventry. By Samuel Buggs, B. D. some- " times fellow of Sidney Suffex college, Cambridge. Lond. 1622." 4to. b.

A catalogue of the MSS. belonging to the school, Cat. MSS. Ang. vol. II. p. 33.

A print of the beautiful cross built after the model of that at Abingdon 1544, at the expence of Sir Wm. Hollis, another mayor of London and native of this county, drawn by H. Beighton 1721, was en-

b Cat. of Harl. pamphlets, N° 280

graved

graved by E. Kirkall. It was a hexagonal pile 57 feet high, each side 7 feet at the bafe, diminifhing in three ftories, with eighteen niches, furnifhed with ftatues of kings and faints, fome of them brought from Whitefriars [c]. Sir William left 200 l. for it, and the undertaker agreed to erect it for 187 l. 6 s. 8 d. [d]. All that remained 1760 was the lower ftory, and part of the fecond, with the ftatue of Henry IV. greatly damaged.

A N. profpect of St. Michael's church, drawn by H. Beighton, engraved by E. Kirkall. Its fteeple, 300 feet high, is one of the moft ftriking inftances of Gothic art and elegance, and was erected towards the end of the 14th century, by two mayors of Coventry, named Botoner, who fpent upon it 100 l. per ann. for more than 22 years: two ladies of the fame family finifhed the fpire 1434, and built the middle aile.

Buck publifhed a large S. view of the city 1731.

A plan of it, with the number of inhabitants in 1748 and 1749, by Samuel Bradford, engraved by Jefferies, with a view of the crofs.

A plan of *Birmingham*, with the S. elevation of St. Martin's and St. Philip's churches, and the number of houfes and inhabitants.

An account of the public buildings there is in the Gentleman's Magazine, for July and Sept. 1764, p. 328 and 431.

A plan and E. profpect of the town, and a N. profpect of St. Philip's church, with a N. profpect of the fquare at the corner, drawn by W. Weftley, engraved by J. Harris. Large E. and S. W. views of the town by Buck 1731.

Ames [e] mentions " A letter, wherein part of the entertainment unto " the queen's majefty at *Killingworth* caftle, in Warwick fheer, in this " foomerz progrefs, 1575, is fignified, from a freend, officer, attend- " ant in coourt, unto his freend, a citizen and merchant of London." Signed at the end " per me R. L. gent. mercer. merchant adventurer, " and clark of the councel chamber door, and alfo keeper of the " fame." P. 44 he calls himfelf Laneham, and p. 34 he gives

[e] The gate of this abbey, founded 1342 by Sir John Poulteney, four times mayor of London, is ftill intire.

[d] See the copy of the agreement in fome of Wanley's collections for this town MS. Harl. 6466.

[e] Hift. of Print. p. 539.

capt.

capt. Cox's f library of the romantic and humorous books of that age. Besides the views and groundplot of this magnificent castle, where chivalry and gallantry made their last efforts, given in Dugdale's Warwickshire when it was almost intire, we have a S. prospect of its ruins by Vivares 174⁶₇, from a drawing by T. Smith, in a set with three more views in other counties. E. views of the castle g and priory by Buck, 1729.

The natural history of *Sutton Coldfield* was published in the Gentleman's Magazine for Sept. and Oct. 1762, p. 401 and 472.

The river *Avon* and the birth place of Shakespeare are celebrated in " Avon, a poem, in 3 parts, [by Mr. Henckell.] Birmingham printed " by John Baskerville 1758." 4to.

The extensive prospect, and memorable battle, of *Edge hill* in " Edge " hill, or the rural prospect delineated and moralized, a poem, in four " books. By Richard Jago, M.A. Lond 1767." 4to.

An account of a supposed shower of wheat [which proved to be ivyberries] in Warwickshire, May 1661, is inserted in the register-book of the Royal Society. Birch's Hist. vol. i. p. 32.

" A brief discourse of certaine bathes or mineral waters in the coun- " tie of Warwick, near unto a village called *Newnham Regis*. By " Walter Bailey h. Lond. 1582."

f This captain Cox, by St. Mary,
Was at Bullen with king Hary;
And (if some do not vary)
Had a goodly library,
By which he was discerned
To be one of the learned
To entertain the queen here
When last she was seen here.
And for the town of Coventry
To act for her soveraignty.——
And for his sake the play
Was call'd for the second day.

B. Johnson's Masque of Owls, at Kenelworth presented by the ghost of capt. Cox mounted on his hobby horse, 1626, in his works, vol. vi. p. 48.

g The W. entrance into the great room of this castle, and a S. E. view of *Chesterton* house in this county, by James Butler, were exhibited in the Strand 1763.

h M. D. of New college, Oxf. 1563, and chief physician to Q. Elizabeth, which is all Wood says of him. Fasti. I. 92. Dr. Short, who mentions this piece, says, " a much larger treatise, full of observations, from a neighbouring gentleman, was promised, and expected; but prevented by death." Hist. of min. waters, p. 42.

" Hydro-

" Hydrologia philofophica : or an account of *Ilmington* waters, in
" Warwickfhire ; with directions for the drinking of the fame. Toge-
" ther with fome experimental obfervations touching the original of
" compound bodies. By Samuel Derham, bachelour in phyfick, lately
" of Magdalen hall. Oxon. Oxford 1685." 8vo.

" An account of an analyfis made on the *Stratford* mineral water,
" comprehending near thirty different experiments, with obfervations
" thereon, and conclufions drawn from the whole. In this work the
" mineral or medicinal contents of that excellent water are faithfully
" and accurately fet forth : its wonderfull virtues and properties are
" proved as well from its contents as its effects, and the great cures it
" has performed are accounted for upon the principles of mechanical
" reafoning ; and laftly it is judicially confidered, and directed to fuch
" difeafes for which it is peculiarly proper and good. By Charles Perry,
" M. D. Northampton 1744." 8vo.

A plan of Tripontium [*Dovebridge*] makes pl. xciv. of Stukeley's
Itinerary.

Other views by Buck, 1729, are
    S. Combe abbey i.
    E. Nun Eaton nunnery.
    E. Maxtoke caftle, and N. W. of the priory.
   S. E. Tamworth caftle

and large ones of Afton hall, the feat of Sir Lifter Holt, bart. and of
Honnington hall, the feat of Sir H. Parker, 1731.

Saxton's map, including Leicefterfhire, and wanting the hundreds,
was engraved by Leon. Tervoort 1576.

Speed's map 1610 has plans of Warwick and Coventry.

Beighton's widow propofed in 1750 to publifh by fubfcription his
furvey of this county k before-mentioned, with the feveral emendations
left by him at his death ; and alfo a fmaller, reduced to a fingle fheet :
but with what fuccefs I have not learned.

Another by T. Kitchin, with views of Guycliff, and Warwick caftle,
and a plan of Kenilworth caftle.

---

i One by King, in the Monafticon, vol. i. p. 883.
 k " Mr. Beighton's map of Warwickfhire is laid down by Englifh meafured miles re-
" duced to horizontal by his own, that is by a very good hand." Ward in Horfley's B. R.
P. 385.   5

WESTMORLAND.

THE antiquities of this county were collected by Thomas Machel, rector of Kirkby-Thore, and left in great confusion to bp. Nicholson, who took care to preserve them, bound in 6 volumes folio. His lordship communicated some of his own observations in this part of his diocese to bp. Gibson. The genealogical history of the eminent families in this county was drawn up by Sir Daniel Fleming of Rydal. It was visited with Cumberland by St. George 1615. Some coins found here, and published by bp. Gibson in p. 814 of his Britannia, induced a learned foreigner to write " De argento Runis seu literis Gothicis in-" signito, quod delineatum in Camdeni Britannia Anglice nunc loquente " et ampliata literato exhibetur orbi, sententia Nicolai Kederi, regii an-" tiquitatum collegii quod Holmiæ est assessoris. Lipsiæ 1703." 4to. In p. 555 of Nº 158 of the Philosophical Transactions is a letter to Sir W. Dugdale from Mr. Machel, March 25, 1684, concerning some Roman antiquities found in his parish ; of which see Horsley, p. 298, and two large fir vessels fixed in the ground as a well ª. Further accounts of Roman antiquities here may be found in the Gentleman's Magazine for Aug. 1738, p. 417, and June 1753, p. 270 : of *Maiden* way and castle, by Mr. Pegge, in that for June 1755, p. 272 : of Roman inscriptions found at *Old Carlisle* in that for Aug. 1755, p. 360 ; given more correctly by T. T. in that for May 1757, p. 220 : of *Willington* bridge over the Lone, with a print, and of a halo seen May 24, 1753, near *Kirby Lonsdale*, in that for Aug. 1753, p. 355. 370, by S. Parrot. In that for May 1754, p. 230, a description of *Kirby Stephen* ; and of a romantic valley near *Wildbore Fell*, by J. Harris, in that for Feb. 1761, p. 72.

" An essay towards a natural history of Westmorland and Cumber-" land, wherein an account is given of their several minerall and sur-

ª Dr. Batteley describes cisterns of oak found at Reculver, Ant. Rut. p. 56. 4to. of others at Canterbury see Somner's Chartham news, p. 5. and at Spalding, Philosophical Transactions, Nº 279.

" face

" face productions; with some directions how to discover mines by the
" external and adjacent strata, &c.   To which is annexed a vindication
" of the philosophical and theological paraphrases of the Mosaick sys-
" tem of the creation. By Thomas Robinson, rector of Ousby in Cum-
" berland. Lond. 1709." 8vo.

Views of Bywell Bay; Winander meer, near Ambleside; Hawswater
lake near Banton; Ulswater, towards Poola-bridge, were engraved by
Chatelain, Canot, and Muller, 1753, from paintings by Bellers: the
figures by Boitard junior.

A plan of Appleby has been taken by Mr. Thompson, printer at
Newcastle.

S. E. Shap abbey: N. E. Appleby: N. W. Pendragon: N. W. Broug-
ham: S. E. Brough: E. Harcla: and E. Kendal castles, by Buck,
1739.

" The N. W. prospect of *Whinfield* forest in the county of Westmorland, belonging to the earl of Thanet, six miles W. of Appleby: with
an exact representation of that most wonderful and surprising large oak
tree[b], which to most persons in the North is well known by the name
of the *Three brethren tree*; with an entertaining historical description
thereof, by Wm. Todd, formerly of Moor-houses in the said county."
Drawn by O. Neale, and engraved by Pranker.

In Nº 454, p. 235, of the Philosophical Transactions is Sir John
Clark's account, in a letter to Roger Gale, of oaks struck with lightning
in Whinfield park, and a stag's horn inclosed in one against which it
was first fixed; with remarks by professor Martyn.

Saxton has included this county in his map of Cumberland, engraved without the hundreds by A. Ryther 1576. Speed has added
the hundreds and a plan of Kendall in his 1610. The same counties
are united in one map for the British Atlas 1760.

---

[b] 270 years old, 42 feet in circumference, and capable of admitting a man on horse-
back to turn about in it.

WILTSHIRE.

WILTSHIRE.

AT a meeting of gentlemen at the Devizes for choosing knights of the shire March 1659, it was proposed, that a survey of this county should be taken, after the manner of Dugdale's Warwickshire. Mr. William Yorke, a counsellor, undertook the middle division, Mr. Aubrey [a] the north, and T. Gore [b] and Jefferey Daniel, esquires, and Sir John Erneley offered their assistance. Judge Nicholas had taken notes of all the antient deeds he met with; but both his and Mr. Yorke's papers seem to have been lost at their deaths, as we learn from Aubrey's Miscellanies on several curious subjects, p. 22. in p. 47 of which is a letter concerning the village of *Newton*. This seems to be the book Aubrey refers to in the preface to his Miscellanies 1696, which he says is left half finished, and devolves the care of it to his friend bp. Tanner. The MS. from whence bp. Gibson inserted some things in his edition of Camden, is intitled " An essay towards the description of the north-" division of Wiltshire, by me John Aubrey, of Easton Pierse." Fol. and reposited in the musæum at Oxford. He designed a naturalhistory of this county, the plan of which, divided into chapters, is among the other MSS. The preface and dedication, with Mr. Ray's letter to him on a perusal of it, are published in p. 403 of the 5th volume of the History and antiquities of Surrey. This he began in 1656 [c].

Bp. Tanner communicated to the publick his scheme of an intended history of Wiltshire, which was to be divided into two books: the first containing the several names of Wiltshire, its bounds, length, breadth, &c. the history of the Britains, Romans, Saxons, and Danes here, in chronological order, with an exact account of all their antiquities found or remaining here. The second was to consist of memorable things since the Conquest, in two parts: the first containing a large history of

[a] Notwithstanding the indifferent opinion Wood had formed of Aubrey's antiquarian abilities, Hearne thinks, if Ashmole had not turned his head as well as his own with astronomy and superstition, he might have drawn up a good account of this county. Account of antiquities about Oxford. Lel. It. II. 70.

[b] Of whom see before p. 21.   [c] See p. 238.

Old

WILTSHIRE.

Old and New Sarum, with their fuburbs; the foundation and endowment
of the cathedral of Old Sarum by bifhops Herman and Ofmund; an
account of the caftle, and its governors, the churches, chapels, and
other memorials: the removal of the town; the rife, progrefs, and
ftate of the new city; its civil government, privileges &c. a hiftory of
the mayors, a particular furvey of every parifh and ftreet; and an account of all churches, religious houfes, hofpitals, halls, &c. therein;
with a full hiftory of the new cathedral and all its appurtenances;
the lives and actions of the bifhops and deans, and catalogues of the
other dignitaries. The fecond part was to treat of the divifions of the
fhire, with refpect to its civil, ecclefiaftical, and military government:
of the hundreds in Domefday book and later records, a catalogue of
the fheriffs, and an account of all the towns and parifhes in each
hundred, their antient poffeffors, their privileges, markets, fairs,
&c. catalogues of all the mayors, bailiffs, recorders, &c. of corporations, &c. the foundations, endowments, ftate, and fuppreffion of all
religious houfes and focieties, hofpitals and free fchools; feries of the
abbots, abbeffes, priors, prioreffes, and mafters: the building of all
the churches and chapels: their dedication, chantries, altars, fhrines,
and epitaphs; with the value of all ecclefiaftical benefices, and a
fucceffion of the incumbents and patrons: the birth-places of all
bifhops, writers, and other eminent men; the lives of the earls of
Wiltfhire and Salifbury, new written. The bifhop profeffed himfelf
unfkilled in natural hiftory: fo that the moft that could be expected
from him (if nobody elfe fet about this department) was, that he would
get all poffible intelligence on the fubject, and then, fubmitting it
to the correction of fome eminent naturalift, infert it in his work.
The whole was to be adorned with an exact map of the county, having
the arms of all the corporations, nobility, and gentry round it, and
particular maps of the hundreds; with the ichnography and profpects
of the city and cathedral of Salifbury, the chief market-towns, religious
houfes, Wilton, Longleat, and other feats; Stonehenge, Abury, and
other remarkable antiquities and all natural rarities; and in the defcription of every parifh the arms and pictures in the church-windows, and
the moft confiderable monuments. His lordfhip communicated many

obfer-

obfervations to bp. Gibfon, and made large collections; but the diftance of his preferments from the county prevented from him from profecuting and finifhing this work. Bagford tells us, he was ready to communicate his materials to any perfon who would undertake it. They are probably among his other valuable collections in the Bodleian library.

Mr. Thomas Rawlinfon had a fair MS. furvey of the manors of Netyllton, Grutleton, Kyngton, Chriftmalford, Wynterbone, Badury [Afhbury in Berkfhire d], Idmyfton, Domfhire, Camely, Nony, Pulle, Brode-winfore, Weft-coker, Efte-ftoke, and Mudford, 9 Hen. VIiI. intitled "Wiltes integra, decima domini regis in com. prædicto."

This county was vifited 1565 by Harvey: 1623 by St. George and Lennard.

The only account of *Salifbury* is " The hiftory and antiquities of the " cathedral church of Salifbury, containing, 1. All the monumental " infcriptions. 2. An account of the refpective dignitaries. 3. A cata- " logue of the feveral miffals, or books of divine fervice, publifhed be- " fore the reformation for the ufe of the church at Sarum. 4. An " architectonical account of Salifbury cathedral, by Sir Chrifto. Wren e. " Lond. 1719." 1723. 8vo. To this work is added a very fcarce piece, which was fupprefled in 1683, occafioned by a controverfy between dean Peirce and bp. Ward, concerning the right of difpofal of the prebends of Sarum: one of which being refufed the dean for his fon, he contended for the king's right of patronage againft the bifhop, but without fuccefs, being at length obliged to afk the bifhop s pardon. Dr. Peirce difcovers a large ftock of learning in this piece; previous to which he had written a narrative of the controverfy, anfwered by the bifhop in a piece not printed, to which the dean replied in this tract intitled, " A vindication of the king's fovereign right; with a " juftification of his royal exercifes thereof, in all caufes, and over all " perfons ecclefiaftical, as well as by confequence over all ecclefiaftical

---

d An extract from it concerning this manor is reprinted in his edition of Afhmole's Antiquities of Berkfhire, I. p. 65.

e From his original MS. in the dean and chapter s regiftry, reprinted in the Parentalia, or Memoirs of the Wren family. 1750. Fol. p. 303.

" bodies

" bodies corporate and cathedrals ; more particularly apply d to the
" king's free-chapel and church of Sarum. Occafioned by the narra-
" tive and collections of Tho. Pierce, D. D. made by the command
" of his majefty's ecclefiaftical commiffioners. By way of reply to Seth
" Ward, lord bifhop of that diocefe."

The only Latin books which Caxton printed were, " Directorium
" facerdotum five ordinale fecundum ufum Sarum, una cum defen-
" fione ejufdem directorii, item tractatus qui dicitur crede michi
" Weftm." Fol. with a calendar prefixed having at the end his mark,
1487. and a prologue. Crede michi expreffes the approbation of this
rule by the church of Salifbury.

The Pfalter and hymns in ufum ecclefiæ Sarum et Eborac, were
printed by Pinfon 1505. 4to. [f]

" Miffale ad ufum infignis & preclare ecclefiæ Sarum," on vellum,
in red and black ink, with mufical notes. Fol. ap. eund. 1520 [g].

A Pfalter in ufum Sarum. Antwerp 1524. 8vo. [h]

Another Latin Pfalter in ufum Sarum, with hymns for York, printed
by John Reynes 1530. 12mo. [i]

" Horæ beatæ Mariæ virg. ad ufum ecclefiæ Sarum, cum multis ac
" variis orationibus multum devotis. 1531. Venundantur in cemiterio
" Sci Pauli, fub interfignio Sci Auguftini." 4to.

" Portiforium five Breviarium percelebris ecclefiæ Sarum," with
Grafton's compartment but not his name, 128 leaves, and mufical
notes, 1554 [k].

The Prymer of Salifbury ufe, &c. Paris 1534. 12mo.

Another in Englifh and Latin, fett forth after the ufe of Sarum.
Rouen 1555. 8vo. [m]. Lond. per Kingfton and Sutton, 1555. 4to.

" Portiforium fecundum ufum Sarum, noviter impreffum, & a plu-
" rimis purgatum mendis, in quo nomen Romano pontifici afcriptum
" omittitur, by Ed. Whytchurch, the king's printer, 1541." 1544 [n].

" Manuale ad ufum percelebris ecclefiæ Sarum. Londini noviter im-
" preffum 1554." 4to. in red and black, with mufical notes : feems
to be printed by John Wayland [o].

---

[f] Ames's Hift. of Print. p. 116. [g] Ib. p. 121. [h] Ib. p. 489. Ib. p. 165.
[k] Ib. p. 204. [l] Ib. p. 496. [m] Ib. p. 516. [n] Ib. p. 205. [o] Ib. p. 213.

" Proceffionale

" Proceffionale ad ufum infignis ecclefiæ Sarifburg. Lond. 1555." 4to.[p]

Among the pofthumous works of John Gregory[q] Lond. 1650, 1661. 1664. 1671. 1683. 4to. is a differtation, intitled, " Epifcopus " puerorum in die innocentium : or, a difcourfe of an antient cuftom " in the church of Sarum, of making an anniverfary bifhop among the " chorifters.". This cuftom was not peculiar to this cathedral or kingdom, but obferved at Canterbury, St. Paul's, Colchefter, and Weftminfter, as well as at Antwerp, &c.

A catalogue of the MSS. in this church is in Cat. MSS. Angliæ, tom. ii. p. 23.

" A feries of particular obfervations, made with great diligence and " care, upon that admirable ftructure the cathedral church at Salif- " bury : calculated for the ufe and amufement of gentlemen and other " curious perfons, as well as for the affiftance of fuch artifts as may be " employed in buildings of the like kind. By all which they will be " enabled to form a right judgement upon this or any other antient " ftructure, either in the Gothick or other ftiles of building. By " Francis Price, author of the Britifh Carpenter [and furveyor to this " cathedral]. Lond. 1753." 4to. To this is prefixed a tranflation of a Latin MS. in the bifhops of Sarum's hands, wrote by William de Wenda, præcentor at the removal from Old Sarum and afterwards dean, giving an account of the building of the prefent church, and pope Honorius's bulls for the fame purpofe. Among the many plates with which the book is illuftrated one is a view of the fcite of Old Sarum : another plan and fection of which, with a view of the caftle and defcription of the whole, was publifhed in one fheet by F. Merry-weather 1761. Three others make pl. lxv. lxxvi. lxvii. of Stukeley's Itinerarium Curiofum.

Among lord Coleraine's county views in the Antiquarian Society's library is a beautiful drawing of the W. front of this cathedral by T Spratt, 1737.

[p] Ames's Catalogue. N° 98.

[q] A learned divine and writer of the laft century, who funk under its perfecution in the prime of life.

[r] Anftis' Black book of the Garter, vol i. p 308, and notes. Blomefield's Hiftory of Norfolk, vol. ii. p. 156

The

The N. S. and E. fides, by Hollar, for the Monafticon, vol. iii. The N. fide by King.

Robert Thacker, who calls himfelf the king's defigner [s], engraved a large print of Salifbury cathedral [t], in four fheets.

A N. E. profpective view of the cathedral church and clofe, 22 inches and an half by 17, drawn by Jackfon, engraved by Fougeron.

An exact copy of an ancient and curious painting, large as life, in Hungerford's chapel, at the E. end of the cathedral, by the fame, engraved by Thomas Langley, 1748.

The E. front of the organ, by John Lyons, engraved by Dewing.

A print of the organ made of the materials left when the great organ was finifhed in 1710, by the fame.

A plan of St. Thomas's church in the city of New Sarum, exactly taken by John Lyons and engraved by Langley 1745, with N. W. and S. E. views of the church.

" The whole cafe of H. Sherfield, efq; recorder of Sarum, for de-
" facing St. Edmund's window, with the learned arguments pro and
con, was publifhed at large 1717." 8vo. Sherfield acted with unwarrantable impetuofity, and was punifhed with unparallelled rigour.

In this hiftory is fome account of the collegiate church and antiquities of Salifbury cathedral, p. 160. with a draught of its feal, of which another, with the reverfe, from the original in the hands of

---

[s] Walpole's Cat. of Engr. p. 70. I have fince found in the Pepyfian library a plan of Greenwich park, dedicated to lord Arlington, intitled, " Vivarium Grenovicanum. R. Thacker del. F. Place fc."

[t] June 4, 1762, the workmen employed in repairing the fpire, found on the top, in a cavity of the capftone, on the S. fide, 'a round leaden box, about five pound weight, with a loofe cover fuppofed to have been originally foldered on, five inches and a half diameter, and two and a half deep; wherein was depofited a neat wooden box and cover, of the fame circular form, four inches and an half diameter, and one inch three quarters deep, with a hole or opening on the fide in this form ◁, about two inches broad, and four holes round the rim, probably defigned to faften the cover on. In this box was only the remains of a piece of filk, or fine linen, fo much decayed that it had the appearance of tinder, of a bark-brown colour; it may have had fome relation to the Virgin Mary, to whom this cathedral is dedicated, or might have contained fome religious relique depofited there on finifhing the fpire to fecure it. The hole on the fide is conjectured to have been left for introducing any future relique, if occafion required. There was no date, infcription, or mark whatever.

" Dr.

Dr. Rawlinſon, was engraved i p. 247 of the Engliſh Topographer, more exactly than that engraved at his expence in p. 283 of the 6th volume of Leland's Collectanea.

" A declaration written by John Ivie the elder, of the city of New
" Sarum, in the county of Wilts, and one of the aldermen, where he
" hath done his true and faithfull ſervice for above forty years for the
" good of the poor and inhabitants thereof; but now ſo it is that not
" only the mayor but myſelf with many other juſtices have been moſt
" falſely and unjuſtly abuſed by the overſeers with others that ſhould
" have had more wit; as theſe inſuing lines will declare much of it,
" but not half. 1661." 4to.

A N. E. view of the city was publiſhed in 1734 by Buck.

A plan of the city, with the adjacent cloſe, church, and river, accurately ſurvey'd by Wm. Naiſh, 1751. At the corners are a N. E. view of the city, and a S. W. one of the church, and courſe of the river Avon between Saliſbury and the ſea, ſurvey'd by T. Naiſh and James Mooring.

Several Roman coins and urns found 1699 at the *Devizes* are mentioned in a letter from Mr. Clark, Philoſophical Tranſactions, N 268, p. 758. Others found there were engraved on a folio ſheet at the expence of Sir Robert Eyre and publiſhed by Mr. William Muſgrave, ſon of Dr. Muſgrave, in a broad ſheet with this ſhort account, " Penates hi ſeſ-
" quimille annos terra abſconditi, Guil. Cadby apud Deviſas olitoris, are inciſi." inſerted in the doctor's Belgium Britannicum, chap. xi.

" Origines Deviſianæ: or the antiquities of the Devizes: in ſome
" familiar letters to a friend, wrote in the years 1750 and 1751. Lond.
" 1754." 8vo. By Dr. John Davis. A ſatire on antiquarians, particularly Dr. Stukeley; whoſe view of this town when the Roman ſtation of Punctuobice makes pl. lxix. of his Itinerary.

Wilton gardens have been engraved in 22 folio copper plates.

The principal front, great gate, and ſections of the dining room by Hulſberg after Campbell.

The ſtone bridge built 1736 was engraved by Fourdrinier, after a painting by R. Morris.

A plan

A plan of the houſe, gardens, and park, with views of the houſe, great bridge, gate, and porters lodge, by Rocque 1754.

A view of the houſe by J. Sullivan 1759.

" A deſcription of the earl of Pembroke's pictures. Now publiſhed " by C. Gambarini of Lucca, being an introduction to his deſign. " Weſtm. 1731." 8vo. He propoſed to engrave the moſt celebrated pictures in Engliſh collections : and the famous family piece here by Vandyk, engraved by Audran jun. [u], was to be ready by Chriſtmas that year, in a ſet with three others of Parmegiano and Schidone, the laſt ſupper by Giorgione, and Titian's family at the duke of Somerſet's, engraved by Baron. Prudhome [x] lived ſeveral years in the town of Wilton, and copied moſt of the principal pictures : at his death, 1726, his drawings were ſold and diſperſed. The antique painting of Rich. II. was engraved by Hollar for Aſhmole's Hiſtory of the order of the garter. Peter healing the lame man by Suavio Lombardo, by himſelf : the murder of Pyrrhus by P. Teſta, by himſelf : a Madonna and Chriſt of Raphael's by Morien : a vintage by ditto, with an Arundellian vaſe, by M. Antonio : taking down Chriſt from the croſs, by M. Angelo, by Beatrichetti : a holy family of L. Caracci, by his nephew Annibal : Rubens's aſſumption by Bolſwert : the upper half of Maezzola's Ceres in mezzotinto ; and the Dedalus and Icarus on the ceiling of the cube room in 1600. Gambarini quotes n old catalogue, which I ſuppoſe is a MS.

Another deſcription of the pictures, ſtatutes, buſtos, baſs relievos, and other curioſities here, was publiſhed by Richard Cowdry. Lond. 1751. 8vo.

" A new deſcription, &c. By James Kennedy, Saliſb. 1758." 8vo.

In this collection of antiques are contained the whole of card. Richlieu's and card. Mazarine's, and the greateſt part of the earl of Arundel's ; beſides ſeveral particular pieces purchaſed at different times. The ſtatues were etched by Carey Creed 1731. 4to. who prefixed this motly advertiſement to his very ſcarce book. " The marble antiqui " ties of the right hon. the earl of Pembroke at Wilton are too many

---

[u] Baron engraved it about the ſame time.
[x] Of him ſee Walpole's Anecd. vol. iii. p. 147.

" to be drawn but by feveral hands, there being of ftatues, buftos,
" bas releivos, and mifcellanies, each relating to a great variety of ufes,
" as appears beft by a book, that is digefted in a fcientifique method,
" with infcriptions, divifions, and illuftrations. I have drawn and
" etched, in imitation of Perrier, all the ftatues; and to make the
" number feventy here are three different poftures of fome of the fta-
" tues by the famous fculptor Cleomenes. Becaufe here are the four
" laft ftatues which was fuppofed to be done by another, thofe who
" have only feventy may alfo add them." Among thefe is the famous
Egyptian pillar erected by J. Cæfar before his temple of Venus Geni-
trix. The Acis and Galatea, pl. 15 and 16, found at Arles, near the
Venus, and highly valued on that account by card. Richeleiu; Cupid
furnifhing water to a bath, pl. 35. and two boys, pl. 55 and 56, don't
occur in the catalogues. Five Sarcophagi in this collection have been
engraved by Salvini, pl. 7, 8, 9, 10. The tomb of Epaphroditus,
while Foucault's property, was illuftrated in a differtion by Montfaucon,
printed in the Memoires de l'Acad. des Infcriptions, and his Antiquity
explained: in which laft is alfo the large relief of a Veftal. The Ifis
and Ofiris are in Gordon's defcription of the mummy, tab. ix. three
views of the fame by Dr. Stukeley, engraved by E. Kirkall, dedicated to
Dr. Mead. The facrifice of Mantheus to Jupiter, with its Bouftrophe-
don infcription, was drawn by J. Lyons and engraved by Tho. Langley;
and before in the Gentleman's Magazine for April 1752, p. 174. The
buft of Marcus Modius, the phyfician, is prefixed to Dr. Stukeley's book
on the fpleen, 1723. A releif reprefenting the antient manner of eating
is in Caftell's villas of the antients. The medals were engraved in a 4to
volume, intitled " Numifmata Pembrochiana, 1746." to which Ames
made an index. One cannot help wifhing the bufts of this valuable collection, among which are feveral uniques z, were alfo communicated
to the world by fome able engraver. Dr. Stukeley had a folio volume
of them, drawn by himfelf, now in the hands of his fon-in-law Mr.
Fleming. Vandergucht engraved from his drawings the ftatues of
Diana Ephefia and Jupiter Ammon a. Drawings of the facrifice of

z Epicurus, Sefoftris, C. and L. Cæfars, Apollonius Tyaneus, Rhemitalces, befides
the fine Julius Cæfar, Cicero, Horace, and many of the emperors and empreffes, not very
common, if there are any duplicates of them.
a This laft is fuppofed to be only a chriftian reprefentation of the good fhepherd.

Y y y																Man-

Mantheus and two other bas releifs, a buft of Achilles, and another head are among lord Coleraine's collections in the Antiquarian Society's library; as alfo feveral drawings of a term of Janus by Vertue.

Stone-henge has engaged the conjectures of many writers. Inigo Jones, who firft after Camden beftowed particular attention on it, fancied it a temple of Cælus built by the Romans. From his undigefted notes his fon-in-law J. Webb, architect to Charles II. compiled " The moft notable antiquity of Great Britain, vulgarlv called Stone- " heng, on Salifbury-plain reftored, by Inigo Jones, efq; architect- " generall to the late king. Lond. 1655." Fol. There were but few copies printed, and moft of them loft in the fire of London. This opinion, which the mere difference of meafures from the Roman fcale would fuffice to confute, was fully confuted in " Chorea Gigantum : " or the moft famous antiquity of Great Britain, vulgarly called Stone- " heng, ftanding on Salifbury plain, reftored to the Danes. By Walter " Charleton, M. D. and phyfician in ordinary to his majefty. Lond: " 1663." 4to. But the doctor was not able to eftablifh his own fyftem ; there being no fuch monuments defcribed among the Gothic nations. Jones's opinion was defended by its editor in " A vindication of Stone- " heng reftored : in which the orders and rules of architecture, obferved " by the antient Romans, are difcufs'd. Together with the cuftoms " and manners of feverall nations of the world in matters of building " of greateft antiquity. As alfo an hiftoricall narration of the moft " memorable actions of the Danes in England. By John Webb, of " Butleigh, in the county of Somerfet, efq; Lond. 1665." Fol. Thefe three pieces were reprinted together in 1725 in folio, with certain memoirs relating to the life of Jones, and his effigies by Hollar, Charlton's by P. Lombart, four new views of Stonehenge in its prefent fituation, with above twenty other copper plates by Edw. Kirkall, and a compleat index to the entire collection. David Loggan engraved W. and S. views of Stonehenge. Boulton in his " Nero Cæfar; 1624." p. 184, fuppofes this work to be the tomb of Boadicia, raifed by her fubjects. Aylett Sammes, an impertinent pedant who knew nothing about antiquities, nor (if we believe Wood [b]) ever heard of the books he quotes, in his " Britannia antiqua illuftrata," fuppofed to be.

[b] Fafti. II. 207.

4

wrote

wrote by his uncle, has a diſtinct chapter c, or " treatiſe of the an-
" tient monument called Stone-henge ;" in which he labours hard to
no purpoſe to prove it a work of the Phænicians, from whom he would
derive all our antiquities. Aubrey, in his MS. " Monumenta Britannica, or a diſcourſe concerning Stonehenge, and Rollricht ſtones in
Oxfordſhire, d" thinks it Britiſh. John Gibbons, in his " Fool's bolt
" ſhotte at Stonage," publiſhed in p. 481 of Hearne's edition of Langtoft's Chronicle. Oxf. 1725. makes it an old Britiſh triumphal trophical
temple, erected to Anaraith, goddeſs of victory, on the defeat of Divitiacus
and his Belgæ, by Stunnings and his Ceangic giants e. . Toland, in his
" Specimen of a critical hiſtory of the Celtic religion," printed in his
works, thought it a cathedral of the druids, long before the coming in of
the Romans f. Wood, the architect, in his " Choir gaure, vulgarly called
" Stonehenge, on Saliſbury plain, deſcribed, reſtored, and explained.
" In a letter to the right hon. Edward late earl of Oxford and Morti-
" mer. Oxf. 1747." 8vo. is of opinion, that it was a temple of the
moon, erected by the druids about 100 years before Chriſt, and ſimilar to that at Stanton Dru in Somerſetſhire. When lord Oxford was
at Bath 1740 Wood having hinted to him his opinion of this laſt pile
of ſtones, was ordered to take a correct plan of it, for his book of
drawings of the like Britiſh antiquities. His diſſertation on the Britiſh
works at Bath and Stanton Dru were incorporated into his Deſcription
of Bath. He conſiders the antient works ſtill remaining at Harptree
on the N ſide of Mendip hills between Stanton Dru and Okey, on
Exmore, at Stonehenge, and at Aubury, as four colleges of druids ;
the firſt, of poets ; the ſecond, of extiſpices ; the third, of divines
and necromancers ; the fourth, of philoſophers, who were to draw

c Page 495.
d Bagford tells us, this MS. was lately in the poſſeſſion of Mr. Aunſham Churchill,
bookſeller, and is ſtill in being, but he ſuſpects without Mr. Gale's annotations, which
it appears Aubrey deſigned to print with it. See a letter to him from Bathurſt 1693,
Wharton's Life of Bathurſt, p. 151.
e Gibbons's other papers are in the Heralds Office, but nothing relative to Stonehenge
except one leaf of extracts from Charlton's book. A. Paſchal had it 1689. and quotes it
in a letter to Aubrey. Miſcel. on ſeveral curious ſubjects. At the time of publication it
belonged to Mr. Weſt. of Baliol. The author ſpeaks of himſelf as living in 1670. If
Hearne had left it in obſcurity the world would ha e been no loſers.
f Dr. Borlaſe doubts whether Toland ever copied or meaſured one monument; and
ſays, his authorities for many extraordinary particulars have never been produced. Pref.
to the Antiquities of Cornwall.

down

down the gods from above. The moſt accurate examiner and deſcriber of this ſtupendous pile, which could have been nothing but a religious, and conſequently a druidical, monument, is Dr. Stukeley, in " Stone- " henge, a temple reſtored to the Britiſh druids. Lond.1740." Fol. ᵍ.

Abury, a ſimilar, but more ſtupendous, work in this county, had been very unſucceſsfully laboured upon by Mr. Twining, in his " Ave- " bury in Wiltſhire, the remain of a Roman work, erected by Veſpa- " tian and Julius Agricola, during their ſeveral commands in Britanny; " a ſhort eſſay, humbly dedicated to the right hon. the earl of Win- " chilſea. Lond. 1723." ʰ. 4to. He took it for a temple of Terminus, and Silbury hill for an honorary monument to the emperor Titus. Dr. Stukeley has fully aſcertained its deſign in his " Abury, a temple of the " Britiſh druids, with ſome others, deſcribed. Wherein is a more par- " ticular account of the firſt and patriarchal religion; and the peopling " the Britiſh iſlands. Volume the ſecond. Lond. 1743." Fol. His two books have been abridged in " An enquiry into the patriarchal and " druidical religion, temples, &c. being the ſubſtance of ſome letters " to Sir Hildebrand Jacobs, bart. wherein the primæval inſtitution and " univerſality of the Chriſtian ſcheme is manifeſted, the principles of " the patriarchs and druids are laid open, and ſhewn to correſpond en- " tirely with each other, and both with the doctrines of Chriſtianity; " the earlieſt antiquities of the Britiſh iſlands are explained, and an " account given of the ſacred ſtructures of the druids; particularly the " ſtupendous work of Abiry, Stonehenge, &c. in Witſhire, are mi- " nutely deſcribed: with an introduction in vindication of the ſeveral

---

ᵍ A pitiful abſtract of which for the uſe of travellers, was publiſhed by Collins, bookſeller at Saliſbury, 1761. 12mo. Dr. Speed, of St. John's college, Oxford, wrote " Stonehenge, a *paſtoral, acted* before Dr. Baylie, the preſident, at his return from " Saliſbury, where he had been inſtalled dean." Ath. Ox. I. 631.

ʰ He determines Abury to be above 700 years older than Stonehenge, the work of the firſt Phænician colony that came hither, and dates its foundation the year of Sarah's death, 1859 years before Chriſt, p. 53. The whole number of ſtones at Stonehenge is 140, but Abury when intire conſiſted of 650 ſtones. " Plains, and hills, valleys, ſprings, and rivers contributing to form a temple three miles in length." p. 101. The only unpubliſhed plate I have found for Abury is a Celtic temple at Winterburn, a little N. of Abury, 22 Aug. 1723, mentioned p. 45. His notion that Perſepolis was the ſame kind of open temple as Stonehenge, only ſquare and ornamented, is very chime- rical. The entrance to the great pagoda of Chiringham, on the Malabar coaſt, of which a drawing was exhibited in Pall Mall this ſpring, bears a great reſemblance to the Perſian palace.

" hiero-

" hieroglyphical figures defcribed and exhibited in the courfe of this
" treatife. By William Cooke, A. M. rector of Oldbury and Did-
" marton in Gloucefterfhire, vicar of Enford in Wiltfhire, and chap-
" lain to the earl of Suffolk. Illuftrated with copper plates. Lond.
" 1754." and 1755. 4to. The plates are the doctor's plans of Abury
and Stonehenge contracted. Had the author been lefs infected with
Hutchinfonianifm, his book would be a ufeful compendium.——If
any man was born for the fervice of antiquity it was Dr. Stukeley.
Benet college, Cambridge, which boafts of having trained the great
Parker to revive the ftudy of antiquity with that of humanity in the
16th century, educated Stukeley in this, to trace our antiquities to
their remoteft origin. Furnifhed with extenfive reading, favoured
with as extenfive correfpondence, he vifited with unwearied affiduity
the greateft part of the kingdom, taking drawings and admeafure-
ments of the monuments on the fpot. He revived the Society of
Antiquarians i 1718, and fuggefted to Mr. Samuel Buck, his fellow
traveller, the ufeful defign of preferving fo many of our antient buildings, which he and his brother have fince fo fuccefsfully executed.
Determined to fathom the utmoft depth of druidical fcience, he almoft loft himfelf in an abyfs which nothing but his ftrong imagina-
tion could have carried him through. The application of his whole
life produced a vaft quantity of drawings and writing, which he propofed to digeft into a work to be intitled " Patriarchal Chriftianity, or
" the chronological hiftory of the origin and progrefs of true religion
" and idolatry, in 5 parts: 1. Canon Mofaicæ chronologiæ; a fyftem
" of chronology from the creation to the exodus. 2. Melchifedec, or
" a delineation of the firft and patriarchal religion. 3. Antient my-
" fteries k, and the rife of idolatry. 4. Hieroglyphics, and the origin
" of writing. 5. The patriarchal hiftory and the deduction of the
" Phænician colonies into Britain, with the origin of the druids. 6.
" The druid temples and religious rites in Britain, particularly an accu-

To which he was many years fecretary. Mr. Fleming has his fcheme of it. The
Doctor was defcended on the father's fide from a very antient family, lords of Great
Stukeley, Huntingdonfhire, and by the mother's from the fame anceftors with Anne Bul-
len, and was born 1687.

k He took free mafonry to be a remain of thefe, and from his initiation into it
thought he acquired additional lights into them.

" rate

" rate defcription of Abury. 7. Of Stonehenge." [1]. Of thefe only the defcriptions of thofe two temples were publifhed. In the preface to the laft work he propofed printing only one volume more, to compleat his argument as far as he had materials, which was to have comprifed the remaining temples [m] he knew of, with the places of fports and games of the antient Britons; and the religion of the druids. He furvived the publication of Abury 22 years, in which time the hiftory of Caraufius and the Britifh kings engroffed his attention. For the firft of thefe whatever obligation hiftory in general has to him, his country has very little : it being no eafy matter to prove his hero was her benefactor. The latter, left at his death ready for the prefs, is now in the hands of his fon-in-law and executor Mr. Fleming, together with all his valuable antiquarian correfpondencies. In the fpring of 1766 his vaft collections, the labour of above fifty years, were difperfed by public auction at Effex houfe. His original drawings of Stonehenge and Abury, many of them unpublifhed, and many firft fketches, fell into my hands; as did alfo a large quantity of other antiquarian drawings; many original ones of his Itinerary, and moft of the unpublifhed plates [u] fpecified in the courfe of this work. His own copies of Stonehenge, Abury, the Itinerary, Richard of Cirencefter, and Caraufius, with large MS. additions, were bought by the bifhop of Hereford.

In the Gentleman's Magazine for April 1744, p. 139, is an account of the chancel of a church lately difcovered under the furface of the earth, with feveral monuments, &c. at *Monkton Farley*, where Hum-

---

[1] See preface to his Stonehenge. In that to his Itinerary, 20 years before, we find his " Hiftory of the antient Celts, particularly the firft inhabitants of Great Britain" for the moft part finifhed. It was then to have confifted of four folio books, with above 300 copper plates, many of which were then engraved.

[m] He divides the druid temples into three forts; round, ferpentine, and alate. The firft are numerous enough : of the fecond we have this at Abury, one at Shap in Weftmoreland, which the doctor juft faw 1725, a third at Claffernefs in Lewis ifland, which he copied and engraved from a drawing of I huyd's. Of the third fort he finds one at Barrow, Lincolnfhire, one on Naveftock common, Effex (if this be really any thing more than a rabbet warren), and fancies the hurlers in Cornwall was a third, but made of ftones, as the others are of earth

Intended for that volume of his Itinerary which he printed, and in which the fubjects are defcribed The indifferent opinion he unjuftly conceived of this, as a hafty juvenile performance, or his attachment to the particular ftudy of druidifm, prevented his giving the world a continuation of it, which he feems to promife in the preface.

phry

phry de Bohun founded a monaftery 1125; and in that for May, p. 271, one of the infcriptions correctly engraved from Ballard's collections 1734. Of a groupe of figures in alabafter, taken out of a barrow on Salifbury plain, and fixed over the chimney of an alehoufe at *Shrawton*, a neighbouring village, fee the fame Magazine for Sept. 1752, p. 408, inferted in the appendix to the 3d vol. of the " Tour through " Great Britain," p. 309, edit. 1753. In that for March 1761, p. 125, an account of a coffin found in *Purton* church. In that for July 1763, p. 324. an account of *Savernake* foreft.

Mr. Rawlinfon had a copy of the charter and ftatutes of the hofpital of *Heightefburie*, founded by Margaret, wife of Sir Robert Hungerford, kt. figned April 8, 1472, and the grant of Edw. IV. April 4, 1472 º. Of *Lacocke* nunnery fee Hearne's hiftory and antiquities of Glaftonbury, p. 331, 332. A S. E. view of it by Buck 1733.

Jof. Glanville wrote " A relation of the famed difturbance at the " houfe of Mr. Mumpeffon of *Tedworth*, occafioned by the beating of " an invifible drum every night for above a year," annexed to his " Blow at modern Sadducifm, 1668." and reprinted under the title of " Palpable evidence of fpirits and witchcraft, in an account of the famed " difturbance, &c." This affair, which paffed for an article of faith in that age, furnifhed the plot for Mr. Addifon's Drummer.

In 1674 was publifhed " The ftrange appearance of the fpirit of " Edw. Aven, late of *Marleborough*, to his own fon, on the 23d, 25th, " and 26th of Nov. laft paft; with his confeffion of money he had " formerly borrowed of Mr. E. L. and forfworn; and alfo of a rob- " bery and murder by him committed 39 years ago: of the truth " whereof the reader may be fatisfied by the carriers of Marleborough " inning at the Rofe at Holbourne bridge, or any other perfons lately " come from thence, having been attefted publicly before the magi- " ftrates of the town. 1674."

" An experimental hiftory of *Road* water in Wiltfhire, with a fhort " mechanical account of its virtues, and of chronical diftempers, in a " letter to the rev. Dr. Durham. By Stephen Williams, M. B. Lond. " 1731." 8vo.

º Engl. Topog. p. 250.

" An

" An hiſtorical account of the cures done by the mineral water
" at *Holt*, with ſome ſhort obſervations concerning its nature, virtues
" and the method of uſing it. 1723." 16 pages 12mo.   Sold at the
old mineral-well in Holt.

" A brief account of the Holt waters, containing one hundred and
" twelve eminent cures, performed by the uſe of the famous mineral
" waters at Holt (near Bath) in Wiltſhire.   Being faithfully collected
" by Henry Eyre, ſworn purveyor to her majeſty for all mineral
" waters.   To which are added, directions for drinking the Holt wa-
" ters, and ſome experimental obſervations on the ſeveral wells. Lond.
" 1731." 12mo.

In p. 281 of N° 186 of the Philoſophical Tranſactions is a letter
from Dr. Cole of Briſtol, concerning a ſuppoſed ſhower of wheat in
this county.

Among the counteſs of Winchelſea's miſcellaneous poems, p. 66, is
" A deſcription of one of the peices of tapiſtry at *Longleat*, made after
" the famous cartons of Raphael, in which Elymas the ſorcerer is mi-
" raculoully ſtruck blind by St. Paul, before Sergius Paulus, the pro-
" conſul of Aſia, inſcribed to the hon. Henry Thynne, under the name
" of Theanor. Lond. 1713." 8vo.   A proſpect of this houſe by John
Sybrecht, ſomewhat in Wouverman's manner, is at Newſted abbey p.

Among lord Coleraine s collections are 11 views of his ſeat at *Longford*, about two miles from Saliſbury, drawn by Rob. Thacker, and engraved by Nicholas Yeates and J. Collins.   The former did the fore front,
the addreſs towards it, the S. ſide, with the flower garden and fountain,
and the backſide next the wallnut-tree court : the latter, a longer view,
the porter's lodge, the ſtables, &c. and the view about the ſtew pond :
a view at an angle, and ichnography of the firſt and ſecond floors have
no name.   Mr. T. Miller exhibited at Spring-gardens this year a drawing of the front of this houſe, now the ſeat of the earl of Radnor.

A print of a moſt curious braſs cup found in a well at *Rudge* near
Marlborough, with the names of five ſtations (one of them mentioned
only by Ravennas) was engraved at the expence of lord Hertford,
and ſince inſerted in Horſley's Brit. R. with an account of it, p. 329.

P Walp. Anecd. of Painting, vol. iii. p. 102.

A print

A print of a Mosaic pavement found in a coppice at Rudge, near Frox-field, 1723, by Vandergucht. Another print, I believe of the same, on two sheets, where it is said to have been found in *Littlecoat* park, in the parish of *Ramsbury*, was engraved by Vertue, with a large account of it by professor Ward.

Other views by Messrs. Buck, 1733, are,

S. W. Malmsbury q abbey.

N. Bradenstoke priory.

S. E. Wardour castle.

Stourhead castle by Campbell.

A view of lord Hertford's house, and the Roman mount and camp at Marlborough, is in plate i. iii. a plan and S. prospect of this town, the antient Cunetio, in pl. lxii. lxiii. of Stukeley's Itinerary: plate ix. exhibits the ruins of king John's palace at Clarendon: pl. xli. Chlorus's camp near this place: pl. xlii. Oldbury camp: pl. xliv. Martinsal hill: p. lxiv. Leucomagus (Great Bedwin): pl. lxviii. Verlucio (Heddington).

Saxton's map of Wiltshire was engraved by R. Hogenbergius 1577, without the hundreds; supplied in Speed's 1610, with a plan of Salisbury and view of Stonehenge.

Another map by E. Bowen.

q King's view of this is most execrable.

WORCESTER.

A Copy of Domefday book relating to this county, on a parchment roll, is mentioned among lord Herbert's MSS. at Jefus Col. Oxf. in Cat. MSS. Ang. tom. i. part i. p. 70, N° 2122. but is now faid to be miflaid. There is another, MS Harl. 1908. Vertue engraved an extract from Domefday relating to *Hambyrie* church, Wyrecefterfhire². The county was vifited 1569 by Rob. Cook: 1634 by —— ——

In the fame college library is an imperfect MS. furvey wrote by Mr. Thomas Abingdon of Hendlip, in this county. What concerns the cathedral was printed from another copy compared with this, under the title of " The antiquities of the cathedral church of Worcefter. By that " learned antiquary, Thomas Abingdon, efq; To which are added, " The antiquities of the cathedral churches of Chichefter and Lich- " feld. Lond. 1717." and 1723. 8vo. The furvey is continued to the time of publication by another hand : the catalogue of the dignitaries and fome other particulars in the introduction are moftly extracted from the papers of Dr. Wm. Hopkins, late prebendary and a curious inquirer into its antiquities, who corrected Gibfon's tranflation of the Chronicon Saxonicum, communicated fome things to Wharton relating to this church, and tranflated Camden's account of this county, adding remarks. Others were communicated by Mr. Oliver. In p. iv. of the introduction is the ftate of this diocefe Edw. I. from a Bodleian MS. A copy of the ftatutes of this church, made 1544, is in Benet Coll. library, N° 23—1, and Mifc. xx. 401. 409. Dean Holand gave the original to card. Pole. A catalogue of the MSS. by Dr. Hopkins, in Cat. MSS. Angl. tom. ii. p. 16.

" Hemingii chartularium ecclefiæ Wigornenfis, ex codice MSto penes " Richardum Graves de Mickleton in agro Glouceftrienfi, armigerum

Walpole's cat. of his works. Not mentioned by Mr. Webb. Quære. If it be that publifhed with the reft of Domefday for the cathedral in Hemingii Chartularium, p. 503 ?

" defcripfit

" defcripfit ediditque Thomas Hearnius : qui & eam partem libri de
" Domefday, quæ ad ecclefiam pertinet Wigornenfem, aliaque ad operis
" (duobus voluminibus comprehenfi) nitorem facientia fubnexuit. Oxon.
" 1723." 8vo. As this church was one of the moft flourifhing in the
whole ifland under the government of our Saxon kings, fo it had the fortune to preferve its charters and other inftruments relating to thofe times
much better than its neighbours. In 1643 Dugdale drew up a catalogue of no lefs than 92 fuch original donations, none whereof fell lower
than the reign of Henry I. To thefe there have been 15 more (now in
the church archives and not mentioned in the Monafticon) added by
Dr. Hickes b, who thinks there are feveral more in Lambarde's MSS. at
Canterbury c. Heming's original Latin tranflation of a fhort Saxon life
of bp. Wulftan, by whofe orders this book was compiled about A. D.
1100, had been publifhed from it in Anglia Sacra d, i. 541. and Dugdale made ufe of collections from it in his Warwickfhire. The original MS. ftolen from Worcefter is in the Cotton library, Tib. A. xiii.
P. Young made extracts and an abridgement of it, both which with a
catalogue of original charters in Worcefter cathedral, and in the hands
of the late lord Somers, who was born here, are annexed to this edition, which may be confidered as a valuable hiftory of this cathedral.
To it are prefixed the old figures of K. Edgar and his wives Ethelfleda
and Ethelfrida over the college gate fronting Edgar's ftreet.

" A furvey of the cathedral-church of Worcefter : with an account
" of the bifhops e thereof, from the foundation of the fee, to the year
" 1600 : alfo an appendix of many original papers and records, never
" before printed. By Wm. Thomas, D. D. rector of St. Nicholas, Wor-
" cefter. Lond. 1727." 4to. with views of the monuments mifer-
ably executed : Abingdon's account of the painted windows is inferted
at large; alfo his furvey of the monuments, with additions, and Heming's Chartulary digefted in order of time. Mr. Thomas was grandfon
of the bifhop of that name who died 1688, juft before his deprivation

---

b Cat. libb. feptr. p. 170—177.   c Nich. Eng. H. L. p. 134.
    d Where are annals of the church to 1308, continued to 1542, p. 469. 531.
    e John Rofs of Warwick wrote a book De epifcopis Vuicenfibus, cited by Whitlock
in Chron. Lich. Wood H. and A. Ox. p. 4. Plot's Staff p. 407. &c. but Tanner
does not fay where it now is.

from

from this fee. He republiſhed Dugdale's Warwickſhire, and we ſhall hear of him again at Malvern. He died 1738. His epitaph in Worceſter cloyſter ſtiles him *Antiquarius celeberrimus.* Tanner f calls him *Vir in antiquitatibus Wigornienſibus verſatiſſimus.* But this his laſt work does him leaſt credit. A more correct as well as more judicious and entertaining account has lately been given to the public in " A ſurvey " of the city of Worceſter; containing the eccleſiaſtical and civil go- " vernment thereof, as originally founded, and the preſent adminiſtra- " tion as ſince reformed: comprehending alſo the moſt material parts of " its hiſtory, from its foundation to the preſent time; extracted from " the beſt authorities: together with an account of whatever is moſt " remarkable for grandeur, elegance, curioſity, or uſe, in this antient " city. The whole embelliſhed with 16 copper plates of perſpective " views of the public buildings, &c. engraved from original drawings " taken on purpoſe for this work. By Valentine Green, of Worceſter. " Worc. 1764." 8vo.

In the Philoſophical Tranſactions, N° 439, p. 136, are Mr. Ward's obſervations on an antient date on Edgar tower near the cathedral g. King John's monument and the college gate make pl. xviii. and xxiii. of Stukeley's Itinerary. A view of the church in the Monaſticon, vol. iii. without Hollar's name. A miſerable view of the church by King; a better drawn by Joſ. Dougharty, engraved by Harris.

Worceſter's elegy and eulogie: or a gratefull acknowledgment of her " benefactors. By J. T. M. A. Lond. 1638. 12mo. The author of this poem was John Toy h, maſter of the free ſchool here, who proba- bly wrote likewiſe " Grammatices Græcæ enchiridion in uſum ſcholæ " collegialis Wigorniæ. Lond. 1650." 8vo.

Another poem is intitled " Vigornia. Lond. 1697." Fol.

A plan of this city was publiſhed 1741.

A large S. W view of it by Buck 1732.

E. and W proſpects 1742.

E. and N. W. views by Chatelain, engraved by A. Walker.

---

f Not. Mon p. 621.

g In ſome late repairs, by a negligence and inattention for which the members of this cathedral are infamous, this date has been thrown back almoſt 50 years.

h Ath. Ox. II. 331.

A tri-

A triumphal arch erected by feveral of the principal members of the conftitution club in this city June 11, 1748, on occafion of fome ufurpations in the city's privileges being checked: engraved by Taylor, with an explanation.

We have an account of both the Benedictine priories founded at *Malvern* within a century after each other, in Abingdon's Antiquities of Worcefter: but a more particular one of the larger and older priory by Dr. Wm. Thomas, in his "Antiquitates prioratus majoris Malverne in agro " Wiccienfi: cum chartis originalibus eafdem illuftrantibus, ex regiftris " fedis epifcopalis Wigornienfis nunc primum editis. Lond. 1725." 8vo. A N. view of this abbey was publifhed by Buck 1731.

In the Philofophical Tranfactions, N° 20, p. 358, and N° 57, p. 1154, is Dr. Beale's account of the medical waters near the foot of Malverne hills, and others in Flint and Somerfetfhire. Dr. John Wall, phyfician at Worcefter, and fellow of Merton, publifhed experiments and obfervations on thefe waters in the fame Tranfactions, vol. xlix. p. 459, and vol. l. p. 23, and fince in an 8vo pamphlet 1756, to the 2d edition of which was added, an appendix containing fome farther particulars relating to their nature and ufes, illuftrated with feveral hiftories of their effects. The 3d edition 1763 was enlarged with an additional appendix containing feveral remarkable hiftories of their effects which came under the author's own obfervation.

A poem on Malvern fpa, 1757, by the rev. Mr. Perry, is inferted in Dodfley's collection of poems, vol. v. p. 84.

An exact plan of *Kidderminfter*, furveyed by John Dogharty, jun. 1753, engraved by Jefferies, in which the new ftreets are inferted as intended to be built.

In p. 34 of Hearne's preface to Leland's Collectanea is the infcription on the offertory bafon at *Soulfton* in *Stamford* parifh.

In the appendix to Heming, N° xi. is a letter from Mr. Graves, giving an account of an infcription in *Perfhore* church for Wm. Newnton, abbot there 1434: and in the preface, p. cv. are the editor's obfervations on the cyricfceate or tythe paid to this church.

An account of the falt fpring at *Draitwich*, by Dr. Wm. Cole, is in N° 142, p. 1059, of the Philofophical Tranfactions; and another by

Dr.

Dr. Lifter in Nº 156. In Nº 139, p. 978, is a letter from Edw. Pitt, alderman of Worcefter, about the Sorbus pyriformis growing in this county; not mentioned by any of our botanifts. In Nº 394, p. 118, Dr. Beard s account of lightning at Worcefter, Jun. 11, 1724.

An E. view of *Hartlebury* caftle by Buck, 1731.

Two views of *Hagley* park by Vivares, from a painting by Smith.

Blackfton cave, and its groundplot, near Bewdley, make pl. xiii. xiv. of Stukeley's Itinerary.

Bewdley, a defcriptive poem in blank verfe, by the rev. Mr. E. Cooper, of Droitwyche; printed in the Grand Magazine, vol. ii. 1759.

Saxton's map of this county was engraved 1577, without the hundreds: added in Speed's, with a plan of the city.

E. Bowen publifhed another map 1756.

YORK-

YORKSHIRE.

ONE cannot approach the borders of this county without paying tribute to the memory of that indefatigable collector of its antiquities Roger Dodfworth, who undertook and executed a work which to the antiquarians of the prefent age would have been the ftone of Tydides: 122 volumes of his own writing, befides original MSS. which he had obtained from feveral hands, making all together 162 volumes folio ᵃ, now lodged in that grand repofitory of our antient muniments the Bodleian library, are lafting memorials what this county owes to him, as the two volumes of the Monafticon (which, tho' publifhed under his and Dugdale's names conjointly, were both collected and written totally by him) will immortalize that extenfive application which has laid the whole kingdom under obligation to it. The patronage of general Fairfax ᵇ (whofe regard to our antiquities, which the rage of his party was fo bitter againft, fhould cover his faults from the eyes of antiquarians) preferved this treafure, and bequeathed it to the library 'tis now lodged in. He was " fon of Matthew Dodfworth, regiftrary of York cathedral, born July 24, 1585, at Newton Grange

ᵃ " I never (fays Hearne, in a tranfport of antiquarian enthufiafm) look upon thefe volumes without the utmoft furprize and wonder; and I cannot but blefs God that he was pleafed out of his infinite goodnefs and mercy to raife up fo pious and diligent a perfon, that fhould by his bleffing fo effectually difcover and preferve fuch a noble treafure of antiquities as is contained in thefe volumes: moft of them written with his own hand, and the genealogical tables, and the notes on them, done with that exquifite care and judgment, that I cannot but think otherwife of this eminent perfon than the author of the Athenæ Oxon. For it plainly appears to me, that his judgment and fagacity were equal to his diligence; and I fee no reafon to doubt but that if he had lived to write the antiquities of Yorkfhire (as he once defigned it) it would have appeared in a very pleafing and entertaining method, and in a proper and elegant ftyle, and fet out with all other becoming advantages." Pref. to Leland's Collect. p. 79.

ᵇ Fairfax preferved the fine windows of this cathedral; and when St. Mary's tower, in which were lodged innumerable records both public and private relating to the northern parts, was blown up during the fiege of York, he gave money to the foldiers that could fave any fcattered papers, many of which are now at Oxford; though Dodfworth had tranfcribed and abridged the greateft part before. Wood's Fafti. II. 11. Th. Tomfon at the hazard of his life faved out of the rubbifh fuch as were legible; which, after paffing through feveral hands, are now the property of Dr. Wm Roundel of York. Burton's preface to his Monafticon.

in

in the parifh of St. Ofwald in Rydale, died Aug. 1654, and was
buried at Rufford; Lancafhire.——of wonderful induftry, but lefs judgment; always collecting and tranfcribing, but never publifhed any
thing c." Wood drew his own character in the firft part of this. Fairfax died 1671; but the MSS. were not brought to Oxford till 1673,
and then in wet weather, when Wood with much ado obtained leave
of the vice-chancellor to have them brought into the muniment room
in the fchool tower, and was a month drying them on the leads.

Before Dodfworth's time T. Talbot, clerk of the Tower records d,
about 1580, made fome collections, which remain in the Cotton library, Vefp. D. 21. One Mr. Jenyngs, an induftrious perfon, who
compiled a ufeful ordinary of arms, now in the Heralds office, and
Mr. Tilleyfon or Tilefon e, the Suffolk antiquary, collected from Dodfworth's papers 12 volumes of notes relating to the following hundreds
and wapentakes: Hangweft, Halikell, in the N. riding; Ainfty,
Barkeftone, Morley, Staincroffe, Claro, Ofgoodcroffe, Strafford, Skir-
rack, Agbridge, Stainbridge, and Evecrofs, in the W. riding, which
with a volume of Yorkfhire pedigrees, ordine alphabetico as far as G,
are in the Harleian library, 793—805.

Dr. Johnfon of Pontfract made large collections from Dodfworth's
papers and other quarters, and communicated many particulars to bp.
Gibfon, who was alfo affifted by Mr. Thorefby, and in the E. Riding
by Mr. John Burnfall of Hull. Mr. Drake tells us the doctor's MSS.
are in fuch an awkward Arabic fcrawl as to be fcarce legible, and that
a fubfcription was propofed fome few years fince to lodge them in the
caftle library, which might have made them more ufeful than they

c Wood's Fafti, II. 14.
d In chartophylacio actuarius. Smith vit. Camd. p. 26. See Camd. Brit. in courts.
The fuperficial imperfect obfervations on Yorkfhire by Wm. Valvafour of Hafelwood,
efq; printed by Hearne in Leland's Collectanea, vi. 300, are hardly worth mentioning.
He fays a coin of Domitian was found at Tadcafter 1658, infcribed C A L C A R A V C I,
rev. figura equeftris fubfcribed COS. V. He has read C A E S A R A V G. F. D O M I-
T I A N V S the wrong way, and placed the confulfhip on the wrong fide: and in this
motley legend he would find Calcaria, the antient name of Tadcafter. We need only
look into Leigh's Natural hiftory of Lancafhire to fee how deficient our antiquarians fixty
years ago were in their medallic knowlege.
e See an account of a MS. by him, intitled " Honours genealogie, or the arms of the
Englifh kings and the degrees of the nobility, 1647." in Ofborne's hands 1787. Brit.
Librarian, p. 105.

can

can be now. The doctor gave out he had fpent thirty years in amaffing materials, and propofed to write the antiquities of the county after
Dugdale's and the natural hiftory after Plott's manner. Wood was informed he grew weary of the work. Nicholfon has left this cenfure
on his labours, that " only death prevented the publication of what its
readers would have been weary of." Dr. Burton informs us [f] he
had the ufe of above 100 folio volumes relating to this county, collected by this indefatigable phyfician [g], and then in the hands of Rich.
Franke of Campfal, efq; recorder of Pontefract and Doncafter, who had
purchafed them. Since his death I am informed they have been lately
brought to London, with a view of felling them by auction. A catalogue of them and others in the doctor's poffeffion was publifhed in
Cat. MSS. Angl. tom. ii. p. 99. Among the reft is mentioned a large
volume of profpects of York, and other towns and caftles, draughts of
Roman and Saxon camps, and views of churches, abbies [h], and feats:
others contain arms, tombs, and monumental infcriptions before the
civil war.

Mr. T. Rawlinfon had an exact MS. catalogue of all the ecclefiaftical dignities and benefices in Yorkfhire, with their valuations and
the names of the patrons and incumbents, 1696, and brought down
later. The fulleft information on the monaftical article may be found
in " Monafticon Eboracenfe: and the ecclefiaftical hiftory of Yorkfhire.
" Containing an account of the firft introduction and progrefs of Chrif-
" tianity in that diocefe, untill the end of William the Conqueror's reign.
" Alfo the defcription of the fituation, fabric, times of endowments of
" all churches, collegiate, conventual, parochial, or of peculiar jurif-
" diction; and of other religious places in that diftrict; and to whofe
" memory they were dedicated; together with an account of fuch
" monuments and infcriptions as are worthy of notice, as well as of

[f] Pref. to his Monafticon.

[g] The doctor had wrote a hiftory of the Talbot family from their Norman anceftor
Richard Talbot to the lord Edw. Talbot, laft earl of Shrewfbury of the houfe of Sheffield. An hiftorical account of the reign of Charles I. after the breaking out of the civil
war. A fhort account of Stephen's reign. His hiftorical account of the family of Bruce
is in the Harleian library, N° 3879.

[h] Kirkall engraved the profpect of *Kirkley*'s abbey, where Robin Hood died, from a
drawing of the doctor's among his Yorkfhire antiquities, p. 54 of his drawings.

" the

" the rife, progrefs, eftablifhment, privileges, and fuppreffion of each
" order, religious or military, fixed therein: with a catalogue of all
" the abbots, and other fuperiors of thofe places, and of all the patrons
" rectors, vicars, cantarifts, &c. of each church, chapel, &c. from
" the earlieft account, down to the prefent time. Collected from the
" beft hiftorians, antient MSS. with above 2000 copies of original
" charters and deeds never yet publifhed. Adorned with copper plates
" reprefenting the ichnographies i of fome of their churches, abbies,
" ruins, &c. and other curious things worthy of obfervation. To
" which is added, a fcheme k and propofals in order to form a fociety
" for compiling a complete civil and natural hiftory of the antient and
" prefent ftate of Yorkfhire: with a chorographical and topographical
" defcription thereof; and for a fet of accurate maps taken from ac-
" tual furveys. To this is fubjoined a fhort hiftorical account of the
" parifh of *Hemingbrough* l, as a fpecimen, fhewing what materials the
" author has collected towards affifting fuch a fociety according to
" the above propofals. By John Burton, M. D. York 1758." Fol.
The fecond volume of this valuable work is expected very foon. The
doctor appears to have the greateft zeal for illuftrating the antiquities of
his native country, and his indefatigable refearches have hitherto met
with due encouragement from thofe who had many valuable materials
in their hands. The late Mr. Conftable, of Burton Conftable, fpared
no expence to procure whatever would illuftrate any branch of the
hiftory of Yorkfhire. Another collector, equally affiduous and judicious,
was Mr. Frank before-mentioned. The regifters of feveral priories are
in the hands of thofe who poffefs the fcites; but none can fhew fo
compleat an affemblage of their records as Fountains abbey, itfelf the
compleateft religious houfe in the county, in the poffeffion of the late
Mr. Meffenger, whofe venerable feat in fuch a neighbourhood cannot
be vifited by antiquarians without envious reverence.

---

i Only the ichnographies of Fountains and Kirkftall are in this volume, where we are
promifed Whitby, Byland, Jorval, and Selby. S. and W. views of the laft by D. King
are in the Monafticon Anglicanum.

k The fame publifhed for Ireland about twenty years fince. The doctor has the fatif-
faction to find his fcheme approved.

l This defcription and the map annexed fhould make fome later defcribers of counties
blufh for their remiffnefs and inattention.

A copy

A copy of Sir Thomas Widdrington's MS. account of the antiquities of the city of York is in the hands of Thomas Fairfax of Menſton, eſq; Sir Thomas married a ſiſter of general Fairfax, from whoſe uncle Charles the Menſton family was deſcended [m], and probably gave or left it to his brother-in-law. He began in Charles the Iſt's time, and after the reſtoration offered to print this work, and dedicate it to the city, who ſeem to have refuſed it on account of the indifference he ſhewed to their intereſts when he repreſented them in Cromwell's parliament. Upon this he is ſaid to have expreſly forbid his deſcendants to publiſh it. Beſides the Menſton MS. there was another copy in the Shaftoe family at Durham, who married a daughter of the author; and Mr. Drake had the uſe of one among the city records, and another from Sir Rich. Smyth of St. Edmund's Bury, which he thinks was prepared by the author himſelf for the preſs, and might have paſſed thro' different hands on the death of lord Fairfax, and diſperſion of his effects.

Chriſtopher Hildyard, eſq; of an antient family in this county, recorder of Heddon and ſteward of St. Mary's court, York, out of zeal for the ſubject, and to aſſiſt a more general hiſtorian publiſhed " A " liſt, or catalogue of all the mayors, and bayliffs, lord-mayors, and " ſheriffs, of the moſt ancient, honourable, noble, and loyall city of " Yorke, from the time of king Edward the Firſt, untill this preſent " year, 1664; being the 16th year of the moſt happy reign of our " moſt gracious ſoveraign lord king Charles the Second. Together " with many, and ſundry remarkable paſſages, which happen'd in their " ſeverall years. Publiſhed by a true lover of antiquity, and a well- " wiſher to the proſperity of the city; together with his hearty deſire " of the reſtoration of its glory, ſplendor, and magnificence. York " 1664." 4to. Mr. Drake ſays [n], " ſome hiſtorical remarks are thinly interſperſed in this piece," which is pretty exact; his preface containing more of the antiquities of York than his whole book. The late induſtrious Mr. Torr copied this book, as he has done ſeveral others which he thought ſcarce, making ſome additions of his own from Camden and others. A copy of this or the original tranſcript was given by the collector, or otherwiſe fell into the hands of the late Mr. Francis Hild-

---

[m] See Thoreſby's Ducat. Leod. p. 68.   [n] Preface.

yard,

yard, bookfeller, who dreffed it up for the prefs, with a pompous title page, and very injudicioufly put Torr's name to it. It were to be wifhed he had informed the public that this was only a copy of his namefake's printed book (fince he muft know it) with a few additions by Mr. Torr. It would have prevented fome peevifh advertifements⁰ between the fon of that great collector and the bookfeller. How this neceffary preface came to be omitted I know not. Mr. Hildyard for the courfe of many years bore a very fair character in his bufinefs, and I cannot fufpect him of having done it with any defign, efpecially when fuch a declaration would rather have cleared up than obftructed the matter on all fides. By this miftake I am obliged to fay, in order to vindicate the memory of a perfon to whofe labours my work is fo greatly obliged, that a " lean catalogue (as bp. Nicholfon juftly calls it) of our mayors and fheriffs, publifhed long ago by another hand ᵖ, is again crept into the world with the name of James Torr," under the title of " The antiquities of York city, and the civil government there-
" of; with a lift of all the mayors and bayliffs, lord-mayors and fhe-
" riffs, from the time of K. Edward the Firft, to this prefent year 1719.
" Collected from the papers of Chriftopher Hildyard, efq; with notes
" and obfervations, and the addition of ancient infcriptions, and coates
" of arms, from grave-ftones and church windows. By James Torr,
" gent. and fince continued to this year prefent 1719. With an appen-
" dix of the dimenfions of York minfter, the names of the founders,
" repairers and benefactors; a catalogue of all the religious houfes,
" chappels and churches, that have been, and at prefent are, in the
" faid city. As alfo the gifts and legacies to the charity fchools, with the
" names of the firft promoters and founders thereof. York 1719." 8vo.
Torr's application and exactnefs in ecclefiaftical antiquities and family

⁰ Nicholas Torr having in the Evening Poft, Nov. 17, 1719, denied that his father had any concern in this work, Hildyard replied, that Mr. James Torr borrowed Chrifto-pher Hildyard's papers of him, which having methodized and confiderably enlarged from monuments, &c. he gave to him to print. Upon this N. Torr in a fecond adver-tifement challenged H. to produce a MS. of the faid book or part of it wrote by Mr. J T. which he affirmed H. had confeffed before fufficient witneffes he could not do : and fo the affair dropt.
ᵖ There is a copy of the firft edition MS. Harl. 6115, with large MS. additions, con-tinuing it to 1677, and an abftract of Widdrington's MS.

defcents

defcents were prodigious. One of his MSS. mentioned by Mr. Drake has this title: "Antiquities ecclefiaftical of the city of York, concerning

churches {parochial / conventual} chapels, hofpitals, gilds,} and in them {chantries and interments,}

alfo churches parochial and conventual within the archdeaconry of the W. riding: collected out of public records and regifters. 1691." This work contains no lefs than 1255 columns in folio, for the moft part clofely writ, in a very fmall but legible hand, with a compleat index. The other archdeaconries are treated in the fame manner in two more volumes, one more contains the peculiars belonging to the church or fee. They were all given to the dean and chapter's library by abp Sharp's ^q executors; and are an index or key to all the records of the archbifhops, deans, and chapters, and all other offices of the church or fee. His authorities are explained in particular marks at the beginning of the volume. They are kept *fub figillo* in the regifter's office: 1500l. have been offered for them to be printed; and the greateft part are included in Dr. Burton's Monafticon. Five MS. volumes in folio are in the poffeffion of his fon Nicholas Torr, of Snydall near Pontefract, efq; intitled, "Englifh nobility and gentry, or fupplemental collections to "Sir Wm. Dugdale's Baronage, carrying on the genealogical defcents "and hiftorical remarks of families therein contained." He has here tranfcribed Dugdale's Baronage throughout, corrected it in many places, added many hiftorical remarks, and enriched it with the genealogies of many families of leffer note, efpecially of the northern gentry; with the coats and different quarterings of the feveral families, and a copious index ^r. If thefe are not fufficient there are above 20 volumes of collections from the regifters of York and Wells, made by Dr. Matthew Hutton, rector of Aynho, Northamptonfhire, who died 1711. Wharton had the ufe of thefe, but does not fay where they were lodged after-

---

^q The archbifhop himfelf had begun a moft ufeful work of collecting the endowments and benefactions to the churches and chapels in his diocefe. His grace's remarks on Englifh, Scotch, and Irifh money were in Thorefby's mufeum, and another copy is in the Harleian library.

^r This intenfe application did not in the leaft injure Mr. Torr's conftitution. He died of a fever, 1699, at the age of 49; and lies in Normanton church, in which parifh Snydall is fituate. See his epitaph in Drake's preface.

wards.

wards [r]. Three 8vo volumes of his tranſcripts from York regiſters are in the Harleian library.

The next account of this city is a uſeful compendium, the work of an induſtrious printer, containing ſome things not in larger hiſtories, intitled, " The antient and modern hiſtory of the famous city of York;
" and in a particular manner of its magnificent cathedral, commonly
" called York-minſter : as alſo an account of St. Mary's abbey, and
" other antient religious houſes and churches; the places whereon
" they ſtood, what orders belonged to them, and the remains of thoſe
" antient buildings that are yet to be ſeen: with a deſcription of thoſe
" churches now in uſe, of their curiouſly painted windows [s], the in-
" ſcriptions carefully collected, and many of them tranſlated: the lives
" of the archbiſhops of this ſee; the government of the northern parts
" under the Romans, eſpecially by the emperors Severus and Con-
" ſtantius, who both dyed in this city: of the kings of England, and
" other illuſtrious perſons, who have honoured York with their pre-
" ſence; an account of the mayors and bayliffs, lord-mayors and
" ſheriffs (with ſeveral remarkable tranſactions not publiſhed before)
" from different MSS. down to the 3d year of the reign of his preſent
" majeſty K. George II. To which is added, a deſcription of the moſt
" noted towns in Yorkſhire, with the antient buildings that have been
" therein, alphabetically digeſted for the delight of the reader; not
" only by the aſſiſtance of antient writers, but from the obſervations
" of ſeveral ingenious perſons in the preſent age. The whole diligently
" collected by T. G. [Thomas Gent]. 1730." 12mo.

But the beſt account of this ſecond city of England is Mr. Francis Drake's " Eboracum: or the hiſtory and antiquities of the city of York,
" from its original to the preſent times. Together with the hiſtory of
" the cathedral church, and the lives of the archbiſhops of that ſee, from
" the firſt introduction of Chriſtianity into the northern parts of this
" iſland, to the preſent ſtate and condition of that magnificent fabrick.
" Collected from authentick MSS. publick records, ancient chronicles,
" and modern hiſtorians; and illuſtrated with copper plates. In two

[r] Pref. to Ang. Sac. i. ad fin.
[s] No city or town in the kingdom can boaſt ſuch a collection of paintings on glaſs as York. Above half of the twenty-three churches can ſhew ſome good remains in the windows, and there are not above ſix or ſeven plain ones out of ſixty-ſeven in the minſter.

2 " books.

" books. Lond. 1736." Fol. Befides the affiftance derived from the collections of Johnfon, Widdrington, Gale, and Torr, Mr. Drake acknowleges fome in the heraldical way from thofe of Henry Keepe, mentioned before at Weftminfter, p. 269, who began an account of York about 1684, and was very particular in his defcription of arms in the windows of the feveral churches: the former part of his work fairly tranfcribed for the prefs was in Roger Gale's mufeum, the materials for the fecond were in the poffeffion of Mr. Adams, late recorder of York. The law part of Mr. Drake's book is chiefly taken from the collections of Mr. Hopkinfon, clerk of the peace to the Weft Riding about 1670, many of whofe MSS. there is reafon to fufpect were imbezzled: the reft were given to the library of Dr. Richardfon of N. Byerley [t].

An abridgement of Drake's hiftory of this church and of Dart's defcription of Canterbury cathedral, with the plates of each work, was publifhed under the title of " An accurate defcription and hiftory of " the metropolitan and cathedral churches of Canterbury and York, " from their firft foundation to the prefent year. Illuftrated with 117 " copper plates, confifting of different views, plans, monuments, an- " tiquities, arms, &c. Lond. 1755." Fol. with an appendix of monuments, erected after it went to the prefs.

Alcuin, one of the politeft fcholars of his age, when divinity was the only ftudy, wrote a poem " De pontificibus & fanctis ecclefiæ Eboracenfis," publifhed by Gale among Script. Hift. Ang. Ox. 1691. i. 703. He begins his ftory with fuch an account of the antient ftate of that city and the firft appearance of Chriftianity among the northern Saxons as Bede, whom he put upon writing an ecclefiaftical hiftory, furnifhed him with; concluding with the death of his patron abp. Eandbald I. One Thomas Stubbs, about 1370, wrote or continued a hiftory of the archbifhops, publifhed by Twifden 1685.

Mr. Samuel Gale had formed a defign of publifhing fomething on the ecclefiaftical antiquities of this city, and from the dean his father's, and his own induftry, he had made a confiderable progrefs. Mr. Drake

---

[t] Thorefby had his collection of pedigrees and defcents of feveral of the W. Riding gentry 1666, continued and enlarged by Rich. Thornton, efq; and himfelf: bought at his fale by Dr. Wilfon.

had

had the ufe of his collections, which a public employment prevented Gale from printing.   Dr. Stukeley had a fmall 4to MS. of his, intitled, " A view of the feveral foundations of York minfter."

Some fuperficial extracts relating to this cathedral were publifhed from Dugdale's papers, at the end of the laft edition of his Hiftory of St. Paul's.

" Miffale ad ufum celeberrimæ ecclefiæ Eboracenfis, optimis carac-
" teribus recenter impreffum, cura pervigili, maximaq. lucubratione,
" mendifq. pluribus emendatum, fumptibus & expenfis Johannis Gacket,
" mercatoris librarii bene me-ti, juxta præfatam ecclefiam commoran-
" tis, A D. decimo fexto fupra millefimum & quingentefimum, die
" vero 5to Feb. completum atq. perfectum." with mufical notes and feveral fine wooden cuts. Fol.   Tho. Rawlinfon, efq; had a book in-titled thus, " Feliciter finiunt feftum vifitationis B. Marie V. fec. ufum " Eborac..noviter impreffi per Urfyn Mylner commorantem in cimi-" tero minfteris S. Petri." 8vo.

In lord Hatton s library was a moft curious MS. containing draughts of all the arms and monuments remaining in and about it, 1641.   A copy of this, very neatly drawn by Sedgwicke, was given by Dugdale to the Herald's office, where it now is.   The great S. window is en-graved from it in Drake's book.

Tho. Gent, finking under age and neceffity, compiled and printed " The moft delectable, fcriptural, and pious hiftory of the famous and " magnificent great eaftern window (according to beautifull portrai-" tures) in St. Peter's cathedral, York : previous thereto is a remark-" able account how the ancient churches were differently erected by " two famous kings; the prefent built by five excellent archbifhops, " one extraordinary bifhop, with others : the names of fepulchred per-" fonages, and important affairs worthy remembrance ; a book which " might be ftyled the hiftory of hiftories.   Succinctly treated of in three " parts u   Likewife is added, a chronological account of fome emi-" nent perfonages there depicted, anciently remarkable for their learn-" ing, virtue, and piety.   Impreffed for the author, in St. Peter's

He divides the windows into the tracery, the panes containing Old Teftament hiftory, and the Revelations.

" gate.

" gate. 1762." 8vo. He had some years before engraved a wooden plate of it. A better drawn by J. Haynes was executed on copper by Toms; and there is a small one in Drake. This window is 75 feet high, and 32 broad, and contains besides the tracery 117 panes, each near a yard square. John Thornton of Coventry performed it for 56l. in three years. He agreed for four shillings a week, and was to have 100 shillings a year, and 10l. at the end for his care.——What would the revivers of Thornton's art charge for such a work!

A platform of the church by E. Barker and J. Nutting.

Chori ecclesiæ cathedralis Eboracensis arcus australis, by Vandergucht.

An inside view of the minster from the W. end by J. Haynes, engraved by J. Harris, 1741.

The S. side of the minster by Hollar, Mon. iii. 129, and two others I believe there.

F. Place drew and etched another.

King engraved the E. W. and S. sides, and S. cross: the three last in his best manner.

A capital view of the W. front, drawn by Joseph Baker, manager of the theatre at York, was engraved by Vivares 1750. The W. front of Lincoln minster, before-mentioned, was done by the same.

J. Harris engraved the chapter house.

Sigill. capituli. ecclesie. beati Petri. Eboraci ad causas. et negocia. penes R. Thoresby, engraved 1719.

The old horn of Ulphus was engraved by Vertue for the Antiquarian Society from a drawing in Sam. Gale's possession, by B. M.

Mr. Tho. Rawlinson had a MS. giving a full account of the several fee-farm rents belonging to the hospital of St. Nicholas in York, seized and alienated at the dissolution, surveyed Michaelmas 1610, and signed Julius Cæsar, a specimen of which was printed in the Antiquities of Surry, vol. ii. p. 189.

A very indifferent S. view of St. Mary's abbey, near this city, by Buck 1721. A better in Gent's history of Kingston. The best by Lodge and Tempesta.

The

The Antiquarian Society have a good drawing of St. Helen's church by J. Haynes.

Mr. Heneage Dering, dean of Rippon, attempted a history of this famous city in verfe, but lived to carry it hardly through the Roman times, in " Reliquiæ Eboracenfes, per H. D. Ripenfem. Eborac. " 1743." 4to.

An account of the fiege 1644 may be feen in " Marfton-moore : five " de obfidione prælioque Eboracenfi carmen, in fex libris. Autore " P. Fyfher. Lond. 1650." 4to.

" The king's noble entertainment at York, with the lord maior of " York his worthy fpeech to the king : as alfo the manner how the " aldermen, fheriffs, citizens, and fundry other gentlemen congratu- " lated his majefty to York : likewife how triumphantly he was enter- " tained with many rich prefents, and how they conducted his ma- " jefty to his caftle. Sent from York by Sir Nath. Rigby to a merchant " of London, March 18, 1641. Lond. 1641." reprinted in Somers' Tracts, 3d col. vol. i. p. 282.

In N° 145 of the Philofophical Tranfactions, 1683, are Dr. Lifter's obfervations upon feveral other antiquities and the ruins of a Roman wall, and multangular tower in York, with a cut. The original draw- ing by Lodge was in Thorefby's mufeum. In p. 1017 of 171 is an ac- count of an antient earthern veffel found near York, and now in the Afhmolean mufeum. In p. 33 of vol. xlviii. is an explanation of a Roman infcription here by Mr. Drake and profeffor Ward. In p. 564 of the fame volume is an account of an earthquake felt at York Apr. 19. 1754.

In the Gentleman's Magazine for April 1740, p. 189, is a Roman altar found near Micklegate. In that for March 1751, p. 102, a draught *y* and Dr. Stukeley's explanation of a bas releif of Mithras, dug up in Micklegate ftreet 1747, firft publifhed in the Philofophical Tranf- actions, N° 493, p. 214, and again in the doctor s Palæographia Bri- tannica, N° iii. 1752. In the fame Magazine for Sept. 1752, p. 402, is a Roman infcription found in the fame ftreet, explained by Mr. Pegge

y In which a little figure ftanding at the head of the horfe is omitted.

in

m that for Nov. following, p. 515; and further commented on by Mr. S. Hill in June 1753, p. 269.

A plan of the gaol in the castle was taken 17 .. to build Newgate according to it.

We have a prospect of the terras walk laid out at the expence of the corporation, taken from the center. By Nathaniel Dráke, and engraved by C. Grignion 1756.

" The S. W. prospect of the antient city of York, with the plattform " of Knavesmire; whereon his majesty K. George the IId's hundred " guineas was run for Aug. 10, 1731. By John Haynes."

A plan of York by John Coffin, engraved by John Haynes 1748, a new edition with amendments, and views of the city-house and fifteen other gentlemen's houses there.

Another plan, surveyed by Peter Chassereau, with improvements, published by John Rocque 1750, adorned with views of the city-house, county hospital, W. view of the cathedral, abp. Bowet's monument, map of the county with Roman roads, gaol, section of the assembly room, Clifford's tower, Thursday-market cross, and the church of Allhallows pavement.

Mr. Wm. Lodge drew and engraved small views of Clifford's tower, and of York from the water-house to the ruins of the manor-house, i. e. a S. view of the city.

A large S. view from Old Baile by S. Buck, engraved by Vandergucht 1736.

A large S. E. prospect of this city by Buck 1745.

A view of it from the river Ouse by Chatelain and Toms 1751.

A perspective view of the inside of the grand assembly room by W. Lindley.

The grand stand erected on Knavesmire for the convenience of seeing the horse races. John Carr inv. and del. P. Fourdrinier sc. with two plans. Another view by W. Lindley.

" *Hallifax* and its gibbet law, placed in a true light. Together with " a description of the town, the nature of the soil, the temper and dis- " position of the people, the antiquity of its customary law, and the

4 B 2

" reason-

" reafonablenefs thereof: with an account of the gentry, and other
" eminent perfons born and inhabiting within the faid town, and the
" liberties thereof: with many other matters and things of great re-
" mark, never before publifhed. To which are added the unparal-
" lelled tragedies committed by Sir John Eland of Eland and his grand
" antagonifts [z]. Lond. 1708." 12mo. [By Wm. Bentley.] To correct this was publifhed " The antiquities of the town of Halifax in
" Yorkfhire. Wherein is given an account of the town, church, and
" 12 chapels, the free grammar fchool; a lift of vicars and fchool
" mafters; the ancient and cuftomary law, called Halifax gibbet-law,
" with the names of the perfons that fuffer'd thereby, and the times
" when; the public charities to church and poor; the men of learn-
" ing, whether natives or inhabitants, together with the moft remark-
" able epitaphs and infcriptions in the church and church yard. The
" whole faithfully collected from printed authors, rolls of courts, re-
" gifters, old wills, and other authentic writings. By the rev. Tho
" Wright, of Halifax. Leedes 1738." 12mo.

The rev. Mr. Watfon is collecting for this part of the county.

Ralph Thorefby, defcended from a family cotemporary with Canute,
and at the conqueft lords of Thorefby in this county, from whence
they took their name, exerted that paffion for antiquities which he inherited from his father in the illuftration of the W. riding, and particularly the town of *Leedes* [a], in his " Ducatus Leodienfis: or, the to-
" pography of the ancient and populous town and parifh of Leedes,
" and parts adjacent, in the weft-riding of the county of York: with

---

[z] The full title of this additional piece is " Revenge upon revenge: or, an hiftorical
" narrative of the tragical practices of Sir John Eland, of Eland, high-fheriff of the
" county of York, committed upon the perfons of Sir Robert Beaumont, and his alli-
" ances, in the reign of Edward the Third, king of England, &c. (15 Edw. III. 1340.)
" Together with an account of the revenge which Adam, the fon of Sir Robert Beau-
" mont, and his accomplices, took upon the perfons of Sir John Eland and his pofterity,
" hereby fully and plainly, as well as impartially reprefented, for the fatisfaction of the
" inquifitive part of the world; the whole being divided into three equal parts. Lond.
" 1708." 12mo.

[a] Where his anceftors had been fettled for feveral defcents, and where himfelf was
born. Roger Dodfworth defcended by the mother's fide from a female of the elder
branch.

" the

" the pedigrees of many of the nobility and gentry, and other matters
" relating to thofe parts; extracted from records, original evidences,
" and MSS. To which is added, at the requeft of feveral learned
" perfons, a catalogue of his mufæum b; with the curiofities, natural
" and artificial, and the antiquities; particularly the Roman, Britifh,
" Saxon, Danifh, Norman, and Scotch coins, with modern medals. Alfo
" a catalogue of MSS. c, the various editions of the Bible, and of books
" publifhed in the infancy of the art of printing; with an account of fome
" unufual accidents that have attended fome perfons, attempted after
" the method of Dr. Plott. Lond. 1715." Fol. To this book is prefixed the moft compleat map that ever was engraved of thefe parts,
and the firft of any part in the north of England, drawn after the new
method for twenty miles round Leeds, like thofe for the like diftance
from London, Oxford, and Cambridge d, and engraved by Sutton Nichols.
The hiftorical part of this treatife, giving a view of the ftate of the
northern parts of the kingdom under the Britons, Romans, and Saxons,
brought down almoft to the end of the.6th century, being left ready
for the prefs, is publifhed in his article in the Biographia Britannica,
n. H.

" Vicaria Leodienfis: or, the hiftory of the church of Leedes in
" Yorkfhire; containing an account of the learned men, bifhops, and
" writers who have been vicars of that populous parifh; with the cata-
" logues of their works, printed and MS.; to which are added the

b His father, a wealthy clothier of Leeds, bought lord Fairfax's valuable library and
cabinet of coins of his heir, for 1851. His lordfhip purchafed the coins of Mr. Stonehoufe, rector of Darfield, and continually added to them. Above 100 were inferted in
Gibfon's edition of the Britannia, with Dr. Walker's notes. When Ralph Thorefby
died, 1725, they were brought to London, and on the death of his eldeft fon, late
rector of Newington, fold by auction March 1764. The printed books (many of them
inriched with Thorefby's MS. notes) were purchafed by T. Payne, bookfeller, at the
Mews gate, and retailed by a marked catalogue. The author's copy of the Ducatus,
full of MS. additions, is in the hands of the bp. of Hereford. The reft of the collection
remaining at Leeds 1734, neglected in a garret, having been refufed by feveral on account of forty copies of the Ducatus infeparable from it, was bought at laft all together by
two bookfellers at Leeds, and afterwards partly by Dr. Burton, author of the Monafticon
Eboracenfe.

c Another catalogue was printed in Cat. MSS. Ang. tom. ii. part i. p. 229

d Duc. Leod p 135. Under it is a map of the navigable courfe of the river Are
from Leedes to the Humber and German ocean.

" lives

" lives of feveral archbifhops of York, and other eminent perfons,
" benefactors to that church; with many other things interfperfed re-
" lating to the city and county of York. And abp. Thorefby's me-
" morable expofition of the decalogue, creed, and lords prayer [e].
" With an appendix of original records and MSS. Lond. 1724. 8vo.

Thorefby was not without merit as an antiquarian. He feems to
have been well fkilled in the Saxon language, and in general to
have applied it happily in his etymologies. What antiquities came in
his way he gives a good account of, and fome idea of the face of the
country. His credulity and want of judgment in collecting his curiofities muft be charged on the infancy of thofe purfuits in the age he
lived in. Tradefcant was the firft Englifh collector in a private rank,
Thorefby the fecond.

F. Place [f] drew and etched the churches and profpect of Leedes in
the Ducatus : and Wm. Lodge drew and engraved the profpect of this
town and Wakefield, with the ruins of Kirkftall and Fountains abbies,
and a map of the wapentakes of Skirack and Morley, in one plate.

A large E. view of Leedes from Chaverler hill by S. Buck, engraved
by Harris. A S. view of this town by Buck was publifhed 1745.

Roger Gale had a hiftory of the church at *Rippon*, wrote by Sir
Thomas Herbert, of which Mr. Drake has publifhed part in his appendix, p. xci. and in p. lxxxvii. part of his hiftory of *Beverley*. Sir Thomas
alfo wrote the hiftory of York and *Southwell*, which are printed in
Latin and Englifh in Leland's Collectanea. He was a great collector
of antient MSS. a fingular lover of antiquities, and affifted Dugdale
in the 3d volume of the Monafticon [g].

[e] Printed from the original in the abp's archives at York. John Thorefby, cardinal
and abp. 1352, was defcended from a younger branch of the fame family, a prelate of
exemplary piety and beneficence ; a generous contributor to his cathedral, of which he
built the choir, and, which is ftill more to his praife, the firft of Wicliffe's friends.
This expofition of the ten commandments, creed, and pater-nofter he obliged the clergy
of his province to read in Englifh, " for comune profet, that the underloutes might be
lered to know God almighten, and fo comme to that bliffe that never more blynnes."
   He was a Yorkfhire gentleman, well acquained with Hollar and Thorefby; and applied himfelf to moft of the beautiful arts. His other drawings have been already fpecified. In Walpole's Cat. of engra. p. 50, are prints of him and Lodge.
[g] Wood's Faft. II. 15. In the Athenæ, II. 690. is a particular detail of his attendance on Cha. I. during the two laft years of his life ; for which Cha. II. created him a
baronet.

In

In Peck's Defiderata Curiofa, vol. ii. book vii. N° 20, p. 56, is the fcheme of a new college (after the manner of an niverfity) defigned at Rippon, dated 4th July, 1604, for which James the Ift's queen (Anne) gave letters patent.

"The antient and modern hiftory of the loyal town of Rippon:
" (introduced by a poem on the furprizing beauties of *Studley* park,
" with a defcription of the venerable ruins of Fountains abbey, written
" by Mr. Peter Aram, and another [h] on the pleafures of a country
" life by a reverend young gentleman), &c. Adorned with many cuts,
" preceded by a S. W. profpect (and a new plan) of Rippon. Befides
" are added, Travels into other parts of Yorkfhire. 1. Beverly; an
" account of its minfter: the feal of St. John: the beauty of St. Mary's:
" and a lift of the mayors of the town fince incorporated. 2. Re-
" marks on Pontefract. 3. Of the church at Wakefield. 4. Thofe
" of Leeds: with a vifit to Kirkftal and Kirkham. 5. An account of
" Keighley. 6. State of Skipton caftle, &c. 7. Knarefborough: of
" the church and its monuments, St. Robert's chapel, &c. 8. Towns
" near York; as Tadcafter, Bilbrough, Bolton-Percy, Howlden, Selby,
" Wiftow, Cawood church and caftle, Acafter and Bifhop's Thorpe,
" Acomb, Nun-monkton, and Skelton, &c. with their antiquity and
" infcriptions. Faithfully and painfully collected by Thomas Gent of
" York. York 1733." 8vo.

A S. E. view of the town by Buck, 1745.

S. and W. views of the minfter when the three fpires were ftanding are in the Monafticon.

Thomas de Caftleford, a Benedictine monk at *Pontfract* about 1520, wrote the hiftory of this town from the Saxon times to his own, which Leland [i] perufed with much fatisfaction, and promifed a larger account in his own work "De civili hiftoria," unfinifhed or loft. Dr. Johnfon wrote a particular detail of its hiftory and antiquities: but the only

[h] Intitled "U-l-thania [Upletham] poetæ rufticantis amœnitates: or a poem on the " pleafures of a country life. A. D. 1733." Upletham is a village of Cleveland, a few miles N. of Gifborough.

[i] De Script. Brit. Tanner.

printed

printed account is that communicated to the compiler of Magna Britannia by Mr. Marmaduke Fothergill, vol. vi. 394

" Pontefract caſtle. An account how it was taken : and how general " Rainſborough was ſurprized in his quarters at Doncaſter, anno 1648, " in a letter to a friend, by capt. Thomas Paulden. Written upon oc- " caſion of prince Eugene's ſurprizing M. Villeroy at Cremona, in the " Savay, 1703." 4to. reprinted in Somers's Tracts, 2d coll. vol. ii. p. 471. It was printed a third time under the title of " An account of " the taking and ſurrendering of Pontefract caſtle, &c. Oxf. 1747." 8vo. The author was engaged in the ſcenes of which he wrote this account when he was 78. Mr. Drake is poſſeſſed of a minute and exact MS. diary of each day's proceedings, by a relation who was in the caſtle all the time.

" An exact relation of the tryal and examination of John Morris, " governor of Pontefract caſtle, at the aſſizes held at York : together " with his ſpeeches, prayers, and other paſſages before his death, Aug. " 23, 1649. Whereunto is added the ſpeech of cornet Blackburne, " executed at the ſame time. Printed in the year 1649." reprinted in Somers's Tracts, 3d coll. vol. ii. p. 476. " The hiſtory of the ſurprize of this caſtle by col. John Morris, governor for K. Charles I. and II. 1648. with the trial of the ſaid col. Morris and cornet Blackburne, with their behaviour and ſpeeches at their execution at York, 23 Aug. 1649." the original writ by Mr. Caſtilion Morris, his ſon, town clerk of Leeds, who died 1702, was given by him to Thoreſby [k], and ſince bought by the rev. Dr. T. Wilſon, prebendary of Weſtminſter. Theſe brave men who ſurprized the caſtle, by a concurrence of ill ſucceſs on their ſovereign's cauſe, held it only nine months ; but in that ſhort time diſtinguiſhed themſelves by a ſecond and almoſt un-parelleled ſurprizal of the parliament's general at Doncaſter. It coſt the parliament near 1800 l. to demoliſh this noble pile ſo diſtin-guiſhed in our ſtory [l]. They granted 1000 l. ariſing from the ſale of the materials to repair the beautiful church, which ſtill remains a ſhell : and, as if Pontefract was to ſhew no evidence of its former

[k] See his Muſeum, No 78.
[l] Gent's Hiſtory of Kingſton, p. 168. n.

ſplendor,

splendor, St. Ofwald's crofs gave place within thefe thirty years to an unmeaning market-houfe.

A view of the caftle in its original ftate was publifhed by the Antiquarian Society 1734; and another by Buck, from a drawing taken during the fiege, and in the hands of R. Gale. Hearne mentions a *picture* of it in the Afhmolean mufeum [m]. The feal of St. John the Evangelift's convent in the caftle was publifhed, with others, by the Antiquarian Society 1741.

There is a plan of this town in two fheets by Paul Jollage; with a S. W. view of All Saints church, others of the market-crofs, the caftle as in 1648, and its ruins, and a S. E. view of St. Giles' church.

A S. E. profpect of Allhallows church in Pontefract, with the parts adjacent from Bagg hills, drawn by J. Marfden, was engraved by Toms 1742. A N. E. profpect of Newhall, near Pontefract, by the fame, 1740.

" Annales Regioduni Hullini: or the hiftory of the royal and beau-
" tifull town of *Kingfton-upon-Hull*, from the original of it, through
" the means of its illuftrious founder K. Edw. I. &c. till this prefent
" year 1735: in which are included all the moft remarkable tranfac-
" tions ecclefiaftical, civil, and military: the erection of churches, con-
" vents, and monafteries, with the names of their founders and bene-
" factors: alfo a fuccinct relation of the De la Pole's family, from the
" firft mayor of that name to his fucceffors who were advanced to be
" earls and dukes of Suffolk: the monuments, infcriptions, &c. in the
" churches of Holy Trinity and St. Mary: the names of the mayors,
" fheriffs, and chamberlains, with what remarkable accidents have
" befallen fome of them in the courfe of their lives: interfperfed with
" a compendium of Britifh hiftory, efpecially what relates to the civil
" wars (for the better illuftration of fuch things as moft particularly
" concerned the town in thofe troublefome times) and fince then,
" with regard to the revolution. Adorned with cuts; as likewife
" various curiofities in antiquity, hiftory, travels, &c. Alfo a neceffary
" and compleat index to the whole. Together with feveral letters
" containing fome accounts of the antiquities of Bridlington, Scar-

[m] Cur. Difc. pref. p. cvi. n.

4 C

" borough,

" borough, Whitby, &c. for the entertainment of the curious travel-
" lers who vifit the N. E. parts of Yorkfhire. Faithfully collected by
" Thomas Gent, compiler of the hiftory of York and the moft re-
" markable places of that large county. York 1735." 8vo.

Among Mr. Warburton's collections were the antiquities of Hull by
the rev. Mr. De la prime and others, 2 vols. Fol. alfo of Rippon, Selby, Doncafter, and the N. Riding, one volume; of Hatfield, one volume; of Headon and the E. Riding, one volume; of York and the
N. Riding, one volume; and one volume of Beverley.

Hollar engraved a view of Hull and the Humber, with a bird's-eye
profpect of Kingfton on Hull, at the lower corner of a fmall map of
Lincolnfhire, with part of York and Nottinghamfhires.

A S. E. view by Buck 1745.

A large S. view of *Wakefield* from Law hill by Buck 1722, the plate
deftroyed. A large S. E. view of All Saints church there, drawn by
W. Beaumont, engraved by J. Sturt, fold by Overton. A perfpective
view of the chapel adjoining to the bridge, built by Edw. IV. in memory of his father Richard duke of York, flain at the battle fought
near this town Dec. 31, 1466, was drawn and publifhed by George
Fleming, painter in Wakefield, engraved by Toms 1743. There is a
better view of it with the town by Lodge in Thorefby's Ducatus, p. 164.

In the Gentleman's Magazine, Dec. 1756, p. 559, is an account of
a great number of groupes in wood and alabafter, found that fpring in
the roof of a chapel in the church, with a drawing of one, reprefenting St. William abp. of York, by Mr. Pegge. His interpretation of
the legend was contefted by Mr. Hugh Worthington in that for Feb.
1757, p. 79, and defended by himfelf in the following one, p. 127.
Another, reprefenting the martyrdom of Amphibalus, was exhibited
and explained in the fame Magazine, June 1759, p. 267. Thefe
figures were fhewn about at the country fairs, and afterwards in London 1759.

" Elevations, fections, and other ornaments of the manfion houfe
" belonging to the corporation of *Doncafter*. By James Payne. Lond.
" 1751." Fol. engraved by Rooker.

A print

A print of the cross, by the Antiquarian Society 1753, from a drawing and account taken before its demolition 1644, originally in lord Fairfax's and Mr. Thoresby's possession, and last in Dr. Rawlinson's. The inscription on it was published in its present state a month before in the Gentleman's Magazine for July 1753, p. 281.

" The survey of the manor of *Sherife Hutton*, in the county of York, with the members belonging to the same, parcell of the possessions of Charles, prince of Wales, duke of Cornwall and of York, and earl of Chester, taken in Julie and August, &c. by John Norden the elder and John the younger, taken by vertue of his Majesty's commission out of the Exchequer, dated the 16 day of June, 22 Jac. I. as well by the perambulation and view of the land, and evidences of the tenantes, as by oathes of those, as touching Sherife Hutton mannor itselfe, that are hereafter named." MS. Harl. 6288. Lodge engraved a small view, and Buck a N. view of this castle 1721.

The seal of *Cottingham* abbey, in the possession of the late Mr. Warburton, was engraved 1720 by the Antiquarian Society [n], who in 1751 published deeds and seals of the abbies of *Meaux* and *Drax*, in the possession of Dr. Rawlinson.

In p. 73——109 of Gent's history of Rippon is inserted the most particular account of *Beverley*. The earl of Northumberland has caused draughts to be made of the Piercy monuments in this church.

In the Cotton library, Otho, C. XVI. and the Harleian, N° 560, is a MS. intitled, " Libertates ecclesiæ S. Joannis de Beverlik cum privilegiis apostolicis & episcopalibus, quas magister Aluredus, sacrista ejusdem ecclesiæ, de Anglico in Latinum transtulit." In this treatise are the Saxon charters granted to this church by Athelstan, Edw. Conf. and William Conq. but incorrectly translated in both copies. Hearne in his edition of this author's annals, Ox. 1726, says, this is no more than the life of St. John of Beverley; but that seems to be there besides. In

---

[n] It has this remarkable inscription: *Ceo est le seil labbe e la covent de Cotingham que vous Thomas Wake singnour de Lidel avoyes founde en lan de lincarnacion* millcccxx *secounde al honour de la vcrai croyz e denre dame e seynt Pere ed seynt Poul.* The house was removed two years after to Haltemprice, or Newton. See Burton, p. 313, and the Wake pedigree in Stukeley's Itin. Cur. p. 9.

the

the catalogue of the Benet Coll. MSS. is "Antiquitates abbatiæ Bever-laci," N. vii. p. 13.

"The prologue, interludes, and epilogue to the Heautontimorou-
"menos of Terence, acted by the young gentlemen of Beverley school
"at Christmas 1756. Lond. 1757." Fol.

King engraved the W. and S. sides of the minster.

A representation or view of the N. front of the great cross aile, which overhung four feet beyond its base, and was brought back into its place by means of the timber-framing here described: published May 17, 1739. Wm. Thornton inv. Edw. Geldart del. P. Fourdri-nier sc.

The N. E. prospect of the minster drawn by the same E. Geldart, who only waits for proper encouragment to engrave a drawing of the W. front; another view of which drawn by N. Hawksmoor was engraved 1716 by M. Vandergucht, on occasion of the ruinous state of the building.

A short account of *Sheffield* was published in the Gentleman's Maga-zine for April 1764, p. 157. and some corrections and additions in that for July, p. 329.

An E. view of the town by Buck 1744.

Of *Richmondshire* we have a good account from materials collected by Roger Gale, and published since his death, under the title of "Regis-
"trum honoris de Richmond, exhibens terrarum & villarum quæ
"quondam fuerunt Edwini comitis infra Richmundshire descriptionem:
"ex libro Domesday in thesauria domini regis: nec non varias ex-
"tentas, feoda comitis, feoda militum, relevia, fines & wardas,
"inquisitiones, compotos, clamea, chartasque ad Richmondiæ comi-
"tatum spectantes. Omnia juxta exemplar antiquum in bibliotheca
"Cottoniana asservatum exarata. Adjiciuntur in appendice chartæ
"aliæ, observationes, plurimæ genealogiæ, & indices ad opus illus-
"trandum necessarii. Lond. 1722." Fol. A copy of this book is in the hands of Mr. Smithson of Moulton in Richmondshire, transcribed with all its errors from the Cotton MS. and two more, containing only the Doomsday part of it, in the Herald's office. A view of the castle as earl Conan left it, with the stations of the several captains of the guard,

guard, and their banners, is engraved from the MS. p. 28. Another
view of the tower built by Conan, at the corner of the map of Rich-
mondſhire. A view of the caſtle by Buck 1721. who alſo publiſhed
two views of the town, of which there is a third in the Regiſtrum,
from the high road to Bedal a mile off, by R. Goſling, engraved by
Huſburg. A plan of the town by Robert Harman, dancing-maſter
there, was engraved 1724, adorned with views of the town, &c. liſts
of the dukes and earls, and arms of the nobility in the ſhire; dedicated
to Sir Ralph Milbank of Staneby in the N. Riding.

The monuments and arms in *Bedal* church make two plates in Gale's
book.

A beautiful view of the ruins of Giſeburn abbey, drawn by Edward
Maſcall, engraved by Hollar 1661, and three ſides of a rich tomb of
the Bruce family, in the church, are in the Monaſticon. ii. 148.

Mr. George Plaxton prepared an account of *Berwick in Elmet*, where
he was rector[o].

In Thoreſby's muſeum, N° 245. was a deſcription of *Kigbley* pariſh,
by Miles Gale, rector. In the ſame collection was a deed of gift of
lands to *Haxey* church, in leſs than 8 lines, ſcarce 4 inches long and
2 broad. Muſ. Thor. p. 554.

A friend of Dr. Rawlinſon's had the original patent for the ſchool
at *Sedburgh*, 5 Edw. VI. (1558.) ſigned at top by the king, at bottom by E. Somerſet, T. Cant. R. Ryche, W. Wilts, J. Bedford, W.
Northton. E. Clynton, T. Darcy. G. Cobham. T. Ely. Kip drew
and engraved an ichnography and platform of the ſchool and maſter's
houſe, as deſigned to be built.

In the notes at the end of Hearne's Liber niger Scac. p. 666, are
printed the will of abp. Rotheram, and the ſtatutes of his college at
Rotheram, from a MS. in Sidney Coll. The latter ſo much damaged
in every leaf as to be of little uſe: only the firſt part is printed. It has
the founder's effigies and arms.

We have ſeveral pieces on the mineral waters of this county; thoſe
of *Knareſborough* are treated of in " Spadacrene Anglica : or the Eng-
" liſh ſpaw fountaine : being a brief treatiſe of the acid or tart foun-

[o] Duc. Leod. p. 234.

" taine

" taine in the foreſt of Knareſborough, in Yorkſhire. Lond. 1626."
1625. 8vo. By Edmund Deane, M. D.

" Cures without care : or a ſummons to all ſuch as find little or no
" help by the uſe of phyſick, to repair to the northern ſpa; wherein
" by many precedents of a few late years it's proved to the world, that
" infirmities of their own nature deſperate and of long continuance
" have received perfect cure by virtue of mineral waters near Knareſ-
" borough, in the W. Riding of Yorkſhire. By Michael Stanhope.
" Lond. 1632."

" The Yorkſhire ſpaw, or a treatiſe of four famous medicinal wells,
" viz. the ſpaw or vitrioline well ; the ſtinking or ſulphur well ; the
" dropping or petrifying well; and St. Mugnus well, near Knareſ-
" borow in Yorkſhire. Together with the cauſes, vertues, and uſe
" thereof. Compoſed by John French ᴾ, Dr. of phyſick. Lond. 1652.
" 1654." 12mo.

" Spadacrene Eboracenſis; or the Yorkſhire ſpaws, near Knareſ-
" burgh : being a deſcription of five famous medicinal wells, viz.
" The ſweet ſpa. 2. The ſulphur or ſtinking well. 3. The dropping
" well. 4. The black ſpring, found out by the author. 5. St. Mag-
" nus's or St. Mungo's well. All which wells, with their ſituation,
" operation, virtues, &c. are deſcribed, together with the hot and
" cold baths ; as likewiſe fume baths. By Geo. Neale, M. D. of
" Leedes," an unfiniſhed piece inſerted in Short's hiſtory of mineral
waters, p. 286—293, notes. No more of the many curious obſervations left by the doctor, who died in 1681, could be found by his ſon,
Dr. John Neale of Doncaſter.

Knareſborough, on the river Nid, drawn and painted by Oram, engraved by E. Rooker 1745.

A S. W. proſpect of the dropping well, as it appeared in the great
froſt Jan. 1739, drawn and engraved by John Haynes.

A view of the petrifying ſpring, commonly called the dropping well,
at Knareſborough, belonging to Sir Henry Slingſby, and ruins of the
caſtle belonging to the earl of Burlington, was engraved 174⁶₇, by
Vivares, from a picture of Smith's.

ᴾ Of whom ſee Athen. Ox. II. 214.

Another

Another view of the caſtle in its original ſtate was publiſhed 1735 by the Antiquarian Society, from an old draught in the dutchy of Lancaſter's office.

A S. view of its ruins by S. Buck 1721.

The life of St. Robert of Knareſborough by one Richard Stodley is in the Harleian library, Nº 3774.

" Piety diſplayed : in the holy life and death of the antient and " celebrated St. Robert, hermit, at Knareſborough. Shewing how he " relinquiſhed the hope of an inheritance, as having been the heir of " his father, who was twice chief magiſtrate of York ; and lived ab- " ſtemiouſly upon herbs, roots, &c, on the narrow banks of the river " Nid, near which in the rocks are to be ſeen his moſt ſolitary cave, " and wonderful chapel, at this very day. Collected from antient and " authentick records. By T. Gent. York." 12mo. A ſmall piece to be bought at the cave.

Of cures by *Gillfoot* or *Guilthwait* ſpa near Rotheram, in Bole hill, whoſe clay, dried and moiſtened into paſte with common water, is an effectual and eaſy cure for corns, ſee p. 144. of the 2d edition of Dr. Joſeph Brown's " account of the wonderfull cures performed by cold " bathing. Lond. 1707." 12mo.

Scarborough ſpaw gave occaſion to a paper war in the laſt century, begun by Dr. Wittie, in his " Scarbrough ſpaw : or, a deſcription of " the nature and vertues of the ſpaw at Scarbrough, Yorkſhire. Alſo, " a treatiſe of the nature and uſe of ſea, rain, dew, ſnow, hail, pond, " lake, ſpring, and river waters. Where more largely the controverſy " among learned writers, about the original of ſprings, is diſcuſſed. " To which is added, a ſhort diſcourſe concerning mineral waters. " Corrected and augmented throughout the whole ; together with an " hiſtorical relation of cures done by theſe waters. By Robert Wittie, " doctor in phyſick. York 1667." 12m. In anſwer to this Dr. Wm. Simpſon publiſhed his " Hydrologia chymica : or, the chymical ana- " tomy of the Scarbrough and other ſpaws in Yorkſhire. Wherein " are interſperſed ſome animadverſions upon Dr. Wittie's lately pub- " liſhed treatiſe of the Scarbrough ſpaw. Alſo a ſhort deſcription of

---

ˢ Short's Hiſtory of mineral waters, p. 16.

" the

" the fpaws at Malton and Knarfbrough. And a difcourfe concern-
" ing the original of hot fprings and other fountains : with the caufe
" and cures of moft of the ftubborneft difeafes (either chronical or
" acute) incident to the body of man. Alfo a vindication of chymi-
" cal phyfick ; where a probable way is propounded for the improve-
" ment of experimental philofophy : with a digreffion concerning an
" univerfal character. Likewife, a fhort account of the principles of
" all concretes, whether vegetable, animal, or mineral. Laftly is fub-
" joyned, an appendix of the original of fprings; with the author's
" ternary of medicines : and the epilogue to the whole, of the effence
" of the Scarbrough fpaw. Lond. 1669." 8vo. Simpfon firft fet up
to practife phyfick in York in oppofition to Wittie, whom he treated
in a very unhandfome manner ; but failing in his defign, he removed
to Wakefield, and fome time after to Leeds, where he fpent the reft of
his days. He affumes the title of chimical phyfician, but was too young
and inexperienced a fcholar to attack a phyfician of fuch abilities and
eminence. He has ftuft his work with many fubjects foreign to it,
of which his digreffion concerning a univerfal character was fcraped
up from his converfation with Dr. Wilkins of Rippon Dr. Wittie replied to him in his " Pyrologia Mimica : or, an anfwer to Hydrologia
" Chymica of William Simpfon, philo-chimico-medicus, in defence
" of Scarbrough fpaw; wherein the five mineral principles of the faid
" fpaw are defended againft all his objections, by plain reafon and ex-
" periments, and further confirmed by a difcovery of Mr. S. his fre-
" quent contradictions and manifeft recantation. Alfo a vindication of
" the rational method and practice of phyfick, called Galenical ; and
" a reconciliation betwixt that and the chymical. Likewife a further
" difcourfe about the original of fprings. Lond. 1669." 8vo. The
doctor, though pretty fharp in fome parts of this anfwer, is moderate,
confidering the fcurrilous treatment he had received from a junior and
inferior ; and though it muft be owned he fhews himfelf through his
whole writings a poor naturalift and no great chymift, he difcovers extenfive well digefted reading, and appears to have been an excellent
practical phyfician, and a careful obferver of the effects of thefe waters.
Simpfon being upbraided with impudence, and want of learning, and a

degree

degree (of which the firft was natural, and the fecond could not be helped in a fhort time) to remedy the third pofted away to fome foreign univerfity, and at his return anfwered Wittie in " Hydrological " effays: or, a vindication of Hydrologia chymica: being a farther " difcovery of the Scarbrough fpaw, and of the right ufe thereof. And " of the fweet fpaw, and fulphur well at Knarfbrough, with a brief " account of the allom-works at Whitby. Together with a return to " fome queries propounded by the ingenious Dr. Daniel Foot, con- " cerning mineral waters. To which is annexed, an anfwer to Dr. " Tunftal's book concerning the Scarbrough fpaw. With an appen- " dix of the anatomy of the German fpaw. And, laftly, obfervations " on the diffeaion of a woman who died of the jaundice. All " grounded upon reafon and experiment, by William Simpfon, doaor " of phyfick, and praaitioner at Wakefield in Yorkfhire. Lond. 1670." 8vo. This is wrote more modeftly and intelligibly, but fome of the chymical cant is ftill retained. In the warmth of the difpute came on the ftage a new champion, Dr. Tunftal of New Coll. Oxford, with an unexpeaed back ftroke on Wittie, whom he upbraids with ignorance of the nature of the waters, want of judgment to try them, inconclu- five arguments and unjuft obfervations; at the fame time attacking Simpfon for his forwardnefs before he had laid in a fufficient ftock of learning. His piece is intitled " Scarbrough fpaw fpagirically anato- " mized: by George Tonftal, doaor of phyfic. Lond. 1672." 8vo. Wittie declined the controverfy after anfwering both his antagonifts in " Scarbrough's fpagyrical anatomizer diffeaed: or, an anfwer to all " that Dr. Tonftall hath objeaed in his book againft Scarbrough fpaw. " The innocency and excellency of that fpaw is further afferted. 1. " Concerning the rife and growth of the art of phyfick. 2. Touching " the caufes of the petrifying property that is in fome fprings; more " efpecially that of the dropping well at Knarefborough. 3. About " the figns, fymptoms and cures of difeafes. As alfo refleaions upon " a late piece, called A vindication of Hydrologia chymica. Lond. " 1672." 12mo. This was quickly followed by a moft fatyrical ill- natured reply from Tonftal, intitled, " A new-years-gift for Dr. " Wittie: or the diffeaor anatomis'd. Lond. 1672." 12mo. dedicated

to

to the Royal Society, to whom the author appeals for a decision of the
controversy. Some sharp reflections were made on it in the next N°
of their Transactions. Simpson and Tonstal were not the only antagonists Wittie had to encounter : for in N° 52 of the Philosophical
Transactions we find him attacked by Dr. Daniel Foot before-
mentioned, chiefly concerning the cause of the sudden loss of the virtues of mineral waters ; and in " Some considerations relating to Dr.
" Wittie's defence of Scarbrough spaw, by Dr. Highmore, in a letter
" to Dr. Beal of Yeavil, Dec. 17, 1669." printed in the Philosophical
Transactions, N° 56. p. 1128 : to both which he returned an answer in
N° 60. His first piece went through several editions before 1678,
when he published it in Latin, greatly enlarged, with this title : " Fons
" Scarburgensis : sive tractatus de omnis aquarum generis origine ac
" usu, particulariter de fonte minerali apud Scarbrough in comitatu
" Eboracensi Angliæ. Item dissertationes variæ tam philosophicæ quam
" medicinales, quas cum sectionum titulis pagina librum proxime præ-
" cedens exhibet. Lond. 1678." 8vo. Simpson published another reply in " The history of the Scarbrough spaw : or, a further discovery
" of the excellent vertues thereof, in the cure of the scurvy, hypo-
" chond. agues, jaundies, dropsie, womens diseases, &c. by many re-
" markable instances ; being a demonstration from the most convin-
" cing arguments, viz. matter of fact. Also a discourse of an artifi-
" cial sulphur-bath, and bath of sea-water, with the uses thereof in
" the cure of many diseases : together with a short account of the rari-
" ties of nature observable at Scarbrough. Lond. 1679." 12mo. Upon
an impartial review of the whole affair, Dr. Short (from whose History
of mineral waters, &c. 1734. 4to. p. 113 to 161, this abstract is taken)
observes it must be allowed that none of the parties engaged in it were
proper and unprejudiced judges : for Wittie could never make good his
assertion by fair experiments, and was prejudiced in favour of the spa
from its advantages to himself, and against his antagonists, who had
also their particular views. Simpson, a bigot to Paracelsian practice
and hot regimen, wanted to disgrace and succeed him. Tonstal had
for two or three seasons attempted to monopolize the place, but being
disappointed grew peevish and abusive, decried the water, and set up

Harrogate

Harrogate againſt it. We hear no more of this ſpa before Dr. Liſter's treatiſe on the medicinal waters of England in 1682. Of him Short ſays, that he was too much attached to his hypotheſes, too remiſs in his examinations, ſcanty in his experiments, and haſty in his con-cluſions.

In this century have appeared " An enquiry into the contents, vir-
" tues, and uſes of the Scarborough ſpaw water, with the method of
" examining any other mineral water. By Peter Shaw, phyſician at
" Scarborough. Lond. 1734." 8vo.

" A diſſertation on the contents, virtues, and uſes of cold and
" hot mineral ſprings, particularly thoſe of Scarborough; in a letter
" to Robert Robinſon, eſq; recorder of that corporation. York.
" 1735." 8vo.

" A compendious treatiſe on the contents, virtues, and uſes of cold and
" hot mineral ſprings in general, particularly the celebrated hot waters
" of Scarborough; with obſervations on their quality and proper direc-
" tions in drinking them. The whole conſiſting of what is chiefly
" uſeful in the works of the moſt celebrated authors who have wrote
" on this ſubject. By John Atkins, ſurgeon. To which are annexed
" the opinion of Sir John Floyer and Dr. Baynard on the great uſe and
" effect of bathing in the ſea. 8vo. Lond. 1737." or ſooner.

In p. 804 of N° 461 of the Philoſophical Tranſactions is an account of an earthquake at Scarborough, by Maurice Johnſon.

The town, with its accommodations, &c. is deſcribed in " A journey from London to Scarborough, in ſeveral letters from a gentleman there, to his friend in London. To which is annexed an account of the na-ture and uſe of the Scarborough ſpaw water, in a ſhort view of the moſt celebrated writers on that ſubject, with obſervations and remarks. Lond. " 1734." 8vo. A print of Dicky Dickinſon, keeper of the wells, is prefixed. Vertue engraved a poor one with verſes round it.

" The Scarborough miſcellany," a collection of various original poems, &c. handed about for ſeveral ſeaſons at Scarborough, begun 1732, and continued for ſeveral ſucceeding years.

A view of Scarborough, with the caſtle, port, and ſpa, by F. Place, engraved by J. Kip 1731.

A view

A view of the caſtle and town ſeen a quarter of a mile from the ſpa was engraved by Buck 1722, from a drawing belonging to Iſ. Bolter eſq; and a larger S. one of the town 1745.

Another perſpective view of the caſtle, port, and ſpa, 2 ſheets.

" The humours of *Harrogate* deſcribed, in a letter to a friend, by " J. E. with notes deſcriptive, hiſtorical, explanatory, critical, and hy- " percritical, by Mart. Scriblerus. Lond. 1763." 4to. A local per- formance, without wit or humour.

" The methods propoſed for making the river Dunn navigable, and " the objections to it anſwered : with an account of the petitioner's " behaviour to the land owners, To which is annexed, a mapp of " the river, and the reaſons lately printed for making it navigable, " with the advantages of it. Lond. 1723." 4to.

In the Philoſophical Collections, N° iv. p. 87, are Dr. Liſter's letter and obſervations about Roman urns found in different parts of York- ſhire, a Roman pottery between *Wilberfoſs* and *Barnby Moor*, ſix miles from York, and another in Lincolnſhire at the ſand hills at *Santon* near *Brigg*. In N° 89, p. 5116, of the Philoſophical Tranſactions is an account of ſome odd muſhrooms found in *Marton* woods, near Craven, by Dr. Liſter. In N° 152, p. 1052, are Mr. D. Colwart's account of the alum works. In N° 160, p. 593, ſeveral inſtances of longevity in Yorkſhire by Dr. Liſter. In N°. 221, p. 266, is Mrs. A. Saville's account of Henry Jenkins at *Bolton*, aged 169, who carried a' horſeload of arrows to Flodden field; was born before regiſters were appointed in churches; remembered the diſſolution, and the abbot of Fountains (who uſed to drink a glaſs heartily with lord Conyers, to whom Jenkins was butler) and at laſt was a fiſherman and beggar 1670: con- firmed by a bill in the Remembrancer's office, N° 222. p. 543. There is a metzotinto print of him without a name. In p. 319 of N° 222 is Thoreſby's account of a Roman pottery on Blackmore, two miles from Leeds, at *Hawcaſterrigg*. In p. 526 of N° 228 is a letter to Dr. Richardſon, concerning ſome ſubterraneous trees dug up at *Youle.* In p. 738 of N° 234 are letters from Mr. Thoreſby to Dr. Liſter and Dr. Gale, 1697, concerning ſome Roman antiquities found at *Boutham- bar*, and ſome moulds for coins at *Thorp*. In p. 310 of N° 244 is his letter to Mr. John Evelyn, about ſome Roman antiquities found in this county,

county, particularly a piece of earthen ware, which he took for part of a coffin fitted by pegs to other ſuch pieces. In N° 249, p. 52, his account of a youth killed by lightning at *Warley*. In p. 73 of N° 250 is Dr. Liſter's account of borings for coal near *Leeds*. In p. 507 of N° 264 is Mr. Thoreſby's account of the effects of lightning near Leeds. In p. 1285 of N° 282 is his letter concerning the veſtigia of a Roman town at *Adell* [Adellocum][q], near Leeds. In p. 1248 of N° 181, and p. 1331 of N° 284, are De la Pryme's relations of waterſpouts on Hatfield chace 1687. In N° 289, p. 1555, his relation of an earthquake at Hull and in Lincolnſhire Dec. 28, 1703. and Thoreſby's account of the ſame at Hull, Beverley, &c. In p. 1864 of N° 296 the latter's account of a leaden and oak coffin found in the Roman burying ground at York. In p. 2127 of N° 303 his account of coins of Wm. the Conq. &c. found in that city; in the ſame number, p. 2145, a Roman inſcription, GENIO LOCI FELICITER, there; and in p. 2149 of Roman coins at *Clifton*. In p. 2194 of N° 305 his letter to Dr. Sloan, concerning two Roman inſcriptions of the ixth legion found at York, inſerted in Hearne's Livy, vi. 181, and Horſley, p. 308, N° viii. In N° 306, p. 2236, he relates an eruption of water in Craven June 1686, mentioned by R. P. vicar of Kildwick, N° 245[r]. In p. 134 of N° 316 is another letter from him to Dr. Sloan, concerning ſome Roman coins found at *Cookridge*. In N° 289, p. 251, a 3d letter about an altar found at Adell, and a ſtorm of thunder, lightning, and rain, Aug. 5. 1708. In p. 314 of N° 320 is a 4th letter, dated Apr. 22, 1709, concerning a Roman altar dug up at Adell. In p. 395. of N° 322 is Hearne's verboſe unſatisfactory diſſertation on the braſs Celts dug up at *Oſmondthick* near *Brambam moor*, in a letter to Thoreſby, printed at the end of Leland's Itin. vol. i. with an extract from Thoreſby's letter. The whole letter is inſerted in vol. iv. p. 5, with Hearne's remarks. In N° 331, p. 322, is Thoreſby's account of a meteor at Leeds May 18, 1710. In p. 514 of N° 335 is a 5th letter, concerning damages by a hail ſtorm at Rotheram June 7, 1711. In p. 167 of N° 337 are ſeveral obſervations in natural hiſtory made at *North Bierly*, by Dr. Richard Richardſon phyſician there, communicated by Dr. Sloan. In N° 372, p. 101,

[q] He takes it for the *Burgidunum* of Domeſday.

[r] Whoſe letter is printed in Birch's Hiſt. of the Royal Society, vol. iv. p. 509.

his

his account of a violent shower of rain at *Ripendon* near Halifax. In N° 437, p. 74, Dr. Cookson's account of lightning at *Wakefield* 1731. In p. 560 of N° 459 the rev. Mr. Kirshaw's account of two pigs of lead inscribed IMP. CAES. DOMITIANO AVG. COS. VII. found near *Ripley*: explained by Mr. Ward, vol. xlix. p. 686: and in p. 612 a description of a large lake called *Malholm Tarn* near *Skipton* in *Craven*, by John Fuller, esq; jun. In p. 124 of N° 479 we have an account of two extraordinary deers horns found in this county. In p. 100 of the same N° are Mr. Knowlton's remarks on the situation of *Delgovitia*; and in p. 541 of N° 483 is a dissertation on the same station by Dr. John Burton of York, who fixes it near *Millington*, with which opinion Mr. Drake concurs in an appendix to the above papers. Besides the maps accompanying the doctor's account, John Haynes of York drew, at the expence of lord Burlington, 1744, " An accurate survey of some stupendous remains of Roman antiquity on the Wolds in Yorkshire, through which some grand military ways to several eminent stations are traced, &c. &c." engraved by Vertue. In p. 498 of vol. xlvii. is an account of vegetable balls in a lake twelve miles W. of *Hull*. In p. 69 of vol. xlix. Mr. Ward's explanation of a Roman inscription found at *Malton* 1753. In p. 688 and 786 of vol. l. an account of the fossil bones of an alligator, found in the allum rock near *Whitby* 1758. inserted with the print in the Gentleman's Magazine, Oct. 1760, p. 452.

An account of the method of working the allom at Whitby is annexed to the several editions of Ray's Collection of English local words.

In p. 36 of Hearne's preface to Leland's Collectanea is an old inscription in *Campsall* church near Pontefract. In the Review of Leland's Itinerary at the end of the 9th vol. p. 142, is a letter from Dr. Richardson to Hearne, giving a short account of sundry British and Roman antiquities in that Riding, particularly at *Kiddale, Halifax, Burstall, Ilkley, Bingley, the Devil's Arrows, Almonbury,* &c. also p. 166, part of another from him, about an epitaph of a prioress at *Kirkleys:* another in p. 194 from Mr. Brockesby, describing the Sunk Island † in

---

† Sunk Island from a waste sand, which appeared only four hours at low water, was in 1666, by col. Gilby, banked in and improved to good pasture ground for cattle, being about nine miles round.

the Humber; of which fee p. 1014 of N° 361 of the Philofophical Tranfactions. A view of the Devil's Arrows, Sept. 14, 1725, by Dr. Stukeley was engraved by Hulett. There are others in Gale's Antoninus and Drake's York; the latter accompanied with particulars about them and *Aldburgh* by Mr. Morris, late rector of that place.

In the Gentleman's Magazine for April 1740, p. 171, is a Roman infcription found at *Netherby* In that for Jan. 1747, p. 23, is an account of the Cell on *Hatfield* wafte, where the hermit William of Lindholme lived, by G. Stovin, with a poem on the hermit by A. De la Pryme. In the fame Magazine for Oct. 1753, p. 456, is the epitaph, &c. of Sir Marmaduke Cunftable at *Flamborough*. In that for July 1754, p. 309, another epitaph at *Wiflow*, with an explanation by Mr. Pegge. An account of *Aughton*, and the Afke family there, may be found in the fame Magazine for Aug. p. 358. and for Sept. p. 407; alfo an infcription at *Morton*, near *Gretabridge*, in that for Nov. p. 494. and a derivation of the name of *Cataract* or *Catterick* in that for Dec. p. 548, the fame year. In that for July 1760, p. 315, is an account of an ebbing well near *Settie*. In thofe for March and April, 1761, p. 126 and 148, is an account of *Ingleborough* mountain. In that for Nov. 1763, p. 531, is a defcription of *Grayfbrooke*, and the plantation at *Wentworth* hall, the feat of the marquis of Rockingham. A drawing was fent to the publifher, who alleged that its fize prevented his making ufe of it. I have feen two fheets of a plan of the gardens, park, plantations, and fifh ponds.

" The praife of Yorkfhire ale, wherein is enumerated feveral forts " of drink, with a difcription of the humours of moft forts of druhck- " ards. To which is added, a Yorkfhire dialogue in its pure natural " dialect, as is now commonly fpoken in the north parts of Yorkfhire. " By G. M. gent. York. 1685." The 3d edition in 1697 had the " Addition of fome obfervations on the dialect and pronuntiation of words in the E. Ryding: together with a collection of fignificant and ufeful proverbs."

A draught of the river Humber, dedicated to the worfhipful company of Trinity-houfe of Kingfton upon Hull, by Robert Mitchell, engraved by T. Mynde.

2

A plan

A plan of the navigation of the Calder from Wakefield to Halifax.

A plan of a Roman Hypocauft or Sudatory, and bath, difcovered in the gardens of Thomas Worfley, efq; at *Hovingham*, in the N. Riding, drawn by Charles Mitley, and engraved by Vertue, with a defcription of it by Mr. F. Drake, was publifhed in one fheet 1745.

A plan of the Roman roads in Yorkfhire was engraved, and dedicated to the Antiquarian Society, by Mr. Drake.

Bramham park, belonging to lord Bingley, is celebrated in a poem addreffed to Robert Lane, efq; written in May 1745. 8vo. A view of it by Hulfberg is engraved by J. Wood : another by Campbell.

Afke, *Swinton*, and *Lazenby* halls were engraved by Mr. Warburton, but never publifhed.

A S. profpect of *Gawthorpe*, near Leeds, the feat of John Boulter, efq; 1721. Another view drawn by Wm. Van Hagen, 1721, engraved by J. Harris 1722.

S. front of *Cufworth*, the feat of Wm. Wrightfon, efq; near Doncafter. Paine, arch. del. J. S. Muller, fc.

Four views of the gardens at *Studley*, viz. the banquetting houfe and round temple; the refervoir and artificial mount, with Fountains abbey; the moon pond and the temple of piety; and the lake and gardens from the park, drawn and engraved by A. Walker 1758.

" *Caftle Howard*, the feat of the right hon. Charles earl of Carlifle ; " to whom the poem is humbly infcribed. Lond. 1732."

A view of the houfe and part of the gardens, drawn and engraved by A. Walker 1758.

Two views of *Stainborough* and *Wentworth* caftle, one of the feats of lord Strafford, by Badeflade and Harris.

A S. W. profpect of *Ackworth* park hall, the feat of Mrs. Mary Lowther, drawn by J. Marfden, engraved by Toms 1729.

Two perfpective views in *Craven*, by Vivares, 1753.

Gordal at *Malham* in Craven, by J. Mafon, after Smith, 1751.

Malham Cove and *Tarn* by Vivares.

The Antiquarian Society have given us views of *Tickhill* and *Sandal* caftles, from old draughts preferved in the Dutchy of Lancafter's office. Buck engraved a S. view of the latter, 1722.

The

The fame Society have four views of *Fountains* abbey: of which there are others publifhed in the Monafticon by King, and in Thoref-by's Ducatus by Lodge A S. view by Buck 1722; and a S. E. view by F. Vivares, from a drawing by T. Smith, 174⁶⁄₇. A correct plan drawn by T. Atkinfon of York, engraved by F. Perry, in Burton's Monafticon.

A S. profpect of *Kirkftall* abbey by Buck 1723. A S. E. profpect of it, drawn by James Walker, and engraved 1744 by H. Gravelot, " a faithful copier of antient buildings, tombs, and profpects; his large print of this abbey fhews how able an engraver he was ᵘ." Another S. E. view by Vivares, from a drawing by Smith, 174⁶. An-other by Oram. A beautiful one by Lodge is in Thorefby's Ducatus Leodenfis, p. 164: copied by B. Cole for Stevens's Monafticon, vol. ii. p.36. A plan of it in Dr. Burton's book by Atkinfon, engraved by R. Ledger.   Dr. Rawlinfon engraved from the originals in his own poffef-fion, 1751 and 1752, an agreement between the abbot of this abbey and the priory of St. Trinity, York, touching lands in the parifh of Leedsˣ: alfo between abbot Maurice, about 1221, and Robert, fon of Rich. de Lofthus, a leafe of a bovate in Lofthus: another between ab-bot John de Bardefay and Thomas Rocheley, touching homage, &c. 1398: a grant to this abbey from Richard Fitz-Robert de Allerton of lands in Allerton, Hedingley, and Ofmundthorp, about 1242: abbot Adam's grant of a yearly penfion to his prior and convent, 1262: R. de Bernes' grant of 10 pence yearly rent-charge on lands in *Calverley*, temp. Hen. III.ʸ, and John Pomeray's confirmation of lands in *Ofgotby* to John Fitz-Nicholas there, temp. Edw. III. Hen. IId's charter of pro-tection, 26 reg. 1180, with his great feal: a grant of lands in Lofthus by Harewood from Hamo de Altaripa to Wm. Hamilton, dean of York, who died 1307: a grant of a mill, &c. in *Heddingley*, &c. from Wm. Pictavienfis to the Templars at London: R. de Burun's con-firmation of lands in *Cotgrave* to the Hofpital of Jerufalem: a charter

---

ᵘ Walpoles cat. of engravers, p. 124.
ˣ Of which fee Burton's Mon. Eboracenfe, p. 294, and Stevens's appendix, p. 257.
ʸ See Burton's Mon. Eboracenfe, p. 294.

of

of lands in *Bleiſtrete*, York, from St. Peter's hoſpital there to *Bolton* abbey, in Stephen's reign.

Views in this county by Meſſrs. Buck, 1721, 1722, 1725, are,.

N. Byland
S. E. Bolton
S. Burſtal
S. Eaſby
N. Egleſton
S. St. Martin's } abbies.
W. Rivaulx
W. Roche [z]
S. Sawley
N. Whitby
W. Mount-grace } priory.
N. Kirkham
S. Coniſborough } caſtles.
S. Harlſey
E. Lady's chapel, near Mount-grace.

A view of the mill at *Blyth*, painted by P. Sandy, was exhibited in Spring-garden 1764; of *Upper Aiſgarth Foſs* in Wentſdale, Richmond-ſhire; *Bolton* caſtle, ditto; and a view near *Whitley*, in the W. riding, 1763. A ſunſet view of *Raywood*, near Caſtle Howard; and a mill at *Kilnſey*, Craven, by Dall, 1766; who exhibited 1767 a view of *Aiſ-garth Foſs*, near Swinnewite.

A large map of his native county was drawn by Saxton 1577, with-out the hundreds, with a plan of York in one corner and a proſpect of Hull in the other, and engraved principally by Auguſtine Ryther; and afterwards 1642. Thoreſby calls this the beſt that ever was made of this county. Others by the ſame hand on a ſmaller ſcale by Wm. Hole.

Speed has a general map of Yorkſhire, and three particular ones of the ridings: at the corner of the N. riding is a plan of York, and at that of the Eaſt, plans of Hull and Richmond.

A new map was engraved by Overton 1728.

---

[z] Other views of it by Meſſrs. Hopkinſon and Sandby appeared at Spring-gardens 1762; and one by Mr. Barret 1767.

" A new.

" A new and correct map of the county of York, in all its divifions, by actual furvey and dimenfuration: with the arms and feats of the nobility and gentry, the diftances in miles and furlongs between each of the market towns, the courfes of the feveral Roman ways, prefent roads, rivers, and rivulets, churches, caftles, religious houfes, ancient baronies, forefts, chaces, parks, woods, mountains, lakes, fields of battle, collieries, copper mines, and lead mines, allom works, or other minerals, fea-coafts, rocks, fands, fhoals, &c. By John Warburton, efq; Somerfet herald of arms and fellow of the Royal Society."

A new and correct map of the fouth part of the county by actual furvey, fhewing the true fituations of the feveral towns, noblemens and gentlemens feats, the courfes of the feveral rivers and rivulets, prefent roads, Roman ways, caftles, antient abbies and priories, woods, hills, lakes, collieries and other minerals. Taken at the coft of the moft hon. Thomas marquis of Rockingham, by J. Dickinfon 1750. 2 fheets. For the marquis's ufe, and not to be fold.

E. Bowen publifhed a general map of the county in concentric circles 1750; another of the N. riding, with a view of York, 1750; and two more of the other ridings, having at the corners views of Hull and Leeds; and an epitomized map of the E. riding by a gentleman refiding in the county, 1753.

Mr. Jefferies is engaged in a furvey of this county, to be ready next year.

W A L E S.

VERY little pains have been taken by natives or neighbours to illuftrate the hiftory or antiquities of this part of the ifland. Yet antiquity is the glory of every Welchman, and the fpirit of competition with the later inhabitants of England one would have expected fhould fire their breafts with a defire to be known and celebrated beyond them. If their anceftors could not fpare time to write about a territory which they could hardly defend, their defcendants with fecure tenure have all the helps a living language and original records can afford. Many very antient MSS. are faid to be ftill remaining in Wales; a good collection of them was made by Mr. Maurice, of Kenvybreach, Denbighfhire, whom bp. Nicholfon calls a notable antiquary, and fince came into the hands of Sir Wm. Williams. Befides the valuable library of Mr. Davies, of Llannerk, in the fame county, there are feveral other confiderable ones [a] The collections of their moft eminent antiquary Edward Lhuyd were laft in the hands of Sir Tho. Seabright, of Beach wood, Hertfordfhire. Lhuyd undertook more for illuftrating this part of the kingdom than any one man befides ever did, or than any one man can be equal to. Yet under certain reftrictions we might wifh to fee fomebody revive the ufeful defign, before time, and a thoufand circumftances fatal to private collections, complete the defolation already too far advanced. The progrefs of antiquarian difcoveries, on which I muft congratulate this age, has not yet, that I know of, been turned into this channel. Mr. Evans, who has opened the poetic treafuries of his country, muft bear the torch before us into the gloom that overfpreads the other provinces of early fcience there.

Wales was divided by its univerfal monarch Roderic Maur, A. D. 870. into three provinces: Deheubarth or Demetia, now South Wales; Gwynedh or Venedotia, now North Wales; and Mathrafal or Powis

[a] See Evans's fpecimens of Welch poetry, app. p. 155.

land,

land, which was foon fwallowed up in the other two. Antient records divide it alfo into N.S. and W. Wales, containing 14 fhires, including thofe of Hereford and Monmouth; the prefent divifion into 12 is but a little older than the reformation. As early as Edw. I. Wales loft its independence. Henry VIII. when he incorporated it with England, abrogated all laws, cuftoms, and tenures not agreeable to thofe of England.

Giraldus Cambrenfis, a native of Pembrokefhire, and archdeacon of St. David's and Brecon, who accompanied Baldwin abp. of Canterbury on a crufading fcheme into Wales 1188, compiled " Itinerarium Cam- " briæ: feu laboriofæ Baldvini, Cantuar. archiepifcopi per Walliam " legationis, accurata defcriptio, auctore Sil. Giraldo Cambrenfe. Cum " annotationibus Davidis Poveli, Sacræ Theologiæ Profefforis. Lond. " 1585." 12mo. with Ponticus Virunnius' Britannicæ Hiftoriæ, lib. 6. by the fame editor; reprinted among Camden's Scriptores Hiftoriæ An- glic. &c. Francf. 1605. Fol. b. To this was annexed the firft book of his Cambriæ defcriptio, or Topographia, with notes by the fame editor. This is generally known by the title " De laudabilibus Walliæ:" the 2d book was publifhed by Wharton, Anglia Sacra, vol. ii. p. 447. intitled, " Giraldi Cambrenfis liber fecundus de defcriptione Walliæ, " feu liber de illaudabilibus Walliæ;" which is divided into ten heads. or chapters. Giraldus made at the fame time " Cambriæ totius map- " pam," or Bale's " Cambriæ mappæ expofitionem," lib. 1. a coloured geographical map, laying down rivers, mountains, and fea-coafts, and the neighbouring places of England, with 43 towns of Wales. A copy of it in red lead is prefixed to the Weftminfter MS. of his Topo- graphia Cambriæ. Giraldus's own account of it is, " Mappam " [Cambriæ] expreffam, quatenus et natale folum non tantum literis, " fed etiam protractionibus quibufdam, & quafi picturis variis, nec in- " competentibus aut indecentibus noftra foret ad unguem opera declara- " tum, brevi in loculo arctoque folio loca quamplurima complectentes, " eademque tamen dilucidè fatis et diftinctè difponentes non abfque " ftudiofo labore propalavimus c." Together with the topography

---

* Bale fplits this into two; " Itinerarium Cambriæ," and " Itinerarium Baldwini," which are the fame; and thus he makes four books inftead of two.

c Catalogue of his own works. Angl. Sac. p. 443.

we

we have a mixture of Popish miracles and tales, which not only divert the reader, but afford an opportunity to the learned publisher of communicating a deal of his own critical knowledge. The description is general, being in the main a panegyric on the soil, and the good humour, strict morals, and exemplary piety of the inhabitants [d]. The faults he charges them with in the 2d book are fickleness, breach of faith, and a marauding spirit; with directions how to subdue and govern them.

David Morgan, treasurer of Landaff 1480, is said by Pitts to have wrote the geography and antiquities of Wales. Tanner and Willis give no account of his works.

"Commentarioli Britannicæ descriptionis fragmentum, auctore
"Humfredo Lhuyd [e], Denbyghiense, Cambro-Britanno. Hujus auc-
"toris diligentiam & judicium lector admirabitur. Coloniae Agrip-
"pinae. 1572." 12mo. It was finished 30 Aug. 1568, while the author lay ill of a violent fever, as appears by the dedication to his dear friend Ortelius, and soon after translated into English by Tho. Twyne, under the title of "The breviary of Britaine, as this most
"noble and renowned island was of auncient time devided into three
"kingdoms, England, Scotland, and Wales. Contaynyng a learned
"discourse of the variable state and alteration thereof, under divers
"as wel natural, as forren princes and conquerours. Together with
"the geographical [f] description of the same, such as nether by elder
"nor later writers, the like hath been set foorth before. Writen in
"Latin by Humfrey Lhuyd of Denbigh, a Cambre Britayne, and
"lately englished by Thomas Twyne, gent. Lond. 1573." 12mo. Reprinted at the end of "The history of Great Britain from the first
"inhabitants thereof, till the death of Cadwalader, last king of the
"Britains; and of the kings of Scotland to Eugene V. as also a short

[d] There are two MS. of this work; one in the library at Westminster, dedicated to Hugh bp. of Lincoln: the other enlarged and dedicated to Stephen abp. of Canterbury. Cott. lib. Dom. A. 1. Giraldus himself calls this "Tam terræ quam morum gentis "illius brevis & compendiosa descriptio."

[e] This noted antiquary, whom Camden calls one of the best, was educated at Oxford, practised physic in Denbigh-castle, and dying 1570, was buried at Whitchurch near Denbigh.

[f] Chiefly etymological. He labours hard to vindicate his countrymen from the unfavourable representation of them by Gildas, as if it was no more than the flourishes of pulpit oratory.

"account

" account of the kings, dukes, and earles of Bretagne, till the duke-
" dom was united to the crown of France, ending with the year of
" our Lord 68 : in which are feveral pieces of Taliefſin, an antient
" Britiſh poet, and a defence of the antiquity of the Scotiſh nation :
" with many other antiquities never before publiſhed in the Engliſh
" tongue.   By John Lewis, efq. barrefter at law ; now firſt publiſhed
" from his original MS. Lond. 1729." Fol. The original Latin
edition of Llwyd's book is ſo full of errors, that it is hardly intelligible.
A new edition of it was publiſhed by the learned Mofes Williams. Lond.
1731. 4to. and Amſt. 1738. with his pieces " De Mona infula," and
" De Britannica arce : accedunt æræ Cambro-Britannicæ," which had
been annexed to " A defcription of Cambria, now called Wales, wrote
" by Sir John Price g, knt. prefixed to the hiſtorie of Cambria, now
" called Wales; a part of the moſt famous yland of Brytaine ; written
" in the Brytiſh language above two hundred years paſt ; tranflated into
" Engliſh by H. Lloyd, gentleman : augmented h out of records and
" beſt approved authors, by David Powell, doctor in divinitie. 1584."
4to.   The defcription of Cambria was reprinted at Oxford 1663, in two
4to ſheets and a half, under the title of " A defcription of Wales ;"
but ſo much altered and difguifed, that many have thought it a different piece.   The hiſtory of Cambria is by Caradoc of Lancarvon, and
this tranflation was republiſhed by Wm. Wynne. Lond. 1697. 8vo.

" The hiſtory of the ancient and moderne eſtate of the principality
" of Wales, dutchy of Cornwall, and earldom of Cheſter.   Collected
" out of the recordes of the Tower of London, and divers ancient
" authors.   By Sir John Dodridge, knt. late one of his majeſtie's judges
" in the King's-bench, and by himfelf dedicated to king James of ever
" bleſſed memory. Lond. 1630." 4to. ſince reprinted in 8vo. 1701.
The 2d edition is intitled " An hiſtorical account, &c. to which is added
the prince of Wales's patent both in Latin and Engliſh ; alfo an account
of his dignity, privileges, arms, rank and titles, and of his ſons and
daughters. Lond. 1714." 8vo.

g Author of " Fides hiſtoriæ Britannicæ:" " Defenfio regis Arthuri :" and a 3d
piece in defence of our hiſtory againſt Polydore Virgil, intitled " Hiſtoriæ Britannicæ
" defenfio," publiſhed 1573 by his fon Dr. Rich. Price.   Ath. Ox. I. 90.
Thefe additions are marked with a cinqfoil. Lhuyd died before it was finiſhed.

2   " Arguments

" Arguments proving the jurifdiction ufed by the prefident and
" counfel in the marches of Wales over the counties of Gloucefter,
" Worcefter, Hereford, and Salop, to be illegal and injurious, and
" a meere incroachment beyond their appointed limits, and the proofe
" is like a threefold corde, not eafily broken, viz. by ftatutes, by law
" books, by records: whereunto is added a catalogue of part of
" the manifeft grievances to which his majefty's fubjects are lyable,
" who live within that jurifdiction. Lond. 1641." 4to.

" Cambria triumphans: or Brittain in its perfect luftre, fhewing
" the origen and antiquity of that illuftrious nation, the fucceffions of
" their kings and princes from the firft to K. Charles of happy me-
" mory: the defcription of the country, the hiftory of the antient
" and modern eftate, the manner of the inveftiture of the princes;
" with the coats of arms of the nobility. By Percy Enderbie, gent.
" Lond. 1661." Fol. The defcription and hiftory are copied, if not
verbally tranfcribed, from Powel: but the hiftory has authorities in
the margin, and comes no lower than 1281. The firft book of the
2d vol. contains the early part of the Welfh hiftory, and a defcription
of Wales: the 3d is the hiftory continued: the 4th contains a lift of
the princes of Wales of Englifh blood, their inveftiture, jurifdiction,
&c. i Wood calls his book juftly enough a fcribble from late authors.

" Britifh antiquities revived: or a friendly conteft touching the fove-
" raignty of the three princes of Wales in antient times, managed with
" certain arguments, whereunto anfwers are applied, by Rob. Vaughan,
" efq. To which is added the pedegree of the right hon. the earl of
" Carbery, lord prefident of Wales: with a fhort account of the five royal
" tribes of Cambria; by the fame author. Oxf. 1662." 4to. Dr. Nicholfon fays this contains " a great many very pretty remarks and difcoveries. The author was patronized by Ufher, to whom he fent his tranflation of Annals of Wales into Englifh for his opinion whether they
were worth printing k. He intended a new edition of Powel's hiftory

i Ath. Ox. II. 518.
k Ufher's letters, p. 261. Among which are feveral letters from Vaughan The abp.
himfelf, in his retirement at St. Donat's, made fome choice collections relative to Britifh
antiquities which were in his chaplain Parr's hands. Life of Ufher, p. 60.

with

with corrections and additions diftinguifhed by this mark [¶]; but being prevented by other engagements, he put his papers into the hands of Thomas Ellis, fellow of Jefus Coll. Oxford, who would have illuftrated the antiquities of his native country, if his employment as college tutor, and difappointments in his expectations of preferment at the reftoration, had not thrown him into a melancholy retirement. However he began to print Powel's work, with his own, and Vaughan's additions; but compleated no more than 128 4to pages, dated 1663, moft of which were fold for wafte paper [l]. Wood and Nicholfon fay a large collection of his MS. papers was fome time in the poffeffion of Sir Wm. Williams. Edw. Lhwyd, who was educated in the fame college, and fucceeded Dr. Plot as keeper of the Afhmolean mufeum, had the ufe of all Vaughan's collections, and with inceffant labour and great exactnefs employed a confiderable part of his life in fearching into the antiquities of the Welfh, had perufed or collected a great deal of antient and valuable matter from their MSS. tranfcribed all the old charters of their monafteries that he could meet with, travelled feveral times over Wales, Cornwall, Scotland, Ireland, Armoric Bretagne, countries inhabited by the fame people, compared their antiquities, and made obfervations on the whole; but died 1709, before he had digefted them into the form of a difcourfe on the antient inhabitants of this ifland. For want of proper encouragement he did very little towards underftanding the Britifh bards, having feen but one of thofe of the 6th cent. and not being able to procure accefs to two of the principal libraries in the country. He communicated many obfervations to bp. Gibfon, whofe edition of the Britannia he revifed [m]; and publifhed " Archæologia Britannica, giving fome account additional " to what has been hitherto publifhed of the languages, hiftories, and " cuftoms of the original inhabitants of Great Britain, from collections " and obfervations in travels through Wales, Cornwall, Bas Bretagne, " Ireland, and Scotland. Vol. i. Gloffography. Oxf. 1707." Fol. [n].

[l] Ath. Ox. II. 518. His additions to the Hiftory of Wales are in Afhmole's mufeum, Nº 663. Ib. p. 372.

[m] Bp. Humphrey's notes on Camden are loft.

[n] Baxter gave an account of it, Philofophical Tranfactions, Nº 311.

He

He left in MS. a Scottiſh or Iriſh-Engliſh dictionary, propoſed to be publiſhed in 1732 by ſubſcription, by Mr. David Malcolme, a miniſter of the church of Scotland, with additions; as alſo the elements of the ſaid language, with neceſſary and uſeful informations for propagating more effectually the Engliſh language, and for promoting the know-ledge of the antient Scottiſh or Iriſh, and very many branches of uſeful and curious learning[o].

" The grievances of his majeſtie's ſubjects reſiding within the prin-
" cipality of Wales, in reſpect of the court of the council in the
" marches of Wales. Lond. 1689." Fol.

" An anſwer to a paper intitled, The grievances of his majeſtie's
" ſubjects reſiding within the principality of Wales, in reſpect of the
" court of the council in the marches of Wales, with the particular
" conveniencies of that court. Lond. 1689." Fol.

" A true (though a ſhort account) of the antient Britons: in reſpect
" to their deſcent, qualities, ſettlement, country, language, learning,
" and religion; with the effigies of Llewylyn ap Griffith, the laſt
" prince of Wales of the Britiſh blood. By J. L. a Cambro-Briton.
" Lond. 1716." 4to.

" The hiſtory of the principality of Wales in three parts. 1. A
" brief account of the antient kings and princes of Britain and Wales,
" till the final extinguiſhing of the royal Britiſh line. 2. Remarks
" upon the lives of all the princes of Wales of the royal families of
" England from K. Edw. I. to Cha. II. 3. Remarkable obſervations
" on the moſt memorable perſons and places in Wales, and of many
" conſiderable tranſactions and paſſages that have happened therein,
" for many hundred years. Together with the natural and artificial
" rarities in the ſeveral counties of that principality. By Robert Bur-
" ton. The 2d edition. Lond. 1730." 12mo. The firſt ſeems to
have been annexed to his " Admirable curioſities, rarities, and won-
" ders in England, Scotland, and Ireland," &c.

For a brief account of plants, natives of this country, ſee " Mer-
' curii botanici pars altera, ſive plantarum gratia ſuſcepti itineris in

---

[o] Carte's account of materials for a hiſtory of England.

" Cam-

" Cambriam five Walliam defcriptio, exhibens reliquarum ftirpium
" noftratium (quæ in priore parte non enumerabantur) catalogum.
" Lond. 1641." 8vo.

" Propofals for enriching the principality of Wales. Humbly fub-
" mitted to the confideration of his countrymen. By Giraldus Cam-
" brenfis. 2d edition. Glocefter 1762." 8vo.

" The worthynes of Wales. A poem. By Thomas Churchyard.
" Lond. 1587." 4to.

" Cambria triumphans; or a panegyric upon Wales. A pindaric
" poem. By Ezechiel Polfted, gent. Lond. 1703." 4to.

" Cambria. A poem. In three books. Illuftrated with notes
" hiftorical, critical, and explanatory. Humbly infcribed to his royal
" highnefs prince George. By Richard Rolt. Lond. 1749." 4to.

We have burlefque defcriptions of this country in " The weftern
" wonder: or O Brazeel, an inchanted ifland, difcovered; with a
" relation of two fhipwrecks in a dreadful fea-ftorm in that difcovery.
" To which is added, a defcription of a place called Montecapernia,
" relating to the nature of the people, their qualities, humours, fafhions,
" religions, &c. Lond. 1674." 4to.

" O Brazeel, or the inchanted ifland: being a particular relation
" of the late difcovery and wonderful difenchantment of an ifland on
" the N. of Ireland: with an account of the riches and commodities
" thereof. Communicated by a letter from Londonderry to a friend
" in London. Lond. 1675." 4to.

" Mufcipula, five Καμβρομυομαχια. Lond. 1709." 8vo. This
poem, which is efteemed a mafter-piece in its kind, was the work of
Mr. Holdfworth of Oxford, and after going through feveral editions, was
at laft inferted in the Mufæ Britannicæ. 1711. 8vo. Several Englifh
verfions came out foon after, intitled " The moufe-trap; or the Welfh-
" man's fcuffle with the mice. Lond. 1709." 8vo. " Taffey's triumph;
" or a new tranflation of Cambro-Muomachia: in imitation of Mil-
" ton, by a gentleman of Oxford. Lond. 1709." 8vo. " The moufe-
" trap; a poem, done from the original Latin, in Milton's ftile. Lond.
" 1715." 8vo. Other tranflations were intitled " Mufcipula, or the
" moufe-trap. A poem in Latin and Englifh; the Latin by E. Holdf-

4 F 2 " worth

" worth of Magdalen coll. Oxon. Tranflated by Sam. Cobb, M. A.
" late of Trinity college, Cambridge. Lond." 8vo. And a 2d edition
in 1720. Another tranflation, 1737, was called " Καμβρομυομαχια,
" or the moufe-trap ; being a tranflation of Mr. Holdfworth's muf-
" cipula :" inferted fince in Dodfley's collection of poems, vol. v.
p. 258. Dr. Cobden publifhed another in his poetical works 1748.
8vo. p. 230. with letters from Mr. Holdfworth.

" The leek. A poem on St. David's day, by N. Griffith, efq.
" Lond. 1719." 2d edit. 1720. Fol.

" Wallography, or the Briton defcribed, being a pleafant relation
" of a journey into Wales ; wherein are fet down feveral remarkable
" paffages that occurred in the way thither, and alfo many choice ob-
" fervables and notable commemorations concerning the ftate and
" condition, the nature, and humorous actions, manners, cuftoms,
" &c. of that country and people; by William Richards [P], a mighty
" lover of Welfh travels. Lond. 1682." 12mo.

" A collection of Welch travels and memoirs of Wales : containing,
" I. The Briton defcribed, or a pleafant relation of D—n S—t's journey
" to that antient kingdom, and remarkable paffages that occurred on
" the way : alfo many choice obfervations and notable commemora-
" tions concerning the ftate and condition, the nature, humours, man-
" ners, cuftoms, and mighty actions of that country and people. II.
" A trip to N. Wales, by a barrifter of the Temple. III. A funeral
" fermon preached by the parfon of Langwillin. IV. The Welfh
" fchool-mafter, by Dr. K——g. V. Mufcipula ; or the Welfh moufe-
" trap, a poem in Latin and Englifh. The whole collected by J. T.
" [John Torbuck] a mighty lover of Welfh travels. Lond." 12mo.
fans date.

Of the mines we have fome account in " A juft and true remon-
" ftrance of his majefty's mines royal in the principality of Wales.
" Lond. 1642." 4to. By Tho. Bufhel, farmer of his majefty's minerals here, of whom before in Oxfordfhire, p. He worked five
mountains in Cardiganfhire, and minted filver enough to cloath the
king's garrifon at Oxford. The fuccefs of the parliament forces in

P Of him fee Ath. Ox. II. 1072,

Wales put an end to his refearches; after the reftoration he went to work in Mendip hills, but died two years after q.

In Dr. Birch's hift. of the Royal Society, IV. 491. is a letter from Mr. Cafwell to Mr. Halley 1686 of the heights of fome Welfh and Shropfhire mountains.

In N⁰ 208 of Phil. Tranf. is Mr. E. Lhwyd's letter to Dr. Lifter concerning locufts lately obferved in Wales. His other obfervations on the natural hiftory of Wales are in N° 334. and on its antiquities N° 335 and 337. In p. 210 of vol. xlix. is an account of the char-fifh in N Wales.

Some inftances of land fwallowed up by the fea in different parts of Wales are collected in the Gentleman s Mag. for Feb. 1751. p. 60.

The firft general map of Wales is Speed's 1610, adorned with views of the four cathedrals, and of Beaumaris, Carnarvan, Harlieg, Cardigan, Penbrok, Carmarthen, Denbigh, Flint, Montgomery, Radnor, Brecknok, and Cardife.

Hollar engraved a map of S. Wales, fans date.

q Ath. Ox. II. 527.

SOUTH

SOUTH WALES.

" God's warning to his people of England, by the great over-
" flowing of the waters or floudes, lately hapned in S. Wales,
" and many other places [a] : wherein is defcribed the great loffes and
" wonderfull damages, that hapned thereby, by the drowning of
" many townes and villages, to the utter undooing of many thoufandes
" of people. Lond. 1607." 4to.

As an article of the natural hiftory of S. Wales one might infert the
feveral accounts of the fimple and antient method of inoculating the
fmall pox, communicated to the world in the Philofophical Tranfactions, N° 262 and 375, by Dr. Williams, and Mr. Wright, furgeon,
at Haverfordweft.   In N° 243, p. 279, is a letter from Edw. Lluyd
about ftones found in S. Wales : and in N° 252, p. 186, his account
of a figured marble or alcyonium there.

In the Harleian library N° 3538 contains Welfh pedigrees and
draughts of fome churches, &c. in S. Wales. N° 3325 is a fhort hiftory of Wales from the year 688 to 936; epitaphs in feveral churches,
principally in Brecknokfhire, and Welfh pedigrees. N° 6823. 6831.
6870. contain the defcents and pedigrees of many of the antient and
prefent nobility and gentry of Wales, from authentic records, infcriptions on grave ftones, collections, and vifitations of all the churches
and places of note in Wales and the neighbouring parts, by Mr. Hugh
Thomas, about 1700.

[a] Gloucefterfhire and Somerfetfhire.

GLAMORGAN-

GLAMORGANSHIRE.

THomas Leyſon, phyſician, of Neath, wrote a Latin poem deſcribing the ſcite and beauty of *St. Donat*'s caſtle in Glamorganſhire, tranſlated into Welſh by his friend Dr. Rheſe : but whether the poem or the tranſlation were ever printed Wood does not tell us[a]. Sir Edw. Stradling of this caſtle, wrote " The winning of the lordſhip of " Glamorgan or Morganwe out of the Welſhmen's hands, &c." of which ſee more in The Hiſtorie of Cambria, p. 122. 141. the genealogical part whereof was compoſed by Sir Edward, whoſe father, Sir John, communicated ſome particulars to Camden. A letter from Mr. Cole of Briſtol to Dr. Plot, about the liquor of ſhell fiſh found near St. Donnets, ſtaining linen, is publiſhed in Birch's Hiſtory of the Royal Society, vol. iv. p. 329—332 [b].

Buck engraved a N. W. view of this caſtle 1740.

The annals of *Margan* abbey, now the beautiful ſeat of lord Manſell, preſerving a fine chapter houſe and other remains, are publiſhed in Gale's Scriptores hiſt. Ang. vol. i. and reach from 1066 to 1232.

" A ſurvey of the cathedral church of *Landaff*; containing the in-
" ſcriptions upon the monuments, with an account of the biſhops and
" other dignitaries belonging to the ſame; what other preferments
" they enjoy'd; and the times of their deceaſe, places of burial, and
" epitaphs. To which is ſubjoind, a large appendix of records, and
" other curious matters relating thereto. Collected by Browne Willis,
" eſq; adorned with draughts [c] of the ſaid church, in order to illuſtrate
" the deſcription thereof. Lond. 1719." 8vo.

The Liber Landaff is frequently quoted by Camden, which ſeems to be the ſame referred to in the Monaſticon, called Teilo, ſaid to be compiled by biſhop Urban, who built the preſent church in the 12th century. The Chronicon eccleſiæ Landavenſis, Cott. Lib. Tit. D. 22. has very little about the ſee. Wharton printed in Anglia Sacra, ii. 662. a

---

[a] Ath. Ox. I. 346.

[b] In Nº 197 of the Philoſophical Tranſactions is Dr. Liſter's account of the Purpura of the antients. Sir Robert Southwell told him it was found in Ireland; and Beaumont found it in Bede, I. c. i.   [c] By Joſeph Lord.

life

life of St. Teliaw, and Hiftoriola ecclef. Landavenfis, prefixed to the above regifter called after his name, different from that in the Monafticon.

A N. view of this church by Buck 1741.

A N. E. view of the abbey and N. W. of the caftle by Buck 1741.

" The advantages of the mineral works at *Neath*. 1720." 8vo.

Edward Lhuyd, when he vifited this county 1696, found on one of the fteps of a tower at *Caerphilly* caftle a number of confufed and fingular marks, which he took for traces of an infcription originally in fome other part of the caftle. He fent the ftone to Oxford, and a tranfcript of the infcription, and certain letters about the caftle, which he calls mafon's marks, to the Royal Society, in whofe Tranfactions, N° 335, p. 500, they are inferted. Mr. J. Sandford took a particular and accurate furvey of this caftle d, which deferves more particular attention. Buck has given a S. E. view of it.

A view

d Inferted in Gibfon's Camden. Mr. Llwyd particularly defcribes a large roon there, which was undoubtedly a hall : but he has brought no arguments to prove it a Roman building. The following account of it from a MS. of the late Mr. William Harris, a minor canon of Landaff, was inferted in the General Evening Poft, June 20, 1767 : " Five computed miles from Cardiff is fituated a Roman ftation, viz. that of Caerphylly, or the Bullæum Silurum of the Itinerary. Mr. Edward Llwyd rightly termed it *Caer-Vol* (Anglicè, Kingfton) in the genitive cafe *Caer-Vyle*. To confirm this etymology, there is a farm-houfe two fhort miles diftant, called *Kaer-Vol*, i. e. the Prince's Field, and in contradiftinction another called *Kaer-Marchog*, i. e. Knight's Field. Not far from Caerphylly, and in the fame hundred, is *Ynis y Bwl* or *y Vol*, the Prince's Ifland, or rather a low, flat fituation, now a farm houfe. In the year 1753 feveral tumuli were opened on *Eglwys Ilan* common, two miles from Caerphylly, in which burnt bones were found, but no coins : the urns which contained them were all broke by the workmen. Antiquarians are furprifed at the filence of hiftorians with regard to this caftle ; when at the fame time it occurs in Wynn's improvement of Caradock of Lancarvan's Hiftory of Wales (printed in 1697) in pages 203. 209. 244. and 247. under the name of *Sengennith* caftle. Now to prove that Sengennith is the fame with Caerphylly caftle I fhall only obferve, that we at this day term Caerphylly hundred, the hundred of Sengennith in Welch ; the North gate of Cardiff town, which leads towards Caerphylly, is called by the Welch *Porth Sengennith* ; and the inhabitants of Lantriffant term the eaft wind *Gwynt Sengennith*, as blowing from that quarter where this hundred is fituate. Whence it had this appellation of Sengennith I am at a lofs to judge, unlefs it were from St. Kenneth or Chineth (Chinedus) from whom Langennith in the weft part of Glamorganfhire, where he lived and erected a fmall religious houfe, took its name. A. D. 1174, prince Rees prevailed with feveral lords of S. Wales to do homage to king Hen. II. at Gloucefter, on St. James's day : of this number were, Morgan ap Caradock ap Jeftyn of Glamorgan, and Griffith ap Ivor ap Meyrick of Sengennith. By the word Caer it is evident this place muft have been fortified by the Romans ; though I never heard of any coins, bricks, or infcribed ftones, or any other remains of thofe people found

there.

A view of the ſtupendous bridge of one arch, 145 feet wide and 35 high, over the river Tave at *Pontytypridd*, with a ſhort hiſtory of it, was inſerted in the Gentleman's Magazine for Dec. 1764, p. 564. A plan and proſpect of it was engraved 1755, and dedicated to lord Windſor. A beautiful view of it by R. Wilſon 1767. The architect William Edwards, a country maſon, raiſed it three times without ſuc-ceſs, till by lightning the abutments, it has ſtood, after a fourth at-tempt, now ten years [e].

In Nº 233, p. 727, of the Philoſophical Tranſactions is Mr. Aubrey's account of a medicated ſpring in *Lancarim* pariſh.

An autumnal view of a waterfall near *Hoath*, by Mr. Lewis, appeared at Spring-gardens 1767.

there. The preſent building was erected 1221 (6 Hen. III.) as appears from Caradock, p. 247, by John Bruce or de Braioſa, the proprietor, which family were lords of Gower-land in this county, and John was ſon-in-law to prince Lewelyn ap Jorwerth. In this age the Flemings were the beſt maſter-builders, and were employed here, as appears by the diſcovery of ſome Flemiſh braſs coins at this place, and likewiſe at Landaff cathe-dral when it was lately repaired. Godwin de Præſulibus mentions bp. Poer, of Saliſbury, ſending abroad for artificers to erect the preſent ſtately cathedral there in the reign of Henry III. When the old free ſchool at Leiceſter was taken down within theſe laſt 20 years, there were found, below the foundations, great numbers of Flemiſh braſs pieces. In p. 244 of Caradock's Chronicle we find that Rees Vychan entirely demoliſhed the old caſtle 1217. The preſent caſtle, within its old deep mote, is not of any great compaſs; Cardiff caſtle within its mote being bigger; but the out-works at Caerphylly are of great extent; thoſe to the eaſt are of later erection, and likewiſe thoſe on the outſide of the old mote: the works that lie to the N. E have a mote of a more modern faſhion before them, and the gate on that ſide appears more recent, and does not run parallel with the inner gate of the caſtle and the eaſtern drawbridge. Theſe additional works probably were erected by the younger Spencer, lord of Glamorgan, who was beſieged in this caſtle by the Queen's and the Barons forces 1326, when he obliged them to raiſe the ſiege. Great part of the out-works ſeems never to have been finiſhed. The noted hanging tower has for ſome years paſt been out of the perpendicular in the middle; the eaſtern part of it projects about ten feet. This caſtle in old Welſh MSS. is termed the *blue caſtle*, from the colour of the ſtone wherewith it is built, as Powis caſtle in Montgomeryſhire is ſtiled the *red caſtle*."

[e] The very antient bridge of old Brioude in Auvergne conſiſts of one ſemicircular arch over the river Allier, 195 feet from pile to pile, and 84 feet high from the water: built of two rows of hewn ſtones, and a mixture of ſmaller ſtones and rubbiſh cemented together. The two ſides are founded on a rock, which makes the arch riſe higher on one ſide than on the other: the breadth of the bridge is only 14 feet, which is juſt the thick-neſs of the wall on each ſide: two perſons at the oppoſite piers below can diſtinctly hear each other whiſper. The bridge, ſuppoſed to have been built by the Romans, gives name to the town which was antiently called Brivas, the old Gauliſh name of a bridge. Montfaucon Antiq. expliq. vol. iv. part II. book i. c. 5.

Views

Views in this county by Meſſrs. Buck, beſides thoſe already mentioned, are two large ones of the towns of Cardiffe and Swanſea ; S. W. Ewenny priory ; and the following caſtles,

N. W. Cardiffe,	S. E. Landlythian,
E. Swanſea,	N. W. Penrice,
N. E. Oyſtermouth,	N. Morlaſhe,
N. E. Pennarth,	N. E. Webley. 1741.
S. Coyty,	

" Glamorgan comitatus auſtralis Cambriæ deſcriptio," by Saxton, 1578, without the hundreds ; added in Speed's " Glamorganſhyre, " with the ſittuations of the chief towne Cardyff and ancient Landaffe " deſcribed. 1610." A late one by T. Kitchin, with a N. W. view of Cardiffe.

CARDIGANSHIRE.

RAY annexed to his Collection of Engliſh local words, 1674. 1691. 1742. an account of the manner of preparing ſilver in Cardiganſhire.

" An eſſay on the value of the mines, late of Sir Carbery Price. By " Wm. Waller, gent. ſteward of the ſaid mines. Writ for the private " ſatisfaction of all the partners. Lond. 1698." 12mo. The ſame author wrote afterwards " A deſcription of theſe mines," with plans. 12mo.

" Some account of mines, and the advantages of them to this king- " dom : with an appendix relating to the mine-adventurers in Wales. " Lond. 1707." 12mo.

" A familiar diſcourſe or dialogue concerning the mine-adventurers. " Lond. 1700. By Mr. Shiers." 12mo. To which is prefixed " An " abſtract of the preſent ſtate of the mines of Bwlk-yr-eſkir-hyr ; and " of the material proceedings of the committee appointed for the " management thereof."

A liſt of the names of the mine-adventurers, printed by Freeman Collins 1700, and Mr. Yalden's " Poems on the mines late Sir Carbery " Price's.

Views by Buck, 1741, S. Cardigan caſtle and priory.
W. Stratflour abbey.
E. Aberyſtwith caſtle.

3

This

This county is included in Saxton's " map of Radnor, Breknok, and " Caermarden shires, Brit. Deheubart. Ang. S.Wales, 1578," without the hundreds: supplied in " Cardigan shyre described, with the due forme " of the shire town as it was surveyed by I. S." [John Speed.] 1710.

A later one by Kitchen.

BRECKNOCKSHIRE.

THERE is a very imperfect geographical description of Breck-nockshire, and of most of its rarities, wonders, and remarkable places; with its history from Meyric, king of Brytan, till 1693. MS. Harl. N° 7017, in a modern hand.

A view in this county was exhibited by Mr. Jones at Spring-gardens 1767.

Buck's views in it, 1741, are Brecknock priory and castle, S. E.; and the castles of Lanthew, S. W.; Blaenlleveny, S.; Penkelly, S.; Crickhowel, S.: Tretŵr, S.; Hay, N.; Brwynllys, N.

Speed made a map with a plan of the town; and there is a later map by Kitchen.

CAERMARTHENSHIRE.

" THE charter of the borough of *Caermarthen*. Caerm. 1765." 8vo.

In the British museum, MS. Harl. 5203, is " John Cade's repre-" sentation of the poor estate of the town of *Kidwillie* to Sir George " Carewe."

In the Philosophical Transactions, N° 416, p. 444, is an account of the effects of lightning in Caermarthenshire, by Mr. Evan Davies.

A large view of the town of Caermarthen by Buck; a smaller S. of its castle, and those of Caerkenin, S. W.ᵃ; Kydwelly, S. E.;

ᵃ Two views of this and Brecknock castle by Mr. Jones were exhibited at Spring-gardens 1766.

Green,

Green, W.; Laugharne, S.E.; Llanſtephan, N.E.; Denefawr. S.
1741.

" Caermarthen, both ſhyre and towne, deſcribed. By John Speed."
1610.   A later map by Kitchen, with a S.E. view of Caermarthen.

PEMBROKESHIRE.

A M.S. Hiſtory of this county, wrote by George Owen, eſq; is or was
lately in the hands of Howel Vaughan of Hengwrt, eſq; There
is another among the Harleian MSS. in the Britiſh muſeum, N° 6824.
Fol. beginning " The firſt book of the deſcription of Penbrokeſhire
" in general, 1603." The table is as follows. " Of the ſituation,
" form, and quantity of Penbrokeſhire, with the longitude and lati-
" tude of the ſame, and of the air of the country and quality of the
" ſoil. chap. 1. Of the antient names of the countrey, and that the
" ſame in antient time was a kingdom, and ſhortly after the Conqueſt
" created an earldom, and then rayſed to the degree of a marqueſdom,
" and what kings, earls, and marquiſſes hath ben of the ſame, and
" whie it is called Little England beyond Wales. c. 2. What nations
" of people inhabited this country in antient time, and from whence
" the now inhabitants are antiently deſcended, and from what coun-
" trie and places, and when and howe they came thither. c. 3. That
" the country is now inhabited by 3 nations, as Welſhmen, the rem-
" nant of the antient Britaignes, and the firſt inhabitants of the coun-
" try, Engliſhmen, brought thither at the conqueſt thereof, and Iriſh-
" men, which doe daylye ferrye over thither out of Ireland ; and the
" languages ſpoken by theſe 3 ſeveral nations. c. 4. Of the conſtitution
" of the bodies of the people, and of the inclination and nature of the
" inhabitants. c. 5. Of the diviſion of the ſaid country in antient tyme
" into cantredes and comotts, how it is divided into the Engliſhrie
" and Welſhrie, and alſo howe the ſame is laſtlie divided into 8 hun-
" dreds. c. 6. Of ſuch commodities as this country chieflye yeeldeth,
" and venteth to other parts, thereby to bringe in money for the ſame.
" c. 7. Of the cheefe wantes and defectes that the county of Pen-
                                                              " broke

" broke naturally hath, and of diverfe inconveniencies in the ftate of
" the county, which by induftry of the people might be redreffed.
" c. 8.　Of the maner of hufbandrie and tillinge of the land, and of
" the natural help and mendmentes the foile itfelf yeeldeth for better-
" ynge and mendynge of the lande, as lyme, 2 kyndes of marle,
" fande, and wort or woade of the fea. c. 9.　Of the maner and order
" of buildings both of townes, caftles, churches, and houfes us'd in
" this county, and of the fundrye forts and quarries of ftone that are
" founde fitte and fervinge for that purpofe. c. 10.　Of caftles, fortes,
" and ftronge holdes in this fhire, and of the citties and townes there-
" of. c. 11.　Of the feveral fortes of fuell that the county yeeldeth.
" c. 12.　Of the cheefe ryvers of this fhire that have theire courfe
" throwe or by the fame ; or that have their rifeinges in the fame, and
" ending in other countreys. c. 13.　Of the cheefe and fpeciall hills
" and mountains of the fhire. c. 14.　Of fault iflands feperated by the
" fea from the mayne, and yet efteemed part thereof, and of diverfe
" rockes and ftones neere the fea fhore, yeelding fowle and other
" comodities, and of two peninfulas or half iflands in this fhire. c. 15.
" Of the feveral fortes of fifh taken in this fhire as well in the frefhe
" ryvers as on the fea coaftes, and of the great plenty thereof. c. 16.
" Of abundance of fowle that the country yeldeth, and the feveral
" fortes and kindes of them. c. 17.　Of the ufuall meafure of lande
" in Penbrokefhire, and howe the fame differs from the common mea-
" fure of the realme, as alfo within itfelf in the fundrie parts thereof.
" c. 18.　Of weights and meafures ufed in Penbrokefhire as well drye
" as liquide. c. 19.　Of faires and markets ufed yeerlye in Penbroke-
" fhire. c. 20.　Of the adminiftration of lawe and juftice within the
" county of Penbroke, as well by the common lawes of this realme, as
" by certaine courtes of equitie, and alfo for caufes maritime, together
" with goverment civil and ecclefiaftical practis'd and us'd by lawe civil
" and canon, and how and where this fhire doth participate therein
" with other countrys of the realm in general, and where it is parti-
" cular to itfelf; and laftly of the government martial and militarie
" there, under the lord lieutenant. c. 21. f. 70.　Of the order and
" forme

" forme of conveyaunce of landes and tenements us'd in antient tyme
" within this county of Penbroke, and of antient wordes and phrafes
" ufed in old tyme, nowe growne out of ufes and not underftood
" of moft people, and how the conveyaunces at this daye differeth
" in forme from that of antient tyme. c. 22. f. 76. Of general and
" particular cuftomes us'd and allow'd of within the county of Pen-
" broke, as well temporal as ecclefiaftical. c. 23. f. 83. That Pen-
" brokefhire was in antient tyme a countye palantyne, not part of the
" principalitie of Wales, and what the principalitie of Wales is, where-
" in is toched howe Wales came to be fubjecte to-the crowne of Eng-
" land. c. 24. f. 85. Of divers famous and learned men that hath
" ben borne or lived in the county of Penbroke, in former tymes,
" whofe workes are left and be yet extante to the pofteritie. c. 15. f. 91.
" Of certaine rare wonders and ftrange things found in Penbrokefhire.
" c. 26. f. 95. Of the worthynes of Penbroke and the people thereof
" in antient tyme, and what benefitte that county hath yelded to the
" realme of England, howe Ireland and the cheefeft parts of Wales was
" firft and cheefly fubdued by it to the crowne of England. c. 27. f. 98.
" Of paftimes and recreations fit for gentlemen which Penbrokefhire
" yeeldeth, and of feates of activitie wherein the antient play called
" *knappan* [a] is defcribed. c. 28. f. 100. The 2d parte of the defcrip-
" tion of Penbrokefhire, wherein is handled the geographical and
" hiftorical defcription of everie hundred, and in the fame of every
" parifh, and therein the townreddes, villages, monafteries, priories,
" caftells, gentlemen's houfes, and other places of note, with fuch mat-
" ters of antiquity as concerneth the fame, found either by antient re-
" cords or writings, teftimony or true tradition by the antient people,
" the antient and modern owners of moft of thefe places, with their
" difcent and arms, with many other notes worthy the knowledge."
In this MS. is a drawing of the great ftone Maen y cromlech on Pen-
try Iwan land: the upper ftone 18 feet long, 9 broad, and 3 thick:
a piece 5 feet by 10 broke off.

[a] Hurling, or toffing and catching a wooden ball, a game very common in the villages
of S Wales.

" A fur-

" A furvey of the cathedral church of *St. David*'s, and the edifices
" belonging to it, as they ftood in the year 1715; to which is added,
" fome memoirs relating thereto, and the country adjacent, from a
" MS. wrote about the latter end of queen Elizabeth's reign b. Toge-
" ther with an account of the archbifhops, bifhops, precentors, chan-
" cellors, treafurers, and archdeacons of the fee of St. David's. Col-
" lected by Browne Willis; efq; illuftrated with draughts, and adapted
" to the faid hiftorical defcription. Lond. 1717." 8vo. The account
of this and Landaff cathedrals were drawn up by Dr. Wm. Wotton,
author of Reflections on antient and modern learning, when he retired
into Wales. Bp. Gibfon began his antiquarian ftudies with tranfcribing
the MSS. and records of this diocefe : and his account was kept there.
MS. Harl. 6260. is a very old book of ftatutes, &c. of this church by
bp. Gervafe 1228. The life of the patron faint and abp. was wrote by
Ricemar, one of his fucceffors, 1085 c, from which Wharton printed
fome extracts, Ang. Sac. ii. 643, and Giraldus's enlargement of it, ib.
p. 628; alfo, p. 514. his piece De jure & ftatu ecclefiæ Menevenfis,
from an original MS. in the Cotton library. Another life of St. David d
and a chronicle of the church are printed there, p. 648, from a Cotton MS. A S. E. view of the church and palace by Buck 1740.

Several grants, &c. of Pembroke priory to St. Alban's abbey are in
the Acts of abbot Whethamftede, publifhed with Otterburne's Chronicle by Hearne. Oxf. 1732. 8vo. p. 311. 314. 323. 523.

" A plain difquifition on the indefpenfible neceffity of fortifying
" and improving *Milford Haven*; containing likewife an attempt to
" demonftrate the advantages that will arife from it to this nation, with
" fome hints on the profecuting fcheme. To which is annexed an
" exact map of the harbour, drawn after a very late furvey. Addreffed
" to a patriot member of parliament. Lond. 1759." 8vo.

b The perfon communicating this MS. whom I take to be Dr. Wotton, from M. N.
the laft letters of his name figned at the end of his letter about it, had it from Mr.
Wm. Lewes, of Llwyn Derew, Caermarthenfhire, a gentleman eminently fkilled in the
antiquities of the Britons, particularly the genealogical; and fuppofes it to have been
written by Mr. Geo. Owen, lord of Kemys hundred, for the ufe of Camden, who acknowleges his affiftance in this county.

c He was fon of Jutien or Sulghum, bifhop of this fee.

d Very little to his credit. Giraldus wrote as a relation.

In N°

In N° 208, p. 45, of the Philofophical Tranfactions is Ed. Llwyd's letter to Dr. Lifter, giving an account of locufts obferved Oct. 20, 1693, in *Marthery* parifh ; and green worms on a hill in *Mean Clochog* parifh 1601. In N° 334 he gives an account of ftrange cranes in Cardiganfhire 1606, and a flock of birds, which he fuppofed Virginia nightingales, in this county, 1694.

Other views in this county by Buck 1740, are two large ones of the towns of Pembroke and Haverfordweft ; fmaller N. W. of Pembroke caftle : thofe of Carew, S E. ; Picton, N. E. ; Mannorbeer, S. E. ; Llehaiden, S. E. ; Tenby town and caftle, E. ; St. Dogmael's priory, S. W. ; Haverfordweft priory, S. E. ; Lantphey court, S. W.

Pembroke town and caftle by Mafon are engraved in one view, and Kilgarran caftle in another by Wilfon.

 " Penbrok comitatus qui inter meridionales Cambriæ provincias
 " hodie cenfetur, olim Demetia, L. Dyfet, B. h. e. occidentalis Wallia,
 " defcriptio," by Saxton, 1578, without the hundreds : added in
 " Penbrokfhyre defcribed, and the fittuations both of Penbroke and
 " St. David's fhewed in due form as they were taken by John Speed,
 " 1610." A later map by Kitchen, with an E. view of Haverfordweft.

R A D N O R S H I R E.

 " A Journey to *Llandrindod* wells in Radnorfhire ; with a particular
 " defcription of thofe wells, the places adjacent, the humours of
 " the company there, &c. being a faithful narrative of every occur-
 " rence worth notice, that happened in a journey to and from thofe wells.
 " To which is added, obfervations and informations to thofe who in-
 " tend vifiting Llandrindod : and to which is prefixed, the Parfon's
 " tale, a poem. By a countryman. The 2d edition, corrected and
 " amended. Lond. 1746." The firft was about 1744. The work of a lawyer, who gave himfelf great airs there, and afterwards drew caricatures of all the characters he converfed with.

A trea-

" A treatife on the medicinal mineral water at Llandrindod in Rad-
" norfhire, South Wales; with fome remarks on mineral and foffil
" mixtures in their native veins and beds, at leaft as far as refpects
" their influence on water. By Diederick Weffel Linden, M. D. Lond.
" 1755." 8vo.

Meffrs. Bucks have given us no views in this county.

Boydel engraved a view of the cataract called *Rhaiadr Fawr*, or
Piftil Rhaiadr', 1750. Another is in the Gentleman's Magazine for
January that year. A third was engraved on a large fheet by J. Lewis.
I think I have feen a fourth.

" The countie of Radnor defcribed, and the fhyre townes fittua-
" tione, 1610." This is Saxton's map augmented by Speed, with the
addition of the hundreds. There is a later one by Kitchen.

NORTH WALES.

CAERNARVONSHIRE.

IN the 6th number of the Bibliotheca literaria, 1722, p. 17—28, Dr. Wotton, after giving an account of Gale's Regiftrum de Richmond, adds a particular defcription of a like work in the Harleian library, known by the title of the " Record of Caernarvon," being an extent of the counties of Caernarvon and Anglefey, in imitation of Domefday, by commots, or half hundreds, and towns, taken chiefly in Edw. IIId's time, though begun by Edw. I. This MS. on vellum is a copy taken in Q. Elizabeth's time from the original record, almoft deftroyed by damp in Caernarvon caftle. The doctor has accompanied his account of it with a curious illuftration of the antient tenures and fervices in N. Wales [a].

" A furvey of the cathedral church of *Bangor*, and the edifices
" belonging to it. Containing an account of all the infcriptions
" on the mouments and grave ftones : the hiftory of the bifhops [b],
" deans, and other dignitaries : their feveral preferments, times of de-
" ceafe, burials, and epitaphs. Together with a large appendix of re-
" cords, and other curious matters relating to Bangor church and
" bifhoprick : as namely, the dedication of all the churches and chapels
" in the diocefe of Bangor ; and defcriptions [c] of *Clynocfawr* church and
" *Bodowen* chapel. To which is alfo fubjoined feveral fupplementary
" additions and records to the like hiftory of St. Afaph cathedral, fome
" time fince publifhed : the dedications of the churches and chapels in

---

[a] His fplendid and valuable edition of Hoel Dha's laws in the original, with a Latin tranflation and notes, was publifhed after his death, Lond. 1730. Fol. Mr. Rowlands mentions two large parchment books of extents in N. Wales, collected by Sir Wm. Gruffyd of Penryn, Chamberlain of N. Wales ; one preferved in the Chamberlain's office, called the Extent of N. Wales, the other in the Auditor's office at London : from thefe and a few other remains Mr. Rowlands collected his obfervations on the antient tenures and fervices, Mona. p. 120—134. Dr. Humphreys, late bp. of Bangor, had a like extent for his diocefe.

[b] A hiftory of the lives of the bifhops of Bangor fince Q. Elizabeth's time is referred to p. 106. as then " drawing for the prefs and near publifhing by J. Le Neve, author of the Fafti Anglicani." Bp. Humphreys fent Wood a lift of the deans from 1500, printed by Hearne at the end of Otterburn's Chronicle.

[c] By Jof. Lord of Caermarthen, who drew the views.

" that

" that diocefe ; and defcriptions of *Gresford,* and *Mould* churches.
" Collected by Brown Willis, efq; illuftrated with draughts of the
" ichnography and upright of Bangor cathedral, and view of Bodowen
" chapel. Lond. 1721." 8vo.

A S. view of this church by King. A view of the town by J. Lewis.
A S. W. view of the church with the palace by Buck, 1742: alfo
Clynnog Vawr abbey, S. E.; and the caftles of Caernarvon, N. W
N. E. and S.; Dolyweddelen with Snowden hill, E.; Dolbadarn with
Snowden hill, E.; Crickiaith, W.; Conway, N. and S.

A view of Conway by J. Lewis. A view of Penmann Mawr and
Snowden, and of Gaunant Mawr, a great waterfall near the latter, by
Boydell, 1750 : alfo N. W. and E. views of Caernarvon, and W. of
Conway caftles.

Caernarvon caftle, Snowden with its environs, and Cader Idris, make
Wilfon's three views for N. Wales.

An account of a great fire of three or four months continuance on
the coaft of Caernarvonfhire, by Lhwyd and Jones, is printed in the
Philofophical Tranfactions, N° 218, p. 213, and Dr. Halley's account
of Snowden hill, N° 229, p. 566.

Dr. Linden's account of a mineral water at *Llangyba* is inferted in
the Gentleman s Magazine, July 1766, p. 328.

Verfes on feeing abp. Williams's monument at Landegay, near Bangor, is in Dodfley's Mifcell. vol. vi. p. 284.

Saxton's map of this county 1578 includes Anglefea, and wants the
hundreds : added in " Caernarvon, both fhyre and fhire-towne, with
" the ancient citie Bangor defcribed. A. D. 1610. By J. Speed."

DENBIGHSHIRE.

DR. Rawlinfon had a MS. hiftory of this county [a].
" Extenta caftri & honoris de Denbigh facta per Hugonem de
" Beckele, 8 Edw. III." [1334.] Harl. MS. 3632. Mr. T. Rawlin-
fon had a fine copy of this, formerly Dudley earl of Leicefter's.

A perambulation and furvey of the lordfhips of *Bromfield* and *Yale,*
parcel of the eftates of Charles prince of Wales, by John Norden, 1620,
is in the Harleian library 3696.

Englifh Topog. p. 273.
4 H 2

" Wonder-

" Wonderfull news from Wales: or a true narrative of an old wo-
" man [Jane Morgan] living near *Lanfelin*, in Denbighfhire, whofe
" memory ferves her truly and perfectly to relate what fhe hath feen
" and done 130 years ago, having now the full number of her teeth;
" though moft of them were loft when fhe was threefcore years and ten.
" She is alfo remembered by fome of 90 years old to be taller than
" fhe is 17 or 18 inches: with feveral other circumftances of her life,
" which fhew her to be the wonder of her age. Lond. 1677." 4to. reprinted in the Harleian Mifcellany, vol. vii. p. 66.

In the Philofophical Tranfactions, Nᵒ 308, p. 2342, is an account
of a hail ftorm near Denbigh, July 16, 1706.

A view of *Llanroft* bridge over the river Conway was inferted in the
Gentleman's Magazine for Feb. 1753, and a defcription of it in the
table of contents.

A W. profpect of *Erthig*, the feat of Sim. York, efq; by Badeflade
and Toms

Three others of *Chirk* caftle by the fame, and a N. one by Meffrs.
Buck: who have alfo publifhed a large one of Wrexham town; E. and
W. of Valle Crucis abbey; Denbigh abbey and caftle, E.; the caftle, E.
and N.: thofe of Dinas Bran, S. E.; Rhuthin, S. W.; and Holt, S.

Two large views of Denbigh and Rhuthin by J. Lewis. N. views of
Denbigh caftle and N. E. of Wrexham church by Boydell, 1750.

A profpect of the N. fide of the church and fteeple of Wrexham by
Thomas Bradfhaw jun.

Denbigh and Flint fhires are united in Saxton's map 1578, engraved
by R. Hogenbergius, without the hundreds, added in Speed's map,
with a plan of Denbigh.

FLINTSHIRE.

" **A** Survey of the cathedral church of *St. Afaph*, and the edifices
" belonging to it; together with an account of all the infcriptions
" on the monuments and grave ftones; the hiftory of the bifhops,
" deans [a], and other dignitaries, as far as they have come to hand from

---

[a] Bifhop Humphrey's catalogue of deans fince 1500 fent to Wood, was printed by
Hearne at the end of Otterburn's Chronicle.

" records,

" records, or are to be met with in any printed hiſtory. To which is
" ſubjoined a large appendix of records, and other curious matters re-
" lating to St. Aſaph church and dioceſe. Collected by Browne Willis,
" eſq; Illuſtrated with draughts of the ichnography and upright of
" the ſaid cathedral. Lond. 1720." 8vo. Bp. Goldwell carried all the
muniments of his church to Rome, except one regiſter called Coch
Aſaph, loſt in the civil war. We have a view of this church by King.
A S. E. view of it with the biſhop's palace by Buck, 1742. A view
of the town by J. Lewis.

The life of St. Winifred, patroneſs of this county, has been frequently written. There is one in the Cotton library, Claud. A. 5. which
ſays nothing of her tranſlation to Shrewſbury. Another in the Bodleian, among Laud's MSS. L. 21. f. 140, wrote by Robert, prior of
Shrewſbury; and ſaid, in a note of Langbaine's [b], to be printed 1633.
A third ſhort life in five chapters by an anonymous compiler, taken
moſtly out of the two foregoing, in a MS. formerly belonging to Ram-
ſey abbey and afterwards to Sir James Ware, from whoſe library Mr.
Dodwell procured a copy for Dr. Humphreys bp. of St. Aſaph [c], who
had fully diſcuſſed this hiſtory. Dodwell ſaw the MS. which was
ſtolen from the bp. who afterwards recovered it, but where it is now
does not appear. Robert Salopienſis's book was abridged by John of
Tinmouth in his Sanctilogium, which Capgrave tranſcribed, as Surius,
Alford, and Creſſy copied it from him. An account of her life [d] was
annexed to the nine leſſons read on her feſtival Nov. 3. in the Sarum
breviary. There is one more in old Engliſh rhyme in the publick
library at Oxford, art. A. 72. f. 189. One J. F. a Jeſuit, tranſlated
Robert's life into Engliſh 1635, adding a preface and concluſion of his
own. This book being much ſought after, and growing ſcarce, was
reprinted 1712, with the addition of ſome modern miracles. Dr.
Fleetwood, who at that time held the ſee of St. Aſaph, and intended
to publiſh the Cotton life in Engliſh with notes, and two eſſays on the

[b] Tanner Bib. Brit. voc. Robertus Salop. He ſeems to mean J. F.'s tranſlation.
[c] See Hearne's pref. to Otterburne, p. 84.
[d] By one Medcalfe. Davies Ath. Britan. I. 284. Mr. Gale ſhewed bp. Fleetwood
another MS. life, taken moſtly out of Robert's, but ſhorter, and differing from it in
many places.

ſuperſtition

ſuperſtition of waters, and the growth of miracles, republiſhed this, under the title of " The life and miracles of St. Wenefrede, together " with her litanies; with ſome hiſtorical obſervations made thereon. " Lond. 1713." 8vo.   At the end is an extract out of the Bodleian poetical life.   Theſe were reprinted in the folio edition of the biſhop's works, Lond. 1737. p. 593—656.   Francis Place drew and etched a N. view of this well and chapel, which P. Tempeſta engraved.   Another was publiſhed by Buck 1742.   A view of the other ſide of it is in Speed's map of the county 1610, as alſo a plan of the towns of Flint and St. Aſaph.   A view of Flint by J. Lewis.

An account of the pariſh of *Hanmer* is inſerted in the Gentleman's Magazine for Nov. 1762. p. 516.

In the Philoſophical Tranſactions, N° 136, p. 895, is an account of ſome very unuſual damps in a coal mine at *Moſtyn*, by Roger Moſtyn, eſq.   In N° 462, p. 24, an account of a gold torquis, wt. 9 oz. found at *Gloddeth*, by Sir Thomas Moſtyn.

A map of *Saltney* marſh engraved by Toms.

A view of *Hawarden* caſtle and park, five miles from Cheſter, the ſeat of Sir John Wynne, bart. by Badeſlade and Toms 1740.   Another S. E. by Buck 1742.   Mr. Barret exhibited a painting of it at Spring-gardens 1765.   Buck's other views are, Baſingwerk abbey, N. W.; Rhuddlan priory, S. W. and caſtle, S. E.; Flint caſtle, S. E.; and Caergwrley caſtle, N. E.   A N. W. view of Rhuddlan caſtle by J. Boydell 1750.

MERIONETHSHIRE.

IN p. 46 of N° 208 of the Philoſophical Tranſactions is E. Lhwyd's account of a fiery exhalation at *Harlech* in Merionethſhire.

A view of Harlech caſtle by J. Lewis.   A N. W. view of it, and S. E. view of Cymner abbey by Buck 1741.

Saxton joined this and the following county in one map 1578, engraved by R. Hogenbergius, without the hundreds; added in " Merio- " nethſhire deſcribed, 1610." By J. Speed, with a plan of Merioneth.

MONT-

MONTGOMERYSHIRE.

J. LEWIS engraved a view of the town of Pool. Buck a S. view of Montgomery and S. E. of Powys caſtle. A painting of the laſt by Marlow appeared at Spring-gardens 1762.

Saxton's Montgomeryſhire deſcribed, augmented by Speed; with a plan of Montgomery.

ANGLESEA.

" DE Mona, druidum inſula antiquitati ſuæ reſtituta: Humph.
" Lluydii epiſtola ad Ortelium." Lond. 1543. 1570. 1573. 4to. and at the end of Ortelius's Theatrum. Antw. 1592. Fol. and together with Lluyd's treatiſe " De armamentario Romano," printed at the end of Sir John Pryſe's Hiſtoriæ Britannicæ defenſio. Lond. 1573. 4to. and annexed to Mr. Williams's correct edition of Lluyd's Deſcriptio Britannica. 1731.

" Mona antiqua reſtaurata: an archæological diſcourſe on the anti-
" quities natural and hiſtorical of the iſle of Angleſey, the antient ſeat
" of the Britiſh druids. In two eſſays. With an appendix, containing
" a comparative table of primitive words and the derivatives of them in
" ſeveral of the tongues of Europe; with remarks upon them. Toge-
" ther with ſome letters, and three catalogues added thereunto. 1. Of
" the members of parliament for the county of Angleſey. 2. Of the
" high ſheriffs: and, 3. Of the beneficed clergy thereof. By Henry
" Rowlands, vicar of Llanidan, in the iſle of Angleſey. Dublin 1723."
4to. As it was very incorrectly printed, and the author died before it came out, a 2d edition was publiſhed 1766 by Dr. Owen of St. Olave's, corrected both in the language and matter, with the addition of notes by the late ingenious Mr. Lewis Morris [a]. At the end of both editions are ſome letters between the author and E. Lluyd on grammatical ſub-

---

[a] Whoſe work, intitled, " Celtic Remains," ſays the editor of this book, will, when-ever publiſhed, exhibit a noble and curious ſpecimen of his great abilities and knowledge of antiquity.—The catalogues are continued, and there is added a deſcription of a druidical circle of ſtones, &c. called the Bride Stones, in *Biddulph* pariſh, Staffordſhire, communicated by Mr. Tho. Mulbon, rector of Congleton, Cheſhire, with a cut.

3   jects.

jeᴄts. Bp. Nicholſon gave an abſtraᴄt of it while in MS. in his Engliſh
hiſt. lib. chap. 2.   The ſecond eſſay clears ſome difficulties in the preceding accounts, enlarging on ſome paſſages thereof, and anſwering
ſome objeᴄtions.   According to this writer's conjeᴄtures (p. 74—77.)
we have an account of Angleſea in the writings of Hecatæus b, who
was cotemporary with Alexander the Great, and in Plutarch de Ora-
culorum defeᴄtu in the ſtory of Demetrius.   Others have contended
as earneſtly for Sweden.   " Mr. Rowlands examined many druid monuments, and deſcribed them as particularly as he could (though his
drawings are extremely ſhort of the reſt of his performance) and gives
many pertinent obſervations on them.   He underſtood the Britiſh and
and the learned languages, and has properly applied both c."

Dr. Stukeley drew and J. Harris engraved the great temple and grove
of the druids at *Frerdrews*.

In Nº 176 of the Philoſophical Tranſaᴄtions we have E. Lhwyd's
account of a ſort of paper made of linum aſbeſtinum, found in *Llan
fair yng Hornway* pariſh.   In Nº 252 his account of a ſort of coral.
In Nº 269 an antient inſcription for Kadran over the S. door of *Llan
Gadwalader* church, inſerted in Rowlands' book, pl. 9. with an exaᴄt
copy of this as well as of the others, and in the 2d edition an additional one for Pabo, pl. 10.   In Nº 369, p. 250, Mr. Rowlands's
account of the ſtocking the river *Mene* with oyſters.   Art. 45 of vol.
li. part ii. is Dr. Rutty's account of the vitriolic waters of *Almwich*.

A view of Beaumares by J. Lewis.   Holyhead collegiate church,
Penmon and Llanddwynwen priories, Beaumaris caſtle from N. and S.
by Buck 1742.

Angleſea, antiently called Mona, deſcribed, 1710. By John Speed;
with a plan of Beaumaris.

All the counties of N. Wales with Angleſea are included together in
a late map for the Britiſh Atlas.

---

b Diod. Sic. book ii. §. 47. which Rowlands quotes, book iii. §. 11. In this Hyper-
borean iſland, which, according to his deſcription of it, muſt have deſerved a place
among the Fortunate Iſlands, Hecatæus ſays the moon appeared at no great diſtance,
and full of certain irregularities like thoſe on the ſurface of the earth, εξοχαι γεωδεις:
Rowlands tranſlates this " the people could ſee the moon as if they had teleſcopes."
c Dr. Borlace pref. to antiquities of Cornwall.

I S L A N D S

ISLANDS on the coasts of England and Wales.

LELAND under the article Portuna (Portland) in his Comment on the Cygnea Cantio, promises a book De insulis Britaniæ adjacentibus.

Peck published in Desid. Cur. vol. xi. N° 12. p. 18. " The history " and antiquities of the Isle of *Man*. By James [Stanley] earl of Derby " and lord of Man, beheaded at Bolton Ap. 1, 1651. with an account " of his many troubles and losses in the civil war, and of his own pro- " ceedings in the Isle of Man during his residence there in 1643 : in- " terspersed with large and excellent advices to his son Charles lord " Strange upon many curious points." from the original MS. all in his own hand writing, in the possession of the hon. Robert Gale, esq; divided into chapters, and illustrated with contents and notes, an introduction and appendix by the editor.

, Annexed to King's Cheshire is " A short treatise of the Isle of " Man, digested into six chapters; containing, 1. A description of the " island. 2. Of the inhabitants. 3. Of the state ecclesiastical. 4. Of " the civil government. 5. Of the trade. 6. Of the strength of " the island. Illustrated with several prospects of the island. By Dan. " King:" who was only publisher. It is dedicated from Middle park, Dec. 1653, to Thomas lord Fairfax, lord of Man and of the Isles, by the author, James Chaloner, younger son of Sir Thomas Chaloner, and one of the three commissioners appointed by Fairfax to survey this island, given him by the parliament, and afterwards made by him governor of Peele castle. He was esteemed an ingenious man, and a singular lover of antiquities. He made divers collections of arms, pedigrees, seals, monuments, &c. which bp. Sanderson had the perusal of. Those for Shropshire and Staffordshire are in the Herald's office, among Vincent's papers. When the government sent to reduce the island 1660 he took poison [a]. A fair MS. of this book in Thoresby's museum was bought by Mr. Edmondson of the Herald's office. Succeeding historians of this island agree that this is the first and best account of it.

[a] Ath. Ox. II. 252.

4 I

" An

" An account of the Ifle of Man, its inhabitants, language, foil, re-
" markable curiofities, the fucceffion of its kings and bifhops down to
" the prefent time. By way of effay. With a voyage to I-Columb-kill.
" By Wm. Sacheverell, efq; late governor of Man. To which is
" added, a differtation about the Mona of Cæfar and Tacitus, and an
" account of the antient druids, &c. By Mr. Thomas Brown, addreffed
" in a letter to his learned friend Mr. A. Sellers. Lond. 1702." 12mo.
The governor is no more than editor of the papers of a gentleman who
has not been fo kind as to tranfmit his name to pofterity, and pretends
to no further fhare than wording and reforming fome few miftakes,
which it is very poffible for a ftranger to make. Sacheverell fpeaks of
fomething on the natural hiftory of this ifland, which he communicated
in a letter to his friend Mr. Addifon of Magdalen Coll. and promifes an
account of the houfe of Derby, if thefe find acceptance in the world.
The great and learned Mr. Blundell of Crofby, who prudently retired
thither during the time of the ufurpation, whereby he preferved both
his perfon and eftate, employed his leifure hours in collecting the
hiftory and antiquities of the ifland. His MS. gave pofterity the cleareft
and moft correct account thereof.

" Memoirs : containing a genealogical and hiftorical account of the
" ancient honourable houfe of Stanley, from the conqueft to the death
" of James late earl Derby, in the year 1735 : alfo a full defcription
" of the Ifle of Man. By John Seacome of Liverpool, gent. Liverp."
4to. undated. This ill printed, ill fpelt, ill written, confufed book
feems partly taken out of bifhop Rutter's MSS. who was tutor to lord
Strange and chaplain in the family at the fiege of Latham houfe, of
which he wrote an account, inferted p. 101.

In the Compleat works of Geo. Waldron, gent. late of Queen's college, Oxf. 1731. Fol. p. 90, is " a defcription of the Ifle of Man, with
fome ufeful and entertaining reflections on the laws, cuftoms, and manners of its inhabitants." I have been told it is printed feparately in 8vo.

" The hiftory and defcription of the Ifle of Man ; viz. its anti-
" quity, hiftory, law, trade, cuftoms, religion, and manners of the
" inhabitants ; animals, minerals, hufbandry, &c. and whatever elfe
" is memorable relating to that country and people : wherein are in-
" ferted many furprifing and entertaining ftories of apparitions, fairies,
" giants,

" giants, &c. believed by the inhabitants as their gospel. Collected
" from original papers and personal knowledge during near twenty
" years residence there. The 2d edit. Lond. 1745." 12mo.

The late truly primitive and amiable bishop of this island Dr. Tho.
Wilson [b], who was so universal a benefactor to his diocese, communicated to bp. Gibson the account of it inserted in his edition of the
Britannia 1722. The see having been antiently suffragan to that of
Drontheim in Norway, he applied to that metropolitan for copies of
deeds, &c. relative to it in his archives; but was informed the antient
archives themselves had been burnt.

A W. prospect of the cathedral was engraved by King.

Since this island has been annexed to the crown of Great Britain there
was published, " A short view of the present state of the Isle of Man :
" humbly submitted to the right hon. the lords of his majesty's board
" of treasury. By an impartial hand. 1767." 8vo. A proposal to re-
dress the grievances of its civil institutions to strangers, and those of its
ecclesiastical government to natives.

· " The most wonderfull and strange finding of a chayre of gold near
" the isle of *Jarsie*; with the true discourse of the death of eight
" several men, and other most rare accidents thereby proceeding.
" Lond. 1595." 4to. :

" Full relation of two journies, the one into the main land of France;
" the other into some of the adjacent islands [Jersey and Guernsey]. In 5
" books. Lond. 1656." 4to. " Survey of the estate of the two islands
" Guernsey and Jersey, with the islands depending, &c. in one book.
" Lond. 1656." 4to. printed with the former, and both published by
Dr. Heylin, because a little before a false copy of them had got abroad
under the title of " France painted to the life," stole by one Lek, a
bookseller, who fathered it in Stationers-hall on one Rich. Bignall [c].

" An account of the isle of Jersey, the greatest of those islands that
" are now the only remainder of the English dominions in France.

---

[b] He died 1755, aged 93. See his life Suppl. to Biographia Brit. where a larger one
preparing by his son, the rector of Walbrook, is referred to, and some Memoirs of him
in a letter to Dr. Cooper, the late learned physician and antiquary of Chester, in the
Chester Courant, Ap. 1, 1755.

[c] Ath. Ox. II. 283.

" With

" With a new and accurate map of the iſland. By Philip Falle, M. A. d
' rector of St. Saviour, and late deputy from the ſtates of the ſaid
' iſland to their majeſties. Lond. 1694." 12mo. This book was largely
quoted by bp. Gibſon. The map by Thomas Lempriere from a ſurvey
of Philip Dumareſq, eſq; was publiſhed by itſelf 1755. The famous
William Prynne wrote a poetical deſcription of mount Orgueil caſtle,
where he was confined two years. Mr. Falle mentions from Brown's
Travels a view of Jerſey in Häer Van Adherſhelm's cabinet at Leipſic,
deſigned by Charles II. who ſurveyed it himſelf while ſheltered in it
before Worceſter fight. Mr. Walpole ſays ᵉ, it is in the Imperial library
at Vienna. Hollar engraved four ſeveral views of Elizabeth caſtle 1650.
A picture of it by Brooking, was engraved by Le Comte.

" Cæſarea: or an account of Jerſey, the greateſt of the iſlands round
" the coaſt of England or the ancient dutchy of Normandy. With an
" appendix of records, &c. an accurate map of the iſland, and a pro-
" ſpect of Elizabeth caſtle. The 2d edition, reviſed and much aug-
" mented. By Phillip Falle, &c. To which are added in a letter to
" the author, remarks on the 19 chapter of the 2d book of Mr. Selden's
" Mare Clauſum. By Philip Morant, M. A. ᶠ 1734." 8vo.

" An hiſtorical account of *Guernſey*, from its firſt ſettlement before
" the Norman conqueſt to the preſent time: giving a particular and
" entertaining deſcription of the iſland, its produce, trade, laws, re-
" venues, privileges, religion, and government in general. To which
" is added remarks on Jerſey and the other iſlands belonging to the
" crown of Great Britain on the French coaſt. The whole interperſed
" with many new and intereſting obſervations worthy of public no-
" tice. By Thomas Dicey, gent. 1751." 12mo.

" Hiſtoire de l'erection originelle de l'avancement & augmentation
" du havre de la ville de St. Pierre port a Guerneſey; avec quelques
" remarques pour juſtifier la proprietè, ou domaine utile que les habi-
" tans de la dite iſle de Güerneſey ont au dit havre," 4to. By William

---

ᵈ He was alſo rector of Shenley, Hertfordſhire, prebend of Durham, and died 7 May,
1742, leaving his fine library to this iſland, of which he was a native. There is a MS.
intitled, " Cæſarea, or a diſcourſe of the iſland of Jerſey." MS. Harl. 5417. Falle quotes
a MS. chronique de l'iſle de Jerſey, written 1585, and a MS. relation de la priſe de
l'iſle & du chateau par les rebelles d'Angleterre, found among Sir Geo. Carteret's papers,
who was governor for K. Charles.

ᵉ Anecd. of Painting, vol. iii. p. 2.   ᶠ Native of this iſland.

Le

le Marchant de l'Hyvreuſe. Dated Longworth, Berkſhire, Feb. 8, 1755. Printed at Oxford.

"Lilium Sarnienſe; or a deſcription of the Guernſay lilly: to which "is added the botanical diſſection of the coffee berry: with figures. "By Dr. James Douglas, honorary fellow of the royal college of phy- "ſicians, London, and F. R. S. Lond. 1725." Fol. The firſt account of this beautiful flower, a native of Japan, and not of the iſland whoſe name it bears, is in James Cornutus's "Canadenſium plantarum, aliarumq; nondum editarum hiſtoria. Par. 1635." 4to. which beſides the plants of Canada includes other curious ones the author met with. John Rea mentions it in his "Complete florilege. Lond. 1665." Fol. and firſt gave it its preſent name, though that of Narciſſus or Lilio-narciſſus Japonicus is ſtill the true botanical one. Succeeding botaniſts have barely mentioned it. Dr. Douglas has entered into a minute examination of it, illuſtrated with very particular and accurate draughts.

"News from the Channel: or, the diſcovery and perfect deſcrip- "tion of the iſle of *Serke*, appertaining to the Engliſh crown, and "never before publickly diſcourſed of: truly ſetting forth the notable "ſtratagem whereby it was firſt taken, the nature of the place and "people; their government, cuſtoms, manufactures, and other par- "ticulars, no leſs neceſſary than pleaſant to be known. In a letter "from a gentleman now inhabiting there, to his kinſman in Lond. "Lond. 1673." 4to. Harleian Miſcellany, vol. 3. p. 480.

G. Vertue engraved, 1725, a plate of eighteen Gauliſh coins of ſilver gilt, found in an earthen urn bound with an iron hoop, in the iſle of Serck 1719. The firſt, with the head of Jupiter, inſcribed on the re- verſe cccc and under a horſeman P. CREPVSI, is a Roman denarius of the Crepuſian family: the reſt have a head inſcribed ATEVLA; on the reverſe a horſe lifting up his head, over him an S, under him a penta- gon or quatrefoil, the legend VLATOS g. The 7th and 17th have the head helmeted, and the inſcription on the reverſe CATOLVCA.

General and particular proſpects of the iſlands of Jerſey, Guernſey, Alderney, Sark, Aurigny, and Jethou, belonging to the Britiſh crown,

g Occo, p. 542, gives from his own cabinet ſuch ſilver medals aſcribed to Attila: but it has been doubted whether theſe and the other aſcribed to that prince are not Gauliſh. It was not the genius of the Hunns to coin their ſpoils into money.

4 in

in the Britiſh Channel, on the coaſt of France, taken on the ſpot by J. H. B. and finiſhed by C. Lempriere.

Three new charts of the iſles of Guernſey, Alderney, &c. by Dobree, 1747.

Carte nouvelle des iſles de Jerſey, Guernſey, and Aurigny, avec un memoire par M. Belin, 1757.

Carte generale des iſles Greneſay, Jerſey, Aurigny, Chauſe, &c. Dediee au roi par le Chev. Beaurain, geographe de ſa majeſte, 1757. 4 ſheets.

A map of the iſlands of Jerſey, Guernſey, Sark, Alderney, and Burhou, for the Britiſh Atlas.

" A natural and hiſtorical account of the iſlands of *Scilly*; deſcrib-" ing their ſituation, number, extent, ſoil, culture, produce, &c. " their importance to the Britiſh trade and navigation, the improve-" ments they are capable of, and directions for all ſhips to avoid " the danger of their rocks. Illuſtrated with a new and correct " draught ʰ of thoſe iſles from an actual ſurvey in the year 1744, in-" cluding the neighbouring ſeas and ſea-coaſts next the land's end of " Cornwall. To which are added the tradition of a tract of land " called Lioneſs, devoured by the ſea, formerly joining thoſe iſles and " Cornwall: of the cauſe, riſe, and diſappearance of ſome iſlands; " and, laſtly, a general account of Cornwall ⁱ. By Robert Heath, an " officer of his majeſty's forces, ſome time in garriſon at Scilly. Lond. " 1750." 8vo.

" Obſervations on the antient and preſent ſtate of the iſlands of " Scilly, and their importance to the trade of Great Britain. In a letter " to the rev. Charles Lyttelton, L. L. D. dean of Exeter, F. R. S. By " Wm. Borlaſe, M. A. F. R. S. 1756." who gave an account of the alterations which theſe iſlands have undergone as to their number, extent, and poſition, ſince the time of the antients who mention them, in a letter to the rev. Dr. Birch, Philoſophical Tranſactions, vol. xlviii. part i. p. 55. The " Petition from the iſland of Silley," printed for T. Banks 1642, and reprinted in Heath's book, p. 212, is only a banter on the times, punning on the name of the iſlands.

ʰ With a view of Agnes light-houſe and St. Mary's caſtle.
ⁱ From Carew. Mr. Heath intended a fuller deſcription of Cornwall, with a new and accurate map.

ANECDOTES

OF

Scottish Topography.

ANECDOTES

OF

SCOTTISH Topography.

WHEN I undertake to give a lift of topographical writers for Scotland I bear in mind the great Camden's caution at the beginning of his account of it, where he modeftly profeffes to have but a flight acquaintance with it.　Sir Robert Sibbald firft began an " Account of the writers antient and modern, printed and MS. which treat of the defcription of North Britain called Scotland, as it was of old, and is now at prefent, with a catalogue of the maps, and profpects, and figures of the antient monuments thereof, fuch as have come to his hands, in feveral languages," printed at Edinb. 1710 [a]; but he ends foon, and refers to the bifhop of Carlifle's Scots Library.　It is no eafy matter to fill up the firft lineaments of his lordfhip's book.　Whether it be for want of materials or application, the nationality of our northern neighbours fuffers the natural and artificial face of their country to lie as undefcribed as their poverty once left it unimproved and unadorned.　The Irifh, their progenitors, have exerted themfelves more to fearch out their antiquities.　Attentive to humanize themfelves and mankind we fee the Scots a nation of philofophers, without an antiquary to lay open to us their original ftate.　Are we to reproach our princes that have left fo little for one to folace himfelf with ?　Shall we fay that the nation, engaged in every kind of war

---

[a] This catalogue is inferted in " A collection of feveral treatifes in folio, concerning " Scotland, as it was of old, and alfo in later times.　By Sir Rob. Sibbald, M.D. Edinb. " 1739." fold feparately or bound together by the bookfellers in Edinburgh and Glafgow. His other pieces in this collection will be fpecified in their feveral departments.

and hoſtility, had no time for inveſtigating thoſe noble monuments their anceſtors in the ſame diſtracted ſtate found time to erect ? Or ſhall we accept Sir Robert Sibbald's apology [b], that " the troubles which aroſe in this country upon the change of religion made his countrymen fall behind others in the ſtudy of antient actions and exploits, while in other parts of learning they yielded to few ?"—Prudes in divinity, metaphyſicians in philoſophy, novices in philology, they aſpire above the ruſt of antiquarian ſcience. By principle averſe to religious magnificence, the ſplendor of the earlier church moulders away unnoticed. Their artiſts, ſeeking fame in England, forget what ſubjects they leave behind them, which few of our countrymen have the hardineſs to viſit: and we have as few ſubjects of the pencil or graver from the N. ſide of the Tweed as if the marches were ſtill infeſted by marauders.

Roman Geography of Scotland.

AGRICOLA's progreſs deſcribed by Tacitus's pen throws great light on the antient geography of Britain. That author's relation of his father-in-law's exploits takes in ſo large a detail of Roman tranſactions in Scotland, that we may place it at the head of a catalogue of topographical writers for this part of the Britiſh dominions. William Barclay, L. L. D. native of this country and profeſſor of law at Pont-a-Mouſſon in Lorrain, where Lipſius ſtudied under him, illuſtrated it with a commentary under the title of " Gul. Barclaii ex 'vita Julii Agricolæ, auctore genero, præmetia [c]." Lipſius highly valued this performance, now extremely ſcarce; of which a few paſſages ſerve as notes to the variorum edition of Tacitus. Dempſter [d] ſeems to have expected greater accuracy from his countryman ; but bp. Nicholſon thinks him ſufficiently excuſed by his abſence from Scotland.

Sir Robert Sibbald, who, as he ſays himſelf [e], firſt broke the ice in the way of writing the antiquities of his country, illuſtrated its Roman hiſtory in the following eſſays.

[b] Pref. to Portus, &c. Tacitus, calls him *John.*
[c] Nich. Sc. hiſt. Lib. p. 1. 2. Gronovius pref. to
[d] Hiſt. Ec. Scot. p. 120.
[e] Pref. to hiſt. inq.

" In-

" Introductio ad historiam rerum a Romanis gestarum in ea borealis
" Britanniæ parte quæ ultra murum Picticum est: in qua veterum in
" hac plaga incolarum nomina & sedes explicantur. Cum tabula ænea
" Britanniæ integræ & Hiberniæ, & una hujus plagæ borealis juxta
" rectum ejus situm; & figura castri Romani Iernensis. Edinb. 1706."
Fol. To this is annexed " Specimen glossarii, de populis & locis
" Britanniæ borealis in explicatione locorum quorundam difficilium
" apud scriptores veteres," in nine sections, with an appendix of antient historians, and another of some places in Buchanan. He intended
to continue this glossary to the times succeeding the Roman, and speaks
of copper plates in it, which do not appear.

" Historical inquiries concerning the Roman monuments and anti-
" quities in the north part of Britain called Scotland: in which there
" is an account of the Roman wall, ports, colonies, and forts, temples,
" altars, sepulchres, and military ways in that country; and of the
" Roman forces lodged there, from the vestiges and inscriptions yet
" remaining; and from the urns, medals, measures, and buckles and
" arms, and such like antiquities found there: with copper cuts of the
" most remarkable of them. Edinb. 1707." Fol.

" Miscellanea quædam eruditæ antiquitatis, qu ad borealem Bri-
" tanniæ majoris partem pertinent, inquibus loci quidam historico-
" rum, variaq. monumenta antiqua illustrantur. Cura Rob. Sibbaldi,
" M. D. eq. aur. Edinb. 1710." Fol. with an appendix about the
friths Bodotria and Tay, and their islands. Of the 11 sections of this
very miscellaneous work the two first relate to the history of Orrok, and
the antiquities found in a cairne there and in other places, with three
cuts; the 3d treats of Cæsar's root called *Chara*, the *Karemile* of the
highlands; the 4th, de elogiis medicinæ indigenæ; the 5th, of fossils,
represented in plate 2; the 6th, of magic, and the druids; the 7th, of
marine animals; the 8th, of the Nautilus; in the 9th, Sir R. Gordon
clears up the vulgar error about the Barnacles; the 10th and 11th are
medical exercitations; the 12th, an essay on the antient temples, followed by another 11th section on medical subjects.

" Commentarius in Julii Agricolæ expeditiones 3. 4. 5. 6. 7. in vita
" ejus, per C. Tacitum generum ejus, descriptas; & in boreali Britan-

4 K 2   " niæ

" niæ parte, quæ Scotia dicitur, geftas : in quo, ex veftigiis caftrorum
" & caftellorum Romanorum, monumentifq. antiquis ibi repertis, tex-
" tus Taciti illuftrantur. Edinb. 1711." Fol.   To this is annexed
" Series rerum a Romanis poft avocatum Agricolam, in Britannia,
" boreali, geftarum f."

" Portus, coloniæ & caftella Romana ad Bodotriam & Taum ; or
" conjectures concerning the Roman ports, colonies and forts on the
" firths, taken from their veftigies and the antiquities found near
" them.   In 3 fections : the 1ft concerning thefe upon the N. coaft
" of Forth ; the 2d concerning thefe upon the S. coaft of Tay ; the 3d
" concerning thefe upon the N. coaft of Tay. Edinb. 1711." Fol.

Sir Robert in his Commentarius takes in the whole ifland, together
with Ireland and the adjacent ifles, not forgetting Thule.   He took
an actual furvey of the fcenes of action defcribed by the Roman hiftorians, and defcribes the monuments remaining.   Mr. Gordon however charges him ᵍ with wrefting in his work the genuine fenfe of
Tacitus and other Roman writers, and contradicting the text ; carrying people and ftations from England to Scotland.

Scarce any two editions of thefe printed pieces agree.   He left in MS.
A work " De Britannicis infulis & Britannia in genere," in 2 books.
" Book i. §. 1. De Britannicis infulis in genere. §. 2. De Britannia in
genere.   §. 3. De origine gentium Britannicarum. §. 4. De exteris qui
Britanniam frequentarint.   Book ii. De divifione Britanniæ in partes
apud authores.   De Albania five Scotia antiqua. §. 1. De Albaniæ
regionibus & infulis, & de populis Albaniæ. §. 2. De origine incolarum Albaniæ & moribus eorum.   Book iii. De Scotia antiqua fpeci-
alius."

" Conjectanea quædam de primis infularum Britannicarum colonis,
" ex fcriptoribus antiquis Græcis & Latinis haufta, de quibus docti
" judicent."

" Caledonia five Scotia antiqua duobus libris.   I. De infulis Britan-
" nicis & de Britannia citeriore feu meridionali intra Hadriani murum.
" II. De ea parte Britanniæ quæ ultra murum Hadriani erat."

---

f The Introductio, Mifcellanea, and Commentarius, with their appendages, and the
Vindiciæ, have one common title of " Tractatus Varii. Edinb. 1711." Fol.

ᵍ It. Sept. p. 43—46. where he makes an appendix to his 4th chap to confute him.

" Cor-

" Cornelii Taciti Britannia, five commentarius in ea quæ a Tacito.
" in fuis fcriptis de Britannia & Britannicis infulis adducuntur."

" Exercitationes hiftoricæ in ea quæ apud Dionem & Herodianum
" aliofq. hiftoricos veteres referuntur de geftis Severi imp. ejufdemq.
" filii Ant. Caracallæ in feptentrionali Britanniæ parte." To which is
added, " Series rerum a Romanis in Britannia geftarum per D. Bucha-
" nanum collecta:" and the fame in chronological order by R. Maule,
and enlarged and continued by Sir Robert. The titles of the feveral
chapters may be feen in his account of the Scottifh writers, and of
thofe of the Taciti Britannia in Nicholfon, p. 3.

Mercator and Sir Robert Gordon in his Theatrum Scotiæ, where he
gives a map of Roman Scotland with notes [h], obferve of Ptolomy [i], that
his account of the antient ftate of Scotland is very juft and accurate if
we change the points of his compafs, and turn the eaft to the north [k].
D. Buchanan and R. Maule [m] did their countrymen the honour to derive
Ptolomy's names from the Hebrew and Celtic. Bp. Nicholfon mentions fome MS. conjectures of Sir Rob. Sibbald's on Ptolomy's Scotland.
Sir John Cunningham, a learned lawyer and antiquary, left fome notes
on this part of Antoninus's Itinerary, which the bifhop fuppofes were in
the hands of his fon Sir William ; but Mr. Gordon could not get a fight
of them.

As Mr. Horfley illuftrated the Roman antiquities of the whole ifland,
Alexander Gordon had before treated of fuch as remain in this part
of it in his " Itinerarium feptentrionale: or a journey through moft of
" the counties of Scotland, and thofe in the N. of England. In two
" parts. Part I. containing an account of all the monuments of Ro-
" man antiquity found and collected in that journey, and exhibited in
" order to illuftrate the Roman hiftory in thefe parts of Britain, from
" the firft invafion by J. Cæfar till J. Agricola's march into Caledonia,

[h] Thefe laft are inferted in Sibbald's Introductio, c. 2.

[i] Honeft Hector Boethius has invented or propagated a pretty legend to give authority
to this part of Ptolomy's Geography, and the good bifhop of Carlifle thought it worth
repeating.

Mr. Pegge in the Gentleman's Magazine, for Dec. 1759, p. 571, helps out the
monk of Ravenna in the fame way.

[i] Preface to Knox's Hiftory, and his notes inferted in Sibbald's Introductio, c. 3.

[m] De Antiq. Gentis Scot. MS. Gordon often quotes him.

" in

" in the reign of Vespasian, and thence more fully to their last aban-
" doning the island, in the reign of Theodosius, jun. with a particular
" description of the Roman walls in Cumberland, Northumberland,
" and Scotland, &c. &c. Part II. An account of the Danish invasions
" on Scotland, and of the monuments erected there, on the different
" defeats of that people. With other curious remains of antiquity never
" before communicated to the publick : the whole illustrated with 66
" copper plates. Lond. 1726." Fol. He made a laborious progress
through almost every part of Scotland for three years successively. His
map of Scotland, shewing the principal Roman works between Tyne and
Tay, is the work of James Mackay. At the end of the whole is an advertisement purporting that Mr. Gordon designed in a few days to publish
proposals for engraving by subscription a compleat view of the Roman
walls in Britain, with those of the emperors Hadrian and Severus in
Cumberland and Northumberland, in a large map near 14 feet by 6 ;
and that of Antoninus Pius in Scotland in another map of 6 feet by 4,
from actual geometrical surveys : the height, thickness, and number
of courses of stones, breadth and depth of the ditches, height and
breadth of the cespititious ramparts, and the appearance of the military
ways, stations, towers, &c. and a compleat perspective view of the
country on both sides : with exact draughts of the inscriptions, &c.
found there, and an English and Latin description at the foot of each
map. As he complains of want of sufficient encouragement to his
book, I am afraid he met with none to his survey, which certainly
was a noble design. Some lovers of antiquity in Holland printing
a Latin translation of his Itinerary about 1730, applied to the author
for additions and corrections ; which he afterwards published in
English 1732. Fol. containing several dissertations on and descriptions
of Roman antiquities discovered in Scotland ⁿ since the publishing the
said Itinerary ; together with observations on other ancient monuments
found in the north of England ᵒ

ᵃ At Middleby.
ᵒ Two inscriptions in Durham library found at Lanchester, illustrated in the Philosophical Transactions by Hunter and Gale.

General

General Geography of Scotland.

IN the king of France's library, MS. Colbert. Nº 3120, is a kind of description of Albany, or Scotland N. of the friths of Clyde and Forth, intitled, " De situ Albaniæ quæ in se figuram hominis habet, quomodo fuit primitus in 7 regionibus divisa, quibusq, nominibus antiquitus sit vocata, & a quibus inhabitata." From the author's assuring his readers that he had part of his information from Andrew bishop of Caithness, who died 1115, it appears to have been wrote about the 12th century. Mr. Innes [a] thinks there is ground to believe it the work of Giraldus Cambrensis, who somewhere observes that he promised a description of Albany or Scotland, and bp. Andrew may have seen him in England in the time of king David, or his grandchildren Malcolm or William. Several passages of it are quoted word for word in Higden's Polychronicon (Ed. Gale, p. 185. 209.) as from Giraldus Cambrensis, now lost; and his calling the bishop Andreas *natione Scotus*, and other expressions prove the author no Scotsman. Camden in the last edition of his description of Scotland gives an extract from it, calling it " a little antient book of the division of Scotland, in lord Burleigh's library:" he quotes also a MS. " De divisione Scotiæ." Q. If the same

Among Ashmole's MSS. is an English description of Scotland, 1641, and among Brian Twyne's in the same museum a MS. called " Mirabilia " Cornubiæ, Hiberniæ, Angliæ, Scotiæ, & Walliæ [b]."

Most of the writers of the Scottish history have prefixed geographical descriptions of the country to their books. The earliest of these is Hector Boethius, whose history was published in the original Latin Paris, ap. Bad. Asc. 1526. Fol. and again there with the addition of an 18th and part of the 19th books by Ferrier. 1574. Fol. A translation of it into Scotch, or rather an abridgement, by John Bellenden, archdeacon of Murray, 1536, was " imprentet in Edinburgh by Thomas Da-

---

[a] " Critical essays on the ancient inhabitants of the northern parts of Britain or Scot-
" land: containing an account of the Romans; of the Britains betwixt the walls; of the
" Caledonians, or Picts; and particularly of the Scots: with an appendix of antient MS.
" pieces. Lond. 1729." 2 vols. 8vo.
Nich. p. 23, Cat. MSS. Ang. tom. i. p. i. 8294, and p. ii. 1730.

vidſon dwelling fornens the Fryere Wynde c." It was tranſlated from both together into Engliſh by Wm. Harriſon, who dying before it was finiſhed, it was enlarged from other authors and completed by F. Thinn, and printed in the firſt volume of Hollinſhed's Chronicle. Sir Robert Sibbald had an old French abridgment of Boethius by Jehan Deſmontier, eſcuyer, intitled, " Summaire de l'origine, deſcription, & merveills d'Eſ-coſſe, avec une petite cronique des roys dudict pays juſques a ce temps. Par. 1538." 8vo Boethius profeſſes great attention to the natural hiſtory; but many of his ſtories may match with the late bp. of Berghen's. Bp. Leſley has corrected ſome of his extravagancies, and adopted others in his deſcription prefixed to his work " De origine, moribus, & rebus " geſtis Scotorum a primordio gentis ad an. 1562. Rom. 1578." 4to.

" Fordun in his 2d book, c. 7—11. has a deſcription which favour-eth of the rudeneſs and drineſs of the writers of that age." Sibbald.

George Buchanan, who has followed the method of the two former hiſtorians, writes with more probability as well as elegance. The two firſt books of his hiſtory are taken up in a deſcription of the ſeveral pro-vinces; and the third is a collection of the Roman accounts of Scot-land. This deſcription was turned into elegant verſe, with good digreſ-ſions, by Andrew Melvin, in his " Scotiæ Topographia," prefixed to the edition of Pont's maps 1655 d. David Buchanan wrote ſeveral ſhort diſ-courſes concerning the antiquities and chorography of Scotland, which Nicholſon ſays were in ſafe cuſtody, in bundles of looſe papers, Latin and Engliſh. Sibbald ſpeaks of them as digeſted into one volume, which he had ſeen in MS. both in Latin and his vulgar language e.

Camden profeſſes only to have run over Scotland f. His account of it was altered in different editions as he received information, and was publiſhed ſeparately from his Britannia by Sir James Dalrymple, bart. clerk of the council, parliament, and ſeſſions. Edinb. 1695. 8vo. but I have not met with it. Beſides the inſertion of many remarks and corrections the editor has continued and enlarged the catalogue of the nobility, and added liſts of the peers, members of parliament, religi-

---

c Nich. p. 109.   d Ib. p. 18.   e Catalogue, p. 5.   Nich. p. 16.
f He refers to ſome curious obſervations on it by one Servatius Riehelius, a Sileſian gentleman, who copied ſome inſcriptions for him.   Stirlingſhire.

4

ous houfes, provincial affemblies, &c. g. A fheet of remarks on Camden by Sir Rob. Gordon was inferted in Bleau's Theatrum Scotiæ, and Sir Rob. Sibbald fent large additions to Gibfon's firft edition, which are fpecified in Sir Robert's catalogue, p. 5.

D. Hume, who from the place of his birth ftiled himfelf Theagrius, wrote " Camdenea five examen nonullorum, a Gul. Camdeno " in Britannia fua pofitorum, præcipue quæ ad irrifionem Scoticæ " gentis pertinent, & eorum & Pictorum falfam originem," in feven chapters. Bp. Nicholfon calls this a fpirited and elegant MS. examination of Camden's mifreprefentations and fneers on the Scots and Picts. Not long after this W. Drummond of Hathornden wrote remarks on fome antient names in which he differed from Camden, intitled, " Nuntius Scoto-Britannus h." which Sir R. Sibbald thinks was the firft draught of his " Pair of fpectacles for Camden to look with upon N. " Britain." Sir R. Gordon alfo refuted Camden in a fheet of Bleau's Theatrum Scotiæ, intitled, " Adnotata ad Scotorum antiquitatem eor- " umq. in Britannia ex Hibernia alterum trajectum, duce Reuthari, " quem Beda Reudam vocat."

" Index locorum, nominum propriorum, gentilitium, vocumq; diffi- " ciliorum quæ in Latinis Scotorum hiftoriis occurrunt. Edinb. 1664." 8vo. By Dr. Chriftopher Irwin, mentioned by Nicholfon as deferving a new impreffion, which it feems to have had in " Hiftoriæ Scoticæ " nomenclatura Latino-vernacula : multis flofculis, ex antiquis Albino- " rum monumentis, & lingua Galeciorum prifca decerptis, adfperfa.; " in gratiam eorum qui Scotorum nomen & veritatis·numen colunt, " Chriftophorus Irwinus, abs Bon-Bofco, aufpice fummo numine, " concinnavit; & Edinbruchii cal. Jan. 1682. imprimi curavit." 12mo.

Andrew Sympfon, a learned epifcopal divine at Edinburgh, drew up a " Villare Scoticum," in imitation of Spelman's Villare Anglicanum ; and an account of the patrons of all the parochial benefices i.

---

g Nich. p. 13. Sir Robert borrowed this title for his work on the antiquities of his country: " Nuncius Scoto-Britannus de defcriptione Scotiæ antiquæ & modernæ. Edinb. " 1683." Fol.

h Nich. p. 14. i Nich. p. 22.

" De-

" Defcrizione del regno di Scozia & delle ifole fue adjacenti da Pa-
" truccio Ubaldini. Antv. 1586." [k]   Ubaldini was a fkilful writer and
illuminator, and perhaps tranflated this from the Latin MS. below [l].

" A modern account of Scotland : being an exact defcription of the
" country, and a true character of the people and their manners.
" Written from thence by an Englifh gentleman. Printed in the year
" 1670." 4to. reprinted in the Harleian Mifcellany, vol. vii. p. 121.
Satyrical [m].

" Scotiæ indiculum ; or the prefent ftate of Scotland ; together with
" divers reflections on the antient ftate thereof. By A. M. Philopatris.
" 1682." 12mo.

Among bp. Corbett's poems. Lond. 1672. 12mo. is a famous one
called " Iter boreale."

" A journey thro' Scotland 1723." 8vo. was the work of J. Macky,
a native, and author of the Journey thro' England before mentioned.

Sir Robert Gordon had notes on feveral parts of the *Highlands* by a
native [n]. " A full defcription of the Highlands of Scotland ; its fitu-
" ation and produce, the manners and cuftoms of the natives, &c. To
" which is annexed a fcheme for making the moft difaffected among
" them become zealoufly affected to his reigning majefty. By John
" Campbell. Lond. 1751." 8vo.

" Letters from a gentleman in the north of Scotland to his friend in
" London ; containing a defcription of a capital town in that northern
" country, with an account of many uncommon cuftoms of the inha-
" bitants : likewife an account of the Highlands, with the cuftoms
" and manners of the Highlanders. To which is added, a letter re-
" lating to the military ways among the mountains began in the year
" 1726. The whole interfperfed with facts and circumftances intirely
" new to the generality of people in England, and little known in the
" fouthern parts of Scotland. In 2 vols. Lond. 1759." 8vo. the 2d edit.

Exact plans of his majefty's great roads thro' the Highlands by And.
Rutherford, 1745.

[k] So Nich. p. 16. but Rawlinfon's Method of ftudying hiftory dates it Ant. 1588. Fol.
[l] In the king's library, 13 A. VIII. in the Britifh Mufeum, is Scotiæ defcriptio a Dei-
donenfi quodam facto, A. D. 1550. & per Petruccium Ubaldinum tranfcripta A, 1576.
[m] Quære, If the *waggifh* defcription of Scotland by Tho. Kirk, efq; of Cookridge
twice printed ? Thorefby had fome of his *more folid* obfervations in his Journal thro'
moft parts of Scotland 1677. Muf. Thorefb. N° 262. .   [n] Nich. p. 20.

Charts.

Charts.

Nich. d'Arville's " Defcription de l'ifle & royaume d'Efcoffe, &
des Hebrides, & des Orchades," was printed among " Mifcel-
" lanea antiqua, containing firft the life and death of king James the
" Vth of Scotland, from the French, &c. Lond. 1710." 12mo. under
the title of the " Navigation of king James V. round Scotland, the
" Orkney ifles, and the Hebrids or Weftern Ifles, under the conduct
" of that excellent pilot Alex. Lindfay; methodized by N. d'Arville,
" the chief cofmographer to the French king: in which is the diftances
" of the havens; the dangers, and how to avoid them; the foundings,
" courfes, the times of full fea, and the courfes of the tides, &c. from
" the mouth of the Humber to Carlifle:. done from the French origi-
" nal, printed at Paris 1583."   Nicholas was invited to England 1546
by our admiral lord Dudley, and by order of Henry II of France went
the year following with 16 galleys, commanded by Stroza, prior of
Capua, and admiral of all the galleys of France, to befiege the caftle of
St. Andrews, held by Beaton's murderers.   James failed with five fhips
of war to Orkney, Sky, and Lewis, where he fettled garrifons, and
feized fome of their chiefs: and after he had founded the remoteft
rocks of his kingdom, he was driven by ftrefs of weather to St. Ninian's
near Whitehorn in Galloway a.   The hydro-graphical chart of the
Scotch coaft and iflands; drawn by Nicholas from this navigation, in
the Paris edition, is omitted in this.   Mr. Adair re-engraved it 1688.
Among the Harleian MSS. Nº 3996, is a very neat 4to one on vellum,
with printed fchemes, intitled, " Navigation de la mer, avec les havres,
" raddes, profondites, dangers, & approchemens des coftes de depuis
" le fleuve Humbre nort; coutoyant alentour du royaulme d'Efcoffe
" tirant aux iles Orchades & Hebrides jufques a la mulle de Gallouuay
" & la riviere de Soluay, premierement compofé par Alex. Lyndefay,
" Efcoffois foubs le commandement du roy d'Efcoffe Jaques cinquiefme
" du nom, & depuis remife en fon entier, avec augmentation et illuf-
" tration de plufieurs figures & defcriptions tres neceffaires pour la navi-

a Drummond's Hift. of Scotland, p. 309.

4 L 2   " gation,

" gation, par Nicholas du Nicholay du Daulphine : geographe du roi. This feems to be d'Arville's under another name. Hearne b fays, the Englifh were formerly fo uncivilized and malicious as to give the name of *hell* to the northern ocean ; by which character it is expreffed in an old very odd map in the Bodleian library.

In Ortelius' Geography is an exact draught of the fea coaft of Scotland by Humphrey Lhuyd, Apr. 5, 1586 c.

A defcription of the fea coafts and iflands of Scotland, with large and exact maps for the ufe of feamen. By John Adair : the 1ft part defcribing the whole eaft coaft from the borders northward to Buchannefs ; with five charts : the 2d was to contain a journal of his voyage to the N. and W. iflands, 1698 ; with his hiftorical and mathematical account of the Roman wall : and the maps were very forward d.

A map of the N. coaft of Britain from Row Stoir of Affynt to Wich in Caithnefs, by a geometrical furvey ; with the harbours, rocks, and an account of the tides in the Pentland firth. Done at the defire of the Philofophical Society at Edinburgh. By Alexander Bryce.

Maps.

IN the Bodleian library, Arch Seld. B. 26. is a beautiful MS. of Harding's Chronicle, at the end of which is a fhort profe defcription of Scotland, with a map, which has but few names, and is filled up with figures of cities and towns e. There is fuch another copy among the Harleian MSS. with a map of Scotland from Carlifle to the water of Tay, and another from thence to Sutherland and Caithnefs. Thefe muft take precedence of all other maps of this kingdom.

The map of Scotland by bifhop Lefley, afterwards abridged for his Hiftory, rank as the firft printed one. It has the bifhop's and the royal arms, and fome account of the country.

A map of the borders of the two kingdoms, taking in feveral whole counties in both, was made on James's acceffion to the Englifh crown : and foon after came out Speed's and Camden's maps of Scotland. The

---

b Notæ in Gul. Neub. p. 749.   c Ames's Hift. of Print p. 580.   d Nich. p. 22. Chapters 18, 19, 20, of J. Marr s navigation in coafting. Aberd. 1683. 8vo. refpect the north feas. Ib. p. 21.   e Cat. MSS. Ang. tom. i. p. 1. Nº 3356. Index to Hearne's Alfred.   Tanner, B. B. p. 378. Lett. to Thorefby. Lel. Itin. p. 81.

firft

firſt is only a general one 1612, with the yles of Orknay at the corner: and a ſhort account at the back. The two in the late editions of Camden are by Andrew Johnſton.

Sir Robert Gordon made an excellent map of Scotland, with its iſles, which he calls " Scotia antiqua, qualis priſcis temporibus, Romanis " præſertim, cognita fuit, quam in lucem eruere conabatur Rob. Gor- " donius a Straloch, M.CVI.LIII." In this he has both the antient and modern names of the counties and people, and annotations on Ptolomy's map. He has alſo given us a map of Albion and Ireland, intitled, " Inſulæ Albion & Hibernia, cum minoribus adjacentibus," and a diſſertation on Thule, where he gives his opinion what the Romans underſtood by the name. This is much the ſame which Bertius gives in his Theatrum geographiæ veteris, where is Ortelius's Britannicarum inſularum typus. There is a later deſcription of our iſlands by Orteiius in Hornius.

The firſt county maps taken with any exactneſs were thoſe by Timothy Pont [f], a complete mathematician, and the firſt projector of a Scotch Atlas. At the expence of Sir John Scot of Scots-Tarvet, director of the Chancery, he perſonally ſurveyed all the counties and iſlands, making draughts on the ſpot, and adding curſory obſervations on the monuments of antiquity and other curioſities [g]. His maps and papers, wanting only the finiſhing hand, were ſent after his death to Sir Robert Gordon of Stralogh, who with his ſon James completed the ſurvey, by the aſſiſtance of Sir John Scot. Theſe 46 maps make the Theatrum Scotiæ inſerted in Bleau's Atlas. Amſt. 1662. Fol. Some of the deſcriptions annexed were drawn up by Sir Robert: others after his deceaſe by D Buchanan. The moſt complete deſcription that Pont left was of Cunningham, of which Sibbald publiſhed an abſtract in his Catalogue of Scotch writers. The firſt publiſher of this Theatre 1655, dedicated it to Cromwell, and omitted ſome of the beſt deſcriptions (particularly thoſe of Aberdeenſhire and Bamf) prefixing G. Buchanan's Dialogue de jure regni ; 19 diſcourſes relating to the general ſtate of the

[f] Son of an eminent divine and lawyer Robert Pont.

[g] From his papers and draught Sir Rob. Sibbald communicated the additional deſcription of the Roman wall in Scotland at the end of Camden. Pont took notes of all the Roman coins, inſcriptions, and other monuments, he met with ; alſo of antient and modern buildings, and natural productions.

kingdom,

kingdom, of which fee Nicholfon, p. 18, precede the maps. Thofe that relate to our fubject are Melvin's Scotiæ topographia; R. Gordon's differtation on Thule: Remarks on a map of old.Scotland; G. Buchanan's defcription in his firft book; and another defcription. Sir Robert Gordon while engaged in this work iffued out queries to the curious in the feveral counties; the anfwers h to which, together with fundry tracts on the Scottifh antiquities, came into Sir R. Sibbald's hands, who had thoughts of communicating to the world their mofb interefting contents.

Sir R. Sibbald had feveral new maps engraved for his works, many of them by Adair i.

The north part of Great Britain. By H. Moll, 1714.

Ditto, two fheets, with views of towns.

A new and exact map of Scotland or N. Britain defcribed, by N. Sanfon, geographer to the French king, tranflated into Englifh at the expence of H. Overton of London, mapfeller, 2 fheets.

A new and correct map of Scotland, drawn from particular furveys made by order of the late duke of Cumberland, &c. divided into fbires, &c. engraved by J. Proctor.

A new map of N. Britain with the iflands thereunto belonging, done from fome late furveys of part of the E. and W. coafts, and from modern accounts of the country and other authorities mentioned in the explanation annexed. By J. Cowley, 1734.

A complete and exact map of the *Lothians*; containing the fhires of Edinburgh, Haddington, and Llinlithgow; with a view of the country from Stirlingfhire to Berwickfhire, in which is marked out the different marches of the rebels and their encampments in thefe counties, being the fulleft and moft particular of any extant: furveyed by Mr. Adair, with fome improvements by a gentleman.

A map of E. Lothian, furveyed by Mr. J. Adair, F. R. S. Mid-Lothian and W. Lothian, by the fame.

A new and correct map of the Lothians from Mr. Adam's obfervations, by John Elphinfton, 1745.

A new and correct Mercator's map of N. Britain, carefully copied from the lateft furveys and maps, with obfervations, by John Elphinftone, efq;

h See Nich. p. 20.   i Nich. p. 25.

principal

principal engineer, 1745. This firft attempt to fettle the geography of Scotland was feverely criticized k by Mr. Jefferys, who propofed, 1746, to engrave, on one fheet of imperial paper, a new map of Scotland, correctly drawn from Mr. Adair's and other later furveys, divided into the proper fhires as they return members to parliament, purfuant to the act of union; with the cities, parliament burghs, prefbyteries, and market towns, which are omitted in all maps yet extant, diftinctly inferted in proper characters; with the king's roads, and a complete lift of all the fhires and burghs, with the number of their reprefentatives; alfo of the provincial fynods, and prefbyteries of the church of Scotland, 1746. To have been delivered in two months.

A general map of Scotland and iflands thereto belonging, from new furveys, the fhires properly divided and fubdivided, the forts lately erected, and roads of communication or military ways carried on by his majefty's command, the times when and places where the moft memorable battles have been fought; likewife the Roman camps, forts, walls, and military ways, the Danifh camps and forts: alfo the feats of the nobility in each fhire diftinguifhed, with feveral other remarkable places that occur in the hiftories of Scotland. By James Dorret, landfurveyor. In four fheets: and reduced, in two and one. Another in one fheet, taken from this.

" Geographia Scotiæ; being a new and correct map of all the coun
" ties and iflands in the kingdom of Scotland; containing the univer
" fities, cities, prefbytery and market towns, rivers, lochs, roads, &c.

k " The projection of a land map fhould certainly be drawn according to the gradual declenfion of the meridians; but Mr. Elphinfton's being made on Mercator's projection, which was defigned merely for fea charts, the whole furface of Scotland is diftorted. and the geography needlefsly confounded. His longitude from Fero and Paris are both computed wrong; the former is a degree too much, and the latter a degree too little: and inftead of making a fcale for every degree, which in that map was quite neceffary, he has inferted none a all. The making his longitude from Paris preferably to London, is a grofs abfurdity in a map reprefenting part of an ifland where London is the metropolis. He difcovers exceffive ignorance of his native country, for among the fhires are omitted Huddington, Edinburgh, Lithgo, Lanerk, Selkirk, Forfar, Kincardin, and Elgin. Nairn is wrong underftood. Roxburghfhire is blundered into Selkirkfhire: many burghs and prefbyteries are forgot, and above fixty rivers left namelefs, particularly Tweed, Tyne, Leith, Amond, Carron, Avon, Forth, Ila, Findorn, Loffie, Navern, Strath, Lauder, Yarrow, Teviot, Annan, Jed, Nith, Etterick, Dun, Dee, Fleet, Girvin, Air, Irwin, Gree, Cart, &c. Nairn is falfly put for Findorn, and the great river Efk for another; with many other faults." Jefferys's propofals.

" with

" with a general map of the whole kingdom, from the lateſt obſerva-
" tions. Lond. 1746." 4to. 1756. 12mo. By T. Kitchin.

A new and accurate map of Scotland or N. Britain, drawn from
ſurveys and the moſt approved maps and charts, exhibiting the king's
roads, &c. By Em. Bowen.

Propoſals for a new ſet of maps of Scotland were advertiſed about
1764 by one Trale; but I believe met with no ſucceſs.

Views.

" THeatrum Scotiæ, containing the proſpects of their majeſties
" caſtles and palaces: together with thoſe of the moſt conſidera-
" ble towns and colleges: the ruins of many ancient abbeys, churches,
" monaſteries, and convents within the ſaid kingdom, all curiouſly en-
" graved on [57] copper plates, with a ſhort deſcription of each place
" by John Slezer, captain of the artillery company and ſurveyor of their
" majeſty's ſtores and magazines in the kingdom of Scotland. Lond.
" 1693." Fol. The deſcriptions drawn up by Sir R. Sibbald were intended to be publiſhed in Latin, but were inaccurately tranſlated into
Engliſh without leave or acknowlegement of the author. To each is
prefixed the arms of the nobleman to whom they were dedicated.
Slezer intended proſpects of all the conſiderable places in Scotland,
in ſeveral volumes, which, as he has executed this, would have been
a valuable work; but he ſeems to have failed of encouragement. Theſe
were republiſhed in the ſame ſize 1718: but as both editions are become ſcarce, I ſhall ſpecify the views in their reſpective counties.

In 1766 were-publiſhed propoſals for printing by ſubſcription, in two
large volumes folio, the plans, elevations, and ſections, of the principal
regular buildings in Scotland, together with ſeveral new deſigns, done
for ſome of the noblemen and gentlemen of that country. To which
will be added the particular ſections of the beſt rooms built in Scotland:
alſo ſome deſigns of buildings for the decoration of parks and gardens.
By the late William Adam, eſq; architect, and continued by his ſon John
Adam, eſq; In 160 copper plates, with 200 folio pages of engravings,
and a deſcription or explanation of the plates in Engliſh and French,
after the manner of Campbell's Vitruvius.

Eccleſiaſtical

Ecclefiaftical Topography.

JOhn Skene, in his book De verborum fignificatione, Edinb. 1597, Fol. and Lond. 1641. 4to. at the end of the ftatutes, mentions an old taxation of benefices called Bagimont, taken by a legate temp. Alexander III. which bp. Nicolfon a fixes to the time of Ed. I. There is a tranfcript of it, with a lift of the greater benefices as affeffed 1561, and a taxation roll of abbey lands 1630, Harl. MS. 4613. The monafteries of Scotland have had far lefs care taken of their hiftories and records than thofe of England. Dugdale b could procure no more than the endowment charters of a few, communicated by Sir James Balfour, who left a fmall folio treatife of his own, which he was pleafed to call " Monafticon Scoticum," though it looks more like an index to fuch a performance. Nicholfon had feen four more books bearing the like titles, two in folio, and the others in quarto c. " In every one of thefe, he fays, the curious antiquary will meet with feveral particulars that are overlooked in Dempfter's Apparatus ad hift. Scot. Bonon. 1622. Fol. A MS. inventory of all the pious donations to churches and hofpitals from the reign of James I. to James VI. was in the hands of Mr. Geo. Martin of Cameron : and in Sir J. Ware's library d are fome notes on the ftate and condition of the bifhopricks and monafteries fince 1212, collected out of the Hiftory of Lanercoft near Carlifle. e" His lordfhip f had feen charters of *St. Andrews* and *Aberdeen* among Sir R. Sibbald's MSS. two parchment regifters of *Arbrothoc* or *Aberbrothoc* abbey in the Advocates library at Edinburgh ; one in 4to, wrote about or before 1400, the other in folio, t. James IV. and the regifter of *Balmerinoc* monaftery in 4to: that of *Cambufkenneth* in the hands of the earl of Marr : that of *Coldingham*, containing the greateft number of original charters g of any religious houfe in Scotland, in the Dean and chapter's

---

a Page 183.   b Mon. Ang. ii. 1051. Tit. C. X. in the Cotton library, contains the names of religious houfes in Scotland t. Eliz.   c Among Sir R. Sibbald's MSS. Cat. MSS. Ang. tom. ii. part. 2. N° 54.   e Nich. p. 219.   f Ib. p. 220, & feq.   g No lefs than 70 of the Scottifh kings, with their feals. Nicholfon has given a lift of the chief in his append. N° 7. MS. Harl. 4623, has a lift of papers in Durham library concerning this abbey, &c.

     library

library at Durham : the " Liber *S.* Mariæ de *Dryburgh*," incorrectly tranfcribed on large Lombard paper, 4to. in the Advocates library [h], where is alfo the chartulary of *Dunfermelin*, in various hands, from the 13th to the 16th century. " Liber monafterii de *Kinlofe*," or hiftory of the abbots and affairs of that religious houfe to 1535 [i], written in Latin by Ferrier, who continued Boethius's hiftory, was tranfcribed by Dr. Jamefon from the original in the author's own hand in the queen of Sweden s library at Rome. *Lindoris* regifter is alfo in the Advocates library : that of *Mailros*, in the hands of the earl of Haddington ; a re-gifter of its charters Fol. MS. Harl. 2160 : that of *Paifley*, in the hands of the earl of Dundonald : that of *Pitweem*, in thofe of Mr. G. Martin of Cameron. The chartulary of *Scone* is in the Advocates library and in that of Sir John Murray of Drumkairn.

" Calculations, with the principles and data on which they are in-
" ftituted, relative to a late act of parliament, intitled, An act for raifing
" and eftablifhing a fund for a provifion for the widows and children
" of the minifters of the church, and of the heads, principals, and
" mafters of the univerfities of Scotland : fhewing the rife and progrefs
" of the fund. Publifhed by order of the truftees nominated by the
" faid act of parliament. Edinb. 1748." Fol.

[h] This library at Edinburgh was founded 1689 by Sir G. Mackenzie, king's advocate in Scotland, and ftored with variety of MSS. relating to Scottifh antiquities, and all forts of books, clafs'd in excellent order planned by him in an elegant Latin oration pro-nounced on the occafion, and afterwards publifhed: Biog. Brit. Mackenzie. A Latin catalogue of the printed books was printed at Edinburgh 1692. 4to. with a learned pre-face by Sir George.—A catalogue of the MSS. would have been more to the purpofe! Mr. Gordon in his Itinerary, p. 119—134. has given a lift of the confular medals in this library, moftly found in the Roman ftations in this kingdom, and collected with variety of others by Mr. James Sutherland, of whom they were purchafed, and who made an-other lift, with an explanation of each.
[i] With fome imperfect additions down to 1545.

Natural Hiſtory.

SIR Andrew Balfour, M. D. made many intereſting diſcoveries and obſervations on the natural hiſtory of his country, and left a noble collection of natural and artificial curioſities in the muſeum that bears his name at Edinburgh; to which his intimate friend and collegue Sir R. Sibbald made conſiderable additions and publiſhed a catalogue of the whole, under the title of " Auctarium muſæi Balfouriani
" e muſeo Sibbaldiano; ſive enumeratio & deſcriptio rerum rariorum,
" tam naturalium quam artificialium, tam domeſticarum quam exotica-
" rum, quas Rob. Sibbaldus, M. D. eq. aur. academiæ Edinburgenæ
" donavit; quæ quaſi manuductio brevis eſt ad hiſtoriam naturalem.
" Edinb. 1697." 8vo. Sir Robert wrote likewiſe, " Memoria Balfou-
" riana, ſive hiſtoria rerum pro literis promovendis geſtarum, a clariſſi-
" mis fratribus Balfouriis, D. Jacobo barone, de Kenard equite, leone,
" rege armorum; & D. Andrea, M. D. eq. aur. Edin. 1699." 8vo.

" Scotia illuſtrata, ſive prodromus hiſtoriæ naturalis, in quo regionis
" natura, incolarum ingenia & mores, morbi, iiſq, medendi methodus
" & medicina indigena accuratè explicantur: & multiplices naturæ
" partus in triplice ejus regno, vegetabili ſcil. animali & minerali, per
" hancce borealem Magnæ Britanniæ partem, quæ antiquiſſimum Sco-
" tiæ regnum conſtituit, undequaq; diffuſi, nunc primum in lucem eru-
" untur, & varii eorum uſus, medici præſertim & mechanici, quos ad
" vitæ cum neceſſitatem tum commoditatem præſtant, cunctis perſpicuè
" exponuntur. Cum figuris æneis. Opus 20 annorum, ſereniſſimi re-
" gis Caroli II: M. B. &c. monarchæ juſſu editum, auctore Roberto
" Sibbaldo, M. D. eq. aur. medico & geographico regio, & regii me-
" dicorum coll. ap. Edinburgum ſocio. Edinb. 1684 [a]." Fol. is an Introduction to a more extenſive work, which was to have comprehended all that related to the antient and preſent ſtate of Scotland. His
" Nuncius Scoto-Britannus de deſcriptione Scotiæ antiquæ & modernæ"
prefixed to it, and printed ſeparately 1683. Fol. [b], gives a compen-

---

[a] It has an Engliſh title, a tranſlation of this, prefixed.

Alſo in Engliſh, intitled, " An account of the Scottiſh Atlas, or the deſcription of
" Scotland antient and modern. Edinb. 1683." Fol.

dious

dious view of his defign. The antient ftate of the country, including antient Britain in general, was to have been wrote in Latin. His dif-courfe on Thule publifhed in Camden was part of it; but was to have received great enlargement in the other work. The 2d part or volume was to have been wrote in Englifh, and to treat on the prefent govern-ment, manners, natural productions, antiquities, &c. He anfwered fome attacks made on this work in " Vindiciæ Scotiæ illuftratæ, " five prodromi naturalis hiftoriæ Scotiæ, contra prodromomaftiges, " fub larva libelli de legibus hiftoriæ naturalis, latentes. Edinb. 1710." Fol. annexed to his Mifcellanea eruditæ antiquitatis, and reprinted 1739. Sir Robert's detached effays in natural hiftory, and the improvements that might be made in Scotland, may be feen in Nicholfon. His " Phalainologia nova, five obfervationes de rarioribus quibufdam balæ-" nis in Scotiæ littus nuper ejectis; in quibus nuper confpectæ balænæ " per genera & fpecies fecundum characteres ab ipfa natura impreffos " diftribuuntur, quædam nunc primum defcribuntur; errores etiam " circa defcriptas deteguntur, & breves de dentium, fpermatis ceti & " ambrægrifeæ ortu, natura & ufu differtationes traduntur," was pub-lifhed Edinb. 1692. 4to. An abftract of it is in p. 972 of N° 205 of the Philofophical Tranfactions. In p. 2314 of N° 308 he tells Sir H. Sloane he was going to publifh his Cœtologia in Latin, in a 2d vol. of his Prodromus, to confift of the fifh and marine animals of Scotland [c]; and the fame letter contains a defcription of the pediculus ceti, a fhell fifh. In N° 222, p. 321, is his letter about Scotch fhells [d]. He pub-lifhed alfo advertifements anent a rare fort of whale that came in near Cramonde 1701, and anent the xiphias or fword-fifh expofed at Edinburgh.

Mr. James Sutherland before-mentioned, overfeer of Balfour's phyfic garden, drew up and publifhed the ftate of it in his " Hortus medicus " Edinburgenfis. Edinb. 1683." 8vo. [e], which had a 2d edit.

Bp. Nicholfon faw a MS. treatife on the metals of Scotland by one Thomas Atkinfon, an Englifhman, affay-mafter of the mint at Edin-

[c] Probably made up of the MS. treatifes enumerated by N ch. p. 29.

[d] Quære, If his Nautilogia.

[e] Nich. p. 32. What Bale, upon the flighteft authority from Boethius, fays of king Jofina's book De herbarum viribus, muft pafs among the inaccuracies of both writers: and as fuch Tanner has not mentioned his majefty's name.

burgh under James VI.. Much is there faid of gold found in Scotland; but moft of the information is borrowed from a parchment MS. left by one Cornelius, a German lapidary, conftituted fuperior of his majefty's gold mines on Q. Elizabeth's recommendation. He firft difcovered fuch mines on Crawford moor, and in thirty days time conveyed into the mint at Edinburgh half a ftone weight of natural gold, or 8 lb. troy, worth 450 l. fterling. He talks of great gold, from the fize of birds eyes to their eggs, found in Glangaber water, worth 6 s. 8 d. per ounce at firft hand. A very modern tranfcript of this tract, whofe author is there called Atchefon, is among the Harl. MSS, N° 4612. Col. J. Borthwick's " Narratio de metallis & mineralibus in Scotia," quoted in Sibbald's Nuncius, p. 11, is only a fhort lift of places where the feveral metals abound.

In the Philofophical Tranfactions, N° 4, p. 53, is Sir Robert Murray's account of the extraordinary weftern tides. In N° 113, p. 337, are Sir George Mackenzie s obfervations on the winds, lakes in Strathkerrie and Straglafh, lake Monar, and Nefs, and a petrifying river in Glevelg. In N° 114, p. 30, fome phænomena in certain lakes by the fame. In p. 396 of N° 117, his remarks on the foil, agriculture, plants, and Molucca beans found in Scotland, and ink made out of the iris paluftris. In N° 137, p. 925, Sir Rob. Murray's paper concerning barnacles, in the fhape of birds, produced in concha anatifera. In N° 142, p. 1069, Sir Geo. Mackenzie's account of the method of making falt in Scotland. In N° 172, p. 1036, Dr. Tancred Robinfon's account of the Scottifh barnacle and French macreufe. In N° 269 Ed. Lhuyd's account of fome Roman, French, and Irifh infcriptions and antiquities found in Scotland and Ireland : many of them inferted in Camden. In N° 330, p. 246, is a letter from George earl of Cromartie to Sir H. Sloane, giving an account of the moffes in Scotland, and his anfwer to it, treating of others in England and Wales. In N° 333, p. 434, Dr. Blair's account of amiantus in the Highlands. In N° 337, p. 93, and 275, Ed. Lhuyd's obfervations in his travels through Wales and Scotland. In Birch's Hiftory of the Royal Society, vol. i. p. 270, 271, are Sir R. Murray's meafures of a gigantic Scotch child, and of a large herring on the Scotch coaft.

" The

" The privileges of the royal boroughs in Scotland" were publifhed by —— Black [f].

The cities and boroughs royal are moft of them defcribed in Latin verfe by Jo. Johnfton, king's profeffor of divinity at St. Andrews, printed at Middleburgh, Zealand, 1642. 12mo. from which Camden has tranfcribed copioufly.

" The ftaple contract, betwixt the royal burrows of Scotland, and
" the city Campvere in Zealand: with the feveral amplifications,
" prolongations; and ratifications thereof. Publifhed by order of the
" general convention of royal burrows, in July 1749. To which is
" prefixed an hiftorical account of the ftaple, by a private gentleman.
" Edinb. 1749." 8vo. This contract was firft entered into 1444, upon the marriage of Mary, fifter of James II. of Scotland, to Wolfred van Borfelen, lord of Campvere, and after feveral intermiffions ratified anew with the late ftadtholder 1748.

Of 31 fhires, into which Scotland is divided, thofe of *BUTE*, *CROMARTY*, and *NAIRN* are the only ones that have no accounts, maps, or views to fhew.

ABERDEENSHIRE.

" BReviarium ad ufum & confuetudinem percelebris ecclefiæ ca-
" thedralis *Aberdonenfis* in Scotia, regnante Jacobo IV. per Will.
" Abirdonenfem epifcopum. 1510." 8vo. in the Advocates library at Edinburgh [g]. Hector Boethius's " Vitæ epifcoporum Murthlacenfium
" & Aberdonenfium: ex prelo Afcenfiano. 1522." 4to. includes a defcription of the college at Aberdeen, and the hiftory of its profeffors, &c. In the library of King's college here [h] is a fair original chartulary from the foundation of the fee to the laft catholic bifhop: alfo original regifters of the cathedral plate, &c. the ftatutes of the church; and the " Statuta generalis ecclefiæ Scoticanæ ;" out of all which Dr. Jamefon compiled a Chartularium ecclefiæ Aberdonenfis, of which bp. Nicholfon, who faw the MS. in the hands of Mr. Thomas Innife, has given an abftract [i].

[f] Worral's Bibliotheca Legum. p. 211.   [g] Ames's Hiftory of Printing, p. 573.   [h] Nich. [i] Ib. p. 213—216.)

" Memorials

" Memorials for the government of the royal burghs in Scotland,
" with a fuccinct furvey of the famous city of Aberdeen, with its fitu-
" ation. defcription, antiquity, fidelity, and loyalty to their fovereigns:
" as alfo the gracious rewards conferred thereon: and the fignal evi-
" dences of honour put upon many chief magiftrates thereof; with a
" catalogue of them fince the city was burned for loyalty about the
" year 1330. Aberd. 1685." 12mo. Bp. Nicholfon [k] fays, there is
in this fmall book a deal of curious remarks in a decent and nervous
ftile. The author affumes the name of Philopoliteius, but his true
name was Skene. Having briefly explained the nature and conftitution of thefe burghs, as diftinct from burghs of barony and regality, he
treats of the offices and qualifications of the magiftrates, deans of gilds,
recorders, &c. and gives abftracts of fome of the laws; but writes more
like a divine or moralift than a man of law or bufinefs. Mr. James
Gordon, fon of Sir Robert, drew a map of New and Old Aberdeen,
with the colleges, port, harbour, and river Dee; and at the fides a
fhort view of the ager Abredonenfis, in Latin and Englifh. Plates
xix and xx in Slezer are views of New and Old Aberdeen.

In pl. lix of Gordon's Itinerary is a carved ftone in *Mar* county, defcribed p. 162.

A view of Mar lodge in Mar foreft, by Mr. Tomkins, was exhibited at Spring-gardens 1767.

" Ane brief defcription of the qualities and effectes of the well of
" the woman-hill [m] befyde Abirdene. A.D. 1580." in one fheet 12mo.
with a pretty border round the margin [n].

Dr. Wm. Barclay, the phyfician, wrote a fmall treatife on the Cal-
lirhóe, commonly called the well of the fpa, or the nymph of Aberdeen. Aberd. 1615. 1670. 18mo.

In N° 222, p. 311, of the Philofophical Tranfactions is an account
of the effects of lightning at Aberdeen. In N° 276, p. 1004, is Mr.
Wilfon's account of amiantus at *Achindore* in this county.

The countefs of Errol defcribed all the remarkables of *Buchan*,
which is principally comprehended in this county. Another defcription
is given of it by Dr. Cockburn: a third (of the north fide of the coaft)

---

[k] Nich. p. 58, 59.   [l] Ib. p. 60.   [m] Alias Wolman or Woolman hill, from a wool-
market antiently kept there.   [n] Ames's Hift. of Printing, p. 586.

5

by Alex. Gaerdon of Troup.   Bp. Nicholſon [o] mentions all thoſe as remaining unpubliſhed in Sir R. Sibbald's poſſeſſion.

In the Gentleman's Magazine for May, 1755, p. 198, is a view and deſcription of the bullers of Buchan, 18 miles N. from Aberdeen and 6 S. from Peterhead.   Plate ii. the ſea proſpect, is not inſerted.

AIRSHIRE.

A Deſcription of the bailiwick of *Carrick* by Mr. Abercromby, miniſter at Maybore, was in Sir R. Gordon's hands [p].   Slezer has two views of *Aire*, pl. xxix. xxx. and of *Corſregal* abbey, pl. xlii.

ARGYLESHIRE.

DR. Stukeley drew and Harris engraved a cairn near *Kilmartin*, in Argileſhire, and in the ſame plate two concentric ſtone walls in a wood called *Coed iſa Plas yn Llanvair Vechan*, and one ſuch wall with a cairn called *Karnedh Vawr* on a mountain in *Hwygyſylchn* pariſh by *Maen y Kampien* and within three arrows flight of *Mein hirion*, *Caernarvonſhire*.   In another plate two ſuch walls diſtinct near *Na Hottre*, a village in *Mayow* county ; a cairn in a circle, two circles, &c. on a hill above the upper end of *Loch Kreigneſs*, in Argileſhire, and two concentric walls at *Klochlynach* in *Dynſarri* near *Benbwyſken*.

A map of ſuch part of his grace the duke of Argyle's heritable dukedom and juſticiary territories, &c. as lie contiguous on the W. coaſt of N. Britain, &c. 1734.

BAMFFSHIRE.

MR. Tomkins exhibited at Spring-gardens 1767 a view of *Rothamy*, on the earl of Fife's eſtate.

BERWICKSHRIE.

A MS. account of Berwickſhire, or the Merſe, by Meſſrs. Elliot and Veech, miniſters there, was in Sir R. Gordon's hands [q].
" An eſſay on the contents and virtues of *Dunſe* ſpa, in a letter to
" my lord ———. By Francis Home, M. D. Edinb. 1751." 8vo.

[o] Nich. p. 59.   [p] Nich. p. 20.   [q] Id. ib.

CAITNESS-

CAITHNESS SHIRE.

BP. Nicholſon had ſeen a dry liſt of the biſhops of *Caithneſs* at the end of a MS. hiſtory of the Sutherland family, by Alex. Roſs, who ſeems to have compiled it [r]. Sir R. Gordon had certain anſwers to his queries about Caithneſs by Mr. Wm. Geddes, miniſter at Wich, and Mr. W. Dundaſs, advocate [s].

CLACMANNANSHIRE.

SLEZER gives a view of *Alloa*, pl. viii.

DUMBARTONSHIRE.

TWO views of *Dumbarton* and one of the caſtle make Slezer's pl. iii. iv. v. A N. view of the caſtle by P. Sandby, 1751.

" The report of John Smeaton, engineer, and F. R. S. concern-
" ing the practicability and expence of joining the rivers *Forth* and
" *Clyde* by a navigable canal, and thereby to join the eaſt ſea and the
" weſt. Addreſſed to the hon. truſtees for fiſheries, manufactures,
" and improvements in Scotland, at whoſe deſire the ſurvey was made;
" with a map of the country, and a plan of the canal. 1767 " The
expence of Mr. Smeaton's plan, 80,000 l. not being encouraged by
government, ſome merchants of Glaſgow and Carron ſubſcribed for a
ſmaller canal, for which a bill is depending in parliament. The greater
utility of the larger cut was vindicated without ſucceſs in " Conſidera-
" tions upon the intended navigable communication between the firths
" of Forth and Clyde. In a letter to the lord provoſt of Edinburgh,
" prefes of the general convention of the royal boroughs of Scotland,
" from a member of the convention, 1767." 4to. enlarging the plan.

A cataract in the Clyde near Lanrig, 50 yards high, is deſcribed in
the Gentleman's Magazine, Apr. 1758, p. 179, with a cut.

A new and exact map of the river Clyde, done by Mr. John Adair,
hydrographer, and F. R. S. and publiſhed for the good of the publick
by George Scott.

[r] Nich. p. 215.　　　　[s] Ib. p. 20.

　　　　DUMFRIES-

DUMFRIESSHIRE.

SIR Robert Gordon had a MS. defcription of this fhire by Dr. Ar-chibald, with his account of the natural produ&ions thereof, and of Galloway: alfo an account of the Stewarty of *Annandale*, with a map, by Mr. Johnfton, minifter; and of the upper part of the Sheriffdom of *Niddifdale*, by Mr. Thomas Black, minifter at Pempont [t].

" *Moffet* well: or a topographico-fpagyrical defcription of the mi-
" neral wells at *Moffet* in Annandale of Scotland: tranflated and much
" enlarged by the author Matthew Mackaile, chyrurgo-medicine: as
" alfo the Oyly well, or topographico-fpagyricall defcription of the
" Oyly well at St. Catharine's chappel, in the paroch of Libberton.
" To thefe is fubjoined a chara&er of Mr. Culpeper, and his writings,
" by the fame author. Edinb. 1664." 12mo. This was firft wrote in Latin 1659. In the Medical effays of 1733 is a difcourfe on the vir-tues and ufes of this water by Mr. Geo. Mulligen, furgeon in Moffat; but not a word of enquiry into its principles. This is followed in the fame year's Effays, by a fet of very curious and ingenious experiments by the learned Dr. Plummer, fellow of the college of phyficians at Edinburgh, and profeffor of medicine in that univerfity [u].

" Experiments and obfervations upon the *Hartfell* fpaw, made at
" Moffat 1750; and an account of its medicinal virtues fo far as
" they have been hitherto difcovered from experience. By Wm. Horfe-
" burg, D. M." make art. xii. of " Effays and obfervations, phyfical
" and literary, read before a fociety in Edinburgh; and publifhed by
" them. Vol. i. 1754." 8vo.

In the Philofophical Tranfa&ions, vol. l. p. 115, is an account of a new difcovered well near Moffat. In vol. xlix. p. 512, an account of the agitation of *Clofeburn* lake, Feb. 1, 1756.

In pl. lvii. lviii. of Gordon's Itinerary is a large obelifk in *Ruthvel* church, Annandale, infcribed partly with Runic and partly with Saxon or Gothic chara&ers, defcribed p. 160.

EDINBURGHSHIRE.

BIfhop Nicholfon had feen two little MSS. afcribed to D. Buchanan, intitled " Edinburgæ & Lethæ defcriptio," and " Provinciæ Edin-
" burgenæ defcriptio [x]."

Nich. p. 20.　[u] Short's Hift. of min. waters, p. 73.　[x] Page 59.

" The

" The hiftory of Edinburgh from its foundation to the prefent time:
" containing a faithful relation of the publick tranfactions of the citi-
" zens; accounts of the feveral parifhes; its governments, civil, eccle-
" fiaftical, and military; incorporations of trade and manufactures;
" courts of juftice; ftate of learning; charitable foundations, &c. with
" the feveral accounts of the parifhes of the Canongate, St. Cuthbert,
" and other diftricts within the fuburbs of Edinburgh. Together with
" the antient and prefent ftate of the town of Leith, and a perambu-
" lation of divers miles round the city. With an alphabetical index.
" In nine books. By William Maitland, F. R. S. author of the Hiftory
" of London. The whole illuftrated with a plan y of the town, and a
" great variety of other fine cuts z of the principal buildings within the
" city and fuburbs. Edinb. 1753." Fol.

Bp. Nicholfon a mentions a MS. tranfcript of the hiftory of St. Giles's
church, Edinburgh.

" The theatre of mortality, or the illuftrious infcriptions extant upon
" the feveral monuments erected over the dead bodies of the fome-
" time honourable perfons buried within the Grey Friars churchyard,
" and other churches and burial places within the city of Edinburgh
" and fuburbs. Collected by R. Monteith, M. A. 1704." 12mo.

" Eloge de la ville d'Edinbourg, divife en quatre chants. Par le
" Sieur de Forbes. A Edinb. 1753." 12mo.

A decreet arbitral made 1583 by James VI. for determining contro-
verfies about the election of magiftrates between the merchants gild
and the 14 companies, was printed under the title of " The fet of the
" city of Edinburgh. Edinb. 1683." 8vo b.

In Churchyard's Chipps, part i. 1575 and 1578, 4to. is a poetical
account of the fiege of Edinburgh caftle by Q. Elizabeth. At Ridlef-
worth hall, Norfolk, is a picture of Sir Wm. Drury, lord chief juftice
of Ireland 1579, by which hangs an old plan of Edinburgh caftle and
two armies before it, and round it " Sir Wm. Drurye, knt. general of
" the Englifhe wanne Edenburghe caftle 1573 c."

In the Gentleman's Magazine 1754, p. 119, fee a journey to Edinburgh, undertaken to trace the meridian of the caftle, by S. G.

---

y By William Edgar, architect, 1742.   z Engraved by Fourdrinier.
a Page 226.   b Id. p. 59.   c Blomfield's Hift. of Norfolk, vol. i. p. 188.

" The

" The hiſtory of the ſtatutes of the Royal Infirmary of Edinburgh.
" Edinb. 1749." 12mo.

" Index plantarum, præcipue officinalium, quæ, in horto medico
" Edinburgenſi, a Carolo Alſton, M. & B. P. medicinæ ſtudioſis de-
" monſtrantur. Edinb. 1749." 12mo.

A fair draught of this city, four feet long, printed in Holland, was
taken by James Gordon, ſon of Sir Robert, who ſurveyed it very accurately, and noted down the names of all places of note [d].

A plan of the city by Wm. Edgar, architeét, 1742, one ſheet.
Another by Rocque.

A S. view of Edinburgh by Hollar, 2 ſheets, ſans date.

Another view by Wm. Lodge [e].

I have four old views of Edinborrowgh Caſtell from the Weſt
porte; the royal palace of Holyrood houſe; Heriot's hoſpital; and the
parliament houſe, by J. G. engraved by F. de Wit at Amſterdam.

Two views of the caſtle by Slezer, pl. i. and ii.

A W. view of the city and E. view of the caſtle by P. Sandby, 1751.

Two engravings; being the plan, elevations, and ſeétions of an intended building for the Regiſter office of Scotland, from a deſign of
James earl of Morton, lord regiſter of Scotland, and preſident of the
Royal Society, to whom it is dedicated, by Robert Baldwin, architeét,
1767.

Slezer has given a view of the beautiful chapel of *Roſlin*, and two of
The Baſs, a fortified rock on this coaſt, pl. liv. lvi. lvii.

A view of *Leith* from the E. road by P. Sandby, 1751.

The caverns at *Hauthornden*, which Dr. Stukeley ſuppoſed a Piétiſh
caſtle, make pl. xxxviii. of his Itinerary.

In the Philoſophical Tranſaétions, N° 495, p. 412, is an account of
the tide in *Forth*.

The river and firth of Forth, engraved by Richard Cooper, Edinb.
1730, dedicated to George earl of Morton by the editor.

E L G I N S H I R E.

SLEZER engraved a view of *Elgin*, pl. xxxvi. and of its cathedral, pl. xxxvii.

[d] Nich. p. 58.　　　　Walp. Cat. of eng. p. 55.

FIFESHIRE.

" THE hiftory, ancient and modern, of the fheriffdoms of Fife
" and Kinrofs; with the defcription of both, and of the firths
" of Forth and Tay, and the iflands in them: in which there is an ac-
" count of the royal feats and caftles; and of the royal burghs and the
" ports; and of the religious houfes and fchools; and of the moft re-
" markable houfes of the nobility and gentry: with an account of the
" natural produfts of the land and waters. By Sir Robert Sibbald,
" doftor of medicin. Edinb. 1710." Fol. republifhed 1739.

Bp. Nicholfon fays, Sir James Balfour wrote a full account of this
fhire, which he fuppofes was ftill among his papers, though he did not
recolleft having feen it [f]. Sibbald made great ufe of it. The Bifhop
had feen a treatife of the original and continuance of the Mackduffs,
thanes of Fife, and a lift of the moft eminent men of the Mackintofh
family: alfo a good rental of the king's revenue here, fuperfcribed
" Inquifitio fafta in curia vice-comitis de Fyffe tenta in prætorio burgi
" de Cupro [Couper] per nob. dom. patricium dom. Lindefay de Byres,
" &c. A. D. 1517." He fays [g], the univerfity has a fufficiency of
records in her archives to clear up her whole hiftory, and that he
faw a fair tranfcript of them taken by Dr. Skene, provoft of St. Salvator's college there.

" Some hiftorical remarks on the city of *St. Andrews* in North Bri-
" tain: with a particular account of the ruinous condition of the har-
" bour in that place; and of what importance the repairing of it will
" be to all concerned in trade and navigation. Lond. 1728." 8vo.
By Wm. Douglas. Dr. Stukeley was told of a Roman pharos here like
that at Dover [h]

In the Britifh mufeum, MS. Harl. 6375, is a 4to written by Mr.
George Martin 1685, intitled, " Reliquiæ D. Andreæ; or the ftate of
the venerable and primitial fee of St. Andrews; containing an account
of the rife, advancement, dignities, honours, jurifdiftions, privileges,
and revolutions of this ancient fee, and of the church benefices of old
depending thereto, and the kirks now belonging to the fame: with fome

[f] Page 57. He refers to Memor. Balfour, p. 49.   [g] Page 227.   [h] Itin. p. 122.

hiftorical

hiftorical memoirs of the moft famous prelates and primates of this fee."
Bp. Nicholfon fays [i], this is a finifhed piece in ten chapters, and that
its few miftakes were corrected by Dr. Jamefon, who was a compleat
mafter of the antiquities of that place.　Dr. Rawlinfon engraved a feal
of abp. Hamilton in his poffeffion, infcribed *Joannes Hammiltoun archi-
epifcopus Sancti Andree* 1555.　Another infcribed *S. comune foci. frm.
predicatorum. civitis. Sancti. Andree :* on which under the figure of our
lady is a fhield with a boar [k] and a faltire in chief : and a 3d with this
legend ; *Sigilli. capit. ecclie. fce. trinitatis. de dunferonelin.*

Slezer engraved the town, cathedral [l], and caftle of St. Andrews,
pl. xiii. xiv. xv. the town and abbey of *Dumferlin*, pl. xlv. xlvi. and
the town and palace of *Falkland*, p. xi. xii.　Sibbald had James Gordon's plans of St. Andrews and Coupar.

　" An effay upon the infcription of Mac Duff's croffe in Fyfe.　By
" J. C. [James Cunningham] [m]. Edinb. 1678." 4to.　This gentleman has made intelligible this antient Saxon infcription, very imperfectly given by Sir Rob. Sibbald from Balfour's papers, difguifed under
a Latin cover [n] now extant only in various tranfcripts, none of which
feem to have preferved the original character.

　In Gordon's Itinerary, pl. lv. fig. 3. and pl. lvi. are two obelifks at
Inverkeithing and near *Forres*, commemorating the laft invafion of
Scotland by the Danes ; and in pl. lx. queen Vanora's grave-ftones at
Miggle, a village four miles from Coupar.

　John Smith, minifter of *Lefley*, defcribed that parifh in Latin, as the
minifter of *Skunie* did his in Englifh.

　" The colde fpring of *Kingborne Craig*, his admirable and new
" tryed properties, fo far foorth as they are found true by experience.
" Written by Patrick Anderfon, doctor of phyfick. Edinb. 1618." 4to.

[i] Page 210.　　[k] Probably the monftrous one killed in this neighbourhood, which
was infefted by them.　See Sibbald, p. 134.　　[l] He makes it exceed St. Peter's and
St. Paul's.　Douglas found it to be 370 feet long, 65 wide, about 100 high : the
tranfepts 180.—It comes neareft, except in height, to Hereford and Wells cathedrals.
[m] He was writer to the fignet, and author of a Latin poetical anfwer (1685) to bp.
Lloyd, who in his hiftorical account of antient church government in Great Britain and
Ireland had fhortned the royal line, and otherwife wronged the Scots.　Nich. p. 138.
[n] Sir Robert gives a verfion of it in more modern Latin and Englifh, from Sir James
Dalrymple's Camden.　Hift. of Fife, p. 99.　Gordon fays the form of this monument,
which is now quite gone, is no where exhibited.　There is a print of it prefixed to Sibbald's Hiftory.

Wm.

Wm. Lodge drew and engraved a view of *Dysart* °.

Sir R. Sibbald says, he employed Adair to make a new survey of this shire, in which he omitted near two presbyteries and all the S. coast W. of Dysart.

FORFARSHIRE.

A Description of this shire by Mr. Aughterlauney, an ingenious gentleman there, was in Sir R. Gordon's hands p. *Angus* was elegantly described in a pure Latin style by Mr. Rob. Edwards, minister at Murress, who also drew an excellent new map of it, both published by the Jansons q. Slezer's views are *Aberbrothic* town and abbey, pl. xl. xli. the towns of *Montross*, *Dundee* (two), and *Brechin*, pl. xxiii. xxxviii. xxxix. liii. In Gordon's Itinerary, pl. liii. liv. lv. are the obelisks erected at *Aberlemmy* and *Camus* on several defeats of the Danes, described p. 149—157; in pl. lv. and lxi. the monument of K. Malcolm's murder in *Glames'* churchyard ; and pl. lix. St. Orland's stone at *Cossens*.

HADDINGTONSHIRE.

IN vol. lii. art. 17, of the Philosophical Transactions is an account by Dr. Pococke, bishop of Ossory, of a rock on the W. side of the entrance of *Dunbar* harbour like the Giants Causeway in Ireland.

Slezer's pl. xxi. is a view of *Haddington*, and pl. xxii. of the coast of Mid-Lothian from Stony-hill.

INVERNESS-SHIRE.

MR. Gordon in his Itinerarium septentrionale, p. 166, pl. lxv. has given a particular description and view of two of the four circular buildings mentioned by Buchanan, book i. and iv r. as in Ross, now in this shire, in the vale of *Glenbeg*. Martin mentions several such in Lewis isle s. Dr. Stukeley had an unpublished plate of that which Gordon calls Castle *Telive*, and he, the giants castle. He makes them

---

° Walp. Cat. of Engr. p. 55.   P Nich. p. 20.   q Ib. p. 56.   r He describes them as resembling Arthur's Oon, which they do not at all.   s. Western isles, p. 8.

druidical

druidical temples; and his sketch of the vale exhibits a circle of stones, with an avenue at the head of a little river [t].

In N° 254, p. 230, of the Philosophical Transactions is an account of loch *Ness*, castle *Urquart*, &c. by James Fraser, minister of Kirkhill near Inverness.

Plan and perspective view of the improved land of *Mingary*, with the improveable bay of *Kilchoan*, drawn from the original survey of *Ardnamurcan*, by J. Cowley.

A map of the improved moss and improveable bay of *Kintra*, drawn from the plan of the survey of *Ardnamurcan*, by J. Cowley, 1734.

A plan of loch *Lunart*, &c. " become famous by the greatest natural improvements this age has produced," surveyed, &c. by A. Bruce, engraved by R. Cooper.

Slezer engraved a view of *Inverness*, pl. xxxiv.

KINROSS-SHIRE.

SIR Robert Sibbald wrote the history and description of this shire incorporated with that of Fife.

KINCARDINSHIRE.

A Note of remarkables in the sheriffdom of *Mernes*, with a particular description of *Dunotter*, by Mr. John Keith, minister there, was among Sir Robert Gordon's papers [u]. Slezer engraved Dunotter castle, pl. xxxi.

KIRKCUDBRIGHTSHIRE.

THE large county of Galloway, now comprehended in this shire and Wigton, was exactly surveyed by Mr. Andrew Symson, sometime minister there, afterwards at Douglas, and last an ejected episcopalian at Edinburgh [x].

---

[t] He says capt. Douglas told him there were vast numbers of stones like Stonehenge, with avenues of stones, all over Scotland.   [u] Nich. p. 20.   [x] Ib. p. 57.

LANERK-

LANERKSHIRE.

SIR William Baillie of Lamentoun, and his namesake of Carphin, drew up an account of the sheriffdom of *Lanerk*: the MS. was in Sir R. Gordon's hands *y*.

" A view of the city of *Glasgow*: or an account of its origin, rise, and
" progress, with a more particular description thereof than has hither-
" to been known. Containing the foundation of the episcopal see, with
" the succession of the bps. and abps. from the year 1122 to the late
" happy revolution ; the erection of the town into a royal burgh, with
" the subsequent grants from the crown thereto ; the account of the
" cathedral church, as well as the other churches of the city, the
" hospitals, halls, streets, lanes, markets, fairs, the several incorpora-
" tions, the sett of the merchants, and deacon-conveeners houses, the
" rise, growth, and progress of trade, the several benefactors to the
" city, the university, the buildings and builders, gardens, and walks
" here, from the time of its foundation to the present time : illus-
" trated with many curious and useful observations and reflections.
" Collected from many antient records, charters, and other antient
" vouchers, and from the best historians and private MSS. By John
" M'Ure, alias Campbel, clerk to the registration of seisins, and other
" evidences for the district of Glasgow. Glasgow 1736." 8vo *z*. The
university of Glasgow received this spring, from the principal of the
Scots college at Paris, an authenticated copy of the chartulary belonging to its cathedral, from the year 1116 to the reformation, carried
over by Beaton, the last Popish archbishop, and lodged by him in the
Scots college. This valuable present is very richly bound in 2 volumes,
quarto. Bishop Nicholson, p. 228, seems to mention such an one at
Glasgow in his time.

Of an earthquake felt at Glasgow and Dumbarton, Dec. 1755, see
Philosophical Transactions, vol. xlviii. art. 67.

Wm. Lodge drew and engraved a view of this city. Slezer has two
more, pl. xvi. xvii. ; one of the college, p. xviii. ; *Hamilton*, pl. xxviii. ;
Bothwell castle, pl. li. Of the last we have S. and N. E. views by P.
Sandby 1751.

Nich. p. 21.   *z* With a miserable mezzotinto of the author by S. Taylor.

Dr. Rawlinson engraved the feal of Alexander Cairncroce, bifhop of Glafgow, infcribed *Pro deo, rege, & ecclefia facra.*

In Birch's Hiftory of the Royal Society, vol. i. p. 137, is Sir Robert Moray's account of an echo near *Rofneath* houfe near Glafgow.

LINLITHGOWSHIRE.

" THE hiftory, ancient and modern, of the fheriffdoms of Linlith-
" gow and Stirling, in which there is an account of the royal
" feats and caftles; and of the royal burghs and the ports; and of the
" religious houfes and hofpitals; and of the moft remarkable houfes
" of the nobility and gentry: with an account of the natural products
" of the land and water. In two books: the 1ft book treateth of
" the fhire of Linlithgow, the 2d of Stirlingfhire. By Sir Robert Sib-
" bald, doctor of medicine. Edinb. 1710." Fol. A map of antient Scotland is prefixed.

Slezer engraved the town and palace of Linlithgow, pl. ix. x.

PEEBLESSHIRE.

SIR Robert Gordon had a defcription of *Tweedale* by Dr. Penny-cuick and Mr. Forbes, and of *Ettrick* foreft by Mr. Elliot.

A map of the barony of *Stobbo*, in the fheriffdom of *Peebles*, now belonging to Charles Murray, efq; with the parks and improvements of Sir A. Murray, by An. Bearhof.

A new and correct map of the fhire of *Peebles* or *Tweedale*, furveyed by Wm. Edgar 1741.

PERTHSHIRE.

SIR Robert Gordon had a defcription of *Strathern* and *Stormont* by John Adair [b].

Slezer's views in this county are *Dunkeld* and *Dumblane*, and their cathedrals, pl. xxiv. xxv. xxvi. xxvii. *Scone* pl. xxxv. and *Perth* pl. xliv

Pl. lx. of Gordon's Itinerary contains a round tower at *Abernethey* and another at *Brechin* in Forfar, like fome in Ireland, and fuppofed to be Pictifh.

[a] Nich. p. 21.   [b] Idem. ib.

Mr.

Mr. Stuart exhibited at Spring-gardens 1765 three paintings of the cascade at the earl of Breadalbane's seat at Teymouth, the duke of Athol's seat at Dunkeld from the E. and the cathedral of Dunkeld. In 1767, part of a lake of 8000 acres belonging to the earl of Breadalbane, and a waterfall fifty feet high, seen from the hermitage in the duke of Athol's gardens at Dunkeld.

Straithern, Stormont, and *Car of Gourie,* with the rivers *Tay* and *Jern,* surveyed and designed by J. Adair.

RENFREWSHIRE.

A MS. description of this shire by Mr. Wm. Dunlop, a curious antiquary and principal of Glasgow college, more complete than two former ones by Shaw of Greenoch and Montgomery of Wetlands, was in the hands of Sir Robert Gordon [c].

Slezer engraved a view of *Paisley* town and abbey. The black books of this and Scone abbey are no more than Fordon's Scotichronicon, with continuation in the 15th century. Sibbald had an abridgement of the first in 16 books, ending with James I.

A relation of the diabolical practices of above twenty wizards and witches in the shire of Renfrew in their trials, &c. 1697. 4to.

" Sadducismus debellatus ; or a true narrative of the sorceries and
" witchcrafts exercised by the devil and his instruments on Mrs. Christian Shaw, daughter of Mr. John Shaw of *Bargarran,* in the county
" of Renfrew, &c. from 1696 to 1697. 1698. with the lawyers arguments on both sides." 4to. two editions. Two died in prison, and five saved themselves by a confession that hanged seven others : the girl recovered and outlived all their united efforts—the last struggles of expiring credulity in this part of the British dominions.

ROSSSHIRE.

SLEZER engraved the town of *Channerie,* pl. xliii. and the town and abbey of *Colross,* pl. xlvii. xlviii.

[c] Nich. p. 20. Sir Robert Sibbald refers to it. Hist. enquiry concerning the Roman monuments, p. 36. [d] Nich. p. 21.

ROXBURGHSHIRE.

MS. defcriptions of Tiviotdale and Roxburgh by lord Jedburgh Sir Wm. Scot of Harden, and Mr. And. Carr of Sinlafs were in Sir Robert Gordon's hands [e].

Dr. Rawlinfon engraved a feal in his own poffeffion infcribed *S. Andree. commendatare. monafterii. de jedburgh.*

Slezer engraved *Dryburg* town and abbey, pl. xxxii. xxxiii. *Kelfo* town and abbey, pl. xlix.. l. and the magnificent abbey of *Mailros*, which one may call the Croyland of Scotland, though it has fhared a better fate.

Gordon, pl. lxiv. gives the remains of a bridge with hollow piers over the Tweed, near Mailros, and the letter'd ftones in *Efkdale.*

SELKIRKSHIRE.

THE fheriffdom of Selkirk was defcribed by Wm. Elliot of Stobbes and Walter Scot of Orkilton. MS. pen. Sir Robert Gordon [f].

STIRLINGSHIRE.

SIR Thomas Hope of Craig hall had in MS. " Proceffus fuper " erectione ecclefiæ collegiatæ de Strivelin [g]. Sir. R. Sibbald's defcription of this county has been already mention d.

" An account of a Roman temple and other antiquities near Gra- " ham's Dike in Scotland," by Dr Stukeley, 1720. 4to. giving a fhort furvey of the Roman wall in Scotland, called by this laft name, built by Lollius Urbicus under Antoninus Pius [h]; and a particular defcription

---

[e] Nich. p. 21.　　　[f] Id. ib.　　　[g] Ib. p. 226.

[h] Of which fee Gordon's 6th chapter, and Horfley, book ii. c. 10. The former, p. 20 68, fuppofe Agricola made a prætentura there before that time; and fhews clearly againft Buchanan, Ufher, Sir Robert Gordon, and Tillemont, that Severus was not the builder of this *turf* wall, but of that *ftone* one in England a little north of Hadrian's turf wall. Antoninus's wall was ruined and rebuilt of turf after the firft legation of the provincial Britons. Bede, book i. p. 12. Gord. p. 58. 63. 111. In his 11th chap. Mr. Gordon defcribes a great ditch called the Catrail, or Picts-work ditch, from Solway frith to near Edinburgh, which he fuppofes the limit of the Caledonians on their peace with Severus.

of

of Arthur's Oon, a round building on the banks of the Carron near Camelon, which the doctor labours hard to ascribe to Agricola, making it a temple in imitation of the Pantheon, and dedicated to Romulus. Notwithstanding he here explodes the notion of Carausius having any hand in it, he took as much pains in his history of that prince to give him the honour of it, pathetically lamenting its demolition a few years ago, when a sacrilegious farmer threw its ruins into a mill-dam, which the floods soon after carried quite away. He has in both works exhibited sections and views of it, from measurements by Mr. Jelf, as has also Gordon, who thought it a chapel to place the ensigns in. Sibbald took it for a temple of Terminus built by Severus; so did Buchanan at first, but afterwards for a trophy or tomb. Horsley thought it a mausoleum, like that of Metella at Rome, called Capo di Bove.

Vorsterman painted a view of *Stirling* castle; the figures by Wych [i]. Slezer engraved views of the town, pl. vi. vii. Sandby a view of the castle 1751.

SUTHERLANDSHIRE.

SIR Robert Gordon had a MS. survey of this shire by Mr. Duglass, chaplain to the earl of Sutherland [k].

WIGTONSHIRE.

A Description of this sheriffdom drawn long since by Sir Andrew Agnew of Lachnaw, and David Dunbar of Baldoon, was in Sir R. Gordon hands [l].

A poem on *Loch Rian*, addressed to the earl of Stair 1734, in the Gentleman's Magazine 1741, p. 269.

[i] Walpole's Anecd. vol. iii. p. 58. n.
[k] Nich. p. 21.   [l] Id. ib.

ISLANDS

ISLANDS on the coaſt of Scotland.

D R. Robert James, the noted antiquary of C. C. Coll. Oxon.
wrote a ſhort deſcription of *Orkney* and the Highlands, now
among his MSS. there [a].   As this work, in four 4to ſheets, includes a deſcription of Shetland, Wales, *Poland*, *Greenland*, and *Guinee*,
it cannot be very copious.

   " Thormondus Torffæus, hiſtoriographer royal of Norway, wrote
" Orcades, ſeu rerum Orcadenſium hiſtoriæ, lib. iii. quorum primus
" præter inſularum ſitum, numerumque, comitum, procerum, incola-
" rumque origines, familias, geſta & viciſſitudines a primis monarchiæ
" Norvegicæ incunabulis ad A. D. 1222, continua fere ſerie exhibet.
" 2dus, primos Orcadum epiſcopos eorumq. ſucceſſores, &, qui poſtea
" vixerunt, comites ſub regibus Norvegiæ fiduciarios, tum etiam quæ de
" rebus Orcadenſibus & Hæbudenſibus exinde ad an. 1469, annotata,
" complectitur.   Utroq. firmiter aſſeritur regum Norvegiæ jus dominii
" in inſulas illas.   Tertius, indefeſſa potentiſſimorum regum Daniæ
" Norvegiæq. ſtudia in jure ſuo repetendo continet, variis documentis
" ex archivis regiis aſſerta. Hafniæ. 1697." Fol.

   Mr. James Wallace, miniſter of Kirkwall, at the requeſt of Sir R.
Sibbald, made collections and a large map of that country for the General
Atlas which his friend had projected.   It was firſt publiſhed and dedicated to Sir Robert by his ſon, the phyſician, Edinb. 1693. 12mo. who
enlarged and reprinted it in his own name under the title of " An ac-
" count of the iſlands of Orkney. By James Wallace, M. D. and
" F. R. S. To which is added, an eſſay concerning the Thule of the
" antients. Lond. 1700." 8vo [b].   Out of theſe and other informations,
and his own obſervations, Sir Robert compoſed a large and finiſhed deſcription of theſe iſlands in 52 chapters, whoſe titles may be ſeen in
Nicholſon, p. 54.   He had alſo a deſcription of them by John Ben,
who lived there 1529, and a ſhort relation of the moſt conſiderable things
in them, by Matthew Mackail [c].   He publiſhed at Edinburgh 1711.

   [a] Cat. MSS. Ang. tom. i. p. 263. Nº 43. Nich. p. 51.
   [b] The eſſay on Thule is Sir Robert Sibbald's, and was in the firſt edition. Sir Robert
Gordon had an account of Orkney from Mr. Wallace, larger than that which has been
printed. Nich. p. 20.   [c] Ib. p. 52.

Fol. from a MS. of Sir Robert Monteith, laird of Egliſha and Gairſa, dated Kirkwall, Sept. 29, 1633, " The deſcription of the iſles of Ork-
" nay and Zetland; with the mapps of them, done from the accurat
" obſervation of the moſt learned who lived in theſe iſles."

" A brief deſcription of Orkney, Zeatland, Pightland firth, and
" Caithneſs, wherein after a ſhort journal of the author's voyage thi-
" ther, theſe northern places are firſt more generally deſcribed; then
" a particular view is given of the ſeveral iſles thereto belonging, toge-
" ther with an account of what is moſt rare and remarkable therein;
" with the author's obſervations thereupon. Edinb. 1701." 12mo. By
John Brand.

" Orcades: or a geographic and hydrographic ſurvey of the Ork-
" neys and Lewis iſlands, in 8 maps, exhibiting the rocks, ſhoals,
" ſoundings, quality of the bottom, diverſities of the coaſt, flowings
" and ſettings of the tides, and diſtant views of the land: alſo an ac-
" count of the Orkney iſlands, the manner of taking the ſurvey, the
" ſtate of the tides, and a particular deſcription of the rocks, ſhoals,
" channels, harbours, anchoring-places, the directions, irregularities,
" and velocities of the ſeveral ſtreams of tide round each iſland. In-
" terſperſed with ſuitable obſervations for ſailors. By Murdoch Mac-
" kenzie. Lond. 1750." Fol.

In N° 1, p. 53, and N° 98, p. 6139, of the Philoſophical Tranſactions are Sir Robert Murray's obſervations on the remarkable current of
the tides about the iſles of Orkney. In N° 137, p. 927, Sir Robert
Murray's deſcription of the iſle of *Hirta* and the Barnacles. In N°
222, p. 298, Sir H. Sloane's reflections on four kinds of Indian beans
found on the Orkney ſhore, three of which grow in Jamaica [d]. In
N° 233, p. 727, Mr. Martin Martin's obſervations on the N. iſlands
of Scotland. In N° 492, p. 144, Mr. Mackenzie's ſtate of the tides
in Orkney.

Sir Rob. Sibbald publiſhed a deſcription of the iſles of *Shetland* different as it ſeems from that of which Nicholſon gives the chapters,
p. 55. It begins with a general account of theſe iſlands, and then

---

[d] Sir G. Mackenzie obſerves, N° 117, that it is very common to find ſuch beans on the ſhore of the W. iſlands.   [e] Nich. p. 20.

each

each are particularly defcribed. Dunrofenefs, c. 1. Fair ifle, c. 2.
Burray, c. 3. Breffay, c. 4. Nofs, c. 5. Waes parifh in Yetland, c. 6.
Daleting, c. 7. Yell, c. 8. Northmaven parifh, c. 9. Unft, c. 10.
The particular advantages of Shetland, and ufefulnefs to Great Britain,
c. 11. Of the firft inhabitants; that thefe iflands are Thulè, &c. c. 12.
Sir Robert's larger differtation on Thule was firft printed at the end of
Wallace's defcription of the Orkney, and in Gibfon's Camden.

In the Philofophical Tranfactions, Nº 473, p. 57, is a defcription
of the ifland of Zetland, in two letters from Mr. Tho. Prefton, 174¾.
Bagford's lift, prefixed to Gibfon's Camden, mentions " A defcription
" of Hethland, and of the fifhery there, by Jo. Smith", and " A table
" of Hethland, with a defcription of it."

" A voyage to Shetland, the Orkneys, and the Weftern Ifles of
" Scotland: giving an account of the laws, cuftoms, antiquities, na-
" tural curiofities, fifheries, &c. of thofe places, particularly the her-
" ring fifheries; with the prefent methods of catching, curing, pack-
" ing, &c. the fingular fincerity, honefty, and temperance of the in-
" habitants; their religious ceremonies, fuperftitions, charms, appari-
" tions, and that amazing faculty of the fecond fight, fo frequent
" among them, by which future events are with certainty foretold.
" 1751." 8vo. A meagre compilation to favour the herring fifhery.

A defcription of Shetland, 1753. 8vo.

" An exact and authentic account of the greateft white-herring-
" fifhery in Scotland carried on yearly in the ifland of Zetland, by the
" Dutch only. The method the Dutch ufe in catching the herrings,
" and an exact account of their way of curing, and lafting, or cafking
" them: and the method laid down, whereby we may eafily engrofs
" that profitable branch of trade into our own hands. To which is
" prefixed, a defcription of the ifland, its fituation, produce, the man-
" ners of the inhabitants, with their method of trading with the Dutch.
" By a gentleman who refided five years on the ifland. Lond. 1750."
8vo.

Sir Robert Gordon had a MS. defcription of the ifles of *Tirecy*, *Conna*,
Colle, and *Columbkill*, by Mr. Frazer, dean of the ifles [e]. Sir Rob. Sib-

---

[e] Nich. p. 20.

2   bald

bald had a MS. account of the Ebudæ, by Donald Monroe, treating of 2io iflands, beginning with Man and ending with Suilfkeray.

At the end of Sacheverell's account of Man is his voyage to I Columb-kill 1688.

In the Gentleman's Magazine, Dec. 1754, p. 566, and Feb. 1755, p. 61, are attempts to prove the antient Emona to have been *Inch-Comb* in the firth of Forth, by G. S. and John Romefcot: Sibbald was of the fame opinion f; but Malcolm Campbell, in the laft of thefe Magazines, removes it to Icolm-kill.

The *Weftern Ifles* were pretty accurately defcribed by Donald Monroe, dean of the ifles, who travelled over them in 1549; from whence G. Buchanan made extracts. Several MS. of his account are mentioned by Nicholfon g, who had feen another defcription of *Hirta* and *Rona* by lord vifcount Tarbet. A fpecimen of the dialect of Irifh ftill ufed here and in the Highlands, is at the end of his Scotch hiftorical library, N° ii. Mr. Wallace promifed a full defcription of thefe iflands, Shetland, and thofe in Edinburgh firth, by his father, with maps of the moft confiderable.

" A defcription of the Weftern iflands of Scotland: containing a
" full account of their fituation, extent, foils, product, harbours, bays,
" tides, anchoring-places, and fifheries; the antient and modern go-
" vernment; religion and cuftoms of the inhabitants, particularly of
" their druids, heathen temples, monafteries, churches, chappels, an-
" tiquities, monuments, forts, caves, and other curiofities of art and
" nature. Of their admirable and expeditious way of curing moft
" difeafes by fimples of their own product. A particular account of
" the fecond fight, or faculty of forefeeing things to come, by way
" of vifion, fo common among them. A brief hint of methods to
" improve trade in that country, both by fea and land. With a
" new map of the whole, defcribing the harbours, anchoring-places,
" and dangerous rocks, for the benefit of failors. To which is added
" a brief defcription of the ifles of Orkneyand Schetland. By M. Mar-
" tin, gent. Lond. 1703." 8vo. The 2d edition, very much corrected,

---

f Sir R. Sibbald's account of Fifefhire, p. ii. c. 2. and Appendix ad Mifc. erud. ant. de Bodotria, p. 104. g P. 55.

was

was printed 1716. 8vo.   In this book is an account and plate of the druids temple at *Claſſerniſs* in Lewis.   Dr. Stukeley had a correct plate of the upright of it.

" A late voyage to *St. Kilda*, the remoteſt of all the Hebrides or
" Weſtern Iſles of Scotland : with a hiſtory of the iſland, natural,
" moral, and topographical ; wherein is an account of their cuſtoms,
" religion, fiſh, fowl, &c. as alſo a relation of a late impoſtor there,
" pretended to be ſent by St. John Baptiſt. By M. Martin, gent. Lond.
" 1698, 1716." 1746. 8vo. The 3d edit. 1749. and 4th, 1753. both
8vo. have the ſame title enlarged : the latter has a map and figures
of the birds prefixed.

" The hiſtory of St. Kilda : containing a deſcription of this remark-
" able iſland ; the manners and cuſtoms of the inhabitants ; the reli-
" gious and pagan antiquities there found ; with many other curious and
" intereſting particulars.   By the rev. Mr. Kenneth Macaulay, miniſter
" of Ardnamurchan, miſſionary to the iſland, from the Society for
" promoting Chriſtian knowledge. Lond. 1764." 8vo. with a map.
This ſeems the moſt authentic and probable account, and is wrote
with a good degree of judgment and learning.

ANECDOTES

ANECDOTES

OF

IRISH Topography.

ANECDOTES

OF

IRISH Topography.

DR. Nicholſon while he was compiling his other hiſtorical libraries collected many materials for an Iriſh one. His appointment to the ſee of Derry, where he ſat eight years, gave him better opportunities for compleating it, though he confeſſes many pieces muſt have eſcaped his notice. The laſt edition of Ware's Iriſh writers has above 400 additional ones: the greater part have devoted their pens to religious ſubjects, controverſy, and lives of ſaints; the reſt are chroniclers; but ſcarce any topographers. This kind of curioſity is of very modern date in Ireland. The ſociety founded by Petty and Molyneux for philoſophical inquiries hardly ſubſiſted five years. The preſent century has thrown more light on the face of the country. The ſociety formed about twenty years ago have given ſpecimens of their abilities, which their country has no reaſon to be aſhamed of:——a plan for writing the deſcriptions of counties, which would more illuſtrate thoſe of England than thoſe which uncertain genealogiſts or unſkilful compilers have obtruded on the public.

Roman Geography of Ireland.

WE can go no further for a deſcription of Ireland among the antient geographers than to Ptolomy, who calls it *Little Britain*, and makes it the next iſland in the world after Great Britain and Tapobranè. A map of it according to him engraved by Hollar is in Ware's

Anti-

Antiquities. All that is faid about Ireland by Strabo, Mela, and Solinus fhews only, as bp. Nicholfon obferves, that they knew not what to fay. The former places it north of Britain, and ingenuoufly confeffes he had received very little information about it. He only learned that it was inhabited by brutifh canibals, and was of an oblong form[a]. Mela and Solinus give the fame reprefentation of the people, and concur in their accounts of the richnefs of its meadows. The firft allows it few birds and no bees[b]: the other adds, that the fea between it and us is navigable only a few days in fummer. Hearne[c] mentions an old MS. of him in the Royal Society's library, that had a whole chapter about Ireland not in the common editions, which, if genuine, and not taken from Giraldus Cambrenfis, would prove it to be known and frequented by the Romans. Mr. Wallace[d] endeavours to prove it was not, and that their Ierne and Hybernia were part of Scotland. Pliny[e] reckons Ireland among the Britifh ifles, Orofius[f] diftinguifhes it from Britain, and fays it is narrower, more temperate and fruitful. He peoples it with Scots, in which he has Claudian[g] and later authors on his fide. Marcianus Heracleota[h] makes it 2170 ftades long, 1834 broad, and from 6845 to 9085 in circumference; and gives it 16 provinces, 15 cities, 5 promontories, and 6 iflands. Tacitus[i] reprefents it as narrower than Britain, the country and people of which greatly refembled thofe of Ireland; but the ports and havens more frequented by merchants, as lying between Britain and Spain, and convenient to Gaul. But though one of its petty princes put himfelf under the protection of Agricola, and that general frequently obferved a fmall force was fufficient to reduce it, it never appears to have been fubject to the Romans, nor have any of their coins or monuments been found there.

---

[a] vi. p. 201. Such is the fenfe Cafaubon gives to προμηκης, μαλλον δε πλατος εχυσα. Perhaps Strabo wrote προμηκης μεν, αλλ' υ πλατlεια υσα. Pliny makes it longer than broad. [b] Mela goes fo far as to fay, that duft or ftones brought from thence will make them forfake their hives. Camden fays they were in his time remarkably plenty.——Bede fays *fcrapings* of Irifh *books* will kill fnakes. St. Nannan, to deliver a village of Connaught from fleas, made an adjoining meadow fo full of them that neither man nor beaft could come near it. Giral. Top. ii. p. 31 [c] Letter to Thorefby at the end of Leland's It. vol. i. p. 106. [f] Hift. of the Orkneys, p. 156, &c. [e] Lib. iv. p. 16. [f] Lib. i. p. 2. [g] Paneg. de 4to Hon. conf. l. 33. [h] In Periplo. [i] Vita Agr, c. 24.

The

The oldeſt [k] deſcriptions of Ireland by its own natives ſeem to be thoſe antient MS. ones which divide it into provinces, with the particular books of Connaught, Munſter, Leinſter, Ulſter, Flatrach, and Uriel in the famous Liber Lechanus, a large collection of old Iriſh treatiſes moſtly hiſtorical [l]. Ware [m] mentions theſe diviſions in a MS. code of the Minorites of Monſernand, t. Ed. I. and the regiſter of Duiſk abbey. Nicholſon [n] ſpeaks of other general deſcriptions in the Cotton library, Jul. F. 6. & Dom. A. 18. but the firſt is only a deſcription of Munſter, art. 76, and the other the maps before-mentioned in England. Treviſa's " Deſcription of Ireland," as well as of Britain, is barely mentioned by Pits and Tanner, without adding whether they now exiſt or not.

Giraldus Cambrenſis, who accompanied prince John, afterwards king of England, in quality of ſecretary and privy counſeller, and refuſed two biſhopricks here, is the firſt that gives any connected account of the country. He wrote beſides a civil hiſtory of tranſactions here, " Topographia Hiberniæ," in 3 books or diſtinctions [o]; the 1ſt treating of the natural hiſtory, the 2d of mirabilia [p], the 3d, the firſt peopling of the iſland, and the manners of the inhabitants [q];

firſt

[k] Staniharſt (Deſc. Hib. c. 7.) and Bale make St. Patrick author of an Odœporicon or Itinerary of Ireland, which is nothing more than a journal of his travels through the iſland—perhaps like thoſe of ſome modern apoſtles !——Inexperienced as the Iriſh were in their own geography, we muſt not forget that Virgil, who at the end of the 8th century, revived and maintained the doctrine of the antipodes againſt Scripture, the antient geographers, the fathers, and the whole world, was their countryman. Pope Zachary threatned him with excommunication; but as his holineſs ſeems to have proceeded on a miſconception of the point, taking the antipodes for another earth and ſolar ſyſtem, the ſentence was not executed.——Of this country too was Johannes Erigena, who oppoſed the doctrine of tranſubſtantiation in the next age. So little do hiſtorians labour to be exact, that this man has been made aſſiſtant to Grimbald in founding the univerſity of Oxford, and been brought to an untimely end by the penknives of his pupils : whereas he was dead ſix years before his nameſake, abbot of Etheling, was invited by Alfred, and twenty years before the ſame abbot was murdered by the contrivance of his monks.

[l] Nich. p. 2 and 38. Once in abp Uſher's library at Trinity Coll. Dublin ; but in James IId's reign ſent to Paris by James Fitzgerald. [m] Antiq. of Ireland and writers, p. 22. [n] Page 3. [o] Not four, as Bale. [p] This ſeems to be alone in the Cotton library, Cleop. D. 5. and bibl. Chandois memb. hiſt. N° 7. 4to. unleſs it is the title of the whole as in the Weſtminſter MS. where *explicit Topologia Hiberniæ.* [q] He begins his firſt preface to his deſcription of Wales, addreſſed to abp. Langton, " Ille ego qui quondam Hyberniæ topographiam cum abditis ſuis & ſecretis

firſt printed by Camden among his Anglica, &c. Francf. 1602. Fol. In his Retractationes, publiſhed by Wharton [r], he apologizes for the many marvellous ſtories he has filled this his firſt [s] work with; aſſuring his readers that he had many of them from perſons of rank in the country, though he took many on report: and St. Auſtin ſays, uncertainties are neither to be poſitively affirmed nor totally rejected. He recited it publickly at Oxford three days ſucceſſively before the poor, the doctors, and the towns-people and univerſity, all of whom he treated [t].——A very good atteſtation in an age that could not contradict him! yet compared by Hearne to Herodotus' recital of his hiſtory at the Olympic games. Wood [u] ſays he made a map of Ireland, which is not in the two Bodleian copies, but is to be found in a much completer at Benet Coll. I. 9. His work was tranſlated into Engliſh by James Walſh [x], an Iriſh ſtudent at Hart hall, Oxf. 1572, and ſoon after by John Stowe, whoſe MS. is in the Harleian library, N° 551. Its many invectives and groſs errors were confuted by Stephen White an Iriſh Jeſuit, whom Uſher calls *virum antiquitatum non ſolum Hiberniæ ſuæ ſed aliarum gentium ſcientiſſimum,* and Ware, *a curious and diligent ſearcher into the antiquities of Ireland.* Philip Sullivan, much inferior to White, anſwered Giraldus in " Zoilomaſtix," which does not appear to have been ever printed. He publiſhed " Hiſtoriæ " catholicæ Hiberniæ compendium. Ulyſſip. 1621. 4to. in 4 vols. the 1ſt treating of the nature and commodities of the country; manners, religion, &c. the reſt are hiſtorical down to 1618. Uſher brands him for an egregious liar, for which the other lays him on in his " Patriciana." He was a ſea captain under Philip king of Spain [y]. John Lynch, titular archdeacon of Tuam and abp. of Killaloe, who had White's unfiniſhed MS. wrote under a feigned name a particular de-

---

ſecretis in 3 diſtinctionibus triennii labore digeſſi, & vaticinalem expugnationis Hibernicæ ſubſequenter hiſtoriam duobus diſtinctionibus biennali labore complevi:" and in his epiſtle to the chapter of Hereford about·his writings (Ang. Sac. ii. 439.) he calls it " opus ab alio non attemptatum." In a letter he wrote to Wm. [Vere] bp. of Hereford about his books, printed in Uſher's Epiſt. Hib. ſylloge, p. 114, he values himſelf upon part of the 3d diſtinction, where he treats of the harp and other muſical inſtruments of the Iriſh.

 [r] Ang. Sac. ii. 455.   [s] Labore primævo.   [t] Cat. of his own works. Hiſt. & ant. Ox. I. p. 56. [u] Hiſt. & ant. Ox. ſub an. 1187.   Ath. Ox. i. 157. [y] Nich. p. 44.

                  tection

tection of Giraldus's errors, called " Cambrenfis everfus, feu potius
" hiftorica fides in rebus Hibernicis G. Cambrenfi abrogata : in quo
" plerafq; jufti hiftorici dotes defiderari, plerofq. nævos ineffe oftendit
" Gratianus Lucius Hibernus, qui etiam aliquot res memorabiles Hi-
" bernicas veteris & novæ memoriæ paffim e re nata huic operi infe-
" ruit. Impreff. 1662. Fol [z]. in which he follows him ftep by ftep,
expofing his ignorance and malice, and charging him with the crime
of Polidore Virgil and Aldus, deftroying many of the Irifh annals he
perufed :——an affertion allowed in either cafe only by thofe whofe
partiality would afcribe more to the Irifh than their due, and unworthy
to be even fuppofed of the great reftorer of claffical literature !——
Giraldus, with all his credulity and prejudices as an hiftorian, appears
to be an honeft man, and, for that time of day, a good fcholar. The
freedom with which he treats the monks, againft whofe hypocrify,
roguery, and ignorance he wrote his Speculum ecclefiæ [a], made them
his inveterate enemies. His franknefs appears in the plainnefs with
which he paints out the faults of his countrymen the Welfh, after
having drawn the better part of their character with equal plainnefs;
and in nothing fo much as the freedom and ferioufnefs with which he
reproved Richard II. when king, for his vices [b]. He loft the bifhopric of
St. David's after actual election bv the venality of his chapter, the dirty
ambition of abp. Walter, and the bafe ingratitude of king John : on
which he refigned his archdeaconry to his nephew. Mortified to the
laft degree at his difappointment he was not content to reprefent Hen. II.
as a deceitful prince, pleafed to difappoint his fervants, but carried his
refentment fo far as to rejoice at the fucceffes of Lewis in England as
his avenger, and this in his Inftitution of a prince, wrote when he
was near 70, and juft before he died.

The defcription of Ireland in Hollinfhed is no more than a tranflation of Giraldus' Topography, with fhort notes by Richard Stanihurft,
popifh archbifhop of Armagh, uncle and predeceffor to Ufher, and fon
of James Stanihurft, recorder of Dublin and fpeaker of the houfe of com-

[z] Ware's Irifh writers, p. 163.   [a] MS. Cott. Tib. B. xiii.   [b] In his letters,
Lel. Coll. II. 109.

mons

mons there c. It is dedicated to Sir Hen. Sidney, lord lieutenant. His four books of the affairs of Ireland in Latin d, with an appendix out of Giraldus, and annotations, were printed by Plantin at Antwerp 1584. 4to.

Camden has given the beſt topographical deſcription of this iſland, improved in bp. Gibſon's editions of his Britannia with notes by Sir Richard Cox, &c. The names of places in Ptolemy e and other old geographers are well explained, the modern ſtate of the five provinces (Leinſter, Munſter, Ulſter, Connaught, and Meath) conciſely and juſtly drawn; and the various cuſtoms of the inhabitants from the earlieſt times to his own properly repreſented. He acknowledges receiving much information from one John Good f, a Romiſh prieſt, educated at Oxford, and ſchoolmaſter at Limerick 1566, whoſe ſhort treatiſe on the then modern cuſtoms of Ireland he inſerted in his later Latin editions g, and in his edition of 1606 is a deſcription of Dublin h, drawn up at his deſire by Uſher, afterwards primate. Flaherty i reflects thus on Camden:

> Perluſtras Anglos oculis, Camdene, duobus;
> Uno oculo Scotos, cæcus Hibernigenas.

How could it be otherwiſe? He never travelled further than the Picts wall; and yet his work would have been incompleat without ſome account of Scotland and Ireland. He therefore took the beſt he could get. Leland, who perſonally perluſtrated only England, ſays not a word of the other two kingdoms.

The Camden of Ireland was Sir James Ware, who collected and preſerved the ſcattered monuments and antiquities of his native country. His purſuit of theſe ſtudies began after he left the univerſity, by the

---

c Ath. Ox. I. 442. He practiſed alchemy at Antwerp till every body was weary of his knaveries, and then took up the profeſſion of phyſic in Spain. Rich's New deſcription of Ireland.

d Addreſſed to his dear brother P. Plunket, baron of Dunſane.

e Sir J. Ware has a chapter explaining them, and another of the antient territories in Ireland.

f Quære, If this be not Tanner's *William* Good?

g Lynch calls theſe vt her low anecdotes. Biſhop Nicholſon ſuppoſes this John mentioned in the Ath. Ox. I. 101.

h Communicated in a letter printed among Camden's, p. 76, including other places in Ireland.   i Ogygia, p. 347.

encouragement of bp. Ufher. When he was juft turned of thirty he publifhed lives of the abps. of Cafhell and Tuam, and of the bifhops of Dublin [k] : about twelve years after [1639] an account of the Irifh writers, 4to. and 1654, when he was 65, difquifitions on the antiquities of Ireland, and a 2d edition augmented 1658, together with Annals of Ireland under Hen. VII [l]. which were fucceeded by feveral hiftorical and other pieces [m]. Many of thefe came out in different volumes, and were collected into one, and tranflated from the original Latin by his fon Robert and others 1705. A completer and far better edition of all his works, except his Annals of Ireland, was publifhed at different times by Walter Harris, efq; [n] in three volumes, Fol. The 1ft contains the ecclefiaftical affairs of this kingdom, adorned with prints of the cathedrals, feals, &c. Dublin 1739. The 2d is a tranflation of his Difquifitions, with eight additional chapters, and other improvements from his own and other papers, diftinguifhed from the reft of the work ; with prints of antiquities, coins, and religious orders. Dubl. 1745. The 3d volume comprehends the Irifh writers, with the addition of near 400 new articles, many from a copy interleaved by the author. Thefe were reprinted in two volumes folio. Dubl. 1764. Sir James found time for thefe ftudies notwithftanding his engagements as auditor-general, at the council-board and in parliament for the univerfity, and the negociations he conducted for Charles I. with the Irifh catholics. When the parliament were mafters of Ireland he retired firft to France [o], and then to England, till the Reftoration reinftated him in thefe and other public charges. He died 1666, aged 73. His MS. collections relative to Ireland were purchafed of his heir by lord Clarendon, when lieutenant 1686, and after his death by the late duke of Chandos [p], whom the public fpirited dean of St. Patrick in vain follicited to depofit them in the public library at Dublin. They have

---

[k] The firft 1626, the other 1628. 4to. all incorporated into his large work containing the lives of the Irifh prelates 1665. Fol.

[l] His Annals under Hen. VIII. Edw. and Mary were publifhed 1664. Fol.

[m] Spencer's View of the ftate of Ireland 1733, Hanmer s Chronicle, and Campion's Hiftory of Ireland.

[n] Who married his great grand-daughter.

[o] He gave his Itinerarium Gallicum to Sir R. Cotton, in whofe library it now is.

[p] See before in Middlefex, p. 265.

4 Q 2

fince

fince fuffered another fate, and been difperfed into more numerous hands. Some part fell into thofe of lord Newport, late chancellor of Ireland ⁑.

Flaherty, who had confiderable knowledge in the hiftory and anti-quities of his country, begins his Ogygia, printed at Lond. 1685. 4to with a topographical account of Ireland, to which he gives this name from Plutarch on the authority of Camden.

John Dymmocks's Treatife of Ireland, infcribed to Sir Edm. Carye; containing a geographical defcription of the kingdom and its five pro-vinces, and an account of Effex's expedition 1599, is among the Har-leian MSS. N⁰ 1291.

Jofias Bodley (younger brother to Sir Thomas) wrote " Obferva-
" tions concerning the fortreffes of Ireland and of the Britifh colonies
" of Ulfter;" and " A jocular defcription of a journey which he
" took to Lecale in Ulfter 1602.' both MSS. in Sir James Ware's
library ʳ.

" A fhort furvey of Ireland, truely difcuffing who it is that hath fo
" armed the hearts of the people with difobedience to the prince: with
" a defcription of the country and the condition of the people, no leffe
" neceffarie and needfull to be refpected by the Englifh, then requifite
" and behoovefull to be reformed in the Irifh. By Barnabe Rych,
" gent. 1609." 4to. This is intitled in the catalogue of Harleian
pamphlets, " A new defcription of Ireland : wherein is defcribed
" the difpofition of the Irifh; whereunto they are inclined : no
" lefs admirable to be perufed, than credible to be believed : neither
" unprofitable nor unpleafant to be read and underftood by thofe
" worthy citizens of London that be now undertakers in Ireland. By
" Barnabe Rich, gent. Lond. 1610." 4to. The author had a captain's commiffion under Sir J. Perrot, and lived 47 years in this kingdom, of which he publifhed a furvey, He laments the barbarifm in
which the people were kept by popery, and the corruptions of their
hiftory by Giraldus and Stanihurft, the later of whom he largely
confutes.

⁑ Pref. to Harris's Hibernica, and Effays on the Irifh hiftorians, in a letter to lord New-port, p. 149.
ʳ Ath. Ox. I. 385.

Laurence

Laurence Echard compiled, " An exact defcription of Ireland. Lond.
" 1691." 12mo. in the form of a geographical dictionary, not mentioned among his works in the Biographia Britanica.

David Rothe, titular bifhop of Offory, of whom his cotemporary
Ufher [s] gives a high character, wrote anonymoufly a treatife   De no-
" minibus Hiberniæ," prefixed to Meffingham's " Florilegium Sanc-
" torum Hiberniæ. Par. 1624." Fol.

" A tour thro Ireland in feveral entertaining letters : wherein the
" prefent ftate of that kingdom is confidered, and the moft noted
" cities, towns, feats, rivers, buildings, &c. are defcribed ; interfperfed
" with obfervations on the manners, cuftoms, antiquities, curiofities,
" and natural hiftory of the country.   To which is prefixed a defcrip-
" tion of the road from London to Holyhead. By two Englifh gen-
" tleman. Lond. 1748." 8vo. firft printed at Dublin 1740, and dedicated to the Philofophical Society.

" Hibernia curiofa.   A letter from a gentleman in Dublin to his friend
" at Dover in Kent, giving a general view of the manners, cuftoms,
" difpofitions, &c. of the inhabitants of Ireland ; with occafional ob
" fervations on the ftate of trade and agriculture in that kingdom : and
" including an account of fome of its moft remarkable natural curiofi-
" ties, fuch as falmon-leaps, waterfalls, cafcades, glynns, lakes, &c.
" with a more particular defcription of the Giants Caufeway in the
" north and of the celebrated lake of Kilarny in the fouth of Ire-
" land, taken from an attentive furvey and examination of the originals.
" Collected in a tour thro' the kingdom in the year 1764, and orna-
" mented with plans of the principal originals, engraved from draw-
" ings taken on the fpot. Lond. [1767.]" 8vo. By Mr. John Bufh, who
promifes a natural hiftory of the whole kingdom. The low wit and
wretched plates are no recommendation of this otherwife ufeful account.

" Letters to the earl of Pomfret, earl of Corke and Orrery, earl of
" Shannon, lord Southwell, &c. &c. written from Leverpoole, Chef-
" ter, Corke, the lake of Killarney, Dublin, Tunbridge wells, and
" Bath : containing obfervations on fuch particulars as were thought

---

[s] *Patriarum antiquitatum indagator diligentiffimus.* Ant. Brit. p. 385.   He wrote
" Hibernia refurgens," and fome other religious tracts in favour of popery in Ireland.

" worthy

" worthy of attention. By Samuel Derrick, efq; mafter of the ceremo-
" nies of Bath and Tunbridge wells.   To which are added, letters to
" lady J—n C—r, defcribing the lake of Killarney and Mucrus gar-
" dens, written by William Ockenden, efq; member for Great Mar-
" low. Lond. 1767." 2 vols. 12mo.

   " Under the guidance and patronage of a gentleman (whom we
are not at liberty to name) a few perfons formed themfelves into a
fociety, in order to collect materials for a book after the method of
Camden's Britannia, to be publifhed under the title of " Hibernia or
" Ireland antient and modern."   For this end they fent circular letters
to many curious and learned gentlemen in the feveral counties, intreat-
ing their affiftance to forward the faid fcheme, which many of them
communicated with freedom and chearfulnefs.   Yet the deficiencies
were fo great, that the fociety judged it neceffary to fend into the
world a rude and premature fkeleton of one particular county t, in order to fhew their defign, and to have an opportunity of publifhing a
table of queries, in order to inftruct every man in the nature of the
enquiries to be made in their refpective neighbourhoods.   But neither
did this method anfwer the purpofes in as compleat a manner as could
be wifhed, and therefore the fociety were obliged to change their plan,
and after as much time as would have compleated the defign over the
whole kingdom they returned in a great meafure to their firft fcheme
of perfonal applications, and refolved to collect as full an account as
poffible of the county of Down, and by the publication of it, to demonftrate that 'tis very far from impoffible to carry on the fame views
through every county of the kingdom ; provided they are undertaken
with a fmall degree of public fpirit u."

Maps.

THE oldeft engraved maps of Ireland feem to be Speed's general
map of the kingdom, and one of the four counties of Leinfter,
Munfter, Connaught, and Ulfter, 1610.

   Thuanus in a letter to Camden, dated Feb. 1605, mentions fome
maps *nuper editæ* x.

---

t Down.   u Pref. to the Antient and prefent ftate of the county of Down 1744.
x Camd. Epift. 69.

   There

There is an old map of Ireland by Woodhoufe 1653 ʸ. Hollar engraved another the fame year, with the four chief cities in a fingle fheet.

Robert Leeth, a perfon fkilful in taking a plot of a country, was fent to take Ulfter 1567 ᶻ.

Sir William Petty, who was fent over as phyfician to the army, and two years after entered into a contract to furvey the lands forfeited in the rebellion 1641, in ten months made an actual furvey of the whole kingdom, and publifhed a fet of accurate maps 1685, intitled, " Hiber-" niæ delineatio quoad hactenus licuit perfectiffima. Studio Gul. Petty, " eq. aur." The province of Leinfter, confifting of 16 counties, each in a diftinct map: that of Munfter, of 6 : Ulfter, 9 : and Connaught 5ᵃ.

Cornelius a Beughem, a modern Dutch chalcographer, publifhed itinerary defcriptions of the roads in Ireland, in a fmall pocket book, written in his own language, under the title of " Polimetria Britan-" nica, dat is, Stedemeting van Groot Britanie, ziinde een korfe aen-" wiizinge hoe wiid, voernamfte ftede in drie koningriiken van Eng-" leand, Schotland, Yreland, van malkanderen leggen. In kooper " gefneden. Amft. 1692. 12mo ᵇ.

Ireland, corrected from the lateft obfervations, divided into its provinces, counties, and baronies, fhewing the principal roads, and the diftances of places in common reputed miles, by infpection, where barracks are erected, &c. By John Senex, F. R. S. Price, and Maxwell. 1712. 2 fheets.

A large map of Ireland by ——— Pratt. Another by Geo. Wildey, 1714.

Another by Moll, with plans of Dublin ᶜ, Corke, &c. He publifhed 20 maps of the provinces and counties, 4to.

A new and accurate map of Ireland, divided into its 4 provinces and 32 counties: alfo diftinct maps of the 4 provinces. All contracted from Sir Wm. Petty's furvey.

ʸ This is placed among 4to printed books in Dr. Rawlinfon's Cat. Nᵒ 329.
ᶻ Ames's Hift. of Printing, p. 540.
ᵃ Another edition has been fince made from the fame plates.
ᵇ Nich. p. 25.
ᶜ Bp. Nicholfon, p. 22. mentions feveral inquifitions, furveys, and leafes in Dublin library, taken about Q. Elizabeth's time.

2   Another

Another from Petty's and later furveys by J. Bayley. One fheet.

A map of Ireland, divided into provinces, counties, baronies, &c. with the poft and other roads, and the inland navigation, by John Rocque. 4 fheets.

Another, with the poft roads agreable to Rocque's Traveller's affiftant thro' Great Britain and Ireland. One fheet.

Nicholfon d mentions feveral charts of the coaftings and ports of Ireland in the Cotton library, Aug. A. 1.

A chart of the coaft of Ireland, with the weftern ports of Great Britain, by Murdoch, from the beft furveys and aftronomical obfervations, engraved by Kitchen.

d Page 24.

Ecclefiaftical Topography.

" IRELAND has been diftinguifhed among other nations by the
title of the Ifland of Saints, for the vigilance of its reformers
from heathenifm, and the perfeverance of the nation for fome centuries in the practice of the ftricteft moral and religious duties [a]." Avi-
enus [b] after earlier writers called it the *holy* ifland many centuries ago.
Was this from the number of their idols or the purity of their manners? Harris fays only for the happy temperature of the climate,
admitting no venomous creature to live in it [c]. One would think this a
mark of happinefs rather than of holinefs! Bolingbrooke's Parifian
doctor was not more out in his conjectures [d].

At the end of the 2d vol of Dugdale's Monafticon is a very fhort
account of fuch religious houfes in Ireland as were cells to others of
the fame order in England, or were founded by Englifhmen, or
whofe lands, regifters, and records fell into private hands there at the
diffolution, communicated by Sir James Ware, who publifhed about
1628, " Cænobia Ciftertienfia Hiberniæ," which Mr. Harris never faw.
He alfo attempted a general catalogue and fhort hiftory of all the Irifh
monafteries, omitting only fuch as were meanly built, or endowed in
the earlier ftate of the church, ranged according to the provinces and
counties. Mr. Harris difpofed this in better order, with great additions. It was before improved in the " Hiftoire monaftique d'Irlande,
" ou l'on voit toutes les abbayes, prieurez, convens, & autres com-
" munautez regulieres qu'il y a eu dans ce royaume, le temps & les titres
" de leur fondation, le nom, & la qualitè des fondateurs ; les villes,
" bourgs, comtez, & provinces ou elles etoient fituees, les differens
" ordres reguliers dont elles dependoient, les circonftances les plus re-
" marquables de leur etabliffement & de leur fuppreffion, avec quan-
" tite de remarques hiftoriques & critiques. a Paris 1690." 12mo.

---

[a] Harris's preface to his edition of Ware.
[b] In his poem De oris maritimis, collected from the moft antient Greek geographers.—
Perhaps Ιεpm had been mifread Ιεpn.
[c] Ware's Antiquities, c. 1
[d] Swift's letters by Hawkefworth, vol. ii. p. 224.

4 R   This

This little piece, whose author's name was Allemand *e*, soon became scarce, and was succeeded by " Monasticon Hibernicum, or the mo-
" nastical history of Ireland : containing, 1. All the abbies, priories,
" nunneries, and other regular communities, which were in that king-
" dom. 2. The time when, and the titles under which, they were
" founded. 3. The name and quality of their founders. 4. The
" provinces, counties, cities, or towns in which they were seated.
" 5. The several regular orders to which they belonged, and the most
" remarkable circumstances relating to their foundation and suppres-
" sion. 6. Historical and critical observations, and draughts of their
" general habits, with a map of Ireland. Lond. 1722." 8vo. This
is neither a translation of the former, though great use has been made
of it, nor were the compiler and the editor the same person.

Sir John Davis left in MS. " A large epistle to Robert earl of Salis-
" bury of the state of the counties of Monaghan, Fermanagh, and
" Cavan; and of the justices of peace and other officers of Ireland : " in
which is " A discourse touching the Corbes and Erenaghs of Ireland *f* "
Abp. Usher wrote a very learned treatise concerning the Herenach,
Termon, and Corban lands, the antient demesns (or mensals, as the
Irish call them) of the Chorepiscopi of both kingdoms, epitomised
in Spelman's Glossary, and Ware's Antiquities. The original MS.
seems to be in Dublin library, with the capitals J. U. 1609, in the
archbishop's own hand writing *g*. Mr. Harris mentions another in the
Lambeth library. His grace employed his skill in ecclesiastical antiquities in further illustrating those of his native country, in " Veterum
" epistolarum Hibernicarum sylloge. 1632 " 4to. a collection of letters
from 592 to 1180, relating to the ecclesiastical discipline and jurisdiction of the Irish church, and his " Britannicarum ecclesiarum antiqui-
" tates. Dub. 1659." 4to. Lond. 1687. Fol. a treasure of British and
Irish ecclesiastical antiquities.

e He promised other works relative to Ireland, but probably died soon.
f Harris's Irish writers p. 333.
g Nich. p. 21.

Natural

Natural Hiſtory.

THE firſt [a] inquirer into the natural hiſtory of Ireland was Dr. Gerard Boate, a Hollander, phyſician to the ſtate there 1649, which poſt he lived to hold but eight months, but compiled his book ſome years before he went over, from materials furniſhed by Sir William and Sir Richard Parſons, and his own brother Dr. Arnold Boate, who practiſed phyſic eight years at Dublin, and ſpent ſome months with him at London in his way to Paris 1644, informing him how to improve certain forfeited lands he had purchaſed in Leinſter and Ulſter. His book is intitled " Ireland's natural hiſtory : being a true and
" ample deſcription of its ſituation, greatneſs, ſhape, and nature ; of
" its hills, woods, heaths, bogs ; of its fruitful parts and profitable
" grounds, with the ſeveral ways of manuring and improving the
" ſame ; with its heads or promontories, harbours, roads, and bayes :
" of its ſprings and fountaines, brookes, rivers, loghs ; of its metalls,
" mineralls, freeſtone, marble, ſea coal, turfs, and other things that
" are taken out of the ground ; and, laſtly, of the nature and tem-
" perature of its air and ſeaſon, and what diſeaſes it is free from or
" ſubject unto : conducing to the advancement of navigation and huſ-
" bandry, and other profitable arts and profeſſions. Written by Gerard
" Boate, late doctor of phyſick to the ſtate in Ireland, and now pub-
" liſhed by Samuel Hartlib, eſq; for the common good of Ireland,
" and more eſpecially for the benefit of the adventurers and planters
therein. Lond. 1652. 12mo [b]." It is not to be wondered that his accounts are ſo imperfect, and his topographical errors ſo numerous ; but rather that a ſtranger to the country ſhould have done ſo well. He intended a 2d and 3d book of the vegetables and animals, and a 4th of the natives, their old faſhions, laws, and cuſtoms, and the attempts of their Engliſh conquerors to civilize and improve both them and their country, which his brother in his letter to Hartlib promiſed

---

[a] We ought to except St. Ruadan in the 6th century, who is ſaid to have written on the ſtrange nature of the Iriſh ſprings, and a wonderful tree. Ware de ſcript. Engl. ed. p. 5. Nich. p. 24. Tanner.

[b] See an abſtract of it in Nich. p. 12, 13.

to

to publiſh. What he publiſhed was afterwards incorporated into a natural hiſtory of Ireland by ſeveral hands. 1726. 4to. the 2d part of which conſiſted of " A collection of ſuch papers as were communicated to the Royal Society referring to ſuch curioſities in Ireland : as alſo a MS. by the abp. of Dublin :" and the 3d part was " A diſcourſe concerning the Daniſh mounts, forts, and towers in Ireland, never before publiſhed." The editor of theſe pieces was Dr. Tho. Molyneux ^c, profeſſor of phyſic in the univerſity of Dublin, phyſician to the ſtate and army in Ireland. Boate's book was tranſlated into French with this title : " Hiſtoire naturelle d'Irlande, contenant une deſcription exacte de ſa " ſituation, de ſa grandeur, de ſa figure, de la nature de ſes mon- " tagnes, de ſes foreſts, de ſes bruyeres, de ſes marais, & de ſes terres " labourables : avec le deſnombrement de ſes caps, de ſes havres, de " ſes rades, des ſes ruiſſeaux, des ſes rivieres, & de ſes lacs, des me- " taux, des mineraux, &c. et enfin de la nature & de la temperature " de ſon air & de ſes ſaiſons, des maladies dont elle eſt exempte, & " de celles a quoy elle eſt ſujette, le tout donnant de grandes lumieres " a la navigation, & a l'agriculture. Traduit de l'Anglois de Gerard " Boate, medecin des derniers eſtats d'Irlande. Par. 1666." 12mo ^d.

The rev. Mr. John Payne is mentioned in Barton s lectures on Lough Neagh, p. 176, as a perſon capable of enlarging the hiſtory of Iriſh gems ; if at hand to communicate his diſcoveries to his acquaintance.

" Synopſis ſtirpium Hibernicarum alphabeticè diſpoſitarum, ſive " commentatio de plantis indigenis, præſertim Dublinienſibus, inſti- " tuta : being a ſhort treatiſe of native plants, eſpecially in the vicinity " of Dublin, with their Latin, Engliſh, and Iriſh names, and an " abridgement of their vertue ; with ſeveral new diſcoveries : with an " appendix of obſervations made upon plants by Dr. Molyneux, phy- " ſician to the ſtate of Ireland. The firſt eſſay of this kind in the ' kingdom of Ireland. Auctore Caleb Threlkeld. M. D. Dublin. ' 1727." 12mo.

^c Younger brother to William, of whom hereafter. Some of his letters are among Locke's. He was created a baronet 1730, and died three years after.
 ^d The tranſlator refers to Sanſon's maps of Ireland, from Camden and Speed.

In

In N° 168, p. 875, of the Philofophical Tranfaᵴtions is Mr. William ᶜ Molyneux's account of the Connaught worm, faid to be the only poifonous animal in the kingdom : he thinks it the elephant caterpillar of Goedart, and that it has no fuch quality. In N° 170, p. 948, is an account of the bogs and loughs in Ireland by Mr. Wm. King, fellow of the Dublin fociety, afterwards archbifhop of Dublin. In N° 177 Mr. William Molyneux's obfervations on the circulation of the blood in the Lacerta aquatica. In N° 198, p. 659, Sir Robert Redding's account of the pearl fifhery at Omagh, in the north of Ireland : Gilbert bifhop of Limerick, about 1094, made Anfelm archbifhop of Canterbury a prefent of Irifh pearls ᶠ. In N° 205, p. 926, are improvements by fowing maize propofed by Sir Rich. Bulkley ᵍ. In N° 220, p. 223, bp. Afhe and Mr. Van's account of butter-dew that fell in the provinces of Munfter and Leinfter. In N° 225, p. 415, Dr. T. Molyneux's account of a non-defcript fcolopendra marina, found in a cod fifh. Mr. Dale, N° 254, p. 51, obferved it was the fea moufe on the Effex coaft, and the phyfalus of Johnfon, &c. Dr. Molyneux, N° 251, p. 157, fhewed this was a miftake, but acknowledged that Bartholine had mentioned the animal in Aᵴta Hafnienfia. In N° 227, p. 489, is Dr. T. Molyneux's difcourfe ʰ on the large horns frequently found underground in Ireland, with a print of a fkull with them

---

ᵉ This gentleman, diftinguifhed by the friendfhip and correfpondence of Mr. Locke, was born at Dublin 1650, and being of a philofophical genius, formed, 1683, a philofophical fociety at Dublin, on the plan of the Royal Society, under the encouragement of Sir Wm. Petty, the firft prefident, himfelf being firft fecretary, in which poft he was fucceeded by Mr. St. Geo. Afhe, profeffor of mathematics in the univerfity of Dublin. The fociety met firft weekly, and their minutes were from time to time communicated to the Royal Society : in the confufion of 1688 they were difperfed, and never refumed their meeting. He publifhed " Dioptrica, 1692." 4to. and " The cafe of Ireland's being bound by aᵴts of parliament in England ftated. 1698." which did not come out till the parliament had eftablifhed the dependency of Ireland. He died of the ftone 1698. His fon Samuel was a great aftronomer, and left his papers to Dr. Smith, of Trinity Coll. Cambridge, who publifhed his treatife of optics. His father Samuel was mafter gunner of Ireland, and publifhed praᵴtical problems in his profeffion. His grandfon Daniel, Ulfter king at arms, called by Sir J. Ware *veneranda antiquitatis cultor*, finifhed Hanmer's Chronicle, which Sir James publifhed.
ᶠ Epift. Hibern. Syll. p. 88.
ᵍ Sir Richard died 1710, a dupe to the French prophets. Harris.
ʰ Inferted with the cut in the Natural hiftory of Ireland, and in Harris's edit. of Ware.

found.

found at Dardiftoun in Meath; from which he concludes that the great American or moofe deer was formerly common there. In N° 234, p. 741, his account of fwarms of beetles infefting part of the province of Connaught in a letter to Dr. St. George, bp of Clogher. In N° 240, p. 184, and N° 261, p. 504 Dr. Plott and Dr. T. Molyneux's account of Edward Mallone, an Irifhman, 19 years old, feven feet fix inches high; his finger fix inches three-quarters long. In N° 243, p. 271, is an extract from the minutes of the philofophical fociety at Oxford, 168¼, concerning Irifh flate, and p. 294, bifhop Afhe's account of the virtues of Mackenboy, Tithimallus Hibernicus, or Irifh fpurge. In N° 261 capt. South's lift of all the feamen, fifhermen, watermen, lightermen, gabbardmen, kielmen, bargemen, boatmen, ferrymen, cottmen, and feafaring-men in Ireland 1697: the number of people in the counties of Armagh, Louth, and Meath, and city of Dublin; and an eftimate of people in Ireland, Jan. 10, 1696, and of Romifh clergy in Ireland April 1698. In N° 269, p. 792, are fome antient infcriptions found in Ireland and Scotland by Edward Lhwyd, inferted in Gibfon's Camden; and in N° 291, p. 1566, his letter to Mr. Dale about chriftalline fhells there. In N° 320, p. 308, Mr. Neve's account of inundations in the north of Ireland 1706. In Nos 335 and 336 his remarks on the natural hiftory and antiquities of Ireland. In N° 337, p. 252, are Mr. Nevill's accounts of urns and fepulchres in an ifland in Donnegal; others near Ban bridge, Down, near Omagh, Cookfton and Dungannon, Tyrone, and near Wattle bridge, Fermanagh. In N° 346, p. 367, an account of large teeth lately dug up at Maghens in the north of Ireland by Mr. F. Nevill, and Dr. Molyneux's remarks on them, addreffed to the abp. of Dublin. In N° 394, p. 122, is Mr. J. Kelly's account of ftrata found in digging for marle, and of horns difcovered in Ireland. In N° 477, p. 531, Mr. Simon's account of lac lunæ, white vitriol, &c. found by him in Ireland. In N° 487, p. 211, Mr. Skelton's account of the camel caterpiller.

" Some thoughts on the tillage of Ireland" were printed at Dublin and London 1738. 8vo.

" A letter to the public concerning bogs. Dubl. 1757." 12mo.

IRELAND was moſt antiently divided under two princes into N. and S. parts, which Bede [a] calls N. and S. Scotts. The diviſion of it into five provinces is firſt mentioned in the Montfernand MS. before referred to. Each province comprehended ſo many cantreds, each cantred (which anſwers to our hundred), 30 townlands, each of which was capable of maintaining 300 cows. Giraldus [b], who divides the province of Munſter into S. and N. and ſays nothing of Meath, gives each cantred 100 towns. Henry II. when he introduced the Engliſh laws into Ireland, A.D. 1172 divided it into ſhires. This diviſion has undergone ſeveral alterations, and does not ſeem to have been finally compleated till the beginning of the laſt century. In Sir James Ware's time there were reckoned only four provinces, LEINSTER, MUNSTER, VLSTER, and CONNAUGHT; Meath being accounted part of Leinſter. Of theſe LEINSTER contained the twelve counties of Dublin, Lowth, Meath, Weſt Meath, Longford, Kildare, King's County, Queen's County, Catherlogh, Kilkenny, Wexford, and Wicklow. MUNSTER, the ſix counties of Waterford, Cork, Kerry, Limerick, Tipperary, and Clare. VLSTER nine; Armagh, Down, Monaghan, Antrim, Donegal, Cavan, Fermanagh, Tyrone, and Londonderry. CONNAUGHT five; Galway, Mayo, Sligo, Roſcommon, and Leitrim. I follow the diviſion by counties ranged alphabetically, as in England and Scotland. Thoſe for which nothing has been done are CATHERLOGH, CAVAN, GALWAY, KING'S, LEITRIM, LONGFORD, MONAGHAN, QUEEN'S, and ROSCOMMON.

A N T R I M.

IN N° 199, p. 708, of the Philoſophical Tranſactions is part of a letter from Sir Rich. Bulkley, F.R.S. to Dr. Liſter, on the Giant's Cauſeway 1693. In N° 211 Dr. T. Molyneux's letter to Dr. Liſter about it, with correct draughts and explanations. In N° 212, p. 170, are Dr. Sam. Foley's [c] remarks on it, with anſwers to Sir R. Bulkley's queries, and Dr. Molyneux's notes. In N° 235 and N° 241 a further

---

[a] Eccleſiaſt. Hiſt. lib. 3. c. 24.   [b] Top. Hiſt. diſt i. c. 6.
[c] Afterwards bp of Down and Connor.

account

account of it by Dr. T. Molyneux, with a correct draught from the N. W. by Mr. Edwin Sandys, 1696. In N° 485, p. 124, and vol. xlviii. part 1, p. 226—238, Dr. Pococke's account of it. Vivares engraved two views of it 174¼, from paintings by Susan Drury. In N° 243 is bishop Ashe's account of a quarry of white marble in this county. In N° 372, p. 89. is a parrhelion, and in N° 395, p. 128, an aurora borealis, seen Sept. 24, 25, 26, 1725, by Arthur Dobbs, esq; of Castle Dobbs.

A R M A G H.

" THE county of Ardmagh is likely to furnish matter for a very " agreeable history, both of natural and civil commerce. There " flourishes the linnen manufacture in beauty and opulence, which has " made great part of the county like a garden. Thro' that county " passes the canal which communicating between the sea and a lake is " now of great utility to the merchants, and will soon be so to the col- " liers when the coal mine near Lough Neagh is fully opened. There " is the ancient and most honourable see, giving the greatest title in " the church of Ireland. There are mountains well worth the exa- " mination of the curious, not horrid and useless, but capable of great " beauty, and likely to be advantageous: from the summits of some of " them (which should rather be called hills than mountains, since a " plough passes over the top and corn grows on them) may be seen a " dozen beautiful lakes as well as the sea; each abounding with fish, " and probably each has marl as well as timber. Here lay the prin- " cipal scenes of action between the earl of Tir-oen and Q. Elizabeth's " generals, their battles have given names to places, and many of their " forts remain." Preface to " Lectures in natural philosophy designed " to be a foundation for reasoning pertinently upon the petrifications, " gems, crystals, and sanative quality of *Lough Neagh* in Ireland, and " intended to be an introduction to the natural history of several coun- " ties, contiguous to that lake, particularly the county of Ardmagh. " By Richard Barton, B. D. author of the analogy of divine wisdom " in the material, sensitive, moral, civil, and spiritual system of things. " Dubl. 1751." 4to. Prefixed to it is a view of part of the lough, the river *Camlin* or *Crumlin*, and the country adjacent, etched by T.

Cham-

Chambars from a painting by Mrs. L. Bufh, almoft from a verbal defcription, and " yet her pencil has come fo near nature, that had fhe " drawn from it," the doctor fays d, " it would have been vain to have " expected that fhe would have excelled it." This book is the effect of fix years enquiry, printed on paper and types made in Ireland, and the plates performed by Irifh artifts. To it is annexed " A dia- " logue concerning fome things of importance to Ireland; particularly " to the county of Armagh, being part of a defign to write the " natural, civil, and ecclefiaftical hiftory of this county," which the editor fome years before engaged in, and took a great deal of pains to this purpofe at the defire of feveral perfons of rank: a good foundation of materials was provided; but fome things neceffary to the defign being likely to prove very expenfive, to which the editor's own fortune was by no means equal, he was forced to content himfelf with this fpecimen of his intention. The rev. Mr. James Hacket, a gentleman of letters and tafte, was appointed affociate in this work; but either forefeeing the expence and labour, without the reafonable profpect of a reward, or defirous to finifh a treatife on the antiquities of Egypt, which he had fome years under confideration, he declined the tafk.

Mrs. Bufh is mentioned in this work e as having painted a volume of perfpective views, which if publifhed would do great credit to the country.

In Nᵒ 158 of the Philofophical Tranfactions, p. 552, is a letter on Lough Neagh, and its petrifying qualities, from Mr. Wm. Molyneux, fecretary to the Dublin Society, to Wm. Mufgrave, L. L. B. fellow of New Coll. Oxford, and fecretary to the Philofophical Society at Oxford for advancement of knowlege; and in Nᵒ 166 is another letter from him, Dublin, Nov. 25, 1684, retracting the feventh and laft paragraph of the former, concerning Lough Neagh ftone, and its non-application to the magnet upon calcination. In Nᵒ 168 his further obfervations. In Nᵒ 174, p. 1108, anfwers to fome queries from Molyneux concerning it by Mr. Edward Smyth, fellow of Trinity Coll. Dublin, afterwards bifhop of Down. In Nᵒ 337, p. 260, are obfervations on this lake by Fr. Nevill, in a letter to the bp. of Clogher.

d Pref. p. xvi. n.   e Page 175.

In p. 305 of Nº 481 a letter from James Simon of Dublin on its petrifying quality and petrifactions; and another from bifhop Berkley who
concurs with him, and mentions ftones fufed and cooled again to
ftone, like the fciara or lava of Etna.   Simon fays he faw in the
church at Fontevraud two pillars each 60 feet high, of one ftone, faid
to have been run.

In Birch's Hiftory of the Royal Society, vol. iv. p. 524, is Dr. Pa-
pin's account of the examination of a piece of iron broke from the petrified wood of this lake.

A S. view of the cathedral of Armagh, drawn by J. Blaymiers, engraved by L. Dempfy, is in Harris's edition of Ware: and the feals of
three archbifhops at the head of the chapter.

A map of the county by J. Rocque in four fheets.

C L A R E.

" A Letter from a clergyman in Ireland, giving an account of
" the taking of great numbers of fifh, and of many fea mon-
" fters, in the county of Clare, in that kingdom, fent to a member of
" the Royal Society at Grefham college.   Publifhed by Henry Davin-
" fon, gent. F. R. S. Lond. 1721." 12mo.

In the Philofophical Tranfactions, Nº 456, p. 360, is Dr. Lucas's
account of *Kilcorney* cave in Burren barony.

The S. profpect of *Killaloe* cathedral by J. Blaymiers and L. Dempfy
is in the laft edition of Ware.

C O R K.

" THE antient and prefent ftate of the county and city of *Cork*,
" in four books.   1. Containing the antient names of the
" territories and inhabitants, with the civil and ecclefiaftical divifions
" thereof.   2. The topography of the county and city of Cork.   3.
" The civil hiftory of the county.   4. The natural hiftory of the
" fame.   The whole illuftrated by remarks on the baronies, parifhes,
" towns, villages, feats, mountains, rivers, medicinal waters, foffils,
" animals, and vegetables, together with a new hydrographical de-
" fcription

" fcription of the fea coafts. To which are added curious notes and
" obfervations relating to the erecting and improvement of feveral arts
" and manufactures, either neglected, or ill profecuted in this county.
" Embellifhed with new and correct maps of the county and city,
" perfpective views of the chief towns, and other capital places.
" Publifhed with the approbation of the Philofophical Society. By
" Charles Smith. Dubl. 1751." 8vo. 2 vols. The xith ch. of b. iv.
contains an account of one William Clarke, an oftified man, of whom
Dr. Edw. Barry a of Dublin (who has the fkeleton) compofed and intends to publifh a learned and accurate tract, with the hiftory of his
life ; the accounts of him by Robert bp. of Cork, dean Copping, and
a lady, in the Philofophical Tranfactions, Nº 461, p. 810—815. being
far from accurate. See alfo Gent. Mag. 1760. p. 325.

" Pietas Corcagienfis : A view of the green coat hofpital, and other
" charitable foundations in the parifh of St. Mary Shandon, Corke ;
" fhewing the feveral fteps that have been taken in erecting and fup-
" porting thofe charities. Publifhed by order of the truftees of that
" hofpital. Cork 1721." 4to. with a S. view of the hofpital, and W.
view of Betridge's and Skiddy's alms houfes, engraved by J. Harris of
Cork.

" The wonderful battle of ftarlings, fought at the city of Cork, in
" Ireland, the 12th and 14th of October 1621. as it hath been cre-
" dibly informed by divers noblemen and others of the faid kingdom,
" &c. Lond. 1622." 4to. reprinted in Morgan's Phœnix Britannicus,
p. 250. Such a battle was feen on the intermediate day by perfons
on the water, between Gravefend and Woolwich.

A plan of the city at the corner of Speed's map of Munfter.

A furvey of the city and fuburbs, by J. Rocque. 1759.

The S. profpect of *Cloyne* cathedral, by J. Blaymiers and J. Haydon,
is in the laft edition of Ware.

In p. 813, Nº 461. of the Philofophical Tranfactions is Robert bp. of
Cork's account of a Frenchman at *Innis*, 70 years old, who faid he
gave fuck to a child : his breafts were very large for a man, his nipple
larger than a woman's. In p. 581 of Nº 471 is a letter from the

---

a Who has wrote feveral elaborate pieces in his profeffion.

fame

fame about the remains of an antient temple like Stonehenge, in *Kilgariffe* parish, 10 miles S. W. of Bandon, and an antient Irish stone hatchet; with a print from a drawing by Miss Anne la Bushe, a relation of his lordship's wife, made from his description. In N° 475, p. 283, are professor Ward's remarks on two dates in Arabic figures in *Cork* friary and *Kilbriton* castle.

In the " Genealogical history of the house of Yvery, with different " branches of Yvery, Lovel, Percival, and Gournay. Lond. 1742." 8vo. 2 volumes, published by the present earl of Egmont, by an example worthy of imitation, are views of three of his lordship's castles in this county; *Kanturk*, a magnificent pile, begun t. Eliz. but left unfinished by an order from the government; *Loghart* near Mallow, and *Liscarrol* b.

Basire engraved for the Antiquarian Society, in a plate with the Shropshire shield, &c. 1763. three brass trumpets found with ten more in a bog between Cork and Mallow c.

Mr. Harris encouraged us to expect a correct map of this county from the physico-historical society at Dublin.

DONNEGAL.

NOTHING has rendered this county so famous as a cave in an island in Logh Derg, formed by the Liffer near its rise, discovered by the patron saint of Ireland, or his name-sake an Irish abbot, native of Nevers, about 400 years after. Ulysses is supposed to have first made it a thoroughfare to hell; and the holy monk obtained by his prayers a constant exhibition of the torments of the wicked in it for the Irish. Pope Alexander VI. 1497, ordered the guardian of the Minorites at Donnegal to demolish it as a fiction: but it was soon restored. The lords justices under James I. drove out the priests, and laid the cave open. A description and print of it are in

b Also a view of *Weston Gordein*, or *in Gordano*, Somersetsh. granted by the Conqueror to Ascelin Govel de Percheval, common ancestor to the families of Lovel and Percival, the monuments of Richard Perceval 1190, and of another Richard Perceval 1483, both there, and the head of Sir Philip Perceval.

c More of the same were found near Carrickfergus in the north of Ireland; two others are lodged in the British Museum; two more were sold among bp. Pococke's curiosities.

Ware's

Ware's antiquities, 1ſt Eng. edit. p. 98. Henry or Hugh, monk of Saltrey, Huntingdonſhire, in Stephen's reign, was the firſt who wrote about it, and what one Owen or Tyndal a ſoldier had ſeen there: his work was publiſhed by Colgan, in his Trias Thaumaturga, p. 273. Meſſingham in Florilegio makes large extracts from it. Bale, Pits, and Nicholſon mention ſome ſuch work in the Cotton library, Dom. A. 4. with a deſcription of Ireland. Cæſarius afterwards propagated the legend d.

"St. Patrick's purgatory, containing the deſcription, originall, pro-
"greſſe and demolition of that ſuperſtitious place. By Henry Jones,
"bp. of Clogher. 1647." 4to.

"The delightful hiſtory of the life and death of St. Patrick, the
"renowned and famous champion of Ireland, containing his heroick
"acts and valorous atchievements in Europe, Aſia, and Africa; with
"other remarkable paſſages from his cradle to his grave. 1685."
12mo.

"The great folly, ſuperſtition, and idolatry of pilgrimages in Ire-
"land, eſpecially of that to St. Patrick's purgatory; together with an

---

d Uſher has proved that this purgatory is not of Patrick's invention, the oldeſt writers of his life ſaying nothing of it, nor, which is of more conſequence, he himſelf in his book de tribus habitaculis, which are heaven, earth, and hell.——Camden, p. 797, ſays ſixty-ſix books were wrote about the life and actions of this famous ſaint, moſt of which were early burnt. Two of the oldeſt were wrote by an Iriſhman; the two next by Probus about 920, falſely aſcribed to Bede his cotemporary, and printed among his works, Baſil. 1563. fol. vol. 3. Thoſe by Patrick's ſucceſſor Benignus, by bp. Kinnan (not in Tanner) by St. Evin or Eyven, by his nephews Luman, Mal, and Patrick, and by Kiaran of Belaigduin, ſeem to be all loſt. The principal one ſtill extant in Meſſingham's Florile-gium was compiled out of the reſt, by Jocelyn, monk of Furnes, but whether in Lan-caſhire or Meath, uncertain. There are others in the Bodleian library, MSS. Digb. N° 34 and 172, and Cott. lib. Vit. E. 7. Abp. Uſher had two MS. lives of him in Latin, and a third in old Iriſh. John Colgan, an Iriſh mendicant, divinity reader in the univerſity of Louvain, publiſhed a long one in three parts, in his "Trias Thauma-"turga: ſive divorum Patricii, Columbæ, & Brigidæ, trium veteris & majoris Scotiæ, "ſeu Hiberniæ, ſanctorum inſulæ, communium patronorum acta. Lovan. 1647." fol. His obituary office is printed among others. Par. 1620. fol. Philip O'Sullivan before-mentioned wrote a full account of his life and miracles, with a deal of abuſe on Engliſh heretics in "Patriciana decas. Matriti. 1629." 4to. in ten books of ten chapters. "Vitæ & miraculorum S. Patricii Hiberniæ apoſtoli epitome in brevi notitia Hiberniæ," by Ric. Archdekin, is at the end of his "Præcipuæ controverſiæ. Lovan. 1671." and enlarged at the end of his "Theologia tripartita univerſa. Antv. 1682." 3 vol. 8vo. Uſher (whoſe uncle Stanihurſt publiſhed two books of his life in Latin, Antv. 1587) intended to collect all the treatiſes truly or falſely fathered on St. Patrick, and print them under the title of "Magno Patricio adſcripta opuſcula," which deſign was executed by Sir James Ware. Lond. 1656. 8vo. with notes.

"account

" account of the lofs that the publick fuftaineth thereby, truly and
" impartially reprefented by J. Richardfon· rector of the parifh of
" Belturbet, alias Armagh ᵉ. Dubl. 1727." 8vo.

Mr. Hewfon, rector of St. Andrews, Dublin, wrote " A defcrip-
" tion of St. Patrick's purgatory in Lough-Derg, and an account of
" the pilgrim's bufinefs there ᶠ." An account of the pilgrimage and
ceremonies ftill fubfifting may be feen in the Gentleman's Magazine,
Feb. 1766, p. 60.

In N.º 337 of the Phil. Tranf. is Mr. Nevill's letter to the bifhop of
Clogher, concerning the urns and fepulchral monuments found near
Caftle-doe in an ifland between Dunfannaghan bay and Kinneveir logh.

Hollar engraved a map of *Ennifhore* [Enifhowen] a province in
Ireland [in this county] with lord Donnegal's head. 1667.

D O W N.

" **A** Topographical and chorographical furvey of the county of
" Down, including fome part of the natural and civil hiftory,
" intended as an effay towards a fuller defcription of the kingdom of
" Ireland than has hitherto appeared, with queries, recommended to
" the curious, to enable them to make proper enquiries in their re-
" fpective neighbourhoods. Dubl. Lond. 1740." 8vo. This is the
fpecimen of the phyfico-hiftorical fociety's attempts to compile a hiftory
of Ireland before-mentioned, p. 670, which not fucceeding, they had
recourfe to circular letters, by which they collected materials for
" The antient and prefent ftate of the county of Down, containing a
" chorographical defcription, with the natural hiftory of the fame.
" Illuftrated by obfervations made on the baronies, parifhes, towns,
" villages, churches, abbies, charter-fchools, mountains, rivers, lakes,
" medicinal and other fprings, &c. with a furvey of the new canal :
" as alfo a new and correct map of the county. Dubl. 1744." 8vo.

ᵉ And dean of Kilmacduac, author of " A propofal for the converfion of the Popifh
" natives of Ireland. Dubl. 1711." 8vo. and " A fhort hiftory of the attempts that
" have been made to convert the Popifh natives of Ireland to the eftablifhed religion :
" with a propofal for their converfion, &c. 1712." 8vo. He was alfo chaplain to the
duke of Ormond, and the bp. of Clogher.

Harris's writers of Ireland, p. 199. Q. if printed.

A 2d edit. Dubl. 1757. 8vo. Whoever casts his eyes on the contents of the chapters will soon perceive this is not a revised edition of the foregoing, but an entire new work.

"A letter sent by J. B. gent. unto his very frende mayster R. C. "esq. wherein is contayned a discourse of the peopling and inhabiting "the cuntrie called the *Ardes*, and other adjacent, in the northe of "Ireland; and taken in hand by Sir Tho. Smith, one of her majesties "privie council, and Tho. Smith, esq. his son. Lond. imprinted by "Binneman, sans dateg." 8vo. Sir Thomas sent his natural and only son on this expedition, and his family take the title of viscount Strangeford from a town opposite to the peninsula of Ardes. It appears from Camden's account of it, in his annals of Elizabeth, A. D. 1572. that this letter was written that year. Mr. Smith being treacherously murdered by one of the natives, the undertaking came to nothing. It cost Sir T. 10,000 l. and James I. granted it to some of the Scotch nobility.

In the Ph. Transf. N° 313, p. 36, is a relation of the strange effects of thunder and lightning at Mrs. Close's house at *New Forge*, Aug. 9, 1707, by Sam. Molyneux, esq.

The Dublin Society published a correct map of the county.

D U B L I N.

THE antient and present state of the city of Dublin ecclesiastical and civil, as also of the county, were under the care of Mr. Harris and two other gentlemen [h], who hoped to put the last hand to it before the end of 1747. The same was said of the natural history undertaken by another member of the society at Dublin, whose abilities in that department were well known. A map of the county was also preparing [i]. As much as Mr. Harris left behind him, collected from many useful and interesting materials in his own possession (particularly

[g] Ames's hist. of printing, p. 328.
[h] One of whom probably was Dr. Smith.
[i] Harris's "Essay on the defects of the histories of Ireland," at the end of his Hibernica, 1746. Fol.

the unfinished and very imperfect k MS. hiſtory of Robert Ware, eſq. youngeſt ſon of the Iriſh antiquary and annaliſt) was publiſhed this year in " The hiſtory and antiquities of the city of Dublin, from the " earlieſt accounts : compiled from authentic memoirs, offices of re- " cord, MS. collections, and other unexceptionable vouchers ; with " an appendix, containing an hiſtory of the cathedrals of Chriſt church " and St. Patrick, the univerſity, the hoſpitals, and other public build- " ings.   Alſo two plans, one of the city as it was in the year 1610, " being the earlieſt extant ; the other as it is at preſent, from the " accurate ſurvey of the late Mr. Rocque l ; with ſeveral other em- " belliſhments m. Lond. 1764." 8vo.

Sir James Ware gave Sir Rob. Cotton a fair chartulary of St. Mary's abbey near Dublin.   He wrote in Latin the lives of the biſhops of the province of Leinſter or Dublin, 1628, 4to. incorporated into his larger hiſtory of Iriſh biſhops.

" The complaints of Dublin ; humbly offered to his excellency " Wm. earl of Harrington, lord lieut. general, and general governor " of Ireland, by Charles Lucas, in behalf of himſelf, and the reſt of " the citizens and inhabitants of the ſaid city. Dubl. 1747." 8vo.

" The great charter of the liberties of this city, tranſcribed and " tranſlated into Engliſh, with explanatory notes, addreſſed to his " majeſty, and preſented to the lords juſtices.   By Charles Lucas, a " free citizen. Dubl. 1749." 8vo.   Henry 2d's charter is the found- ation of the liberties of this city n.

Sir Wm. Petty publiſhed obſervations upon the Dublin bills of mor- tality 1681, and the ſtate of that city. Lond. 1683. 8vo. 1686. 12mo. and further obſervations upon the Dublin bills ; or accounts of the houſes, hearths, baptiſms, and burials in that city. Lond. 1686. 8vo. Theſe were reprinted, with his eſſays in political arithmetic, 1682. 1699. 1755. 8vo.

In Nº 127 of the Phil. Tranſ. is a relation of an aurora borealis at Dublin, by an unknown hand. In p. 192 of Nº 182, Dr. Wm.

---

l. So Harris calls it.   Iriſh writers, p. 257.
l Corrected to 1765.
m Miſerable engravings of the public buildings.
n Harris's Hiſtory of Dubl. p. 14.

Moly-

Molyneux's letter to Mr. Halley on the tides of the port of Dublin. In N° 209, p. 105, Dr. T. Molyneux's account of a general cough, and other epidemic diftempers in Dublin. In N° 364, p. 21, a luminous appearance in the air, by Ph. Percival, efq. In N° 368, p. 180, an account of an aurora borealis feen at Dublin, Feb. 6, 1720, by J. W.

" The charter of his majefty K. Geo. II. for erecting and endowing " St. Patrick's hofpital, founded by the laft will of the rev. Dr. Jona- " than Swift, late dean of St. Patrick's, Dublin, for the reception of " ideots, lunatics, and incurables. Printed by order of the truftees. " Dubl. 1746." 8vo.

" Verfes on the intended hofpital for incurables at Dublin. Lond. " 1744."

" The Liffy : a fable in imitation of the metamorphofis of Ovid, " addrefft to a young lady. With an epiftle dedicatory, in which is " contained an effay upon the metamorphofis of Ovid. By ****** " ****, efq. Dubl. 1726." 8vo. reprinted 1732. 8vo.

Tho. Fich, fub-prior of Trinity church, Dublin, wrote a hiftory and obituary of the church in the 10th century [p].

" Tranflation of the charter and ftatutes of Trinity college, Dublin, " together with the library ftatutes and rules of the univerfity ; to " which is added the expences for a degree. By Rob. Bolton, A. B. " Dubl. 1753." 8vo.

A comparifon between Effex-bridge and Weftminfter-bridge [q] in the Gentleman's Magazine for 1761, p. 609.

A map of the city and fuburbs of Dublin, alfo the abp. and earl of Meath's liberties, from an actual furvey made by Cha. Brookin, 1728.

A new and correct map of the bay and harbour of Dublin, with a fmall plan of the city, 1728.

---

[p] Ath. Ox. I. 11. Ware, p. 816.

[q] The former was built on the plan of the latter, but in a fmaller and better proportion. Effex-bridge, fo called from Arthur earl of Effex, in whofe lieutenancy it was firft built 1676, was rebuilt 1753, by Geo. Semple, in a year and half, and at the expence of 20661 l. Weftminfter-bridge was 11 years and three quarters about, and coft above ten times as much (218800 l.) An eaft elevation and fection of the foundation of Effex-bridge is in Harris's Hiftory of Dublin.

An

An exact furvey of the city, harbour, bay, and environs of Dublin, on the fame fcale as thofe of London, Paris, and Rome, by J. Rocque: with views of Kildare-houfe, the barracks, and the royal hofpital, drawn by G. Smith; and a fmall plan of Dublin [r], 1610, with the fpelling as then, in four fheets.

An exact furvey of the city and fuburbs, in which is expreffed the ground-plot of all the publick buildings, dwelling houfes, ware-houfes, ftables, courts, yards, &c. by J. Rocque, 1756. in four fheets, and reduced to one, with an index of the ftreets.

The environs of Dublin, in four fheets, containing the harbour, bay, and foundings at low water, by the fame.

The fame contracted, etched by A. Dury and engraved by P. Halquin. Dub. 1757.

A new and exact plan of this city and fuburbs from an actual furvey, with a N. view of it, the companies arms, and elevations of the principal buildings, 3 fheets. Ditto on 2, with only the view of Dublin.

The S. and S. E. profpects of St. Patrick's cathedral, and the N. fide of Trinity church, Dublin, engraved by Dheulland, are in the laft edition of Ware.

John Tuder drew and engraved fix views in Dublin: the city from the Magazine-hill; the Cuftom-houfe and Effex-bridge; the Library and Trinity college; the Parliament-houfe and College-green; the Upper Caftle court; and the Barracks. There are fix perfpective views in Dublin, by Jefferies, 1753.

Views of *Black rock* and *Howth*, painted by Wm. Jones of Dublin, were engraved by Giles King 1745.

J. Rocque publifhed a map of this county in four fheets; reduced to one.

FERMANAGH.

IN the Philofophical Tranfactions, N° 337, p. 278, is an extract of a letter from F. Nevil, efq; to the bp. of Clogher, about a quarry of white marble difcovered by him in this county, on the N. fide of Calcagh, in *Kilafher* parifh.

[r] By J. Speed, at the corner of his map of Leinfter.

5

KERRY.

K E R R Y.

" THE antient and prefent ftate of the county of Kerry; being
" a natural, civil, ecclefiaftical, hiftorical, and topographical
" defcription thereof. Illuftrated with remarks made on the baronies,
" parifhes, towns, villages, feats, mountains, rivers, harbours, bays,
" roads, medicinal waters, foffils, animals, and vegetables; with notes
" and obfervations on the further improvements of this part of Ireland.
" Embellifhed with a large map of the county from an actual furvey,
" a perfpective view of the lake of Killarney, and other plates; under-
" taken with the approbation of the phyfico-hiftorical fociety, by
" Charles Smith, author of the natural and civil hiftories of the coun-
" ties of Cork and Waterford. Dubl. 1756." 8vo.

At the end of Barton's lectures in natural philofophy, &c. before-
mentioned, are " Some remarks towards a full defcription of upper
" and lower Lough Lene, near Killarney, in the county of Kerry.
" Dubl. 1751." 4to. with a view of the lake, etched by C. Spooner.
This defcription was inferted in the Gent. Mag. for Nov. 1750. p. 505.
Other defcriptions of this moft beautiful natural fcenery are in Bufh's
and Derrick's letters lately publifhed : the beft account in the latter is
drawn up by Mr. Okendon.

K I L D A R E.

THE S. profpect of *Kildare* cathedral, with its ruins, engraved
by L. Dempfy, is in the laft edition of Ware.

The Salmon leap at *Leixlip*, the feat of Wm. Conolly, efq. painted
by Wm. Jones of Dublin, was engraved by Giles King 1745. Another
view painted by J. Tudor, engraved by John Brook.

KILKENNY.

KILKENNY.

A Survey of the city of *Kilkenny*, by J. Rocque, 1758.
A S. E. profpect and ground-plan of the cathedral, byD heu-land, in the laft edition of Ware.

LIMERICK.

" A Journal of three months campaign of his majefty in Ireland,
" together with a true and perfect diary of the fiege of *Lime-*
" *rick*. By Sam. Mullenaux, M. D. 1690." 4to.

" A diary of the fiege and furrender of Limerick; with the articles
" at large, both civil and military, publifhed by authority. Lond. 1692."
4to. reprinted in the Harleian Mifcellany, vi. 479.

" An impartial journal of the fiege of Limerick" is annexed to
W. Griffyth, efq's " Villare Hibernicum, or an exact account of all
" provinces, &c. in Ireland reduced by K. William."——4to.

A plan of the town at the corner of Speed's map'of Munfter.

In N° 233, p. 714, of the Philofophical Tranfactions is a defcription
of the bog of *Kapanihane* on the eftate of Brook Bridges, efq. in the
county of Limerick near Charleville, with an account of its motion
June 7, 1697, in the afternoon, which lafted about half an hour: by
Mr. Wm. Molyneux, who alfo communicated Mr. Honohane's account
of it.

In Birch's Hiftory of the Royal Society, iv. 448. is a letter from
Mr. St. George Afhe to Mr. Afton, fec. to the Royal Society, of the
Shannon running backwards for 24 miles from the fea by floods with-
out tides.

The S. profpect of Limerick cathedral by L. Dempfy. is in the laft
edition of Ware.

LONDONDERRY.

" A True account of the fiege of *Londonderry*. By the rev. Mr.
" George Walker, rector of Donoghmoore, in the county of
" Tirone, and late governor of Derry, in Ireland. The fecond edition
" corrected. Lond. 1689." 4to. This being attacked by fome who
envied him the glory of that brave defence, he wrote " A vindication
" of a true account, &c. Lond. 1689." 4to.

" An apology for the failures charged on the rev. Mr. Walker's
" printed account of the late fiege of Londonderry, in a letter to the
" undertakers of a more accurate account of that fiege. 1689." 4to.
by an anonymous writer.

" Reflections on a paper pretending to be An apology, &c. 1689."
4to.

" A narrative of the fiege of London-derry: or, the late memorable
" tranfactions of that city, faithfully reprefented, to rectifie the mif-
" takes and fupply the omiffions of Mr. Walker's account. By John
" Mackenzie, chaplain to a regiment there during the fiege. The
" moft material paffages relating to other parts of Ulfter and Sligo are
" alfo inferted from the memoirs of fuch as were chiefly concerned
" in them. Lond. 1690." 4to. To this a friend of Walker writ an
anfwer, under the title of " Mr. John Mackenzy's narrative of the
" fiege of Londonderry a falfe libel, in defence of Dr. Geo. Walker.
" Lond. 1690." 4to. The doctor acquired fuch a military tafte by
this gallant atchievement, that he facrificed his life at the battle of the
Boyne: it was thought, had he lived, he would have been promoted to
the fee of Derry, vacant by the death of bp. Hopkins three days before ᵉ.
The late Dr. Brown, who did all he could to reform and revive us,
republifhed his account of this fiege. Lond. 1758. 8vo. " as a ufeful
" leffon to the prefent times, with a prefatory addrefs to the public."

" A vindication of the rev. Mr. Alexander Ofborne, in reference to
" the affairs of the north of Ireland, in which fome miftakes concern-
" ing him (in the printed account of the fiege of Derry, the obferva-

ᵉ Harris's writers, p. 205.

" tions

" tions on it, and Mr. Walker's vindication of it) are rectified, and a
" brief relation of those affairs is given so far as Mr. Osborne and other
" non-conformist ministers in the north were concerned in them.
" Written at Mr. Osborne's request by his friend Mr. John Boyse.
" 1690." 4to. Osborne was a meddling presbyterian minister, a spy
upon the whole north of Ireland, and would admit none to fight for
the protestant religion till they had taken the covenant [t].

A new and exact map of Londonderry and Culmore, first drawn
with great exactness by capt. Macullach, who was there in the siege [u].

In N° 3 of the Philosophical Collections is an account of an inundation near Londonderry, June 26, 1680, by Dr. Hook. In N° 314,
p. 59, of the Transactions is the abp. of Dublin's account of manuring
lands with sea shells as practised on the coasts of Londonderry and Donnegal. In N° 320, p. 308, is a letter from Mr. Neve of Maghrafelt
to Mr. Wm. Derham, F. R. S. giving an account of an inundation
thereabout Oct. 7. 1706, and another in Antrim July 3, 1707, and
of an aurora borealis Nov. 16, 1707.

The S. and E. sides of Derry cathedral are in the last edition of
Ware.

L O U T H.

" **L**Outhiana: or an introduction to the antiquities of Ireland. In
" upwards of 90 [x] views and plans; representing, with proper
" explanations, the principal ruins, curiosities, and antient dwellings
" in the county of Louth. Divided into three books. Taken upon
" the spot, by Tho. Wright, author of the physical and mathematical
" elements of astronomy, &c. engraved by P. Fourdrinier. Lond.
" 1748." 4to. The 2d edit. 1758, revised and corrected, with some
few additions by the author. Book i. contains views and plans of the
most remarkable bodes, forts, and mounts, in 20 plates. B. ii. the
principal castles, keeps, and towers, in 24 plates. B. iii. a collection
of Danish and Druidical remains, in 22 plates.

---

[t] See Walker's Account of the siege.   [u] In the first edition of Walker's Account.
[x] The plates in the three books are 66: which with the frontispiece and eight head
and tail pieces make only 75: so that we must reckon fig. 1 and 2 in several plates to
make up 90.

Dundugan

Dundugan fort is alſo given in the Gent. Mag. 1752, p. 319.

An inſcription on a croſs at *Munſter-boys* near Drogheda, by E. Lhwyd, in Philoſophical Tranſactions, N° 269, p. 790. in Gibſon's Camden, and in the Louthiana, book iii. pl. 11, 12, 13.

A deſcription of an old Britiſh fort or Iriſh monument at *New-Grange* near Drogheda, in a Letter from Ed. Lhwyd to Rowlands. Mona Ant. p. 338, and to Dr. Molyneux in the Philoſophical Tranſactions, N° 335, p. 503, and N° 336, p. 524, and inſerted in the latter's diſcourſe concerning the Daniſh monuments, and in Harris's edition of Ware, p. 146, with a plan.

Dr. Stukeley cauſed to be engraved two plates, containing the mount of New-Grange (near which are four other mounts, three leſſer, and the fourth as big) a circle in the ſame field, two other circles (one incloſing a mount) ſome other irregular ſtone monuments, and a circle called *Ger Craw*, with certain ſtones in its neighbourhood.

Dr. Nicholas Bernard wrote " A letter from the ſiege of *Drogheda* " to a friend in London, Jan. 7, 1641." and " The whole proceedings " of the ſiege of Drogheda in Ireland : with a thankful remembrance " of its wonderful delivery, raiſed, with God's aſſiſtance, by the prayers " and ſole valour of the beſieged. With a relation of ſuch paſſages " as have fallen out there, and in the parts near adjoining. Dublin " 1642." 4to. reprinted 1736. 4to. The author who was chaplain to abp. Uſher, and dean of Ardagh or Kilmore, was in the town all the time, and in great danger y. Dr. Nicholſon ſays the MS. of the laſt piece was 1724 in the hands of lord Ferrard, whoſe grandfather Sir Henry Titchburn commanded the garriſon and defended the place againſt O Neal z,

A monument to K. William on the river Boyne, invented by J. la Cordi, and engraved by Vivares. " Gulielmi redemptoris monumentum accipe, cui titulum a Boyna dedit amor Gulielmi.

> For ever ſacred and immortal ſtream
> Preſerve this marble rais'd to William's name :

---

y Wood's Faſti. I. 224.   z P. 26.

> So fhall we thee the king of rivers own
> Where Stewart loft and William won a crown."

An obelifk erected on the field of battle makes the frontifpiece to Wright's book.

M A Y O.

DR. Stukeley caufed to be engraved in one plate four circles of ftones, two of them double, half a mile off *King*, in a field on the right fide of the road to Ballinrope, in this county. In another plate a circle of ftones, 29 paces diameter, on a mountain near the famous fortification at *Dyneyeguill* near Ballinrope, but in *Inys-kynhaim* parifh: In the fame plate was a circle called *Karrachan*, by *Lochbury* in Mull: another by Mawnog Grigog, in *Penmorva* parifh, Carnarvonfhire: and a triple one, with two great ftones in the centre, at *Mynyd Carreg*, in the parifh of Llan Gyudyern, ten yards diameter, the higheft ftone not three feet [a].

M E A T H.

WOOD [b] mentions " Catalogus epifcoporum Midenfium a Si- " mone de Rupeforte Anglorum primo qui fedem illam ob- " tinuit ufq; ad Hug. Inge cui coævus fuit," by Geo. Cogley, no- tary public and regifter of the bifhop's court at Meath about 1528.

---

[a] I have one of his plates of Celtic fepulchres at *Eglwys Gleminog* on the top of *Arennig Vaur*, in *Llanykil* parifh, *Merionethfhire*; with *Karnedh Hengum*, about a quar- ter of a mile S. E. from *Dynas Gortyn*, both in the parifh of *Llan Aber Meir*; and feveral Coiten Arthurs: another plate of circles, ftones, and cairns, *Kairn mawr*, and fome on the road fide between *Bwnahyrin* and *Clochan Cantyr*: a third of fuch monuments in Germany (in Drent, near Helmftad, and near Bulk in Halfatia) dedicated to Keyfler: and another of the like near Roefchild, in the way to Frederickfburgh, prope vicum Hobifh veteris marchiæ, in Seland near the highway to the village of Birkis; befides drawings of others in Sweden, and a kind of Coit y Arthur near Poitiers.

[b] Ath. Ox. I. 11.

In

In Harris's edition of Ware, p. 165, is a plate exhibiting a N. W. view and a plan of the 11 churches in one churchyard at *Clonmacnois*, N. and W. doors of Temple Macdermot (one of them), the arch of a nunnery chapel adjoining, N. prospect of the bishop's palace, and four views of two crosses.

An inscription copied by Ed. Lhuyd at Clonmacnois abbey is inserted in the Philosophical Transactions, Nº 269, p. 790, and in Gibson's Camden.

S L I G O.

ADraught and account of an antient sepulchre, discovered 1640 in a hill at Sligo, a mile from Castle Conner; drawn by Dr. Miles Symner, an able mathematician, is in Ware's Antiquities, p. 152, Harris's edition, p. 138.

T I P P E R A R Y.

" ATrue account of divers most strange and prodigious appari-
" tions seen in the air at *Poins-town* in the county of Tipperary,
" in Ireland, March the second, 167$\frac{8}{9}$, attested by 16 persons that
" were eye-witnesses. Published at Dublin, and thence communi-
" cated hither. Lond. 1679." 4to. These wonderful sights were ships, forts, dogs, bulls, &c. fighting in the air about sunset, most probably only meteors, or clouds of a singular form.

In Nº 238 of the Philosophical Transactions is part of a letter from Dr. Francis Vaughan, physician at Tipperary, to Mr. Ray, concerning the poisonous qualities of hemlock water-drop wort, confirmed by the latter.

The S. prospect of *Cashell* cathedral, by Dheuland, is in the last edition of Ware.

4 U

TYRONE.

T Y R O N E.

IN Nº 337, p. 250, of the Philofophical Tranfactions is Mr. Nevill's account of trumpets, and other antiquities found in the lower barony, of Dungannon; and p. 267 the bp. of Clogher's account of the finking of part of a hill near *Clogher*. In vol. xlviii. art. 1. is an account of an extraordinary ftream of wind which fhot through part of the parifh. of *Termonomungan* and *Urney*, in this county, Oct. 11, 1752, by Wm. Henry, D. D. rector of Urney.

W E S T   M E A T H.

A Defcripton of Weft Meath by Sir Henry Piers of Trifternaugh;, in the faid county, bart. done at the requeft of Dr. Anthony Dopping, bifhop of Meath, 1681-97, was given to Thorefby by his grandfon Sir Henry Piers ͨ.

W A T E R F O R D:

" THE antient and prefent ftate of the county and city of Water-
" ford: being a natural, civil, ecclefiaftical, hiftorical and topo-
" graphical defcription thereof. Illuftrated by remarks made on the
" baronies, parifhes, towns, villages, mountains, rivers, medicinal
" waters, foffils, animals and vegetables; with fome hints relating to
" agriculture, and other ufeful improvements. With feveral notes and
" obfervations: together with new and correct maps of the city and
" county; and embellifhed with perfpective views of the city of Water-
" ford, and of the towns of Lifmore and Dungarvan. Publifhed with
" the approbation of the phyfico-hiftorical fociety. By Charles Smith.
" Dubl. 1751." Printed in 1746, but not brought over to England
till 1751. Mr. Doyl's chart of *Tramore* bay and *Waterford* harbour,
an exact furvey done with great nicety, is reduced into the map of the
county.

ͨ See his Mufæum, Nº 244.

" Magna

" Magna charta libertatum civitatis Waterford, Timotheo Cuning-
" ham editore. Dubl. 1752." 8vo.

In the Philofophical Tranfactions, N° 176, p. 1202, is a letter from
Mr. St. George Afhe, fecretary of the Dublin fociety, concerning a girl
at Waterford who had feveral horny excrefcencies on her joints.

The S. E. and N. W. profpects and the ichnography of Waterford
cathedral by Dheuland, and the S. view of Lifmore cathedral by J.
Blaymiers and J. Haydon, are in the laft edition of Ware.

WEXFORD.

BOnaventure Baron, divinity reader at St. Ifidore's college, Rome,
where he died 1696, wrote " Obfidio & expugnatio arcis *Dun-
cannon* fub Thoma Preftono," which is all Mr. Harris fays of it [d].

WICKLOW.

IN the Philofophical Tranfactions, vol. xlvii. art. 84, is a letter from
Dr. Henry to lord Cadogan, concerning copper fprings in this
county : a fecond letter from the fame in vol. xlviii. art. 12, and another from John Bond, M. D. in the fame volume, art. 28.

Mr. Barrett exhibited at Spring-gardens 1764 a view of the waterfall at Powerfcourt, and another in the Dargell, both in lord Powerfcourt's eftate.

A N. profpect of *Bleffingtown*, a feat belonging to the earl of Blef-
ingtown. Jo. Tudor, pinxit, John Brookes, exc.

[d] Irifh writers, p. 353

ADDITIONS

ADDITIONS

AND

CORRECTIONS.

PAGE 22, *line 7 from the bottom, for* Nº 965 and 966, *read* 964 and 965.

P. 24. " Anglicæ defcriptionis compendium per Gul. Paradinum Cuyfellienfem. Par. 1545." 12mo.

P. 30. " A book of the names of all the parifhes in England and Wales, with county mapps. Lond. 1657." 4to.

P. 31. *add to note* k. It is a large map dedicated to Charles II. and has this infcription, " Angliæ totius tabula, diftantiis notioribus in itinerantium ufum accomodata. Johannes Adamus defcripfit, Thomas Burnford lineas, ellipfes, & circulos fculpfit.

P. 32. In the Philofophical Tranfactions, Nº 352, p. 589, is Dr. Mufgrave's Differtation de Britannia quondam pene infulâ.

P. 35. Ogilby's plates were corrected and improved by Senex 1719.

P. 42. Ortelius recommended one Doetecum of Haerlem to reduce certain maps of Britain, made by himfelf, after Camden had corrected them for his Britannia. [Camdeni. Ep. 29.] The edition of 1600 was the firft that had maps, and thofe only two general ones. In the fame collection is a letter from Camden to Jodocus Hondius, informing him that he had recommended him to Speed, whom he calls *fumme induftrius.* Ep. 63.

R. 42.

P. 42. " The fhires of England and Wales defcribed by C. Saxton,
" being the beft and moft original mapps, with many additions and
" corrections, viz. the hundreds, roads, &c. by Ph. Lea: alfo the
" new furveys of Ogilby, Seller, &c. Sold by Ph. Lea, globemaker,
" in Cheapfide, near Friday Street." Fol. The map of Ireland is
abridged from Petty, that of Scotland from Gordon. Bagford fuppofes Wolfe the printer firft defigned a map of England by the fketches
he had taken from Leland's New year's gift, though nothing of this
nature was done till Saxton.

P. 43. Hollar's Quarter mafters map has been retouched by Jefferies.

P. 44. A correct map of South Britain by Charles Price, with alphabetical lifts at the fides, in 3 fheets and 2 fheets. 1712. Alfo in 2
fheets, with tables; and a map of Great Britain in 2 fheets.

The following, which, in the great variety of fingle maps of England, efcaped my fearch, muft be added to thofe already enumerated.

The great roads of England. Sold by George Wildey, printfeller,
at the toyfhop at the W. end of St. Paul's.

The roads, with the meafured diftances according to Ogilby, and
an accurate delineation of the fea-coafts and rivers, laid down by De-
larochette and engraved by T. Kitchen. $5\frac{1}{2}$ feet fquare.

England, Scotland, and Ireland, with fo much of Germany as includes the electorate of Hanover, and the dutchies of Bremen and
Verden, with the contiguous ftates, by John Senex, F. R. S. 9 fheets.
$6\frac{1}{2}$ feet by $5\frac{1}{2}$.

England and Wales, fhewing its antient and prefent government, as
in the Saxon heptarchy, and as now in counties, diocefes, and circuits,
great and crofs roads, with meafured miles according to Ogilby: 6
feet fquare.

England and Wales by John Rocque.

England and Wales fully defcribed, with the meafured and computed miles, tables of members and diftances from London.

A new and correct map of Great Britain and Ireland, with views of
his majefty's palaces in England, &c.

A new and correct map of the roads of England, &c. by Emanuel
Bowen. 1748.

A new

A new and correct poft map of England and Wales by ditto, 1 fheet.

A new and correct map of England and Wales, with the roads, the arms of the cities and boroughs, lifts of fairs, boroughs, navigable places, and views of London, Briftol, Newcaftle, Hull, Liverpool, Yarmouth, Portfmouth, and Plymouth. 3 fheets.

A new and exact map of Great Britain, or England and Scotland, from the lateft and beft obfervations on the poft roads. 2 fheets.

A new and accurate map of Great Britain and Ireland, from the lateft furveys and aftronomical obfervations, with views of the principal towns in each kingdom. 2 fheets.

A new and correct map of England and Wales, with an alphabetical table, and the bifhops and deans: to which is added, Geography epitomized. 3 fheets. Ditto, 2 fheets.

A new and correct poft map of the great crofs roads throughout England and Wales, with the meafured diftances, engraved by Rich. Bennett. 1763, with views of the fea ports as before. 2 fheets. The fame on one fheet, without views.

A new and accurate map of England and Wales, by J. Ellis, 1 fheet.

A new traveller's guide through England and Wales. one fheet.

The traveller's guide or Ogilby's roads epitomized, a fet of tables of roads in one fheet:

A moft accurate map of the Englifh and Welfh roads by T. Kitchen. one fheet:

England defcribed, or Ogilby epitomized, a pocket map of roads. one fheet.

A map of roads in England and Wales by Senex. one fheet.

P. 45. The Englifh Atlas, by Bowen, Kitchen, and others, confifts of 47 maps, befides general ones of the three kingdoms; with a general defcription of the counties, and hiftorical extracts relative to trade, &c. Thefe have been fpecified in each county. The Royal Englifh Atlas, by the fame hands, confifts only of 44 maps and a general one of England, fmaller folio, to be had fingly at one fhilling,. as the others at 1 s. 6 d. Mr. Bowen, reduced by family extravagances and almoft blind through age, had begun to engrave them on a long quarto, in eighteenpenny numbers of three maps each; but dying May 1767, before

before he had finished above three or four numbers, they are continued by his son.

P. 59. King's views of the churches, &c. were executed in a set for Overton. 1672: there is another set of perspective views of all the cathedrals in England and Wales, with the collegiate churches of Westminster, Manchester, Southwell, and St. George's, Windsor; with an account of their foundations, first bishops, parishes in each bishopric, and their arms.

P. 63. " Caroli Claromontii doct. medici, nob. Lotharing. de aere, " locis & aquis terræ Angliæ, deque morbis Anglorum vernaculis. " Cum observationibus, ratiocinatione & curandi modo illustratis. " Lond. 1672." 12mo. At the end are " Observationes medicæ " Cambro-Britannicæ." Twenty-six cases during his two years practice in South Wales.

P. 71. The British Zoology is just reprinted in 2 vols. 8vo. " with 18 copper plates of animals, omitted in the former edition. Class 1. Quadrupeds. Class 2. Birds. With an appendix, an essay on birds of passage, and an index. 1768."

P. 72. The first part of Lister de fontibus was reprinted at Frankfort and Leipsic. 1684. 12mo.

P. 74. Dr. Short's history of mineral waters was reprinted, with a continuation, in 2 vols. 4to. 1740.

P. 76. Collections for a history of BEDFORD by John Pomfret, Rougecroix pursuivant, and Torr's account of *Woburne* abbey, were sold at Warburton's sale.——J. Rocque engraved a plan of *Wrest* house and gardens, with views at the sides, 1734.——Jefferies has published an actual survey of the county, in eight sheets.

P. 78. Warburton had some collections for BERKSHIRE by Dr. Plott.——An appendix to Pote's history and antiquities of *Windsor* was published 1762, continuing the knights to the last installment, with an alphabetical index of them from the first institution, and of all the plates of arms.

" An historical account of the knights of the most noble order of " the garter, from its first institution in the year 1350 to the present " time, by John Buswell, one of the gentlemen of his majesty's chapel
" royal

" royal and of his majefty's free chapel of St. George at Windfor.
" Lond. 1757."——Mr. Walpole fays, Wren drew a view of Windfor,
engraved by Hollar. Anecd. vol. iii. p. 91. Two neat views of Wind-
for by Vofterman are among the pictures there. Peter Vanderbank
engraved Verrios cielings of the prefence-chamber, king's clofet, &c.
Cat. of eng. p. 89.——A profpective view of the palace and town of
Windfor, 2 fheets.——" The laft horfe-race run before Charles II. by
" Dorfett ferry near Windfor, drawn from the place and defigned by
" F. Barlow. 1687."——In the Philofophical Tranfactions, N° 483,
p. 458, is Dr. Hill's account of the earth called Windfor loam, dug at
Hedgerley.——Jefferies publifhed a plan of the country round *Padworth,*
the feat of the late R. Griffiths, efq,——" Ecclefia parochialis de *Coxwell*
" *magna,* in com. Bercherienfi ab auftro vifa: aviorum cinerum cryp-
" tam ita fervari voluit. Ed. Rowe Mores, arm. 1755."

T. Jefferies propofed to engrave by fubfcription a map of the county
of BUCKINGHAM, from a fcale of one inch to a mile : wherein will
be accurately delineated the boroughs, market towns, villages, nobility
and gentries feats, woods, &c. drawn from an accurate furvey taken
by himfelf. It was to have come out Oct. 1766.

CAMBRIDGESHIRE.] A beautiful elevation of the tower and fpire of
St. Mary's church at *Whittlefea,* engraved by Lamborne, from a drawing by J. Heins 1763.——John Chapman has juft engraved a plan of
Newmarket in one fheet; with the Heath, in two fheets, expreffing
the feveral courfes, ftands, roads, and every thing remarkable on it,
from an actual furvey.

A fmall bronze buft found in digging the foundations of the new
bridge near Magdalen Coll. was engraved by Benazech, in 3 views,
for Dr. Stukeley, who perfuaded himfelf it reprefented *Oriuna,* and belonged to a ftandard pole.——" The hiftory and antiquities of the univerfity" had a new title page printed for it by Warcus, bookfeller in
London.

Randall Catheral, an eminent and expert antiquary, native of CHE-
SHIRE, made large collections for it and Oxfordfhire, in which laft he
fettled, and died 1725. An extract from his book of the antiquities and
gentry of this county is in MS Harl. 1988.——Hollar engraved a fmall

map

map of Chefhire 1670.——A S. E. profpect of the city of *Chefter*, lieut. Jof. Winder del. J. Evans fc. 2 fheets.——A view of the abbey fquare, with views of the work-houfe, bluecoat hofpital, and infirmary, by the fame.——The outfide front of the Roman gate of the Watling ftreet, called Eaft gate, at Chefter, as ftanding 2 Aug. 1725, drawn by Dr. Stukeley, was engraved by Sturt.——A Roman tile, reprefenting a retia-rius, found at Chefter 1738, by the Antiquarian Society.——" Il Pen-
" ferofo: an evening's contemplation in St. John's church-yard, Chefter.
" A rhapfody written more than twenty years ago, and now firft pub-
" lifhed, illuftrated with notes hiftorical and explanatory. Addreffed to
" the rev. John Allen, M. A. fenior fellow of Trinity Coll. Camb. and
" rector of Torporley in Chefhire. Lond. 1767." 4to. This poetical antiquary, the late Dr. Wm. Cowper, phyfician at Chefter, who died Oct. 1767, while he was preparing a memorial of his native city, here takes a view of fome of the moft remarkable places around it, diftin-guifhed by memorable perfonages and events.

" The new-cut canal, intended for improving the navigation of the city of Chefter, with the low lands adjacent to the river Dee, compared with the Welland, alias Spalding river, now filted up, and Deeping fens adjacent, now drowned. Alfo arguments to prove, that as the river Welland and Deeping fenns were deftroyed by imbanking falt marfhes, and making that river narrow, fo the river Dee and the low lands adjacent will be deftroyed, if the white fands and falt marfhes be imbanked and the river made narrow, as propofed in Mr. Grundy's book. To which is added, reafons and experiments, fhewing why a flat and fenny country cannot be drowned through a fewer that has but four inches in each mile; with a refutation of Mr. Grundy's de-monftration, by which he endeavours to prove that it can. Done for the ufe of drainers. With a defence of thofe gentlemen who have been undertakers to drain Deeping fenns againft the reflections of Mr. Grundy; in which is fhewed the true caufe of the great decay of late years of navigation and draining in the rivers of Wifbech, Spalding, Bourn, and Bofton, which all fall into the fame bay: alfo experiments and reafons agreeing with Sir I. Newton's theory of the tides, relating to the practice of taking a level by the high-water mark of a fpring tide,

tide, occafioned by Mr. Grundy's affertion that that method is founded upon falfe principles; with confiderations on his method of taking the level of the country about Spalding with an inftrument called a fpirit level, at upwards of 2500 ftations. Chefter." [1736. By T. Badeflade.] Fol. To this are added " Philofophical and mathematical reafons humbly offered to the confideration of the publick, to prove that the prefent works, executing at Chefter, to recover and preferve the navigation of the river Dee, muft intirely deftroy the fame. With fome remarks on Mr. Badeflade's reafons, &c. thereon." [By John Grundy.]

" Reafons humbly offered to the confideration of the public; fhewing how the works now executing by virtue of an act of parliament, to recover and preferve the navigation of the river Dee, will deftroy the navigation, and occafion the drowning all the low lands adjacent to the faid river. From obfervations made on the fpot; or from inftances of the ruinous effects like works have had at the ports of Lyn, Rye, Wifbech, and Spalding: with an appendix, illuftrated with a map of the river Dee, Lyn, Rye, Wifbech, all drawn by hand. Chefter." Fol. 2d edit. [by Thomas Badeflade.] He had prepared a fcheme to preferve the navigation of the Dee; and was writing a hiftory of our ports.

P. 124. Mr. Warburton had a vifitation of CORNWALL by R. Cooke, Clarencieux, and Edm. Knyght, Chefter, 1556: another of Devon and Cornwall by Wm. Tong, Norroy, 1530.

" The voice of the Lord in the temple, or a moft ftrange and won-
" derfull relation of God's great power, providence, and mercy in
" fending very ftrange founds, fires, and a fiery ball into the church
" of *Anthony* in Cornwall, neere Plimouth, on Whitfunday laft 1640,
" to the fcorching and aftonifhing of 14 feveral perfons, who were
" fmitten, and likewife to the great terrour of all the other people
" then prefent, being about 200 perfons, the truth whereof will be
" maintained by the oathes of the fame perfons, having been examined
" by Richard Carew of Anthony, efq; and Arthur Backe, vicar of
" Anthony. Lond. 1640." 4to.

In the Philofophical Tranfactions, Nᵒ 401 and 403 are Dr. F. Nicholl's obfervations on mines in Cornwall. In vol. lvi. art. 7, two letters from Dr. Borlafe to Mr. Da Cofta, about a fpecimen of native tin, the

exiftence

exiftence of which has always been denied.——" The reafons of Henry Jones, efq; for building a mould or pier in Whitefand bay at the land's end ;" with a plan.

Bp. Nicholfon affifted bp. Gibfon in his account of CUMBERLAND. The Britifh circus, note *y*. p. 132, is defcribed in Stukeley's Stonehenge, p. 43 ; and this and the camp feem to be mentioned in Todd's letter about the medicinal fpring.——Peak and Toms engraved after Bellers a view of *Kefwic* town and vale from Caftle head cragg, and another of *Armathwaite* bay.——T. Jefferies propofed to engrave a map of this county from an actual furvey by Mr. Elliot, on a fcale of one mile to an inch, to be delivered June 1767.

Vertue had feen a pocket-book almoft full of fketches and views of DERBYSHIRE, the Peak, Chatfworth, &c. very freely touched, and in imitation of Salvator Rofa, by Philip Boul. Anecd. of Paint. vol. iii. p. 118.

" A letter to a friend on the mineral cuftoms of Derbyfhire; in " which the queftion relative to the claim of the duty of lot on fmitham " is occafionally confidered. By a Derbyfhire working miner. 1766." 8vo. oppofing this new duty of one-third on this particular affortment of lead ore.——In the Philofophical Tranfactions, N° 117, p. 391, and N° 119, p. 450, is Mr. Jeffop's account of the various forts of damps in the mines. In N° 487, p. 320, a beautiful nautilus from *Poole's hole* is defcribed.——A general view of *Chatfworth* houfe and gardens, by A. Walker.——A S. view of All Saints church at *Derby*, rebuilt to the old tower. Ja. Gibbs del. H. Hulfberg fc.

P. 134. l. 24. for N° 406 read N° 407.

P. 139. Dr. Mufgrave furnifhed bifhop Gibfon with obfervations on: DEVONSHIRE.

" Two moft ftrange births. Lond. 1608." 4to. at *Modbury* and *Plymouth*. Cat. of Harleian pamphlets, N° 529.——Warburton had fome curious notes on the monuments in Devonfhire, in the hand of lord William Howard of Naworth, temp. Elizabeth.

" An effay concerning the caufe of the endemial colic of Devon-" fhire, which was read in the theatre of the college of phyficians in " London June 29, 1767. By George Baker, fellow of the college of

" phyficians

" phyficians and of the Royal Society, and phyfician to her majefty's
" houfhold. Lond. 1767." 8vo   Dr. Baker afcribes this diforder to
the particles of lead which pais into the cyder from the pounds in
which it is preffed.   The fact was denied in " Some obfervations on
" Dr. Baker s effay on the endemial colic of Devonfhire.   By Francis
" Geach, furgeon at Plymouth and F. R. S.   To which are added,
" fome remarks on the fame fubject by the rev. Mr. Alcock. 1767."
8vo.   This tract fuppofing the lead to have been only fome fhot left in
the bottles, that objection is removed in " An anfwer to the obferva-
" tions of Mr. Geach, and to the curfory remarks of Mr. Alcock,
" &c. in a letter from Dr. Saunders [who affifted in the analvfis] to
" Dr. Baker. 1767." 8vo.

" Obfervations on the air and epidemic difeafes from the beginning
" of the year 1738 to the end of the year 1748. 2 vols. by John
" Huxham, M. D. F. R. S. and now tranflated from the original by
" his fon John Coram Huxham, M. A. Lond. 1767." 8vo.

" A plain and eafie method ; fhewing how the office of overfeer of
" the poor may be managed, whereby it may be 9000l. per ann. ad-
" vantage to the county of Devon, without abating the weekly relief
" of any poor, or doing a penny damage to any perfon.   By Richard
" Dunning, gent, Lond. 1685." 4to.

" The meffage fent by the kyng's majeftie to certain of his people
" affembled in Devonfhire."   A mild rational expoftulation with the
malecontents of 1549, printed by Grafton 1549. 12mo. Harl. Cat.
of pamphlets.

P. 142. l. 2. for 2d and 3d editions read 3d, 4th, and 5th. l. 3, for
1723 read 1724.——" The life and death of Mr. Ignatius Jurdain,
" one of the aldermen of the city of Exeter, who departed this life
" July 15, 1640, drawn up and publifhed by Ferd. Nicholls, minifter
" of the gofpel at Mary Arches, Exon.   The 2d edition, enlarged by
" the author. Lond. 1655." fmall 12mo.——A letter about finding
bifhop Bitton's body in the choir of the cathedral, Gent. Mag. Aug.
1763, p. 396.——Rocque's plan of Exeter is reduced in one fheet.   He
likewife engraved a view of the citadel of *Plymonth*.——In the Philofophical Tranfactions, N° 395, are Dr. Huxham and Dr. Hallet's ob--
fervationss

fervations on the aurora borealis at Plymouth and Exeter 1726. In
N° 474, p. 204, the former's account of a fine ſtalactites found at *Cat-
down* rocks near Plymouth; now in the Royal Society's muſeum.   N°
424, p. 301, is Mr. Joſeph Atwell's account of the intermitting ſpring
called *Laywell*, near Brixam, deſcribed by Dr. Oliver at Torbay ——
" Reaſons for making a mould or harbour in Torbay, humbly ſub-
" mitted to both houſes of parliament. By Arthur Robinſon, eſq;"
with a plan.

P. 146. l. 28. for *Bartow* read *Barlow*. P. 149. l. 2. read *Etricke
and Mr. Bennet.*——A plan of *Blandford*, by Wm. Baſtard, engraved by
T. Bowles, for Overton, 1731.——In the Gentleman's Magazine, April
and May 1767, Mr. Hutchins's account of *Kingbarrow*, near Wareham; and deſcription and views of *Aggleſton* barrow, in the iſle of
Purbeck.   This name he certainly ſtrains in ſuppoſing it Heilig ſtone :
it may rather be a corruption of *Agger* ſtone, q. d. the ſtone on the
barrow, or the monument of *Egil.*——In that for March, 1768, his
account of *Blagden* pits, *Kimeridge* coals, &c.

Dr. Smith aſſiſted bp. Gibſon in the biſhopric of DVRHAM.   A copy
of the Britannia with his additions is now in the hands of John Williams, eſq; of Killingworth, Northumberland.

P. 156. Note ʳ, read Dom. A. vii. many of the names are wrote in
gold and ſilver letters.——A beautiful view of the inſide of the cathedral, by Mr. Ebdon, exhibited at Spring-gardens 1767, is now engraving.

P. 159. l. 9. for *feet* read *yards*.   Mr. Lambert exhibited a view
of this fall at Spring-gardens 1762.——I have another W view of
Hilton caſtle, with a different account under it, and dedicated as the
other, but without a name.   I take it however to be Buck's.——T. Jefferies advertiſed Oct. 1766, propoſals for engraving a new map of the
county from a ſcale of one inch to a mile, from an accurate ſurvey, by
capt. Armſtrong, to be ready in the ſpring 1767.

ESSEX.] " A new and exact proſpect of *Colcheſter*, taken from the
N. part 1724, by John Pryer." 2 ſheets, with views of the caſtle, St.
John's gate, St. Botolph's priory, and St. Anne's chapel.——The Anti-
quarian Society have a drawing of the inſide of the caſtle. W. by J.
Morley,

Morley, 1745.——An infcription lately found at Colchefter was engraved at the expence of Mr. Grey.——A plan of Colchefter, by Sparrow, with views at the fides, is engraving by Rooker.——Dr. Stukeley devifed and engraved a plan of Cæfaromagus, which he fays is *Chelmsford*, as built by Cunobeline in honour of Auguftus. ——His plan of Colchefter calls that town *Camulodunum Colonia*.——Rocque engraved a plan of lord Tylney's houfe and gardens at *Wanfted*, with views at the fides, 2 fheets, 1735. In the back ground of a fmall whole length of Q. Elizabeth at Welbec, by De Heere, is a view of the old houfe. Walp. Anecd. i. 135.——Tho. Sparrow, land-furveyor, is engraving a map of this county, on a fcale of one inch to a mile : in which is expreffed the exact geometrical fituation of every place remarkable or curious in the faid county, by an actual furvey, as towns, villages, all main and crofs roads, lanes, hills, vallies, rivers, brooks, bridges, fords, ferries, mills, toll-bars, mile-ftones, direction-pofts, large inns, Roman roads, ruins, woods, heaths, commons, parks, churches, noblemens and gentlemens feats, with the divifion of the hundreds and parifhes.

P. 172. Bp. Gibfon had many particulars about GLOUCESTERSHIRE from one Mr. Aftry.——A neat account of *Fairford* windows with a view of the church was printed at Cirencefter 1763. 12mo.——A large witch elm at *Stoke Gifford* is engraved and defcribed in the Gentleman's Magazine, Nov. 1766.

HAMPSHIRE.] " Foffilia Hahtonienfia ; or Hampfhire foffils. 1767." 4to. Of thefe curious foffil-fhells, collected out of the cliffs between Chrift church and Lymington, and prefented to the Britifh Mufeum by G. Brander, efq; very few are known to be natives of our own, or indeed of any of the European fhores ; the greater part, upon a comparifon with the recent, are wholly unknown to us. The copper-plates are exact draughts, engraved from the originals, by the late Mr. Green. To the figures are annexed a fcientific Latin defcription by Dr. Solander, (who is now compofing a fcientific catalogue of all the natural productions in the Britifh Mufeum) and a prefatory account of thefe phenomena in Latin and Englifh. In the defcriptiones fpeciminum the fpecies are defcribed promifcuoufly, and even the different fpecies of the fame genus fcattered about the work. 1767. 4to.

Henry

Henry Worfeley, efq; communicated many particulars about this county to bifhop Gibfon. See the lift of his MSS. in Cat. MSS. Ang. tom. xi. 211.——" A correct plan of the city of *Winchefter*, and the adjacent parts, with the Heffian camp, by order of count Ifenburg. By F. W. Baur, engineer. 1756."——Lowth's life of Wykeham was reprinted 1759. 8vo. with additions.——" A view and plan of the camp in the ifle of *Wight*, by A. Menageott and Chriftopher Seton. 1741." Another view of Carifbrook caftle, by ditto. 1741.——A profpect of *Portfmouth*, by ditto. 174⅞.——In N° 410 of the Philofophical Tranf-actions, p. 137, Mr. Derham's account of an aurora borealis at *Red-bridge* Oct. 13, 1728. In N° 444, p. 362, Dr. Baylies's account of an earthquake at *Havant* Oct. 25, 1735.——A 7th edition of " Batt upon Batt" was printed by Cooper in London. 8vo. undated.——*Montague town*, five miles from Southampton and five from Lymington. This plate of two fea baths defigned to be built on the manor of *Bewley* in Hants is dedicated to John duke of Montague by W. Williams.

Hereford.] P. 190. " The life and gefts of S. Thomas Cantilupe, " bp. of Hereford and fometime lord chancellor of England, extracted " out of the authentique records of his cathedral as to the maine part, " Anonymus, M. Paris, Capgrave, Harpsfield, and others. Collected " by R. S. S. J. at Gant. 1674." 12mo.

" Old Meg of Herefordfhire for a mayd-marian, and Hereford towne " for a morris-dance: or 12 morris-dancers in Herefordfhire of 1200 " years old. Lond. 1609." 4to. dedicated to that renowned old Hall, taberer of Herefordfhire, and to his invincible weather-beaten, nut-browne taber, being old and found 30 years and upwards. Serjeant Hofkins, who entertained James I. on his progrefs here, to fhew how healthy and long-lived the inhabitants were, affembled thefe 12 old men and women, whofe ages together amounted to above 1200, to dance before him.

P. 192. l. 9. read, *Hollar engraved the N. and W. fides for the Monafticon, vol. iii. and Vertue three feals of the Bohun family, one of the dean, two of the dean and chapter (temp. Hen. III. and a later) and thofe of the bifhops, &c.* l. 3. from the bottom, read 8vo. P. 193. l. 4. read *relation of the knavery of.* l. 6. for *caftle* read *gaol.*

l. 10.

l. 10. for *and* read *an.* l. 12. for *issue* read *arise.* l. 15. for *sans date* read *Lond.* 1679. 4*to.*——In the Philosophical Transactions, N° 20. is an account of some sanative waters in this county. Bagford's list.—— Harris engraved a view of *Shobdon* court.——Gibson's view of *Door,* &c. p. 176, should have been placed in this county.

HERTFORDSHIRE.] A good plan of *St. Albans,* by John Oliver, is in Chauncey's history. Another by I. Andrews and M. Wren was published 1766, also one of Hertford by the same.——" Observations on a particular kind of scarlet fever that lately prevailed in and about S. Albans. In a letter to Dr. Mead, by Nathaniel Cotton, M. D. Lond. 1749." 4to.

Dr. Stukeley mentions the *Royston* Gymnasium in his Stonehenge, p. 43.

Mr. Walpole describes a very curious picture, probably by Steenwyck, at earl Poulet's at Hinton St. George, representing an inside view of *Theobalds,* with figures of the King and Queen, William earl of Pembroke, and Philip earl of Montgomery, probably copied from Vandyk by Polenberg, or Van Bassan. Anecd. of Paint. ii. 103.

P. 202. l. 6. N° 11. is a distinct book. l. 16. add, Lond. 1712. 8vo. l. 17. for *witches* read *witchcraft.*

An actual survey of the county by I. Andrews and A. Dury. 1766.

HUNTINGDONSHIRE.] Bishop Gibson had many particulars from one Mr. Astry.——Dr. Layard's account of the *Somersham* water was published 1767. 8vo. His and Dr. Morris's experiments on this water are inserted in the Philosophical Transactions, vol. lvi. art. 3. The pamphlet contains only some history, list of subscribers, rules and directions for drinking the waters.

KENT.] P. 214. The very large additions said by bp. Kennet to be left by Somner in his copy of his Antiquities of *Canterbury,* in the church library, are little more than corrections of the press and some transpositions, and are all inserted in Batteley's edition; in which the views and plans are by Hollar and Kip; the few monuments wretchedly executed. Batteley in his preface gives an account of all Somner's MSS. relative to Canterbury. The Saxon annals are a transcript of a Cottonian MS. intitled, Chronica Saxonica Abingdoniæ ad an. 1066.

4 Y

Estrey's

Eftrey's catalogue of priors of Chrift church is in Ang. Sac. i. 83. In Batteley's book is a plan of the city, engraved by order of the corporation 1703, with views of the two croffes.

" A plan of the antient city of Canterbury, fhewing the feveral precinéts and liberties within the faid city which are exempt from its jurifdiction, together with the remains of St. Auftin's monaftery, carefully furveyed and delineated by W. and H. Doidge, land furveyors, April 1752. J. Hilton fc."

Dr. Harris frequently quotes bp. Williams's ecclefiaftical map of the diocefe of Canterbury.——Johnfon made a draught of the cathedral, which hangs on the library ftairs. Walp. Anecd. ii. 123.

" Charter of the fhipwrights of *Redrith.* Lond. 1677." 4to.

P. 221. " Grants of ballaftage to the corporation of Trinity-houfe; Lond. 1738." 12mo. Trinity-houfe alms-houfes at Deptford were engraved by S. Gribelin. 1701.——" The anfwer of the mafter, war-
" dens, and affiftants of the corporation and hofpital of Trinity-houfe,
" humbly offered concerning certain pretended abufes complained of
" by fome mafters of fhips trading to Newcaftle and Sunderland." 4to.
fans date.——A view of *Purfleet* by H. Bell and H. Jones.

P. 224. " *Tunbridge* wells : or a direétory for the drinking of thofe
" waters. Shewing; 1. their nature and virtues. 2. The difeafes in
" which they are moft beneficial. 3. The time, manner, and order
" of drinking them. 4. The preparation of the body required.
" 5. The diet proper to be ufed by all mineral-water drinkers. By
" Lewis Roufe, M. D. To which are annexed two traéts. I. Mr.
" Boyle's obfervations upon Tunbridge and other mineral waters. II. A
" phyfico-mechanical differtation on water in general, proving it to be
" the beft fpecifick for the cure of all difeafes, with a particular account
" of the virtues of the German waters. Made Englifh from the La-
" tin original. Lond. 1725." 12mo.

" Fax fonte accenfa; fire out of water: or, an endeavour to kindle
" devotion, from the confideration of the fountains God hath made.
" Defigned for the benefit of thofe who ufe the waters of Tunbridg-
" wells, the Bath, Epfom, Scarborough, Chigwell, Aftrop, Northall,
" &c. Two fermons preached at New chappel by Tunbridg-wells,
" with

" with devout meditations of cardinal Bellarmin upon fountains of wa-
" ters. Alfo fome forms of meditations, prayers, and thankfgivings,
" fuited to the occafion, by Anthony Walker, D. D. Lond. 1684."
12mo.

" Tunbridge epiftles from lady Margaret to the countefs of B.
" 1767." 4to. in imitation of the Bath Guide.

" Copy of Sir William Boreman's ordinances and ftatutes for the
" government of a fchool by him founded at *Greenwich.* Lond. 1701."
——A general view of the hofpital from the river, the hall and chapel,
and plan of the whole, by Gribelin.

" State of *Bromley* college in Kent, by archdeacon Denne. 1735."
Fol.

" This winter's wonder: or a true relation of a calamitous accident
" at *Bennenden*, in the county of Kent; how the church and feveral
" houfes were deftroy'd by thunder and lighning on the 29 of Dec.
" laft, being Sabbath day: with a perfect account of many confider-
" able damages in feveral counties in England, as Wofterfhire, Glofter-
" fhire, Yorkfhire, Newcaftle, the fenns in Lincolnfhire, Cambridge-
" fhire, and Suffolk have fuftained by great floods and inundations of
" waters, &c. 167$\frac{2}{1}$." 4to.

P. 227. Dr. Harris fays, " Sir John Spilman in Charles Ift's reign
fet up on the river Darent the firft paper mill that ever was built in
England. That prince granted him a patent and a falary of 200 l. a
year." He adds, " that he brought over in his portmanteau two lime
trees, perhaps the firft ever planted in England, which he fet at Dartford, and they thrived exceedingly. Sir Edw. Spilman, his relation,
has a Dutch epitaph in the chancel," p. 92. The doctor certainly
brings the eftablifhment half a century too low. Wood, Tanner, and
the catalogue of the Harleian pamphlets are my vouchers.

P. 229. Sackette's letter to Batteley, dated Folkftone Nov. 8, 1702,
about the church and pharos at *Dover* caftle, are in the appendix to
Batteley's Canterbury, N° i. a.——In the Gentleman's Magazine, Oct.
1767, p. 499, is a defcription of Q. Elizabeth's pocket piftol in Dover
caftle by D. H.——l. 9. read, Mr. Barrell's account; and l. 10. Dr. R.
Nefbitt's account. N° 462. p. 47. Mr. H. Miles's account of parhelia

feen

ſeen in Kent Dec. 19, 1741. N° 496. Dr. Mortimer's deſcription of a nodulus with lines found at *Shepey*.

P. 231. " A chart of the entrance of the rivers Thames and *Medway* and places adjacent, with the floating light at the Nore ſand; ſurveyed by capt. John Mitchell, engraved by Toms, and dedicated to Sir Charles Wager, by David Avery."

" A brief account of the proceedings of the truſtees appointed by act of parliament for building a harbour at *Ramſgate*, together with ſome conſiderations in vindication of the ſafety and uſefullneſs of the harbour on their preſent plan." 8vo.——" A true ſtate of facts relating to Ramſgate harbour." 4to. ——" A ſeaman's plain anſwer to every thing that may ſeem material in the landman's pamphlett relating to the contracting Ramſgate harbour." Fol.——" State of the expence of building Ramſgate harbour on the contracted plan." a folio ſheet.—— " Narrative of facts and obſervations thereon which induced many truſtees to be againſt contracting Ramſgate harbour, and againſt taking up of works built agreeable to the direction of the board of truſtees. a folio ſheet.——" Report, and eſtimate ſubjoined, relating to the harbour of Ramſgate, an. 1755-6." Fol.——" A plan of the pier and harbour, with the additions propoſed to enlarge it."

Dr. Packe's ſon at Canterbury has his father's large maps which were printed off.——John Andrews and A. Dury, who publiſhed the ſurvey of Hertfordſhire, have undertaken a topographical map of Kent, in 25 ſheets of imperial paper, on a ſcale of two inches to a mile; and reduced to one ſheet, to ſerve as an index to the other. Theſe mapmakers are extremely inaccurate in their orthography.

LANCASHIRE.] P. 232. Dr. Peploe's caſe was printed at Cambridge the ſame year as at Oxford.——A plan of the towns of *Mancheſter* and *Salford*, by R. Caſſon and J. Berry, with a S. proſpect of the towns, and views of Chriſt church, Trinity church, St. Anne's chapel and ſquare, the college, exchange, key, and long-room, and nine private houſes, on 2 ſheets.——G. Thornton engraved the Exchange, built by Sir Oſwald Moſely 1729.——A N. proſpect of St. Anne's chapel. 1732.

A plan

A plan and account of the duke of Bridgewater's navigation, and a view of an aqueduct in the Gentleman's Mag. Jan. 1766. p. 231.

A correct plan of *Liverpool*, on one sheet of imperial Atlas paper; shewing all the streets, lanes, and allies, with the docks and basons, and a short historical account of the town. This survey was taken by order of the corporation in June 1765, by Mr. John Eyes, and engraved by Thomas Kitchen.

P. 236. l. 25. for *a well and earth*, r. *the burning well.*—P. 237. l. 8. for *an account*, read *Mr. Hopkin's account.* l. 11. after Church town, add, by Mr. Richmond. N° 496. p. 535. Mr. Platt's account of a nodule found at *Ardwick.* P. 238. l. 15. after 4to. add, " De-" clarations of popish impostures." P. 239. l. 3. for *Aston* read *Lister.* l. 29. read, " A brief narrative of the Surrey dæmoniac, with a vindication of the same as no impostor. 1698." and " The Lanca-shire Levite. 1698."

LEICESTERSHIRE.] P. 241. Mr. Rogers, archdeacon of Leicester, communicated many particulars to bp. Gibson.—*Rawdikes* is mentioned in Stukeley's Stonehenge, p. 43. Among his unpublished plates is a prospect of *Burrow hill* (Vernometum) from the Leicester road, engraved by Kirkall. 1722.——Thomas Roberts engraved a plan of *Leicester.* 1741.

" The history of the rise and progress of the charitable foundations " at *Church-Langton:* together with the different deeds of trust of that " establishment. By the rev. Mr. Hanbury. London printed for the " benefit of the charity. 1767." 8vo. The rector of this town, with a firmness of mind equal to the benevolence of his heart, seems to have brought to the utmost degree of maturity and stability human affairs are capable of this singular undertaking of raising from a plantation of all the various trees, plants, &c. the world produces, a yearly fund of near 10,000 l. sufficient to relieve the distressed, instruct the ignorant, assist the curious, adorn the parish, and benefit this and the neighbouring county of Rutland, as long as integrity and public spirit subsist in Britain, or dare to defy singularity and censure. This generous design claims a place here on a double account. We antiquarians have great obligations to this liberal founder, who has appropriated

part

part of this fund to the compiling and publishing a history of every county of England by a professor appointed on purpose. An Essay "on planting," printed at Oxford 1758, 8vo. was his first publication. He proposes speedily to publish, for the benefit of the charity, "A complete body of planting and gardening," in 2 volumes, folio. Price 4 guineas.

LINCOLNSHIRE.] P. 245. Among bp. More's MSS. is John Norden's "Abstract of the general survey of the soke of *Kirketon of Lindesay*, in the county of Lincoln, with all the manors, townships, lands, and tenements within or belonging to the same, being part of the duchy of Cornwall, taken 1610." Cat. MSS. Ang. N° 819.

"Statutes and constitutions for the government of an infirmary or hospital to be established at *Lincoln*, for the sick and lame poor in the county and city of Lincoln. 1745." 8vo.

N. S. E. W. and inside views, and a plan of the nave and choir of the cathedral, by Hollar, are in the Monasticon, iii. 256.——There is a better view of St. Leonard's hospital *(Stamford)* in Peck's Annals. ——Howgrave, who was an apothecary at Stamford, in his preface ridicules a penny history of Stamford bull runnings, by Peck.

The best views of *Croyland* are S. and W. ones by Millecent, engraved by Kirkall and Vandergucht: by the same are *Barling* abbey, *Tatterfal* castle, and 4 more, making a set. The Antiquarian Society have an upright and sections of the British tower at *Boston*, now in the hands of the corporation, drawn 1734 by W. Stennet.——Three of Dr. Stukeley's unpublished plates exhibit *Aukborough* (Aquis), *Brigcasterton* from the Hermen street, and *Ancaster*.

"Instructions for jurymen on the commission of sewers at Spalding, concerning Lovewell's works, and the river Glean. Lond. 1664." 8vo.

MIDDLESEX.] P. 259. dele lines 11 and 12.——P. 262, Toms engraved a view of St. Pancras wells, with 5 stones voided by Mr. Harrod of Hedge-row, Islington, after drinking them a few days.——Vanfoon, a flower painter under Charles II. designed to introduce all the medicinal plants at *Chelsea* in his large pictures, but soon grew tired of the work. There is another view, sections, and plan of the greenhouse.

houfe.——A furvey of the low grounds about *Wapping* in difpute between lady Ivie and the dean of St. Paul's.

" A fcheme for the better fupplying this metropolis with fweet and
" wholefome water from the river *Coln*, moft humbly offered to the
" confideration of parliament, the nobility, gentry, and inhabitants of
" the weft end of the town in particular, by Wm. Efford, gent. Lond.
" 1764." 4to. with a map of the river from Denham to the Thames.

P. 265. l. 11. for *John Bridges of Lincoln's inn, efq*; read *Duke of
Chandos.*——S. Nicholls engraved a defign of the buildings begun at
Marybone 1719.——A map of the country 20 miles round Lond n,
by Ph. Lea.——P. 272. A S. E. view of Weftminfter abbey by Weft
and Toms 1739. l. 27. for *that formerly occupied the fcite of* read *now
concealed by*—l. 34. for 1615 read 1685.——P. 273. There are two
old views of King-ftreet gate in the Pepyfian library, and an old print
of the houfe of lords with Elizabeth on the throne.——Add to note d,
Mr. Walpole fays, Ryther *made* them.—Add to note g, Mr. Walpole's
Cat. of Engr. p. 34, mentions James and Charles I. fitting in parliament by Thomas Cockfon. Quære, if thefe ?

P. 274. Bafire has juft engraved for the Antiquarian Society the
beautiful window at St. Margaret's, of which they have a drawing by
Vertue.——" The pardon grauntyd to the fraternyte of feynt Cornelys
at Weftmynfter, that vicet gyve or fende to it. The fume of indulgence cometh in the yere to 2740 dayes for ever to endure."

P. 275. In the Pepyfian library is Hollar's draught of Jones' defign
for the banqueting houfe. The original fketch for the middle compartment is at Houghton. John Skillman between 1660 and 1670 engraved the facade of Albemarle houfe, and a view of the banqueting
houfe. Walp. Cat. of Engr. p. 70. Skillman's name with *S. C.* and a
line through it for his mark, is to a view of Clarendon houfe. J. Spilberg. del. & ex. in the Pepyfian library. " Veue & perfpective du
palais du roy d'Angleterre a Londres qui fapelle Whithall. Silveftre fc.
Ifrael exc. Cum priv. reg." The Antiquarian Society have a drawing
of James IId's ftatue in Privy gardens by Vertue.

P. 276. Dr. Stukeley took a draught of the ruinous ichnography of
Whitehall, June 14, 1718, the week before it was totally deftroyed,

inferted.

inferted in his Itinerary, pl. viii.——l. 21. for *Streete* read *Streel*.—The new building for the Treafury, defigned and engraved by Kent 1734. —A plan and elevation of the fcreen before the Admiralty by Mr. Adams, who defigned it.

P. 277. In the Pepyfian library is a drawing of the remains of Charing crofs, being only a fquare fhaft mounted on 8 fteps. The Antiquarian Society have another of it intire. Hollar engraved the equeftrian ftatue. In the Pepyfian library is the popifh chapel at St. James, built for Mary, James IId's queen, 1688.—The chapel, with the marriage of the late prince of Orange, decorated and drawn by Kent, was engraved by Rigaud 1733. Arlington houfe by Kip and by S. Nicolls. The gardens at Carlton houfe by Woolet.

P. 278. l. 1. add, by N. Hawkfmoor, efq; P. 286. l. 4. for *Stillin-fleet*, read *Stillingfleet*. l. 5. after cafes, add, 1704. 8vo. P. 293. l. 6. from the bottom, for *modeftly* read *moderately*. l. 4. add, Lond. 1672. l. 3. for *An* read *Another*. laft l. for *thereof. By* read *thereof.* 1682. *By* —and for 1686 read 1683. P. 294. l. 28. add, 1682. 8vo. the 4th edition. 1755. To the laft was annexed, Memoirs of the author's life.

P. 287. " The London and Weftminfter guide through the cities and fuburbs. 1768." 12mo.——London was vifited 1634 by Henry St. George; and with Middlefex by Sir E. Byfhee 1660.

P. 298. l. 7, 8. read " London's deliverance predicted: in a fhort difcourfe, fhewing the caufes of plagues in general, and the probable time (God not contradicting the courfe of fecond caufes) when this prefent peft may abate. By John Gadbury, Φιλομαϑης. 1665." 4to.

To the tracts on the plague add the 13 following.——" Certain ne-
" ceffary directions as well for the cure of the plague as for preventing
" the infection: with many eafie medicines of fmall charge, very pro-
" fitable to his majefty's fubjects. Set down by the colledge of phyfi-
" cians, by the king's majefty's fpecial command. 1665." 4to———
" Orders conceived and publifhed by the lord mayor and aldermen
" of the city of London, concerning the infection of the plague.
" Printed by James Flefher, printer to the hon. city of Lond." 4to.
————" Cautionary rules for preventing the ficknefs; publifhed by
" order of the lord mayor. 1665." 4to. [By Dr. Humphrey Brooke.]
————" The

———" The meanes of preventing, and preferving from, and curing of
" that moft contagious difeafe called the plague : with the peftilential
" feavers, and the fearfull fymptomes, and accidents, incident there-
" unto. Alfo fome prayers, and meditations upon death. 1665." 4to.

———" Health better than wealth : or Mr. Culpepper's famous re-
" medies for cure of the fad and difmal peftilence, and for prevent-
" ing the further infection, and increafe thereof : as alfo his treatife
" touching the fhutting up of houfes : the chief caufes of this lament-
" able difeafe : the conjunctions of the fuperior planets; the effects
" and events thereof: the 12 figns of one infected, either for tokens,
" rifings, or carbuncles ; and the onely ways and means (with God's
" affiftance) to cure the fame. Likewife, his feveral arguments,
" proving the peft not infectious : the 12 figns that appear before fo
" great a judgment : and the prophetical obfervations of Mr. Lille and
" Mr. Booker, in the year 1644, touching the fucceeding of an au-
" tumnal plague. With that moft excellent electuary invented by the
" renowned king of Pontus, and ufed by the emperor Charles V. in
" times of ficknefs. With directions for all people infected or not in-
" fected how to make the fame. Publifhed for the good and benefit
" both of town and country. 1665." 4to. 6 pages.——" Directions
" for the prevention and cure of the plague. Fitted for the poorer
" fort. 1665." 4to.——" Υγιεινη, or a plain and practical difcourfe
" upon the firft of the 6 non-naturals, viz. Air : with cautionary
" rules and directions for the prefervation of people in this time of
" ficknefs. Very neceffary for the gentry and citizens that are now in
" the country, to perufe before they come into London. By Thomas
" Cock. 1665." 4to. ——" A brief treatife of the nature, caufes,
" fignes, prefervation from and cure of the peftilence. Collected by
" W. Kemp, Mr. of arts. 1665." 4to.——" The fhutting up infected
" houfes as it is practifed in England, foberly debated. By way of
" addrefs from the poor fouls that are vifited to their brethren that are
" free. With objections on the wayes whereby the prefent infection
" hath fpread. As alfo a certain method of diet, attendance, lodging,
" and phyfick, experimented in the recovery of fick perfons. 1665."
4to.——" A difcourfe of the plague : containing the nature, caufes,

4 Z

" figns,

" figns, and prefages of the peftilence in general. Together with the
" ftate of the prefent contagion. Alfo moft rational prefervatives for
" families, and choice curative medicines both for rich and poor. With
" feveral waies for purifying the air in houfes, ftreets, &c. Publifhed
" for the benefit of this great city and fuburbs. By Gideon Harvey.
" M. D. 1665." 4to.——" Golgotha; or a looking-glafs for London
" and the fuburbs thereof. Shewing the caufes, nature, and efficacy
" of the prefent plagues; and the moft hopefull way for healing.
" With an humble witnefs againft the cruel advice and practice of
" fhutting-up *unto oppreffion:* both now and formerly experienced
" to encreafe, rather than prevent the fpreading thereof. By J. V
" grieved for the poor, who perifh daily thereby. 1665." 4to.——
" Prefervatives againft the plague, or directions and advertifements
" for this time of peftilential contagion. With certain inftructions
" for the poorer fort of people when they fhall be vifited: and alfo
" a caveat to thofe that were about their necks impoifoned amulets
" as a prefervative againft that ficknefs. Publifhed in behoofe of the
" city of London now vifited, and all other parts of the ifland that
" may or fhall hereafter be vifited. By Francis Herring, Dr. in phy-
" fick. 1665." 4to.——" A mite caft into the treafury of the famous
" city of London: being a brief and methodical difcourfe of the na-
" ture, caufes, fymptomes, remedies, and prefervation from the plague,
" in this calamitous year 1665. Digefted into aphorifmes, by Theo-
" philus Garencieres, Dr. in phyfick. 1665." 4to.

P. 299. l. 12. dele, The 2d edit.

P. 302. " An account of the burning the city of London, as it was
" publifhed by the fpecial authority of the king and council in the year
" 1666. To which is added, the opinion of Dr. Kennet, the prefent
" bp. of Peterborough, as publifh'd by his lordfhip's order, and that
" of Dr. Eachard, relating thereunto. With a faithful relation of the
" prophecy of Thomas Ebbit, a quaker, who publickly foretold the
" burning of the faid city. From all which it plainly appears, that the
" papifts had no hand in that dreadfull conflagration. Very ufeful for
" all thofe who keep the annual folemn faft on that occafion. Lond.
" 1720." 8vo.

Read

Read l. 23. " שרדיבהיה, or the burning of London in the year
" 1666, commemorated and improved in a cx difcourfes, meditations,
" and contemplations, divided into 4 parts. By Samuel Rolle, minifter
" of the word, and fometime fellow of Trinity college in Cambridge.
" Lond. 1667." 12mo.

P. 304. l. 12. There is another copy, MS. Harl. 335; but Wanley
fays, many ftatutes in it are not Niger's.

P. 305. Dr. Warner had before printed " A fcheme of a fund for
the better maintenance of the widows and children of the clergy.
Lond. 1752." 8vo.

P. 308. add, " The 2d part of Fact againft fcandal, in anfwer to
a pamphlet, intitled, A continuation of frauds and abufes at St. Paul's.
Lond. 1713." 8vo.

P. 309. Ecclefiæ cath. S. Pauli, Lond. ab occidente defcriptio orthographica, ex autographo architecti. S. Gribelin fc. 1702.——A fection
of the choir, decorated agreeable to Sir C. Wren's original defign, engraved by Rooker, publifhed by S. Wale and J. Gwyn, the proprietors.

P. 310. l. 5. add, Another with the queen's ftatue by Hulfberg.
1713. l. 16. for *a general* read *an infide*. l. 21. add, J. Harris engraved the chapter houfe.——G. F. Blondel, architect, propofes to publifh by fubfcription two mezzotinto infide views of St. Stephen's Walbrook, and St. Paul's, from original drawings in his majefty's collection, in a fet with two others of St. Peter's at Rome, and the Invalids
at Paris.

P. 311. " A view of the altar piece lately erected in the church of
St. James, Clerkenwell, with a letter to the bp. of London by Thomas
Watfon, with remarks; and bp. Fleetwood's account of the rife and
progrefs of placing pictures and images in churches; as the whole was
publifhed in the Old Whig, Oct. 30. 1735." One fheet.

" A letter to an inhabitant of St. Andrew's, Holborn, about new
ceremonies in the church. Lond. 17 . . ." 8vo.

P. 312. A plan and elevation of Bow church by Hulfberg. St. Anthony, vulg. St. Antholin, and St. Dunftan's in the eaft, by Overton,
large. A large elevation and fection of St. Bride's, the hand unknown,
in the Antiquarian Society's library. St. Clement's Danes by Kip.

E. and

E. and S. W. profpects of St. Leonard's Shoreditch, by B. Lens 1735, another by Toms 1740.

P. 314. James Maurer drew, and Vivares and Fourdrinier engraved, 1741—1744, a number of fmall views of London and Middlefex. Boydel and Chatelain have fince done the fame. Thofe by the laft are fifty views of churches, &c. about fix or eight miles round London. The churches and public buildings in London are done for Overton in a number of compartments. Profpects of remarkable places in and about London by Robert Morden, fold by Ph. Lea. Fifhmongers-hall by B. Lens.

P. 315. The third edition of Woodward's letter 1723 is intituled " Remarks upon the antient and prefent ftate of London, occafioned " by fome Roman coins and other antiquities lately difcovered."

P. 317. Sir Hans Sloane in the Philofophical Tranfactions, N° 403, 404, gives a particular account of elephants bones in his poffeffion found in London, Northamptonfhire, and Gloucefterfhire.

P. 319. MS. Harl. 4015 is a regifter of charters of St. Giles's hof-pital.——The monument of Rahere, engraved by Hulet, with a defcrip-tion is in the Gentleman's Magazine, Oct. 1767, p. 502.——l. 26. *for* *this* read *St. Bartholomew's*.——A plan, fection, and elevation of the new buildings at St. Bartholomew's hofpital.——" Directions and prayers Guy's hofpital. 1738." 12mo.

P. 322. A view of the Foundling hofpital. Theod Jacobfon, arm. inv. Jeremiah Robinfon del. A. Roberts, fc.

P. 323. l. 19. add, who publifhed " A letter to R. Dingley, efq; being a propofal for the relief and employment of friendlefs girls and repenting proftitutes. Lond. 1758." 4to. and " Serious confiderations on the falutary defign of an act of parliament for a regular uniform of parifh poor [infants] in all the parifhes within the bills of mortality, &c."

P. 324. l. 6. add, By Dr. Lardner. l. 10. add, by Mr. Jerning-ham.——" The king and council's letters relating to the college of phyficians, and a fhort account of the privileges of their royal founda-tion. Lond. 1688." 4to.

P. 325.

P. 325. Holbein's capital picture of Hen. VIII. giving the surgeons company their charter is engraved by Baron.

P. 328. " Memoirs of the Royal Society, being a new abridgement of the Philosophical Transactions, giving an account of the undertakings, studies, and labours of the learned and ingenious in many considerable parts of the world, from the first institution of that illustrious society in the year 1665, under their royal founder king Charles II. to the year 1735 inclusive. Disposed under proper general heads, with a translation of the Latin tracts from their originals: the whole regularly abridged, the order of time observed, the theoretical parts applied to practical uses, and an explanation of the terms of art as they occur in the course of the work: being a work of general use to the public, and worthy the perusal of all mathematicians, artificers, tradesmen, &c. for their improvement in various branches of business. By Mr. Benj. Baddam [a printer.] Illustrated with copper plates. Lond. 1738." 8 vols. 8vo.

P. 331. after l. 3. add, It was sent to Peiresc to be printed in a tetrapla by F. Fronton. See Camd. epist. p. 206. 212. 217. 221. 269. 309. 374.——P. 332. l. 16. for *present* read *late*.

P. 333. " Letters on the British Museum. 1767." 12mo. Trifling description with trifling remarks.——P. 334. A S. view of the Temple church, by W. Emmitt.——P. 337. " The charter and laws of the Loriner's company. Lond. 1743." 8vo.

P. 338. There were pageants exhibited when Hen. IIId's queen, Eleanor, rode through the city to her coronation 1236, and for Edw. Ist's victory over the Scots 1298. Strype.

P. 341. l. 15. for 1690 read 1660. l. pen. read Mr. *Thomas* Stevenson; and add a note, Of him see Walp. Anecd. iii. 49.

P. 342. " London's great jubilee restored and performed on Tuesd.
" Oct. the 29th, 1689, for the entertainment of the right hon. Sir
" Tho. Pilkington, kt. lord mayor of the city of London; containing
" a description of the several pageants, and speeches, together with a
" song for the entertainment of their majesties, who with their royal
" highnesses the prince and princess of Denmark honoured his lord-
" ship this year with their presence. All set forth at the proper cost
" and

" and charge of the right worſhipful the company of ſkinners, by
" M. T. [Matthew Taubman.] 1689." Reprinted in Somers's tracts,
2d col. vol. iii. p. 33. See another 3d col. vol. i.

P. 343. l. 3. add, and a 3d in that of the Antiquarian Society.

R. 344. l. 16. *Mauron*, add a note, Mr. Walpole, Anecd. iii. 128.
calls him *Laroon*. I have ſpelt it as it ſtands in the Pepyſian ſet.

P. 346. Claud David of Burgundy publiſhed a print, from a model
of a fountain, with the ſtatues of Q. Anne, duke of Marlborough on
horſeback, and ſeveral river gods, deſigned to be erected at the conduit
in Cheapſide : under the print, Opus equitis Cl. David, comitatus Bur-
gundiæ. Walp. Eng. 116.——Add to note ᵇ. La Serre's hiſtory of her
journey to and reception in England, is a pompous folio, with curious
prints of towns, ſeats, and St. James's palace at that time. Hollar engraved 6 plates for it. Vertue's Life of Hollar, p. 16.

P. 347. l. 27. for *poetical* read *poems on*.

P. 349. l. ult. after Thames, add, March 8, 1725.

P. 350. l. 2. for *p.* 136 read *p.* 198.——Add to note ⁱ, Their brother
or father Peter painted theſe ſubjects. Mr. Walpole never ſaw but 2,
and ſays, the ſet is 8 : that in the Pepyſian library conſiſts of but 7.
Vertue mentions a large picture by Roderigo of the king's cavalcade
through the city gates the day before his coronation, painted 1662.
Some of the plates to Ogilby's Eſop among Hollar's are by the ſame,
but poorly done. Anecd. iii. 54.

P. 351. " The conſtitutions of the company of watermen and
" lightermen, as amended by the right hon. the court of lord mayor
" and aldermen, and afterwards confirmed by lord chief juſtice Parker :
" to which is prefixed a table of the contents of thoſe bye-laws, and
" thereunto annexed an abſtract of the reſpective duties of the rulers.
" Lond. 1730." 8vo.

P. 352. The W. front of St. George's church, Southwark. Price
arch. P. Fourdrinier ſc.

P. 354. l. 27. after 1560, add, on wood. P. 357. note ᶻ read ʸ.
Note ᶻ read *p.* 133. P. 359. note, for 26. 29. 33. read 28. 29. 35.

P. 360. " A proſpect of London and Weſtminſter, by Kip, in 12
ſheets."——A perſpective plan in the Antiquarian Society's library.——

3   A pro-

A profpect of London and Weftminfter and St. James's park, by J. Kip, dedicated to Q. Caroline when princefs of Wales. I think on 2 fheets.

P. 362. l. 13. for 1743 read 1745; and add, in 16 fheets.

P. 366. Norfolk was vifited 1563 by Harvey: 1589 by Cooke: 1613 by Raven.——Martin Booth, bookfeller at Norwich, lately begun to publifh in octavo numbers a hiftory of the city and county of Norwich; which neither found nor deferved encouragement.

P. 368. l. 1. for *p.* 430 read 420. l. 6. for *Norvicus* read *Angli Norvicus.* l. 7. dele, Kettus. l. 8. dele, five. After London, add, ap. Binneman. l. 9. for *This* read *the firft of thefe editions.* l. 10. for *and " Al.* read *and the latter " Al.* l. 11. for *it* read *both.* l. 12. after Lyne, add, and Remigius Hogenbergius, fervants. l. 15. for 1582 read 1580. l. 22. after Norwich, add, and a catalogue of the feveral governors thereof from the dayes of king Edred, with the fucceffion of the bifhops, &c. P. 369. l. 6. read, of his grandfon Owen.——reprinted 1721, with a new preface.

P. 370. Vertue mentions a plan of Norwich cathedral, by Hollar. Quære, if in the Monafticon?——Mackerell's Hiftory of Lynne was reprinted 1768 by F. Newberry, bookfeller in London.——In a catalogue of books by Booth, above-mentioned, 1767, was a MS. defcription of St. Peter's Mancroft, by Mr. Mackerell.

P. 371. after Corbridge, add, 1727, engraved by J. Harris.

P. 372. Linn market place, J. Bell del. & exc.——Lynn regis, Hen. Bell del. N. Donne fc. & exc. W. profpect of Lynn, by Hen. Bell. Chart of the jurifdiction of the admiralty of King's Lynn, from Stapleware up to the long fand and down to the fea, taken when the bounds were gone in the mayoralty of Hen. Bell, 1693.

P. 374. " Mr. Humph. Smith's fcheme for the draining of the S. " and middle levels of the fens. Aug. 28, 1729." a folio fheet.

P. 375 *. l. 9. add, and *Dereham* abbey, mifprinted Denham.—— Le Neve engraved a grant from William abbot of *Holme* and his convent to William Baffet. fans date. Lewis on feals, p. 625. This was probably William Baffet, abbot from 1127 to 1137.——P. 383, l. 8. 17 5 read 1755.

The

The Antiquarian Society have drawings of Geddington and Queen croffes, and of a Roman urn and coins found 1753 in *Sowthorpe* pit, near *Bernack* in NORTHAMPTONSHIRE: a proof that thefe famous quarries, which furnifhed ftone for Peterborough, Ramfey, St. Edmund's Bury, and other abbey churches, were known to the Romans. ——Buck miftakes for a priory the antient manfion houfe of the Longuevilles at *Little Billing*. See Hiftory of Northamptonfhire, p. 409. This and the fragment of Longefpee's houfe, now or late at Canford, Dorfet, are the only fpecimens of our early manfion houfes not caftellated that I have heard of.——Two unpublifhed plates of Dr. Stukeley's were profpects of Benavona, 1725, Fletcher fc. and of *Caftor* (Durobrivis) 1724, Kirkall fc.

Propofals are now circulated for printing by fubfcription, in 2 vols. 4to. The natural hiftory and antiquities of NORTHUMBERLAND, and of fo much of the county of DURHAM as lies between the rivers Tyne and Tweed, commonly called North Bifhoprick. By John Wallis, A. M. To be delivered before December 1768.

P. 386. l. penult. after church, add, drawn by William Horfeley. And l. the laft, for *Talbot* read *Crew*.

P. 387. A large S. view of *Newcaftle* from Gatefide fteeple, by Buck. l. pen. add Dublin. 1664. 12mo. the title fomewhat different.

P. 390. the article about *Fatfield* collery fhould have been inferted in *Durham*. l. 23. add, illuftrated by the like found near Bath, in that for Jan. 1768, p. 18.——" A perfpective view of *Dilfton hall*, once the feat of the unfortunate James earl of Derwentwater." Thomas Oliver, of Hexham del. Spilfbury fc. 1766.

NOTTINGHAMSHIRE.] P. 393. " Appendix to the queries con-
" cerning the ftatute of 11th and 12th of William III. to enable juftices
" of peace to build and repair goals in their refpective counties; re-
" vived and continued 10th Anne, and made perpetual 6th of his pre-
" fent majefty K. George. Nott. 1724." 4to.—" Reafons for repeal-
" ing the order of feffions made by the juftices of peace for the coun-
" ty of Nottingham at Rufford, 24 April, 1724, for joining with the
" corporation of Nottingham in building a county hall in the market-
" place, Nottingham; with propofals for repairing, enlarging, and
" amending

" amending the old county halls, and making them convenient with
" grand jury, petit jury rooms, and workhoufe adjoining, whereby the
" county may fave 3 or 4000 l. By Julius Hutchinfon, efq; one of
" the juftices."

" A difcourfe addreffed to the inhabitants of *Newark*, againft the
" mifapplication of public charities, and enforced from the following
" text, Ecclus. vi. 1. By the rev. Bernard Wilfon, D. D. vicar of
" Newark and prebend of Worcefter. To which is added a more
" full and true account of the very confiderable and numerous bene-
" factions left to the town of Newark than has hitherto been pub-
" lifhed. Lond. 1768." 4to.

OXFORDSHIRE.] P. 395. another unpublifhed plate of Dr. Stukeley
is Ælia caftra *(Alcefter.)*——P. 396. The chapel, N. fide of *Sanford*
houfe, and other old buildings at Sanford, were engraved by B. Cole.
1722. The Confeffor's chapel at *Iflip* is in the preface to Hearne's
Curious Difcourfes.———B. Green engraved fmall views of Godftow
nunnery, friar Bacon's ftudy, and Oxford from Elsfield.

" Tragi-comædia : being a brief relation of the ftrange and won-
" derfull hand of God difcovered at *Witney*, in a comedy acted there
" Feb. 3, where there were fome flaine, many hurt, with many other
" remarkable paffages : together with what was preached in three fer-
" mons on that occafion, from Rom. i. 18. both which may ferve as
" fome check to the growing atheifm of the prefent age. By John
" Rowe of C. C. C. in Oxford, lecturer in the town of Witney. Oxf.
" 1652." 4to. Enthufiaftic nonfenfe.

" W. Whately's fermon, and account of the fire at *Banbury*, which
" burned 103 houfes, &c. Lond. 1630." 4to.

P. 400. dele the fecond line of note ᵐ, except the reference.

P. 402. l. 16. add, In vol. lvii. art. 19. is Mr. Frankcombe's account
of fome uncommon foffils, fuppofed to be the upper jaw of a marine
animal found at Shotover, and in Glouceftershire.———The front and
E. fide of *Blenheim* houfe, with the bridge, and plans of the vaults
and firft ftory, were engraved in one fheet, by H. Terafon. The
bridge again, on a larger fcale, by Van Gunft.——" Blenheim. Lond.
1728." Fol. a poem.——A plan of lord North's gardens at *Wroxton*,

by Francis Booth, engraved by James Green.——" The Veſtry, a poem.
By an overſeer of the poor of the pariſh of St. Peter le Bailey, Oxford.
Oxf. 1767." 4to. about pariſh buſineſs or miſmanagement: ſatirizing a
pariſhioner who objected to an aſſeſſment and abuſed the veſtry.

P. 403. Thomas Jefferies propoſed to engrave a new map of the
county of Oxford, from a ſcale of one inch to a mile: wherein will
be accurately delineated the boroughs, market towns, villages, ſeats of
the nobility and gentry, woods, rivers, &c. from an accurate ſurvey
taken by himſelf. To be delivered in January 1767.

P. 404. l. 10. after 1713, add, at the end of Dodwell de parma eq.
Collegiorum.——Note y read *grandfather* John.

P. 406. l. 4. after 1608, add, 4to.

P. 411. The univerſity have engaged Mr. Swinton to methodize Dr.
Rawlinſon's Continuation of the Athenæ.

P. 415. " The new Oxford guide. 1759." with cuts. 12mo.

P. 422. note b. Dr. Stukeley ſays, the antique ſtatues at Thorpe
near Peterborough came out of the Arundel collection. Itin. Cur. p. 79.
The fragments in Cuper's gardens have been purchaſed, and removed
to Beconsfield (Buck's) and Fawley court (Oxfordſhire).

P. 424. B. Green etched the head of Cicero, in a round.

P. 429. " Corpus ſtatutorum Univerſitatis Oxonienſis, ſive pandectes
conſtitutionum academicarum e libris publicis & regiſtris univerſitatis
conſarcinatus. Ox. 1768." 4to.

P. 430. The catalogue of graduates has been continued to 1760.

P. 431. Robert Whittleſey was the republiſher of Aggas' plan.

P. 439. The author of the Vindication of the Mallard of All Souls
having levelled his ſatire at ſuch as purſue the ſtudy of antiquity in an
extravagant manner, was anſwered in a folio ſheet, intitled " Propoſals
for printing by ſubſcription the Hiſtory of the Mallardians," divided into
ſeveral chapters, treating his ſociety as a ſet of ſtupid bon vivans; with
the figure of a cat, ſaid to have been ſtarved in the college library: on
which he put out a 2d edition of his pamphlet, with additions.

P. 440. The plan, &c. belong to Magdalen college.

P. 447. " Oratiuncula habita in domo convocationis Oxon. die
" Oct. 27, 1756. Publicavit & illuſtravit notis criticis, politicis & ſa-
" tiricis J. C. prof. reg. Ox. Lond. 1757." 4to.

P. 455.

P. 455. " Advice to the inhabitants of *Wem*, in Salop, on the fire there. By Andrew Parſons. 1677." 8vo.——In the Harleian library is a MS. hiſtory of *Ludlow*.

P. 457. note d, after 1662, add, 1680: for *Mr.* read *Mrs.* and add, It was tranſlated into French and Portugueſe. Wood Ath. Ox. II. 73.

P. 458. Turner's " Treatiſe of the rare treaſure of Engliſhe bathes, ſet forth for the benefit of the poorer ſort of people, who are not able to go to the phyſitians, by Wm. Bremer, practitioner in phyſicke and chyrurgerie," was inſerted in the Engliſhman's treaſure, with Vicary's anatomy. Lond. 1633. 4to. part v. p. 79—95.

P. 466. l. 17 and 25. for *Quincy* read *Quinton*.

P. 469. art. 21. of the Philoſophical Tranſactions, vol lvii. is a letter from John Howard, eſq; to Mr. Canton, containing obſervations on the heat of Bath waters: art. 22. Mr. Canton's remarks on the heat of Briſtol waters.

P. 470. Dodwell's explanation of Vitalis' epitaph is in Engliſh at the end of Hearne's life of Alfred. The lower half of the equeſtrian figure, which Dr. Muſgrave laboured ſo hard to prove to be Geta, ſeems to have been found 1736, with the inſcription L. VITELLIVS MANIAI. F. TANCINVS, &c.——Harris engraved for Dr. Stukeley a plate of the inſcriptions, reliefs, &c. at Bath.

P. 472. l. 15. for 1757 read 1767.

P. 475. " An exact delineation of the famous city of Briſtol, and ſuburbs; together with all the high wayes, thoroughfare ſtreets, lanes, and publick paſſages therein contained: compoſed by a ſcale ichnographically deſcribed, engraven and publiſhed by James Millard, cittizen and inhabitant there." with views of the public buildings, &c. at the ſides; among others, the caſtle before its demolition 1656. The laſt view is dated 1710.

P. 477. l. penult. after incorrectly put a *comma* inſtead of a *point*.

P. 485. Propoſals are now circulated for printing by ſubſcription " A general hiſtory of Staffordſhire; comprehending its antiquities, natural hiſtory, hiſtorical accounts of families, preſent ſtate of the manufactures, public works, produce, &c. Illuſtrated with views of the public buildings, principal ſeats of the nobility and gentry, ſome remains of

antiquity,

antiquity, and the subjects of natural history, and an improved map of the county. Compiled from the manuscripts of the late learned and ingenious Dr. Wilkes, of Willenhall, in the said county, with considerable additions, by the rev. Thomas Feilde, M. A. head master of the free grammar-school at Brewood, in the same county."

P. 489. Mynde engraved for Dr. Huddesford the monument of Sir John Hanbury of *Hanbury*, from a drawing by Ashmole, in his museum, N° 7058.

P. 492. l. 8. for *Sir* read *St.*——P. 493. l. 15. for *M.* read *Mr.*

P. 497. This pot, with the inscription explained by Gagnier, was engraved in Anglia Judaica. 1736. 4to. by Dr. Tovey, who thinks it a vessel to contain records, like the earthen one Jerem. xxxi. 14. and the brass ones called εχινοι in Aristophanes. Schol. Kust. p. 327.

P. 508. " Hortus *Kewensis*, sistens herbas exoticas, indigenasq. ra-
" riores in area botanica hortorum augustissimæ principissæ Cambriæ
" dotissæ, apud Kew, in com. Surreiano cultas, methodo florali nova
" dispositas. Auctore Johanne Hill, M. D. Lond. 1768." 8vo.

P. 512. l. antep. add, Mr. Vines inserted an illustration of this account in that for Oct. p. 498; and in that for June 1768, p. 284, a comparison between Sussex and Dorsetshire antiquities.

P. 515. l. 14. after 8vo. add, By the rev. Mr. Jackson, schoolmaster of Coventry, and Samuel Carte.——P. 516. " The workes of G. Gascoigne, esq; the pleasures at Kenelworth castle when Q. Elizabeth was entertained. Lond. impr. by Abel Jeffes 1587." 4to.

P. 518. " Short remarks on Dr. Perry's analysis made on the Strat-
" ford mineral water, with a short essay, by way of appendix, towards
" a more perfect examination into the same waters. By Wm. Baylies,
" jun. Stratford upon Avon. 1745." 8vo.

P. 520. T. Jefferies proposes to engrave a new survey of WEST-MORELAND, on a scale of one inch to a mile, by Mr. Ainslie; but fixes no time of delivery.

P. 524. l. 2, 3, 4, 5. read thus, " Upon occasion of the dean of Sa-
" rum's Narrative, and collections made by the order and command of
" the most noble and most hon. the lords commissioners appointed by
" the king's majesty for ecclesiastical promotions, by way of reply unto

" the

" the anfwer of the lord bifhop of that diocefe, prefented to the afore-
" faid moft hon. lords. Printed only to fave the labour of tranfcribing
" feveral copies, and to prevent miftakes," &c.

 After l. 11. add, " Miffale fec. uf. ecc. Sarum Anglicane. Venet.
" ap. Joan. Bertzog de Landoia. 1494." 12mo.——" Breviarii fec.
" morem Sarum pars æftivalis ap. eund. 1495." 12mo.——" Miffale
" ad uf. infignis ac preclare ecc. Sarum confummatum in alma Pari-
" fiorum academia. 1516." 8vo.——" Enchiridion preclare ecc. Sarum
" Paris. ap. T. Kerver. 1513. 1528.——Horæ B. M. V ad uf ecc. Sarum.
" 1530. Lond. in cimiterio divi Pauli apud Joh. Renis, fub interfignio
" Sci Gregorii."——Ditto, novo impreff. 1555. Lond. in ædibus Rob.
" Toy. 12mo.——" Portiforium feu breviarium ad ufum eccl. Sarifburi-
" enfis, caftigatum, fuppletum, marginalibus quotationibus adornatum,
" ac nunc primum ad veriffimum ordinalis exemplar in fuum ordi-
" nem a peritiffimis viris redactum. Pars hiemalis. Lond. 1555." 4to.
" Pars æftivalis" is undated.——" Miffale ad ufum eccl. Sarifburienfis.
" 1553." Printed by Robert Valentin.——" Sacra inftitutio baptizandi,
" matrimonium celebrandi, infirmos unguendi, mortuos fepeliendi,
" ac alii nonulli ritus ecclefiaftici juxta uf. ec. Sar. Duaci. 1604."——
The oldeft regifter of this church is or was in the hands of Mr. Nafh,
a Wiltfhire clergyman.

 P. 532. add to note g. " A vindication of the antiquity of Stone-
" henge. Salifb. 1730." 8vo. with a poem, by a neighbouring clergyman.

 P. 538. head title to be WORCESTERSHIRE.——Mr. Taylor is now
taking a furvey of this county.

 P. 544. YORKSHIRE was vifited 1530 by T. Tong: 1584 by
Glover: 1575 by Flower: 1665 by Dugdale.——Wanley, in a note
in his copy of Nicholfon's Englifh hiftorical library, now in the
Bodleian library, fays, Dodfworth's Yorkfhire was tranfcribed by two
clergymen, Tillotfon and Tenifon, in divers folio volumes, in the
Harleian library.

 P. 553. l. 24. after 1719. add, for the Antiquarian Society.——l. 31
for 189 read 188. iii. 315.

P. 555.

P. 555. " Ichnography and ground plot of the city of Yorke, furveyed by, Benedict Horfley of the city of Yorke, 1694." publifhed 1697. I think Drake's plan is an improved copy of this.

P. 560. l. 2. after Fothergill, add, His fine library, including a moft valuable collection of MSS. efpecially in the ritual and liturgical way, on which he intended to have written fomething, is in York cathedral. See an account of him in Drake's York, p. 379.——l. 25. for *T.* read *C.*

P. 565. l. 6. for *Hufburg* read *Hulfburg.*

P. 571. " The town, harbour, and fpaw of Scarborough by John Setterington." 2 fheets.

P. 575. l. 6, 7. the Netherby article belongs to Cumberland.

P. 577. l. 1. after have, add, publifhed.

P. 583. Lewis dedicates his book to Henry prince of Wales, fon of James I. He promifes an ecclefiaftical hiftory of Britain. His civil one is worth little. The editor has inferted after the firft book, Lluyd's own tranflation of the Welfh preface to his Archæologia: at the end of which Lluyd promifes an hiftorical dictionary of Britifh perfons and places mentioned in antient records. It feems to have been ready for prefs, but he could not fix the time of publication.——l. 11. after arce, add, " five armamentario Romano."——Thefe æræ, wrote in Welfh 400 years ago, were tranflated into Englifh by R. Vaughan, of Hengwrt, who added notes as far as A. D. 811. Williams tranflated both into Latin, and continued the notes.

P. 586. In the Philofophical Tranfaction, vol. lvii. art. 23. is an account of fome particular fifh in Wales by the hon. Daines Barrington.

P. 592. l. 4. read view of *Neath* abbey.——Mr. Harris' MS. mentioned in the note is in the Antiquarian Society's library.——Mr. Anftis had a 4to volume of collections by Geo Owen of Henllys, in Pembrokefhire, efq; 1602. intitled, " The number of hundreds, caftells, &c. in all the fhires of Wales, with the names of the chief gentry, &c. nature of the foile, qualitie of the people, &c. &c."

P. 594. " The mine-adventure; or an expedient, fit, for compofing " all differences between the partners of the mines late of Sir Carbery " Pryfe. 2dly, For eftablifhing a new method for the management " thereof, and thereby (inftead of an arbitrary power over the mines

" and

" and ſtock of all the partners in one perſon) ſettling an equal and fair
" conſtitution for every perſon concerned. 3dly, For granting ſeveral
" charities out of the ſame to the poor of every county in England and
" Wales, without prejudice to the partners. 4thly, For enabling the
" partners to employ a much greater ſtock therein, and conſequently
" (in the ſame proportion) to advance the gain and profits thereof.
" 5thly, For diſcharging all debts, duties, and demands chargeable
" upon the mines, originally occaſioned by ſeveral expenſive law ſuits
" between the ſaid Sir C. Pryſe and the patentees of royal mines. And,
" 6thly, for raiſing a large ſtock of 20000 l. (clear of all manner of
" incumbrances) for the working and carrying on the ſaid mineral
" works, to the great advantage of the king and kingdom. Propoſed
" by Sir Humphry Mackworth, peruſed and ſettled by eminent council
" in the law, and finally eſtabliſhed in two indentures, made and ex-
" ecuted by the preſent partners, and which ſhall be inrolled in the
" high court of chancery. Lond. 1698." Fol. 16 pages. The indentures make 20 pages more. There is an abſtract in 2 pages, and one
in 4, with views of the mines.

P. 601. " An experimental and practical enquiry into the ophthal-
" mic, antiſcrophulous, and nervous properties of the mineral waters of
" *Llangybi* in Carnarvonſhire. To which is annexed, An eſſay on the
" prize queſtion propoſed by the Royal Academy of *Bourdeaux*, for
" the year 1767, on the ſubject of analizing mineral waters. By Die-
" derick Weſſel Linden, M. D. 1767."———The 4th view of Piſtil
Rhaidr is by J. Green and J. Evans, 1753.

P. 603. Dr. Stukeley drew and J. Harris engraved in one plate two
concentric circles of ſtones in a wood called *Coed iſa*, by Plas yn Llanvair Vechan, and another with a carn, called *Karnedh vawr*, in Hwy-
gyfylchen pariſh, by Maen y Campien, and within three arrows flight
of Mein hirion.——P. 606. l. 7. for *this* read *her*.——An antient monument called Maen Achwynfan (the ſtone of lamentation) on Sir R.
Moſtyn's eſtate near Gelli chapel, Whiteford pariſh, with 2 others in
Diſert churchyard, drawn by Watkin Williams 1759, engraved by
Major.——P. 608. l. 14. for *Frerdrews* read *Trerdrew*.——P. 609.
l. 6. for *xi.* read. *II.*——P. 610. l. 31. read, reprinted ſeparately.

P. 619. l. 20. for *qu* read *quæ*. l. 21. read, in quibus.

P. 632. In the 2d edition of Slezer's Theatrum is added a large view of Edinburgh, and a smaller of lord Loudun's house, besides considerable additions to the descriptions.

P. 634. " An impartial account of the rise, progress, and nature " of the scheme for augmenting the livings of the Scots clergy. In " a letter to the publisher of the printed collection of papers relative " to that affair. Edin. 1751." 4to. This scheme warmly agitated in their synods 1748, 1749, came to nothing.

P. 637. " De Volucri arborea absq. patre & matre in insulis Or- " cadum, formâ anserculorum proveniente, authore Mich. Maiero. " Francf. 1619." 12mo.

P. 641. Wm. Edgar drew a map of *Stirlingshire*, 1745. from whence a general one of the county between the Forth and Clyde shewing the course of the intended canal, was extracted by Mr. Smeaton, engraved by A..Bell.——" Reflections on inland navigations : " and a new method proposed for executing the intended navigation " betwixt the Forth and the Clyde in a compleat manner, at an ex- " pence one-third less than what that work has hitherto been estimated " at. The same method applied to almost all rivers and rivulets, by " which Great Britain and Ireland might have, at a very easy expence, " above 5000 miles of new inland navigation. Lond. 1768.' 8vo. "

P. 643. l. 16. for *The* read *An*.——l. 20. after collected, add, and englished.——Robert Monteith was the Weever of Scotland, and published 1713, " A further collection of funeral inscriptions over Scot- " land, gathered from Edinburgh, Dundee, Aberdeen, &c. &c. and " several other places elsewhere. Whereto are subjoined some on the " passion and death of Christ, Mary Q. of Scots, James and Charles I. " with foreign epitaphs, antient and modern, christian and heathenish, " acrostichal, monostichal, teleostical, chronological and dialogical, " rhythmical, jocose, enigmatical; some in most elegant prose; seve- " rals upon the ruines of Greece, Troy and Rome ; and upon the " death of sundrie creatures." 8vo.

P. 644. There is a prospect of Edinburgh, with Neptune on the fore ground, by Thomas Jameson. Walp. addit. to his Anecdotes.

P. 656.

P. 656. Smith's defcription of Hetland, a defcription of the iflands of Orkney and Shetland, &c. makes the 6th book of " England's improvement, revived by Capt. John Smith. 1671." 4to.

P. 657. A S. E. view of the cathedral in *Icolmkill*, drawn on the fpot and etched by lord Cardrofs. 1761.

P. 668. " A geographical defcription of the kingdom of Ireland. Lond. 1642." 4to.

P. 670. " Speed reprefented fome rivers and lakes more truly than fome modern geographers. Riccioli in his Geographia Reformata was the firft that placed the towns of Ireland in their true latitudes. Sir Wm. Petty's Surveys, as far as they go, are tolerably exact as to diftances and fituations, but neither the latitudes nor roads are expreffed, nor is the fea coaft exactly drawn ; his defign being only to take an account of the forfeited lands, many other tracts are left blank, and from fuch a furvey his maps were formed. The plates of all the barony maps, in number 252, were taken on board a fhip in queen Anne's wars by a French privateer, and are faid to be now in the king of France's library." Smith's preface to his Hiftory of Cork.

P. 673. To the 2d edition of " Hartlib's Legacie, or enlargement of the difcourfe of the Brabant and Flaunder's hufbandry," is added " An interrogatory, relating more particularly to the hufbandry and naturall hiftory of Ireland. Lond. 1652." 4to.

P. 674. The editor of the Monafticon Hibernicum was captain Stevens, who continued Dugdale's Monafticon.

P. 676. The Natural hiftory was reprinted 1755, with a new preface and index of chapters.——l. 7. read, publifhed by Dr. Thomas, &c.

P. 683. l. 5. for *capital places* read *copper plates*. l. 6. for *philofophical* read *phyfico-hiftorical*. l. 7. for 175 read 1750.——The views are drawn by Anthony Chearnly, gent. and engraved by T. Chambars. ——Smith quotes Dr. Rogers's " Effay on the endemical difeafes of Cork."

P. 686. l. 25. after natural, add, and civil.

P. 688. A map of the city and fuburbs of Dublin, and alfo the archbifhop and earl of Meath's liberties, with the bounds of each

5 B

parifh,

parifh, drawn from an actual furvey (with a N. profpect of the city, and a view of the poor-houfe) printed for Overton, and dedicated to lord Carteret, then lieutenant, without any furveyor's name.

P. 693. l. 4. for 2*d* read 3*d*.

P. 694. l. 9. after fiege, add, is prefixed to all the editions of Walker's account. Another map and defcription of the town is added to " A true and impartial account of the moft material paffages in Ire-" land fince Dec. 1688, &c. 1689." 4to.

P. 137. " The river *Dove:* a lyric paftoral. By Samuel Bentley. " Lond. 1768." 4to. A defcription of Dovedale by the courfe of the river.

P. 153. l. 20. read, After his death 1703 it was printed under, &c.

P. 155. " The antiquities of the abbey or cathedral church of " *Durham:* alfo a particular defcription of the county palatine of " Durham, compiled from the beft authorities and original MSS. " To which is added, the fucceffion of the bifhops, deans, arch-" deacons, and prebends: the bifhop's courts and his officers; and " the caftles and manfion houfes of the nobility and gentry; with " other particulars. Newcaftle 1767." 12mo. The defcription of the cathedral is the old one reprinted: that of the county taken from Magna Britannia, with no material additions.

P. 157. l. penult, for 1721 read 1711.

P. 162. Morant's Hiftory of Effex, including a new edition of his Hiftory of Colchefter, is now completed.

P. 167. l. 25. for 1745 read 1645.

P. 172. Atkin's Gloucefterfhire is juft republifhed, without any im-provement but a correction of literal errors, by Mr. Herbert, formerly printfeller on London-bridge, who has all the original plates.

P. 184. " The Southampton Guide, or an account of the antient " and prefent ftate of that town. To which is added, a defcription of " the Ifle of Wight, Netley abbey, &c. Southampt. 1768." 12mo.

P. 187. laft line, and p. 188. line 1, 2, 3, read, This date profef-for Ward, N° 474. p. 79. takes to be the characters in a wooden mo-

del;

del of a window in a ftable, reprefenting the names of Jefus and John, and an emblem of the trinity.——Add in the fame page, " Hoglandiæ " defcriptio. Lond. 1710." 8vo.——" The honorable entertainment " given to the Queen's majeftie in progrefs at *Elvetham* in Hampfhire " by the earl of Hertford 1591. Lond. printed by J. Wolfe 1591." with the family arms prefixed, and a map and defcription of the great pond at Elvetham, and the properties which it contains, coloured. The only copy Wanley ever faw is in the public library at Cambridge.

P. 308. l. 5. for II. read I.

P. 318. l. 22. dele *late.*——l. 29. dele the firft inverted comma's.

P. 334. l. 1. read, plates of the arms in the feveral halls. P. 330 and 340, for *laft fpring* read 1765.

P. 365. Edward Garvey propofes publifhing by fubfcription four views of *Piercefield*, in *Monmouthfhire*, the feat of Valentine Morris, efq; together with two views of Rome and the lake Albano: painted by himfelf.

P. 377. note b, for *Survey* read *Surrey.*

P. 430. l. 15. *beadles* fhould be placed after *fuperior.*

P. 433. " The proceedings of the vifitors of Univerfity college, " with regard to the late difputed election of a mafter, vindicated. " Oxf. 1723." 2 fheets, fol..

P. 441. l. 10. after remarks, add, upon the King's authority in ec- clefiaftical cafes, according —

P. 456. " A medicinal and experimental hiftory and analyfis of the " *Hanly's* fpa, faline. purging, and chalybeate waters, near Shrewfbury, " &c. By D. W. Linden. Lond. 1768." 8vo.

P. 464. line 32. read, gaVDIo.

P. 477. l. 1. for *monument* read *monaftery.*

P. 547. line 29, and p. 548. line 13. dele the inverted commas.

P. 551. " An accurate defcription and hiftory of the cathedral and " metropolitical church of St. Peter, York, from its firft foundation to " the prefent year. Illuftrated with copper plates, confifting of different " views, plans, &c. and tranflations of all the Latin epitaphs. To " which are added, Catalogues of the archbifhops, deans, fubdeans,. " chancellors, treafurers, precentors, and fuccentors. York 1768." 12mo. A pocket companion, compiled from Drake, with his plates.

2   A fecond

A second part, containing the antiquities, &c. of the see, the privileges of the chapter, and the lives of the archbishops and deans is preparing with all possible expedition.

P. 624. l. 29, 30. read, under the title of " A second edition of " Camden's description of Scotland, containing a supplement of those " peers, or lords of parliament, who were mentioned in the first edi- " tion, and an account of those since raised to, and further advanced " in the degree of peerage, until the year 1694." The editor has corrected only errors of press, but continued ———

P. 625. Dele line 2d and half line 1st.—Add, note b, Nich. p. 14. Sir Robert.——Dele, note b, Nich. p. 14. *below.*

P. 536. and p. 649. for *this spring*, read 1767.

INDEX.

INDEX.

5 B   Atkins,

I N D E X.

Booth,

I N D E X.

INDEX.

I N D E X.

Conyers,

INDEX.

I N D E X.

I N D E X.

I N D E X.

5 C 2

Grene-

I N D E X.

INDEX.

Johnson,

I N D E X.

Kitchen,

INDEX.

Martin-

INDEX.

2

Morris,

I N D E X.

Oram,

I N D E X.

I N D E X.

Ph.

I N D E X.

Phil.

Ph.

INDEX.

INDEX.

I N D E X.

INDEX.

I N D E X.

Spilberg,

I N D E X.

INDEX.

Tucker,

I N D E X.

2

Walker,

INDEX.

Willis,

INDEX.

Lightning Source UK Ltd.
Milton Keynes UK
UKOW02f2033170214

226638UK00002B/8/P